About Pearson

Pearson is the world's learning company, with presence across 70 countries worldwide. Our unique insights and world-class expertise comes from a long history of working closely with renowned teachers, authors and thought leaders, as a result of which, we have emerged as the preferred choice for millions of teachers and learners across the world.

We believe learning opens up opportunities, creates fulfilling careers and hence better lives. We hence collaborate with the best of minds to deliver you class-leading products, spread across the Higher Education and K12 spectrum.

Superior learning experience and improved outcomes are at the heart of everything we do. This product is the result of one such effort.

Your feedback plays a critical role in the evolution of our products and you can contact us – reachus@pearson.com. We look forward to it.

Digital Image Processing

FOURTH
EDITION

Digital Image Processing

4

FOURTH
EDITION

Rafael C. Gonzalez

University of Tennessee

Richard E. Woods

Interapptics

 Pearson

MATLAB is a registered trademark of The MathWorks, Inc., 1 Apple Hill Drive, Natick, MA 01760-2098.

Authorized adaptation from the United States edition, entitled *Digital Image Processing: Global Edition*, *4th Edition*, ISBN 9781292223049 by Rafael C. Gonzalez and Richard E. Woods, published by Pearson Education Inc., Copyright © 2018.

Indian Subcontinent Adaptation
Copyright © 2018 Pearson India Education Services Pvt. Ltd

ISBN 978-93-530-6298-9

First Impression, 2019
Sixth Impression, 2022
Seventh Impression, 2023

This edition is manufactured in India and is authorized for sale only in India, Bangladesh, Bhutan, Pakistan, Nepal, Sri Lanka and the Maldives. Circulation of this edition outside of these territories is UNAUTHORIZED.

Published by Pearson India Education Services Pvt. Ltd, CIN: U72200TN2005PTC057128.

Head Office: 1st Floor, Berger Tower, Plot No. C-001A/2, Sector16B, Noida 201301 U.P., India.

Registered Office: 7th Floor, SDB2, ODC 7, 8 & 9, Survey No.01 ELCOT IT/ ITES SEZ, Sholinganallur, Chennai – 600119, Tamil Nadu, India.
Website: in.pearson.com, Email: companysecretary.india@pearson.com

Printed in India at Sai Printo Pack Pvt Ltd

To Connie, Ralph, and Rob
and
To Janice, David, and Jonathan

Contents

4 Filtering in the Frequency Domain 203

5 Image Restoration and Reconstruction 317

6 Color Image Processing 399

7 Wavelet and Other Image Transforms   463

8 Image Compression and Watermarking   539

9 Morphological Image Processing   635

Preface

When something can be read without effort, great effort has gone into its writing.

Enrique Jardiel Poncela

This edition of *Digital Image Processing* is a major revision of the book. As in the 1977 and 1987 editions by Gonzalez and Wintz, and the 1992, 2002, and 2008 editions by Gonzalez and Woods, this sixth-generation edition was prepared with students and instructors in mind. The principal objectives of the book continue to be to provide an introduction to basic concepts and methodologies applicable to digital image processing, and to develop a foundation that can be used as the basis for further study and research in this field. To achieve these objectives, we focused again on material that we believe is fundamental and whose scope of application is not limited to the solution of specialized problems. The mathematical complexity of the book remains at a level well within the grasp of college seniors and first-year graduate students who have introductory preparation in mathematical analysis, vectors, matrices, probability, statistics, linear systems, and computer programming.

One of the principal reasons this book has been the world leader in its field for 40 years is the level of attention we pay to the changing educational needs of our readers. The present edition is based on an extensive survey that involved faculty, students, and independent readers of the book in 150 institutions from 30 countries. The survey revealed a need for coverage of new material that has matured since the last edition of the book. The principal findings of the survey indicated a need for:

- Expanded coverage of the fundamentals of spatial filtering.
- A more comprehensive and cohesive coverage of image transforms.
- A more complete presentation of finite differences, with a focus on edge detection.
- A discussion of clustering, superpixels, and their use in region segmentation.
- Coverage of maximally stable extremal regions.
- Expanded coverage of feature extraction to include the Scale Invariant Feature Transform (SIFT).
- Expanded coverage of neural networks to include deep neural networks, back-propagation, deep learning, and, especially, deep convolutional neural networks.
- More homework exercises at the end of the chapters.

The new and reorganized material that resulted in the present edition is our attempt at providing a reasonable balance between rigor, clarity of presentation, and the findings of the survey. In addition to new material, earlier portions of the text were updated and clarified. This edition contains 241 new images, 72 new drawings, and 135 new exercises.

New to This Edition

The highlights of this edition are as follows.

Chapter 1: Some figures were updated, and parts of the text were rewritten to correspond to changes in later chapters.

Chapter 2: Many of the sections and examples were rewritten for clarity. We added 14 new exercises.

Chapter 3: Fundamental concepts of spatial filtering were rewritten to include a discussion on separable filter kernels, expanded coverage of the properties of low-pass Gaussian kernels, and expanded coverage of highpass, bandreject, and bandpass filters, including numerous new examples that illustrate their use. In addition to revisions in the text, including 6 new examples, the chapter has 59 new images, 2 new line drawings, and 15 new exercises.

Chapter 4: Several of the sections of this chapter were revised to improve the clarity of presentation. We replaced dated graphical material with 35 new images and 4 new line drawings. We added 21 new exercises.

Chapter 5: Revisions to this chapter were limited to clarifications and a few corrections in notation. We added 6 new images and 14 new exercises,

Chapter 6: Several sections were clarified, and the explanation of the CMY and CMYK color models was expanded, including 2 new images.

Chapter 7: This is a new chapter that brings together wavelets, several new transforms, and many of the image transforms that were scattered throughout the book. The emphasis of this new chapter is on the presentation of these transforms from a unified point of view. We added 24 new images, 20 new drawings, and 25 new exercises.

Chapter 8: The material was revised with numerous clarifications and several improvements to the presentation.

Chapter 9: Revisions of this chapter included a complete rewrite of several sections, including redrafting of several line drawings. We added 16 new exercises.

Chapter 10: Several of the sections were rewritten for clarity. We updated the chapter by adding coverage of finite differences, K-means clustering, superpixels, and graph cuts. The new topics are illustrated with 4 new examples. In total, we added 29 new images, 3 new drawings, and 6 new exercises.

Chapter 11: The chapter was updated with numerous topics, beginning with a more detailed classification of feature types and their uses. In addition to improvements in the clarity of presentation, we added coverage of slope change codes, expanded the explanation of skeletons, medial axes, and the distance transform, and added several new basic descriptors of compactness, circularity, and eccentricity. New material includes coverage of the Harris-Stephens corner detector, and a presentation of maximally stable extremal regions. A major addition to the chapter is a comprehensive discussion dealing with the Scale-Invariant Feature Transform (SIFT). The new material is complemented by 65 new images, 15 new drawings, and 12 new exercises.

Chapter 12: This chapter underwent a major revision to include an extensive rewrite of neural networks and deep learning, an area that has grown significantly since the last edition of the book. We added a comprehensive discussion on fully connected, deep neural networks that includes derivation of backpropagation starting from basic principles. The equations of backpropagation were expressed in "traditional" scalar terms, and then generalized into a compact set of matrix equations ideally suited for implementation of deep neural nets. The effectiveness of fully connected networks was demonstrated with several examples that included a comparison with the Bayes classifier. One of the most-requested topics in the survey was coverage of deep convolutional neural networks. We added an extensive section on this, following the same blueprint we used for deep, fully connected nets. That is, we derived the equations of backpropagation for convolutional nets, and showed how they are different from "traditional" backpropagation. We then illustrated the use of convolutional networks with simple images, and applied them to large image databases of numerals and natural scenes. The written material is complemented by 23 new images, 28 new drawings, and 12 new exercises.

This edition of *Digital Image Processing* is a reflection of how the educational needs of our readers have changed since 2008. As is usual in an endeavor such as this, progress in the field continues after work on the manuscript stops. One of the reasons why this book has been so well accepted since it first appeared in 1977 is its continued emphasis on fundamental concepts that retain their relevance over time. This approach, among other things, attempts to provide a measure of stability in a rapidly evolving body of knowledge. We have tried to follow the same principle in preparing this edition of the book.

R.C.G.
R.E.W.

Acknowledgments

We are indebted to a number of individuals in academic circles, industry, and government who have contributed to this edition of the book. In particular, we wish to extend our appreciation to Hairong Qi and her students, Zhifei Zhang and Chengcheng Li, for their valuable review of the material on neural networks, and for their help in generating examples for that material. We also want to thank Ernesto Bribiesca Correa for providing and reviewing material on slope chain codes, and Dirk Padfield for his many suggestions and review of several chapters in the book. We appreciate Michel Kocher's many thoughtful comments and suggestions over the years on how to improve the book. Thanks also to Steve Eddins for his suggestions on MATLAB and related software issues.

Numerous individuals have contributed to material carried over from the previous to the current edition of the book. Their contributions have been important in so many different ways that we find it difficult to acknowledge them in any other way but alphabetically. We thank Mongi A. Abidi, Yongmin Kim, Bryan Morse, Andrew Oldroyd, Ali M. Reza, Edgardo Felipe Riveron, Jose Ruiz Shulcloper, and Cameron H.G. Wright for their many suggestions on how to improve the presentation and/or the scope of coverage in the book. We are also indebted to Naomi Fernandes at the MathWorks for providing us with MATLAB software and support that were important in our ability to create many of the examples and experimental results included in this edition of the book.

A significant percentage of the new images used in this edition (and in some cases their history and interpretation) were obtained through the efforts of individuals whose contributions are sincerely appreciated. In particular, we wish to acknowledge the efforts of Serge Beucher, Uwe Boos, Michael E. Casey, Michael W. Davidson, Susan L. Forsburg, Thomas R. Gest, Daniel A. Hammer, Zhong He, Roger Heady, Juan A. Herrera, John M. Hudak, Michael Hurwitz, Chris J. Johannsen, Rhonda Knighton, Don P. Mitchell, A. Morris, Curtis C. Ober, David. R. Pickens, Michael Robinson, Michael Shaffer, Pete Sites, Sally Stowe, Craig Watson, David K. Wehe, and Robert A. West. We also wish to acknowledge other individuals and organizations cited in the captions of numerous figures throughout the book for their permission to use that material.

We also thank Scott Disanno, Michelle Bayman, Rose Kernan, and Julie Bai for their support and significant patience during the production of the book.

R.C.G.
R.E.W.

About the Authors

RAFAEL C. GONZALEZ

R. C. Gonzalez received the B.S.E.E. degree from the University of Miami in 1965 and the M.E. and Ph.D. degrees in electrical engineering from the University of Florida, Gainesville, in 1967 and 1970, respectively. He joined the Electrical and Computer Science Department at the University of Tennessee, Knoxville (UTK) in 1970, where he became Associate Professor in 1973, Professor in 1978, and Distinguished Service Professor in 1984. He served as Chairman of the department from 1994 through 1997. He is currently a Professor Emeritus at UTK.

Gonzalez is the founder of the Image & Pattern Analysis Laboratory and the Robotics & Computer Vision Laboratory at the University of Tennessee. He also founded Perceptics Corporation in 1982 and was its president until 1992. The last three years of this period were spent under a full-time employment contract with Westinghouse Corporation, who acquired the company in 1989.

Under his direction, Perceptics became highly successful in image processing, computer vision, and laser disk storage technology. In its initial ten years, Perceptics introduced a series of innovative products, including: The world's first commercially available computer vision system for automatically reading license plates on moving vehicles; a series of large-scale image processing and archiving systems used by the U.S. Navy at six different manufacturing sites throughout the country to inspect the rocket motors of missiles in the Trident II Submarine Program; the market-leading family of imaging boards for advanced Macintosh computers; and a line of trillion-byte laser disk products.

He is a frequent consultant to industry and government in the areas of pattern recognition, image processing, and machine learning. His academic honors for work in these fields include the 1977 UTK College of Engineering Faculty Achievement Award; the 1978 UTK Chancellor's Research Scholar Award; the 1980 Magnavox Engineering Professor Award; and the 1980 M.E. Brooks Distinguished Professor Award. In 1981 he became an IBM Professor at the University of Tennessee and in 1984 he was named a Distinguished Service Professor there. He was awarded a Distinguished Alumnus Award by the University of Miami in 1985, the Phi Kappa Phi Scholar Award in 1986, and the University of Tennessee's Nathan W. Dougherty Award for Excellence in Engineering in 1992.

Honors for industrial accomplishment include the 1987 IEEE Outstanding Engineer Award for Commercial Development in Tennessee; the 1988 Albert Rose National Award for Excellence in Commercial Image Processing; the 1989 B. Otto Wheeley Award for Excellence in Technology Transfer; the 1989 Coopers and Lybrand Entrepreneur of the Year Award; the 1992 IEEE Region 3 Outstanding Engineer Award; and the 1993 Automated Imaging Association National Award for Technology Development.

Gonzalez is author or co-author of over 100 technical articles, two edited books, and four textbooks in the fields of pattern recognition, image processing, and robotics. His books are used in over 1000 universities and research institutions throughout the world. He is listed in the prestigious *Marquis Who's Who in America*, *Marquis Who's Who in Engineering*, *Marquis Who's Who in the World*, and in 10 other national and international biographical citations. He is the co-holder of two U.S. Patents, and has been an associate editor of the *IEEE Transactions on Systems, Man and Cybernetics*, and the *International Journal of Computer and Information Sciences*. He is a member of numerous professional and honorary societies, including Tau Beta Pi, Phi Kappa Phi, Eta Kappa Nu, and Sigma Xi. He is a Fellow of the IEEE.

RICHARD E. WOODS

R. E. Woods earned his B.S., M.S., and Ph.D. degrees in Electrical Engineering from the University of Tennessee, Knoxville in 1975, 1977, and 1980, respectively. He became an Assistant Professor of Electrical Engineering and Computer Science in 1981 and was recognized as a Distinguished Engineering Alumnus in 1986.

A veteran hardware and software developer, Dr. Woods has been involved in the founding of several high-technology startups, including Perceptics Corporation, where he was responsible for the development of the company's quantitative image analysis and autonomous decision-making products; MedData Interactive, a high-technology company specializing in the development of handheld computer systems for medical applications; and Interapptics, an internet-based company that designs desktop and handheld computer applications.

Dr. Woods currently serves on several nonprofit educational and media-related boards, including Johnson University, and was recently a summer English instructor at the Beijing Institute of Technology. He is the holder of a U.S. Patent in the area of digital image processing and has published two textbooks, as well as numerous articles related to digital signal processing. Dr. Woods is a member of several professional societies, including Tau Beta Pi, Phi Kappa Phi, and the IEEE.

Digital Image
Processing

4

FOURTH
EDITION

 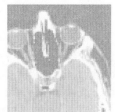 

Introduction

One picture is worth more than ten thousand words.

Anonymous

Preview

Interest in digital image processing methods stems from two principal application areas: improvement of pictorial information for human interpretation, and processing of image data for tasks such as storage, transmission, and extraction of pictorial information. This chapter has several objectives: (1) to define the scope of the field that we call image processing; (2) to give a historical perspective of the origins of this field; (3) to present an overview of the state of the art in image processing by examining some of the principal areas in which it is applied; (4) to discuss briefly the principal approaches used in digital image processing; (5) to give an overview of the components contained in a typical, general-purpose image processing system; and (6) to provide direction to the literature where image processing work is reported. The material in this chapter is extensively illustrated with a range of images that are representative of the images we will be using throughout the book.

Upon completion of this chapter, readers should:

- Understand the concept of a digital image.

- Have a broad overview of the historical underpinnings of the field of digital image processing.

- Understand the definition and scope of digital image processing.

- Know the fundamentals of the electromagnetic spectrum and its relationship to image generation.

- Be aware of the different fields in which digital image processing methods are applied.

- Be familiar with the basic processes involved in image processing.

- Be familiar with the components that make up a general-purpose digital image processing system.

- Be familiar with the scope of the literature where image processing work is reported.

1.1 WHAT IS DIGITAL IMAGE PROCESSING?

An image may be defined as a two-dimensional function, $f(x, y)$, where x and y are *spatial* (plane) coordinates, and the amplitude of f at any pair of coordinates (x, y) is called the *intensity* or *gray level* of the image at that point. When x, y, and the intensity values of f are all finite, discrete quantities, we call the image a *digital image*. The field of *digital image processing* refers to processing digital images by means of a digital computer. Note that a digital image is composed of a finite number of elements, each of which has a particular location and value. These elements are called *picture elements*, *image elements*, *pels*, and *pixels*. *Pixel* is the term used most widely to denote the elements of a digital image. We will consider these definitions in more formal terms in Chapter 2.

Vision is the most advanced of our senses, so it is not surprising that images play the single most important role in human perception. However, unlike humans, who are limited to the visual band of the electromagnetic (EM) spectrum, imaging machines cover almost the entire EM spectrum, ranging from gamma to radio waves. They can operate on images generated by sources that humans are not accustomed to associating with images. These include ultrasound, electron microscopy, and computer-generated images. Thus, digital image processing encompasses a wide and varied field of applications.

There is no general agreement among authors regarding where image processing stops and other related areas, such as *image analysis* and *computer vision*, start. Sometimes, a distinction is made by defining image processing as a discipline in which both the input and output of a process are images. We believe this to be a limiting and somewhat artificial boundary. For example, under this definition, even the trivial task of computing the average intensity of an image (which yields a single number) would not be considered an image processing operation. On the other hand, there are fields such as computer vision whose ultimate goal is to use computers to emulate human vision, including learning and being able to make inferences and take actions based on visual inputs. This area itself is a branch of *artificial intelligence* (AI) whose objective is to emulate human intelligence. The field of AI is in its earliest stages of infancy in terms of development, with progress having been much slower than originally anticipated. The area of image analysis (also called *image understanding*) is in between image processing and computer vision.

There are no clear-cut boundaries in the continuum from image processing at one end to computer vision at the other. However, one useful paradigm is to consider three types of computerized processes in this continuum: low-, mid-, and high-level processes. Low-level processes involve primitive operations such as image preprocessing to reduce noise, contrast enhancement, and image sharpening. A low-level process is characterized by the fact that both its inputs and outputs are images. Mid-level processing of images involves tasks such as segmentation (partitioning an image into regions or objects), description of those objects to reduce them to a form suitable for computer processing, and classification (recognition) of individual objects. A mid-level process is characterized by the fact that its inputs generally are images, but its outputs are attributes extracted from those images (e.g., edges, contours, and the identity of individual objects). Finally, higher-level processing involves "making sense" of an ensemble of recognized objects, as in image analysis, and, at the far end of the continuum, performing the cognitive functions normally associated with human vision.

Based on the preceding comments, we see that a logical place of overlap between image processing and image analysis is the area of recognition of individual regions or objects in an image. Thus, what we call in this book *digital image processing* encompasses processes whose inputs and outputs are images and, in addition, includes processes that extract attributes from images up to, and including, the recognition of individual objects. As an illustration to clarify these concepts, consider the area of automated analysis of text. The processes of acquiring an image of the area containing the text, preprocessing that image, extracting (segmenting) the individual characters, describing the characters in a form suitable for computer processing, and recognizing those individual characters are in the scope of what we call digital image processing in this book. Making sense of the content of the page may be viewed as being in the domain of image analysis and even computer vision, depending on the level of complexity implied by the statement "making sense of." As will become evident shortly, digital image processing, as we have defined it, is used routinely in a broad range of areas of exceptional social and economic value. The concepts developed in the following chapters are the foundation for the methods used in those application areas.

1.2 THE ORIGINS OF DIGITAL IMAGE PROCESSING

One of the earliest applications of digital images was in the newspaper industry, when pictures were first sent by submarine cable between London and New York. Introduction of the Bartlane cable picture transmission system in the early 1920s reduced the time required to transport a picture across the Atlantic from more than a week to less than three hours. Specialized printing equipment coded pictures for cable transmission, then reconstructed them at the receiving end. Figure 1.1 was transmitted in this way and reproduced on a telegraph printer fitted with typefaces simulating a halftone pattern.

Some of the initial problems in improving the visual quality of these early digital pictures were related to the selection of printing procedures and the distribution of

FIGURE 1.1 A digital picture produced in 1921 from a coded tape by a telegraph printer with special typefaces. (McFarlane.) [References in the bibliography at the end of the book are listed in alphabetical order by authors' last names.]

FIGURE 1.2
A digital picture
made in 1922 from
a tape punched
after the signals
had crossed the
Atlantic twice.
(McFarlane.)

intensity levels. The printing method used to obtain Fig. 1.1 was abandoned toward
the end of 1921 in favor of a technique based on photographic reproduction made
from tapes perforated at the telegraph receiving terminal. Figure 1.2 shows an image
obtained using this method. The improvements over Fig. 1.1 are evident, both in
tonal quality and in resolution.

The early Bartlane systems were capable of coding images in five distinct levels of
gray. This capability was increased to 15 levels in 1929. Figure 1.3 is typical of the type
of images that could be obtained using the 15-tone equipment. During this period,
introduction of a system for developing a film plate via light beams that were modulated by the coded picture tape improved the reproduction process considerably.

Although the examples just cited involve digital images, they are not considered
digital image processing results in the context of our definition, because digital computers were not used in their creation. Thus, the history of digital image processing
is intimately tied to the development of the digital computer. In fact, digital images
require so much storage and computational power that progress in the field of digital image processing has been dependent on the development of digital computers
and of supporting technologies that include data storage, display, and transmission.

FIGURE 1.3
Unretouched
cable picture of
Generals Pershing
(right) and Foch,
transmitted in
1929 from
London to New
York by 15-tone
equipment.
(McFarlane.)

The concept of a computer dates back to the invention of the abacus in Asia Minor, more than 5000 years ago. More recently, there have been developments in the past two centuries that are the foundation of what we call a computer today. However, the basis for what we call a *modern* digital computer dates back to only the 1940s, with the introduction by John von Neumann of two key concepts: (1) a memory to hold a stored program and data, and (2) conditional branching. These two ideas are the foundation of a central processing unit (CPU), which is at the heart of computers today. Starting with von Neumann, there were a series of key advances that led to computers powerful enough to be used for digital image processing. Briefly, these advances may be summarized as follows: (1) the invention of the transistor at Bell Laboratories in 1948; (2) the development in the 1950s and 1960s of the high-level programming languages COBOL (Common Business-Oriented Language) and FORTRAN (Formula Translator); (3) the invention of the integrated circuit (IC) at Texas Instruments in 1958; (4) the development of operating systems in the early 1960s; (5) the development of the microprocessor (a single chip consisting of a CPU, memory, and input and output controls) by Intel in the early 1970s; (6) the introduction by IBM of the personal computer in 1981; and (7) progressive miniaturization of components, starting with large-scale integration (LI) in the late 1970s, then very-large-scale integration (VLSI) in the 1980s, to the present use of ultra-large-scale integration (ULSI) and experimental nonotechnologies. Concurrent with these advances were developments in the areas of mass storage and display systems, both of which are fundamental requirements for digital image processing.

The first computers powerful enough to carry out meaningful image processing tasks appeared in the early 1960s. The birth of what we call digital image processing today can be traced to the availability of those machines, and to the onset of the space program during that period. It took the combination of those two developments to bring into focus the potential of digital image processing for solving problems of practical significance. Work on using computer techniques for improving images from a space probe began at the Jet Propulsion Laboratory (Pasadena, California) in 1964, when pictures of the moon transmitted by *Ranger 7* were processed by a computer to correct various types of image distortion inherent in the on-board television camera. Figure 1.4 shows the first image of the moon taken by *Ranger 7* on July 31, 1964 at 9:09 A.M. Eastern Daylight Time (EDT), about 17 minutes before impacting the lunar surface (the markers, called *reseau marks*, are used for geometric corrections, as discussed in Chapter 2). This also is the first image of the moon taken by a U.S. spacecraft. The imaging lessons learned with *Ranger 7* served as the basis for improved methods used to enhance and restore images from the Surveyor missions to the moon, the *Mariner* series of flyby missions to Mars, the *Apollo* manned flights to the moon, and others.

In parallel with space applications, digital image processing techniques began in the late 1960s and early 1970s to be used in medical imaging, remote Earth resources observations, and astronomy. The invention in the early 1970s of *computerized axial tomography* (CAT), also called *computerized tomography* (CT) for short, is one of the most important events in the application of image processing in medical diagnosis. Computerized axial tomography is a process in which a ring of detectors

FIGURE 1.4
The first picture
of the moon by
a U.S. spacecraft.
Ranger 7 took
this image on
July 31, 1964 at
9:09 A.M. EDT,
about 17 minutes
before impacting
the lunar surface.
(Courtesy of
NASA.)

encircles an object (or patient) and an X-ray source, concentric with the detector ring, rotates about the object. The X-rays pass through the object and are collected at the opposite end by the corresponding detectors in the ring. This procedure is repeated the source rotates. Tomography consists of algorithms that use the sensed data to construct an image that represents a "slice" through the object. Motion of the object in a direction perpendicular to the ring of detectors produces a set of such slices, which constitute a three-dimensional (3-D) rendition of the inside of the object. Tomography was invented independently by Sir Godfrey N. Hounsfield and Professor Allan M. Cormack, who shared the 1979 Nobel Prize in Medicine for their invention. It is interesting to note that X-rays were discovered in 1895 by Wilhelm Conrad Roentgen, for which he received the 1901 Nobel Prize for Physics. These two inventions, nearly 100 years apart, led to some of the most important applications of image processing today.

From the 1960s until the present, the field of image processing has grown vigorously. In addition to applications in medicine and the space program, digital image processing techniques are now used in a broad range of applications. Computer procedures are used to enhance the contrast or code the intensity levels into color for easier interpretation of X-rays and other images used in industry, medicine, and the biological sciences. Geographers use the same or similar techniques to study pollution patterns from aerial and satellite imagery. Image enhancement and restoration procedures are used to process degraded images of unrecoverable objects, or experimental results too expensive to duplicate. In archeology, image processing methods have successfully restored blurred pictures that were the only available records of rare artifacts lost or damaged after being photographed. In physics and related fields, computer techniques routinely enhance images of experiments in areas such as high-energy plasmas and electron microscopy. Similarly successful applications of image processing concepts can be found in astronomy, biology, nuclear medicine, law enforcement, defense, and industry.

These examples illustrate processing results intended for human interpretation. The second major area of application of digital image processing techniques mentioned at the beginning of this chapter is in solving problems dealing with machine perception. In this case, interest is on procedures for extracting information from an image, in a form suitable for computer processing. Often, this information bears little resemblance to visual features that humans use in interpreting the content of an image. Examples of the type of information used in machine perception are statistical moments, Fourier transform coefficients, and multidimensional distance measures. Typical problems in machine perception that routinely utilize image processing techniques are automatic character recognition, industrial machine vision for product assembly and inspection, military recognizance, automatic processing of fingerprints, screening of X-rays and blood samples, and machine processing of aerial and satellite imagery for weather prediction and environmental assessment. The continuing decline in the ratio of computer price to performance, and the expansion of networking and communication bandwidth via the internet, have created unprecedented opportunities for continued growth of digital image processing. Some of these application areas will be illustrated in the following section.

1.3 EXAMPLES OF FIELDS THAT USE DIGITAL IMAGE PROCESSING ◼

Today, there is almost no area of technical endeavor that is not impacted in some way by digital image processing. We can cover only a few of these applications in the context and space of the current discussion. However, limited as it is, the material presented in this section will leave no doubt in your mind regarding the breadth and importance of digital image processing. We show in this section numerous areas of application, each of which routinely utilizes the digital image processing techniques developed in the following chapters. Many of the images shown in this section are used later in one or more of the examples given in the book. Most images shown are digital images.

The areas of application of digital image processing are so varied that some form of organization is desirable in attempting to capture the breadth of this field. One of the simplest ways to develop a basic understanding of the extent of image processing applications is to categorize images according to their source (e.g., X-ray, visual, infrared, and so on). The principal energy source for images in use today is the electromagnetic energy spectrum. Other important sources of energy include acoustic, ultrasonic, and electronic (in the form of electron beams used in electron microscopy). Synthetic images, used for modeling and visualization, are generated by computer. In this section we will discuss briefly how images are generated in these various categories, and the areas in which they are applied. Methods for converting images into digital form will be discussed in the next chapter.

Images based on radiation from the EM spectrum are the most familiar, especially images in the X-ray and visual bands of the spectrum. Electromagnetic waves can be conceptualized as propagating sinusoidal waves of varying wavelengths, or they can be thought of as a stream of massless particles, each traveling in a wavelike pattern and moving at the speed of light. Each massless particle contains a certain amount (or bundle) of energy. Each bundle of energy is called a *photon*. If spectral

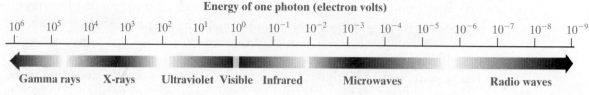

Energy of one photon (electron volts)

FIGURE 1.5 The electromagnetic spectrum arranged according to energy per photon.

bands are grouped according to energy per photon, we obtain the spectrum shown in Fig. 1.5, ranging from gamma rays (highest energy) at one end to radio waves (lowest energy) at the other. The bands are shown shaded to convey the fact that bands of the EM spectrum are not distinct, but rather transition smoothly from one to the other.

GAMMA-RAY IMAGING

Major uses of imaging based on gamma rays include nuclear medicine and astronomical observations. In nuclear medicine, the approach is to inject a patient with a radioactive isotope that emits gamma rays as it decays. Images are produced from the emissions collected by gamma-ray detectors. Figure 1.6(a) shows an image of a complete bone scan obtained by using gamma-ray imaging. Images of this sort are used to locate sites of bone pathology, such as infections or tumors. Figure 1.6(b) shows another major modality of nuclear imaging called *positron emission tomography* (PET). The principle is the same as with X-ray tomography, mentioned briefly in Section 1.2. However, instead of using an external source of X-ray energy, the patient is given a radioactive isotope that emits positrons as it decays. When a positron meets an electron, both are annihilated and two gamma rays are given off. These are detected and a tomographic image is created using the basic principles of tomography. The image shown in Fig. 1.6(b) is one sample of a sequence that constitutes a 3-D rendition of the patient. This image shows a tumor in the brain and another in the lung, easily visible as small white masses.

A star in the constellation of Cygnus exploded about 15,000 years ago, generating a superheated, stationary gas cloud (known as the Cygnus Loop) that glows in a spectacular array of colors. Figure 1.6(c) shows an image of the Cygnus Loop in the gamma-ray band. Unlike the two examples in Figs. 1.6(a) and (b), this image was obtained using the natural radiation of the object being imaged. Finally, Fig. 1.6(d) shows an image of gamma radiation from a valve in a nuclear reactor. An area of strong radiation is seen in the lower left side of the image.

X-RAY IMAGING

X-rays are among the oldest sources of EM radiation used for imaging. The best known use of X-rays is medical diagnostics, but they are also used extensively in industry and other areas, such as astronomy. X-rays for medical and industrial imaging are generated using an X-ray tube, which is a vacuum tube with a cathode and anode. The cathode is heated, causing free electrons to be released. These electrons flow at high speed to the positively charged anode. When the electrons strike a

a b
c d

FIGURE 1.6
Examples of
gamma-ray
imaging.
(a) Bone scan.
(b) PET image.
(c) Cygnus Loop.
(d) Gamma radia-
tion (bright spot)
from a reactor
valve.
(Images
courtesy of
(a) G.E. Medical
Systems; (b) Dr.
Michael E. Casey,
CTI PET Systems;
(c) NASA;
(d) Professors
Zhong He and
David K. Wehe,
University of
Michigan.)

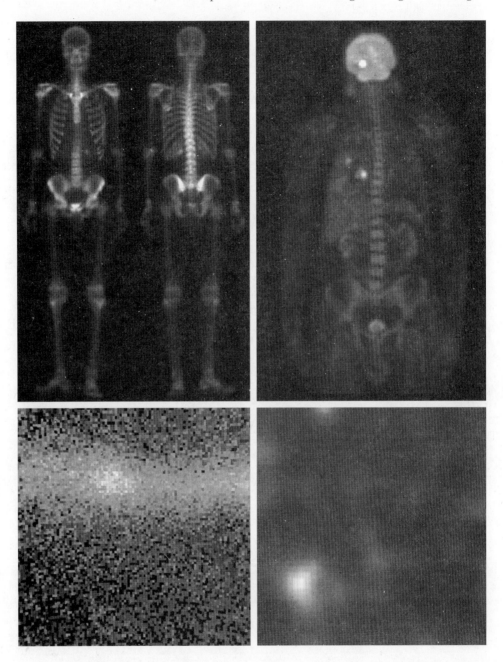

nucleus, energy is released in the form of X-ray radiation. The energy (penetrat-
ing power) of X-rays is controlled by a voltage applied across the anode, and by a
current applied to the filament in the cathode. Figure 1.7(a) shows a familiar chest
X-ray generated simply by placing the patient between an X-ray source and a film
sensitive to X-ray energy. The intensity of the X-rays is modified by absorption as
they pass through the patient, and the resulting energy falling on the film develops it,
much in the same way that light develops photographic film. In digital radiography,

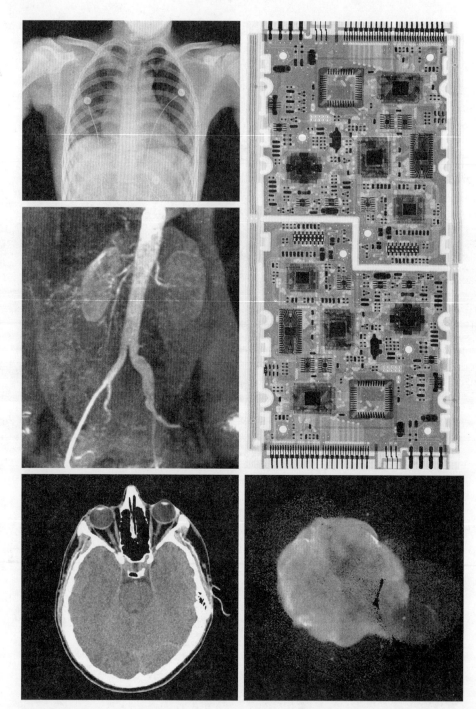

a	d
c	
b	e

FIGURE 1.7
Examples of
X-ray imaging.
(a) Chest X-ray.
(b) Aortic
angiogram.
(c) Head CT.
(d) Circuit boards.
(e) Cygnus Loop.
(Images courtesy
of (a) and (c) Dr.
David R. Pickens,
Dept. of
Radiology &
Radiological
Sciences,
Vanderbilt
University
Medical Center;
(b) Dr. Thomas
R. Gest, Division
of Anatomical
Sciences, Univ. of
Michigan Medical
School;
(d) Mr. Joseph
E. Pascente, Lixi,
Inc.; and
(e) NASA.)

digital images are obtained by one of two methods: (1) by digitizing X-ray films; or; (2) by having the X-rays that pass through the patient fall directly onto devices (such as a phosphor screen) that convert X-rays to light. The light signal in turn is captured by a light-sensitive digitizing system. We will discuss digitization in more detail in Chapters 2 and 4.

Angiography is another major application in an area called contrast enhancement radiography. This procedure is used to obtain images of blood vessels, called *angiograms*. A catheter (a small, flexible, hollow tube) is inserted, for example, into an artery or vein in the groin. The catheter is threaded into the blood vessel and guided to the area to be studied. When the catheter reaches the site under investigation, an X-ray contrast medium is injected through the tube. This enhances the contrast of the blood vessels and enables a radiologist to see any irregularities or blockages. Figure 1.7(b) shows an example of an aortic angiogram. The catheter can be seen being inserted into the large blood vessel on the lower left of the picture. Note the high contrast of the large vessel as the contrast medium flows up in the direction of the kidneys, which are also visible in the image. As we will discuss further in Chapter 2, angiography is a major area of digital image processing, where image subtraction is used to further enhance the blood vessels being studied.

Another important use of X-rays in medical imaging is computerized axial tomography (CAT). Due to their resolution and 3-D capabilities, CAT scans revolutionized medicine from the moment they first became available in the early 1970s. As noted in Section 1.2, each CAT image is a "slice" taken perpendicularly through the patient. Numerous slices are generated as the patient is moved in a longitudinal direction. The ensemble of such images constitutes a 3-D rendition of the inside of the body, with the longitudinal resolution being proportional to the number of slice images taken. Figure 1.7(c) shows a typical CAT slice image of a human head.

Techniques similar to the ones just discussed, but generally involving higher energy X-rays, are applicable in industrial processes. Figure 1.7(d) shows an X-ray image of an electronic circuit board. Such images, representative of literally hundreds of industrial applications of X-rays, are used to examine circuit boards for flaws in manufacturing, such as missing components or broken traces. Industrial CAT scans are useful when the parts can be penetrated by X-rays, such as in plastic assemblies, and even large bodies, such as solid-propellant rocket motors. Figure 1.7(e) shows an example of X-ray imaging in astronomy. This image is the Cygnus Loop of Fig. 1.6(c), but imaged in the X-ray band.

IMAGING IN THE ULTRAVIOLET BAND

Applications of ultraviolet "light" are varied. They include lithography, industrial inspection, microscopy, lasers, biological imaging, and astronomical observations. We illustrate imaging in this band with examples from microscopy and astronomy.

Ultraviolet light is used in fluorescence microscopy, one of the fastest growing areas of microscopy. Fluorescence is a phenomenon discovered in the middle of the nineteenth century, when it was first observed that the mineral fluorspar fluoresces when ultraviolet light is directed upon it. The ultraviolet light itself is not visible, but when a photon of ultraviolet radiation collides with an electron in an atom of a fluorescent material, it elevates the electron to a higher energy level. Subsequently, the excited electron relaxes to a lower level and emits light in the form of a lower-energy photon in the visible (red) light region. Important tasks performed with a fluorescence microscope are to use an excitation light to irradiate a prepared specimen, and then to separate the much weaker radiating fluorescent light from the brighter

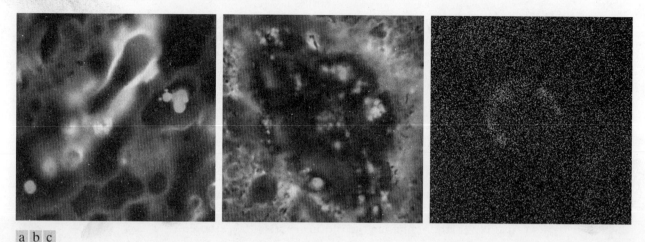

FIGURE 1.8 Examples of ultraviolet imaging. (a) Normal corn. (b) Corn infected by smut. (c) Cygnus Loop. (Images (a) and (b) courtesy of Dr. Michael W. Davidson, Florida State University, (c) NASA.)

excitation light. Thus, only the emission light reaches the eye or other detector. The resulting fluorescing areas shine against a dark background with sufficient contrast to permit detection. The darker the background of the nonfluorescing material, the more efficient the instrument.

Fluorescence microscopy is an excellent method for studying materials that can be made to fluoresce, either in their natural form (primary fluorescence) or when treated with chemicals capable of fluorescing (secondary fluorescence). Figures 1.8(a) and (b) show results typical of the capability of fluorescence microscopy. Figure 1.8(a) shows a fluorescence microscope image of normal corn, and Fig. 1.8(b) shows corn infected by "smut," a disease of cereals, corn, grasses, onions, and sorghum that can be caused by any one of more than 700 species of parasitic fungi. Corn smut is particularly harmful because corn is one of the principal food sources in the world. As another illustration, Fig. 1.8(c) shows the Cygnus Loop imaged in the high-energy region of the ultraviolet band.

IMAGING IN THE VISIBLE AND INFRARED BANDS

Considering that the visual band of the electromagnetic spectrum is the most familiar in all our activities, it is not surprising that imaging in this band outweighs by far all the others in terms of breadth of application. The infrared band often is used in conjunction with visual imaging, so we have grouped the visible and infrared bands in this section for the purpose of illustration. We consider in the following discussion applications in light microscopy, astronomy, remote sensing, industry, and law enforcement.

Figure 1.9 shows several examples of images obtained with a light microscope. The examples range from pharmaceuticals and microinspection to materials characterization. Even in microscopy alone, the application areas are too numerous to detail here. It is not difficult to conceptualize the types of processes one might apply to these images, ranging from enhancement to measurements.

a b c
d e f

FIGURE 1.9
Examples of light
microscopy images.
(a) Taxol (anticancer
agent), magnified
250×.
(b) Cholesterol—
40×.
(c) Microprocessor—60×.
(d) Nickel oxide
thin film—600×.
(e) Surface of audio
CD—1750×.
(f) Organic superconductor— 450×.
(Images courtesy of
Dr. Michael W.
Davidson, Florida
State University.)

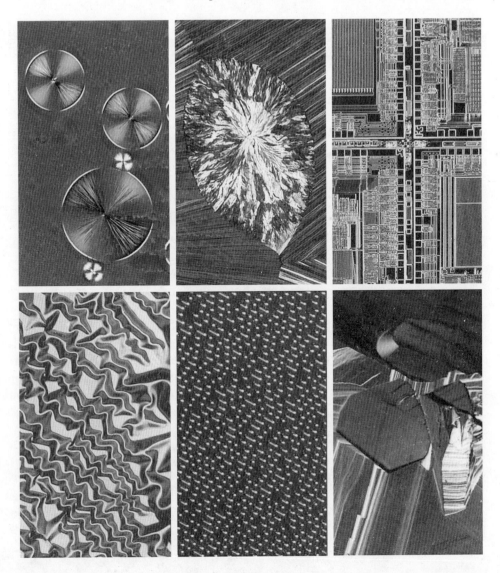

Another major area of visual processing is remote sensing, which usually includes several bands in the visual and infrared regions of the spectrum. Table 1.1 shows the so-called *thematic bands* in NASA's LANDSAT satellites. The primary function of LANDSAT is to obtain and transmit images of the Earth from space, for purposes of monitoring environmental conditions on the planet. The bands are expressed in terms of wavelength, with $1\,\mu$m being equal to 10^{-6} m (we will discuss the wavelength regions of the electromagnetic spectrum in more detail in Chapter 2). Note the characteristics and uses of each band in Table 1.1.

In order to develop a basic appreciation for the power of this type of multispectral imaging, consider Fig. 1.10, which shows one image for each of the spectral bands in Table 1.1. The area imaged is Washington D.C., which includes features such as buildings, roads, vegetation, and a major river (the Potomac) going though the city.

TABLE 1.1
Thematic bands of NASA's LANDSAT satellite.

Band No.	Name	Wavelength (μm)	Characteristics and Uses
1	Visible blue	0.45–0.52	Maximum water penetration
2	Visible green	0.53–0.61	Measures plant vigor
3	Visible red	0.63–0.69	Vegetation discrimination
4	Near infrared	0.78–0.90	Biomass and shoreline mapping
5	Middle infrared	1.55–1.75	Moisture content: soil/vegetation
6	Thermal infrared	10.4–12.5	Soil moisture; thermal mapping
7	Short-wave infrared	2.09–2.35	Mineral mapping

Images of population centers are used over time to assess population growth and shift patterns, pollution, and other factors affecting the environment. The differences between visual and infrared image features are quite noticeable in these images. Observe, for example, how well defined the river is from its surroundings in Bands 4 and 5.

Weather observation and prediction also are major applications of multispectral imaging from satellites. For example, Fig. 1.11 is an image of Hurricane Katrina, one of the most devastating storms in recent memory in the Western Hemisphere. This image was taken by a National Oceanographic and Atmospheric Administration (NOAA) satellite using sensors in the visible and infrared bands. The eye of the hurricane is clearly visible in this image.

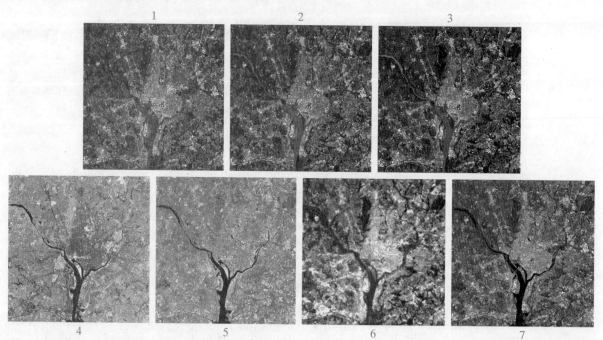

FIGURE 1.10 LANDSAT satellite images of the Washington, D.C. area. The numbers refer to the thematic bands in Table 1.1. (Images courtesy of NASA.)

FIGURE 1.11
Satellite image of Hurricane Katrina taken on August 29, 2005. (Courtesy of NOAA.)

Figures 1.12 and 1.13 show an application of infrared imaging. These images are part of the Nighttime Lights of the World data set, which provides a global inventory of human settlements. The images were generated by an infrared imaging system mounted on a NOAA/DMSP (Defense Meteorological Satellite Program) satellite. The infrared system operates in the band 10.0 to 13.4 μm, and has the unique capability to observe faint sources of visible, near infrared emissions present on the Earth's surface, including cities, towns, villages, gas flares, and fires. Even without formal training in image processing, it is not difficult to imagine writing a computer program that would use these images to estimate the relative percent of total electrical energy used by various regions of the world.

A major area of imaging in the visible spectrum is in automated visual inspection of manufactured goods. Figure 1.14 shows some examples. Figure 1.14(a) is a controller board for a CD-ROM drive. A typical image processing task with products such as this is to inspect them for missing parts (the black square on the top, right quadrant of the image is an example of a missing component).

Figure 1.14(b) is an imaged pill container. The objective here is to have a machine look for missing, incomplete, or deformed pills. Figure 1.14(c) shows an application in which image processing is used to look for bottles that are not filled up to an acceptable level. Figure 1.14(d) shows a clear plastic part with an unacceptable number of air pockets in it. Detecting anomalies like these is a major theme of industrial inspection that includes other products, such as wood and cloth. Figure 1.14(e) shows a batch of cereal during inspection for color and the presence of anomalies such as burned flakes. Finally, Fig. 1.14(f) shows an image of an intraocular implant (replacement lens for the human eye). A "structured light" illumination technique was used to highlight deformations toward the center of the lens, and other imperfections. For example, the markings at 1 o'clock and 5 o'clock are tweezer damage. Most of the other small speckle detail is debris. The objective in this type of inspection is to find damaged or incorrectly manufactured implants automatically, prior to packaging.

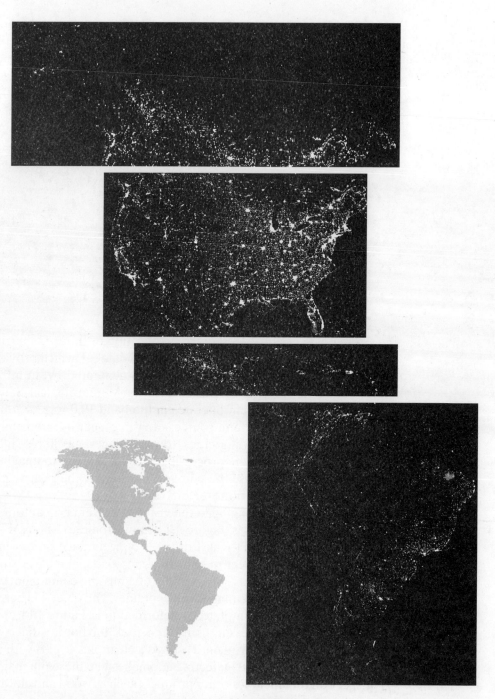

Figure 1.15 illustrates some additional examples of image processing in the visible spectrum. Figure 1.15(a) shows a thumb print. Images of fingerprints are routinely processed by computer, either to enhance them or to find features that aid in the automated search of a database for potential matches. Figure 1.15(b) shows an image of paper currency. Applications of digital image processing in this area

FIGURE 1.13
Infrared
satellite images
of the remaining
populated parts
of the world. The
small shaded map
is provided for
reference.
(Courtesy of
NOAA.)

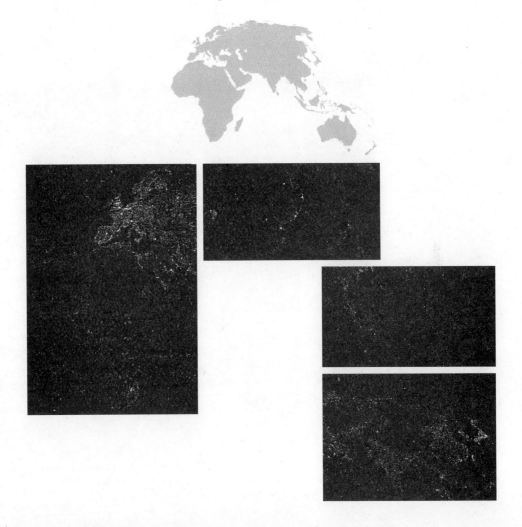

include automated counting and, in law enforcement, the reading of the serial number for the purpose of tracking and identifying currency bills. The two vehicle images shown in Figs. 1.15(c) and (d) are examples of automated license plate reading. The light rectangles indicate the area in which the imaging system detected the plate. The black rectangles show the results of automatically reading the plate content by the system. License plate and other applications of character recognition are used extensively for traffic monitoring and surveillance.

IMAGING IN THE MICROWAVE BAND

The principal application of imaging in the microwave band is radar. The unique feature of imaging radar is its ability to collect data over virtually any region at any time, regardless of weather or ambient lighting conditions. Some radar waves can penetrate clouds, and under certain conditions, can also see through vegetation, ice, and dry sand. In many cases, radar is the only way to explore inaccessible regions of the Earth's surface. An imaging radar works like a flash camera in that it provides its own illumination (microwave pulses) to illuminate an area on the ground and

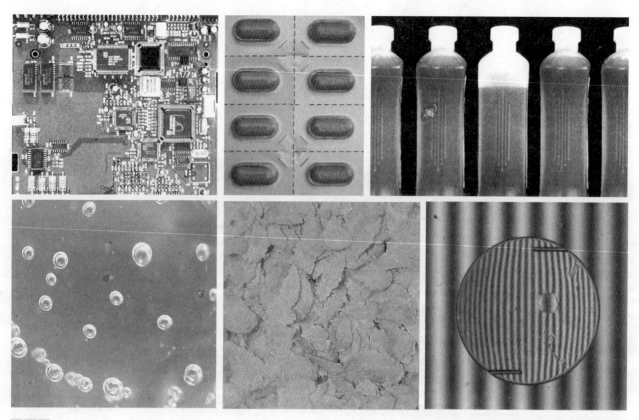

a b c
d e f

FIGURE 1.14 Some examples of manufactured goods checked using digital image processing. (a) Circuit board controller. (b) Packaged pills. (c) Bottles. (d) Air bubbles in a clear plastic product. (e) Cereal. (f) Image of intraocular implant. (Figure (f) courtesy of Mr. Pete Sites, Perceptics Corporation.)

take a snapshot image. Instead of a camera lens, a radar uses an antenna and digital computer processing to record its images. In a radar image, one can see only the microwave energy that was reflected back toward the radar antenna.

Figure 1.16 shows a spaceborne radar image covering a rugged mountainous area of southeast Tibet, about 90 km east of the city of Lhasa. In the lower right corner is a wide valley of the Lhasa River, which is populated by Tibetan farmers and yak herders, and includes the village of Menba. Mountains in this area reach about 5800 m (19,000 ft) above sea level, while the valley floors lie about 4300 m (14,000 ft) above sea level. Note the clarity and detail of the image, unencumbered by clouds or other atmospheric conditions that normally interfere with images in the visual band.

IMAGING IN THE RADIO BAND

As in the case of imaging at the other end of the spectrum (gamma rays), the major applications of imaging in the radio band are in medicine and astronomy. In medicine, radio waves are used in magnetic resonance imaging (MRI). This technique places a

a b
c
d

FIGURE 1.15
Some additional examples of imaging in the visible spectrum. (a) Thumb print. (b) Paper currency. (c) and (d) Automated license plate reading. (Figure (a) courtesy of the National Institute of Standards and Technology. Figures (c) and (d) courtesy of Dr. Juan Herrera, Perceptics Corporation.)

patient in a powerful magnet and passes radio waves through the individual's body in short pulses. Each pulse causes a responding pulse of radio waves to be emitted by the patient's tissues. The location from which these signals originate and their strength are determined by a computer, which produces a two-dimensional image of a section of the patient. MRI can produce images in any plane. Figure 1.17 shows MRI images of a human knee and spine.

The rightmost image in Fig. 1.18 is an image of the Crab Pulsar in the radio band. Also shown for an interesting comparison are images of the same region, but taken in most of the bands discussed earlier. Observe that each image gives a totally different "view" of the pulsar.

OTHER IMAGING MODALITIES

Although imaging in the electromagnetic spectrum is dominant by far, there are a number of other imaging modalities that are also important. Specifically, we discuss

FIGURE 1.16
Spaceborne radar
image of
mountainous
region in
southeast Tibet.
(Courtesy of
NASA.)

in this section acoustic imaging, electron microscopy, and synthetic (computer-generated) imaging.

Imaging using "sound" finds application in geological exploration, industry, and medicine. Geological applications use sound in the low end of the sound spectrum (hundreds of Hz) while imaging in other areas use ultrasound (millions of Hz). The most important commercial applications of image processing in geology are in mineral and oil exploration. For image acquisition over land, one of the main approaches is to use a large truck and a large flat steel plate. The plate is pressed on the ground by

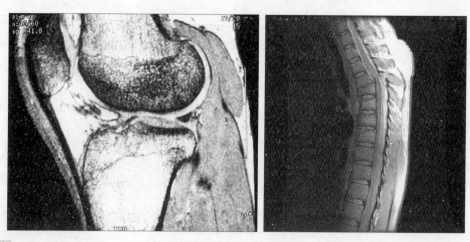

a b

FIGURE 1.17 MRI images of a human (a) knee, and (b) spine. (Figure (a) courtesy of Dr. Thomas R. Gest, Division of Anatomical Sciences, University of Michigan Medical School, and (b) courtesy of Dr. David R. Pickens, Department of Radiology and Radiological Sciences, Vanderbilt University Medical Center.)

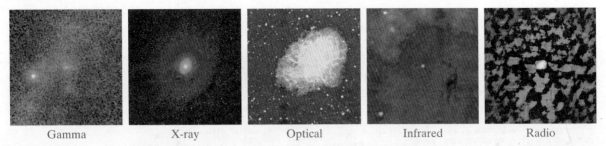

| Gamma | X-ray | Optical | Infrared | Radio |

FIGURE 1.18 Images of the Crab Pulsar (in the center of each image) covering the electromagnetic spectrum. (Courtesy of NASA.)

the truck, and the truck is vibrated through a frequency spectrum up to 100 Hz. The strength and speed of the returning sound waves are determined by the composition of the Earth below the surface. These are analyzed by computer, and images are generated from the resulting analysis.

For marine image acquisition, the energy source consists usually of two air guns towed behind a ship. Returning sound waves are detected by hydrophones placed in cables that are either towed behind the ship, laid on the bottom of the ocean, or hung from buoys (vertical cables). The two air guns are alternately pressurized to ~2000 psi and then set off. The constant motion of the ship provides a transversal direction of motion that, together with the returning sound waves, is used to generate a 3-D map of the composition of the Earth below the bottom of the ocean.

Figure 1.19 shows a cross-sectional image of a well-known 3-D model against which the performance of seismic imaging algorithms is tested. The arrow points to a hydrocarbon (oil and/or gas) trap. This target is brighter than the surrounding layers because the change in density in the target region is larger. Seismic interpreters look for these "bright spots" to find oil and gas. The layers above also are bright, but their brightness does not vary as strongly across the layers. Many seismic reconstruction algorithms have difficulty imaging this target because of the faults above it.

Although ultrasound imaging is used routinely in manufacturing, the best known applications of this technique are in medicine, especially in obstetrics, where fetuses are imaged to determine the health of their development. A byproduct of this

FIGURE 1.19 Cross-sectional image of a seismic model. The arrow points to a hydrocarbon (oil and/or gas) trap. (Courtesy of Dr. Curtis Ober, Sandia National Laboratories.)

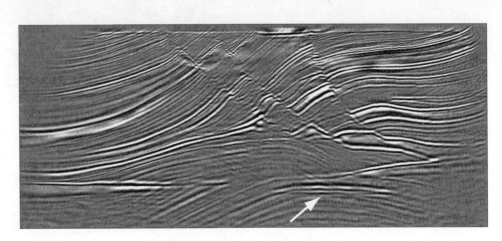

examination is determining the sex of the baby. Ultrasound images are generated using the following basic procedure:

1. The ultrasound system (a computer, ultrasound probe consisting of a source, a receiver, and a display) transmits high-frequency (1 to 5 MHz) sound pulses into the body.

2. The sound waves travel into the body and hit a boundary between tissues (e.g., between fluid and soft tissue, soft tissue and bone). Some of the sound waves are reflected back to the probe, while some travel on further until they reach another boundary and are reflected.

3. The reflected waves are picked up by the probe and relayed to the computer.

4. The machine calculates the distance from the probe to the tissue or organ boundaries using the speed of sound in tissue (1540 m/s) and the time of each echo's return.

5. The system displays the distances and intensities of the echoes on the screen, forming a two-dimensional image.

In a typical ultrasound image, millions of pulses and echoes are sent and received each second. The probe can be moved along the surface of the body and angled to obtain various views. Figure 1.20 shows several examples of medical uses of ultrasound.

We continue the discussion on imaging modalities with some examples of electron microscopy. Electron microscopes function as their optical counterparts, except

a b
c d

FIGURE 1.20
Examples of ultrasound imaging. (a) A fetus. (b) Another view of the fetus. (c) Thyroids. (d) Muscle layers showing lesion. (Courtesy of Siemens Medical Systems, Inc., Ultrasound Group.)

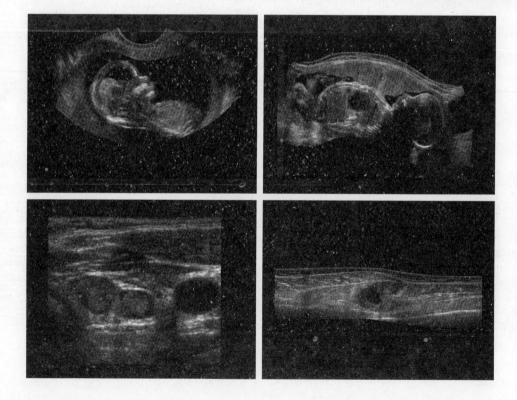

that they use a focused beam of electrons instead of light to image a specimen. The operation of electron microscopes involves the following basic steps: A stream of electrons is produced by an electron source and accelerated toward the specimen using a positive electrical potential. This stream is confined and focused using metal apertures and magnetic lenses into a thin, monochromatic beam. This beam is focused onto the sample using a magnetic lens. Interactions occur inside the irradiated sample, affecting the electron beam. These interactions and effects are detected and transformed into an image, much in the same way that light is reflected from, or absorbed by, objects in a scene. These basic steps are carried out in all electron microscopes.

A *transmission electron microscope* (TEM) works much like a slide projector. A projector transmits a beam of light through a slide; as the light passes through the slide, it is modulated by the contents of the slide. This transmitted beam is then projected onto the viewing screen, forming an enlarged image of the slide. TEMs work in the same way, except that they shine a beam of electrons through a specimen (analogous to the slide). The fraction of the beam transmitted through the specimen is projected onto a phosphor screen. The interaction of the electrons with the phosphor produces light and, therefore, a viewable image. A *scanning electron microscope* (SEM), on the other hand, actually scans the electron beam and records the interaction of beam and sample at each location. This produces one dot on a phosphor screen. A complete image is formed by a raster scan of the beam through the sample, much like a TV camera. The electrons interact with a phosphor screen and produce light. SEMs are suitable for "bulky" samples, while TEMs require very thin samples.

Electron microscopes are capable of very high magnification. While light microscopy is limited to magnifications on the order of $1000\times$, electron microscopes can achieve magnification of $10,000 \times$ or more. Figure 1.21 shows two SEM images of specimen failures due to thermal overload.

We conclude the discussion of imaging modalities by looking briefly at images that are not obtained from physical objects. Instead, they are generated by computer. Fractals are striking examples of computer-generated images. Basically, a fractal is nothing more than an iterative reproduction of a basic pattern according to some mathematical rules. For instance, tiling is one of the simplest ways to generate a fractal image. A square can be subdivided into four square subregions, each of which can be further subdivided into four smaller square regions, and so on. Depending on the complexity of the rules for filling each subsquare, some beautiful tile images can be generated using this method. Of course, the geometry can be arbitrary. For instance, the fractal image could be grown radially out of a center point. Figure 1.22(a) shows a fractal grown in this way. Figure 1.22(b) shows another fractal (a "moonscape") that provides an interesting analogy to the images of space used as illustrations in some of the preceding sections.

A more structured approach to image generation by computer lies in 3-D modeling. This is an area that provides an important intersection between image processing and computer graphics, and is the basis for many 3-D visualization systems (e.g., flight simulators). Figures 1.22(c) and (d) show examples of computer-generated images. Because the original object is created in 3-D, images can be generated in any

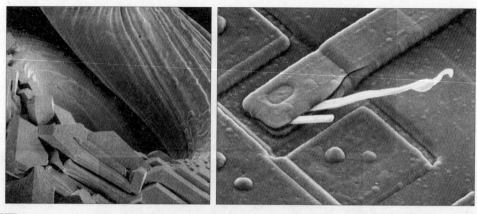

a b

FIGURE 1.21 (a) $250\times$ SEM image of a tungsten filament following thermal failure (note the shattered pieces on the lower left). (b) $2500\times$ SEM image of a damaged integrated circuit. The white fibers are oxides resulting from thermal destruction. (Figure (a) courtesy of Mr. Michael Shaffer, Department of Geological Sciences, University of Oregon, Eugene; (b) courtesy of Dr. J. M. Hudak, McMaster University, Hamilton, Ontario, Canada.)

perspective from plane projections of the 3-D volume. Images of this type can be used for medical training and for a host of other applications, such as criminal forensics and special effects.

a b
c d

FIGURE 1.22
(a) and (b) Fractal images.
(c) and (d) Images generated from 3-D computer models of the objects shown. (Figures (a) and (b) courtesy of Ms. Melissa D. Binde, Swarthmore College; (c) and (d) courtesy of NASA.)

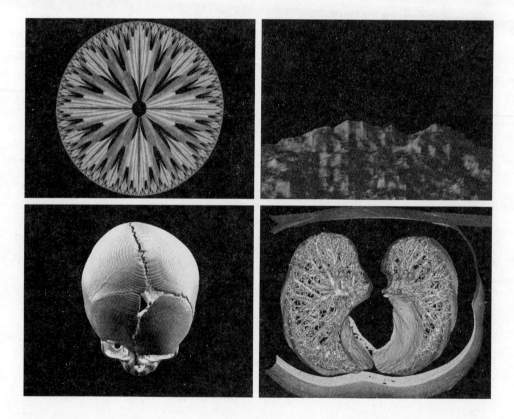

1.4 FUNDAMENTAL STEPS IN DIGITAL IMAGE PROCESSING ▪▪▪▪▪

It is helpful to divide the material covered in the following chapters into the two broad categories defined in Section 1.1: methods whose input and output are images, and methods whose inputs may be images, but whose outputs are attributes extracted from those images. This organization is summarized in Fig. 1.23. The diagram does not imply that every process is applied to an image. Rather, the intention is to convey an idea of all the methodologies that can be applied to images for different purposes, and possibly with different objectives. The discussion in this section may be viewed as a brief overview of the material in the remainder of the book.

Image acquisition is the first process in Fig. 1.23. The discussion in Section 1.3 gave some hints regarding the origin of digital images. This topic will be considered in much more detail in Chapter 2, where we also introduce a number of basic digital image concepts that are used throughout the book. Acquisition could be as simple as being given an image that is already in digital form. Generally, the image acquisition stage involves preprocessing, such as scaling.

Image enhancement is the process of manipulating an image so the result is more suitable than the original for a specific application. The word *specific* is important here, because it establishes at the outset that enhancement techniques are problem oriented. Thus, for example, a method that is quite useful for enhancing X-ray images may not be the best approach for enhancing satellite images taken in the infrared band of the electromagnetic spectrum.

There is no general "theory" of image enhancement. When an image is processed for visual interpretation, the viewer is the ultimate judge of how well a particular

FIGURE 1.23
Fundamental steps in digital image processing. The chapter(s) indicated in the boxes is where the material described in the box is discussed.

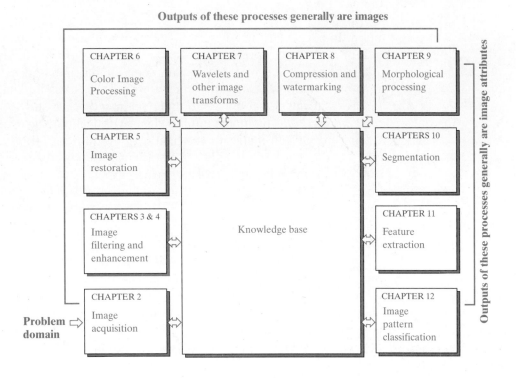

Outputs of these processes generally are images

| CHAPTER 6 Color Image Processing | CHAPTER 7 Wavelets and other image transforms | CHAPTER 8 Compression and watermarking | CHAPTER 9 Morphological processing |

CHAPTER 5 Image restoration

CHAPTERS 10 Segmentation

CHAPTERS 3 & 4 Image filtering and enhancement

Knowledge base

CHAPTER 11 Feature extraction

Problem domain ⇨

CHAPTER 2 Image acquisition

CHAPTER 12 Image pattern classification

Outputs of these processes generally are image attributes

method works. Enhancement techniques are so varied, and use so many different image processing approaches, that it is difficult to assemble a meaningful body of techniques suitable for enhancement in one chapter without extensive background development. For this reason, and also because beginners in the field of image processing generally find enhancement applications visually appealing, interesting, and relatively simple to understand, we will use image enhancement as examples when introducing new concepts in parts of Chapter 2 and in Chapters 3 and 4. The material in the latter two chapters span many of the methods used traditionally for image enhancement. Therefore, using examples from image enhancement to introduce new image processing methods developed in these early chapters not only saves having an extra chapter in the book dealing with image enhancement but, more importantly, is an effective approach for introducing newcomers to the details of processing techniques early in the book. However, as you will see in progressing through the rest of the book, the material developed in Chapters 3 and 4 is applicable to a much broader class of problems than just image enhancement.

Image restoration is an area that also deals with improving the appearance of an image. However, unlike enhancement, which is subjective, image restoration is objective, in the sense that restoration techniques tend to be based on mathematical or probabilistic models of image degradation. Enhancement, on the other hand, is based on human subjective preferences regarding what constitutes a "good" enhancement result.

Color image processing is an area that has been gaining in importance because of the significant increase in the use of digital images over the internet. Chapter 6 covers a number of fundamental concepts in color models and basic color processing in a digital domain. Color is used also as the basis for extracting features of interest in an image.

Wavelets are the foundation for representing images in various degrees of resolution. In particular, this material is used in the book for image data compression and for pyramidal representation, in which images are subdivided successively into smaller regions. The material in Chapters 4 and 5 is based mostly on the Fourier transform. In addition to wavelets, we will also discuss in Chapter 7 a number of other transforms that are used routinely in image processing.

Compression, as the name implies, deals with techniques for reducing the storage required to save an image, or the bandwidth required to transmit it. Although storage technology has improved significantly over the past decade, the same cannot be said for transmission capacity. This is true particularly in uses of the internet, which are characterized by significant pictorial content. Image compression is familiar (perhaps inadvertently) to most users of computers in the form of image file extensions, such as the jpg file extension used in the JPEG (Joint Photographic Experts Group) image compression standard.

Morphological processing deals with tools for extracting image components that are useful in the representation and description of shape. The material in this chapter begins a transition from processes that output images to processes that output image attributes, as indicated in Section 1.1.

Segmentation partitions an image into its constituent parts or objects. In general, autonomous segmentation is one of the most difficult tasks in digital image processing. A rugged segmentation procedure brings the process a long way toward successful solution of imaging problems that require objects to be identified individually. On the other hand, weak or erratic segmentation algorithms almost always guarantee eventual failure. In general, the more accurate the segmentation, the more likely automated object classification is to succeed.

Feature extraction almost always follows the output of a segmentation stage, which usually is raw pixel data, constituting either the boundary of a region (i.e., the set of pixels separating one image region from another) or all the points in the region itself. Feature extraction consists of feature detection and feature description. *Feature detection* refers to finding the features in an image, region, or boundary. *Feature description* assigns quantitative attributes to the detected features. For example, we might detect corners in a region, and describe those corners by their orientation and location; both of these descriptors are quantitative attributes. Feature processing methods discussed in this chapter are subdivided into three principal categories, depending on whether they are applicable to boundaries, regions, or whole images. Some features are applicable to more than one category. Feature descriptors should be as insensitive as possible to variations in parameters such as scale, translation, rotation, illumination, and viewpoint.

Image pattern classification is the process that assigns a label (e.g., "vehicle") to an object based on its feature descriptors. In the last chapter of the book, we will discuss methods of image pattern classification ranging from "classical" approaches such as *minimum-distance*, *correlation*, and *Bayes classifiers*, to more modern approaches implemented using *deep neural networks*. In particular, we will discuss in detail *deep convolutional neural networks*, which are ideally suited for image processing work.

So far, we have said nothing about the need for prior knowledge or about the interaction between the knowledge base and the processing modules in Fig. 1.23. *Knowledge* about a problem domain is coded into an image processing system in the form of a knowledge database. This knowledge may be as simple as detailing regions of an image where the information of interest is known to be located, thus limiting the search that has to be conducted in seeking that information. The knowledge base can also be quite complex, such as an interrelated list of all major possible defects in a materials inspection problem, or an image database containing high-resolution satellite images of a region in connection with change-detection applications. In addition to guiding the operation of each processing module, the knowledge base also controls the interaction between modules. This distinction is made in Fig. 1.23 by the use of double-headed arrows between the processing modules and the knowledge base, as opposed to single-headed arrows linking the processing modules.

Although we do not discuss image display explicitly at this point, it is important to keep in mind that viewing the results of image processing can take place at the output of any stage in Fig. 1.23. We also note that not all image processing applications require the complexity of interactions implied by Fig. 1.23. In fact, not even all those modules are needed in many cases. For example, image enhancement for human visual interpretation seldom requires use of any of the other stages in Fig. 1.23. In general, however, as the complexity of an image processing task increases, so does the number of processes required to solve the problem.

1.5 COMPONENTS OF AN IMAGE PROCESSING SYSTEM

As recently as the mid-1980s, numerous models of image processing systems being sold throughout the world were rather substantial peripheral devices that attached to equally substantial host computers. Late in the 1980s and early in the 1990s, the market shifted to image processing hardware in the form of single boards designed to be compatible with industry standard buses and to fit into engineering workstation cabinets and personal computers. In the late 1990s and early 2000s, a new class of add-on boards, called graphics processing units (GPUs) were introduced for work on 3-D applications, such as games and other 3-D graphics applications. It was not long before GPUs found their way into image processing applications involving large-scale matrix implementations, such as training deep convolutional networks. In addition to lowering costs, the market shift from substantial peripheral devices to add-on processing boards also served as a catalyst for a significant number of new companies specializing in the development of software written specifically for image processing.

The trend continues toward miniaturizing and blending of general-purpose small computers with specialized image processing hardware and software. Figure 1.24 shows the basic components comprising a typical general-purpose system used for digital image processing. The function of each component will be discussed in the following paragraphs, starting with image sensing.

Two subsystems are required to acquire digital images. The first is a physical *sensor* that responds to the energy radiated by the object we wish to image. The second, called a *digitizer*, is a device for converting the output of the physical sensing device into digital form. For instance, in a digital video camera, the sensors (CCD chips) produce an electrical output proportional to light intensity. The digitizer converts these outputs to digital data. These topics will be covered in Chapter 2.

Specialized image processing hardware usually consists of the digitizer just mentioned, plus hardware that performs other primitive operations, such as an *arithmetic logic unit* (ALU), that performs arithmetic and logical operations in parallel on entire images. One example of how an ALU is used is in averaging images as quickly as they are digitized, for the purpose of noise reduction. This type of hardware sometimes is called a *front-end subsystem*, and its most distinguishing characteristic is speed. In other words, this unit performs functions that require fast data throughputs (e.g., digitizing and averaging video images at 30 frames/s) that the typical main computer cannot handle. One or more GPUs (see above) also are common in image processing systems that perform intensive matrix operations.

The *computer* in an image processing system is a general-purpose computer and can range from a PC to a supercomputer. In dedicated applications, sometimes custom computers are used to achieve a required level of performance, but our interest here is on general-purpose image processing systems. In these systems, almost any well-equipped PC-type machine is suitable for off-line image processing tasks.

Software for image processing consists of specialized modules that perform specific tasks. A well-designed package also includes the capability for the user to write code that, as a minimum, utilizes the specialized modules. More sophisticated

FIGURE 1.24
Components of a
general-purpose
image processing
system.

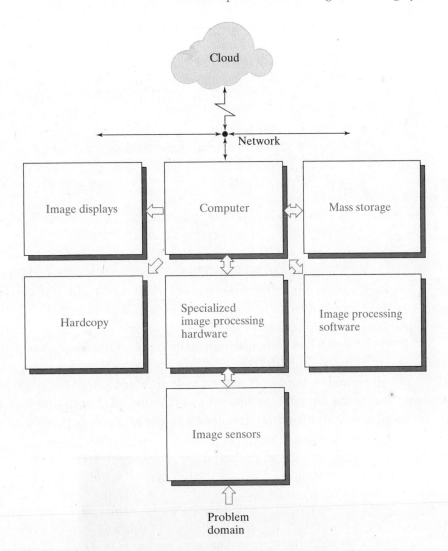

software packages allow the integration of those modules and general-purpose
software commands from at least one computer language. Commercially available
image processing software, such as the well-known MATLAB® Image Processing
Toolbox, is also common in a well-equipped image processing system.

Mass storage is a must in image processing applications. An image of size 1024×1024
pixels, in which the intensity of each pixel is an 8-bit quantity, requires one megabyte
of storage space if the image is not compressed. When dealing with image databases
that contain thousands, or even millions, of images, providing adequate storage in
an image processing system can be a challenge. Digital storage for image processing
applications falls into three principal categories: (1) short-term storage for use during processing; (2) on-line storage for relatively fast recall; and (3) archival storage,
characterized by infrequent access. Storage is measured in bytes (eight bits), Kbytes
(10^3 bytes), Mbytes (10^6 bytes), Gbytes (10^9 bytes), and Tbytes (10^{12} bytes).

One method of providing short-term storage is computer memory. Another is by specialized boards, called *frame buffers*, that store one or more images and can be accessed rapidly, usually at video rates (e.g., at 30 complete images per second). The latter method allows virtually instantaneous image *zoom*, as well as *scroll* (vertical shifts) and *pan* (horizontal shifts). Frame buffers usually are housed in the specialized image processing hardware unit in Fig. 1.24. On-line storage generally takes the form of magnetic disks or optical-media storage. The key factor characterizing on-line storage is frequent access to the stored data. Finally, archival storage is characterized by massive storage requirements but infrequent need for access. Magnetic tapes and optical disks housed in "jukeboxes" are the usual media for archival applications.

Image displays in use today are mainly color, flat screen monitors. Monitors are driven by the outputs of image and graphics display cards that are an integral part of the computer system. Seldom are there requirements for image display applications that cannot be met by display cards and GPUs available commercially as part of the computer system. In some cases, it is necessary to have stereo displays, and these are implemented in the form of headgear containing two small displays embedded in goggles worn by the user.

Hardcopy devices for recording images include laser printers, film cameras, heat-sensitive devices, ink-jet units, and digital units, such as optical and CD-ROM disks. Film provides the highest possible resolution, but paper is the obvious medium of choice for written material. For presentations, images are displayed on film transparencies or in a digital medium if image projection equipment is used. The latter approach is gaining acceptance as the standard for image presentations.

Networking and *cloud* communication are almost default functions in any computer system in use today. Because of the large amount of data inherent in image processing applications, the key consideration in image transmission is *bandwidth*. In dedicated networks, this typically is not a problem, but communications with remote sites via the internet are not always as efficient. Fortunately, transmission bandwidth is improving quickly as a result of optical fiber and other broadband technologies. Image data compression continues to play a major role in the transmission of large amounts of image data.

Summary, References, and Further Reading

The main purpose of the material presented in this chapter is to provide a sense of perspective about the origins of digital image processing and, more important, about current and future areas of application of this technology. Although the coverage of these topics in this chapter was necessarily incomplete due to space limitations, it should have left you with a clear impression of the breadth and practical scope of digital image processing. As we proceed in the following chapters with the development of image processing theory and applications, numerous examples are provided to keep a clear focus on the utility and promise of these techniques. Upon concluding the study of the final chapter, a reader of this book will have arrived at a level of understanding that is the foundation for most of the work currently underway in this field.

In past editions, we have provided a long list of journals and books to give readers an idea of the breadth of the image processing literature, and where this literature is reported. The list has been updated, and it has become so extensive that it is more practical to include it in the book website: *www.ImageProcessingPlace.com*, in the section entitled *Publications*.

Digital Image Fundamentals

Those who wish to succeed must ask the right preliminary questions.

Aristotle

Preview

This chapter is an introduction to a number of basic concepts in digital image processing that are used throughout the book. Section 2.1 summarizes some important aspects of the human visual system, including image formation in the eye and its capabilities for brightness adaptation and discrimination. Section 2.2 discusses light, other components of the electromagnetic spectrum, and their imaging characteristics. Section 2.3 discusses imaging sensors and how they are used to generate digital images. Section 2.4 introduces the concepts of uniform image sampling and intensity quantization. Additional topics discussed in that section include digital image representation, the effects of varying the number of samples and intensity levels in an image, the concepts of spatial and intensity resolution, and the principles of image interpolation. Section 2.5 deals with a variety of basic relationships between pixels. Finally, Section 2.6 is an introduction to the principal mathematical tools we use throughout the book. A second objective of that section is to help you begin developing a "feel" for how these tools are used in a variety of basic image processing tasks.

Upon completion of this chapter, readers should:

■ Have an understanding of some important functions and limitations of human vision.

■ Be familiar with the electromagnetic energy spectrum, including basic properties of light.

■ Know how digital images are generated and represented.

■ Understand the basics of image sampling and quantization.

■ Be familiar with spatial and intensity resolution and their effects on image appearance.

■ Have an understanding of basic geometric relationships between image pixels.

■ Be familiar with the principal mathematical tools used in digital image processing.

■ Be able to apply a variety of introductory digital image processing techniques.

47

2.1 ELEMENTS OF VISUAL PERCEPTION

Although the field of digital image processing is built on a foundation of mathematics, human intuition and analysis often play a role in the choice of one technique versus another, and this choice often is made based on subjective, visual judgments. Thus, developing an understanding of basic characteristics of human visual perception as a first step in our journey through this book is appropriate. In particular, our interest is in the elementary mechanics of how images are formed and perceived by humans. We are interested in learning the physical limitations of human vision in terms of factors that also are used in our work with digital images. Factors such as how human and electronic imaging devices compare in terms of resolution and ability to adapt to changes in illumination are not only interesting, they are also important from a practical point of view.

STRUCTURE OF THE HUMAN EYE

Figure 2.1 shows a simplified cross section of the human eye. The eye is nearly a sphere (with a diameter of about 20 mm) enclosed by three membranes: the *cornea* and *sclera* outer cover; the *choroid*; and the *retina*. The cornea is a tough, transparent tissue that covers the anterior surface of the eye. Continuous with the cornea, the sclera is an opaque membrane that encloses the remainder of the optic globe.

The choroid lies directly below the sclera. This membrane contains a network of blood vessels that serve as the major source of nutrition to the eye. Even superficial

FIGURE 2.1
Simplified diagram of a cross section of the human eye.

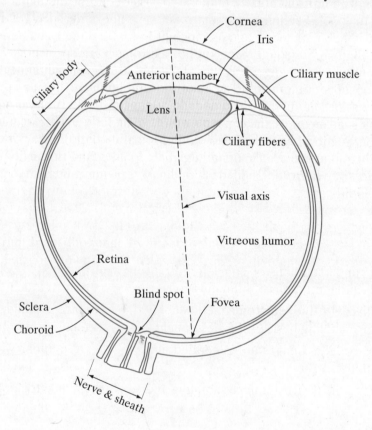

injury to the choroid can lead to severe eye damage as a result of inflammation that restricts blood flow. The choroid coat is heavily pigmented, which helps reduce the amount of extraneous light entering the eye and the backscatter within the optic globe. At its anterior extreme, the choroid is divided into the *ciliary body* and the *iris*. The latter contracts or expands to control the amount of light that enters the eye. The central opening of the iris (the *pupil*) varies in diameter from approximately 2 to 8 mm. The front of the iris contains the visible pigment of the eye, whereas the back contains a black pigment.

The *lens* consists of concentric layers of fibrous cells and is suspended by fibers that attach to the ciliary body. It is composed of 60% to 70% water, about 6% fat, and more protein than any other tissue in the eye. The lens is colored by a slightly yellow pigmentation that increases with age. In extreme cases, excessive clouding of the lens, referred to as *cataracts*, can lead to poor color discrimination and loss of clear vision. The lens absorbs approximately 8% of the visible light spectrum, with higher absorption at shorter wavelengths. Both infrared and ultraviolet light are absorbed by proteins within the lens and, in excessive amounts, can damage the eye.

The innermost membrane of the eye is the *retina*, which lines the inside of the wall's entire posterior portion. When the eye is focused, light from an object is imaged on the retina. Pattern vision is afforded by discrete light receptors distributed over the surface of the retina. There are two types of receptors: *cones* and *rods*. There are between 6 and 7 million cones in each eye. They are located primarily in the central portion of the retina, called the *fovea*, and are highly sensitive to color. Humans can resolve fine details because each cone is connected to its own nerve end. Muscles rotate the eye until the image of a region of interest falls on the fovea. Cone vision is called *photopic* or *bright-light* vision.

The number of rods is much larger: Some 75 to 150 million are distributed over the retina. The larger area of distribution, and the fact that several rods are connected to a single nerve ending, reduces the amount of detail discernible by these receptors. Rods capture an overall image of the field of view. They are not involved in color vision, and are sensitive to low levels of illumination. For example, objects that appear brightly colored in daylight appear as colorless forms in moonlight because only the rods are stimulated. This phenomenon is known as *scotopic* or *dim-light* vision.

Figure 2.2 shows the density of rods and cones for a cross section of the right eye, passing through the region where the optic nerve emerges from the eye. The absence of receptors in this area causes the so-called *blind spot* (see Fig. 2.1). Except for this region, the distribution of receptors is radially symmetric about the fovea. Receptor density is measured in degrees from the visual axis. Note in Fig. 2.2 that cones are most dense in the center area of the fovea, and that rods increase in density from the center out to approximately 20° off axis. Then, their density decreases out to the periphery of the retina.

The fovea itself is a circular indentation in the retina of about 1.5 mm in diameter, so it has an area of approximately 1.77 mm^2. As Fig. 2.2 shows, the density of cones in that area of the retina is on the order of 150,000 elements per mm^2. Based on these figures, the number of cones in the fovea, which is the region of highest acuity

FIGURE 2.2
Distribution of
rods and cones in
the retina.

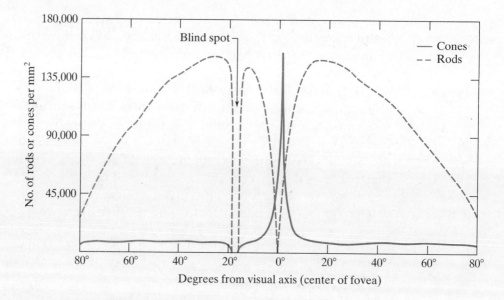

in the eye, is about 265,000 elements. Modern electronic imaging chips exceed this number by a large factor. While the ability of humans to integrate intelligence and experience with vision makes purely quantitative comparisons somewhat superficial, keep in mind for future discussions that electronic imaging sensors can easily exceed the capability of the eye in resolving image detail.

IMAGE FORMATION IN THE EYE

In an ordinary photographic camera, the lens has a fixed focal length. Focusing at various distances is achieved by varying the distance between the lens and the imaging plane, where the film (or imaging chip in the case of a digital camera) is located. In the human eye, the converse is true; the distance between the center of the lens and the imaging sensor (the retina) is fixed, and the focal length needed to achieve proper focus is obtained by varying the shape of the lens. The fibers in the ciliary body accomplish this by flattening or thickening the lens for distant or near objects, respectively. The distance between the center of the lens and the retina along the visual axis is approximately 17 mm. The range of focal lengths is approximately 14 mm to 17 mm, the latter taking place when the eye is relaxed and focused at distances greater than about 3 m. The geometry in Fig. 2.3 illustrates how to obtain the dimensions of an image formed on the retina. For example, suppose that a person is looking at a tree 15 m high at a distance of 100 m. Letting h denote the height of that object in the retinal image, the geometry of Fig. 2.3 yields $15/100 = h/17$ or $h = 2.5$ mm. As indicated earlier in this section, the retinal image is focused primarily on the region of the fovea. Perception then takes place by the relative excitation of light receptors, which transform radiant energy into electrical impulses that ultimately are decoded by the brain.

BRIGHTNESS ADAPTATION AND DISCRIMINATION

Because digital images are displayed as sets of discrete intensities, the eye's ability to discriminate between different intensity levels is an important consideration

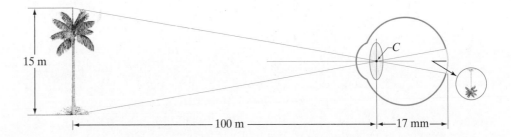

FIGURE 2.3
Graphical representation of the eye looking at a palm tree. Point C is the focal center of the lens.

in presenting image processing results. The range of light intensity levels to which the human visual system can adapt is enormous—on the order of 10^{10}— from the scotopic threshold to the glare limit. Experimental evidence indicates that *subjective brightness* (intensity as perceived by the human visual system) is a logarithmic function of the light intensity incident on the eye. Figure 2.4, a plot of light intensity versus subjective brightness, illustrates this characteristic. The long solid curve represents the range of intensities to which the visual system can adapt. In photopic vision alone, the range is about 10^6. The transition from scotopic to photopic vision is gradual over the approximate range from 0.001 to 0.1 millilambert (−3 to −1 mL in the log scale), as the double branches of the adaptation curve in this range show.

The key point in interpreting the impressive dynamic range depicted in Fig. 2.4 is that the visual system cannot operate over such a range *simultaneously*. Rather, it accomplishes this large variation by changing its overall sensitivity, a phenomenon known as *brightness adaptation*. The total range of distinct intensity levels the eye can discriminate simultaneously is rather small when compared with the total adaptation range. For a given set of conditions, the current sensitivity level of the visual system is called the *brightness adaptation level*, which may correspond, for example,

FIGURE 2.4
Range of subjective brightness sensations showing a particular adaptation level, B_a.

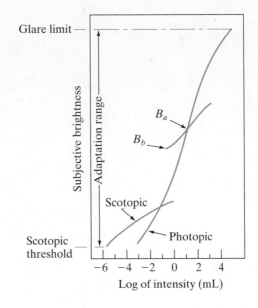

to brightness B_a in Fig. 2.4. The short intersecting curve represents the range of subjective brightness that the eye can perceive when adapted to *this* level. This range is rather restricted, having a level B_b at, and below which, all stimuli are perceived as indistinguishable blacks. The upper portion of the curve is not actually restricted but, if extended too far, loses its meaning because much higher intensities would simply raise the adaptation level higher than B_a.

The ability of the eye to discriminate between *changes* in light intensity at any specific adaptation level is of considerable interest. A classic experiment used to determine the capability of the human visual system for brightness discrimination consists of having a subject look at a flat, uniformly illuminated area large enough to occupy the entire field of view. This area typically is a diffuser, such as opaque glass, illuminated from behind by a light source, I, with variable intensity. To this field is added an increment of illumination, ΔI, in the form of a short-duration flash that appears as a circle in the center of the uniformly illuminated field, as Fig. 2.5 shows.

If ΔI is not bright enough, the subject says "no," indicating no perceivable change. As ΔI gets stronger, the subject may give a positive response of "yes," indicating a perceived change. Finally, when ΔI is strong enough, the subject will give a response of "yes" all the time. The quantity $\Delta I_c/I$, where ΔI_c is the increment of illumination discriminable 50% of the time with background illumination I, is called the *Weber ratio*. A small value of $\Delta I_c/I$ means that a small percentage change in intensity is discriminable. This represents "good" brightness discrimination. Conversely, a large value of $\Delta I_c/I$ means that a large percentage change in intensity is required for the eye to detect the change. This represents "poor" brightness discrimination.

A plot of $\Delta I_c/I$ as a function of $\log I$ has the characteristic shape shown in Fig. 2.6. This curve shows that brightness discrimination is poor (the Weber ratio is large) at low levels of illumination, and it improves significantly (the Weber ratio decreases) as background illumination increases. The two branches in the curve reflect the fact that at low levels of illumination vision is carried out by the rods, whereas, at high levels, vision is a function of cones.

If the background illumination is held constant and the intensity of the other source, instead of flashing, is now allowed to vary incrementally from never being perceived to always being perceived, the typical observer can discern a total of one to two dozen different intensity changes. Roughly, this result is related to the number of different intensities a person can see at any one *point* or *small area* in a monochrome image. This does not mean that an image can be represented by such a small number of intensity values because, as the eye roams about the image, the average

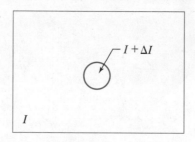

FIGURE 2.5
Basic experimental setup used to characterize brightness discrimination.

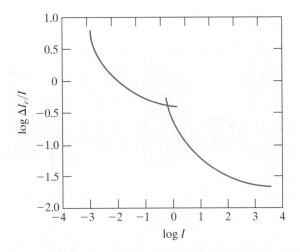

FIGURE 2.6
A typical plot of the Weber ratio as a function of intensity.

background changes, thus allowing a *different* set of incremental changes to be detected at each new adaptation level. The net result is that the eye is capable of a broader range of *overall* intensity discrimination. In fact, as we will show in Section 2.4, the eye is capable of detecting objectionable effects in monochrome images whose overall intensity is represented by fewer than approximately two dozen levels.

Two phenomena demonstrate that perceived brightness is not a simple function of intensity. The first is based on the fact that the visual system tends to undershoot or overshoot around the boundary of regions of different intensities. Figure 2.7(a) shows a striking example of this phenomenon. Although the intensity of the stripes

FIGURE 2.7
Illustration of the Mach band effect. Perceived intensity is not a simple function of actual intensity.

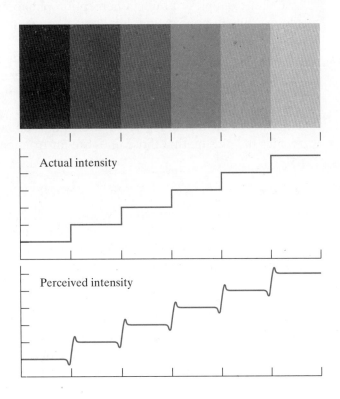

a b c

FIGURE 2.8 Examples of simultaneous contrast. All the inner squares have the same intensity, but they appear progressively darker as the background becomes lighter.

is constant [see Fig. 2.7(b)], we actually perceive a brightness pattern that is strongly scalloped near the boundaries, as Fig. 2.7(c) shows. These perceived scalloped bands are called *Mach bands* after Ernst Mach, who first described the phenomenon in 1865.

The second phenomenon, called *simultaneous contrast*, is that a region's perceived brightness does not depend only on its intensity, as Fig. 2.8 demonstrates. All the center squares have exactly the same intensity, but each appears to the eye to become darker as the background gets lighter. A more familiar example is a piece of paper that looks white when lying on a desk, but can appear totally black when used to shield the eyes while looking directly at a bright sky.

Other examples of human perception phenomena are *optical illusions*, in which the eye fills in nonexisting details or wrongly perceives geometrical properties of objects. Figure 2.9 shows some examples. In Fig. 2.9(a), the outline of a square is seen clearly, despite the fact that no lines defining such a figure are part of the image. The same effect, this time with a circle, can be seen in Fig. 2.9(b); note how just a few lines are sufficient to give the illusion of a complete circle. The two horizontal line segments in Fig. 2.9(c) are of the same length, but one appears shorter than the other. Finally, all long lines in Fig. 2.9(d) are equidistant and parallel. Yet, the crosshatching creates the illusion that those lines are far from being parallel.

2.2 LIGHT AND THE ELECTROMAGNETIC SPECTRUM

The electromagnetic spectrum was introduced in Section 1.3. We now consider this topic in more detail. In 1666, Sir Isaac Newton discovered that when a beam of sunlight passes through a glass prism, the emerging beam of light is not white but consists instead of a continuous spectrum of colors ranging from violet at one end to red at the other. As Fig. 2.10 shows, the range of colors we perceive in visible light is a small portion of the electromagnetic spectrum. On one end of the spectrum are radio waves with wavelengths billions of times longer than those of visible light. On the other end of the spectrum are gamma rays with wavelengths millions of times smaller than those of visible light. We showed examples in Section 1.3 of images in most of the bands in the EM spectrum.

a b
c d

FIGURE 2.9 Some well-known optical illusions.

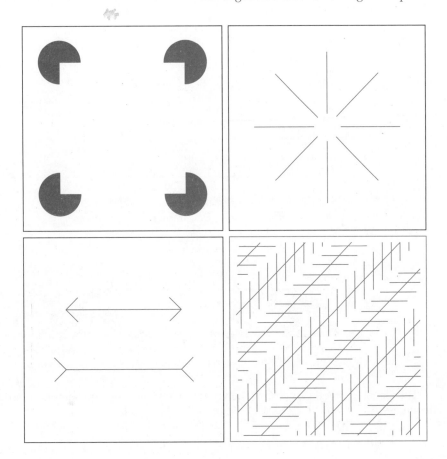

The electromagnetic spectrum can be expressed in terms of wavelength, frequency, or energy. Wavelength (λ) and frequency (ν) are related by the expression

$$\lambda = \frac{c}{\nu} \qquad (2\text{-}1)$$

where c is the speed of light (2.998×10^8 m/s). Figure 2.11 shows a schematic representation of one wavelength.

The energy of the various components of the electromagnetic spectrum is given by the expression

$$E = h\nu \qquad (2\text{-}2)$$

where h is Planck's constant. The units of wavelength are meters, with the terms *microns* (denoted μm and equal to 10^{-6} m) and *nanometers* (denoted nm and equal to 10^{-9} m) being used just as frequently. Frequency is measured in *Hertz* (Hz), with one Hz being equal to one cycle of a sinusoidal wave per second. A commonly used unit of energy is the *electron-volt*.

Electromagnetic waves can be visualized as propagating sinusoidal waves with wavelength λ (Fig. 2.11), or they can be thought of as a stream of massless particles,

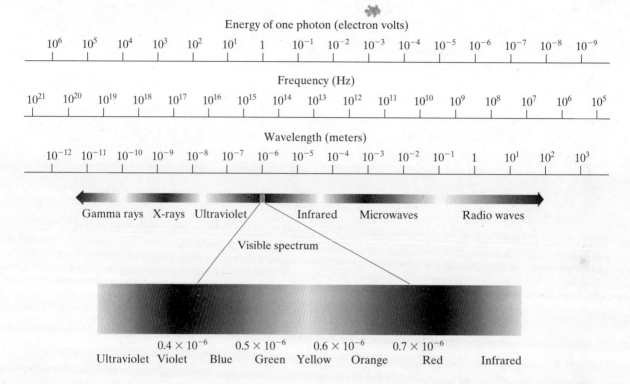

FIGURE 2.10 The electromagnetic spectrum. The visible spectrum is shown zoomed to facilitate explanations, but note that it encompasses a very narrow range of the total EM spectrum.

each traveling in a wavelike pattern and moving at the speed of light. Each mass-less particle contains a certain amount (or bundle) of energy, called a *photon*. We see from Eq. (2-2) that energy is proportional to frequency, so the higher-frequency (shorter wavelength) electromagnetic phenomena carry more energy per photon. Thus, radio waves have photons with low energies, microwaves have more energy than radio waves, infrared still more, then visible, ultraviolet, X-rays, and finally gamma rays, the most energetic of all. High-energy electromagnetic radiation, especially in the X-ray and gamma ray bands, is particularly harmful to living organisms.

Light is a type of electromagnetic radiation that can be sensed by the eye. The visible (color) spectrum is shown expanded in Fig. 2.10 for the purpose of discussion (we will discuss color in detail in Chapter 6). The visible band of the electromagnetic spectrum spans the range from approximately 0.43 μm (violet) to about 0.79 μm (red). For convenience, the color spectrum is divided into six broad regions: violet, blue, green, yellow, orange, and red. No color (or other component of the

FIGURE 2.11
Graphical
representation of
one wavelength.

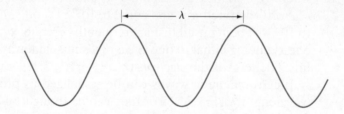

electromagnetic spectrum) ends abruptly; rather, each range blends smoothly into the next, as Fig. 2.10 shows.

The colors perceived in an object are determined by the nature of the light *reflected* by the object. A body that reflects light relatively balanced in all visible wavelengths appears white to the observer. However, a body that favors reflectance in a limited range of the visible spectrum exhibits some shades of color. For example, green objects reflect light with wavelengths primarily in the 500 to 570 nm range, while absorbing most of the energy at other wavelengths.

Light that is void of color is called *monochromatic* (or *achromatic*) light. The only attribute of monochromatic light is its intensity. Because the intensity of monochromatic light is perceived to vary from black to grays and finally to white, the term *gray level* is used commonly to denote monochromatic intensity (we use the terms *intensity* and *gray level* interchangeably in subsequent discussions). The range of values of monochromatic light from black to white is usually called the *gray scale*, and monochromatic images are frequently referred to as *grayscale images*.

Chromatic (color) light spans the electromagnetic energy spectrum from approximately 0.43 to 0.79 μm, as noted previously. In addition to frequency, three other quantities are used to describe a chromatic light source: radiance, luminance, and brightness. *Radiance* is the total amount of energy that flows from the light source, and it is usually measured in watts (W). *Luminance*, measured in lumens (lm), gives a measure of the amount of energy an observer *perceives* from a light source. For example, light emitted from a source operating in the far infrared region of the spectrum could have significant energy (radiance), but an observer would hardly perceive it; its luminance would be almost zero. Finally, as discussed in Section 2.1, *brightness* is a subjective descriptor of light perception that is practically impossible to measure. It embodies the achromatic notion of intensity and is one of the key factors in describing color sensation.

In principle, if a sensor can be developed that is capable of detecting energy radiated in a band of the electromagnetic spectrum, we can image events of interest in that band. Note, however, that the wavelength of an electromagnetic wave required to "see" an object must be of the same size as, or smaller than, the object. For example, a water molecule has a diameter on the order of 10^{-10} m. Thus, to study these molecules, we would need a source capable of emitting energy in the far (high-energy) ultraviolet band or soft (low-energy) X-ray bands.

Although imaging is based predominantly on energy from electromagnetic wave radiation, this is not the only method for generating images. For example, we saw in Section 1.3 that sound reflected from objects can be used to form ultrasonic images. Other sources of digital images are electron beams for electron microscopy, and software for generating synthetic images used in graphics and visualization.

2.3 IMAGE SENSING AND ACQUISITION

Most of the images in which we are interested are generated by the combination of an "illumination" source and the reflection or absorption of energy from that source by the elements of the "scene" being imaged. We enclose *illumination* and *scene* in quotes to emphasize the fact that they are considerably more general than the familiar situation in which a visible light source illuminates a familiar 3-D scene. For example, the illumination may originate from a source of electromagnetic energy, such as a radar, infrared, or X-ray system. But, as noted earlier, it could originate from less traditional sources, such as ultrasound or even a computer-generated illumination pattern. Similarly, the scene elements could be familiar objects, but they can just as easily be molecules, buried rock formations, or a human brain. Depending on the nature of the source, illumination energy is reflected from, or transmitted through, objects. An example in the first category is light reflected from a planar surface. An example in the second category is when X-rays pass through a patient's body for the purpose of generating a diagnostic X-ray image. In some applications, the reflected or transmitted energy is focused onto a photo converter (e.g., a phosphor screen) that converts the energy into visible light. Electron microscopy and some applications of gamma imaging use this approach.

Figure 2.12 shows the three principal sensor arrangements used to transform incident energy into digital images. The idea is simple: Incoming energy is transformed into a voltage by a combination of the input electrical power and sensor material that is responsive to the type of energy being detected. The output voltage waveform is the response of the sensor, and a digital quantity is obtained by digitizing that response. In this section, we look at the principal modalities for image sensing and generation. We will discuss image digitizing in Section 2.4.

IMAGE ACQUISITION USING A SINGLE SENSING ELEMENT

Figure 2.12(a) shows the components of a single sensing element. A familiar sensor of this type is the photodiode, which is constructed of silicon materials and whose output is a voltage proportional to light intensity. Using a filter in front of a sensor improves its selectivity. For example, an optical green-transmission filter favors light in the green band of the color spectrum. As a consequence, the sensor output would be stronger for green light than for other visible light components.

In order to generate a 2-D image using a single sensing element, there has to be relative displacements in both the x- and y-directions between the sensor and the area to be imaged. Figure 2.13 shows an arrangement used in high-precision scanning, where a film negative is mounted onto a drum whose mechanical rotation provides displacement in one dimension. The sensor is mounted on a lead screw that provides motion in the perpendicular direction. A light source is contained inside the drum. As the light passes through the film, its intensity is modified by the film density before it is captured by the sensor. This "modulation" of the light intensity causes corresponding variations in the sensor voltage, which are ultimately converted to image intensity levels by digitization.

This method is an inexpensive way to obtain high-resolution images because mechanical motion can be controlled with high precision. The main disadvantages of this method are that it is slow and not readily portable. Other similar mechanical arrangements use a flat imaging bed, with the sensor moving in two linear directions. These types of mechanical digitizers sometimes are referred to as *transmission microdensitometers*. Systems in which light is reflected from the medium, instead of passing through it, are called *reflection microdensitometers*. Another example of imaging with a single sensing element places a laser source coincident with the

a
b
c

FIGURE 2.12
(a) Single sensing element.
(b) Line sensor.
(c) Array sensor.

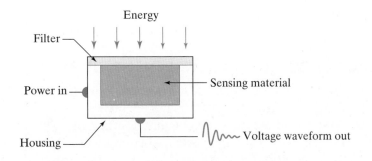

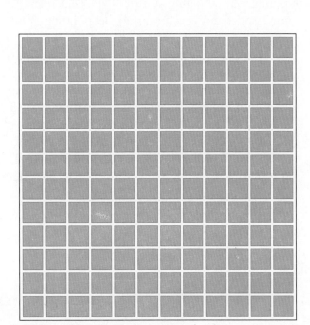

FIGURE 2.13
Combining a single sensing element with mechanical motion to generate a 2-D image.

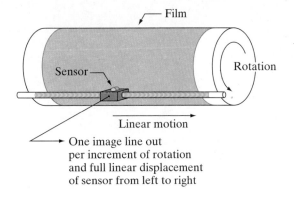

sensor. Moving mirrors are used to control the outgoing beam in a scanning pattern and to direct the reflected laser signal onto the sensor.

IMAGE ACQUISITION USING SENSOR STRIPS

A geometry used more frequently than single sensors is an in-line sensor strip, as in Fig. 2.12(b). The strip provides imaging elements in one direction. Motion perpendicular to the strip provides imaging in the other direction, as shown in Fig. 2.14(a). This arrangement is used in most flat bed scanners. Sensing devices with 4000 or more in-line sensors are possible. In-line sensors are used routinely in airborne imaging applications, in which the imaging system is mounted on an aircraft that flies at a constant altitude and speed over the geographical area to be imaged. One-dimensional imaging sensor strips that respond to various bands of the electromagnetic spectrum are mounted perpendicular to the direction of flight. An imaging strip gives one line of an image at a time, and the motion of the strip relative to the scene completes the other dimension of a 2-D image. Lenses or other focusing schemes are used to project the area to be scanned onto the sensors.

Sensor strips in a ring configuration are used in medical and industrial imaging to obtain cross-sectional ("slice") images of 3-D objects, as Fig. 2.14(b) shows. A rotating X-ray source provides illumination, and X-ray sensitive sensors opposite the source collect the energy that passes through the object. This is the basis for medical and industrial computerized axial tomography (CAT) imaging, as indicated in Sections 1.2 and 1.3. The output of the sensors is processed by reconstruction algorithms whose objective is to transform the sensed data into meaningful cross-sectional images (see Section 5.11). In other words, images are not obtained directly

a b

FIGURE 2.14
(a) Image acquisition using a linear sensor strip. (b) Image acquisition using a circular sensor strip.

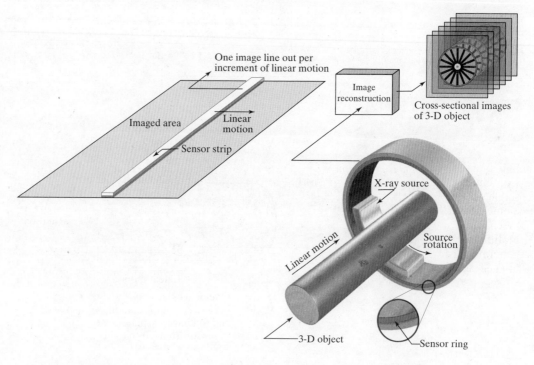

One image line out per increment of linear motion

Imaged area

Linear motion

Sensor strip

Image reconstruction

Cross-sectional images of 3-D object

X-ray source

Source rotation

Linear motion

3-D object

Sensor ring

from the sensors by motion alone; they also require extensive computer processing. A 3-D digital volume consisting of stacked images is generated as the object is moved in a direction perpendicular to the sensor ring. Other modalities of imaging based on the CAT principle include magnetic resonance imaging (MRI) and positron emission tomography (PET). The illumination sources, sensors, and types of images are different, but conceptually their applications are very similar to the basic imaging approach shown in Fig. 2.14(b).

IMAGE ACQUISITION USING SENSOR ARRAYS

Figure 2.12(c) shows individual sensing elements arranged in the form of a 2-D array. Electromagnetic and ultrasonic sensing devices frequently are arranged in this manner. This is also the predominant arrangement found in digital cameras. A typical sensor for these cameras is a CCD (charge-coupled device) array, which can be manufactured with a broad range of sensing properties and can be packaged in rugged arrays of 4000×4000 elements or more. CCD sensors are used widely in digital cameras and other light-sensing instruments. The response of each sensor is proportional to the integral of the light energy projected onto the surface of the sensor, a property that is used in astronomical and other applications requiring low noise images. Noise reduction is achieved by letting the sensor integrate the input light signal over minutes or even hours. Because the sensor array in Fig. 2.12(c) is two-dimensional, its key advantage is that a complete image can be obtained by focusing the energy pattern onto the surface of the array. Motion obviously is not necessary, as is the case with the sensor arrangements discussed in the preceding two sections.

In some cases, the source is imaged directly, as in obtaining images of the sun.

Figure 2.15 shows the principal manner in which array sensors are used. This figure shows the energy from an illumination source being reflected from a scene (as mentioned at the beginning of this section, the energy also could be transmitted through the scene). The first function performed by the imaging system in Fig. 2.15(c) is to collect the incoming energy and focus it onto an image plane. If the illumination is light, the front end of the imaging system is an optical lens that projects the viewed scene onto the focal plane of the lens, as Fig. 2.15(d) shows. The sensor array, which is coincident with the focal plane, produces outputs proportional to the integral of the light received at each sensor. Digital and analog circuitry sweep these outputs and convert them to an analog signal, which is then digitized by another section of the imaging system. The output is a digital image, as shown diagrammatically in Fig. 2.15(e). Converting images into digital form is the topic of Section 2.4.

A SIMPLE IMAGE FORMATION MODEL

As introduced in Section 1.1, we denote images by two-dimensional functions of the form $f(x, y)$. The value of f at spatial coordinates (x, y) is a scalar quantity whose physical meaning is determined by the source of the image, and whose values are proportional to energy radiated by a physical source (e.g., electromagnetic waves). As a consequence, $f(x, y)$ must be nonnegative[†] and finite; that is,

---

[†] Image intensities can become negative during processing, or as a result of interpretation. For example, in radar images, objects moving toward the radar often are interpreted as having negative velocities while objects moving away are interpreted as having positive velocities. Thus, a velocity image might be coded as having both positive and negative values. When storing and displaying images, we normally scale the intensities so that the smallest negative value becomes 0 (see Section 2.6 regarding intensity scaling).

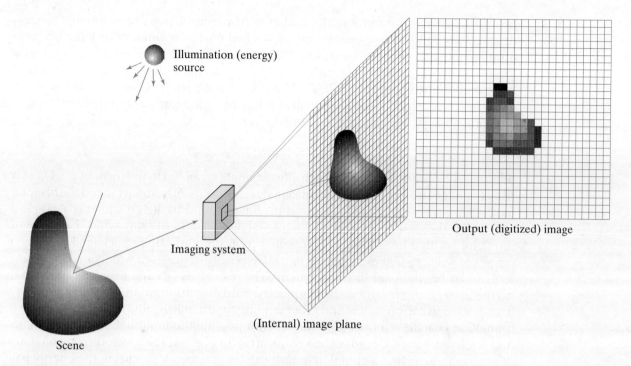

Illumination (energy) source

Output (digitized) image

Imaging system

(Internal) image plane

Scene

a
b c d e

FIGURE 2.15 An example of digital image acquisition. (a) Illumination (energy) source. (b) A scene. (c) Imaging system. (d) Projection of the scene onto the image plane. (e) Digitized image.

$$0 \le f(x, y) < \infty \tag{2-3}$$

Function $f(x, y)$ is characterized by two components: (1) the amount of source illumination incident on the scene being viewed, and (2) the amount of illumination reflected by the objects in the scene. Appropriately, these are called the *illumination* and *reflectance* components, and are denoted by $i(x, y)$ and $r(x, y)$, respectively. The two functions combine as a product to form $f(x, y)$:

$$f(x, y) = i(x, y)r(x, y) \tag{2-4}$$

where

$$0 \le i(x, y) < \infty \tag{2-5}$$

and

$$0 \le r(x, y) \le 1 \tag{2-6}$$

Thus, reflectance is bounded by 0 (total absorption) and 1 (total reflectance). The nature of $i(x, y)$ is determined by the illumination source, and $r(x, y)$ is determined by the characteristics of the imaged objects. These expressions are applicable also to images formed via transmission of the illumination through a medium, such as a chest X-ray. In this case, we would deal with a *transmissivity* instead of a *reflectivity* function, but the limits would be the same as in Eq. (2-6), and the image function formed would be modeled as the product in Eq. (2-4).

EXAMPLE 2.1:   Some typical values of illumination and reflectance.

The following numerical quantities illustrate some typical values of illumination and reflectance for visible light. On a clear day, the sun may produce in excess of $90,000$ lm/m^2 of illumination on the surface of the earth. This value decreases to less than $10,000$ lm/m^2 on a cloudy day. On a clear evening, a full moon yields about 0.1 lm/m^2 of illumination. The typical illumination level in a commercial office is about $1,000$ lm/m^2. Similarly, the following are typical values of $r(x,y)$: 0.01 for black velvet, 0.65 for stainless steel, 0.80 for flat-white wall paint, 0.90 for silver-plated metal, and 0.93 for snow.

Let the intensity (gray level) of a monochrome image at any coordinates (x, y) be denoted by

$$\ell = f(x, y) \tag{2-7}$$

From Eqs. (2-4) through (2-6) it is evident that ℓ lies in the range

$$L_{min} \le \ell \le L_{max} \tag{2-8}$$

In theory, the requirement on L_{min} is that it be nonnegative, and on L_{max} that it be finite. In practice, $L_{min} = i_{min} r_{min}$ and $L_{max} = i_{max} r_{max}$. From Example 2.1, using average office illumination and reflectance values as guidelines, we may expect $L_{min} \approx 10$ and $L_{max} \approx 1000$ to be typical indoor values in the absence of additional illumination. The units of these quantities are lum/m^2. However, actual units seldom are of interest, except in cases where photometric measurements are being performed.

The interval $[L_{min}, L_{max}]$ is called the *intensity* (or *gray*) *scale*. Common practice is to shift this interval numerically to the interval $[0, 1]$, or $[0, C]$, where $\ell = 0$ is considered black and $\ell = 1$ (or C) is considered white on the scale. All intermediate values are shades of gray varying from black to white.

2.4 IMAGE SAMPLING AND QUANTIZATION ▨

The discussion of sampling in this section is of an intuitive nature. We will discuss this topic in depth in Chapter 4.

As discussed in the previous section, there are numerous ways to acquire images, but our objective in all is the same: to generate digital images from sensed data. The output of most sensors is a continuous voltage waveform whose amplitude and spatial behavior are related to the physical phenomenon being sensed. To create a digital image, we need to convert the continuous sensed data into a digital format. This requires two processes: *sampling* and *quantization*.

BASIC CONCEPTS IN SAMPLING AND QUANTIZATION

Figure 2.16(a) shows a continuous image f that we want to convert to digital form. An image may be continuous with respect to the x- and y-coordinates, and also in

a b
c d

FIGURE 2.16
(a) Continuous image. (b) A scan line showing intensity variations along line *AB* in the continuous image. (c) Sampling and quantization. (d) Digital scan line. (The black border in (a) is included for clarity. It is not part of the image).

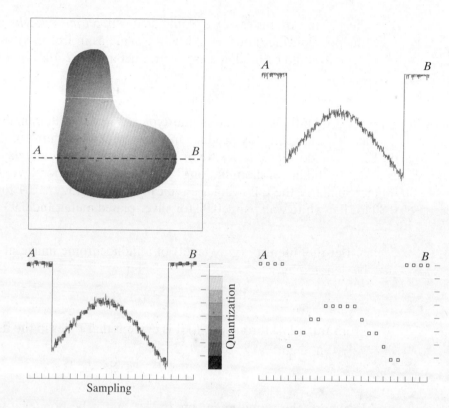

amplitude. To digitize it, we have to sample the function in both coordinates and also in amplitude. Digitizing the coordinate values is called *sampling*. Digitizing the amplitude values is called *quantization*.

The one-dimensional function in Fig. 2.16(b) is a plot of amplitude (intensity level) values of the continuous image along the line segment *AB* in Fig. 2.16(a). The random variations are due to image noise. To sample this function, we take equally spaced samples along line *AB*, as shown in Fig. 2.16(c). The samples are shown as small dark squares superimposed on the function, and their (discrete) spatial locations are indicated by corresponding tick marks in the bottom of the figure. The set of dark squares constitute the *sampled* function. However, the *values* of the samples still span (vertically) a continuous range of intensity values. In order to form a digital function, the intensity values also must be converted (*quantized*) into *discrete* quantities. The vertical gray bar in Fig. 2.16(c) depicts the intensity scale divided into eight discrete intervals, ranging from black to white. The vertical tick marks indicate the specific value assigned to each of the eight intensity intervals. The continuous intensity levels are quantized by assigning one of the eight values to each sample, depending on the vertical proximity of a sample to a vertical tick mark. The digital samples resulting from both sampling and quantization are shown as white squares in Fig. 2.16(d). Starting at the top of the continuous image and carrying out this procedure downward, line by line, produces a two-dimensional digital image. It is implied in Fig. 2.16 that, in addition to the number of discrete levels used, the accuracy achieved in quantization is highly dependent on the noise content of the sampled signal.

a b

FIGURE 2.17
(a) Continuous
image projected
onto a sensor
array. (b) Result
of image sampling
and quantization.

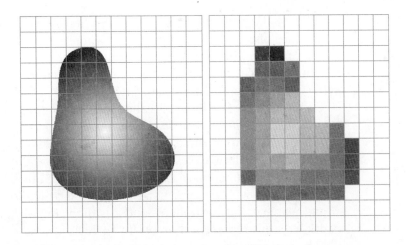

In practice, the method of sampling is determined by the sensor arrangement used to generate the image. When an image is generated by a single sensing element combined with mechanical motion, as in Fig. 2.13, the output of the sensor is quantized in the manner described above. However, spatial sampling is accomplished by selecting the number of individual mechanical increments at which we activate the sensor to collect data. Mechanical motion can be very exact so, in principle, there is almost no limit on how fine we can sample an image using this approach. In practice, limits on sampling accuracy are determined by other factors, such as the quality of the optical components used in the system.

When a sensing strip is used for image acquisition, the number of sensors in the strip establishes the samples in the resulting image in one direction, and mechanical motion establishes the number of samples in the other. Quantization of the sensor outputs completes the process of generating a digital image.

When a sensing array is used for image acquisition, no motion is required. The number of sensors in the array establishes the limits of sampling in both directions. Quantization of the sensor outputs is as explained above. Figure 2.17 illustrates this concept. Figure 2.17(a) shows a continuous image projected onto the plane of a 2-D sensor. Figure 2.17(b) shows the image after sampling and quantization. The quality of a digital image is determined to a large degree by the number of samples and discrete intensity levels used in sampling and quantization. However, as we will show later in this section, image content also plays a role in the choice of these parameters.

REPRESENTING DIGITAL IMAGES

Let $f(s, t)$ represent a *continuous* image function of two continuous variables, s and t. We convert this function into a *digital image* by sampling and quantization, as explained in the previous section. Suppose that we sample the continuous image into a digital image, $f(x, y)$, containing M rows and N columns, where (x, y) are discrete coordinates. For notational clarity and convenience, we use integer values for these discrete coordinates: $x = 0, 1, 2, \ldots, M - 1$ and $y = 0, 1, 2, \ldots, N - 1$. Thus, for example, the value of the digital image at the origin is $f(0,0)$, and its value at the next coordinates along the first row is $f(0,1)$. Here, the notation $(0, 1)$ is used to denote the second sample along the first row. It *does not* mean that these are the values of the physical coordinates when the image was sampled. In general, the value of a digital image at any coordinates (x, y) is denoted $f(x, y)$, where x and y are integers. When we need to refer to specific coordinates (i, j), we use the notation $f(i, j)$, where the arguments are integers. The section of the real plane spanned by the coordinates of an image is called the *spatial domain*, with x and y being referred to as *spatial variables* or *spatial coordinates*.

Figure 2.18 shows three ways of representing $f(x, y)$. Figure 2.18(a) is a plot of the function, with two axes determining spatial location and the third axis being the values of f as a function of x and y. This representation is useful when working with grayscale sets whose elements are expressed as triplets of the form (x, y, z), where x and y are spatial coordinates and z is the value of f at coordinates (x, y). We will work with this representation briefly in Section 2.6.

The representation in Fig. 2.18(b) is more common, and it shows $f(x, y)$ as it would appear on a computer display or photograph. Here, the intensity of each point in the display is proportional to the value of f at that point. In this figure, there are only three equally spaced intensity values. If the intensity is normalized to the interval $[0, 1]$, then each point in the image has the value $0, 0.5$, or 1. A monitor or printer converts these three values to black, gray, or white, respectively, as in Fig. 2.18(b). This type of representation includes color images, and allows us to view results at a glance.

As Fig. 2.18(c) shows, the third representation is an array (matrix) composed of the numerical values of $f(x, y)$. This is the representation used for computer processing. In equation form, we write the representation of an $M \times N$ numerical array as

$$f(x, y) = \begin{bmatrix} f(0,0) & f(0,1) & \cdots & f(0, N-1) \\ f(1,0) & f(1,1) & \cdots & f(1, N-1) \\ \vdots & \vdots & & \vdots \\ f(M-1,0) & f(M-1,1) & \cdots & f(M-1, N-1) \end{bmatrix} \qquad (2\text{-}9)$$

The right side of this equation is a digital image represented as an array of real numbers. Each element of this array is called an *image element, picture element, pixel,* or *pel*. We use the terms *image* and *pixel* throughout the book to denote a digital image and its elements. Figure 2.19 shows a graphical representation of an image array, where the x- and y-axis are used to denote the rows and columns of the array. Specific pixels are values of the array at a fixed pair of coordinates. As mentioned earlier, we generally use $f(i, j)$ when referring to a pixel with coordinates (i, j).

We can also represent a digital image in a traditional matrix form:

$$\mathbf{A} = \begin{bmatrix} a_{0,0} & a_{0,1} & \cdots & a_{0,N-1} \\ a_{1,0} & a_{1,1} & \cdots & a_{1,N-1} \\ \vdots & \vdots & & \vdots \\ a_{M-1,0} & a_{M-1,1} & \cdots & a_{M-1,N-1} \end{bmatrix} \qquad (2\text{-}10)$$

Clearly, $a_{ij} = f(i, j)$, so Eqs. (2-9) and (2-10) denote identical arrays.

a
b c

FIGURE 2.18
(a) Image plotted
as a surface.
(b) Image displayed
as a visual intensity
array. (c) Image
shown as a 2-D nu-
merical array. (The
numbers 0, .5, and
1 represent black,
gray, and white,
respectively.)

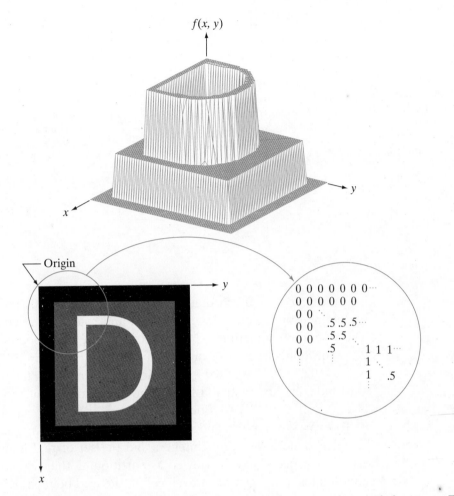

As Fig. 2.19 shows, we define the *origin* of an image at the top left corner. This is a convention based on the fact that many image displays (e.g., TV monitors) sweep an image starting at the top left and moving to the right, one row at a time. More important is the fact that the first element of a matrix is by convention at the top left of the array. Choosing the origin of $f(x, y)$ at that point makes sense mathematically because digital images in reality are matrices. In fact, as you will see, sometimes we use x and y interchangeably in equations with the *rows* (r) and *columns* (c) of a matrix.

It is important to note that the representation in Fig. 2.19, in which the positive x-axis extends downward and the positive y-axis extends to the right, is precisely the right-handed Cartesian coordinate system with which you are familiar,[†] but shown rotated by 90° so that the origin appears on the top, left.

[†]Recall that a right-handed coordinate system is such that, when the index of the right hand points in the direction of the positive x-axis and the middle finger points in the (perpendicular) direction of the positive y-axis, the thumb points up. As Figs. 2.18 and 2.19 show, this indeed is the case in our image coordinate system. In practice, you will also find implementations based on a left-handed system, in which the x- and y-axis are interchanged from the way we show them in Figs. 2.18 and 2.19. For example, MATLAB uses a left-handed system for image processing. Both systems are perfectly valid, provided they are used consistently.

FIGURE 2.19
Coordinate convention used to represent digital images. Because coordinate values are integers, there is a one-to-one correspondence between x and y and the rows (r) and columns (c) of a matrix.

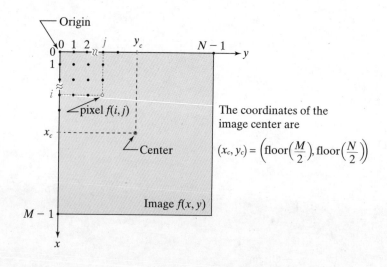

The *center* of an $M \times N$ digital image with origin at $(0,0)$ and range to $(M-1, N-1)$ is obtained by dividing M and N by 2 and rounding *down* to the nearest integer. This operation sometimes is denoted using the floor operator, $\lfloor \cdot \rfloor$, as shown in Fig. 2.19. This holds true for M and N even *or* odd. For example, the center of an image of size 1023×1024 is at $(511, 512)$. Some programming languages (e.g., MATLAB) start indexing at 1 instead of at 0. The center of an image in that case is found at $(x_c, y_c) = (\text{floor}(M/2) + 1, \text{floor}(N/2) + 1)$.

To express sampling and quantization in more formal mathematical terms, let Z and R denote the set of integers and the set of real numbers, respectively. The sampling process may be viewed as partitioning the xy-plane into a grid, with the coordinates of the center of each cell in the grid being a pair of elements from the Cartesian product Z^2 (also denoted $Z \times Z$) which, as you may recall, is the set of all ordered pairs of elements (z_i, z_j) with z_i and z_j being integers from set Z. Hence, $f(x, y)$ is a digital image if (x, y) are integers from Z^2 and f is a function that assigns an intensity value (that is, a real number from the set of real numbers, R) to each distinct pair of coordinates (x, y). This functional assignment is the quantization process described earlier. If the intensity levels also are integers, then $R = Z$, and a digital image becomes a 2-D function whose coordinates and amplitude values are integers. This is the representation we use in the book.

Image digitization requires that decisions be made regarding the values for M, N, and for the number, L, of discrete intensity levels. There are no restrictions placed on M and N, other than they have to be positive integers. However, digital storage and quantizing hardware considerations usually lead to the number of intensity levels, L, being an integer power of two; that is

$$L = 2^k \tag{2-11}$$

where k is an integer. We assume that the discrete levels are equally spaced and that they are integers in the range $[0, L-1]$.

The *floor* of z, sometimes denoted $\lfloor z \rfloor$, is the largest integer that is less than or equal to z. The *ceiling* of z, denoted $\lceil z \rceil$, is the smallest integer that is greater than or equal to z.

See Eq. (2-41) in Section 2.6 for a formal definition of the Cartesian product.

FIGURE 2.20
An image exhibiting saturation and noise. Saturation is the highest value beyond which all intensity values are clipped (note how the entire saturated area has a high, constant intensity level). Visible noise in this case appears as a grainy texture pattern. The dark background is noisier, but the noise is difficult to see.

Sometimes, the range of values spanned by the gray scale is referred to as the *dynamic range*, a term used in different ways in different fields. Here, we define the dynamic range of an imaging system to be the ratio of the maximum measurable intensity to the minimum detectable intensity level in the system. As a rule, the upper limit is determined by *saturation* and the lower limit by *noise*, although noise can be present also in lighter intensities. Figure 2.20 shows examples of saturation and slight visible noise. Because the darker regions are composed primarily of pixels with the minimum detectable intensity, the background in Fig. 2.20 is the noisiest part of the image; however, dark background noise typically is much harder to see.

The dynamic range establishes the lowest and highest intensity levels that a system can represent and, consequently, that an image can have. Closely associated with this concept is *image contrast*, which we define as the difference in intensity between the highest and lowest intensity levels in an image. The *contrast ratio* is the ratio of these two quantities. When an appreciable number of pixels in an image have a high dynamic range, we can expect the image to have high contrast. Conversely, an image with low dynamic range typically has a dull, washed-out gray look. We will discuss these concepts in more detail in Chapter 3.

The number, b, of bits required to store a digital image is

$$b = M \times N \times k \tag{2-12}$$

When $M = N$, this equation becomes

$$b = N^2 k \tag{2-13}$$

FIGURE 2.21
Number of megabytes required to store images for various values of N and k.

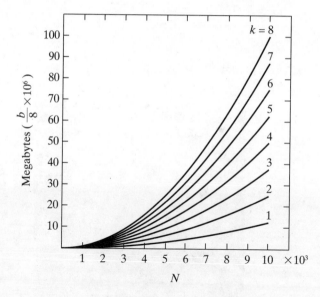

Figure 2.21 shows the number of megabytes required to store square images for various values of N and k (as usual, one byte equals 8 bits and a megabyte equals 10^6 bytes).

When an image can have 2^k possible intensity levels, it is common practice to refer to it as a "k-bit image," (e.g., a 256-level image is called an *8-bit image*). Note that storage requirements for large 8-bit images (e.g., $10,000 \times 10,000$ pixels) are not insignificant.

LINEAR VS. COORDINATE INDEXING

The convention discussed in the previous section, in which the location of a pixel is given by its 2-D coordinates, is referred to as *coordinate indexing*, or *subscript indexing*. Another type of indexing used extensively in programming image processing algorithms is *linear indexing*, which consists of a 1-D string of nonnegative integers based on computing offsets from coordinates $(0,0)$. There are two principal types of linear indexing, one is based on a row scan of an image, and the other on a column scan.

Figure 2.22 illustrates the principle of linear indexing based on a column scan. The idea is to scan an image column by column, starting at the origin and proceeding down and then to the right. The linear index is based on counting pixels as we scan the image in the manner shown in Fig. 2.22. Thus, a scan of the first (leftmost) column yields linear indices 0 through $M - 1$. A scan of the second column yields indices M through $2M - 1$, and so on, until the last pixel in the last column is assigned the linear index value $MN - 1$. Thus, a linear index, denoted by α, has one of MN possible values: $0, 1, 2, \ldots, MN - 1$, as Fig. 2.22 shows. The important thing to notice here is that each pixel is assigned a linear index value that identifies it uniquely.

The formula for generating linear indices based on a column scan is straightforward and can be determined by inspection. For any pair of coordinates (x, y), the corresponding linear index value is

$$\alpha = My + x \tag{2-14}$$

FIGURE 2.22
Illustration of column scanning for generating linear indices. Shown are several 2-D coordinates (in parentheses) and their corresponding linear indices.

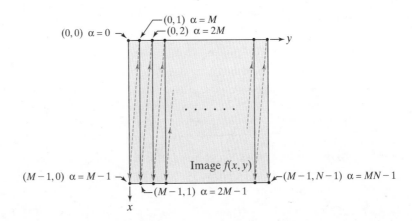

Conversely, the coordinate indices for a given linear index value α are given by the equations[†]

$$x = \alpha \bmod M \qquad (2\text{-}15)$$

and

$$y = (\alpha - x)/M \qquad (2\text{-}16)$$

Recall that $\alpha \bmod M$ means "the remainder of the division of α by M." This is a formal way of stating that row numbers repeat themselves at the start of every column. Thus, when $\alpha = 0$, the remainder of the division of 0 by M is 0, so $x = 0$. When $\alpha = 1$, the remainder is 1, and so $x = 1$. You can see that x will continue to be equal to α until $\alpha = M - 1$. When $\alpha = M$ (which is at the beginning of the second column), the remainder is 0, and thus $x = 0$ again, and it increases by 1 until the next column is reached, when the pattern repeats itself. Similar comments apply to Eq. (2-16). See Problem 2.11 for a derivation of the preceding two equations.

SPATIAL AND INTENSITY RESOLUTION

Intuitively, *spatial resolution* is a measure of the smallest discernible detail in an image. Quantitatively, spatial resolution can be stated in several ways, with *line pairs per unit distance*, and *dots (pixels) per unit distance* being common measures. Suppose that we construct a chart with alternating black and white vertical lines, each of width W units (W can be less than 1). The width of a *line pair* is thus $2W$, and there are $W/2$ line pairs per unit distance. For example, if the width of a line is 0.1 mm, there are 5 line pairs per unit distance (i.e., per mm). A widely used definition of image resolution is the largest number of *discernible* line pairs per unit distance (e.g., 100 line pairs per mm). Dots per unit distance is a measure of image resolution used in the printing and publishing industry. In the U.S., this measure usually is expressed as *dots per inch* (dpi). To give you an idea of quality, newspapers are printed with a

---

[†]When working with modular number systems, it is more accurate to write $x \equiv \alpha \bmod M$, where the symbol $\equiv$ means *congruence*. However, our interest here is just on converting from linear to coordinate indexing, so we use the more familiar equal sign.

resolution of 75 dpi, magazines at 133 dpi, glossy brochures at 175 dpi, and the book page at which you are presently looking was printed at 2400 dpi.

To be meaningful, measures of spatial resolution must be stated with respect to spatial units. Image size by itself does not tell the complete story. For example, to say that an image has a resolution of 1024×1024 pixels is not a meaningful statement without stating the spatial dimensions encompassed by the image. Size by itself is helpful only in making comparisons between imaging capabilities. For instance, a digital camera with a 20-megapixel CCD imaging chip can be expected to have a higher capability to resolve detail than an 8-megapixel camera, assuming that both cameras are equipped with comparable lenses and the comparison images are taken at the same distance.

Intensity resolution similarly refers to the smallest *discernible* change in intensity level. We have considerable discretion regarding the number of spatial samples (pixels) used to generate a digital image, but this is not true regarding the number of intensity levels. Based on hardware considerations, the number of intensity levels usually is an integer power of two, as we mentioned when discussing Eq. (2-11). The most common number is 8 bits, with 16 bits being used in some applications in which enhancement of specific intensity ranges is necessary. Intensity quantization using 32 bits is rare. Sometimes one finds systems that can digitize the intensity levels of an image using 10 or 12 bits, but these are not as common.

Unlike spatial resolution, which must be based on a per-unit-of-distance basis to be meaningful, it is common practice to refer to the number of bits used to quantize intensity as the "*intensity resolution*." For example, it is common to say that an image whose intensity is quantized into 256 levels has 8 bits of intensity resolution. However, keep in mind that *discernible* changes in intensity are influenced also by noise and saturation values, and by the capabilities of human perception to analyze and interpret details in the context of an entire scene (see Section 2.1). The following two examples illustrate the effects of spatial and intensity resolution on discernible detail. Later in this section, we will discuss how these two parameters interact in determining perceived image quality.

EXAMPLE 2.2: Effects of reducing the spatial resolution of a digital image.

Figure 2.23 shows the effects of reducing the spatial resolution of an image. The images in Figs. 2.23(a) through (d) have resolutions of 930, 300, 150, and 72 dpi, respectively. Naturally, the lower resolution images are smaller than the original image in (a). For example, the original image is of size 2136×2140 pixels, but the 72 dpi image is an array of only 165×166 pixels. In order to facilitate comparisons, all the smaller images were zoomed back to the original size (the method used for zooming will be discussed later in this section). This is somewhat equivalent to "getting closer" to the smaller images so that we can make comparable statements about visible details.

There are some small visual differences between Figs. 2.23(a) and (b), the most notable being a slight distortion in the seconds marker pointing to 60 on the right side of the chronometer. For the most part, however, Fig. 2.23(b) is quite acceptable. In fact, 300 dpi is the typical minimum image spatial resolution used for book publishing, so one would not expect to see much difference between these two images. Figure 2.23(c) begins to show visible degradation (see, for example, the outer edges of the chronometer

a b
c d

FIGURE 2.23
Effects of
reducing spatial
resolution. The
images shown
are at:
(a) 930 dpi,
(b) 300 dpi,
(c) 150 dpi, and
(d) 72 dpi.

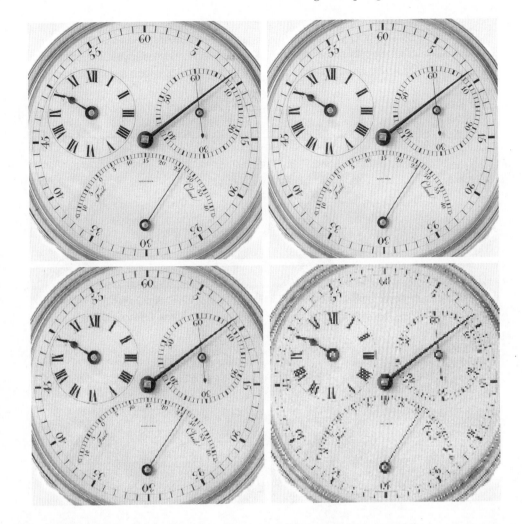

case and compare the seconds marker with the previous two images). The numbers also show visible degradation. Figure 2.23(d) shows degradation that is visible in most features of the image. When printing at such low resolutions, the printing and publishing industry uses a number of techniques (such as locally varying the pixel size) to produce much better results than those in Fig. 2.23(d). Also, as we will show later in this section, it is possible to improve on the results of Fig. 2.23 by the choice of interpolation method used.

EXAMPLE 2.3: Effects of varying the number of intensity levels in a digital image.

Figure 2.24(a) is a 774×640 CT projection image, displayed using 256 intensity levels (see Chapter 1 regarding CT images). The objective of this example is to reduce the number of intensities of the image from 256 to 2 in integer powers of 2, while keeping the spatial resolution constant. Figures 2.24(b) through (d) were obtained by reducing the number of intensity levels to 128, 64, and 32, respectively (we will discuss in Chapter 3 how to reduce the number of levels).

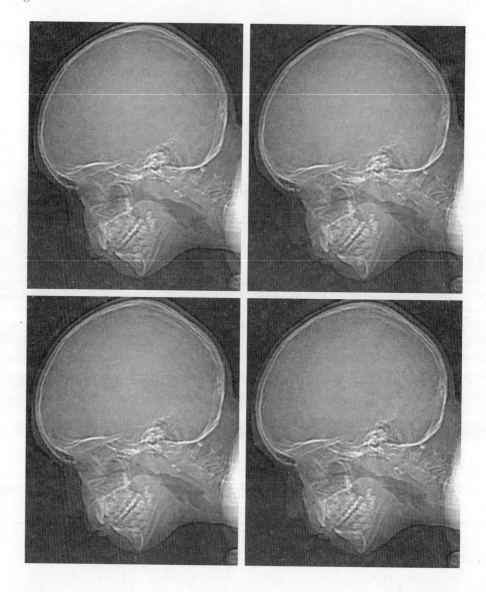

a b
c d

FIGURE 2.24
(a) 774×640,
256-level image.
(b)-(d) Image
displayed in 128,
64, and 32 inten-
sity levels, while
keeping the
spatial resolution
constant.
(Original image
courtesy of the
Dr. David R.
Pickens,
Department of
Radiology &
Radiological
Sciences,
Vanderbilt
University
Medical Center.)

The 128- and 64-level images are visually identical for all practical purposes. However, the 32-level image in Fig. 2.24(d) has a set of almost imperceptible, very fine ridge-like structures in areas of constant intensity. These structures are clearly visible in the 16-level image in Fig. 2.24(e). This effect, caused by using an insufficient number of intensity levels in smooth areas of a digital image, is called *false contouring*, so named because the ridges resemble topographic contours in a map. False contouring generally is quite objectionable in images displayed using 16 or fewer uniformly spaced intensity levels, as the images in Figs. 2.24(e)-(h) show.

As a very rough guideline, and assuming integer powers of 2 for convenience, images of size 256×256 pixels with 64 intensity levels, and printed on a size format on the order of 5×5 cm, are about the lowest spatial and intensity resolution images that can be expected to be reasonably free of objectionable sampling distortions and false contouring.

e f
g h

FIGURE 2.24
(*Continued*)
(e)-(h) Image
displayed in 16, 8,
4, and 2 intensity
levels.

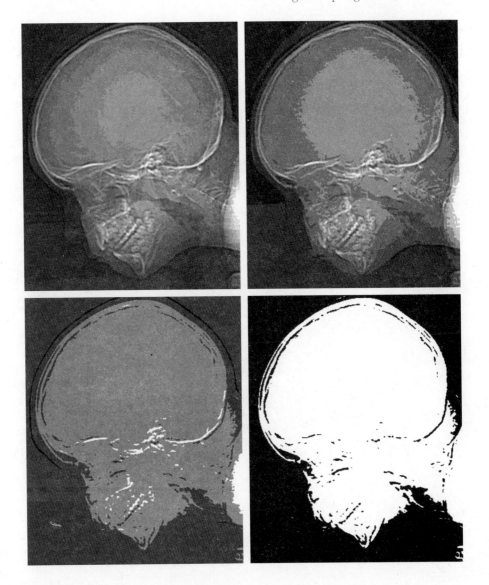

The results in Examples 2.2 and 2.3 illustrate the effects produced on image quality by varying spatial and intensity resolution independently. However, these results did not consider any relationships that might exist between these two parameters. An early study by Huang [1965] attempted to quantify experimentally the effects on image quality produced by the interaction of these two variables. The experiment consisted of a set of subjective tests. Images similar to those shown in Fig. 2.25 were used. The woman's face represents an image with relatively little detail; the picture of the cameraman contains an intermediate amount of detail; and the crowd picture contains, by comparison, a large amount of detail.

Sets of these three types of images of various sizes and intensity resolution were generated by varying N and k [see Eq. (2-13)]. Observers were then asked to rank

a b c

FIGURE 2.25 (a) Image with a low level of detail. (b) Image with a medium level of detail. (c) Image with a relatively large amount of detail. (Image (b) courtesy of the Massachusetts Institute of Technology.)

them according to their subjective quality. Results were summarized in the form of so-called *isopreference curves* in the Nk-plane. (Figure 2.26 shows average isopreference curves representative of the types of images in Fig. 2.25.) Each point in the Nk-plane represents an image having values of N and k equal to the coordinates of that point. Points lying on an isopreference curve correspond to images of equal subjective quality. It was found in the course of the experiments that the isopreference curves tended to shift right and upward, but their shapes in each of the three image categories were similar to those in Fig. 2.26. These results were not unexpected, because a shift up and right in the curves simply means larger values for N and k, which implies better picture quality.

FIGURE 2.26
Representative
isopreference
curves for the
three types of
images in
Fig. 2.25.

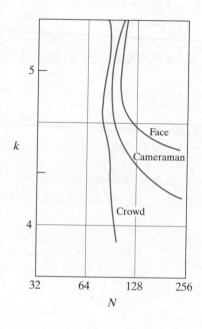

Observe that isopreference curves tend to become more vertical as the detail in the image increases. This result suggests that for images with a large amount of detail only a few intensity levels may be needed. For example, the isopreference curve in Fig. 2.26 corresponding to the crowd is nearly vertical. This indicates that, for a fixed value of N, the perceived quality for this type of image is nearly independent of the number of intensity levels used (for the range of intensity levels shown in Fig. 2.26). The perceived quality in the other two image categories remained the same in some intervals in which the number of samples was increased, but the number of intensity levels actually decreased. The most likely reason for this result is that a decrease in k tends to increase the apparent contrast, a visual effect often perceived as improved image quality.

IMAGE INTERPOLATION

Interpolation is used in tasks such as zooming, shrinking, rotating, and geometrically correcting digital images. Our principal objective in this section is to introduce interpolation and apply it to image resizing (shrinking and zooming), which are basically image resampling methods. Uses of interpolation in applications such as rotation and geometric corrections will be discussed in Section 2.6.

Interpolation is the process of using known data to estimate values at unknown locations. We begin the discussion of this topic with a short example. Suppose that an image of size 500×500 pixels has to be enlarged 1.5 times to 750×750 pixels. A simple way to visualize zooming is to create an imaginary 750×750 grid with the same pixel spacing as the original image, then shrink it so that it exactly overlays the original image. Obviously, the pixel spacing in the shrunken 750×750 grid will be less than the pixel spacing in the original image. To assign an intensity value to any point in the overlay, we look for its closest pixel in the underlying original image and assign the intensity of that pixel to the new pixel in the 750×750 grid. When intensities have been assigned to all the points in the overlay grid, we expand it back to the specified size to obtain the resized image.

The method just discussed is called *nearest neighbor interpolation* because it assigns to each new location the intensity of its nearest neighbor in the original image (see Section 2.5 regarding neighborhoods). This approach is simple but, it has the tendency to produce undesirable artifacts, such as severe distortion of straight edges. A more suitable approach is *bilinear interpolation*, in which we use the four nearest neighbors to estimate the intensity at a given location. Let (x, y) denote the coordinates of the location to which we want to assign an intensity value (think of it as a point of the grid described previously), and let $v(x, y)$ denote that intensity value. For bilinear interpolation, the assigned value is obtained using the equation

$$v(x, y) = ax + by + cxy + d \tag{2-17}$$

Contrary to what the name suggests, bilinear interpolation is *not* a linear operation because it involves multiplication of coordinates (which is not a linear operation). See Eq. (2-17).

where the four coefficients are determined from the four equations in four unknowns that can be written using the *four* nearest neighbors of point (x, y). Bilinear interpolation gives much better results than nearest neighbor interpolation, with a modest increase in computational burden.

The next level of complexity is *bicubic interpolation*, which involves the sixteen nearest neighbors of a point. The intensity value assigned to point (x, y) is obtained using the equation

$$v(x, y) = \sum_{i=0}^{3} \sum_{j=0}^{3} a_{ij} x^i y^j \qquad (2\text{-}18)$$

The sixteen coefficients are determined from the sixteen equations with sixteen unknowns that can be written using the sixteen nearest neighbors of point (x, y). Observe that Eq. (2-18) reduces in form to Eq. (2-17) if the limits of both summations in the former equation are 0 to 1. Generally, bicubic interpolation does a better job of preserving fine detail than its bilinear counterpart. Bicubic interpolation is the standard used in commercial image editing applications, such as Adobe Photoshop and Corel Photopaint.

Although images are displayed with integer coordinates, it is possible during processing to work with *subpixel accuracy* by increasing the size of the image using interpolation to "fill the gaps" between pixels in the original image.

EXAMPLE 2.4: Comparison of interpolation approaches for image shrinking and zooming.

Figure 2.27(a) is the same as Fig. 2.23(d), which was obtained by reducing the resolution of the 930 dpi image in Fig. 2.23(a) to 72 dpi (the size shrank from 2136×2140 to 165×166 pixels) and then zooming the reduced image back to its original size. To generate Fig. 2.23(d) we used nearest neighbor interpolation both to shrink and zoom the image. As noted earlier, the result in Fig. 2.27(a) is rather poor. Figures 2.27(b) and (c) are the results of repeating the same procedure but using, respectively, bilinear and bicubic interpolation for both shrinking and zooming. The result obtained by using bilinear interpolation is a significant improvement over nearest neighbor interpolation, but the resulting image is blurred slightly. Much sharper results can be obtained using bicubic interpolation, as Fig. 2.27(c) shows.

a b c

FIGURE 2.27 (a) Image reduced to 72 dpi and zoomed back to its original 930 dpi using nearest neighbor interpolation. This figure is the same as Fig. 2.23(d). (b) Image reduced to 72 dpi and zoomed using bilinear interpolation. (c) Same as (b) but using bicubic interpolation.

It is possible to use more neighbors in interpolation, and there are more complex techniques, such as using *splines* or *wavelets*, that in some instances can yield better results than the methods just discussed. While preserving fine detail is an exceptionally important consideration in image generation for 3-D graphics (for example, see Hughes and Andries [2013]), the extra computational burden seldom is justifiable for general-purpose digital image processing, where bilinear or bicubic interpolation typically are the methods of choice.

2.5 SOME BASIC RELATIONSHIPS BETWEEN PIXELS

In this section, we discuss several important relationships between pixels in a digital image. When referring in the following discussion to particular pixels, we use lower-case letters, such as p and q.

NEIGHBORS OF A PIXEL

A pixel p at coordinates (x, y) has two horizontal and two vertical neighbors with coordinates

$$(x+1, y), (x-1, y), (x, y+1), (x, y-1)$$

This set of pixels, called the 4-*neighbors* of p, is denoted $N_4(p)$.

The four *diagonal* neighbors of p have coordinates

$$(x+1, y+1), (x+1, y-1), (x-1, y+1), (x-1, y-1)$$

and are denoted $N_D(p)$. These neighbors, together with the 4-neighbors, are called the 8-*neighbors* of p, denoted by $N_8(p)$. The set of image locations of the neighbors of a point p is called the *neighborhood* of p. The neighborhood is said to be *closed* if it contains p. Otherwise, the neighborhood is said to be *open*.

ADJACENCY, CONNECTIVITY, REGIONS, AND BOUNDARIES

Let V be the set of intensity values used to define adjacency. In a binary image, $V = \{1\}$ if we are referring to adjacency of pixels with value 1. In a grayscale image, the idea is the same, but set V typically contains more elements. For example, if we are dealing with the adjacency of pixels whose values are in the range 0 to 255, set V could be any subset of these 256 values. We consider three types of adjacency:

1. 4-*adjacency*. Two pixels p and q with values from V are 4-adjacent if q is in the set $N_4(p)$.
2. 8-*adjacency*. Two pixels p and q with values from V are 8-adjacent if q is in the set $N_8(p)$.
3. *m-adjacency* (also called *mixed adjacency*). Two pixels p and q with values from V are *m*-adjacent if

(a) q is in $N_4(p)$, *or*

(b) q is in $N_D(p)$ *and* the set $N_4(p) \cap N_4(q)$ has no pixels whose values are from V.

We use the symbols $\cap$ and $\cup$ to denote set intersection and union, respectively. Given sets A and B, recall that their intersection is the set of elements that are members of both A and B. The union of these two sets is the set of elements that are members of A, of B, or of both. We will discuss sets in more detail in Section 2.6.

Mixed adjacency is a modification of 8-adjacency, and is introduced to eliminate the ambiguities that may result from using 8-adjacency. For example, consider the pixel arrangement in Fig. 2.28(a) and let $V = \{1\}$. The three pixels at the top of Fig. 2.28(b) show multiple (ambiguous) 8-adjacency, as indicated by the dashed lines. This ambiguity is removed by using m-adjacency, as in Fig. 2.28(c). In other words, the center and upper-right diagonal pixels are not m-adjacent because they do not satisfy condition (b).

A *digital path* (or *curve*) from pixel p with coordinates (x_0, y_0) to pixel q with coordinates (x_n, y_n) is a sequence of distinct pixels with coordinates

$$(x_0, y_0), (x_1, y_1), \ldots, (x_n, y_n)$$

where points (x_i, y_i) and (x_{i-1}, y_{i-1}) are adjacent for $1 \leq i \leq n$. In this case, n is the *length* of the path. If $(x_0, y_0) = (x_n, y_n)$ the path is a *closed* path. We can define 4-, 8-, or m-paths, depending on the type of adjacency specified. For example, the paths in Fig. 2.28(b) between the top right and bottom right points are 8-paths, and the path in Fig. 2.28(c) is an m-path.

Let S represent a subset of pixels in an image. Two pixels p and q are said to be *connected in S* if there exists a path between them consisting entirely of pixels in S. For any pixel p in S, the set of pixels that are connected to it in S is called a *connected component* of S. If it only has one component, and that component is connected, then S is called a *connected set*.

Let R represent a subset of pixels in an image. We call R a *region* of the image if R is a connected set. Two regions, R_i and R_j are said to be *adjacent* if their union forms a connected set. Regions that are not adjacent are said to be *disjoint*. We consider 4- and 8-adjacency when referring to regions. For our definition to make sense, the type of adjacency used must be specified. For example, the two regions of 1's in Fig. 2.28(d) are adjacent only if 8-adjacency is used (according to the definition in the previous

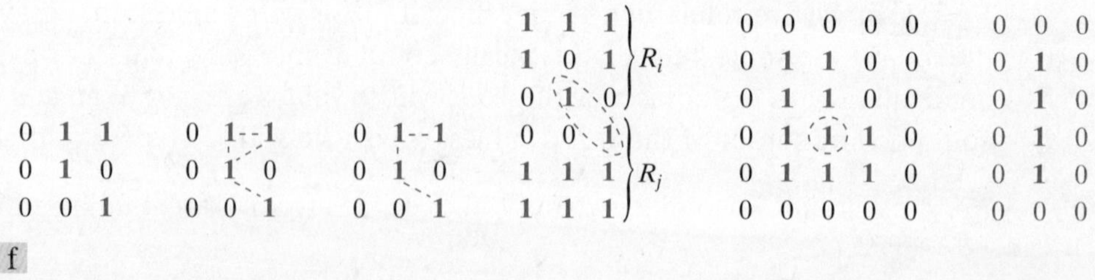

a b c d e f

FIGURE 2.28 (a) An arrangement of pixels. (b) Pixels that are 8-adjacent (adjacency is shown by dashed lines). (c) m-adjacency. (d) Two regions (of 1's) that are 8-adjacent. (e) The circled point is on the boundary of the 1-valued pixels only if 8-adjacency between the region and background is used. (f) The inner boundary of the 1-valued region does not form a closed path, but its outer boundary does.

paragraph, a 4-path between the two regions does not exist, so their union is not a connected set).

Suppose an image contains K disjoint regions, $R_k, k = 1, 2, \ldots, K$, none of which touches the image border.[†] Let R_u denote the union of all the K regions, and let $(R_u)^c$ denote its complement (recall that the *complement* of a set A is the set of points that are not in A). We call all the points in R_u the *foreground*, and all the points in $(R_u)^c$ the *background* of the image.

The *boundary* (also called the *border* or *contour*) of a region R is the set of pixels in R that are adjacent to pixels in the complement of R. Stated another way, the border of a region is the set of pixels in the region that have at least one background neighbor. Here again, we must specify the connectivity being used to define adjacency. For example, the point circled in Fig. 2.28(e) is not a member of the border of the 1-valued region if 4-connectivity is used between the region and its background, because the only possible connection between that point and the background is diagonal. As a rule, adjacency between points in a region and its background is defined using 8-connectivity to handle situations such as this.

The preceding definition sometimes is referred to as the *inner border* of the region to distinguish it from its *outer border*, which is the corresponding border in the background. This distinction is important in the development of border-following algorithms. Such algorithms usually are formulated to follow the outer boundary in order to guarantee that the result will form a closed path. For instance, the inner border of the 1-valued region in Fig. 2.28(f) is the region itself. This border does not satisfy the definition of a closed path. On the other hand, the outer border of the region does form a closed path around the region.

If R happens to be an entire image, then its *boundary* (or *border*) is defined as the set of pixels in the first and last rows and columns of the image. This extra definition is required because an image has no neighbors beyond its border. Normally, when we refer to a region, we are referring to a subset of an image, and any pixels in the boundary of the region that happen to coincide with the border of the image are included implicitly as part of the region boundary.

The concept of an *edge* is found frequently in discussions dealing with regions and boundaries. However, there is a key difference between these two concepts. The boundary of a finite region forms a closed path and is thus a "global" concept. As we will discuss in detail in Chapter 10, edges are formed from pixels with derivative values that exceed a preset threshold. Thus, an edge is a "local" concept that is based on a measure of intensity-level discontinuity at a point. It is possible to link edge points into edge segments, and sometimes these segments are linked in such a way that they correspond to boundaries, but this is not always the case. The one exception in which edges and boundaries correspond is in binary images. Depending on the type of connectivity and edge operators used (we will discuss these in Chapter 10), the edge extracted from a binary region will be the same as the region boundary. This is

---

[†] We make this assumption to avoid having to deal with special cases. This can be done without loss of generality because if one or more regions touch the border of an image, we can simply pad the image with a 1-pixel-wide border of background values.

intuitive. Conceptually, until we arrive at Chapter 10, it is helpful to think of edges as intensity discontinuities, and of boundaries as closed paths.

DISTANCE MEASURES

For pixels p, q, and s, with coordinates (x, y), (u, v), and (w, z), respectively, D is a *distance function* or *metric* if

(a) $D(p,q) \geq 0$ $(D(p,q) = 0$ iff $p = q)$,

(b) $D(p,q) = D(q,p)$, and

(c) $D(p,s) \leq D(p,q) + D(q,s)$.

The *Euclidean distance* between p and q is defined as

$$D_e(p,q) = \left[(x-u)^2 + (y-v)^2\right]^{\frac{1}{2}} \qquad (2\text{-}19)$$

For this distance measure, the pixels having a distance less than or equal to some value r from (x, y) are the points contained in a disk of radius r centered at (x, y).

The D_4 *distance*, (called the *city-block distance*) between p and q is defined as

$$D_4(p,q) = |x - u| + |y - v| \qquad (2\text{-}20)$$

In this case, pixels having a D_4 distance from (x, y) that is less than or equal to some value d form a diamond centered at (x, y). For example, the pixels with D_4 distance ≤ 2 from (x, y) (the center point) form the following contours of constant distance:

```
        2
      2 1 2
    2 1 0 1 2
      2 1 2
        2
```

The pixels with $D_4 = 1$ are the 4-neighbors of (x, y).

The D_8 *distance* (called the *chessboard distance*) between p and q is defined as

$$D_8(p,q) = \max(|x - u|, |y - v|) \qquad (2\text{-}21)$$

In this case, the pixels with D_8 distance from (x, y) less than or equal to some value d form a square centered at (x, y). For example, the pixels with D_8 distance ≤ 2 form the following contours of constant distance:

```
    2 2 2 2 2
    2 1 1 1 2
    2 1 0 1 2
    2 1 1 1 2
    2 2 2 2 2
```

The pixels with $D_8 = 1$ are the 8-neighbors of the pixel at (x, y).

Note that the D_4 and D_8 distances between p and q are independent of any paths that might exist between these points because these distances involve only the coordinates of the points. In the case of m-adjacency, however, the D_m distance between two points is defined as the shortest m-path between the points. In this case, the distance between two pixels will depend on the values of the pixels along the path, as well as the values of their neighbors. For instance, consider the following arrangement of pixels and assume that p, p_2, and p_4 have a value of 1, and that p_1 and p_3 can be 0 or 1:

$$
\begin{matrix}
 & p_3 & p_4 \\
p_1 & p_2 & \\
p & &
\end{matrix}
$$

Suppose that we consider adjacency of pixels valued 1 (i.e., $V = \{1\}$). If p_1 and p_3 are 0, the length of the shortest m-path (the D_m distance) between p and p_4 is 2. If p_1 is 1, then p_2 and p will no longer be m-adjacent (see the definition of m-adjacency given earlier) and the length of the shortest m-path becomes 3 (the path goes through the points $p\,p_1p_2p_4$). Similar comments apply if p_3 is 1 (and p_1 is 0); in this case, the length of the shortest m-path also is 3. Finally, if both p_1 and p_3 are 1, the length of the shortest m-path between p and p_4 is 4. In this case, the path goes through the sequence of points $p\,p_1p_2p_3p_4$.

2.6 INTRODUCTION TO THE BASIC MATHEMATICAL TOOLS USED IN DIGITAL IMAGE PROCESSING

You may find it helpful to download and study the review material dealing with probability, vectors, linear algebra, and linear systems. The review is available in the Tutorials section of the book website.

This section has two principal objectives: (1) to introduce various mathematical tools we use throughout the book; and (2) to help you begin developing a "feel" for how these tools are used by applying them to a variety of basic image-processing tasks, some of which will be used numerous times in subsequent discussions.

ELEMENTWISE VERSUS MATRIX OPERATIONS

An *elementwise operation* involving one or more images is carried out on a *pixel-by-pixel* basis. We mentioned earlier in this chapter that images can be viewed equivalently as matrices. In fact, as you will see later in this section, there are many situations in which operations between images are carried out using matrix theory. It is for this reason that a clear distinction must be made between elementwise and matrix operations. For example, consider the following 2×2 images (matrices):

$$
\begin{bmatrix} a_{11} & a_{12} \\ a_{21} & a_{22} \end{bmatrix} \quad \text{and} \quad \begin{bmatrix} b_{11} & b_{12} \\ b_{21} & b_{22} \end{bmatrix}
$$

The elementwise product of two matrices is also called the *Hadamard product* of the matrices.

The *elementwise product* (often denoted using the symbol $\odot$ or $\otimes$) of these two images is

The symbol $\ominus$ is often used to denote *elementwise division*.

$$
\begin{bmatrix} a_{11} & a_{12} \\ a_{21} & a_{22} \end{bmatrix} \odot \begin{bmatrix} b_{11} & b_{12} \\ b_{21} & b_{22} \end{bmatrix} = \begin{bmatrix} a_{11}b_{11} & a_{12}b_{12} \\ a_{21}b_{21} & a_{22}b_{22} \end{bmatrix}
$$

That is, the elementwise product is obtained by multiplying pairs of *corresponding* pixels. On the other hand, the *matrix product* of the images is formed using the rules of matrix multiplication:

$$\begin{bmatrix} a_{11} & a_{12} \\ a_{21} & a_{22} \end{bmatrix} \begin{bmatrix} b_{11} & b_{12} \\ b_{21} & b_{22} \end{bmatrix} = \begin{bmatrix} a_{11}b_{11} + a_{12}b_{21} & a_{11}b_{12} + a_{12}b_{22} \\ a_{21}b_{11} + a_{22}b_{21} & a_{21}b_{12} + a_{22}b_{22} \end{bmatrix}$$

We assume elementwise operations throughout the book, unless stated otherwise. For example, when we refer to raising an image to a power, we mean that each individual pixel is raised to that power; when we refer to dividing an image by another, we mean that the division is between corresponding pixel pairs, and so on. The terms *elementwise addition* and *subtraction* of two images are redundant because these are elementwise operations by definition. However, you may see them used sometimes to clarify notational ambiguities.

LINEAR VERSUS NONLINEAR OPERATIONS

One of the most important classifications of an image processing method is whether it is linear or nonlinear. Consider a general operator, $\mathcal{H}$, that produces an output image, $g(x, y)$, from a given input image, $f(x, y)$:

$$\mathcal{H}[f(x, y)] = g(x, y) \tag{2-22}$$

Given two arbitrary constants, a and b, and two arbitrary images $f_1(x, y)$ and $f_2(x, y)$, $\mathcal{H}$ is said to be a *linear operator* if

$$\mathcal{H}[af_1(x, y) + bf_2(x, y)] = a\mathcal{H}[f_1(x, y)] + b\mathcal{H}[f_2(x, y)]$$
$$= ag_1(x, y) + bg_2(x, y) \tag{2-23}$$

This equation indicates that the output of a linear operation applied to the sum of two inputs is the same as performing the operation individually on the inputs and then summing the results. In addition, the output of a linear operation on a constant multiplied by an input is the same as the output of the operation due to the original input multiplied by that constant. The first property is called the property of *additivity,* and the second is called the property of *homogeneity*. By definition, an operator that fails to satisfy Eq. (2-23) is said to be *nonlinear*.

As an example, suppose that $\mathcal{H}$ is the sum operator, Σ. The function performed by this operator is simply to sum its inputs. To test for linearity, we start with the left side of Eq. (2-23) and attempt to prove that it is equal to the right side:

These are image summations, not the sums of all the elements of an image.

$$\sum[af_1(x, y) + bf_2(x, y)] = \sum af_1(x, y) + \sum bf_2(x, y)$$
$$= a\sum f_1(x, y) + b\sum f_2(x, y)$$
$$= ag_1(x, y) + bg_2(x, y)$$

where the first step follows from the fact that summation is distributive. So, an expansion of the left side is equal to the right side of Eq. (2-23), and we conclude that the sum operator is linear.

On the other hand, suppose that we are working with the max operation, whose function is to find the maximum value of the pixels in an image. For our purposes here, the simplest way to prove that this operator is nonlinear is to find an example that fails the test in Eq. (2-23). Consider the following two images

$$f_1 = \begin{bmatrix} 0 & 2 \\ 2 & 3 \end{bmatrix} \quad \text{and} \quad f_2 = \begin{bmatrix} 6 & 5 \\ 4 & 7 \end{bmatrix}$$

and suppose that we let $a = 1$ and $b = -1$. To test for linearity, we again start with the left side of Eq. (2-23):

$$\max \left\{ (1) \begin{bmatrix} 0 & 2 \\ 2 & 3 \end{bmatrix} + (-1) \begin{bmatrix} 6 & 5 \\ 4 & 7 \end{bmatrix} \right\} = \max \left\{ \begin{bmatrix} -6 & -3 \\ -2 & -4 \end{bmatrix} \right\}$$

$$= -2$$

Working next with the right side, we obtain

$$(1)\max \left\{ \begin{bmatrix} 0 & 2 \\ 2 & 3 \end{bmatrix} \right\} + (-1)\max \left\{ \begin{bmatrix} 6 & 5 \\ 4 & 7 \end{bmatrix} \right\} = 3 + (-1)7 = -4$$

The left and right sides of Eq. (2-23) are not equal in this case, so we have proved that the max operator is nonlinear.

As you will see in the next three chapters, linear operations are exceptionally important because they encompass a large body of theoretical and practical results that are applicable to image processing. The scope of nonlinear operations is considerably more limited. However, you will encounter in the following chapters several nonlinear image processing operations whose performance far exceeds what is achievable by their linear counterparts.

ARITHMETIC OPERATIONS

Arithmetic operations between two images $f(x, y)$ and $g(x, y)$ are denoted as

$$\begin{aligned} s(x, y) &= f(x, y) + g(x, y) \\ d(x, y) &= f(x, y) - g(x, y) \\ p(x, y) &= f(x, y) \times g(x, y) \\ v(x, y) &= f(x, y) \div g(x, y) \end{aligned} \tag{2-24}$$

These are elementwise operations which, as noted earlier in this section, means that they are performed between corresponding pixel pairs in f and g for $x = 0, 1, 2, \ldots, M-1$ and $y = 0, 1, 2, \ldots, N-1$. As usual, M and N are the row and column sizes of the images. Clearly, s, d, p, and v are images of size $M \times N$ also. Note that image arithmetic in the manner just defined involves images of the same size. The following examples illustrate the important role of arithmetic operations in digital image processing.

EXAMPLE 2.5: Using image addition (averaging) for noise reduction.

Suppose that $g(x,y)$ is a corrupted image formed by the addition of noise, $\eta(x,y)$, to a *noiseless* image $f(x,y)$; that is,

$$g(x,y) = f(x,y) + \eta(x,y) \tag{2-25}$$

where the assumption is that at every pair of coordinates (x,y) the noise is uncorrelated[†] and has zero average value. We assume also that the noise and image values are uncorrelated (this is a typical assumption for additive noise). The objective of the following procedure is to reduce the noise content of the output image by adding a set of noisy input images, $\{g_i(x,y)\}$. This is a technique used frequently for image enhancement.

If the noise satisfies the constraints just stated, it can be shown (Problem 2.26) that if an image $\bar{g}(x,y)$ is formed by averaging K different noisy images,

$$\bar{g}(x,y) = \frac{1}{K}\sum_{i=1}^{K} g_i(x,y) \tag{2-26}$$

then it follows that

$$E\{\bar{g}(x,y)\} = f(x,y) \tag{2-27}$$

and

$$\sigma^2_{\bar{g}(x,y)} = \frac{1}{K}\sigma^2_{\eta(x,y)} \tag{2-28}$$

where $E\{\bar{g}(x,y)\}$ is the expected value of $\bar{g}(x,y)$, and $\sigma^2_{\bar{g}(x,y)}$ and $\sigma^2_{\eta(x,y)}$ are the variances of $\bar{g}(x,y)$ and $\eta(x,y)$, respectively, all at coordinates (x,y). These variances are arrays of the same size as the input image, and there is a scalar variance value for each pixel location.

The standard deviation (square root of the variance) at any point (x,y) in the average image is

$$\sigma_{\bar{g}(x,y)} = \frac{1}{\sqrt{K}}\sigma_{\eta(x,y)} \tag{2-29}$$

As K increases, Eqs. (2-28) and (2-29) indicate that the variability (as measured by the variance or the standard deviation) of the pixel values at each location (x,y) decreases. Because $E\{\bar{g}(x,y)\} = f(x,y)$, this means that $\bar{g}(x,y)$ approaches the noiseless image $f(x,y)$ as the number of noisy images used in the averaging process increases. In order to avoid blurring and other artifacts in the output (average) image, it is necessary that the images $g_i(x,y)$ be *registered* (i.e., spatially aligned).

An important application of image averaging is in the field of astronomy, where imaging under very low light levels often cause sensor noise to render individual images virtually useless for analysis (lowering the temperature of the sensor helps reduce noise). Figure 2.29(a) shows an 8-bit image of the Galaxy Pair NGC 3314, in which noise corruption was simulated by adding to it Gaussian noise with zero mean and a standard deviation of 64 intensity levels. This image, which is representative of noisy astronomical images taken under low light conditions, is useless for all practical purposes. Figures 2.29(b) through (f) show the results of averaging 5, 10, 20, 50, and 100 images, respectively. We see from Fig. 2.29(b) that an average of only 10 images resulted in some visible improvement. According to Eq.

[†]The variance of a random variable z with mean $\bar{z}$ is defined as $E\{(z-\bar{z})^2\}$, where $E\{\cdot\}$ is the expected value of the argument. The covariance of two random variables z_i and z_j is defined as $E\{(z_i - \bar{z}_i)(z_j - \bar{z}_j)\}$. If the variables are uncorrelated, their covariance is 0, and vice versa. (Do not confuse correlation and statistical independence. If two random variables are statistically independent, their correlation is zero. However, the converse is not true in general.)

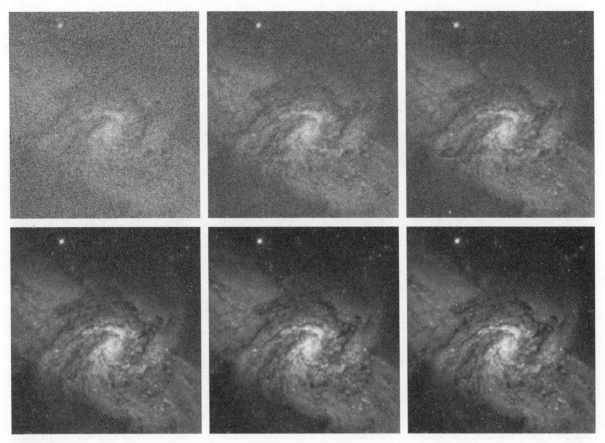

a b c
d e f

FIGURE 2.29 (a) Image of Galaxy Pair NGC 3314 corrupted by additive Gaussian noise. (b)-(f) Result of averaging 5, 10, 20, 50, and 1,00 noisy images, respectively. All images are of size 566×598 pixels, and all were scaled so that their intensities would span the full $[0, 255]$ intensity scale. (Original image courtesy of NASA.)

(2-29), the standard deviation of the noise in Fig. 2.29(b) is less than half $(1/\sqrt{5} = 0.45)$ the standard deviation of the noise in Fig. 2.29(a), or $(0.45)(64) \approx 29$ intensity levels. Similarly, the standard deviations of the noise in Figs. 2.29(c) through (f) are 0.32, 0.22, 0.14, and 0.10 of the original, which translates approximately into 20, 14, 9, and 6 intensity levels, respectively. We see in these images a progression of more visible detail as the standard deviation of the noise decreases. The last two images are visually identical for all practical purposes. This is not unexpected, as the difference between the standard deviations of their noise level is only about 3 intensity levels According to the discussion in connection with Fig. 2.5, this difference is below what a human generally is able to detect.

EXAMPLE 2.6: Comparing images using subtraction.

Image subtraction is used routinely for enhancing differences between images. For example, the image in Fig. 2.30(b) was obtained by setting to zero the least-significant bit of every pixel in Fig. 2.30(a). Visually, these images are indistinguishable. However, as Fig. 2.30(c) shows, subtracting one image from

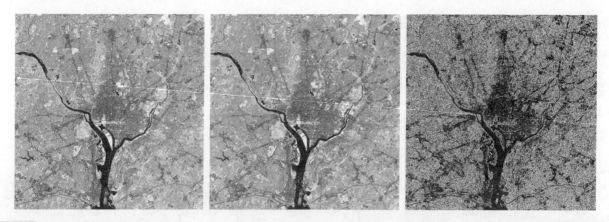

a b c

FIGURE 2.30 (a) Infrared image of the Washington, D.C. area. (b) Image resulting from setting to zero the least significant bit of every pixel in (a). (c) Difference of the two images, scaled to the range [0, 255] for clarity. (Original image courtesy of NASA.)

the other clearly shows their differences. Black (0) values in the difference image indicate locations where there is no difference between the images in Figs. 2.30(a) and (b).

We saw in Fig. 2.23 that detail was lost as the resolution was reduced in the chronometer image shown in Fig. 2.23(a). A vivid indication of image change as a function of resolution can be obtained by displaying the differences between the original image and its various lower-resolution counterparts. Figure 2.31(a) shows the difference between the 930 dpi and 72 dpi images. As you can see, the differences are quite noticeable. The intensity at any point in the difference image is proportional to the magnitude of the numerical difference between the two images at that point. Therefore, we can analyze which areas of the original image are affected the most when resolution is reduced. The next two images in Fig. 2.31 show proportionally less overall intensities, indicating smaller differences between the 930 dpi image and 150 dpi and 300 dpi images, as expected.

a b c

FIGURE 2.31 (a) Difference between the 930 dpi and 72 dpi images in Fig. 2.23. (b) Difference between the 930 dpi and 150 dpi images. (c) Difference between the 930 dpi and 300 dpi images.

As a final illustration, we discuss briefly an area of medical imaging called *mask mode radiography*, a commercially successful and highly beneficial use of image subtraction. Consider image differences of the form

$$g(x,y) = f(x,y) - h(x,y) \tag{2-30}$$

In this case $h(x,y)$, the *mask*, is an X-ray image of a region of a patient's body captured by an intensified TV camera (instead of traditional X-ray film) located opposite an X-ray source. The procedure consists of injecting an X-ray contrast medium into the patient's bloodstream, taking a series of images called *live images* [samples of which are denoted as $f(x,y)$] of the same anatomical region as $h(x,y)$, and subtracting the mask from the series of incoming live images after injection of the contrast medium. The net effect of subtracting the mask from each sample live image is that the areas that are different between $f(x,y)$ and $h(x,y)$ appear in the output image, $g(x,y)$, as enhanced detail. Because images can be captured at TV rates, this procedure outputs a video showing how the contrast medium propagates through the various arteries in the area being observed.

Figure 2.32(a) shows a mask X-ray image of the top of a patient's head prior to injection of an iodine medium into the bloodstream, and Fig. 2.32(b) is a sample of a live image taken after the medium was

a b
c d

FIGURE 2.32
Digital subtraction angiography.
(a) Mask image.
(b) A live image.
(c) Difference between (a) and (b). (d) Enhanced difference image.
(Figures (a) and (b) courtesy of the Image Sciences Institute, University Medical Center, Utrecht, The Netherlands.)

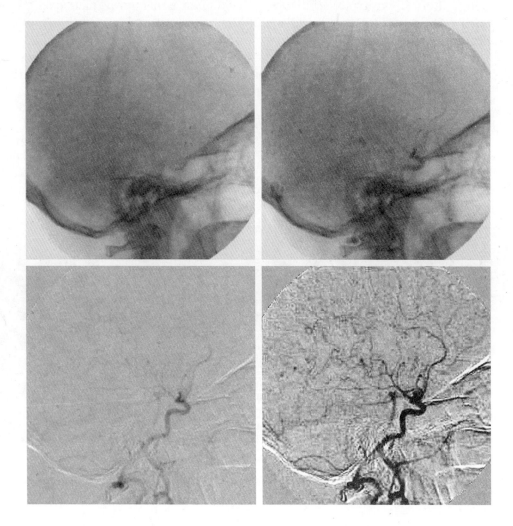

injected. Figure 2.32(c) is the difference between (a) and (b). Some fine blood vessel structures are visible in this image. The difference is clear in Fig. 2.32(d), which was obtained by sharpening the image and enhancing its contrast (we will discuss these techniques in the next chapter). Figure 2.32(d) is a "snapshot" of how the medium is propagating through the blood vessels in the subject's brain.

EXAMPLE 2.7: Using image multiplication and division for shading correction and for masking.

An important application of image multiplication (and division) is *shading correction*. Suppose that an imaging sensor produces images that can be modeled as the product of a "perfect image," denoted by $f(x, y)$, times a shading function, $h(x, y)$; that is, $g(x, y) = f(x, y)h(x, y)$. If $h(x, y)$ is known or can be estimated, we can obtain $f(x, y)$ (or an estimate of it) by multiplying the sensed image by the inverse of $h(x, y)$ (i.e., dividing g by h using elementwise division). If access to the imaging system is possible, we can obtain a good approximation to the shading function by imaging a target of constant intensity. When the sensor is not available, we often can estimate the shading pattern directly from a shaded image using the approaches discussed in Sections 3.5 and 9.8. Figure 2.33 shows an example of shading correction using an estimate of the shading pattern. The corrected image is not perfect because of errors in the shading pattern (this is typical), but the result definitely is an improvement over the shaded image in Fig. 2.33 (a). See Section 3.5 for a discussion of how we estimated Fig. 2.33 (b). Another use of image multiplication is in *masking*, also called *region of interest* (ROI), operations. As Fig. 2.34 shows, the process consists of multiplying a given image by a mask image that has 1's in the ROI and 0's elsewhere. There can be more than one ROI in the mask image, and the shape of the ROI can be arbitrary.

A few comments about implementing image arithmetic operations are in order before we leave this section. In practice, most images are displayed using 8 bits (even 24-bit color images consist of three separate 8-bit channels). Thus, we expect image values to be in the range from 0 to 255. When images are saved in a standard image format, such as TIFF or JPEG, conversion to this range is automatic. When image values exceed the allowed range, clipping or scaling becomes necessary. For example, the values in the difference of two 8-bit images can range from a minimum of −255

a b c

FIGURE 2.33 Shading correction. (a) Shaded test pattern. (b) Estimated shading pattern. (c) Product of (a) by the reciprocal of (b). (See Section 3.5 for a discussion of how (b) was estimated.)

a b c

FIGURE 2.34 (a) Digital dental X-ray image. (b) ROI mask for isolating teeth with fillings (white corresponds to 1 and black corresponds to 0). (c) Product of (a) and (b).

to a maximum of 255, and the values of the sum of two such images can range from 0 to 510. When converting images to eight bits, many software applications simply set all negative values to 0 and set to 255 all values that exceed this limit. Given a digital image g resulting from one or more arithmetic (or other) operations, an approach guaranteeing that the full range of a values is "captured" into a fixed number of bits is as follows. First, we perform the operation

$$g_m = g - \min(g) \tag{2-31}$$

which creates an image whose minimum value is 0. Then, we perform the operation

These are elementwise subtraction and division.

$$g_s = K\left[g_m / \max(g_m)\right] \tag{2-32}$$

which creates a scaled image, g_s, whose values are in the range $[0, K]$. When working with 8-bit images, setting $K = 255$ gives us a scaled image whose intensities span the full 8-bit scale from 0 to 255. Similar comments apply to 16-bit images or higher. This approach can be used for all arithmetic operations. When performing division, we have the extra requirement that a small number should be added to the pixels of the divisor image to avoid division by 0.

SET AND LOGICAL OPERATIONS

In this section, we discuss the basics of set theory. We also introduce and illustrate some important set and logical operations.

Basic Set Operations

A *set* is a collection of distinct objects. If a is an *element* of set A, then we write

$$a \in A \tag{2-33}$$

Similarly, if a is not an element of A we write

$$a \notin A \tag{2-34}$$

The set with no elements is called the *null* or *empty set*, and is denoted by $\varnothing$.

A set is denoted by the contents of two braces: $\{\,\bullet\,\}$. For example, the expression

$$C = \left\{ c \mid c = -d, \, d \in D \right\}$$

means that C is the set of elements, c, such that c is formed by multiplying each of the elements of set D by -1.

If every element of a set A is also an element of a set B, then A is said to be a *subset* of B, denoted as

$$A \subseteq B \tag{2-35}$$

The *union* of two sets A and B, denoted as

$$C = A \cup B \tag{2-36}$$

is a set C consisting of elements belonging *either* to A, to B, *or* to *both*. Similarly, the *intersection* of two sets A and B, denoted by

$$D = A \cap B \tag{2-37}$$

is a set D consisting of elements belonging to *both* A and B. Sets A and B are said to be *disjoint* or *mutually exclusive* if they have no elements in common, in which case,

$$A \cap B = \varnothing \tag{2-38}$$

The *sample space*, Ω, (also called the *set universe*) is the set of all possible set elements in a given application. By definition, these set elements are members of the sample space for that application. For example, if you are working with the set of real numbers, then the sample space is the real line, which contains all the real numbers. In image processing, we typically define Ω to be the rectangle containing all the pixels in an image.

The *complement* of a set A is the set of elements that are not in A:

$$A^c = \left\{ w \mid w \notin A \right\} \tag{2-39}$$

The *difference* of two sets A and B, denoted $A - B$, is defined as

$$A - B = \left\{ w \mid w \in A, w \notin B \right\} = A \cap B^c \tag{2-40}$$

This is the set of elements that belong to A, but not to B. We can define A^c in terms of Ω and the set difference operation; that is, $A^c = \Omega - A$. Table 2.1 shows several important set properties and relationships.

Figure 2.35 shows diagrammatically (in so-called *Venn diagrams*) some of the set relationships in Table 2.1. The shaded areas in the various figures correspond to the set operation indicated above or below the figure. Figure 2.35(a) shows the sample set, Ω. As no earlier, this is the set of all possible elements in a given application. Figure 2.35(b) shows that the complement of a set A is the set of all elements in Ω that are not in A, which agrees with our earlier definition. Observe that Figs. 2.35(e) and (g) are identical, which proves the validity of Eq. (2-40) using Venn diagrams. This

TABLE 2.1
Some important set operations and relationships.

Description	Expressions
Operations between the sample space and null sets	$\Omega^c = \emptyset$; $\emptyset^c = \Omega$; $\Omega \cup \emptyset = \Omega$; $\Omega \cap \emptyset = \emptyset$
Union and intersection with the null and sample space sets	$A \cup \emptyset = A$; $A \cap \emptyset = \emptyset$; $A \cup \Omega = \Omega$; $A \cap \Omega = A$
Union and intersection of a set with itself	$A \cup A = A$; $A \cap A = A$
Union and intersection of a set with its complement	$A \cup A^c = \Omega$; $A \cap A^c = \emptyset$
Commutative laws	$A \cup B = B \cup A$ $A \cap B = B \cap A$
Associative laws	$(A \cup B) \cup C = A \cup (B \cup C)$ $(A \cap B) \cap C = A \cap (B \cap C)$
Distributive laws	$(A \cup B) \cap C = (A \cap C) \cup (B \cap C)$ $(A \cap B) \cup C = (A \cup C) \cap (B \cup C)$
DeMorgan's laws	$(A \cup B)^c = A^c \cap B^c$ $(A \cap B)^c = A^c \cup B^c$

is an example of the usefulness of Venn diagrams for proving equivalences between set relationships.

When applying the concepts just discussed to image processing, we let sets represent objects (regions) in a binary image, and the elements of the sets are the (x, y) coordinates of those objects. For example, if we want to know whether two objects, A and B, of a binary image overlap, all we have to do is compute $A \cap B$. If the result is not the empty set, we know that some of the elements of the two objects overlap. Keep in mind that the only way that the operations illustrated in Fig. 2.35 can make sense in the context of image processing is if the images containing the sets are binary, in which case we can talk about set membership based on coordinates, the assumption being that all members of the sets have the same intensity value (typically denoted by 1). We will discuss set operations involving binary images in more detail in the following section and in Chapter 9.

The preceding concepts are not applicable when dealing with grayscale images, because we have not defined yet a mechanism for assigning intensity values to the pixels resulting from a set operation. In Sections 3.8 and 9.6 we will define the union and intersection operations for grayscale values as the maximum and minimum of corresponding pixel pairs, respectively. We define the *complement* of a grayscale image as the pairwise differences between a constant and the intensity of every pixel in the image. The fact that we deal with corresponding pixel pairs tells us that grayscale set operations are elementwise operations, as defined earlier. The following example is a brief illustration of set operations involving grayscale images. We will discuss these concepts further in the two sections just mentioned.

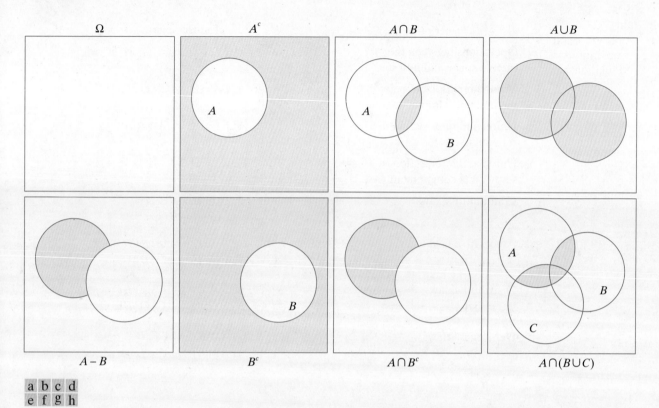

FIGURE 2.35 Venn diagrams corresponding to some of the set operations in Table 2.1. The results of the operations, such as A^c, are shown shaded. Figures (e) and (g) are the same, proving via Venn diagrams that $A - B = A \cap B^c$ [see Eq. (2-40)].

EXAMPLE 2.8: Illustration of set operations involving grayscale images.

Let the elements of a grayscale image be represented by a set A whose elements are triplets of the form (x, y, z), where x and y are spatial coordinates, and z denotes intensity values. We define the *complement* of A as the set

$$A^c = \left\{(x, y, K - z) \,\middle|\, (x, y, z) \in A\right\}$$

which is the set of pixels of A whose intensities have been subtracted from a constant K. This constant is equal to the maximum intensity value in the image, $2^k - 1$, where k is the number of bits used to represent z. Let A denote the 8-bit grayscale image in Fig. 2.36(a), and suppose that we want to form the negative of A using grayscale set operations. The negative is the set complement, and this is an 8-bit image, so all we have to do is let $K = 255$ in the set defined above:

$$A^c = \left\{(x, y, 255 - z) \,\middle|\, (x, y, z) \in A\right\}$$

Figure 2.36(b) shows the result. We show this only for illustrative purposes. Image negatives generally are computed using an intensity transformation function, as discussed later in this section.

FIGURE 2.36
Set operations involving grayscale images. (a) Original image. (b) Image negative obtained using grayscale set complementation. (c) The union of image (a) and a constant image. (Original image courtesy of G.E. Medical Systems.)

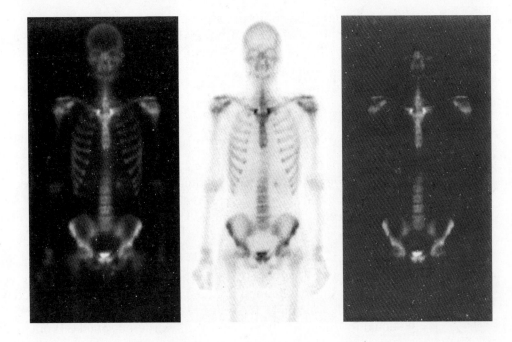

The *union* of two grayscale sets A and B with the same number of elements is defined as the set

$$A \cup B = \left\{ \max_z(a, b) \mid a \in A, b \in B \right\}$$

where it is understood that the max operation is applied to pairs of corresponding elements. If A and B are grayscale images of the same size, we see that their the union is an array formed from the maximum intensity between pairs of spatially corresponding elements. As an illustration, suppose that A again represents the image in Fig. 2.36(a), and let B denote a rectangular array of the same size as A, but in which all values of z are equal to 3 times the mean intensity, $\bar{z}$, of the elements of A. Figure 2.36(c) shows the result of performing the set union, in which all values exceeding $3\bar{z}$ appear as values from A and all other pixels have value $3\bar{z}$, which is a mid-gray value.

We follow convention in using the symbol $\times$ to denote the Cartesian product. This is not to be confused with our use of the same symbol throughout the book to denote the size of an M-by-N image (i.e., $M \times N$).

Before leaving the discussion of sets, we introduce some additional concepts that are used later in the book. The *Cartesian product* of two sets X and Y, denoted $X \times Y$, is the set of *all* possible ordered pairs whose first component is a member of X and whose second component is a member of Y. In other words,

$$X \times Y = \left\{ (x, y) \mid x \in X \text{ and } y \in Y \right\} \tag{2-41}$$

For example, if X is a set of M equally spaced values on the x-axis and Y is a set of N equally spaced values on the y-axis, we see that the Cartesian product of these two sets define the coordinates of an M-by-N rectangular array (i.e., the coordinates of an image). As another example, if X and Y denote the specific x- and y-coordinates of a group of 8-connected, 1-valued pixels in a binary image, then set $X \times Y$ represents the region (object) comprised of those pixels.

A *relation* (or, more precisely, a *binary relation*) on a set A is a collection of ordered pairs of elements from A. That is, a binary relation is a subset of the Cartesian product $A \times A$. A binary relation between *two* sets, A and B, is a subset of $A \times B$.

A *partial order* on a set S is a relation $\mathcal{R}$ on S such that $\mathcal{R}$ is:

(a) *reflexive:* for any $a \in S$, $a\mathcal{R}a$;

(b) *transitive:* for any $a, b, c \in S$, $a\mathcal{R}b$ and $b\mathcal{R}c$ implies that $a\mathcal{R}c$;

(c) *antisymmetric:* for any $a, b \in S$, $a\mathcal{R}b$ and $b\mathcal{R}a$ implies that $a = b$.

where, for example, $a\mathcal{R}b$ reads "a is related to b." This means that a and b are in set $\mathcal{R}$, which itself is a subset of $S \times S$ according to the preceding definition of a relation. A set with a partial order is called a *partially ordered set*.

Let the symbol $\preceq$ denote an ordering relation. An expression of the form

$$a_1 \preceq a_2 \preceq a_3 \preceq \cdots \preceq a_n$$

reads: a_1 precedes a_2 or is the same as a_2, a_2 precedes a_3 or is the same as a_3, and so on. When working with numbers, the symbol $\preceq$ typically is replaced by more traditional symbols. For example, the set of real numbers ordered by the relation "less than or equal to" (denoted by $\leq$) is a partially ordered set (see Problem 2.33). Similarly, the set of natural numbers, paired with the relation "divisible by" (denoted by $\div$), is a partially ordered set.

Of more interest to us later in the book are strict orderings. A *strict ordering* on a set S is a relation $\mathcal{R}$ on S, such that $\mathcal{R}$ is:

(a) *antireflexive:* for any $a \in S$, $\neg a\mathcal{R}a$;

(b) *transitive:* for any $a, b, c \in S$, $a\mathcal{R}b$ and $b\mathcal{R}c$ implies that $a\mathcal{R}c$.

where $\neg a\mathcal{R}a$ means that a is *not related* to a. Let the symbol $\prec$ denote a strict ordering relation. An expression of the form

$$a_1 \prec a_2 \prec a_3 \prec \cdots \prec a_n$$

reads a_1 precedes a_2, a_2 precedes a_3, and so on. A set with a strict ordering is called a *strict-ordered set*.

As an example, consider the set composed of the English alphabet of lowercase letters, $S = \{a, b, c, \cdots, z\}$. Based on the preceding definition, the ordering

$$a \prec b \prec c \prec \cdots \prec z$$

is strict because no member of the set can precede itself (antireflexivity) and, for any three letters in S, if the first precedes the second, and the second precedes the third, then the first precedes the third (transitivity). Similarly, the set of integers paired with the relation "less than ($<$)" is a strict-ordered set.

Logical Operations

Logical operations deal with TRUE (typically denoted by 1) and FALSE (typically denoted by 0) variables and expressions. For our purposes, this means binary images composed of *foreground* (1-valued) pixels, and a *background* composed of 0-valued pixels.

We work with set and logical operators on binary images using one of two basic approaches: (1) we can use the *coordinates* of individual regions of foreground pixels in a single image as sets, or (2) we can work with one or more images of the same size and perform logical operations between corresponding pixels in those arrays.

In the first category, a binary image can be viewed as a Venn diagram in which the coordinates of individual regions of 1-valued pixels are treated as sets. The union of these sets with the set composed of 0-valued pixels comprises the set universe, Ω. In this representation, we work with single images using all the set operations defined in the previous section. For example, given a binary image with two 1-valued regions, R_1 and R_2, we can determine if the regions overlap (i.e., if they have at least one pair of coordinates in common) by performing the set intersection operation $R_1 \cap R_2$ (see Fig. 2.35). In the second approach, we perform logical operations on the pixels of one binary image, or on the corresponding pixels of two or more binary images of the same size.

Logical operators can be defined in terms of truth tables, as Table 2.2 shows for two logical variables a and b. The logical AND operation (also denoted $\wedge$) yields a 1 (TRUE) only when both *a and b* are 1. Otherwise, it yields 0 (FALSE). Similarly, the logical OR ($\vee$) yields 1 when both *a or b* or *both* are 1, and 0 otherwise. The NOT ($\sim$) operator is self explanatory. When applied to two binary images, AND and OR operate on pairs of corresponding pixels between the images. That is, they are elementwise operators (see the definition of elementwise operators given earlier in this chapter) in this context. The operators AND, OR, and NOT are *functionally complete*, in the sense that they can be used as the basis for constructing any other logical operator.

Figure 2.37 illustrates the logical operations defined in Table 2.2 using the second approach discussed above. The NOT of binary image B_1 is an array obtained by changing all 1-valued pixels to 0, and vice versa. The AND of B_1 and B_2 contains a 1 at all spatial locations where the corresponding elements of B_1 and B_2 are 1; the operation yields 0's elsewhere. Similarly, the OR of these two images is an array that contains a 1 in locations where the corresponding elements of B_1, or B_2, or *both*, are 1. The array contains 0's elsewhere. The result in the fourth row of Fig. 2.37 corresponds to the set of 1-valued pixels in B_1 but not in B_2. The last row in the figure is the XOR (exclusive OR) operation, which yields 1 in the locations where the corresponding elements of B_1 or B_2, (but *not both*) are 1. Note that the logical

TABLE 2.2
Truth table defining the logical operators AND($\wedge$), OR($\vee$), and NOT($\sim$).

a	b	a AND b	a OR b	NOT(a)
0	0	0	0	1
0	1	0	1	1
1	0	0	1	0
1	1	1	1	0

FIGURE 2.37
Illustration of
logical operations
involving
foreground
(white) pixels.
Black represents
binary 0's and
white binary 1's.
The dashed lines
are shown for
reference only.
They are not part
of the result.

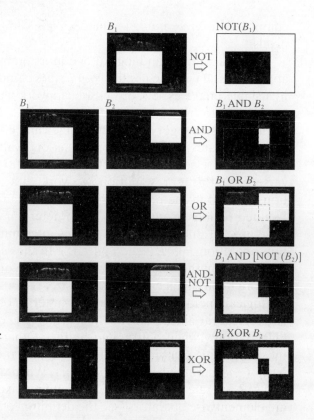

expressions in the last two rows of Fig. 2.37 were constructed using operators from Table 2.2; these are examples of the functionally complete nature of these operators.

We can arrive at the same results in Fig. 2.37 using the first approach discussed above. To do this, we begin by labeling the individual 1-valued regions in each of the two images (in this case there is only one such region in each image). Let A and B denote the *set of coordinates* of all the 1-valued pixels in images B_1 and B_2, respectively. Then we form a *single* array by ORing the two images, while keeping the labels A and B. The result would look like the array B_1 OR B_2 in Fig. 2.37, but with the two white regions labeled A and B. In other words, the resulting array would look like a Venn diagram. With reference to the Venn diagrams and set operations defined in the previous section, we obtain the results in the rightmost column of Fig. 2.37 using set operations as follows: $A^c =$ NOT(B_1), $A \cap B = B_1$ AND B_2, $A \cup B = B_1$ OR B_2, and similarly for the other results in Fig. 2.37. We will make extensive use in Chapter 9 of the concepts developed in this section.

SPATIAL OPERATIONS

Spatial operations are performed directly on the pixels of an image. We classify spatial operations into three broad categories: (1) single-pixel operations, (2) neighborhood operations, and (3) geometric spatial transformations.

Single-Pixel Operations

The simplest operation we perform on a digital image is to alter the intensity of its pixels individually using a transformation function, T, of the form:

$$s = T(z) \tag{2-42}$$

where z is the intensity of a pixel in the original image and s is the (mapped) intensity of the corresponding pixel in the processed image. For example, Fig. 2.38 shows the transformation used to obtain the *negative* (sometimes called the *complement*) of an 8-bit image. This transformation could be used, for example, to obtain the negative image in Fig. 2.36, instead of using sets.

Our use of the word "negative" in this context refers to the digital equivalent of a photographic negative, not to the numerical negative of the pixels in the image.

Neighborhood Operations

Let S_{xy} denote the set of coordinates of a neighborhood (see Section 2.5 regarding neighborhoods) centered on an arbitrary point (x, y) in an image, f. Neighborhood processing generates a corresponding pixel at the same coordinates in an output (processed) image, g, such that the value of that pixel is determined by a specified operation on the neighborhood of pixels in the input image with coordinates in the set S_{xy}. For example, suppose that the specified operation is to compute the average value of the pixels in a rectangular neighborhood of size $m \times n$ centered on (x, y). The coordinates of pixels in this region are the elements of set S_{xy}. Figures 2.39(a) and (b) illustrate the process. We can express this averaging operation as

$$g(x, y) = \frac{1}{mn} \sum_{(r,c) \in S_{xy}} f(r, c) \tag{2-43}$$

where r and c are the row and column coordinates of the pixels whose coordinates are in the set S_{xy}. Image g is created by varying the coordinates (x, y) so that the center of the neighborhood moves from pixel to pixel in image f, and then repeating the neighborhood operation at each new location. For instance, the image in Fig. 2.39(d) was created in this manner using a neighborhood of size 41×41. The

FIGURE 2.38
Intensity transformation function used to obtain the digital equivalent of photographic negative of an 8-bit image..

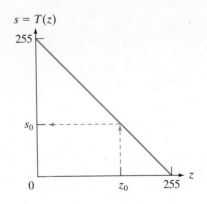

a b
c d

FIGURE 2.39
Local averaging using neighborhood processing. The procedure is illustrated in (a) and (b) for a rectangular neighborhood. (c) An aortic angiogram (see Section 1.3). (d) The result of using Eq. (2-43) with $m = n = 41$. The images are of size 790×686 pixels. (Original image courtesy of Dr. Thomas R. Gest, Division of Anatomical Sciences, University of Michigan Medical School.)

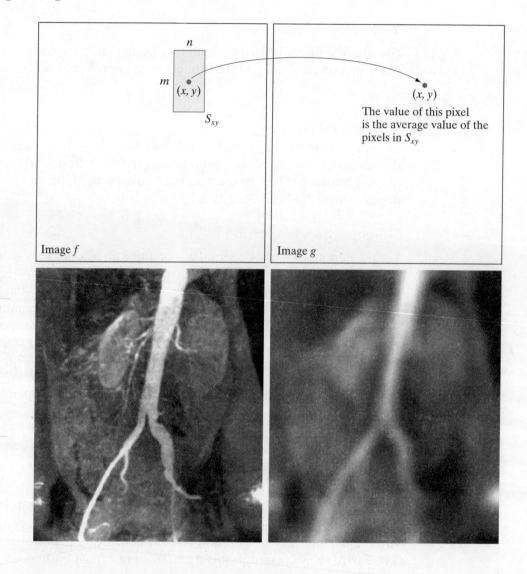

net effect is to perform local blurring in the original image. This type of process is used, for example, to eliminate small details and thus render "blobs" corresponding to the largest regions of an image. We will discuss neighborhood processing in Chapters 3 and 5, and in several other places in the book.

Geometric Transformations

We use geometric transformations modify the spatial arrangement of pixels in an image. These transformations are called *rubber-sheet transformations* because they may be viewed as analogous to "printing" an image on a rubber sheet, then stretching or shrinking the sheet according to a predefined set of rules. Geometric transformations of digital images consist of two basic operations:

1. Spatial transformation of coordinates.
2. Intensity interpolation that assigns intensity values to the spatially transformed pixels.

The transformation of coordinates may be expressed as

$$\begin{bmatrix} x' \\ y' \end{bmatrix} = \mathbf{T} \begin{bmatrix} x \\ y \end{bmatrix} = \begin{bmatrix} t_{11} & t_{12} \\ t_{21} & t_{22} \end{bmatrix} \begin{bmatrix} x \\ y \end{bmatrix} \tag{2-44}$$

where (x, y) are pixel coordinates in the original image and (x', y') are the corresponding pixel coordinates of the transformed image. For example, the transformation $(x', y') = (x/2, y/2)$ shrinks the original image to half its size in both spatial directions.

Our interest is in so-called *affine transformations*, which include scaling, translation, rotation, and shearing. The key characteristic of an affine transformation in 2-D is that it preserves points, straight lines, and planes. Equation (2-44) can be used to express the transformations just mentioned, except translation, which would require that a constant 2-D vector be added to the right side of the equation. However, it is possible to use homogeneous coordinates to express all four affine transformations using a single 3×3 matrix in the following general form:

$$\begin{bmatrix} x' \\ y' \\ 1 \end{bmatrix} = \mathbf{A} \begin{bmatrix} x \\ y \\ 1 \end{bmatrix} = \begin{bmatrix} a_{11} & a_{12} & a_{13} \\ a_{21} & a_{22} & a_{23} \\ 0 & 0 & 1 \end{bmatrix} \begin{bmatrix} x \\ y \\ 1 \end{bmatrix} \tag{2-45}$$

This transformation can *scale*, *rotate*, *translate*, or *sheer* an image, depending on the values chosen for the elements of matrix $\mathbf{A}$. Table 2.3 shows the matrix values used to implement these transformations. A significant advantage of being able to perform all transformations using the unified representation in Eq. (2-45) is that it provides the framework for concatenating a sequence of operations. For example, if we want to resize an image, rotate it, and move the result to some location, we simply form a 3×3 matrix equal to the product of the scaling, rotation, and translation matrices from Table 2.3 (see Problems 2.36 and 2.37).

The preceding transformation moves the coordinates of pixels in an image to new locations. To complete the process, we have to assign intensity values to those locations. This task is accomplished using *intensity interpolation*. We already discussed this topic in Section 2.4. We began that discussion with an example of zooming an image and discussed the issue of intensity assignment to new pixel locations. Zooming is simply scaling, as detailed in the second row of Table 2.3, and an analysis similar to the one we developed for zooming is applicable to the problem of assigning intensity values to the relocated pixels resulting from the other transformations in Table 2.3. As in Section 2.4, we consider nearest neighbor, bilinear, and bicubic interpolation techniques when working with these transformations.

We can use Eq. (2-45) in two basic ways. The first, is a *forward mapping*, which consists of scanning the pixels of the input image and, at each location (x, y), computing the spatial location (x', y') of the corresponding pixel in the output image using Eq. (2-45) directly. A problem with the forward mapping approach is that two or more pixels in the input image can be transformed to the same location in the output image, raising the question of how to combine multiple output values into a single output pixel value. In addition, it is possible that some output locations may not be assigned a pixel at all. The second approach, called *inverse mapping*, scans the output pixel locations and, at each location (x', y'), computes the corresponding location in the input image using $(x, y) = A^{-1}(x', y')$. It then interpolates (using one of the techniques discussed in Section 2.4) among the nearest input pixels to determine the intensity of the output pixel value. Inverse mappings are more efficient to implement than forward mappings, and are used in numerous commercial implementations of spatial transformations (for example, MATLAB uses this approach).

TABLE 2.3
Affine transformations based on Eq. (2-45).

Transformation Name	Affine Matrix, A	Coordinate Equations	Example
Identity	$\begin{bmatrix} 1 & 0 & 0 \\ 0 & 1 & 0 \\ 0 & 0 & 1 \end{bmatrix}$	$x' = x$ $y' = y$	
Scaling/Reflection (For reflection, set one scaling factor to −1 and the other to 0)	$\begin{bmatrix} c_x & 0 & 0 \\ 0 & c_y & 0 \\ 0 & 0 & 1 \end{bmatrix}$	$x' = c_x x$ $y' = c_y y$	
Rotation (about the origin)	$\begin{bmatrix} \cos\theta & -\sin\theta & 0 \\ \sin\theta & \cos\theta & 0 \\ 0 & 0 & 1 \end{bmatrix}$	$x' = x\cos\theta - y\sin\theta$ $y' = x\sin\theta + y\cos\theta$	
Translation	$\begin{bmatrix} 1 & 0 & t_x \\ 0 & 1 & t_y \\ 0 & 0 & 1 \end{bmatrix}$	$x' = x + t_x$ $y' = y + t_y$	
Shear (vertical)	$\begin{bmatrix} 1 & s_v & 0 \\ 0 & 1 & 0 \\ 0 & 0 & 1 \end{bmatrix}$	$x' = x + s_v y$ $y' = y$	
Shear (horizontal)	$\begin{bmatrix} 1 & 0 & 0 \\ s_h & 1 & 0 \\ 0 & 0 & 1 \end{bmatrix}$	$x' = x$ $y' = s_h x + y$	

EXAMPLE 2.9: Image rotation and intensity interpolation.

The objective of this example is to illustrate image rotation using an affine transform. Figure 2.40(a) shows a simple image and Figs. 2.40(b)–(d) are the results (using inverse mapping) of rotating the original image by −21° (in Table 2.3, clockwise angles of rotation are negative). Intensity assignments were computed using nearest neighbor, bilinear, and bicubic interpolation, respectively. A key issue in image rotation is the preservation of straight-line features. As you can see in the enlarged edge sections in Figs. 2.40(f) through (h), nearest neighbor interpolation produced the most jagged edges and, as in Section 2.4, bilinear interpolation yielded significantly improved results. As before, using bicubic interpolation produced slightly better results. In fact, if you compare the progression of enlarged detail in Figs. 2.40(f) to (h), you can see that the transition from white (255) to black (0) is smoother in the last figure because the edge region has more values, and the distribution of those values is better balanced. Although the small intensity differences resulting from bilinear and bicubic interpolation are not always noticeable in human visual analysis, they can be important in processing image data, such as in automated edge following in rotated images.

The size of the spatial rectangle needed to contain a rotated image is larger than the rectangle of the original image, as Figs. 2.41(a) and (b) illustrate. We have two options for dealing with this: (1) we can crop the rotated image so that its size is equal to the size of the original image, as in Fig. 2.41(c), or we can keep the larger image containing the full rotated original, an Fig. 2.41(d). We used the first option in Fig. 2.40 because the rotation did not cause the object of interest to lie outside the bounds of the original rectangle. The areas in the rotated image that do not contain image data must be filled with some value, 0 (black) being the most common. Note that counterclockwise angles of rotation are considered positive. This is a result of the way in which our image coordinate system is set up (see Fig. 2.19), and the way in which rotation is defined in Table 2.3.

Image Registration

Image registration is an important application of digital image processing used to align two or more images of the same scene. In image registration, we have available an *input* image and a *reference* image. The objective is to transform the input image geometrically to produce an output image that is aligned (registered) with the reference image. Unlike the discussion in the previous section where transformation functions are known, the geometric transformation needed to produce the output, registered image generally is not known, and must be estimated.

Examples of image registration include aligning two or more images taken at approximately the same time, but using different imaging systems, such as an MRI (magnetic resonance imaging) scanner and a PET (positron emission tomography) scanner. Or, perhaps the images were taken at different times using the same instruments, such as satellite images of a given location taken several days, months, or even years apart. In either case, combining the images or performing quantitative analysis and comparisons between them requires compensating for geometric distortions caused by differences in viewing angle, distance, orientation, sensor resolution, shifts in object location, and other factors.

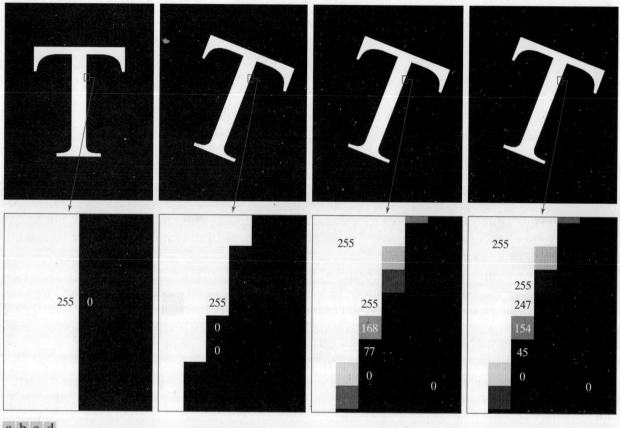

a b c d
e f g h

FIGURE 2.40 (a) A 541×421 image of the letter T. (b) Image rotated $-21°$ using nearest-neighbor interpolation for intensity assignments. (c) Image rotated $-21°$ using bilinear interpolation. (d) Image rotated $-21°$ using bicubic interpolation. (e)-(h) Zoomed sections (each square is one pixel, and the numbers shown are intensity values).

One of the principal approaches for solving the problem just discussed is to use *tie points* (also called *control points*). These are corresponding points whose locations are known precisely in the input and reference images. Approaches for selecting tie points range from selecting them interactively to using algorithms that detect these points automatically. Some imaging systems have physical artifacts (such as small metallic objects) embedded in the imaging sensors. These produce a set of known points (called *reseau marks* or *fiducial marks*) directly on all images captured by the system. These known points can then be used as guides for establishing tie points.

The problem of estimating the transformation function is one of modeling. For example, suppose that we have a set of four tie points each in an input and a reference image. A simple model based on a bilinear approximation is given by

$$x = c_1 v + c_2 w + c_3 vw + c_4 \tag{2-46}$$

and

a b
c d

FIGURE 2.41
(a) A digital image.
(b) Rotated image (note the counterclockwise direction for a positive angle of rotation).
(c) Rotated image cropped to fit the same area as the original image.
(d) Image enlarged to accommodate the entire rotated image.

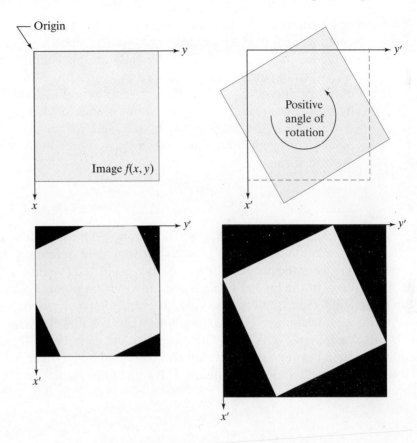

$$y = c_5 v + c_6 w + c_7 vw + c_8 \tag{2-47}$$

During the estimation phase, (v, w) and (x, y) are the coordinates of tie points in the input and reference images, respectively. If we have four pairs of corresponding tie points in both images, we can write eight equations using Eqs. (2-46) and (2-47) and use them to solve for the eight unknown coefficients, c_1 through c_8.

Once we have the coefficients, Eqs. (2-46) and (2-47) become our vehicle for transforming all the pixels in the input image. The result is the desired registered image. After the coefficients have been computed, we let (v, w) denote the coordinates of each pixel in the input image, and (x, y) become the corresponding coordinates of the output image. The same set of coefficients, c_1 through c_8, are used in computing all coordinates (x, y); we just step through all (v, w) in the input image to generate the corresponding (x, y) in the output, registered image. If the tie points were selected correctly, this new image should be registered with the reference image, within the accuracy of the bilinear approximation model.

In situations where four tie points are insufficient to obtain satisfactory registration, an approach used frequently is to select a larger number of tie points and then treat the quadrilaterals formed by groups of four tie points as subimages. The subimages are processed as above, with all the pixels within a quadrilateral being transformed using the coefficients determined from the tie points corresponding to that quadrilateral. Then we move to another set of four tie points and repeat the procedure until all quadrilateral regions have been processed. It is possible to use more complex regions than quadrilaterals, and to employ more complex models, such as polynomials fitted by least squares algorithms. The number of control points and sophistication of the model required to solve a problem is dependent on the severity of the geometric distortion. Finally, keep in mind that the transformations defined by Eqs. (2-46) and (2-47), or any other model for that matter, only map the spatial coordinates of the pixels in the input image. We still need to perform intensity interpolation using any of the methods discussed previously to assign intensity values to the transformed pixels.

EXAMPLE 2.10: Image registration.

Figure 2.42(a) shows a reference image and Fig. 2.42(b) shows the same image, but distorted geometrically by vertical and horizontal shear. Our objective is to use the reference image to obtain tie points and then use them to register the images. The tie points we selected (manually) are shown as small white squares near the corners of the images (we needed only four tie points because the distortion is linear shear in both directions). Figure 2.42(c) shows the registration result obtained using these tie points in the procedure discussed in the preceding paragraphs. Observe that registration was not perfect, as is evident by the black edges in Fig. 2.42(c). The difference image in Fig. 2.42(d) shows more clearly the slight lack of registration between the reference and corrected images. The reason for the discrepancies is error in the manual selection of the tie points. It is difficult to achieve perfect matches for tie points when distortion is so severe.

VECTOR AND MATRIX OPERATIONS

Multispectral image processing is a typical area in which vector and matrix operations are used routinely. For example, you will learn in Chapter 6 that color images are formed in RGB color space by using red, green, and blue component images, as Fig. 2.43 illustrates. Here we see that *each* pixel of an RGB image has three components, which can be organized in the form of a column vector

$$\mathbf{z} = \begin{bmatrix} z_1 \\ z_2 \\ z_3 \end{bmatrix} \tag{2-48}$$

where z_1 is the intensity of the pixel in the red image, and z_2 and z_3 are the corresponding pixel intensities in the green and blue images, respectively. Thus, an RGB color image of size $M \times N$ can be represented by three component images of this size, or by a total of MN vectors of size 3×1. A general multispectral case involving n component images (e.g., see Fig. 1.10) will result in n-dimensional vectors:

Recall that an n-dimensional vector can be thought of as a point in n-dimensional Euclidean space.

$$\mathbf{z} = \begin{bmatrix} z_1 \\ z_2 \\ \vdots \\ z_n \end{bmatrix} \tag{2-49}$$

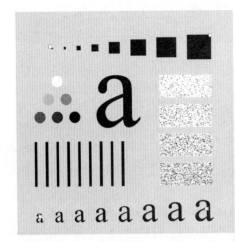

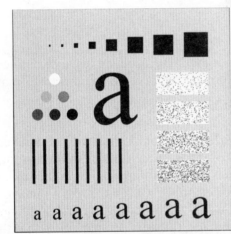

a b
c d

FIGURE 2.42
Image registration. (a) Reference image. (b) Input (geometrically distorted image). Corresponding tie points are shown as small white squares near the corners. (c) Registered (output) image (note the errors in the border). (d) Difference between (a) and (c), showing more registration errors.

We will use this type of vector representation throughout the book.

The *inner product* (also called the *dot product*) of two n-dimensional column vectors $\mathbf{a}$ and $\mathbf{b}$ is defined as

The product $\mathbf{ab}^T$ is called the *outer product* of $\mathbf{a}$ and $\mathbf{b}$. It is a matrix of size $n \times n$.

$$\mathbf{a} \cdot \mathbf{b} \triangleq \mathbf{a}^T \mathbf{b}$$
$$= a_1 b_1 + a_2 b_2 + \cdots + a_n b_n \tag{2-50}$$
$$= \sum_{i=1}^{n} a_i b_i$$

where T indicates the transpose. The *Euclidean vector norm*, denoted by $\|\mathbf{z}\|$, is defined as the square root of the inner product:

$$\|\mathbf{z}\| = \left(\mathbf{z}^T \mathbf{z}\right)^{\frac{1}{2}} \tag{2-51}$$

FIGURE 2.43
Forming a vector from corresponding pixel values in three RGB component images.

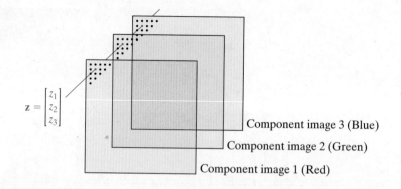

$$\mathbf{z} = \begin{bmatrix} z_1 \\ z_2 \\ z_3 \end{bmatrix}$$

Component image 3 (Blue)

Component image 2 (Green)

Component image 1 (Red)

We recognize this expression as the length of vector $\mathbf{z}$.

We can use vector notation to express several of the concepts discussed earlier. For example, the Euclidean distance, $D(\mathbf{z}, \mathbf{a})$, between points (vectors) $\mathbf{z}$ and $\mathbf{a}$ in n-dimensional space is defined as the Euclidean vector norm:

$$D(\mathbf{z}, \mathbf{a}) = \|\mathbf{z} - \mathbf{a}\| = \left[(\mathbf{z} - \mathbf{a})^T (\mathbf{z} - \mathbf{a}) \right]^{\frac{1}{2}}$$

$$= \left[(z_1 - a_1)^2 + (z_2 - a_2)^2 + \cdots + (z_n - a_n)^2 \right]^{\frac{1}{2}}$$

(2-52)

This is a generalization of the 2-D Euclidean distance defined in Eq. (2-19).

Another advantage of pixel vectors is in linear transformations, represented as

$$\mathbf{w} = \mathbf{A}(\mathbf{z} - \mathbf{a})$$

(2-53)

where $\mathbf{A}$ is a matrix of size $m \times n$, and $\mathbf{z}$ and $\mathbf{a}$ are column vectors of size $n \times 1$.

As noted in Eq. (2-10), entire images can be treated as matrices (or, equivalently, as vectors), a fact that has important implication in the solution of numerous image processing problems. For example, we can express an image of size $M \times N$ as a column vector of dimension $MN \times 1$ by letting the first M elements of the vector equal the first column of the image, the next M elements equal the second column, and so on. With images formed in this manner, we can express a broad range of linear processes applied to an image by using the notation

$$\mathbf{g} = \mathbf{Hf} + \mathbf{n}$$

(2-54)

where $\mathbf{f}$ is an $MN \times 1$ vector representing an input image, $\mathbf{n}$ is an $MN \times 1$ vector representing an $M \times N$ noise pattern, $\mathbf{g}$ is an $MN \times 1$ vector representing a processed image, and $\mathbf{H}$ is an $MN \times MN$ matrix representing a linear process applied to the input image (see the discussion earlier in this chapter regarding linear processes). It is possible, for example, to develop an entire body of generalized techniques for image restoration starting with Eq. (2-54), as we discuss in Section 5.9. We will mention the use of matrices again in the following section, and show other uses of matrices for image processing in numerous chapters in the book.

IMAGE TRANSFORMS

All the image processing approaches discussed thus far operate directly on the pixels of an input image; that is, they work directly in the spatial domain. In some cases, image processing tasks are best formulated by transforming the input images, carrying the specified task in a *transform domain*, and applying the inverse transform to return to the spatial domain. You will encounter a number of different transforms as you proceed through the book. A particularly important class of 2-D *linear transforms*, denoted $T(u,v)$, can be expressed in the general form

$$T(u,v) = \sum_{x=0}^{M-1}\sum_{y=0}^{N-1} f(x,y)r(x,y,u,v) \tag{2-55}$$

where $f(x,y)$ is an input image, $r(x,y,u,v)$ is called a *forward transformation kernel*, and Eq. (2-55) is evaluated for $u = 0,1,2,\ldots,M-1$ and $v = 0,1,2,\ldots,N-1$. As before, x and y are spatial variables, while M and N are the row and column dimensions of f. Variables u and v are called the *transform variables*. $T(u,v)$ is called the *forward transform* of $f(x,y)$. Given $T(u,v)$, we can recover $f(x,y)$ using the *inverse transform* of $T(u,v)$:

$$f(x,y) = \sum_{u=0}^{M-1}\sum_{v=0}^{N-1} T(u,v)s(x,y,u,v) \tag{2-56}$$

for $x = 0,1,2,\ldots,M-1$ and $y = 0,1,2,\ldots,N-1$, where $s(x,y,u,v)$ is called an *inverse transformation kernel*. Together, Eqs. (2-55) and (2-56) are called a *transform pair*.

Figure 2.44 shows the basic steps for performing image processing in the linear transform domain. First, the input image is transformed, the transform is then modified by a predefined operation and, finally, the output image is obtained by computing the inverse of the modified transform. Thus, we see that the process goes from the spatial domain to the transform domain, and then back to the spatial domain.

The forward transformation kernel is said to be *separable* if

$$r(x,y,u,v) = r_1(x,u)r_2(y,v) \tag{2-57}$$

In addition, the kernel is said to be *symmetric* if $r_1(x,u)$ is functionally equal to $r_2(y,v)$, so that

$$r(x,y,u,v) = r_1(x,u)r_1(y,v) \tag{2-58}$$

Identical comments apply to the inverse kernel.

The nature of a transform is determined by its kernel. A transform of particular importance in digital image processing is the *Fourier transform*, which has the following forward and inverse kernels:

$$r(x,y,u,v) = e^{-j2\pi(ux/M + vy/N)} \tag{2-59}$$

and

$$s(x,y,u,v) = \frac{1}{MN} e^{j2\pi(ux/M + vy/N)} \tag{2-60}$$

FIGURE 2.44
General approach
for working in the
linear transform
domain.

The exponential terms
in the Fourier transform
kernels can be expanded
as sines and cosines of
various frequencies. As
a result, the domain of
the Fourier transform
is called the *frequency
domain.*

respectively, where $j = \sqrt{-1}$, so these kernels are complex functions. Substituting the preceding kernels into the general transform formulations in Eqs. (2-55) and (2-56) gives us the *discrete Fourier transform pair*:

$$T(u,v) = \sum_{x=0}^{M-1} \sum_{y=0}^{N-1} f(x,y) e^{-j2\pi(ux/M \,+\, vy/N)} \tag{2-61}$$

and

$$f(x,y) = \frac{1}{MN} \sum_{u=0}^{M-1} \sum_{v=0}^{N-1} T(u,v) e^{j2\pi(ux/M \,+\, vy/N)} \tag{2-62}$$

It can be shown that the Fourier kernels are separable and symmetric (Problem 2.39), and that separable and symmetric kernels allow 2-D transforms to be computed using 1-D transforms (see Problem 2.40). The preceding two equations are of fundamental importance in digital image processing, as you will see in Chapters 4 and 5.

EXAMPLE 2.11: Image processing in the transform domain.

Figure 2.45(a) shows an image corrupted by periodic (sinusoidal) interference. This type of interference can be caused, for example, by a malfunctioning imaging system; we will discuss it in Chapter 5. In the spatial domain, the interference appears as waves of intensity. In the frequency domain, the interference manifests itself as bright bursts of intensity, whose location is determined by the frequency of the sinusoidal interference (we will discuss these concepts in much more detail in Chapters 4 and 5). Typically, the bursts are easily observable in an image of the magnitude of the Fourier transform, $|T(u,v)|$. With reference to the diagram in Fig. 2.44, the corrupted image is $f(x,y)$, the transform in the leftmost box is the Fourier transform, and Fig. 2.45(b) is $|T(u,v)|$ displayed as an image. The bright dots shown are the bursts of intensity mentioned above. Figure 2.45(c) shows a mask image (called a *filter*) with white and black representing 1 and 0, respectively. For this example, the operation in the second box of Fig. 2.44 is to multiply the filter by the transform to remove the bursts associated with the interference. Figure 2.45(d) shows the final result, obtained by computing the inverse of the modified transform. The interference is no longer visible, and previously unseen image detail is now made quite clear. Observe, for example, the fiducial marks (faint crosses) that are used for image registration, as discussed earlier.

When the forward and inverse kernels of a transform are separable and symmetric, and $f(x,y)$ is a square image of size $M \times M$, Eqs. (2-55) and (2-56) can be expressed in matrix form:

a b
c d

FIGURE 2.45
(a) Image corrupted by sinusoidal interference.
(b) Magnitude of the Fourier transform showing the bursts of energy caused by the interference (the bursts were enlarged for display purposes).
(c) Mask used to eliminate the energy bursts.
(d) Result of computing the inverse of the modified Fourier transform. (Original image courtesy of NASA.)

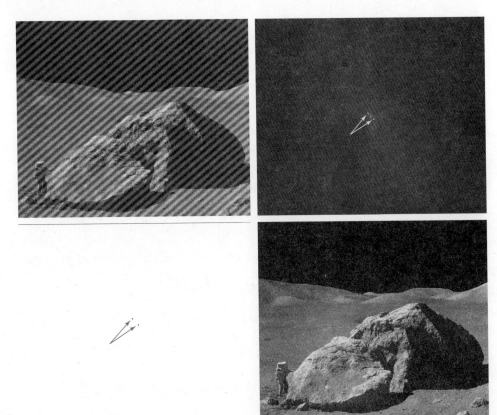

$$\mathbf{T} = \mathbf{AFA} \tag{2-63}$$

where $\mathbf{F}$ is an $M \times M$ matrix containing the elements of $f(x, y)$ [see Eq. (2-9)], $\mathbf{A}$ is an $M \times M$ matrix with elements $a_{ij} = r_1(i, j)$, and $\mathbf{T}$ is an $M \times M$ transform matrix with elements $T(u, v)$, for $u, v = 0, 1, 2, \dots, M - 1$.

To obtain the inverse transform, we pre- and post-multiply Eq. (2-63) by an inverse transformation matrix $\mathbf{B}$:

$$\mathbf{BTB} = \mathbf{BAFAB} \tag{2-64}$$

If $\mathbf{B} = \mathbf{A}^{-1}$,

$$\mathbf{F} = \mathbf{BTB} \tag{2-65}$$

indicating that $\mathbf{F}$ or, equivalently, $f(x, y)$, can be recovered completely from its forward transform. If $\mathbf{B}$ is not equal to $\mathbf{A}^{-1}$, Eq. (2-65) yields an approximation:

$$\hat{\mathbf{F}} = \mathbf{BAFAB} \tag{2-66}$$

In addition to the Fourier transform, a number of important transforms, including the *Walsh*, *Hadamard*, *discrete cosine*, *Haar*, and *slant* transforms, can be expressed in the form of Eqs. (2-55) and (2-56), or, equivalently, in the form of Eqs. (2-63) and (2-65). We will discuss these and other types of image transforms in later chapters.

IMAGE INTENSITIES AS RANDOM VARIABLES

You may find it useful to consult the tutorials section in the book website for a brief review of probability.

We treat image intensities as random quantities in numerous places in the book. For example, let z_i, $i = 0,1,2,\ldots,L-1$, denote the values of all possible intensities in an $M \times N$ digital image. The probability, $p(z_k)$, of intensity level z_k occurring in the image is estimated as

$$p(z_k) = \frac{n_k}{MN} \tag{2-67}$$

where n_k is the number of times that intensity z_k occurs in the image and MN is the total number of pixels. Clearly,

$$\sum_{k=0}^{L-1} p(z_k) = 1 \tag{2-68}$$

Once we have $p(z_k)$, we can determine a number of important image characteristics. For example, the mean (average) intensity is given by

$$m = \sum_{k=0}^{L-1} z_k p(z_k) \tag{2-69}$$

Similarly, the variance of the intensities is

$$\sigma^2 = \sum_{k=0}^{L-1} (z_k - m)^2 p(z_k) \tag{2-70}$$

The variance is a measure of the spread of the values of z about the mean, so it is a useful measure of image contrast. In general, the nth central moment of random variable z about the mean is defined as

$$\mu_n(z) = \sum_{k=0}^{L-1} (z_k - m)^n p(z_k) \tag{2-71}$$

We see that $\mu_0(z) = 1$, $\mu_1(z) = 0$, and $\mu_2(z) = \sigma^2$. Whereas the mean and variance have an immediately obvious relationship to visual properties of an image, higher-order moments are more subtle. For example, a positive third moment indicates that the intensities are biased to values higher than the mean, a negative third moment would indicate the opposite condition, and a zero third moment would tell us that the intensities are distributed approximately equally on both sides of the mean. These features are useful for computational purposes, but they do not tell us much about the appearance of an image in general.

As you will see in subsequent chapters, concepts from probability play a central role in a broad range of image processing applications. For example, Eq. (2-67) is utilized in Chapter 3 as the basis for image enhancement techniques based on histograms. In Chapter 5, we use probability to develop image restoration algorithms, in Chapter 10 we use probability for image segmentation, in Chapter 11 we use it to describe texture, and in Chapter 12 we use probability as the basis for deriving optimum pattern recognition algorithms.

Summary, References, and Further Reading

The material in this chapter is the foundation for the remainder of the book. For additional reading on visual perception, see Snowden et al. [2012], and the classic book by Cornsweet [1970]. Born and Wolf [1999] discuss light in terms of electromagnetic theory. A basic source for further reading on image sensing is Trussell and Vrhel [2008]. The image formation model discussed in Section 2.3 is from Oppenheim et al. [1968]. The IES Lighting Handbook [2011] is a reference for the illumination and reflectance values used in that section. The concepts of image sampling introduced in Section 2.4 will be covered in detail in Chapter 4. The discussion on experiments dealing with the relationship between image quality and sampling is based on results from Huang [1965]. For further reading on the topics discussed in Section 2.5, see Rosenfeld and Kak [1982], and Klette and Rosenfeld [2004].

See Castleman [1996] for additional reading on linear systems in the context of image processing. The method of noise reduction by image averaging was first proposed by Kohler and Howell [1963]. See Ross [2014] regarding the expected value of the mean and variance of the sum of random variables. See Schröder [2010] for additional reading on logic and sets. For additional reading on geometric spatial transformations see Wolberg [1990] and Hughes and Andries [2013]. For further reading on image registration see Goshtasby [2012]. Bronson and Costa [2009] is a good reference for additional reading on vectors and matrices. See Chapter 4 for a detailed treatment of the Fourier transform, and Chapters 7, 8, and 11 for details on other image transforms. For details on the software aspects of many of the examples in this chapter, see Gonzalez, Woods, and Eddins [2009].

Problems

Solutions to the problems marked with an asterisk (*) are in the DIP4E Student Support Package (consult the book website: www.ImageProcessingPlace.com).

2.1 When you enter a dark theatre on a bright day, it takes an appreciable interval of time before you can see well enough to find an empty seat. Which of the visual process discussed in Section 2.1 is responsible for this?

2.2* Using the background information provided in Section 2.1, and thinking purely in geometrical terms, estimate the diameter of the smallest printed dot that the eye can discern if the page on which the dot is printed is 0.25 m away from the eyes. Assume for simplicity that the visual system ceases to detect the dot when the image of the dot on the fovea becomes smaller than the diameter of one receptor (cone) in that area of the retina. Assume further that the fovea can be modeled as a square array of dimension 1.5 mm on the side, and that the cones and spaces between the cones are distributed uniformly throughout this array.

2.3 Although it is not shown in Fig 2.10, alternating current is part of the electromagnetic spectrum. Commercial alternating current in the United States has a frequency of 50 Hz. What is the wavelength in kilometers of this component of the spectrum?

2.4 You are hired to design the front end of an imaging system for studying the shapes of cells, bacteria, viruses, and proteins. The front end consists in this case of the illumination source(s) and corresponding imaging camera(s). The diameters of circles required to fully enclose individual specimens in each of these categories are 50, 1, 0.1, and 0.01 μm, respectively. In order to perform automated analysis, the smallest detail discernible on a specimen must be 0.001 μm.

(a)* Can you solve the imaging aspects of this problem with a single sensor and camera? If your answer is yes, specify the illumination wavelength band and the type of camera needed. By "type," we mean the band of the electromagnetic spectrum to which the camera is most sensitive (e.g., infrared).

(b) If your answer in (a) is no, what type of illumination sources and corresponding imaging sensors would you recommend? Specify the light sources and cameras as requested in part (a). Use the minimum number of illumination sources and cameras needed to solve the problem. (*Hint:* From the discussion in

Section 2.2, the illumination required to "see" an object must have a wavelength the same size or smaller than the object.)

2.5 You are preparing a report and have to insert in it an image of size 2048×2048 pixels.

(a)*Assuming no limitations on the printer, what would the resolution in line pairs per mm have to be for the image to fit in a space of size 5×5 cm?

(b) What would the resolution have to be in dpi for the image to fit in 2×2 inches?

2.6* A CCD camera chip of dimensions 5×5 mm and 1024×1024 sensing elements, is focused on square, flat area, located 0.3 m away. The camera is equipped with a 30-mm lens. How many line pairs per mm will this camera be able to resolve? (*Hint*: Model the imaging process as in Fig. 2.3, with the focal length of the camera lens substituting for the focal length of the eye.)

2.7 An automobile manufacturer is automating the placement of certain components on the bumpers of a limited-edition line of sports cars. The components are color-coordinated, so the assembly robots need to know the color of each car in order to select the appropriate bumper component. Models come in only four colors: blue, green, red, and white. You are hired to propose a solution based on imaging. How would you solve the problem of determining the color of each car, keeping in mind that cost is the most important consideration in your choice of components?

2.8* Suppose that a given automated imaging application requires a minimum resolution of 5 line pairs per mm to be able to detect features of interest in objects viewed by the camera. The distance between the focal center of the camera lens and the area to be imaged is 1 m. The area being imaged is 0.5×0.5 m. You have available a 200 mm lens, and your job is to pick an appropriate CCD imaging chip. What is the minimum number of sensing elements and square size, $d \times d$, of the CCD chip that will meet the requirements of this application? (*Hint:* Model the imaging process as in Fig. 2.3, and assume for simplicity that the imaged area is square.)

2.9 A common measure of transmission for digital data is the *baud rate,* defined as symbols (bits in our case) per second. As a minimum, transmission is accomplished in packets consisting of a start bit, a byte (8 bits) of information, and a stop bit. Using these facts, answer the following:

(a)* How many seconds would it take to transmit a sequence of 200 images of size 1280×960 pixels with 256 intensity levels using a 3 M-baud (10^6 bits/sec) modem? (This is a representative medium speed for a DSL (Digital Subscriber Line) residential line.

(b) What would the time be using a 30 G-baud (10^6 bits/sec) modem? (This is a representative medium speed for a commercial line.)

2.10* High-definition television (HDTV) generates images with 1125 horizontal TV lines interlaced (i.e., where every other line is "painted" on the screen in each of two fields, each field being 1/60th of a second in duration). The width-to-height aspect ratio of the images is 16:9. The fact that the number of horizontal lines is fixed determines the vertical resolution of the images. A company has designed a system that extracts digital images from HDTV video. The resolution of each horizontal line in their system is proportional to vertical resolution of HDTV, with the proportion being the width-to-height ratio of the images. Each pixel in the color image has 24 bits of intensity, 8 bits each for a red, a green, and a blue component image. These three "primary" images form a color image. How many bits would it take to store the images extracted from a 2.5-hour HDTV movie?

2.11 When discussing linear indexing in Section 2.4, we arrived at the linear index in Eq. (2-14) by inspection. The same argument used there can be extended to a 3-D array with coordinates x, y, and z, and corresponding dimensions M, N, and P. The linear index for any (x, y, z) is

$$s = x + M(y + Nz)$$

Start with this expression and

(a)* Derive Eq. (2-15).

(b) Derive Eq. (2-16).

2.12* Suppose that a flat area with center at (x_0, y_0) is illuminated by a light source with intensity distribution

$$i(x, y) = Ke^{-[(x-x_0)^2 + (y-y_0)^2]}$$

Assume for simplicity that the reflectance of the area is constant and equal to 1.0, and let $K = 255$. If the intensity of the resulting image is quantized using k bits, and the eye can detect an abrupt change of eight intensity levels between adjacent pixels, what is the highest value of k that will cause visible false contouring?

2.13 Sketch the image in Problem 2.12 for $k = 2$.

2.14 Consider the two image subsets, S_1 and S_2 in the following figure. With reference to Section 2.5, and assuming that $V = \{1\}$, determine whether these two subsets are:

(a)* 4-adjacent.

(b) 8-adjacent.

(c) m-adjacent.

	S_1					S_2			
0	0	1	0	0	0	0	0	1	0
1	0	0	1	0	0	1	0	0	1
0	0	0	1	0	1	1	0	0	1
0	0	1	1	1	0	0	0	0	0
1	0	1	1	1	0	0	1	1	0

2.15* Develop an algorithm for converting a one-pixel-thick 8-path to a 4-path.

2.16 Develop an algorithm for converting a one-pixel-thick m-path to a 4-path.

2.17 Refer to the discussion toward the end of Section 2.5, where we defined the background of an image as $(R_u)^c$, the complement of the union of all the regions in the image. In some applications, it is advantageous to define the background as the subset of pixels of $(R_u)^c$ that are not *hole* pixels (informally, think of holes as sets of background pixels surrounded by foreground pixels). How would you modify the definition to exclude hole pixels from $(R_u)^c$? An answer such as "the background is the subset of pixels of $(R_u)^c$ that are not hole pixels" is not acceptable. (*Hint:* Use the concept of connectivity.)

2.18 Consider the image segment shown in the figure that follows.

(a)*As in Section 2.5, let $V = \{0,1\}$ be the set of intensity values used to define adjacency. Compute the lengths of the shortest 4-, 8-, and m-path between p and q in the following image. If a particular path does not exist between these two points, explain why.

2	2	1	1 (q)
2	2	0	2
1	2	1	1
(p) 1	0	1	3

(b) Repeat (a) but using $V = \{1,2\}$.

2.19 Consider two points p and q.

(a)* State the condition(s) under which the D_4 distance between p and q is equal to the shortest 4-path between these points.

(b) Is this path unique?

2.20 Repeat problem 2.19 for the D_8 distance.

2.21 Consider two 2×2 images f and g of the same size. What is the difference between element wise and matrix product of these images discussed in Section 2.6? Can either of the two images can be first in forming the product.

2.22* In the next chapter, we will deal with operators whose function is to compute the sum of pixel values in a small subimage area, S_{xy}, as in Eq. (2-43). Show that these are linear operators.

2.23 Refer to Eq. (2-24) in answering the following:

(a)* Show that image summation is a linear operation.

(b) Show that image subtraction is a linear operation.

(c)* Show that image multiplication is a nonlinear operation.

(d) Show that image division is a nonlinear operation.

2.24 The median, ζ, of a set of numbers is such that half the values in the set are below ζ and the other half are above it. For example, the median of the set of values $\{2,3,8,20,21,25,31\}$ is 20. Show that an operator that computes the median of a subimage area, S, is nonlinear. (*Hint:* It is sufficient to show that ζ fails the linearity test for a simple numerical example.)

2.25* How is image averaging used for noise reduction in images? Write an important application of image averaging.

2.26 With reference to Example 2.5:

(a)* Prove the validity of Eq. (2-27).

(b) Prove the validity of Eq. (2-28).

For part (b) you will need the following facts from probability: (1) the variance of a constant times a random variable is equal to the constant squared times the variance of the random variable. (2) The variance of the sum of uncorrelated random variables is equal to the sum of the variances of the individual random variables.

2.27 Consider two 8-bit images whose intensity levels span the full range from 0 to 255.

(a)* Discuss the limiting effect of repeatedly subtracting image (2) from image (1). Assume that the results have to be represented also in eight bits.

(b) Would reversing the order of the images yield a different result?

2.28* Image subtraction is used often in industrial applications for detecting missing components in product assembly. The approach is to store a "golden" image that corresponds to a correct assembly; this image is then subtracted from incoming images of the same product. *Ideally,* the differences would be zero if the new products are assembled correctly. Difference images for products with missing components would be nonzero in the area where they differ from the golden image. What conditions do you think have to be met in practice for this method to work?

2.29 With reference to Eq. (2-32),

(a)* Give a general formula for the value of K as a function of the number of bits, k, in an image, such that K results in a scaled image whose intensities span the full k-bit range.

(b) Find K for 16- and 32-bit images.

2.30 Give Venn diagrams for the following expressions:

(a)* $(A \cap B) - (A \cap B \cup C)$

(b) $(A \cap C) \cup (A \cap B)$

(c) $C - [(A \cap C) - (A \cap B \cap C)]$

(d) $A - A \cap (B \cup C)$; Given that $B \cap C = \emptyset$

2.31 Use Venn diagrams to prove the validity of the following expressions:

(a)* $(A \cap B) \cup [(A \cap C) - A \cap B \cap C] = A \cap (B \cup C)$

(b) $(A \cup B \cup C)^c = A^c \cap B^c \cap C^c$

(c) $(A \cup C)^c \cap B = (B - A) - C$

(d) $(A \cap B \cap C)^c = A^c \cup B^c \cup C^c$

2.32 Give expressions (in terms of sets A, B, and C) for the sets shown shaded in the following figures. The shaded areas in each figure constitute one set, so give only one expression for each of the four figures.

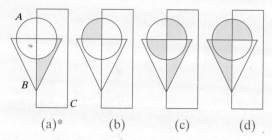

(a)*   (b)   (c)   (d)

2.33 With reference to the discussion on sets in Section 2.6, do the following:

(a)* Let S be a set of real numbers ordered by the relation "less than or equal to" ($\leq$). Show that S is a partially ordered set; that is, show that the reflexive, transitive, and antisymmetric properties hold.

(b)* Show that changing the relation "less than or equal to" to "less than" ($<$) produces a strict ordered set.

(c) Now let S be the set of lower-case letters in the English alphabet. Show that, under ($<$), S is a strict ordered set.

2.34 For any nonzero integers m and n, we say that m is divisible by n, written m/n, if there exists an integer k such that $kn = m$. For example, 42 (m) is divisible by 7 (n) because there exists an integer $k = 6$ such that $kn = m$. Show that the set of positive integers is a partially ordered set under the relation "divisible by." In other words, do the following:

(a)* Show that the property of reflectivity holds under this relation.

(b) Show that the property of transitivity holds.

(c) Show that anti symmetry holds.

2.35 In general, what would the resulting image, $g(x,y)$, look like if we modified Eq. (2-43), as follows:

$$g(x,y) = \frac{1}{mn} \sum_{(r,c) \in S_{xy}} T[f(r,c)]$$

where T is the intensity transformation function in Fig. 2.38(b)?

2.36 With reference to Table 2.3, provide single, composite transformation functions for performing the following operations:

(a)* Scaling and translation.

(b)* Scaling, translation, and rotation.

(c) Vertical shear, scaling, translation, and rotation.

(d) Does the order of multiplication of the individual matrices to produce a single transformations make a difference? Give an example based on a scaling/translation transformation to support your answer.

2.37 We know from Eq. (2-45) that an affine transformation of coordinates is given by

$$\begin{bmatrix} x' \\ y' \\ 1 \end{bmatrix} = \mathbf{A} \begin{bmatrix} x \\ y \\ 1 \end{bmatrix} = \begin{bmatrix} a_{11} & a_{12} & a_{13} \\ a_{21} & a_{22} & a_{23} \\ 0 & 0 & 1 \end{bmatrix} \begin{bmatrix} x \\ y \\ 1 \end{bmatrix}$$

where (x', y') are the transformed coordinates, (x, y) are the original coordinates, and the elements of $\mathbf{A}$ are given in Table 2.3 for various types of transformations. The inverse transformation, $\mathbf{A}^{-1}$, to go from the transformed back to the original coordinates is just as important for performing inverse mappings.

(a)* Find the inverse scaling transformation.

(b) Find the inverse translation transformation.

(c) Find the inverse vertical and horizontal shearing transformations.

(d)* Find the inverse rotation transformation.

(e)* Show a composite inverse translation/rotation transformation.

2.38 What are the equations, analogous to Eqs. (2-46) and (2-47), that would result from using triangular instead of quadrilateral regions?

2.39 Do the following.

(a)* Prove that the Fourier kernel in Eq. (2-59) is separable and symmetric.

(b) Repeat (a) for the kernel in Eq. (2-60).

2.40* Show that 2-D transforms with separable, symmetric kernels can be computed by: (1) computing 1-D transforms along the individual rows (columns) of the input image; and (2) computing 1-D transforms along the columns (rows) of the result from step (1).

2.41 A plant produces miniature polymer squares that have to undergo 100% visual inspection. Inspection is semi-automated. At each inspection station, a robot places each polymer square over an optical system that produces a magnified image of the square. The image completely fills a viewing screen of size 80×80 mm. Defects appear as dark circular blobs, and the human inspector's job is to look at the screen and reject any sample that has one or more dark blobs with a diameter of 0.8 mm or greater, as measured on the scale of the screen. The manufacturing manager believes that if she can find a way to fully automate the process, profits will increase by 50%, and success in this project will aid her climb up the corporate ladder. After extensive investigation, the manager decides that the way to solve the problem is to view each inspection screen with a CCD TV camera and feed the output of the camera into an image processing system capable of detecting the blobs, measuring their diameter, and activating the accept/reject button previously operated by a human inspector. She is able to find a suitable system, provided that the smallest defect occupies an area of at least 2×2 pixels in the digital image. The manager hires you to help her specify the camera and lens system to satisfy this requirement, using off-the-shelf components. Available off-the-shelf lenses have focal lengths that are integer multiples of 25 mm or 35 mm, up to 200 mm. Available cameras yield image sizes of 512×512, 1024×1024, or 2048×2048 pixels. The *individual* imaging elements in these cameras are squares measuring $8 \times 8 \ \mu$m, and the spaces between imaging elements are $2 \ \mu$m. For this application, the cameras cost much more than the lenses, so you should use the lowest-resolution camera possible, consistent with a suitable lens. As a consultant, you have to provide a written recommendation, showing in reasonable detail the analysis that led to your choice of components. Use the imaging geometry suggested in Problem 2.6.

3

Intensity Transformations and Spatial Filtering

It makes all the difference whether one sees darkness through the light or brightness through the shadows.

David Lindsay

Preview

The term *spatial domain* refers to the image plane itself, and image processing methods in this category are based on direct manipulation of pixels in an image. This is in contrast to image processing in a transform domain which, as we will discuss in Chapters 4 and 6, involves first transforming an image into the transform domain, doing the processing there, and obtaining the inverse transform to bring the results back into the spatial domain. Two principal categories of spatial processing are intensity transformations and spatial filtering. Intensity transformations operate on single pixels of an image for tasks such as contrast manipulation and image thresholding. Spatial filtering performs operations on the neighborhood of every pixel in an image. Examples of spatial filtering include image smoothing and sharpening. In the sections that follow, we discuss a number of "classical" techniques for intensity transformations and spatial filtering.

Upon completion of this chapter, readers should:

- Understand the meaning of spatial domain processing, and how it differs from transform domain processing.

- Be familiar with the principal techniques used for intensity transformations.

- Understand the physical meaning of image histograms and how they can be manipulated for image enhancement.

- Understand the mechanics of spatial filtering, and how spatial filters are formed.

- Understand the principles of spatial convolution and correlation.

- Be familiar with the principal types of spatial filters, and how they are applied.

- Be aware of the relationships between spatial filters, and the fundamental role of lowpass filters.

- Understand how to use combinations of enhancement methods in cases where a single approach is insufficient.

119

3.1 BACKGROUND

All the image processing techniques discussed in this chapter are implemented in the spatial domain, which we know from the discussion in Section 2.4 is the plane containing the pixels of an image. Spatial domain techniques operate directly on the pixels of an image, as opposed, for example, to the frequency domain (the topic of Chapter 4) in which operations are performed on the Fourier transform of an image, rather than on the image itself. As you will learn in progressing through the book, some image processing tasks are easier or more meaningful to implement in the spatial domain, while others are best suited for other approaches.

THE BASICS OF INTENSITY TRANSFORMATIONS AND SPATIAL FILTERING

The spatial domain processes we discuss in this chapter are based on the expression

$$g(x, y) = T[f(x, y)] \tag{3-1}$$

where $f(x, y)$ is an input image, $g(x, y)$ is the output image, and T is an operator on f defined over a neighborhood of point (x, y). The operator can be applied to the pixels of a single image (our principal focus in this chapter) or to the pixels of a set of images, such as performing the elementwise sum of a sequence of images for noise reduction, as discussed in Section 2.6. Figure 3.1 shows the basic implementation of Eq. (3-1) on a single image. The point (x_0, y_0) shown is an arbitrary location in the image, and the small region shown is a *neighborhood* of (x_0, y_0), as explained in Section 2.6. Typically, the neighborhood is rectangular, centered on (x_0, y_0), and much smaller in size than the image.

The process that Fig. 3.1 illustrates consists of moving the center of the neighborhood from pixel to pixel, and applying the operator T to the pixels in the neighborhood to yield an output value at that location. Thus, for any specific location (x_0, y_0),

FIGURE 3.1
A 3×3 neighborhood about a point (x_0, y_0) in an image. The neighborhood is moved from pixel to pixel in the image to generate an output image. Recall from Chapter 2 that the value of a pixel at location (x_0, y_0) is $f(x_0, y_0)$, the value of the image at that location.

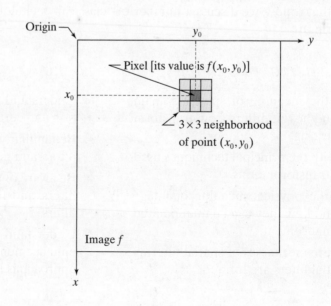

the value of the output image g at those coordinates is equal to the result of applying T to the neighborhood with origin at (x_0, y_0) in f. For example, suppose that the neighborhood is a square of size 3×3 and that operator T is defined as "compute the average intensity of the pixels in the neighborhood." Consider an arbitrary location in an image, say (100,150). The result at that location in the output image, $g(100,150)$, is the sum of $f(100,150)$ and its 8-neighbors, divided by 9. The center of the neighborhood is then moved to the next adjacent location and the procedure is repeated to generate the next value of the output image g. Typically, the process starts at the top left of the input image and proceeds pixel by pixel in a horizontal (vertical) scan, one row (column) at a time. We will discuss this type of neighborhood processing beginning in Section 3.4.

The smallest possible neighborhood is of size 1×1. In this case, g depends only on the value of f at a single point (x, y) and T in Eq. (3-1) becomes an *intensity* (also called a *gray-level,* or *mapping*) *transformation function* of the form

$$s = T(r) \tag{3-2}$$

where, for simplicity in notation, we use s and r to denote, respectively, the intensity of g and f at any point (x, y). For example, if $T(r)$ has the form in Fig. 3.2(a), the result of applying the transformation to every pixel in f to generate the corresponding pixels in g would be to produce an image of higher contrast than the original, by darkening the intensity levels below k and brightening the levels above k. In this technique, sometimes called *contrast stretching* (see Section 3.2), values of r lower than k reduce (darken) the values of s, toward black. The opposite is true for values of r higher than k. Observe how an intensity value r_0 is mapped to obtain the corresponding value s_0. In the limiting case shown in Fig. 3.2(b), $T(r)$ produces a two-level (binary) image. A mapping of this form is called a *thresholding function*. Some fairly simple yet powerful processing approaches can be formulated with intensity transformation functions. In this chapter, we use intensity transformations principally for image enhancement. In Chapter 10, we will use them for image segmentation. Approaches whose results depend only on the intensity at a point sometimes are called *point processing* techniques, as opposed to the *neighborhood processing* techniques discussed in the previous paragraph.

Depending on the size of a neighborhood and its location, part of the neighborhood may lie outside the image. There are two solutions to this: (1) to ignore the values outside the image, or (2) to pad image, as discussed in Section 3.4. The second approach is preferred.

a b

FIGURE 3.2
Intensity transformation functions.
(a) Contrast stretching function.
(b) Thresholding function.

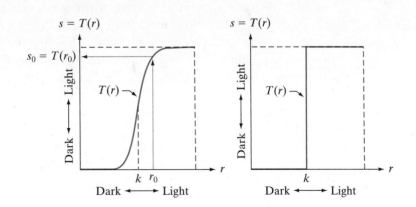

ABOUT THE EXAMPLES IN THIS CHAPTER

Although intensity transformation and spatial filtering methods span a broad range of applications, most of the examples in this chapter are applications to image enhancement. *Enhancement* is the process of manipulating an image so that the result is more suitable than the original for a specific application. The word *specific* is important, because it establishes at the outset that enhancement techniques are problem-oriented. Thus, for example, a method that is quite useful for enhancing X-ray images may not be the best approach for enhancing infrared images. There is no general "theory" of image enhancement. When an image is processed for visual interpretation, the viewer is the ultimate judge of how well a particular method works. When dealing with machine perception, enhancement is easier to quantify. For example, in an automated character-recognition system, the most appropriate enhancement method is the one that results in the best recognition rate, leaving aside other considerations such as computational requirements of one method versus another. Regardless of the application or method used, image enhancement is one of the most visually appealing areas of image processing. Beginners in image processing generally find enhancement applications interesting and relatively simple to understand. Therefore, using examples from image enhancement to illustrate the spatial processing methods developed in this chapter not only saves having an extra chapter in the book dealing with image enhancement but, more importantly, is an effective approach for introducing newcomers to image processing techniques in the spatial domain. As you progress through the remainder of the book, you will find that the material developed in this chapter has a scope that is much broader than just image enhancement.

3.2 SOME BASIC INTENSITY TRANSFORMATION FUNCTIONS

Intensity transformations are among the simplest of all image processing techniques. As noted in the previous section, we denote the values of pixels, before and after processing, by r and s, respectively. These values are related by a transformation T, as given in Eq. (3-2), that maps a pixel value r into a pixel value s. Because we deal with digital quantities, values of an intensity transformation function typically are stored in a table, and the mappings from r to s are implemented via table lookups. For an 8-bit image, a lookup table containing the values of T will have 256 entries.

As an introduction to intensity transformations, consider Fig. 3.3, which shows three basic types of functions used frequently in image processing: linear (negative and identity transformations), logarithmic (log and inverse-log transformations), and power-law (nth power and nth root transformations). The identity function is the trivial case in which the input and output intensities are identical.

IMAGE NEGATIVES

The negative of an image with intensity levels in the range $[0, L-1]$ is obtained by using the negative transformation function shown in Fig. 3.3, which has the form:

$$s = L - 1 - r \qquad (3-3)$$

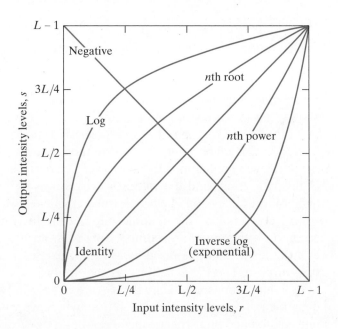

Reversing the intensity levels of a digital image in this manner produces the equivalent of a photographic negative. This type of processing is used, for example, in enhancing white or gray detail embedded in dark regions of an image, especially when the black areas are dominant in size. Figure 3.4 shows an example. The original image is a digital mammogram showing a small lesion. Despite the fact that the visual content is the same in both images, some viewers find it easier to analyze the fine details of the breast tissue using the negative image.

a b

FIGURE 3.4
(a) A
digital
mammogram.
(b) Negative
image obtained
using Eq. (3-3).
(Image (a)
Courtesy of
General Electric
Medical Systems.)

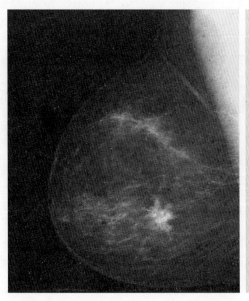
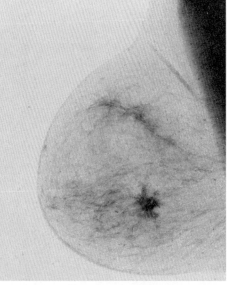

LOG TRANSFORMATIONS

The general form of the log transformation in Fig. 3.3 is

$$s = c \log(1 + r) \tag{3-4}$$

where c is a constant and it is assumed that $r \geq 0$. The shape of the log curve in Fig. 3.3 shows that this transformation maps a narrow range of low intensity values in the input into a wider range of output levels. For example, note how input levels in the range $[0, L/4]$ map to output levels to the range $[0, 3L/4]$. Conversely, higher values of input levels are mapped to a narrower range in the output. We use a transformation of this type to expand the values of dark pixels in an image, while compressing the higher-level values. The opposite is true of the inverse log (exponential) transformation.

Any curve having the general shape of the log function shown in Fig. 3.3 would accomplish this spreading/compressing of intensity levels in an image, but the power-law transformations discussed in the next section are much more versatile for this purpose. The log function has the important characteristic that it compresses the dynamic range of pixel values. An example in which pixel values have a large dynamic range is the Fourier spectrum, which we will discuss in Chapter 4. It is not unusual to encounter spectrum values that range from 0 to 10^6 or higher. Processing numbers such as these presents no problems for a computer, but image displays cannot reproduce faithfully such a wide range of values. The net effect is that intensity detail can be lost in the display of a typical Fourier spectrum.

Figure 3.5(a) shows a Fourier spectrum with values in the range 0 to 1.5×10^6. When these values are scaled linearly for display in an 8-bit system, the brightest pixels dominate the display, at the expense of lower (and just as important) values of the spectrum. The effect of this dominance is illustrated vividly by the relatively small area of the image in Fig. 3.5(a) that is not perceived as black. If, instead of displaying the values in this manner, we first apply Eq. (3-4) (with $c = 1$ in this case) to the spectrum values, then the range of values of the result becomes 0 to 6.2. Transforming values in this way enables a greater range of intensities to be shown on the display. Figure 3.5(b) shows the result of scaling the intensity range linearly to the

a b

FIGURE 3.5
(a) Fourier spectrum displayed as a grayscale image.
(b) Result of applying the log transformation in Eq. (3-4) with $c = 1$. Both images are scaled to the range $[0, 255]$.

interval $[0, 255]$ and showing the spectrum in the same 8-bit display. The level of detail visible in this image as compared to an unmodified display of the spectrum is evident from these two images. Most of the Fourier spectra in image processing publications, including this book, have been scaled in this manner.

POWER-LAW (GAMMA) TRANSFORMATIONS

Power-law transformations have the form

$$s = cr^\gamma \tag{3-5}$$

where c and γ are positive constants. Sometimes Eq. (3-5) is written as $s = c(r + \varepsilon)^\gamma$ to account for offsets (that is, a measurable output when the input is zero). However, offsets typically are an issue of display calibration, and as a result they are normally ignored in Eq. (3-5). Figure 3.6 shows plots of s as a function of r for various values of γ. As with log transformations, power-law curves with fractional values of γ map a narrow range of dark input values into a wider range of output values, with the opposite being true for higher values of input levels. Note also in Fig. 3.6 that a family of transformations can be obtained simply by varying γ. Curves generated with values of $\gamma > 1$ have exactly the opposite effect as those generated with values of $\gamma < 1$. When $c = \gamma = 1$ Eq. (3-5) reduces to the identity transformation.

The response of many devices used for image capture, printing, and display obey a power law. By convention, the exponent in a power-law equation is referred to as *gamma* [hence our use of this symbol in Eq. (3-5)]. The process used to correct these power-law response phenomena is called *gamma correction* or *gamma encoding*. For example, cathode ray tube (CRT) devices have an intensity-to-voltage response that is a power function, with exponents varying from approximately 1.8 to 2.5. As the curve for $\gamma = 2.5$ in Fig. 3.6 shows, such display systems would tend to produce

FIGURE 3.6
Plots of the gamma equation $s = cr^\gamma$ for various values of γ ($c = 1$ in all cases). Each curve was scaled *independently* so that all curves would fit in the same graph. Our interest here is on the *shapes* of the curves, not on their relative values.

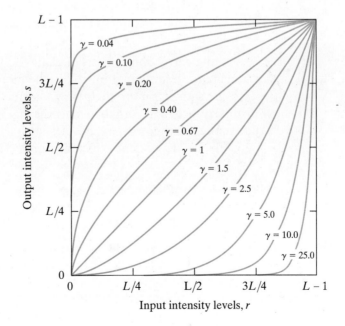

FIGURE 3.7
(a) Intensity ramp image. (b) Image as viewed on a simulated monitor with a gamma of 2.5. (c) Gamma-corrected image. (d) Corrected image as viewed on the same monitor. Compare (d) and (a).

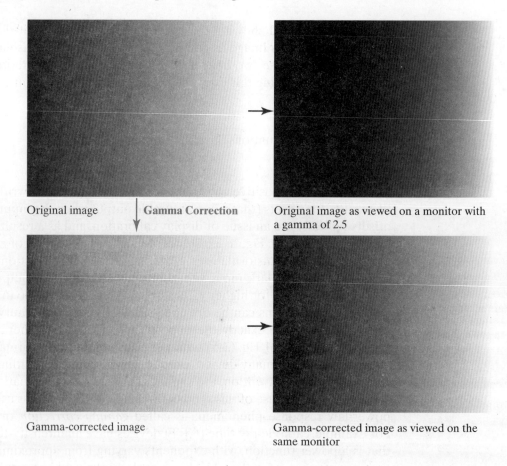

Original image | **Gamma Correction** | Original image as viewed on a monitor with a gamma of 2.5

Gamma-corrected image | Gamma-corrected image as viewed on the same monitor

images that are darker than intended. Figure 3.7 illustrates this effect. Figure 3.7(a) is an image of an intensity ramp displayed in a monitor with a gamma of 2.5. As expected, the output of the monitor appears darker than the input, as Fig. 3.7(b) shows.

Sometimes, a higher gamma makes the displayed image look better to viewers than the original because of an increase in contrast. However, the objective of gamma correction is to produce a faithful display of an input image.

In this case, gamma correction consists of using the transformation $s = r^{1/2.5} = r^{0.4}$ to preprocess the image before inputting it into the monitor. Figure 3.7(c) is the result. When input into the same monitor, the gamma-corrected image produces an output that is close in appearance to the original image, as Fig. 3.7(d) shows. A similar analysis as above would apply to other imaging devices, such as scanners and printers, the difference being the device-dependent value of gamma (Poynton [1996]).

EXAMPLE 3.1 : Contrast enhancement using power-law intensity transformations.

In addition to gamma correction, power-law transformations are useful for general-purpose contrast manipulation. Figure 3.8(a) shows a magnetic resonance image (MRI) of a human upper thoracic spine with a fracture dislocation. The fracture is visible in the region highlighted by the circle. Because the image is predominantly dark, an expansion of intensity levels is desirable. This can be accomplished using a power-law transformation with a fractional exponent. The other images shown in the figure were obtained by processing Fig. 3.8(a) with the power-law transformation function of Eq. (3-5). The values

a b
c d

FIGURE 3.8
(a) Magnetic resonance image (MRI) of a fractured human spine (the region of the fracture is enclosed by the circle). (b)–(d) Results of applying the transformation in Eq. (3-5) with $c = 1$ and $\gamma = 0.6, 0.4,$ and 0.3, respectively. (Original image courtesy of Dr. David R. Pickens, Department of Radiology and Radiological Sciences, Vanderbilt University Medical Center.)

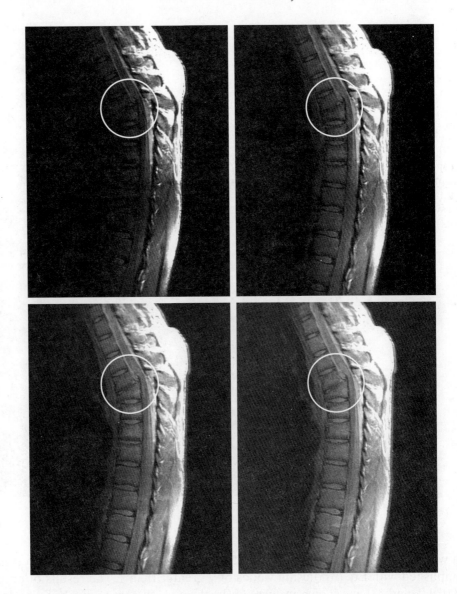

of gamma corresponding to images (b) through (d) are 0.6, 0.4, and 0.3, respectively ($c = 1$ in all cases). Observe that as gamma decreased from 0.6 to 0.4, more detail became visible. A further decrease of gamma to 0.3 enhanced a little more detail in the background, but began to reduce contrast to the point where the image started to have a very slight "washed-out" appearance, especially in the background. The best enhancement in terms of contrast and discernible detail was obtained with $\gamma = 0.4$. A value of $\gamma = 0.3$ is an approximate limit below which contrast in this particular image would be reduced to an unacceptable level.

EXAMPLE 3.2: Another illustration of power-law transformations.

Figure 3.9(a) shows the opposite problem of that presented in Fig. 3.8(a). The image to be processed now

FIGURE 3.9
(a) Aerial image.
(b)–(d) Results
of applying the
transformation
in Eq. (3-5) with
$\gamma = 3.0, 4.0$, and
5.0, respectively.
($c = 1$ in all cases.)
(Original image
courtesy of
NASA.)

has a washed-out appearance, indicating that a compression of intensity levels is desirable. This can be accomplished with Eq. (3-5) using values of γ greater than 1. The results of processing Fig. 3.9(a) with $\gamma = 3.0, 4.0$, and 5.0 are shown in Figs. 3.9(b) through (d), respectively. Suitable results were obtained using gamma values of 3.0 and 4.0. The latter result has a slightly more appealing appearance because it has higher contrast. This is true also of the result obtained with $\gamma = 5.0$. For example, the airport runways near the middle of the image appears clearer in Fig. 3.9(d) than in any of the other three images.

PIECEWISE LINEAR TRANSFORMATION FUNCTIONS

An approach complementary to the methods discussed in the previous three sections is to use piecewise linear functions. The advantage of these functions over those discussed thus far is that the form of piecewise functions can be arbitrarily complex. In fact, as you will see shortly, a practical implementation of some important transformations can be formulated only as piecewise linear functions. The main disadvantage of these functions is that their specification requires considerable user input.

Contrast Stretching

Low-contrast images can result from poor illumination, lack of dynamic range in the imaging sensor, or even the wrong setting of a lens aperture during image acquisition. *Contrast stretching* expands the range of intensity levels in an image so that it spans the ideal full intensity range of the recording medium or display device.

Figure 3.10(a) shows a typical transformation used for contrast stretching. The locations of points (r_1, s_1) and (r_2, s_2) control the shape of the transformation function. If $r_1 = s_1$ and $r_2 = s_2$ the transformation is a linear function that produces no changes in intensity. If $r_1 = r_2$, $s_1 = 0$, and $s_2 = L-1$ the transformation becomes a *thresholding function* that creates a binary image [see Fig. 3.2(b)]. Intermediate values of (r_1, s_1) and (s_2, r_2) produce various degrees of spread in the intensity levels of the output image, thus affecting its contrast. In general, $r_1 \le r_2$ and $s_1 \le s_2$ is assumed so that the function is single valued and monotonically increasing. This preserves the order of intensity levels, thus preventing the creation of intensity artifacts. Figure 3.10(b) shows an 8-bit image with low contrast. Figure 3.10(c) shows the result of contrast stretching, obtained by setting $(r_1, s_1) = (r_{min}, 0)$ and $(r_2, s_2) = (r_{max}, L-1)$, where r_{min} and r_{max} denote the minimum and maximum intensity levels in the input

a b
c d

FIGURE 3.10
Contrast stretching.
(a) Piecewise linear transformation function. (b) A low-contrast electron microscope image of pollen, magnified 700 times.
(c) Result of contrast stretching.
(d) Result of thresholding.
(Original image courtesy of Dr. Roger Heady, Research School of Biological Sciences, Australian National University, Canberra, Australia.)

a b

FIGURE 3.11
(a) This transformation function highlights range $[A, B]$ and reduces all other intensities to a lower level.
(b) This function highlights range $[A, B]$ and leaves other intensities unchanged.

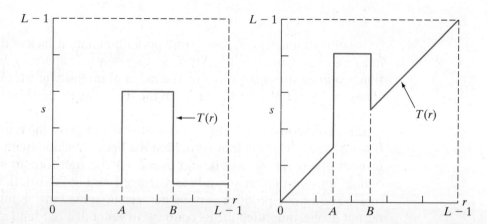

image, respectively. The transformation stretched the intensity levels linearly to the full intensity range, $[0, L - 1]$. Finally, Fig. 3.10(d) shows the result of using the thresholding function, with $(r_1, s_1) = (m, 0)$ and $(r_2, s_2) = (m, L - 1)$, where m is the mean intensity level in the image.

Intensity-Level Slicing

There are applications in which it is of interest to highlight a specific range of intensities in an image. Some of these applications include enhancing features in satellite imagery, such as masses of water, and enhancing flaws in X-ray images. The method, called *intensity-level slicing*, can be implemented in several ways, but most are variations of two basic themes. One approach is to display in one value (say, white) all the values in the range of interest and in another (say, black) all other intensities. This transformation, shown in Fig. 3.11(a), produces a binary image. The second approach, based on the transformation in Fig. 3.11(b), brightens (or darkens) the desired range of intensities, but leaves all other intensity levels in the image unchanged.

EXAMPLE 3.3: Intensity-level slicing.

Figure 3.12(a) is an aortic angiogram near the kidney area (see Section 1.3 for details on this image). The objective of this example is to use intensity-level slicing to enhance the major blood vessels that appear lighter than the background, as a result of an injected contrast medium. Figure 3.12(b) shows the result of using a transformation of the form in Fig. 3.11(a). The selected band was near the top of the intensity scale because the range of interest is brighter than the background. The net result of this transformation is that the blood vessel and parts of the kidneys appear white, while all other intensities are black. This type of enhancement produces a binary image, and is useful for studying the shape characteristics of the flow of the contrast medium (to detect blockages, for example).

If interest lies in the actual intensity values of the region of interest, we can use the transformation of the form shown in Fig. 3.11(b). Figure 3.12(c) shows the result of using such a transformation in which a band of intensities in the mid-gray region around the mean intensity was set to black, while all other intensities were left unchanged. Here, we see that the gray-level tonality of the major blood vessels and part of the kidney area were left intact. Such a result might be useful when interest lies in measuring the actual flow of the contrast medium as a function of time in a sequence of images.

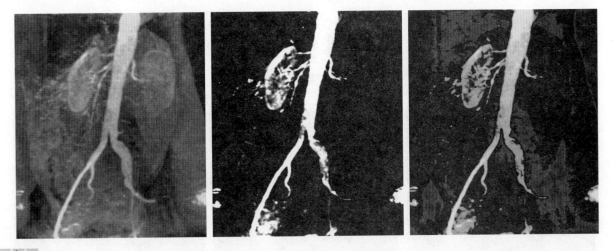

a b c

FIGURE 3.12 (a) Aortic angiogram. (b) Result of using a slicing transformation of the type illustrated in Fig. 3.11(a), with the range of intensities of interest selected in the upper end of the gray scale. (c) Result of using the transformation in Fig. 3.11(b), with the selected range set near black, so that the grays in the area of the blood vessels and kidneys were preserved. (Original image courtesy of Dr. Thomas R. Gest, University of Michigan Medical School.)

Bit-Plane Slicing

Pixel values are integers composed of bits. For example, values in a 256-level gray-scale image are composed of 8 bits (one byte). Instead of highlighting intensity-level ranges, as 3.3, we could highlight the contribution made to total image appearance by specific bits. As Fig. 3.13 illustrates, an 8-bit image may be considered as being composed of eight one-bit planes, with plane 1 containing the lowest-order bit of all pixels in the image, and plane 8 all the highest-order bits.

Figure 3.14(a) shows an 8-bit grayscale image and Figs. 3.14(b) through (i) are its eight one-bit planes, with Fig. 3.14(b) corresponding to the highest-order bit. Observe that the four higher-order bit planes, especially the first two, contain a significant amount of the visually-significant data. The lower-order planes contribute to more subtle intensity details in the image. The original image has a gray border whose intensity is 194. Notice that the corresponding borders of some of the bit

FIGURE 3.13
Bit-planes of an
8-bit image.

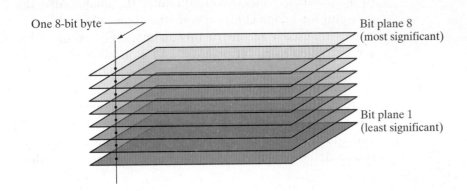

One 8-bit byte

Bit plane 8
(most significant)

Bit plane 1
(least significant)

a b c
d e f
g h i

FIGURE 3.14 (a) An 8-bit gray-scale image of size 550×1192 pixels. (b) through (i) Bit planes 8 through 1, with bit plane 1 corresponding to the least significant bit. Each bit plane is a binary image..

planes are black (0), while others are white (1). To see why, consider a pixel in, say, the middle of the lower border of Fig. 3.14(a). The corresponding pixels in the bit planes, starting with the highest-order plane, have values 1 1 0 0 0 0 1 0, which is the binary representation of decimal 194. The value of any pixel in the original image can be similarly reconstructed from its corresponding binary-valued pixels in the bit planes by converting an 8-bit binary sequence to decimal.

The binary image for the 8th bit plane of an 8-bit image can be obtained by thresholding the input image with a transformation function that maps to 0 intensity values between 0 and 127, and maps to 1 values between 128 and 255. The binary image in Fig. 3.14(b) was obtained in this manner. It is left as an exercise (see Problem 3.3) to obtain the transformation functions for generating the other bit planes.

Decomposing an image into its bit planes is useful for analyzing the relative importance of each bit in the image, a process that aids in determining the adequacy of the number of bits used to quantize the image. Also, this type of decomposition is useful for image compression (the topic of Chapter 8), in which fewer than all planes are used in reconstructing an image. For example, Fig. 3.15(a) shows an image reconstructed using bit planes 8 and 7 of the preceding decomposition. The reconstruction is done by multiplying the pixels of the nth plane by the constant 2^{n-1}. This converts the nth significant binary bit to decimal. Each bit plane is multiplied by the corresponding constant, and all resulting planes are added to obtain the grayscale image. Thus, to obtain Fig. 3.15(a), we multiplied bit plane 8 by 128, bit plane 7 by 64, and added the two planes. Although the main features of the original image were restored, the reconstructed image appears flat, especially in the background. This

a b c **FIGURE 3.15** Image reconstructed from bit planes: (a) 8 and 7; (b) 8, 7, and 6; (c) 8, 7, 6, and 5.

is not surprising, because two planes can produce only four distinct intensity levels. Adding plane 6 to the reconstruction helped the situation, as Fig. 3.15(b) shows. Note that the background of this image has perceptible false contouring. This effect is reduced significantly by adding the 5th plane to the reconstruction, as Fig. 3.15(c) illustrates. Using more planes in the reconstruction would not contribute significantly to the appearance of this image. Thus, we conclude that, in this example, storing the four highest-order bit planes would allow us to reconstruct the original image in acceptable detail. Storing these four planes instead of the original image requires 50% less storage.

3.3 HISTOGRAM PROCESSING

Let r_k, for $k = 0, 1, 2, \ldots, L-1$, denote the intensities of an L-level digital image, $f(x, y)$. The *unnormalized histogram* of f is defined as

$$h(r_k) = n_k \quad \text{for } k = 0, 1, 2, \ldots, L-1 \tag{3-6}$$

where n_k is the number of pixels in f with intensity r_k, and the subdivisions of the intensity scale are called *histogram bins*. Similarly, the *normalized histogram* of f is defined as

$$p(r_k) = \frac{h(r_k)}{MN} = \frac{n_k}{MN} \tag{3-7}$$

where, as usual, M and N are the number of image rows and columns, respectively. Mostly, we work with normalized histograms, which we refer to simply as *histograms* or *image histograms*. The sum of $p(r_k)$ for all values of k is always 1. The components of $p(r_k)$ are estimates of the probabilities of intensity levels occurring in an image. As you will learn in this section, histogram manipulation is a fundamental tool in image processing. Histograms are simple to compute and are also suitable for fast hardware implementations, thus making histogram-based techniques a popular tool for real-time image processing.

Histogram shape is related to image appearance. For example, Fig. 3.16 shows images with four basic intensity characteristics: dark, light, low contrast, and high contrast; the image histograms are also shown. We note in the dark image that the most populated histogram bins are concentrated on the lower (dark) end of the intensity scale. Similarly, the most populated bins of the light image are biased toward the higher end of the scale. An image with low contrast has a narrow histo-

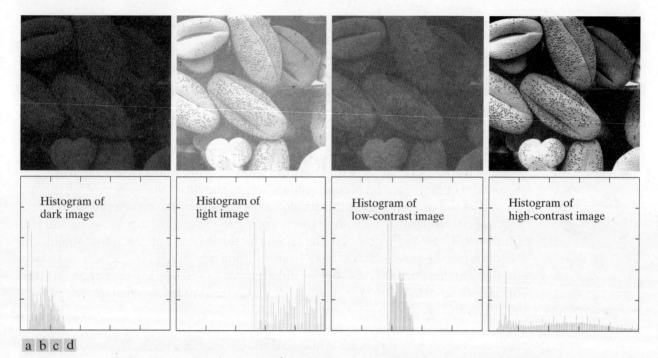

a b c d

FIGURE 3.16 Four image types and their corresponding histograms. (a) dark; (b) light; (c) low contrast; (d) high contrast. The horizontal axis of the histograms are values of r_k and the vertical axis are values of $p(r_k)$.

gram located typically toward the middle of the intensity scale, as Fig. 3.16(c) shows. For a monochrome image, this implies a dull, washed-out gray look. Finally, we see that the components of the histogram of the high-contrast image cover a wide range of the intensity scale, and the distribution of pixels is not too far from uniform, with few bins being much higher than the others. Intuitively, it is reasonable to conclude that an image whose pixels tend to occupy the entire range of possible intensity levels and, in addition, tend to be distributed uniformly, will have an appearance of high contrast and will exhibit a large variety of gray tones. The net effect will be an image that shows a great deal of gray-level detail and has a high dynamic range. As you will see shortly, it is possible to develop a transformation function that can achieve this effect automatically, using only the histogram of an input image.

HISTOGRAM EQUALIZATION

Assuming initially continuous intensity values, let the variable r denote the intensities of an image to be processed. As usual, we assume that r is in the range $[0, L-1]$, with $r = 0$ representing black and $r = L-1$ representing white. For r satisfying these conditions, we focus attention on transformations (intensity mappings) of the form

$$s = T(r) \qquad 0 \le r \le L-1 \tag{3-8}$$

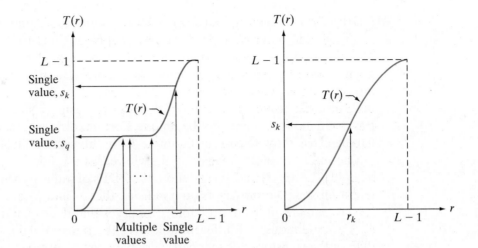

a b

FIGURE 3.17
(a) Monotonic increasing function, showing how multiple values can map to a single value. (b) Strictly monotonic increasing function. This is a one-to-one mapping, both ways.

that produce an output intensity value, s, for a given intensity value r in the input image. We assume that

(a) $T(r)$ is a monotonic[†] increasing function in the interval $0 \leq r \leq L - 1$; and
(b) $0 \leq T(r) \leq L - 1$ for $0 \leq r \leq L - 1$.

In some formulations to be discussed shortly, we use the inverse transformation

$$r = T^{-1}(s) \qquad 0 \leq s \leq L - 1 \tag{3-9}$$

in which case we change condition (a) to:

(a′) $T(r)$ is a *strictly* monotonic increasing function in the interval $0 \leq r \leq L - 1$.

The condition in (a) that $T(r)$ be monotonically increasing guarantees that output intensity values will never be less than corresponding input values, thus preventing artifacts created by reversals of intensity. Condition (b) guarantees that the range of output intensities is the same as the input. Finally, condition (a′) guarantees that the mappings from s back to r will be one-to-one, thus preventing ambiguities.

Figure 3.17(a) shows a function that satisfies conditions (a) and (b). Here, we see that it is possible for multiple input values to map to a single output value and still satisfy these two conditions. That is, a monotonic transformation function performs a one-to-one or many-to-one mapping. This is perfectly fine when mapping from r to s. However, Fig. 3.17(a) presents a problem if we wanted to recover the values of r uniquely from the mapped values (inverse mapping can be visualized by reversing the direction of the arrows). This would be possible for the inverse mapping of s_k in Fig. 3.17(a), but the inverse mapping of s_q is a range of values, which, of course, prevents us in general from recovering the original value of r that resulted in s_q. As Fig.

[†]A function $T(r)$ is a *monotonic increasing* function if $T(r_2) \geq T(r_1)$ for $r_2 > r_1$. $T(r)$ is a *strictly monotonic increasing* function if $T(r_2) > T(r_1)$ for $r_2 > r_1$. Similar definitions apply to a monotonic decreasing function.

3.17(b) shows, requiring that $T(r)$ be strictly monotonic guarantees that the inverse mappings will be *single valued* (i.e., the mapping is one-to-one in both directions). This is a theoretical requirement that will allow us to derive some important histogram processing techniques later in this chapter. Because images are stored using integer intensity values, we are forced to round all results to their nearest integer values. This often results in strict monotonicity not being satisfied, which implies inverse transformations that may not be unique. Fortunately, this problem is not difficult to handle in the discrete case, as Example 3.7 in this section illustrates.

The intensity of an image may be viewed as a random variable in the interval $[0, L-1]$. Let $p_r(r)$ and $p_s(s)$ denote the PDFs of intensity values r and s in two different images. The subscripts on p indicate that p_r and p_s are different functions. A fundamental result from probability theory is that if $p_r(r)$ and $T(r)$ are known, and $T(r)$ is continuous and differentiable over the range of values of interest, then the PDF of the transformed (mapped) variable s can be obtained as

$$p_s(s) = p_r(r)\left|\frac{dr}{ds}\right| \tag{3-10}$$

Thus, we see that the PDF of the output intensity variable, s, is determined by the PDF of the input intensities and the transformation function used [recall that r and s are related by $T(r)$].

A transformation function of particular importance in image processing is

$$s = T(r) = (L-1)\int_0^r p_r(w)\,dw \tag{3-11}$$

where w is a dummy variable of integration. The integral on the right side is the *cumulative distribution function* (CDF) of random variable r. Because PDFs always are positive, and the integral of a function is the area under the function, it follows that the transformation function of Eq. (3-11) satisfies condition (a). This is because the area under the function cannot decrease as r increases. When the upper limit in this equation is $r = (L-1)$ the integral evaluates to 1, as it must for a PDF. Thus, the maximum value of s is $L-1$, and condition (b) is satisfied also.

We use Eq. (3-10) to find the $p_s(s)$ corresponding to the transformation just discussed. We know from Leibniz's rule in calculus that the derivative of a definite integral with respect to its upper limit is the integrand evaluated at the limit. That is,

$$\frac{ds}{dr} = \frac{dT(r)}{dr}$$

$$= (L-1)\frac{d}{dr}\left[\int_0^r p_r(w)\,dw\right] \tag{3-12}$$

$$= (L-1)p_r(r)$$

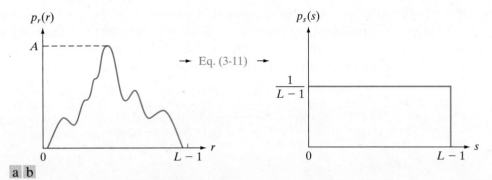

a b

FIGURE 3.18 (a) An arbitrary PDF. (b) Result of applying Eq. (3-11) to the input PDF. The resulting PDF is always uniform, independently of the shape of the input.

Substituting this result for dr/ds in Eq. (3-10), and noting that all probability values are positive, gives the result

$$p_s(s) = p_r(r) \left| \frac{dr}{ds} \right|$$

$$= p_r(r) \left| \frac{1}{(L-1)p_r(r)} \right| \tag{3-13}$$

$$= \frac{1}{L-1} \qquad 0 \le s \le L-1$$

We recognize the form of $p_s(s)$ in the last line of this equation as a *uniform* probability density function. Thus, performing the intensity transformation in Eq. (3-11) yields a random variable, s, characterized by a uniform PDF. What is important is that $p_s(s)$ in Eq. (3-13) will *always* be uniform, *independently* of the form of $p_r(r)$. Figure 3.18 and the following example illustrate these concepts.

EXAMPLE 3.4: Illustration of Eqs. (3-11) and (3-13).

Suppose that the (continuous) intensity values in an image have the PDF

$$p_r(r) = \begin{cases} \dfrac{2r}{(L-1)^2} & \text{for } 0 \le r \le L-1 \\ 0 & \text{otherwise} \end{cases}$$

From Eq. (3-11)

$$s = T(r) = (L-1) \int_0^r p_r(w)\,dw = \frac{2}{L-1} \int_0^r w\,dw = \frac{r^2}{L-1}$$

Suppose that we form a new image with intensities, s, obtained using this transformation; that is, the s values are formed by squaring the corresponding intensity values of the input image, then dividing them by $L-1$. We can verify that the PDF of the intensities in the new image, $p_s(s)$, is uniform by substituting $p_r(r)$ into Eq. (3-13), and using the fact that $s = r^2/(L-1)$; that is,

$$p_s(s) = p_r(r) \left| \frac{dr}{ds} \right| = \frac{2r}{(L-1)^2} \left| \left[\frac{ds}{dr} \right]^{-1} \right|$$

$$= \frac{2r}{(L-1)^2} \left| \left[\frac{d}{dr} \frac{r^2}{L-1} \right]^{-1} \right| = \frac{2r}{(L-1)^2} \left| \frac{(L-1)}{2r} \right| = \frac{1}{L-1}$$

The last step follows because r is nonnegative and $L > 1$. As expected, the result is a uniform PDF.

For discrete values, we work with probabilities and summations instead of probability density functions and integrals (but the requirement of monotonicity stated earlier still applies). Recall that the probability of occurrence of intensity level r_k in a digital image is approximated by

$$p_r(r_k) = \frac{n_k}{MN} \tag{3-14}$$

where MN is the total number of pixels in the image, and n_k denotes the number of pixels that have intensity r_k. As noted in the beginning of this section, $p_r(r_k)$, with $r_k \in [0, L-1]$, is commonly referred to as a normalized image histogram.

The discrete form of the transformation in Eq. (3-11) is

$$s_k = T(r_k) = (L-1) \sum_{j=0}^{k} p_r(r_j) \quad k = 0, 1, 2, \ldots, L-1 \tag{3-15}$$

where, as before, L is the number of possible intensity levels in the image (e.g., 256 for an 8-bit image). Thus, a processed (output) image is obtained by using Eq. (3-15) to map each pixel in the input image with intensity r_k into a corresponding pixel with level s_k in the output image, This is called a *histogram equalization* or *histogram linearization* transformation. It is not difficult to show (see Problem 3.9) that this transformation satisfies conditions (a) and (b) stated previously in this section.

EXAMPLE 3.5: Illustration of the mechanics of histogram equalization.

It will be helpful to work through a simple example. Suppose that a 3-bit image ($L = 8$) of size 64×64 pixels ($MN = 4096$) has the intensity distribution in Table 3.1, where the intensity levels are integers in the range $[0, L-1] = [0, 7]$. The histogram of this image is sketched in Fig. 3.19(a). Values of the histogram equalization transformation function are obtained using Eq. (3-15). For instance,

$$s_0 = T(r_0) = 7 \sum_{j=0}^{0} p_r(r_j) = 7p_r(r_0) = 1.33$$

TABLE 3.1
Intensity distribution and histogram values for a 3-bit, 64×64 digital image.

r_k	n_k	$p_r(r_k) = n_k/MN$
$r_0 = 0$	790	0.19
$r_1 = 1$	1023	0.25
$r_2 = 2$	850	0.21
$r_3 = 3$	656	0.16
$r_4 = 4$	329	0.08
$r_5 = 5$	245	0.06
$r_6 = 6$	122	0.03
$r_7 = 7$	81	0.02

Similarly, $s_1 = T(r_1) = 3.08$, $s_2 = 4.55$, $s_3 = 5.67$, $s_4 = 6.23$, $s_5 = 6.65$, $s_6 = 6.86$, and $s_7 = 7.00$. This transformation function has the staircase shape shown in Fig. 3.19(b).

At this point, the s values are fractional because they were generated by summing probability values, so we round them to their nearest integer values in the range $[0, 7]$:

$$s_0 = 1.33 \rightarrow 1 \quad s_2 = 4.55 \rightarrow 5 \quad s_4 = 6.23 \rightarrow 6 \quad s_6 = 6.86 \rightarrow 7$$
$$s_1 = 3.08 \rightarrow 3 \quad s_3 = 5.67 \rightarrow 6 \quad s_5 = 6.65 \rightarrow 7 \quad s_7 = 7.00 \rightarrow 7$$

These are the values of the equalized histogram. Observe that the transformation yielded only five distinct intensity levels. Because $r_0 = 0$ was mapped to $s_0 = 1$, there are 790 pixels in the histogram equalized image with this value (see Table 3.1). Also, there are 1023 pixels with a value of $s_1 = 3$ and 850 pixels with a value of $s_2 = 5$. However, both r_3 and r_4 were mapped to the same value, 6, so there are $(656 + 329) = 985$ pixels in the equalized image with this value. Similarly, there are $(245 + 122 + 81) = 448$ pixels with a value of 7 in the histogram equalized image. Dividing these numbers by $MN = 4096$ yielded the equalized histogram in Fig. 3.19(c).

Because a histogram is an approximation to a PDF, and no new allowed intensity levels are created in the process, perfectly flat histograms are rare in practical applications of histogram equalization using the method just discussed. Thus, unlike its continuous counterpart, it cannot be proved in general that discrete histogram equalization using Eq. (3-15) results in a uniform histogram (we will introduce later in

a b c

FIGURE 3.19
Histogram equalization.
(a) Original histogram.
(b) Transformation function.
(c) Equalized histogram.

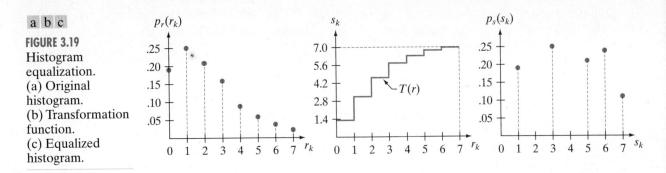

this section an approach for removing this limitation). However, as you will see shortly, using Eq. (3-15) has the general tendency to spread the histogram of the input image so that the intensity levels of the equalized image span a wider range of the intensity scale. The net result is contrast enhancement.

We discussed earlier the advantages of having intensity values that span the entire gray scale. The method just derived produces intensities that have this tendency, and also has the advantage that it is fully automatic. In other words, the process of histogram equalization consists entirely of implementing Eq. (3-15), which is based on information that can be extracted directly from a given image, without the need for any parameter specifications. This automatic, "hands-off" characteristic is important.

The inverse transformation from s back to r is denoted by

$$r_k = T^{-1}(s_k) \tag{3-16}$$

It can be shown (see Problem 3.9) that this inverse transformation satisfies conditions (a') and (b) defined earlier *only* if *all* intensity levels are present in the input image. This implies that none of the bins of the image histogram are empty. Although the inverse transformation is not used in histogram equalization, it plays a central role in the histogram-matching scheme developed after the following example.

EXAMPLE 3.6: Histogram equalization.

The left column in Fig. 3.20 shows the four images from Fig. 3.16, and the center column shows the result of performing histogram equalization on each of these images. The first three results from top to bottom show significant improvement. As expected, histogram equalization did not have much effect on the fourth image because its intensities span almost the full scale already. Figure 3.21 shows the transformation functions used to generate the equalized images in Fig. 3.20. These functions were generated using Eq. (3-15). Observe that transformation (4) is nearly linear, indicating that the inputs were mapped to nearly equal outputs. Shown is the mapping of an input value r_k to a corresponding output value s_k. In this case, the mapping was for image 1 (on the top left of Fig. 3.21), and indicates that a dark value was mapped to a much lighter one, thus contributing to the brightness of the output image.

The third column in Fig. 3.20 shows the histograms of the equalized images. While all the histograms are different, the histogram-equalized images themselves are visually very similar. This is not totally unexpected because the basic difference between the images on the left column is one of contrast, not content. Because the images have the same content, the increase in contrast resulting from histogram equalization was enough to render any intensity differences between the equalized images visually indistinguishable. Given the significant range of contrast differences in the original images, this example illustrates the power of histogram equalization as an adaptive, autonomous contrast-enhancement tool.

HISTOGRAM MATCHING (SPECIFICATION)

As explained in the last section, histogram equalization produces a transformation function that seeks to generate an output image with a uniform histogram. When automatic enhancement is desired, this is a good approach to consider because the

FIGURE 3.20 Left column: Images from Fig. 3.16. Center column: Corresponding histogram-equalized images. Right column: histograms of the images in the center column (compare with the histograms in Fig. 3.16).

FIGURE 3.21
Transformation functions for histogram equalization. Transformations (1) through (4) were obtained using Eq. (3-15) and the histograms of the images on the left column of Fig. 3.20. Mapping of one intensity value r_k in image 1 to its corresponding value s_k is shown.

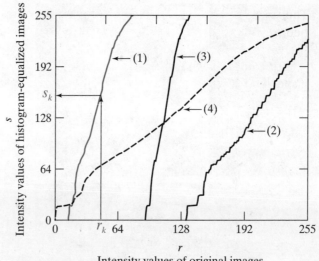

results from this technique are predictable and the method is simple to implement. However, there are applications in which histogram equalization is not suitable. In particular, it is useful sometimes to be able to specify the shape of the histogram that we wish the processed image to have. The method used to generate images that have a specified histogram is called *histogram matching* or *histogram specification*.

Consider for a moment continuous intensities r and z which, as before, we treat as random variables with PDFs $p_r(r)$ and $p_z(z)$, respectively. Here, r and z denote the intensity levels of the input and output (processed) images, respectively. We can estimate $p_r(r)$ from the given input image, and $p_z(z)$ is the *specified* PDF that we wish the output image to have.

Let s be a random variable with the property

$$s = T(r) = (L-1)\int_0^r p_r(w)\,dw \tag{3-17}$$

where w is dummy variable of integration. This is the same as Eq. (3-11), which we repeat here for convenience.

Define a function G on variable z with the property

$$G(z) = (L-1)\int_0^z p_z(v)\,dv = s \tag{3-18}$$

where v is a dummy variable of integration. It follows from the preceding two equations that $G(z) = s = T(r)$ and, therefore, that z must satisfy the condition

$$z = G^{-1}(s) = G^{-1}\big[T(r)\big] \tag{3-19}$$

The transformation function $T(r)$ can be obtained using Eq. (3-17) after $p_r(r)$ has been estimated using the input image. Similarly, function $G(z)$ can be obtained from Eq. (3-18) because $p_z(z)$ is given.

Equations (3-17) through (3-19) imply that an image whose intensity levels have a specified PDF can be obtained using the following procedure:

1. Obtain $p_r(r)$ from the input image to use in Eq. (3-17).
2. Use the specified PDF, $p_z(z)$, in Eq. (3-18) to obtain the function $G(z)$.
3. Compute the inverse transformation $z = G^{-1}(s)$; this is a mapping from s to z, the latter being the values that have the specified PDF.
4. Obtain the output image by first equalizing the input image using Eq. (3-17); the pixel values in this image are the s values. For each pixel with value s in the equalized image, perform the inverse mapping $z = G^{-1}(s)$ to obtain the corresponding pixel in the output image. When all pixels have been processed with this transformation, the PDF of the output image, $p_z(z)$, will be equal to the specified PDF.

Because s is related to r by $T(r)$, it is possible for the mapping that yields z from s to be expressed directly in terms of r. In general, however, finding analytical expressions for G^{-1} is not a trivial task. Fortunately, this is not a problem when working with discrete quantities, as you will see shortly.

As before, we have to convert the continuous result just derived into a discrete form. This means that we work with histograms instead of PDFs. As in histogram equalization, we lose in the conversion the ability to be able to guarantee a result that will have the exact specified histogram. Despite this, some very useful results can be obtained even with approximations.

The discrete formulation of Eq. (3-17) is the histogram equalization transformation in Eq. (3-15), which we repeat here for convenience:

$$s_k = T(r_k) = (L-1)\sum_{j=0}^{k} p_r(r_j) \quad k = 0,1,2,\ldots,L-1 \qquad (3\text{-}20)$$

where the components of this equation are as before. Similarly, given a specific value of s_k, the discrete formulation of Eq. (3-18) involves computing the transformation function

$$G(z_q) = (L-1)\sum_{i=0}^{q} p_z(z_i) \qquad (3\text{-}21)$$

for a value of q so that

$$G(z_q) = s_k \qquad (3\text{-}22)$$

where $p_z(z_i)$ is the ith value of the specified histogram. Finally, we obtain the desired value z_q from the inverse transformation:

$$z_q = G^{-1}(s_k) \tag{3-23}$$

When performed over all pixels, this is a mapping from the s values in the histogram-equalized image to the corresponding z values in the output image.

In practice, there is no need to compute the inverse of G. Because we deal with intensity levels that are integers, it is a simple matter to compute all the possible values of G using Eq. (3-21) for $q = 0, 1, 2, \ldots, L-1$. These values are rounded to their nearest integer values spanning the range $[0, L-1]$ and stored in a lookup table. Then, given a particular value of s_k, we look for the closest match in the table. For example, if the 27th entry in the table is the closest value to s_k, then $q = 26$ (recall that we start counting intensities at 0) and z_{26} is the best solution to Eq. (3-23). Thus, the given value s_k would map to z_{26}. Because the z's are integers in the range $[0, L-1]$, it follows that $z_0 = 0$, $z_{L-1} = L-1$, and, in general, $z_q = q$. Therefore, z_{26} would equal intensity value 26. We repeat this procedure to find the mapping from each value s_k to the value z_q that is its closest match in the table. These mappings are the solution to the histogram-specification problem.

Given an input image, a specified histogram, $p_z(z_i)$, $i = 0, 1, 2, \ldots, L-1$, and recalling that the s_k's are the values resulting from Eq. (3-20), we may summarize the procedure for discrete histogram specification as follows:

1. Compute the histogram, $p_r(r)$, of the input image, and use it in Eq. (3-20) to map the intensities in the input image to the intensities in the histogram-equalized image. Round the resulting values, s_k, to the integer range $[0, L-1]$.

2. Compute all values of function $G(z_q)$ using the Eq. (3-21) for $q = 0, 1, 2, \ldots, L-1$, where $p_z(z_i)$ are the values of the specified histogram. Round the values of G to integers in the range $[0, L-1]$. Store the rounded values of G in a lookup table.

3. For every value of s_k, $k = 0, 1, 2, \ldots, L-1$, use the stored values of G from Step 2 to find the corresponding value of z_q so that $G(z_q)$ is closest to s_k. Store these mappings from s to z. When more than one value of z_q gives the same match (i.e., the mapping is not unique), choose the smallest value by convention.

4. Form the histogram-specified image by mapping every equalized pixel with value s_k to the corresponding pixel with value z_q in the histogram-specified image, using the mappings found in Step 3.

As in the continuous case, the intermediate step of equalizing the input image is conceptual. It can be skipped by combining the two transformation functions, T and G^{-1}, as Example 3.7 below shows.

We mentioned at the beginning of the discussion on histogram equalization that, in addition to condition (b), inverse functions (G^{-1} in the present discussion) have to be strictly monotonic to satisfy condition (a'). In terms of Eq. (3-21), this means that none of the values $p_z(z_i)$ in the specified histogram can be zero (see Problem 3.9). When this condition is not satisfied, we use the "work-around" procedure in Step 3. The following example illustrates this numerically.

EXAMPLE 3.7: Illustration of the mechanics of histogram specification.

Consider the 64×64 hypothetical image from Example 3.5, whose histogram is repeated in Fig. 3.22(a). It is desired to transform this histogram so that it will have the values specified in the second column of Table 3.2. Figure 3.22(b) shows this histogram.

The first step is to obtain the histogram-equalized values, which we did in Example 3.5:

$$s_0 = 1; \quad s_1 = 3; \quad s_2 = 5; \quad s_3 = 6; \quad s_4 = 6; \quad s_5 = 7; \quad s_6 = 7; \quad s_7 = 7$$

In the next step, we compute the values of $G(z_q)$ using the values of $p_z(z_q)$ from Table 3.2 in Eq. (3-21):

$$G(z_0) = 0.00 \quad G(z_2) = 0.00 \quad G(z_4) = 2.45 \quad G(z_6) = 5.95$$
$$G(z_1) = 0.00 \quad G(z_3) = 1.05 \quad G(z_5) = 4.55 \quad G(z_7) = 7.00$$

As in Example 3.5, these fractional values are rounded to integers in the range $[0,7]$:

$$\begin{aligned}
G(z_0) &= 0.00 \rightarrow 0 & G(z_4) &= 2.45 \rightarrow 2 \\
G(z_1) &= 0.00 \rightarrow 0 & G(z_5) &= 4.55 \rightarrow 5 \\
G(z_2) &= 0.00 \rightarrow 0 & G(z_6) &= 5.95 \rightarrow 6 \\
G(z_3) &= 1.05 \rightarrow 1 & G(z_7) &= 7.00 \rightarrow 7
\end{aligned}$$

These results are summarized in Table 3.3. The transformation function, $G(z_q)$, is sketched in Fig. 3.23(c). Because its first three values are equal, G is not strictly monotonic, so condition (a') is violated. Therefore, we use the approach outlined in Step 3 of the algorithm to handle this situation. According to this step, we find the smallest value of z_q so that the value $G(z_q)$ is the closest to s_k. We do this for every value of

a b
c d

FIGURE 3.22
(a) Histogram of a 3-bit image.
(b) Specified histogram.
(c) Transformation function obtained from the specified histogram.
(d) Result of histogram specification. Compare the histograms in (b) and (d).

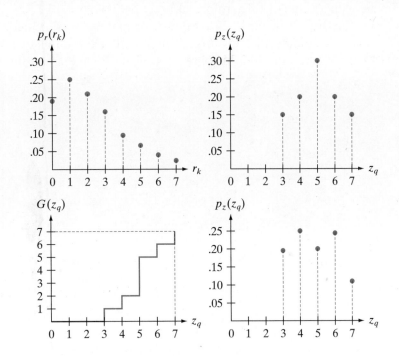

TABLE 3.2
Specified and
actual histograms
(the values in
the third column
are computed in
Example 3.7).

z_q	Specified $p_z(z_q)$	Actual $p_z(z_q)$
$z_0 = 0$	0.00	0.00
$z_1 = 1$	0.00	0.00
$z_2 = 2$	0.00	0.00
$z_3 = 3$	0.15	0.19
$z_4 = 4$	0.20	0.25
$z_5 = 5$	0.30	0.21
$z_6 = 6$	0.20	0.24
$z_7 = 7$	0.15	0.11

s_k to create the required mappings from s to z. For example, $s_0 = 1$, and we see that $G(z_3) = 1$, which is a perfect match in this case, so we have the correspondence $s_0 \rightarrow z_3$. Every pixel whose value is 1 in the histogram equalized image would map to a pixel valued 3 in the histogram-specified image. Continuing in this manner, we arrive at the mappings in Table 3.4.

In the final step of the procedure, we use the mappings in Table 3.4 to map every pixel in the histogram equalized image into a corresponding pixel in the newly created histogram-specified image. The values of the resulting histogram are listed in the third column of Table 3.2, and the histogram is shown in Fig. 3.22(d). The values of $p_z(z_q)$ were obtained using the same procedure as in Example 3.5. For instance, we see in Table 3.4 that $s_k = 1$ maps to $z_q = 3$, and there are 790 pixels in the histogram-equalized image with a value of 1. Therefore, $p_z(z_3) = 790/4096 = 0.19$.

Although the final result in Fig. 3.22(d) does not match the specified histogram exactly, the general trend of moving the intensities toward the high end of the intensity scale definitely was achieved. As mentioned earlier, obtaining the histogram-equalized image as an intermediate step is useful for

TABLE 3.3
Rounded values
of the
transformation
function $G(z_q)$.

z_q	$G(z_q)$
$z_0 = 0$	0
$z_1 = 1$	0
$z_2 = 2$	0
$z_3 = 3$	1
$z_4 = 4$	2
$z_5 = 5$	5
$z_6 = 6$	6
$z_7 = 7$	7

TABLE 3.4
Mapping of
values s_k into
corresponding
values z_q.

s_k	$\rightarrow$	z_q
1	$\rightarrow$	3
3	$\rightarrow$	4
5	$\rightarrow$	5
6	$\rightarrow$	6
7	$\rightarrow$	7

explaining the procedure, but this is not necessary. Instead, we could list the mappings from the r's to the s's and from the s's to the z's in a three-column table. Then, we would use those mappings to map the original pixels directly into the pixels of the histogram-specified image.

EXAMPLE 3.8: Comparison between histogram equalization and histogram specification.

Figure 3.23(a) shows an image of the Mars moon, Phobos, taken by NASA's Mars Global Surveyor. Figure 3.23(b) shows the histogram of Fig. 3.23(a). The image is dominated by large, dark areas, resulting in a histogram characterized by a large concentration of pixels in the dark end of the gray scale. At first glance, one might conclude that histogram equalization would be a good approach to enhance this image, so that details in the dark areas become more visible. It is demonstrated in the following discussion that this is not so.

Figure 3.24(a) shows the histogram equalization transformation [Eq. (3-20)] obtained using the histogram in Fig. 3.23(b). The most relevant characteristic of this transformation function is how fast it rises from intensity level 0 to a level near 190. This is caused by the large concentration of pixels in the input histogram having levels near 0. When this transformation is applied to the levels of the input image to obtain a histogram-equalized result, the net effect is to map a very narrow interval of dark pixels into the

a b

FIGURE 3.23
(a) An image, and
(b) its histogram.

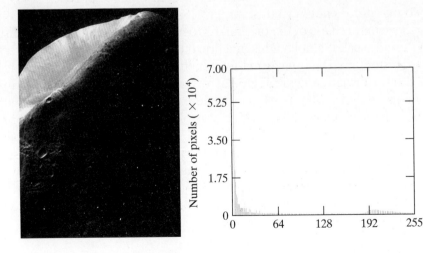

a b
c

FIGURE 3.24
(a) Histogram
equalization
transformation
obtained using
the histogram
in Fig. 3.23(b).
(b) Histogram
equalized image.
(c) Histogram of
equalized image.

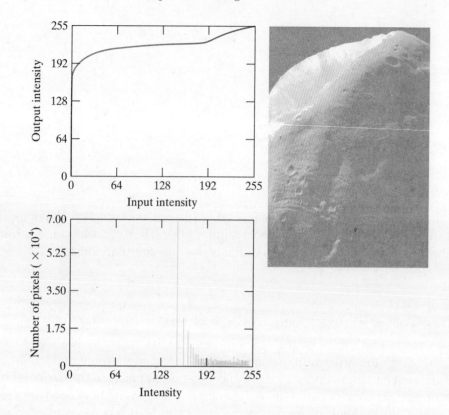

upper end of the gray scale of the output image. Because numerous pixels in the input image have levels precisely in this interval, we would expect the result to be an image with a light, washed-out appearance. As Fig. 3.24(b) shows, this is indeed the case. The histogram of this image is shown in Fig. 3.24(c). Note how all the intensity levels are biased toward the upper one-half of the gray scale.

Because the problem with the transformation function in Fig. 3.24(a) was caused by a large concentration of pixels in the original image with levels near 0, a reasonable approach is to modify the histogram of that image so that it does not have this property. Figure 3.25(a) shows a manually specified function that preserves the general shape of the original histogram, but has a smoother transition of levels in the dark region of the gray scale. Sampling this function into 256 equally spaced discrete values produced the desired specified histogram. The transformation function, $G(z_q)$, obtained from this histogram using Eq. (3-21) is labeled transformation (1) in Fig. 3.25(b). Similarly, the inverse transformation $G^{-1}(s_k)$, from Eq. (3-23) (obtained using the step-by-step procedure discussed earlier) is labeled transformation (2) in Fig. 3.25(b). The enhanced image in Fig. 3.25(c) was obtained by applying transformation (2) to the pixels of the histogram-equalized image in Fig. 3.24(b). The improvement of the histogram-specified image over the result obtained by histogram equalization is evident by comparing these two images. It is of interest to note that a rather modest change in the original histogram was all that was required to obtain a significant improvement in appearance. Figure 3.25(d) shows the histogram of Fig. 3.25(c). The most distinguishing feature of this histogram is how its low end has shifted right toward the lighter region of the gray scale (but not excessively so), as desired.

FIGURE 3.25
Histogram
specification.
(a) Specified histogram.
(b) Transformation
$G(z_q)$, labeled (1),
and $G^{-1}(s_k)$,
labeled (2).
(c) Result of
histogram
specification.
(d) Histogram of
image (c).

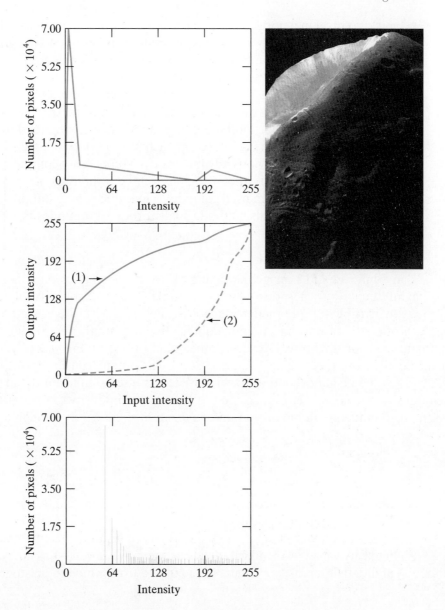

LOCAL HISTOGRAM PROCESSING

The histogram processing methods discussed thus far are *global*, in the sense that pixels are modified by a transformation function based on the intensity distribution of an entire image. This global approach is suitable for overall enhancement, but generally fails when the objective is to enhance details over small areas in an image. This is because the number of pixels in small areas have negligible influence on the computation of global transformations. The solution is to devise transformation functions based on the intensity distribution of pixel neighborhoods.

The histogram processing techniques previously described can be adapted to local enhancement. The procedure is to define a neighborhood and move its center from pixel to pixel in a horizontal or vertical direction. At each location, the histogram of the points in the neighborhood is computed, and either a histogram equalization or histogram specification transformation function is obtained. This function is used to map the intensity of the pixel centered in the neighborhood. The center of the neighborhood is then moved to an adjacent pixel location and the procedure is repeated. Because only one row or column of the neighborhood changes in a one-pixel translation of the neighborhood, updating the histogram obtained in the previous location with the new data introduced at each motion step is possible (see Problem 3.14). This approach has obvious advantages over repeatedly computing the histogram of all pixels in the neighborhood region each time the region is moved one pixel location. Another approach used sometimes to reduce computation is to utilize nonoverlapping regions, but this method usually produces an undesirable "blocky" effect.

EXAMPLE 3.9: Local histogram equalization.

Figure 3.26(a) is an 8-bit, 512×512 image consisting of five black squares on a light gray background. The image is slightly noisy, but the noise is imperceptible. There are objects embedded in the dark squares, but they are invisible for all practical purposes. Figure 3.26(b) is the result of global histogram equalization. As is often the case with histogram equalization of smooth, noisy regions, this image shows significant enhancement of the noise. However, other than the noise, Fig. 3.26(b) does not reveal any new significant details from the original. Figure 3.26(c) was obtained using local histogram equalization of Fig. 3.26(a) with a neighborhood of size 3×3. Here, we see significant detail within all the dark squares. The intensity values of these objects are too close to the intensity of the dark squares, and their sizes are too small, to influence global histogram equalization significantly enough to show this level of intensity detail.

USING HISTOGRAM STATISTICS FOR IMAGE ENHANCEMENT

Statistics obtained directly from an image histogram can be used for image enhancement. Let r denote a discrete random variable representing intensity values in the range $[0, L-1]$, and let $p(r_i)$ denote the normalized histogram component corresponding to intensity value r_i. As indicated earlier, we may view $p(r_i)$ as an estimate of the probability that intensity r_i occurs in the image from which the histogram was obtained.

a b c

FIGURE 3.26
(a) Original image. (b) Result of global histogram equalization. (c) Result of local histogram equalization.

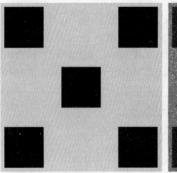  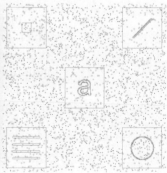

See the tutorials section in the book website for a review of probability.

For an image with intensity levels in the range $[0, L-1]$, the nth moment of r about its mean, m, is defined as

$$\mu_n = \sum_{i=0}^{L-1} (r_i - m)^n p(r_i) \tag{3-24}$$

where m is given by

We follow convention in using m for the mean value. Do not confuse it with our use of the same symbol to denote the number of rows in an $m \times n$ neighborhood.

$$m = \sum_{i=0}^{L-1} r_i p(r_i) \tag{3-25}$$

The mean is a measure of average intensity and the variance (or standard deviation, σ), given by

$$\sigma^2 = \mu_2 = \sum_{i=0}^{L-1} (r_i - m)^2 p(r_i) \tag{3-26}$$

is a measure of image contrast.

We consider two uses of the mean and variance for enhancement purposes. The *global* mean and variance [Eqs. (3-25) and (3-26)] are computed over an entire image and are useful for gross adjustments in overall intensity and contrast. A more powerful use of these parameters is in local enhancement, where the *local* mean and variance are used as the basis for making changes that depend on image characteristics in a neighborhood about each pixel in an image.

Let (x, y) denote the coordinates of any pixel in a given image, and let S_{xy} denote a neighborhood of specified size, centered on (x, y). The mean value of the pixels in this neighborhood is given by the expression

$$m_{S_{xy}} = \sum_{i=0}^{L-1} r_i p_{S_{xy}}(r_i) \tag{3-27}$$

where $p_{S_{xy}}$ is the histogram of the pixels in region S_{xy}. This histogram has L bins, corresponding to the L possible intensity values in the input image. However, many of the bins will have 0 counts, depending on the size of S_{xy}. For example, if the neighborhood is of size 3×3 and $L = 256$, only between 1 and 9 of the 256 bins of the histogram of the neighborhood will be nonzero (the maximum number of possible *different* intensities in a 3×3 region is 9, and the minimum is 1). These non-zero values will correspond to the number of different intensities in S_{xy}.

The variance of the pixels in the neighborhood is similarly given by

$$\sigma^2_{S_{xy}} = \sum_{i=0}^{L-1} (r_i - m_{S_{xy}})^2 p_{S_{xy}}(r_i) \tag{3-28}$$

As before, the local mean is a measure of average intensity in neighborhood S_{xy}, and the local variance (or standard deviation) is a measure of intensity contrast in that neighborhood.

As the following example illustrates, an important aspect of image processing using the local mean and variance is the flexibility these parameters afford in developing simple, yet powerful enhancement rules based on statistical measures that have a close, predictable correspondence with image appearance.

EXAMPLE 3.10: Local enhancement using histogram statistics.

Figure 3.27(a) is the same image as Fig. 3.26(a), which we enhanced using local histogram equalization. As noted before, the dark squares contain embedded symbols that are almost invisible. As before, we want to enhance the image to bring out these hidden features.

We can use the concepts presented in this section to formulate an approach for enhancing low-contrast details embedded in a background of similar intensity. The problem at hand is to enhance the low-contrast detail in the dark areas of the image, while leaving the light background unchanged.

A method used to determine whether an area is relatively light or dark at a point (x, y) is to compare the average local intensity, $m_{S_{xy}}$, to the average image intensity (the global mean), denoted by m_G. We obtain m_G using Eq. (3-25) with the histogram of the entire image. Thus, we have the first element of our enhancement scheme: We will consider the pixel at (x, y) as a candidate for processing if $k_0 m_G \leq m_{S_{xy}} \leq k_1 m_G$, where k_0 and k_1 are nonnegative constants and $k_0 < k_1$. For example, if our focus is on areas that are darker than one-quarter of the mean intensity, we would choose $k_0 = 0$ and $k_1 = 0.25$.

Because we are interested in enhancing areas that have low contrast, we also need a measure to determine whether the contrast of an area makes it a candidate for enhancement. We consider the pixel at (x, y) as a candidate if $k_2 \sigma_G \leq \sigma_{S_{xy}} \leq k_3 \sigma_G$, where σ_G is the global standard deviation obtained with Eq. (3-26) using the histogram of the entire image, and k_2 and k_3 are nonnegative constants, with $k_2 < k_3$. For example, to enhance a dark area of low contrast, we might choose $k_2 = 0$ and $k_3 = 0.1$. A pixel that meets all the preceding conditions for local enhancement is processed by multiplying it by a specified constant, C, to increase (or decrease) the value of its intensity level relative to the rest of the image. Pixels that do not meet the enhancement conditions are not changed.

We summarize the preceding approach as follows. Let $f(x, y)$ denote the value of an image at any image coordinates (x, y), and let $g(x, y)$ be the corresponding value in the enhanced image at those coordinates. Then,

$$g(x, y) = \begin{cases} Cf(x, y) & \text{if } k_0 m_G \leq m_{S_{xy}} \leq k_1 m_G \text{ AND } k_2 \sigma_G \leq \sigma_{S_{xy}} \leq k_3 \sigma_G \\ f(x, y) & \text{otherwise} \end{cases} \quad (3\text{-}29)$$

a b

FIGURE 3.27
(a) Original image. (b) Result of local enhancement based on local histogram statistics. Compare (b) with Fig. 3.26(c).

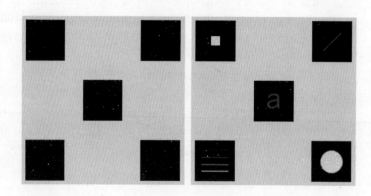

for $x = 0, 1, 2, \ldots, M-1$ and $y = 0, 1, 2, \ldots, N-1$, where, as indicated above, C, k_0, k_1, k_2, and k_3 are specified constants, m_G is the global mean of the input image, and σ_G is its standard deviation. Parameters $m_{S_{xy}}$ and $\sigma_{S_{xy}}$ are the local mean and standard deviation, respectively, which change for every location (x, y). As usual, M and N are the number of rows and columns in the input image.

Factors such as the values of the global mean and variance relative to values in the areas to be enhanced play a key role in selecting the parameters in Eq. (3-29), as does the range of differences between the intensities of the areas to be enhanced and their background. In the case of Fig. 3.27(a), $m_G = 161$, $\sigma_G = 103$, the maximum intensity values of the image and areas to be enhanced are 228 and 10, respectively, and the minimum values are 0 in both cases.

We would like for the maximum value of the enhanced features to be the same as the maximum value of the image, so we select $C = 22.8$. The areas to be enhanced are quite dark relative to the rest of the image, and they occupy less than a third of the image area; thus, we expect the mean intensity in the dark areas to be much less than the global mean. Based on this, we let $k_0 = 0$ and $k_1 = 0.1$. Because the areas to be enhanced are of very low contrast, we let $k_2 = 0$. For the upper limit of acceptable values of standard deviation we set $k_3 = 0.1$, which gives us one-tenth of the global standard deviation. Figure 3.27(b) is the result of using Eq. (3-29) with these parameters. By comparing this figure with Fig. 3.26(c), we see that the method based on local statistics detected the same hidden features as local histogram equalization. But the present approach extracted significantly more detail. For example, we see that all the objects are solid, but only the boundaries were detected by local histogram equalization. In addition, note that the intensities of the objects are not the same, with the objects in the top-left and bottom-right being brighter than the others. Also, the horizontal rectangles in the lower left square evidently are of different intensities. Finally, note that the background in both the image and dark squares in Fig. 3.27(b) is nearly the same as in the original image; by comparison, the same regions in Fig. 3.26(c) exhibit more visible noise and have lost their gray-level content. Thus, the additional complexity required to use local statistics yielded results in this case that are superior to local histogram equalization.

3.4 FUNDAMENTALS OF SPATIAL FILTERING

In this section, we discuss the use of spatial filters for image processing. Spatial filtering is used in a broad spectrum of image processing applications, so a solid understanding of filtering principles is important. As mentioned at the beginning of this chapter, the filtering examples in this section deal mostly with image enhancement. Other applications of spatial filtering are discussed in later chapters.

The name *filter* is borrowed from frequency domain processing (the topic of Chapter 4) where "filtering" refers to passing, modifying, or rejecting specified frequency components of an image. For example, a filter that passes low frequencies is called a *lowpass filter*. The net effect produced by a lowpass filter is to smooth an image by blurring it. We can accomplish similar smoothing directly on the image itself by using *spatial filters*.

Spatial filtering modifies an image by replacing the value of each pixel by a function of the values of the pixel and its neighbors. If the operation performed on the image pixels is linear, then the filter is called a *linear spatial filter*. Otherwise, the filter is a *nonlinear spatial filter*. We will focus attention first on linear filters and then introduce some basic nonlinear filters. Section 5.3 contains a more comprehensive list of nonlinear filters and their application.

See Section 2.6 regarding linearity.

THE MECHANICS OF LINEAR SPATIAL FILTERING

A linear spatial filter performs a sum-of-products operation between an image f and a *filter kernel*, w. The kernel is an array whose size defines the neighborhood of operation, and whose coefficients determine the nature of the filter. Other terms used to refer to a spatial filter kernel are *mask*, *template*, and *window*. We use the term *filter kernel* or simply *kernel*.

Figure 3.28 illustrates the mechanics of linear spatial filtering using a 3×3 kernel. At any point (x, y) in the image, the response, $g(x, y)$, of the filter is the sum of products of the kernel coefficients and the image pixels encompassed by the kernel:

$$g(x,y) = w(-1,-1)f(x-1, y-1) + w(-1,0)f(x-1, y) + \ldots$$
$$+ w(0,0)f(x,y) + \ldots + w(1,1)f(x+1, y+1) \tag{3-30}$$

As coordinates x and y are varied, the center of the kernel moves from pixel to pixel, generating the filtered image, g, in the process.[†]

Observe that the center coefficient of the kernel, $w(0,0)$, aligns with the pixel at location (x, y). For a kernel of size $m \times n$, we assume that $m = 2a + 1$ and $n = 2b + 1$, where a and b are nonnegative integers. This means that our focus is on kernels of odd size in both coordinate directions. In general, linear spatial filtering of an image of size $M \times N$ with a kernel of size $m \times n$ is given by the expression

It certainly is possible to work with kernels of even size, or mixed even and odd sizes. However, working with odd sizes simplifies indexing and is also more intuitive because the kernels have centers falling on integer values, and they are spatially symmetric.

$$g(x,y) = \sum_{s=-a}^{a} \sum_{t=-b}^{b} w(s,t)f(x+s, y+t) \tag{3-31}$$

where x and y are varied so that the center (origin) of the kernel visits every pixel in f once. For a fixed value of (x, y), Eq. (3-31) implements the *sum of products* of the form shown in Eq. (3-30), but for a kernel of arbitrary odd size. As you will learn in the following section, this equation is a central tool in linear filtering.

SPATIAL CORRELATION AND CONVOLUTION

Spatial correlation is illustrated graphically in Fig. 3.28, and it is described mathematically by Eq. (3-31). Correlation consists of moving the center of a kernel over an image, and computing the sum of products at each location. The mechanics of *spatial convolution* are the same, except that the correlation kernel is rotated by 180°. Thus, when the values of a kernel are symmetric about its center, correlation and convolution yield the same result. The reason for rotating the kernel will become clear in the following discussion. The best way to explain the differences between the two concepts is by example.

We begin with a 1-D illustration, in which case Eq. (3-31) becomes

$$g(x) = \sum_{s=-a}^{a} w(s)f(x+s) \tag{3-32}$$

[†] A filtered pixel value typically is assigned to a corresponding location in a new image created to hold the results of filtering. It is seldom the case that filtered pixels replace the values of the corresponding location in the original image, as this would change the content of the image while filtering is being performed.

FIGURE 3.28
The mechanics of linear spatial filtering using a 3×3 kernel. The pixels are shown as squares to simplify the graphics. Note that the origin of the image is at the top left, but the origin of the kernel is at its center. Placing the origin at the center of spatially symmetric kernels simplifies writing expressions for linear filtering.

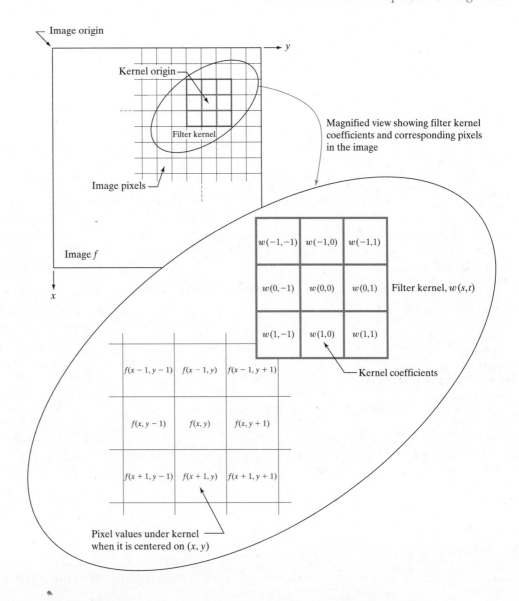

Figure 3.29(a) shows a 1-D function, f, and a kernel, w. The kernel is of size 1×5, so $a = 2$ and $b = 0$ in this case. Figure 3.29(b) shows the starting position used to perform correlation, in which w is positioned so that its center coefficient is coincident with the origin of f.

The first thing we notice is that part of w lies outside f, so the summation is undefined in that area. A solution to this problem is to *pad* function f with enough 0's on either side. In general, if the kernel is of size $1 \times m$, we need $(m-1)/2$ zeros on either side of f in order to handle the beginning and ending configurations of w with respect to f. Figure 3.29(c) shows a properly padded function. In this starting configuration, all coefficients of the kernel overlap valid values.

Zero padding is not the only padding option, as we will discuss in detail later in this chapter.

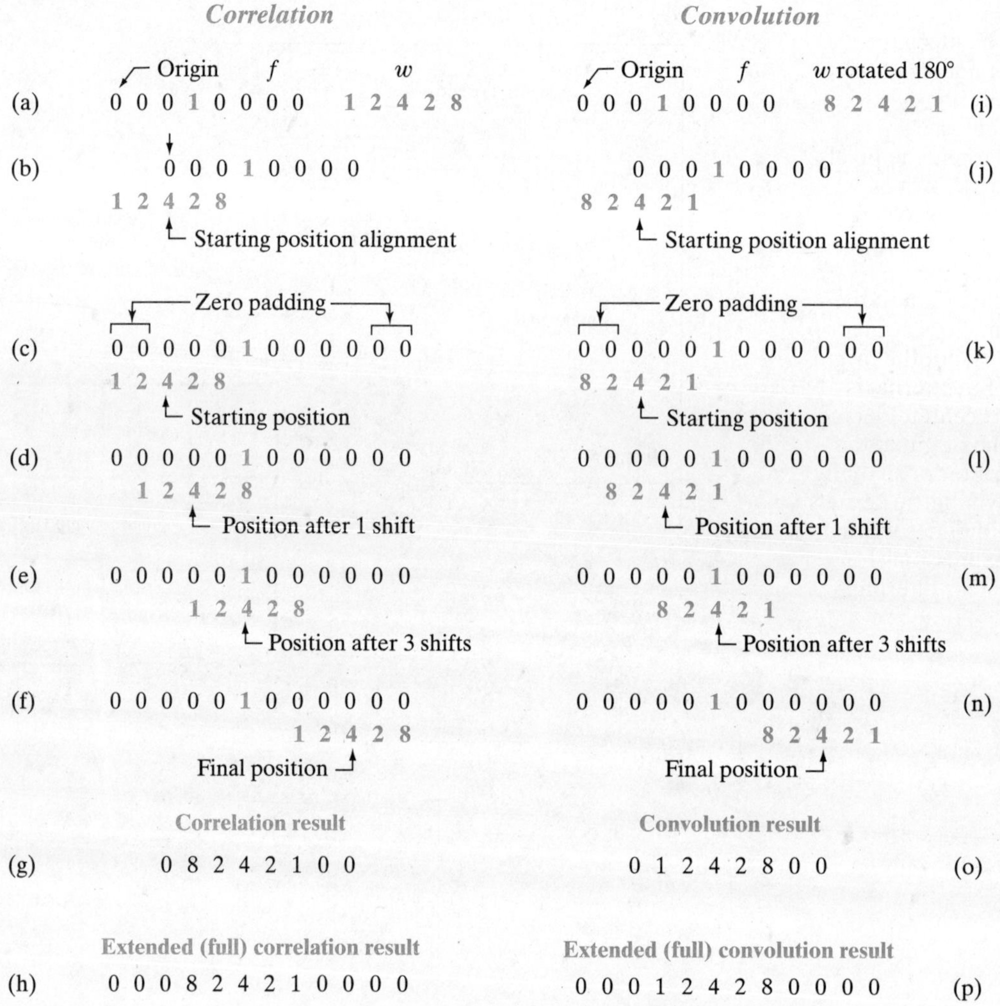

FIGURE 3.29
Illustration of 1-D correlation and convolution of a kernel, w, with a function f consisting of a discrete unit impulse. Note that correlation and convolution are functions of the variable x, which acts to *displace* one function with respect to the other. For the extended correlation and convolution results, the starting configuration places the right-most element of the kernel to be coincident with the origin of f. Additional padding must be used.

Correlation

(a)   Origin f w
       0 0 0 1 0 0 0 0   1 2 4 2 8

(b)   0 0 0 1 0 0 0 0
           1 2 4 2 8
             └─ Starting position alignment

(c)   ┌─── Zero padding ───┐
       0 0 0 0 0 1 0 0 0 0 0 0
       1 2 4 2 8
           └─ Starting position

(d)   0 0 0 0 0 1 0 0 0 0 0 0
         1 2 4 2 8
             └─ Position after 1 shift

(e)   0 0 0 0 0 1 0 0 0 0 0 0
           1 2 4 2 8
               └─ Position after 3 shifts

(f)   0 0 0 0 0 1 0 0 0 0 0 0
               1 2 4 2 8
       Final position ─┘

Correlation result

(g)   0 8 2 4 2 1 0 0

Extended (full) correlation result

(h)   0 0 0 8 2 4 2 1 0 0 0 0

Convolution

(i)   Origin f w rotated 180°
       0 0 0 1 0 0 0 0   8 2 4 2 1

(j)   0 0 0 1 0 0 0 0
           8 2 4 2 1
             └─ Starting position alignment

(k)   ┌─── Zero padding ───┐
       0 0 0 0 0 1 0 0 0 0 0 0
       8 2 4 2 1
           └─ Starting position

(l)   0 0 0 0 0 1 0 0 0 0 0 0
         8 2 4 2 1
             └─ Position after 1 shift

(m)   0 0 0 0 0 1 0 0 0 0 0 0
           8 2 4 2 1
               └─ Position after 3 shifts

(n)   0 0 0 0 0 1 0 0 0 0 0 0
               8 2 4 2 1
       Final position ─┘

Convolution result

(o)   0 1 2 4 2 8 0 0

Extended (full) convolution result

(p)   0 0 0 1 2 4 2 8 0 0 0 0

The first correlation value is the sum of products in this initial position, computed using Eq. (3-32) with $x = 0$:

$$g(0) = \sum_{s=-2}^{2} w(s)f(s+0) = 0$$

This value is in the leftmost location of the correlation result in Fig. 3.29(g).

To obtain the second value of correlation, we shift the relative positions of w and f one pixel location to the right [i.e., we let $x = 1$ in Eq. (3-32)] and compute the sum of products again. The result is $g(1) = 8$, as shown in the leftmost, nonzero location in Fig. 3.29(g). When $x = 2$, we obtain $g(2) = 2$. When $x = 3$, we get $g(3) = 4$ [see Fig. 3.29(e)]. Proceeding in this manner by varying x one shift at a time, we "build" the correlation result in Fig. 3.29(g). Note that it took 8 values of x (i.e., $x = 0, 1, 2, …, 7$) to fully shift w past f so the *center* coefficient in w visited *every* pixel in f. Sometimes, it is useful to have every element of w visit every pixel in f. For this, we have to start with the rightmost element of w coincident with the origin of f, and end with the leftmost element of w being coincident the last element of f (additional padding would be required). Figure Fig. 3.29(h) shows the result of this *extended*, or *full*, correlation. As Fig. 3.29(g) shows, we can obtain the "standard" correlation by cropping the full correlation in Fig. 3.29(h).

There are two important points to note from the preceding discussion. First, correlation is a function of *displacement* of the filter kernel relative to the image. In other words, the first value of correlation corresponds to zero displacement of the kernel, the second corresponds to one unit displacement, and so on.[†] The second thing to notice is that correlating a kernel w with a function that contains all 0's and a single 1 yields a *copy* of w, but *rotated* by 180°. A function that contains a single 1 with the rest being 0's is called a *discrete unit impulse*. Correlating a kernel with a discrete unit impulse yields a *rotated* version of the kernel at the location of the impulse.

Rotating a 1-D kernel by 180° is equivalent to flipping the kernel about its axis.

The right side of Fig. 3.29 shows the sequence of steps for performing convolution (we will give the equation for convolution shortly). The only difference here is that the kernel is *pre-rotated* by 180° prior to performing the shifting/sum of products operations. As the convolution in Fig. 3.29(o) shows, the result of pre-rotating the kernel is that now we have an *exact* copy of the kernel at the location of the unit impulse. In fact, a foundation of linear system theory is that convolving a function with an impulse yields a copy of the function at the location of the impulse. We will use this property extensively in Chapter 4.

The 1-D concepts just discussed extend easily to images, as Fig. 3.30 shows. For a kernel of size $m \times n$, we pad the image with a minimum of $(m-1)/2$ rows of 0's at the top and bottom and $(n-1)/2$ columns of 0's on the left and right. In this case, m and n are equal to 3, so we pad f with one row of 0's above and below and one column of 0's to the left and right, as Fig. 3.30(b) shows. Figure 3.30(c) shows the initial position of the kernel for performing correlation, and Fig. 3.30(d) shows the final result after the center of w visits every pixel in f, computing a sum of products at each location. As before, the result is a copy of the kernel, rotated by 180°. We will discuss the extended correlation result shortly.

In 2-D, rotation by 180° is equivalent to flipping the kernel about one axis and then the other.

For convolution, we pre-rotate the kernel as before and repeat the sliding sum of products just explained. Figures 3.30(f) through (h) show the result. You see again that convolution of a function with an impulse copies the function to the location of the impulse. As noted earlier, correlation and convolution yield the same result if the kernel values are symmetric about the center.

The concept of an impulse is fundamental in linear system theory, and is used in numerous places throughout the book. A *discrete impulse of strength (amplitude) A* located at coordinates (x_0, y_0) is defined as

$$\delta(x - x_0, y - y_0) = \begin{cases} A & \text{if } x = x_0 \text{ and } y = y_0 \\ 0 & \text{otherwise} \end{cases} \tag{3-33}$$

[†] In reality, we are shifting f to the left of w every time we increment x in Eq. (3-32). However, it is more intuitive to think of the smaller kernel moving right over the larger array f. The motion of the two is relative, so either way of looking at the motion is acceptable. The reason we increment f and not w is that indexing the equations for correlation and convolution is much easier (and clearer) this way, especially when working with 2-D arrays.

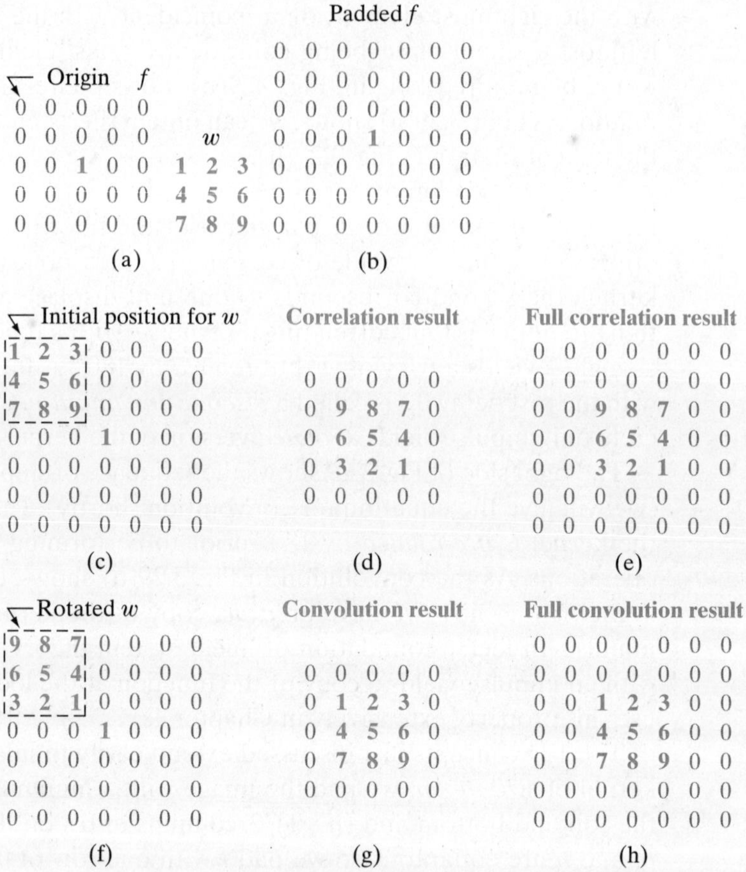

FIGURE 3.30
Correlation
(middle row) and
convolution (last
row) of a 2-D
kernel with an
image consisting
of a discrete unit
impulse. The 0's
are shown in gray
to simplify visual
analysis. Note that
correlation and
convolution are
functions of x and
y. As these
variable change,
they
displace one
function with
respect to the
other. See the
discussion of Eqs.
(3-36) and (3-37)
regarding full
correlation and
convolution.

Padded f

0	0	0	0	0	0	0
0	0	0	0	0	0	0
0	0	0	0	0	0	0
0	0	0	1	0	0	0
0	0	0	0	0	0	0
0	0	0	0	0	0	0
0	0	0	0	0	0	0

Origin f

0	0	0	0	0
0	0	0	0	0
0	0	1	0	0
0	0	0	0	0
0	0	0	0	0

w

1	2	3
4	5	6
7	8	9

(a) (b)

Initial position for w

1	2	3	0	0	0	0
4	5	6	0	0	0	0
7	8	9	0	0	0	0
0	0	0	1	0	0	0
0	0	0	0	0	0	0
0	0	0	0	0	0	0
0	0	0	0	0	0	0

Correlation result

0	0	0	0	0
0	9	8	7	0
0	6	5	4	0
0	3	2	1	0
0	0	0	0	0

Full correlation result

0	0	0	0	0	0	0
0	0	0	0	0	0	0
0	0	9	8	7	0	0
0	0	6	5	4	0	0
0	0	3	2	1	0	0
0	0	0	0	0	0	0
0	0	0	0	0	0	0

(c) (d) (e)

Rotated w

9	8	7	0	0	0	0
6	5	4	0	0	0	0
3	2	1	0	0	0	0
0	0	0	1	0	0	0
0	0	0	0	0	0	0
0	0	0	0	0	0	0
0	0	0	0	0	0	0

Convolution result

0	0	0	0	0
0	1	2	3	0
0	4	5	6	0
0	7	8	9	0
0	0	0	0	0

Full convolution result

0	0	0	0	0	0	0
0	0	0	0	0	0	0
0	0	1	2	3	0	0
0	0	4	5	6	0	0
0	0	7	8	9	0	0
0	0	0	0	0	0	0
0	0	0	0	0	0	0

(f) (g) (h)

Recall that $A = 1$ for a unit impulse.

For example, the unit impulse in Fig. 3.29(a) is given by $\delta(x - 3)$ in the 1-D version of the preceding equation. Similarly, the impulse in Fig. 3.30(a) is given by $\delta(x - 2, y - 2)$ [remember, the origin is at $(0,0)$].

Summarizing the preceding discussion in equation form, the correlation of a kernel w of size $m \times n$ with an image $f(x, y)$, denoted as $(w \star f)(x, y)$, is given by Eq. (3-31), which we repeat here for convenience:

$$(w \star f)(x, y) = \sum_{s=-a}^{a} \sum_{t=-b}^{b} w(s,t)f(x+s, y+t) \tag{3-34}$$

Because our kernels do not depend on (x, y), we will sometimes make this fact explicit by writing the left side of the preceding equation as $w \star f(x, y)$. Equation (3-34) is evaluated for all values of the displacement variables x and y so that the center point of w visits every pixel in f,[†] where we assume that f has been padded appropriately.

[†] As we mentioned earlier, the *minimum* number of required padding elements for a 2-D correlation is $(m-1)/2$ rows above and below f, and $(n-1)/2$ columns on the left and right. With this padding, and assuming that f is of size $M \times N$, the values of x and y required to obtain a complete correlation are $x = 0, 1, 2, \ldots, M-1$ and $y = 0, 1, 2, \ldots, N-1$. This assumes that the starting configuration is such that the *center* of the kernel coincides with the *origin* of the image, which we have defined to be at the top, left (see Fig. 2.19).

As explained earlier, $a = (m-1)/2$, $b = (n-1)/2$, and we assume that m and n are odd integers.

In a similar manner, the *convolution* of a kernel w of size $m \times n$ with an image $f(x,y)$, denoted by $(w \star f)(x,y)$, is defined as

$$(w \star f)(x,y) = \sum_{s=-a}^{a} \sum_{t=-b}^{b} w(s,t)f(x-s, y-t) \tag{3-35}$$

where the minus signs align the coordinates of f and w when one of the functions is rotated by 180° (see Problem 3.17). This equation implements the sum of products process to which we refer throughout the book as *linear spatial filtering*. That is, linear spatial filtering and spatial convolution are synonymous.

Because convolution is commutative (see Table 3.5), it is immaterial whether w or f is rotated, but rotation of the kernel is used by convention. Our kernels do not depend on (x,y), a fact that we sometimes make explicit by writing the left side of Eq. (3-35) as $w \star f(x,y)$. When the meaning is clear, we let the dependence of the previous two equations on x and y be implied, and use the simplified notation $w \star f$ and $w \star f$. As with correlation, Eq. (3-35) is evaluated for all values of the displacement variables x and y so that the center of w visits every pixel in f, which we assume has been padded. The values of x and y needed to obtain a full convolution are $x = 0, 1, 2, \ldots, M-1$ and $y = 0, 1, 2, \ldots, N-1$. The size of the result is $M \times N$.

We can define correlation and convolution so that *every* element of w (instead of just its center) visits *every* pixel in f. This requires that the starting configuration be such that the right, lower corner of the kernel coincides with the origin of the image. Similarly, the ending configuration will be with the top left corner of the kernel coinciding with the lower right corner of the image. If the kernel and image are of sizes $m \times n$ and $M \times N$, respectively, the padding would have to increase to $(m-1)$ padding elements above and below the image, and $(n-1)$ elements to the left and right. Under these conditions, the size of the resulting full correlation or convolution array will be of size $S_v \times S_h$, where (see Figs. 3.30(e) and (h), and Problem 3.19),

$$S_v = m + M - 1 \tag{3-36}$$

and

$$S_h = n + N - 1 \tag{3-37}$$

Often, spatial filtering algorithms are based on correlation and thus implement Eq. (3-34) instead. To use the algorithm for correlation, we input w into it; for convolution, we input w rotated by 180°. The opposite is true for an algorithm that implements Eq. (3-35). Thus, either Eq. (3-34) or Eq. (3-35) can be made to perform the function of the other by rotating the filter kernel. Keep in mind, however, that the *order* of the functions input into a correlation algorithm *does* make a difference, because correlation is neither commutative nor associative (see Table 3.5).

TABLE 3.5
Some fundamental properties of convolution and correlation. A dash means that the property does not hold.

Property	Convolution	Correlation
Commutative	$f \star g = g \star f$	—
Associative	$f \star (g \star h) = (f \star g) \star h$	—
Distributive	$f \star (g + h) = (f \star g) + (f \star h)$	$f \star (g + h) = (f \star g) + (f \star h)$

Because the values of these kernels are symmetric about the center, no rotation is required before convolution.

Figure 3.31 shows two kernels used for smoothing the intensities of an image. To filter an image using one of these kernels, we perform a convolution of the kernel with the image in the manner just described. When talking about filtering and kernels, you are likely to encounter the terms *convolution filter, convolution mask,* or *convolution kernel* to denote filter kernels of the type we have been discussing. Typically, these terms are used in the literature to denote a spatial filter kernel, and not to imply necessarily that the kernel is used for convolution. Similarly, "convolving a kernel with an image" often is used to denote the sliding, sum-of-products process we just explained, and does not necessarily differentiate between correlation and convolution. Rather, it is used generically to denote either of the two operations. This imprecise terminology is a frequent source of confusion. In this book, when we use the term *linear spatial filtering,* we mean *convolving a kernel with an image.*

Sometimes an image is filtered (i.e., convolved) sequentially, in stages, using a different kernel in each stage. For example, suppose than an image f is filtered with a kernel w_1, the result filtered with kernel w_2, that result filtered with a third kernel, and so on, for Q stages. Because of the commutative property of convolution, this multistage filtering can be done in a single filtering operation, $w \star f$, where

We could not write a similar equation for correlation because it is not commutative.

$$w = w_1 \star w_2 \star w_3 \star \cdots \star w_Q \tag{3-38}$$

The size of w is obtained from the sizes of the individual kernels by successive applications of Eqs. (3-36) and (3-37). If all the individual kernels are of size $m \times n$, it follows from these equations that w will be of size $W_v \times W_h$, where

$$W_v = Q \times (m - 1) + m \tag{3-39}$$

and

$$W_h = Q \times (n - 1) + n \tag{3-40}$$

These equations assume that every value of a kernel visits every value of the array resulting from the convolution in the previous step. That is, the initial and ending configurations, are as described in connection with Eqs. (3-36) and (3-37).

a b

FIGURE 3.31
Examples of smoothing kernels: (a) is a *box* kernel; (b) is a *Gaussian* kernel.

$$\frac{1}{9} \times \begin{array}{|c|c|c|} \hline 1 & 1 & 1 \\ \hline 1 & 1 & 1 \\ \hline 1 & 1 & 1 \\ \hline \end{array}$$

$$\frac{1}{4.8976} \times \begin{array}{|c|c|c|} \hline 0.3679 & 0.6065 & 0.3679 \\ \hline 0.6065 & 1.0000 & 0.6065 \\ \hline 0.3679 & 0.6065 & 0.3679 \\ \hline \end{array}$$

SEPARABLE FILTER KERNELS

As noted in Section 2.6, a 2-D function $G(x, y)$ is said to be *separable* if it can be written as the product of two 1-D functions, $G_1(x)$ and $G_2(x)$; that is, $G(x, y) = G_1(x)G_2(y)$. A spatial filter kernel is a matrix, and a separable kernel is a matrix that can be expressed as the outer product of two vectors. For example, the 2×3 kernel

$$w = \begin{bmatrix} 1 & 1 & 1 \\ 1 & 1 & 1 \end{bmatrix}$$

is separable because it can be expressed as the outer product of the vectors

$$\mathbf{c} = \begin{bmatrix} 1 \\ 1 \end{bmatrix} \quad \text{and} \quad \mathbf{r} = \begin{bmatrix} 1 \\ 1 \\ 1 \end{bmatrix}$$

That is,

$$\mathbf{c}\,\mathbf{r}^T = \begin{bmatrix} 1 \\ 1 \end{bmatrix}\begin{bmatrix} 1 & 1 & 1 \end{bmatrix} = \begin{bmatrix} 1 & 1 & 1 \\ 1 & 1 & 1 \end{bmatrix} = w$$

A separable kernel of size $m \times n$ can be expressed as the outer product of two vectors, $\mathbf{v}$ and $\mathbf{w}$:

$$w = \mathbf{v}\mathbf{w}^T \tag{3-41}$$

where $\mathbf{v}$ and $\mathbf{w}$ are vectors of size $m \times 1$ and $n \times 1$, respectively. For a square kernel of size $m \times m$, we write

$$w = \mathbf{v}\mathbf{v}^T \tag{3-42}$$

It turns out that the product of a column vector and a row vector is the same as the 2-D convolution of the vectors (see Problem 3.24).

The importance of separable kernels lies in the computational advantages that result from the associative property of convolution. If we have a kernel w that can be decomposed into two simpler kernels, such that $w = w_1 \star w_2$, then it follows from the commutative and associative properties in Table 3.5 that

$$w \star f = (w_1 \star w_2) \star f = (w_2 \star w_1) \star f = w_2 \star (w_1 \star f) = (w_1 \star f) \star w_2 \tag{3-43}$$

This equation says that convolving a separable kernel with an image is the same as convolving w_1 with f first, and then convolving the result with w_2.

For an image of size $M \times N$ and a kernel of size $m \times n$, implementation of Eq. (3-35) requires on the order of $MNmn$ multiplications and additions. This is because it follows directly from that equation that *each* pixel in the output (filtered) image depends on *all* the coefficients in the filter kernel. But, if the kernel is separable and we use Eq. (3-43), then the first convolution, $w_1 \star f$, requires on the order of

MNm multiplications and additions because w_1 is of size $m \times 1$. The result is of size $M \times N$, so the convolution of w_2 with the result requires MNn such operations, for a total of $MN(m + n)$ multiplication and addition operations. Thus, the *computational advantage* of performing convolution with a separable, as opposed to a nonseparable, kernel is defined as

$$C = \frac{MNmn}{MN(m + n)} = \frac{mn}{m + n} \tag{3-44}$$

For a kernel of modest size, say 11×11, the computational advantage (and thus execution-time advantage) is a respectable 5.2. For kernels with hundreds of elements, execution times can be reduced by a factor of a hundred or more, which is significant. We will illustrate the use of such large kernels in Example 3.16.

We know from matrix theory that a matrix resulting from the product of a column vector and a row vector *always* has a rank of 1. By definition, a separable kernel is formed by such a product. Therefore, to determine if a kernel is separable, all we have to do is determine if its rank is 1. Typically, we find the rank of a matrix using a pre-programmed function in the computer language being used. For example, if you use MATLAB, function rank will do the job.

Once you have determined that the rank of a kernel matrix is 1, it is not difficult to find two vectors $\mathbf{v}$ and $\mathbf{w}$ such that their outer product, $\mathbf{vw}^T$, is equal to the kernel. The approach consists of only three steps:

1. Find any nonzero element in the kernel and let E denote its value.
2. Form vectors $\mathbf{c}$ and $\mathbf{r}$ equal, respectively, to the column and row in the kernel containing the element found in Step 1.
3. With reference to Eq. (3-41), let $\mathbf{v} = \mathbf{c}$ and $\mathbf{w}^T = \mathbf{r}/E$.

The reason why this simple three-step method works is that the rows and columns of a matrix whose rank is 1 are linearly dependent. That is, the rows differ only by a constant multiplier, and similarly for the columns. It is instructive to work through the mechanics of this procedure using a small kernel (see Problems 3.20 and 3.22).

As we explained above, the objective is to find two 1-D kernels, w_1 and w_2, in order to implement 1-D convolution. In terms of the preceding notation, $w_1 = \mathbf{c} = \mathbf{v}$ and $w_2 = \mathbf{r}/E = \mathbf{w}^T$. For circularly symmetric kernels, the column through the center of the kernel describes the entire kernel; that is, $w = \mathbf{vv}^T/c$, where c is the value of the center coefficient. Then, the 1-D components are $w_1 = \mathbf{v}$ and $w_2 = \mathbf{v}^T/c$.

As we will discuss later in this chapter, the only kernels that are separable *and* whose values are circularly symmetric about the center are Gaussian kernels, which have a nonzero center coefficient (i.e., $c > 0$ for these kernels).

SOME IMPORTANT COMPARISONS BETWEEN FILTERING IN THE SPATIAL AND FREQUENCY DOMAINS

Although filtering in the frequency domain is the topic of Chapter 4, we introduce at this junction some important concepts from the frequency domain that will help you master the material that follows.

The tie between spatial- and frequency-domain processing is the *Fourier transform*. We use the Fourier transform to go from the spatial to the frequency domain;

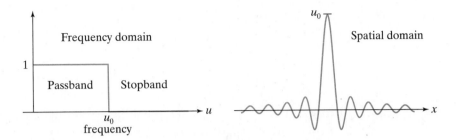

a b
FIGURE 3.32
(a) Ideal 1-D low-pass filter transfer function in the frequency domain. (b) Corresponding filter kernel in the spatial domain.

to return to the spatial domain we use the *inverse Fourier transform*. This will be covered in detail in Chapter 4. The focus here is on two fundamental properties relating the spatial and frequency domains:

1. Convolution, which is the basis for filtering in the spatial domain, is equivalent to multiplication in the frequency domain, and vice versa.

2. An impulse of strength A in the spatial domain is a constant of value A in the frequency domain, and vice versa.

See the explanation of Eq. (3-33) regarding impulses.

As explained in Chapter 4, a function (e.g., an image) satisfying some mild conditions can be expressed as the sum of sinusoids of different frequencies and amplitudes. Thus, the *appearance* of an image depends on the frequencies of its sinusoidal components—change the frequencies of those components, and you will change the appearance of the image. What makes this a powerful concept is that it is possible to associate certain frequency bands with image characteristics. For example, regions of an image with intensities that vary slowly (e.g., the walls in an image of a room) are characterized by sinusoids of low frequencies. Similarly, edges and other sharp intensity transitions are characterized by high frequencies. Thus, reducing the high-frequency components of an image will tend to blur it.

Linear filtering is concerned with finding suitable ways to modify the frequency content of an image. In the spatial domain we do this via convolution filtering. In the frequency domain we do it with multiplicative filters. The latter is a much more intuitive approach, which is one of the reasons why it is virtually impossible to truly understand spatial filtering without having at least some rudimentary knowledge of the frequency domain.

An example will help clarify these ideas. For simplicity, consider a 1-D function (such as an intensity scan line through an image) and suppose that we want to eliminate all its frequencies above a cutoff value, u_0, while "passing" all frequencies below that value. Figure 3.32(a) shows a frequency-domain filter function for doing this. (The term *filter transfer function* is used to denote filter functions in the frequency domain—this is analogous to our use of the term "filter kernel" in the spatial domain.) Appropriately, the function in Fig. 3.32(a) is called a *lowpass* filter transfer function. In fact, this is an *ideal* lowpass filter function because it eliminates *all* frequencies above u_0, while passing all frequencies below this value.[†] That is, the

As we did earlier with spatial filters, when the meaning is clear we use the term *filter* interchangeably with *filter transfer function* when working in the frequency domain.

[†]All the frequency domain filters in which we are interested are symmetrical about the origin and encompass both positive and negative frequencies, as we will explain in Section 4.3 (see Fig. 4.8). For the moment, we show only the right side (positive frequencies) of 1-D filters for simplicity in this short explanation.

transition of the filter between low and high frequencies is instantaneous. Such filter functions are not realizable with physical components, and have issues with "ringing" when implemented digitally. However, ideal filters are very useful for illustrating numerous filtering phenomena, as you will learn in Chapter 4.

To lowpass-filter a spatial signal in the frequency domain, we first convert it to the frequency domain by computing its Fourier transform, and then *multiply* the result by the filter transfer function in Fig. 3.32(a) to eliminate frequency components with values higher than u_0. To return to the spatial domain, we take the inverse Fourier transform of the filtered signal. The result will be a blurred spatial domain function.

Because of the duality between the spatial and frequency domains, we can obtain the same result in the spatial domain by *convolving* the equivalent spatial domain filter kernel with the input spatial function. The equivalent spatial filter kernel is the inverse Fourier transform of the frequency-domain filter transfer function. Figure 3.32(b) shows the spatial filter kernel corresponding to the frequency domain filter transfer function in Fig. 3.32(a). The ringing characteristics of the kernel are evident in the figure. A central theme of digital filter design theory is obtaining faithful (and practical) approximations to the sharp cut off of ideal frequency domain filters while reducing their ringing characteristics.

A WORD ABOUT HOW SPATIAL FILTER KERNELS ARE CONSTRUCTED

We consider three basic approaches for constructing spatial filters in the following sections of this chapter. One approach is based on formulating filters based on mathematical properties. For example, a filter that computes the average of pixels in a neighborhood blurs an image. Computing an average is analogous to integration. Conversely, a filter that computes the local derivative of an image sharpens the image. We give numerous examples of this approach in the following sections.

A second approach is based on sampling a 2-D spatial function whose shape has a desired property. For example, we will show in the next section that samples from a Gaussian function can be used to construct a weighted-average (lowpass) filter. These 2-D spatial functions sometimes are generated as the inverse Fourier transform of 2-D filters specified in the frequency domain. We will give several examples of this approach in this and the next chapter.

A third approach is to design a spatial filter with a specified frequency response. This approach is based on the concepts discussed in the previous section, and falls in the area of digital filter design. A 1-D spatial filter with the desired response is obtained (typically using filter design software). The 1-D filter values can be expressed as a vector **v**, and a 2-D separable kernel can then be obtained using Eq. (3-42). Or the 1-D filter can be rotated about its center to generate a 2-D kernel that approximates a circularly symmetric function. We will illustrate these techniques in Section 3.7.

3.5 SMOOTHING (LOWPASS) SPATIAL FILTERS

Smoothing (also called *averaging*) spatial filters are used to reduce sharp transitions in intensity. Because random noise typically consists of sharp transitions in intensity, an obvious application of smoothing is noise reduction. Smoothing prior to image resampling to reduce aliasing, as will be discussed in Section 4.5, is also a common application. Smoothing is used to reduce irrelevant detail in an image, where "irrelevant" refers to pixel regions that are small with respect to the size of the filter kernel. Another application is for smoothing the false contours that result from using an insufficient number of intensity levels in an image, as discussed in Section 2.4. Smoothing filters are used in combination with other techniques for image enhancement, such as the histogram processing techniques discussed in Section 3.3, and unsharp masking, as discussed later in this chapter. We begin the discussion of smoothing filters by considering linear smoothing filters in some detail. We will introduce nonlinear smoothing filters later in this section.

As we discussed in Section 3.4, linear spatial filtering consists of convolving an image with a filter kernel. Convolving a smoothing kernel with an image blurs the image, with the degree of blurring being determined by the size of the kernel and the values of its coefficients. In addition to being useful in countless applications of image processing, lowpass filters are fundamental, in the sense that other important filters, including sharpening (highpass), bandpass, and bandreject filters, can be derived from lowpass filters, as we will show in Section 3.7.

We discuss in this section lowpass filters based on *box* and *Gaussian* kernels, both of which are separable. Most of the discussion will center on Gaussian kernels because of their numerous useful properties and breadth of applicability. We will introduce other smoothing filters in Chapters 4 and 5.

BOX FILTER KERNELS

The simplest, separable lowpass filter kernel is the *box kernel*, whose coefficients have the same value (typically 1). The name "box kernel" comes from a constant kernel resembling a box when viewed in 3-D. We showed a 3×3 box filter in Fig. 3.31(a). An $m \times n$ box filter is an $m \times n$ array of 1's, with a normalizing constant in front, whose value is 1 divided by the sum of the values of the coefficients (i.e., $1/mn$ when all the coefficients are 1's). This normalization, which we apply to all lowpass kernels, has two purposes. First, the average value of an area of constant intensity would equal that intensity in the filtered image, as it should. Second, normalizing the kernel in this way prevents introducing a *bias* during filtering; that is, the sum of the pixels in the original and filtered images will be the same (see Problem 3.31). Because in a box kernel all rows and columns are identical, the rank of these kernels is 1, which, as we discussed earlier, means that they are separable.

EXAMPLE 3.11: Lowpass filtering with a box kernel.

Figure 3.33(a) shows a test pattern image of size 1024×1024 pixels. Figures 3.33(b)-(d) are the results obtained using box filters of size $m \times m$ with $m = 3, 11$, and 21, respectively. For $m = 3$, we note a slight overall blurring of the image, with the image features whose sizes are comparable to the size of the kernel being affected significantly more. Such features include the thinner lines in the image and the noise pixels contained in the boxes on the right side of the image. The filtered image also has a thin gray border, the result of zero-padding the image prior to filtering. As indicated earlier, padding extends the boundaries of an image to avoid undefined operations when parts of a kernel lie outside the border of

a b
c d

FIGURE 3.33
(a) Test pattern of size 1024×1024 pixels.
(b)-(d) Results of lowpass filtering with box kernels of sizes 3×3, 11×11, and 21×21, respectively.

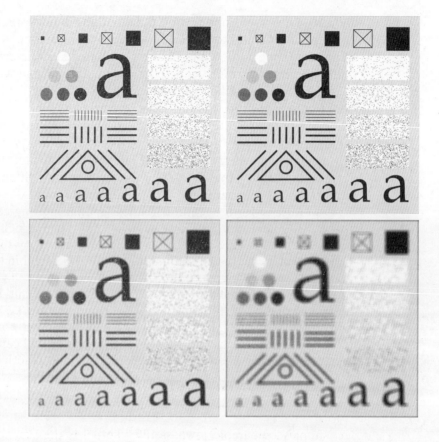

the image during filtering. When zero (black) padding is used, the net result of smoothing at or near the border is a dark gray border that arises from including black pixels in the averaging process. Using the 11×11 kernel resulted in more pronounced blurring throughout the image, including a more prominent dark border. The result with the 21×21 kernel shows significant blurring of all components of the image, including the loss of the characteristic shape of some components, including, for example, the small square on the top left and the small character on the bottom left. The dark border resulting from zero padding is proportionally thicker than before. We used zero padding here, and will use it a few more times, so that you can become familiar with its effects. In Example 3.14 we discuss two other approaches to padding that eliminate the dark-border artifact that usually results from zero padding.

LOWPASS GAUSSIAN FILTER KERNELS

Because of their simplicity, box filters are suitable for quick experimentation and they often yield smoothing results that are visually acceptable. They are useful also when it is desired to reduce the effect of smoothing on edges (see Example 3.13). However, box filters have limitations that make them poor choices in many applications. For example, a defocused lens is often modeled as a lowpass filter, but box filters are poor approximations to the blurring characteristics of lenses (see Problem 3.33). Another limitation is the fact that box filters favor blurring along perpendicular directions. In applications involving images with a high level of detail, or with strong geometrical components, the directionality of box filters often produces undesirable results. (Example 3.13 illustrates this issue.) These are but two applications in which box filters are not suitable.

The kernels of choice in applications such as those just mentioned are *circularly symmetric* (also called *isotropic*, meaning their response is independent of orientation). As it turns out, Gaussian kernels of the form

$$w(s,t) = G(s,t) = Ke^{-\frac{s^2+t^2}{2\sigma^2}} \tag{3-45}$$

are the *only* circularly symmetric kernels that are also separable (Sahoo [1990]). Thus, because Gaussian kernels of this form are separable, Gaussian filters enjoy the same computational advantages as box filters, but have a host of additional properties that make them ideal for image processing, as you will learn in the following discussion. Variables s and t in Eq. (3-45), are real (typically discrete) numbers.

By letting $r = [s^2 + t^2]^{1/2}$ we can write Eq. (3-45) as

$$G(r) = Ke^{-\frac{r^2}{2\sigma^2}} \tag{3-46}$$

This equivalent form simplifies derivation of expressions later in this section. This form also reminds us that the function is circularly symmetric. Variable r is the distance from the center to any point on function G. Figure 3.34 shows values of r for several kernel sizes using integer values for s and t. Because we work generally with odd kernel sizes, the centers of such kernels fall on integer values, and it follows that all values of r^2 are integers also. You can see this by squaring the values in Fig. 3.34

Our interest here is strictly on the bell shape of the Gaussian function; thus, we dispense with the traditional multiplier of the Gaussian PDF and use a general constant, K, instead. Recall that σ controls the "spread" of a Gaussian function about its mean.

FIGURE 3.34
Distances from the center for various sizes of square kernels.

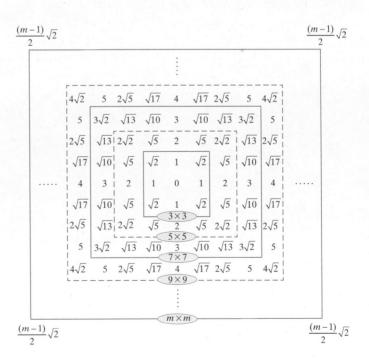

(for a formal proof, see Padfield [2011]). Note in particular that the distance squared to the corner points for a kernel of size $m \times m$ is

$$r_{max}^2 = \left[\frac{(m-1)}{2} \sqrt{2} \right]^2 = \frac{(m-1)^2}{2} \tag{3-47}$$

The kernel in Fig. 3.31(b) was obtained by sampling Eq. (3-45) (with $K = 1$ and $\sigma = 1$). Figure 3.35(a) shows a perspective plot of a Gaussian function, and illustrates that the samples used to generate that kernel were obtained by specifying values of s and t, then "reading" the values of the function at those coordinates. These values are the coefficients of the kernel. Normalizing the kernel by dividing its coefficients by the sum of the coefficients completes the specification of the kernel. The reasons for normalizing the kernel are as discussed in connection with box kernels. Because Gaussian kernels are separable, we could simply take samples along a cross section through the center and use the samples to form vector **v** in Eq. (3-42), from which we obtain the 2-D kernel.

Separability is one of many fundamental properties of circularly symmetric Gaussian kernels. For example, we know that the values of a Gaussian function at a distance larger than 3σ from the mean are small enough that they can be ignored. This means that if we select the size of a Gaussian kernel to be $\lceil 6\sigma \rceil \times \lceil 6\sigma \rceil$ (the notation $\lceil c \rceil$ is used to denote the *ceiling* of c; that is, the smallest integer not less than c), we are assured of getting essentially the same result as if we had used an arbitrarily large Gaussian kernel. Viewed another way, this property tells us that there is nothing to be gained by using a Gaussian kernel larger than $\lceil 6\sigma \rceil \times \lceil 6\sigma \rceil$ for image processing. Because typically we work with kernels of odd dimensions, we would use the smallest *odd* integer that satisfies this condition (e.g., a 43×43 kernel if $\sigma = 7$).

Two other fundamental properties of Gaussian functions are that the product and convolution of two Gaussians are Gaussian functions also. Table 3.6 shows the mean and standard deviation of the product and convolution of two 1-D Gaussian functions, f and g (remember, because of separability, we only need a 1-D Gaussian to form a circularly symmetric 2-D function). The mean and standard deviation com-

a b

FIGURE 3.35
(a) Sampling a Gaussian function to obtain a discrete Gaussian kernel. The values shown are for $K = 1$ and $\sigma = 1$. (b) Resulting 3×3 kernel [this is the same as Fig. 3.31(b)].

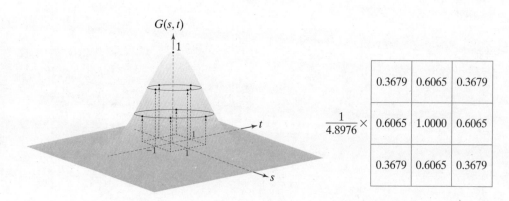

TABLE 3.6 Mean and standard deviation of the product ($\times$) and convolution ($\star$) of two 1-D Gaussian functions, f and g. These results generalize directly to the product and convolution of more than two 1-D Gaussian functions (see Problem 3.25).

	f	g	$f \times g$	$f \star g$
Mean	m_f	m_g	$m_{f \times g} = \dfrac{m_f \sigma_g^2 + m_g \sigma_f^2}{\sigma_f^2 + \sigma_g^2}$	$m_{f \star g} = m_f + m_g$
Standard deviation	σ_f	σ_g	$\sigma_{f \times g} = \sqrt{\dfrac{\sigma_f^2 \sigma_g^2}{\sigma_f^2 + \sigma_g^2}}$	$\sigma_{f \star g} = \sqrt{\sigma_f^2 + \sigma_g^2}$

pletely define a Gaussian, so the parameters in Table 3.6 tell us all there is to know about the functions resulting from multiplication and convolution of Gaussians. As indicated by Eqs. (3-45) and (3-46), Gaussian kernels have zero mean, so our interest here is in the standard deviations.

The convolution result is of particular importance in filtering. For example, we mentioned in connection with Eq. (3-43) that filtering sometimes is done in successive stages, and that the same result can be obtained by one stage of filtering with a composite kernel formed as the convolution of the individual kernels. If the kernels are Gaussian, we can use the result in Table 3.6 (which, as noted, generalizes directly to more than two functions) to compute the standard deviation of the composite kernel (and thus completely define it) without actually having to perform the convolution of all the individual kernels.

EXAMPLE 3.12: Lowpass filtering with a Gaussian kernel.

To compare Gaussian and box kernel filtering, we repeat Example 3.11 using a Gaussian kernel. Gaussian kernels have to be larger than box filters to achieve the same degree of blurring. This is because, whereas a box kernel assigns the same weight to all pixels, the values of Gaussian kernel coefficients (and hence their effect) decreases as a function of distance from the kernel center. As explained earlier, we use a size equal to the closest odd integer to $\lceil 6\sigma \rceil \times \lceil 6\sigma \rceil$. Thus, for a Gaussian kernel of size 21×21, which is the size of the kernel we used to generate Fig. 3.33(d), we need $\sigma = 3.5$. Figure 3.36(b) shows the result of lowpass filtering the test pattern with this kernel. Comparing this result with Fig. 3.33(d), we see that the Gaussian kernel resulted in significantly less blurring. A little experimentation would show that we need $\sigma = 7$ to obtain comparable results. This implies a Gaussian kernel of size 43×43. Figure 3.36(c) shows the results of filtering the test pattern with this kernel. Comparing it with Fig. 3.33(d), we see that the results indeed are very close.

We mentioned earlier that there is little to be gained by using a Gaussian kernel larger than $\lceil 6\sigma \rceil \times \lceil 6\sigma \rceil$. To demonstrate this, we filtered the test pattern in Fig. 3.36(a) using a Gaussian kernel with $\sigma = 7$ again, but of size 85×85. Figure 3.37(a) is the same as Fig. 3.36(c), which we generated using the smallest odd kernel satisfying the $\lceil 6 \rceil \times \lceil 6 \rceil$ condition (43×43, for $\sigma = 7$). Figure 3.37(b) is the result of using the 85×85 kernel, which is double the size of the other kernel. As you can see, not discernible additional

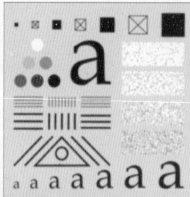

a b c

FIGURE 3.36 (a) A test pattern of size 1024×1024. (b) Result of lowpass filtering the pattern with a Gaussian kernel of size 21×21, with standard deviations $\sigma = 3.5$. (c) Result of using a kernel of size 43×43, with $\sigma = 7$. This result is comparable to Fig. 3.33(d). We used $K = 1$ in all cases.

blurring occurred. In fact, the difference image in Fig 3.37(c) indicates that the two images are nearly identical, their maximum difference being 0.75, which is less than one level out of 256 (these are 8-bit images).

EXAMPLE 3.13: Comparison of Gaussian and box filter smoothing characteristics.

The results in Examples 3.11 and 3.12 showed little visual difference in blurring. Despite this, there are some subtle differences that are not apparent at first glance. For example, compare the large letter "a" in Figs. 3.33(d) and 3.36(c); the latter is much smoother around the edges. Figure 3.38 shows this type of different behavior between box and Gaussian kernels more clearly. The image of the rectangle was

a b c

FIGURE 3.37 (a) Result of filtering Fig. 3.36(a) using a Gaussian kernels of size 43×43, with $\sigma = 7$. (b) Result of using a kernel of 85×85, with the same value of σ. (c) Difference image.

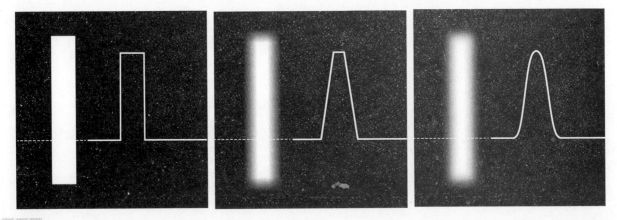

a b c

FIGURE 3.38 (a) Image of a white rectangle on a black background, and a horizontal intensity profile along the scan line shown dotted. (b) Result of smoothing this image with a box kernel of size 71×71, and corresponding intensity profile. (c) Result of smoothing the image using a Gaussian kernel of size 151×151, with $K = 1$ and $\sigma = 25$. Note the smoothness of the profile in (c) compared to (b). The image and rectangle are of sizes 1024×1024 and 768×128 pixels, respectively.

smoothed using a box and a Gaussian kernel with the sizes and parameters listed in the figure. These parameters were selected to give blurred rectangles of approximately the same width and height, in order to show the effects of the filters on a comparable basis. As the intensity profiles show, the box filter produced linear smoothing, with the transition from black to white (i.e., at an edge) having the shape of a ramp. The important features here are hard transitions at the onset and end of the ramp. We would use this type of filter when less smoothing of edges is desired. Conversely, the Gaussian filter yielded significantly smoother results around the edge transitions. We would use this type of filter when generally uniform smoothing is desired.

As the results in Examples 3.11, 3.12, and 3.13 show, zero padding an image introduces dark borders in the filtered result, with the thickness of the borders depending on the size and type of the filter kernel used. Earlier, when discussing correlation and convolution, we mentioned two other methods of image padding: *mirror* (also called *symmetric*) *padding*, in which values outside the boundary of the image are obtained by mirror-reflecting the image across its border; and *replicate padding*, in which values outside the boundary are set equal to the nearest image border value. The latter padding is useful when the areas near the border of the image are constant. Conversely, mirror padding is more applicable when the areas near the border contain image details. In other words, these two types of padding attempt to "extend" the characteristics of an image past its borders.

Figure 3.39 illustrates these padding methods, and also shows the effects of more aggressive smoothing. Figures 3.39(a) through 3.39(c) show the results of filtering Fig. 3.36(a) with a Gaussian kernel of size 187×187 elements with $K = 1$ and $\sigma = 31$, using zero, mirror, and replicate padding, respectively. The differences between the borders of the results with the zero-padded image and the other two are obvious,

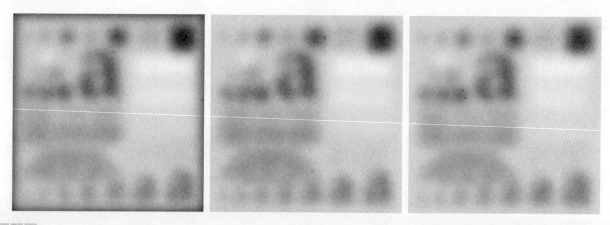

a b c

FIGURE 3.39 Result of filtering the test pattern in Fig. 3.36(a) using (a) zero padding, (b) mirror padding, and (c) replicate padding. A Gaussian kernel of size 187×187, with $K = 1$ and $\sigma = 31$ was used in all three cases.

and indicate that mirror and replicate padding yield more visually appealing results by eliminating the dark borders resulting from zero padding.

EXAMPLE 3.14:   Smoothing performance as a function of kernel and image size.

The amount of relative blurring produced by a smoothing kernel of a given size depends directly on image size. To illustrate, Fig. 3.40(a) shows the same test pattern used earlier, but of size 4096×4096 pixels, four times larger in each dimension than before. Figure 3.40(b) shows the result of filtering this image with the same Gaussian kernel and padding used in Fig. 3.39(b). By comparison, the former image shows considerably less blurring for the same size filter. In fact, Fig. 3.40(b) looks more like the image

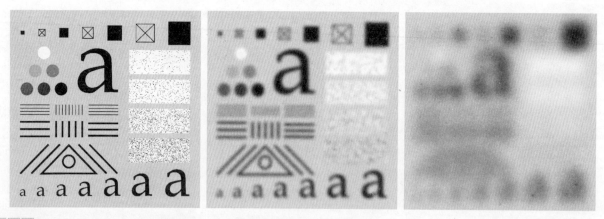

a b c

FIGURE 3.40 (a) Test pattern of size 4096×4096 pixels. (b) Result of filtering the test pattern with the same Gaussian kernel used in Fig. 3.39. (c) Result of filtering the pattern using a Gaussian kernel of size 745×745 elements, with $K = 1$ and $\sigma = 124$. Mirror padding was used throughout.

in Fig. 3.36(d), which was filtered using a 43×43 Gaussian kernel. In order to obtain results that are comparable to Fig. 3.39(b) we have to increase the size and standard deviation of the Gaussian kernel by four, the same factor as the increase in image dimensions. This gives a kernel of (odd) size 745×745 (with $K = 1$ and $\sigma = 124$). Figure 3.40(c) shows the result of using this kernel with mirror padding. This result is quite similar to Fig. 3.39(b). After the fact, this may seem like a trivial observation, but you would be surprised at how frequently not understanding the relationship between kernel size and the size of objects in an image can lead to ineffective performance of spatial filtering algorithms.

EXAMPLE 3.15: Using lowpass filtering and thresholding for region extraction.

Figure 3.41(a) is a 2566×2758 Hubble Telescope image of the *Hickson Compact Group* (see figure caption), whose intensities were scaled to the range $[0, 1]$. Our objective is to illustrate lowpass filtering combined with intensity thresholding for eliminating irrelevant detail in this image. In the present context, "irrelevant" refers to pixel regions that are small compared to kernel size.

Figure 3.41(b) is the result of filtering the original image with a Gaussian kernel of size 151×151 (approximately 6% of the image width) and standard deviation $\sigma = 25$. We chose these parameter values in order generate a sharper, more selective Gaussian kernel shape than we used in earlier examples. The filtered image shows four predominantly bright regions. We wish to extract only those regions from the image. Figure 3.41(c) is the result of thresholding the filtered image with a threshold $T = 0.4$ (we will discuss threshold selection in Chapter 10). As the figure shows, this approach effectively extracted the four regions of interest, and eliminated details deemed irrelevant in this application.

EXAMPLE 3.16: Shading correction using lowpass filtering.

One of the principal causes of image shading is nonuniform illumination. *Shading correction* (also called *flat-field correction*) is important because shading is a common cause of erroneous measurements, degraded performance of automated image analysis algorithms, and difficulty of image interpretation

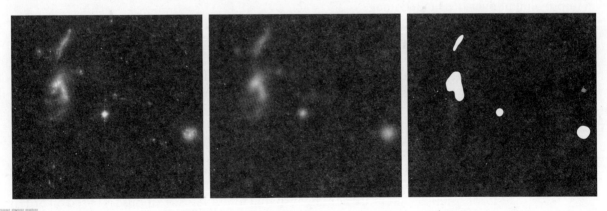

a b c

FIGURE 3.41 (a) A 2566×2758 Hubble Telescope image of the *Hickson Compact Group*. (b) Result of lowpass filtering with a Gaussian kernel. (c) Result of thresholding the filtered image (intensities were scaled to the range $[0, 1]$). The Hickson Compact Group contains dwarf galaxies that have come together, setting off thousands of new star clusters. (Original image courtesy of NASA.)

a b c

FIGURE 3.42 (a) Image shaded by a shading pattern oriented in the −45° direction. (b) Estimate of the shading patterns obtained using lowpass filtering. (c) Result of dividing (a) by (b). (See Section 9.8 for a morphological approach to shading correction).

by humans. We introduced shading correction in Example 2.7, where we corrected a shaded image by dividing it by the shading pattern. In that example, the shading pattern was given. Often, that is not the case in practice, and we are faced with having to estimate the pattern directly from available samples of shaded images. Lowpass filtering is a rugged, simple method for estimating shading patterns.

Consider the 2048×2048 checkerboard image in Fig. 3.42(a), whose inner squares are of size 128×128 pixels. Figure 3.42(b) is the result of lowpass filtering the image with a 512×512 Gaussian kernel (four times the size of the squares), $K = 1$, and $\sigma = 128$ (equal to the size of the squares). This kernel is just large enough to blur-out the squares (a kernel three times the size of the squares is too small to blur them out sufficiently). This result is a good approximation to the shading pattern visible in Fig. 3.42(a). Finally, Fig. 3.42(c) is the result of dividing (a) by (b). Although the result is not perfectly flat, it definitely is an improvement over the shaded image.

In the discussion of separable kernels in Section 3.4, we pointed out that the computational advantage of separable kernels can be significant for large kernels. It follows from Eq. (3-44) that the computational advantage of the kernel used in this example (which of course is separable) is 262 to 1. Thinking of computation time, if it took 30 sec to process a set of images similar to Fig. 3.42(b) using the two 1-D separable components of the Gaussian kernel, it would have taken 2.2 hrs to achieve the same result using a nonseparable lowpass kernel, or if we had used the 2-D Gaussian kernel directly, without decomposing it into its separable parts.

ORDER-STATISTIC (NONLINEAR) FILTERS

Order-statistic filters are nonlinear spatial filters whose response is based on ordering (ranking) the pixels contained in the region encompassed by the filter. Smoothing is achieved by replacing the value of the center pixel with the value determined by the ranking result. The best-known filter in this category is the *median filter*, which, as its name implies, replaces the value of the center pixel by the median of the intensity values in the neighborhood of that pixel (the value of the center pixel is included in computing the median). Median filters provide excellent noise reduction capabilities for certain types of random noise, with considerably less blurring than linear smoothing filters of similar size. Median filters are particularly effective in the presence of *impulse noise* (sometimes called *salt-and-pepper noise,* when it manisfests itself as white and black dots superimposed on an image).

The *median*, ξ, of a set of values is such that half the values in the set are less than or equal to ξ and half are greater than or equal to ξ. In order to perform median filtering at a point in an image, we first sort the values of the pixels in the neighborhood, determine their median, and assign that value to the pixel in the filtered image corresponding to the center of the neighborhood. For example, in a 3×3 neighborhood the median is the 5th largest value, in a 5×5 neighborhood it is the 13th largest value, and so on. When several values in a neighborhood are the same, all equal values are grouped. For example, suppose that a 3×3 neighborhood has values (10, 20, 20, 20, 15, 20, 20, 25, 100). These values are sorted as (10, 15, 20, 20, 20, 20, 20, 25, 100), which results in a median of 20. Thus, the principal function of median filters is to force points to be more like their neighbors. Isolated clusters of pixels that are light or dark with respect to their neighbors, and whose area is less than $m^2/2$ (one-half the filter area), are forced by an $m \times m$ median filter to have the value of the median intensity of the pixels in the neighborhood (see Problem 3.36).

The median filter is by far the most useful order-statistic filter in image processing, but is not the only one. The median represents the 50th percentile of a ranked set of numbers, but ranking lends itself to many other possibilities. For example, using the 100th percentile results in the so-called *max filter*, which is useful for finding the brightest points in an image or for eroding dark areas adjacent to light regions. The response of a 3×3 max filter is given by $R = \max\{z_k \mid k = 1, 2, 3, \ldots, 9\}$. The 0th percentile filter is the *min filter*, used for the opposite purpose. Median, max, min, and several other nonlinear filters will be considered in more detail in Section 5.3.

EXAMPLE 3.17: Median filtering.

Figure 3.43(a) shows an X-ray image of a circuit board heavily corrupted by salt-and-pepper noise. To illustrate the superiority of median filtering over lowpass filtering in situations such as this, we show in Fig. 3.43(b) the result of filtering the noisy image with a Gaussian lowpass filter, and in Fig. 3.43(c) the result of using a median filter. The lowpass filter blurred the image and its noise reduction performance was poor. The superiority in all respects of median over lowpass filtering in this case is evident.

3.6 SHARPENING (HIGHPASS) SPATIAL FILTERS

Sharpening highlights transitions in intensity. Uses of image sharpening range from electronic printing and medical imaging to industrial inspection and autonomous guidance in military systems. In Section 3.5, we saw that image blurring could be accomplished in the spatial domain by pixel averaging (smoothing) in a neighborhood. Because averaging is analogous to integration, it is logical to conclude that sharpening can be accomplished by spatial differentiation. In fact, this is the case, and the following discussion deals with various ways of defining and implementing operators for sharpening by digital differentiation. The strength of the response of

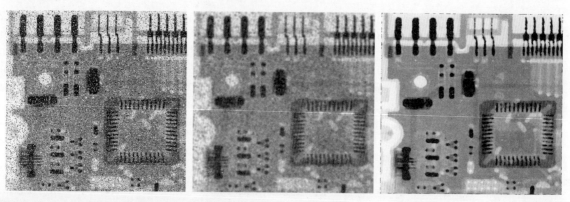

a b c

FIGURE 3.43 (a) X-ray image of a circuit board, corrupted by salt-and-pepper noise. (b) Noise reduction using a 19×19 Gaussian lowpass filter kernel with $\sigma = 3$. (c) Noise reduction using a 7×7 median filter. (Original image courtesy of Mr. Joseph E. Pascente, Lixi, Inc.)

a derivative operator is proportional to the magnitude of the intensity discontinuity at the point at which the operator is applied. Thus, image differentiation enhances edges and other discontinuities (such as noise) and de-emphasizes areas with slowly varying intensities. As noted in Section 3.5, smoothing is often referred to as lowpass filtering, a term borrowed from frequency domain processing. In a similar manner, sharpening is often referred to as *highpass* filtering. In this case, high frequencies (which are responsible for fine details) are passed, while low frequencies are attenuated or rejected.

FOUNDATION

In the two sections that follow, we will consider in some detail sharpening filters that are based on first- and second-order derivatives, respectively. Before proceeding with that discussion, however, we stop to look at some of the fundamental properties of these derivatives in a digital context. To simplify the explanation, we focus attention initially on one-dimensional derivatives. In particular, we are interested in the behavior of these derivatives in areas of constant intensity, at the onset and end of discontinuities (*step* and *ramp discontinuities*), and along *intensity ramps*. As you will see in Chapter 10, these types of discontinuities can be used to model noise points, lines, and edges in an image.

Derivatives of a digital function are defined in terms of differences. There are various ways to define these differences. However, we require that any definition we use for a *first derivative:*

1. Must be zero in areas of constant intensity.
2. Must be nonzero at the onset of an intensity step or ramp.
3. Must be nonzero along intensity ramps.

Similarly, any definition of a *second derivative*

1. Must be zero in areas of constant intensity.

2. Must be nonzero at the onset *and* end of an intensity step or ramp.

3. Must be zero along intensity ramps.

We are dealing with digital quantities whose values are finite. Therefore, the maximum possible intensity change also is finite, and the shortest distance over which that change can occur is between adjacent pixels.

A basic definition of the *first-order* derivative of a one-dimensional function $f(x)$ is the difference

We will return to Eq. (3-48) in Section 10.2 and show how it follows from a Taylor series expansion. For now, we accept it as a definition.

$$\frac{\partial f}{\partial x} = f(x+1) - f(x) \tag{3-48}$$

We used a partial derivative here in order to keep the notation consistent when we consider an image function of two variables, $f(x, y)$, at which time we will be dealing with partial derivatives along the two spatial axes. Clearly, $\partial f / \partial x = df / dx$ when there is only one variable in the function; the same is true for the second derivative.

We define the *second-order* derivative of $f(x)$ as the difference

$$\frac{\partial^2 f}{\partial x^2} = f(x+1) + f(x-1) - 2f(x) \tag{3-49}$$

These two definitions satisfy the conditions stated above, as we illustrate in Fig. 3.44, where we also examine the similarities and differences between first- and second-order derivatives of a digital function.

The values denoted by the small squares in Fig. 3.44(a) are the intensity values along a horizontal intensity profile (the dashed line connecting the squares is included to aid visualization). The actual numerical values of the scan line are shown inside the small boxes in 3.44(b). As Fig. 3.44(a) shows, the scan line contains three sections of constant intensity, an intensity ramp, and an intensity step. The circles indicate the onset or end of intensity transitions. The first- and second-order derivatives, computed using the two preceding definitions, are shown below the scan line values in Fig. 3.44(b), and are plotted in Fig. 3.44(c). When computing the first derivative at a location x, we subtract the value of the function at that location from the next point, as indicated in Eq. (3-48), so this is a "look-ahead" operation. Similarly, to compute the second derivative at x, we use the previous and the next points in the computation, as indicated in Eq. (3-49). To avoid a situation in which the previous or next points are outside the range of the scan line, we show derivative computations in Fig. 3.44 from the second through the penultimate points in the sequence.

As we traverse the profile from left to right we encounter first an area of constant intensity and, as Figs. 3.44(b) and (c) show, both derivatives are zero there, so condition (1) is satisfied by both. Next, we encounter an intensity ramp followed by a step, and we note that the first-order derivative is nonzero at the onset of the ramp and the step; similarly, the second derivative is nonzero at the onset and end of both the ramp and the step; therefore, property (2) is satisfied by both derivatives. Finally, we

FIGURE 3.44
(a) A section of a horizontal scan line from an image, showing ramp and step edges, as well as constant segments.
(b) Values of the scan line and its derivatives.
(c) Plot of the derivatives, showing a zero crossing. In (a) and (c) points were joined by dashed lines as a visual aid.

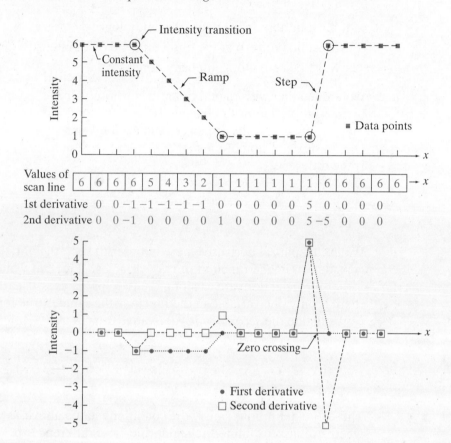

see that property (3) is satisfied also by both derivatives because the first derivative is nonzero and the second is zero along the ramp. Note that the sign of the second derivative changes at the onset and end of a step or ramp. In fact, we see in Fig. 3.44(c) that in a step transition a line joining these two values crosses the horizontal axis midway between the two extremes. This *zero crossing* property is quite useful for locating edges, as you will see in Chapter 10.

Edges in digital images often are ramp-like transitions in intensity, in which case the first derivative of the image would result in thick edges because the derivative is nonzero along a ramp. On the other hand, the second derivative would produce a double edge one pixel thick, separated by zeros. From this, we conclude that the second derivative enhances fine detail much better than the first derivative, a property ideally suited for sharpening images. Also, second derivatives require fewer operations to implement than first derivatives, so our initial attention is on the former.

USING THE SECOND DERIVATIVE FOR IMAGE SHARPENING—THE LAPLACIAN

We will return to the second derivative in Chapter 10, where we use it extensively for image segmentation.

In this section we discuss the implementation of 2-D, second-order derivatives and their use for image sharpening. The approach consists of defining a discrete formulation of the second-order derivative and then constructing a filter kernel based on that formulation. As in the case of Gaussian lowpass kernels in Section 3.5, we are interested here in isotropic kernels, whose response is independent of the direction of intensity discontinuities in the image to which the filter is applied.

It can be shown (Rosenfeld and Kak [1982]) that the simplest isotropic derivative operator (kernel) is the *Laplacian*, which, for a function (image) $f(x, y)$ of two variables, is defined as

$$\nabla^2 f = \frac{\partial^2 f}{\partial x^2} + \frac{\partial^2 f}{\partial y^2} \tag{3-50}$$

Because derivatives of any order are linear operations, the Laplacian is a linear operator. To express this equation in discrete form, we use the definition in Eq. (3-49), keeping in mind that we now have a second variable. In the x-direction, we have

$$\frac{\partial^2 f}{\partial x^2} = f(x + 1, y) + f(x - 1, y) - 2f(x, y) \tag{3-51}$$

and, similarly, in the y-direction, we have

$$\frac{\partial^2 f}{\partial y^2} = f(x, y + 1) + f(x, y - 1) - 2f(x, y) \tag{3-52}$$

It follows from the preceding three equations that the discrete Laplacian of two variables is

$$\nabla^2 f(x, y) = f(x + 1, y) + f(x - 1, y) + f(x, y + 1) + f(x, y - 1) - 4f(x, y) \tag{3-53}$$

This equation can be implemented using convolution with the kernel in Fig. 3.45(a); thus, the filtering mechanics for image sharpening are as described in Section 3.5 for lowpass filtering; we are simply using different coefficients here.

The kernel in Fig. 3.45(a) is isotropic for rotations in increments of 90° with respect to the x- and y-axes. The diagonal directions can be incorporated in the definition of the digital Laplacian by adding four more terms to Eq. (3-53). Because each diagonal term would contains a $-2f(x, y)$ term, the total subtracted from the differ-

0	1	0
1	−4	1
0	1	0

1	1	1
1	−8	1
1	1	1

0	−1	0
−1	4	−1
0	−1	0

−1	−1	−1
−1	8	−1
−1	−1	−1

a b c d

FIGURE 3.45 (a) Laplacian kernel used to implement Eq. (3-53). (b) Kernel used to implement an extension of this equation that includes the diagonal terms. (c) and (d) Two other Laplacian kernels.

ence terms now would be $-8f(x, y)$. Figure 3.45(b) shows the kernel used to implement this new definition. This kernel yields isotropic results in increments of 45°. The kernels in Figs. 3.45(c) and (d) also are used to compute the Laplacian. They are obtained from definitions of the second derivatives that are the negatives of the ones we used here. They yield equivalent results, but the difference in sign must be kept in mind when combining a Laplacian-filtered image with another image.

Because the Laplacian is a derivative operator, it highlights sharp intensity transitions in an image and de-emphasizes regions of slowly varying intensities. This will tend to produce images that have grayish edge lines and other discontinuities, all superimposed on a dark, featureless background. Background features can be "recovered" while still preserving the sharpening effect of the Laplacian by adding the Laplacian image to the original. As noted in the previous paragraph, it is important to keep in mind which definition of the Laplacian is used. If the definition used has a negative center coefficient, then we *subtract* the Laplacian image from the original to obtain a sharpened result. Thus, the basic way in which we use the Laplacian for image sharpening is

$$g(x, y) = f(x, y) + c\left[\nabla^2 f(x, y)\right] \tag{3-54}$$

where $f(x, y)$ and $g(x, y)$ are the input and sharpened images, respectively. We let $c = -1$ if the Laplacian kernels in Fig. 3.45(a) or (b) is used, and $c = 1$ if either of the other two kernels is used.

EXAMPLE 3.18: Image sharpening using the Laplacian.

Figure 3.46(a) shows a slightly blurred image of the North Pole of the moon, and Fig. 3.46(b) is the result of filtering this image with the Laplacian kernel in Fig. 3.45(a) directly. Large sections of this image are black because the Laplacian image contains both positive and negative values, and all negative values are clipped at 0 by the display.

Figure 3.46(c) shows the result obtained using Eq. (3-54), with $c = -1$, because we used the kernel in Fig. 3.45(a) to compute the Laplacian. The detail in this image is unmistakably clearer and sharper than in the original image. Adding the Laplacian to the original image restored the overall intensity variations in the image. Adding the Laplacian increased the contrast at the locations of intensity discontinuities. The net result is an image in which small details were enhanced and the background tonality was reasonably preserved. Finally, Fig. 3.46(d) shows the result of repeating the same procedure but using the kernel in Fig. 3.45(b). Here, we note a significant improvement in sharpness over Fig. 3.46(c). This is not unexpected because using the kernel in Fig. 3.45(b) provides additional differentiation (sharpening) in the diagonal directions. Results such as those in Figs. 3.46(c) and (d) have made the Laplacian a tool of choice for sharpening digital images.

Because Laplacian images tend to be dark and featureless, a typical way to scale these images for display is to use Eqs. (2-31) and (2-32). This brings the most negative value to 0 and displays the full range of intensities. Figure 3.47 is the result of processing Fig. 3.46(b) in this manner. The dominant features of the image are edges and sharp intensity discontinuities. The background, previously black, is now gray as a result of scaling. This grayish appearance is typical of Laplacian images that have been scaled properly.

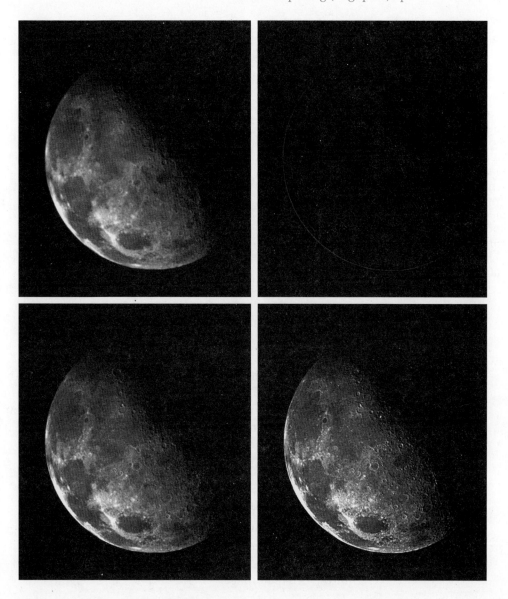

a b
c d

FIGURE 3.46
(a) Blurred image of the North Pole of the moon.
(b) Laplacian image obtained using the kernel in Fig. 3.45(a).
(c) Image sharpened using Eq. (3-54) with $c = -1$.
(d) Image sharpened using the same procedure, but with the kernel in Fig. 3.45(b).
(Original image courtesy of NASA.)

Observe in Fig. 3.45 that the coefficients of each kernel sum to zero. Convolution-based filtering implements a sum of products, so when a derivative kernel encompasses a constant region in a image, the result of convolution in that location must be zero. Using kernels whose coefficients sum to zero accomplishes this.

In Section 3.5, we normalized smoothing kernels so that the sum of their coefficients would be one. Constant areas in images filtered with these kernels would be constant also in the filtered image. We also found that the sum of the pixels in the original and filtered images were the same, thus preventing a bias from being introduced by filtering (see Problem 3.31). When convolving an image with a kernel

FIGURE 3.47
The Laplacian image from Fig. 3.46(b), scaled to the full $[0, 255]$ range of intensity values. Black pixels correspond to the most negative value in the unscaled Laplacian image, grays are intermediate values, and white pixels corresponds to the highest positive value.

whose coefficients sum to zero, it turns out that the pixels of the filtered image *will sum to zero also* (see Problem 3.32). This implies that images filtered with such kernels will have negative values, and sometimes will require additional processing to obtain suitable visual results. Adding the filtered image to the original, as we did in Eq. (3-54), is an example of such additional processing.

UNSHARP MASKING AND HIGHBOOST FILTERING

Subtracting an unsharp (smoothed) version of an image from the original image is process that has been used since the 1930s by the printing and publishing industry to sharpen images. This process, called *unsharp masking*, consists of the following steps:

The photographic process of unsharp masking is based on creating a blurred positive and using it along with the original negative to create a sharper image. Our interest is in the *digital* equivalent of this process.

1. Blur the original image.

2. Subtract the blurred image from the original (the resulting difference is called the *mask*.)

3. Add the mask to the original.

Letting $\bar{f}(x, y)$ denote the blurred image, the mask in equation form is given by:

$$g_{\text{mask}}(x, y) = f(x, y) - \bar{f}(x, y) \tag{3-55}$$

Then we add a weighted portion of the mask back to the original image:

$$g(x, y) = f(x, y) + k\, g_{\text{mask}}(x, y) \tag{3-56}$$

a
b
c
d

FIGURE 3.48
1-D illustration of
the mechanics of
unsharp masking.
(a) Original
signal. (b) Blurred
signal with original
shown dashed for
reference.
(c) Unsharp mask.
(d) Sharpened
signal, obtained by
adding (c) to (a).

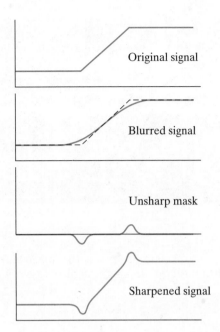

Original signal

Blurred signal

Unsharp mask

Sharpened signal

where we included a weight, k ($k \geq 0$), for generality. When $k = 1$ we have unsharp masking, as defined above. When $k > 1$, the process is referred to as *highboost filtering*. Choosing $k < 1$ reduces the contribution of the unsharp mask.

Figure 3.48 illustrates the mechanics of unsharp masking. Part (a) is a horizontal intensity profile across a vertical ramp edge that transitions from dark to light. Figure 3.48(b) shows the blurred scan line superimposed on the original signal (shown dashed). Figure 3.48(c) is the mask, obtained by subtracting the blurred signal from the original. By comparing this result with the section of Fig. 3.44(c) corresponding to the ramp in Fig. 3.44(a), we note that the unsharp mask in Fig. 3.48(c) is similar to what we would obtain using a second-order derivative. Figure 3.48(d) is the final sharpened result, obtained by adding the mask to the original signal. The points at which a change of slope occurs in the signal are now emphasized (sharpened). Observe that negative values were added to the original. Thus, it is possible for the final result to have negative intensities if the original image has any zero values, or if the value of k is chosen large enough to emphasize the peaks of the mask to a level larger than the minimum value in the original signal. Negative values cause dark halos around edges that can become objectionable if k is too large.

EXAMPLE 3.19: Unsharp masking and highboost filtering.

Figure 3.49(a) shows a slightly blurred image of white text on a dark gray background. Figure 3.49(b) was obtained using a Gaussian smoothing filter of size 31×31 with $\sigma = 5$. As explained in our earlier discussion of Gaussian lowpass kernels, the size of the kernel we used here is the smallest odd integer no less than $6\sigma \times 6\sigma$. Figure 3.49(c) is the unsharp mask, obtained using Eq. (3-55). To obtain the im-

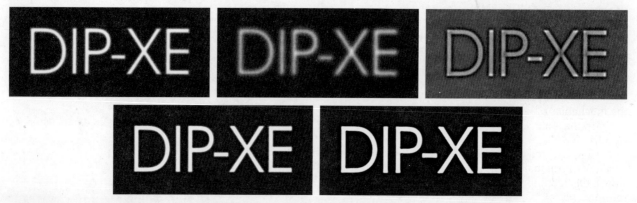

a b c
d e

FIGURE 3.49 (a) Original image of size 600×259 pixels. (b) Image blurred using a 31×31 Gaussian lowpass filter with $\sigma = 5$. (c) Mask. (d) Result of unsharp masking using Eq. (3-56) with $k = 1$. (e) Result of highboost filtering with $k = 4.5$.

age in Fig. 3.49(d) was used the unsharp masking expression room Eq. (3-56) with $k = 1$. This image is significantly sharper than the original image in Fig. 3.49(a), but we can do better, as we show in the following paragraph.

Figure 3.49(e) shows the result of using Eq. (3-56) with $k = 4.5$. This value is almost at the extreme of what we can use without introducing some serious artifacts in the image. The artifacts are dark, almost black, halos around the border of the characters. This is caused by the lower "blip" in Fig. 3.48(d) becoming negative, as we explained earlier. When scaling the image so that it only has positive values for display, the negative values are either clipped at 0, or scaled so that the most negative values become 0, depending on the scaling method used. In either case, the blips will be the darkest values in the image.

The results in Figs. 3.49(d) and 3.49(e) would be difficult to generate using the traditional film photography explained earlier, and it illustrates the power and versatility of image processing in the context of digital photography.

USING FIRST-ORDER DERIVATIVES FOR IMAGE SHARPENING—THE GRADIENT

We will discuss the gradient in more detail in Section 10.2. Here, we are interested only in using it for image sharpening.

First derivatives in image processing are implemented using the magnitude of the gradient. The *gradient* of an image f at coordinates (x, y) is defined as the two-dimensional column vector

$$\nabla f \equiv \text{grad}(f) = \begin{bmatrix} g_x \\ g_y \end{bmatrix} = \begin{bmatrix} \dfrac{\partial f}{\partial x} \\ \dfrac{\partial f}{\partial y} \end{bmatrix} \tag{3-57}$$

This vector has the important geometrical property that it points in the direction of the greatest rate of change of f at location (x, y).

The *magnitude* (*length*) of vector ∇f, denoted as $M(x, y)$ (the vector norm notation $\|\nabla f\|$ is also used frequently), where

$$M(x, y) = \|\nabla f\| = \mathrm{mag}\,(\nabla f) = \sqrt{g_x^2 + g_y^2} \tag{3-58}$$

is the *value* at (x, y) of the *rate of change* in the direction of the gradient vector. Note that $M(x, y)$ is an image of the same size as the original, created when x and y are allowed to vary over all pixel locations in f. It is common practice to refer to this image as the *gradient image* (or simply as the *gradient* when the meaning is clear).

Because the components of the gradient vector are derivatives, they are linear operators. However, the magnitude of this vector is not, because of the squaring and square root operations. On the other hand, the partial derivatives in Eq. (3-57) are not rotation invariant, but the magnitude of the gradient vector is.

In some implementations, it is more suitable computationally to approximate the squares and square root operations by absolute values:

The vertical bars denote absolute values.

$$M(x, y) \approx |g_x| + |g_y| \tag{3-59}$$

This expression still preserves the relative changes in intensity, but the isotropic property is lost in general. However, as in the case of the Laplacian, the isotropic properties of the discrete gradient defined in the following paragraph are preserved only for a limited number of rotational increments that depend on the kernels used to approximate the derivatives. As it turns out, the most popular kernels used to approximate the gradient are isotropic at multiples of $90°$. These results are independent of whether we use Eq. (3-58) or (3-59), so nothing of significance is lost in using the latter equation if we choose to do so.

As in the case of the Laplacian, we now define discrete approximations to the preceding equations, and from these formulate the appropriate kernels. In order to simplify the discussion that follows, we will use the notation in Fig. 3.50(a) to denote the intensities of pixels in a 3×3 region. For example, the value of the center point, z_5, denotes the value of $f(x, y)$ at an arbitrary location, (x, y); z_1 denotes the value of $f(x - 1, y - 1)$; and so on. As indicated in Eq. (3-48), the simplest approximations to a first-order derivative that satisfy the conditions stated at the beginning of this section are $g_x = (z_8 - z_5)$ and $g_y = (z_6 - z_5)$. Two other definitions, proposed by Roberts [1965] in the early development of digital image processing, use cross differences:

$$g_x = (z_9 - z_5) \quad \text{and} \quad g_y = (z_8 - z_6) \tag{3-60}$$

If we use Eqs. (3-58) and (3-60), we compute the gradient image as

$$M(x, y) = \left[(z_9 - z_5)^2 + (z_8 - z_6)^2 \right]^{1/2} \tag{3-61}$$

a
b c
d e

FIGURE 3.50
(a) A 3×3 region
of an image,
where the zs are
intensity values.
(b)–(c) Roberts
cross-gradient
operators.
(d)–(e) Sobel
operators. All the
kernel
coefficients sum
to zero, as expect-
ed of a derivative
operator.

z_1	z_2	z_3
z_4	z_5	z_6
z_7	z_8	z_9

| -1 | 0 |
| 0 | 1 |

| 0 | -1 |
| 1 | 0 |

-1	-2	-1
0	0	0
1	2	1

-1	0	1
-2	0	2
-1	0	1

If we use Eqs. (3-59) and (3-60), then

$$M(x, y) \approx |z_9 - z_5| + |z_8 - z_6| \tag{3-62}$$

where it is understood that x and y vary over the dimensions of the image in the manner described earlier. The difference terms needed in Eq. (3-60) can be implemented using the two kernels in Figs. 3.50(b) and (c). These kernels are referred to as the *Roberts cross-gradient operators*.

As noted earlier, we prefer to use kernels of odd sizes because they have a unique, (integer) center of spatial symmetry. The smallest kernels in which we are interested are of size 3×3. Approximations to g_x and g_y using a 3×3 neighborhood centered on z_5 are as follows:

$$g_x = \frac{\partial f}{\partial x} = (z_7 + 2z_8 + z_9) - (z_1 + 2z_2 + z_3) \tag{3-63}$$

and

$$g_y = \frac{\partial f}{\partial y} = (z_3 + 2z_6 + z_9) - (z_1 + 2z_4 + z_7) \tag{3-64}$$

These equations can be implemented using the kernels in Figs. 3.50(d) and (e). The difference between the third and first rows of the 3×3 image region approximates the partial derivative in the x-direction, and is implemented using the kernel in Fig. 3.50(d).

The difference between the third and first columns approximates the partial derivative in the y-direction and is implemented using the kernel in Fig. 3.50(e). The partial derivatives at all points in an image are obtained by convolving the image with these kernels. We then obtain the magnitude of the gradient as before. For example, substituting g_x and g_y into Eq. (3-59) yields

$$M(x,y) = \left[g_x^2 + g_y^2 \right]^{\frac{1}{2}} = \left\{ \left[(z_7 + 2z_8 + z_9) - (z_1 + 2z_2 + z_3) \right]^2 \right.$$
$$\left. + \left[(z_3 + 2z_6 + z_9) - (z_1 + 2z_4 + z_7) \right]^2 \right\}^{\frac{1}{2}} \tag{3-65}$$

This equation indicates that the value of M at any image coordinates (x,y) is given by squaring values of the convolution of the two kernels with image f at those coordinates, summing the two results, and taking the square root.

The kernels in Figs. 3.50(d) and (e) are called the *Sobel operators*. The idea behind using a weight value of 2 in the center coefficient is to achieve some smoothing by giving more importance to the center point (we will discuss this in more detail in Chapter 10). The coefficients in all the kernels in Fig. 3.50 sum to zero, so they would give a response of zero in areas of constant intensity, as expected of a derivative operator. As noted earlier, when an image is convolved with a kernel whose coefficients sum to zero, the elements of the resulting filtered image sum to zero also, so images convolved with the kernels in Fig. 3.50 will have negative values in general.

The computations of g_x and g_y are linear operations and are implemented using convolution, as noted above. The nonlinear aspect of sharpening with the gradient is the computation of $M(x,y)$ involving squaring and square roots, or the use of absolute values, all of which are nonlinear operations. These operations are performed after the linear process (convolution) that yields g_x and g_y.

EXAMPLE 3.20: Using the gradient for edge enhancement.

The gradient is used frequently in industrial inspection, either to aid humans in the detection of defects or, what is more common, as a preprocessing step in automated inspection. We will have more to say about this in Chapter 10. However, it will be instructive now to consider a simple example to illustrate how the gradient can be used to enhance defects and eliminate slowly changing background features.

Figure 3.51(a) is an optical image of a contact lens, illuminated by a lighting arrangement designed to highlight imperfections, such as the two edge defects in the lens boundary seen at 4 and 5 o'clock. Figure 3.51(b) shows the gradient obtained using Eq. (3-65) with the two Sobel kernels in Figs. 3.50(d) and (e). The edge defects are also quite visible in this image, but with the added advantage that constant or slowly varying shades of gray have been eliminated, thus simplifying considerably the computational task required for automated inspection. The gradient can be used also to highlight small specs that may not be readily visible in a gray-scale image (specs like these can be foreign matter, air pockets in a supporting solution, or miniscule imperfections in the lens). The ability to enhance small discontinuities in an otherwise flat gray field is another important feature of the gradient.

a b

FIGURE 3.51
(a) Image of a
contact lens (note
defects on the
boundary at 4 and
5 o'clock).
(b) Sobel gradient.
(Original image
courtesy of
Perceptics
Corporation.)

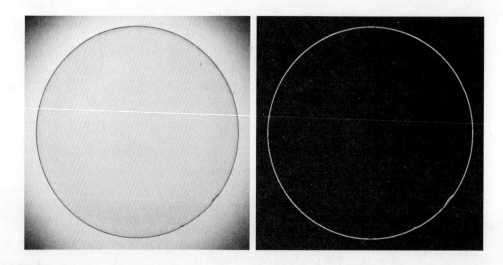

3.7 HIGHPASS, BANDREJECT, AND BANDPASS FILTERS FROM LOW-PASS FILTERS

Spatial and frequency-domain linear filters are classified into four broad categories: lowpass and highpass filters, which we introduced in Sections 3.5 and 3.6, and *bandpass* and *bandreject* filters, which we introduce in this section. We mentioned at the beginning of Section 3.5 that the other three types of filters can be constructed from lowpass filters. In this section we explore methods for doing this. Also, we illustrate the third approach discussed at the end of Section 3.4 for obtaining spatial filter kernels. That is, we use a filter design software package to generate 1-D filter functions. Then, we use these to generate 2-D separable filters functions either via Eq.(3-42), or by rotating the 1-D functions about their centers to generate 2-D kernels. The rotated versions are approximations of circularly symmetric (isotropic) functions.

Figure 3.52(a) shows the transfer function of a 1-D ideal lowpass filter in the frequency domain [this is the same as Fig. 3.32(a)]. We know from earlier discussions in this chapter that lowpass filters attenuate or delete high frequencies, while passing low frequencies. A *highpass filter* behaves in exactly the opposite manner. As Fig. 3.52(b) shows, a highpass filter deletes or attenuates all frequencies below a cutoff value, u_0, and passes all frequencies above this value. Comparing Figs. 3.52(a) and (b), we see that a highpass filter transfer function is obtained by subtracting a lowpass function from 1. This operation is in the frequency domain. As you know from Section 3.4, a constant in the frequency domain is an impulse in the spatial domain. Thus, we obtain a highpass filter kernel in the spatial domain by subtracting a lowpass filter kernel from a unit impulse with the same center as the kernel. An image filtered with this kernel is the same as an image obtained by subtracting a lowpass-filtered image from the original image. The unsharp mask defined by Eq. (3-55) is precisely this operation. Therefore, Eqs. (3-54) and (3-56) implement equivalent operations (see Problem 3.42).

Figure 3.52(c) shows the transfer function of a bandreject filter. This transfer function can be constructed from the sum of a lowpass and a highpass function with

Recall from the discussion of Eq. (3-33) that a unit impulse is an array of 0's with a single 1.

a b
c d

FIGURE 3.52
Transfer functions of ideal 1-D filters in the frequency domain (u denotes frequency).
(a) Lowpass filter.
(b) Highpass filter.
(c) Bandreject filter.
(d) Bandpass filter.
(As before, we show only positive frequencies for simplicity.)

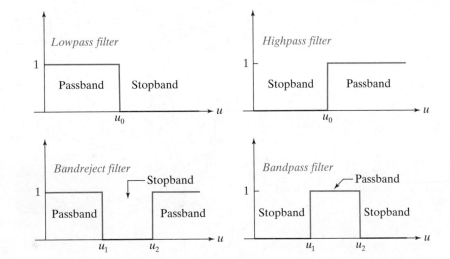

different cut-off frequencies (the highpass function can be constructed from a *different* lowpass function). The bandpass filter transfer function in Fig. 3.52(d) can be obtained by subtracting the bandreject function from 1 (a unit impulse in the spatial domain). Bandreject filters are also referred to as *notch* filters, but the latter tend to be more locally oriented, as we will show in Chapter 4. Table 3.7 summarizes the preceding discussion.

The key point in Fig. 3.52 and Table 3.7 is that all transfer functions shown can be obtained starting with a lowpass filter transfer function. This is important. It is important also to realize that we arrived at this conclusion via simple graphical interpretations in the frequency domain. To arrive at the same conclusion based on convolution in the spatial domain would be a much harder task.

EXAMPLE 3.21: Lowpass, highpass, bandreject, and bandpass filtering.

In this example we illustrate how we can start with a 1-D lowpass filter transfer function generated using a software package, and then use that transfer function to generate spatial filter kernels based on the concepts introduced in this section. We also examine the spatial filtering properties of these kernels.

TABLE 3.7
Summary of the four principal spatial filter types expressed in terms of low-pass filters. The centers of the unit impulse and the filter kernels coincide.

Filter type	Spatial kernel in terms of lowpass kernel, lp
Lowpass	$lp(x,y)$
Highpass	$hp(x,y) = \delta(x,y) - lp(x,y)$
Bandreject	$br(x,y) = lp_1(x,y) + hp_2(x,y)$
	$\quad = lp_1(x,y) + \big[\delta(x,y) - lp_2(x,y)\big]$
Bandpass	$bp(x,y) = \delta(x,y) - br(x,y)$
	$\quad = \delta(x,y) - \Big[lp_1(x,y) + \big[\delta(x,y) - lp_2(x,y)\big]\Big]$

FIGURE 3.53
A zone plate
image of size
597×597 pixels.

Figure 3.53 shows a so-called *zone plate* image that is used frequently for testing the characteristics of filtering approaches. There are various versions of zone plates; the one in Fig. 3.53 was generated using the equation

$$z(x, y) = \frac{1}{2}\left[1 + \cos\left(x^2 + y^2\right)\right] \tag{3-66}$$

with x and y varying in the range $[-8.2, 8.2]$, in increments of 0.0275. This resulted in an image of size 597×597 pixels. The bordering black region was generated by setting to 0 all pixels with distance greater than 8.2 from the image center. The key characteristic of a zone plate is that its spatial frequency increases as a function of distance from the center, as you can see by noting that the rings get narrower the further they are from the center. This property makes a zone plate an ideal image for illustrating the behavior of the four filter types just discussed.

Figure 3.54(a) shows a 1-D, 128-element spatial lowpass filter function designed using MATLAB [compare with Fig. 3.32(b)]. As discussed earlier, we can use this 1-D function to construct a 2-D, separable lowpass filter kernel based on Eq. (3-42), or we can rotate it about its center to generate a 2-D, isotropic kernel. The kernel in Fig. 3.54(b) was obtained using the latter approach. Figures 3.55(a) and (b) are the results of filtering the image in Fig. 3.53 with the separable and isotropic kernels, respectively. Both filters passed the low frequencies of the zone plate while attenuating the high frequencies significantly. Observe, however, that the separable filter kernel produced a "squarish" (non-radially symmetric) result in the passed frequencies. This is a consequence of filtering the image in perpendicular directions with a separable kernel that is not isotropic. Using the isotropic kernel yielded a result that is uniform in all radial directions. This is as expected, because both the filter and the image are isotropic.

a b

FIGURE 3.54
(a) A 1-D spatial
lowpass filter
function. (b) 2-D
kernel obtained
by rotating the
1-D profile about
its center.

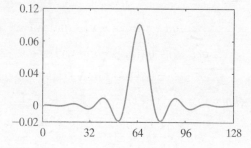

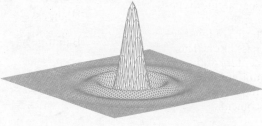

a b

FIGURE 3.55
(a) Zone plate image filtered with a separable lowpass kernel. (b) Image filtered with the isotropic lowpass kernel in Fig. 3.54(b).

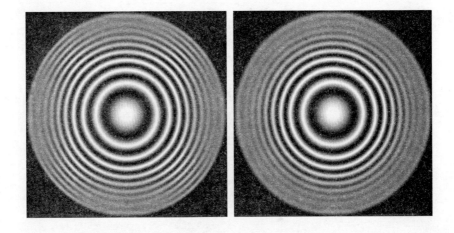

Figure 3.56 shows the results of filtering the zone plate with the four filters described in Table 3.7. We used the 2-D lowpass kernel in Fig. 3.54(b) as the basis for the highpass filter, and similar lowpass kernels for the bandreject filter. Figure 3.56(a) is the same as Fig. 3.55(b), which we repeat for convenience. Figure 3.56(b) is the highpass-filtered result. Note how effectively the low frequencies were filtered out. As is true of highpass-filtered images, the black areas were caused by negative values being clipped at 0 by the display. Figure 3.56(c) shows the same image scaled using Eqs. (2-31) and (2-32). Here we see clearly that only high frequencies were passed by the filter. Because the highpass kernel was constructed using the same lowpass kernel that we used to generate Fig. 3.56(a), it is evident by comparing the two results that the highpass filter passed the frequencies that were attenuated by the lowpass filter.

Figure 3.56(d) shows the bandreject-filtered image, in which the attenuation of the mid-band of frequencies is evident. Finally, Fig. 33.56(e) shows the result of bandpass filtering. This image also has negative values, so it is shown scaled in Fig. 3.56(f). Because the bandpass kernel was constructed by subtracting the bandreject kernel from a unit impulse, we see that the bandpass filter passed the frequencies that were attenuated by the bandreject filter. We will give additional examples of bandpass and bandreject filtering in Chapter 4.

3.8 COMBINING SPATIAL ENHANCEMENT METHODS

With a few exceptions, such as combining blurring with thresholding (Fig. 3.41), we have focused attention thus far on individual spatial-domain processing approaches. Frequently, a given task will require application of several complementary techniques in order to achieve an acceptable result. In this section, we illustrate how to combine several of the approaches developed thus far in this chapter to address a difficult image enhancement task.

The image in Fig. 3.57(a) is a nuclear whole body bone scan, used to detect diseases such as bone infections and tumors. Our objective is to enhance this image by sharpening it and by bringing out more of the skeletal detail. The narrow dynamic range of the intensity levels and high noise content make this image difficult to enhance. The strategy we will follow is to utilize the Laplacian to highlight fine detail, and the gradient to enhance prominent edges. For reasons that will be explained shortly, a smoothed version of the gradient image will be used to mask the Laplacian

In this context, masking refers to multiplying two images, as in Fig. 2.34. This is not be confused with the mask used in unsharp masking.

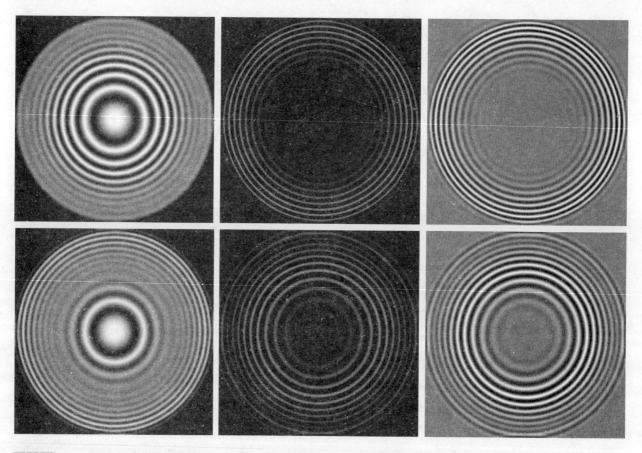

a b c
d e f

FIGURE 3.56
Spatial filtering of the zone plate image. (a) Lowpass result; this is the same as Fig. 3.55(b). (b) Highpass result. (c) Image (b) with intensities scaled. (d) Bandreject result. (e) Bandpass result. (f) Image (e) with intensities scaled.

image. Finally, we will attempt to increase the dynamic range of the intensity levels by using an intensity transformation.

Figure 3.57(b) shows the Laplacian of the original image, obtained using the kernel in Fig. 3.45(d). This image was scaled (for display only) using the same technique as in Fig. 3.47. We can obtain a sharpened image at this point simply by adding Figs. 3.57(a) and (b), according to Eq. (3-54). Just by looking at the noise level in Fig. 3.57(b), we would expect a rather noisy sharpened image if we added Figs. 3.57(a) and (b). This is confirmed by the result in Fig. 3.57(c). One way that comes immediately to mind to reduce the noise is to use a median filter. However, median filtering is an aggressive nonlinear process capable of removing image features. This is unacceptable in medical image processing.

An alternate approach is to use a mask formed from a smoothed version of the gradient of the original image. The approach is based on the properties of first- and

a b
c d

FIGURE 3.57
(a) Image of whole body bone scan.
(b) Laplacian of (a).
(c) Sharpened image obtained by adding (a) and (b).
(d) Sobel gradient of image (a). (Original image courtesy of G.E. Medical Systems.)

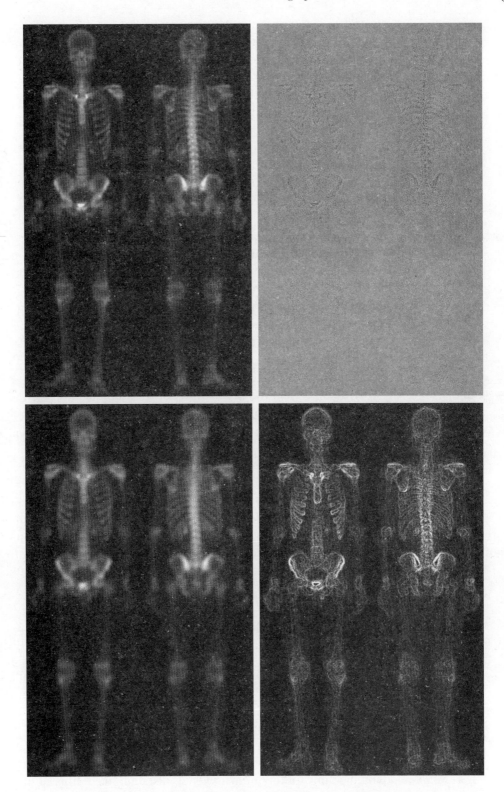

second-order derivatives we discussed when explaining Fig. 3.44. The Laplacian, is a second-order derivative operator and has the definite advantage that it is superior for enhancing fine detail. However, this causes it to produce noisier results than the gradient. This noise is most objectionable in smooth areas, where it tends to be more visible. The gradient has a stronger response in areas of significant intensity transitions (ramps and steps) than does the Laplacian. The response of the gradient to noise and fine detail is lower than the Laplacian's and can be lowered further by smoothing the gradient with a lowpass filter. The idea, then, is to smooth the gradient and multiply it by the Laplacian image. In this context, we may view the smoothed gradient as a mask image. The product will preserve details in the strong areas, while reducing noise in the relatively flat areas. This process can be interpreted roughly as combining the best features of the Laplacian and the gradient. The result is added to the original to obtain a final sharpened image.

Figure 3.57(d) shows the Sobel gradient of the original image, computed using Eq. (3-59). Components g_x and g_y were obtained using the kernels in Figs. 3.50(d) and (e), respectively. As expected, the edges are much more dominant in this image than in the Laplacian image. The smoothed gradient image in Fig. 3.57(e) was obtained by using a box filter of size 5×5. The fact that Figs. 3.57(d) and (e) are much brighter than Fig. 3.57(b) is further evidence that the gradient of an image with significant edge content has values that are higher in general than in a Laplacian image.

Figure 3.57(f) shows the product of the Laplacian and smoothed gradient image. Note the dominance of the strong edges and the relative lack of visible noise, which is the reason for masking the Laplacian with a smoothed gradient image. Adding the product image to the original resulted in the sharpened image in Fig. 3.57(g). The increase in sharpness of detail in this image over the original is evident in most parts of the image, including the ribs, spinal cord, pelvis, and skull. This type of improvement would not have been possible by using the Laplacian or the gradient alone.

The sharpening procedure just discussed did not affect in an appreciable way the dynamic range of the intensity levels in an image. Thus, the final step in our enhancement task is to increase the dynamic range of the sharpened image. As we discussed in some detail in Sections 3.2 and 3.3, there are several intensity transformation functions that can accomplish this objective. Histogram processing is not a good approach on images whose histograms are characterized by dark and light components, which is the case here. The dark characteristics of the images with which we are dealing lend themselves much better to a power-law transformation. Because we wish to spread the intensity levels, the value of γ in Eq. (3-5) has to be less than 1. After a few trials with this equation, we arrived at the result in Fig. 3.57(h), obtained with $\gamma = 0.5$ and $c = 1$. Comparing this image with Fig. 3.57(g), we note that significant new detail is visible in Fig. 3.57(h). The areas around the wrists, hands, ankles, and feet are good examples of this. The skeletal bone structure also is much more pronounced, including the arm and leg bones. Note the faint definition of the outline of the body, and of body tissue. Bringing out detail of this nature by expanding the dynamic range of the intensity levels also enhanced noise, but Fig. 3.57(h) is a significant visual improvement over the original image.

e f
g h

FIGURE 3.57
(Continued)
(e) Sobel image
smoothed with a
5×5 box filter.
(f) Mask image
formed by the
product of (b)
and (e).
(g) Sharpened
image obtained
by the adding
images (a) and (f).
(h) Final result
obtained by
applying a power-
law transformation
to (g). Compare
images (g) and (h)
with (a). (Original
image courtesy
of G.E. Medical
Systems.)

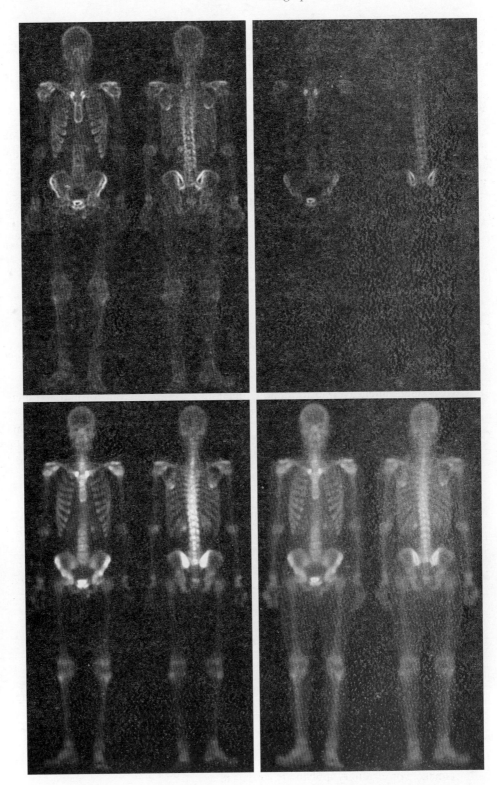

Summary, References, and Further Reading

The material in this chapter is representative of current techniques used for intensity transformations and spatial filtering. The topics were selected for their value as fundamental material that would serve as a foundation in an evolving field. Although most of the examples used in this chapter deal with image enhancement, the techniques presented are perfectly general, and you will encounter many of them again throughout the remaining chapters in contexts unrelated to enhancement.

The material in Section 3.1 is from Gonzalez [1986]. For additional reading on the material in Section 3.2, see Schowengerdt [2006] and Poyton [1996]. Early references on histogram processing (Section 3.3) are Gonzalez and Fittes [1977], and Woods and Gonzalez [1981]. Stark [2000] gives some interesting generalizations of histogram equalization for adaptive contrast enhancement.

For complementary reading on linear spatial filtering (Sections 3.4-3.7), see Jain [1989], Rosenfeld and Kak [1982], Schowengerdt [2006], Castleman [1996], and Umbaugh [2010]. For an interesting approach for generating Gaussian kernels with integer coefficients see Padfield [2011]. The book by Pitas and Venetsanopoulos [1990] is a good source for additional reading on median and other nonlinear spatial filters.

For details on the software aspects of many of the examples in this chapter, see Gonzalez, Woods, and Eddins [2009].

Problems

Solutions to the problems marked with an asterisk (*) are in the DIP4E Student Support Package (consult the book website: www.ImageProcessingPlace.com).

3.1 Give a single intensity transformation function for spreading the intensities of an image so the lowest intensity is 0 and the highest is $L-1$.

3.2 Exponentials of the form $e^{(-ar^2)}$, with a positive constant, are useful for constructing smooth intensity transformation functions. Start with this basic function and construct transformation functions having the general shapes shown in the following figures.

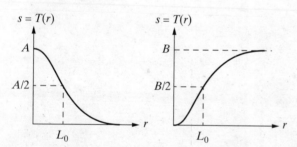

3.3 Do the following:

(a)* Propose a *set* of intensity-slicing transformation functions capable of producing all the individual bit planes of an 8-bit monochrome image. For example, applying to an image a

transformation function with the property $T(r) = 0$ if r is 0 or even, and $T(r) = 1$ if r is odd, produces an image of the least significant bit plane (see Fig. 3.13). (*Hint:* Use an 8-bit truth table to determine the form of each transformation function.)

(b) How many intensity transformation functions would there be for 16-bit images?

(c) Is the basic approach in (a) limited to images in which the number of intensity levels is an integer power of 2, or is the method general for any number of *integer* intensity levels?

(d) If the method is general, how would it be different from your solution in (a)?

3.4 Do the following:

(a) How is it useful to decompose an image into its bit planes?

(b) Find all the bit planes of the following 4-bit image:

0	3	7	8
1	1	2	2
3	14	15	13
4	6	9	11

3.5 In general:

(a)* What effect would setting to zero the lower-order bit planes have on the histogram of an image?

(b) What would be the effect on the histogram if we set to zero the higher-order bit planes instead?

3.6 How is discrete histogram equalization technique different from its continuous counterpart?

3.7 Suppose that a digital image with continuous intensity values is subjected to histogram equalization. State the conditions that the transformation function should satisfy. What do these conditions guarantee?

3.8 Assuming continuous values, show by an example that it is possible to have a case in which the transformation function given in Eq. (3-11) satisfies conditions (a) and (b) discussed in Section 3.3, but its inverse may fail condition (a').

3.9 Do the following:

(a) Show that the discrete transformation function given in Eq. (3-15) for histogram equalization satisfies conditions (a) and (b) stated at the beginning of Section 3.3.

(b)* Show that the inverse discrete transformation in Eq. (3-16) satisfies conditions (a') and (b) in Section 3.3 *only if* none of the intensity levels r_k, $k = 0, 1, 2, \ldots, L-1$, are missing in the original image.

3.10 Two images, $f(x, y)$ and $g(x, y)$ have unnormalized histograms h_f and h_g. Give the conditions (on the values of the pixels in f and g) under which you can determine the histograms of images formed as follows:

(a)* $f(x, y) + g(x, y)$

(b) $f(x, y) - g(x, y)$

(c) $f(x, y) \times g(x, y)$

(d) $f(x, y) \div g(x, y)$

Show how the histograms would be formed in each case. The arithmetic operations are element-wise operations, as defined in Section 2.6.

3.11 Assume continuous intensity values, and suppose that the intensity values of an image have the PDF $p_r(r) = 2r/(L-1)^2$ for $0 \le r \le L-1$, and

$p_r(r) = 0$ for other values of r.

(a)* Find the transformation function that will map the input intensity values, r, into values, s, of a histogram-equalized image.

(b)* Find the transformation function that (when applied to the histogram-equalized intensities, s) will produce an image whose intensity PDF is $p_z(z) = 3z^2/(L-1)^3$ for $0 \le z \le L-1$ and $p_z(z) = 0$ for other values of z.

(c) Express the transformation function from (b) directly in terms of r, the intensities of the input image.

3.12 An image with intensities in the range [0,1] has the PDF, $p_r(r)$, shown in the following figure. It is desired to transform the intensity levels of this image so that they will have the specified $p_z(z)$ shown in the figure. Assume continuous quantities, and find the transformation (expressed in terms of r and z) that will accomplish this.

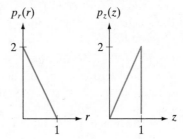

3.13* The discrete formulation of function $G(z)$ [from Eq. (3-18)] involves computing the transformation function $G(z_q)$ [from Eq. (3-21)] and inverse transformation $G^{-1}(s_k)$ [from Eq. 3-23]. Is it required in practice to compute the inverse of G?

3.14* The local histogram processing method discussed in Section 3.3 requires that a histogram be computed at each neighborhood location. Propose a method for updating the histogram from one neighborhood to the next, rather than computing a new histogram each time.

3.15 When do spatial correlation and convolution yield the same result?

3.16 You are given a computer chip that is capable of performing linear filtering in real time, but you are not told whether the chip performs correlation or convolution. Give the details of a test you would perform to determine which of the two operations the chip performs.

3.17* We mentioned in Section 3.4 that to perform convolution we rotate the kernel by 180°. The rotation is "built" into Eq. (3-35). Figure 3.28 corresponds to correlation. Draw the part of the figure enclosed by the large ellipse, but with w rotated 180°. Expand Eq. (3-35) for a general 3×3 kernel and show that the result of your expansion corresponds to your figure. This shows graphically that convolution and correlation differ by the rotation of the kernel.

3.18 You are given the following kernel and image:

$$w = \begin{bmatrix} 1 & 2 & 1 \\ 2 & 4 & 2 \\ 1 & 2 & 1 \end{bmatrix} \quad f = \begin{bmatrix} 0 & 0 & 0 & 0 & 0 \\ 0 & 0 & 1 & 0 & 0 \\ 0 & 0 & 1 & 0 & 0 \\ 0 & 0 & 1 & 0 & 0 \\ 0 & 0 & 0 & 0 & 0 \end{bmatrix}$$

(a)* Give a sketch of the area encircled by the large ellipse in Fig. 3.28 when the kernel is centered at point (2,3) (2nd row, 3rd col) of the image shown above. Show specific values of w and f.

(b)* Compute the convolution $w \star f$ using the *minimum* zero padding needed. Show the details of your computations when the kernel is centered on point (2,3) of f; and then show the final full convolution result.

(c) Repeat (b), but for correlation, $w \star f$.

3.19* Prove the validity of Eqs. (3-36) and (3-37).

3.20 The kernel, w, in Problem 3.18 is separable.

(a)* By inspection, find two kernels, w_1 and w_2 so that $w = w_1 \star w_2$.

(b) Using the image in Problem 3.18, compute $w_1 \star f$ using the *minimum* zero padding (see Fig. 3.30). Show the details of your computation when the kernel is centered at point (2,3) (2nd row, 3rd col) of f and then show the full convolution.

(c) Compute the convolution of w_2 with the result from (b). Show the details of your computation when the kernel is centered at point (3,3) of the result from (b), and then show the full convolution. Compare with the result in Problem 3.18(b).

3.21 Given the following kernel and image:

$$w = \begin{bmatrix} 1 & 2 & 1 \\ 2 & 4 & 2 \\ 1 & 2 & 1 \end{bmatrix} \quad f = \begin{bmatrix} 1 & 1 & 1 & 1 & 1 \\ 1 & 1 & 1 & 1 & 1 \\ 1 & 1 & 1 & 1 & 1 \\ 1 & 1 & 1 & 1 & 1 \\ 1 & 1 & 1 & 1 & 1 \end{bmatrix}$$

(a) Give the convolution of the two.

(b) Does your result have a bias?

3.22 Answer the following:

(a)* If $v = \begin{bmatrix} 1 & 3 & 1 \end{bmatrix}^T$ and $w^T = \begin{bmatrix} 1 & 2 & 2 & 3 \end{bmatrix}$, is the kernel formed by vw^T separable?

(b) The following kernel is separable. Find w_1 and w_2 such that $w = w_1 \star w_2$.

$$w = \begin{bmatrix} 2 & 1 & 1 \\ 4 & 2 & 2 \end{bmatrix}$$

3.23 Do the following:

(a)* Provide the form of the Gaussian kernel, $G(s, t)$ which is separable. What are two other fundamental properties of these kernels?

3.24* Show that the product of a column vector with a row vector is equivalent to the 2-D convolution of the two vectors. The vectors do not have to be of the same length. You may use a graphical approach (as in Fig. 3.30) to support the explanation of your proof.

3.25 Given K, 1-D Gaussian kernels, $g_1, g_2, \ldots, g_K$, with arbitrary means and standard deviations:

(a)* Determine what the entries in the third column of Table 3.6 would be for the product $g_1 \times g_2 \times \cdots \times g_K$.

(b) What would the fourth column look like for the convolution $g_1 \star g_2 \star \cdots \star g_K$?

(*Hint:* It is easier to work with the variance; the standard deviation is just the square root of your result.)

3.26 The two images shown in the following figure are quite different, but their histograms are the same. Suppose that each image is blurred using a 3×3 box kernel.

(a)* Would the histograms of the blurred images still be equal? Explain.

(b) If your answer is no, either sketch the two histograms or give two tables detailing the histogram components.

3.27 An image is filtered four times using a Gaussian kernel of size 3×3 with a standard deviation of 1.0. Because of the associative property of convolution, we know that equivalent results can be obtained using a single Gaussian kernel formed by convolving the individual kernels.

    (a) * What is the size of the single Gaussian kernel?

    (b) What is its standard deviation?

3.28 An image is filtered with three Gaussian lowpass kernels of sizes 3×3, 5×5, and 7×7, and standard deviations 1.0, 2 and 2, respectively. A composite filter, w, is formed as the convolution of these three filters.

    (a) * Is the resulting filter Gaussian? Explain.

    (b) What is its standard deviation?

    (c) What is its size?

3.29 * Discuss the limiting effect of repeatedly filtering an image with a 3×3 lowpass filter kernel. You may ignore border effects.

3.30 Fig. 3.42(b) is the result of lowpass filtering with a 512×512 Gaussian kernel. Discuss the computational advantage of using such as a large separable kernel.

3.31 * An image is filtered with a kernel whose coefficients sum to 1. Show that the sum of the pixel values in the original and filtered images is the same.

3.32 An image is filtered with a kernel whose coefficients sum to 0. Show that the sum of the pixel values in the filtered image also is 0.

3.33 A single point of light can be modeled by a digital image consisting of all 0's, with a 1 in the location of the point of light. If you view a single point of

light through a defocused lens, it will appear as a fuzzy blob whose size depends on the amount by which the lens is defocused. We mentioned in Section 3.5 that filtering an image with a box kernel is a poor model for a defocused lens, and that a better approximation is obtained with a Gaussian kernel. Using the single-point-of-light analogy, explain why this is so.

3.34 In the original image used to generate the three blurred images shown, the vertical bars are 5 pixels wide, 100 pixels high, and their separation is 20 pixels. The image was blurred using square box kernels of sizes 23, 25, and 45 elements on the side, respectively. The vertical bars on the left, lower part of (a) and (c) are blurred, but a clear separation exists between them.

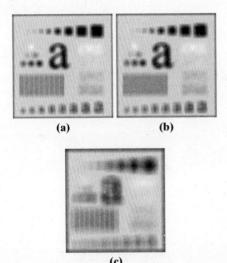

(a)   **(b)**

(c)

However, the bars have merged in image (b), despite the fact that the kernel used to generate this image is much smaller than the kernel that produced image (c). Explain the reason for this.

3.35 Consider an application such as in Fig. 3.41, in which it is desired to eliminate objects smaller than those enclosed by a square of size $q \times q$ pixels. Suppose that we want to reduce the average intensity of those objects to one-tenth of their original average value. In this way, their intensity will be closer to the intensity of the background and they can be eliminated by thresholding. Give the (odd) size of the smallest box kernel that will yield the desired reduction in average intensity in only one pass of the kernel over the image.

3.36 With reference to order-statistic filters (see Section 3.5):

(a)* We mentioned that isolated clusters of dark or light (with respect to the background) pixels whose area is less than one-half the area of a median filter are forced to the median value of the neighbors by the filter. Assume a filter of size $n \times n$ (n odd) and explain why this is so.

(b) Consider an image having various sets of pixel clusters. Assume that all points in a cluster are lighter or darker than the background (but not both simultaneously in the same cluster), and that the area of each cluster is less than or equal to $n^2/2$. In terms of n, under what condition would one or more of these clusters cease to be isolated in the sense described in part (a)?

3.37 Do the following:

(a)* What is median filter? Determine the median of a 7×7 neighborhood.

(b) What is the difference between *max* filter and *min* filter?

3.38 What is the use of applying a Laplacian kernel and a smoothing kernel to an image? In which order these operations should be applied?

3.39* Show that the Laplacian defined in Eq. (3-50) is isotropic (invariant to rotation). Assume continuous quantities. From Table 2.3, coordinate rotation by an angle θ is given by

$$x' = x\cos\theta - y\sin\theta \text{ and } y' = x\sin\theta + y\cos\theta$$

where (x, y) and (x', y') are the unrotated and rotated coordinates, respectively.

3.40* You saw in Fig. 3.46 the Laplacian kernels with a negative and positive center coefficient. What is the difference between the two?

3.41* What is unsharp masking? How is unsharp masking performed?

3.42 Show that subtracting the Laplacian from an image gives a result that is proportional to the unsharp mask in Eq. (3-55). Use the definition for the Laplacian given in Eq. (3-53).

3.43 Do the following:

(a)* Show that the magnitude of the gradient given in Eq. (3-58) is an isotropic operation (see the statement of Problem 3.39).

(b) Show that the isotropic property is lost in general if the gradient is computed using Eq. (3-59).

3.44 Are any of the following highpass (sharpening) kernels separable? For those that are, find vectors **v** and **w** such that $\mathbf{vw}^T$ equals the kernel(s).

(a) The Laplacian kernels in Figs. 3.45(a) and (b).

(b) The Roberts cross-gradient kernels shown in Figs. 3.50(b) and (c).

(c)* The Sobel kernels in Figs. 3.50(d) and (e).

3.45 In a character recognition application, text pages are reduced to binary using a thresholding transformation function of the form in Fig. 3.2(b). This is followed by a procedure that thins the characters until they become strings of binary 1's on a background of 0's. Due to noise, binarization and thinning result in broken strings of characters with gaps ranging from 1 to 3 pixels. One way to "repair" the gaps is to run a smoothing kernel over the binary image to blur it, and thus create bridges of nonzero pixels between gaps.

(a)* Give the (odd) size of the smallest box kernel capable of performing this task.

(b) After bridging the gaps, the image is thresholded to convert it back to binary form. For your answer in (a), what is the minimum value of the threshold required to accomplish this, without causing the segments to break up again?

3.46 A manufacturing company purchased an imaging system whose function is to either smooth or sharpen images. The results of using the system on the manufacturing floor have been poor, and the plant manager suspects that the system is not smoothing and sharpening images the way it should. You are hired as a consultant to determine if the system is performing these functions properly. How would you determine if the system is working correctly? (*Hint:* Study the statements of Problems 3.31 and 3.32).

3.47 A CCD TV camera is used to perform a long-term study by observing the same area 24 hours a day, for 30 days. Digital images are captured and transmitted to a central location every 5 minutes. The illumination of the scene changes from natural daylight to artificial lighting. At no time is the scene without illumination, so it is always possible to obtain an acceptable image. Because the range of illumination is such that it is always in the linear operating range of the camera, it is decided not to employ any compensating mechanisms on the camera itself. Rather, it is decided to use image processing techniques to post-process, and thus normalize, the images to the equivalent of constant illumination. Propose a method to do this. You are at liberty to use any method you wish, but state clearly all the assumptions you made in arriving at your design.

4 Filtering in the Frequency Domain

Filter: A device or material for suppressing or minimizing waves or oscillations of certain frequencies.

Frequency: The number of times that a periodic function repeats the same sequence of values during a unit variation of the independent variable.

Webster's New Collegiate Dictionary

Preview

After a brief historical introduction to the Fourier transform and its importance in image processing, we start from basic principles of function sampling, and proceed step-by-step to derive the one- and two-dimensional discrete Fourier transforms. Together with convolution, the Fourier transform is a staple of frequency-domain processing. During this development, we also touch upon several important aspects of sampling, such as aliasing, whose treatment requires an understanding of the frequency domain and thus are best covered in this chapter. This material is followed by a formulation of filtering in the frequency domain, paralleling the spatial filtering techniques discussed in Chapter 3. We conclude the chapter with a derivation of the equations underlying the fast Fourier transform (FFT), and discuss its computational advantages. These advantages make frequency-domain filtering practical and, in many instances, superior to filtering in the spatial domain.

Upon completion of this chapter, readers should:

- Understand the meaning of frequency domain filtering, and how it differs from filtering in the spatial domain.
- Be familiar with the concepts of sampling, function reconstruction, and aliasing.
- Understand convolution in the frequency domain, and how it is related to filtering.
- Know how to obtain frequency domain filter functions from spatial kernels, and vice versa.
- Be able to construct filter transfer functions directly in the frequency domain.

- Understand why image padding is important.
- Know the steps required to perform filtering in the frequency domain.
- Understand when frequency domain filtering is superior to filtering in the spatial domain.
- Be familiar with other filtering techniques in the frequency domain, such as unsharp masking and homomorphic filtering.
- Understand the origin and mechanics of the fast Fourier transform, and how to use it effectively in image processing.

4.1 BACKGROUND

We begin the discussion with a brief outline of the origins of the Fourier transform and its impact on countless branches of mathematics, science, and engineering.

A BRIEF HISTORY OF THE FOURIER SERIES AND TRANSFORM

The French mathematician Jean Baptiste Joseph Fourier was born in 1768 in the town of Auxerre, about midway between Paris and Dijon. The contribution for which he is most remembered was outlined in a memoir in 1807, and later published in 1822 in his book, *La Théorie Analitique de la Chaleur* (*The Analytic Theory of Heat*). This book was translated into English 55 years later by Freeman (see Freeman [1878]). Basically, Fourier's contribution in this field states that any periodic function can be expressed as the sum of sines and/or cosines of different frequencies, each multiplied by a different coefficient (we now call this sum a *Fourier series*). It does not matter how complicated the function is; if it is periodic and satisfies some mild mathematical conditions, it can be represented by such a sum. This is taken for granted now but, at the time it first appeared, the concept that complicated functions could be represented as a sum of simple sines and cosines was not at all intuitive (see Fig. 4.1). Thus, it is not surprising that Fourier's ideas were met initially with skepticism.

Functions that are not periodic (but whose area under the curve is finite) can be expressed as the integral of sines and/or cosines multiplied by a weighting function. The formulation in this case is the *Fourier transform*, and its utility is even greater than the Fourier series in many theoretical and applied disciplines. Both representations share the important characteristic that a function, expressed in either a Fourier series or transform, can be reconstructed (recovered) completely via an inverse process, with no loss of information. This is one of the most important characteristics of these representations because it allows us to work in the *Fourier domain* (generally called the *frequency domain*) and then return to the original domain of the function without losing any information. Ultimately, it is the utility of the Fourier series and transform in solving practical problems that makes them widely studied and used as fundamental tools.

The initial application of Fourier's ideas was in the field of heat diffusion, where they allowed formulation of differential equations representing heat flow in such a way that solutions could be obtained for the first time. During the past century, and especially in the past 60 years, entire industries and academic disciplines have flourished as a result of Fourier's initial ideas. The advent of digital computers and the "discovery" of a fast Fourier transform (FFT) algorithm in the early 1960s revolutionized the field of signal processing. These two core technologies allowed for the first time practical processing of a host of signals of exceptional importance, ranging from medical monitors and scanners to modern electronic communications.

As you learned in Section 3.4, it takes on the order of $MNmn$ operations (multiplications and additions) to filter an $M \times N$ image with a kernel of size $m \times n$ elements. If the kernel is separable, the number of operations is reduced to $MN(m + n)$. In Section 4.11, you will learn that it takes on the order of $2MN \log_2 MN$ operations to perform the equivalent filtering process in the frequency domain, where the 2 in front arises from the fact that we have to compute a forward and an inverse FFT.

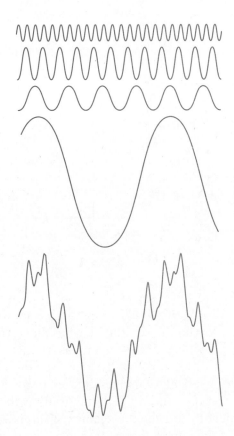

To get an idea of the relative computational advantages of filtering in the frequency versus the spatial domain, consider square images and kernels, of sizes $M \times M$ and $m \times m$, respectively. The *computational advantage* (as a function of kernel size) of filtering one such image with the FFT as opposed to using a nonseparable kernel is defined as

$$
\begin{aligned}
C_n(m) &= \frac{M^2 m^2}{2M^2 \log_2 M^2} \\
&= \frac{m^2}{4 \log_2 M}
\end{aligned}
$$

(4-1)

If the kernel is separable, the advantage becomes

$$
\begin{aligned}
C_s(m) &= \frac{2M^2 m}{2M^2 \log_2 M^2} \\
&= \frac{m}{2 \log_2 M}
\end{aligned}
$$

(4-2)

In either case, when $C(m) > 1$ the advantage (in terms of fewer computations) belongs to the FFT approach; otherwise the advantage favors spatial filtering.

FIGURE 4.2
(a) Computational advantage of the FFT over non-separable spatial kernels.
(b) Advantage over separable kernels. The numbers for $C(m)$ in the inset tables are not to be multiplied by the factors of 10 shown for the curves.

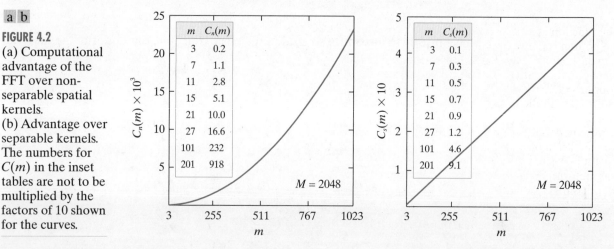

The computational advantages given by Eqs. (4-1) and (4-2) do not take into account the fact that the FFT performs operations between complex numbers, and other secondary (but small in comparison) computations discussed later in the chapter. Thus, comparisons should be interpreted only as guidelines,

Figure 4.2(a) shows a plot of $C_n(m)$ as a function of m for an image of intermediate size ($M = 2048$). The inset table shows a more detailed look for smaller kernel sizes. As you can see, the FFT has the advantage for kernels of sizes 7×7 and larger. The advantage grows rapidly as a function of m, being over 200 for $m = 101$, and close to 1000 for $m = 201$. To give you a feel for the meaning of this advantage, if filtering a bank of images of size 2048×2048 takes 1 minute with the FFT, it would take on the order of 17 hours to filter the same set of images with a nonseparable kernel of size 201×201 elements. This is a significant difference, and is a clear indicator of the importance of frequency-domain processing using the FFT.

In the case of separable kernels, the computational advantage is not as dramatic, but it is still meaningful. The "cross over" point now is around $m = 27$, and when $m = 101$ the difference between frequency- and spatial-domain filtering is still manageable. However, you can see that with $m = 201$ the advantage of using the FFT approaches a factor of 10, which begins to be significant. Note in both graphs that the FFT is an overwhelming favorite for large spatial kernels.

Our focus in the sections that follow is on the Fourier transform and its properties. As we progress through this chapter, it will become evident that Fourier techniques are useful in a broad range of image processing applications. We conclude the chapter with a discussion of the FFT.

ABOUT THE EXAMPLES IN THIS CHAPTER

As in Chapter 3, most of the image filtering examples in this chapter deal with image enhancement. For example, smoothing and sharpening are traditionally associated with image enhancement, as are techniques for contrast manipulation. By its very nature, beginners in digital image processing find enhancement to be interesting and relatively simple to understand. Therefore, using examples from image enhancement in this chapter not only saves having an extra chapter in the book but, more importantly, is an effective tool for introducing newcomers to filtering techniques in the frequency domain. We will use frequency domain processing methods for other applications in Chapters 5, 7, 8, 10, and 11.

4.2 PRELIMINARY CONCEPTS

We pause briefly to introduce several of the basic concepts that underlie the material in later sections.

COMPLEX NUMBERS

A complex number, C, is defined as

$$C = R + jI \tag{4-3}$$

where R and I are real numbers and $j = \sqrt{-1}$. Here, R denotes the *real part* of the complex number and I its *imaginary part*. Real numbers are a subset of complex numbers in which $I = 0$. The *conjugate* of a complex number C, denoted C^*, is defined as

$$C^* = R - jI \tag{4-4}$$

Complex numbers can be viewed geometrically as points on a plane (called the *complex plane*) whose abscissa is the *real axis* (values of R) and whose ordinate is the *imaginary axis* (values of I). That is, the complex number $R + jI$ is point (R, I) in the coordinate system of the complex plane.

Sometimes it is useful to represent complex numbers in polar coordinates,

$$C = |C|(\cos\theta + j\sin\theta) \tag{4-5}$$

where $|C| = \sqrt{R^2 + I^2}$ is the length of the vector extending from the origin of the complex plane to point (R, I), and θ is the angle between the vector and the real axis. Drawing a diagram of the real and complex axes with the vector in the first quadrant will show that $\tan\theta = (I/R)$ or $\theta = \arctan(I/R)$. The arctan function returns angles in the range $[-\pi/2, \pi/2]$. But, because I and R can be positive and negative independently, we need to be able to obtain angles in the full range $[-\pi, \pi]$. We do this by keeping track of the sign of I and R when computing θ. Many programming languages do this automatically via so called *four-quadrant arctangent functions*. For example, MATLAB provides the function **atan2(Imag, Real)** for this purpose.

Using *Euler's formula*,

$$\boxed{e^{j\theta} = \cos\theta + j\sin\theta} \tag{4-6}$$

where $e = 2.71828...$, gives the following familiar representation of complex numbers in polar coordinates,

$$C = |C|e^{j\theta} \tag{4-7}$$

where $|C|$ and θ are as defined above. For example, the polar representation of the complex number $1 + j2$ is $\sqrt{5}e^{j\theta}$, where $\theta = 63.4°$ or 1.1 radians. The preceding equations are applicable also to complex functions. A complex function, $F(u)$, of a real variable u, can be expressed as the sum $F(u) = R(u) + jI(u)$, where $R(u)$ and $I(u)$ are the real and imaginary component functions of $F(u)$. As previously noted, the complex conjugate is $F^*(u) = R(u) - jI(u)$, the magnitude is $|F(u)| = [R(u)^2 + I(u)^2]^{1/2}$, and the angle is $\theta(u) = \arctan[I(u)/R(u)]$. We will return to complex functions several times in the course of this and the next chapter.

FOURIER SERIES

As indicated in the previous section, a function $f(t)$ of a continuous variable, t, that is periodic with a period, T, can be expressed as the sum of sines and cosines multiplied by appropriate coefficients. This sum, known as a *Fourier series*, has the form

$$f(t) = \sum_{n=-\infty}^{\infty} c_n e^{j\frac{2\pi n}{T}t} \tag{4-8}$$

where

$$c_n = \frac{1}{T}\int_{-T/2}^{T/2} f(t)e^{-j\frac{2\pi n}{T}t}\,dt \qquad \text{for } n = 0, \pm 1, \pm 2,\ldots \tag{4-9}$$

are the coefficients. The fact that Eq. (4-8) is an expansion of sines and cosines follows from Euler's formula, Eq. (4-6).

IMPULSES AND THEIR SIFTING PROPERTIES

Central to the study of linear systems and the Fourier transform is the concept of an impulse and its sifting property. A *unit impulse* of a continuous variable t, located at $t = 0$, and denoted $\delta(t)$, is defined as

An impulse is not a function in the usual sense. A more accurate name is a *distribution* or *generalized function*. However, one often finds in the literature the names *impulse function*, *delta function*, and *Dirac delta function*, despite the misnomer.

$$\delta(t) = \begin{cases} \infty & \text{if } t = 0 \\ 0 & \text{if } t \neq 0 \end{cases} \tag{4-10}$$

and is constrained to satisfy the identity

$$\int_{-\infty}^{\infty} \delta(t)\,dt = 1 \tag{4-11}$$

Physically, if we interpret t as time, an impulse may be viewed as a spike of infinity amplitude and zero duration, having unit area. An impulse has the so-called *sifting property* with respect to integration,

To *sift* means literally to separate, or to separate out, by putting something through a sieve.

$$\int_{-\infty}^{\infty} f(t)\delta(t)\,dt = f(0) \tag{4-12}$$

provided that $f(t)$ is continuous at $t = 0$, a condition typically satisfied in practice. Sifting simply yields the *value* of the function $f(t)$ at the *location* of the impulse (i.e., at $t = 0$ in the previous equation). A more general statement of the sifting property involves an impulse located at an arbitrary point, t_0, denoted as, $\delta(t - t_0)$. In this case,

$$\int_{-\infty}^{\infty} f(t)\delta(t - t_0)\,dt = f(t_0) \tag{4-13}$$

which simply gives the value of the function at the location of the im
example, if $f(t) = \cos(t)$, using the impulse $\delta(t - \pi)$ in Eq. (4-13) yields the result
$f(\pi) = \cos(\pi) = -1$. The power of the sifting concept will become evident shortly.

Of particular interest later in this section is an *impulse train*, $s_{\Delta T}(t)$, defined as the sum of infinitely many impulses ΔT units apart:

$$s_{\Delta T}(t) = \sum_{k=-\infty}^{\infty} \delta(t - k\Delta T) \qquad (4\text{-}14)$$

Figure 4.3(a) shows a single impulse located at $t = t_0$, and Fig. 4.3(b) shows an impulse train. Impulses for continuous variables are denoted by up-pointing arrows to simulate infinite height and zero width. For discrete variables the height is finite, as we will show next.

Let x represent a *discrete* variable. As you learned in Chapter 3, the unit discrete impulse, $\delta(x)$, serves the same purposes in the context of discrete systems as the impulse $\delta(t)$ does when working with continuous variables. It is defined as

$$\delta(x) = \begin{cases} 1 & \text{if } x = 0 \\ 0 & \text{if } x \neq 0 \end{cases} \qquad (4\text{-}15)$$

Clearly, this definition satisfies the discrete equivalent of Eq. (4-11):

$$\sum_{x=-\infty}^{\infty} \delta(x) = 1 \qquad (4\text{-}16)$$

The sifting property for discrete variables has the form

$$\sum_{x=-\infty}^{\infty} f(x)\delta(x) = f(0) \qquad (4\text{-}17)$$

FIGURE 4.3
(a) Continuous impulse located at $t = t_0$. (b) An impulse train consisting of continuous impulses. (c) Unit discrete impulse located at $x = x_0$. (d) An impulse train consisting of discrete unit impulses.

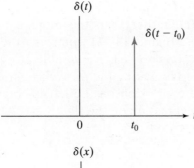
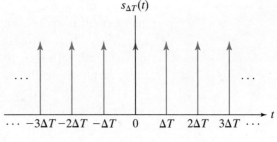
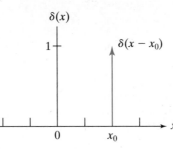
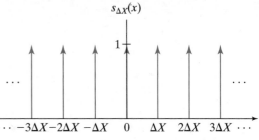

or, more generally using a discrete impulse located at $x = x_0$ (see Eq. 3-33),

$$\sum_{x=-\infty}^{\infty} f(x)\delta(x - x_0) = f(x_0) \tag{4-18}$$

As before, we see that the sifting property yields the value of the function at the location of the impulse. Figure 4.3(c) shows the unit discrete impulse diagrammatically, and Fig. 4.3(d) shows a train of discrete unit impulses, Unlike its continuous counterpart, the discrete impulse is an ordinary function.

THE FOURIER TRANSFORM OF FUNCTIONS OF ONE CONTINUOUS VARIABLE

The *Fourier transform* of a continuous function $f(t)$ of a continuous variable, t, denoted $\Im\{f(t)\}$, is defined by the equation

$$\Im\{f(t)\} = \int_{-\infty}^{\infty} f(t)e^{-j2\pi\mu t}\,dt \tag{4-19}$$

where μ is a continuous variable also.[†] Because t is integrated out, $\Im\{f(t)\}$ is a function only of μ. That is $\Im\{f(t)\} = F(\mu)$; therefore, we write the Fourier transform of $f(t)$ as

$$F(\mu) = \int_{-\infty}^{\infty} f(t)e^{-j2\pi\mu t}\,dt \tag{4-20}$$

Conversely, given $F(\mu)$, we can obtain $f(t)$ back using the *inverse Fourier transform*, written as

Equation (4-21) indicates the important fact mentioned in Section 4.1 that a function can be recovered from its transform.

$$f(t) = \int_{-\infty}^{\infty} F(\mu)e^{j2\pi\mu t}\,d\mu \tag{4-21}$$

where we made use of the fact that variable μ is integrated out in the inverse transform and wrote simply $f(t)$, rather than the more cumbersome notation $f(t) = \Im^{-1}\{F(\mu)\}$. Equations (4-20) and (4-21) comprise the so-called *Fourier transform pair*, often denoted as $f(t) \Leftrightarrow F(\mu)$. The double arrow indicates that the expression on the right is obtained by taking the *forward* Fourier transform of the expression on the left, while the expression on the left is obtained by taking the *inverse* Fourier transform of the expression on the right.

Using Euler's formula, we can write Eq. (4-20) as

Because t is integrated out in this equation, the only variable left is μ, which is the frequency of the sine and cosine terms.

$$F(\mu) = \int_{-\infty}^{\infty} f(t)\big[\cos(2\pi\mu t) - j\sin(2\pi\mu t)\big]\,dt \tag{4-22}$$

[†]Conditions for the existence of the Fourier transform are complicated to state in general (Champeney [1987]), but a sufficient condition for its existence is that the integral of the absolute value of $f(t)$, or the integral of the square of $f(t)$, be finite. Existence is seldom an issue in practice, except for idealized signals, such as sinusoids that extend forever. These are handled using generalized impulses. Our primary interest is in the discrete Fourier transform pair which, as you will see shortly, is guaranteed to exist for all finite functions.

If $f(t)$ is real, we see that its transform in general is complex. Note that the Fourier transform is an expansion of $f(t)$ multiplied by sinusoidal terms whose frequencies are determined by the values of μ. Thus, because the only variable left after integration is frequency, we say that the domain of the Fourier transform is the *frequency domain*. We will discuss the frequency domain and its properties in more detail later in this chapter. In our discussion, t can represent any continuous variable, and the units of the frequency variable μ depend on the units of t. For example, if t represents time in seconds, the units of μ are cycles/sec or Hertz (Hz). If t represents distance in meters, then the units of μ are cycles/meter, and so on. In other words, the units of the frequency domain are cycles per unit of the independent variable of the input function.

EXAMPLE 4.1: Obtaining the Fourier transform of a simple continuous function.

The Fourier transform of the function in Fig. 4.4(a) follows from Eq. (4-20):

$$F(\mu) = \int_{-\infty}^{\infty} f(t)e^{-j2\pi\mu t}dt = \int_{-W/2}^{W/2} Ae^{-j2\pi\mu t}dt$$

$$= \frac{-A}{j2\pi\mu}\left[e^{-j2\pi\mu t}\right]_{-W/2}^{W/2} = \frac{-A}{j2\pi\mu}\left[e^{-j\pi\mu W} - e^{j\pi\mu W}\right]$$

$$= \frac{A}{j2\pi\mu}\left[e^{j\pi\mu W} - e^{-j\pi\mu W}\right]$$

$$= AW\frac{\sin(\pi\mu W)}{(\pi\mu W)}$$

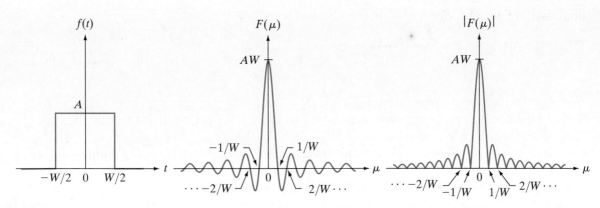

a b c

FIGURE 4.4 (a) A box function, (b) its Fourier transform, and (c) its spectrum. All functions extend to infinity in both directions. Note the inverse relationship between the width, W, of the function and the zeros of the transform.

where we used the trigonometric identity $\sin\theta = (e^{j\theta} - e^{-j\theta})/2j$. In this case, the complex terms of the Fourier transform combined nicely into a real sine function. The result in the last step of the preceding expression is known as the *sinc* function, which has the general form

$$\text{sinc}(m) = \frac{\sin(\pi m)}{(\pi m)} \tag{4-23}$$

where $\text{sinc}(0) = 1$ and $\text{sinc}(m) = 0$ for all other *integer* values of m. Figure 4.4(b) shows a plot of $F(\mu)$.

In general, the Fourier transform contains complex terms, and it is customary for display purposes to work with the magnitude of the transform (a real quantity), which is called the *Fourier spectrum* or the *frequency spectrum*:

$$|F(\mu)| = AW\left|\frac{\sin(\pi\mu W)}{(\pi\mu W)}\right|$$

Figure 4.4(c) shows a plot of $|F(\mu)|$ as a function of frequency. The key properties to note are (1) that the locations of the zeros of both $F(\mu)$ and $|F(\mu)|$ are inversely proportional to the width, W, of the "box" function; (2) that the height of the lobes decreases as a function of distance from the origin; and (3) that the function extends to infinity for both positive and negative values of μ. As you will see later, these properties are quite helpful in interpreting the spectra of two dimensional Fourier transforms of images.

EXAMPLE 4.2: Fourier transform of an impulse and an impulse train.

The Fourier transform of a unit impulse located at the origin follows from Eq. (4-20):

$$\Im\{\delta(t)\} = F(\mu) = \int_{-\infty}^{\infty} \delta(t)e^{-j2\pi\mu t}dt = \int_{-\infty}^{\infty} e^{-j2\pi\mu t}\delta(t)dt = e^{-j2\pi\mu}$$

where we used the sifting property from Eq. (4-12). Thus, we see that the Fourier transform of an impulse located at the origin of the spatial domain is a constant in the frequency domain (we discussed this briefly in Section 3.4 in connection with Fig. 3.30).

Similarly, the Fourier transform of an impulse located at $t = t_0$ is

$$\Im\{\delta(t - t_0)\} = F(\mu) = \int_{-\infty}^{\infty} \delta(t - t_0)e^{-j2\pi\mu t}dt = \int_{-\infty}^{\infty} e^{-j2\pi\mu t}\delta(t - t_0)dt = e^{-j2\pi\mu t_0}$$

where we used the sifting property from Eq. (4-13). The term $e^{-j2\pi\mu t_0}$ represents a unit circle centered on the origin of the complex plane, as you can easily see by using Euler's formula to expand the exponential into its sine and cosine components.

In Section 4.3, we will use the Fourier transform of a periodic impulse train. Obtaining this transform is not as straightforward as we just showed for individual impulses. However, understanding how to derive the transform of an impulse train is important, so we take the time to derive it here. We start by noting that the only basic difference in the form of Eqs. (4-20) and (4-21) is the sign of the exponential. Thus, if a function $f(t)$ has the Fourier transform $F(\mu)$, then evaluating this function at t, $F(t)$, must have the transform $f(-\mu)$. Using this *symmetry* property and given, as we showed above, that the Fourier transform of an impulse $\delta(t - t_0)$ is $e^{-j2\pi\mu t_0}$, it follows that the function $e^{-j2\pi\mu t_0}$ has the transform

$\delta(-\mu - t_0)$. By letting $-t_0 = a$, it follows that the transform of $e^{j2\pi at}$ is $\delta(-\mu + a) = \delta(\mu - a)$, where the last step is true because δ is zero unless $\mu = a$, which is the same condition for either $\delta(-\mu + a)$ or $\delta(\mu - a)$.

The impulse train $s_{\Delta T}(t)$ in Eq. (4-14) is periodic with period ΔT, so it can be expressed as a Fourier series:

$$s_{\Delta T}(t) = \sum_{n=-\infty}^{\infty} c_n e^{j\frac{2\pi n}{\Delta T}t}$$

where

$$c_n = \frac{1}{\Delta T} \int_{-\Delta T/2}^{\Delta T/2} s_{\Delta T}(t) e^{-j\frac{2\pi n}{\Delta T}t} dt$$

With reference to Fig. 4.3(b), we see that the integral in the interval $[-\Delta T/2, \Delta T/2]$ encompasses only the impulse located at the origin. Therefore, the preceding equation becomes

$$c_n = \frac{1}{\Delta T} \int_{-\Delta T/2}^{\Delta T/2} \delta(t) e^{-j\frac{2\pi n}{\Delta T}t} dt = \frac{1}{\Delta T} e^0 = \frac{1}{\Delta T}$$

where we used the sifting property of $\delta(t)$. The Fourier series then becomes

$$s_{\Delta T}(t) = \frac{1}{\Delta T} \sum_{n=-\infty}^{\infty} e^{j\frac{2\pi n}{\Delta T}t}$$

Our objective is to obtain the Fourier transform of this expression. Because summation is a linear process, obtaining the Fourier transform of a sum is the same as obtaining the sum of the transforms of the individual components of the sum. These components are exponentials, and we established earlier in this example that

$$\Im\left\{e^{j\frac{2\pi n}{\Delta T}t}\right\} = \delta\left(\mu - \frac{n}{\Delta T}\right)$$

So, $S(\mu)$, the Fourier transform of the periodic impulse train, is

$$S(\mu) = \Im\{s_{\Delta T}(t)\} = \Im\left\{\frac{1}{\Delta T}\sum_{n=-\infty}^{\infty} e^{j\frac{2\pi n}{\Delta T}t}\right\} = \frac{1}{\Delta T}\Im\left\{\sum_{n=-\infty}^{\infty} e^{j\frac{2\pi n}{\Delta T}t}\right\} = \frac{1}{\Delta T}\sum_{n=-\infty}^{\infty} \delta\left(\mu - \frac{n}{\Delta T}\right)$$

This fundamental result tells us that the Fourier transform of an impulse train with period ΔT is also an impulse train, whose period is $1/\Delta T$. This *inverse proportionality* between the periods of $s_{\Delta T}(t)$ and $S(\mu)$ is analogous to what we found in Fig. 4.4 in connection with a box function and its transform. This inverse relationship plays a fundamental role in the remainder of this chapter.

CONVOLUTION

As in Section 3.4, the fact that convolution of a function with an impulse shifts the origin of the function to the location of the impulse is also true for continuous convolution. (See Figs. 3.29 and 3.30.)

We showed in Section 3.4 that convolution of two functions involves flipping (rotating by 180°) one function about its origin and sliding it past the other. At each displacement in the sliding process, we perform a computation, which, for discrete variables, is a sum of products [see Eq. (3-35)]. In the present discussion, we are interested in the convolution of two *continuous* functions, $f(t)$ and $h(t)$, of one continuous variable, t, so we have to use integration instead of a summation. The convolution of these two functions, denoted as before by the operator ★, is defined as

$$(f \star h)(t) = \int_{-\infty}^{\infty} f(\tau)h(t-\tau)d\tau \qquad (4\text{-}24)$$

where the minus sign accounts for the flipping just mentioned, t is the *displacement* needed to slide one function past the other, and τ is a dummy variable that is integrated out. We assume for now that the functions extend from $-\infty$ to ∞.

We illustrated the basic mechanics of convolution in Section 3.4, and we will do so again later in this chapter and in Chapter 5. At the moment, we are interested in finding the Fourier transform of Eq. (4-24). We start with Eq. (4-19):

$$\Im\{(f \star h)(t)\} = \int_{-\infty}^{\infty} \left[\int_{-\infty}^{\infty} f(\tau)h(t-\tau)d\tau \right] e^{-j2\pi\mu t} dt$$

$$= \int_{-\infty}^{\infty} f(\tau) \left[\int_{-\infty}^{\infty} h(t-\tau) e^{-j2\pi\mu t} dt \right] d\tau$$

The term inside the brackets is the Fourier transform of $h(t-\tau)$. We will show later in this chapter that $\Im\{h(t-\tau)\} = H(\mu)e^{-j2\pi\mu\tau}$, where $H(\mu)$ is the Fourier transform of $h(t)$. Using this in the preceding equation gives us

$$\Im\{(f \star h)(t)\} = \int_{-\infty}^{\infty} f(\tau) \left[H(\mu)e^{-j2\pi\mu\tau} \right] d\tau$$

$$= H(\mu) \int_{-\infty}^{\infty} f(\tau)e^{-j2\pi\mu\tau} d\tau$$

$$= H(\mu)F(\mu)$$

$$= (H \cdot F)(\mu)$$

Remember, convolution is commutative, so the order of the functions in convolution expressions does not matter.

where "·" indicates multiplication. As noted earlier, if we refer to the domain of t as the spatial domain, and the domain of μ as the frequency domain, the preceding equation tells us that the Fourier transform of the convolution of two functions in the spatial domain is equal to the product in the frequency domain of the Fourier transforms of the two functions. Conversely, if we have the product of the two transforms, we can obtain the convolution in the spatial domain by computing the inverse Fourier transform. In other words, $f \star h$ and $H \cdot F$ are a Fourier transform *pair*. This result is one-half of the *convolution theorem* and is written as

$$(f \star h)(t) \Leftrightarrow (H \cdot F)(\mu) \qquad (4\text{-}25)$$

As noted earlier, the double arrow indicates that the expression on the right is obtained by taking the *forward* Fourier transform of the expression on the left, while the expression on the left is obtained by taking the *inverse* Fourier transform of the expression on the right.

Following a similar development would result in the other half of the convolution theorem:

$$(f \cdot h)(t) \Leftrightarrow (H \star F)(\mu) \tag{4-26}$$

These two expressions also hold for discrete variables, with the exception that the right side of Eq. (4-26) is multiplied by (1/*M*), where *M* is the number of discrete samples (see Problem 4.18).

which states that convolution in the frequency domain is analogous to multiplication in the spatial domain, the two being related by the forward and inverse Fourier transforms, respectively. As you will see later in this chapter, the convolution theorem is the foundation for filtering in the frequency domain.

4.3 SAMPLING AND THE FOURIER TRANSFORM OF SAMPLED FUNCTIONS

In this section, we use the concepts from Section 4.2 to formulate a basis for expressing sampling mathematically. Starting from basic principles, this will lead us to the Fourier transform of sampled functions. That is, the discrete Fourier transform.

SAMPLING

Continuous functions have to be converted into a sequence of discrete values before they can be processed in a computer. This requires sampling and quantization, as introduced in Section 2.4. In the following discussion, we examine sampling in more detail.

Consider a continuous function, $f(t)$, that we wish to sample at uniform intervals, ΔT, of the independent variable t (see Fig. 4.5). We assume initially that the function extends from $-\infty$ to ∞ with respect to t. One way to model sampling is to multiply $f(t)$ by a sampling function equal to a train of impulses ΔT units apart. That is,

Taking samples ΔT units apart implies a *sampling rate* equal to $1/\Delta T$. If the units of ΔT are seconds, then the sampling rate is in samples/s. If the units of ΔT are meters, then the sampling rate is in samples/m, and so on.

$$\tilde{f}(t) = f(t)s_{\Delta T}(t) = \sum_{n=-\infty}^{\infty} f(t)\delta(t - n\Delta T) \tag{4-27}$$

where $\tilde{f}(t)$ denotes the sampled function. Each component of this summation is an impulse weighted by the value of $f(t)$ at the location of the impulse, as Fig. 4.5(c) shows. The *value* of each sample is given by the "strength" of the weighted impulse, which we obtain by integration. That is, the value, f_k, of an arbitrary sample in the sampled sequence is given by

$$\begin{aligned} f_k &= \int_{-\infty}^{\infty} f(t)\delta(t - k\Delta T)\,dt \\ &= f(k\Delta T) \end{aligned} \tag{4-28}$$

where we used the sifting property of δ in Eq. (4-13). Equation (4-28) holds for any integer value $k = \ldots, -2, -1, 0, 1, 2, \ldots$. Figure 4.5(d) shows the result, which consists of equally spaced samples of the original function.

a
b
c
d

FIGURE 4.5
(a) A continuous function. (b) Train of impulses used to model sampling. (c) Sampled function formed as the product of (a) and (b). (d) Sample values obtained by integration and using the sifting property of impulses. (The dashed line in (c) is shown for reference. It is not part of the data.)

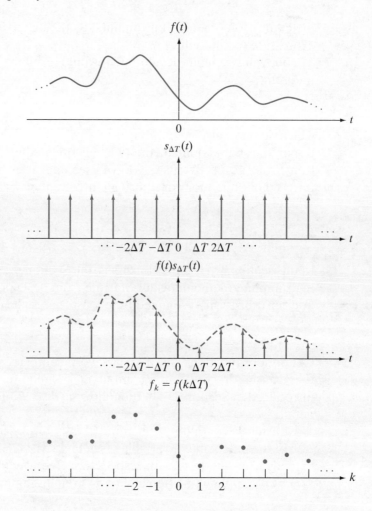

THE FOURIER TRANSFORM OF SAMPLED FUNCTIONS

Let $F(\mu)$ denote the Fourier transform of a continuous function $f(t)$. As discussed in the previous section, the corresponding sampled function, $\tilde{f}(t)$, is the product of $f(t)$ and an impulse train. We know from the convolution theorem that the Fourier transform of the product of two functions in the spatial domain is the convolution of the transforms of the two functions in the frequency domain. Thus, the Fourier transform of the sampled function is:

$$\tilde{F}(\mu) = \Im\{\tilde{f}(t)\} = \Im\{f(t)s_{\Delta T}(t)\}$$
$$= (F \star S)(\mu)$$

(4-29)

where, from Example 4.2,

$$S(\mu) = \frac{1}{\Delta T} \sum_{n=-\infty}^{\infty} \delta\left(\mu - \frac{n}{\Delta T}\right)$$

(4-30)

is the Fourier transform of the impulse train $s_{\Delta T}(t)$. We obtain the convolution of $F(\mu)$ and $S(\mu)$ directly from the 1-D definition of convolution in Eq. (4-24):

$$\tilde{F}(\mu) = (F \star S)(\mu) = \int_{-\infty}^{\infty} F(\tau) S(\mu - \tau) d\tau$$

$$= \frac{1}{\Delta T} \int_{-\infty}^{\infty} F(\tau) \sum_{n=-\infty}^{\infty} \delta\left(\mu - \tau - \frac{n}{\Delta T}\right) d\tau$$

$$= \frac{1}{\Delta T} \sum_{n=-\infty}^{\infty} \int_{-\infty}^{\infty} F(\tau) \delta\left(\mu - \tau - \frac{n}{\Delta T}\right) d\tau \tag{4-31}$$

$$= \frac{1}{\Delta T} \sum_{n=-\infty}^{\infty} F\left(\mu - \frac{n}{\Delta T}\right)$$

where the final step follows from the sifting property of the impulse, Eq. (4-13).

The summation in the last line of Eq. (4-31) shows that the Fourier transform $\tilde{F}(\mu)$ of the sampled function $\tilde{f}(t)$ is an *infinite*, *periodic* sequence of *copies* of the transform of the original, continuous function. The separation between copies is determined by the value of $1/\Delta T$. Observe that although $\tilde{f}(t)$ is a sampled function, its transform, $\tilde{F}(\mu)$, is *continuous* because it consists of copies of $F(\mu)$, which is a continuous function.

Figure 4.6 is a graphical summary of the preceding results.[†] Figure 4.6(a) is a sketch of the Fourier transform, $F(\mu)$, of a function $f(t)$, and Fig. 4.6(b) shows the transform, $\tilde{F}(\mu)$, of the sampled function, $\tilde{f}(t)$. As mentioned in the previous section, the quantity $1/\Delta T$ is the *sampling rate* used to generate the sampled function. So, in Fig. 4.6(b) the sampling rate was high enough to provide sufficient separation between the periods, and thus preserve the integrity (i.e., perfect copies) of $F(\mu)$. In Fig. 4.6(c), the sampling rate was just enough to preserve $F(\mu)$, but in Fig. 4.6(d), the sampling rate was below the minimum required to maintain distinct copies of $F(\mu)$, and thus failed to preserve the original transform. Figure 4.6(b) is the result of an *over-sampled* signal, while Figs. 4.6(c) and (d) are the results of *critically sampling* and *under-sampling* the signal, respectively. These concepts are the basis that will help you grasp the fundamentals of the sampling theorem, which we discuss next.

THE SAMPLING THEOREM

We introduced the idea of sampling intuitively in Section 2.4. Now we consider sampling formally, and establish the conditions under which a continuous function can be recovered uniquely from a set of its samples.

A function $f(t)$ whose Fourier transform is zero for values of frequencies outside a finite interval (band) $[-\mu_{max}, \mu_{max}]$ about the origin is called a *band-limited* function. Figure 4.7(a), which is a magnified section of Fig. 4.6(a), is such a function. Similarly, Fig. 4.7(b) is a more detailed view of the transform of the critically sampled

---

[†]For the sake of clarity in sketches of Fourier transforms in Fig. 4.6, and other similar figures in this chapter, we ignore the fact that Fourier transforms typically are complex functions. Our interest here is on concepts.

a
b
c
d

FIGURE 4.6
(a) Illustrative
sketch of the
Fourier transform
of a band-limited
function.
(b)–(d) Trans-
forms of the
corresponding
sampled functions
under the
conditions of
over-sampling,
critically
sampling, and
under-sampling,
respectively.

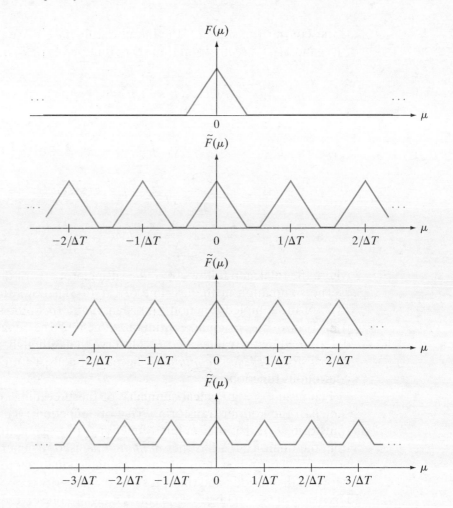

function [see Fig. 4.6(c)]. A higher value of ΔT would cause the periods in $\tilde{F}(\mu)$ to merge; a lower value would provide a clean separation between the periods.

We can recover $f(t)$ from its samples if we can isolate a single copy of $F(\mu)$ from the periodic sequence of copies of this function contained in $\tilde{F}(\mu)$, the transform of the sampled function $\tilde{f}(t)$. Recall from the discussion in the previous section that $\tilde{F}(\mu)$ is a *continuous*, *periodic* function with period $1/\Delta T$. Therefore, all we need is one complete period to characterize the entire transform. In other words, we can recover $f(t)$ from that single period by taking its inverse Fourier transform.

Extracting from $\tilde{F}(\mu)$ a single period that is equal to $F(\mu)$ is possible if the separation between copies is sufficient (see Fig. 4.6). In terms of Fig. 4.7(b), sufficient separation is guaranteed if $1/2\Delta T > \mu_{\max}$ or

$$\frac{1}{\Delta T} > 2\mu_{\max} \tag{4-32}$$

Remember, the sampling
rate is the number of
samples taken per unit of
the independent variable.

This equation indicates that a continuous, band-limited function can be recovered completely from a set of its samples if the samples are acquired at a rate exceeding

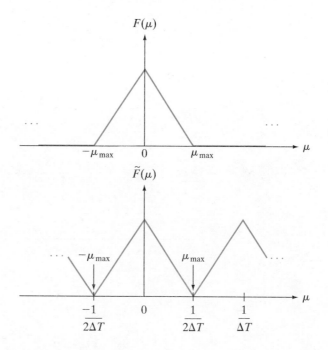

a
b

FIGURE 4.7
(a) Illustrative sketch of the Fourier transform of a band-limited function.
(b) Transform resulting from critically sampling that band-limited function.

twice the highest frequency content of the function. This exceptionally important result is known as the *sampling theorem*.[†] We can say based on this result that no information is lost if a continuous, band-limited function is represented by samples acquired at a rate greater than twice the highest frequency content of the function. Conversely, we can say that the *maximum* frequency that can be "captured" by sampling a signal at a rate $1/\Delta T$ is $\mu_{max} = 1/2\Delta T$. A sampling rate *exactly* equal to twice the highest frequency is called the *Nyquist rate*. Sampling at exactly the Nyquist rate sometimes is sufficient for perfect function recovery, but there are cases in which this leads to difficulties, as we will illustrate later in Example 4.3. This is the reason why the sampling theorem specifies that sampling must exceed the Nyquist rate.

Figure 4.8 illustrates the procedure for recovering $F(\mu)$ from $\tilde{F}(\mu)$ when a function is sampled at a rate higher than the Nyquist rate. The function in Fig. 4.8(b) is defined by the equation

The ΔT in Eq. (4-33) cancels out the $1/\Delta T$ in Eq. (4-31).

$$H(\mu) = \begin{cases} \Delta T & -\mu_{max} \le \mu \le \mu_{max} \\ 0 & \text{otherwise} \end{cases} \tag{4-33}$$

When multiplied by the periodic sequence in Fig. 4.8(a), this function isolates the period centered on the origin. Then, as Fig. 4.8(c) shows, we obtain $F(\mu)$ by multiplying $\tilde{F}(\mu)$ by $H(\mu)$:

[†]The sampling theorem is a cornerstone of digital signal processing theory. It was first formulated in 1928 by Harry Nyquist, a Bell Laboratories scientist and engineer. Claude E. Shannon, also from Bell Labs, proved the theorem formally in 1949. The renewed interest in the sampling theorem in the late 1940s was motivated by the emergence of early digital computing systems and modern communications, which created a need for methods dealing with digital (sampled) data.

a
b
c

FIGURE 4.8
(a) Fourier transform of a sampled, band-limited function.
(b) Ideal lowpass filter transfer function.
(c) The product of (b) and (a), used to extract one period of the infinitely periodic sequence in (a).

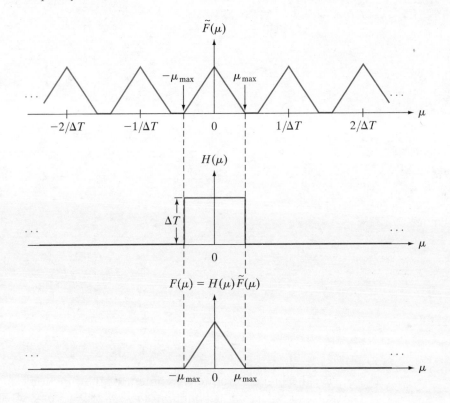

$$F(\mu) = H(\mu)\tilde{F}(\mu) \tag{4-34}$$

Once we have $F(\mu)$, we can recover $f(t)$ using the inverse Fourier transform:

$$f(t) = \int_{-\infty}^{\infty} F(\mu)e^{j2\pi\mu t}d\mu \tag{4-35}$$

Equations (4-33) through (4-35) prove that, theoretically, it is possible to recover a band-limited function from samples obtained at a rate exceeding twice the highest frequency content of the function. As we will discuss in the following section, the requirement that $f(t)$ must be band-limited implies in general that $f(t)$ must extend from $-\infty$ to ∞, a condition that cannot be met in practice. As you will see shortly, having to limit the duration of a function prevents perfect recovery of the function from its samples, except in some special cases.

In Fig. 3.32 we sketched the radial cross sections of filter transfer functions using only positive frequencies, for simplicity. Now you can see that frequency domain filter functions encompass both positive and negative frequencies.

Function $H(\mu)$ is called a *lowpass filter* because it passes frequencies in the low end of the frequency range, but it eliminates (filters out) higher frequencies. It is called also an *ideal lowpass filter* because of its instantaneous transitions in amplitude (between 0 and ΔT at location $-\mu_{\max}$ and the reverse at $\mu_{\max}$), a characteristic that cannot be implemented physically in hardware. We can simulate ideal filters in software, but even then there are limitations (see Section 4.8). Because they are instrumental in recovering (reconstructing) the original function from its samples, filters used for the purpose just discussed are also called *reconstruction filters*.

ALIASING

Literally, the word *alias* means "a false identity." In the field of signal processing, aliasing refers to sampling phenomena that cause different signals to become indistinguishable from one another after sampling; or, viewed another way, for one signal to "masquerade" as another.

Conceptually, the relationship between sampling and aliasing is not difficult to grasp. The foundation of aliasing phenomena as it relates to sampling is that we can describe a digitized function *only* by the values of its samples. This means that it is possible for two (or more) totally *different* continuous functions to coincide at the values of their respective samples, but we would have no way of knowing the characteristics of the functions between those samples. To illustrate, Fig. 4.9 shows two completely different sine functions sampled at the same rate. As you can see in Figs. 4.9(a) and (c), there are numerous places where the sampled values are the same in the two functions, resulting in identical sampled functions, as Figs. 4.9(b) and (d) show.

Two continuous functions having the characteristics just described are called an *aliased pair*, and such pairs are indistinguishable after sampling. Note that the reason these functions are aliased is because we used a sampling rate that is too coarse. That is, the functions were *under-sampled*. It is intuitively obvious that if sampling were refined, more and more of the differences between the two continuous functions would be revealed in the sampled signals. The principal objective of the following discussion is to answer the question: What is the minimum sampling rate required to avoid (or reduce) aliasing? This question has both a theoretical and a practical answer and, in the process of arriving at the answers, we will establish the conditions under which aliasing occurs.

We can use the tools developed earlier in this section to formally answer the question we just posed. All we have to do is ask it in a different form: What happens

Although we show sinusoidal functions for simplicity, aliasing occurs between any arbitrary signals whose values are the same at the sample points.

a b
c d

FIGURE 4.9
The functions in (a) and (c) are totally different, but their digitized versions in (b) and (d) are identical. Aliasing occurs when the samples of two or more functions coincide, but the functions are different elsewhere.

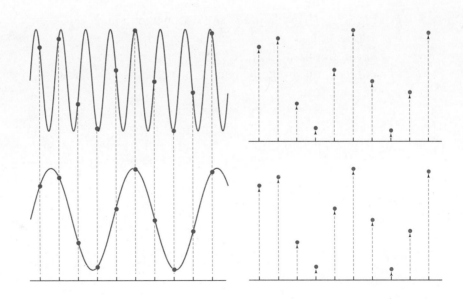

if a band-limited function is sampled at less than the Nyquist rate (i.e., at less than twice its highest frequency)? This is precisely the under-sampled situation discussed earlier in this section and mentioned in the previous paragraph.

Figure 4.10(a) is the same as Fig. 4.6(d); it shows schematically the Fourier transform of an under-sampled, band-limited function. This figure illustrates that the net effect of lowering the sampling rate below the Nyquist rate is that the periods of the Fourier transform now overlap, and it becomes impossible to isolate a single period of the transform, regardless of the filter used. For instance, using the ideal lowpass filter in Fig. 4.10(b) would result in a transform that is corrupted by frequencies from adjacent periods, as Fig. 4.10(c) shows. The inverse transform would then yield a function, $f_a(t)$, different from the original. That is, $f_a(t)$ would be an aliased function because it would contain frequency components not present in the original. Using our earlier terminology, $f_a(t)$ would masquerade as a different function. It is possible for aliased functions to bear no resemblance whatsoever to the functions from which they originated.

If we cannot isolate one period of the transform, we cannot recover the signal without aliasing,

Unfortunately, except in some special cases mentioned below, aliasing is always present in sampled signals. This is because, even if the original sampled function is band-limited, infinite frequency components are introduced the moment we limit the duration of the function, which we always have to do in practice. As an illustration, suppose that we want to limit the duration of a band-limited function, $f(t)$, to a finite interval, say $[0, T]$. We can do this by multiplying $f(t)$ by the function

$$h(t) = \begin{cases} 1 & 0 \le t \le T \\ 0 & \text{otherwise} \end{cases} \tag{4-36}$$

This function has the same basic shape as Fig. 4.4(a), whose Fourier transform, $H(\mu)$, has frequency components extending to infinity in both directions, as Fig. 4.4(b) shows. From the convolution theorem, we know that the transform of the product $h(t)f(t)$ is the convolution in the frequency domain of the transforms $F(\mu)$ and $H(\mu)$. Even if $F(\mu)$ is band-limited, convolving it with $H(\mu)$, which involves sliding one function across the other, will yield a result with frequency components extending to infinity in both directions (see Problem 4.12). From this we conclude that no function of *finite* duration can be band-limited. Conversely, a function that is band-limited must extend from $-\infty$ to ∞.[†]

Although aliasing is an inevitable fact of working with sampled records of finite length, the effects of aliasing can be reduced by smoothing (lowpass filtering) the input function to attenuate its higher frequencies. This process, called *anti-aliasing*, has to be done *before* the function is sampled because aliasing is a sampling issue that cannot be "undone after the fact" using computational techniques.

[†]An important special case is when a function that extends from $-\infty$ to ∞ is band-limited *and* periodic. In this case, the function can be truncated and still be band-limited, *provided* that the truncation encompasses *exactly* an integral number of periods. A single truncated period (and thus the function) can be represented by a set of discrete samples satisfying the sampling theorem, taken over the truncated interval.

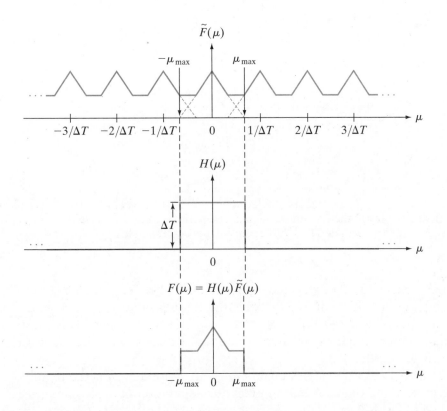

a
b
c

FIGURE 4.10 (a) Fourier transform of an under-sampled, band-limited function. (Interference between adjacent periods is shown dashed). (b) The same ideal lowpass filter used in Fig. 4.8. (c) The product of (a) and (b). The interference from adjacent periods results in aliasing that prevents perfect recovery of $F(\mu)$ and, consequently, of $f(t)$.

<hr>

EXAMPLE 4.3: Aliasing.

Figure 4.11 shows a classic illustration of aliasing. A pure sine wave extending infinitely in both directions has a single frequency so, obviously, it is band-limited. Suppose that the sine wave in the figure (ignore the large dots for now) has the equation $f(t) = \sin(\pi t)$, and that the horizontal axis corresponds to time, t, in seconds. The function crosses the axis at $t = 0, \pm 1, \pm 2, \dots$.

Recall that a function $f(t)$ is *periodic* with *period P* if $f(t + P) = f(t)$ for all values of t. The period is the number (including fractions) of units of the independent variable that it takes for the function to complete one cycle. The *frequency* of a *periodic* function is the number of periods (cycles) that the function completes in one unit of the independent variable. Thus, the frequency of a periodic function is the *reciprocal* of the period. As before, the sampling rate is the number of samples taken per unit of the independent variable.

In the present example, the independent variable is time, and its units are seconds. The period, P, of $\sin(\pi t)$ is 2 s, and its frequency is $1/P$, or $1/2$ cycles/s. According to the sampling theorem, we can recover this signal from a set of its samples if the sampling rate exceeds twice the highest frequency of the signal. This means that a sampling rate greater than 1 sample/s ($2 \times 1/2 = 1$) is required to

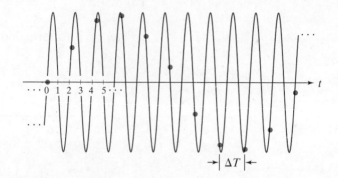

FIGURE 4.11 Illustration of aliasing. The under-sampled function (dots) looks like a sine wave having a frequency much lower than the frequency of the continuous signal. The period of the sine wave is 2 s, so the zero crossings of the horizontal axis occur every second. ΔT is the separation between samples.

recover the signal. Viewed another way, the separation, ΔT, between samples has to be less than 1 s. Observe that sampling this signal at *exactly* twice the frequency (1 sample/s), with samples taken at $t = 0, \pm 1, \pm 2, \ldots$, results in $\ldots \sin(-\pi), \sin(0), \sin(\pi) \ldots$, all of which are 0. This illustrates the reason why the sampling theorem requires a sampling rate that exceeds twice the highest frequency of the function, as mentioned earlier.

The large dots in Fig. 4.11 are samples taken uniformly at a rate *below* the required 1 sample/s (i.e., the samples are taken *more* than 1 s apart; in fact, the separation between samples exceeds 2 s). The sampled signal *looks* like a sine wave, but its frequency is about one-tenth the frequency of the original function. This sampled signal, having a frequency well below anything present in the original continuous function, is an example of aliasing. If the signal had been sampled at a rate slightly exceeding the Nyquist rate, the samples would not look like a sine wave at all (see Problem 4.6).

Figure 4.11 also illustrates how aliasing can be extremely problematic in musical recordings by introducing frequencies not present in the original sound. In order to mitigate this, signals with frequencies above half the sampling rate *must* be filtered out to reduce the effect of aliased signals introduced into digital recordings. This is the reason why digital recording equipment contains lowpass filters specifically designed to remove frequency components above half the sampling rate used by the equipment.

If we were given just the samples in Fig. 4.11, another issue illustrating the seriousness of aliasing is that we would have no way of knowing that these samples are not a true representation of the original function. As you will see later in this chapter, aliasing in images can produce similarly misleading results.

FUNCTION RECONSTRUCTION (RECOVERY) FROM SAMPLED DATA

In this section, we show that reconstructing a function from a set of its samples reduces in practice to interpolating between the samples. Even the simple act of displaying an image requires reconstruction of the image from its samples by the display medium. Therefore, it is important to understand the fundamentals of sampled data reconstruction. Convolution is central to developing this understanding, demonstrating again the importance of this concept.

The discussion of Fig. 4.8 and Eq. (4-34) outlines the procedure for perfect recovery of a band-limited function from its samples using frequency domain methods.

Using the convolution theorem, we can obtain the equivalent result in the spatial domain. From Eq. (4-34), $F(\mu) = H(\mu)\tilde{F}(\mu)$, so it follows that

$$
\begin{aligned}
f(t) &= \mathfrak{J}^{-1}\{F(\mu)\} \\
&= \mathfrak{J}^{-1}\{H(\mu)\tilde{F}(\mu)\} \\
&= h(t) \star \tilde{f}(t)
\end{aligned}
\tag{4-37}
$$

where, as before, $\tilde{f}(t)$ denotes the sampled function, and the last step follows from the convolution theorem, Eq. (4-25). It can be shown (see Problem 4.13), that substituting Eq. (4-27) for $\tilde{f}(t)$ into Eq. (4-37), and then using Eq. (4-24), leads to the following spatial domain expression for $f(t)$:

$$
f(t) = \sum_{n=-\infty}^{\infty} f(n\Delta T)\,\mathrm{sinc}\big[(t - n\Delta T)/\Delta T\big]
\tag{4-38}
$$

where the sinc function is defined in Eq. (4-23). This result is not unexpected because the inverse Fourier transform of the ideal (box) filter, $H(\mu)$, is a sinc function (see Example 4.1). Equation (4-38) shows that the perfectly reconstructed function, $f(t)$, is an infinite sum of sinc functions weighted by the sample values. It has the important property that the reconstructed function is identically equal to the sample values at multiple integer increments of ΔT. That is, for any $t = k\Delta T$, where k is an integer, $f(t)$ is equal to the kth sample, $f(k\Delta T)$. This follows from Eq. (4-38) because $\mathrm{sinc}(0) = 1$ and $\mathrm{sinc}(m) = 0$ for any other integer value of m. Between sample points, values of $f(t)$ are *interpolations* formed by the sum of the sinc functions.

See Section 2.4 regarding interpolation.

Equation (4-38) requires an infinite number of terms for the interpolations between samples. In practice, this implies that we have to look for approximations that are *finite* interpolations between the samples. As we discussed in Section 2.6, the principal interpolation approaches used in image processing are nearest-neighbor, bilinear, and bicubic interpolation. We will discuss the effects of interpolation on images in Section 4.5.

4.4 THE DISCRETE FOURIER TRANSFORM OF ONE VARIABLE

One of the principal goals of this chapter is the derivation of the *discrete Fourier transform* (DFT) starting from basic principles. The material up to this point may be viewed as the foundation of those basic principles, so now we have in place the necessary tools to derive the DFT.

OBTAINING THE DFT FROM THE CONTINUOUS TRANSFORM OF A SAMPLED FUNCTION

As we discussed in Section 4.3, the Fourier transform of a sampled, band-limited function extending from $-\infty$ to ∞ is a *continuous, periodic* function that also extends from $-\infty$ to ∞. In practice, we work with a finite number of samples, and the objective of this section is to derive the DFT of such finite sample sets.

Equation (4-31) gives the transform, $\tilde{F}(\mu)$, of sampled data in terms of the transform of the original function, but it does not give us an expression for $\tilde{F}(\mu)$ in terms of the sampled function $\tilde{f}(t)$ itself. We find that expression directly from the definition of the Fourier transform in Eq. (4-19):

$$\tilde{F}(\mu) = \int_{-\infty}^{\infty} \tilde{f}(t)e^{-j2\pi\mu t}dt \tag{4-39}$$

By substituting Eq. (4-27) for $\tilde{f}(t)$, we obtain

$$\tilde{F}(\mu) = \int_{-\infty}^{\infty} \tilde{f}(t)e^{-j2\pi\mu t}dt = \int_{-\infty}^{\infty}\sum_{n=-\infty}^{\infty}f(t)\delta(t-n\Delta T)e^{-j2\pi\mu t}dt$$

$$= \sum_{n=-\infty}^{\infty}\int_{-\infty}^{\infty}f(t)\delta(t-n\Delta T)e^{-j2\pi\mu t}dt \tag{4-40}$$

$$= \sum_{n=-\infty}^{\infty}f_n e^{-j2\pi\mu n\Delta T}$$

The last step follows from Eq. (4-28) and the sifting property of the impulse. Although f_n is a discrete function, its Fourier transform, $\tilde{F}(\mu)$, is continuous and infinitely periodic with period $1/\Delta T$, as we know from Eq. (4-31). Therefore, all we need to characterize $\tilde{F}(\mu)$ is one period, and sampling one period of this function is the basis for the DFT.

Suppose that we want to obtain M equally spaced samples of $\tilde{F}(\mu)$ taken over the one period interval from $\mu = 0$ to $\mu = 1/\Delta T$ (see Fig. 4.8). This is accomplished by taking the samples at the following frequencies:

$$\mu = \frac{m}{M\Delta T} \qquad m = 0, 1, 2, ..., M-1 \tag{4-41}$$

Substituting this result for μ into Eq. (4-40) and letting F_m denote the result yields

$$F_m = \sum_{n=0}^{M-1}f_n e^{-j2\pi mn/M} \qquad m = 0, 1, 2, ..., M-1 \tag{4-42}$$

This expression is the *discrete Fourier transform* we are seeking.[†] Given a set $\{f_m\}$ consisting of M samples of $f(t)$, Eq. (4-42) yields a set $\{F_m\}$ of M complex values corresponding to the discrete Fourier transform of the input sample set. Conversely,

---

[†]Referring back to Fig. 4.6(b), note that the interval $[0, 1/\Delta T]$ over which we sampled one period of $\tilde{F}(\mu)$ covers two adjacent half periods of the transform (but with the lowest half of period appearing at higher frequencies). This means that the data in F_m requires re-ordering to obtain samples that are ordered from the lowest to the highest frequency of the period. This is the price paid for the notational convenience of taking the samples at $m = 0, 1, 2, ..., M-1$, instead of using samples on either side of the origin, which would require the use of negative notation. The procedure used to order the transform data will be discussed in Section 4.6.

given $\{F_m\}$, we can recover the sample set $\{f_m\}$ by using the *inverse discrete Fourier transform* (IDFT)

$$f_n = \frac{1}{M} \sum_{m=0}^{M-1} F_m e^{j2\pi mn/M} \quad n = 0, 1, 2, \ldots, M-1 \tag{4-43}$$

It is not difficult to show (see Problem 4.15) that substituting Eq. (4-43) for f_n into Eq. (4-42) gives the identity $F_m \equiv F_m$. Similarly, substituting Eq. (4-42) into Eq. (4-43) for F_m yields $f_n \equiv f_n$. This implies that Eqs. (4-42) and (4-43) constitute a *discrete Fourier transform pair*. Furthermore, these identities indicate that the forward and inverse Fourier transforms exist for any set of samples whose values are finite. Note that neither expression depends explicitly on the sampling interval ΔT, nor on the frequency intervals of Eq. (4-41). Therefore, the DFT pair is applicable to *any* finite set of discrete samples taken uniformly.

We used m and n in the preceding development to denote discrete variables because it is typical to do so for derivations. However, it is more intuitive, especially in two dimensions, to use the notation x and y for image coordinate variables and u and v for frequency variables, where these are understood to be integers.[†] Then, Eqs. (4-42) and (4-43) become

$$F(u) = \sum_{x=0}^{M-1} f(x) e^{-j2\pi ux/M} \quad u = 0, 1, 2, \ldots, M-1 \tag{4-44}$$

and

$$f(x) = \frac{1}{M} \sum_{u=0}^{M-1} F(u) e^{j2\pi ux/M} \quad x = 0, 1, 2, \ldots, M-1 \tag{4-45}$$

where we used functional notation instead of subscripts for simplicity. Comparing Eqs. (4-42) through (4-45), you can see that $F(u) \equiv F_m$ and $f(x) \equiv f_n$. From this point on, we use Eqs. (4-44) and (4-45) to denote the 1-D DFT pair. As in the continuous case, we often refer to Eq. (4-44) as the *forward* DFT of $f(x)$, and to Eq. (4-45) as the *inverse* DFT of $F(u)$. As before, we use the notation $f(x) \Leftrightarrow F(u)$ to denote a Fourier transform pair. Sometimes you will encounter in the literature the $1/M$ term in front of Eq. (4-44) instead. That does not affect the proof that the two equations form a Fourier transform pair (see Problem 4.15).

Knowledge that $f(x)$ and $F(u)$ are a transform pair is useful in proving relationships between functions and their transforms. For example, you are asked in Problem 4.17 to show that $f(x - x_0) \Leftrightarrow F(u) e^{-j2\pi ux_0/M}$ is a Fourier transform pair. That is, you have to show that the DFT of $f(x - x_0)$ is $F(u) e^{-j2\pi ux_0/M}$ and, conversely, that the *inverse* DFT of $F(u) e^{-j2\pi ux_0/M}$ is $f(x - x_0)$. Because this is done by substituting

[†]We have been careful in using t for *continuous* spatial variables and μ for the corresponding *continuous* frequency variables. From this point on, we will use x and u to denote 1-D *discrete* spatial and frequency variables, respectively. When working in 2-D, we will use (t, z), and (μ, ν), to denote continuous spatial and frequency domain variables, respectively. Similarly, we will use (x, y) and (u, v) to denote their discrete counterparts.

directly into Eqs. (4-44) and (4-45), and you will have proved already that these two equations constitute a Fourier transform pair (Problem 4.15), if you prove that one side of "⇔" is the DFT (IDFT) of the other, then it must be true the other side is the IDFT (DFT) of the side you just proved. It turns out that having the option to prove one side or the other often simplifies proofs significantly. This is true also of the 1-D continuous and 2-D continuous and discrete Fourier transform pairs.

It can be shown (see Problem 4.16) that both the forward and inverse discrete transforms are infinitely periodic, with period M. That is,

$$F(u) = F(u + kM) \tag{4-46}$$

and

$$f(x) = f(x + kM) \tag{4-47}$$

where k is an integer.

The discrete equivalent of the 1-D convolution in Eq. (4-24) is

$$f(x) \star h(x) = \sum_{m=0}^{M-1} f(m)h(x - m) \quad x = 0, 1, 2, \ldots, M - 1 \tag{4-48}$$

Because in the preceding formulations the functions are periodic, their convolution also is periodic. Equation (4-48) gives one period of the periodic convolution. For this reason, this equation often is referred to as *circular convolution*. This is a direct result of the periodicity of the DFT and its inverse. This is in contrast with the convolution you studied in Section 3.4, in which values of the displacement, x, were determined by the requirement of sliding one function completely past the other, and were not fixed to the range $[0, M - 1]$ as in circular convolution. We will discuss this difference and its significance in Section 4.6 and in Fig. 4.27.

Finally, we point out that the convolution theorem given in Eqs. (4-25) and (4-26) is applicable also to discrete variables, with the exception that the right side of Eq. (4-26) is multiplied by $1/M$ (Problem 4.18).

RELATIONSHIP BETWEEN THE SAMPLING AND FREQUENCY INTERVALS

If $f(x)$ consists of M samples of a function $f(t)$ taken ΔT units apart, the length of the record comprising the set $\{f(x)\}, x = 0, 1, 2, \ldots, M - 1$, is

$$T = M\Delta T \tag{4-49}$$

The corresponding spacing, Δu, in the frequency domain follows from Eq. (4-41):

$$\Delta u = \frac{1}{M\Delta T} = \frac{1}{T} \tag{4-50}$$

The entire frequency range spanned by the M components of the DFT is then

$$R = M\Delta u = \frac{1}{\Delta T} \qquad (4\text{-}51)$$

Thus, we see from Eqs. (4-50) and (4-51) that the resolution in frequency, Δu, of the DFT depends inversely on the length (duration, if t is time) of the record, T, over which the continuous function, $f(t)$, is sampled; and the range of frequencies spanned by the DFT depends on the sampling interval ΔT. Keep in mind these *inverse* relationships between Δu and ΔT.

EXAMPLE 4.4: The mechanics of computing the DFT.

Figure 4.12(a) shows four samples of a continuous function, $f(t)$, taken ΔT units apart. Figure 4.12(b) shows the samples in the x-domain. The values of x are 0, 1, 2, and 3, which refer to the number of the samples in sequence, counting up from 0. For example, $f(2) = f(t_0 + 2\Delta T)$, the third sample of $f(t)$.

From Eq. (4-44), the first value of $F(u)$ [i.e., $F(0)$] is

$$F(0) = \sum_{x=0}^{3} f(x) = \left[f(0) + f(1) + f(2) + f(3)\right] = 1 + 2 + 4 + 4 = 11$$

The next value of $F(u)$ is

$$F(1) = \sum_{x=0}^{3} f(x)e^{-j2\pi(1)x/4} = 1e^{0} + 2e^{-j\pi/2} + 4e^{-j\pi} + 4e^{-j3\pi/2} = -3 + 2j$$

Similarly, $F(2) = -(1 + 0j)$ and $F(3) = -(3 + 2j)$. Observe that *all* values of $f(x)$ are used in computing *each* value of $F(u)$.

If we were given $F(u)$ instead, and were asked to compute its inverse, we would proceed in the same manner, but using the inverse Fourier transform. For instance,

$$f(0) = \frac{1}{4}\sum_{u=0}^{3} F(u)e^{j2\pi u(0)} = \frac{1}{4}\sum_{u=0}^{3} F(u) = \frac{1}{4}[11 - 3 + 2j - 1 - 3 - 2j] = \frac{1}{4}[4] = 1$$

which agrees with Fig. 4.12(b). The other values of $f(x)$ are obtained in a similar manner.

---

a b

FIGURE 4.12
(a) A continuous function sampled ΔT units apart.
(b) Samples in the x-domain. Variable t is continuous, while x is discrete.

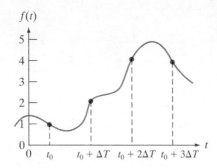 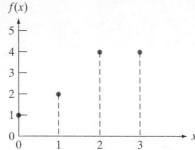

4.5 EXTENSIONS TO FUNCTIONS OF TWO VARIABLES

In the following discussion we extend to two variables the concepts introduced in the previous sections of this chapter.

THE 2-D IMPULSE AND ITS SIFTING PROPERTY

The impulse, $\delta(t,z)$, of two continuous variables, t and z, is defined as before:

$$\delta(t,z) = \begin{cases} 1 & \text{if } t = z = 0 \\ 0 & \text{otherwise} \end{cases} \tag{4-52}$$

and

$$\int_{-\infty}^{\infty} \int_{-\infty}^{\infty} \delta(t,z)\,dt\,dz = 1 \tag{4-53}$$

As in the 1-D case, the 2-D impulse exhibits the *sifting property* under integration,

$$\int_{-\infty}^{\infty} \int_{-\infty}^{\infty} f(t,z)\delta(t,z)\,dt\,dz = f(0,0) \tag{4-54}$$

or. more generally for an impulse located at (t_0, z_0),

$$\int_{-\infty}^{\infty} \int_{-\infty}^{\infty} f(t,z)\delta(t - t_0, z - z_0)\,dt\,dz = f(t_0, z_0) \tag{4-55}$$

As before, we see that the sifting property yields the value of the function at the location of the impulse.

For discrete variables x and y, the 2-D discrete unit impulse is defined as

$$\delta(x,y) = \begin{cases} 1 & \text{if } x = y = 0 \\ 0 & \text{otherwise} \end{cases} \tag{4-56}$$

and its sifting property is

$$\sum_{x=-\infty}^{\infty} \sum_{y=-\infty}^{\infty} f(x,y)\delta(x,y) = f(0,0) \tag{4-57}$$

where $f(x,y)$ is a function of discrete variables x and y. For an impulse located at coordinates (x_0, y_0) (see Fig. 4.13) the sifting property is

$$\sum_{x=-\infty}^{\infty} \sum_{y=-\infty}^{\infty} f(x,y)\delta(x - x_0, y - y_0) = f(x_0, y_0) \tag{4-58}$$

When working with an image of finite dimensions, the limits in the two preceding equations are replaced by the dimensions of the image.

FIGURE 4.13
2-D unit discrete impulse. Variables x and y are discrete, and δ is zero everywhere except at coordinates (x_0, y_0), where its value is 1.

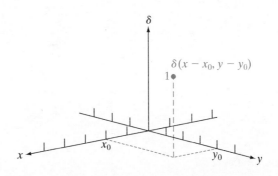

THE 2-D CONTINUOUS FOURIER TRANSFORM PAIR

Let $f(t,z)$ be a continuous function of two continuous variables, t and z. The two-dimensional, continuous Fourier transform pair is given by the expressions

$$F(\mu,\nu) = \int_{-\infty}^{\infty} \int_{-\infty}^{\infty} f(t,z) e^{-j2\pi(\mu t + \nu z)} \, dt \, dz \tag{4-59}$$

and

$$f(t,z) = \int_{-\infty}^{\infty} \int_{-\infty}^{\infty} F(\mu,\nu) e^{j2\pi(\mu t + \nu z)} \, d\mu \, d\nu \tag{4-60}$$

where μ and ν are the frequency variables. When referring to images, t and z are interpreted to be continuous *spatial* variables. As in the 1-D case, the domain of the variables μ and ν defines the *continuous frequency domain*.

EXAMPLE 4.5: Obtaining the Fourier transform of a 2-D box function.

Figure 4.14(a) shows the 2-D equivalent of the 1-D box function in Example 4.1. Following a procedure similar to the one used in that example gives the result

$$F(\mu,\nu) = \int_{-\infty}^{\infty} \int_{-\infty}^{\infty} f(t,z) e^{-j2\pi(\mu t + \nu z)} \, dt \, dz = \int_{-T/2}^{T/2} \int_{-Z/2}^{Z/2} A e^{-j2\pi(\mu t + \nu z)} \, dt \, dz$$

$$= ATZ \left[\frac{\sin(\pi\mu T)}{(\pi\mu T)} \right] \left[\frac{\sin(\pi\nu Z)}{(\pi\nu Z)} \right]$$

Figure 4.14(b) shows a portion of the spectrum about the origin. As in the 1-D case, the locations of the zeros in the spectrum are inversely proportional to the values of T and Z. In this example, T is larger than Z, so the spectrum is the more "contracted" along the μ-axis.

2-D SAMPLING AND THE 2-D SAMPLING THEOREM

In a manner similar to the 1-D case, sampling in two dimensions can be modeled using a sampling function (i.e., a 2-D impulse train):

a b

FIGURE 4.14
(a) A 2-D function
and (b) a section
of its spectrum.
The box is longer
along the *t*-axis,
so the spectrum is
more contracted
along the μ-axis.

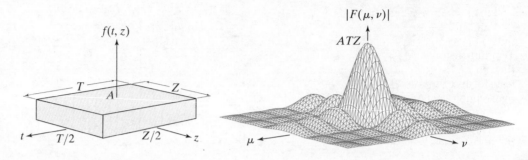

$$s_{\Delta T \Delta Z}(t,z) = \sum_{m=-\infty}^{\infty} \sum_{n=-\infty}^{\infty} \delta(t - m\Delta T, z - n\Delta Z) \qquad (4\text{-}61)$$

where ΔT and ΔZ are the separations between samples along the *t*- and *z*-axis of the continuous function $f(t,z)$. Equation (4-61) describes a set of periodic impulses extending infinitely along the two axes (see Fig. 4.15). As in the 1-D case illustrated in Fig. 4.5, multiplying $f(t,z)$ by $s_{\Delta T \Delta Z}(t,z)$ yields the sampled function.

Function $f(t,z)$ is said to be *band limited* if its Fourier transform is 0 outside a rectangle established in the frequency domain by the intervals $\left[-\mu_{max}, \mu_{max} \right]$ and $\left[-\nu_{max}, \nu_{max} \right]$; that is,

$$F(\mu,\nu) = 0 \quad \text{for } |\mu| \geq \mu_{max} \text{ and } |\nu| \geq \nu_{max} \qquad (4\text{-}62)$$

The *two-dimensional sampling theorem* states that a continuous, band-limited function $f(t,z)$ can be recovered with no error from a set of its samples if the sampling intervals are

$$\Delta T < \frac{1}{2\mu_{max}} \qquad (4\text{-}63)$$

and

$$\Delta Z < \frac{1}{2\nu_{max}} \qquad (4\text{-}64)$$

or, expressed in terms of the sampling rate, if

FIGURE 4.15
2-D impulse train.

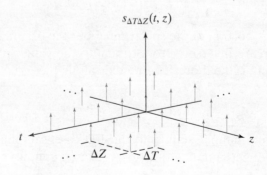

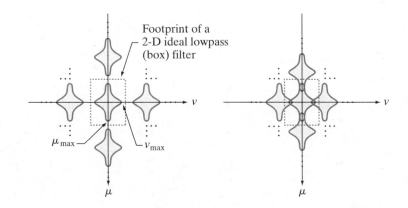

a b

FIGURE 4.16
Two-dimensional Fourier transforms of (a) an over-sampled, and (b) an under-sampled, band-limited function.

$$\frac{1}{\Delta T} > 2\mu_{max} \qquad (4\text{-}65)$$

and

$$\frac{1}{\Delta Z} > 2\nu_{max} \qquad (4\text{-}66)$$

Stated another way, we say that no information is lost if a 2-D, band-limited, continuous function is represented by samples acquired at rates greater than twice the highest frequency content of the function in both the μ- and ν-directions.

Figure 4.16 shows the 2-D equivalents of Figs. 4.6(b) and (d). A 2-D ideal filter transfer function has the form illustrated in Fig. 4.14(a) (but in the frequency domain). The dashed portion of Fig. 4.16(a) shows the location of the filter function to achieve the necessary isolation of a single period of the transform for reconstruction of a band-limited function from its samples, as in Fig. 4.8. From Fig 4.10, we know that if the function is under-sampled, the periods overlap, and it becomes impossible to isolate a single period, as Fig. 4.16(b) shows. Aliasing would result under such conditions.

ALIASING IN IMAGES

In this section, we extend the concept of aliasing to images, and discuss in detail several aspects of aliasing related to image sampling and resampling.

Extensions from 1-D Aliasing

As in the 1-D case, a continuous function $f(t, z)$ of two continuous variables, t and z, can be band-limited in general only if it extends infinitely in both coordinate directions. The very act of limiting the spatial duration of the function (e.g., by multiplying it by a box function) introduces corrupting frequency components extending to infinity in the frequency domain, as explained in Section 4.3 (see also Problem 4.12). Because we cannot sample a function infinitely, aliasing is always present in digital images, just as it is present in sampled 1-D functions. There are two principal manifestations of aliasing in images: spatial aliasing and temporal aliasing. *Spatial aliasing* is caused by under-sampling, as discussed in Section 4.3, and tends to be more visible (and objectionable) in images with repetitive patterns. *Temporal aliasing* is related to time intervals between images of a sequence of dynamic images. One of the most common examples of temporal aliasing is the "wagon wheel" effect, in which wheels with spokes in a sequence of images (for example, in a movie) appear to be rotating backwards. This is caused by the frame rate being too low with respect to the speed of wheel rotation in the sequence, and is similar to the phenomenon described in Fig. 4.11, in which under sampling produced a signal that appeared to be of much lower frequency than the original.

Our focus in this chapter is on spatial aliasing. The key concerns with spatial aliasing in images are the introduction of artifacts such as jaggedness in line features, spurious highlights, and the appearance of frequency patterns not present in the original image. Just as we used Fig. 4.9 to explain aliasing in 1-D functions, we can develop an intuitive grasp of the nature of aliasing in images using some simple graphics. The sampling grid in the center section of Fig. 4.17 is a 2-D representation of the impulse train in Fig. 4.15. In the grid, the little white squares correspond to the location of the impulses (where the image is sampled) and black represents the separation between samples. Superimposing the sampling grid on an image is analogous to multiplying the image by an impulse train, so the same sampling concepts we discussed in connection with the impulse train in Fig. 4.15 are applicable here. The focus now is to analyze graphically the interaction between sampling rate (the separation of the sampling points in the grid) and the frequency of the 2-D signals being sampled.

Figure 4.17 shows a sampling grid partially overlapping three 2-D signals (regions of an image) of low, mid, and high spatial frequencies (relative to the separation between sampling cells in the grid). Note that the level of spatial "detail" in the regions is proportional to frequency (i.e., higher-frequency signals contain more bars). The sections of the regions inside the sampling grip are rough manifestations of how they would appear after sampling. As expected, all three digitized regions

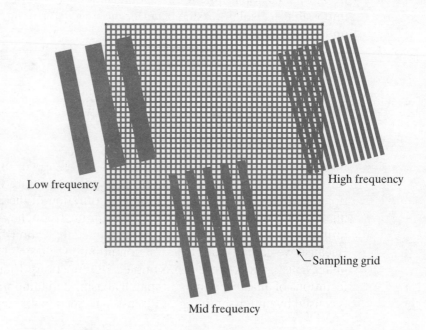

FIGURE 4.17
Various aliasing effects resulting from the interaction between the frequency of 2-D signals and the sampling rate used to digitize them. The regions outside the sampling grid are continuous and free of aliasing.

Low frequency

High frequency

Sampling grid

Mid frequency

exhibit aliasing to some degree, but the effects are dramatically different, worsening as the discrepancy between detail (frequency) and sampling rate increases. The low-frequency region is rendered reasonably well, with some mild jaggedness around the edges. The jaggedness increases as the frequency of the region increases to the mid-range because the sampling rate is the same. This edge distortion (appropriately called *jaggies*) is common in images with strong line and/or edge content.

The digitized high-frequency region in the top right of Fig. 4.17 exhibits totally different and somewhat surprising behavior. Additional stripes (of lower frequency) appear in the digitized section, and these stripes are rotated significantly with respect to the direction of the stripes in the continuous region. These stripes are an alias of a totally different signal. As the following example shows, this type of behavior can result in images that appear "normal" and yet bear no relation to the original.

EXAMPLE 4.6: Aliasing in images.

Consider an imaging system that is perfect, in the sense that it is noiseless and produces an exact digital image of what it sees, but the number of samples it can take is fixed at 96×96 pixels. For simplicity, assume that pixels are little squares of unit width and length. We want to use this system to digitize checkerboard images of alternating black and white squares. Checkerboard images can be interpreted as periodic, extending infinitely in both dimensions, where one period is equal to adjacent black/white pairs. If we specify "valid" digitized images as being those extracted from an infinite sequence in such a way that the image contains an integer multiple of periods, then, based on our earlier comments, we know that properly sampled periodic images will be free of aliasing. In the present example, this means that the sizes of the squares must be such that dividing 96 by the size yields an even number. This will give an integer number of periods (pairs of black/white squares). The smallest size of squares under the stated conditions is 1 pixel.

The principal objective of this example is to examine what happens when checkerboard images with squares of sizes less than 1 pixel on the side are presented to the system. This will correspond to the undersampled case discussed earlier, which will result in aliasing. A horizontal or vertical scan line of the checkerboard images results in a 1-D square wave, so we can focus the analysis on 1-D signals.

To understand the capabilities of our imaging system in terms of sampling, recall from the discussion of the 1-D sampling theorem that, given the sampling rate, the maximum frequency allowed before aliasing occurs in the sampled signal has to be less than one-half the sampling rate. Our sampling rate is fixed, at one sample per unit of the independent variable (the units are pixels). Therefore, the maximum frequency our signal can have in order to avoid aliasing is 1/2 cycle/pixel.

We can arrive at the same conclusion by noting that the most demanding image our system can handle is when the squares are 1 unit (pixel) wide, in which case the period (cycle) is two pixels. The frequency is the reciprocal of the period, or 1/2 cycle/pixel, as in the previous paragraph.

Figures 4.18(a) and (b) show the result of sampling checkerboard images whose squares are of sizes 16×16 and 6×6 pixels, respectively. The frequencies of scan lines in either direction of these two images are 1/32 and 1/6 cycles/pixel. These are well below the 1/2 cycles/pixel allowed for our system. Because, as mentioned earlier, the images are perfectly registered in the field of view of the system, the results are free of aliasing, as expected.

When the size of the squares is reduced to slightly less than one pixel, a severely aliased image results, as Fig. 4.18(c) shows (the squares used were approximately of size 0.95×0.95 pixels). Finally, reducing

FIGURE 4.18
Aliasing. In (a) and (b) the squares are of sizes 16 and 6 pixels on the side. In (c) and (d) the squares are of sizes 0.95 and 0.48 pixels, respectively. Each small square in (c) is one pixel. Both (c) and (d) are aliased. Note how (d) masquerades as a "normal" image.

the size of the squares to slightly less than 0.5 pixels on the side yielded the image in Fig. 4.18(d). In this case, the aliased result looks like a normal checkerboard pattern. In fact, this image would result from sampling a checkerboard image whose squares are 12 pixels on the side. This last image is a good reminder that aliasing can create results that may be visually quite misleading.

The effects of aliasing can be reduced by slightly defocusing the image to be digitized so that high frequencies are attenuated. As explained in Section 4.3, anti-aliasing filtering has to be done at the "front-end," *before* the image is sampled. There are no such things as after-the-fact software anti-aliasing filters that can be used to reduce the effects of aliasing caused by violations of the sampling theorem. Most commercial digital image manipulation packages do have a feature called "anti-aliasing." However, as illustrated in Example 4.8 below, this term is related to blurring a digital image to reduce additional aliasing artifacts caused by resampling. The term does not apply to reducing aliasing in the original sampled image. A significant number of commercial digital cameras have true anti-aliasing filtering built in, either in the lens or on the surface of the sensor itself. Even nature uses this approach to reduce the effects of aliasing in the human eye, as the following example shows.

EXAMPLE 4.7: Nature obeys the limits of the sampling theorem.

When discussing Figs. 2.1 and 2.2, we mentioned that cones are the sensors responsible for sharp vision. Cones are concentrated in the fovea, in line with the visual axis of the lens, and their concentration is measured in degrees off that axis. A standard test of visual acuity (the ability to resolve fine detail) in humans is to place a pattern of alternating black and white stripes in one degree of the visual field. If the total number of stripes exceeds 120 (i.e., a frequency of 60 cycles/degree), experimental evidence shows that the observer will perceive the image as a single gray mass. That is, the lens in the eye automatically lowpass filters spatial frequencies higher than 60 cycles/degree. Sampling in the eye is done by the cones, so, based on the sampling theorem, we would expect the eye to have on the order of 120 cones/degree in order to avoid the effects of aliasing. As it turns out, that is exactly what we have!

Image Resampling and Interpolation

As in the 1-D case, perfect reconstruction of a band-limited image function from a set of its samples requires 2-D convolution in the spatial domain with a sinc function. As explained in Section 4.3, this theoretically perfect reconstruction requires interpolation using infinite summations which, in practice, forces us to look for approximate interpolation methods. One of the most common applications of 2-D interpolation in image processing is in image resizing (zooming and shrinking). Zooming may be viewed as over-sampling, while shrinking may be viewed as under-sampling. The key difference between these two operations and the sampling concepts discussed in previous sections is that we are applying zooming and shrinking to digital images.

We introduced interpolation in Section 2.4. Our interest there was to illustrate the performance of nearest neighbor, bilinear, and bicubic interpolation. In this section, the focus is on sampling and anti-aliasing issues. Aliasing generally is introduced when an image is scaled, either by zooming or by shrinking. For example, a special case of nearest neighbor interpolation is zooming by *pixel replication*, which we use to increase the size of an image an integer number of times. To double the size of an image, we duplicate each column. This doubles the image size in the horizontal direction. Then, we duplicate each row of the enlarged image to double the size in the vertical direction. The same procedure is used to enlarge the image any integer number of times. The intensity level assignment of each pixel is predetermined by the fact that new locations are exact duplicates of old locations. In this crude method of enlargement, one of the principal aliasing effects is the introduction of jaggies on straight lines that are not horizontal or vertical. The effects of aliasing in image enlargement often are reduced significantly by using more sophisticated interpolation, as we discussed in Section 2.4. We show in the following example that aliasing can also be a serious problem in image shrinking.

EXAMPLE 4.8: Illustration of aliasing in resampled natural images.

The effects of aliasing generally are worsened when the size of a digital image is reduced. Figure 4.19(a) is an image containing regions purposely selected to illustrate the effects of aliasing (note the thinly spaced parallel lines in all garments worn by the subject). There are no objectionable aliasing artifacts in Fig. 4.19(a), indicating that the sampling rate used initially was sufficient to mitigate visible aliasing.

In Fig. 4.19(b), the image was reduced to 33% of its original size using row/column deletion. The effects of aliasing are quite visible in this image (see, for example, the areas around scarf and the subject's knees). Images (a) and (b) are shown in the same size because the reduced image was brought back to its original size by pixel replication (the replication did not alter appreciably the effects of aliasing just discussed.

The digital "equivalent" of the defocusing of continuous images mentioned earlier for reducing aliasing, is to attenuate the high frequencies of a *digital* image by smoothing it with a lowpass filter before resampling. Figure 4.19(c) was processed in the same manner as Fig. 4.19(b), but the original image was smoothed using a 5×5 spatial averaging filter (see Section 3.5) before reducing its size. The improvement over Fig. 4.19(b) is evident. The image is slightly more blurred than (a) and (b), but aliasing is no longer objectionable.

a b c

FIGURE 4.19 Illustration of aliasing on resampled natural images. (a) A digital image of size 772×548 pixels with visually negligible aliasing. (b) Result of resizing the image to 33% of its original size by pixel deletion and then restoring it to its original size by pixel replication. Aliasing is clearly visible. (c) Result of blurring the image in (a) with an averaging filter prior to resizing. The image is slightly more blurred than (b), but aliasing is not longer objectionable. (Original image courtesy of the Signal Compression Laboratory, University of California, Santa Barbara.)

The term *moiré* is a French word (not the name of a person) that appears to have originated with weavers, who first noticed what appeared to be interference patterns visible on some fabrics. The root of the word is from the word *mohair*, a cloth made from Angora goat hairs.

Aliasing and Moiré Patterns

In optics, a *moiré pattern* is a secondary, visual phenomenon produced, for example, by superimposing two gratings of approximately equal spacing. These patterns are common, everyday occurrences. For instance, we see them in overlapping insect window screens and on the interference between TV raster lines and striped or highly textured materials in the background, or worn by individuals. In digital image processing, moiré-like patterns arise routinely when sampling media print, such as newspapers and magazines, or in images with periodic components whose spacing is comparable to the spacing between samples. It is important to note that moiré patterns are more general than sampling artifacts. For instance, Fig. 4.20 shows the moiré effect using vector drawings that have not been digitized. Separately, the patterns are clean and void of interference. However, the simple acts of superimposing one pattern on the other creates a pattern with frequencies not present in either of the original patterns. Note in particular the moiré effect produced by two patterns of dots, as this is the effect of interest in the following discussion.

EXAMPLE 4.9: Sampling printed media.

Newspapers and other printed materials use so called *halftone dots*, which are black dots or ellipses whose sizes and various grouping schemes are used to simulate gray tones. As a rule, the following numbers are typical: newspapers are printed using 75 halftone dots per inch (dpi), magazines use 133 dpi, and

FIGURE 4.20
Examples of
the moiré effect.
These are vector
drawings, not
digitized patterns.
Superimposing
one pattern on the
other is analogous
to multiplying the
patterns.

high-quality brochures use 175 dpi. Figure 4.21 shows what happens when a newspaper image is (under) sampled at 75 dpi. The sampling lattice (which is oriented vertically and horizontally) and dot patterns on the newspaper image (oriented at ±45°) interact to create a uniform moiré-like pattern that makes the image look blotchy. (We will discuss a technique in Section 4.10 for reducing the effects of moiré patterns in under-sampled print media.)

FIGURE 4.21
A newspaper
image digitized at
75 dpi. Note the
moiré-like pattern
resulting from
the interaction
between the ±45°
orientation of the
half-tone dots and
the north-south
orientation of the
sampling elements
used to digitized
the image.

THE 2-D DISCRETE FOURIER TRANSFORM AND ITS INVERSE

A development similar to the material in Sections 4.3 and 4.4 would yield the following 2-D discrete Fourier transform (DFT):

$$F(u,v) = \sum_{x=0}^{M-1} \sum_{y=0}^{N-1} f(x,y) e^{-j2\pi(ux/M + vy/N)} \tag{4-67}$$

where $f(x,y)$ is a digital image of size $M \times N$. As in the 1-D case, Eq. (4-67) must be evaluated for values of the discrete variables u and v in the ranges $u = 0, 1, 2, \ldots, M - 1$ and $v = 0, 1, 2, \ldots, N - 1$.[†]

Given the transform $F(u,v)$, we can obtain $f(x,y)$ by using the *inverse discrete Fourier transform* (IDFT):

Sometimes you will find in the literature the $1/MN$ constant in front of the DFT instead of the IDFT. At times, the square root of this constant is included in front of the forward and inverse transforms, thus creating a more symmetrical pair. Any of these formulations is correct, provided they are used consistently.

$$f(x,y) = \frac{1}{MN} \sum_{u=0}^{M-1} \sum_{v=0}^{N-1} F(u,v) e^{j2\pi(ux/M + vy/N)} \tag{4-68}$$

for $x = 0, 1, 2, \ldots, M - 1$ and $y = 0, 1, 2, \ldots, N - 1$. As in the 1-D case, [Eqs. (4-44) and (4-45)], Eqs. (4-67) and (4-68) constitute a 2-D *discrete Fourier transform pair*, $f(x,y) \Leftrightarrow F(u,v)$. (The proof is a straightforward extension of the 1-D case in Problem 4.15.) The rest of this chapter is based on properties of these two equations and their use for image filtering in the frequency domain. The comments made in connection with Eqs. (4-44) and (4-45) are applicable to Eqs. (4-67) and (4-68); that is, knowing that $f(x,y)$ and $F(u,v)$ are a Fourier transform pair can be quite useful in proving relationships between functions and their transforms.

4.6 SOME PROPERTIES OF THE 2-D DFT AND IDFT ▬▬▬▬

In this section, we introduce several properties of the 2-D discrete Fourier transform and its inverse.

RELATIONSHIPS BETWEEN SPATIAL AND FREQUENCY INTERVALS

The relationships between spatial sampling and the corresponding frequency domain intervals are as explained in Section 4.4. Suppose that a continuous function $f(t,z)$ is sampled to form a digital image, $f(x,y)$, consisting of $M \times N$ samples taken in the t- and z-directions, respectively. Let ΔT and ΔZ denote the separations between samples (see Fig. 4.15). Then, the separations between the corresponding discrete, frequency domain variables are given by

$$\Delta u = \frac{1}{M \Delta T} \tag{4-69}$$

[†]As mentioned in Section 4.4, keep in mind that in this chapter we use (t,z) and (μ,ν) to denote 2-D *continuous* spatial and frequency-domain variables. In the 2-D *discrete* case, we use (x,y) for spatial variables and (u,v) for frequency-domain variables, all of which are discrete.

and

$$\Delta v = \frac{1}{N\Delta Z} \tag{4-70}$$

respectively. Note the important property that the separations between samples in the frequency domain are inversely proportional both to the spacing between spatial samples *and* to the number of samples.

TRANSLATION AND ROTATION

The validity of the following Fourier transform pairs can be demonstrated by direct substitution into Eqs. (4-67) and (4-68) (see Problem 4.27):

Recall that we use the symbol "⇔" to denote Fourier transform pairs. That is, the term on the right is the transform of the term on the left, and the term on the left is the inverse Fourier transform of the term on the right.

$$f(x,y)e^{j2\pi(u_0 x/M + v_0 y/N)} \Leftrightarrow F(u - u_0, v - v_0) \tag{4-71}$$

and

$$f(x - x_0, y - y_0) \Leftrightarrow F(u,v)e^{-j2\pi(x_0 u/M + y_0 v/N)} \tag{4-72}$$

That is, multiplying $f(x,y)$ by the exponential shown shifts the origin of the DFT to (u_0, v_0) and, conversely, multiplying $F(u,v)$ by the negative of that exponential shifts the origin of $f(x,y)$ to (x_0, y_0). As we illustrate in Example 4.13, translation has no effect on the magnitude (spectrum) of $F(u,v)$.

Using the polar coordinates

$$x = r\cos\theta \qquad y = r\sin\theta \qquad u = \omega\cos\varphi \qquad v = \omega\sin\varphi$$

results in the following transform pair:

$$f(r, \theta + \theta_0) \Leftrightarrow F(\omega, \varphi + \theta_0) \tag{4-73}$$

which indicates that rotating $f(x,y)$ by an angle θ_0 rotates $F(u,v)$ by the same angle. Conversely, rotating $F(u,v)$ rotates $f(x,y)$ by the same angle.

PERIODICITY

As in the 1-D case, the 2-D Fourier transform and its inverse are infinitely periodic in the u and v directions; that is,

$$F(u,v) = F(u + k_1 M, v) = F(u, v + k_2 N) = F(u + k_1 M, v + k_2 N) \tag{4-74}$$

and

$$f(x,y) = f(x + k_1 M, y) = f(x, y + k_2 N) = f(x + k_1 M, y + k_2 N) \tag{4-75}$$

where k_1 and k_2 are integers.

The periodicities of the transform and its inverse are important issues in the implementation of DFT-based algorithms. Consider the 1-D spectrum in Fig. 4.22(a). As explained in Section 4.4 [see the footnote to Eq. (4-42)], the transform data in the interval from 0 to $M - 1$ consists of two half periods meeting at point $M/2$, but with

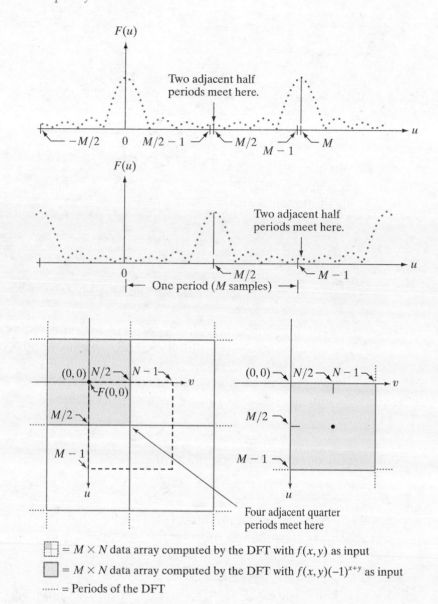

FIGURE 4.22
Centering the
Fourier transform.
(a) A 1-D DFT
showing an infinite
number of peri-
ods. (b) Shifted
DFT obtained
by multiplying
$f(x)$ by $(-1)^x$
before computing
$F(u)$. (c) A 2-D
DFT showing an
infinite number of
periods. The area
within the dashed
rectangle is the
data array, $F(u,v)$,
obtained with
Eq. (4-67) with
an image $f(x,y)$
as the input. This
array consists of
four quarter peri-
ods. (d) Shifted
array obtained
by multiplying
$f(x,y)$ by $(-1)^{x+y}$
before computing
$F(u,v)$. The data
now contains one
complete, centered
period, as in (b).

the lower part of the period appearing at higher frequencies. For display and filtering purposes, it is more convenient to have in this interval a complete period of the
transform in which the data are contiguous and ordered properly, as in Fig. 4.22(b).
It follows from Eq. (4-71) that

$$f(x)e^{j2\pi(u_0 x/M)} \Leftrightarrow F(u - u_0)$$

In other words, multiplying $f(x)$ by the exponential term shown shifts the transform
data so that the origin, $F(0)$, is moved to u_0. If we let $u_0 = M/2$, the exponential
term becomes $e^{j\pi x}$, which is equal to $(-1)^x$ because x is an integer. In this case,

$$f(x)(-1)^x \iff F(u - M/2)$$

That is, multiplying $f(x)$ by $(-1)^x$ shifts the data so that $F(u)$ is centered on the interval $[0, M-1]$, which corresponds to Fig. 4.22(b), as desired.

In 2-D the situation is more difficult to graph, but the principle is the same, as Fig. 4.22(c) shows. Instead of two half periods, there are now four quarter periods meeting at the point $(M/2, N/2)$. As in the 1-D case, we want to shift the data so that $F(0,0)$ is at $(M/2, N/2)$. Letting $(u_0, v_0) = (M/2, N/2)$ in Eq. (4-71) results in the expression

$$f(x,y)(-1)^{x+y} \iff F(u - M/2, v - N/2) \tag{4-76}$$

Using this equation shifts the data so that $F(0,0)$ is moved to the center of the *frequency rectangle* (i.e., the rectangle defined by the intervals $[0, M-1]$ and $[0, N-1]$ in the frequency domain). Figure 4.22(d) shows the result.

Keep in mind that in all our discussions, coordinate values in both the spatial and frequency domains are integers. As we explained in Section 2.4 (see Fig. 2.19) if, as in our case), the origin of an $M \times N$ image or transform is at $(0,0)$, then the center of that image or transform is at $(\text{floor}(M/2), \text{floor}(N/2))$. This expression is applicable to both even and odd values of M and N. For example, the center of an array of size 20×15 is at point $(10,7)$. Because we start counting from 0, these are the 11th and 8th points in the first and second coordinate axes of the array, respectively.

SYMMETRY PROPERTIES

An important result from functional analysis is that any real *or* complex function, $w(x,y)$, can be expressed as the sum of an even and an odd part, each of which can be real or complex:

$$w(x,y) = w_e(x,y) + w_o(x,y) \tag{4-77}$$

where the *even* and *odd* parts are defined as

$$w_e(x,y) \triangleq \frac{w(x,y) + w(-x,-y)}{2} \tag{4-78}$$

and

$$w_o(x,y) \triangleq \frac{w(x,y) - w(-x,-y)}{2} \tag{4-79}$$

for all valid values of x and y. Substituting Eqs. (4-78) and (4-79) into Eq. (4-77) gives the identity $w(x,y) \equiv w(x,y)$, thus proving the validity of the latter equation. It follows from the preceding definitions that

$$w_e(x,y) = w_e(-x,-y) \tag{4-80}$$

and

$$w_o(x, y) = -w_o(-x, -y) \tag{4-81}$$

In the context of this discussion, the *locations* of elements in a sequence are denoted by integers. Therefore, the same observations made a few paragraphs back about the centers of arrays of even and odd *sizes* are applicable to sequences. But, do not confuse the concepts of even/odd *numbers* and even/odd *functions*.

Even functions are said to be *symmetric* and odd functions *antisymmetric*. Because all indices in the DFT and IDFT are nonnegative integers, when we talk about symmetry (antisymmetry) we are referring to symmetry (antisymmetry) about the *center point* of a sequence, in which case the definitions of even and odd become:

$$w_e(x, y) = w_e(M - x, N - y) \tag{4-82}$$

and

$$w_o(x, y) = -w_o(M - x, N - y) \tag{4-83}$$

for $x = 0, 1, 2, \ldots, M - 1$ and $y = 0, 1, 2, \ldots, N - 1$. As usual, M and N are the number of rows and columns of a 2-D array.

We know from elementary mathematical analysis that the product of two even or two odd functions is even, and that the product of an even and an odd function is odd. In addition, the only way that a discrete function can be odd is if all its samples sum to zero. These properties lead to the important result that

To convince yourself that the samples of an odd function sum to zero, sketch one period of a 1-D sine wave about the origin or any other interval spanning one period.

$$\sum_{x=0}^{M-1} \sum_{y=0}^{N-1} w_e(x, y) w_o(x, y) = 0 \tag{4-84}$$

for any two discrete even and odd functions w_e and w_o. In other words, because the argument of Eq. (4-84) is odd, the result of the summations is 0. The functions can be real or complex.

EXAMPLE 4.10: Even and odd functions.

Although evenness and oddness are visualized easily for continuous functions, these concepts are not as intuitive when dealing with discrete sequences. The following illustrations will help clarify the preceding ideas. Consider the 1-D sequence

$$f = \{f(0), f(1), f(2), f(3)\} = \{2, 1, 1, 1\}$$

in which $M = 4$. To test for evenness, the condition $f(x) = f(4 - x)$ must be satisfied for $x = 0, 1, 2, 3$. That is, we require that

$$f(0) = f(4), \quad f(1) = f(3), \quad f(2) = f(2), \quad f(3) = f(1)$$

Because $f(4)$ is outside the range being examined and can be any value, the value of $f(0)$ is immaterial in the test for evenness. We see that the next three conditions are satisfied by the values in the array, so the sequence is even. In fact, we conclude that *any* 4-point even sequence has to have the form

$$\{a, b, c, b\}$$

That is, only the second and last points must be equal in a 4-point even sequence. In general, when M is an even number, a 1-D even sequence has the property that the points at locations 0 and $M/2$ have arbitrary values. When M is odd, the first point of an even sequence is still arbitrary, but the others form pairs with equal values.

Odd sequences have the interesting property that their first term, $w_o(0,0)$, is always 0, a fact that follows directly from Eq. (4-79). Consider the 1-D sequence

$$g = \{g(0), g(1), g(2), g(3)\} = \{0, -1, 0, 1\}$$

We can confirm that this is an odd sequence by noting that the terms in the sequence satisfy the condition $g(x) = -g(4 - x)$ for $x = 1,2,3$. All we have to do for $x = 0$ is to check that $g(0) = 0$. We check the other terms using the definition. For example, $g(1) = -g(3)$. Any 4-point odd sequence has the form

$$\{0, -b, 0, b\}$$

In general, when M is an even number, a 1-D odd sequence has the property that the points at locations 0 and $M/2$ are always zero. When M is odd, the first term still has to be 0, but the remaining terms form pairs with equal value but opposite signs.

The preceding discussion indicates that evenness and oddness of sequences depend also on the length of the sequences. For example, we showed already that the sequence $\{0, -1, 0, 1\}$ is odd. However, the sequence $\{0, -1, 0, 1, 0\}$ is neither odd nor even, although the "basic" structure appears to be odd. This is an important issue in interpreting DFT results. We will show later in this section that the DFTs of even and odd functions have some very important characteristics. Thus, it often is the case that understanding when a function is odd or even plays a key role in our ability to interpret image results based on DFTs.

The same basic considerations hold in 2-D. For example, the 6×6 2-D array with center at location $(3,3)$, shown bold in the figure [remember, we start counting at $(0,0)$],

$$
\begin{array}{cccccc}
0 & 0 & 0 & 0 & 0 & 0 \\
0 & 0 & 0 & 0 & 0 & 0 \\
0 & 0 & -1 & 0 & 1 & 0 \\
0 & 0 & -2 & \mathbf{0} & 2 & 0 \\
0 & 0 & -1 & 0 & 1 & 0 \\
0 & 0 & 0 & 0 & 0 & 0 \\
\end{array}
$$

is odd, as you can prove using Eq. (4-83). However, adding another row or column of 0's would give a result that is neither odd nor even. In general, inserting a 2-D array of *even dimensions* into a larger array of zeros, *also* of even dimensions, preserves the symmetry of the smaller array, provided that the centers coincide. Similarly, a 2-D array of *odd dimensions* can be inserted into a larger array of zeros of *odd dimensions* without affecting the symmetry. Note that the inner structure of the preceding array is a Sobel kernel (see Fig. 3.50). We return to this kernel in Example 4.15, where we embed it in a larger array of zeros for filtering purposes.

Conjugate symmetry is also called *hermitian symmetry*. The term *antihermitian* is used sometimes to refer to conjugate antisymmetry.

Armed with the preceding concepts, we can establish a number of important symmetry properties of the DFT and its inverse. A property used frequently is that the Fourier transform of a *real* function, $f(x, y)$, is *conjugate symmetric*:

$$F^{*}(u,v) = F(-u,-v) \qquad (4\text{-}85)$$

We show the validity of this equation as follows:

$$
\begin{aligned}
F^{*}(u,v) &= \left[\sum_{x=0}^{M-1} \sum_{y=0}^{N-1} f(x,y) e^{-j2\pi(ux/M + vy/N)} \right]^{*} \\
&= \sum_{x=0}^{M-1} \sum_{y=0}^{N-1} f^{*}(x,y) e^{j2\pi(ux/M + vy/N)} \\
&= \sum_{x=0}^{M-1} \sum_{y=0}^{N-1} f(x,y) e^{-j2\pi([-u]x/M + [-v]y/N)} \\
&= F(-u,-v)
\end{aligned}
$$

where the third step follows from the fact that $f(x,y)$ is real. A similar approach can be used to prove that, if $f(x,y)$ is *imaginary*, its Fourier transform is conjugate *antisymmetric*; that is, $F^{*}(-u,-v) = -F(u,v)$.

Table 4.1 lists symmetries and related properties of the DFT that are useful in digital image processing. Recall that the double arrows indicate Fourier transform pairs; that is, for any row in the table, the properties on the right are satisfied by the Fourier transform of the function having the properties listed on the left, and vice versa. For example, entry 5 reads: The DFT of a real function $f(x,y)$, in which (x,y)

TABLE 4.1
Some symmetry properties of the 2-D DFT and its inverse. $R(u,v)$ and $I(u,v)$ are the real and imaginary parts of $F(u,v)$, respectively. Use of the word *complex* indicates that a function has nonzero real and imaginary parts.

	Spatial Domain†		Frequency Domain†
1)	$f(x,y)$ real	$\Leftrightarrow$	$F^{*}(u,v) = F(-u,-v)$
2)	$f(x,y)$ imaginary	$\Leftrightarrow$	$F^{*}(-u,-v) = -F(u,v)$
3)	$f(x,y)$ real	$\Leftrightarrow$	$R(u,v)$ even; $I(u,v)$ odd
4)	$f(x,y)$ imaginary	$\Leftrightarrow$	$R(u,v)$ odd; $I(u,v)$ even
5)	$f(-x,-y)$ real	$\Leftrightarrow$	$F^{*}(u,v)$ complex
6)	$f(-x,-y)$ complex	$\Leftrightarrow$	$F(-u,-v)$ complex
7)	$f^{*}(x,y)$ complex	$\Leftrightarrow$	$F^{*}(-u,-v)$ complex
8)	$f(x,y)$ real and even	$\Leftrightarrow$	$F(u,v)$ real and even
9)	$f(x,y)$ real and odd	$\Leftrightarrow$	$F(u,v)$ imaginary and odd
10)	$f(x,y)$ imaginary and even	$\Leftrightarrow$	$F(u,v)$ imaginary and even
11)	$f(x,y)$ imaginary and odd	$\Leftrightarrow$	$F(u,v)$ real and odd
12)	$f(x,y)$ complex and even	$\Leftrightarrow$	$F(u,v)$ complex and even
13)	$f(x,y)$ complex and odd	$\Leftrightarrow$	$F(u,v)$ complex and odd

†Recall that $x, y, u,$ and v are *discrete* (integer) variables, with x and u in the range $[0, M-1]$, and y and v in the range $[0, N-1]$. To say that a complex function is *even* means that its real *and* imaginary parts are even, and similarly for an *odd* complex function. As before, "$\Leftrightarrow$" indicates a Fourier transform pair.

is replaced by $(-x,-y)$, is $F^*(u,v)$, the complex conjugate of the DFT of $f(x,y)$. Conversely, the IDFT of $F^*(u,v)$ is $f(-x,-y)$.

EXAMPLE 4.11: 1-D illustrations of the properties in Table 4.1.

The 1-D sequences (functions) and their transforms in Table 4.2 are short examples of the properties listed in Table 4.1. For example, in property 3 we see that a real function with elements $\{1, 2, 3, 4\}$ has a Fourier transform whose real part, $\{10, -2, -2, -2\}$, is even and whose imaginary part, $\{0, 2, 0, -2\}$, is odd. Property 8 tells us that a real even function has a transform that is real and even also. Property 12 shows that an even complex function has a transform that is also complex and even. The other listings in the table are analyzed in a similar manner.

EXAMPLE 4.12: Proving some of the DFT symmetry properties from Table 4.1.

In this example, we prove several of the properties in Table 4.1 to help you develop familiarity with manipulating these important properties, and to establish a basis for solving some of the problems at the end of the chapter. We prove only the properties on the right given the properties on the left. The converse is proved in a manner similar to the proofs we give here.

Consider property 3, which reads: If $f(x,y)$ is a real function, the real part of its DFT is even and the imaginary part is odd. We prove this property as follows: $F(u,v)$ is complex in general, so it can be expressed as the sum of a real and an imaginary part: $F(u,v) = R(u,v) + jI(u,v)$. Then, $F^*(u,v) = R(u,v) - jI(u,v)$. Also, $F(-u,-v) = R(-u,-v) + jI(-u,-v)$. But, as we proved earlier for Eq. (4-85), if $f(x,y)$ is real then $F^*(u,v) = F(-u,-v)$, which, based on the preceding two equations, means that $R(u,v) = R(-u,-v)$ and $I(u,v) = -I(-u,-v)$. In view of the definitions in Eqs. (4-80) and (4-81), this proves that R is an even function and that I is an odd function.

Next, we prove property 8. If $f(x,y)$ is real, we know from property 3 that the real part of $F(u,v)$ is even, so to prove property 8 all we have to do is show that if $f(x,y)$ is real and even then the imaginary part of $F(u,v)$ is 0 (i.e., F is real). The steps are as follows:

TABLE 4.2 1-D examples of some of the properties in Table 4.1.	**Property**	$f(x)$		$F(u)$
	3	$\{1, 2, 3, 4\}$	$\Leftrightarrow$	$\{(10+0j),(-2+2j),(-2+0j),(-2-2j)\}$
	4	$\{1j, 2j, 3j, 4j\}$	$\Leftrightarrow$	$\{(0+2.5j),(.5-.5j),(0-.5j),(-.5-.5j)\}$
	8	$\{2, 1, 1, 1\}$	$\Leftrightarrow$	$\{5, 1, 1, 1\}$
	9	$\{0, -1, 0, 1\}$	$\Leftrightarrow$	$\{(0+0j),(0+2j),(0+0j),(0-2j)\}$
	10	$\{2j, 1j, 1j, 1j\}$	$\Leftrightarrow$	$\{5j, j, j, j\}$
	11	$\{0j, -1j, 0j, 1j\}$	$\Leftrightarrow$	$\{0, -2, 0, 2\}$
	12	$\{(4+4j),(3+2j),(0+2j),(3+2j)\}$	$\Leftrightarrow$	$\{(10+10j),(4+2j),(-2+2j),(4+2j)\}$
	13	$\{(0+0j),(1+1j),(0+0j),(-1-j)\}$	$\Leftrightarrow$	$\{(0+0j),(2-2j),(0+0j),(-2+2j)\}$

$$\Im\{f(x,y)\} = F(u,v) = \sum_{x=0}^{M-1}\sum_{y=0}^{N-1} f(x,y)e^{-j2\pi(ux/M + vy/N)}$$

$$= \sum_{x=0}^{M-1}\sum_{y=0}^{N-1} [f_r(x,y)]e^{-j2\pi(ux/M + vy/N)}$$

$$= \sum_{x=0}^{M-1}\sum_{y=0}^{N-1} [f_r(x,y)]e^{-j2\pi(ux/M)}e^{-j2\pi(vy/N)}$$

We can expand the last line of this expression in terms of even and odd parts

$$F(u,v) = \sum_{x=0}^{M-1}\sum_{y=0}^{N-1} [\text{even}][\text{even} - j\text{odd}][\text{even} - j\text{odd}]$$

$$= \sum_{x=0}^{M-1}\sum_{y=0}^{N-1} [\text{even}][\text{even}\cdot\text{even} - 2j\text{even}\cdot\text{odd} - \text{odd}\cdot\text{odd}]$$

$$= \sum_{x=0}^{M-1}\sum_{y=0}^{N-1} [\text{even}\cdot\text{even}] - 2j\sum_{x=0}^{M-1}\sum_{y=0}^{N-1}[\text{even}\cdot\text{odd}] - \sum_{x=0}^{M-1}\sum_{y=0}^{N-1}[\text{even}\cdot\text{even}]$$

$$= \text{real.}$$

The first step follows from Euler's equation, and the fact that the cos and sin are even and odd functions, respectively. We also know from property 8 that, in addition to being real, $f(x,y)$ is an even function. The only term in the penultimate line containing imaginary components is the second term, which is 0 according to Eq. (4-84). Therefore, if $f(x,y)$ is real and even, then $F(u,v)$ is real. As noted earlier, $F(u,v)$ is even also because $f(x,y)$ is real. This concludes the proof.

Finally, we demonstrate the validity of property 6. From the definition of the DFT,

$$\Im\{f(-x,-y)\} = \sum_{x=0}^{M-1}\sum_{y=0}^{N-1} f(-x,-y)e^{-j2\pi(ux/M+vy/N)}$$

We are not making a change of variable here. We are evaluating the DFT of $f(-x,-y)$, so we simply insert this function into the equation, as we would any other function. Because of periodicity, $f(-x,-y) = f(M-x, N-y)$. If we now define $m = M - x$ and $n = N - y$, then

$$\Im\{f(-x,-y)\} = \sum_{m=0}^{M-1}\sum_{n=0}^{N-1} f(m,n)e^{-j2\pi(u[M-m]/M+v[N-n]/N)}$$

To convince yourself that the summations are correct, try a 1-D transform and expand a few terms by hand. Because $\exp[-j2\pi(\text{integer})] = 1$, it follows that

$$\Im\{f(-x,-y)\} = \sum_{m=0}^{M-1}\sum_{n=0}^{N-1} f(m,n)e^{j2\pi(mu/M+vn/N)} = F(-u,-v)$$

This concludes the proof.

FOURIER SPECTRUM AND PHASE ANGLE

Because the 2-D DFT is complex in general, it can be expressed in polar form:

$$F(u,v) = R(u,v) + jI(u,v)$$
$$= |F(u,v)|e^{j\phi(u,v)} \tag{4-86}$$

where the magnitude

$$|F(u,v)| = \left[R^2(u,v) + I^2(u,v) \right]^{1/2} \tag{4-87}$$

is called the *Fourier* (or *frequency*) *spectrum*, and

$$\phi(u,v) = \arctan\left[\frac{I(u,v)}{R(u,v)} \right] \tag{4-88}$$

is the *phase angle* or *phase spectrum*. Recall from the discussion in Section 4.2 that the arctan must be computed using a four-quadrant arctangent function, such as MATLAB's **atan2(Imag, Real)** function.

Finally, the *power spectrum* is defined as

$$P(u,v) = |F(u,v)|^2$$
$$= R^2(u,v) + I^2(u,v) \tag{4-89}$$

As before, R and I are the real and imaginary parts of $F(u,v)$, and all computations are carried out for the discrete variables $u = 0, 1, 2, \ldots, M-1$ and $v = 0, 1, 2, \ldots, N-1$. Therefore, $|F(u,v)|$, $\phi(u,v)$, and $P(u,v)$ are arrays of size $M \times N$.

The Fourier transform of a real function is conjugate symmetric [see Eq. (4-85)], which implies that the spectrum has *even* symmetry about the origin:

$$|F(u,v)| = |F(-u,-v)| \tag{4-90}$$

The phase angle exhibits *odd* symmetry about the origin:

$$\phi(u,v) = -\phi(-u,-v) \tag{4-91}$$

It follows from Eq. (4-67) that

$$F(0,0) = \sum_{x=0}^{M-1} \sum_{y=0}^{N-1} f(x,y)$$

which indicates that the zero-frequency term of the DFT is proportional to the average of $f(x,y)$. That is,

$$F(0,0) = MN \frac{1}{MN} \sum_{x=0}^{M-1} \sum_{y=0}^{N-1} f(x,y) \tag{4-92}$$
$$= MN\bar{f}$$

where $\bar{f}$ (a scalar) denotes the average value of $f(x, y)$. Then,

$$|F(0,0)| = MN \, |\bar{f}| \tag{4-93}$$

Because the proportionality constant MN usually is large, $|F(0,0)|$ typically is the largest component of the spectrum by a factor that can be several orders of magnitude larger than other terms. Because frequency components u and v are zero at the origin, $F(0,0)$ sometimes is called the *dc component* of the transform. This terminology is from electrical engineering, where "dc" signifies direct current (i.e., current of zero frequency).

EXAMPLE 4.13: The spectrum of a rectangle.

Figure 4.23(a) shows an image of a rectangle and Fig. 4.23(b) shows its spectrum, whose values were scaled to the range $[0, 255]$ and displayed in image form. The origins of both the spatial and frequency domains are at the top left. This is the right-handed coordinate system convention we defined in Fig. 2.19. Two things are apparent in Fig. 4.23(b). As expected, the area around the origin of the transform contains the highest values (and thus appears brighter in the image). However, note that the four corners

a b
c d

FIGURE 4.23
(a) Image.
(b) Spectrum, showing small, bright areas in the four corners (you have to look carefully to see them).
(c) Centered spectrum.
(d) Result after a log transformation. The zero crossings of the spectrum are closer in the vertical direction because the rectangle in (a) is longer in that direction. The right-handed coordinate convention used in the book places the origin of the spatial and frequency domains at the top left (see Fig. 2.19).

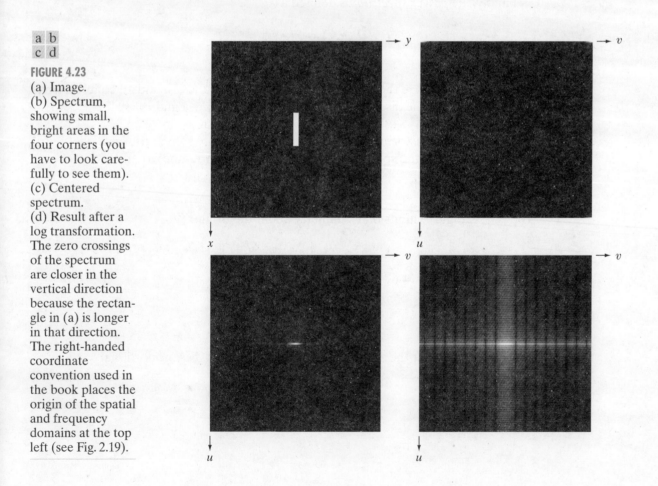

a b
c d

FIGURE 4.24
(a) The rectangle
in Fig. 4.23(a)
translated.
(b) Corresponding
spectrum.
(c) Rotated
rectangle.
(d) Corresponding
 spectrum.
The spectrum of
the translated
rectangle is
identical to the
spectrum of the
original image in
Fig. 4.23(a).

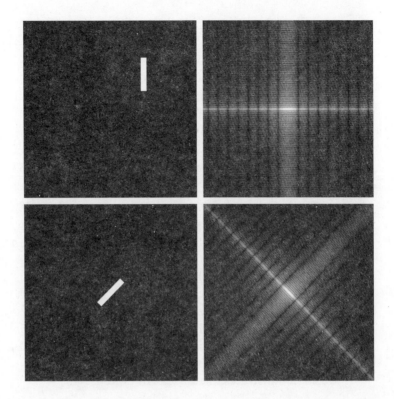

of the spectrum contain similarly high values. The reason is the periodicity property discussed in the previous section. To center the spectrum, we simply multiply the image in (a) by $(-1)^{x+y}$ before computing the DFT, as indicated in Eq. (4-76). Figure 4.23(c) shows the result, which clearly is much easier to visualize (note the symmetry about the center point). Because the dc term dominates the values of the spectrum, the dynamic range of other intensities in the displayed image are compressed. To bring out those details, we used the log transformation defined in Eq. (3-4) with $c = 1$. Figure 4.23(d) shows the display of $\log(1 + |F(u,v)|)$. The increased rendition of detail is evident. Most spectra shown in this and subsequent chapters are scaled in this manner.

It follows from Eqs. (4-72) and (4-73) that the spectrum is insensitive to image translation (the absolute value of the exponential term is 1), but it rotates by the same angle of a rotated image. Figure 4.24 illustrates these properties. The spectrum in Fig. 4.24(b) is identical to the spectrum in Fig. 4.23(d).

a b c

FIGURE 4.25
Phase angle
images of
(a) centered,
(b) translated,
and (c) rotated
rectangles.

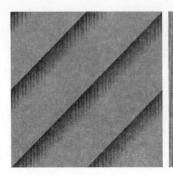  

Clearly, the images in Figs. 4.23(a) and 4.24(a) are different so, if their Fourier spectra are the same, then, based on Eq. (4-86), their phase angles must be different. Figure 4.25 confirms this. Figures 4.25(a) and (b) are the phase angle arrays (shown as images) of the DFTs of Figs. 4.23(a) and 4.24(a). Note the lack of similarity between the phase images, in spite of the fact that the only differences between their corresponding images is simple translation. In general, visual analysis of phase angle images yields little intuitive information. For instance, because of its 45° orientation, one would expect intuitively that the phase angle in Fig. 4.25(a) should correspond to the rotated image in Fig. 4.24(c), rather than to the image in Fig. 4.23(a). In fact, as Fig. 4.25(c) shows, the phase angle of the rotated image has a strong orientation that is much less than 45°.

The components of the spectrum of the DFT determine the amplitudes of the sinusoids that combine to form an image. At any given frequency in the DFT of an image, a large amplitude implies a greater prominence of a sinusoid of that frequency in the image. Conversely, a small amplitude implies that less of that sinusoid is present in the image. Although, as Fig. 4.25 shows, the contribution of the phase components is less intuitive, it is just as important. The phase is a measure of displacement of the various sinusoids with respect to their origin. Thus, while the magnitude of the 2-D DFT is an array whose components determine the intensities in the image, the corresponding phase is an array of angles that carry much of the information about where discernible objects are located in the image. The following example illustrates these ideas in more detail.

EXAMPLE 4.14: Contributions of the spectrum and phase angle to image formation.

Figure 4.26(b) shows as an image the phase-angle array, $\phi(u,v)$, of the DFT of Fig. 4.26(a), computed using Eq. (4-88). Although there is no detail in this array that would lead us by visual analysis to associate it with the structure of its corresponding image, the information in this array is crucial in determining shape features of the image. To illustrate this, we reconstructed the boy's image using only its phase angle. The reconstruction consisted of computing the inverse DFT of Eq. (4-86) using $\phi(u,v)$, but setting $|F(u,v)| = 1$. Figure Fig. 4.26(c) shows the result (the original result had much less contrast than is shown; to bring out details important in this discussion, we scaled the result using Eqs. (2-31) and (2-32), and then enhanced it using histogram equalization). However, even after enhancement, it is evident that much of the intensity information has been lost (remember, that information is carried by the spectrum, which we did not use in the reconstruction). However, the *shape* features in 4.26(c) are unmistakably from Fig. 4.26(a). This illustrates vividly the importance of the phase angle in determining shape characteristics in an image.

Figure 4.26(d) was obtained by computing the inverse DFT Eq. (4-86), but using only the spectrum. This means setting the exponential term to 1, which in turn implies setting the phase angle to 0. The result is not unexpected. It contains only intensity information, with the dc term being the most dominant. There is no shape information in the image because the phase was set to zero.

Finally, Figs. 4.26(e) and (f) show yet again the dominance of the phase in determining the spatial feature content of an image. Figure 4.26(e) was obtained by computing the inverse DFT of Eq. (4-86) using the spectrum of the rectangle from Fig. 4.23(a) and the phase angle from the boy's image. The boy's features clearly dominate this result. Conversely, the rectangle dominates Fig. 4.26(f), which was computed using the spectrum of the boy's image and the phase angle of the rectangle.

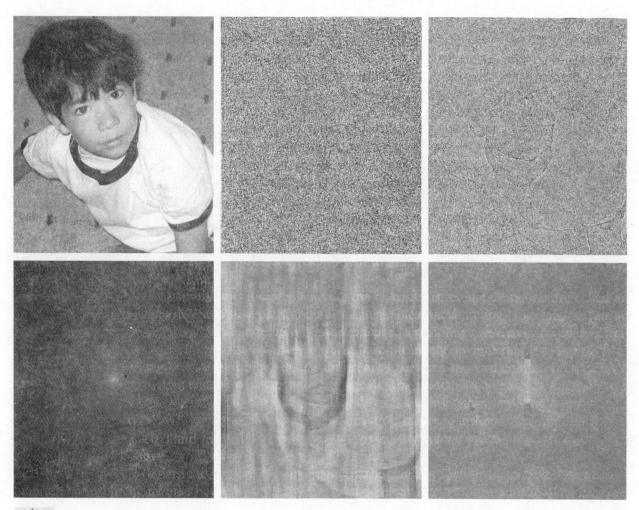

a b c
d e f

FIGURE 4.26 (a) Boy image. (b) Phase angle. (c) Boy image reconstructed using only its phase angle (all shape features are there, but the intensity information is missing because the spectrum was not used in the reconstruction). (d) Boy image reconstructed using only its spectrum. (e) Boy image reconstructed using its phase angle and the spectrum of the rectangle in Fig. 4.23(a). (f) Rectangle image reconstructed using its phase and the spectrum of the boy's image.

THE 2-D DISCRETE CONVOLUTION THEOREM

You will find it helpful to review Eq. (4-48), and the comments made there regarding circular convolution, as opposed to the convolution we studied in Section 3.4.

Extending Eq. (4-48) to two variables results in the following expression for 2-D *circular convolution*:

$$(f \star h)(x,y) = \sum_{m=0}^{M-1}\sum_{n=0}^{N-1} f(m,n)h(x-m,y-n) \qquad (4-94)$$

for $x = 0, 1, 2, \ldots, M-1$ and $y = 0, 1, 2, \ldots, N-1$. As in Eq. (4-48), Eq. (4-94) gives one period of a 2-D periodic sequence. The 2-D convolution theorem is give by

$$(f \star h)(x,y) \Leftrightarrow (F \cdot H)(u,v) \qquad (4-95)$$

and, conversely,

$$(f \cdot h)(x, y) \Leftrightarrow \frac{1}{MN}(F \star H)(u, v) \tag{4-96}$$

The function products
are elementwise products,
as defined in Section 2.6.

where F and H are the Fourier transforms of f and h, respectively, obtained using Eq. (4-67). As before, the double arrow is used to indicate that the left and right sides of the expressions constitute a Fourier transform pair. Our interest in the remainder of this chapter is in Eq. (4-95), which states that the Fourier transform of the spatial convolution of f and h, is the product of their transforms. Similarly, the inverse DFT of the product $(F \cdot H)(u, v)$ yields $(f \star h)(x, y)$.

Equation (4-95) is the foundation of linear filtering in the frequency domain and, as we will explain in Section 4.7, is the basis for all the filtering techniques discussed in this chapter. As you will recall from Chapter 3, spatial convolution is the foundation for spatial filtering, so Eq. (4-95) is the tie that establishes the equivalence between spatial and frequency-domain filtering, as we have mentioned several times before.

Ultimately, we are interested in the results of convolution in the spatial domain, where we analyze images. However, the convolution theorem tell us that we have two ways of computing the spatial convolution of two functions. We can do it directly in the spatial domain with Eq. (3-35), using the approach described in Section 3.4 or, according to Eq. (4-95), we can compute the Fourier transform of each function, multiply the transforms, and compute the inverse Fourier transform. Because we are dealing with discrete quantities, computation of the Fourier transforms is carried out using a DFT algorithm. This automatically implies periodicity, which means that when we take the inverse Fourier transform of the product of the two transforms we would get a circular (i.e., periodic) convolution, one period of which is given by Eq. (4-94). The question is: under what conditions will the direct spatial approach and the inverse Fourier transform method yield the same result? We arrive at the answer by looking at a 1-D example first, and then extending the results to two variables.

We will discuss efficient
ways for computing the
DFT in Section 4.11.

The left column of Fig. 4.27 implements convolution of two functions, f and h, using the 1-D equivalent of Eq. (3-35), which, because the two functions are of same size, is written as

$$(f \star h)(x) = \sum_{m=0}^{399} f(x) h(x - m)$$

Recall from our explanation of Figs. 3.29 and 3.30 that the procedure consists of (1) rotating (flipping) h by 180°, [see Fig. 4.27(c)], (2) translating the resulting function by an amount x [Fig. 4.27(d)], and (3) for *each* value x of translation, computing the entire sum of products in the right side of the equation. In terms of Fig. 4.27, this means multiplying the function in Fig. 4.27(a) by the function in Fig. 4.27(d) for *each* value of x. The displacement x ranges over all values required to completely slide h across f. Figure 4.27(e) shows the convolution of these two functions. As you know, convolution is a function of the displacement variable, x, and the range of x required in this example to completely slide h past f is from 0 to 799.

FIGURE 4.27
Left column:
Spatial
convolution
computed with
Eq. (3-35), using
the approach
discussed in
Section 3.4.
Right column:
Circular
convolution. The
solid line in (j)
is the result we
would obtain
using the DFT,
or, equivalently,
Eq. (4-48). This
erroneous result
can be remedied
by using zero
padding.

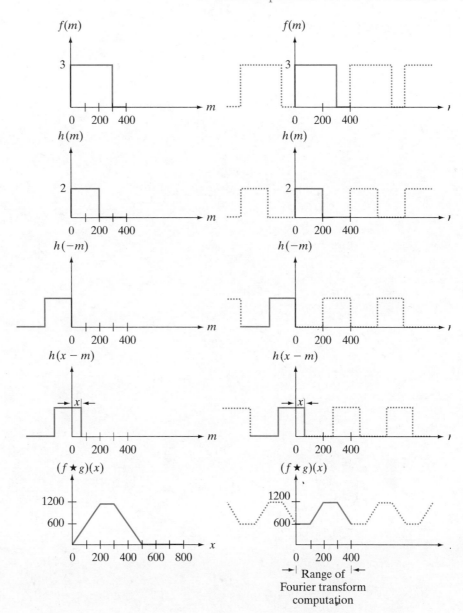

If we use the DFT and the convolution theorem to try to obtain the same result as in the left column of Fig. 4.27, we must take into account the periodicity inherent in the expression for the DFT. This is equivalent to convolving the two periodic functions in Figs. 4.27(f) and (g) (i.e., as Eqs. (4-46) and (4-47) indicate, the functions their transforms have implied periodicity). The convolution procedure is the same as we just discussed, but the two functions now are periodic. Proceeding with these two functions as in the previous paragraph would yield the result in Fig. 4.27(j), which obviously is incorrect. Because we are convolving two periodic functions, the convolution itself is periodic. The closeness of the periods in Fig. 4.27 is such that they interfere with each other to cause what is commonly referred to as *wraparound error*. According to the convolution theorem, if we had computed the DFT of the two 400-point functions, f and h, multiplied the two transforms, and then computed the inverse DFT, we would have obtained the erroneous 400-point segment of the periodic convolution shown as a solid line in Fig. 4.27(j) (remember the limits of the 1-D DFT are $u = 0, 1, 2, \ldots, M - 1$). This is also the result we would obtain if we used Eq. (4-48) [the 1-D equivalent of Eq. (4-94)] to compute one period of the circular convolution.

Fortunately, the solution to the wraparound error problem is simple. Consider two functions, $f(x)$ and $h(x)$ composed of A and B samples, respectively. It can be shown (Brigham [1988]) that if we append zeros to both functions so that they have the same length, denoted by P, then wraparound is avoided by choosing

$$P \geq A + B - 1 \tag{4-97}$$

In our example, each function has 400 points, so the minimum value we could use is $P = 799$, which implies that we would append 399 zeros to the trailing edge of each function. This procedure is called *zero padding*, as we discussed in Section 3.4. As an exercise, you should convince yourself that if the periods of the functions in Figs. 4.27(f) and (g) were lengthened by appending to each period at least 399 zeros, the result would be a periodic convolution in which each period is identical to the correct result in Fig. 4.27(e). Using the DFT via the convolution theorem would result in a 799-point spatial function identical to Fig. 4.27(e). The conclusion, then, is that to obtain the same convolution result between the "straight" representation of the convolution equation approach in Chapter 3, and the DFT approach, functions in the latter must be padded prior to computing their transforms.

The padding zeros could be appended also at the beginning of the functions, or they could be divided between the beginning and end of the functions. It is simpler to append them at the end.

Visualizing a similar example in 2-D is more difficult, but we would arrive at the same conclusion regarding wraparound error and the need for appending zeros to the functions. Let $f(x, y)$ and $h(x, y)$ be two image arrays of sizes $A \times B$ and $C \times D$ pixels, respectively. Wraparound error in their circular convolution can be avoided by padding these functions with zeros, as follows:

We use zero-padding here for simplicity. Recall from the discussion of Fig. 3.39 that replicate and mirror padding generally yield better results.

$$f_p(x, y) = \begin{cases} f(x, y) & 0 \leq x \leq A - 1 \text{ and } 0 \leq y \leq B - 1 \\ 0 & A \leq x \leq P \text{ or } B \leq y \leq Q \end{cases} \tag{4-98}$$

and

$$h_p(x, y) = \begin{cases} h(x, y) & 0 \leq x \leq C - 1 \text{ and } 0 \leq y \leq D - 1 \\ 0 & C \leq x \leq P \text{ or } D \leq y \leq Q \end{cases} \tag{4-99}$$

with

$$P \geq A + C - 1 \tag{4-100}$$

and

$$Q \geq B + D - 1 \qquad (4\text{-}101)$$

The resulting padded images are of size $P \times Q$. If both arrays are of the same size, $M \times N$, then we require that $P \geq 2M - 1$ and $Q \geq 2N - 1$. As a rule, DFT algorithms tend to execute faster with arrays of even size, so it is good practice to select P and Q as the smallest even integers that satisfy the preceding equations. If the two arrays are of the same size, this means that P and Q are selected as:

$$P = 2M \qquad (4\text{-}102)$$

and

$$Q = 2N \qquad (4\text{-}103)$$

Figure 4.31 in the next section illustrates the effects of wraparound error on images.

The two functions in Figs. 4.27(a) and (b) conveniently become zero before the end of the sampling interval. If one or both of the functions were not zero at the end of the interval, then a discontinuity would be created when zeros were appended to the function to eliminate wraparound error. This is analogous to multiplying a function by a box, which in the frequency domain would imply convolution of the original transform with a sinc function (see Example 4.1). This, in turn, would create so-called *frequency leakage*, caused by the high-frequency components of the sinc function. Leakage produces a blocky effect on images. Although leakage can never be totally eliminated, it can be reduced significantly by multiplying the sampled function by another function that tapers smoothly to near zero at both ends of the sampled record. This idea is to dampen the sharp transitions (and thus the high frequency components) of the box. This approach, called *windowing* or *apodizing*, is an important consideration when fidelity in image reconstruction (as in high-definition graphics) is desired.

A simple apodizing function is a triangle, centered on the data record, which tapers to 0 at both ends of the record. This is called a *Bartlett window*. Other common windows are the Gaussian, the *Hamming* and the *Hann* windows.

SUMMARY OF 2-D DISCRETE FOURIER TRANSFORM PROPERTIES

Table 4.3 summarizes the principal DFT definitions introduced in this chapter. We will discuss the separability property in Section 4.11, where we also show how to obtain the inverse DFT using a forward transform algorithm. Correlation will be discussed in detail Chapter 12.

Table 4.4 summarizes some important DFT pairs. Although our focus is on discrete functions, the last two entries in the table are Fourier transform pairs that can be derived only for continuous variables (note the use of continuous variable notation). We include them here because, with proper interpretation, they are quite useful in digital image processing. The differentiation pair can be used to derive the frequency-domain equivalent of the Laplacian defined in Eq. (3-50) (see Problem 4.52). The Gaussian pair is discussed in Section 4.7. Tables 4.1, 4.3 and 4.4 provide a summary of properties useful when working with the DFT. Many of these properties are key elements in the development of the material in the rest of this chapter, and some are used in subsequent chapters.

Summary of DFT definitions and corresponding expressions.

	Name	Expression(s)
1)	Discrete Fourier transform (DFT) of $f(x,y)$	$F(u,v) = \sum_{x=0}^{M-1}\sum_{y=0}^{N-1} f(x,y)e^{-j2\pi(ux/M+vy/N)}$
2)	Inverse discrete Fourier transform (IDFT) of $F(u,v)$	$f(x,y) = \dfrac{1}{MN}\sum_{u=0}^{M-1}\sum_{v=0}^{N-1} F(u,v)e^{j2\pi(ux/M+vy/N)}$
3)	Spectrum	$\lvert F(u,v)\rvert = \left[R^2(u,v) + I^2(u,v)\right]^{1/2}$ $R = \text{Real}(F);\ I = \text{Imag}(F)$
4)	Phase angle	$\phi(u,v) = \tan^{-1}\left[\dfrac{I(u,v)}{R(u,v)}\right]$
5)	Polar representation	$F(u,v) = \lvert F(u,v)\rvert e^{j\phi(u,v)}$
6)	Power spectrum	$P(u,v) = \lvert F(u,v)\rvert^2$
7)	Average value	$\bar{f} = \dfrac{1}{MN}\sum_{x=0}^{M-1}\sum_{y=0}^{N-1} f(x,y) = \dfrac{1}{MN}F(0,0)$
8)	Periodicity (k_1 and k_2 are integers)	$F(u,v) = F(u+k_1 M, v) = F(u, v+k_2 N)$ $\qquad = F(u+k_1, v+k_2 N)$ $f(x,y) = f(x+k_1 M, y) = f(x, y+k_2 N)$ $\qquad = f(x+k_1 M, y+k_2 N)$
9)	Convolution	$(f \star h)(x,y) = \sum_{m=0}^{M-1}\sum_{n=0}^{N-1} f(m,n)h(x-m, y-n)$
10)	Correlation	$(f \star h)(x,y) = \sum_{m=0}^{M-1}\sum_{n=0}^{N-1} f^*(m,n)h(x+m, y+n)$
11)	Separability	The 2-D DFT can be computed by computing 1-D DFT transforms along the rows (columns) of the image, followed by 1-D transforms along the columns (rows) of the result. See Section 4.11.
12)	Obtaining the IDFT using a DFT algorithm	$MNf^*(x,y) = \sum_{u=0}^{M-1}\sum_{v=0}^{N-1} F^*(u,v)e^{-j2\pi(ux/M+vy/N)}$ This equation indicates that inputting $F^*(u,v)$ into an algorithm that computes the forward transform (right side of above equation) yields $MNf^*(x,y)$. Taking the complex conjugate and dividing by MN gives the desired inverse. See Section 4.11.

	Name	**DFT Pairs**

TABLE 4.4
Summmary of DFT pairs. The closed-form expressions in 12 and 13 are valid only for continuous variables. They can be used with discrete variables by sampling the continuous expressions.

1)	Symmetry properties	See Table 4.1
2)	Linearity	$af_1(x,y) + bf_2(x,y) \Leftrightarrow aF_1(u,v) + bF_2(u,v)$
3)	Translation (general)	$f(x,y)e^{j2\pi(u_0x/M + v_0y/N)} \Leftrightarrow F(u-u_0, v-v_0)$ $f(x-x_0, y-y_0) \Leftrightarrow F(u,v)e^{-j2\pi(ux_0/M + vy_0/N)}$
4)	Translation to center of the frequency rectangle, $(M/2, N/2)$	$f(x,y)(-1)^{x+y} \Leftrightarrow F(u-M/2, v-N/2)$ $f(x-M/2, y-N/2) \Leftrightarrow F(u,v)(-1)^{u+v}$
5)	Rotation	$f(r, \theta + \theta_0) \Leftrightarrow F(\omega, \varphi + \theta_0)$ $r = \sqrt{x^2 + y^2} \quad \theta = \tan^{-1}(y/x) \quad \omega = \sqrt{u^2 + v^2} \quad \varphi = \tan^{-1}(v/u)$
6)	Convolution theorem[†]	$f \star h(x,y) \Leftrightarrow (F \cdot H)(u,v)$ $(f \cdot h)(x,y) \Leftrightarrow (1/MN)[(F \star H)(u,v)]$
7)	Correlation theorem[†]	$(f \star h)(x,y) \Leftrightarrow (F^* \cdot H)(u,v)$ $(f^* \cdot h)(x,y) \Leftrightarrow (1/MN)[(F \star H)(u,v)]$
8)	Discrete unit impulse	$\delta(x,y) \Leftrightarrow 1$ $1 \Leftrightarrow MN\delta(u,v)$
9)	Rectangle	$\text{rec}[a,b] \Leftrightarrow ab\dfrac{\sin(\pi ua)}{(\pi ua)}\dfrac{\sin(\pi vb)}{(\pi vb)}e^{-j\pi(ua+vb)}$
10)	Sine	$\sin(2\pi u_0 x/M + 2\pi v_0 y/N) \Leftrightarrow \dfrac{jMN}{2}[\delta(u+u_0, v+v_0) - \delta(u-u_0, v-v_0)]$
11)	Cosine	$\cos(2\pi u_0 x/M + 2\pi v_0 y/N) \Leftrightarrow \dfrac{1}{2}[\delta(u+u_0, v+v_0) + \delta(u-u_0, v-v_0)]$

The following Fourier transform pairs are derivable only for continuous variables, denoted as before by t and z for spatial variables and by μ and ν for frequency variables. These results can be used for DFT work by sampling the continuous forms.

12)	Differentiation (the expressions on the right assume that $f(\pm\infty, \pm\infty) = 0$.	$\left(\dfrac{\partial}{\partial t}\right)^m \left(\dfrac{\partial}{\partial z}\right)^n f(t,z) \Leftrightarrow (j2\pi\mu)^m(j2\pi\nu)^n F(\mu,\nu)$ $\dfrac{\partial^m f(t,z)}{\partial t^m} \Leftrightarrow (j2\pi\mu)^m F(\mu,\nu); \quad \dfrac{\partial^n f(t,z)}{\partial z^m} \Leftrightarrow (j2\pi\nu)^n F(\mu,\nu)$
13)	Gaussian	$A2\pi\sigma^2 e^{-2\pi^2\sigma^2(t^2+z^2)} \Leftrightarrow Ae^{-(\mu^2+\nu^2)/2\sigma^2}$ \quad (A is a constant)

[†]Assumes that $f(x,y)$ and $h(x,y)$ have been properly padded. Convolution is associative, commutative, and distributive (see Table 3.5). Correlation is distributive (see Table 3.5). The products are elementwise products (see Section 2.6).

4.7 THE BASICS OF FILTERING IN THE FREQUENCY DOMAIN

In this section, we lay the groundwork for all the filtering techniques discussed in the remainder of the chapter.

ADDITIONAL CHARACTERISTICS OF THE FREQUENCY DOMAIN

We begin by observing in Eq. (4-67) that *each* term of $F(u,v)$ contains *all* values of $f(x,y)$, modified by the values of the exponential terms. Thus, with the exception of trivial cases, it is usually impossible to make direct associations between specific components of an image and its transform. However, some general statements can be made about the relationship between the frequency components of the Fourier transform and spatial features of an image. For instance, because frequency is directly related to spatial rates of change, it is not difficult intuitively to associate frequencies in the Fourier transform with patterns of intensity variations in an image. We showed in Section 4.6 that the slowest varying frequency component $(u = v = 0)$ is proportional to the average intensity of an image. As we move away from the origin of the transform, the low frequencies correspond to the slowly varying intensity components of an image. In an image of a room, for example, these might correspond to smooth intensity variations on the walls and floor. As we move further away from the origin, the higher frequencies begin to correspond to faster and faster intensity changes in the image. These are the edges of objects and other components of an image characterized by abrupt changes in intensity.

Filtering techniques in the frequency domain are based on modifying the Fourier transform to achieve a specific objective, and then computing the inverse DFT to get us back to the spatial domain, as introduced in Section 2.6. It follows from Eq. (4-87) that the two components of the transform to which we have access are the transform magnitude (spectrum) and the phase angle. We learned in Section 4.6 that visual analysis of the phase component generally is not very useful. The spectrum, however, provides some useful guidelines as to the gross intensity characteristics of the image from which the spectrum was generated. For example, consider Fig. 4.28(a), which is a scanning electron microscope image of an integrated circuit, magnified approximately 2500 times.

Aside from the interesting construction of the device itself, we note two principal features in this image: strong edges that run approximately at ±45°, and two white, oxide protrusions resulting from thermally induced failure. The Fourier spectrum in Fig. 4.28(b) shows prominent components along the ±45° directions that correspond to the edges just mentioned. Looking carefully along the vertical axis in Fig. 4.28(b), we see a vertical component of the transform that is off-axis, slightly to the left. This component was caused by the edges of the oxide protrusions. Note how the angle of the frequency component with respect to the vertical axis corresponds to the inclination (with respect to the horizontal axis of the image) of the long white element. Note also the zeros in the vertical frequency component, corresponding to the narrow vertical span of the oxide protrusions.

These are typical of the types of associations we can make in general between the frequency and spatial domains. As we will show later in this chapter, even these types of gross associations, coupled with the relationships mentioned previously

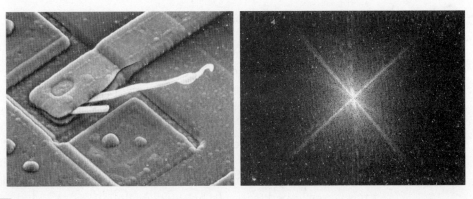

a b

FIGURE 4.28 (a) SEM image of a damaged integrated circuit. (b) Fourier spectrum of (a). (Original image courtesy of Dr. J. M. Hudak, Brockhouse Institute for Materials Research, McMaster University, Hamilton, Ontario, Canada.)

between frequency content and rate of change of intensity levels in an image, can lead to some very useful results. We will show in Section 4.8 the effects of modifying various frequency ranges in the transform of Fig. 4.28(a).

FREQUENCY DOMAIN FILTERING FUNDAMENTALS

Filtering in the frequency domain consists of modifying the Fourier transform of an image, then computing the inverse transform to obtain the spatial domain representation of the processed result. Thus, given (a padded) digital image, $f(x, y)$, of size $P \times Q$ pixels, the basic filtering equation in which we are interested has the form:

$$g(x, y) = \text{Real}\left\{\mathfrak{I}^{-1}\left[H(u, v)F(u, v)\right]\right\} \tag{4-104}$$

where $\mathfrak{I}^{-1}$ is the IDFT, $F(u, v)$ is the DFT of the input image, $f(x, y)$, $H(u, v)$ is a *filter transfer function* (which we often call just a *filter* or *filter function*), and $g(x, y)$ is the *filtered (output) image*. Functions F, H, and g are arrays of size $P \times Q$, the same as the padded input image. The product $H(u, v)F(u, v)$ is formed using elementwise multiplication, as defined in Section 2.6. The filter transfer function modifies the transform of the input image to yield the processed output, $g(x, y)$. The task of specifying $H(u, v)$ is simplified considerably by using functions that are symmetric about their center, which requires that $F(u, v)$ be centered also. As explained in Section 4.6, this is accomplished by multiplying the input image by $(-1)^{x+y}$ prior to computing its transform.[†]

> If H is real and symmetric and f is real (as is typically the case), then the IDFT in Eq. (4-104) should yield real quantities in theory. In practice, the inverse often contains parasitic complex terms from roundoff error and other computational inaccuracies. Thus, it is customary to take the real part of the IDFT to form g.

[†] Some software implementations of the 2-D DFT (e.g., MATLAB) do not center the transform. This implies that filter functions must be arranged to correspond to the same data format as the uncentered transform (i.e., with the origin at the top left). The net result is that filter transfer functions are more difficult to generate and display. We use centering in our discussions to aid in visualization, which is crucial in developing a clear understanding of filtering concepts. Either method can be used in practice, provided that consistency is maintained.

We are now in a position to consider filtering in detail. One of the simplest filter transfer functions we can construct is a function $H(u,v)$ that is 0 at the center of the (centered) transform, and 1's elsewhere. This filter would reject the dc term and "pass" (i.e., leave unchanged) all other terms of $F(u,v)$ when we form the product $H(u,v)F(u,v)$. We know from property 7 in Table 4.3 that the dc term is responsible for the average intensity of an image, so setting it to zero will reduce the average intensity of the output image to zero. Figure 4.29 shows the result of this operation using Eq. (4-104). As expected, the image became much darker. An average of zero implies the existence of negative intensities. Therefore, although it illustrates the principle, Fig. 4.29 is not a true representation of the original, as all negative intensities were clipped (set to 0) by the display.

As noted earlier, low frequencies in the transform are related to slowly varying intensity components in an image, such as the walls of a room or a cloudless sky in an outdoor scene. On the other hand, high frequencies are caused by sharp transitions in intensity, such as edges and noise. Therefore, we would expect that a function $H(u,v)$ that attenuates high frequencies while passing low frequencies (called a *lowpass filter*, as noted before) would blur an image, while a filter with the opposite property (called a *highpass filter*) would enhance sharp detail, but cause a reduction in contrast in the image. Figure 4.30 illustrates these effects. For example, the first column of this figure shows a lowpass filter transfer function and the corresponding filtered image. The second column shows similar results for a highpass filter. Note the similarity between Figs. 4.30(e) and Fig. 4.29. The reason is that the highpass filter function shown eliminates the dc term, resulting in the same basic effect that led to Fig. 4.29. As illustrated in the third column, adding a small constant to the filter does not affect sharpening appreciably, but it does prevent elimination of the dc term and thus preserves tonality.

Equation (4-104) involves the product of two functions in the frequency domain which, by the convolution theorem, implies convolution in the spatial domain. We know from the discussion in Section 4.6 that we can expect wraparound error if the functions in question are not padded. Figure 4.31 shows what happens when we

FIGURE 4.29
Result of filtering the image in Fig. 4.28(a) with a filter transfer function that sets to 0 the dc term, $F(P/2,Q/2)$, in the centered Fourier transform, while leaving all other transform terms unchanged.

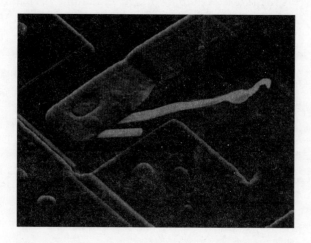

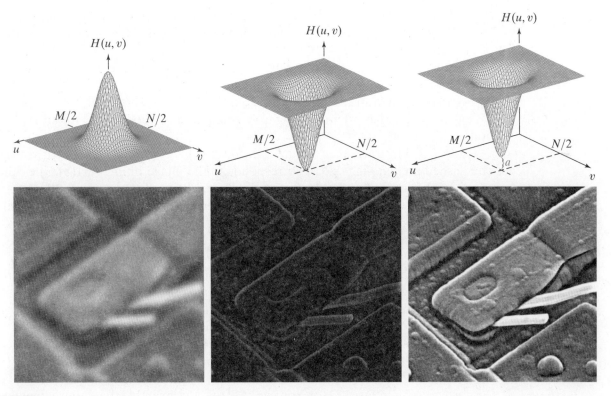

a b c
d e f

FIGURE 4.30 Top row: Frequency domain filter transfer functions of (a) a lowpass filter, (b) a highpass filter, and (c) an offset highpass filter. Bottom row: Corresponding filtered images obtained using Eq. (4-104). The offset in (c) is $a = 0.85$, and the height of $H(u,v)$ is 1. Compare (f) with Fig. 4.28(a).

a b c

FIGURE 4.31 (a) A simple image. (b) Result of blurring with a Gaussian lowpass filter without padding. (c) Result of lowpass filtering with zero padding. Compare the vertical edges in (b) and (c).

apply Eq. (4-104) without padding. Figure 4.31(a) shows a simple image, and Fig. 4.31(b) is the result of lowpass filtering the image with a Gaussian lowpass filter of the form shown in Fig. 4.30(a). As expected, the image is blurred. However, the blurring is not uniform; the top white edge is blurred, but the sides are not. Padding the input image with zeros according to Eqs. (4-98) and (4-99) before applying Eq. (4-104) resulted in the filtered image in Fig. 4.31(c). This result is as expected, with a uniform dark border resulting from zero padding (see Fig. 3.33 for an explanation of this effect).

Figure 4.32 illustrates the reason for the discrepancy between Figs. 4.31(b) and (c). The dashed area in Fig. 4.32(a) corresponds to the image in Fig. 4.31(a). The other copies of the image are due to the implied periodicity of the image (and its transform) implicit when we use the DFT, as explained in Section 4.6. Imagine convolving the spatial representation of the blurring filter (i.e., the corresponding spatial kernel) with this image. When the kernel is centered on the top of the dashed image, it will encompass part of the image and also part of the bottom of the periodic image immediately above it. When a dark and a light region reside under the filter, the result is a mid-gray, blurred output. However, when the kernel is centered on the top right side of the image, it will encompass only light areas in the image and its right region. Because the average of a constant value is that same value, filtering will have no effect in this area, giving the result in Fig. 4.31(b). Padding the image with 0's creates a uniform border around each image of the periodic sequence, as Fig. 4.32(b) shows. Convolving the blurring kernel with the padded "mosaic" of Fig. 4.32(b) gives the correct result in Fig. 4.31(c). You can see from this example that failure to pad an image prior to filtering can lead to unexpected results.

Thus far, the discussion has centered on padding the input image. However, Eq. (4-104) also involves a filter transfer function that can be specified either in the

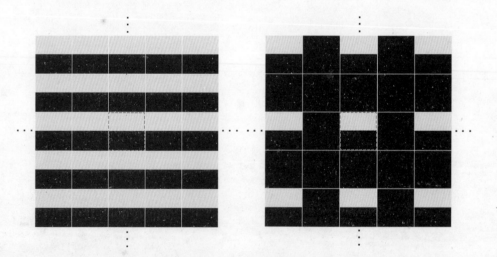

a b

FIGURE 4.32 (a) Image periodicity without image padding. (b) Periodicity after padding with 0's (black). The dashed areas in the center correspond to the image in Fig. 4.31(a). Periodicity is inherent when using the DFT. (The thin white lines in both images are superimposed for clarity; they are not part of the data.)

spatial or in the frequency domain. But padding is done in the spatial domain, which raises an important question about the relationship between *spatial* padding and filter functions specified directly in the frequency domain.

It would be reasonable to conclude that the way to handle padding of a frequency domain transfer function is to construct the function the same size as the unpadded image, compute the IDFT of the function to obtain the corresponding spatial representation, pad that representation in the spatial domain, and then compute its DFT to return to the frequency domain. The 1-D example in Fig. 4.33 illustrates the pitfalls in this approach.

Figure 4.33(a) shows a 1-D ideal lowpass filter transfer function in the frequency domain. The function is real and has even symmetry, so we know from property 8 in Table 4.1 that its IDFT will be real and symmetric also. Figure 4.33(b) shows the result of multiplying the elements of the transfer function by $(-1)^u$ and computing its IDFT to obtain the corresponding spatial filter kernel. The result is shown in Fig. 4.33(b). It is evident in this figure that the extremes of this spatial function are not zero. Zero-padding the function would create two discontinuities, as Fig. 4.33(c) shows. To return to the frequency domain, we compute the forward DFT of the spatial, padded function. As Fig. 4.33(d) shows, the discontinuities in the padded function caused ringing in its frequency domain counterpart.

Padding the two ends of a function is the same as padding one end, provided that the total number of zeros is the same.

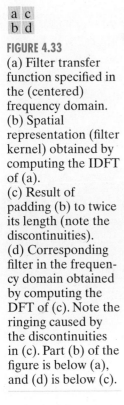

a c
b d

FIGURE 4.33
(a) Filter transfer function specified in the (centered) frequency domain.
(b) Spatial representation (filter kernel) obtained by computing the IDFT of (a).
(c) Result of padding (b) to twice its length (note the discontinuities).
(d) Corresponding filter in the frequency domain obtained by computing the DFT of (c). Note the ringing caused by the discontinuities in (c). Part (b) of the figure is below (a), and (d) is below (c).

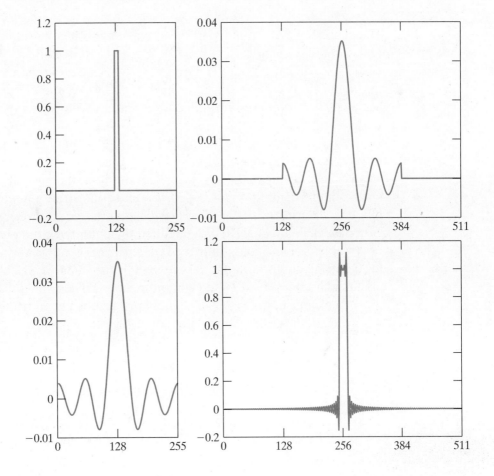

The preceding results tell us that we cannot pad the spatial representation of a frequency domain transfer function in order to avoid wraparound error. Our objective is to work with specified filter shapes in the frequency domain without having to be concerned with truncation issues. An alternative is to pad images and then create the desired filter transfer function directly in the frequency domain, this function being of the same size as the padded images (remember, images and filter transfer functions must be of the same size when using the DFT). Of course, this will result in wraparound error because no padding is used for the filter transfer function, but this error is mitigated significantly by the separation provided by padding the image, and it is preferable to ringing. Smooth transfer functions (such as those in Fig. 4.30) present even less of a problem. Specifically, then, the approach we will follow in this chapter is to pad images to size $P \times Q$ and construct filter transfer functions of the same dimensions directly in the frequency domain. As explained earlier, P and Q are given by Eqs. (4-100) and (4-101).

We conclude this section by analyzing the phase angle of filtered images. We can express the DFT in terms of its real and imaginary parts: $F(u,v) = R(u,v) + jI(u,v)$. Equation (4-104) then becomes

$$g(x,y) = \Im^{-1}\left[H(u,v)R(u,v) + jH(u,v)I(u,v)\right] \qquad (4\text{-}105)$$

The phase angle is computed as the arctangent of the ratio of the imaginary and the real parts of a complex number [see Eq. (4-88)]. Because $H(u,v)$ multiplies both R and I, it will cancel out when this ratio is formed. Filters that affect the real and imaginary parts equally, and thus have no effect on the phase angle, are appropriately called *zero-phase-shift* filters. These are the only types of filters considered in this chapter.

The importance of the phase angle in determining the spatial structure of an image was vividly illustrated in Fig. 4.26. Thus, it should be no surprise that even small changes in the phase angle can have dramatic (and usually undesirable) effects on the filtered output. Figures 4.34(b) and (c) illustrate the effect of changing the phase angle array of the DFT of Fig. 4.34(a) (the $|F(u,v)|$ term was not changed in either case). Figure 4.34(b) was obtained by multiplying the phase angle, $\phi(u,v)$, in Eq. (4-86) by −1 and computing the IDFT. The net result is a reflection of every pixel in the image about both coordinate axes. Figure 4.34(c) was obtained by multiplying the phase term by 0.25 and computing the IDFT. Even a scale change rendered the image almost unrecognizable. These two results illustrate the advantage of using frequency-domain filters that do not alter the phase angle.

SUMMARY OF STEPS FOR FILTERING IN THE FREQUENCY DOMAIN

The process of filtering in the frequency domain can be summarized as follows:

1. Given an input image $f(x,y)$ of size $M \times N$, obtain the padding sizes P and Q using Eqs. (4-102) and (4-103); that is, $P = 2M$ and $Q = 2N$.

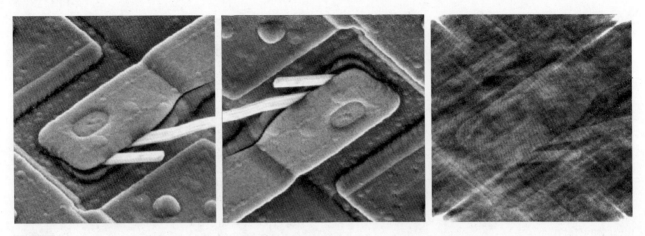

a b c

FIGURE 4.34 (a) Original image. (b) Image obtained by multiplying the phase angle array by −1 in Eq. (4-86) and computing the IDFT. (c) Result of multiplying the phase angle by 0.25 and computing the IDFT. The magnitude of the transform, $|F(u,v)|$, used in (b) and (c) was the same.

2. Form a padded[†] image $f_p(x, y)$ of size $P \times Q$ using zero-, mirror-, or replicate padding (see Fig. 3.39 for a comparison of padding methods).

3. Multiply $f_p(x, y)$ by $(-1)^{x+y}$ to center the Fourier transform on the $P \times Q$ frequency rectangle.

4. Compute the DFT, $F(u, v)$, of the image from Step 3.

5. Construct a real, symmetric filter transfer function, $H(u, v)$, of size $P \times Q$ with center at $(P/2, Q/2)$.

See Section 2.6 for a definition of elementwise operations.

6. Form the product $G(u, v) = H(u, v)F(u, v)$ using elementwise multiplication; that is, $G(i, k) = H(i, k)F(i, k)$ for $i = 0, 1, 2, \ldots, M - 1$ and $k = 0, 1, 2, \ldots, N - 1$.

7. Obtain the filtered image (of size $P \times Q$) by computing the IDFT of $G(u, v)$:

$$g_p(x, y) = \left(\text{real}\left[\mathfrak{I}^{-1}\{G(u, v)\} \right] \right)(-1)^{x+y}$$

8. Obtain the final filtered result, $g(x, y)$, of the same size as the input image, by extracting the $M \times N$ region from the top, left quadrant of $g_p(x, y)$.

We will discuss the construction of filter transfer functions (Step 5) in the following sections of this chapter. In theory, the IDFT in Step 7 should be real because $f(x, y)$ is real and $H(u, v)$ is real and symmetric. However, parasitic complex terms in the IDFT resulting from computational inaccuracies are not uncommon. Taking the real part of the result takes care of that. Multiplication by $(-1)^{x+y}$ cancels out the multiplication by this factor in Step 3.

[†] Sometimes we omit padding when doing "quick" experiments to get an idea of filter performance, or when trying to determine quantitative relationships between spatial features and their effect on frequency domain components, particularly in band and notch filtering, as explained later in Section 4.10 and in Chapter 5.

a b c
d e f
g h

FIGURE 4.35
(a) An $M \times N$ image, f.
(b) Padded image, f_p of size $P \times Q$.
(c) Result of multiplying f_p by $(-1)^{x+y}$.
(d) Spectrum of F. (e) Centered Gaussian lowpass filter transfer function, H, of size $P \times Q$.
(f) Spectrum of the product HF.
(g) Image g_p, the real part of the IDFT of HF, multiplied by $(-1)^{x+y}$.
(h) Final result, g, obtained by extracting the first M rows and N columns of g_p.

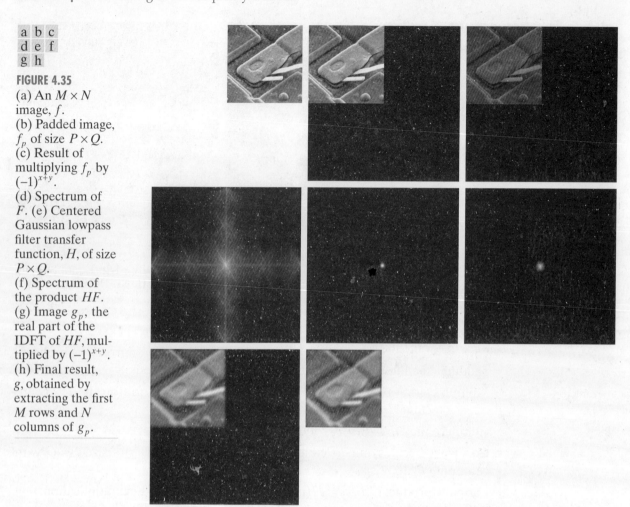

Figure 4.35 illustrates the preceding steps using zero padding. The figure legend explains the source of each image. If enlarged, Fig. 4.35(c) would show black dots interleaved in the image because negative intensities, resulting from the multiplication of f_p by $(-1)^{x+y}$, are clipped at 0 by the display. Note in Fig. 4.35(h) the characteristic dark border of by lowpass filtered images obtained using zero padding.

CORRESPONDENCE BETWEEN FILTERING IN THE SPATIAL AND FREQUENCY DOMAINS

See Section 2.6 for a definition of elementwise operations.

As mentioned several times before, the link between filtering in the spatial and frequency domains is the convolution theorem. Earlier in this section, we defined filtering in the frequency domain as the elementwise product of a filter transfer function, $H(u,v)$, and $F(u,v)$, the Fourier transform of the input image. Given $H(u,v)$, suppose that we want to find its equivalent kernel in the spatial domain. If we let $f(x,y) = \delta(x,y)$, it follows from Table 4.4 that $F(u,v) = 1$. Then, from Eq. (4-104), the filtered output is $\Im^{-1}\{H(u,v)\}$. This expression as the inverse transform of the frequency domain filter transfer function, which is the corresponding kernel in the spatial domain. Conversely, it follows from a similar analysis and the convolution theorem that, given a spatial filter kernel, we obtain its frequency domain representation by taking the forward Fourier transform of the kernel. Therefore, the two filters form a Fourier transform pair:

$$h(x, y) \Leftrightarrow H(u, v) \qquad (4\text{-}106)$$

where $h(x, y)$ is the spatial kernel. Because this kernel can be obtained from the response of a frequency domain filter to an impulse, $h(x, y)$ sometimes is referred to as the *impulse response* of $H(u, v)$. Also, because all quantities in a discrete implementation of Eq. (4-106) are finite, such filters are called *finite impulse response* (FIR) filters. These are the only types of linear spatial filters considered in this book.

We discussed spatial convolution in Section 3.4, and its implementation in Eq. (3-35), which involved convolving functions of different sizes. When we use the DFT to compute the transforms used in the convolution theorem, it is implied that we are convolving periodic functions of the *same* size, as explained in Fig. 4.27. For this reason, as explained earlier, Eq. (4-94) is referred to as *circular convolution*.

When computational speed, cost, and size are important parameters, spatial convolution filtering using Eq. (3-35) is well suited for small kernels using hardware and/or firmware, as explained in Section 4.1. However, when working with general-purpose machines, frequency-domain methods in which the DFT is computed using a fast Fourier transform (FFT) algorithm can be hundreds of times faster than using spatial convolution, depending on the size of the kernels used, as you saw in Fig. 4.2. We will discuss the FFT and its computational advantages in Section 4.11.

Filtering concepts are more intuitive in the frequency domain, and filter design often is easier there. One way to take advantage of the properties of both domains is to specify a filter in the frequency domain, compute its IDFT, and then use the properties of the resulting, full-size spatial kernel as a guide for constructing smaller kernels. This is illustrated next (keep in mind that the Fourier transform and its inverse are linear processes (see Problem 4.24), so the discussion is limited to linear filtering). In Example 4.15, we illustrate the converse, in which a spatial kernel is given, and we obtain its full-size frequency domain representation. This approach is useful for analyzing the behavior of small spatial kernels in the frequency domain.

Frequency domain filters can be used as guides for specifying the coefficients of some of the small kernels we discussed in Chapter 3. Filters based on Gaussian functions are of particular interest because, as noted in Table 4.4, both the forward and inverse Fourier transforms of a Gaussian function are real Gaussian functions. We limit the discussion to 1-D to illustrate the underlying principles. Two-dimensional Gaussian transfer functions are discussed later in this chapter.

Let $H(u)$ denote the 1-D frequency domain Gaussian transfer function

$$H(u) = Ae^{-u^2/2\sigma^2} \qquad (4\text{-}107)$$

As mentioned in Table 4.4, the forward and inverse Fourier transforms of Gaussians are valid only for continuous variables. To use discrete formulations, we sample the continuous forms.

where σ is the standard deviation of the Gaussian curve. The kernel in the spatial domain is obtained by taking the inverse DFT of $H(u)$ (see Problem 4.48):

$$h(x) = \sqrt{2\pi}\,\sigma A\, e^{-2\pi^2\sigma^2 x^2} \qquad (4\text{-}108)$$

These two equations are important for two reasons: (1) They are a Fourier transform pair, both components of which are Gaussian *and* real. This facilitates analysis because we do not have to be concerned with complex numbers. In addition, Gaussian curves are intuitive and easy to manipulate. (2) The functions behave reciprocally. When $H(u)$ has a broad profile (large value of σ), $h(x)$ has a narrow profile, and vice versa. In fact, as σ approaches infinity, $H(u)$ tends toward a constant function and $h(x)$ tends toward an impulse, which implies no filtering in either domain.

Figures 4.36(a) and (b) show plots of a Gaussian lowpass filter transfer function in the frequency domain and the corresponding function in the spatial domain. Suppose that we want to use the shape of $h(x)$ in Fig. 4.36(b) as a guide for specifying the coefficients of a small kernel in the spatial domain. The key characteristic of the function in Fig. 4.36(b) is that all its values are positive. Thus, we conclude that we can implement lowpass filtering in the spatial domain by using a kernel with all positive coefficients (as we did in Section 3.5). For reference, Fig. 4.36(b) also shows two of the kernels discussed in that section. Note the reciprocal relationship between the width of the Gaussian functions, as discussed in the previous paragraph. The narrower the frequency domain function, the more it will attenuate the low frequencies, resulting in increased blurring. In the spatial domain, this means that a larger kernel must be used to increase blurring, as we illustrated in Example 3.11.

As you know from Section 3.7, we can construct a highpass filter from a lowpass filter by subtracting a lowpass function from a constant. We working with Gaussian functions, we can gain a little more control over filter function shape by using a so-called *difference of Gaussians*, which involves two lowpass functions. In the frequency domain, this becomes

$$H(u) = Ae^{-u^2/2\sigma_1^2} - Be^{-u^2/2\sigma_2^2} \tag{4-109}$$

with $A \geq B$ and $\sigma_1 > \sigma_2$. The corresponding function in the spatial domain is

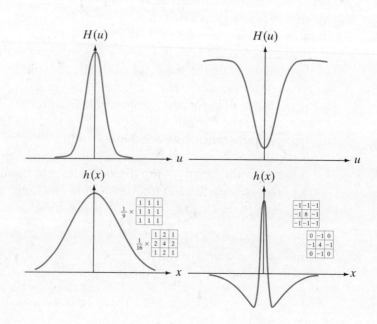

a c
b d

FIGURE 4.36
(a) A 1-D Gaussian lowpass transfer function in the frequency domain.
(b) Corresponding kernel in the spatial domain. (c) Gaussian highpass transfer function in the frequency domain.
(d) Corresponding kernel. The small 2-D kernels shown are kernels we used in Chapter 3.

$$h(x) = \sqrt{2\pi}\sigma_1 Ae^{-2\pi^2\sigma_1^2 x^2} - \sqrt{2\pi}\sigma_2 Be^{-2\pi^2\sigma_2^2 x^2} \qquad (4\text{-}110)$$

Figures 4.36(c) and (d) show plots of these two equations. We note again the reciprocity in width, but the most important feature here is that $h(x)$ has a positive center term with negative terms on either side. The small kernels shown in Fig. 4.36(d), which we used in Chapter 3 for sharpening, "capture" this property, and thus illustrate how knowledge of frequency domain filtering can be used as the basis for choosing coefficients of spatial kernels.

Although we have gone through significant effort to get here, be assured that it is impossible to truly understand filtering in the frequency domain without the foundation we have just established. In practice, the frequency domain can be viewed as a "laboratory" in which we take advantage of the correspondence between frequency content and image appearance. As will be demonstrated numerous times later in this chapter, some tasks that would be exceptionally difficult to formulate directly in the spatial domain become almost trivial in the frequency domain. Once we have selected a specific filter transfer function via experimentation in the frequency domain, we have the option of implementing the filter directly in that domain using the FFT, or we can take the IDFT of the transfer function to obtain the equivalent spatial domain function. As we showed in Fig. 4.36, one approach is to specify a small spatial kernel that attempts to capture the "essence" of the *full* filter function in the spatial domain. A more formal approach is to design a 2-D digital filter by using approximations based on mathematical or statistical criteria, as we discussed in Section 3.7.

EXAMPLE 4.15: Obtaining a frequency domain transfer function from a spatial kernel.

In this example, we start with a spatial kernel and show how to generate its corresponding filter transfer function in the frequency domain. Then, we compare the filtering results obtained using frequency domain and spatial techniques. This type of analysis is useful when one wishes to compare the performance of a given kernel against one or more "full" filter candidates in the frequency domain, or to gain a deeper understanding about the performance of a kernel in the spatial domain. To keep matters simple, we use the 3×3 vertical Sobel kernel from Fig. 3.50(e). Figure 4.37(a) shows a 600×600-pixel image, $f(x,y)$, that we wish to filter, and Fig. 4.37(b) shows its spectrum.

Figure 4.38(a) shows the Sobel kernel, $h(x,y)$ (the perspective plot is explained below). Because the input image is of size 600×600 pixels and the kernel is of size 3×3, we avoid wraparound error in the frequency domain by padding f and h with zeros to size 602×602 pixels, according to Eqs. (4-100) and (4-101). At first glance, the Sobel kernel appears to exhibit odd symmetry. However, its first element is not 0, as required by Eq. (4-81). To convert the kernel to the smallest size that will satisfy Eq. (4-83), we have to add to it a leading row and column of 0's, which turns it into an array of size 4×4. We can embed this array into a larger array of zeros and still maintain its odd symmetry if the larger array is of even dimensions (as is the 4×4 kernel) *and* their centers coincide, as explained in Example 4.10. The preceding comments are an important aspect of filter generation. If we preserve the odd symmetry with respect to the padded array in forming $h_p(x,y)$, we know from property 9 in Table 4.1 that $H(u,v)$ will be purely imaginary. As we show at the end of this example, this will yield results that are identical to filtering the image spatially using the original kernel $h(x,y)$. If the symmetry were not preserved, the results would no longer be the same.

a b

FIGURE 4.37
(a) Image of a
building, and
(b) its Fourier
spectrum.

The procedure used to generate $H(u,v)$ is: (1) multiply $h_p(x,y)$ by $(-1)^{x+y}$ to center the frequency domain filter; (2) compute the forward DFT of the result in (1) to generate $H(u,v)$; (3) set the real part of $H(u,v)$ to 0 to account for parasitic real parts (we know that H has to be purely imaginary because h_p is real and odd); and (4) multiply the result by $(-1)^{u+v}$. This last step reverses the multiplication of $H(u,v)$ by $(-1)^{u+v}$, which is implicit when $h(x,y)$ was manually placed in the center of $h_p(x,y)$. Figure 4.38(a) shows a perspective plot of $H(u,v)$, and Fig. 4.38(b) shows $H(u,v)$ as an image. Note the antisymmetry in this image about its center, a result of $H(u,v)$ being odd. Function $H(u,v)$ is used as any other frequency domain filter transfer function. Figure 4.38(c) is the result of using the filter transfer function just obtained to filter the image in Fig. 4.37(a) in the frequency domain, using the step-by-step filtering procedure outlined earlier. As expected from a derivative filter, edges were enhanced and all the constant intensity areas were reduced to zero (the grayish tone is due to scaling for display). Figure 4.38(d) shows the result of filtering the same image in the spatial domain with the Sobel kernel $h(x,y)$, using the procedure discussed in Section 3.6. The results are identical.

4.8 IMAGE SMOOTHING USING LOWPASS FREQUENCY DOMAIN FILTERS

The remainder of this chapter deals with various filtering techniques in the frequency domain, beginning with lowpass filters. Edges and other sharp intensity transitions (such as noise) in an image contribute significantly to the high frequency content of its Fourier transform. Hence, smoothing (blurring) is achieved in the frequency domain by high-frequency attenuation; that is, by *lowpass* filtering. In this section, we consider three types of lowpass filters: *ideal*, *Butterworth*, and *Gaussian*. These three categories cover the range from very sharp (ideal) to very smooth (Gaussian) filtering. The shape of a Butterworth filter is controlled by a parameter called the *filter order*. For large values of this parameter, the Butterworth filter approaches the ideal filter. For lower values, the Butterworth filter is more like a Gaussian filter. Thus, the Butterworth filter provides a transition between two "extremes." All filtering in this section follows the procedure outlined in the previous section, so all filter transfer functions, $H(u,v)$, are understood to be of size $P \times Q$; that is, the discrete

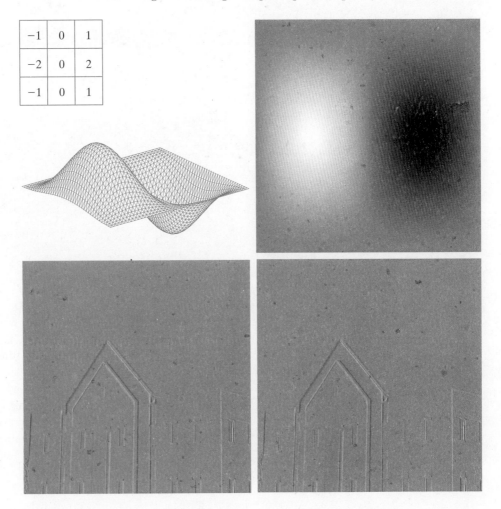

−1	0	1
−2	0	2
−1	0	1

a b
c d

FIGURE 4.38
(a) A spatial kernel and perspective plot of its corresponding frequency domain filter transfer function.
(b) Transfer function shown as an image.
(c) Result of filtering Fig. 4.37(a) in the frequency domain with the transfer function in (b).
(d) Result of filtering the same image in the spatial domain with the kernel in (a). The results are identical.

frequency variables are in the range $u = 0, 1, 2, \ldots, P - 1$ and $v = 0, 1, 2, \ldots, Q - 1$, where P and Q are the padded sizes given by Eqs. (4-100) and (4-101).

IDEAL LOWPASS FILTERS

A 2-D lowpass filter that passes without attenuation all frequencies within a circle of radius from the origin, and "cuts off" all frequencies outside this, circle is called an *ideal lowpass filter* (ILPF); it is specified by the transfer function

$$H(u,v) = \begin{cases} 1 & \text{if } D(u,v) \le D_0 \\ 0 & \text{if } D(u,v) > D_0 \end{cases} \qquad (4\text{-}111)$$

where D_0 is a positive constant, and $D(u,v)$ is the distance between a point (u,v) in the frequency domain and the center of the $P \times Q$ frequency rectangle; that is,

$$D(u,v) = \left[(u - P/2)^2 + (v - Q/2)^2 \right]^{1/2} \qquad (4\text{-}112)$$

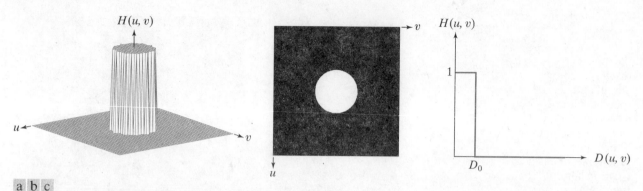

a b c

FIGURE 4.39 (a) Perspective plot of an ideal lowpass-filter transfer function. (b) Function displayed as an image. (c) Radial cross section.

where, as before, P and Q are the padded sizes from Eqs. (4-102) and (4-103). Figure 4.39(a) shows a perspective plot of transfer function $H(u,v)$ and Fig. 4.39(b) shows it displayed as an image. As mentioned in Section 4.3, the name *ideal* indicates that all frequencies on or inside a circle of radius D_0 are passed without attenuation, whereas all frequencies outside the circle are completely attenuated (filtered out). The ideal lowpass filter transfer function is radially symmetric about the origin. This means that it is defined completely by a radial cross section, as Fig. 4.39(c) shows. A 2-D representation of the filter is obtained by rotating the cross section 360°.

For an ILPF cross section, the point of transition between the values $H(u,v) = 1$ and $H(u,v) = 0$ is called the *cutoff frequency*. In Fig. 4.39, the cutoff frequency is D_0. The sharp cutoff frequency of an ILPF cannot be realized with electronic components, although they certainly can be simulated in a computer (subject to the constrain that the fastest possible transition is limited by the distance between pixels).

The lowpass filters in this chapter are compared by studying their behavior as a function of the same cutoff frequencies. One way to establish standard cutoff frequency loci using circles that enclose specified amounts of total *image power* P_T, which we obtain by summing the components of the power spectrum of the padded images at each point (u,v), for $u = 0, 1, 2, \ldots, P-1$ and $v = 0, 1, 2, \ldots, Q-1$; that is,

$$P_T = \sum_{u=0}^{P-1} \sum_{v=0}^{Q-1} P(u,v) \tag{4-113}$$

where $P(u,v)$ is given by Eq. (4-89). If the DFT has been centered, a circle of radius D_0 with origin at the center of the frequency rectangle encloses α percent of the power, where

$$\alpha = 100 \left[\sum_u \sum_v P(u,v) / P_T \right] \tag{4-114}$$

and the summation is over values of (u,v) that lie inside the circle or on its boundary.

Figures 4.40(a) and (b) show a test pattern image and its spectrum. The circles superimposed on the spectrum have radii of 10, 30, 60, 160, and 460 pixels,

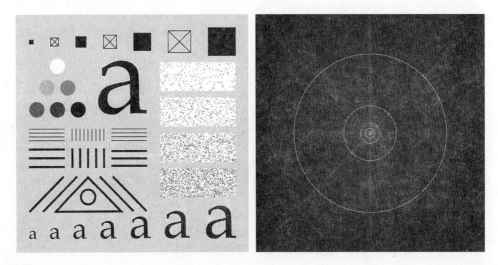

a b

FIGURE 4.40 (a) Test pattern of size 688×688 pixels, and (b) its spectrum. The spectrum is double the image size as a result of padding, but is shown half size to fit. The circles have radii of 10, 30, 60, 160, and 460 pixels with respect to the full-size spectrum. The radii enclose 86.9, 92.8, 95.1, 97.6, and 99.4% of the padded image power, respectively.

respectively, and enclosed the percentages of total power listed in the figure caption. The spectrum falls off rapidly, with close to 87% of the total power being enclosed by a relatively small circle of radius 10. The significance of this will become evident in the following example.

EXAMPLE 4.16: Image smoothing in the frequency domain using lowpass filters.

Figure 4.41 shows the results of applying ILPFs with cutoff frequencies at the radii shown in Fig. 4.40(b). Figure 4.41(b) is useless for all practical purposes, unless the objective of blurring is to eliminate all detail in the image, except the "blobs" representing the largest objects. The severe blurring in this image is a clear indication that most of the sharp detail information in the image is contained in the 13% power removed by the filter. As the filter radius increases, less and less power is removed, resulting in less blurring. Note that the images in Figs. 4.41(c) through (e) contain significant "ringing," which becomes finer in texture as the amount of high frequency content removed decreases. Ringing is visible even in the image in which only 2% of the total power was removed [Fig. 4.41(e)]. This ringing behavior is a characteristic of ideal filters, as we have mentioned several times before. Finally, the result for $\alpha = 99.4\%$ in Fig. 4.41(f) shows very slight blurring and almost imperceptible ringing but, for the most part, this image is close to the original. This indicates that little edge information is contained in the upper 0.6% of the spectrum power removed by the ILPF.

It is clear from this example that ideal lowpass filtering is not practical. However, it is useful to study the behavior of ILPFs as part of our development of filtering concepts. Also, as shown in the discussion that follows, some interesting insight is gained by attempting to explain the ringing property of ILPFs in the spatial domain.

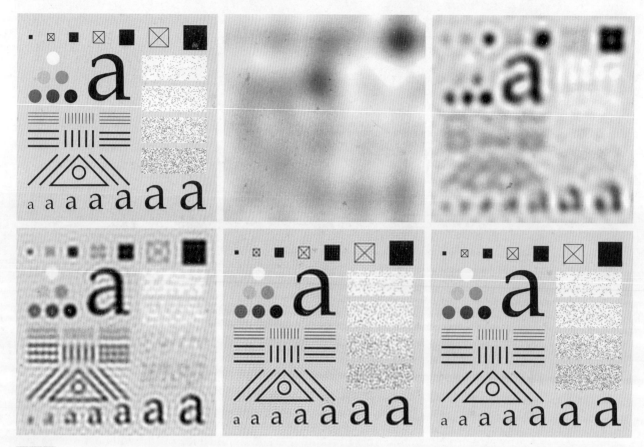

a b c
d e f

FIGURE 4.41 (a) Original image of size 688×688 pixels. (b)–(f) Results of filtering using ILPFs with cutoff frequencies set at radii values 10, 30, 60, 160, and 460, as shown in Fig. 4.40(b). The power removed by these filters was 13.1, 7.2, 4.9, 2.4, and 0.6% of the total, respectively. We used mirror padding to avoid the black borders characteristic of zero padding, as illustrated in Fig. 4.31(c).

The blurring and ringing properties of ILPFs can be explained using the convolution theorem. Figure 4.42(a) shows an image of a frequency-domain ILPF transfer function of radius 15 and size 1000×1000 pixels. Figure 4.42(b) is the spatial representation, $h(x, y)$, of the ILPF, obtained by taking the IDFT of (a) (note the ringing). Figure 4.42(c) shows the intensity profile of a line passing through the center of (b). This profile resembles a sinc function.[†] Filtering in the spatial domain is done by convolving the function in Fig. 4.42(b) with an image. Imagine each pixel in an image as being a discrete impulse whose strength is proportional to the intensity of the image at that location. Convolving this sinc-like function with an impulse copies (i.e., shifts the origin of) the function to the location of the impulse. That is, convolution

---

[†]Although this profile resembles a sinc function, the transform of an ILPF is actually a Bessel function whose derivation is beyond the scope of this discussion. The important point to keep in mind is that the inverse proportionality between the "width" of the filter function in the frequency domain, and the "spread" of the width of the lobes in the spatial function, still holds.

a b c

FIGURE 4.42
(a) Frequency domain ILPF transfer function.
(b) Corresponding spatial domain kernel function.
(c) Intensity profile of a horizontal line through the center of (b).

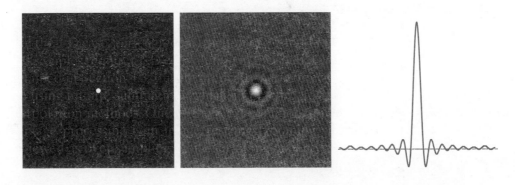

makes a copy of the function in Fig. 4.42(b) centered on each pixel location in the image. The center lobe of this spatial function is the principal cause of blurring, while the outer, smaller lobes are mainly responsible for ringing. Because the "spread" of the spatial function is inversely proportional to the radius of $H(u,v)$, the larger D_0 becomes (i,e, the more frequencies that are passed), the more the spatial function approaches an impulse which, in the limit, causes no blurring at all when convolved with the image. The converse happens as D_0 becomes smaller. This type of reciprocal behavior should be routine to you by now. In the next two sections, we show that it is possible to achieve blurring with little or no ringing, an important objective in lowpass filtering.

GAUSSIAN LOWPASS FILTERS

Gaussian lowpass filter (GLPF) transfer functions have the form

$$H(u,v) = e^{-D^2(u,v)/2\sigma^2} \tag{4-115}$$

where, as in Eq. (4-112), $D(u,v)$ is the distance from the center of the $P \times Q$ frequency rectangle to any point, (u,v), contained by the rectangle. Unlike our earlier expressions for Gaussian functions, we do not use a multiplying constant here in order to be consistent with the filters discussed in this and later sections, whose highest value is 1. As before, σ is a measure of spread about the center. By letting $\sigma = D_0$, we can express the Gaussian transfer function in the same notation as other functions in this section:

$$H(u,v) = e^{-D^2(u,v)/2D_0^2} \tag{4-116}$$

where D_0 is the cutoff frequency. When $D(u,v) = D_0$, the GLPF transfer function is down to 0.607 of its maximum value of 1.0.

From Table 4.4, we know that the inverse Fourier transform of a frequency-domain Gaussian function is Gaussian also. This means that a spatial Gaussian filter kernel, obtained by computing the IDFT of Eq. (4-115) or (4-116), will have no ringing. As property 13 of Table 4.4 shows, the same inverse relationship explained earlier for ILPFs is true also of GLPFs. Narrow Gaussian transfer functions in the frequency domain imply broader kernel functions in the spatial domain, and vice

FIGURE 4.43 (a) Perspective plot of a GLPF transfer function. (b) Function displayed as an image. (c) Radial cross sections for various values of D_0.

versa. Figure 4.43 shows a perspective plot, image display, and radial cross sections of a GLPF transfer function.

EXAMPLE 4.17: Image smoothing in the frequency domain using Gaussian lowpass filters.

Figure 4.44 shows the results of applying the GLPF of Eq. (4-116) to Fig. 4.44(a), with D_0 equal to the five radii in Fig. 4.40(b). Compared to the results obtained with an ILPF (Fig. 4.41), we note a smooth transition in blurring as a function of increasing cutoff frequency. The GLPF achieved slightly less smoothing than the ILPF. The key difference is that we are assured of no ringing when using a GLPF. This is an important consideration in practice, especially in situations in which any type of artifact is unacceptable, as in medical imaging. In cases where more control of the transition between low and high frequencies about the cutoff frequency are needed, the Butterworth lowpass filter discussed next presents a more suitable choice. The price of this additional control over the filter profile is the possibility of ringing, as you will see shortly.

BUTTERWORTH LOWPASS FILTERS

The transfer function of a Butterworth lowpass filter (BLPF) of order n, with cutoff frequency at a distance D_0 from the center of the frequency rectangle, is defined as

$$H(u,v) = \frac{1}{1 + \left[D(u,v)/D_0\right]^{2n}} \tag{4-117}$$

where $D(u,v)$ is given by Eq. (4-112). Figure 4.45 shows a perspective plot, image display, and radial cross sections of the BLPF function. Comparing the cross section plots in Figs. 4.39, 4.43, and 4.45, we see that the BLPF function can be controlled to approach the characteristics of the ILPF using higher values of n, and the GLPF for lower values of n, while providing a smooth transition in from low to high frequencies. Thus, we can use a BLPF to approach the sharpness of an ILPF function with considerably less ringing.

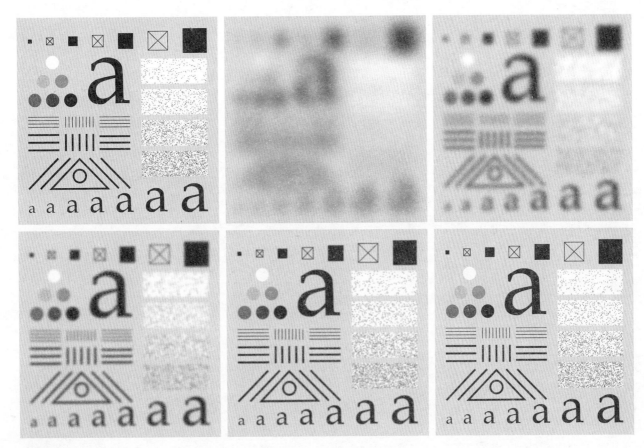

a b c
d e f

FIGURE 4.44 (a) Original image of size 688×688 pixels. (b)–(f) Results of filtering using GLPFs with cutoff frequencies at the radii shown in Fig. 4.40. Compare with Fig. 4.41. We used mirror padding to avoid the black borders characteristic of zero padding.

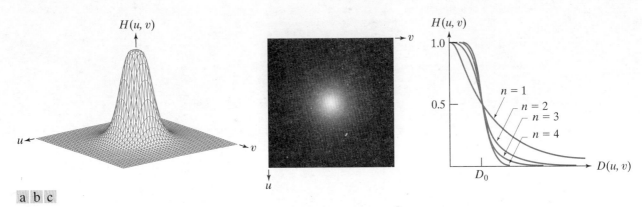

a b c

FIGURE 4.45 (a) Perspective plot of a Butterworth lowpass-filter transfer function. (b) Function displayed as an image. (c) Radial cross sections of BLPFs of orders 1 through 4.

EXAMPLE 4.18: Image smoothing using a Butterworth lowpass filter.

Figures 4.46(b)-(f) show the results of applying the BLPF of Eq. (4-117) to Fig. 4.46(a), with cutoff frequencies equal to the five radii in Fig. 4.40(b), and with $n = 2.25$. The results in terms of blurring are between the results obtained with using ILPFs and GLPFs. For example, compare Fig. 4.46(b), with Figs. 4.41(b) and 4.44(b). The degree of blurring with the BLPF was less than with the ILPF, but more than with the GLPF.

The kernels in Figs. 4.47(a) through (d) were obtained using the procedure outlined in the explanation of Fig. 4.42.

The spatial domain kernel obtainable from a BLPF of order 1 has no ringing. Generally, ringing is imperceptible in filters of order 2 or 3, but can become significant in filters of higher orders. Figure 4.47 shows a comparison between the spatial representation (i.e., spatial kernels) corresponding to BLPFs of various orders (using a cutoff frequency of 5 in all cases). Shown also is the intensity profile along

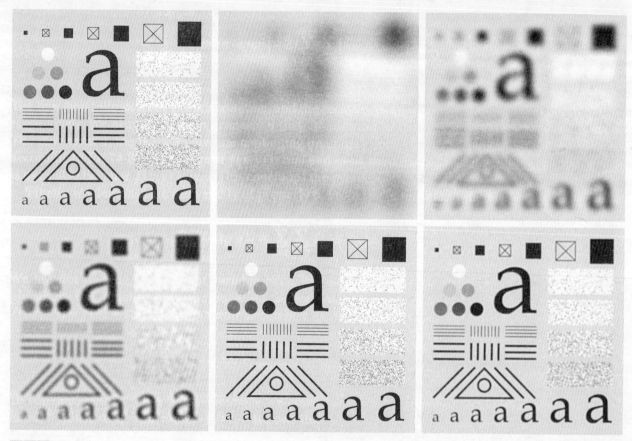

a b c
d e f

FIGURE 4.46 (a) Original image of size 688×688 pixels. (b)–(f) Results of filtering using BLPFs with cutoff frequencies at the radii shown in Fig. 4.40 and $n = 2.25$. Compare with Figs. 4.41 and 4.44. We used mirror padding to avoid the black borders characteristic of zero padding.

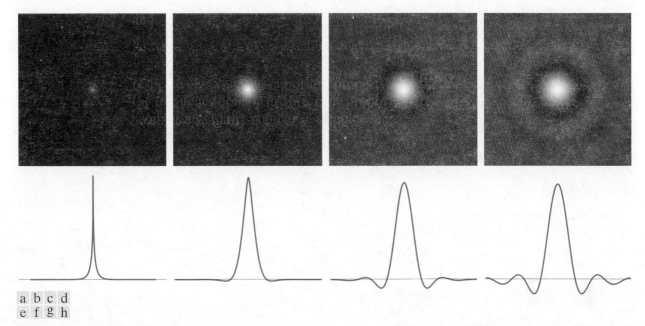

a b c d
e f g h

FIGURE 4.47 (a)–(d) Spatial representations (i.e., spatial kernels) corresponding to BLPF transfer functions of size 1000×1000 pixels, cut-off frequency of 5, and order 1, 2, 5, and 20, respectively. (e)–(h) Corresponding intensity profiles through the center of the filter functions.

a horizontal scan line through the center of each spatial kernel. The kernel corresponding to the BLPF of order 1 [see Fig. 4.47(a)] has neither ringing nor negative values. The kernel corresponding to a BLPF of order 2 does show mild ringing and small negative values, but they certainly are less pronounced than would be the case for an ILPF. As the remaining images show, ringing becomes significant for higher-order filters. A BLPF of order 20 has a spatial kernel that exhibits ringing characteristics similar to those of the ILPF (in the limit, both filters are identical). BLPFs of orders 2 to 3 are a good compromise between effective lowpass filtering and acceptable spatial-domain ringing. Table 4.5 summarizes the lowpass filter transfer functions discussed in this section.

ADDITIONAL EXAMPLES OF LOWPASS FILTERING

In the following discussion, we show several practical applications of lowpass filtering in the frequency domain. The first example is from the field of machine perception with application to character recognition; the second is from the printing and publishing industry; and the third is related to processing satellite and aerial images. Similar results can be obtained using the lowpass spatial filtering techniques discussed in Section 3.5. We use GLPFs in all examples for consistency, but similar results can be obtained using BLPFs. Keep in mind that images are padded to double size for filtering, as indicated by Eqs. (4-102) and (4-103), and filter transfer functions have to match padded-image size. The values of D_0 used in the following examples reflect this doubled filter size.

TABLE 4.5
Lowpass filter transfer functions. D_0 is the cutoff frequency, and n is the order of the Butterworth filter.

Ideal	Gaussian	Butterworth
$H(u,v) = \begin{cases} 1 & \text{if } D(u,v) \leq D_0 \\ 0 & \text{if } D(u,v) > D_0 \end{cases}$	$H(u,v) = e^{-D^2(u,v)/2D_0^2}$	$H(u,v) = \dfrac{1}{1 + \left[D(u,v)/D_0\right]^{2n}}$

Figure 4.48 shows a sample of text of low resolution. One encounters text like this, for example, in fax transmissions, duplicated material, and historical records. This particular sample is free of additional difficulties like smudges, creases, and torn sections. The magnified section in Fig. 4.48(a) shows that the characters in this document have distorted shapes due to lack of resolution, and many of the characters are broken. Although humans fill these gaps visually without difficulty, machine recognition systems have real difficulties reading broken characters. One approach for handling this problem is to bridge small gaps in the input image by blurring it. Figure 4.48(b) shows how well characters can be "repaired" by this simple process using a Gaussian lowpass filter with $D_0 = 120$. It is typical to follow the type of "repair" just described with additional processing, such as thresholding and thinning, to yield cleaner characters. We will discuss thinning in Chapter 9 and thresholding in Chapter 10.

We will cover unsharp masking in the frequency domain in Section 4.9.

Lowpass filtering is a staple in the printing and publishing industry, where it is used for numerous preprocessing functions, including unsharp masking, as discussed in Section 3.6. "Cosmetic" processing is another use of lowpass filtering prior to printing. Figure 4.49 shows an application of lowpass filtering for producing a smoother, softer-looking result from a sharp original. For human faces, the typical objective is to reduce the sharpness of fine skin lines and small blemishes. The magnified sections in Figs. 4.49(b) and (c) clearly show a significant reduction in fine skin lines around the subject's eyes. In fact, the smoothed images look quite soft and pleasing.

Figure 4.50 shows two applications of lowpass filtering on the same image, but with totally different objectives. Figure 4.50(a) is an 808×754 segment of a very high

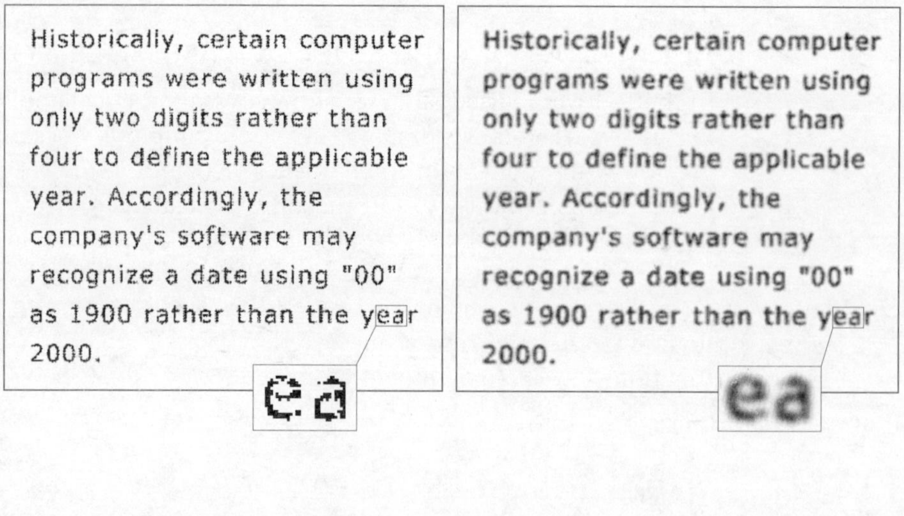

a b

FIGURE 4.48
(a) Sample text of low resolution (note the broken characters in the magnified view). (b) Result of filtering with a GLPF, showing that gaps in the broken characters were joined.

a b c

FIGURE 4.49 (a) Original 785×732 image. (b) Result of filtering using a GLPF with $D_0 = 150$. (c) Result of filtering using a GLPF with $D_0 = 130$. Note the reduction in fine skin lines in the magnified sections in (b) and (c).

resolution radiometer (VHRR) image showing part of the Gulf of Mexico (dark) and Florida (light) (note the horizontal sensor scan lines). The boundaries between bodies of water were caused by loop currents. This image is illustrative of remotely sensed images in which sensors have the tendency to produce pronounced scan lines along the direction in which the scene is being scanned. (See Example 4.24 for an

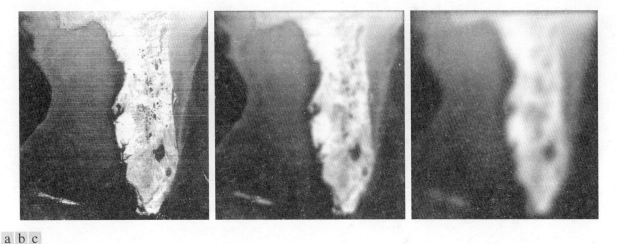

a b c

FIGURE 4.50 (a) 808×754 satellite image showing prominent horizontal scan lines. (b) Result of filtering using a GLPF with $D_0 = 50$. (c) Result of using a GLPF with $D_0 = 20$. (Original image courtesy of NOAA.)

illustration of imaging conditions that can lead for such degradations.) Lowpass filtering is a crude (but simple) way to reduce the effect of these lines, as Fig. 4.50(b) shows (we consider more effective approaches in Sections 4.10 and 5.4). This image was obtained using a GLFP with $D_0 = 50$. The reduction in the effect of the scan lines in the smoothed image can simplify the detection of macro features, such as the interface boundaries between ocean currents.

Figure 4.50(c) shows the result of significantly more aggressive Gaussian lowpass filtering with $D_0 = 20$. Here, the objective is to blur out as much detail as possible while leaving large features recognizable. For instance, this type of filtering could be part of a preprocessing stage for an image analysis system that searches for features in an image bank. An example of such features could be lakes of a given size, such as Lake Okeechobee in the lower eastern region of Florida, shown in Fig. 4.50(c) as a nearly round dark region surrounded by a lighter region. Lowpass filtering helps to simplify the analysis by averaging out features smaller than the ones of interest.

4.9 IMAGE SHARPENING USING HIGHPASS FILTERS

We showed in the previous section that an image can be smoothed by attenuating the high-frequency components of its Fourier transform. Because edges and other abrupt changes in intensities are associated with high-frequency components, image sharpening can be achieved in the frequency domain by highpass filtering, which attenuates low-frequencies components without disturbing high-frequencies in the Fourier transform. As in Section 4.8, we consider only zero-phase-shift filters that are radially symmetric. All filtering in this section is based on the procedure outlined in Section 4.7, so all images are assumed be padded to size $P \times Q$ [see Eqs. (4-102) and (4-103)], and filter transfer functions, $H(u,v)$, are understood to be centered, discrete functions of size $P \times Q$.

In some applications of highpass filtering, it is advantageous to enhance the high-frequencies of the Fourier transform.

IDEAL, GAUSSIAN, AND BUTTERWORTH HIGHPASS FILTERS FROM LOWPASS FILTERS

As was the case with kernels in the spatial domain (see Section 3.7), subtracting a lowpass filter transfer function from 1 yields the corresponding highpass filter transfer function in the frequency domain:

$$H_{HP}(u,v) = 1 - H_{LP}(u,v) \tag{4-118}$$

where $H_{LP}(u,v)$ is the transfer function of a lowpass filter. Thus, it follows from Eq. (4-111) that an ideal highpass filter (IHPF) transfer function is given by

$$H(u,v) = \begin{cases} 0 & \text{if } D(u,v) \le D_0 \\ 1 & \text{if } D(u,v) > D_0 \end{cases} \tag{4-119}$$

where, as before, $D(u,v)$ is the distance from the center of the $P \times Q$ frequency rectangle, as given in Eq. (4-112). Similarly, it follows from Eq. (4-116) that the transfer function of a Gaussian highpass filter (GHPF) transfer function is given by

FIGURE 4.51
Top row:
Perspective plot,
image, and, radial
cross section of
an IHPF transfer
function. Middle
and bottom
rows: The same
sequence for
GHPF and BHPF
transfer functions.
(The thin image
borders were
added for clarity.
They are not part
of the data.)

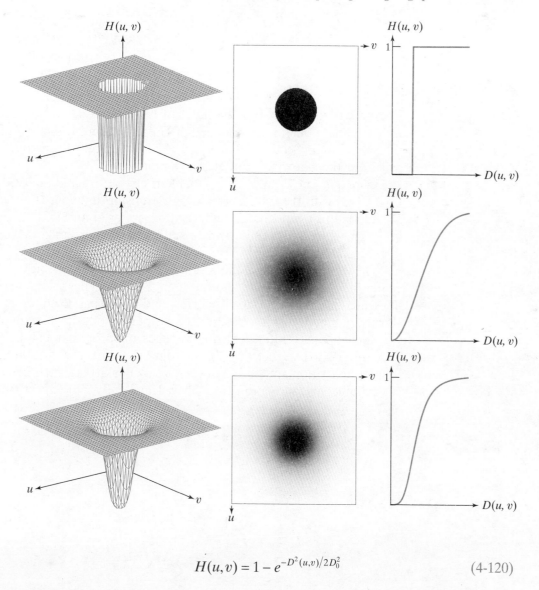

$$H(u,v) = 1 - e^{-D^2(u,v)/2D_0^2} \qquad (4\text{-}120)$$

and, from Eq. (4-117), that the transfer function of a Butterworth highpass filter (BHPF) is

$$H(u,v) = \frac{1}{1 + \left[D_0/D(u,v)\right]^{2n}} \qquad (4\text{-}121)$$

Figure 4.51 shows 3-D plots, image representations, and radial cross sections for the preceding transfer functions. As before, we see that the BHPF transfer function in the third row of the figure represents a transition between the sharpness of the IHPF and the broad smoothness of the GHPF transfer function.

It follows from Eq. (4-118) that the spatial kernel corresponding to a highpass filter transfer function in the frequency domain is given by

$$h_{HP}(x,y) = \Im^{-1}\big[H_{HP}(u,v)\big]$$
$$= \Im^{-1}\big[1 - H_{LP}(u,v)\big] \qquad (4\text{-}122)$$
$$= \delta(x,y) - h_{LP}(x,y)$$

where we used the fact that the IDFT of 1 in the frequency domain is a unit impulse in the spatial domain (see Table 4.4). This equation is precisely the foundation for the discussion in Section 3.7, in which we showed how to construct a highpass kernel by subtracting a lowpass kernel from a unit impulse.

Recall that a unit impulse in the spatial domain is an array of 0's with a 1 in the center.

Figure 4.52 shows highpass spatial kernels constructed in just this manner, using Eq. (4-122) with ILPF, GLPF, and BLPF transfer functions (the values of M, N, and D_0 used in this figure are the same as those we used for Fig. 4.42, and the BLPF is of order 2). Figure 4.52(a) shows the resulting ideal highpass kernel obtained using Eq. (4-122), and Fig. 4.52(b) is a horizontal intensity profile through the center of the kernel. The center element of the profile is a unit impulse, visible as a bright dot in the center of Fig. 4.52(a). Note that this highpass kernel has the same ringing properties illustrated in Fig. 4.42(b) for its corresponding lowpass counterpart. As you will see shortly, ringing is just as objectionable as before, but this time in images sharpened with ideal highpass filters. The other images and profiles in Fig. 4.52 are for Gaussian and Butterworth kernels. We know from Fig. 4.51 that GHPF transfer functions in the frequency domain tend to have a broader "skirt" than Butterworth functions of comparable size and cutoff frequency. Thus, we would expect Butterworth spatial

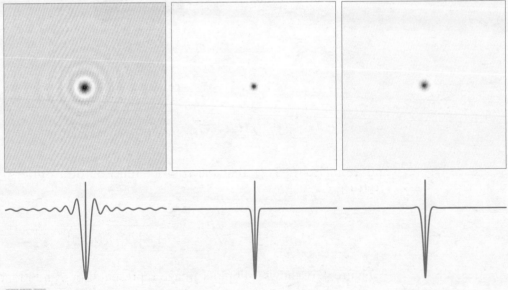

a b c
d e f

FIGURE 4.52 (a)–(c): Ideal, Gaussian, and Butterworth highpass spatial kernels obtained from IHPF, GHPF, and BHPF frequency-domain transfer functions. (The thin image borders are not part of the data.) (d)–(f): Horizontal intensity profiles through the centers of the kernels.

TABLE 4.6
Highpass filter transfer functions. D_0 is the cutoff frequency and n is the order of the Butterworth transfer function.

Ideal	Gaussian	Butterworth
$H(u,v) = \begin{cases} 0 & \text{if } D(u,v) \le D_0 \\ 1 & \text{if } D(u,v) > D_0 \end{cases}$	$H(u,v) = 1 - e^{-D^2(u,v)/2D_0^2}$	$H(u,v) = \dfrac{1}{1 + \left[D_0/D(u,v)\right]^{2n}}$

kernels to be "broader" than comparable Gaussian kernels, a fact that is confirmed by the images and their profiles in Figs. 4.52. Table 4.6 summarizes the three highpass filter transfer functions discussed in the preceding paragraphs.

EXAMPLE 4.19: Highpass filtering of the character test pattern.

The first row of Fig. 4.53 shows the result of filtering the test pattern in Fig. 4.37(a) using IHPF, GHPF, and BHPF transfer functions with $D_0 = 60$ [see Fig. 4.37(b)] and $n = 2$ for the Butterworth filter. We know from Chapter 3 that highpass filtering produces images with negative values. The images in Fig. 4.53 are not scaled, so the negative values are clipped by the display at 0 (black). The key objective of highpass filtering is to sharpen. Also, because the highpass filters used here set the DC term to zero, the images have essentially no tonality, as explained earlier in connection with Fig. 4.30.

Our main objective in this example is to compare the behavior of the three highpass filters. As Fig. 4.53(a) shows, the ideal highpass filter produced results with severe distortions caused by ringing. For example, the blotches inside the strokes of the large letter "a" are ringing artifacts. By comparison, neither Figs. 4.53(b) or (c) have such distortions. With reference to Fig. 4.37(b), the filters removed or attenuated approximately 95% of the image energy. As you know, removing the lower frequencies of an image reduces its gray-level content significantly, leaving mostly edges and other sharp transitions, as is evident in Fig. 4.53. The details you see in the first row of the figure are contained in only the upper 5% of the image energy.

The second row, obtained with $D_0 = 160$, is more interesting. The remaining energy of those images is about 2.5%, or half, the energy of the images in the first row. However, the difference in fine detail is striking. See, for example, how much cleaner the boundary of the large "a" is now, especially in the Gaussian and Butterworth results. The same is true for all other details, down to the smallest objects. This is the type of result that is considered acceptable when detection of edges and boundaries is important.

Figure 4.54 shows the images in the second row of Fig. 4.53, scaled using Eqs. (2-31) and (2-32) to display the full intensity range of both positive and negative intensities. The ringing in Fig. 4.54(a) shows the inadequacy of ideal highpass filters. In contrast, notice the smoothness of the background on the other two images, and the crispness of their edges.

EXAMPLE 4.20: Using highpass filtering and thresholding for image enhancement.

Figure 4.55(a) is a 962×1026 image of a thumbprint in which smudges (a typical problem) are evident. A key step in automated fingerprint recognition is enhancement of print ridges and the reduction of smudges. In this example, we use highpass filtering to enhance the ridges and reduce the effects of

a b c
d e f

FIGURE 4.53 Top row: The image from Fig. 4.40(a) filtered with IHPF, GHPF, and BHPF transfer functions using $D_0 = 60$ in all cases ($n = 2$ for the BHPF). Second row: Same sequence, but using $D_0 = 160$.

a b c

FIGURE 4.54 The images from the second row of Fig. 4.53 scaled using Eqs. (2-31) and (2-32) to show both positive and negative values.

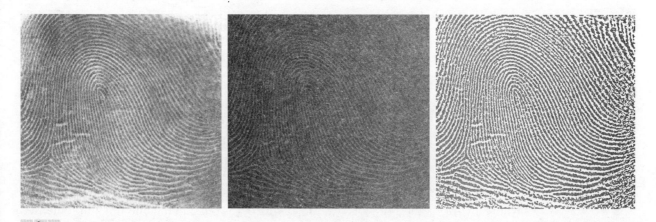

a b c

FIGURE 4.55 (a) Smudged thumbprint. (b) Result of highpass filtering (a). (c) Result of thresholding (b). (Original image courtesy of the U.S. National Institute of Standards and Technology.)

smudging. Enhancement of the ridges is accomplished by the fact that their boundaries are characterized by high frequencies, which are unchanged by a highpass filter. On the other hand, the filter reduces low frequency components, which correspond to slowly varying intensities in the image, such as the background and smudges. Thus, enhancement is achieved by reducing the effect of all features except those with high frequencies, which are the features of interest in this case.

Figure 4.55(b) is the result of using a Butterworth highpass filter of order 4 with a cutoff frequency of 50. A fourth-order filter provides a sharp (but smooth) transition from low to high frequencies, with filtering characteristics between an ideal and a Gaussian filter. The cutoff frequency chosen is about 5% of the long dimension of the image. The idea is for D_0 to be close to the origin so that low frequencies are attenuated but not completely eliminated, except for the DC term which is set to 0, so that tonality differences between the ridges and background are not lost completely. Choosing a value for D_0 between 5% and 10% of the long dimension of the image is a good starting point. Choosing a large value of D_0 would highlight fine detail to such an extent that the definition of the ridges would be affected. As expected, the highpass filtered image has negative values, which are shown as black by the display.

A simple approach for highlighting sharp features in a highpass-filtered image is to threshold it by setting to black (0) all negative values and to white (1) the remaining values. Figure 4.55(c) shows the result of this operation. Note how the ridges are clear, and how the effect of the smudges has been reduced considerably. In fact, ridges that are barely visible in the top, right section of the image in Fig. 4.55(a) are nicely enhanced in Fig. 4.55(c). An automated algorithm would find it much easier to follow the ridges on this image than it would on the original.

THE LAPLACIAN IN THE FREQUENCY DOMAIN

In Section 3.6, we used the Laplacian for image sharpening in the spatial domain. In this section, we revisit the Laplacian and show that it yields equivalent results using frequency domain techniques. It can be shown (see Problem 4.52) that the Laplacian can be implemented in the frequency domain using the filter transfer function

$$H(u,v) = -4\pi^2(u^2 + v^2) \tag{4-123}$$

or, with respect to the center of the frequency rectangle, using the transfer function

$$H(u,v) = -4\pi^2 \left[(u - P/2)^2 + (v - Q/2)^2 \right]$$
$$= -4\pi^2 D^2(u,v)$$

(4-124)

where $D(u,v)$ is the distance function defined in Eq. (4-112). Using this transfer function, the Laplacian of an image, $f(x,y)$, is obtained in the familiar manner:

$$\nabla^2 f(x,y) = \mathfrak{S}^{-1} \left[H(u,v) F(u,v) \right]$$

(4-125)

where $F(u,v)$ is the DFT of $f(x,y)$. As in Eq. (3-54), enhancement is implemented using the equation

$$g(x,y) = f(x,y) + c\nabla^2 f(x,y)$$

(4-126)

Here, $c = -1$ because $H(u,v)$ is negative. In Chapter 3, $f(x,y)$ and $\nabla^2 f(x,y)$ had comparable values. However, computing $\nabla^2 f(x,y)$ with Eq. (4-125) introduces DFT scaling factors that can be several orders of magnitude larger than the maximum value of f. Thus, the differences between f and its Laplacian must be brought into comparable ranges. The easiest way to handle this problem is to normalize the values of $f(x,y)$ to the range $[0,1]$ (before computing its DFT) and divide $\nabla^2 f(x,y)$ by its maximum value, which will bring it to the approximate range $[-1,1]$. (Remember, the Laplacian has negative values.) Equation (4-126) can then be used.

We can write Eq. (4-126) directly in the frequency domain as

$$g(x,y) = \mathfrak{S}^{-1} \left\{ F(u,v) - H(u,v) F(u,v) \right\}$$
$$= \mathfrak{S}^{-1} \left\{ [1 - H(u,v)] F(u,v) \right\}$$
$$= \mathfrak{S}^{-1} \left\{ \left[1 + 4\pi^2 D^2(u,v) \right] F(u,v) \right\}$$

(4-127)

Although this result is elegant, it has the same scaling issues just mentioned, compounded by the fact that the normalizing factor is not as easily computed. For this reason, Eq. (4-126) is the preferred implementation in the frequency domain, with $\nabla^2 f(x,y)$ computed using Eq. (4-125) and scaled using the approach mentioned in the previous paragraph.

EXAMPLE 4.21: Image sharpening in the frequency domain using the Laplacian.

Figure 4.56(a) is the same as Fig. 3.46(a), and Fig. 4.56(b) shows the result of using Eq. (4-126), in which the Laplacian was computed in the frequency domain using Eq. (4-125). Scaling was done as described in connection with Eq. (4-126). We see by comparing Figs. 4.56(b) and 3.46(d) that the frequency-domain result is superior. The image in Fig. 4.56(b) is much sharper, and shows details that are barely visible in 3.46(d), which was obtained using the Laplacian kernel in Fig. 3.45(b), with a -8 in the center. The significant improvement achieved in the frequency domain is not unexpected. The spatial Laplacian kernel

a b

FIGURE 4.56
(a) Original, blurry image.
(b) Image enhanced using the Laplacian in the frequency domain. Compare with Fig. 3.46(d). (Original image courtesy of NASA.)

encompasses a very small neighborhood, while the formulation in Eqs. (4-125) and (4-126) encompasses the entire image.

UNSHARP MASKING, HIGH-BOOST FILTERING, AND HIGH-FREQUENCY-EMPHASIS FILTERING

In this section, we discuss frequency domain formulations of the unsharp masking and high-boost filtering image sharpening techniques introduced in Section 3.6. Using frequency domain methods, the mask defined in Eq. (3-55) is given by

$$g_{\text{mask}}(x, y) = f(x, y) - f_{\text{LP}}(x, y) \tag{4-128}$$

with

$$f_{\text{LP}}(x, y) = \mathfrak{S}^{-1}\left[H_{\text{LP}}(u, v) F(u, v)\right] \tag{4-129}$$

where $H_{\text{LP}}(u, v)$ is a lowpass filter transfer function, and $F(u, v)$ is the DFT of $f(x, y)$. Here, $f_{\text{LP}}(x, y)$ is a smoothed image analogous to $\bar{f}(x, y)$ in Eq. (3-55). Then, as in Eq. (3-56),

$$g(x, y) = f(x, y) + k g_{\text{mask}}(x, y) \tag{4-130}$$

This expression defines *unsharp masking* when $k = 1$ and high-boost filtering when $k > 1$. Using the preceding results, we can express Eq. (4-130) entirely in terms of frequency domain computations involving a lowpass filter:

$$g(x, y) = \mathfrak{S}^{-1}\left\{\left(1 + k\left[1 - H_{\text{LP}}(u, v)\right]\right) F(u, v)\right\} \tag{4-131}$$

We can express this result in terms of a highpass filter using Eq. (4-118):

$$g(x,y) = \Im^{-1}\left\{\left[1 + kH_{HP}(u,v)\right]F(u,v)\right\} \quad\quad (4\text{-}132)$$

The expression contained within the square brackets is called a *high-frequency-emphasis filter transfer function*. As noted earlier, highpass filters set the dc term to zero, thus reducing the average intensity in the filtered image to 0. The high-frequency-emphasis filter does not have this problem because of the 1 that is added to the highpass filter transfer function. Constant k gives control over the proportion of high frequencies that influences the final result. A slightly more general formulation of high-frequency-emphasis filtering is the expression

$$g(x,y) = \Im^{-1}\left\{\left[k_1 + k_2 H_{HP}(u,v)\right]F(u,v)\right\} \quad\quad (4\text{-}133)$$

where $k_1 \geq 0$ offsets the value the transfer function so as not to zero-out the dc term [see Fig. 4.30(c)], and $k_2 > 0$ controls the contribution of high frequencies.

EXAMPLE 4.22: Image enhancement using high-frequency-emphasis filtering.

Figure 4.57(a) shows a 503×720-pixel chest X-ray image with a narrow range of intensity levels. The objective of this example is to enhance the image using high-frequency-emphasis filtering. X-rays cannot be focused in the same manner that optical lenses can, and the resulting images generally tend to be slightly blurred. Because the intensities in this particular image are biased toward the dark end of the

a b
c d

FIGURE 4.57
(a) A chest X-ray.
(b) Result of filtering with a GHPF function.
(c) Result of high-frequency-emphasis filtering using the same GHPF. (d) Result of performing histogram equalization on (c). (Original image courtesy of Dr. Thomas R. Gest, Division of Anatomical Sciences, University of Michigan Medical School.)

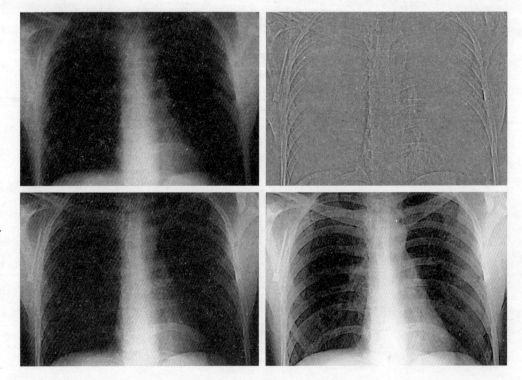

gray scale, we also take this opportunity to give an example of how spatial domain processing can be used to complement frequency-domain filtering.

Image artifacts, such as ringing, are unacceptable in medical image processing, so we use a Gaussian highpass filter transfer function. Because the spatial representation of a GHPF function is Gaussian also, we know that ringing will not be an issue. The value chosen for D_0 should provide enough filtering to sharpen boundaries while at the same time not over-sharpening minute details (such as noise). We used $D_0 = 70$, approximately 10% of the long image dimension, but other similar values would work also. Figure 4.57(b) is the result of highpass filtering the original image (scaled as the images in Fig. 4.54). As expected, the image is rather featureless, but the important boundaries (e.g., the edges of the ribs) are clearly delineated. Figure 4.57(c) shows the advantage of high-frequency-emphasis filtering, where we used Eq. (4-133) with $k_1 = 0.5$ and $k_2 = 0.75$. Although the image is still dark, the gray-level tonality has been restored, with the added advantage of sharper features.

As we discussed in Section 3.3, an image characterized by intensity levels in a narrow range of the gray scale is an ideal candidate for histogram equalization. As Fig. 4.57(d) shows, this was indeed an appropriate method to further enhance the image. Note the clarity of the bone structure and other details that simply are not visible in any of the other three images. The final enhanced image is a little noisy, but this is typical of X-ray images when their gray scale is expanded. The result obtained using a combination of high-frequency-emphasis and histogram equalization is superior to the result that would be obtained by using either method alone.

HOMOMORPHIC FILTERING

The illumination-reflectance model introduced in Section 2.3 can be used to develop a frequency domain procedure for improving the appearance of an image by simultaneous intensity range compression and contrast enhancement. From the discussion in that section, an image $f(x, y)$ can be expressed as the product of its illumination, $i(x, y)$, and reflectance, $r(x, y)$, components:

$$f(x, y) = i(x, y)r(x, y) \qquad (4\text{-}134)$$

This equation cannot be used directly to operate on the frequency components of illumination and reflectance because the Fourier transform of a product is not the product of the transforms:

$$\Im[f(x, y)] \neq \Im[i(x, y)]\Im[r(x, y)] \qquad (4\text{-}135)$$

However, suppose that we define

If $f(x, y)$ has any zero values, a 1 must be added to the image to avoid having to deal with ln(0). The 1 is then subtracted from the final result.

$$\begin{aligned} z(x, y) &= \ln f(x, y) \\ &= \ln i(x, y) + \ln r(x, y) \end{aligned} \qquad (4\text{-}136)$$

Then,

$$\begin{aligned} \Im[z(x, y)] &= \Im[\ln f(x, y)] \\ &= \Im[\ln i(x, y)] + \Im[\ln r(x, y)] \end{aligned} \qquad (4\text{-}137)$$

or

$$Z(u,v) = F_i(u,v) + F_r(u,v) \tag{4-138}$$

where $F_i(u,v)$ and $F_r(u,v)$ are the Fourier transforms of $\ln i(x,y)$ and $\ln r(x,y)$, respectively.

We can filter $Z(u,v)$ using a filter transfer function $H(u,v)$ so that

$$
\begin{aligned}
S(u,v) &= H(u,v)Z(u,v) \\
&= H(u,v)F_i(u,v) + H(u,v)F_r(u,v)
\end{aligned}
\tag{4-139}
$$

The filtered image in the spatial domain is then

$$
\begin{aligned}
s(x,y) &= \mathfrak{S}^{-1}\big[S(u,v)\big] \\
&= \mathfrak{S}^{-1}\big[H(u,v)F_i(u,v)\big] + \mathfrak{S}^{-1}\big[H(u,v)F_r(u,v)\big]
\end{aligned}
\tag{4-140}
$$

By defining

$$i'(x,y) = \mathfrak{S}^{-1}\big[H(u,v)F_i(u,v)\big] \tag{4-141}$$

and

$$r'(x,y) = \mathfrak{S}^{-1}\big[H(u,v)F_r(u,v)\big] \tag{4-142}$$

we can express Eq. (4-140) in the form

$$s(x,y) = i'(x,y) + r'(x,y) \tag{4-143}$$

Finally, because $z(x,y)$ was formed by taking the natural logarithm of the input image, we reverse the process by taking the exponential of the filtered result to form the output image:

$$
\begin{aligned}
g(x,y) &= e^{s(x,y)} \\
&= e^{i'(x,y)}e^{r'(x,y)} \\
&= i_0(x,y)r_0(x,y)
\end{aligned}
\tag{4-144}
$$

where

$$i_0(x,y) = e^{i'(x,y)} \tag{4-145}$$

and

$$r_0(x,y) = e^{r'(x,y)} \tag{4-146}$$

are the illumination and reflectance components of the output (processed) image.

Figure 4.58 is a summary of the filtering approach just derived. This method is based on a special case of a class of systems known as *homomorphic systems*. In this particular application, the key to the approach is the separation of the illumination

FIGURE 4.58
Summary of steps in homomorphic filtering.

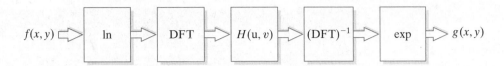

and reflectance components achieved in the form shown in Eq. (4-138). The *homomorphic filter transfer function*, $H(u,v)$, then can operate on these components separately, as indicated by Eq. (4-139).

The illumination component of an image generally is characterized by slow spatial variations, while the reflectance component tends to vary abruptly, particularly at the junctions of dissimilar objects. These characteristics lead to associating the low frequencies of the Fourier transform of the logarithm of an image with illumination, and the high frequencies with reflectance. Although these associations are rough approximations, they can be used to advantage in image filtering, as illustrated in Example 4.23.

A good deal of control can be gained over the illumination and reflectance components with a homomorphic filter. This control requires specification of a filter transfer function $H(u,v)$ that affects the low- and high-frequency components of the Fourier transform in different, controllable ways. Figure 4.59 shows a cross section of such a function. If the parameters γ_L and γ_H are chosen so that $\gamma_L < 1$ and $\gamma_H \geq 1$, the filter function in Fig. 4.59 will attenuate the contribution made by the low frequencies (illumination) and amplify the contribution made by high frequencies (reflectance). The net result is simultaneous dynamic range compression and contrast enhancement.

The shape of the function in Fig. 4.59 can be approximated using a highpass filter transfer function. For example, using a slightly modified form of the GHPF function yields the homomorphic function

A BHPF function would work well too, with the added advantage of more control over the sharpness of the transition between γ_L and γ_H. The disadvantage is the possibility of ringing for high values of n.

$$H(u,v) = (\gamma_H - \gamma_L)\left[1 - e^{-cD^2(u,v)/D_0^2}\right] + \gamma_L \tag{4-147}$$

where $D(u,v)$ is defined in Eq. (4-112) and constant c controls the sharpness of the slope of the function as it transitions between γ_L and γ_H. This filter transfer function is similar to the high-frequency-emphasis function discussed in the previous section.

FIGURE 4.59
Radial cross section of a homomorphic filter transfer function..

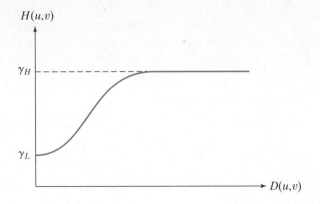

a b

FIGURE 4.60
(a) Full body PET
scan. (b) Image
enhanced using
homomorphic
filtering. (Original
image courtesy
of Dr. Michael E.
Casey, CTI Pet
Systems.)

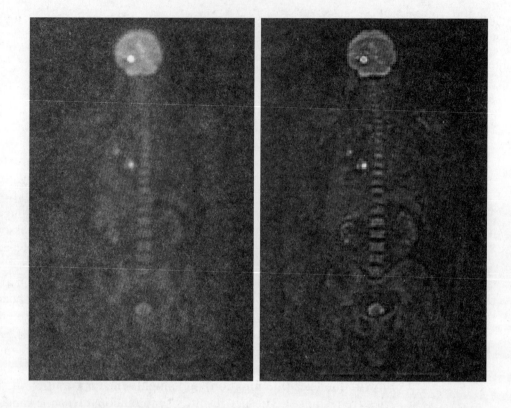

EXAMPLE 4.23: Homomorphic filtering.

Figure 4.60(a) shows a full body PET (Positron Emission Tomography) scan of size 1162×746 pixels. The image is slightly blurred and many of its low-intensity features are obscured by the high intensity of the "hot spots" dominating the dynamic range of the display. (These hot spots were caused by a tumor in the brain and one in the lungs.) Figure 4.60(b) was obtained by homomorphic filtering Fig. 4.60(a) using the filter transfer function in Eq. (4-147) with $\gamma_L = 0.4$, $\gamma_H = 3.0$, $c = 5$, and $D_0 = 20$. A radial cross section of this function looks just like Fig. 4.59, but with a much sharper slope, and the transition between low and high frequencies much closer to the origin.

Note in Fig. 4.60(b) how much sharper the hot spots, the brain, and the skeleton are in the processed image, and how much more detail is visible in this image, including, for example, some of the organs, the shoulders, and the pelvis region. By reducing the effects of the dominant illumination components (the hot spots), it became possible for the dynamic range of the display to allow lower intensities to become more visible. Similarly, because the high frequencies are enhanced by homomorphic filtering, the reflectance components of the image (edge information) were sharpened considerably. The enhanced image in Fig. 4.60(b) is a significant improvement over the original.

4.10 SELECTIVE FILTERING

The filters discussed in the previous two sections operate over the entire frequency rectangle. There are applications in which it is of interest to process specific bands of frequencies or small regions of the frequency rectangle. Filters in the first category are called *band filters*. If frequencies in the band are filtered out, the band filter is called a *bandreject* filter; similarly, if the frequencies are passed, the filter is called a *bandpass* filter. Filters in the second category are called *notch filters*. These filters are further qualified as being *notch reject* or *notch pass* filters, depending on whether frequencies in the notch areas are rejected or passed.

BANDREJECT AND BANDPASS FILTERS

As you learned in Section 3.7, bandpass and bandreject filter transfer functions in the frequency domain can be constructed by combining lowpass and highpass filter transfer functions, with the latter also being derivable from lowpass functions (see Fig. 3.52). In other words, lowpass filter transfer functions are the basis for forming highpass, bandreject, and bandpass filter functions. Furthermore, a bandpass filter transfer function is obtained from a bandreject function in the same manner that we obtained a highpass from a lowpass transfer function:

$$H_{\text{BP}}(u,v) = 1 - H_{\text{BR}}(u,v) \tag{4-148}$$

Figure 4.61(a) shows how to construct an ideal bandreject filter (IBRF) transfer function. It consists of an ILPF and an IHPF function with different cutoff frequencies. When dealing with bandpass functions, the parameters of interest are the width, W, and the center, C_0, of the band. An equation for the IBRF function is easily obtained by inspection from Fig. 4.61(a), as the leftmost entry in Table 4.7 shows. The key requirements of a bandpass transfer function are: (1) the values of the function must be in the range $[0, 1]$; (2) the value of the function must be zero at a distance C_0 from the origin (center) of the function; and (3) we must be able to specify a value for W. Clearly, the IBRF function just developed satisfies these requirements.

Adding lowpass and highpass transfer functions to form Gaussian and Butterworth bandreject functions presents some difficulties. For example, Fig. 4.61(b) shows a bandpass function formed as the sum of lowpass and highpass Gaussian functions with different cutoff points. Two problems are immediately obvious: we have no direct control over W, and the value of $H(u,v)$ is not 0 at C_0. We could

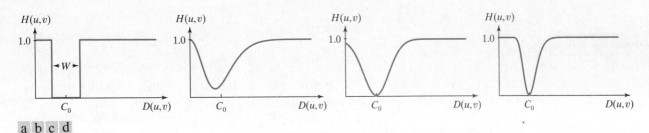

a b c d

FIGURE 4.61 Radial cross sections. (a) Ideal bandreject filter transfer function. (b) Bandreject transfer function formed by the sum of Gaussian lowpass and highpass filter functions. (The minimum is not 0 and does not align with C_0.) (c) Radial plot of Eq. (4-149). (The minimum is 0 and is properly aligned with C_0, but the value at the origin is not 1.) (d) Radial plot of Eq. (4-150); this Gaussian-shape plot meets all the requirements of a bandreject filter transfer function.

TABLE 4.7
Bandreject filter transfer functions. C_0 is the center of the band, W is the width of the band, and $D(u,v)$ is the distance from the center of the transfer function to a point (u,v) in the frequency rectangle.

Ideal (IBRF)	Gaussian (GBRF)	Butterworth (BBRF)
$H(u,v) = \begin{cases} 0 & \text{if } C_0 - \dfrac{W}{2} \le D(u,v) \le C_0 + \dfrac{W}{2} \\ 1 & \text{otherwise} \end{cases}$	$H(u,v) = 1 - e^{-\left[\frac{D^2(u,v) - C_0^2}{D(u,v)W}\right]^2}$	$H(u,v) = \dfrac{1}{1 + \left[\dfrac{D(u,v)W}{D^2(u,v) - C_0^2}\right]^{2n}}$

offset the function and scale it so that values fall in the range $[0,1]$, but finding an analytical solution for the point where the lowpass and highpass Gaussian functions intersect is impossible, and this intersection would be required to solve for the cutoff points in terms of C_0. The only alternatives are trial-and-error or numerical methods.

Fortunately, instead of adding lowpass and highpass transfer function, an alternative is to modify the expressions for the Gaussian and Butterworth highpass transfer functions so that they will satisfy the three requirements stated earlier. We illustrate the procedure for a Gaussian function. In this case, we begin by changing the point at which $H(u,v) = 0$ from $D(u,v) = 0$ to $D(u,v) = C_0$ in Eq. (4-120):

$$H(u,v) = 1 - e^{-\left[\frac{(D(u,v) - C_0)^2}{W^2}\right]} \tag{4-149}$$

A plot of this function [Fig. 4.61(c)] shows that, below C_0, the function behaves as a lowpass Gaussian function, at C_0 the function will always be 0, and for values higher than C_0 the function behaves as a highpass Gaussian function. Parameter W is proportional to the standard deviation and thus controls the "width" of the band. The only problem remaining is that the function is not always 1 at the origin. A simple modification of Eq. (4-149) removes this shortcoming:

The overall ratio in this equation is squared so that, as the distance increases, Eqs. (4-149) and (4-150) behave approximately the same.

$$H(u,v) = 1 - e^{-\left[\frac{D^2(u,v) - C_0^2}{D(u,v)W}\right]^2} \tag{4-150}$$

Now, the exponent is infinite when $D(u,v) = 0$, which makes the exponential term go to zero and $H(u,v) = 1$ at the origin, as desired. In this modification of Eq. (4-149), the basic Gaussian shape is preserved and the three requirements stated earlier are satisfied. Figure 4.61(d) shows a plot of Eq. (4-150). A similar analysis leads to the form of a Butterworth bandreject filter transfer function shown in Table 4.7.

Figure 4.62 shows perspective plots of the filter transfer functions just discussed. At first glance the Gaussian and Butterworth functions appear to be about the same, but, as before, the behavior of the Butterworth function is between the ideal and Gaussian functions. As Fig. 4.63 shows, this is easier to see by viewing the three filter

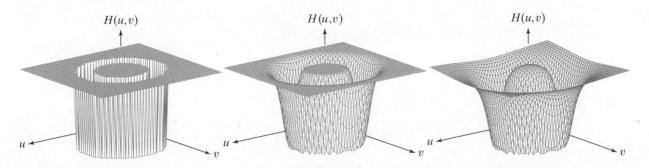

a b c

FIGURE 4.62 Perspective plots of (a) ideal, (b) modified Gaussian, and (c) modified Butterworth (of order 1) bandreject filter transfer functions from Table 4.7. All transfer functions are of size 512×512 elements, with $C_0 = 128$ and $W = 60$.

functions as images. Increasing the order of the Butterworth function would bring it closer to the ideal bandreject transfer function.

NOTCH FILTERS

Notch filters are the most useful of the selective filters. A notch filter rejects (or passes) frequencies in a predefined neighborhood of the frequency rectangle. Zero-phase-shift filters must be symmetric about the origin (center of the frequency rectangle), so a notch filter transfer function with center at (u_0, v_0) must have a corresponding notch at location $(-u_0, -v_0)$. *Notch reject* filter transfer functions are constructed as products of highpass filter transfer functions whose centers have been translated to the centers of the notches. The general form is:

$$H_{\text{NR}}(u,v) = \prod_{k=1}^{Q} H_k(u,v) H_{-k}(u,v) \tag{4-151}$$

where $H_k(u,v)$ and $H_{-k}(u,v)$ are highpass filter transfer functions whose centers are at (u_k, v_k) and $(-u_k, -v_k)$, respectively. These centers are specified with respect to the center of the frequency rectangle, $(M/2, N/2)$, where, as usual, M and N are the

a b c

FIGURE 4.63
(a) The ideal,
(b) Gaussian, and
(c) Butterworth
bandpass transfer
functions from
Fig. 4.62, shown
as images. (The
thin border lines
are not part of the
image data.)

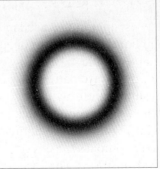

number of rows and columns in the input image. Thus, the distance computations for each filter transfer function are given by

$$D_k(u,v) = \left[(u - M/2 - u_k)^2 + (v - N/2 - v_k)^2 \right]^{1/2} \tag{4-152}$$

and

$$D_{-k}(u,v) = \left[(u - M/2 + u_k)^2 + (v - N/2 + v_k)^2 \right]^{1/2} \tag{4-153}$$

For example, the following is a Butterworth notch reject filter transfer function of order n, containing three notch pairs:

$$H_{\mathrm{NR}}(u,v) = \prod_{k=1}^{3} \left[\frac{1}{1 + \left[D_{0k}/D_k(u,v) \right]^n} \right] \left[\frac{1}{1 + \left[D_{0k}/D_{-k}(u,v) \right]^n} \right] \tag{4-154}$$

where $D_k(u,v)$ and $D_{-k}(u,v)$ are given by Eqs. (4-152) and (4-153). The constant D_{0k} is the same for each pair of notches, but it can be different for different pairs. Other notch reject filter functions are constructed in the same manner, depending on the highpass filter function chosen. As with the filters discussed earlier, a notch pass filter transfer function is obtained from a notch reject function using the expression

$$H_{\mathrm{NP}}(u,v) = 1 - H_{\mathrm{NR}}(u,v) \tag{4-155}$$

As the next two examples show, one of the principal applications of notch filtering is for selectively modifying local regions of the DFT. Often, this type of processing is done interactively, working directly with DFTs obtained without padding. The advantages of working interactively with actual DFTs (as opposed to having to "translate" from padded to actual frequency values) generally outweigh any wraparound errors that may result from not using padding in the filtering process. If necessary, after an acceptable solution is obtained, a final result using padding can be generated by adjusting all filter parameters to compensate for the padded DFT size. The following two examples were done without padding. To get an idea of how DFT values change as a function of padding, see Problem 4.42.

EXAMPLE 4.24: Using notch filtering to remove moiré patterns from digitized printed media images.

Figure 4.64(a) is the scanned newspaper image used in Fig. 4.21, showing a prominent moiré pattern, and Fig. 4.64(b) is its spectrum. The Fourier transform of a pure sine, which is a periodic function, is a pair of conjugate symmetric impulses (see Table 4.4). The symmetric "impulse-like" bursts in Fig. 4.64(b) are a result of the near periodicity of the moiré pattern. We can attenuate these bursts by using notch filtering.

Figure 4.64(c) shows the result of multiplying the DFT of Fig. 4.64(a) by a Butterworth notch reject transfer function with $D_0 = 9$ and $n = 4$ for all notch pairs (the centers of the notches are coincide with the centers of the black circular regions in the figure). The value of the radius was selected (by visual inspection of the spectrum) to encompass the energy bursts completely, and the value of n was selected to produce notches with sharp transitions. The locations of the center of the notches were determined

a b
c d

FIGURE 4.64
(a) Sampled
newspaper
image showing a
moiré pattern.
(b) Spectrum.
(c) Fourier
transform
multiplied by
a Butterworth
notch reject filter
transfer function.
(d) Filtered image.

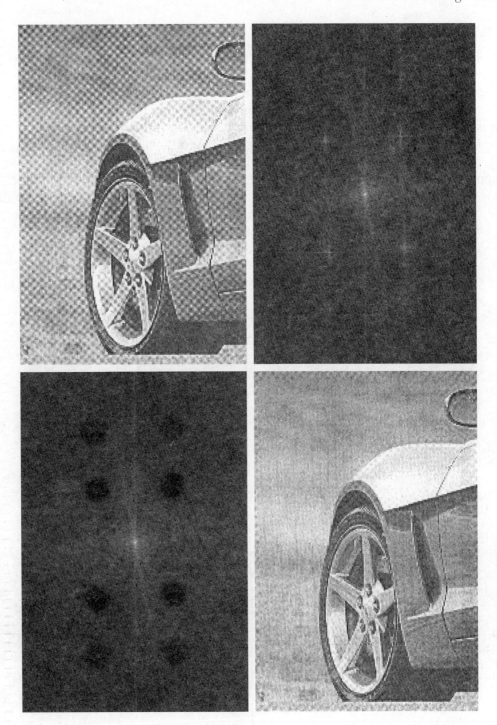

interactively from the spectrum. Figure 4.64(d) shows the result obtained with this filter transfer function, using the filtering procedure outlined in Section 4.7. The improvement is significant, considering the low resolution and degree of degradation of the original image.

EXAMPLE 4.25: Using notch filtering to remove periodic interference.

Figure 4.65(a) shows an image of part of the rings surrounding the planet Saturn. This image was captured by *Cassini*, the first spacecraft to enter the planet's orbit. The nearly sinusoidal pattern visible in the image was caused by an AC signal superimposed on the camera video signal just prior to digitizing the image. This was an unexpected problem that corrupted some images from the mission. Fortunately, this type of interference is fairly easy to correct by postprocessing. One approach is to use notch filtering.

Figure 4.65(b) shows the DFT spectrum. Careful analysis of the vertical axis reveals a series of small bursts of energy near the origin which correspond to the nearly sinusoidal interference. A simple approach is to use a narrow notch rectangle filter starting with the lowest frequency burst, and extending for the remainder of the vertical axis. Figure 4.65(c) shows the transfer function of such a filter (white represents 1 and black 0). Figure 4.65(d) shows the result of processing the corrupted image with this filter. This result is a significant improvement over the original image.

To obtain and image of just the interference pattern, we isolated the frequencies in the vertical axis using a notch pass transfer function, obtained by subtracting the notch reject function from 1 [see Fig. 4.66(a)]. Then, as Fig. 4.66(b) shows, the IDFT of the filtered image is the spatial interference pattern.

a b
c d

FIGURE 4.65
(a) Image of Saturn rings showing nearly periodic interference.
(b) Spectrum. (The bursts of energy in the vertical axis near the origin correspond to the interference pattern).
(c) A vertical notch reject filter transfer function.
(d) Result of filtering. (The thin black border in (c) is not part of the data.) (Original image courtesy of Dr. Robert A. West, NASA/JPL.)

a b

FIGURE 4.66
(a) Notch pass filter function used to isolate the vertical axis of the DFT of Fig. 4.65(a).
(b) Spatial pattern obtained by computing the IDFT of (a).

4.11 THE FAST FOURIER TRANSFORM

We have focused attention thus far on theoretical concepts and on examples of filtering in the frequency domain. One thing that should be clear by now is that computational requirements in this area of image processing are not trivial. Thus, it is important to develop a basic understanding of methods by which Fourier transform computations can be simplified and speeded up. This section deals with these issues.

SEPARABILITY OF THE 2-D DFT

As mentioned in Table 4.3, the 2-D DFT is separable into 1-D transforms. We can write Eq. (4-67) as

$$F(u,v) = \sum_{x=0}^{M-1} e^{-j2\pi ux/M} \sum_{y=0}^{N-1} f(x,y)e^{-j2\pi vy/N}$$

$$= \sum_{x=0}^{M-1} F(x,v)e^{-j2\pi ux/M} \tag{4-156}$$

where

$$F(x,v) = \sum_{y=0}^{N-1} f(x,y)e^{-j2\pi vy/N} \tag{4-157}$$

For one value of x, and for $v = 0, 1, 2, \ldots, N-1$, we see that $F(x,v)$ is the 1-D DFT of *one* row of $f(x,y)$. By varying x from 0 to $M-1$ in Eq. (4-157), we compute a set of 1-D DFTs for all rows of $f(x,y)$. The computations in Eq. (4-156) similarly are 1-D transforms of the columns of $F(x,v)$. Thus, we conclude that the 2-D DFT of $f(x,y)$ can be obtained by computing the 1-D transform of each row of $f(x,y)$ and then computing the 1-D transform along each column of the result. This is an important simplification because we have to deal only with one variable at a time. A similar development applies to computing the 2-D IDFT using the 1-D IDFT. However, as we show in the following section, we can compute the IDFT using an algorithm

We could have formulated the preceding two equations to show that a 2-D DFT can be obtained by computing the 1-D DFT of each *column* of the input image followed by 1-D computations on the rows of the result.

designed to compute the forward DFT, so all 2-D Fourier transform computations are reduced to multiple passes of a 1-D algorithm designed for computing the 1-D DFT.

COMPUTING THE IDFT USING A DFT ALGORITHM

Taking the complex conjugate of both sides of Eq. (4-68) and multiplying the results by MN yields

$$MNf^*(x,y) = \sum_{u=0}^{M-1} \sum_{v=0}^{N-1} F^*(u,v)e^{-j2\pi(ux/M + vy/N)} \tag{4-158}$$

But, we recognize the form of the right side of this result as the DFT of $F^*(u,v)$. Therefore, Eq. (4-158) indicates that if we substitute $F^*(u,v)$ into an algorithm designed to compute the 2-D forward Fourier transform, the result will be $MNf^*(x,y)$. Taking the complex conjugate and dividing this result by MN yields $f(x,y)$, which is the inverse of $F(u,v)$.

Computing the 2-D inverse from a 2-D forward DFT algorithm that is based on successive passes of 1-D transforms (as in the previous section) is a frequent source of confusion involving the complex conjugates and multiplication by a constant, neither of which is done in the 1-D algorithms. The key concept to keep in mind is that we simply input $F^*(u,v)$ into whatever forward algorithm we have. The result will be $MNf^*(x,y)$. All we have to do with this result to obtain $f(x,y)$ is to take its complex conjugate and divide it by the constant MN. Of course, when $f(x,y)$ is real, as typically is the case, then $f^*(x,y) = f(x,y)$.

THE FAST FOURIER TRANSFORM (FFT)

Work in the frequency domain would not be practical if we had to implement Eqs. (4-67) and (4-68) directly. Brute-force implementation of these equations requires on the order of $(MN)^2$ multiplications and additions. For images of moderate size (say, 2048×2048 pixels), this means on the order of 17 trillion multiplications and additions for just one 2-D DFT, excluding the exponentials, which could be computed once and stored in a look-up table. Without the discovery of the *fast Fourier transform* (FFT), which reduces computations to the order of $MN \log_2 MN$ multiplications and additions, it is safe to say that the material presented in this chapter would be of little practical value. The computational reductions afforded by the FFT are impressive indeed. For example, computing the 2-D FFT of a 2048×2048 image would require on the order of 92 million multiplication and additions, which is a significant reduction from the one trillion computations mentioned above.

Although the FFT is a topic covered extensively in the literature on signal processing, this subject matter is of such significance in our work that this chapter would be incomplete if we did not provide an introduction explaining why the FFT works as it does. The algorithm we selected to accomplish this objective is the so-called *successive-doubling method*, which was the original algorithm that led to the birth of an entire industry. This particular algorithm assumes that the number of samples is an integer power of 2, but this is not a general requirement of other approaches

(Brigham [1988]).We know from the previous section that 2-D DFTs can be implemented by successive passes of the 1-D transform, so we need to focus only on the FFT of one variable.

In derivations of the FFT, it is customary to express Eq. (4-44) in the form

$$F(u) = \sum_{x=0}^{M-1} f(x) W_M^{ux} \tag{4-159}$$

for $u = 0, 1, 2, \ldots, M-1$, where

$$W_M = e^{-j2\pi/M} \tag{4-160}$$

and M is assumed to be of the form

$$M = 2^p \tag{4-161}$$

where p is a positive integer. Then it follows that M can be expressed as

$$M = 2K \tag{4-162}$$

with K being a positive integer also. Substituting Eq. (4-162) into Eq. (4-159) yields

$$
\begin{aligned}
F(u) &= \sum_{x=0}^{2K-1} f(x) W_{2K}^{ux} \\
&= \sum_{x=0}^{K-1} f(2x) W_{2K}^{u(2x)} + \sum_{x=0}^{K-1} f(2x+1) W_{2K}^{u(2x+1)}
\end{aligned}
\tag{4-163}
$$

However, it can be shown using Eq. (4-160) that $W_{2K}^{2ux} = W_K^{ux}$, so Eq. (4-163) can be written as

$$F(u) = \sum_{x=0}^{K-1} f(2x) W_K^{ux} + \sum_{x=0}^{K-1} f(2x+1) W_K^{ux} W_{2K}^u \tag{4-164}$$

Defining

$$F_{\text{even}}(u) = \sum_{x=0}^{K-1} f(2x) W_K^{ux} \tag{4-165}$$

for $u = 0, 1, 2, \ldots, K-1$, and

$$F_{\text{odd}}(u) = \sum_{x=0}^{K-1} f(2x+1) W_K^{ux} \tag{4-166}$$

for $u = 0, 1, 2, \ldots, K-1$, reduces Eq. (4-164) to

$$F(u) = F_{\text{even}}(u) + F_{\text{odd}}(u) W_{2K}^u \tag{4-167}$$

Also, because $W_M^{u+K} = W_K^u$ and $W_{2K}^{u+K} = -W_{2K}^u$, it follows that

$$F(u+K) = F_{even}(u) - F_{odd}(u)W_{2K}^u \qquad (4\text{-}168)$$

Analysis of Eqs. (4-165) through (4-168) reveals some important (and surprising) properties of these expressions. An M-point DFT can be computed by dividing the original expression into two parts, as indicated in Eqs. (4-167) and (4-168). Computing the first half of $F(u)$ requires evaluation of the two $(M/2)$-point transforms given in Eqs. (4-165) and (4-166). The resulting values of $F_{even}(u)$ and $F_{odd}(u)$ are then substituted into Eq. (4-167) to obtain $F(u)$ for $u = 0, 1, 2, \ldots, (M/2-1)$. The other half then follows directly from Eq. (4-168) *without* additional transform evaluations.

It is of interest to examine the computational implications of the preceding procedure. Let $m(p)$ and $a(p)$ represent the number of complex multiplications and additions, respectively, required to implement the method. As before, the number of samples is 2^p, where p is a positive integer. Suppose first that $p = 1$ so that the number of samples is two. A two-point transform requires the evaluation of $F(0)$; then $F(1)$ follows from Eq. (4-168). To obtain $F(0)$ requires computing $F_{even}(0)$ and $F_{odd}(0)$. In this case $K = 1$ and Eqs. (4-165) and (4-166) are one-point transforms. However, because the DFT of a single sample point is the sample itself, no multiplications or additions are required to obtain $F_{even}(0)$ and $F_{odd}(0)$. One multiplication of $F_{odd}(0)$ by W_2^0 and one addition yields $F(0)$ from Eq. (4-167). Then $F(1)$ follows from Eq. (4-168) with one more addition (subtraction is considered to be the same as addition). Because $F_{odd}(0)W_2^0$ has been computed already, the total number of operations required for a two-point transform consists of $m(1) = 1$ multiplication and $a(1) = 2$ additions.

The next allowed value for p is 2. According to the preceding development, a four-point transform can be divided into two parts. The first half of $F(u)$ requires evaluation of two, two-point transforms, as given in Eqs. (4-165) and (4-166) for $K = 2$. A two-point transform requires $m(1)$ multiplications and $a(1)$ additions. Therefore, evaluation of these two equations requires a total of $2m(1)$ multiplications and $2a(1)$ additions. Two further multiplications and additions are necessary to obtain $F(0)$ and $F(1)$ from Eq. (4-167). Because $F_{odd}(u)W_{2K}^u$ has been computed already for $u = \{0,1\}$, two more additions give $F(2)$ and $F(3)$. The total is then $m(2) = 2m(1) + 2$ and $a(2) = 2a(1) + 4$.

When p is equal to 3, two four-point transforms are needed to evaluate $F_{even}(u)$ and $F_{odd}(u)$. They require $2m(2)$ multiplications and $2a(2)$ additions. Four more multiplications and eight more additions yield the complete transform. The total then is then $m(3) = 2m(2) + 4$ multiplication and $a(3) = 2a(2) + 8$ additions.

Continuing this argument for any positive integer p leads to recursive expressions for the number of multiplications and additions required to implement the FFT:

$$m(p) = 2m(p-1) + 2^{p-1} \qquad p \geq 1 \qquad (4\text{-}169)$$

and

$$\mathfrak{a}(p) = 2\mathfrak{a}(p-1) + 2^p \qquad p \geq 1 \tag{4-170}$$

where $\mathfrak{m}(0) = 0$ and $\mathfrak{a}(0) = 0$ because the transform of a single point does not require any multiplication or additions.

The method just developed is called the *successive doubling FFT algorithm* because it is based on computing a two-point transform from two one-point transforms, a four-point transform from two two-point transforms, and so on, for any M equal to an integer power of 2. It is left as an exercise (see Problem 4.63) to show that

$$\mathfrak{m}(p) = \frac{1}{2} M \log_2 M \tag{4-171}$$

and

$$\mathfrak{a}(n) = M \log_2 M \tag{4-172}$$

where $M = 2^p$.

The computational advantage of the FFT over a direct implementation of the 1-D DFT is defined as

$$C(M) = \frac{M^2}{M \log_2 M} \\ = \frac{M}{\log_2 M} \tag{4-173}$$

where M^2 is the number of operations required for a "brute force" implementation of the 1-D DFT. Because it is assumed that $M = 2^p$, we can write Eq. (4-173) in terms of p:

$$C(p) = \frac{2^p}{p} \tag{4-174}$$

A plot of this function (Fig. 4.67) shows that the computational advantage increases rapidly as a function of p. For example, when $p = 15$ (32,768 points), the FFT has nearly a 2,200 to 1 advantage over a brute-force implementation of the DFT. Thus, we would expect that the FFT can be computed nearly 2,200 times faster than the DFT on the same machine. As you learned in Section 4.1, the FFT also offers significant computational advantages over spatial filtering, with the cross-over between the two approaches being for relatively small kernels.

There are many excellent sources that cover details of the FFT so we will not dwell on this topic further (see, for example, Brigham [1988]). Most comprehensive signal and image processing software packages contain generalized implementations of the FFT that do not require the number of points to be an integer power

FIGURE 4.67
Computational
advantage of the
FFT over a direct
implementation
of the 1-D DFT.
The number of
samples is $M = 2^p$.
The computational
advantage increases
rapidly as a
function of p.

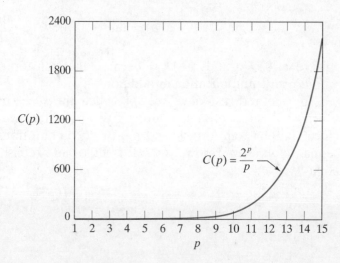

$$C(p) = \frac{2^p}{p}$$

of 2 (at the expense of slightly less efficient computation). Free FFT programs also
are readily available, principally over the internet.

Summary, References, and Further Reading

The material in this chapter is a progression from sampling to the Fourier transform, and then to filtering in the
frequency domain. Some of the concepts, such as the sampling theorem, make very little sense if not explained in
the context of the frequency domain. The same is true of effects such as aliasing. Thus, the material developed in
the preceding sections is a solid foundation for understanding the fundamentals of 2-D digital signal processing. We
took special care to develop the material starting with basic principles, so that any reader with a modest mathematical background would be in a position not only to absorb the material, but also to apply it.

For complementary reading on the 1-D and 2-D continuous Fourier transforms, see the books by Bracewell
[1995, 2003]. These two books, together with Castleman [1996], Petrou and Petrou [2010], Brigham [1988], and Smith
[2003], provide additional background for the material in Sections 4.2 through 4.6. Sampling phenomena such as
aliasing and moiré patterns are topics amply illustrated in books on computer graphics, as exemplified by Hughes
and Andries [2013]. For additional general background on the material in Sections 4.7 through 4.11 see Hall [1979],
Jain [1989], Castleman [1996], and Pratt [2014]. For details on the software aspects of many of the examples in this
chapter, see Gonzalez, Woods, and Eddins [2009].

Problems

*Solutions to the problems marked with an asterisk (*) are in the DIP4E Student Support Package (consult the book
website: www.ImageProcessingPlace.com)*

4.1   Answer the following:

  (a)* Give an equation similar to Eq. (4-10), but
      for an impulse located at $t = t_0$.

  (b)   Repeat for Eq. (4-15).

  (c)* Is it correct to say that $\delta(t - a) = \delta(a - t)$ in
      general? Explain.

4.2   Repeat Example 4.1, but using the function
      $f(t) = A$ for $0 \le t < W$ and $f(t) = 0$ for all other
      values of t. Explain the reason for any differences
      between your results and the results in the example.

4.3   Write equation for the sifting property of the:

  (a)* Continuous impulse located at $t = t_0$.

  (b)   Discrete impulse located at $t = t_0$.

4.4* Use the sifting property of the impulse to show that convolving a 1-D continuous function, $f(t)$, with an impulse located at t_0 shifts the function so that its origin is moved to the location of the impulse (if the impulse is at the origin, the function is not shifted).

4.5* What do you mean by aliasing? When are two continuous function called an aliased pair?

4.6 With reference to Fig. 4.11:

(a)* Redraw the figure, showing what the dots would look like for a sampling rate that exceeds the Nyquist rate slightly.

(b) What is the *approximate* sampling rate represented by the large dots in Fig. 4.11?

(c) *Approximately*, what would be the lowest sampling rate that you would use so that (1) the Nyquist rate is satisfied, and (2) the samples look like a sine wave?

4.7 As the figure below shows, the Fourier transform of a "tent" function (on the left) is a squared sinc function (on the right). Advance an argument that shows that the Fourier transform of a tent function can be obtained from the Fourier transform of a box function. (*Hint:* the tent itself can be generated by convolving two equal boxes.)

4.8* Show that $\Im\{e^{j2\pi t_0 t}\} = \delta(\mu - t_0)$, where t_0 is a constant. (*Hint:* Study Example 4.2.)

4.9 Show that the following expressions are true. (*Hint:* Make use of the solution to Problem 4.8):

(a)* $\Im\{\cos(2\pi\mu_0 t)\} = \frac{1}{2}[\delta(\mu - \mu_0) + \delta(\mu + \mu_0)]$

(b) $\Im\{\sin(2\pi nt)\} = \frac{j}{2}[\delta(\mu + n) - \delta(\mu - n)]$

4.10 Consider the function $f(t) = \sin(2\pi nt)$, where n is an integer. Its Fourier transform, $F(\mu)$, is purely imaginary (see Problem 4.9). Because the transform, $\tilde{F}(\mu)$, of sampled data consists of periodic copies of $F(\mu)$, it follows that $\tilde{F}(\mu)$ will also be purely imaginary. Draw a diagram similar to Fig. 4.6, and answer the following questions based on your diagram (assume that sampling starts at $t = 0$).

(a)* What is the period of $f(t)$?

(b)* What is the frequency of $f(t)$?

(c)* What would the sampled function and its Fourier transform look like in general if $f(t)$ is sampled at a rate higher than the Nyquist rate?

(d) What would the sampled function look like in general if $f(t)$ is sampled at a rate lower than the Nyquist rate?

(e) What would the sampled function look like if $f(t)$ is sampled at the Nyquist rate, with samples taken at $t = 0, \pm\Delta T, \pm 2\Delta T, \dots$?

4.11* Prove the validity of the convolution theorem of one continuous variable, as given in Eqs. (4-25) and (4-26).

4.12 We explained in the paragraph after Eq. (4-36) that arbitrarily limiting the duration of a band-limited function by multiplying it by a box function would cause the function to cease being band limited. Show graphically why this is so by limiting the duration of the function $f(t) = \cos(2\pi\mu_0 t)$ [the Fourier transform of this function is given in Problem 4.9(a)]. (*Hint:* The transform of a box function is given in Example 4.1. Use that result in your solution, and also the fact that convolution of a function with an impulse shifts the function to the location of the impulse, in the sense discussed in the solution of Problem 4.4.)

4.13* Complete the steps that led from Eq. (4-37) to Eq. (4-38).

4.14 Show that $\tilde{F}(\mu)$ in Eq. (4-40) is infinitely periodic in both directions, with period $1/\Delta T$.

4.15 Do the following:

(a) Show that Eqs. (4-42) and (4-43) are a Fourier transform pair: $f_n \Leftrightarrow F_m$.

(b)* Show that Eqs. (4-44) and (4-45) also are a Fourier transform pair: $f(x) \Leftrightarrow F(u)$.

You will need the following orthogonality property in both parts of this problem:

$$\sum_{x=0}^{M-1} e^{j2\pi rx/M} e^{-j2\pi ux/M} = \begin{cases} M & \text{if } r = u \\ 0 & \text{otherwise} \end{cases}$$

4.16 Show that both $F(u)$ and $f(x)$ in Eqs. (4-44) and (4-45) are infinitely periodic with period M; that is,

$F(u) = F(u + kM)$ and $f(x) = f(x + M)$, where k is an integer. [See Eqs. (4-46) and (4-47).]

4.17 Demonstrate the validity of the translation (shift) properties of the following 1-D, discrete Fourier transform pairs. (*Hint:* It is easier in part (b) to work with the IDFT.)

(a)* $f(x)e^{j2\pi u_0 x/M} \Leftrightarrow F(u - u_0)$

(b) $f(x - x_0) \Leftrightarrow F(u)e^{-j2\pi u x_0/M}$

4.18 Show that the 1-D convolution theorem given in Eqs. (4-25) and (4-26) also holds for discrete variables, but with the right side of Eq. (4-26) multiplied by $1/M$. That is, show that

(a)* $(f \star h)(x) \Leftrightarrow (F \cdot H)(u)$, and

(b) $(f \cdot h)(x) \Leftrightarrow \dfrac{1}{M}(F \star H)(u)$

4.19* Extend the expression for 1-D convolution [see Eq. (4-48)] to two discrete variables. Use x and y for the variables on the left side of the expression and m and n for the variables on the right side.

4.20 Consider a checkerboard image in which each square is 1×1 mm. Assuming that the image extends infinitely in both the coordinate directions, what is the minimum sampling rate (in samples/mm) required to avoid aliasing.

4.21 The image on the left in the figure below consists of alternating stripes of black/white, each stripe

being two pixels wide. The image on the right is the Fourier spectrum of the image on the left, showing the dc term and the frequency terms corresponding to the stripes. (Remember, the spectrum is symmetric so all components, other than the dc term, appear in two symmetric locations.)

(a)* Suppose that the stripes of an image of the same size are four pixels wide. Sketch what the spectrum of the image would look like, including only the dc term and the two high-

est-value frequency terms, which correspond to the two spikes in the spectrum above.

(b) Why are the components of the spectrum limited to the horizontal axis?

(c) What would the spectrum look like for an image of the same size but having stripes that are one pixel wide? Explain the reason for your answer.

(d) Are the dc terms in (a) and (c) the same, or are they different? Explain.

4.22 A high-technology company specializes in developing imaging systems for digitizing images of commercial cloth. The company has a new order for 1,000 systems for digitizing cloth consisting of repeating black and white vertical stripes, each of width 2 cm. Optical and mechanical engineers have already designed the front-end optics and mechanical positioning mechanisms so that you are guaranteed that every image your system digitizes starts with a complete black vertical stripe and ends with a complete white stripe. Every image acquired will contain exactly 250 vertical stripes. Noise and optical distortions are negligible. Having learned of your success in taking an image processing course, the company employs you to specify the resolution of the imaging chip to be used in the new system. The optics can be adjusted to project the field of view accurately onto the area defined by the size of the chip you specify. Your design will be implemented in hundreds of locations, so cost is an important consideration. What resolution chip (in terms of number of imaging elements per horizontal line) would you specify to avoid aliasing?

4.23* Briefly describe the most common application of 2-D interpolation in image processing. Discuss the process of zooming an image by pixel replication.

4.24 With reference to the discussion on linearity in Section 2.6, demonstrate that

(a)* The 1-D continuous Fourier transform is a linear operator.

(b) The 1-D DFT is a linear operator also.

4.25 With reference to Eq. (4-85) and Table 4.1, prove the following:

(a)* The Fourier transform of a real function, $f(x, y)$, is conjugate symmetric.

(b) The Fourier transform of an imaginary function, $f(x,y)$, is conjugate antisymmetric.

4.26 Show the validity of the following 2-D *continuous* Fourier transform pairs.

(a)* $\delta(t,z) \Leftrightarrow 1$

(b)* $1 \Leftrightarrow \delta(\mu,\nu)$

(c)* $\delta(t-t_0, z-z_0) \Leftrightarrow e^{-j2\pi(t_0\mu + z_0\nu)}$

(d) $e^{j2\pi(t_0 t + z_0 z)} \Leftrightarrow \delta(\mu - t_0, \nu - z_0)$

(e)* $\cos(2\pi\mu_0 t + 2\pi\nu_0 z) \Leftrightarrow$
$$(1/2)\big[\delta(\mu-\mu_0, \nu-\nu_0) + \delta(\mu+\mu_0, \nu+\nu_0)\big]$$

(f) $\sin(2\pi\mu_0 t + 2\pi\nu_0 z) \Leftrightarrow$
$$(1/2j)\big[\delta(\mu-\mu_0, \nu-\nu_0) - \delta(\mu+\mu_0, \nu+\nu_0)\big]$$

4.27 With reference to Eqs. (4-71) and (4-72), demonstrate the validity of the following translation (shifting) properties of 2-D, *discrete* Fourier transform pairs from Table 4.4. (*Hint:* Study the solutions to Problem 4.17.)

(a) $f(x,y)e^{j2\pi(u_0 x/M + v_0 y/N)} \Leftrightarrow F(u-u_0, v-v_0)$

(b)* $f(x-x_0, y-y_0) \Leftrightarrow F(u,v)e^{-j2\pi(x_0 u/M + y_0 v/N)}$

4.28 Show the validity of the following 2-D *discrete* Fourier transform pairs from Table 4.4:

(a)* $\delta(x,y) \Leftrightarrow 1$

(b)* $1 \Leftrightarrow MN\delta(u,v)$

(c) $\delta(x-x_0, y-y_0) \Leftrightarrow e^{-j2\pi(ux_0/M + vy_0/N)}$

(d)* $e^{j2\pi(u_0 x/M + v_0 y/N)} \Leftrightarrow MN\delta(u-u_0, v-v_0)$

(e) $\cos(2\pi\mu_0 x/M + 2\pi\nu_0 y/N) \Leftrightarrow$
$$(MN/2)\big[\delta(u+\mu_0, v+\nu_0) + \delta(u-\mu_0, v-\nu_0)\big]$$

(f)* $\sin(2\pi\mu_0 x/M + 2\pi\nu_0 y/N) \Leftrightarrow$
$$(jMN/2)\big[\delta(u+\mu_0, v+\nu_0) - \delta(u-\mu_0, v-\nu_0)\big]$$

4.29 Show that the DFT of the discrete function $f(x,y) = 1$ is
$$\Im\{1\} = \delta(u,v) = \begin{cases} 1 & \text{if } u=v=0 \\ 0 & \text{otherwise} \end{cases}$$

4.30 What is period and frequency of each of following digital sequences (*Hint:* Think of these as square waves.)

(a)* $0\,1\,0\,1\,0\,1\,0\,1\ldots$

(b) $0\,0\,1\,0\,0\,1\,0\,0\,1\ldots$

(c) $0\,0\,1\,1\,0\,0\,1\,1\,0\,0\,1\,1\ldots$

4.31 With reference to the 1-D sequences in Example 4.10:

(a)* Write the property of an even sequence, when M is even?

(b) Write the property of an odd sequence, when M is even?

4.32 We mentioned in Example 4.10 that embedding a 2-D array of even (odd) dimensions into a larger array of zeros of even (odd) dimensions keeps the symmetry of the original array, provided that the centers coincide. Show that this is true also for the following 1-D arrays (i.e., show that the larger arrays have the same symmetry as the smaller arrays). For arrays of even length, use arrays of 0's ten elements long. For arrays of odd lengths, use arrays of 0's nine elements long.

(a)* $\{a, b, c, c, b\}$

(b) $\{0, -b, -c, 0, c, b\}$

(c) $\{a, b, c, d, c, b\}$

(d) $\{0, -b, -c, c, b\}$

4.33 In Example 4.10 we showed a Sobel kernel embedded in a field of zeros. The kernel is of size 3×3 and its structure appears to be odd. However, its first element is -1, and we know that in order to be odd, the first (top, left) element a 2-D array must be zero. Show the smallest field of zeros in which you can embed the Sobel kernel so that it satisfies the condition of oddness.

4.34 Do the following:

(a)* Show that the 6×6 array in Example 4.10 is odd.

(b) What would happen if the minus signs are changed to pluses?

(c) Explain why, as stated at the end of the example, adding to the array another row of 0's on the top and column of 0's to the left would give a result that is neither even nor odd.

(d) Suppose that the row is added to the bottom and the column to the right? Would that change your answer in (c)?

4.35 The following problems are related to the properties in Table 4.1.

(a)* Demonstrate the validity of property 3.

(b)* Demonstrate the validity of property 4.

(c) Demonstrate the validity of property 5.

(d)* Demonstrate the validity of property 7.

(e) Demonstrate the validity of property 10.

4.36 You know from Table 4.3 that the dc term, $F(0,0)$, of a DFT is proportional to the average value of its corresponding spatial image. Assume that the image is of size $M \times N$. Suppose that you pad the image with zeros to size $P \times Q$, where P and Q are given in Eqs. (4-102) and (4-103). Let $F_p(0,0)$ denote the dc term of the DFT of the padded function.

(a)* What is the ratio of the average values of the original and padded images?

(b) Is $F_p(0,0) = F(0,0)$? Support your answer mathematically.

4.37 Demonstrate the validity of the linearity property (entry 2) in Table 4.4

4.38 With reference to the 2-D discrete convolution theorem in Eqs. (4-95) and (4-96) (entry 6 in Table 4.4), show that

(a) $(f \star h)(x,y) \Leftrightarrow (F \cdot H)(u,v)$

(b)* $(f \cdot h)(x,y) \Leftrightarrow (1/MN)[(F \star H)(u,v)]$

(*Hint:* Study the solution to Problem 4.18.)

4.39 With reference to the 2-D discrete correlation theorem (entry 7 in Table 4.4), show that

(a)* $(f \star h)(x,y) \Leftrightarrow (F^* \cdot H)(u,v)$

(b) $(f^* \cdot h)(x,y) \Leftrightarrow (1/MN)[(F \star H)(u,v)]$

4.40* Demonstrate validity of the differentiation pairs in entry 12 of Table 4.4.

4.41 We discussed in Section 4.6 the need for image padding when filtering in the frequency domain. We showed in that section that images could be padded by appending zeros to the ends of rows and columns in the image (see the following image, on the left). Do you think it would make a difference if we centered the image and surrounded it by a border of zeros instead (see image on the right), but without changing the total number of zeros used? Explain.

4.42* The two Fourier spectra shown are of the same image. The spectrum on the left corresponds to the original image, and the spectrum on the right was obtained after the image was padded with zeros. Explain the significant increase in signal strength along the vertical and horizontal axes of the spectrum shown on the right.

4.43 Consider the images shown. The image on the right was obtained by: (a) multiplying the image on the left by $(-1)^{x+y}$; (b) computing the DFT; (c) taking the complex conjugate of the transform; (d) computing the inverse DFT; and (e) multiplying the real part of the result by $(-1)^{x+y}$. Explain (mathematically) why the image on the right appears as it does.

4.44* The image in Fig. 4.34(b) was obtained by multiplying by −1 the phase angle of the image in Fig. 4.34(a), and then computing the IDFT. With reference to Eq. (4-86) and entry 5 in Table 4.1, explain why this operation caused the image to be reflected about both coordinate axes.

4.45 In Fig. 4.34(b) we saw that multiplying the phase angle by −1 flipped the image with respect to both coordinate axes. Suppose that instead we multiplied the magnitude of the transform by −1 and then took the inverse DFT using the equation: $g(x,y) = \Im^{-1}\{-|F(u,v)|e^{j\phi(u,v)}\}$.

    (a)* What would be the difference between the two images $g(x,y)$ and $f(x,y)$? [Remember, $F(u,v)$ is the DFT of $f(x,y)$.]

    (b) Assuming that they are both 8-bit images, what would $g(x,y)$ look like in terms of $f(x,y)$ if we scaled the intensity values of $g(x,y)$ using Eqs. (2-31) and (2-32), with $K = 255$?

4.46 What are three types of lowpass filters discussed in Section 4.8? Describe each of these filters.

4.47* Consider a 3×3 spatial kernel that averages the four closest neighbors of a point (x,y), but excludes the point itself from the average.

    (a) Find the equivalent filter transfer function, $H(u,v)$, in the frequency domain.

    (b) Show that your result is a lowpass filter transfer function.

4.48* A continuous Gaussian lowpass filter in the continuous frequency domain has the transfer function

$$H(\mu,\nu) = Ae^{-(\mu^2+\nu^2)/2\sigma^2}$$

Show that the corresponding filter kernel in the continuous spatial domain is

$$h(t,z) = A2\pi\sigma^2 e^{-2\pi^2\sigma^2(t^2+z^2)}$$

4.49 Given an image of size $M \times N$, you are asked to perform an experiment that consists of repeatedly lowpass filtering the image in the frequency domain using a Gaussian lowpass filter transfer function with a cutoff frequency, D_0. You may ignore computational round-off errors.

    (a)* Let K denote the number of applications of the filter. Can you predict (without doing the experiment) what the result (image) will be for a sufficiently large value of K? If so, what is that result?

    (b) Let c_{min} denote the smallest positive number representable in the machine in which the proposed experiment will be conducted (any number $< c_{min}$ is automatically set to 0). Derive an expression (in terms of c_{min}) for the minimum value of K that will guarantee the result that you predicted in (a).

4.50 As explained in Section 3.6, first-order derivatives can be approximated by the spatial differences $g_x = \partial f(x,y)/\partial x = f(x+1,y) - f(x,y)$ and $g_y = \partial f(x,y)/\partial y = f(x,y+1) - f(x,y)$.

    (a) Find the equivalent filter transfer functions $H_x(u,v)$ and $H_y(u,v)$ in the frequency domain.

    (b) Show that these are highpass filter transfer functions.

(*Hint:* Study the solution to Problem 4.47.)

4.51 Find the equivalent frequency-domain filter transfer function for the Laplacian kernel shown in Fig. 3.45(a). Show that your result behaves as a highpass filter transfer function. (*Hint:* Study the solution to Problem 4.47.)

4.52 Do the following:

    (a) Show that the Laplacian of a continuous function $f(t,z)$ of two continuous variables, t and z, satisfies the following Fourier transform pair:

$$\nabla^2 f(t,z) \Leftrightarrow -4\pi^2(\mu^2+\nu^2)F(\mu,\nu)$$

    (*Hint:* See Eq. (3-50) and study entry 12 in Table 4.4.)

    (b)* The result in (a) is valid only for continuous variables. How would you implement the continuous frequency domain transfer function $H(\mu,\nu) = -4\pi^2(\mu^2+\nu^2)$ for discrete variables?

    (c) As you saw in Example 4.21, the Laplacian result in the frequency domain was similar to the result in Fig. 3.46(d), which was obtained using a spatial kernel with a center coefficient equal to −8. Explain why the frequency domain result was not similar instead to the result in Fig. 3.46(c), which was obtained using a kernel with a center coefficient of −4.

4.53* Explain the reason why Fourier transform cannot be used to compute (or partially compute) the magnitude of the gradient [Eq. (3-58)] for use in the image differentiation.

4.54 As explained in Eq. (4-118), it is possible to obtain the transfer function of a highpass filter from the transfer function of a lowpass filter by subtracting the latter from 1. What is the highpass spatial kernel corresponding to the lowpass Gaussian transfer function given in Problem 4.48?

4.55 Describe the steps required to perform filtering in the frequency domain.

4.56* Show how the Butterworth highpass filter transfer function in Eq. (4-121) follows from its lowpass counterpart in Eq. (4-117).

4.57 Consider the hand X-ray images shown below. The image on the right was obtained by lowpass

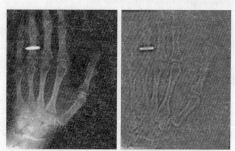

(Original image courtesy of Dr. Thomas R. Gest, Division of Anatomical Sciences, University of Michigan Medical School.)

filtering the image on the left with a Gaussian lowpass filter, and then highpass filtering the result with a Gaussian highpass filter. The images are of size 420×344 pixels and $D_0 = 25$ was used for both filter transfer functions.

(a)* Explain why the center part of the finger ring in the figure on the right appears so bright and solid, considering that the dominant characteristic of the filtered image consists of edges of the fingers and wrist bones, with darker areas in between. In other words, would you not expect the highpass filter to render the constant area inside the ring as

dark, since a highpass filter eliminates the dc term and reduces low frequencies?

(b) Do you think the result would have been different if the order of the filtering process had been reversed?

4.58 Consider the sequence of images shown below. The image on the top left is a segment of an X-ray image of a commercial printed circuit board. The images following it are, respectively, the results of subjecting the image to 1, 10, and 100 passes of a Gaussian highpass filter with $D_0 = 30$. The images are of size 330×334 pixels, with each pixel being represented by 8 bits of gray. The images were scaled for display, but this has no effect on the problem statement.

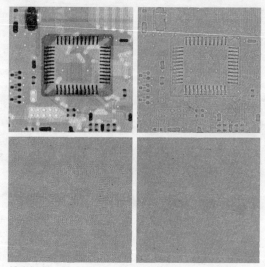

(Original image courtesy of Mr. Joseph E. Pascente, Lixi, Inc.)

(a) It appears from the images that changes will cease to take place after a finite number of passes. Show whether or not this is the case. You may ignore computational round-off errors. Let c_{min} denote the smallest positive number representable in the machine in which the computations are conducted.

(b) If you determined in (a) that changes would cease after a finite number of iterations, determine the minimum value of that number.

(*Hint:* Study the solution to Problem 4.49.)

4.59 As illustrated in Fig. 4.57, combining high-frequency emphasis and histogram equalization is an effective method for achieving edge sharpening and contrast enhancement.

(a)* Show whether or not it matters which process is applied first.

(b) If the order does matter, give a rationale for using one or the other method first.

4.60 Discuss the homomorphic filtering approach. Also, give summary of steps in homomorphic filtering.

4.61 Suppose that you are given a set of images generated by an experiment dealing with the analysis of stellar events. Each image contains a set of bright, widely scattered dots corresponding to stars in a sparsely occupied region of the universe. The problem is that the stars are barely visible as a result of superimposed illumination from atmospheric dispersion. If these images are modeled as the product of a constant illumination component with a set of impulses, give an enhancement procedure based on homomorphic filtering designed to bring out the image components due to the stars themselves.

4.62 How would you generate an image of only the interference pattern visible in Fig. 4.64(a)?

4.63* Show the validity of Eqs. (4-171) and (4-172). (*Hint:* Use proof by induction.)

4.64 A skilled medical technician is assigned the job of inspecting a set of images generated by an electron microscope experiment. In order to simplify the inspection task, the technician decides to use digital image enhancement and, to this end, examines a set of representative images and finds the following problems: (1) bright, isolated dots that are of no interest; (2) lack of sharpness; (3) not enough contrast in some images; and (4) shifts in the average intensity to values other than A_0, which is the average value required to perform correctly certain intensity measurements. The technician wants to correct these problems and then display in white all intensities in a band between intensities I_1 and I_2, while keeping normal tonality in the remaining intensities. Propose a sequence of processing steps that the technician can follow to achieve the desired goal. You may use techniques from both Chapters 3 and 4.

5

Image Restoration and Reconstruction

Things which we see are not themselves what we see . . .
It remains completely unknown to us what the objects may be
by themselves and apart from the receptivity of our senses.
We know only but our manner of perceiving them.

Immanuel Kant

Preview

As in image enhancement, the principal goal of restoration techniques is to improve an image in some predefined sense. Although there are areas of overlap, image enhancement is largely a subjective process, while image restoration is for the most part an objective process. Restoration attempts to recover an image that has been degraded by using a priori knowledge of the degradation phenomenon. Thus, restoration techniques are oriented toward modeling the degradation and applying the inverse process in order to recover the original image. In this chapter, we consider linear, space invariant restoration models that are applicable in a variety of restoration situations. We also discuss fundamental techniques of image reconstruction from projections, and their application to computed tomography (CT), one of the most important commercial applications of image processing, especially in health care.

Upon completion of this chapter, readers should:

■ Be familiar with the characteristics of various noise models used in image processing, and how to estimate from image data the parameters that define those models.

■ Be familiar with linear, nonlinear, and adaptive spatial filters used to restore (denoise) images that have been degraded only by noise.

■ Know how to apply notch filtering in the frequency domain for removing periodic noise in an image.

■ Understand the foundation of linear, space invariant system concepts, and how they can

be applied in formulating image restoration solutions in the frequency domain.

■ Be familiar with direct inverse filtering and its limitations.

■ Understand minimum mean-square-error (Wiener) filtering and its advantages over direct inverse filtering.

■ Understand constrained, least-squares filtering.

■ Be familiar with the fundamentals of image reconstruction from projections, and their application to computed tomography.

317

5.1 A MODEL OF THE IMAGE DEGRADATION/RESTORATION PROCESS

In this chapter, we model image degradation as an operator $\mathcal{H}$ that, together with an additive noise term, operates on an input image $f(x, y)$ to produce a degraded image $g(x, y)$ (see Fig. 5.1). Given $g(x, y)$, some knowledge about $\mathcal{H}$, and some knowledge about the additive noise term $\eta(x, y)$, the objective of restoration is to obtain an estimate $\hat{f}(x, y)$ of the original image. We want the estimate to be as close as possible to the original image and, in general, the more we know about $\mathcal{H}$ and η, the closer $\hat{f}(x, y)$ will be to $f(x, y)$.

We will show in Section 5.5 that, if $\mathcal{H}$ is a linear, position-invariant operator, then the degraded image is given in the spatial domain by

$$g(x, y) = (h \star f)(x, y) + \eta(x, y) \tag{5-1}$$

where $h(x, y)$ is the spatial representation of the degradation function. As in Chapters 3 and 4, the symbol "$\star$" indicates convolution. It follows from the convolution theorem that the equivalent of Eq. (5-1) in the frequency domain is

$$G(u, v) = H(u, v)F(u, v) + N(u, v) \tag{5-2}$$

where the terms in capital letters are the Fourier transforms of the corresponding terms in Eq. (5-1). These two equations are the foundation for most of the restoration material in this chapter.

In the following three sections, we work only with degradations caused by noise. Beginning in Section 5.5 we look at several methods for image restoration in the presence of both $\mathcal{H}$ and η.

5.2 NOISE MODELS

The principal sources of noise in digital images arise during image acquisition and/or transmission. The performance of imaging sensors is affected by a variety of environmental factors during image acquisition, and by the quality of the sensing elements themselves. For instance, in acquiring images with a CCD camera, light levels and sensor temperature are major factors affecting the amount of noise in the resulting image. Images are corrupted during transmission principally by interference in the transmission channel. For example, an image transmitted using a wireless network might be corrupted by lightning or other atmospheric disturbance.

FIGURE 5.1
A model of the image degradation/ restoration process.

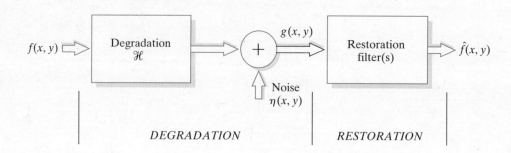

SPATIAL AND FREQUENCY PROPERTIES OF NOISE

Relevant to our discussion are parameters that define the spatial characteristics of noise, and whether the noise is correlated with the image. Frequency properties refer to the frequency content of noise in the Fourier (frequency) domain discussed in detail in Chapter 4. For example, when the Fourier spectrum of noise is constant, the noise is called *white noise*. This terminology is a carryover from the physical properties of white light, which contains all frequencies in the visible spectrum in equal proportions.

With the exception of spatially periodic noise, we assume in this chapter that noise is independent of spatial coordinates, and that it is uncorrelated with respect to the image itself (that is, there is no correlation between pixel values and the values of noise components). Although these assumptions are at least partially invalid in some applications (quantum-limited imaging, such as in X-ray and nuclear-medicine imaging, is a good example), the complexities of dealing with spatially dependent and correlated noise are beyond the scope of our discussion.

SOME IMPORTANT NOISE PROBABILITY DENSITY FUNCTIONS

You may find it helpful to take a look at the Tutorials section of the book website for a brief review of probability.

In the discussion that follows, we shall be concerned with the statistical behavior of the intensity values in the noise component of the model in Fig. 5.1. These may be considered random variables, characterized by a probability density function (PDF), as noted briefly as noted earlier. The noise component of the model in Fig. 5.1 is an image, $\eta(x, y)$, of the same size as the input image. We create a noise image for simulation purposes by generating an array whose intensity values are random numbers with a specified probability density function. This approach is true for all the PDFs to be discussed shortly, with the exception of salt-and-pepper noise, which is applied differently. The following are among the most common noise PDFs found in image processing applications.

Gaussian Noise

Because of its mathematical tractability in both the spatial and frequency domains, Gaussian noise models are used frequently in practice. In fact, this tractability is so convenient that it often results in Gaussian models being used in situations in which they are marginally applicable at best.

The PDF of a *Gaussian* random variable, z, is defined by the following familiar expression:

$$p(z) = \frac{1}{\sqrt{2\pi}\sigma} e^{-\frac{(z - \bar{z})^2}{2\sigma^2}} \qquad -\infty < z < \infty \qquad (5\text{-}3)$$

where z represents intensity, $\bar{z}$ is the mean (average) value of z, and σ is its standard deviation. Figure 5.2(a) shows a plot of this function. We know that for a Gaussian random variable, the probability that values of z are in the range $\bar{z} \pm \sigma$ is approximately 0.68; the probability is about 0.95 that the values of z are in the range $\bar{z} \pm 2\sigma$.

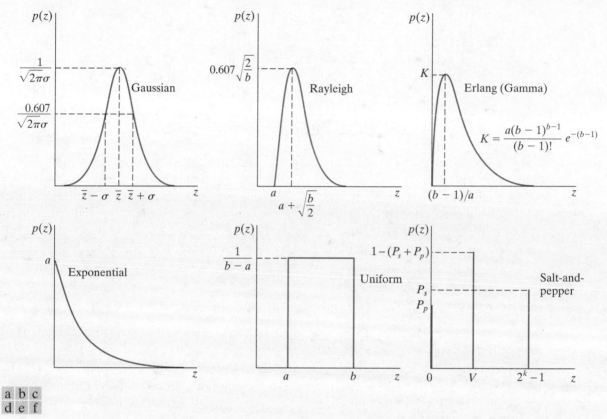

a b c
d e f

FIGURE 5.2 Some important probability density functions.

Rayleigh Noise

The PDF of *Rayleigh* noise is given by

$$
p(z) = \begin{cases} \dfrac{2}{b}(z - a)e^{-(z - a)^2/b} & z \geq a \\ 0 & z < a \end{cases}
\tag{5-4}
$$

The mean and variance of z when this random variable is characterized by a Rayleigh PDF are

$$
\bar{z} = a + \sqrt{\pi b/4}
\tag{5-5}
$$

and

$$
\sigma^2 = \frac{b(4 - \pi)}{4}
\tag{5-6}
$$

Figure 5.2(b) shows a plot of the Rayleigh density. Note the displacement from the origin, and the fact that the basic shape of the density is skewed to the right. The Rayleigh density can be quite useful for modeling the shape of skewed histograms.

Erlang (Gamma) Noise

The PDF of Erlang noise is

$$p(z) = \begin{cases} \dfrac{a^b z^{b-1}}{(b-1)!} e^{-az} & z \geq 0 \\ 0 & z < 0 \end{cases} \tag{5-7}$$

where the parameters are such that $a > b$, b is a positive integer, and "!" indicates factorial. The mean and variance of z are

$$\bar{z} = \frac{b}{a} \tag{5-8}$$

and

$$\sigma^2 = \frac{b}{a^2} \tag{5-9}$$

Figure 5.2(c) shows a plot of this density. Although Eq. (5-9) often is referred to as the *gamma* density, strictly speaking this is correct only when the denominator is the gamma function, $\Gamma(b)$. When the denominator is as shown, the density is more appropriately called the *Erlang* density.

Exponential Noise

The PDF of *exponential* noise is given by

$$p(z) = \begin{cases} ae^{-az} & z \geq 0 \\ 0 & z < 0 \end{cases} \tag{5-10}$$

where $a > 0$. The mean and variance of z are

$$\bar{z} = \frac{1}{a} \tag{5-11}$$

and

$$\sigma^2 = \frac{1}{a^2} \tag{5-12}$$

Note that this PDF is a special case of the Erlang PDF with $b = 1$. Figure 5.2(d) shows a plot of the exponential density function.

Uniform Noise

The PDF of *uniform* noise is

$$p(z) = \begin{cases} \dfrac{1}{b-a} & a \leq z \leq b \\ 0 & \text{otherwise} \end{cases} \tag{5-13}$$

The mean and variance of z are

$$\overline{z} = \frac{a + b}{2} \tag{5-14}$$

and

$$\sigma^2 = \frac{(b - a)^2}{12} \tag{5-15}$$

Figure 5.2(e) shows a plot of the uniform density.

Salt-and-Pepper Noise

If k represents the number of bits used to represent the intensity values in a digital image, then the range of possible intensity values for that image is $[0, 2^k - 1]$ (e.g., $[0,255]$ for an 8-bit image). The PDF of *salt-and-pepper* noise is given by

When image intensities are scaled to the range $[0, 1]$, we replace by 1 the value of salt in this equation. V then becomes a fractional value in the open interval $(0, 1)$.

$$p(z) = \begin{cases} P_s & \text{for } z = 2^k - 1 \\ P_p & \text{for } z = 0 \\ 1 - (P_s + P_p) & \text{for } z = V \end{cases} \tag{5-16}$$

where V is any integer value in the range $0 < V < 2^k - 1$.

Let $\eta(x, y)$ denote a salt-and-pepper noise image, whose intensity values satisfy Eq. (5-16). Given an image, $f(x, y)$, of the same size as $\eta(x, y)$, we corrupt it with salt-and-pepper noise by assigning a 0 to all locations in f where a 0 occurs in η. Similarly, we assign a value of $2^k - 1$ to all location in f where that value appears in η. Finally, we leave unchanged all location in f where V occurs in η.

If neither P_s nor P_p is zero, and especially if they are equal, noise values satisfying Eq. (5-16) will be white ($2^k - 1$) or black (0), and will resemble salt and pepper granules distributed randomly over the image; hence the name of this type of noise. Other names you will find used in the literature are *bipolar impulse noise* (*unipolar* if either P_s or P_p is 0), *data-drop-out noise*, and *spike noise*. We use the terms impulse and salt-and-pepper noise interchangeably.

The probability, P, that a pixel is corrupted by salt or pepper noise is $P = P_s + P_p$. It is common terminology to refer to P as the *noise density*. If, for example, $P_s = 0.02$ and $P_p = 0.01$, then $P = 0.03$ and we say that approximately 2% of the pixels in an image are corrupted by salt noise, 1% are corrupted by pepper noise, and the noise density is 3%, meaning that approximately 3% of the pixels in the image are corrupted by salt-and-pepper noise.

Although, as you have seen, salt-and-pepper noise is specified by the probability of each, and not by the mean and variance, we include the latter here for completeness. The mean of salt-and-pepper noise is given by

$$\overline{z} = (0)P_p + K(1 - P_s - P_p) + (2^k - 1)P_s \tag{5-17}$$

and the variance by

$$\sigma^2 = (0 - \bar{z})^2 P_p + (K - \bar{z})^2 (1 - P_s - P_p) + (2^k - 1)^2 P_s \qquad (5\text{-}18)$$

where we have included 0 as a value explicit in both equations to indicate that the value of pepper noise is assumed to be zero.

As a group, the preceding PDFs provide useful tools for modeling a broad range of noise corruption situations found in practice. For example, Gaussian noise arises in an image due to factors such as electronic circuit noise and sensor noise caused by poor illumination and/or high temperature. The Rayleigh density is helpful in characterizing noise phenomena in range imaging. The exponential and gamma densities find application in laser imaging. Impulse noise is found in situations where quick transients, such as faulty switching, take place during imaging. The uniform density is perhaps the least descriptive of practical situations. However, the uniform density is quite useful as the basis for numerous random number generators that are used extensively in simulations (Gonzalez, Woods, and Eddins [2009]).

EXAMPLE 5.1: Noisy images and their histograms.

Figure 5.3 shows a test pattern used for illustrating the noise models just discussed. This is a suitable pattern to use because it is composed of simple, constant areas that span the gray scale from black to near white in only three increments. This facilitates visual analysis of the characteristics of the various noise components added to an image.

Figure 5.4 shows the test pattern after addition of the six types of noise in Fig. 5.2. Below each image is the histogram computed directly from that image. The parameters of the noise were chosen in each case so that the histogram corresponding to the three intensity levels in the test pattern would start to merge. This made the noise quite visible, without obscuring the basic structure of the underlying image.

We see a close correspondence in comparing the histograms in Fig. 5.4 with the PDFs in Fig. 5.2. The histogram for the salt-and-pepper example does not contain a specific peak for V because, as you will recall, V is used only during the creation of the noise image to leave values in the original image unchanged. Of course, in addition to the salt and pepper peaks, there are peaks for the other intensities in the image. With the exception of slightly different overall intensity, it is difficult to differentiate

FIGURE 5.3
Test pattern used to illustrate the characteristics of the PDFs from Fig. 5.2.

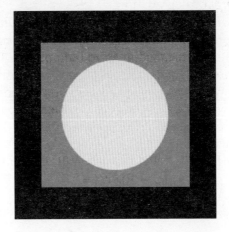

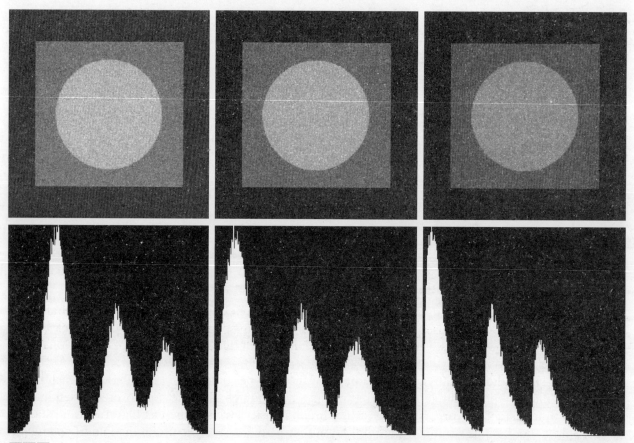

a b c
d e f

FIGURE 5.4 Images and histograms resulting from adding Gaussian, Rayleigh, and Erlanga noise to the image in Fig. 5.3.

visually between the first five images in Fig. 5.4, even though their histograms are significantly different. The salt-and-pepper appearance of the image in Fig. 5.4(i) is the only one that is visually indicative of the type of noise causing the degradation.

PERIODIC NOISE

Periodic noise in images typically arises from electrical or electromechanical interference during image acquisition. This is the only type of spatially dependent noise we will consider in this chapter. As we will discuss in Section 5.4, periodic noise can be reduced significantly via frequency domain filtering. For example, consider the image in Fig. 5.5(a). This image is corrupted by additive (spatial) sinusoidal noise. The Fourier transform of a pure sinusoid is a pair of conjugate impulses[†] located at

---

† Be careful not to confuse the term *impulse* in the frequency domain with the use of the same term in impulse noise discussed earlier, which is in the spatial domain.

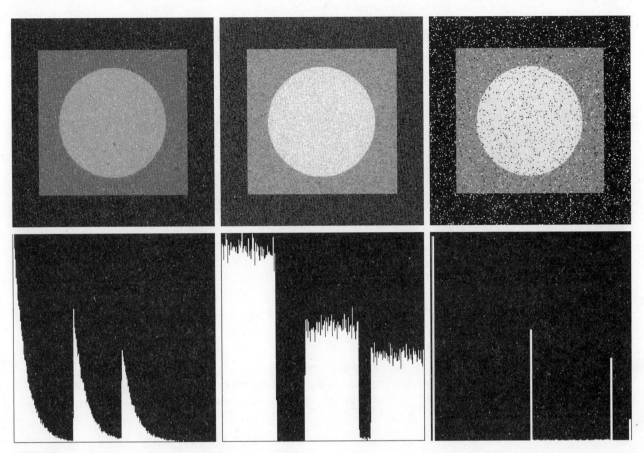

g h i
j k l

FIGURE 5.4 (*continued*) Images and histograms resulting from adding exponential, uniform, and salt-and-pepper noise to the image in Fig. 5.3. In the salt-and-pepper histogram, the peaks in the origin (zero intensity) and at the far end of the scale are shown displaced slightly so that they do not blend with the page background.

the conjugate frequencies of the sine wave (see Table 4.4). Thus, if the amplitude of a sine wave in the spatial domain is strong enough, we would expect to see in the spectrum of the image a pair of impulses for each sine wave in the image. As shown in Fig. 5.5(b), this is indeed the case. Eliminating or reducing these impulses in the frequency domain will eliminate or reduce the sinusoidal noise in the spatial domain. We will have much more to say in Section 5.4 about this and other examples of periodic noise.

ESTIMATING NOISE PARAMETERS

The parameters of periodic noise typically are estimated by inspection of the Fourier spectrum. Periodic noise tends to produce frequency spikes that often can be detected even by visual analysis. Another approach is to attempt to infer the periodicity

FIGURE 5.5
(a) Image
corrupted by
additive
sinusoidal noise.
(b) Spectrum
showing two
conjugate
impulses caused
by the sine wave.
(Original
image courtesy of
NASA.)

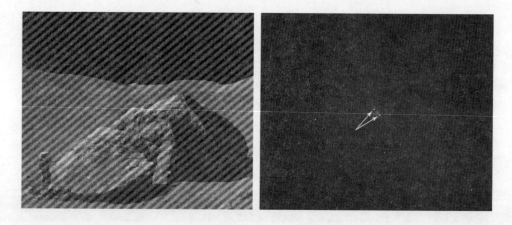

of noise components directly from the image, but this is possible only in simplistic cases. Automated analysis is possible in situations in which the noise spikes are either exceptionally pronounced, or when knowledge is available about the general location of the frequency components of the interference (see Section 5.4).

The parameters of noise PDFs may be known partially from sensor specifications, but it is often necessary to estimate them for a particular imaging arrangement. If the imaging system is available, one simple way to study the characteristics of system noise is to capture a set of "flat" images. For example, in the case of an optical sensor, this is as simple as imaging a solid gray board that is illuminated uniformly. The resulting images typically are good indicators of system noise.

When only images already generated by a sensor are available, it is often possible to estimate the parameters of the PDF from small patches of reasonably constant background intensity. For example, the vertical strips shown in Fig. 5.6 were cropped from the Gaussian, Rayleigh, and uniform images in Fig. 5.4. The histograms shown were calculated using image data from these small strips. The histograms in Fig. 5.4 that correspond to the histograms in Fig. 5.6 are the ones in the middle of the group of three in Figs. 5.4(d), (e), and (k). We see that the shapes of these histograms correspond quite closely to the shapes of the corresponding histograms in Fig. 5.6. Their heights are different due to scaling, but the shapes are unmistakably similar.

The simplest use of the data from the image strips is for calculating the mean and variance of intensity levels. Consider a strip (subimage) denoted by S, and let $p_S(z_i)$, $i = 0, 1, 2, \ldots, L - 1$, denote the probability estimates (normalized histogram values) of the intensities of the pixels in S, where L is the number of possible intensities in the entire image (e.g., 256 for an 8-bit image). As in Eqs. (2-69) and (2-70), we estimate the mean and variance of the pixel values in S as follows:

$$\bar{z} = \sum_{i=0}^{L-1} z_i p_S(z_i) \tag{5-19}$$

and

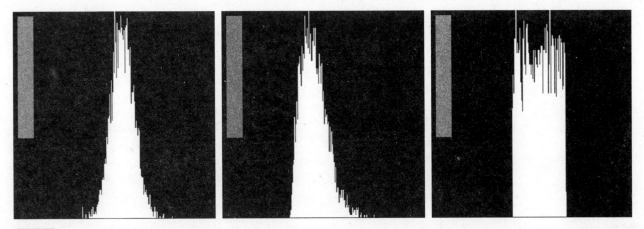

a b c

FIGURE 5.6 Histograms computed using small strips (shown as inserts) from (a) the Gaussian, (b) the Rayleigh, and (c) the uniform noisy images in Fig. 5.4.

$$\sigma^2 = \sum_{i=0}^{L-1} (z_i - \overline{z})^2 \, p_S(z_i) \tag{5-20}$$

The shape of the histogram identifies the closest PDF match. If the shape is approximately Gaussian, then the mean and variance are all we need because the Gaussian PDF is specified completely by these two parameters. For the other shapes discussed earlier, we use the mean and variance to solve for the parameters a and b. Impulse noise is handled differently because the estimate needed is of the actual probability of occurrence of white and black pixels. Obtaining this estimate requires that both black and white pixels be visible, so a mid-gray, relatively constant area is needed in the image in order to be able to compute a meaningful histogram of the noise. The heights of the peaks corresponding to black and white pixels are the estimates of P_a and P_b in Eq. (5-16).

5.3 RESTORATION IN THE PRESENCE OF NOISE ONLY—SPATIAL FILTERING

When an image is degraded only by additive noise, Eqs. (5-1) and (5-2) become

$$g(x,y) = f(x,y) + \eta(x,y) \tag{5-21}$$

and

$$G(u,v) = F(u,v) + N(u,v) \tag{5-22}$$

The noise terms generally are unknown, so subtracting them from $g(x,y)$ $[G(u,v)]$ to obtain $f(x,y)$ $[F(u,v)]$ typically is not an option. In the case of periodic noise, sometimes it is possible to estimate $N(u,v)$ from the spectrum of $G(u,v)$, as noted in Section 5.2. In this case $N(u,v)$ can be subtracted from $G(u,v)$ to obtain an estimate of the original image, but this type of knowledge is the exception, rather than the rule.

Spatial filtering is the method of choice for estimating $f(x,y)$ [i.e., *denoising* image $g(x,y)$] in situations when only additive random noise is present. Spatial filtering was discussed in detail in Chapter 3. With the exception of the nature of the computation performed by a specific filter, the mechanics for implementing all the filters that follow are exactly as discussed in Sections 3.4 through 3.7.

MEAN FILTERS

In this section, we discuss briefly the noise-reduction capabilities of the spatial filters introduced in Section 3.5 and develop several other filters whose performance is in many cases superior to the filters discussed in that section.

Arithmetic Mean Filter

The *arithmetic mean filter* is the simplest of the mean filters (the arithmetic mean filter is the same as the box filter we discussed in Chapter 3). Let S_{xy} represent the set of coordinates in a rectangular subimage window (neighborhood) of size $m \times n$, centered on point (x,y). The arithmetic mean filter computes the average value of the corrupted image, $g(x,y)$, in the area defined by S_{xy}. The value of the restored image $\hat{f}$ at point (x,y) is the arithmetic mean computed using the pixels in the region defined by S_{xy}. In other words,

We assume that m and n are odd integers. The *size* of a mean filter is the same as the size of neighborhood S_{xy}; that is, $m \times n$.

$$\hat{f}(x,y) = \frac{1}{mn} \sum_{(r,c) \in S_{xy}} g(r,c) \tag{5-23}$$

where, as in Eq. (2-43), r and c are the row and column coordinates of the pixels contained in the neighborhood S_{xy}. This operation can be implemented using a spatial kernel of size $m \times n$ in which all coefficients have value $1/mn$. A mean filter smooths local variations in an image, and noise is reduced as a result of blurring.

Geometric Mean Filter

An image restored using a *geometric mean filter* is given by the expression

$$\hat{f}(x,y) = \left[\prod_{(r,c) \in S_{xy}} g(r,c) \right]^{\frac{1}{mn}} \tag{5-24}$$

where Π indicates multiplication. Here, *each* restored pixel is given by the product of *all* the pixels in the subimage area, raised to the power $1/mn$. As Example 5.2 below illustrates, a geometric mean filter achieves smoothing comparable to an arithmetic mean filter, but it tends to lose less image detail in the process.

Harmonic Mean Filter

The *harmonic mean* filtering operation is given by the expression

$$\hat{f}(x,y) = \frac{mn}{\displaystyle\sum_{(r,c)\in S_{xy}} \frac{1}{g(r,c)}} \tag{5-25}$$

The harmonic mean filter works well for salt noise, but fails for pepper noise. It does well also with other types of noise like Gaussian noise.

Contraharmonic Mean Filter

The *contraharmonic mean filter* yields a restored image based on the expression

$$\hat{f}(x,y) = \frac{\displaystyle\sum_{(r,c)\in S_{xy}} g(r,c)^{Q+1}}{\displaystyle\sum_{(r,c)\in S_{xy}} g(r,c)^{Q}} \tag{5-26}$$

where Q is called the *order* of the filter. This filter is well suited for reducing or virtually eliminating the effects of salt-and-pepper noise. For positive values of Q, the filter eliminates pepper noise. For negative values of Q, it eliminates salt noise. It cannot do both simultaneously. Note that the contraharmonic filter reduces to the arithmetic mean filter if $Q = 0$, and to the harmonic mean filter if $Q = -1$.

EXAMPLE 5.2: Image denoising using spatial mean filters.

Figure 5.7(a) shows an 8-bit X-ray image of a circuit board, and Fig. 5.7(b) shows the same image, but corrupted with additive Gaussian noise of zero mean and variance of 400. For this type of image, this is a significant level of noise. Figures 5.7(c) and (d) show, respectively, the result of filtering the noisy image with an arithmetic mean filter of size 3×3 and a geometric mean filter of the same size. Although both filters did a reasonable job of attenuating the contribution due to noise, the geometric mean filter did not blur the image as much as the arithmetic filter. For instance, the connector fingers at the top of the image are sharper in Fig. 5.7(d) than in (c). The same is true in other parts of the image.

Figure 5.8(a) shows the same circuit image, but corrupted now by pepper noise with probability of 0.1. Similarly, Fig. 5.8(b) shows the image corrupted by salt noise with the same probability. Figure 5.8(c) shows the result of filtering Fig. 5.8(a) using a contraharmonic mean filter with $Q = 1.5$, and Fig. 5.8(d) shows the result of filtering Fig. 5.8(b) with $Q = -1.5$. Both filters did a good job of reducing the effect of the noise. The positive-order filter did a better job of cleaning the background, at the expense of slightly thinning and blurring the dark areas. The opposite was true of the negative order filter.

In general, the arithmetic and geometric mean filters (particularly the latter) are well suited for random noise like Gaussian or uniform noise. The contraharmonic filter is well suited for impulse noise, but it has the disadvantage that it must be known whether the noise is dark or light in order to select the proper sign for Q. The results of choosing the wrong sign for Q can be disastrous, as Fig. 5.9 shows. Some of the filters discussed in the following sections eliminate this shortcoming.

a b
c d

FIGURE 5.7
(a) X-ray image of circuit board. (b) Image corrupted by additive Gaussian noise. (c) Result of filtering with an arithmetic mean filter of size 3×3. (d) Result of filtering with a geometric mean filter of the same size. (Original image courtesy of Mr. Joseph E. Pascente, Lixi, Inc.)

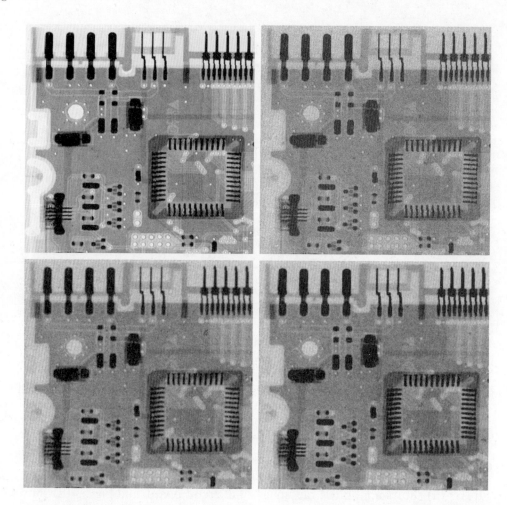

ORDER-STATISTIC FILTERS

We introduced order-statistic filters in Section 3.6. We now expand the discussion in that section and introduce some additional order-statistic filters. As noted in Section 3.6, order-statistic filters are spatial filters whose response is based on ordering (ranking) the values of the pixels contained in the neighborhood encompassed by the filter. The ranking result determines the response of the filter.

Median Filter

The best-known order-statistic filter in image processing is the *median filter*, which, as its name implies, replaces the value of a pixel by the median of the intensity levels in a predefined neighborhood of that pixel:

$$\hat{f}(x, y) = \underset{(r,c) \in S_{xy}}{\text{median}} \{g(r, c)\} \tag{5-27}$$

where, as before, S_{xy} is a subimage (neighborhood) centered on point (x, y). The value of the pixel at (x, y) is included in the computation of the median. Median filters

a b
c d

FIGURE 5.8
(a) Image corrupted by pepper noise with a probability of 0.1. (b) Image corrupted by salt noise with the same probability. (c) Result of filtering (a) with a 3×3 contra-harmonic filter $Q = 1.5$. (d) Result of filtering (b) with $Q = -1.5$.

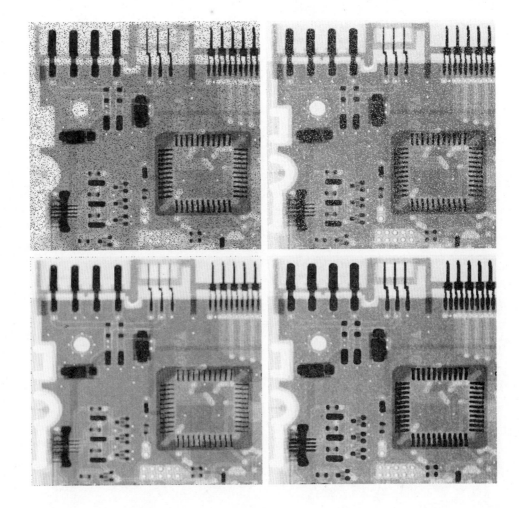

a b

FIGURE 5.9
Results of selecting the wrong sign in contraharmonic filtering.
(a) Result of filtering Fig. 5.8(a) with a contraharmonic filter of size 3×3 and $Q = -1.5$.
(b) Result of filtering Fig. 5.8(b) using $Q = 1.5$.

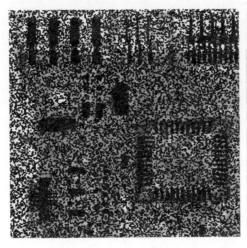
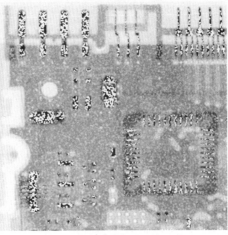

are quite popular because, for certain types of random noise, they provide excellent noise-reduction capabilities, with considerably less blurring than linear smoothing filters of similar size. Median filters are particularly effective in the presence of both bipolar and unipolar impulse noise, as Example 5.3 below shows. Computation of the median and implementation of this filter are discussed in Section 3.6.

Max and Min Filters

Although the median filter is by far the order-statistic filter most used in image processing, it is by no means the only one. The median represents the 50th percentile of a ranked set of numbers, but you will recall from basic statistics that ranking lends itself to many other possibilities. For example, using the 100th percentile results in the so-called *max filter*, given by

$$\hat{f}(x,y) = \max_{(r,c)\in S_{xy}} \{g(r,c)\} \tag{5-28}$$

This filter is useful for finding the brightest points in an image or for eroding dark regions adjacent to bright areas. Also, because pepper noise has very low values, it is reduced by this filter as a result of the max selection process in the subimage area S_{xy}.

The 0th percentile filter is the *min filter*:

$$\hat{f}(x,y) = \min_{(r,c)\in S_{xy}} \{g(r,c)\} \tag{5-29}$$

This filter is useful for finding the darkest points in an image or for eroding light regions adjacent to dark areas. Also, it reduces salt noise as a result of the min operation.

Midpoint Filter

The *midpoint filter* computes the midpoint between the maximum and minimum values in the area encompassed by the filter:

$$\hat{f}(x,y) = \frac{1}{2}\left[\max_{(r,c)\in S_{xy}} \{g(r,c)\} + \min_{(r,c)\in S_{xy}} \{g(r,c)\} \right] \tag{5-30}$$

Note that this filter combines order statistics and averaging. It works best for randomly distributed noise, like Gaussian or uniform noise.

Alpha-Trimmed Mean Filter

Suppose that we delete the $d/2$ lowest and the $d/2$ highest intensity values of $g(r,c)$ in the neighborhood S_{xy}. Let $g_R(r,c)$ represent the remaining $mn - d$ pixels in S_{xy}. A filter formed by averaging these remaining pixels is called an *alpha-trimmed mean filter*. The form of this filter is

$$\hat{f}(x,y) = \frac{1}{mn - d} \sum_{(r,c) \in S_{xy}} g_R(r,c) \qquad (5\text{-}31)$$

where the value of d can range from 0 to $mn - 1$. When $d = 0$ the alpha-trimmed filter reduces to the arithmetic mean filter discussed earlier. If we choose $d = mn - 1$, the filter becomes a median filter. For other values of d, the alpha-trimmed filter is useful in situations involving multiple types of noise, such as a combination of salt-and-pepper and Gaussian noise.

EXAMPLE 5.3: Image denoising using order-statistic filters.

Figure 5.10(a) shows the circuit board image corrupted by salt-and-pepper noise with probabilities $P_s = P_p = 0.1$. Figure 5.10(b) shows the result of median filtering with a filter of size 3×3. The improvement over Fig. 5.10(a) is significant, but several noise points still are visible. A second pass [on the image in Fig. 5.10(b)] with the median filter removed most of these points, leaving only few, barely visible noise points. These were removed with a third pass of the filter. These results are good examples of the power of median filtering in handling impulse-like additive noise. Keep in mind that repeated passes of a median filter will blur the image, so it is desirable to keep the number of passes as low as possible.

Figure 5.11(a) shows the result of applying the max filter to the pepper noise image of Fig. 5.8(a). The filter did a reasonable job of removing the pepper noise, but we note that it also removed (set to a light intensity level) some dark pixels from the borders of the dark objects. Figure 5.11(b) shows the result of applying the min filter to the image in Fig. 5.8(b). In this case, the min filter did a better job than the max filter on noise removal, but it removed some white points around the border of light objects. These made the light objects smaller and some of the dark objects larger (like the connector fingers in the top of the image) because white points around these objects were set to a dark level.

The alpha-trimmed filter is illustrated next. Figure 5.12(a) shows the circuit board image corrupted this time by additive, uniform noise of variance 800 and zero mean. This is a high level of noise corruption that is made worse by further addition of salt-and-pepper noise with $P_s = P_p = 0.1$, as Fig. 5.12(b) shows. The high level of noise in this image warrants use of larger filters. Figures 5.12(c) through (f) show the results, respectively, obtained using arithmetic mean, geometric mean, median, and alpha-trimmed mean (with $d = 6$) filters of size 5×5. As expected, the arithmetic and geometric mean filters (especially the latter) did not do well because of the presence of impulse noise. The median and alpha-trimmed filters performed much better, with the alpha-trimmed filter giving slightly better noise reduction. For example, note in Fig. 5.12(f) that the fourth connector finger from the top left is slightly smoother in the alpha-trimmed result. This is not unexpected because, for a high value of d, the alpha-trimmed filter approaches the performance of the median filter, but still retains some smoothing capabilities.

ADAPTIVE FILTERS

Once selected, the filters discussed thus far are applied to an image without regard for how image characteristics vary from one point to another. In this section, we take a look at two *adaptive* filters whose behavior changes based on statistical characteristics of the image inside the filter region defined by the $m \times n$ rectangular neighborhood S_{xy}. As the following discussion shows, adaptive filters are capable of performance superior to that of the filters discussed thus far. The price paid for improved

a b
c d

FIGURE 5.10
(a) Image corrupted by salt-and- pepper noise with probabilities $P_s = P_p = 0.1$.
(b) Result of one pass with a median filter of size 3×3. (c) Result of processing (b) with this filter.
(d) Result of processing (c) with the same filter.

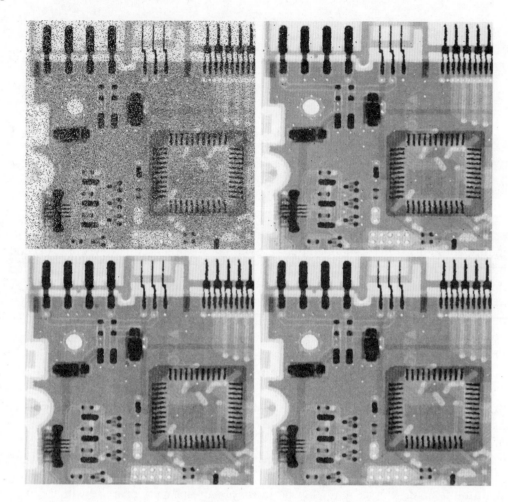

a b

FIGURE 5.11
(a) Result of filtering Fig. 5.8(a) with a max filter of size 3×3.
(b) Result of filtering Fig. 5.8(b) with a min filter of the same size.

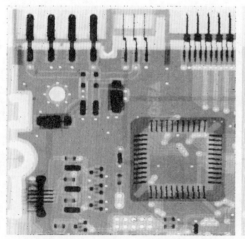
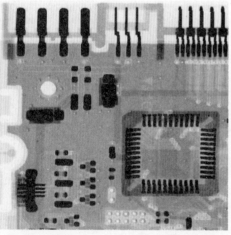

a b
c d
e f

FIGURE 5.12
(a) Image
corrupted by
additive uniform
noise. (b) Image
additionally
corrupted by
additive salt-and-
pepper noise.
(c)-(f) Image (b)
filtered with a
5×5:
(c) arithmetic
mean filter;
(d) geometric
mean filter;
(e) median filter;
(f) alpha-trimmed
mean filter, with
$d = 6$.

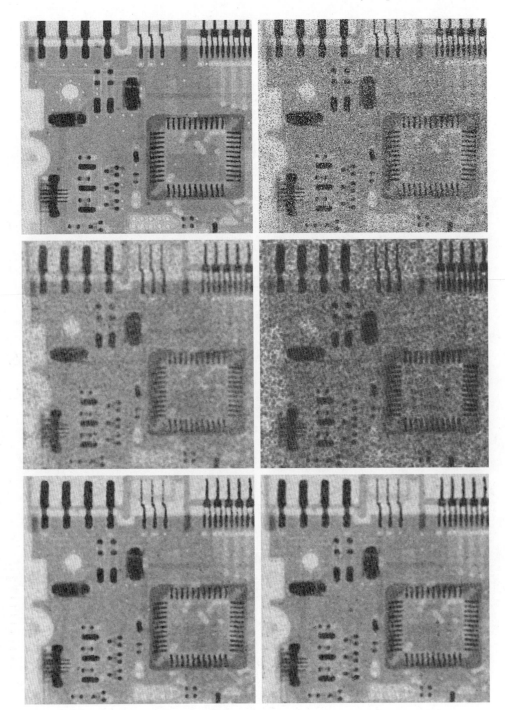

filtering power is an increase in filter complexity. Keep in mind that we still are dealing with the case in which the degraded image is equal to the original image plus noise. No other types of degradations are being considered yet.

Adaptive, Local Noise Reduction Filter

The simplest statistical measures of a random variable are its mean and variance. These are reasonable parameters on which to base an adaptive filter because they are quantities closely related to the appearance of an image. The mean gives a measure of average intensity in the region over which the mean is computed, and the variance gives a measure of image contrast in that region.

Our filter is to operate on a neighborhood, S_{xy}, centered on coordinates (x, y). The response of the filter at (x, y) is to be based on the following quantities: $g(x, y)$, the value of the noisy image at (x, y); σ_η^2, the variance of the noise; $\bar{z}_{S_{xy}}$, the local average intensity of the pixels in S_{xy}; and $\sigma_{S_{xy}}^2$, the local variance of the intensities of pixels in S_{xy}. We want the behavior of the filter to be as follows:

1. If σ_η^2 is zero, the filter should return simply the value of g at (x, y). This is the trivial, zero-noise case in which g is equal to f at (x, y).

2. If the local variance $\sigma_{S_{xy}}^2$ is high relative to σ_η^2, the filter should return a value close to g at (x, y). A high local variance typically is associated with edges, and these should be preserved.

3. If the two variances are equal, we want the filter to return the arithmetic mean value of the pixels in S_{xy}. This condition occurs when the local area has the same properties as the overall image, and local noise is to be reduced by averaging.

An adaptive expression for obtaining $\hat{f}(x, y)$ based on these assumptions may be written as

$$\hat{f}(x, y) = g(x, y) - \frac{\sigma_\eta^2}{\sigma_{S_{xy}}^2}\left[g(x, y) - \bar{z}_{S_{xy}}\right] \tag{5-32}$$

The only quantity that needs to be known a priori is σ_η^2, the variance of the noise corrupting image $f(x, y)$. This is a constant that can be estimated from sample noisy images using Eq. (3-26). The other parameters are computed from the pixels in neighborhood S_{xy} using Eqs. (3-27) and (3-28).

An assumption in Eq. (5-32) is that the ratio of the two variances does not exceed 1, which implies that $\sigma_\eta^2 \leq \sigma_{S_{xy}}^2$. The noise in our model is additive and position independent, so this is a reasonable assumption to make because S_{xy} is a subset of $g(x, y)$. However, we seldom have exact knowledge of σ_η^2. Therefore, it is possible for this condition to be violated in practice. For that reason, a test should be built into an implementation of Eq. (5-32) so that the ratio is set to 1 if the condition $\sigma_\eta^2 > \sigma_{S_{xy}}^2$ occurs. This makes this filter nonlinear. However, it prevents nonsensical results (i.e., negative intensity levels, depending on the value of $\bar{z}_{S_{xy}}$) due to a potential lack of knowledge about the variance of the image noise. Another approach is to allow the negative values to occur, and then rescale the intensity values at the end. The result then would be a loss of dynamic range in the image.

EXAMPLE 5.4: Image denoising using adaptive, local noise-reduction filtering.

Figure 5.13(a) shows the circuit-board image, corrupted this time by additive Gaussian noise of zero mean and a variance of 1000. This is a significant level of noise corruption, but it makes an ideal test bed on which to compare relative filter performance. Figure 5.13(b) is the result of processing the noisy image with an arithmetic mean filter of size 7×7. The noise was smoothed out, but at the cost of significant blurring. Similar comments apply to Fig. 5.13(c), which shows the result of processing the noisy image with a geometric mean filter, also of size 7×7. The differences between these two filtered images are analogous to those we discussed in Example 5.2; only the degree of blurring is different.

Figure 5.13(d) shows the result of using the adaptive filter of Eq. (5-32) with $\sigma_\eta^2 = 1000$. The improvements in this result compared with the two previous filters are significant. In terms of overall noise reduction, the adaptive filter achieved results similar to the arithmetic and geometric mean filters. However, the image filtered with the adaptive filter is much sharper. For example, the connector fingers at the top of the image are significantly sharper in Fig. 5.13(d). Other features, such as holes and the eight legs of the dark component on the lower left-hand side of the image, are much clearer in Fig. 5.13(d). These results are typical of what can be achieved with an adaptive filter. As mentioned earlier, the price paid for the improved performance is additional filter complexity.

a b
c d

FIGURE 5.13
(a) Image corrupted by additive Gaussian noise of zero mean and a variance of 1000.
(b) Result of arithmetic mean filtering.
(c) Result of geometric mean filtering.
(d) Result of adaptive noise-reduction filtering. All filters used were of size 7×7.

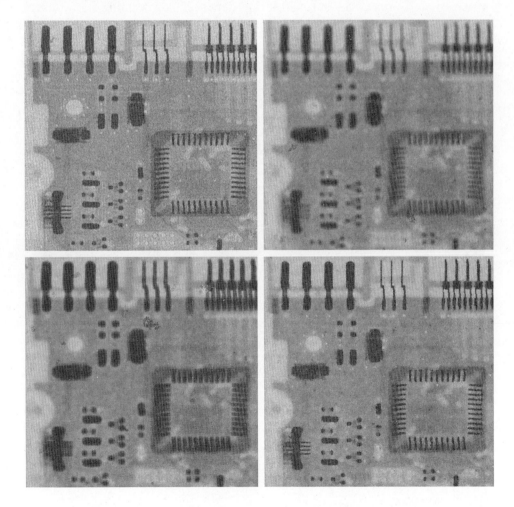

The preceding results used a value for σ_η^2 that matched the variance of the noise exactly. If this quantity is not known, and the estimate used is too low, the algorithm will return an image that closely resembles the original because the corrections will be smaller than they should be. Estimates that are too high will cause the ratio of the variances to be clipped at 1.0, and the algorithm will subtract the mean from the image more frequently than it would normally. If negative values are allowed and the image is rescaled at the end, the result will be a loss of dynamic range, as mentioned previously.

Adaptive Median Filter

The median filter in Eq. (5-27) performs well if the spatial density of the salt-and-pepper noise is low (as a rule of thumb, P_s and P_p less than 0.2). We show in the following discussion that adaptive median filtering can handle noise with probabilities larger than these. An additional benefit of the adaptive median filter is that it seeks to preserve detail while simultaneously smoothing non-impulse noise, something that the "traditional" median filter does not do. As in all the filters discussed in the preceding sections, the adaptive median filter also works in a rectangular neighborhood, S_{xy}. Unlike those filters, however, the adaptive median filter changes (increases) the size of S_{xy} during filtering, depending on certain conditions to be listed shortly. Keep in mind that the output of the filter is a single value used to replace the value of the pixel at (x, y), the point on which region S_{xy} is centered at a given time.

We use the following notation:

$$z_{\min} = \text{minimum intensity value in } S_{xy}$$
$$z_{\max} = \text{maximum intensity value in } S_{xy}$$
$$z_{\text{med}} = \text{median of intensity values in } S_{xy}$$
$$z_{xy} = \text{intensity at coordinates } (x, y)$$
$$S_{\max} = \text{maximum allowed size of } S_{xy}$$

The adaptive median-filtering algorithm uses two processing levels, denoted level A and level B, at each point (x, y):

$$\text{Level } A: \quad \text{If } z_{\min} < z_{\text{med}} < z_{\max}, \text{ go to Level } B$$
$$\text{Else, increase the size of } S_{xy}$$
$$\text{If } S_{xy} \leq S_{\max}, \text{ repeat level } A$$
$$\text{Else, output } z_{\text{med}}.$$
$$\text{Level } B: \quad \text{If } z_{\min} < z_{xy} < z_{\max}, \text{ output } z_{xy}$$
$$\text{Else output } z_{\text{med}}.$$

where S_{xy} and $S_{\max}$ are odd, positive integers greater than 1. Another option in the last step of level A is to output z_{xy} instead of z_{med}. This produces a slightly less blurred result, but can fail to detect salt (pepper) noise embedded in a constant background having the same value as pepper (salt) noise.

This algorithm has three principal objectives: to remove salt-and-pepper (impulse) noise, to provide smoothing of other noise that may not be impulsive, and to reduce distortion, such as excessive thinning or thickening of object boundaries. The values z_{min} and z_{max} are considered statistically by the algorithm to be "impulse-like" noise components in region S_{xy}, even if these are not the lowest and highest possible pixel values in the image.

With these observations in mind, we see that the purpose of level A is to determine if the median filter output, z_{med}, is an impulse (salt *or* pepper) or not. If the condition $z_{min} < z_{med} < z_{max}$ holds, then z_{med} cannot be an impulse for the reason mentioned in the previous paragraph. In this case, we go to level B and test to see if the point in the center of the neighborhood is itself an impulse (recall that (x, y) is the location of the point being processed, and z_{xy} is its intensity). If the condition $z_{min} < z_{xy} < z_{max}$ is true, then the pixel at z_{xy} cannot be the intensity of an impulse for the same reason that z_{med} was not. In this case, the algorithm outputs the unchanged pixel value, z_{xy}. By not changing these "intermediate-level" points, distortion is reduced in the filtered image. If the condition $z_{min} < z_{xy} < z_{max}$ is false, then either $z_{xy} = z_{min}$ or $z_{xy} = z_{max}$. In either case, the value of the pixel is an extreme value and the algorithm outputs the median value, z_{med}, which we know from level A is not a noise impulse. The last step is what the standard median filter does. The problem is that the standard median filter replaces every point in the image by the median of the corresponding neighborhood. This causes unnecessary loss of detail.

Continuing with the explanation, suppose that level A *does* find an impulse (i.e., it fails the test that would cause it to branch to level B). The algorithm then increases the size of the neighborhood and repeats level A. This looping continues until the algorithm either finds a median value that is not an impulse (and branches to stage B), or the maximum neighborhood size is reached. If the maximum size is reached, the algorithm returns the value of z_{med}. Note that there is no guarantee that this value is not an impulse. The smaller the noise probabilities P_a and/or P_b are, or the larger S_{max} is allowed to be, the less likely it is that a premature exit will occur. This is plausible. As the density of the noise impulses increases, it stands to reason that we would need a larger window to "clean up" the noise spikes.

Every time the algorithm outputs a value, the center of neighborhood S_{xy} is moved to the next location in the image. The algorithm then is reinitialized and applied to the pixels in the new region encompassed by the neighborhood. As indicated in Problem 3.37, the median value can be updated iteratively from one location to the next, thus reducing computational load.

EXAMPLE 5.5: Image denoising using adaptive median filtering.

Figure 5.14(a) shows the circuit-board image corrupted by salt-and-pepper noise with probabilities $P_s = P_p = 0.25$, which is 2.5 times the noise level used in Fig. 5.10(a). Here the noise level is high enough to obscure most of the detail in the image. As a basis for comparison, the image was filtered first using a 7×7 median filter, the smallest filter required to remove most visible traces of impulse noise in this case. Figure 5.14(b) shows the result. Although the noise was effectively removed, the filter caused significant

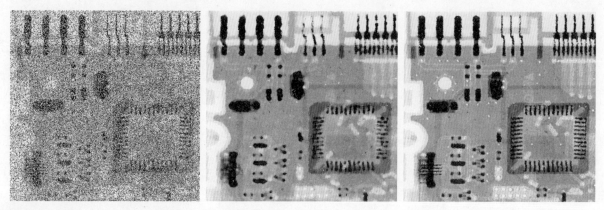

a b c

FIGURE 5.14 (a) Image corrupted by salt-and-pepper noise with probabilities $P_s = P_p = 0.25$. (b) Result of filtering with a 7×7 median filter. (c) Result of adaptive median filtering with $S_{\max} = 7$.

loss of detail in the image. For instance, some of the connector fingers at the top of the image appear distorted or broken. Other image details are similarly distorted.

Figure 5.14(c) shows the result of using the adaptive median filter with $S_{\max} = 7$. Noise removal performance was similar to the median filter. However, the adaptive filter did a much better job of preserving sharpness and detail. The connector fingers are less distorted, and some other features that were either obscured or distorted beyond recognition by the median filter appear sharper and better defined in Fig. 5.14(c). Two notable examples are the feed-through small white holes throughout the board, and the dark component with eight legs in the bottom, left quadrant of the image.

Considering the high level of noise in Fig. 5.14(a), the adaptive algorithm performed quite well. The choice of maximum allowed size for S_{xy} depends on the application, but a reasonable starting value can be estimated by experimenting with various sizes of the standard median filter first. This will establish a visual baseline regarding expectations on the performance of the adaptive algorithm.

5.4 PERIODIC NOISE REDUCTION USING FREQUENCY DOMAIN FILTERING

Periodic noise can be analyzed and filtered quite effectively using frequency domain techniques. The basic idea is that periodic noise appears as concentrated bursts of energy in the Fourier transform, at locations corresponding to the frequencies of the periodic interference. The approach is to use a selective filter (see Section 4.10) to isolate the noise. The three types of selective filters (bandreject, bandpass, and notch) were discussed in detail in Section 4.10. There is no difference between how these filters were used in Chapter 4, and the way they are used for image restoration. In restoration of images corrupted by periodic interference, the tool of choice is a notch filter. In the following discussion we will expand on the notch filtering approach introduced in Section 4.10, and also develop a more powerful optimum notch filtering method.

MORE ON NOTCH FILTERING

As explained in Section 4.10, notch reject filter transfer functions are constructed as products of highpass filter transfer functions whose centers have been translated to the centers of the notches. The general form of a notch filter transfer function is

$$H_{\mathrm{NR}}(u,v) = \prod_{k=1}^{Q} H_k(u,v) H_{-k}(u,v) \tag{5-33}$$

where $H_k(u,v)$ and $H_{-k}(u,v)$ are highpass filter transfer functions whose centers are at (u_k, v_k) and $(-u_k, -v_k)$, respectively.[†] These centers are specified with respect to the center of the frequency rectangle, $[\mathrm{floor}(M/2), \mathrm{floor}(N/2)]$, where, as usual, M and N are the number of rows and columns in the input image. Thus, the distance computations for the filter transfer functions are given by

$$D_k(u,v) = \left[(u - M/2 - u_k)^2 + (v - N/2 - v_k)^2 \right]^{1/2} \tag{5-34}$$

and

$$D_{-k}(u,v) = \left[(u - M/2 + u_k)^2 + (v - N/2 + v_k)^2 \right]^{1/2} \tag{5-35}$$

For example, the following is a Butterworth notch reject filter transfer function of order n with three notch pairs:

$$H_{\mathrm{NR}}(u,v) = \prod_{k=1}^{3} \left[\frac{1}{1 + \left[D_{0k}/D_k(u,v) \right]^n} \right] \left[\frac{1}{1 + \left[D_{0k}/D_{-k}(u,v) \right]^n} \right] \tag{5-36}$$

Because notches are specified as symmetric pairs, the constant D_{0k} is the same for each pair. However, this constant can be different from one pair to another. Other notch reject filter functions are constructed in the same manner, depending on the highpass filter function chosen. As explained in Section 4.10, a notch pass filter transfer function is obtained from a notch reject function using the expression

$$H_{\mathrm{NP}}(u,v) = 1 - H_{\mathrm{NR}}(u,v) \tag{5-37}$$

where $H_{NP}(u,v)$ is the transfer function of the notch pass filter corresponding to the notch reject filter with transfer function $H_{NR}(u,v)$. Figure 5.15 shows perspective plots of the transfer functions of ideal, Gaussian, and Butterworth notch reject filters with one notch pair. As we discussed in Chapter 4, we see again that the shape of the Butterworth transfer function represents a transition between the sharpness of the ideal function and the broad, smooth shape of the Gaussian transfer function.

As we show in the second part of the following example, we are not limited to notch filter transfer functions of the form just discussed. We can construct notch

---

† Remember, frequency domain transfer functions are symmetric about the center of the frequency rectangle, so the notches are specified as symmetric pairs. Also, recall from Section 4.10 that we use unpadded images when working with notch filters in order to simplify the specification of notch locations.

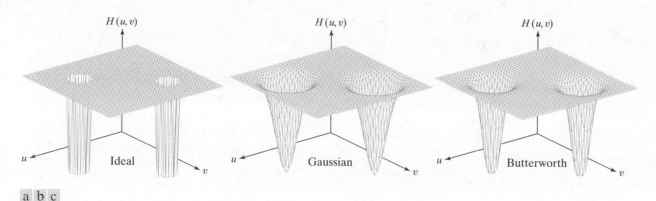

FIGURE 5.15 Perspective plots of (a) ideal, (b) Gaussian, and (c) Butterworth notch reject filter transfer functions.

filters of arbitrary shapes, provided that they are zero-phase-shift functions, as defined in Section 4.7.

EXAMPLE 5.6: Image denoising (interference reduction) using notch filtering.

Figure 5.16(a) is the same as Fig. 2.45(a), which we used in Section 2.6 to introduce the concept of filtering in the frequency domain. We now look in more detail at the process of denoising this image, which is corrupted by a single, 2-D additive sine wave. You know from Table 4.4 that the Fourier transform of a pure sine wave is a pair of complex, conjugate impulses, so we would expect the spectrum to have a pair of bright dots at the frequencies of the sine wave. As Fig. 5.16(b) shows, this is indeed is the case. Because we can determine the location of these impulses accurately, eliminating them is a simple task, consisting of using a notch filter transfer function whose notches coincide with the location of the impulses.

Figure 5.16(c) shows an ideal notch reject filter transfer function, which is an array of 1's (shown in white) and two small circular regions of 0's (shown in black). Figure 5.16(d) shows the result of filtering the noisy image this transfer function. The sinusoidal noise was virtually eliminated, and a number of details that were previously obscured by the interference are clearly visible in the filtered image (see, for example, the thin fiducial marks and the fine detail in the terrain and rock formations). As we showed in Example 4.25, obtaining an image of the interference pattern is straightforward. We simply turn the reject filter into a pass filter by subtracting it from 1, and filter the input image with it. Figure 5.17 shows the result.

Figure 5.18(a) shows the same image as Fig. 4.50(a), but covering a larger area (the interference pattern is the same). When we discussed lowpass filtering of that image in Chapter 4, we indicated that there were better ways to reduce the effect of the scan lines. The notch filtering approach that follows reduces the scan lines significantly, without introducing blurring. Unless blurring is desirable for reasons we discussed in Section 4.9, notch filtering generally gives much better results.

Just by looking at the nearly horizontal lines of the noise pattern in Fig. 5.18(a), we expect its contribution in the frequency domain to be concentrated along the vertical axis of the DFT. However, the noise is not dominant enough to have a clear pattern along this axis, as is evident in the spectrum shown in Fig. 5.18(b). The approach to follow in cases like this is to use a narrow, rectangular notch filter function that extends along the vertical axis, and thus eliminates all components of the interference along that axis. We do not filter near the origin to avoid eliminating the dc term and low frequencies,

a b
c d

FIGURE 5.16
(a) Image corrupted by sinusoidal interference.
(b) Spectrum showing the bursts of energy caused by the interference. (The bursts were enlarged for display purposes.)
(c) Notch filter (the radius of the circles is 2 pixels) used to eliminate the energy bursts. (The thin borders are not part of the data.)
(d) Result of notch reject filtering. (Original image courtesy of NASA.)

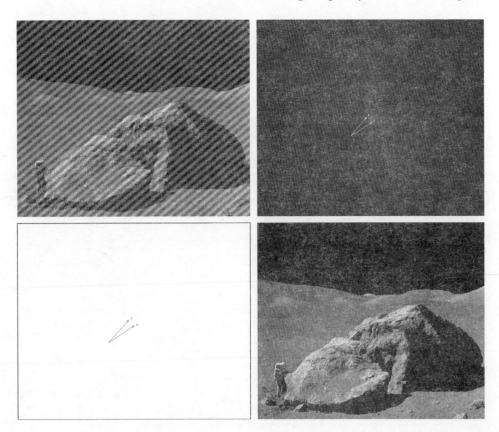

which, as you know from Chapter 4, are responsible for the intensity differences between smooth areas. Figure 5.18(c) shows the filter transfer function we used, and Fig. 5.18(d) shows the filtered result. Most of the fine scan lines were eliminated or significantly attenuated. In order to get an image of the noise pattern, we proceed as before by converting the reject filter into a pass filter, and then filtering the input image with it. Figure 5.19 shows the result.

FIGURE 5.17
Sinusoidal pattern extracted from the DFT of Fig. 5.16(a) using a notch pass filter.

FIGURE 5.18
(a) Satellite image of Florida and the Gulf of Mexico. (Note horizontal sensor scan lines.) (b) Spectrum of (a). (c) Notch reject filter transfer function. (The thin black border is not part of the data.) (d) Filtered image. (Original image courtesy of NOAA.)

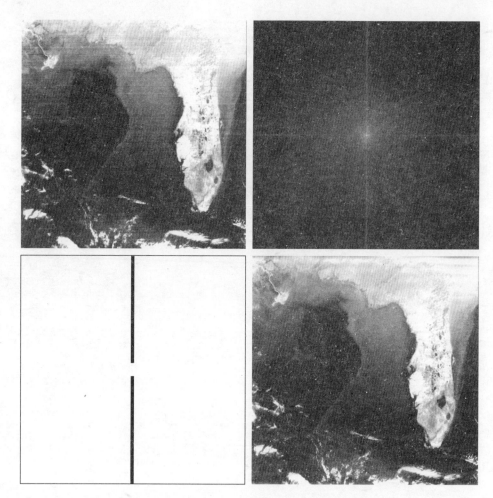

FIGURE 5.19
Noise pattern extracted from Fig. 5.18(a) by notch pass filtering.

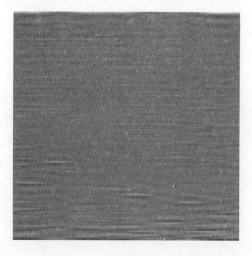

OPTIMUM NOTCH FILTERING

In the examples of notch filtering given thus far, the interference patterns have been simple to identify and characterize in the frequency domain, leading to the specification of notch filter transfer functions that also are simple to define heuristically.

When several interference components are present, heuristic specifications of filter transfer functions are not always acceptable because they may remove too much image information in the filtering process (a highly undesirable feature when images are unique and/or expensive to acquire). In addition, the interference components generally are not single-frequency bursts. Instead, they tend to have broad skirts that carry information about the interference pattern. These skirts are not always easily detectable from the normal transform background. Alternative filtering methods that reduce the effect of these degradations are quite useful in practice. The method discussed next is optimum, in the sense that it minimizes local variances of the restored estimate $\hat{f}(x, y)$.

The procedure consists of first isolating the principal contributions of the interference pattern and then subtracting a variable, weighted portion of the pattern from the corrupted image. Although we develop the procedure in the context of a specific application, the basic approach is general and can be applied to other restoration tasks in which multiple periodic interference is a problem.

We begin by extracting the principal frequency components of the interference pattern. As before, we do this by placing a notch pass filter transfer function, $H_{\text{NP}}(u, v)$, at the location of each spike. If the filter is constructed to pass only components associated with the interference pattern, then the Fourier transform of the interference noise pattern is given by the expression

$$N(u, v) = H_{\text{NP}}(u, v) G(u, v) \tag{5-38}$$

where, as usual, $G(u, v)$ is the DFT of the corrupted image.

Specifying $H_{\text{NP}}(u, v)$ requires considerable judgment about what is or is not an interference spike. For this reason, the notch pass filter generally is constructed interactively by observing the spectrum of $G(u, v)$ on a display. After a particular filter function has been selected, the corresponding noise pattern in the spatial domain is obtained using the familiar expression

$$\eta(x, y) = \Im^{-1}\left\{H_{\text{NP}}(u, v) G(u, v)\right\} \tag{5-39}$$

Because the corrupted image is assumed to be formed by the addition of the uncorrupted image $f(x, y)$ and the interference, $\eta(x, y)$, if the latter were known completely, subtracting the pattern from $g(x, y)$ to obtain $f(x, y)$ would be a simple matter. The problem, of course, is that this filtering procedure usually yields only an approximation of the true noise pattern. The effect of incomplete components not present in the estimate of $\eta(x, y)$ can be minimized by subtracting from $g(x, y)$ a *weighted* portion of $\eta(x, y)$ to obtain an estimate of $f(x, y)$:

$$\hat{f}(x, y) = g(x, y) - w(x, y)\eta(x, y) \tag{5-40}$$

where, as before, $\hat{f}(x,y)$ is the estimate of $f(x,y)$ and $w(x,y)$ is to be determined. This function is called a *weighting* or *modulation function*, and the objective of the procedure is to select $w(x,y)$ so that the result is optimized in some meaningful way. One approach is to select $w(x,y)$ so that the variance of $\hat{f}(x,y)$ is minimized over a specified neighborhood of every point (x,y).

Consider a neighborhood S_{xy} of (odd) size $m \times n$, centered on (x,y). The "local" variance of $\hat{f}(x,y)$ at point (x,y) can be estimated using the samples in S_{xy}, as follows:

$$\sigma^2(x,y) = \frac{1}{mn} \sum_{(r,c) \in S_{xy}} [\hat{f}(r,c) - \bar{\hat{f}}]^2 \tag{5-41}$$

where $\bar{\hat{f}}$ is the average value of $\hat{f}$ in neighborhood S_{xy}; that is,

$$\bar{\hat{f}} = \frac{1}{mn} \sum_{(r,c) \in S_{xy}} \hat{f}(r,c) \tag{5-42}$$

Points on or near the edge of the image can be treated by considering partial neighborhoods or by padding the border with 0's.

Substituting Eq. (5-40) into Eq. (5-41) we obtain

$$\sigma^2(x,y) = \frac{1}{mn} \sum_{(r,c) \in S_{xy}} \left\{ [g(r,c) - w(r,c)\eta(r,c)] - [\bar{g} - \overline{w\eta}] \right\}^2 \tag{5-43}$$

where $\bar{g}$ and $\overline{w\eta}$ denote the average values of g and of the product $w\eta$ in neighborhood S_{xy}, respectively.

If we assume that w is approximately constant in S_{xy} we can replace $w(r,c)$ by the value of w at the center of the neighborhood:

$$w(r,c) = w(x,y) \tag{5-44}$$

Because $w(x,y)$ is assumed to be constant in S_{xy}, it follows that $\bar{w} = w(x,y)$ and, therefore, that

$$\overline{w\eta} = w(x,y)\bar{\eta} \tag{5-45}$$

in S_{xy}, where $\bar{\eta}$ is the average value of η in the neighborhood. Using these approximations, Eq. (5-43) becomes

$$\sigma^2(x,y) = \frac{1}{mn} \sum_{(r,c) \in S_{xy}} \left\{ [g(r,c) - w(x,y)\eta(r,c)] - [\bar{g} - w(x,y)\bar{\eta}] \right\}^2 \tag{5-46}$$

To minimize $\sigma^2(x, y)$ with respect to $w(x, y)$ we solve

$$\frac{\partial \sigma^2(x, y)}{\partial w(x, y)} = 0 \tag{5-47}$$

for $w(x, y)$. The result is (see Problem 5.17):

$$w(x, y) = \frac{\overline{g\eta} - \overline{g}\,\overline{\eta}}{\overline{\eta^2} - \overline{\eta}^2} \tag{5-48}$$

To obtain the value of the restored image at point (x, y) we use this equation to compute $w(x, y)$ and then substitute it into Eq. (5-40). To obtain the complete restored image, we perform this procedure at every point in the noisy image, g.

EXAMPLE 5.7: Denoising (interference removal) using optimum notch filtering.

Figure 5.20(a) shows a digital image of the Martian terrain taken by the Mariner 6 spacecraft. The image is corrupted by a semi-periodic interference pattern that is considerably more complex (and much more subtle) than those we have studied thus far. The Fourier spectrum of the image, shown in Fig. 5.20(b), has a number of "starlike" bursts of energy caused by the interference. As expected, these components are more difficult to detect than those we have seen before. Figure 5.21 shows the spectrum again, but without centering. This image offers a somewhat clearer view of the interference components because the more prominent dc term and low frequencies are "out of way," in the top left of the spectrum.

Figure 5.22(a) shows the spectrum components that, in the judgement of an experienced image analyst, are associated with the interference. Applying a notch pass filter to these components and using Eq. (5-39) yielded the spatial noise pattern, $\eta(x, y)$, shown in Fig. 5.22(b). Note the similarity between this pattern and the structure of the noise in Fig. 5.20(a).

a b

FIGURE 5.20
(a) Image of the Martian terrain taken by Mariner 6.
(b) Fourier spectrum showing periodic interference.
(Courtesy of NASA.)

FIGURE 5.21
Uncentered
Fourier spectrum
of the image
in Fig. 5.20(a).
(Courtesy of
NASA.)

Finally, Fig. 5.23 shows the restored image, obtained using Eq. (5-40) with the interference pattern just discussed. Function $w(x, y)$ was computed using the procedure explained in the preceding paragraphs. As you can see, the periodic interference was virtually eliminated from the noisy image in Fig. 5.20(a).

5.5 LINEAR, POSITION-INVARIANT DEGRADATIONS

The input-output relationship in Fig. 5.1 before the restoration stage is expressed as

$$g(x, y) = \mathcal{H}[f(x, y)] + \eta(x, y) \tag{5-49}$$

For the moment, let us assume that $\eta(x, y) = 0$ so that $g(x, y) = \mathcal{H}[f(x, y)]$. Based on the discussion in Section 2.6, $\mathcal{H}$ is *linear* if

a b

FIGURE 5.22
(a) Fourier spec-
trum of $N(u, v)$,
and
(b) corresponding
spatial noise
interference
pattern, $\eta(x, y)$.
(Courtesy of
NASA.)

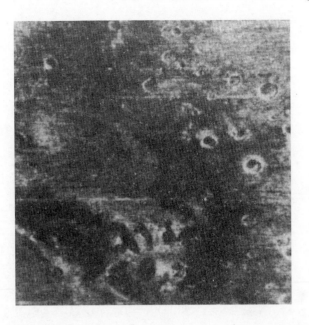

$$\mathcal{H}\big[af_1(x,y) + bf_2(x,y)\big] = a\mathcal{H}\big[f_1(x,y)\big] + b\mathcal{H}\big[f_2(x,y)\big] \qquad (5\text{-}50)$$

where a and b are scalars and $f_1(x,y)$ and $f_2(x,y)$ are any two input images.

If $a = b = 1$, Eq. (5-50) becomes

$$\mathcal{H}\big[f_1(x,y) + f_2(x,y)\big] = \mathcal{H}\big[f_1(x,y)\big] + \mathcal{H}\big[f_2(x,y)\big] \qquad (5\text{-}51)$$

which is called the property of *additivity*. This property says that, if $\mathcal{H}$ is a linear operator, the response to a sum of two inputs is equal to the sum of the two responses.

With $f_2(x,y) = 0$, Eq. (5-50) becomes

$$\mathcal{H}\big[af_1(x,y)\big] = a\mathcal{H}\big[f_1(x,y)\big] \qquad (5\text{-}52)$$

which is called the property of *homogeneity*. It says that the response to a constant multiple of any input is equal to the response to that input multiplied by the same constant. Thus, a linear operator possesses both the property of additivity and the property of homogeneity.

An operator having the input-output relationship $g(x,y) = \mathcal{H}\big[f(x,y)\big]$ is said to be *position* (or *space*) *invariant* if

$$\mathcal{H}\big[f(x-\alpha, y-\beta)\big] = g(x-\alpha, y-\beta) \qquad (5\text{-}53)$$

for any $f(x,y)$ and any two scalars α and β. This definition indicates that the response at any point in the image depends only on the *value* of the input at that point, not on its *position*.

Using the sifting property of the 2-D continuous impulse [see Eq. (4-55)], we can write $f(x,y)$ as

$$f(x, y) = \int_{-\infty}^{\infty} \int_{-\infty}^{\infty} f(\alpha, \beta)\delta(x - \alpha, y - \beta)\,d\alpha\,d\beta \tag{5-54}$$

Assuming again that $\eta(x, y) = 0$, substituting this equation into Eq. (5-49) yields

$$g(x, y) = \mathcal{H}[f(x, y)] = \mathcal{H}\left[\int_{-\infty}^{\infty} \int_{-\infty}^{\infty} f(\alpha, \beta)\delta(x - \alpha, y - \beta)\,d\alpha\,d\beta\right] \tag{5-55}$$

If $\mathcal{H}$ is a linear operator and we extend the additivity property to integrals, then

$$g(x, y) = \int_{-\infty}^{\infty} \int_{-\infty}^{\infty} \mathcal{H}[f(\alpha, \beta)\delta(x - \alpha, y - \beta)]\,d\alpha\,d\beta \tag{5-56}$$

Because $f(\alpha, \beta)$ is independent of x and y, and using the homogeneity property, it follows that

$$g(x, y) = \int_{-\infty}^{\infty} \int_{-\infty}^{\infty} f(\alpha, \beta)\mathcal{H}[\delta(x - \alpha, y - \beta)]\,d\alpha\,d\beta \tag{5-57}$$

The term

$$h(x, \alpha, y, \beta) = \mathcal{H}[\delta(x - \alpha, y - \beta)] \tag{5-58}$$

is called the *impulse response* of $\mathcal{H}$. In other words, if $\eta(x, y) = 0$ in Eq. (5-49), then $h(x, \alpha, y, \beta)$ is the response of $\mathcal{H}$ to an impulse at coordinates (x, y). In optics, the impulse becomes a point of light and $h(x, \alpha, y, \beta)$ is commonly referred to as the *point spread function* (PSF). This name is based on the fact that all physical optical systems blur (spread) a point of light to some degree, with the amount of blurring being determined by the quality of the optical components.

Substituting Eq. (5-58) into Eq. (5-57) we obtain the expression

$$g(x, y) = \int_{-\infty}^{\infty} \int_{-\infty}^{\infty} f(\alpha, \beta)h(x, \alpha, y, \beta)\,d\alpha\,d\beta \tag{5-59}$$

which is called the *superposition* (or *Fredholm*) *integral of the first kind*. This expression is a fundamental result that is at the core of linear system theory. It states that if the response of $\mathcal{H}$ to an impulse is known, the response to *any* input $f(\alpha, \beta)$ can be calculated using Eq. (5-59). In other words, a linear system $\mathcal{H}$ is *characterized completely* by its impulse response.

If $\mathcal{H}$ is position invariant, then it follows from Eq. (5-53) that

$$\mathcal{H}[\delta(x - \alpha, y - \beta)] = h(x - \alpha, y - \beta) \tag{5-60}$$

In this case, Eq. (5-59) reduces to

$$g(x, y) = \int_{-\infty}^{\infty} \int_{-\infty}^{\infty} f(\alpha, \beta)h(x - \alpha, y - \beta)\,d\alpha\,d\beta \tag{5-61}$$

This expression is the *convolution integral* introduced for one variable in Eq. (4-24) and extended to 2-D in Problem 4.19. Equation (5-61) tells us that the output of a linear, position invariant system to *any* input, is obtained by convolving the input and the system's impulse response.

In the presence of additive noise, the expression of the linear degradation model [Eq. (5-59)] becomes

$$g(x, y) = \int_{-\infty}^{\infty} \int_{-\infty}^{\infty} f(\alpha, \beta) h(x, \alpha, y, \beta) \, d\alpha \, d\beta + \eta(x, y) \qquad (5\text{-}62)$$

If $\mathcal{H}$ is position invariant, then this equation becomes

$$g(x, y) = \int_{-\infty}^{\infty} \int_{-\infty}^{\infty} f(\alpha, \beta) h(x - \alpha, y - \beta) \, d\alpha \, d\beta + \eta(x, y) \qquad (5\text{-}63)$$

The values of the noise term $\eta(x, y)$ are random, and are assumed to be independent of position. Using the familiar notation for convolution introduced in Chapters 3 and 4, we can write Eq. (5-63) as

$$g(x, y) = (h \star f)(x, y) + \eta(x, y) \qquad (5\text{-}64)$$

or, using the convolution theorem, we write the equivalent result in the frequency domain as

$$G(u, v) = H(u, v) F(u, v) + N(u, v) \qquad (5\text{-}65)$$

These two expressions agree with Eqs. (5-1) and (5-2). Keep in mind that, for discrete quantities, all products are elementwise products, as defined in Section 2.6.

In summary, the preceding discussion indicates that a linear, spatially invariant degradation system with additive noise can be modeled in the spatial domain as the convolution of an image with the system's degradation (point spread) function, followed by the addition of noise. Based on the convolution theorem, the same process can be expressed in the frequency domain as the product of the transforms of the image and degradation, followed by the addition of the transform of the noise. When working in the frequency domain, we make use of an FFT algorithm. However, unlike in Chapter 4, we do not use image padding in the implementation of any of the frequency domain restoration filters discussed in this chapter. The reason is that in restoration work we usually have access only to degraded images. For padding to be effective, it would have to be applied to images before they were degraded, a condition that obviously cannot be met in practice. If we had access to the original images, then restoration would be a mute point.

Many types of degradations can be approximated by linear, position-invariant processes. The advantage of this approach is that the extensive tools of linear system theory then become available for the solution of image restoration problems.

Nonlinear and position-dependent techniques, although more general (and usually more accurate), introduce difficulties that often have no known solution or are very difficult to solve computationally. This chapter focuses on linear, space-invariant restoration techniques. Because degradations are modeled as being the result of convolution, and restoration seeks to find filters that apply the process in reverse, the term *image deconvolution* is used frequently to signify linear image restoration. Similarly, the filters used in the restoration process often are called *deconvolution filters*.

5.6 ESTIMATING THE DEGRADATION FUNCTION

There are three principal ways to estimate the degradation function for use in image restoration: (1) observation, (2) experimentation, and (3) mathematical modeling. These methods are discussed in the following sections. The process of restoring an image by using a degradation function that has been estimated by any of these approaches sometimes is called *blind deconvolution*, to emphasize the fact that the true degradation function is seldom known completely.

ESTIMATION BY IMAGE OBSERVATION

Suppose that we are given a degraded image without any knowledge about the degradation function $\mathcal{H}$. Based on the assumption that the image was degraded by a linear, position-invariant process, one way to estimate $\mathcal{H}$ is to gather information from the image itself. For example, if the image is blurred, we can look at a small rectangular section of the image containing sample structures, like part of an object and the background. In order to reduce the effect of noise, we would look for an area in which the signal content is strong (e.g., an area of high contrast). The next step would be to process the subimage to arrive at a result that is as unblurred as possible.

Let the observed subimage be denoted by $g_s(x, y)$, and let the processed subimage (which in reality is our estimate of the original image in that area) be denoted by $\hat{f}_s(x, y)$. Then, assuming that the effect of noise is negligible because of our choice of a strong-signal area, it follows from Eq. (5-65) that

$$H_s(u,v) = \frac{G_s(u,v)}{\hat{F}_s(u,v)} \tag{5-66}$$

From the characteristics of this function, we then deduce the complete degradation function $H(u, v)$ based on our assumption of position invariance. For example, suppose that a radial plot of $H_s(u, v)$ has the approximate shape of a Gaussian curve. We can use that information to construct a function $H(u, v)$ on a larger scale, but having the same basic shape. We then use $H(u, v)$ in one of the restoration approaches to be discussed in the following sections. Clearly, this is a laborious process used only in very specific circumstances, such as restoring an old photograph of historical value.

ESTIMATION BY EXPERIMENTATION

If equipment similar to the equipment used to acquire the degraded image is available, it is possible in principle to obtain an accurate estimate of the degradation. Images similar to the degraded image can be acquired with various system settings

a b

FIGURE 5.24
Estimating a
degradation by
impulse
characterization.
(a) An impulse
of light (shown
magnified).
(b) Imaged
(degraded)
impulse.

until they are degraded as closely as possible to the image we wish to restore. Then
the idea is to obtain the impulse response of the degradation by imaging an impulse
(small dot of light) using the same system settings. As noted in Section 5.5, a linear,
space-invariant system is characterized completely by its impulse response.

An impulse is simulated by a bright dot of light, as bright as possible to reduce the
effect of noise to negligible values. Then, recalling that the Fourier transform of an
impulse is a constant, it follows from Eq. (5-65) that

$$H(u,v) = \frac{G(u,v)}{A} \tag{5-67}$$

where, as before, $G(u,v)$ is the Fourier transform of the observed image, and A is a
constant describing the strength of the impulse. Figure 5.24 shows an example.

ESTIMATION BY MODELING

Degradation modeling has been used for many years because of the insight it affords
into the image restoration problem. In some cases, the model can even take into
account environmental conditions that cause degradations. For example, a degradation model proposed by Hufnagel and Stanley [1964] is based on the physical characteristics of atmospheric turbulence. This model has a familiar form:

$$H(u,v) = e^{-k(u^2 + v^2)^{5/6}} \tag{5-68}$$

where k is a constant that depends on the nature of the turbulence. With the exception of the 5/6 power in the exponent, this equation has the same form as the Gaussian lowpass filter transfer function discussed in Section 4.8. In fact, the Gaussian
LPF is used sometimes to model mild, uniform blurring. Figure 5.25 shows examples
obtained by simulating blurring an image using Eq. (5-68) with values $k = 0.0025$

a b
c d

FIGURE 5.25
Modeling
turbulence.
(a) No visible
turbulence.
(b) Severe
turbulence,
$k = 0.0025$.
(c) Mild
turbulence,
$k = 0.001$.
(d) Low
turbulence,
$k = 0.00025$.
All images are
of size 480×480
pixels.
(Original
image courtesy of
NASA.)

(severe turbulence), $k = 0.001$ (mild turbulence), and $k = 0.00025$ (low turbulence). We restore these images using various methods later in this chapter.

Another approach used frequently in modeling is to derive a mathematical model starting from basic principles. We illustrate this procedure by treating in some detail the case in which an image has been blurred by uniform linear motion between the image and the sensor during image acquisition. Suppose that an image $f(x, y)$ undergoes planar motion and that $x_0(t)$ and $y_0(t)$ are the time-varying components of motion in the x- and y-directions, respectively. We obtain the total exposure at any point of the recording medium (say, film or digital memory) by integrating the instantaneous exposure over the time interval during which the imaging system shutter is open.

Assuming that shutter opening and closing takes place instantaneously, and that the optical imaging process is perfect, lets us isolate the effects due to image motion. Then, if T is the duration of the exposure, it follows that

$$g(x,y) = \int_0^T f[x - x_0(t), y - y_0(t)]dt \qquad (5\text{-}69)$$

where $g(x,y)$ is the blurred image.

The continuous Fourier transform of this expression is

$$G(u,v) = \int_{-\infty}^{\infty} \int_{-\infty}^{\infty} g(x,y)e^{-j2\pi(ux+vy)}dx\,dy \qquad (5\text{-}70)$$

Substituting Eq. (5-69) into Eq. (5-70) yields

$$G(u,v) = \int_{-\infty}^{\infty} \int_{-\infty}^{\infty} \left[\int_0^T f[x - x_0(t), y - y_0(t)]dt \right] e^{-j2\pi(ux+vy)}dx\,dy \qquad (5\text{-}71)$$

Reversing the order of integration results in the expression

$$G(u,v) = \int_0^T \left[\int_{-\infty}^{\infty} \int_{-\infty}^{\infty} f[x - x_0(t), y - y_0(t)]e^{-j2\pi(ux+vy)}dx\,dy \right]dt \qquad (5\text{-}72)$$

The term inside the outer brackets is the Fourier transform of the displaced function $f\left[x - x_0(t), y - y_0(t)\right]$. Using entry 3 in Table 4.4 then yields the expression

$$G(u,v) = \int_0^T F(u,v)e^{-j2\pi[ux_0(t)+vy_0(t)]}dt$$
$$= F(u,v)\int_0^T e^{-j2\pi[ux_0(t)+vy_0(t)]}dt \qquad (5\text{-}73)$$

By defining

$$H(u,v) = \int_0^T e^{-j2\pi[ux_0(t)+vy_0(t)]}dt \qquad (5\text{-}74)$$

we can express Eq. (5-73) in the familiar form

$$G(u,v) = H(u,v)F(u,v) \qquad (5\text{-}75)$$

If the motion variables $x_0(t)$ and $y_0(t)$ are known, the transfer function $H(u,v)$ can be obtained directly from Eq. (5-74). As an illustration, suppose that the image in question undergoes uniform linear motion in the x-direction only (i.e., $y_0(t) = 0$), at a rate $x_0(t) = at/T$. When $t = T$, the image has been displaced by a total distance a. With $y_0(t) = 0$, Eq. (5-74) yields

$$H(u,v) = \int_0^T e^{-j2\pi ux_0(t)}dt = \int_0^T e^{-j2\pi uat/T}dt$$
$$= \frac{T}{\pi ua}\sin(\pi ua)e^{-j\pi ua} \qquad (5\text{-}76)$$

FIGURE 5.26
(a) Original image. (b) Result of blurring using the function in Eq. (5-77) with $a = b = 0.1$ and $T = 1$.

If we allow the y-component to vary as well, with the motion given by $y_0(t) = bt/T$, then the degradation function becomes

$$H(u,v) = \frac{T}{\pi(ua + vb)} \sin\left[\pi(ua + vb)\right] e^{-j\pi(ua + vb)} \tag{5-77}$$

To generate a discrete filter transfer function of size $M \times N$, we sample this equation for $u = 0, 1, 2, \ldots, M - 1$ and $v = 0, 1, 2, \ldots, N - 1$.

EXAMPLE 5.8: Image blurring caused by motion.

Figure 5.26(b) is an image blurred by computing the Fourier transform of the image in Fig. 5.26(a), multiplying the transform by $H(u,v)$ from Eq. (5-77), and taking the inverse transform. The images are of size 688×688 pixels, and we used $a = b = 0.1$ and $T = 1$ in Eq. (5-77). As we will discuss in Sections 5.8 and 5.9, recovery of the original image from its blurred counterpart presents some interesting challenges, particularly when noise is present in the degraded image. As mentioned at the end of Section 5.5, we perform all DFT computations without padding.

5.7 INVERSE FILTERING

The material in this section is our first step in studying restoration of images degraded by a degradation function $\mathcal{H}$, which is given, or is obtained by a method such as those discussed in the previous section. The simplest approach to restoration is direct inverse filtering, where we compute an estimate, $\hat{F}(u,v)$, of the transform of the original image by dividing the transform of the degraded image, $G(u,v)$, by the degradation transfer function:

$$\hat{F}(u,v) = \frac{G(u,v)}{H(u,v)} \tag{5-78}$$

The division is elementwise, as defined in Section 2.6 and in connection with Eq. (5-65). Substituting the right side of Eq. (5-2) for $G(u,v)$ in Eq. (5-78) yields

$$\hat{F}(u,v) = F(u,v) + \frac{N(u,v)}{H(u,v)} \qquad (5\text{-}79)$$

This is an interesting expression. It tells us that, even if we know the degradation function, we cannot recover the undegraded image [the inverse Fourier transform of $F(u,v)$] exactly because $N(u,v)$ is not known. There is more bad news. If the degradation function has zero or very small values, then the ratio $N(u,v)/H(u,v)$ could easily dominate the term $F(u,v)$. In fact, this is frequently the case, as you will see shortly.

One approach to get around the zero or small-value problem is to limit the filter frequencies to values near the origin. From the discussion of Eq. (4-92), we know that $H(0,0)$ is usually the highest value of $H(u,v)$ in the frequency domain. Thus, by limiting the analysis to frequencies near the origin, we reduce the likelihood of encountering zero values. The following example illustrates this approach.

EXAMPLE 5.9: Image deblurring by inverse filtering.

The image in Fig. 5.25(b) was inverse filtered with Eq. (5-78) using the exact inverse of the degradation function that generated that image. That is, the degradation function used was

$$H(u,v) = e^{-k\left[(u\,+\,M/2)^2 + (v\,-\,N/2)^2\right]^{5/6}}$$

with $k = 0.0025$. The $M/2$ and $N/2$ constants are offset values; they center the function so that it will correspond with the centered Fourier transform, as discussed in the previous chapter. (Remember, we do not use padding with these functions.) In this case, $M = N = 480$. We know that a Gaussian function has no zeros, so that will not be a concern here. However, despite this, the degradation values became so small that the result of full inverse filtering [Fig. 5.27(a)] is useless. The reasons for this poor result are as discussed in connection with Eq. (5-79).

Figures 5.27(b) through (d) show the results of cutting off values of the ratio $G(u,v)/H(u,v)$ outside a radius of 40, 70, and 85, respectively. The cut off was implemented by applying to the ratio a Butterworth lowpass function of order 10. This provided a sharp (but smooth) transition at the desired radius. Radii near 70 yielded the best visual results [Fig. 5.27(c)]. Radii below 70 resulted in blurred images, as in Fig. 5.27(b), which was obtained using a radius of 40. Values above 70 started to produce degraded images, as illustrated in Fig. 5.27(d), which was obtained using a radius of 85. The image content is almost visible in this image behind a "curtain" of noise, but the noise definitely dominates the result. Further increases in radius values produced images that looked more and more like Fig. 5.27(a).

The results in the preceding example are illustrative of the poor performance of direct inverse filtering in general. The basic theme of the three sections that follow is how to improve on direct inverse filtering.

a b
c d

FIGURE 5.27
Restoring
Fig. 5.25(b)
using Eq. (5-78).
(a) Result of using
the full filter.
(b) Result with H
cut off outside a
radius of 40.
(c) Result with H
cut off outside a
radius of 70.
(d) Result with H
cut off outside a
radius of 85.

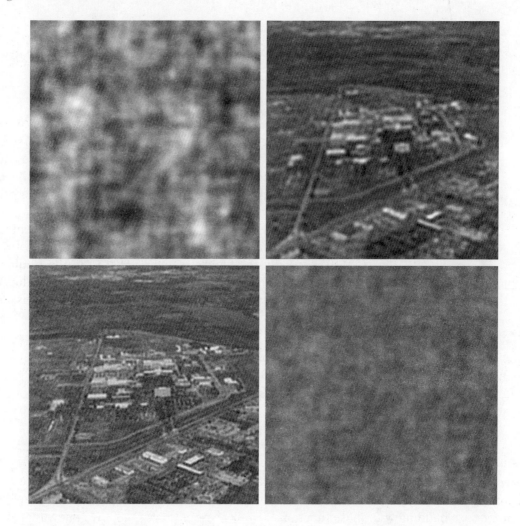

5.8 MINIMUM MEAN SQUARE ERROR (WIENER) FILTERING

The inverse filtering approach discussed in the previous section makes no explicit provision for handling noise. In this section, we discuss an approach that incorporates both the degradation function and statistical characteristics of noise into the restoration process. The method is founded on considering images and noise as random variables, and the objective is to find an estimate $\hat{f}$ of the uncorrupted image f such that the mean square error between them is minimized. This error measure is defined as

$$e^2 = E\left\{(f - \hat{f})^2\right\}$$

(5-80)

where $E\{\cdot\}$ is the expected value of the argument. We assume that the noise and the image are uncorrelated, that one or the other has zero mean, and that the intensity levels in the estimate are a linear function of the levels in the degraded image. Based on these assumptions, the minimum of the error function in Eq. (5-80) is given in the frequency domain by the expression

$$\hat{F}(u,v) = \left[\frac{H^*(u,v)S_f(u,v)}{S_f(u,v)|H(u,v)|^2 + S_\eta(u,v)} \right] G(u,v)$$

$$= \left[\frac{H^*(u,v)}{|H(u,v)|^2 + S_\eta(u,v)/S_f(u,v)} \right] G(u,v) \qquad (5\text{-}81)$$

$$= \left[\frac{1}{H(u,v)} \frac{|H(u,v)|^2}{|H(u,v)|^2 + S_\eta(u,v)/S_f(u,v)} \right] G(u,v)$$

where we used the fact that the product of a complex quantity with its conjugate is equal to the magnitude of the complex quantity squared. This result is known as the *Wiener filter*, after N. Wiener [1942], who first proposed the concept in the year shown. The filter, which consists of the terms inside the brackets, also is commonly referred to as the *minimum mean square error filter* or the *least square error filter*. We include references at the end of the chapter to sources containing detailed derivations of the Wiener filter. Note from the first line in Eq. (5-81) that the Wiener filter does not have the same problem as the inverse filter with zeros in the degradation function, unless the entire denominator is zero for the same value(s) of u and v.

The terms in Eq. (5-81) are as follows:

1. $\hat{F}(u,v)$ = Fourier transform of the estimate of the undegraded image.

2. $G(u,v)$ = Fourier transform of the degraded image.

3. $H(u,v)$ = degradation transfer function (Fourier transform of the spatial degradation).

4. $H^*(u,v)$ = complex conjugate of $H(u,v)$.

5. $|H(u,v)|^2 = H^*(u,v)H(u,v)$.

6. $S_\eta(u,v) = |N(u,v)|^2$ = power spectrum of the noise [see Eq. (4-89)][†]

7. $S_f(u,v) = |F(u,v)|^2$ = power spectrum of the undegraded image.

The restored image in the spatial domain is given by the inverse Fourier transform of the frequency-domain estimate $\hat{F}(u,v)$. Note that if the noise is zero, then the noise power spectrum vanishes and the Wiener filter reduces to the inverse filter. Also, keep in mind the discussion at the end of Section 5.5 regarding the fact that all transform work in this chapter is done without padding.

[†] The term $|N(u,v)|^2$ also is referred to as the *autocorrelation* of the noise. This term comes from the correlation theorem (first line of entry 7 in Table 4.4). When the two functions are the same, correlation becomes *autocorrelation* and the right side of that entry becomes $H^*(u,v)H(u,v)$, which is equal to $|H(u,v)|^2$. Similar comments apply to $|F(u,v)|^2$, which is the autocorrelation of the image. We will discuss correlation in more detail in Chapter 12.

A number of useful measures are based on the power spectra of noise and of the undegraded image. One of the most important is the *signal-to-noise ratio*, approximated using frequency domain quantities such as

$$\text{SNR} = \sum_{u=0}^{M-1}\sum_{v=0}^{N-1}|F(u,v)|^2 \Big/ \sum_{u=0}^{M-1}\sum_{v=0}^{N-1}|N(u,v)|^2 \tag{5-82}$$

This ratio gives a measure of the level of information-bearing signal power (i.e., of the original, undegraded image) to the level of noise power. An image with low noise would tend to have a high SNR and, conversely, the same image with a higher level of noise would have a lower SNR. This ratio is an important measure used in characterizing the performance of restoration algorithms.

The *mean square error* given in statistical form in Eq. (5-80) can be approximated also in terms of a summation involving the original and restored images:

$$\text{MSE} = \frac{1}{MN}\sum_{x=0}^{M-1}\sum_{y=0}^{N-1}[f(x,y)-\hat{f}(x,y)]^2 \tag{5-83}$$

In fact, if one considers the restored image to be "signal" and the difference between this image and the original to be "noise," we can define a signal-to-noise ratio in the spatial domain as

$$\text{SNR} = \sum_{x=0}^{M-1}\sum_{y=0}^{N-1}\hat{f}(x,y)^2 \Big/ \sum_{x=0}^{M-1}\sum_{y=0}^{M-1}\left[f(x,y)-\hat{f}(x,y)\right]^2 \tag{5-84}$$

The closer f and $\hat{f}$ are, the larger this ratio will be. Sometimes the square root of the preceding two measures is used instead, in which case they are referred to as the *root-mean-square-error* and the *root-mean-square-signal-to-noise ratio*, respectively. As we have mentioned before, keep in mind that quantitative measures do not necessarily relate well to perceived image quality.

When dealing with white noise, the spectrum is a constant, which simplifies things considerably. However, the power spectrum of the undegraded image seldom is known. An approach frequently used when these quantities are not known, or cannot be estimated, is to approximate Eq. (5-81) by the expression

$$\hat{F}(u,v) = \left[\frac{1}{H(u,v)}\frac{|H(u,v)|^2}{|H(u,v)|^2 + K}\right]G(u,v) \tag{5-85}$$

where K is a specified constant that is added to all terms of $|H(u,v)|^2$. The following examples illustrate the use of this expression.

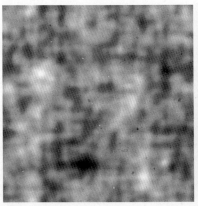  

a b c

FIGURE 5.28 Comparison of inverse and Wiener filtering. (a) Result of full inverse filtering of Fig. 5.25(b). (b) Radially limited inverse filter result. (c) Wiener filter result.

EXAMPLE 5.10: Comparison of deblurring by inverse and Wiener filtering.

Figure 5.28 illustrates the advantage of Wiener filtering over direct inverse filtering. Figure 5.28(a) is the full inverse-filtered result from Fig. 5.27(a). Similarly, Fig. 5.28(b) is the radially limited inverse filter result of Fig, 5.27(c). These images are duplicated here for convenience in making comparisons. Figure 5.28(c) shows the result obtained using Eq. (5-85) with the degradation function used in Example 5.9. The value of K was chosen interactively to yield the best visual results. The advantage of Wiener filtering over the direct inverse approach is evident in this example. By comparing Figs. 5.25(a) and 5.28(c), we see that the Wiener filter yielded a result very close in appearance to the original, undegraded image.

EXAMPLE 5.11: More deblurring examples using Wiener filtering.

The first row of Fig. 5.29 shows, from left to right, the blurred image of Fig. 5.26(b) heavily corrupted by additive Gaussian noise of zero mean and variance of 650; the result of direct inverse filtering; and the result of Wiener filtering. The Wiener filter of Eq. (5-85) was used, with $H(u, v)$ from Example 5.8, and with K chosen interactively to give the best possible visual result. As expected, direct inverse filtering produced an unusable image. Note that the noise in the inverse filtered image is so strong that it masks completely the content of the image. The Wiener filter result is by no means perfect, but it does give us a hint as to image content. The text can be read with moderate effort.

The second row of Fig. 5.29 shows the same sequence just discussed, but with the level of the noise variance reduced by one order of magnitude. This reduction had little effect on the inverse filter, but the Wiener results are considerably improved. For example, the text is much easier to read now. In the third row of Fig. 5.29, the noise variance was reduced more than five orders of magnitude from the first row. In fact, image in Fig. 5.29(g) has no visible noise. The inverse filter result is interesting in this case. The noise is still quite visible, but the text can be seen through a "curtain" of noise (see Problem 5.30). The Wiener filter result in Fig. 5.29(i) is excellent, being quite close visually to the original image in Fig.

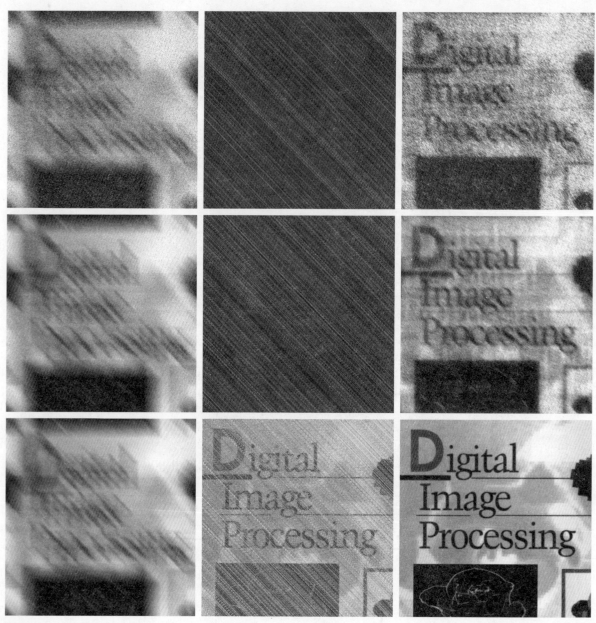

a b c
d e f
g h i

FIGURE 5.29 (a) 8-bit image corrupted by motion blur and additive noise. (b) Result of inverse filtering. (c) Result of Wiener filtering. (d)–(f) Same sequence, but with noise variance one order of magnitude less. (g)–(i) Same sequence, but noise variance reduced by five orders of magnitude from (a). Note in (h) how the deblurred image is quite visible through a "curtain" of noise.

5.26(a). In practice, the results of restoration filtering are seldom this close to the original images. This example, and Example 5.12 in the next section, were idealized slightly to focus on the effects of noise on restoration algorithms.

5.9 CONSTRAINED LEAST SQUARES FILTERING

The problem of having to know something about the degradation function H is common to all methods discussed in this chapter. However, the Wiener filter presents an additional difficulty: the power spectra of the undegraded image and noise must be known also. We showed in the previous section that in some cases it is possible to achieve acceptable results using the approximation in Eq. (5-85), but a constant value for the ratio of the power spectra is not always a suitable solution.

The method discussed in this section requires knowledge of only the mean and variance of the noise. As discussed in Section 5.2, these parameters generally can be calculated from a given degraded image, so this is an important advantage. Another difference is that the Wiener filter is based on minimizing a statistical criterion and, as such, it is optimal in an average sense. The algorithm presented in this section has the notable feature that it yields an optimal result for each image to which it is applied. Of course, it is important to keep in mind that these optimality criteria, although they are comforting from a theoretical point of view, are not related to the dynamics of visual perception. As a result, the choice of one algorithm over the other will almost always be determined by the perceived visual quality of the resulting images.

By using the definition of convolution given in Eq. (4-94), and as explained in Section 2.6, we can express Eq. (5-64) in vector-matrix form:

$$\mathbf{g} = \mathbf{H}\mathbf{f} + \boldsymbol{\eta} \tag{5-86}$$

For example, suppose that $g(x, y)$ is of size $M \times N$. We can form the first N elements of vector $\mathbf{g}$ by using the image elements in the first row of $g(x, y)$, the next N elements from the second row, and so on. The dimensionality of the resulting vector will be $MN \times 1$. These are also the dimensions of $\mathbf{f}$ and $\boldsymbol{\eta}$, as these vectors are formed in the same manner. Matrix $\mathbf{H}$ then has dimensions $MN \times MN$. Its elements are given by the elements of the convolution in Eq. (4-94).

It would be reasonable to arrive at the conclusion that the restoration problem can now be reduced to simple matrix manipulations. Unfortunately, this is not the case. For instance, suppose that we are working with images of medium size, say $M = N = 512$. Then the vectors in Eq. (5-86) would be of dimension $262,144 \times 1$ and matrix $\mathbf{H}$ would be of dimension $262,144 \times 262,144$. Manipulating vectors and matrices of such sizes is not a trivial task. The problem is complicated further by the fact that $\mathbf{H}$ is highly sensitive to noise (after the experiences we had with the effect of noise in the previous two sections, this should not be a surprise). The key advantage of formulating the restoration problem in matrix form is that it facilitates derivation of restoration algorithms.

See Gonzalez and Woods [1992] for an entire chapter devoted to the topic of algebraic techniques for image restoration.

Although we do not fully derive the method of constrained least squares that we are about to present, this method has its roots in a matrix formulation. We give references at the end of the chapter to sources where derivations are covered in detail. Central to the method is the issue of the sensitivity of **H** to noise. One way to reduce the effects of noise sensitivity, is to base optimality of restoration on a measure of smoothness, such as the second derivative of an image (our old friend, the Laplacian). To be meaningful, the restoration must be constrained by the parameters of the problems at hand. Thus, what is desired is to find the minimum of a criterion function, C, defined as

$$C = \sum_{x=0}^{M-1} \sum_{y=0}^{N-1} \left[\nabla^2 f(x, y) \right]^2 \tag{5-87}$$

subject to the constraint

$$\left\| \mathbf{g} - \mathbf{H}\hat{\mathbf{f}} \right\|^2 = \left\| \boldsymbol{\eta} \right\|^2 \tag{5-88}$$

where $\| \mathbf{a} \|^2 \triangleq \mathbf{a}^T \mathbf{a}$ is the Euclidean norm (see Section 2.6), and $\hat{\mathbf{f}}$ is the estimate of the undegraded image. The Laplacian operator ∇^2 is defined in Eq. (3-50).

The frequency domain solution to this optimization problem is given by the expression

The quantity in brackets is the transfer function of the constrained least squares filter. Note that it reduces to the inverse filter transfer function when $\gamma = 0$.

$$\hat{F}(u,v) = \left[\frac{H^*(u,v)}{\left| H(u,v) \right|^2 + \gamma \left| P(u,v) \right|^2} \right] G(u,v) \tag{5-89}$$

where γ is a parameter that must be adjusted so that the constraint in Eq. (5-88) is satisfied, and $P(u,v)$ is the Fourier transform of the function

$$p(x,y) = \begin{bmatrix} 0 & -1 & 0 \\ -1 & 4 & -1 \\ 0 & -1 & 0 \end{bmatrix} \tag{5-90}$$

We recognize this function as a Laplacian kernel from Fig. 3.45. Note that Eq. (5-89) reduces to inverse filtering if $\gamma = 0$.

Functions $P(u,v)$ and $H(u,v)$ must be of the same size. If H is of size $M \times N$, this means that $p(x,y)$ must be embedded in the center of an $M \times N$ array of zeros. In order to preserve the even symmetry of $p(x,y)$, M and N must be even integers, as explained in Examples 4.10 and 4.15. If a given degraded image from which H is obtained is not of even dimensions, then a row and/or column, as appropriate, must be deleted before computing H for use in Eq. (5-89).

EXAMPLE 5.12: Comparison of deblurring by Wiener and constrained least squares filtering.

Figure 5.30 shows the result of processing Figs. 5.29(a), (d), and (g) with constrained least squares filters, in which the values of γ were selected manually to yield the best visual results. This is the same procedure we used to generate the Wiener filter results in Fig. 5.29(c), (f), and (i). By comparing the constrained least squares and Wiener results, we see that the former yielded better results (especially in terms of noise reduction) for the high- and medium-noise cases, with both filters generating essentially

a b c

FIGURE 5.30 Results of constrained least squares filtering. Compare (a), (b), and (c) with the Wiener filtering results in Figs. 5.29(c), (f), and (i), respectively.

equal results for the low-noise case. This is not surprising because parameter γ in Eq. (5-89) is a true scalar, whereas the value of K in Eq. (5-85) is a scalar approximation to the ratio of two unknown frequency domain *functions* of size $M \times N$. Thus, it stands to reason that a result based on manually selecting γ would be a more accurate estimate of the undegraded image. As in Example 5.11, the results in this example are better than one normally finds in practice. Our focus here was on the effects of noise blurring on restoration. As noted earlier, you will encounter situations in which the restoration solutions are not quite as close to the original images as we have shown in these two examples.

As discussed in the preceding example, it is possible to adjust the parameter γ interactively until acceptable results are achieved. However, if we are interested in mathematical optimality, then this parameter must be adjusted so that the constraint in Eq. (5-88) is satisfied. A procedure for computing γ by iteration is as follows.

Define a "residual" vector $\mathbf{r}$ as

$$\mathbf{r} = \mathbf{g} - \mathbf{H}\hat{\mathbf{f}} \qquad (5\text{-}91)$$

From Eq. (5-89), we see that $\hat{F}(u,v)$ (and by implication $\hat{\mathbf{f}}$) is a function of γ. Then it follows that $\mathbf{r}$ also is a function of this parameter. It can be shown (Hunt [1973], Gonzalez and Woods [1992]) that

$$\phi(\gamma) = \mathbf{r}^T \mathbf{r}$$
$$= \|\mathbf{r}\|^2 \qquad (5\text{-}92)$$

is a monotonically increasing function of γ. What we want to do is adjust γ so that

$$\|\mathbf{r}\|^2 = \|\boldsymbol{\eta}\|^2 \pm \alpha \qquad (5\text{-}93)$$

where α is an accuracy factor. In view of Eq. (5-91), if $\|\mathbf{r}\|^2 = \|\boldsymbol{\eta}\|^2$, the constraint in Eq. (5-88) will be strictly satisfied.

Because $\phi(\gamma)$ is monotonic, finding the desired value of γ is not difficult. One approach is to

1. Specify an initial value of γ.

2. Compute $\|\mathbf{r}\|^2$.

3. Stop if Eq. (5-93) is satisfied; otherwise return to Step 2 after increasing γ if $\|\mathbf{r}\|^2 < (\|\boldsymbol{\eta}\|^2 - \alpha)$ or decreasing γ if $\|\mathbf{r}\|^2 > (\|\boldsymbol{\eta}\|^2 + \alpha)$. Use the new value of γ in Eq. (5-89) to recompute the optimum estimate $\hat{F}(u,v)$.

Other procedures, such as a Newton–Raphson algorithm, can be used to improve the speed of convergence.

In order to use this algorithm, we need the quantities $\|\mathbf{r}\|^2$ and $\|\boldsymbol{\eta}\|^2$. To compute $\|\mathbf{r}\|^2$, we note from Eq. (5-91) that

$$R(u,v) = G(u,v) - H(u,v)F(u,v) \tag{5-94}$$

from which we obtain $r(x,y)$ by computing the inverse Fourier transform of $R(u,v)$. Then, from the definition of the Euclidean norm, it follows that

$$\|\mathbf{r}\|^2 = \mathbf{r}^T\mathbf{r} = \sum_{x=0}^{M-1}\sum_{y=0}^{N-1} r^2(x,y) \tag{5-95}$$

Computation of $\|\boldsymbol{\eta}\|^2$ leads to an interesting result. First, consider the variance of the noise over the entire image, which we estimate from the samples using the expression

$$\sigma_\eta^2 = \frac{1}{MN}\sum_{x=0}^{M-1}\sum_{y=0}^{N-1}\left[\eta(x,y) - \bar{\eta}\right]^2 \tag{5-96}$$

where

$$\bar{\eta} = \frac{1}{MN}\sum_{x=0}^{M-1}\sum_{y=0}^{N-1}\eta(x,y) \tag{5-97}$$

is the sample mean. With reference to the *form* of Eq. (5-95), we note that the double summation in Eq. (5-96) is proportional to $\|\boldsymbol{\eta}\|^2$. This leads to the expression

$$\|\boldsymbol{\eta}\|^2 = MN\left[\sigma_\eta^2 + \bar{\eta}^2\right] \tag{5-98}$$

This is a most useful result. It tells us that we can estimate the unknown quantity $\|\boldsymbol{\eta}\|^2$ by having knowledge of only the mean and variance of the noise. These quantities are not difficult to estimate (see Section 5.2), assuming that the noise and image

a b

FIGURE 5.31
(a) Iteratively
determined
constrained
least squares
restoration of
Fig. 5.25(b), using
correct noise
parameters. (b)
Result obtained
with wrong noise
parameters.

intensity values are not correlated. This is an assumption of all the methods discussed in this chapter.

EXAMPLE 5.13: Iterative estimation of the optimum constrained least squares filter.

Figure 5.31(a) shows the result obtained using the algorithm just described to estimate the optimum filter for restoring Fig. 5.25(b). The initial value used for γ was 10^{-5}, the correction factor for adjusting γ was 10^{-6}, and the value for α was 0.25. The noise parameters specified were the same used to generate Fig. 5.25(a): a noise variance of 10^{-5}, and zero mean. The restored result is comparable to Fig. 5.28(c), which was obtained by Wiener filtering with K manually specified for best visual results. Figure 5.31(b) shows what can happen if the wrong estimate of noise parameters are used. In this case, the noise variance specified was 10^{-2} and the mean was left at 0. The result in this case is considerably more blurred.

5.10 GEOMETRIC MEAN FILTER

It is possible to generalize slightly the Wiener filter discussed in Section 5.8. The generalization is in the form of the so-called *geometric mean filter*:

$$\hat{F}(u,v) = \left[\frac{H^*(u,v)}{|H(u,v)|^2} \right]^{\alpha} \left[\frac{H^*(u,v)}{|H(u,v)|^2 + \beta \left[\dfrac{S_{\eta}(u,v)}{S_f(u,v)} \right]} \right]^{1-\alpha} G(u,v) \qquad (5\text{-}99)$$

where α and β are nonnegative, real constants. The geometric mean filter transfer function consists of the two expressions in brackets raised to the powers α and $1 - \alpha$, respectively.

When $\alpha = 1$ the geometric mean filter reduces to the inverse filter. With $\alpha = 0$ the filter becomes the so-called *parametric Wiener filter*, which reduces to the "standard"

Wiener filter when $\beta = 1$. If $\alpha = 1/2$, the filter becomes a product of the two quantities raised to the same power, which is the definition of the geometric mean, thus giving the filter its name. With $\beta = 1$, as α increases above $1/2$, the filter performance will tend more toward the inverse filter. Similarly, when α decreases below $1/2$, the filter will behave more like a Wiener filter. When $\alpha = 1/2$ and $\beta = 1$ the filter is commonly referred to as a *spectrum equalization filter*. Equation (5-99) is useful when implementing restoration filters because it represents a family of filters combined into a single expression.

5.11 IMAGE RECONSTRUCTION FROM PROJECTIONS ▮▮▮▮▮▮

In the previous sections of this chapter we discussed techniques for restoring degraded images. In this section, we examine the problem of *reconstructing* an image from a series of projections, with a focus on X-ray *computed tomography* (CT). This is the earliest and still the most-widely used type of CT, and is currently one of the principal applications of digital image processing in medicine.

As noted in Chapter 1, the term *computerized axial tomography* (CAT) is used interchangeably to denote CT.

INTRODUCTION

The reconstruction problem is simple in principle, and can be explained qualitatively in a straightforward, intuitive manner, without using equations (we will deal with the math later in this section. To begin, consider Fig. 5.32(a), which consists of a single object on a uniform background. In order to bring physical meaning to the following explanation, suppose that this image is a *cross-section* of a 3-D region of a human body. Assume also that the background in the image represents soft, uniform tissue, while the round object is a tumor, also uniform, but with higher X-ray absorption characteristics.

Suppose next that we pass a thin, flat beam of X-rays from left to right (through the plane of the image), as Fig. 5.32(b) shows, and assume that the energy of the beam is absorbed more by the object than by the background, as typically is the case. Using a strip of X-ray absorption detectors on the other side of the region will yield the signal (*absorption profile*) shown, whose amplitude (intensity) is proportional to absorption.[†] We may view any point in the signal as the sum of the absorption values across the single ray in the beam corresponding spatially to that point (such a sum often is referred to as a *raysum*). At this juncture, all the information we have about the object is this 1-D absorption signal.

We have no way of determining from a single projection whether we are dealing with a single object, or a multitude of objects along the path of the beam, but we begin the reconstruction by creating an *image* based only on this information. The approach is to project the 1-D signal *back* in the opposite direction from which the beam came, as Fig. 5.32(c) shows. The process of backprojecting a 1-D signal across a 2-D area sometimes is referred to as *smearing* the projection back across the area. In

---

[†] A treatment of the physics of X-ray sources and detectors is beyond the scope of our discussion, which focuses on the image processing aspects of CT. See Prince and Links [2006] for an excellent introduction to the physics of X-ray image formation.

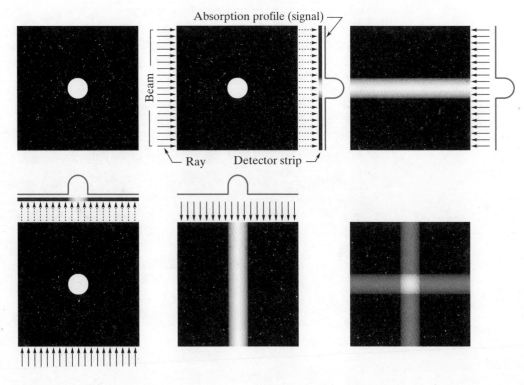

a b c
d e f

FIGURE 5.32
(a) Flat region
with a single
object. (b) Parallel
beam, detector
strip, and profile of
sensed 1-D
absorption signal.
(c) Result of back-
projecting the
absorption profile.
(d) Beam and
detectors rotated
by 90°.
(e) Backprojection.
(f) The sum of (c)
and (e), inten-
sity-scaled. The
intensity where the
backprojections
intersect is twice
the intensity of the
individual back-
projections.

terms of digital images, this means duplicating the same 1-D signal across the image, perpendicularly to the direction of the beam. For example, Fig. 5.32(c) was created by duplicating the 1-D signal in all columns of the reconstructed image. For obvious reasons, the approach just described is called *backprojection*.

Next, suppose that we rotate the position of the source-detector pair by 90°, as in Fig. 5.32(d). Repeating the procedure explained in the previous paragraph yields a backprojection image in the vertical direction, as Fig. 5.32(e) shows. We continue the reconstruction by *adding* this result to the previous backprojection, resulting in Fig. 5.32(f). Now, we begin to suspect that the object of interest is contained in the square shown, whose amplitude is twice the amplitude of the individual backprojections because the signals were added. We should be able to learn more about the shape of the object in question by taking more views in the manner just described, as Fig. 5.33 shows. As the number of projections increases, the amplitude strength of non-intersecting backprojections decreases relative to the strength of regions in which multiple backprojections intersect. The net effect is that brighter regions will dominate the result, and backprojections with few or no intersections will fade into the background as the image is scaled for display.

Figure 5.33(f), which was formed from 32 backprojections, illustrates this concept. Note, however, that while this reconstructed image is a reasonably good approximation to the shape of the original object, the image is blurred by a "halo" effect, the formation of which can be seen in progressive stages in Fig. 5.33. For example, the halo in Fig. 5.33(e) appears as a "star" whose intensity is lower than that of the

FIGURE 5.33
(a) Same as
Fig. 5.32(a).
(b)-(e) Recon-
struction using 1,
2, 3, and 4 back-
projections 45°
apart.
(f) Reconstruction
with 32 backpro-
jections 5.625°
apart (note the
blurring).

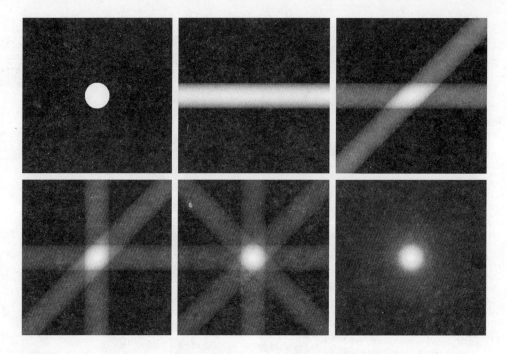

object, but higher than the background. As the number of views increases, the shape of the halo becomes circular, as in Fig. 5.33(f). Blurring in CT reconstruction is an important issue, whose solution is addressed later in this section. Finally, we conclude from the discussion of Figs. 5.32 and 5.33 that backprojections 180° apart are mirror images of each other, so we have to consider only angle increments halfway around a circle in order to generate all the backprojections required for reconstruction.

EXAMPLE 5.14: Backprojections of a planar region containing two objects.

Figure 5.34 illustrates reconstruction using backprojections on a region that contains two objects with different absorption properties (the larger object has higher absorption). Figure 5.34(b) shows the result of using one backprojection. We note three principal features in this figure, from bottom to top: a thin horizontal gray band corresponding to the unoccluded portion of the small object, a brighter (more absorption) band above it corresponding to the area shared by both objects, and an upper band corre- sponding to the rest of the elliptical object. Figures 5.34(c) and (d) show reconstruction using two projec- tions 90° apart and four projections 45° apart, respectively. The explanation of these figures is similar to the discussion of Figs. 5.33(c) through (e). Figures 5.34(e) and (f) show more accurate reconstructions using 32 and 64 backprojections, respectively. The last two results are quite close visually, and they both show the blurring problem mentioned earlier.

PRINCIPLES OF X-RAY COMPUTED TOMOGRAPHY (CT)

As with the Fourier transform discussed in the last chapter, the basic mathematical concepts required for CT were in place many years before the availability of digital

a b c
d e f

FIGURE 5.34
(a) Two objects with different absorption characteristics.
(b)–(d) Reconstruction using 1, 2, and 4 backprojections, 45° apart.
(e) Reconstruction with 32 backprojections, 5.625° apart.
(f) Reconstruction with 64 backprojections, 2.8125° apart.

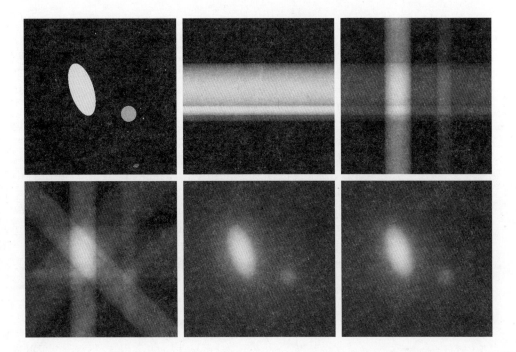

computers made them practical. The theoretical foundation of CT dates back to Johann Radon, a mathematician from Vienna who derived a method in 1917 for projecting a 2-D object along parallel rays, as part of his work on line integrals (the method now is referred to as the *Radon transform*, a topic we will discuss shortly). Forty-five years later, Allan M. Cormack, a physicist at Tufts University, partially "rediscovered" these concepts and applied them to CT. Cormack published his initial findings in 1963 and 1964 and showed how his results could be used to reconstruct cross-sectional images of the body from X-ray images taken in different angular directions. He gave the mathematical formulae needed for the reconstruction and built a CT prototype to show the practicality of his ideas. Working independently, electrical engineer Godfrey N. Hounsfield and his colleagues at EMI in London formulated a similar solution and built the first medical CT machine. Cormack and Hounsfield shared the 1979 Nobel Prize in Medicine for their contributions to medical uses of tomography.

The goal of X-ray computed tomography is to obtain a 3-D representation of the internal structure of an object by X-raying the object from many different directions. Imagine a traditional chest X-ray, obtained by placing the subject against an X-ray sensitive plate and "illuminating" the individual with an X-ray beam in the form of a cone. The X-ray plate would produce an image whose intensity at a point would be proportional to the X-ray energy impinging on that point after it passed through the subject. This image is the 2-D equivalent of the projections we discussed in the previous section. We could back-project this entire image and create a 3-D volume. Repeating this process through many angles and adding the backprojections would result in 3-D rendition of the structure of the chest cavity. Computed tomography attempts to get that same information (or localized parts of it) by generating slices through the body. A 3-D representation then can be obtained by stacking the slices. A CT implementation is much more economical because the number of detectors required to obtain a high resolution slice is much smaller than the number of detectors needed to generate a complete 2-D projection of the same resolution. Computational burden and X-ray dosages are similarly reduced, making the 1-D projection CT a more practical approach.

First-generation (G1) CT scanners employ a "pencil" X-ray beam and a single detector, as Fig. 5.35(a) shows. For a given angle of rotation, the source/detector pair is translated incrementally along the linear direction shown. A projection (like the ones in Fig. 5.32), is generated by measuring the output of the detector at each increment of translation. After a complete linear translation, the source/detector assembly is rotated and the procedure is repeated to generate another projection at a different angle. The procedure is repeated for all desired angles in the range [0°, 180°] to generate a complete set of projections images, from which one final cross-sectional image (a slice through the 3-D object) is obtained, as explained in the

a b
c d

FIGURE 5.35
Four generations of CT scanners. The dotted arrow lines indicate incremental linear motion. The dotted arrow arcs indicate incremental rotation. The cross-mark on the subject's head indicates linear motion perpendicular to the plane of the paper. The double arrows in (a) and (b) indicate that the source/detector unit is translated and then brought back into its original position.

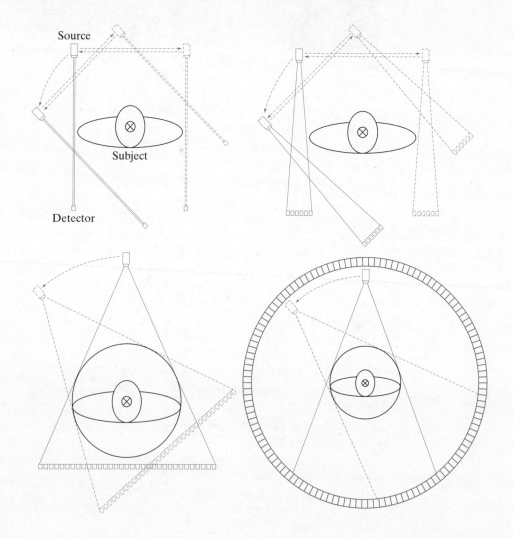

previous section. A set of cross sectional images (slices) is generated by moving the subject incrementally (after each complete scan) past the source/detector plane (the cross-mark on the head of the subject indicates motion in a direction perpendicular to the plane of the source/detector pair). Stacking these images computationally produces a 3-D volume of a section of the body. G1 scanners are no longer manu-factured for medical imaging, but, because they produce a parallel-ray beam (as in Fig. 5.32), their geometry is the one used predominantly for introducing the funda-mentals of CT imaging, and serves as the starting point for deriving the equations necessary to implement image reconstruction from projections.

Second-generation (G2) CT scanners [Fig. 5.35(b)] operate on the same principle as G1 scanners, but the beam used is in the shape of a fan. This allows the use of mul-tiple detectors, thus requiring fewer translations of the source/detector pair.

Third-generation (G3) scanners are a significant improvement over the earlier two generations of CT geometries. As Fig. 5.35(c) shows, G3 scanners employ a bank of detectors long enough (on the order of 1000 individual detectors) to cover the entire field of view of a wider beam. Consequently, each increment of angle produces an entire projection, eliminating the need to translate the source/detector pair, as in G1 and G2 scanners.

Fourth-generation (G4) scanners go a step further. By employing a circular ring of detectors (on the order of 5000 individual detectors), only the source has to rotate. The key advantage of G3 and G4 scanners is speed; key disadvantages are cost and greater X-ray scatter. The latter implies higher X-ray doses than G1 and G2 scanners to achieve comparable signal-to-noise characteristics.

Newer scanning modalities are beginning to be adopted. For example, *fifth-gener-ation (G5) CT scanners*, also known as *electron beam computed tomography (EBCT) scanners*, eliminate all mechanical motion by employing electron beams controlled electromagnetically. By striking tungsten anodes that encircle the patient, these beams generate X-rays that are then shaped into a fan beam that passes through the patient and excites a ring of detectors, as in G4 scanners.

The conventional manner in which CT images are obtained is to keep the patient stationary during the scanning time required to generate one image. Scanning is then halted while the position of the patient is incremented in the direction perpendicu-lar to the imaging plane, using a motorized table. The next image is then obtained and the procedure is repeated for the number of increments required to cover a specified section of the body. Although an image may be obtained in less than one second, there are procedures (e.g., abdominal and chest scans) that require patient to hold their breath during image acquisition. Completing these procedures for, say, 30 images, may require several minutes. An approach for which use is increasing is *helical CT*, sometimes referred to as *sixth-generation (G6) CT*. In this approach, a G3 or G4 scanner is configured using so-called *slip rings* that eliminate the need for electrical and signal cabling between the source/detectors and the processing unit. The source/detector pair then rotates continuously through 360° while the patient is moved at a constant speed along the axis perpendicular to the scan. The result is a continuous helical volume of data that is then processed to obtain individual slice images.

Seventh-generation (G7) scanners (also called *multislice CT scanners*) are emerging in which "thick" fan beams are used in conjunction with parallel banks of detectors to collect volumetric CT data simultaneously. That is, 3-D cross-sectional "slabs," rather than single cross-sectional images are generated per X-ray burst. In addition to a significant increase in detail, this approach has the advantage that it utilizes X-ray tubes more economically, thus reducing cost and potentially reducing dosage.

In the following discussion, we develop the mathematical tools necessary for formulating image projection and reconstruction algorithms. Our focus is on the image-processing fundamentals that underpin all the CT approaches just discussed. Information regarding the mechanical and source/detector characteristics of CT systems is provided in the references cited at the end of the chapter.

PROJECTIONS AND THE RADON TRANSFORM

Next, we develop in detail the mathematics needed for image reconstruction in the context of X-ray computed tomography. The same basic principles apply to other CT imaging modalities, such as SPECT (single photon emission tomography), PET (positron emission tomography), MRI (magnetic resonance imaging), and some modalities of ultrasound imaging.

Throughout this section, we follow CT convention and place the origin of the xy-plane in the center, instead of at our customary top left corner (see Section 2.4). Both are right-handed coordinate systems, the only difference being that our image coordinate system has no negative axes. We can account for the difference with a simple translation of the origin, so both representations are interchangeable.

A straight line in Cartesian coordinates can be described either by its *slope-intercept* form, $y = ax + b$, or, as in Fig. 5.36, by its *normal* representation:

$$x\cos\theta + y\sin\theta = \rho \tag{5-100}$$

The projection of a *parallel-ray beam* can be modeled by a set of such lines, as Fig. 5.37 shows. An arbitrary *point* at coordinates (ρ_j, θ_k) in the projection profile is given by the raysum along the line $x\cos\theta_k + y\sin\theta_k = \rho_j$. Working with continuous quantities for the moment, the *raysum* is a line integral, given by

$$g(\rho_j, \theta_k) = \int_{-\infty}^{\infty}\int_{-\infty}^{\infty} f(x,y)\delta(x\cos\theta_k + y\sin\theta_k - \rho_j)\,dx\,dy \tag{5-101}$$

where we used the properties of the impulse, δ, discussed in Section 4.5. In other words, the right side of Eq. (5-101) is zero unless the argument of δ is zero, indicating

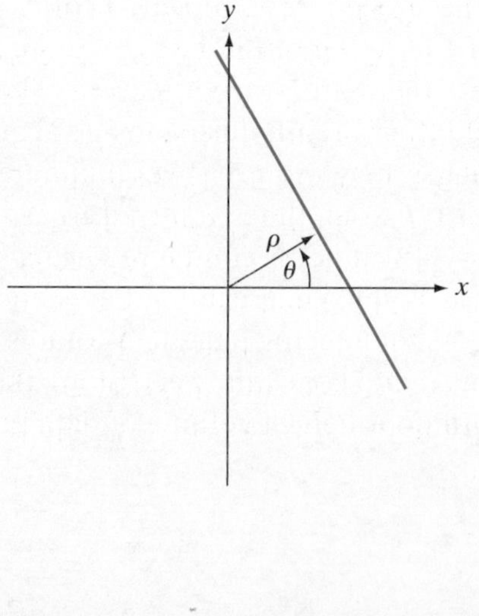

FIGURE 5.36 Normal representation of a line.

FIGURE 5.37
Geometry of a
parallel-ray beam.

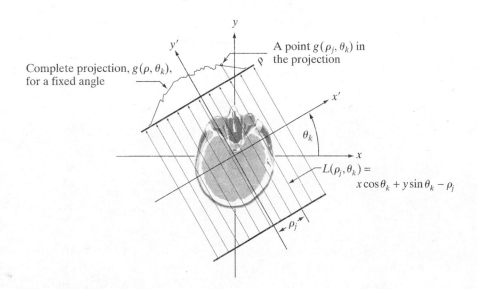

that the integral is computed only along the line $x\cos\theta_k + y\sin\theta_k = \rho_j$. If we consider all values of ρ and θ, the preceding equation generalizes to

$$g(\rho, \theta) = \int_{-\infty}^{\infty} \int_{-\infty}^{\infty} f(x,y)\delta(x\cos\theta + y\sin\theta - \rho)\,dx\,dy \qquad (5\text{-}102)$$

This equation, which gives the projection (line integral) of $f(x,y)$ along an arbitrary line in the xy-plane, is the *Radon transform* mentioned earlier. The notation $\mathfrak{R}\{f(x,y)\}$ or $\mathfrak{R}\{f\}$ is used sometimes in place of $g(\rho, \theta)$ in Eq. (5-102) to denote the Radon transform of $f(x,y)$, but the type of notation used in Eq. (5-102) is more customary. As will become evident in the discussion that follows, the Radon transform is the cornerstone of reconstruction from projections, with computed tomography being its principal application in the field of image processing.

In the discrete case,[†] the Radon transform of Eq. (5-102) becomes

$$g(\rho, \theta) = \sum_{x=0}^{M-1} \sum_{y=0}^{N-1} f(x,y)\delta(x\cos\theta + y\sin\theta - \rho) \qquad (5\text{-}103)$$

where x, y, and are now discrete variables, and M and N are the dimensions of a rectangular area over which the transform is applied. If we fix θ and allow ρ to vary, we see that (5-103) simply sums the pixels of $f(x,y)$ along the line defined by the specified values of these two parameters. Incrementing through all values of ρ

[†] In Chapter 4, we exercised great care in denoting continuous image coordinates by (t, z) and discrete coordinates by (x, y). At that time, the distinction was important because we were developing basic concepts to take us from continuous to sampled quantities. In the present discussion, we go back and forth so many times between continuous and discrete coordinates that adhering to this convention is likely to generate unnecessary confusion. For this reason, and also to follow the published literature in this field (e.g., see Prince and Links [2006]), we let the context determine whether coordinates (x, y) are continuous or discrete. When they are continuous, you will see integrals; otherwise, you will see summations.

required to span the $M \times N$ area (with θ fixed) yields *one* projection. Changing θ and repeating this procedure yields another projection, and so forth. This is precisely how the projections in Figs. 5.32-5.34 were generated.

EXAMPLE 5.15: Using the Radon transform to obtain the projection of a circular region.

Before proceeding, we illustrate how to use the Radon transform to obtain an analytical expression for the projection of the circular object in Fig. 5.38(a):

$$f(x,y) = \begin{cases} A & x^2 + y^2 \leq r^2 \\ 0 & \text{otherwise} \end{cases}$$

where A is a constant and r is the radius of the object. We assume that the circle is centered on the origin of the xy-plane. Because the object is circularly symmetric, its projections are the same for all angles, so all we have to do is obtain the projection for $\theta = 0°$. Equation (5-102) then becomes

$$g(\rho, \theta) = \int_{-\infty}^{\infty} \int_{-\infty}^{\infty} f(x,y)\delta(x - \rho)\,dx\,dy$$

$$= \int_{-\infty}^{\infty} f(\rho, y)\,dy$$

where the second expression follows from Eq. (4-13). As noted earlier, this is a line integral (along the line $L(\rho, 0)$ in this case). Also, note that $g(\rho, \theta) = 0$ when $|\rho| > r$. When $|\rho| \leq r$ the integral is evaluated from $y = -(r^2 - \rho^2)^{1/2}$ to $y = (r^2 - \rho^2)^{1/2}$. Therefore,

a
b

FIGURE 5.38
(a) A disk and,
(b) a plot of its Radon transform, derived analytically. Here we were able to plot the transform because it depends only on one variable. When g depends on both ρ and θ, the Radon transform becomes an image whose axes are ρ and θ, and the intensity of a pixel is proportional to the value of g at the location of that pixel.

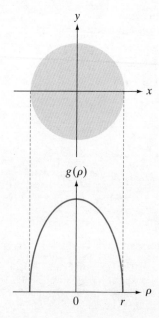

$$g(\rho, \theta) = \int_{-\sqrt{r^2-\rho^2}}^{\sqrt{r^2-\rho^2}} f(\rho, y)\, dy$$

$$= \int_{-\sqrt{r^2-\rho^2}}^{\sqrt{r^2-\rho^2}} A\, dy$$

Carrying out the integration yields

$$g(\rho, \theta) = g(\rho) = \begin{cases} 2A\sqrt{r^2 - \rho^2} & |\rho| \leq r \\ 0 & \text{otherwise} \end{cases}$$

where we used the fact that $g(\rho, \theta) = 0$ when $|\rho| > r$. Figure 5.38(b) shows a plot of this result. Note that $g(\rho, \theta) = g(\rho)$; that is, g is independent of θ because the object is symmetric about the origin.

To generate arrays with rows of the same size, the minimum dimension of the ρ-axis in sinograms corresponds to the largest dimension encountered during projection. For example, the minimum size of a sinogram of a square of size $M \times M$ obtained using increments of $1°$ is $180 \times Q$ where Q is the smallest integer greater than $\sqrt{2}\, M$.

When the Radon transform, $g(\rho, \theta)$, is displayed as an image with ρ and θ as rectilinear coordinates, the result is called a *sinogram*, similar in concept to displaying the Fourier spectrum. Like the Fourier transform, a sinogram contains the data necessary to reconstruct $f(x, y)$. Unlike the Fourier transform, however, $g(\rho, \theta)$ is always a real function. As is the case with displays of the Fourier spectrum, sinograms can be readily interpreted for simple regions, but become increasingly difficult to "read" as the region being projected becomes more complex. For example, Fig. 5.39(b) is the sinogram of the rectangle on the left. The vertical and horizontal axes correspond to θ and ρ, respectively. Thus, the bottom row is the projection of the rectangle in the horizontal direction (i.e., $\theta = 0°$), and the middle row is the projection in the vertical direction (($\theta = 90°$). The fact that the nonzero portion of the bottom row is smaller than the nonzero portion of the middle row tells us that the object is narrower in the horizontal direction. The fact that the sinogram is symmetric in both directions about the center of the image tells us that we are dealing with an object that is symmetric and parallel to the x and y axes. Finally, the sinogram is smooth, indicating that the object has a uniform intensity. Other than these types of general observations, we cannot say much more about this sinogram.

Figure 5.39(c) is an image of the *Shepp-Logan phantom* (Shepp and Logan [1974]), a widely used synthetic image designed to simulate the absorption of major areas of the brain, including small tumors. The sinogram of this image is considerably more difficult to interpret, as Fig. 5.39(d) shows. We still can infer some symmetry properties, but that is about all we can say. Visual analyses of sinograms are of limited practical use, but they can be helpful in tasks such as algorithm development.

BACKPROJECTIONS

To obtain a formal expression for a backprojected image from the Radon transform, let us begin with a *single* point, $g(\rho_j, \theta_k)$, of the complete projection, $g(\rho, \theta_k)$, for a fixed value of rotation, θ_k (see Fig. 5.37). Forming part of an image by backprojecting this single point is nothing more than copying the line $L(\rho_j, \theta_k)$ onto the image,

a b
c d

FIGURE 5.39
Two images and their sinograms (Radon transforms). Each row of a sinogram is a projection along the corresponding angle on the vertical axis. (Note that the horizontal axis of the sinograms are values of ρ.) Image (c) is called the *Shepp-Logan phantom*. In its original form, the contrast of the phantom is quite low. It is shown enhanced here to facilitate viewing.

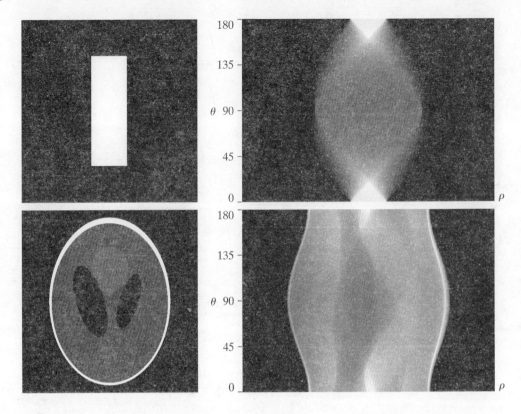

where the value (intensity) of each point in that line is $g(\rho_j, \theta_k)$. Repeating this process of all values of ρ_j in the projected signal (but keeping the value of θ fixed at θ_k) results in the following expression:

$$f_{\theta_k}(x,y) = g(\rho, \theta_k)$$
$$= g(x\cos\theta_k + y\sin\theta_k, \theta_k)$$

for the image due to backprojecting the projection obtained with a fixed angle, θ_k, as in Fig. 5.32(b). This equation holds for an arbitrary value of θ_k, so we may write in general that the image formed from a *single* backprojection obtained at an angle θ is given by

$$f_\theta(x,y) = g(x\cos\theta + y\sin\theta, \theta) \tag{5-104}$$

We form the final image by integrating over all the backprojected images:

$$f(x,y) = \int_0^\pi f_\theta(x,y)\,d\theta \tag{5-105}$$

In the discrete case, the integral becomes a sum of all the backprojected images:

$$f(x, y) = \sum_{\theta=0}^{\pi} f_\theta(x, y) \qquad (5\text{-}106)$$

where, x, y, and θ are now discrete quantities. As mentioned earlier, the projections at 0° and 180° are mirror images of each other, so the summations are carried out to the last angle increment before 180°. For example, if 0.5° increments are being used, the summation is from 0° to 179.5° in half-degree increments. A backprojected image formed in the manner just described sometimes is referred to as a *laminogram*. It is understood implicitly that a laminogram is only an approximation to the image from which the projections were generated, a fact that is illustrated in the following example.

EXAMPLE 5.16: Obtaining backprojected images from sinograms.

Equation (5-106) was used to generate the backprojected images in Figs. 5.32 through 5.34, from projections obtained with Eq. (5-103). Similarly, these equations were used to generate Figs. 5.40(a) and (b), which show the backprojected images corresponding to the sinograms in Figs. 5.39(b) and (d), respectively. As with the earlier figures, we note a significant amount of blurring, so it is obvious that a straight use of Eqs. (5-103) and (5-106) will not yield acceptable results. Early, experimental CT systems were based on these equations. However, as you will see later in our discussion, significant improvements in reconstruction are possible by reformulating the backprojection approach.

THE FOURIER-SLICE THEOREM

In this section, we derive a fundamental equation that establishes a relationship between the 1-D Fourier transform of a projection and the 2-D Fourier transform of the region from which the projection was obtained. This relationship is the basis for reconstruction methods capable of dealing with the blurring problems we have encountered thus far.

The 1-D Fourier transform of a projection with respect to ρ is

This equation has the same form as Eq. (4-20).

$$G(\omega, \theta) = \int_{-\infty}^{\infty} g(\rho, \theta) e^{-j2\pi\omega\rho} \, d\rho \qquad (5\text{-}107)$$

a b

FIGURE 5.40
Backprojections of the sinograms in Fig. 5.39.

where ω is the frequency variable, and it is understood that this expression is based on a fixed value of θ. Substituting Eq. (5-102) for $g(\rho, \theta)$ we obtain

$$
\begin{aligned}
G(\omega, \theta) &= \int_{-\infty}^{\infty} \int_{-\infty}^{\infty} \int_{-\infty}^{\infty} f(x, y)\delta(x\cos\theta + y\sin\theta - \rho)e^{-j2\pi\omega\rho} \, dx \, dy \, d\rho \\
&= \int_{-\infty}^{\infty} \int_{-\infty}^{\infty} f(x, y)\left[\int_{-\infty}^{\infty} \delta(x\cos\theta + y\sin\theta - \rho)e^{-j2\pi\omega\rho} \, d\rho \right] dx \, dy \qquad (5\text{-}108) \\
&= \int_{-\infty}^{\infty} \int_{-\infty}^{\infty} f(x, y)e^{-j2\pi\omega(x\cos\theta + y\sin\theta)} \, dx \, dy
\end{aligned}
$$

where the last step follows from the sifting property of the impulse discussed in Chapter 4. By letting $u = \omega\cos\theta$ and $v = \omega\sin\theta$, we can write Eq. (5-108) as

$$
G(\omega, \theta) = \left[\int_{-\infty}^{\infty} \int_{-\infty}^{\infty} f(x, y)e^{-j2\pi(ux + vy)} \, dx \, dy \right]_{u=\omega\cos\theta; \, v=\omega\sin\theta} \qquad (5\text{-}109)
$$

We recognize this expression as the 2-D Fourier transform of $f(x, y)$ [see Eq. (4-59)] evaluated at the values of u and v indicated. That is,

$$
\begin{aligned}
G(\omega, \theta) &= \left[F(u, v) \right]_{u=\omega\cos\theta; \, v=\omega\sin\theta} \\
&= F(\omega\cos\theta, \omega\sin\theta)
\end{aligned} \qquad (5\text{-}110)
$$

where, as usual, $F(u, v)$ denotes the 2-D Fourier transform of $f(x, y)$.

The result in Eq. (5-110) is known as the *Fourier-slice theorem* (or the *projection-slice theorem*). It states that the Fourier transform of a projection is a *slice* of the 2-D Fourier transform of the region from which the projection was obtained. The reason for this terminology can be explained with the aid of Fig. 5.41. As this figure shows, the 1-D Fourier transform of an arbitrary projection is obtained by extracting the values of $F(u, v)$ along a line oriented at the same angle as the angle used in generating the projection.

In principle, we could obtain $f(x, y)$ simply by obtaining the inverse Fourier transform of $F(u, v)$. However, this is expensive computationally, as it involves obtained the inverse of a 2-D transform. The approach discussed in the following section is much more efficient.

RECONSTRUCTION USING PARALLEL-BEAM FILTERED BACKPROJECTIONS

As we saw in Figs. 5.33, 5.34, and 5.40, obtaining backprojections directly yields unacceptably blurred results. Fortunately, there is a straightforward solution to this problem based simply on filtering the projections before computing the backprojections. From Eq. (4-60), the 2-D inverse Fourier transform of $F(u, v)$ is

FIGURE 5.41
Illustration of the Fourier-slice theorem. The 1-D Fourier transform of a projection is a slice of the 2-D Fourier transform of the region from which the projection was obtained. Note the correspondence of the angle θ in the two figures.

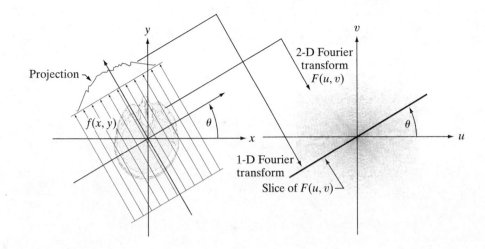

The relationship $dudv = \omega d\omega d\theta$ is from basic integral calculus, where the Jacobian is used as the basis for a change of variables.

$$f(x,y) = \int_{-\infty}^{\infty} \int_{-\infty}^{\infty} F(u,v)e^{j2\pi(ux + vy)}du\,dv \tag{5-111}$$

If, as in Eqs. (5-109) and (5-110), we let $u = \omega\cos\theta$ and $v = \omega\sin\theta$, then the differentials become $dudv = \omega d\omega d\theta$, and we can express Eq. (5-111) in polar coordinates:

$$f(x,y) = \int_{0}^{2\pi} \int_{0}^{\infty} F(\omega\cos\theta, \omega\sin\theta)e^{j2\pi\omega(x\cos\theta + y\sin\theta)}\omega d\omega\,d\theta \tag{5-112}$$

Then, using the Fourier slice theorem,

$$f(x,y) = \int_{0}^{2\pi} \int_{0}^{\infty} G(\omega, \theta)e^{j2\pi\omega(x\cos\theta + y\sin\theta)}\omega d\omega\,d\theta \tag{5-113}$$

By splitting this integral into two expressions, one for θ in the range $0°$ to $180°$ and the other in the range $180°$ to $360°$, and using the fact that $G(\omega, \theta + 180°) = G(-\omega, \theta)$ (see Problem 5.46), we can express Eq. (5-113) as

$$f(x,y) = \int_{0}^{\pi} \int_{-\infty}^{\infty} |\omega|G(\omega, \theta)e^{j2\pi\omega(x\cos\theta + y\sin\theta)}d\omega\,d\theta \tag{5-114}$$

The term $x\cos\theta + y\sin\theta$ is a constant with respect to ω, and we recognize it as ρ from Eq. (5-100). Therefore, we can write Eq. (5-114) as

$$f(x,y) = \int_{0}^{\pi}\left[\int_{-\infty}^{\infty} |\omega|G(\omega,\theta)e^{j2\pi\omega\rho}d\omega\right]_{\rho=x\cos\theta + y\sin\theta} d\theta \tag{5-115}$$

The inner expression is in the form of an *inverse* 1-D Fourier transform [see Eq. (4-21)], with the added term $|\omega|$ which, based on the discussion in Section 4.7, we recognize as a 1-D filter transfer function. Observe that $|\omega|$ is a *ramp* function [see Fig. 5.42(a)]. This function is not integrable because its amplitude extends to $+\infty$ in both directions, so the inverse Fourier transform is undefined. Theoretically, this is handled by methods such as using so-called *generalized delta functions*. In practice, the approach is to *window* the ramp so that it becomes zero outside of a defined frequency interval. That is, a window *band-limits* the ramp filter transfer function.

The simplest approach to band-limit a function is to use a box in the frequency domain. However, as we saw in Fig. 4.4, a box has undesirable ringing properties. This is demonstrated by Figs. 5.42(b) and (c). The former shows a plot of the ramp transfer function after it was band-limited by a box window, and the latter shows its spatial domain representation, obtained by computing its inverse Fourier transform. As expected, the resulting windowed filter exhibits noticeable ringing in the spatial domain. We know from Chapter 4 that filtering in the frequency domain is equivalent to convolution in the spatial domain, so spatial filtering with a function that exhibits ringing will produce a result corrupted by ringing also. Windowing with a smooth function helps this situation. An *M*-point discrete window function used frequently for implementations with the 1-D FFT is given by

$$H(\omega) = \begin{cases} c + (c - 1)\cos\dfrac{2\pi\omega}{M} & 0 \le \omega \le (M - 1) \\ 0 & \text{otherwise} \end{cases} \qquad (5\text{-}116)$$

When $c = 0.54$, this function is called the *Hamming window* (named after Richard Hamming) and, when $c = 0.5$ it is called the *Hann window* (named after Julius von Hann). The key difference between the Hamming and Hann windows is that the

The ramp filter often is referred to as the *Ram-Lak filter*, after Ramachandran and Lakshminarayanan [1971] who generally are credited with having been first to suggest it.

Sometimes the Hann window is referred to as the *Hanning* window in analogy to the Hamming window. However, this terminology is incorrect and is a frequent source of confusion.

a b c
d e f

FIGURE 5.42
(a) Frequency domain ramp filter transfer function. (b) Function after band-limiting it with a box filter. (c) Spatial domain representation. (d) Hamming windowing function. (e) Windowed ramp filter, formed as the product of (b) and (d). (f) Spatial representation of the product. (Note the decrease in ringing.)

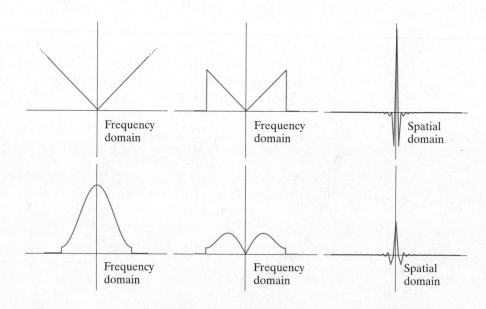

end points are zero in the latter. The difference between the two generally is visually imperceptible in image processing applications.

Figure 5.42(d) is a plot of the Hamming window, and Fig. 5.42(e) shows the product of this window and the band-limited ramp filter transfer function in Fig. 5.42(b). Figure 5.42(f) shows the representation of the product in the spatial domain, obtained as usual by computing the inverse FFT. It is evident by comparing this figure and Fig. 5.42(c) that ringing was reduced in the windowed ramp (the ratios of the peak to trough in Figs. 5.42(c) and (f) are 2.5 and 3.4, respectively). On the other hand, because the width of the central lobe in Fig. 5.42(f) is slightly wider than in Fig. 5.42(c), we would expect backprojections based on using a Hamming window to have less ringing, but be slightly more blurred. As Example 5.17 below shows, this is indeed the case.

Recall from Eq. (5-107) that $G(\omega, \theta)$ is the 1-D Fourier transform of $g(\rho, \theta)$, which is a *single* projection obtained at a fixed angle, θ. Equation (5-115) states that the *complete*, backprojected image $f(x, y)$ is obtained as follows:

1. Compute the 1-D Fourier transform of each projection.

2. Multiply each 1-D Fourier transform by the filter transfer function $|\omega|$ which, as explained above, has been multiplied by a suitable (e.g., Hamming) window.

3. Obtain the inverse 1-D Fourier transform of each resulting filtered transform.

4. Integrate (sum) all the 1-D inverse transforms from Step 3.

Because a filter function is used, this image reconstruction approach is appropriately called *filtered backprojection*. In practice, the data are discrete, so all frequency domain computations are carried out using a 1-D FFT algorithm, and filtering is implemented using the same basic procedure explained in Chapter 4 for 2-D functions. Alternatively, we can implement filtering in the spatial domain using convolution, as explained later.

The preceding discussion addresses the windowing aspects of filtered backprojections. As with any sampled data system, we also need to be concerned about sampling rates. We know from Chapter 4 that the selection of sampling rates has a profound influence on image processing results. In the present discussion, there are two sampling considerations. The first is the number of rays used, which determines the number of samples in each projection. The second is the number of rotation angle increments, which determines the number of reconstructed images (whose sum yields the final image). Under-sampling results in aliasing which, as we saw in Chapter 4, can manifest itself as artifacts in the image, such as streaks. We address CT sampling issues in more detail later in our discussion.

EXAMPLE 5.17: Image reconstruction using filtered backprojections.

The focus of this example is to show reconstruction using filtered backprojections, first with a box-limited ramp transfer function and then using a ramp limited by a Hamming window. These filtered backprojections are compared against the results of "raw" backprojections from Fig. 5.40. In order to focus on the difference due only to filtering, the results in this example were generated with 0.5° increments of rotation, the same we used to generate Fig. 5.40. The separation between rays was one pixel in both cases. The images in both examples are of size 600×600 pixels, so the length of the diagonal is $\sqrt{2} \times 600 \approx 849$. Consequently, 849 rays were used to provide coverage of the entire region when the angle of rotation was 45° and 135°.

Figure 5.43(a) shows the rectangle reconstructed using a ramp function band-limited by a box. The most vivid feature of this result is the absence of any visually detectable blurring. However, as expected, ringing is present, visible as faint lines, especially around the corners of the rectangle. These lines are more visible in the zoomed section in Fig. 5.43(c). Using a Hamming window on the ramp helped considerably with the ringing problem, at the expense of slight blurring, as Figs. 5.43(b) and (d) show. The improvements (even with the box-windowed ramp) over Fig. 5.40(a) are evident. The phantom image does not have transitions that are as sharp and prominent as the rectangle so ringing, even with the box-windowed ramp, is imperceptible in this case, as you can see in Fig. 5.44(a). Using a Hamming window resulted in a slightly smoother image, as Fig. 5.44(b) shows. Both of these results are considerable improvements over Fig. 5.40(b), illustrating again the significant advantage inherent in the filtered backprojection approach.

In most applications of CT (especially in medicine), artifacts such as ringing are a serious concern, so significant effort is devoted to minimizing them. Tuning the filtering algorithms and, as explained earlier, using a large number of detectors are among the design considerations that help reduce these effects.

The preceding discussion is based on obtaining filtered backprojections via an FFT implementation. However, we know from the convolution theorem in Chapter 4 that equivalent results can be obtained using spatial convolution. In particular, note

a b
c d

FIGURE 5.43
Filtered backprojections of the rectangle using (a) a ramp filter, and (b) a Hamming windowed ramp filter. The second row shows zoomed details of the images in the first row. Compare with Fig. 5.40(a).

a b

FIGURE 5.44
Filtered backpro-
jections of the
head phantom
using (a) a ramp
filter, and (b) a
Hamming
windowed ramp
filter. Compare
with Fig. 5.40(b)

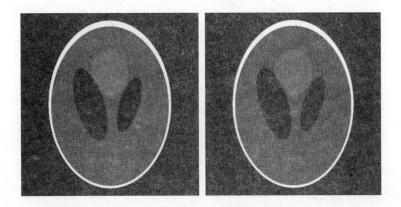

that the term inside the brackets in Eq. (5-115) is the inverse Fourier transform of the product of two frequency domain functions which, according to the convolution theorem, we know to be equal to the convolution of the spatial representations (inverse Fourier transforms) of these two functions. In other words, letting $s(\rho)$ denote the inverse Fourier transform of $|\omega|$,[†] we write Eq. (5-115) as

$$
\begin{aligned}
f(x,y) &= \int_0^\pi \left[\int_{-\infty}^\infty |\omega| G(\omega, \theta) e^{j2\pi\omega\rho} d\omega \right]_{\rho = x\cos\theta + y\sin\theta} d\theta \\
&= \int_0^\pi \left[s(\rho) \star g(\rho, \theta) \right]_{\rho = x\cos\theta + y\sin\theta} d\theta \qquad (5\text{-}117)\\
&= \int_0^\pi \left[\int_{-\infty}^\infty g(\rho, \theta) s(x\cos\theta + y\sin\theta - \rho) d\rho \right] d\theta
\end{aligned}
$$

where, as in Chapter 4, "$\star$" denotes convolution. The second line follows from the first for the reasons explained in the previous paragraph. The third line (including the $-\rho$) follows from the definition of convolution in Eq. (4-24).

The last two lines of Eq. (5-117) say the same thing: individual backprojections at an angle θ can be obtained by convolving the corresponding projection, $g(\rho, \theta)$, and the inverse Fourier transform of the ramp filter transfer function, $s(\rho)$. As before, the complete backprojected image is obtained by integrating (summing) all the individual backprojected images. With the exception of roundoff differences in computation, the results of using convolution will be identical to the results using the FFT. In actual CT implementations, convolution generally turns out to be more efficient computationally, so most modern CT systems use this approach. The Fourier transform does play a central role in theoretical formulations and algorithm development (for example, CT image processing in MATLAB is based on the FFT). Also, we note that there is no need to store all the backprojected images during reconstruction.

[†] If a windowing function, such as a Hamming window, is used, then the inverse Fourier transform is performed on the windowed ramp.

Instead, a single running sum is updated with the latest backprojected image. At the end of the procedure, the running sum will equal the sum total of all the backprojections.

Finally, we point out that, because the ramp filter (even when it is windowed) zeros the dc term in the frequency domain, each backprojection image will have zero average value (see Fig. 4.29). This means that the pixels in each backprojection image will have negative and positive values. When all the backprojections are added to form the final image, some negative locations may become positive and the average value may not be zero, but typically, the final image will still have negative pixels.

There are several ways to handle this problem. The simplest approach, when there is no knowledge regarding what the average values should be, is to accept the fact that negative values are inherent in the approach and scale the result using the procedure described in Eqs. (2-31) and (2-32). This is the approach followed in this section. When knowledge about what a "typical" average value should be is available, that value can be added to the filter transfer function in the frequency domain, thus offsetting the ramp and preventing zeroing the dc term [see Fig. 4.30(c)]. When working in the spatial domain with convolution, the very act of truncating the length of the spatial filter kernel (inverse Fourier transform of the ramp) prevents it from having a zero average value, thus avoiding the zeroing problem altogether.

RECONSTRUCTION USING FAN-BEAM FILTERED BACKPROJECTIONS

The discussion thus far has centered on parallel beams. Because of its simplicity and intuitiveness, this is the imaging geometry used traditionally to introduce computed tomography. However, more modern CT systems use a fan-beam geometry (see Fig. 5.35), which is the topic of the following discussion.

Figure 5.45 shows a basic fan-beam imaging geometry in which the detectors are arranged on a circular arc and the angular increments of the source are assumed to be equal. Let $p(\alpha, \beta)$ denote a fan-beam projection, where α is the angular position of a particular detector measured with respect to the *center ray*, and β is the angular displacement of the source, measured with respect to the y-axis, as shown in the figure. We also note in Fig. 5.45 that a ray in the fan beam can be represented as a line, $L(\rho, \theta)$, in normal form, which is the approach we used to represent a ray in the parallel-beam imaging geometry discussed earlier. This allows us to utilize parallel-beam results as the starting point for deriving the corresponding equations for the fan-beam geometry. We proceed to show this by deriving the fan-beam filtered backprojection based on convolution.[†]

We begin by noticing in Fig. 5.45 that the parameters of line $L(\rho, \theta)$ are related to the parameters of a fan-beam ray by

$$\theta = \beta + \alpha \tag{5-118}$$

[†] The Fourier-slice theorem was derived for a parallel-beam geometry and is not directly applicable to fan beams. However, Eqs. (5-118) and (5-119) provide the basis for converting a fan-beam geometry to a parallel-beam geometry, thus allowing us to use the filtered parallel backprojection approach developed in the previous section, for which the slice theorem is applicable. We will discuss this in more detail at the end of this section.

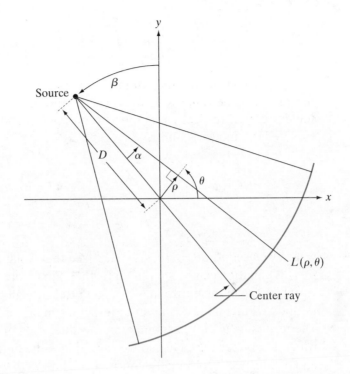

FIGURE 5.45
Basic fan-beam geometry. The line passing through the center of the source and the origin (assumed here to be the center of rotation of the source) is called the *center ray*.

and

$$\rho = D \sin \alpha \qquad (5\text{-}119)$$

where D is the distance from the center of the source to the origin of the xy-plane.

The convolution backprojection formula for the parallel-beam imaging geometry is given by Eq. (5-117). Without loss of generality, suppose that we focus attention on objects that are encompassed within a circular area of radius T about the origin of the xy-plane. Then $g(\rho, \theta) = 0$ for $|\rho| > T$ and Eq. (5-117) becomes

$$f(x,y) = \frac{1}{2} \int_0^{2\pi} \int_{-T}^{T} g(\rho, \theta) s(x \cos \theta + y \sin \theta - \rho) d\rho \, d\theta \qquad (5\text{-}120)$$

where we used the fact mentioned earlier that projections 180° apart are mirror images of each other. In this way, the limits of the outer integral in Eq. (5-120) are made to span a full circle, as required by a fan-beam arrangement in which the detectors are arranged in a circle.

We are interested in integrating with respect to α and β. To do this, we change to polar coordinates, (r, φ). That is, we let $x = r \cos \varphi$ and $y = r \sin \varphi$, from which it follows that

$$\begin{aligned} x \cos \theta + y \sin \theta &= r \cos \varphi \cos \theta + r \sin \varphi \sin \theta \\ &= r \cos(\theta - \varphi) \end{aligned} \qquad (5\text{-}121)$$

Using this result we can express Eq. (5-120) as

$$f(x,y) = \frac{1}{2} \int_0^{2\pi} \int_{-T}^{T} g(\rho, \theta) s(r\cos(\theta - \varphi) - \rho) d\rho \, d\theta \qquad (5\text{-}122)$$

This expression is nothing more than the parallel-beam reconstruction formula written in polar coordinates. However, integration still is with respect to ρ and θ. To integrate with respect to α and β requires a transformation of coordinates using Eqs. (5-118) and (5-119):

$$f(r,\varphi) = \frac{1}{2} \int_{-\alpha}^{2\pi-\alpha} \int_{\sin^{-1}(-T/D)}^{\sin^{-1}(T/D)} g(D\sin\alpha, \alpha + \beta)$$
$$s(r\cos(\beta + \alpha - \varphi) - D\sin\alpha)D\cos\alpha \, d\alpha \, d\beta \qquad (5\text{-}123)$$

where we used $d\rho \, d\theta = D\cos\alpha \, d\alpha \, d\beta$ [see the explanation of Eq. (5-112)].

This equation can be simplified further. First, note that the limits $-\alpha$ to $2\pi - \alpha$ for variable β span the entire range of 360°. Because all functions of β are periodic with period 2π, the limits of the outer integral can be replaced by 0 and 2π, respectively. The term $\sin^{-1}(T/D)$ has a maximum value, α_m, corresponding to $|\rho| > T$, beyond which $g = 0$ (see Fig. 5.46), so we can replace the limits of the inner integral by $-\alpha_m$ and α_m, respectively. Finally, consider the line $L(\rho, \theta)$ in Fig. 5.45. A raysum of a fan beam along this line must equal the raysum of a parallel beam along the same line. This follows from the fact that a raysum is a sum of all values along a line, so the result must be the same for a given ray, regardless of the coordinate system is which it is expressed. This is true of any raysum for corresponding values of (α, β) and (ρ, θ). Thus, letting $p(\alpha, \beta)$ denote a fan-beam projection, it follows that $p(\alpha, \beta) = g(\rho, \theta)$ and, from Eqs. (5-118) and (5-119), that $p(\alpha, \beta) = g(D\sin\alpha, \alpha + \beta)$. Incorporating these observations into Eq. (5-123) results in the expression

$$f(r,\varphi) = \frac{1}{2} \int_0^{2\pi} \int_{-\alpha_m}^{\alpha_m} p(\alpha, \beta) s[r\cos(\beta + \alpha - \varphi) - D\sin\alpha]D\cos\alpha \, d\alpha \, d\beta \quad (5\text{-}124)$$

This is the fundamental fan-beam *reconstruction formula* based on filtered backprojections.

Equation (5-124) can be manipulated further to put it in a more familiar convolution form. With reference to Fig. 5.47, it can be shown (see Problem 5.47) that

$$r\cos(\beta + \alpha - \varphi) - D\sin\alpha = R\sin(\alpha' - \alpha) \qquad (5\text{-}125)$$

where R is the distance from the source to an arbitrary point in a fan ray, and α' is the angle between this ray and the center ray. Note that R and α' are determined by the values of r, φ, and β. Substituting Eq. (5-125) into Eq. (5-124) yields

$$f(r,\varphi) = \frac{1}{2} \int_0^{2\pi} \int_{-\alpha_m}^{\alpha_m} p(\alpha, \beta) s(R\sin[\alpha' - \alpha]) D\cos\alpha \, d\alpha \, d\beta \qquad (5\text{-}126)$$

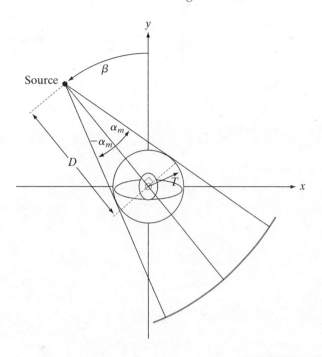

It can be shown (see Problem 5.48) that

$$s(R \sin \alpha) = \left[\frac{\alpha}{R \sin \alpha} \right]^2 s(\alpha) \qquad (5\text{-}127)$$

Using this expression, we can write Eq. (5-126) as

$$f(r, \varphi) = \frac{1}{2} \int_0^{2\pi} \frac{1}{R^2} \left[\int_{-\alpha_m}^{\alpha_m} q(\alpha, \beta) h(\alpha' - \alpha) d\alpha \right] d\beta \qquad (5\text{-}128)$$

where

$$h(\alpha) = \frac{1}{2} \left[\frac{\alpha}{\sin \alpha} \right]^2 s(\alpha) \qquad (5\text{-}129)$$

and

$$q(\alpha, \beta) = p(\alpha, \beta) D \cos \alpha \qquad (5\text{-}130)$$

We recognize the inner integral in Eq. (5-128) as a convolution expression, thus showing that the image reconstruction formula in Eq. (5-124) can be implemented as the convolution of functions $q(\alpha, \beta)$ and $h(\alpha)$. Unlike the reconstruction formula for parallel projections, reconstruction based on fan-beam projections involves a term $1/R^2$, which is a weighting factor inversely proportional to the distance from the source. The computational details of implementing Eq. (5-128) are beyond the scope of the present discussion (see Kak and Slaney [2001] for a detailed treatment of this subject).

FIGURE 5.47
Polar
representation of
an arbitrary point
on a ray of a fan
beam.

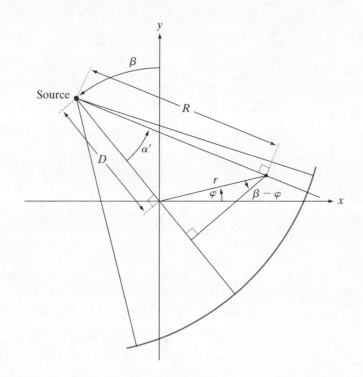

Instead of implementing Eq. (5-128) directly, an approach used often, particularly in software simulations, is to: (1) convert a fan-beam geometry to a parallel-beam geometry using Eqs. (5-118) and (5-119), and (2) use the parallel-beam reconstruction approach developed earlier. We conclude this section with an example of how to do this. As noted earlier, a fan-beam projection, p, taken at angle β has a corresponding parallel-beam projection, g, taken at a corresponding angle θ and, therefore,

$$p(\alpha, \beta) = g(\rho, \theta)$$
$$= g(D\sin\alpha, \alpha + \beta) \tag{5-131}$$

where the last line follows from Eqs. (5-118) and (5-119).

Let $\Delta\beta$ denote the angular increment between successive fan-beam projections, and let $\Delta\alpha$ be the angular increment between rays, which determines the number of samples in each projection. We impose the restriction that

$$\Delta\beta = \Delta\alpha = \gamma \tag{5-132}$$

Then, $\beta = m\gamma$ and $\alpha = n\gamma$ for some integer values of m and n, and we can write Eq. (5-131) as

$$p(n\gamma, m\gamma) = g\big(D\sin n\gamma, (m + n)\gamma\big) \tag{5-133}$$

This equation indicates that the nth ray in the mth radial projection is equal to the nth ray in the $(m + n)$th parallel projection. The $D\sin n\gamma$ term on the right side of Eq. (5-133) implies that parallel projections converted from fan-beam projections are not sampled uniformly, an issue that can lead to blurring, ringing, and aliasing artifacts if the sampling intervals $\Delta\alpha$ and $\Delta\beta$ are too coarse, as the following example illustrates.

EXAMPLE 5.18: Image reconstruction using filtered fan backprojections.

Figure 5.48(a) shows the results of: (1) generating fan projections of the rectangle image with $\Delta\alpha = \Delta\beta = 1°$, (2) converting each fan ray to the corresponding parallel ray using Eq. (5-133), and (3) using the filtered backprojection approach developed earlier for parallel rays. Figures 5.48(b) through (d) show the results using $0.5°, 0.25°$, and $0.125°$ increments of $\Delta\alpha$ and $\Delta\beta$. A Hamming window was used in all cases. We used this variety of angle increments to illustrate the effects of under-sampling.

The result in Fig. 5.48(a) is a clear indication that $1°$ increments are too coarse, as blurring and ringing are quite evident. The result in Fig. 5.48(b) is interesting, in the sense that it compares poorly with Fig. 5.43(b), which we generated using the same angle increment of $0.5°$. In fact, as Fig. 5.48(c) shows, even with angle increments of $0.25°$ the reconstruction still is not as good as in Fig. 5.43(b). We have to use angle increments on the order of $0.125°$ before the two results become comparable, as Fig. 5.48(d) shows. This angle increment results in projections with $180 \times (1/0.125) = 1440$ samples, which is close to double the 849 rays used in the parallel projections of Example 5.17. Thus, it is not unexpected that the results are close in appearance when using $\Delta\alpha = 0.125°$.

Similar results were obtained with the head phantom, except that aliasing in this case is much more visible as sinusoidal interference. We see in Fig. 5.49(c) that even with $\Delta\alpha = \Delta\beta = 0.25°$ significant distortion still is present, especially in the periphery of the ellipse. As with the rectangle, using increments of $0.125°$ finally produced results that are comparable with the backprojected image of the head phantom

a b
c d

FIGURE 5.48
Reconstruction of the rectangle image from filtered fan backprojections.
(a) $1°$ increments of α and β.
(b) $0.5°$ increments.
(c) $0.25°$ increments.
(d) $0.125°$ increments.
Compare (d) with Fig. 5.43(b).

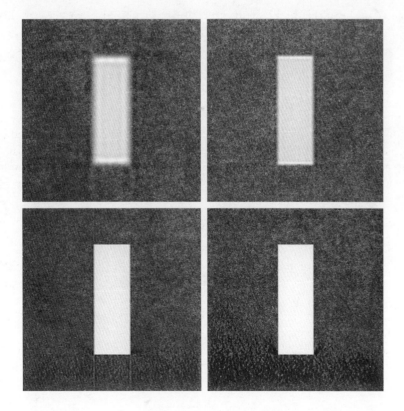

FIGURE 5.49
Reconstruction of
the head phantom
image from filtered
fan backprojections.
(a) 1° increments of
α and β.
(b) 0.5° increments.
(c) 0.25° increments.
(d) 0.125° incre-
ments.
Compare (d) with
Fig. 5.44(b).

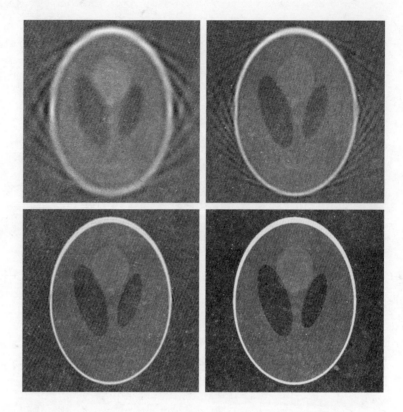

in Fig. 5.44(b). These results illustrate one of the principal reasons why thousands of detectors have to be used in the fan-beam geometry of modern CT systems in order to reduce aliasing artifacts.

Summary, References, and Further Reading

The restoration results in this chapter are based on the assumption that image degradation can be modeled as a linear, position invariant process followed by additive noise that is not correlated with image values. Even when these assumptions are not entirely valid, it is often possible to obtain useful results by using the methods developed in the preceding sections. Our treatment of image reconstruction from projections, though introductory, is the foundation for the image-processing aspects of this field. As noted in Section 5.11, computed tomography (CT) is the main application area of image reconstruction from projections. Although we focused on X-ray tomography, the principles established in Section 5.11 are applicable in other CT imaging modalities, such as SPECT (single photon emission tomography), PET (positron emission tomography), MRI (magnetic resonance imaging), and some modalities of ultrasound imaging.

For additional reading on the material in Section 5.1 see Pratt [2014]. The books by Ross [2014], and by Montgomery and Runger [2011], are good sources for a more in-depth discussion of probability density functions and their properties (Section 5.2). See Umbaugh [2010] for complementary reading on the material in Section 5.3, and Eng and Ma [2001, 2006] regarding adaptive median filtering. The filters in Section 5.4 are direct extensions of the material in Chapter 4. The material in Section 5.5 is fundamental linear system theory; for more advanced reading on this topic see Hespanha [2009]. The topic of estimating image degradation functions (Section 5.6) is fundamental in the field of image restoration. Some of the early techniques for estimating the degradation function are given in Andrews and Hunt [1977], Rosenfeld and Kak [1982]. More recent methods are discussed by Gunturk and Li [2013].

There are two major approaches to the methods developed in Sections 5.7–5.10. One is based on a general formulation using matrix theory, as introduced by Andrews and Hunt [1977] and by Gonzalez and Woods [1992]. This approach is elegant and general, but it tends to be difficult for first-time readers. Approaches based on frequency domain filtering (the approach we followed in this chapter) are easier to follow by newcomers to image restoration, but lack the unifying mathematical rigor of the matrix approach. Both approaches arrive at the same results, but our experience in teaching this material in a variety of settings indicates that students first entering this field favor the latter approach by a significant margin. Complementary readings for our coverage of these filtering concepts are Castleman [1996], Umbaugh [2010], Petrou and Petrou [2010] and Gunturk and Li [2013]. For additional reading on the material in Section 5.11 see Kak and Slaney [2001], Prince and Links [2006], and Buzug [2008]. For details on the software aspects of many of the examples in this chapter, see Gonzalez, Woods, and Eddins [2009].

Problems

Solutions to the problems marked with an asterisk (*) are in the DIP4E Student Support Package (consult the book website: www.ImageProcessingPlace.com).

5.1* The white bars in the test pattern shown are 7 pixels wide and 210 pixels high. The separation between bars is 17 pixels. What would this image look like after application of

    (a) A 3×3 arithmetic mean filter?

    (b) A 7×7 arithmetic mean filter?

    (c) A 9×9 arithmetic mean filter?

Note: This problem and the ones that follow it, related to filtering this image, may seem a bit tedious. However, they are worth the effort, as they help develop a real understanding of how these filters work. After you understand how a particular filter affects the image, your answer can be a brief verbal description of the result. For example, "the resulting image will consist of vertical bars 3 pixels wide and 206 pixels high." Be sure to describe any deformation of the bars, such as rounded corners. You may ignore image border effects, in which the filter neighborhoods only partially contain image pixels.

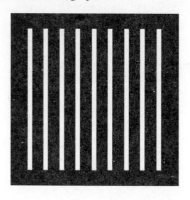

5.2 Repeat Problem 5.1 using a geometric mean filter.

5.3* Repeat Problem 5.1 using a harmonic mean filter.

5.4 Repeat Problem 5.1 using a contraharmonic mean filter with $Q = 1$.

5.5* Repeat Problem 5.1 using a contraharmonic mean filter with $Q = -1$.

5.6 Repeat Problem 5.1 using a median filter.

5.7* Repeat Problem 5.1 using a max filter.

5.8 Repeat Problem 5.1 using a min filter.

5.9* Repeat Problem 5.1 using a midpoint filter.

5.10 In answering the following, refer to the contraharmonic filter in Eq. (5-26):

    (a)* What does the filter do is Q is positive?

    (b) What does the filter do if Q is negative?

    (c)* Discuss the behaviour of the filter when $Q = 0$ or $Q = -1$.

    (d) Discuss (for positive and negative Q) the behaviour of the filter in areas of constant intensity levels.

5.11 What is median filter? How does it function? Why are median filters popular in image processing as compared to other order-statistic filters?

5.12 With reference to the alpha-trimmed filter defined in Eq. (5-31)]:

    (a)* Discuss the behavior of the filter on setting $d = 0$ or $d = mn - 1$.

    (b) For other values of d, how is the filter useful?

5.13 With reference to Table 4.7, give equations for the transfer functions of:

(a) An ideal bandreject filter.

(b)*A Gaussian bandreject filter.

(c) A Butterworth bandreject filter.

5.14 With reference to Eq. (5-33), obtain equations for:

(a)*An ideal notch filter transfer function.

(b) A Gaussian notch filter transfer function.

(c) A Butterworth notch filter transfer function.

5.15 Show that the Fourier transform of the 2-D continuous sine function

$$f(x,y) = A\sin(u_0 x + v_0 y)$$

is the pair of conjugate impulses

$$F(u,v) = \frac{-jA}{2}\left[\delta\left(u - \frac{u_0}{2\pi}, v - \frac{v_0}{2\pi}\right) - \delta\left(u + \frac{u_0}{2\pi}, v + \frac{v_0}{2\pi}\right)\right]$$

5.16 The two subimages shown were extracted from the top right corners of Figs. 5.7(c) and (d), respectively. Thus, the subimage on the left is the result of using an arithmetic mean filter of size 3×3; the other subimage is the result of using a geometric mean filter of the same size.

(a)* Explain why the subimage obtained with geometric mean filtering is less blurred.

(b)* Explain why the black components in the right image are thicker.

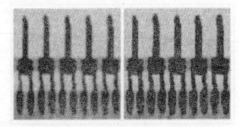

5.17* Start with Eq. (5-46) and derive Eq. (5-48).

5.18 An industrial plant manager has been promoted to a new position. His first responsibility is to characterize an image filtering system left by his predecessor. In reading the documentation, the manager discovers that his predecessor established that the system is linear and position invariant. Furthermore, he learns that experiments conducted under negligible-noise conditions resulted in an impulse response that could be expressed analytically in the frequency domain as

$$H(u,v) = e^{-[u^2/150 + v^2/150]} + 1$$
$$- e^{-[(u - 50)^2/150 + (v - 50)^2/150]}$$

The manager is not a technical person, so he employs you as a consultant to determine what, if anything, he needs to do to complete the characterization of the system. He also wants to know the function that the system performs. What (if anything) does the manager need to do to complete the characterization of his system? What filtering function does the system perform?

5.19 A linear, space invariant system has the impulse response

$$h(x,y) = \delta(x - a, y - b)$$

where a and b are constants, and x and y are discrete quantities. Answer the following, assuming negligible noise in each case.

(a)*What is the system transfer function in the frequency domain?

(b)*What would the spatial domain system response be to a constant input, $f(x,y) = K$?

(c) What would the spatial domain system response be to an impulse input, $f(x,y) = \delta(x,y)$?

5.20* Assuming now that x and y are continuous quantities, show how you would solve Problems 5.19(b) and (c) using Eq. (5-61) directly. [*Hint:* Take a look at the solution to Problem 4.1(c).]

5.21* Consider a linear, position invariant image degradation system with impulse response

$$h(x,y) = e^{-\left[(x-\alpha)^2 + (y-\beta)^2\right]}$$

where x and y are continuous variables. Suppose that the input to the system is a binary image consisting of a white vertical line of infinitesimal width located at $x = a$, on a black background. Such an image can be modeled as $f(x,y) = \delta(x - a)$. Assume negligible noise and use Eq. (5-61) to find the output image, $g(x,y)$.

5.22 What are the three principal ways to estimate the degradation function for use in image restoration? Why is the process of restoring an image by using a degradation function is called blind deconvolution?

5.23 The image shown consists of two infinitesimally thin white lines on a black background, intersecting at some point in the image. The image is input into a linear, position invariant system with the impulse response given in Problem 5.21. Assuming continuous variables and negligible noise, find an expression for the output image, $g(x,y)$. (*Hint:* Review linear operations in Section 2.6.)

5.24 Sketch (with arrow lines showing the direction of blur) what the image in Fig. 5.26(a) would look like if it were blurred using the transfer function in Eq. (5-77)

   (a)* With $a = -0.1$ and $b = 0.1$.

   (b) With $a = 0$ and $b = -0.1$.

5.25* During acquisition, an image undergoes uniform linear motion in the vertical direction for a time T_1. The direction of motion then switches to the horizontal direction for a time interval T_2. Assuming that the time it takes the image to change directions is negligible, and that shutter opening and closing times are negligible also, give an expression for the blurring function, $H(u,v)$.

5.26 During acquisition, an image undergoes uniform linear motion in the vertical direction for a time T. The direction of motion then switches 180° in the opposite direction for a time T. Assume that the time it takes the image to change directions is negligible, and that shutter opening and closing times are negligible also. Is the final image blurred, or did the reversal in direction "undo" the first blur? Obtain the overall blurring function $H(u,v)$ first, and then use it as the basis for your answer.

5.27* Consider image blurring caused by uniform acceleration in the *x*-direction. If the image is at rest at time $t = 0$ and accelerates with a uniform accel-

eration $x_0(t) = at^2$ for a time T, find the blurring function $H(u,v)$. You may assume that shutter opening and closing times are negligible.

5.28 A space probe is designed to transmit images of a planet as it approaches it for landing. During the last stages of landing, one of the control thrusters fails, resulting in rotation of the craft about its vertical axis. The images sent during the last two seconds prior to landing are blurred as a consequence of this circular motion. The camera is located in the bottom of the probe, along its vertical axis, and pointing down. Fortunately, the rotation of the craft is also about its vertical axis, so the images are blurred by uniform rotational motion. During the acquisition time of each image, the craft rotation was $\pi/12$ radians. The image acquisition process can be modeled as an ideal shutter that is open only during the time the craft rotated $\pi/12$ radians. You may assume that the vertical motion was negligible during the image acquisition. Formulate a solution for restoring the images. You do not have to solve the problem, just give an outline of how you would solve it using the methods discussed in Section 5.6 through 5.9. (*Hint*: Consider using polar coordinates. The blur will then appear as one-dimensional, uniform motion blur along the θ-axis.)

5.29* The image that follows is a blurred, 2-D projection of a volumetric rendition of a heart. It is known that each of the cross hairs on the right bottom part of the image was (before blurring) 4 pixels wide, 20 pixels long, and had an intensity value of 255. Provide a step-by-step procedure indicating how you would use the information just given to obtain the blurring function $H(u,v)$.

(Original image courtesy of GE Medical Systems.)

5.30 The image in Fig. 5.29(h) was obtained by inverse-filtering the image in Fig. 5.29(g), which is a blurred image that, in addition, is corrupted by additive Gaussian noise. The blurring itself is corrected by the inverse filter, as is evident in Fig. 5.29(h). However, the restored image has a strong streak pattern that is not apparent in Fig. 5.29(g) [for example, compare the area of constant white in the top right of Fig. 5.29(g) with the corresponding are in Fig. 5.29(h)]. Explain how this pattern originated.

5.31 A certain X-ray imaging geometry produces a blurring degradation that can be modeled as the convolution of the sensed image with the spatial, circularly symmetric function

$$h(x,y) = \frac{x^2 + y^2 - 2\sigma^2}{\sigma^4} e^{-(x^2 + y^2)/2\sigma^2}$$

Assuming continuous variables, show that the degradation in the frequency domain is given by the expression

$$H(u,v) = -8\pi^4\sigma^2(u^2 + v^2)e^{-2\pi^2\sigma^2(u^2+v^2)}$$

(*Hint:* Refer to the discussion of the Laplacian in Section 4.9, entry 13 in Table 4.4, and review Problem 4.52.)

5.32* Using the transfer function in Problem 5.31, give the expression for a Wiener filter transfer function, assuming that the ratio of power spectra of the noise and undegraded images is a constant.

5.33 Given $p(x,y)$ in Eq. (5-90), show that

$$P(u,v) = 4 - 2\cos(2\pi u/M) - 2\cos(2\pi v/N)$$

(*Hint:* Study the solution to Problem 4.47.)

5.34 Show how Eq. (5-98) follows from Eqs. (5-96) and (5-97).

5.35 Show that the transfer function of the constrained least squares filter [Eq. (5-89)] reduces to an inverse filter when $\gamma = 0$.

5.36* Assume that the model in Fig. 5.1 is linear and position invariant, and that the noise and image are uncorrelated. Show that the power spectrum of the output is

$$|G(u,v)|^2 = |H(u,v)|^2 |F(u,v)|^2 + |N(u,v)|^2$$

[*Hint:* Refer to Eqs. (5-65) and (4-89).]

5.37 Cannon [1974] suggested a restoration filter $R(u,v)$ satisfying the condition

$$\left|\hat{F}(u,v)\right|^2 = |R(u,v)|^2 |G(u,v)|^2$$

The restoration filter is based on the premise of forcing the power spectrum of the restored image, $\left|\hat{F}(u,v)\right|^2$, to equal the spectrum of the original image, $|F(u,v)|^2$. Assume that the image and noise are uncorrelated,

(a)* Find $R(u,v)$ in terms of $|F(u,v)|^2$, $|H(u,v)|^2$, and $|N(u,v)|^2$. (*Hint:* Take a look at Fig. 5.1, Eq. (5-65), and Problem 5.36.)

(b) Use your result from (a) to state a result in a form similar to the last line of Eq. (5-81), and using the same terms.

5.38 Show that, when $\alpha = 0$ and $\beta = 1$ in Eq. (5-99), the geometric mean filter reduces to the Wiener filter.

5.39* A professor of archeology doing research on currency exchange practices during the Roman Empire recently became aware that four Roman coins crucial to his research are listed in the holdings of the British Museum in London. Unfortunately, he was told after arriving there that the coins had been recently stolen. Further research on his part revealed that the museum keeps photographs of every item for which it is responsible. Unfortunately, the photos of the coins in question are blurred to the point where the date and other small markings are not readable. The cause of the blurring was the camera being out of focus when the pictures were taken. As an image processing expert and friend of the professor, you are asked as a favor to determine whether computer processing can be utilized to restore the images to the point where the professor can read the markings. You are told that the original camera used to take the photos is still available, as are other representative coins of the same era. Propose a step-by-step solution to this problem.

5.40 An astronomer is working with an optical telescope. The telescope lenses focus images onto a high-resolution, CCD imaging array, and the images are then converted by the telescope electronics into digital images. Working late one evening, the astronomer notices that her new images are noisy and blurry. The manufacturer tells the astronomer that the unit is operating within specifications. Trying to improve the situation by conducting controlled lab experiments with the lenses and imaging sensors is not possible because of the size and weight of the telescope components. Having heard about your success in restoring the Roman coins, the astronomer calls you to help her formulate a digital image processing solution for sharpening her images. How would you go about solving this problem, given that the only images you can obtain are images of stellar bodies? (*Hint:* A single, bright star that appears as a point of light in the field of view can be used to approximate an impulse.)

5.41* Sketch the Radon transform of the $M \times M$ binary image shown below, which consists of two white pixels (dots) along the diagonal. Assume a parallel-beam geometry, and label quantitatively all the important elements of your sketch.

5.42* A Sketch a cross section of the Radon transform of the following white disk image containing a smaller black disk in its center. (*Hint:* Take a look at Fig. 5.38.)

5.43 Show that the Radon transform [Eq. (5-102)] of the shape $f(x, y) = A \exp(x^2 - y^2)$ is given by $g(\rho, \theta) = A\sqrt{\pi} \exp(\rho^2)$.

5.44 Do the following:

(a)* Show that the Radon transform [Eq. (5-102)] of the unit impulse $\delta(x, y)$ is a straight vertical line passing through the origin of the $\rho\theta$-plane .

(b) Show that the radon transform of the impulse $\delta(x - x_0, y - y_0)$ is a sinusoidal curve in the $\rho\theta$-plane.

5.45 Prove the validity of the following properties of the Radon transform [Eq. (5-102)]:

(a)* *Linearity:* The Radon transform is a linear operator. (See Section 2.6 regarding linearity.)

(b) *Translation property:* The radon transform of $f(x - x_0, y - y_0)$ is $g(\rho - x_0 \cos\theta - y_0 \sin\theta, \theta)$.

(c)* *Convolution property:* The Radon transform of the convolution of two functions is equal to the convolution of the Radon transforms of the two functions.

5.46 Provide the steps that lead from Eq. (5-113) to Eq. (5-114). [*Hint:* $G(\omega, \theta + 180°) = G(-\omega, \theta)$.]

5.47* Prove the validity of Eq. (5-125).

5.48 Prove the validity of Eq. (5-127).

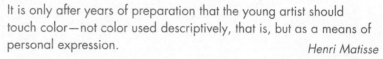

Color Image Processing

It is only after years of preparation that the young artist should touch color—not color used descriptively, that is, but as a means of personal expression.

Henri Matisse

For a long time I limited myself to one color—as a form of discipline.

Pablo Picasso

Preview

Using color in image processing is motivated by two principal factors. First, color is a powerful descriptor that often simplifies object identification and extraction from a scene. Second, humans can discern thousands of color shades, compared to only about two dozen shades of gray. The latter factor is particularly important in manual image analysis. Color image processing is divided into two major areas: *pseudo-* and *full-color* processing. In the first category, the issue is one of assigning color(s) to a particular grayscale intensity or range of intensities. In the second, images typically are acquired using a full-color sensor, such as a digital camera, or color scanner. Until just a few years ago, most digital color image processing was done at the pseudo- or reduced-color level. However, because color sensors and processing hardware have become available at reasonable prices, full-color image processing techniques are now used in a broad range of applications. In the discussions that follow, it will become evident that some of the grayscale methods covered in previous chapters are applicable also to color images.

Upon completion of this chapter, readers should:

- Understand the fundamentals of color and the color spectrum.

- Be familiar with several of the color models used in digital image processing.

- Know how to apply basic techniques in pseudo-color image processing, including intensity slicing and intensity-to-color transformations.

- Be familiar with how to determine if a grayscale method is extendible to color images.

- Understand the basics of working with full-color images, including color transformations, color complements, and tone/color corrections.

- Be familiar with the role of noise in color image processing.

- Know how to perform spatial filtering on color images.

- Understand the advantages of using color in image segmentation.

399

6.1 COLOR FUNDAMENTALS

Although the process employed by the human brain in perceiving and interpreting color is a physiopsychological phenomenon that is not fully understood, the physical nature of color can be expressed on a formal basis supported by experimental and theoretical results.

In 1666, Sir Isaac Newton discovered that when a beam of sunlight passes through a glass prism, the emerging light is not white, but consists instead of a continuous spectrum of colors ranging from violet at one end to red at the other. As Fig. 6.1 shows, the color spectrum may be divided into six broad regions: violet, blue, green, yellow, orange, and red. When viewed in full color (see Fig. 6.2), no color in the spectrum ends abruptly; rather, each color blends smoothly into the next.

Basically, the colors that humans and some other animals perceive in an object are determined by the nature of the light reflected from the object. As illustrated in Fig. 6.2, visible light is composed of a relatively narrow band of frequencies in the electromagnetic spectrum. A body that reflects light that is balanced in all visible wavelengths appears white to the observer. However, a body that favors reflectance in a limited range of the visible spectrum exhibits some shades of color. For example, green objects reflect light with wavelengths primarily in the 500 to 570 nm range, while absorbing most of the energy at other wavelengths.

Characterization of light is central to the science of color. If the light is *achromatic* (void of color), its only attribute is its *intensity*, or amount. Achromatic light is what you see on movie films made before the 1930s. As defined in Chapter 2, and used numerous times since, the term *gray (or intensity) level* refers to a scalar measure of intensity that ranges from black, to grays, and finally to white.

Chromatic light spans the electromagnetic spectrum from approximately 400 to 700 nm. Three basic quantities used to describe the quality of a chromatic light source are: radiance, luminance, and brightness. *Radiance* is the total amount of energy that flows from the light source, and it is usually measured in watts (W). *Luminance*, measured in lumens (lm), is a measure of the amount of energy that an observer *perceives* from a light source. For example, light emitted from a source operating in the far infrared region of the spectrum could have significant energy (radiance), but an observer would hardly perceive it; its luminance would be almost zero. Finally, *brightness* is a subjective descriptor that is practically impossible to measure. It embodies the achromatic notion of intensity, and is one of the key factors in describing color sensation.

FIGURE 6.1
Color spectrum seen by passing white light through a prism. (Courtesy of the General Electric Co., Lighting Division.)

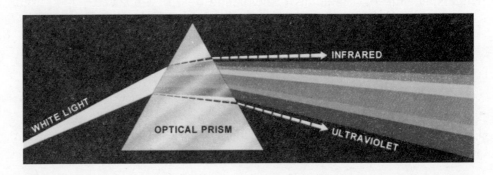

FIGURE 6.2
Wavelengths compris-
ing the visible range
of the electromagnetic
spectrum. (Courtesy of
the General Electric
Co., Lighting Division.)

FIGURE 6.2
Wavelengths compris-
ing the visible range
of the electromagnetic
spectrum. (Courtesy of
the General Electric
Co., Lighting Division.)

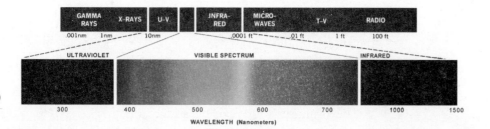

As noted in Section 2.1, cones are the sensors in the eye responsible for color vision. Detailed experimental evidence has established that the 6 to 7 million cones in the human eye can be divided into three principal sensing categories, corresponding roughly to red, green, and blue. Approximately 65% of all cones are sensitive to red light, 33% are sensitive to green light, and only about 2% are sensitive to blue. However, the blue cones are the most sensitive. Figure 6.3 shows average experimental curves detailing the absorption of light by the red, green, and blue cones in the eye. Because of these absorption characteristics, the human eye sees colors as variable combinations of the so-called *primary colors*: *red* (R), *green* (G), and *blue* (B).

For the purpose of standardization, the CIE (Commission Internationale de l'Eclairage—the International Commission on Illumination) designated in 1931 the following specific wavelength values to the three primary colors: blue = 435.8 nm, green = 546.1 nm, and red = 700 nm. This standard was set before results such as those in Fig. 6.3 became available in 1965. Thus, the CIE standards correspond only approximately with experimental data. It is important to keep in mind that defining three specific primary color wavelengths for the purpose of standardization does *not*

FIGURE 6.3
Absorption of
light by the red,
green, and blue
cones in the
human eye as a
function of
wavelength.

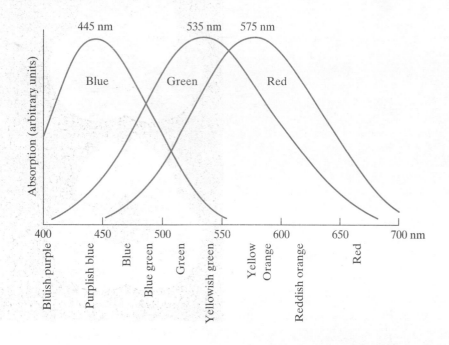

mean that these three fixed RGB components acting alone can generate all spectrum colors. Use of the word *primary* has been widely misinterpreted to mean that the three standard primaries, when mixed in various intensity proportions, can produce all visible colors. As you will see shortly, this interpretation is not correct unless the wavelength also is allowed to vary, in which case we would no longer have three fixed primary colors.

The primary colors can be added together to produce the *secondary* colors of light—*magenta* (red plus blue), *cyan* (green plus blue), and *yellow* (red plus green). Mixing the three primaries, or a secondary with its opposite primary color, in the right intensities produces white light. This result is illustrated in Fig. 6.4(a), which shows also the three primary colors and their combinations to produce the secondary colors of light.

Differentiating between the primary colors of light and the primary colors of pigments or colorants is important. In the latter, a primary color is defined as one that subtracts or absorbs a primary color of light, and reflects or transmits the other two. Therefore, the primary colors of pigments are magenta, cyan, and yellow, and the secondary colors are red, green, and blue. These colors are shown in Fig. 6.4(b). A proper combination of the three pigment primaries, or a secondary with its opposite primary, produces black.

Color television reception is an example of the additive nature of light colors. The interior of CRT (cathode ray tube) color TV screens used well into the 1990s is composed of a large array of triangular dot patterns of electron-sensitive phosphor. When excited, each dot in a triad produces light in one of the primary colors. The

In practice, pigments seldom are pure. This results in a muddy brown instead of black when primaries, or primaries and secondaries, are combined. We will discuss this issue in Section 6.2

FIGURE 6.4
Primary and secondary colors of light and pigments. (Courtesy of the General Electric Co., Lighting Division.)

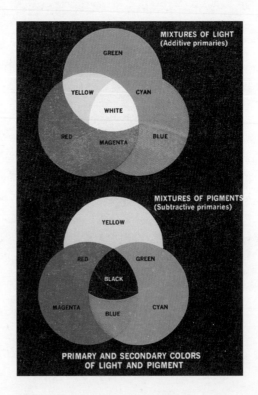

intensity of the red-emitting phosphor dots is modulated by an electron gun inside the tube, which generates pulses corresponding to the "red energy" seen by the TV camera. The green and blue phosphor dots in each triad are modulated in the same manner. The effect, viewed on the television receiver, is that the three primary colors from each phosphor triad are received and "added" together by the color-sensitive cones in the eye and perceived as a full-color image. Thirty successive image changes per second in all three colors complete the illusion of a continuous image display on the screen.

CRT displays started being replaced in the late 1990s by flat-panel digital technologies, such as liquid crystal displays (LCDs) and plasma devices. Although they are fundamentally different from CRTs, these and similar technologies use the same principle in the sense that they all require three subpixels (red, green, and blue) to generate a single color pixel. LCDs use properties of polarized light to block or pass light through the LCD screen and, in the case of active matrix display technologies, thin film transistors (TFTs) are used to provide the proper signals to address each pixel on the screen. Light filters are used to produce the three primary colors of light at each pixel triad location. In plasma units, pixels are tiny gas cells coated with phosphor to produce one of the three primary colors. The individual cells are addressed in a manner analogous to LCDs. This individual pixel triad coordinate addressing capability is the foundation of digital displays.

The characteristics generally used to distinguish one color from another are brightness, hue, and saturation. As indicated earlier in this section, brightness embodies the achromatic notion of intensity. *Hue* is an attribute associated with the dominant wavelength in a mixture of light waves. Hue represents dominant color as perceived by an observer. Thus, when we call an object red, orange, or yellow, we are referring to its hue. *Saturation* refers to the relative purity or the amount of white light mixed with a hue. The pure spectrum colors are fully saturated. Colors such as pink (red and white) and lavender (violet and white) are less saturated, with the degree of saturation being inversely proportional to the amount of white light added.

Hue and saturation taken together are called *chromaticity* and, therefore, a color may be characterized by its brightness and chromaticity. The amounts of red, green, and blue needed to form any particular color are called the *tristimulus* values, and are denoted, X, Y, and Z, respectively. A color is then specified by its *trichromatic coefficients*, defined as

$$x = \frac{X}{X + Y + Z} \tag{6-1}$$

$$y = \frac{Y}{X + Y + Z} \tag{6-2}$$

and

$$z = \frac{Z}{X + Y + Z} \tag{6-3}$$

Our use of x, y, and z in this context follows convention. These should not be confused with our use of (x, y) throughout the book to denote spatial coordinates.

We see from these equations that

$$x + y + z = 1 \tag{6-4}$$

For any wavelength of light in the visible spectrum, the tristimulus values needed to produce the color corresponding to that wavelength can be obtained directly from curves or tables that have been compiled from extensive experimental results (Poynton [1996, 2012]).

Another approach for specifying colors is to use the CIE *chromaticity diagram* (see Fig. 6.5), which shows color composition as a function of x (red) and y (green). For any value of x and y, the corresponding value of z (blue) is obtained from Eq. (6-4) by noting that $z = 1 - (x + y)$. The point marked green in Fig. 6.5, for example, has approximately 62% green and 25% red content. It follows from Eq. (6-4) that the composition of blue is approximately 13%.

The positions of the various spectrum colors—from violet at 380 nm to red at 780 nm—are indicated around the boundary of the tongue-shaped chromaticity diagram. These are the pure colors shown in the spectrum of Fig. 6.2. Any point not actually on the boundary, but within the diagram, represents some mixture of the pure spectrum colors. The *point of equal energy* shown in Fig. 6.5 corresponds to equal fractions of the three primary colors; it represents the CIE standard for white light. Any point located on the boundary of the chromaticity chart is fully saturated. As a point leaves the boundary and approaches the point of equal energy, more white light is added to the color, and it becomes less saturated. The saturation at the point of equal energy is zero.

The chromaticity diagram is useful for color mixing because a straight-line segment joining any two points in the diagram defines all the different color variations that can be obtained by combining these two colors additively. Consider, for example, a straight line drawn from the red to the green points shown in Fig. 6.5. If there is more red than green light, the exact point representing the new color will be on the line segment, but it will be closer to the red point than to the green point. Similarly, a line drawn from the point of equal energy to any point on the boundary of the chart will define all the shades of that particular spectrum color.

Extending this procedure to three colors is straightforward. To determine the range of colors that can be obtained from any three given colors in the chromaticity diagram, we simply draw connecting lines to each of the three color points. The result is a triangle, and any color inside the triangle, or on its boundary, can be produced by various combinations of the three vertex colors. A triangle with vertices at any three fixed colors cannot enclose the entire color region in Fig. 6.5. This observation supports graphically the remark made earlier that not all colors can be obtained with three single, *fixed* primaries, because three colors form a triangle.

The triangle in Fig. 6.6 shows a representative range of colors (called the *color gamut*) produced by RGB monitors. The shaded region inside the triangle illustrates the color gamut of today's high-quality color printing devices. The boundary of the color printing gamut is irregular because color printing is a combination of additive and subtractive color mixing, a process that is much more difficult to control than

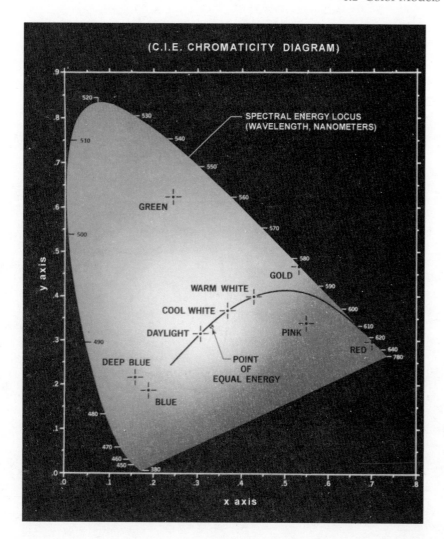

that of displaying colors on a monitor, which is based on the addition of three highly controllable light primaries.

6.2 COLOR MODELS

The purpose of a *color model* (also called a *color space* or *color system*) is to facilitate the specification of colors in some standard way. In essence, a color model is a specification of (1) a coordinate system, and (2) a subspace within that system, such that each color in the model is represented by a single point contained in that subspace.

Most color models in use today are oriented either toward hardware (such as for color monitors and printers) or toward applications, where color manipulation is a goal (the creation of color graphics for animation is an example of the latter). In terms of digital image processing, the hardware-oriented models most commonly used in practice are the RGB (red, green, blue) model for color monitors and a

FIGURE 6.6
Illustrative color
gamut of color
monitors
(triangle) and
color printing
devices (shaded
region).

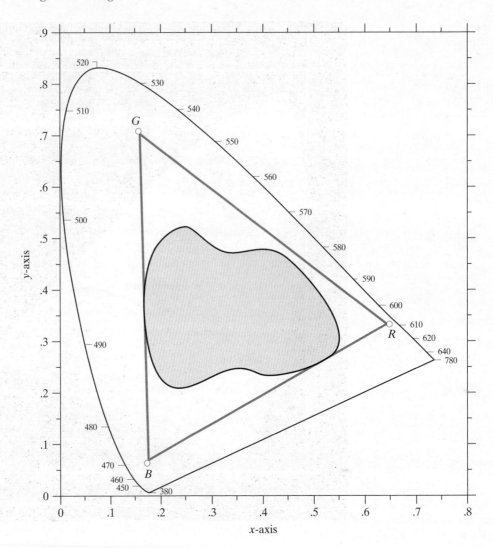

broad class of color video cameras; the CMY (cyan, magenta, yellow) and CMYK (cyan, magenta, yellow, black) models for color printing; and the HSI (hue, saturation, intensity) model, which corresponds closely with the way humans describe and interpret color. The HSI model also has the advantage that it decouples the color and gray-scale information in an image, making it suitable for many of the gray-scale techniques developed in this book. There are numerous color models in use today. This is a reflection of the fact that color science is a broad field that encompasses many areas of application. It is tempting to dwell on some of these models here, simply because they are interesting and useful. However, keeping to the task at hand, we focus attention on a few models that are representative of those used in image processing. Having mastered the material in this chapter, you will have no difficulty in understanding additional color models in use today.

FIGURE 6.7
Schematic of the RGB color cube. Points along the main diagonal have gray values, from black at the origin to white at point $(1, 1, 1)$.

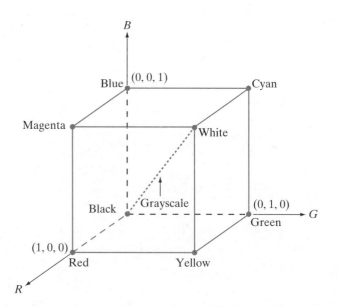

THE RGB COLOR MODEL

In the RGB model, each color appears in its primary spectral components of red, green, and blue. This model is based on a Cartesian coordinate system. The color subspace of interest is the cube shown in Fig. 6.7, in which RGB primary values are at three corners; the secondary colors cyan, magenta, and yellow are at three other corners; black is at the origin; and white is at the corner farthest from the origin. In this model, the grayscale (points of equal RGB values) extends from black to white along the line joining these two points. The different colors in this model are points on or inside the cube, and are defined by vectors extending from the origin. For convenience, the assumption is that all color values have been normalized so the cube in Fig. 6.7 is the unit cube. That is, all values of R, G, and B in this representation are assumed to be in the range $[0, 1]$. Note that the RGB primaries can be interpreted as unit vectors emanating from the origin of the cube.

Images represented in the RGB color model consist of three component images, one for each primary color. When fed into an RGB monitor, these three images combine on the screen to produce a composite color image, as explained in Section 6.1. The number of bits used to represent each pixel in RGB space is called the *pixel depth*. Consider an RGB image in which each of the red, green, and blue images is an 8-bit image. Under these conditions, each RGB *color pixel* [that is, a triplet of values (R, G, B)] has a depth of 24 bits (3 image planes times the number of bits per plane). The term *full-color* image is used often to denote a 24-bit RGB color image. The total number of possible colors in a 24-bit RGB image is $(2^8)^3 = 16,777,216$. Figure 6.8 shows the 24-bit RGB color cube corresponding to the diagram in Fig. 6.7. Note also that for digital images, the range of values in the cube are scaled to the

FIGURE 6.8
A 24-bit RGB
color cube.

numbers representable by the number bits in the images. If, as above, the primary images are 8-bit images, the limits of the cube along each axis becomes [0, 255]. Then, for example, white would be at point [255, 255, 255] in the cube.

EXAMPLE 6.1 : Generating a cross-section of the RGB color cube and its thee hidden planes.

The cube in Fig. 6.8 is a solid, composed of the $(2^8)^3$ colors mentioned in the preceding paragraph. A useful way to view these colors is to generate color planes (faces or cross sections of the cube). This is done by fixing one of the three colors and allowing the other two to vary. For instance, a cross-sectional plane through the center of the cube and parallel to the GB-plane in Fig. 6.8 is the plane (127, G, B) for $G, B = 0,1,2,...,255$. Figure 6.9(a) shows that an image of this cross-sectional plane is generated by feeding the three individual component images into a color monitor. In the component images, 0 represents black and 255 represents white. Observe that each component image into the monitor is a grayscale image. The monitor does the job of combining the intensities of these images to generate an RGB image. Figure 6.9(b) shows the three hidden surface planes of the cube in Fig. 6.8, generated in a similar manner.

Acquiring a color image is the process shown in Fig. 6.9(a) in reverse. A color image can be acquired by using three filters, sensitive to red, green, and blue, respectively. When we view a color scene with a monochrome camera equipped with one of these filters, the result is a monochrome image whose intensity is proportional to the response of that filter. Repeating this process with each filter produces three monochrome images that are the RGB component images of the color scene. In practice, RGB color image sensors usually integrate this process into a single device. Clearly, displaying these three RGB component images as in Fig. 6.9(a) would yield an RGB color rendition of the original color scene.

THE CMY AND CMYK COLOR MODELS

As indicated in Section 6.1, cyan, magenta, and yellow are the secondary colors of light or, alternatively, they are the primary colors of pigments. For example, when a surface coated with cyan pigment is illuminated with white light, no red light is reflected from the surface. That is, cyan subtracts red light from reflected white light, which itself is composed of equal amounts of red, green, and blue light.

Most devices that deposit colored pigments on paper, such as color printers and copiers, require CMY data input or perform an RGB to CMY conversion internally. This conversion is performed using the simple operation

a
b

FIGURE 6.9
(a) Generating
the RGB image of
the cross-sectional
color plane
(127, G, B).
(b) The three
hidden surface
planes in the color
cube of Fig. 6.8.

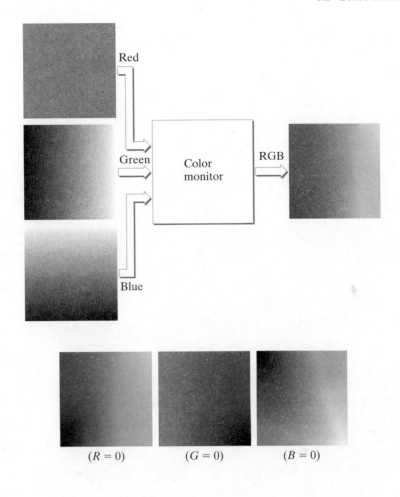

Equation (6-5), as well as
all other equations in this
section, are applied on a
pixel-by-pixel basis.

$$\begin{bmatrix} C \\ M \\ Y \end{bmatrix} = \begin{bmatrix} 1 \\ 1 \\ 1 \end{bmatrix} - \begin{bmatrix} R \\ G \\ B \end{bmatrix} \qquad (6\text{-}5)$$

where the assumption is that all RGB color values have been normalized to the
range [0, 1]. Equation (6-5) demonstrates that light reflected from a surface coated
with pure cyan does not contain red (that is, $C = 1 - R$ in the equation). Similarly,
pure magenta does not reflect green, and pure yellow does not reflect blue. Equation
(6-5) also reveals that RGB values can be obtained easily from a set of CMY values
by subtracting the individual CMY values from 1.

According to Fig. 6.4, equal amounts of the pigment primaries, cyan, magenta, and
yellow, should produce black. In practice, because C, M, and Y inks seldom are pure
colors, combining these colors for printing black produces instead a muddy-looking
brown. So, in order to produce true black (which is the predominant color in printing), a fourth color, *black*, denoted by K, is added, giving rise to the CMYK color
model. The black is added in just the proportions needed to produce true black. Thus,

when publishers talk about "four-color printing," they are referring to the three CMY colors, plus a portion of black.

The conversion from CMY to CMYK begins by letting

$$K = \min(C, M, Y) \tag{6-6}$$

If $K = 1$, then we have pure black, with no color contributions, from which it follows that

$$C = 0 \tag{6-7}$$

$$M = 0 \tag{6-8}$$

$$Y = 0 \tag{6-9}$$

The C, M, and Y on the right side of Eqs. (6-6)-(6-12) are in the CMY color system. The C, M, and Y on left of Eqs. (6-7)-(6-12) are in the CMYK system.

Otherwise,

$$C = (C - K)/(1 - K) \tag{6-10}$$

$$M = (M - K)/(1 - K) \tag{6-11}$$

$$Y = (Y - K)/(1 - K) \tag{6-12}$$

where all values are assumed to be in the range [0, 1]. The conversions from CMYK back to CMY are:

The C, M, Y, and K on the right side of Eqs. (6-13)-(6-15) are in the CMYK color system. The C, M, and Y on the left of these equations are in the CMY system.

$$C = C * (1 - K) + K \tag{6-13}$$

$$M = M * (1 - K) + K \tag{6-14}$$

$$Y = Y * (1 - Y) + K \tag{6-15}$$

As noted at the beginning of this section, all operations in the preceding equations are performed on a pixel-by-pixel basis. Because we can use Eq. (6-5) to convert both ways between CMY and RGB, we can use that equation as a "bridge" to convert between RGB and CMYK, and vice versa.

It is important to keep in mind that all the conversions just presented to go between RGB, CMY, and CMYK are based on the preceding relationships as a group. There are many other ways to convert between these color models, so you cannot mix approaches and expect to get meaningful results. Also, colors seen on monitors generally appear much different when printed, unless these devices are calibrated (see the discussion of a device-independent color model later in this section). The same holds true in general for colors converted from one model to another. However, our interest in this chapter is not on color fidelity; rather, we are interested in using the properties of color models to facilitate image processing tasks, such as region detection.

THE HSI COLOR MODEL

As we have seen, creating colors in the RGB, CMY, and CMYK models, and changing from one model to the other, is straightforward. These color systems are ideally suited for hardware implementations. In addition, the RGB system matches nicely with the fact that the human eye is strongly perceptive to red, green, and blue primaries. Unfortunately, the RGB, CMY, and other similar color models are not well suited for describing colors in terms that are practical for human interpretation. For example, one does not refer to the color of an automobile by giving the percentage of each of the primaries composing its color. Furthermore, we do not think of color images as being composed of three primary images that combine to form a single image.

When humans view a color object, we describe it by its hue, saturation, and brightness. Recall from the discussion in Section 6.1 that hue is a color attribute that describes a pure color (pure yellow, orange, or red), whereas saturation gives a measure of the degree to which a pure color is diluted by white light. Brightness is a subjective descriptor that is practically impossible to measure. It embodies the achromatic notion of *intensity* and is one of the key factors in describing color sensation. We do know that intensity (gray level) is a most useful descriptor of achromatic images. This quantity definitely is measurable and easily interpretable. The model we are about to present, called the *HSI* (hue, saturation, intensity) *color model*, decouples the intensity component from the color-carrying information (hue and saturation) in a color image. As a result, the HSI model is a useful tool for developing image processing algorithms based on color descriptions that are natural and intuitive to humans, who, after all, are the developers and users of these algorithms. We can summarize by saying that RGB is ideal for image color generation (as in image capture by a color camera or image display on a monitor screen), but its use for color description is much more limited. The material that follows provides an effective way to do this.

We know from Example 6.1 that an RGB color image is composed three grayscale intensity images (representing red, green, and blue), so it should come as no surprise that we can to extract intensity from an RGB image. This becomes clear if we take the color cube from Fig. 6.7 and stand it on the black, $(0, 0, 0)$, vertex, with the white, $(1, 1, 1)$, vertex directly above it [see Fig. 6.10(a)]. As noted in our discussion of Fig. 6.7, the intensity (gray) scale is along the line joining these two vertices. In Figs. 6.10(a) and (b), the line (intensity axis) joining the black and white vertices is vertical. Thus, if we wanted to determine the intensity component of any color point in Fig. 6.10, we would simply define a plane that contains the color point and, at the same time, is perpendicular to the intensity axis. The intersection of the plane with the intensity axis would give us a point with intensity value in the range $[0, 1]$. A little thought would reveal that the saturation (purity) of a color increases as a function of distance from the intensity axis. In fact, the saturation of points on the intensity axis is zero, as evidenced by the fact that all points along this axis are gray.

Hue can be determined from an RGB value also. To see how, consider Fig. 6.10(b), which shows a plane defined by three points (black, white, and cyan). The fact that

a b

FIGURE 6.10
Conceptual
relationships
between the RGB
and HSI color
models.

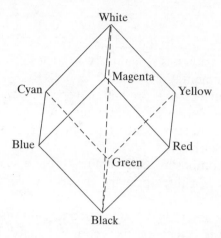
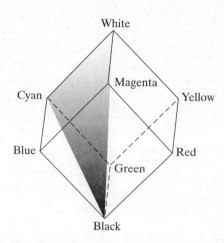

the black and white points are contained in the plane tells us that the intensity axis also is contained in the plane. Furthermore, we see that *all* points contained in the plane segment defined by the intensity axis and the boundaries of the cube have the *same* hue (cyan in this case). We could arrive at the same conclusion by recalling from Section 6.1 that all colors generated by three colors lie in the triangle defined by those colors. If two of those points are black and white, and the third is a color point, all points on the triangle would have the same hue, because the black and white components cannot change the hue (of course, the intensity and saturation of points in this triangle would be different). By rotating the shaded plane about the vertical intensity axis, we would obtain different hues. From these concepts, we arrive at the conclusion that the hue, saturation, and intensity values required to form the HSI space can be obtained from the RGB color cube. That is, we can convert any RGB point to a corresponding point in the HSI color space by working out the formulas that describe the reasoning outlined in the preceding discussion.

The key point regarding the cube arrangement in Fig. 6.10, and its corresponding HSI color space, is that the HSI space is represented by a vertical intensity axis, and the locus of color points that lie on planes perpendicular to that axis. As the planes move up and down the intensity axis, the boundaries defined by the intersection of each plane with the faces of the cube have either a triangular or a hexagonal shape. This can be visualized much more readily by looking at the cube straight down its grayscale axis, as shown in Fig. 6.11(a). We see that the primary colors are separated by 120°. The secondary colors are 60° from the primaries, which means that the angle between secondaries is 120° also. Figure 6.11(b) shows the same hexagonal shape and an arbitrary color point (shown as a dot). The hue of the point is determined by an angle from some reference point. Usually (but not always) an angle of 0° from the red axis designates 0 hue, and the hue increases counterclockwise from there. The saturation (distance from the vertical axis) is the length of the vector from the origin to the point. Note that the origin is defined by the intersection of the color plane with the vertical intensity axis. The important components of the HSI color space are the vertical intensity axis, the length of the vector to a color point, and the

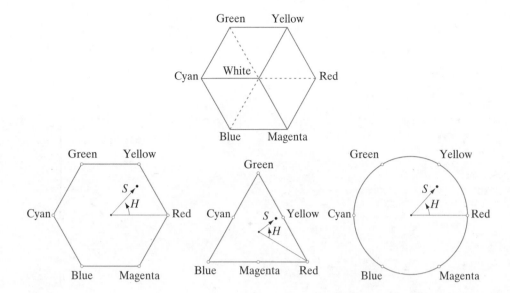

a
b c d

FIGURE 6.11
Hue and saturation in the HSI color model. The dot is any color point. The angle from the red axis gives the hue. The length of the vector is the saturation. The intensity of all colors in any of these planes is given by the position of the plane on the vertical intensity axis.

angle this vector makes with the red axis. Therefore, it is not unusual to see the HSI planes defined in terms of the hexagon just discussed, a triangle, or even a circle, as Figs. 6.11(c) and (d) show. The shape chosen does not matter because any one of these shapes can be warped into one of the other two by a geometric transformation. Figure 6.12 shows the HSI model based on color triangles, and on circles.

Converting Colors from RGB to HSI

Given an image in RGB color format, the H component of each RGB pixel is obtained using the equation

Computations from RGB to HSI and back are carried out on a pixel-by-pixel basis. We omitted the dependence of the conversion equations on (x, y) for notational clarity.

$$H = \begin{cases} \theta & \text{if } B \leq G \\ 360 - \theta & \text{if } B > G \end{cases} \tag{6-16}$$

with[†]

$$\theta = \cos^{-1}\left\{ \frac{\frac{1}{2}\left[(R - G) + (R - B)\right]}{\left[(R - G)^2 + (R - B)(G - B)\right]^{1/2}} \right\} \tag{6-17}$$

The saturation component is given by

$$S = 1 - \frac{3}{(R + G + B)}\left[\min(R, G, B)\right] \tag{6-18}$$

[†] It is good practice to add a small number in the denominator of this expression to avoid dividing by 0 when $R = G = B$, in which case θ will be 90°. Note that when all RGB components are equal, Eq. (6-18) gives $S = 0$. In addition, the conversion from HSI back to RGB in Eqs. (6-20) through (6-30) will give $R = G = B = I$, as expected, because, when $R = G = B$, we are dealing with a grayscale image.

FIGURE 6.12
The HSI color
model based on
(a) triangular, and
(b) circular color
planes. The
triangles and
circles are
perpendicular to
the vertical
intensity axis.

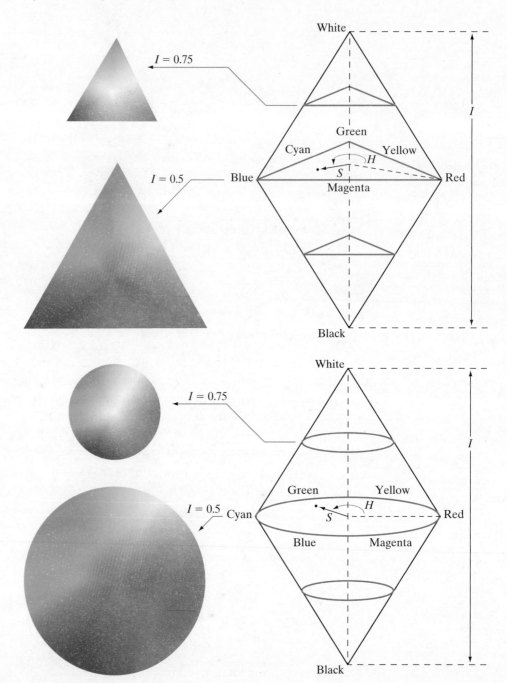

Finally, the intensity component is obtained from the equation

$$I = \frac{1}{3}(R + G + B) \tag{6-19}$$

These equations assume that the RGB values have been normalized to the range [0, 1], and that angle θ is measured with respect to the red axis of the HSI space, as in Fig. 6.11. Hue can be normalized to the range [0, 1] by dividing by 360° all values resulting from Eq. (6-16). The other two HSI components already are in this range if the given RGB values are in the interval [0, 1].

The results in Eqs. (6-16) through (6-19) can be derived from the geometry in Figs. 6.10 and 6.11. The derivation is tedious and would not add significantly to the present discussion. You can find the proof for these equations (and for the equations that follow for HSI to RGB conversion) in the *Tutorials* section of the book website.

Converting Colors from HSI to RGB

Given values of HSI in the interval [0, 1], we now want to find the corresponding RGB values in the same range. The applicable equations depend on the values of H. There are three sectors of interest, corresponding to the 120° intervals in the separation of primaries (see Fig. 6.11). We begin by multiplying H by 360°, which returns the hue to its original range of [0°, 360°].

RG sector $(0° \leq H < 120°)$: When H is in this sector, the RGB components are given by the equations

$$B = I(1 - S) \tag{6-20}$$

$$R = I\left[1 + \frac{S \cos H}{\cos(60° - H)}\right] \tag{6-21}$$

and

$$G = 3I - (R + B) \tag{6-22}$$

GB sector $(120° \leq H < 240°)$: If the given value of H is in this sector, we first subtract 120° from it:

$$H = H - 120° \tag{6-23}$$

Then, the RGB components are

$$R = I(1 - S) \tag{6-24}$$

$$G = I\left[1 + \frac{S \cos H}{\cos(60° - H)}\right] \tag{6-25}$$

and

$$B = 3I - (R + G) \tag{6-26}$$

BR sector $(240° \leq H \leq 360°)$: Finally, if H is in this range, we subtract 240° from it:

$$H = H - 240° \tag{6-27}$$

Then, the RGB components are

$$G = I(1 - S) \tag{6-28}$$

$$B = I\left[1 + \frac{S \cos H}{\cos(60° - H)}\right] \tag{6-29}$$

and

$$R = 3I - (G + B) \tag{6-30}$$

We discuss several uses of these equations in the following sections.

EXAMPLE 6.2:   The HSI values corresponding to the image of the RGB color cube.

Figure 6.13 shows the hue, saturation, and intensity images for the RGB values in Fig. 6.8. Figure 6.13(a) is the hue image. Its most distinguishing feature is the discontinuity in value along a 45° line in the front (red) plane of the cube. To understand the reason for this discontinuity, refer to Fig. 6.8, draw a line from the red to the white vertices of the cube, and select a point in the middle of this line. Starting at that point, draw a path to the right, following the cube around until you return to the starting point. The major colors encountered in this path are yellow, green, cyan, blue, magenta, and back to red. According to Fig. 6.11, the values of hue along this path should increase from 0° to 360° (i.e., from the lowest to highest

a b c

FIGURE 6.13 HSI components of the image in Fig. 6.8: (a) hue, (b) saturation, and (c) intensity images.

possible values of hue). This is precisely what Fig. 6.13(a) shows, because the lowest value is represented as black and the highest value as white in the grayscale. In fact, the hue image was originally normalized to the range [0, 1] and then scaled to 8 bits; that is, we converted it to the range [0, 255], for display.

The saturation image in Fig. 6.13(b) shows progressively darker values toward the white vertex of the RGB cube, indicating that colors become less and less saturated as they approach white. Finally, every pixel in the intensity image shown in Fig. 6.13(c) is the average of the RGB values at the corresponding pixel in Fig. 6.8.

Manipulating HSI Component Images

In the following discussion, we take a look at some simple techniques for manipulating HSI component images. This will help you develop familiarity with these comonents, and deepen your understanding of the HSI color model. Figure 6.14(a) shows an image composed of the primary and secondary RGB colors. Figures 6.14(b) through (d) show the H, S, and I components of this image, generated using Eqs. (6-16) through (6-19). Recall from the discussion earlier in this section that the gray-level values in Fig. 6.14(b) correspond to angles; thus, for example, because red corresponds to 0°, the red region in Fig. 6.14(a) is mapped to a black region in the hue image. Similarly, the gray levels in Fig. 6.14(c) correspond to saturation (they were scaled to [0, 255] for display), and the gray levels in Fig. 6.14(d) are average intensities.

To change the individual color of any region in the RGB image, we change the values of the corresponding region in the hue image of Fig. 6.14(b). Then we convert

a b
c d

FIGURE 6.14
(a) RGB image
and the
components of
its corresponding
HSI image:
(b) hue,
(c) saturation, and
(d) intensity.

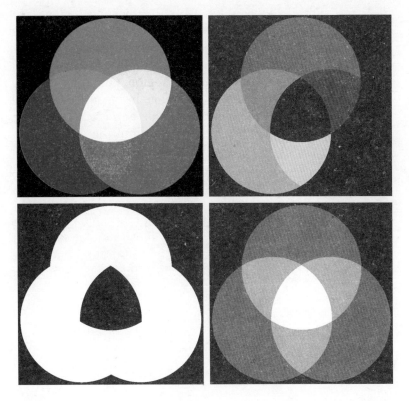

a b
c d

FIGURE 6.15
(a)-(c) Modified
HSI component
images.
(d) Resulting RGB
image. (See Fig.
6.14 for the original
HSI images.)

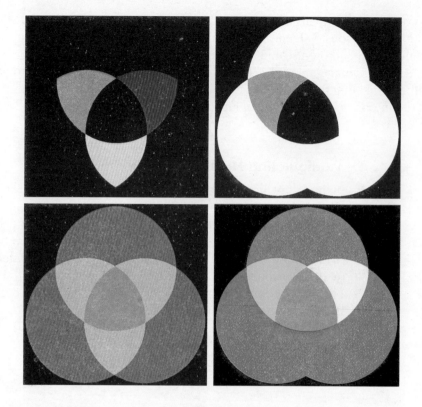

the new H image, along with the unchanged S and I images, back to RGB using the procedure explained in Eqs. (6-20) through (6-30). To change the saturation (purity) of the color in any region, we follow the same procedure, except that we make the changes in the saturation image in HSI space. Similar comments apply to changing the average intensity of any region. Of course, these changes can be made simultaneously. For example, the image in Fig. 6.15(a) was obtained by changing to 0 the pixels corresponding to the blue and green regions in Fig. 6.14(b). In Fig. 6.15(b), we reduced by half the saturation of the cyan region in component image S from Fig. 6.14(c). In Fig. 6.15(c), we reduced by half the intensity of the central white region in the intensity image of Fig. 6.14(d). The result of converting this modified HSI image back to RGB is shown in Fig. 6.15(d). As expected, we see in this figure that the outer portions of all circles are now red; the purity of the cyan region was diminished, and the central region became gray rather than white. Although these results are simple, they clearly illustrate the power of the HSI color model in allowing independent control over hue, saturation, and intensity. These are quantities with which humans are quite familiar when describing colors.

A DEVICE INDEPENDENT COLOR MODEL

As noted earlier, humans see a broad spectrum of colors and color shades. However, color perception differs between individuals. Not only that, but color across devices such as monitors and printers can vary significantly unless these devices are properly calibrated.

Color transformations can be performed on most desktop computers. In conjunction with digital cameras, flatbed scanners, and ink-jet printers, they turn a personal computer into a *digital darkroom*. Also, commercial devices exist that use a combination of spectrometer measurements and software to develop color profiles that can then be loaded on monitors and printers to calibrate their color responses.

The effectiveness of the transformations examined in this section is judged ultimately in print. Because these transformations are developed, refined, and evaluated on monitors, it is necessary to maintain a high degree of color consistency between the monitors used and the eventual output devices. This is best accomplished with a device-independent color model that relates the color gamuts (see Section 6.1) of the monitors and output devices, as well as any other devices being used, to one another. The success of this approach depends on the quality of the color profiles used to map each device to the model, as well as the model itself. The model of choice for many color management systems (CMS) is the CIE $L*a*b*$ model, also called CIELAB (CIE [1978], Robertson [1977]).

The $L*a*b*$ color components are given by the following equations:

$$L* = 116 \cdot h\left(\frac{Y}{Y_W}\right) - 16 \tag{6-31}$$

$$a* = 500\left[h\left(\frac{X}{X_W}\right) - h\left(\frac{Y}{Y_W}\right)\right] \tag{6-32}$$

and

$$b* = 200\left[h\left(\frac{Y}{Y_W}\right) - h\left(\frac{Z}{Z_W}\right)\right] \tag{6-33}$$

where

$$h(q) = \begin{cases} \sqrt[3]{q} & q > 0.008856 \\ 7.787q + 16/116 & q \leq 0.008856 \end{cases} \tag{6-34}$$

and X_W, Y_W, and Z_W are reference white tristimulus values—typically the white of a perfectly reflecting diffuser under CIE standard D65 illumination (defined by $x = 0.3127$ and $y = 0.3290$ in the CIE chromaticity diagram of Fig. 6.5). The $L*a*b*$ color space is *colorimetric* (i.e., colors perceived as matching are encoded identically), *perceptually uniform* (i.e., color differences among various hues are perceived uniformly—see the classic paper by MacAdams [1942]), and *device independent*. While $L*a*b*$ colors are not directly displayable (conversion to another color space is required), the $L*a*b*$ gamut encompasses the entire visible spectrum and can represent accurately the colors of any display, print, or input device. Like the HSI system, the $L*a*b*$ system is an excellent decoupler of intensity (represented by lightness $L*$) and color (represented by $a*$ for red minus green and $b*$ for green minus blue), making it useful in both image manipulation (tone and contrast editing) and image compression applications. Studies indicate that the degree to which the lightness information is separated from the color information in the $L*a*b*$ system is greater than in any other color system (see Kasson and Plouffe [1972]). The principal benefit of calibrated imaging systems is that they allow tonal and color imbalances to be corrected interactively and independently—that is, in two sequential operations. Before color irregularities, like over- and under-saturated colors, are resolved, problems involving the image's tonal range are corrected. The tonal range of an image, also called its *key type*, refers to its general distribution of color intensities. Most of the information in high-key images is concentrated at high (or light) intensities; the colors of low-key images are located predominantly at low intensities; middle-key images lie in between. As in the monochrome case, it is often desirable to distribute the intensities of a color image equally between the highlights and the shadows. In Section 6.4, we give examples showing a variety of color transformations for the correction of tonal and color imbalances.

6.3 PSEUDOCOLOR IMAGE PROCESSING

Pseudocolor (sometimes called *false color*) image processing consists of assigning colors to gray values based on a specified criterion. The term pseudo or false color is used to differentiate the process of assigning colors to achromatic images from the processes associated with true color images, a topic discussed starting in Section 6.4. The principal use of pseudocolor is for human visualization and interpretation of grayscale events in an image or sequence of images. As noted at the beginning of this chapter, one of the principal motivations for using color is the fact that humans can discern thousands of color shades and intensities, compared to less than two dozen shades of gray.

INTENSITY SLICING AND COLOR CODING

The techniques of *intensity* (sometimes called *density*) *slicing* and color coding are the simplest and earliest examples of pseudocolor processing of digital images. If an image is interpreted as a 3-D function [see Fig. 2.18(a)], the method can be viewed as one of placing planes parallel to the coordinate plane of the image; each plane then "slices" the function in the area of intersection. Figure 6.16 shows an example of using a plane at $f(x, y) = l_i$ to slice the image intensity function into two levels.

If a different color is assigned to each side of the plane in Fig. 6.16, any pixel whose intensity level is above the plane will be coded with one color, and any pixel below the plane will be coded with the other. Levels that lie on the plane itself may be arbitrarily assigned one of the two colors, or they could be given a third color to highlight all the pixels at that level. The result is a two- (or three-) color image whose relative appearance can be controlled by moving the slicing plane up and down the intensity axis.

In general, the technique for multiple colors may be summarized as follows. Let $[0, L-1]$ represent the grayscale, let level l_0 represent black $[f(x, y) = 0]$, and level l_{L-1} represent white $[f(x, y) = L-1]$. Suppose that P planes perpendicular to the intensity axis are defined at levels $l_1, l_2, ..., l_P$. Then, assuming that $0 < P < L-1$, the P planes partition the grayscale into $P+1$ intervals, $I_1, I_2, ..., I_{P+1}$. Intensity to color assignments at each pixel location (x, y) are made according to the equation

FIGURE 6.16
Graphical
interpretation of
the intensity-
slicing technique.

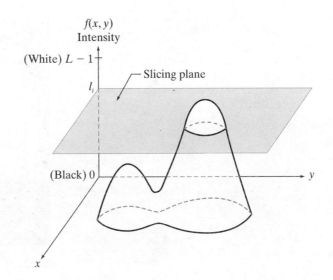

$$\text{if } f(x,y) \in I_k, \text{ let } f(x,y) = c_k \tag{6-35}$$

where c_k is the color associated with the kth intensity interval I_k, defined by the planes at $l = k - 1$ and $l = k$.

Figure 6.16 is not the only way to visualize the method just described. Figure 6.17 shows an equivalent approach. According to the mapping in this figure, any image intensity below level l_i is assigned one color, and any level above is assigned another. When more partitioning levels are used, the mapping function takes on a staircase form.

EXAMPLE 6.3: Intensity slicing and color coding.

A simple but practical use of intensity slicing is shown in Fig. 6.18. Figure 6.18(a) is a grayscale image of the Picker Thyroid Phantom (a radiation test pattern), and Fig. 6.18(b) is the result of intensity slicing this image into eight colors. Regions that appear of constant intensity in the grayscale image are actually quite variable, as shown by the various colors in the sliced image. For instance, the left lobe is a dull gray in the grayscale image, and picking out variations in intensity is difficult. By contrast, the color image

FIGURE 6.17
An alternative
representation of
the intensity-
slicing technique.

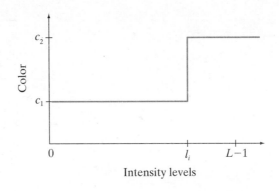

a b

FIGURE 6.18
(a) Grayscale image of the Picker Thyroid Phantom.
(b) Result of intensity slicing using eight colors. (Courtesy of Dr. J. L. Blankenship, Oak Ridge National Laboratory.)

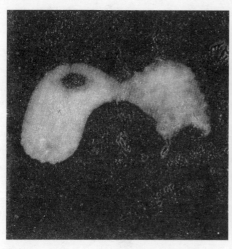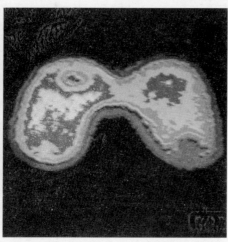

clearly shows eight different regions of constant intensity, one for each of the colors used. By varying the number of colors and the span of the intensity intervals, one can quickly determine the characteristics of intensity variations in a grayscale image. This is particularly true in situations such as the one shown here, in which the object of interest has uniform texture with intensity variations that are difficult to analyze visually. This example also illustrates the comments made in Section 6.1 about the eye's superior capability for detecting different color shades.

In the preceding simple example, the grayscale was divided into intervals and a different color was assigned to each, with no regard for the meaning of the gray levels in the image. Interest in that case was simply to view the different gray levels constituting the image. Intensity slicing assumes a much more meaningful and useful role when subdivision of the grayscale is based on physical characteristics of the image. For instance, Fig. 6.19(a) shows an X-ray image of a weld (the broad, horizontal dark region) containing several cracks and porosities (the bright streaks running horizontally through the middle of the image). When there is a porosity or crack in a weld, the full strength of the X-rays going through the object saturates the imaging sensor on the other side of the object. Thus, intensity values of 255 in an 8-bit image coming from such a system automatically imply a problem with the weld. If human visual analysis is used to inspect welds (still a common procedure today), a simple color coding that assigns

a b

FIGURE 6.19
(a) X-ray image of a weld.
(b) Result of color coding. (Original image courtesy of X-TEK Systems, Ltd.)

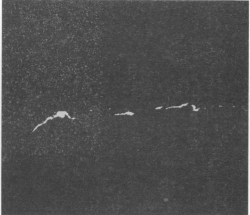

one color to level 255 and another to all other intensity levels can simplify the inspector's job considerably. Figure 6.19(b) shows the result. No explanation is required to arrive at the conclusion that human error rates would be lower if images were displayed in the form of Fig. 6.19(b), instead of the form in Fig. 6.19(a). In other words, if an intensity value, or range of values, one is looking for is known, intensity slicing is a simple but powerful aid in visualization, especially if numerous images have to be inspected on a routine basis.

EXAMPLE 6.4: Use of color to highlight rainfall levels.

Measurement of rainfall levels, especially in the tropical regions of the Earth, is of interest in diverse applications dealing with the environment. Accurate measurements using ground-based sensors are difficult and expensive to acquire, and total rainfall figures are even more difficult to obtain because a significant portion of precipitation occurs over the ocean. One approach for obtaining rainfall figures remotely is to use satellites. The TRMM (Tropical Rainfall Measuring Mission) satellite utilizes, among others, three sensors specially designed to detect rain: a precipitation radar, a microwave imager, and a visible and infrared scanner (see Sections 1.3 and 2.3 regarding image sensing modalities).

The results from the various rain sensors are processed, resulting in estimates of average rainfall over a given time period in the area monitored by the sensors. From these estimates, it is not difficult to generate grayscale images whose intensity values correspond directly to rainfall, with each pixel representing a physical land area whose size depends on the resolution of the sensors. Such an intensity image is shown in Fig. 6.20(a), where the area monitored by the satellite is the horizontal band highlighted in the middle of the picture (these are tropical regions). In this particular example, the rainfall values are monthly averages (in inches) over a three-year period.

Visual examination of this picture for rainfall patterns is difficult and prone to error. However, suppose that we code intensity levels from 0 to 255 using the colors shown in Fig. 6.20(b). In this mode of intensity slicing, each slice is one of the colors in the color band. Values toward the blues signify low values of rainfall, with the opposite being true for red. Note that the scale tops out at pure red for values of rainfall greater than 20 inches. Figure 6.20(c) shows the result of color coding the grayscale image with the color map just discussed. The results are much easier to interpret, as shown in this figure and in the zoomed area of Fig. 6.20(d). In addition to providing global coverage, this type of data allows meteorologists to calibrate ground-based rain monitoring systems with greater precision than ever before.

INTENSITY TO COLOR TRANSFORMATIONS

Other types of transformations are more general, and thus are capable of achieving a wider range of pseudocolor enhancement results than the simple slicing technique discussed in the preceding section. Figure 6.21 shows an approach that is particularly attractive. Basically, the idea underlying this approach is to perform three independent transformations on the intensity of input pixels. The three results are then fed separately into the red, green, and blue channels of a color monitor. This method produces a composite image whose color content is modulated by the nature of the transformation functions.

The method for intensity slicing discussed in the previous section is a special case of the technique just described. There, piecewise linear functions of the intensity levels (see Fig. 6.17) are used to generate colors. On the other hand, the method

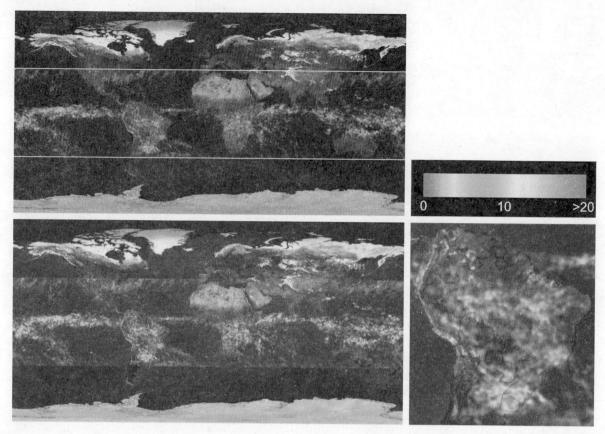

a b
c d

FIGURE 6.20 (a) Grayscale image in which intensity (in the horizontal band shown) corresponds to average monthly rainfall. (b) Colors assigned to intensity values. (c) Color-coded image. (d) Zoom of the South American region. (Courtesy of NASA.)

FIGURE 6.21
Functional block diagram for pseudocolor image processing. Images f_R, f_G, and f_B are fed into the corresponding red, green, and blue inputs of an RGB color monitor.

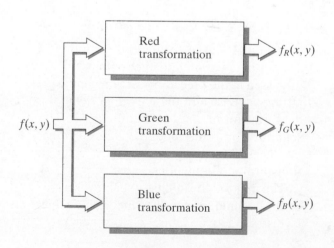

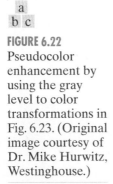

FIGURE 6.22
Pseudocolor
enhancement by
using the gray
level to color
transformations in
Fig. 6.23. (Original
image courtesy of
Dr. Mike Hurwitz,
Westinghouse.)

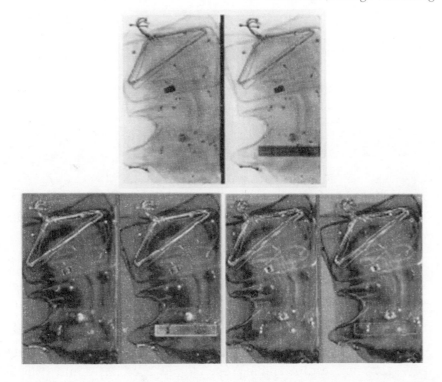

discussed in this section can be based on smooth, nonlinear functions, which gives the technique considerable flexibility.

EXAMPLE 6.5: Using pseudocolor to highlight explosives in X-ray images.

Figure 6.22(a) shows two monochrome images of luggage obtained from an airport X-ray scanning system. The image on the left contains ordinary articles. The image on the right contains the same articles, as well as a block of simulated plastic explosives. The purpose of this example is to illustrate the use of intensity to color transformations to facilitate detection of the explosives.

Figure 6.23 shows the transformation functions used. These sinusoidal functions contain regions of relatively constant value around the peaks as well as regions that change rapidly near the valleys. Changing the phase and frequency of each sinusoid can emphasize (in color) ranges in the grayscale. For instance, if all three transformations have the same phase and frequency, the output will be a grayscale image. A small change in the phase between the three transformations produces little change in pixels whose intensities correspond to peaks in the sinusoids, especially if the sinusoids have broad profiles (low frequencies). Pixels with intensity values in the steep section of the sinusoids are assigned a much stronger color content as a result of significant differences between the amplitudes of the three sinusoids caused by the phase displacement between them.

The image in Fig. 6.22(b) was obtained using the transformation functions in Fig. 6.23(a), which shows the gray-level bands corresponding to the explosive, garment bag, and background, respectively. Note that the explosive and background have quite different intensity levels, but they were both coded with approximately the same color as a result of the periodicity of the sine waves. The image in Fig. 6.22(c) was obtained with the transformation functions in Fig. 6.23(b). In this case, the explosives and garment bag intensity bands were mapped by similar transformations, and thus received essentially the same

FIGURE 6.23
Transformation functions used to obtain the pseudocolor images in Fig. 6.22.

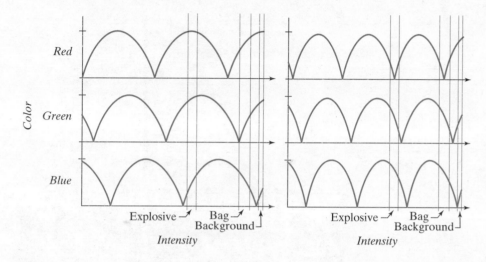

color assignments. Note that this mapping allows an observer to "see" through the explosives. The background mappings were about the same as those used for Fig. 6.22(b), producing almost identical color assignments for the two pseudocolor images.

The approach in Fig. 6.21 is based on a single grayscale image. Often, it is of interest to combine several grayscale images into a single color composite, as illustrated in Fig. 6.24. A frequent use of this approach is in multispectral image processing, where different sensors produce individual grayscale images, each in a different spectral band (see Example 6.6 below). The types of additional processing shown in Fig. 6.24 can be techniques such as color balancing and spatial filtering, as discussed later in this chapter. When coupled with background knowledge about the physical characteristics of each band, color-coding in the manner just explained is a powerful aid for human visual analysis of complex multispectral images.

EXAMPLE 6.6: Color coding of multispectral images.

Figures 6.25(a) through (d) show four satellite images of the Washington, D.C., area, including part of the Potomac River. The first three images are in the visible red (R), green (G), and blue (B) bands, and

FIGURE 6.24
A pseudocolor coding approach using multiple grayscale images. The inputs are grayscale images. The outputs are the three components of an RGB composite image.

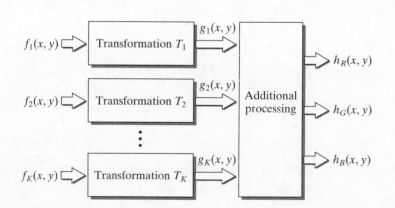

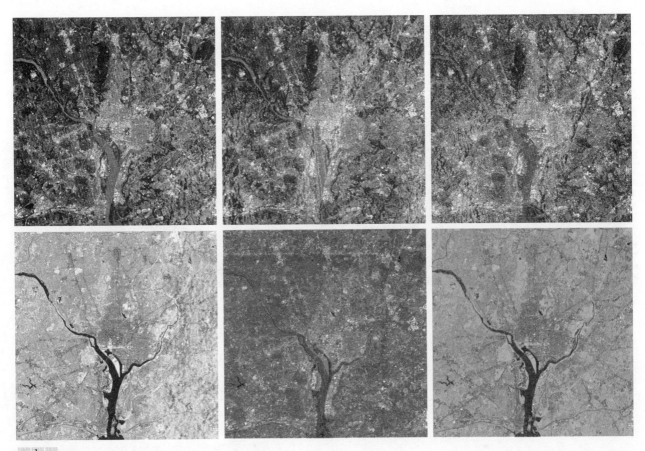

a b c
d e f

FIGURE 6.25 (a)–(d) Red (R), green (G), blue (B), and near-infrared (IR) components of a LANDSAT multispectral image of the Washington, D.C. area. (e) RGB color composite image obtained using the IR, G, and B component images. (f) RGB color composite image obtained using the R, IR, and B component images. (Original multispectral images courtesy of NASA.)

the fourth is in the near infrared (IR) band (see Table 1.1 and Fig. 1.10). The latter band is responsive to the biomass content of a scene, and we want to use this fact to create a composite RGB color image in which vegetation is emphasized and the other components of the scene are displayed in more muted tones.

Figure 6.25(e) is an RGB composite obtained by replacing the red image by infrared. As you see, vegetation shows as a bright red, and the other components of the scene, which had a weaker response in the near-infrared band, show in pale shades of blue-green. Figure 6.25(f) is a similar image, but with the green replaced by infrared. Here, vegetation shows in a bright green color, and the other components of the scene show in purplish color shades, indicating that their major components are in the red and blue bands. Although the last two images do not introduce any new physical information, these images are much easier to interpret visually once it is known that the dominant component of the images are pixels of areas heavily populated by vegetation.

The type of processing just illustrated uses the physical characteristics of a single band in a multispectral image to emphasize areas of interest. The same approach can help visualize events of interest

a
b

FIGURE 6.26
(a) Pseudocolor
rendition of
Jupiter Moon Io.
(b) A close-up.
(Courtesy of
NASA.)

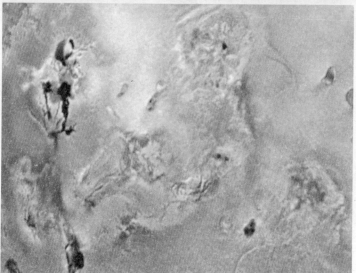

in complex images in which the events are beyond human visual sensing capabilities. Figure 6.26 is an excellent illustration of this. These are images of the Jupiter moon Io, shown in pseudocolor by combining several of the sensor images from the Galileo spacecraft, some of which are in spectral regions not visible to the eye. However, by understanding the physical and chemical processes likely to affect sensor response, it is possible to combine the sensed images into a meaningful pseudocolor map. One way to combine the sensed image data is by how they show either differences in surface chemical composition or changes in the way the surface reflects sunlight. For example, in the pseudocolor image in Fig. 6.26(b), bright red depicts material newly ejected from an active volcano on Io, and the surrounding yellow materials are older sulfur deposits. This image conveys these characteristics much more readily than would be possible by analyzing the component images individually.

6.4 BASICS OF FULL-COLOR IMAGE PROCESSING

In this section, we begin the study of processing methods for full-color images. The techniques developed in the sections that follow are illustrative of how full-color images are handled for a variety of image processing tasks. Full-color image processing approaches fall into two major categories. In the first category, we process each grayscale component image individually, then form a composite color image from the individually processed components. In the second category, we work with color pixels directly. Because full-color images have at least three components, color pixels are vectors. For example, in the RGB system, each color point can be interpreted as a vector extending from the origin to that point in the RGB coordinate system (see Fig. 6.7).

Let **c** represent an arbitrary vector in RGB color space:

$$\mathbf{c} = \begin{bmatrix} c_R \\ c_G \\ c_B \end{bmatrix} = \begin{bmatrix} R \\ G \\ B \end{bmatrix} \tag{6-36}$$

This equation indicates that the components of **c** are the RGB components of a color image at a point. We take into account the fact that the colors of the pixels in an image are a function of spatial coordinates (x, y) by using the notation

Although an RGB image is composed of three grayscale component images, pixels in all three images are registered spatially. That is, a *single* pair of spatial coordinates, (x, y), addresses the *same* pixel location in all three images, as illustrated in Fig. 6.27(b) below.

$$\mathbf{c}(x, y) = \begin{bmatrix} c_R(x, y) \\ c_G(x, y) \\ c_B(x, y) \end{bmatrix} = \begin{bmatrix} R(x, y) \\ G(x, y) \\ B(x, y) \end{bmatrix} \tag{6-37}$$

For an image of size $M \times N$, there are MN such vectors, $\mathbf{c}(x, y)$, for $x = 0, 1, 2, \ldots, M - 1$ and $y = 0, 1, 2, \ldots, N - 1$.

Equation (6-37) depicts a vector whose components are *spatial* variables x and y. This is a frequent source of confusion that can be avoided by focusing on the fact that our interest lies in spatial processes. That is, we are interested in image processing techniques formulated in x and y. The fact that the pixels are now color pixels introduces a factor that, in its easiest formulation, allows us to process a color image by processing each of its component images separately, using standard grayscale image processing methods. However, the results of individual color component processing are not always equivalent to direct processing in color vector space, in which case we must use approaches for processing the elements of color points directly. When these points have more than two components, we call them *voxels*. We use the terms vectors, points, and voxels interchangeably when the meaning is clear that we are referring to images composed of more than one 2-D image.

In order for per-component-image and vector-based processing to be equivalent, two conditions have to be satisfied: first, the process has to be applicable to both vectors and scalars; second, the operation on each component of a vector (i.e., each voxel) must be independent of the other components. As an illustration, Fig. 6.27 shows spatial neighborhood processing of grayscale and full-color images. Suppose

FIGURE 6.27
Spatial
neighborhoods
for grayscale
and RGB color
images. Observe
in (b) that a *single*
pair of spatial
coordinates, (x, y),
addresses the
same spatial
location in all
three images.

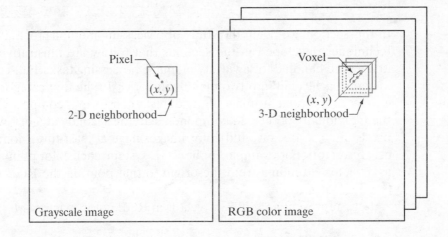

that the process is neighborhood averaging. In Fig. 6.27(a), averaging would be done by summing the intensities of all the pixels in the 2-D neighborhood, then dividing the result by the total number of pixels in the neighborhood. In Fig. 6.27(b), averaging would be done by summing all the voxels in the 3-D neighborhood, then dividing the result by the total number of voxels in the neighborhood. Each of the three component of the average voxel is the sum of the pixels in the single image neighborhood centered on that location. But the same result would be obtained if the averaging were done on the pixels of each image, independently, and then the sum of the three values were added for each. Thus, spatial neighborhood averaging can be carried out on a per-component-image or directly on RGB image voxels. The results would be the same. In the following sections we develop methods for which the per-component-image approach is suitable, and methods for which it is not.

6.5 COLOR TRANSFORMATIONS

The techniques described in this section, collectively called *color transformations*, deal with processing the components of a color image within the context of a *single* color model, as opposed to color transformations *between* color models, as in Section 6.2.

FORMULATION

As with the intensity transformation techniques of Chapter 3, we model color transformations for multispectral images using the general expression

$$s_i = T_i(r_i) \qquad i = 1, 2, \ldots, n \tag{6-38}$$

where n is the total number of component images, r_i are the intensity values of the input component images, s_i are the spatially corresponding intensities in the output component images, and T_i are a set of *transformation* or *color mapping functions* that operate on r_i to produce s_i. Equation (6-38) is applied individually to all pixels in the input image. For example, in the case of RGB color images, $n = 3$, r_1, r_2, r_3 are the intensities values at a point in the input components images, and s_1, s_2, s_3 are the corresponding transformed pixels in the output image. The fact that i is also a subscript on T means that, in principle, we can implement a different transformation for each input component image.

As an illustration, the first row of Fig. 6.28 shows a full color CMYK image of a simple scene, and the second row shows its four component images, all normalized to the range $[0, 1]$. We see that the strawberries are composed of large amounts of magenta and yellow because the images corresponding to these two CMYK components are the brightest. Black is used sparingly and is generally confined to the coffee and shadows within the bowl of strawberries. The fourth row shows the equivalent RGB images obtained from the CMYK images using Eqs. (6-13)-(6-15). Here we see that the strawberries contain a large amount of red and very little (although some) green and blue. From the RGB images, we obtained the CMY images in the third row using Eq. (6-5). Note that these CMY images are slightly different from the CMY images in the row above them. This is because the CMY images in these two systems are different as a result of using K in one of them. The last row of Fig. 6.28 shows the HSI components, obtained from the RGB images using Eqs. (6-16)-(6-19). As expected, the intensity (I) component is a grayscale rendition of the full-color original. The saturation image (S) is as expected also. The strawberries are relatively pure in color; as a result, they show the highest saturation (least dilution by white light) values of any of the other elements of the image. Finally, we note some difficulty in interpreting the values of the hue (H) component image. The problem is that (1) there is a discontinuity in the HSI model where $0°$ and $360°$ meet [see Fig. 6.13(a)], and (2) hue is undefined for a saturation of 0 (i.e., for white, black, and pure grays). The discontinuity of the model is most apparent around the strawberries, which are depicted in gray level values near both black (0) and white (1). The result is an unexpected mixture of highly contrasting gray levels to represent a single color—red.

We can apply Eq. (6-38) to any of the color-space component images in Fig. 6.28. In theory, any transformation can be performed in any color model. In practice, however, some operations are better suited to specific models. For a given transformation, the effects of converting between representations must be factored into the decision regarding the color space in which to implement it. For example, suppose that we wish to modify the intensity of the full-color image in the first row of Fig. 6.28 by a constant value, k in the range $[0, 1]$. In the HSI color space we need to modify only the intensity component image:

$$s_3 = kr_3 \tag{6-39}$$

and we let $s_1 = r_1$ and $s_2 = r_2$. In terms of our earlier discussion note that we are using two different transformation functions: T_1 and T_2 are identity transformations, and T_3 is a constant transformation.

In the RGB color space we need to modify all three components by the same constant transformation:

$$s_i = kr_i \quad i = 1, 2, 3 \tag{6-40}$$

Full color image

Cyan   Magenta   Yellow   Black

Cyan   Magenta   Yellow

Red   Green   Blue

Hue   Saturation   Intensity

FIGURE 6.28 A full-color image and its various color-space components. (Original image courtesy of MedData Interactive.)

The CMY space requires a similar set of linear transformations (see Problem 6.16):

$$s_i = kr_i + (1 - k) \quad i = 1,2,3 \tag{6-41}$$

Similarly, the transformations required to change the intensity of the CMYK image is given by

$$s_i = \begin{cases} r_i & i = 1,2,3 \\ kr_i + (1-k) & i = 4 \end{cases} \tag{6-42}$$

This equation tells us that to change the intensity of a CMYK image, we only change the fourth (K) component.

Figure 6.29(b) shows the result of applying the transformations in Eqs. (6-39) through (6-42) to the full-color image of Fig. 6.28, using $k = 0.7$. The mapping functions themselves are shown graphically in Figs. 6.29(c) through (h). Note that the mapping function for CMYK consist of two parts, as do the functions for HSI; one of the transformations handles one component, and the other does the rest. Although

a b
c d e f g h

FIGURE 6.29 Adjusting the intensity of an image using color transformations. (a) Original image. (b) Result of decreasing its intensity by 30% (i.e., letting $k = 0.7$). (c) The required RGB mapping function. (d)–(e) The required CMYK mapping functions. (f) The required CMY mapping function. (g)–(h) The required HSI mapping functions. (Original image courtesy of MedData Interactive.)

we used several different transformations, the net result of changing the intensity of the color by a constant value was the same for all.

It is important to note that each transformation defined in Eqs. (6-39) through (6-42) depends only on one component within its color space. For example, the red output component, s_1, in Eq. (6-40) is independent of the green (r_2) and blue (r_3) inputs; it depends only on the red (r_1) input. Transformations of this type are among the simplest and most frequently used color processing tools. They can be carried out on a per-color-component basis, as mentioned at the beginning of our discussion. In the remainder of this section, we will examine several such transformations and discuss a case in which the component transformation functions are dependent on all the color components of the input image and, therefore, cannot be done on an individual color-component basis.

COLOR COMPLEMENTS

The *color circle* (also called the *color wheel*) shown in Fig. 6.30 originated with Sir Isaac Newton, who in the seventeenth century created its first form by joining the ends of the color spectrum. The color circle is a visual representation of colors that are arranged according to the chromatic relationship between them. The circle is formed by placing the primary colors equidistant from each other. Then, the secondary colors are placed between the primaries, also in an equidistant arrangement. The net result is that hues directly opposite one another on the color circle are *complements*. Our interest in complements stems from the fact that they are analogous to the grayscale negatives we studied in Section 3.2. As in the grayscale case, color complements are useful for enhancing detail that is embedded in dark regions of a color image—particularly when the regions are dominant in size. The following example illustrates some of these concepts.

FIGURE 6.30
Color complements on the color circle.

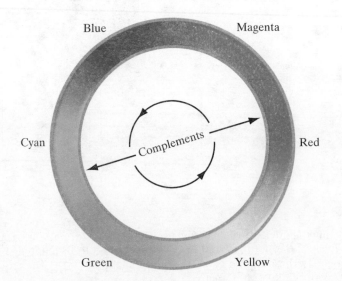

Figures 6.31(a) and (c) show the full-color image from Fig. 6.28 and its color complement. The RGB transformations used to compute the complement are plotted in Fig. 6.31(b). They are identical to the grayscale negative transformation defined in Section 3.2. Note that the complement is reminiscent of conventional photographic color film negatives. Reds of the original image are replaced by cyans in the complement. When the original image is black, the complement is white, and so on. Each of the hues in the complement image can be predicted from the original image using the color circle of Fig. 6.30, and each of the RGB component transforms involved in the computation of the complement is a function of only the corresponding input color component.

Unlike the intensity transformations of Fig. 6.29, the RGB complement transformation functions used in this example do not have a straightforward HSI equivalent. It is left as an exercise (see Problem 6.19) to show that the saturation component of the complement cannot be computed from the saturation component of the input image alone. Figure 6.31(d) shows an approximation of the complement using the hue, saturation, and intensity transformations in Fig. 6.31(b). The saturation component of the input image is unaltered; it is responsible for the visual differences between Figs. 6.31(c) and (d).

a b
c d

FIGURE 6.31
Color complement transformations.
(a) Original image.
(b) Complement transformation functions.
(c) Complement of (a) based on the RGB mapping functions. (d) An approximation of the RGB complement using HSI transformations.

COLOR SLICING

Highlighting a specific range of colors in an image is useful for separating objects from their surroundings. The basic idea is either to: (1) display the colors of interest so that they stand out from the background; or (2) use the region defined by the colors as a mask for further processing. The most straightforward approach is to extend the intensity slicing techniques of Section 3.2. However, because a color pixel is an n-dimensional quantity, the resulting color transformation functions are more complicated than their grayscale counterparts in Fig. 3.11. In fact, the required transformations are more complex than the color component transforms considered thus far. This is because all practical color-slicing approaches require each pixel's transformed color components to be a function of all n original pixel's color components.

One of the simplest ways to "slice" a color image is to map the colors outside some range of interest into a nonprominent neutral color. If the colors of interest are enclosed by a cube (or *hypercube* for $n > 3$) of width W and centered at a prototypical (e.g., average) color with components $(a_1, a_2, \ldots, a_n)$, the necessary set of transformations are given by

$$s_i = \begin{cases} 0.5 & \text{if}\left[\left|r_j - a_j\right| > \dfrac{W}{2}\right]_{\text{any } 1 \le j \le n} \\ r_i & \text{otherwise} \end{cases} \quad i = 1, 2, \ldots, n \tag{6-43}$$

These transformations highlight the colors around the prototype by forcing all other colors to the midpoint of the reference color space (this is an arbitrarily chosen neutral point). For the RGB color space, for example, a suitable neutral point is middle gray or color $(0.5, 0.5, 0.5)$.

If a sphere is used to specify the colors of interest, Eq. (6-43) becomes

$$s_i = \begin{cases} 0.5 & \text{if} \quad \displaystyle\sum_{j=1}^{n}\left(r_j - a_j\right)^2 > R_0^2 \\ r_i & \text{otherwise} \end{cases} \quad i = 1, 2, \ldots, n \tag{6-44}$$

Here, R_0 is the radius of the enclosing sphere (or hypersphere for $n > 3$) and $(a_1, a_2, \ldots, a_n)$ are the components of its center (i.e., the prototypical color). Other useful variations of Eqs. (6-43) and (6-44) include implementing multiple color prototypes and reducing the intensity of the colors outside the region of interest—rather than setting them to a neutral constant.

EXAMPLE 6.8: Color slicing.

Equations (6-43) and (6-44) can be used to separate the strawberries in Fig. 6.29(a) from their sepals, cup, bowl, and other background elements. Figures 6.32(a) and (b) show the results of using both transformations. In each case, a prototype red with RGB color coordinate $(0.6863, 0.1608, 0.1922)$ was selected from the most prominent strawberry. Parameters W and R_0 were chosen so that the highlighted region would not expand to other portions of the image. The actual values used, $W = 0.2549$ and $R_0 = 0.1765$, were determined interactively. Note that the sphere-based transformation of Eq. (6-44) performed slightly better, in the sense that it includes more of the strawberries' red areas. A sphere of radius 0.1765 does not

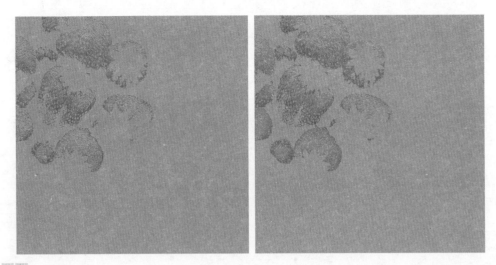

a b

FIGURE 6.32 Color-slicing transformations that detect (a) reds within an RGB cube of width $W = 0.2549$ centered at $(0.6863, 0.1608, 0.1922)$, and (b) reds within an RGB sphere of radius 0.1765 centered at the same point. Pixels outside the cube and sphere were replaced by color $(0.5, 0.5, 0.5)$.

completely enclose a cube of width 0.2549, but it is not small enough to be completely enclosed by the cube either. In Section 6.7, and later in Chapter 10, you will learn more advanced techniques for using color and other multispectral information to extract objects from their background.

TONE AND COLOR CORRECTIONS

Problems involving an image's tonal range need to be corrected before color irregularities, such as over- and under-saturated colors, can be resolved. The tonal range of an image, also called its *key type*, refers to its general distribution of color intensities. Most of the information in *high-key* images is concentrated at high (or light) intensities; the colors of *low-key* images are located predominantly at low intensities; and *middle-key* images lie in between. As in the grayscale case, it is often desirable to distribute the intensities of a color image equally between the highlights and the shadows. The following examples illustrate a variety of color transformations for the correction of tonal and color imbalances.

EXAMPLE 6.9: Tonal transformations.

Transformations for modifying image tones normally are selected interactively. The idea is to adjust experimentally the image's brightness and contrast to provide maximum detail over a suitable range of intensities. The colors themselves are not changed. In the RGB and CMY(K) spaces, this means mapping all the color components, except K, with the same transformation function (see Fig. 6.29); in the HSI color space, only the intensity component is modified, as noted in the previous section.

Figure 6.33 shows typical RGB transformations used for correcting three common tonal imbalances—flat, light, and dark images. The S-shaped curve in the first row of the figure is ideal for boosting contrast

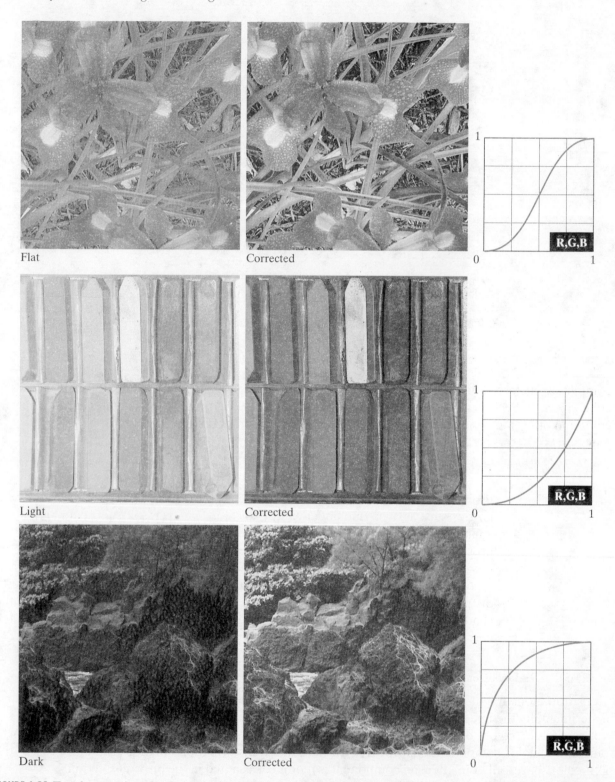

Flat   Corrected

Light   Corrected

Dark   Corrected

FIGURE 6.33 Tonal corrections for flat, light (high key), and dark (low key) color images. Adjusting the red, green, and blue components equally does not always alter the image hues significantly.

[see Fig. 3.2(a)]. Its midpoint is anchored so that highlight and shadow areas can be lightened and darkened, respectively. (The inverse of this curve can be used to correct excessive contrast.) The transformations in the second and third rows of the figure correct light and dark images, and are reminiscent of the power-law transformations in Fig. 3.6. Although the color components are discrete, as are the actual transformation functions, the transformation functions themselves are displayed and manipulated as continuous quantities—typically constructed from piecewise linear or higher order (for smoother mappings) polynomials. Note that the keys of the images in Fig. 6.33 are visually evident; they could also be determined using the histograms of the images' color components.

EXAMPLE 6.10: Color balancing.

Any color imbalances are addressed after the tonal characteristics of an image have been corrected. Although color imbalances can be determined directly by analyzing a known color in an image with a color spectrometer, accurate visual assessments are possible when white areas, where the RGB or CMY(K) components should be equal, are present. As Fig. 6.34 shows, skin tones are excellent subjects for visual color assessments because humans are highly perceptive of proper skin color. Vivid colors, such as bright red objects, are of little value when it comes to visual color assessment.

There are a variety of ways to correct color imbalances. When adjusting the color components of an image, it is important to realize that every action affects its overall color balance. That is, the perception of one color is affected by its surrounding colors. The color wheel of Fig. 6.30 can be used to predict how one color component will affect others. Based on the color wheel, for example, the proportion of any color can be increased by decreasing the amount of the opposite (or complementary) color in the image. Similarly, it can be increased by raising the proportion of the two immediately adjacent colors or decreasing the percentage of the two colors adjacent to the complement. Suppose, for instance, that there is too much magenta in an RGB image. It can be decreased: (1) by removing both red and blue, or (2) by adding green.

Figure 6.34 shows the transformations used to correct simple CMYK output imbalances. Note that the transformations depicted are the functions required for correcting the images; the inverses of these functions were used to generate the associated color imbalances. Together, the images are analogous to a color ring-around print of a darkroom environment and are useful as a reference tool for identifying color printing problems. Note, for example, that too much red can be due to excessive magenta (per the bottom left image) or too little cyan (as shown in the rightmost image of the second row).

HISTOGRAM PROCESSING OF COLOR IMAGES

Unlike the interactive enhancement approaches of the previous section, the gray-level histogram processing transformations of Section 3.3 can be applied to color images in an automated way. Recall that histogram equalization automatically determines a transformation that seeks to produce an image with a uniform histogram of intensity values. We showed in Section 3.3 that histogram processing can be quite successful at handling low-, high-, and middle-key images (for example, see Fig. 3.20). As you might suspect, it is generally unwise to histogram equalize the component images of a color image independently. This results in erroneous color. A more logical approach is to spread the color intensities uniformly, leaving the colors themselves (e.g., hues) unchanged. The following example shows that the HSI color space is ideally suited to this type of approach.

Original/Corrected

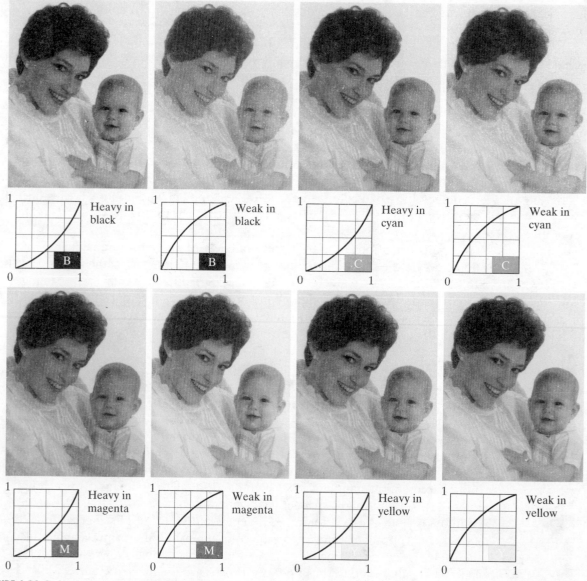

FIGURE 6.34 Color balancing a CMYK image.

a b
c d

FIGURE 6.35
Histogram
equalization
(followed by
saturation
adjustment) in the
HSI color space.

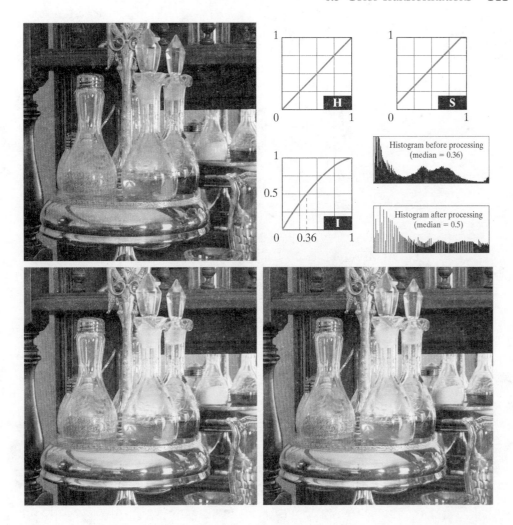

EXAMPLE 6.11 : Histogram equalization in the HSI color space.

Figure 6.35(a) shows a color image of a caster stand containing cruets and shakers whose intensity component spans the entire (normalized) range of possible values, [0, 1]. As can be seen in the histogram of its intensity component prior to processing [see Fig. 6.35(b)], the image contains a large number of dark colors that reduce the median intensity to 0.36. Histogram equalizing the intensity component, without altering the hue and saturation, resulted in the image shown in Fig. 6.35(c). Note that the overall image is significantly brighter, and that several moldings and the grain of the wooden table on which the caster is sitting are now visible. Figure 6.35(b) shows the intensity histogram of the new image, as well as the intensity transformation used to equalize the intensity component [see Eq. (3-15)].

Although intensity equalization did not alter the values of hue and saturation of the image, it did impact the overall color perception. Note, in particular, the loss of vibrancy in the oil and vinegar in the cruets. Figure 6.35(d) shows the result of partially correcting this by increasing the image's saturation component, subsequent to histogram equalization, using the transformation in Fig. 6.35(b). This type of adjustment is common when working with the intensity component in HSI space because changes in intensity usually affect the relative appearance of colors in an image.

6.6 COLOR IMAGE SMOOTHING AND SHARPENING

The next step beyond transforming each pixel of a color image without regard to its neighbors (as in the previous section) is to modify its value based on the characteristics of the surrounding pixels. In this section, the basics of this type of neighborhood processing will be illustrated within the context of color image smoothing and sharpening.

COLOR IMAGE SMOOTHING

With reference to Fig. 6.27(a) and the discussion in Sections 3.4 and 3.5, grayscale image smoothing can be viewed as a spatial filtering operation in which the coefficients of the filtering kernel have the same value. As the kernel is slid across the image to be smoothed, each pixel is replaced by the average of the pixels in the neighborhood encompassed by the kernel. As Fig. 6.27(b) shows, this concept is easily extended to the processing of full-color images. The principal difference is that instead of scalar intensity values, we must deal with component vectors of the form given in Eq. (6-37).

Let S_{xy} denote the set of coordinates defining a neighborhood centered at (x, y) in an RGB color image. The average of the RGB component vectors in this neighborhood is

$$\bar{\mathbf{c}}(x, y) = \frac{1}{K} \sum_{(s,t) \in S_{xy}} \mathbf{c}(s, t) \tag{6-45}$$

It follows from Eq. (6-37) and the properties of vector addition that

$$\bar{\mathbf{c}}(x, y) = \begin{bmatrix} \dfrac{1}{K} \sum\limits_{(s,t) \in S_{xy}} R(s, t) \\ \dfrac{1}{K} \sum\limits_{(s,t) \in S_{xy}} G(s, t) \\ \dfrac{1}{K} \sum\limits_{(s,t) \in S_{xy}} B(s, t) \end{bmatrix} \tag{6-46}$$

We recognize the components of this vector as the scalar images that would be obtained by independently smoothing each plane of the original RGB image using conventional grayscale neighborhood processing. Thus, we conclude that smoothing by neighborhood averaging can be carried out on a per-color-plane basis. The result is the same as when the averaging is performed using RGB color vectors.

a b
c d

FIGURE 6.36
(a) RGB image.
(b) Red
component image.
(c)Green
component.
(d) Blue
component.

EXAMPLE 6.12: Color image smoothing by neighborhood averaging.

Consider the RGB color image in Fig. 6.36(a). Its three component images are shown in Figs. 6.36(b) through (d). Figures 6.37(a) through (c) show the HSI components of the image. Based on the discussion in the previous paragraph, we smoothed each component image of the RGB image in Fig. 6.36 independently using a 5×5 averaging kernel. We then combined the individually smoothed images to form the smoothed, full-color RGB result in Fig. 6.38(a). Note that this image appears as we would expect from performing a spatial smoothing operation, as in the examples given in Section 3.5.

In Section 6.2, we mentioned that an important advantage of the HSI color model is that it decouples intensity and color information. This makes it suitable for many grayscale processing techniques and suggests that it might be more efficient to smooth only the intensity component of the HSI representation in Fig. 6.37. To illustrate the merits and/or consequences of this approach, we next smooth only the intensity component (leaving the hue and saturation components unmodified) and convert the processed result to an RGB image for display. The smoothed color image is shown in Fig. 6.38(b). Note

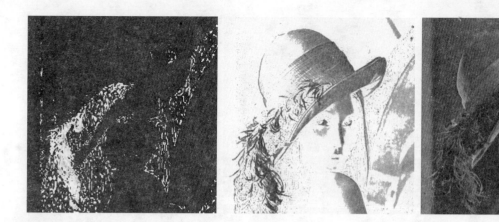

a b c

FIGURE 6.37 HSI components of the RGB color image in Fig. 6.36(a). (a) Hue. (b) Saturation. (c) Intensity.

that it is similar to Fig. 6.38(a), but, as you can see from the difference image in Fig. 6.38(c), the two smoothed images are not identical. This is because in Fig. 6.38(a) the color of each pixel is the average color of the pixels in the neighborhood. On the other hand, by smoothing only the intensity component image in Fig. 6.38(b), the hue and saturation of each pixel was not affected and, therefore, the pixel colors did not change. It follows from this observation that the difference between the two smoothing approaches would become more pronounced as a function of increasing kernel size.

COLOR IMAGE SHARPENING

In this section we consider image sharpening using the Laplacian (see Section 3.6). From vector analysis, we know that the Laplacian of a vector is defined as a vector

a b c

FIGURE 6.38 Image smoothing with a 5×5 averaging kernel. (a) Result of processing each RGB component image. (b) Result of processing the intensity component of the HSI image and converting to RGB. (c) Difference between the two results.

whose components are equal to the Laplacian of the individual scalar components of the input vector. In the RGB color system, the Laplacian of vector **c** in Eq. (6-37) is

$$\nabla^2 \left[\mathbf{c}(x,y) \right] = \begin{bmatrix} \nabla^2 R(x,y) \\ \nabla^2 G(x,y) \\ \nabla^2 B(x,y) \end{bmatrix} \tag{6-47}$$

which, as in the previous section, tells us that we can compute the Laplacian of a full-color image by computing the Laplacian of each component image separately.

EXAMPLE 6.13: Image sharpening using the Laplacian.

Figure 6.39(a) was obtained using Eq. (3-54) and the kernel in Fig. 3.45(c) to compute the Laplacians of the RGB component images in Fig. 6.36. These results were combined to produce the sharpened full-color result. Figure 6.39(b) shows a similarly sharpened image based on the HSI components in Fig. 6.37. This result was generated by combining the Laplacian of the intensity component with the unchanged hue and saturation components. The difference between the RGB and HSI sharpened images is shown in Fig. 6.39(c). The reason for the discrepancies between the two images is as in Example 6.12.

6.7 USING COLOR IN IMAGE SEGMENTATION

Segmentation is a process that partitions an image into regions. Although segmentation is the topic of Chapters 10 and 11, we consider color segmentation briefly here for the sake of continuity. You will have no difficulty following the discussion.

a b c

FIGURE 6.39 Image sharpening using the Laplacian. (a) Result of processing each RGB channel. (b) Result of processing the HSI intensity component and converting to RGB. (c) Difference between the two results.

SEGMENTATION IN HSI COLOR SPACE

If we wish to segment an image based on color and, in addition, we want to carry out the process on individual planes, it is natural to think first of the HSI space because color is conveniently represented in the hue image. Typically, saturation is used as a masking image in order to isolate further regions of interest in the hue image. The intensity image is used less frequently for segmentation of color images because it carries no color information. The following example is typical of how segmentation is performed in the HSI color space.

EXAMPLE 6.14: Segmenting a color image in HSI color space.

Suppose that it is of interest to segment the reddish region in the lower left of the image in Fig. 6.40(a). Figures 6.40(b) through (d) are its HSI component images. Note by comparing Figs. 6.40(a) and (b) that the region in which we are interested has relatively high values of hue, indicating that the colors are on the blue-magenta side of red (see Fig. 6.11). Figure 6.40(e) shows a binary mask generated by thresholding the saturation image with a threshold equal to 10% of the maximum value in that image. Any pixel value greater than the threshold was set to 1 (white). All others were set to 0 (black).

Figure 6.40(f) is the product of the mask with the hue image, and Fig. 6.40(g) is the histogram of the product image (note that the grayscale is in the range [0, 1]). We see in the histogram that high values (which are the values of interest) are grouped at the very high end of the grayscale, near 1.0. The result of thresholding the product image with threshold value of 0.9 resulted in the binary image in Fig. 6.40(h). The spatial location of the white points in this image identifies the points in the original image that have the reddish hue of interest. This was far from a perfect segmentation because there are points in the original image that we certainly would say have a reddish hue, but that were not identified by this segmentation method. However, it can be determined by experimentation that the regions shown in white in Fig. 6.40(h) are about the best this method can do in identifying the reddish components of the original image. The segmentation method discussed in the following section is capable of yielding better results.

SEGMENTATION IN RGB SPACE

Although working in HSI space is more intuitive in the sense of colors being represented in a more familiar format, segmentation is one area in which better results generally are obtained by using RGB color vectors (see Fig. 6.7). The approach is straightforward. Suppose that the objective is to segment objects of a specified color range in an RGB image. Given a set of sample color points representative of the colors of interest, we obtain an estimate of the "average" color that we wish to segment. Let this average color be denoted by the RGB vector $\mathbf{a}$. The objective of segmentation is to classify each RGB pixel in a given image as having a color in the specified range or not. In order to perform this comparison, it is necessary to have a measure of similarity. One of the simplest measures is the Euclidean distance. Let $\mathbf{z}$ denote an arbitrary point in RGB space. We say that $\mathbf{z}$ is similar to $\mathbf{a}$ if the distance between them is less than a specified threshold, D_0. The Euclidean distance between $\mathbf{z}$ and $\mathbf{a}$ is given by

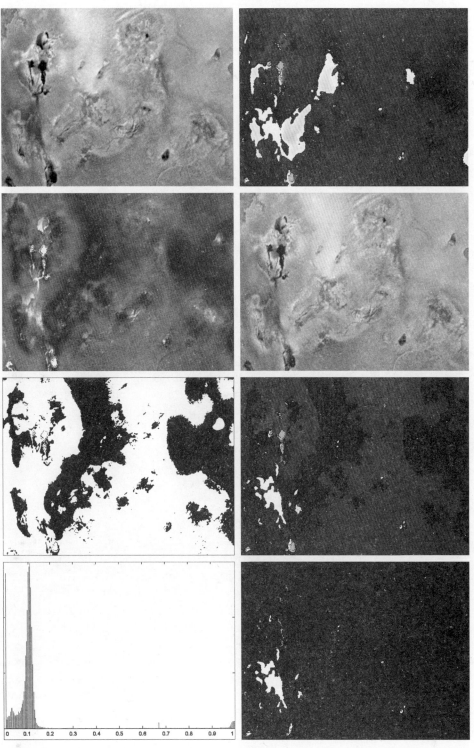

FIGURE 6.40 Image segmentation in HSI space. (a) Original. (b) Hue. (c) Saturation. (d) Intensity. (e) Binary saturation mask (black = 0). (f) Product of (b) and (e). (g) Histogram of (f). (h) Segmentation of red components from (a).

FIGURE 6.41
Three approaches for enclosing data regions for RGB vector segmentation.

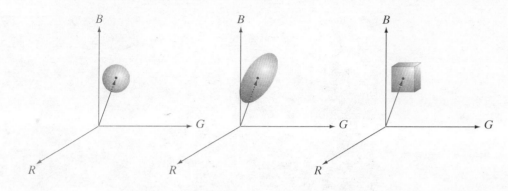

$$D(\mathbf{z}, \mathbf{a}) = \parallel \mathbf{z} - \mathbf{a} \parallel$$

$$= \left[(\mathbf{z} - \mathbf{a})^T (\mathbf{z} - \mathbf{a}) \right]^{\frac{1}{2}} \tag{6-48}$$

$$= \left[(\mathbf{z}_R - \mathbf{a}_R)^2 + (\mathbf{z}_G - \mathbf{a}_G)^2 + (\mathbf{z}_B - \mathbf{a}_B)^2 \right]^{\frac{1}{2}}$$

where the subscripts R, G, and B denote the RGB components of vectors $\mathbf{a}$ and $\mathbf{z}$. The locus of points such that $D(\mathbf{z}, \mathbf{a}) \leq D_0$ is a solid sphere of radius D_0, as illustrated in Fig. 6.41(a). Points contained within the sphere satisfy the specified color criterion; points outside the sphere do not. Coding these two sets of points in the image with, say, black and white, produces a binary segmented image.

A useful generalization of Eq. (6-48) is a distance measure of the form

This equation is called the *Mahalanobis distance*. You are seeing it used here for *multivariate thresholding* (see Section 10.3 regarding thresholding).

$$D(\mathbf{z}, \mathbf{a}) = \left[(\mathbf{z} - \mathbf{a})^T \mathbf{C}^{-1} (\mathbf{z} - \mathbf{a}) \right]^{\frac{1}{2}} \tag{6-49}$$

where $\mathbf{C}$ is the covariance matrix (see Section 11.5) of the samples chosen to be representative of the color range we wish to segment. The locus of points such that $D(\mathbf{z}, \mathbf{a}) \leq D_0$ describes a solid 3-D elliptical body [Fig. 6.41(b)] with the important property that its principal axes are oriented in the direction of maximum data spread. When $\mathbf{C} = \mathbf{I}$, the 3×3 identity matrix, Eq. (6-49) reduces to Eq. (6-48). Segmentation is as described in the preceding paragraph.

Because distances are positive and monotonic, we can work with the distance squared instead, thus avoiding square root computations. However, implementing Eq. (6-48) or (6-49) is computationally expensive for images of practical size, even if the square roots are not computed. A compromise is to use a bounding box, as illustrated in Fig. 6.41(c). In this approach, the box is centered on $\mathbf{a}$, and its dimensions along each of the color axes is chosen proportional to the standard deviation of the samples along each of the axis. We use the sample data to compute the standard deviations, which are the parameters used for segmentation with this approach. Given an arbitrary color point, we segment it by determining whether or not it is on the surface or inside the box, as with the distance formulations. However, determining whether a color point is inside or outside a box is much simpler computationally when compared to a spherical or elliptical enclosure. Note that the preceding discussion is a generalization of the color-slicing method introduced in Section 6.5.

EXAMPLE 6.15: Color segmentation in RGB color space.

The rectangular region shown Fig. 6.42(a) contains samples of reddish colors we wish to segment out of the color image. This is the same problem we considered in Example 6.14 using hue, but now we approach the problem using RGB color vectors. The approach followed was to compute the mean vector **a** using the color points contained within the rectangle in Fig. 6.42(a), and then to compute the standard deviation of the red, green, and blue values of those samples. A box was centered at **a**, and its dimensions along each of the RGB axes were selected as 1.25 times the standard deviation of the data along the corresponding axis. For example, let σ_R denote the standard deviation of the red components of the sample

a
b

FIGURE 6.42
Segmentation in RGB space.
(a) Original image with colors of interest shown enclosed by a rectangle.
(b) Result of segmentation in RGB vector space. Compare with Fig. 6.40(h).

points. Then the dimensions of the box along the R-axis extended from $(a_R - 1.25\sigma_R)$ to $(a_R + 1.25\sigma_R)$, where a_R is the red component of average vector **a**. Figure 6.42(b) shows the result of coding each point in the color image as white if it was on the surface or inside the box, and as black otherwise. Note how the segmented region was generalized from the color samples enclosed by the rectangle. In fact, by comparing Figs. 6.42(b) and 6.40(h), we see that segmentation in the RGB vector space yielded results that are much more accurate, in the sense that they correspond much more closely with what we would define as "reddish" points in the original color image. This result is not unexpected, because in the RGB space we used three color variables, as opposed to just one in the HSI space.

COLOR EDGE DETECTION

As we will discuss in Section 10.2, edge detection is an important tool for image segmentation. In this section, we are interested in the issue of computing edges on individual component images, as opposed to computing edges directly in color vector space.

We introduced edge detection by gradient operators in Section 3.6, when discussing image sharpening. Unfortunately, the gradient discussed there is not defined for vector quantities. Thus, we know immediately that computing the gradient on individual images and then using the results to form a color image will lead to erroneous results. A simple example will help illustrate the reason why.

Consider the two $M \times M$ color images (M odd) in Figs. 6.43(d) and (h), composed of the three component images in Figs. 6.43(a) through (c) and (e) through (g), respectively. If, for example, we compute the gradient image of each of the component images using Eq. (3-58), then add the results to form the two corresponding RGB gradient images, the value of the gradient at point $[(M+1)/2, (M+1)/2]$ would be the same in both cases. Intuitively, we would expect the gradient at that point to be stronger for the image in Fig. 6.43(d) because the edges of the R, G, and B images are in the same direction in that image, as opposed to the image in Fig. 6.43(h), in which only two of the edges are in the same direction. Thus we see from this simple example that processing the three individual planes to form a composite gradient image can yield erroneous results. If the problem is one of just detecting edges, then the individual-component approach can yield acceptable results. If accuracy is an issue, however, then obviously we need a new definition of the gradient applicable to vector quantities. We discuss next a method proposed by Di Zenzo [1986] for doing this.

The problem at hand is to define the gradient (magnitude and direction) of the vector **c** in Eq. (6-37) at any point (x, y). As we just mentioned, the gradient we studied in Section 3.6 is applicable to a *scalar* function $f(x, y)$; it is not applicable to vector functions. The following is one of the various ways in which we can extend the concept of a gradient to vector functions. Recall that for a scalar function $f(x, y)$, the gradient is a vector pointing in the direction of maximum rate of change of f at coordinates (x, y).

Let **r**, **g**, and **b** be unit vectors along the R, G, and B axis of RGB color space (see Fig. 6.7), and define the vectors

a b c d
e f g h

FIGURE 6.43 (a)–(c) R, G, and B component images, and (d) resulting RGB color image. (e)–(g) R, G, and B component images, and (h) resulting RGB color image.

$$\mathbf{u} = \frac{\partial R}{\partial x}\mathbf{r} + \frac{\partial G}{\partial x}\mathbf{g} + \frac{\partial B}{\partial x}\mathbf{b} \qquad (6\text{-}50)$$

and

$$\mathbf{v} = \frac{\partial R}{\partial y}\mathbf{r} + \frac{\partial G}{\partial y}\mathbf{g} + \frac{\partial B}{\partial y}\mathbf{b} \qquad (6\text{-}51)$$

Let the quantities g_{xx}, g_{yy}, and g_{xy} be defined in terms of the dot product of these vectors, as follows:

$$g_{xx} = \mathbf{u} \cdot \mathbf{u} = \mathbf{u}^T\mathbf{u} = \left|\frac{\partial R}{\partial x}\right|^2 + \left|\frac{\partial G}{\partial x}\right|^2 + \left|\frac{\partial B}{\partial x}\right|^2 \qquad (6\text{-}52)$$

$$g_{yy} = \mathbf{v} \cdot \mathbf{v} = \mathbf{v}^T\mathbf{v} = \left|\frac{\partial R}{\partial y}\right|^2 + \left|\frac{\partial G}{\partial y}\right|^2 + \left|\frac{\partial B}{\partial y}\right|^2 \qquad (6\text{-}53)$$

and

$$g_{xy} = \mathbf{u} \cdot \mathbf{v} = \mathbf{u}^T\mathbf{v} = \frac{\partial R}{\partial x}\frac{\partial R}{\partial y} + \frac{\partial G}{\partial x}\frac{\partial G}{\partial y} + \frac{\partial B}{\partial x}\frac{\partial B}{\partial y} \qquad (6\text{-}54)$$

Keep in mind that R, G, and B, and consequently the g's, are functions of x and y. Using this notation, it can be shown (Di Zenzo [1986]) that the direction of maximum rate of change of $\mathbf{c}(x, y)$ is given by the angle

$$\theta(x, y) = \frac{1}{2}\tan^{-1}\left[\frac{2g_{xy}}{g_{xx} - g_{yy}}\right] \qquad (6\text{-}55)$$

and that the value of the rate of change at (x, y) in the direction of $\theta(x, y)$ is given by

$$F_\theta(x, y) = \left\{\frac{1}{2}\left[\left(g_{xx} + g_{yy}\right) + \left(g_{xx} - g_{yy}\right)\cos 2\theta(x, y) + 2g_{xy}\sin 2\theta(x, y)\right]\right\}^{\frac{1}{2}} \qquad (6\text{-}56)$$

Because $\tan(\alpha) = \tan(\alpha \pm \pi)$, if θ_0 is a solution to Eq. (6-55), so is $\theta_0 \pm \pi/2$. Furthermore, $F_\theta = F_{\theta+\pi}$, so F has to be computed only for values of θ in the half-open interval $[0, \pi)$. The fact that Eq. (6-55) gives two values 90° apart means that this equation associates with each point (x, y) a pair of orthogonal directions. Along one of those directions F is maximum, and it is minimum along the other. The derivation of these results is rather lengthy, and we would gain little in terms of the fundamental objective of our current discussion by detailing it here. Consult the paper by Di Zenzo [1986] for details. The Sobel operators discussed in Section 3.6 can be used to compute the partial derivatives required for implementing Eqs. (6-52) through (6-54).

EXAMPLE 6.16: Edge detection in RGB vector space.

Figure 6.44(b) is the gradient of the image in Fig. 6.44(a), obtained using the vector method just discussed. Figure 6.44(c) shows the image obtained by computing the gradient of each RGB component image and forming a composite gradient image by adding the corresponding values of the three component images at each coordinate (x, y). The edge detail of the vector gradient image is more complete than the detail in the individual-plane gradient image in Fig. 6.44(c); for example, see the detail around the subject's right eye. The image in Fig. 6.44(d) shows the difference between the two gradient images at each point (x, y). It is important to note that both approaches yielded reasonable results. Whether the extra detail in Fig. 6.44(b) is worth the added computational burden over the Sobel operator computations can only be determined by the requirements of a given problem. Figure 6.45 shows the three component gradient images, which, when added and scaled, were used to obtain Fig. 6.44(c).

6.8 NOISE IN COLOR IMAGES

The noise models discussed in Section 5.2 are applicable to color images. Usually, the noise content of a color image has the same characteristics in each color channel, but it is possible for color channels to be affected differently by noise. One possibility is for the electronics of a particular channel to malfunction. However, different noise levels are more likely caused by differences in the relative strength of illumination available to each of the color channels. For example, use of a red filter in a CCD camera will reduce the strength of illumination detected by the red sensing elements. CCD sensors are noisier at lower levels of illumination, so the resulting red com-

a b
c d

FIGURE 6.44
(a) RGB image.
(b) Gradient
computed in RGB
color vector space.
(c) Gradient
image formed by
the elementwise
sum of three indi-
vidual
gradient images,
each computed
using the Sobel
operators.
(d) Difference
between (b) and
(c).

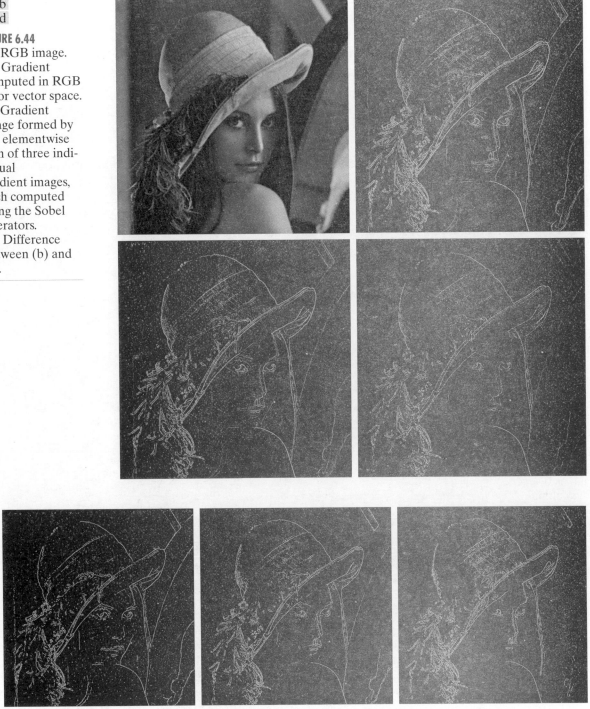

a b c

FIGURE 6.45 Component gradient images of the color image in Fig. 6.44. (a) Red component, (b) green component, and (c) blue component. These three images were added and scaled to produce the image in Fig. 6.44(c).

ponent of an RGB image would tend to be noisier than the other two component images in this situation.

In this example, we take a brief look at noise in color images and how noise carries over when converting from one color model to another. Figures 6.46(a) through (c) show the three color planes of an RGB image corrupted by additive Gaussian noise, and Fig. 6.46(d) is the composite RGB image. Note that fine grain noise such as this tends to be less visually noticeable in a color image than it is in a grayscale image. Figures 6.47(a) through (c) show the result of converting the RGB image in Fig. 6.46(d) to HSI. Compare these results with the HSI components of the original image (see Fig. 6.37) and note how significantly degraded the hue and saturation components of the noisy image are. This was caused by the nonlinearity of the cos and min operations in Eqs. (6-17) and (6-18), respectively. On the other hand, the intensity component in Fig. 6.47(c) is slightly smoother than any of the three noisy RGB component images. This is because the intensity image is the average of the RGB images, as indicated in Eq. (6-19). (Recall the discussion in Section 2.6 regarding the fact that image averaging reduces random noise.)

a b
c d

FIGURE 6.46
(a)–(c) Red, green, and blue 8-bit component images corrupted by additive Gaussian noise of mean 0 and standard deviation of 28 intensity levels. (d) Resulting RGB image. [Compare (d) with Fig. 6.44(a).]

a b c

FIGURE 6.47 HSI components of the noisy color image in Fig. 6.46(d). (a) Hue. (b) Saturation. (c) Intensity.

In cases when, say, only one RGB channel is affected by noise, conversion to HSI spreads the noise to all HSI component images. Figure 6.48 shows an example. Figure 6.48(a) shows an RGB image whose green component image is corrupted by salt-and-pepper noise, with a probability of either salt or pepper equal to 0.05. The HSI component images in Figs. 6.48(b) through (d) show clearly how the noise spread from the green RGB channel to all the HSI images. Of course, this is not unexpected because computation of the HSI components makes use of all RGB components, as discussed in Section 6.2.

As is true of the processes we have discussed thus far, filtering of full-color images can be carried out on a per-image basis, or directly in color vector space, depending on the process. For example, noise reduction by using an averaging filter is the process discussed in Section 6.6, which we know gives the same result in vector space as it does if the component images are processed independently. However, other filters cannot be formulated in this manner. Examples include the class of order statistics filters discussed in Section 5.3. For instance, to implement a median filter in color vector space it is necessary to find a scheme for ordering vectors in a way that the median makes sense. While this was a simple process when dealing with scalars, the process is considerably more complex when dealing with vectors. A discussion of vector ordering is beyond the scope of our discussion here, but the book by Plataniotis and Venetsanopoulos [2000] is a good reference on vector ordering and some of the filters based on the concept of ordering.

6.9 COLOR IMAGE COMPRESSION

Because the number of bits required to represent color is typically three to four times greater than the number employed in the representation of gray levels, data compression plays a central role in the storage and transmission of color images. With respect to the RGB, CMY(K), and HSI images of the previous sections, the data that are the object of any compression are the components of each color pixel (e.g., the red, green, and blue components of the pixels in an RGB image); they are

a b
c d

FIGURE 6.48
(a) RGB image
with green plane
corrupted by salt-
and-pepper noise.
(b) Hue
component of
HSI image.
(c) Saturation
component.
(d) Intensity
component.

the means by which the color information is conveyed. Compression is the process of reducing or eliminating redundant and/or irrelevant data. Although compression is the topic of Chapter 8, we illustrate the concept briefly in the following example using a color image.

EXAMPLE 6.18: An example of color image compression.

Figure 6.49(a) shows a 24-bit RGB full-color image of an iris, in which 8 bits each are used to represent the red, green, and blue components. Figure 6.49(b) was reconstructed from a compressed version of the image in (a) and is, in fact, a compressed and subsequently decompressed approximation of it. Although the compressed image is not directly displayable—it must be decompressed before input to a color monitor—the compressed image contains only 1 data bit (and thus 1 storage bit) for every 230 bits of data in the original image (you will learn about the origin of these numbers in Chapter 8). Suppose that the image is of size $2000 \times 3000 = 6 \cdot 10^6$ pixels. The image is 24 bits/pixel, so it storage size is $144 \cdot 10^6$ bits.

a
b

FIGURE 6.49
Color image
compression.
(a) Original RGB
image.
(b) Result of
compressing, then
decompressing
the image in (a).

Suppose that you are sitting at an airport waiting for your flight, and want to upload 100 such images using the airport's public WiFi connection. At a (relatively high) upload speed of $10 \cdot 10^6$ bits/sec, it would take you about 24 min to upload your images. In contrast, the compressed images would take about 6 sec to upload. Of course, the transmitted data would have to be decompressed at the other end for viewing, but the decompression can be done in a matter of seconds. Note that the reconstructed approximation image is slightly blurred. This is a characteristic of many lossy compression techniques; it can be reduced or eliminated by changing the level of compression. The JPEG 2000 compression algorithm used to generate Fig. 6.49(b) is described in detail in Section 8.2.

Summary, References, and Further Reading

The material in this chapter is an introduction to color image processing and covers topics selected to provide a solid background in the techniques used in this branch of image processing. Our treatment of color fundamentals and color models was prepared as foundation material for a field that is wide in technical scope and areas of application. In particular, we focused on color models that we felt are not only useful in digital image processing but provide also the tools necessary for further study in this area of image processing. The discussion of pseudocolor and full-color processing on an individual image basis provides a tie to techniques that were covered in some detail in Chapters 3 through 5. The material on color vector spaces is a departure from methods that we had studied before and highlights some important differences between grayscale and full-color processing. Our treatment of noise in color images also points out that the vector nature of the problem, along with the fact that color images are routinely transformed from one working space to another, has implications on the issue of how to reduce noise in these images. In some cases, noise filtering can be done on a per-image basis, but others, such as median filtering, require special treatment to reflect the fact that color pixels are vector quantities, as mentioned earlier. Although segmentation is the topic of Chapters 10 and 11, and image data compression is the topic of Chapter 8, we introduced them briefly in the context of color image processing.

For a comprehensive reference on the science of color, see Malacara [2011]. Regarding the physiology of color, see Snowden et al. [2012]. These two references, together with the book by Kuehni [2012], provide ample supplementary material for the discussion in Section 6.1. For further reading on color models (Section 6.2), see Fortner and Meyer [1997], Poynton [1996], and Fairchild [1998]. For a detailed derivation of the equations for the HSI model see the paper by Smith [1978] or consult the book website. The topic of pseudocolor (Section 6.3) is closely tied to the general area of image data visualization. Wolff and Yaeger [1993] is a good basic reference on the use of pseudocolor. See also Telea [2008]. For additional reading on the material in Sections 6.4 and 6.5, see Plataniotis and Venetsanopoulos [2000]. The material on color image filtering (Section 6.6) is based on the vector formulation introduced in Section 6.4 and on our discussion of spatial filtering in Chapter 3. The area of color image segmentation (Section 6.7) is of significant current interest. For an overview of current trends in this field see the survey by Vantaram and Saber [2012]. For more advanced color image processing techniques than those discussed in this chapter see Fernandez-Maloigne [2012]. The discussion in Section 6.8 is based on the noise models introduced in Section 5.2. References on color image compression (Section 6.9) are listed at the end of Chapter 8. For details of software implementation of many of the techniques discussed in this chapter, see Gonzalez, Woods, and Eddins [2009].

Problems

Solutions to the problems marked with an asterisk (*) are in the DIP4E Student Support Package (consult the book website: www.ImageProcessingPlace.com).

6.1 What are the characteristics generally used to distinguish one color from another? Give the percentages of red (X), green (Y), and blue (Z) light required to generate the point labeled "green" in CIE *chromaticity diagram* in Fig. 6.5.

6.2* Consider any two valid colors c_1 and c_2 with coordinates (x_1, y_1) and (x_2, y_2) in the chromaticity diagram of Fig. 6.5. Derive the necessary general expression(s) for computing the relative percentages of colors c_1 and c_2 composing any color that is known to lie on the straight line joining these two colors.

6.3 Consider any three valid colors c_1, c_2, and c_3 with coordinates (x_1, y_1), (x_2, y_2), and (x_3, y_3), in the chromaticity diagram of Fig. 6.5. Derive the necessary general expression(s) for computing the relative percentages of c_1, c_2, and c_3 composing a color that is known to lie within the triangle whose vertices are at the coordinates of c_1, c_2, and c_3.

6.4* The color gamut of a monitor can be displayed as a triangular region within the CIE diagram, whereas the color gamut of a high-quality color-printing device is displayed as the irregular region inside the triangle. Why?

6.5 The R, G, and B component images of an RGB image have the horizontal intensity profiles shown in the following diagram. What color would a person see in the middle column of this image?

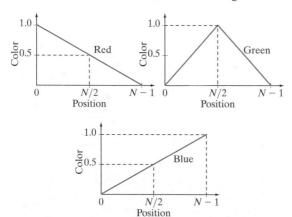

6.6* Sketch the RGB components of the following image as they would appear on a monochrome monitor. All colors are at maximum intensity and saturation. In working this problem, consider the gray border as part of the image.

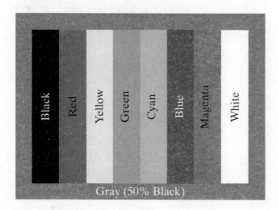

6.7 What is the total number of colors in a 24-bit RGB image?

6.8 Consider the RGB cube in Fig. 6.8 and answer each of the following questions.

(a)* Describe how the gray levels vary in each of the R, G, and B primary images that make up the front face of the color cube (this is the face closer to you). Assume that each component image is an 8-bit image.

(b) Suppose that we replace every color in the RGB cube by its CMY color. This new cube is displayed on an RGB monitor. Label with a color name the eight vertices of the new cube that you would see on the screen.

(c) What can you say about the colors on the edges of the RGB color cube regarding saturation?

6.9 Do the following.

(a)* Sketch the CMY components of the image in Problem 6.6 as they would appear on a monochrome monitor.

(b) If the CMY components sketched in (a) are fed into the red, green, and blue inputs of a color monitor, respectively, describe the appearance of the resulting image.

6.10* Sketch the HSI components of the image in Problem 6.6 as they would appear on a monochrome monitor.

6.11 Propose a method for generating a color band similar to the one shown in the zoomed section entitled *Visible Spectrum* in Fig. 6.2. Note that the band starts at a dark purple on the left and proceeds toward pure red on the right. (*Hint:* Use the HSI color model.)

6.12* Propose a method for generating a color version of the image shown diagrammatically in Fig. 6.11(c). Give your answer in the form of a flow chart. Assume that the intensity value is fixed and given. (*Hint:* Use the HSI color model.)

6.13 Consider the following image composed of solid color squares. For discussing your answer, choose a gray scale consisting of eight shades of gray, 0 through 7, where 0 is black and 7 is white. Suppose that the image is converted to HSI color space. In answering the following questions, use specific numbers for the gray shades if using numbers makes sense. Otherwise, the relationships "same as," "lighter than," or "darker than" are sufficient. If you cannot assign a specific gray level or one of these relationships to the image you are discussing, give the reason.

(a)* Sketch the hue image.

(b) Sketch the saturation image.

(c) Sketch the intensity image.

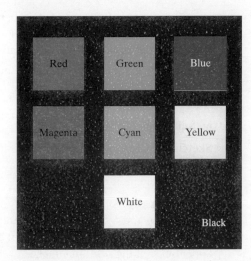

6.14 The following 8-bit images are the H, S, and I component images from Fig. 6.14. The numbers indicate gray-level values. Answer the following questions, explaining the basis for your answer in each. If it is not possible to answer a question based on the given information, state why you cannot do so.

(a)* Give the gray-level values of all regions in the hue image.

(b) Give the gray-level value of all regions in the saturation image.

(c) Give the gray-level values of all regions in the intensity image.

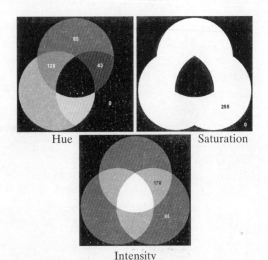

6.15* Compute the $L * a * b *$ components of the image in Problem 6.6 assuming:

$$\begin{bmatrix} X \\ Y \\ Z \end{bmatrix} = \begin{bmatrix} 0.588 & 0.179 & 0.183 \\ 0.29 & 0.606 & 0.105 \\ 0 & 0.068 & 1.021 \end{bmatrix} \begin{bmatrix} R \\ G \\ B \end{bmatrix}$$

This matrix equation defines the tristimulus values of the colors generated by the standard National Television System Committee (NTSC) color TV phosphors viewed under *D65* standard illumination (Benson [1985]).

6.16* What are three basic quantities used to describe the quality of a chromatic light source? Explain.

6.17 Explain hue and saturation. What does HSI color model stands for and what it represents?

6.18 Refer to Fig. 6.25 in answering the following:

(a)* Why does the image in Fig. 6.25(e) exhibit predominantly red tones?

(b)* Suggest an automated procedure for coding the water in Fig. 6.25 in a bright-blue color.

(c) Suggest an automated procedure for coding the predominantly man-made components in a bright yellow color. [*Hint:* Work with Fig. 6.25(e).]

6.19* What are color complements? Considering the color circle in Fig. 6.32, identify the complements of the colors Red, Yellow, and Green.

6.20 Explain the shape of the hue transformation function for the image complement approximation in Fig. 6.31(b) using the HSI color model.

6.21* Differentiate between CMY and CMYK model.

6.22 Draw the general shape of the transformation functions used to correct excessive contrast in the RGB color space.

6.23* Assume that the monitor and printer of an imaging system are imperfectly calibrated. An image that looks balanced on the monitor appears green in print. Describe general transformations that might correct the imbalance.

6.24* Given an image in the RGB, CMY, or CMYK color system, how would you implement the color equivalent of gray-scale histogram matching (specification) from Section 3.3?

6.25 Consider the following 500×500 RGB image, in which the squares are fully saturated red, green, and blue, and each of the colors is at maximum intensity. An HSI image is generated from this image. Answer the following questions.

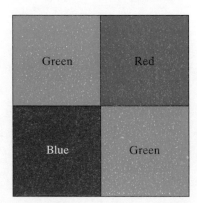

(a) Describe the appearance of each HSI component image.

(b)* The saturation component of the HSI image is smoothed using an averaging kernel of size 125×125. Describe the appearance of the result. (You may ignore image border effects in the filtering operation.)

(c) Repeat (b) for the hue image.

6.26 Answer the following.

(a)* Refer to the discussion in Section 6.7 about segmentation in the RGB color space. Give a procedure (in flow chart form) for determining whether a color vector (point) z is inside a cube with sides W, centered at an average color vector a. Distance computations are not allowed.

(b) If the box is aligned with the axes this process also can be implemented on an image-by-image basis. Show how you would do it.

6.27 Justify the statement

Determining whether a color point is inside or outside a box is much simpler computationally when compared to a spherical or elliptical enclosure.

6.28 Sketch the surface in RGB space for the points that satisfy the equation

$$D(\mathbf{z}, \mathbf{a}) = \left[(\mathbf{z} - \mathbf{a})^T \mathbf{C}^{-1} (\mathbf{z} - \mathbf{a}) \right]^{\frac{1}{2}} = D_0$$

where D_0 is a positive constant. Assume that $\mathbf{a} = \mathbf{0}$, and that

$$\mathbf{C} = \begin{bmatrix} 8 & 0 & 0 \\ 0 & 1 & 0 \\ 0 & 0 & 1 \end{bmatrix}$$

6.29 Refer to the discussion on color edge detection in Section 6.7. One might think that a logical approach for defining the gradient of an RGB image at any point (x, y) would be to compute the gradient vector (see Section 3.6) of each component image and then form a gradient vector for the color image by summing the three individual gradient vectors. Unfortunately, this method can at times yield erroneous results. Specifically, it is possible for a color image with clearly defined edges to have a zero gradient if this method were used. Give an example of such an image. (*Hint:* To simplify your analysis, set one of the color planes to a constant value.)

7 Wavelet and Other Image Transforms

Do not conform any longer to the pattern of this world, but be transformed by the renewing of your mind.

Romans 12:2

Preview

The discrete Fourier transform of Chapter 4 is a member of an important class of linear transforms that include the Hartley, sine, cosine, Walsh-Hadamard, Slant, Haar, and wavelet transforms. These transforms, which are the subject of this chapter, decompose functions into weighted sums of orthogonal or biorthogonal basis functions, and can be studied using the tools of linear algebra and functional analysis. When approached from this point of view, images are vectors in the vector space of all images. Basis functions determine the nature and usefulness of image transforms. Transforms are the coefficients of linear expansions. And for a given image and transform (or set of basis functions), both the orthogonality of the basis functions and the coefficients of the resulting transform are computed using inner products. All of an image's transforms are equivalent in the sense that they contain the same information and total energy. They are reversible and differ only in the way that the information and energy is distributed among the transform's coefficients.

Upon competion of this chapter, readers should:

- Understand image transforms in the context of series expansions.

- Be familiar with a variety of important image transforms and transform basis functions.

- Know the difference between orthogonal and biorthogonal basis functions.

- Be able to construct the transformation matrices of the discrete Fourier, Hartley, sine, cosine, Walsh-Hadamard, Slant, and Haar transforms.

- Be able to compute traditional image transforms, like the Fourier and Haar transforms, using elementary matrix operations.

- Understand the time-frequency plane and its relationship to wavelet transforms.

- Be able to compute 1-D and 2-D fast wavelet transforms (FWTs) using filter banks.

- Understand wavelet packet representations.

- Be familiar with the use of discrete orthogonal transforms in image processing.

7.1 PRELIMINARIES

Consult the Tutorials section of the book website for a brief tutorial on vectors and matrices.

In linear algebra and functional analysis, a *vector space* (or more formally an *abstract vector space*) is a set of mathematical objects or entities, called *vectors*, that can be added together and multiplied by *scalars*. An *inner product space* is an abstract vector space over a field of numbers, together with an *inner product function* that maps two vectors of the vector space to a scalar of the number field such that

(a) $\langle u, v \rangle = \langle v, u \rangle^*$

(b) $\langle u + v, w \rangle = \langle u, w \rangle + \langle v, w \rangle$

(c) $\langle \alpha u, v \rangle = \alpha \langle u, v \rangle$

(d) $\langle v, v \rangle \geq 0$ and $\langle v, v \rangle = 0$ if and only if $v = 0$

In Chapter 2, the inner product of two column vectors, **u** and **v**, is denoted **u** · **v** [see Eq. (2-50)]. In this chapter, $\langle \mathbf{u}, \mathbf{v} \rangle$ is used to denote inner products within any inner product space satisfying conditions (a)–(d), including the Euclidean inner product space and real-valued column vectors of Chapter 2.

where u, v, and w are vectors, α is a scalar, and $\langle \ldots \rangle$ denotes the inner product operation. A simple example of a vector space is the set of directed line segments in two dimensions, where the line segments are represented mathematically as 2×1 column vectors, and the addition of vectors is the arithmetic equivalent of combining the line segments in a head to tail manner. An example of an inner product space is the set of real numbers **R** combined with inner product function $\langle u, v \rangle = uv$, where the "vectors" are real numbers, the inner product function is multiplication, and axioms (a) through (d) above correspond to the commutative, distributive, associative, and "positivity of even powers" properties of multiplication, respectively.

Three inner product spaces are of particular interest in this chapter:

Euclidean space $\mathbf{R}^N$ is an infinite set containing all real N-tuples.

1. *Euclidean* space $\mathbf{R}^N$ over real number field **R** with *dot* or *scalar* inner product

$$\langle \mathbf{u}, \mathbf{v} \rangle = \mathbf{u}^T \mathbf{v} = u_0 v_0 + u_1 v_1 + \ldots + u_{N-1} v_{N-1} = \sum_{i=0}^{N-1} u_i v_i \qquad (7\text{-}1)$$

where **u** and **v** are $N \times 1$ column vectors.

A complex vector space with an inner product is called a *complex inner product space* or *unitary* space.

2. *Unitary* space $\mathbf{C}^N$ over complex number field **C** with inner product function

$$\langle \mathbf{u}, \mathbf{v} \rangle = \mathbf{u}^{*T} \mathbf{v} = \sum_{i=0}^{N-1} u_i^* v_i = \langle \mathbf{v}, \mathbf{u} \rangle^* \qquad (7\text{-}2)$$

where * denotes the complex conjugate operation, and **u** and **v** are complex-valued $N \times 1$ column vectors.

The notation $C[a, b]$ is also used in the literature.

3. Inner product space $C([a, b])$, where the vectors are continuous functions on the interval $a \leq x \leq b$ and the inner product function is the *integral inner product*

$$\langle f(x), g(x) \rangle = \int_a^b f^*(x) g(x) dx \qquad (7\text{-}3)$$

Equations (7-4) through (7-15) are valid for all inner product spaces, including those defined by Eqs. (7-1) to (7-3).

In all three inner product spaces, the *norm* or *length* of vector z, denoted as $\|z\|$, is

$$\|z\| = \sqrt{\langle z, z \rangle} \qquad (7\text{-}4)$$

and the *angle* between two nonzero vectors z and w is

$$\theta = \cos^{-1}\frac{\langle z, w \rangle}{\|z\|\|w\|} \tag{7-5}$$

If the norm of z is 1, z is said to be *normalized*. If $\langle z, w \rangle = 0$ in Eq. (7-5), $\theta = 90°$ and z and w are said to be *orthogonal*. A natural consequence of these definitions is that a set of nonzero vectors $w_0, w_1, w_2, \ldots$ is mutually or pairwise orthogonal if and only if

$$\langle w_k, w_l \rangle = 0 \quad \text{for } k \neq l \tag{7-6}$$

They are an *orthogonal basis* of the inner product space that they are said to *span*. If the *basis vectors* are normalized, they are an *orthonormal basis* and

$$\langle w_k, w_l \rangle = \delta_{kl} = \begin{cases} 0 & \text{for } k \neq l \\ 1 & \text{for } k = l \end{cases} \tag{7-7}$$

Similarly, a set of vectors $w_0, w_1, w_2, \ldots$ and a complementary set of *dual vectors* $\widetilde{w}_0, \widetilde{w}_1, \widetilde{w}_2, \ldots$ are said to be *biorthogonal* and a *biorthogonal basis* of the vector space that they span if

$$\langle \widetilde{w}_k, w_l \rangle = 0 \quad \text{for } k \neq l \tag{7-8}$$

They are a *biorthonormal basis* if and only if

$$\langle \widetilde{w}_k, w_l \rangle = \delta_{kl} = \begin{cases} 0 & \text{for } k \neq l \\ 1 & \text{for } k = l \end{cases} \tag{7-9}$$

As a mechanism for concisely describing an infinite set of vectors, the basis of an inner product space is one of the most useful concepts in linear algebra. The following derivation, which relies on the orthogonality of basis vectors, is foundational to the matrix-based transforms of the next section. Let $W = \{w_0, w_1, w_2, \ldots\}$ be an orthogonal basis of inner product space V, and let $z \in V$. Vector z can then be expressed as the following linear combination of basis vectors

$$z = \alpha_0 w_0 + \alpha_1 w_1 + \alpha_2 w_2 + \ldots \tag{7-10}$$

whose inner product with basis vector w_i is

$$\begin{aligned} \langle w_i, z \rangle &= \langle w_i, \alpha_0 w_0 + \alpha_1 w_1 + \alpha_2 w_2 + \ldots \rangle \\ &= \alpha_0 \langle w_i, w_0 \rangle + \alpha_1 \langle w_i, w_1 \rangle + \ldots + \alpha_i \langle w_i, w_i \rangle + \ldots \end{aligned} \tag{7-11}$$

Since the w_i are mutually orthogonal, the inner products on the right side of Eq. (7-11) are 0 unless the subscripts of the vectors whose inner products are being computed

---

While you must always take the context into account, we generally use the word "vector" for vectors in an abstract sense. A vector can be an $N \times 1$ matrix (i.e., column vector) or a continuous function.

Recall from linear algebra that a *basis* of a vector space is a set of linearly independent vectors for which any vector in the space can be written uniquely as a linear combination of basis vectors. The linear combinations are the *span* of the basis vectors. A set of vectors is *linearly independent* if no vector in the set can be written as a linear combination of the others.

While you must always take to the context into account, we often use the phrase "orthogonal basis" or "orthogonal transform" to refer to any basis or transform that is orthogonal, orthonormal, biorthogonal, or biorthonormal.

match [see Eq. (7-7)]. Thus, the only nonzero term is $\alpha_i \langle w_i, w_i \rangle$. Eliminating the zero terms and dividing both sides of the equation by $\langle w_i, w_i \rangle$ gives

$$\alpha_i = \frac{\langle w_i, z \rangle}{\langle w_i, w_i \rangle} \tag{7-12}$$

which reduces to

$$\alpha_i = \langle w_i, z \rangle \tag{7-13}$$

if the norms of the basis vectors are 1. A similar derivation, which is left as an exercise for the reader, yields

$$\alpha_i = \frac{\langle \tilde{w}_i, z \rangle}{\langle \tilde{w}_i, w_i \rangle} \tag{7-14}$$

and

$$\alpha_i = \langle \tilde{w}_i, z \rangle \tag{7-15}$$

for biorthogonal and biorthonormal basis vectors, respectively. Note when a basis and its dual are identical, biorthogonality reduces to orthogonality.

EXAMPLE 7.1: Vector norms and angles.

The norm of vector $f(x) = \cos x$ of inner product space $C([0, 2\pi])$ is

$$\|f(x)\| = \sqrt{\langle f(x), f(x) \rangle} = \left[\int_0^{2\pi} \cos^2 x \, dx \right]^{\frac{1}{2}} = \left[\frac{1}{2} x + \frac{1}{4} \sin(2x) \Big|_0^{2\pi} \right]^{\frac{1}{2}} = \sqrt{\pi}$$

The angle between vectors $\mathbf{z} = \begin{bmatrix} 1 & 1 \end{bmatrix}^T$ and $\mathbf{w} = \begin{bmatrix} 1 & 0 \end{bmatrix}^T$ of Euclidean inner product space $\mathbf{R}^2$ is

$$\theta = \cos^{-1} \left(\frac{\langle \mathbf{z}, \mathbf{w} \rangle}{\|\mathbf{z}\| \|\mathbf{w}\|} \right) = \cos^{-1} \left(\frac{1}{\sqrt{2}} \right) = 45°$$

These results follow from Eqs. (7-1), (7-3), (7-4) and (7-5).

7.2 MATRIX-BASED TRANSFORMS

In mathematics, the word *transform* is used to denote a change in form without an accompanying change in value.

The 1-D discrete Fourier transform of Chapter 4 is one of a class of important transforms that can be expressed in terms of the general relation

$$T(u) = \sum_{x=0}^{N-1} f(x) r(x, u) \tag{7-16}$$

where x is a *spatial variable*, $T(u)$ is the transform of $f(x)$, $r(x,u)$ is a *forward transformation kernel*, and integer u is a *transform variable* with values in the range $0,1,...,N-1$. Similarly, the inverse transform of $T(u)$ is

$$f(x) = \sum_{u=0}^{N-1} T(u)s(x,u) \tag{7-17}$$

where $s(x,u)$ is an *inverse transformation kernel* and x takes on values in the range $0,1,...,N-1$. Transformation kernels $r(x,u)$ and $s(x,u)$ in Eqs. (7-16) and (7-17), which depend only on indices x and u and not on the values of $f(x)$ and $T(u)$, determine the nature and usefulness of the *transform pair* that they define.

Equation (7-17) is depicted graphically in Fig. 7.1. Note that $f(x)$ is a weighted sum of N inverse kernel functions (i.e., $s(x,u)$ for $u = 0,1,...,N-1$) and that $T(u)$ for $u = 0,1,...,N-1$ are the weights. All N $s(x,u)$ contribute to the value of $f(x)$ at every x. If we expand the right side of Eq. (7-17) to obtain

$$f(x) = T(0)s(x,0) + T(1)s(x,1) + ... + T(N-1)s(x,N-1) \tag{7-18}$$

it is immediately apparent that the computation depicted in Fig. 7.1 is a *linear expansion* like that of Eq. (7-10)—with the $s(x,u)$ and $T(u)$ in Eq. (7-18) taking the place of the w_i (i.e., the basis vectors) and the α_i in Eq. (7-10). If we assume the $s(x,u)$ in Eq. (7-18) are orthonormal basis vectors of an inner product space, Eq. (7-13) tells us that

$$T(u) = \langle s(x,u), f(x) \rangle \tag{7-19}$$

and transform $T(u)$ for $u = 0,1,...,N-1$ can be computed via inner products.

FIGURE 7.1
A graphical illustration of Eq. (7-18).

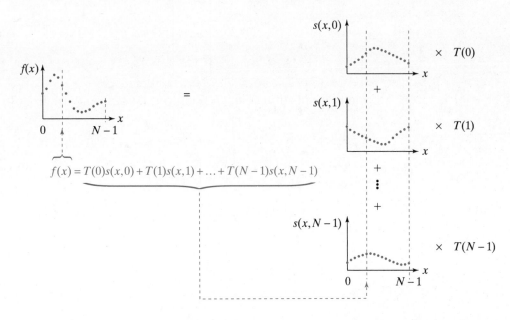

$$f(x) = T(0)s(x,0) + T(1)s(x,1) + ... + T(N-1)s(x,N-1)$$

We are now ready to express Eqs. (7-16) and (7-17) in matrix form. We begin by defining functions $f(x)$, $T(u)$, and $s(x,u)$ as column vectors

We will often use subscripts to denote the elements of a matrix or vector. Thus, f_0 denotes the first element of column vector $\mathbf{f}$, which is $f(0)$, and $s_{3,0}$ denotes the first element of column vector $\mathbf{s}_3$, which is $s(0,3)$.

$$\mathbf{f} = \begin{bmatrix} f(0) \\ f(1) \\ \vdots \\ f(N-1) \end{bmatrix} = \begin{bmatrix} f_0 \\ f_1 \\ \vdots \\ f_{N-1} \end{bmatrix} \tag{7-20}$$

$$\mathbf{t} = \begin{bmatrix} T(0) \\ T(1) \\ \vdots \\ T(N-1) \end{bmatrix} = \begin{bmatrix} t_0 \\ t_1 \\ \vdots \\ t_{N-1} \end{bmatrix} \tag{7-21}$$

and

$$\mathbf{s}_u = \begin{bmatrix} s(0,u) \\ s(1,u) \\ \vdots \\ s(N-1,u) \end{bmatrix} = \begin{bmatrix} s_{u,0} \\ s_{u,1} \\ \vdots \\ s_{u,N-1} \end{bmatrix} \quad \text{for } u = 0,1,\ldots,N-1 \tag{7-22}$$

and using them to rewrite Eq. (7-19) as

$$T(u) = \langle \mathbf{s}_u, \mathbf{f} \rangle \quad \text{for } u = 0,1,\ldots,N-1 \tag{7-23}$$

Combining the N basis vectors of the transform in an $N \times N$ *transformation matrix*

$$\mathbf{A} = \begin{bmatrix} \mathbf{s}_0^T \\ \mathbf{s}_1^T \\ \vdots \\ \mathbf{s}_{N-1}^T \end{bmatrix} = \begin{bmatrix} \mathbf{s}_0 & \mathbf{s}_1 & \cdots & \mathbf{s}_{N-1} \end{bmatrix}^T \tag{7-24}$$

By employing Eq. (7-1), we assume the most common case of real-valued basis vectors. Equation (7-2) must be used for a complex inner product space.

we can then substitute Eq. (7-23) into Eq. (7-21) and use Eq. (7-1) to get

$$
\begin{aligned}
\mathbf{t} &= \begin{bmatrix} \langle \mathbf{s}_0, \mathbf{f} \rangle \\ \langle \mathbf{s}_1, \mathbf{f} \rangle \\ \vdots \\ \langle \mathbf{s}_{N-1}, \mathbf{f} \rangle \end{bmatrix} = \begin{bmatrix} s_{0,0}f_0 + s_{1,0}f_1 + \ldots + s_{N-1,0}f_{N-1} \\ s_{0,1}f_0 + s_{1,1}f_1 + \ldots + s_{N-1,1}f_{N-1} \\ \vdots \\ s_{0,N-1}f_0 + s_{1,N-1}f_1 + \ldots + s_{N-1,N-1}f_{N-1} \end{bmatrix} \\[2mm]
&= \begin{bmatrix} s_{0,0} & s_{1,0} & \cdots & s_{N-1,0} \\ s_{0,1} & s_{1,1} & & \\ \vdots & & \ddots & s_{N-1,N-2} \\ s_{0,N-1} & & s_{N-2,N-1} & s_{N-1,N-1} \end{bmatrix} \begin{bmatrix} f_0 \\ f_1 \\ \vdots \\ f_{N-1} \end{bmatrix}
\end{aligned}
\tag{7-25}
$$

or

$$\mathbf{t} = \mathbf{Af} \tag{7-26}$$

The inverse of this equation follows from the observation that

$$\mathbf{AA}^T = \begin{bmatrix} \mathbf{s}_0^T \\ \mathbf{s}_1^T \\ \vdots \\ \mathbf{s}_{N-1}^T \end{bmatrix} \begin{bmatrix} \mathbf{s}_0 & \mathbf{s}_1 & \cdots & \mathbf{s}_{N-1} \end{bmatrix}$$

$$= \begin{bmatrix} \mathbf{s}_0^T\mathbf{s}_0 & \mathbf{s}_0^T\mathbf{s}_1 & \cdots & \mathbf{s}_0^T\mathbf{s}_{N-1} \\ \mathbf{s}_1^T\mathbf{s}_0 & \mathbf{s}_1^T\mathbf{s}_1 & & \vdots \\ \vdots & & \ddots & \\ \mathbf{s}_{N-1}^T\mathbf{s}_0 & \cdots & & \mathbf{s}_{N-1}^T\mathbf{s}_{N-1} \end{bmatrix} \tag{7-27}$$

$$= \begin{bmatrix} \langle \mathbf{s}_0,\mathbf{s}_0 \rangle & \langle \mathbf{s}_0,\mathbf{s}_1 \rangle & \cdots & \langle \mathbf{s}_0,\mathbf{s}_{N-1} \rangle \\ \langle \mathbf{s}_1,\mathbf{s}_0 \rangle & \langle \mathbf{s}_1,\mathbf{s}_1 \rangle & & \vdots \\ \vdots & & \ddots & \\ \langle \mathbf{s}_{N-1},\mathbf{s}_0 \rangle & \cdots & & \langle \mathbf{s}_{N-1},\mathbf{s}_{N-1} \rangle \end{bmatrix}$$

$$= \begin{bmatrix} 1 & 0 & \cdots & 0 \\ 0 & 1 & & \vdots \\ \vdots & & \ddots & \\ 0 & \cdots & & 1 \end{bmatrix} = \mathbf{I}$$

where the last two steps are a consequence of Eqs. (7-1) and (7-7), respectively. Since $\mathbf{AA}^T = \mathbf{I}$, premultiplying Eq. (7-26) by $\mathbf{A}^T$ and simplifying gives $\mathbf{f} = \mathbf{A}^T\mathbf{t}$. Thus, Eqs. (7-16) and (7-17) become the matrix-based transform pair

$$\mathbf{t} = \mathbf{Af} \tag{7-28}$$

and

$$\mathbf{f} = \mathbf{A}^T\mathbf{t} \tag{7-29}$$

It is important to remember that, in the derivation of Eqs. (7-28) and (7-29), we assumed the N transform basis vectors (i.e., the $\mathbf{s}_u$ for $u = 0, 1, ..., N-1$) of transformation matrix $\mathbf{A}$ are real and orthonormal. In accordance with Eq. (7-7),

$$\langle \mathbf{s}_k,\mathbf{s}_l \rangle = \mathbf{s}_k^T\mathbf{s}_l = \delta_{kl} = \begin{cases} 0 & k \neq l \\ 1 & k = l \end{cases} \tag{7-30}$$

The assumed orthonormality allows forward transforms to be computed without explicit reference to a forward transformation kernel—that is, $\mathbf{t} = \mathbf{Af}$ where $\mathbf{A}$ is a function of the inverse transformation kernal $s(x,u)$ alone. It is left as an exercise for the reader (see Problem 7.3) to show that for real orthonormal basis vectors, $r(x,u) = s(x,u)$.

Because the basis vectors of $\mathbf{A}$ are real and orthonormal, the transform defined in Eq. (7-28) is called an *orthogonal transform*. It preserves inner products—i.e., $\langle \mathbf{f}_1, \mathbf{f}_2 \rangle = \langle \mathbf{t}_1, \mathbf{t}_2 \rangle = \langle \mathbf{Af}_1, \mathbf{Af}_2 \rangle$—and thus the distances and angles between vectors before and after transformation. Both the rows and the columns of $\mathbf{A}$ are orthonormal bases and $\mathbf{AA}^T = \mathbf{A}^T\mathbf{A} = \mathbf{I}$, so $\mathbf{A}^{-1} = \mathbf{A}^T$. The result is that Eqs. (7-28) and (7-29) are a *reversible transform pair*. Substituting Eq. (7-29) into (7-28) yields $\mathbf{t} = \mathbf{Af} = \mathbf{AA}^T\mathbf{t} = \mathbf{t}$, while substituting Eq. (7-28) into (7-29) gives $\mathbf{f} = \mathbf{A}^T\mathbf{t} = \mathbf{A}^T\mathbf{AF} = \mathbf{f}$.

For 2-D square arrays or images, Eqs. (7-16) and (7-17) become

Equations (7-31) and (7-32) are simplified versions of Eqs. (2-55) and (2-56) with $M = N$.

$$T(u,v) = \sum_{x=0}^{N-1}\sum_{y=0}^{N-1} f(x,y)r(x,y,u,v) \tag{7-31}$$

and

$$f(x,y) = \sum_{u=0}^{N-1}\sum_{v=0}^{N-1} T(u,v)s(x,y,u,v) \tag{7-32}$$

where $r(x,y,u,v)$ and $s(x,y,u,v)$ are forward and inverse transformation kernels, respectively. Transform $T(u,v)$ and inverse transformation kernel $s(x,y,u,v)$ again can be viewed as weighting coefficients and basis vectors, respectively, with Eq. (7-32) defining a linear expansion of $f(x,y)$. As was noted in Chapter 2, forward transformation kernel $r(x,y,u,v)$ is *separable* if

$$r(x,y,u,v) = r_1(x,u)r_2(y,v) \tag{7-33}$$

and *symmetric* if r_1 is functionally equal to r_2 so

$$r(x,y,u,v) = r_1(x,u)r_1(y,v) \tag{7-34}$$

Substitute s for r in Eqs. (7-33) and (7-34) for separable and separable symmetric inverse kernals, respectively.

If the transformation kernels are real and orthonormal, and both r and s are separable and symmetric, the matrix equivalents of Eqs. (7-31) and (7-32) are

$$\mathbf{T} = \mathbf{AFA}^T \tag{7-35}$$

and

$$\mathbf{F} = \mathbf{A}^T\mathbf{TA} \tag{7-36}$$

where $\mathbf{F}$ is an $N \times N$ matrix containing the elements of $f(x,y)$, $\mathbf{T}$ is its $N \times N$ transform, and $\mathbf{A}$ is as previously defined in Eq. (7-24). The pre- and post-multiplications of $\mathbf{F}$ by $\mathbf{A}$ and $\mathbf{A}^T$ in Eq. (7-35) compute the column and row transforms of $\mathbf{F}$, respectively. This, in effect, breaks the 2-D transform into two 1-D transforms, mirroring the process described in Section 4.11 for the 2-D DFT.

EXAMPLE 7.2:   A simple orthogonal transformation.

Consider the 2-element basis vectors

$$\mathbf{s}_0 = \frac{1}{\sqrt{2}}\begin{bmatrix}1\\1\end{bmatrix} \quad \text{and} \quad \mathbf{s}_1 = \frac{1}{\sqrt{2}}\begin{bmatrix}1\\-1\end{bmatrix}$$

and note they are orthonormal in accordance with Eq. (7-30):

$$\langle \mathbf{s}_0, \mathbf{s}_1 \rangle = \mathbf{s}_0^T \mathbf{s}_1 = \frac{1}{2}\begin{bmatrix}1 & 1\end{bmatrix}\begin{bmatrix}1\\-1\end{bmatrix} = \frac{1}{2}(1-1) = 0$$

$$\langle \mathbf{s}_1, \mathbf{s}_0 \rangle = \mathbf{s}_1^T \mathbf{s}_0 = \frac{1}{2}\begin{bmatrix}1 & -1\end{bmatrix}\begin{bmatrix}1\\1\end{bmatrix} = \frac{1}{2}(1-1) = 0$$

$$\langle \mathbf{s}_0, \mathbf{s}_0 \rangle = \mathbf{s}_0^T \mathbf{s}_0 = \frac{1}{2}\begin{bmatrix}1 & 1\end{bmatrix}\begin{bmatrix}1\\1\end{bmatrix} = \frac{1}{2}(1+1) = 1$$

$$\langle \mathbf{s}_1, \mathbf{s}_1 \rangle = \mathbf{s}_1^T \mathbf{s}_1 = \frac{1}{2}\begin{bmatrix}1 & -1\end{bmatrix}\begin{bmatrix}1\\-1\end{bmatrix} = \frac{1}{2}(1+1) = 1$$

Substitution of $\mathbf{s}_0$ and $\mathbf{s}_1$ into Eq. (7-24) with $N = 2$ yields transformation matrix

$$\mathbf{A} = \begin{bmatrix}\mathbf{s}_0 & \mathbf{s}_1\end{bmatrix}^T = \frac{1}{\sqrt{2}}\begin{bmatrix}1 & 1\\1 & -1\end{bmatrix} \tag{7-37}$$

and the transform of 2×2 matrix

$$\mathbf{F} = \begin{bmatrix}20 & 63\\21 & 128\end{bmatrix}$$

follows from Eq. (7-35):

$$\mathbf{T} = \left(\frac{1}{\sqrt{2}}\right)^2 \begin{bmatrix}1 & 1\\1 & -1\end{bmatrix}\begin{bmatrix}20 & 63\\21 & 128\end{bmatrix}\begin{bmatrix}1 & 1\\1 & -1\end{bmatrix}^T$$

$$= \frac{1}{2}\begin{bmatrix}41 & 191\\-1 & -65\end{bmatrix}\begin{bmatrix}1 & 1\\1 & -1\end{bmatrix} = \frac{1}{2}\begin{bmatrix}232 & -150\\-66 & 64\end{bmatrix}$$

$$= \begin{bmatrix}116 & -75\\-33 & 32\end{bmatrix}$$

In accordance with Eq. (7-36), the inverse of transform $\mathbf{T}$ is

$$\mathbf{F} = \left(\frac{1}{\sqrt{2}}\right)^2 \begin{bmatrix}1 & 1\\1 & -1\end{bmatrix}^T \begin{bmatrix}116 & -75\\-33 & 32\end{bmatrix}\begin{bmatrix}1 & 1\\1 & -1\end{bmatrix} = \frac{1}{2}\begin{bmatrix}83 & -43\\149 & -107\end{bmatrix}\begin{bmatrix}1 & 1\\1 & -1\end{bmatrix} = \begin{bmatrix}20 & 63\\21 & 128\end{bmatrix}$$

Finally, we note **A** is an orthogonal transformation matrix for which

$$\mathbf{AA}^T = \frac{1}{\sqrt{2}}\begin{bmatrix} 1 & 1 \\ 1 & -1 \end{bmatrix}\frac{1}{\sqrt{2}}\begin{bmatrix} 1 & 1 \\ 1 & -1 \end{bmatrix}^T = \frac{1}{2}\begin{bmatrix} 2 & 0 \\ 0 & 2 \end{bmatrix} = \begin{bmatrix} 1 & 0 \\ 0 & 1 \end{bmatrix} = \mathbf{I}$$

and $\mathbf{A}^{-1} = \mathbf{A}^T$. It is also interesting to note Eq. (7-37) is the transformation matrix of the discrete *Fourier, Hartley, Cosine, Sin, Walsh-Hadamard, Slant,* and *Haar* transforms for 1- and 2-D inputs of size 2×1 and 2×2, respectively. These transforms are discussed in detail in Sections 7.6 through 7.9.

Although formulated for real orthonormal bases and square arrays, Eqs. (7-35) and (7-36) can be modified to accomodate a variety of situations, including rectangular arrays, complex-valued basis vectors, and biorthonormal bases.

RECTANGULAR ARRAYS

When the arrays to be transformed are rectangular, as opposed to square, Eqs. (7-35) and (7-36) become

$$\mathbf{T} = \mathbf{A}_M \mathbf{F} \mathbf{A}_N^T \tag{7-38}$$

and

$$\mathbf{F} = \mathbf{A}_M^T \mathbf{T} \mathbf{A}_N \tag{7-39}$$

where $\mathbf{F}$, $\mathbf{A}_M$, and $\mathbf{A}_N$ are of size $M \times N$, $M \times M$, and $N \times N$, respectively. Both $\mathbf{A}_M$ and $\mathbf{A}_N$ are defined in accordance with Eq. (7-24).

EXAMPLE 7.3:   **Computing the transform of a rectangular array.**

A simple transformation in which M and N are 2 and 3, respectively, is

$$\mathbf{T} = \mathbf{A}_2 \mathbf{F} \mathbf{A}_3^T = \frac{1}{\sqrt{2}}\begin{bmatrix} 1 & 1 \\ 1 & -1 \end{bmatrix}\begin{bmatrix} 5 & 100 & 44 \\ 6 & 103 & 40 \end{bmatrix}\frac{1}{\sqrt{3}}\begin{bmatrix} 1 & 1 & 1 \\ 1 & 0.366 & -1.366 \\ 1 & -1.366 & 0.366 \end{bmatrix}^T$$

$$= \frac{1}{\sqrt{6}}\begin{bmatrix} 11 & 203 & 84 \\ -1 & -3 & 4 \end{bmatrix}\begin{bmatrix} 1 & 1 & 1 \\ 1 & 0.366 & -1.366 \\ 1 & -1.366 & 0.366 \end{bmatrix} = \begin{bmatrix} 121.6580 & -12.0201 & -96.1657 \\ 0 & -3.0873 & 1.8624 \end{bmatrix}$$

where matrices $\mathbf{F}$, $\mathbf{A}_2$, and $\mathbf{A}_3$ are as defined in the first step of the computation. As would be expected, 2×3 output transform $\mathbf{T}$ is the same size as $\mathbf{F}$. It is left as an exercise for the reader (see Problem 7.5) to show that $\mathbf{A}_3$ is an orthogonal transformation matrix, and that the transformation is reversible using Eq. (7-39). The orthonormality of $\mathbf{A}_2$ was established in Example 7.2.

COMPLEX ORTHONORMAL BASIS VECTORS

Complex-valued basis vectors are orthonormal if and only if

$$\langle \mathbf{s}_k, \mathbf{s}_l \rangle = \langle \mathbf{s}_l, \mathbf{s}_k \rangle^* = \mathbf{s}_k^{*T} \mathbf{s}_l = \delta_{kl} = \begin{cases} 0 & k \neq l \\ 1 & k = l \end{cases} \tag{7-40}$$

where * denotes the complex conjugate operation. When basis vectors are complex, as opposed to real-valued, Eqs. (7-35) and (7-36) become

$$\mathbf{T} = \mathbf{AFA}^T \tag{7-41}$$

and

$$\mathbf{F} = \mathbf{A}^{*T} \mathbf{TA}^* \tag{7-42}$$

Orthogonal transforms are a special case of unitary transforms in which the expansion functions are real-valued. Both transforms preserve inner products.

respectively. Transformation matrix $\mathbf{A}$ is then called a *unitary matrix* and Eqs. (7-41) and (7-42) are a *unitary transform* pair. An important and useful property of $\mathbf{A}$ is that $\mathbf{A}^{*T}\mathbf{A} = \mathbf{AA}^{*T} = \mathbf{A}^*\mathbf{A}^T = \mathbf{A}^T\mathbf{A}^* = \mathbf{I}$, so $\mathbf{A}^{-1} = \mathbf{A}^{*T}$. The 1-D counterparts of Eq. (7-41) and (7-42) are:

$$\mathbf{t} = \mathbf{Af} \tag{7-43}$$

$$\mathbf{f} = \mathbf{A}^{*T}\mathbf{t} \tag{7-44}$$

EXAMPLE 7.4:   A transform with complex-valued basis vectors.

Unlike orthogonal transformation matrices, where the inverse of the transformation matrix is its transpose, the inverse of unitary transformation matrix

$$\mathbf{A} = \frac{1}{\sqrt{3}} \begin{bmatrix} 1 & 1 & 1 \\ 1 & -0.5 - j0.866 & -0.5 + j0.866 \\ 1 & -0.5 + j0.866 & -0.5 - j0.866 \end{bmatrix} \tag{7-45}$$

is its conjugate transpose. Thus,

$$\mathbf{A}^{*T}\mathbf{A} = \frac{1}{\sqrt{3}} \begin{bmatrix} 1 & 1 & 1 \\ 1 & -0.5 - j0.866 & -0.5 + j0.866 \\ 1 & -0.5 + j0.866 & -0.5 - j0.866 \end{bmatrix}^{*T} \frac{1}{\sqrt{3}} \begin{bmatrix} 1 & 1 & 1 \\ 1 & -0.5 - j0.866 & -0.5 + j0.866 \\ 1 & -0.5 + j0.866 & -0.5 - j0.866 \end{bmatrix}$$

$$= \frac{1}{3} \begin{bmatrix} 1 & 1 & 1 \\ 1 & -0.5 + j0.866 & -0.5 - j0.866 \\ 1 & -0.5 - j0.866 & -0.5 + j0.866 \end{bmatrix} \begin{bmatrix} 1 & 1 & 1 \\ 1 & -0.5 - j0.866 & -0.5 + j0.866 \\ 1 & -0.5 + j0.866 & -0.5 - j0.866 \end{bmatrix}$$

$$= \frac{1}{3} \begin{bmatrix} 3 & 0 & 0 \\ 0 & 3 & 0 \\ 0 & 0 & 3 \end{bmatrix} = \mathbf{I}$$

where $j = \sqrt{-1}$ and matrix $\mathbf{A}$ is a unitary matrix that can be used in Eqs. (7-41) through (7-44). It is easy to show (see Problem 7.4) that when $\mathbf{A}^{*T}\mathbf{A} = \mathbf{I}$, the basis vectors in $\mathbf{A}$ satisfy Eq. (7-40) and are thus orthonormal.

BIORTHONORMAL BASIS VECTORS

Expansion functions $\mathbf{s}_0, \mathbf{s}_1, \ldots, \mathbf{s}_{N-1}$ in Eq. (7-24) are *biorthonormal* if there exists a set of *dual expansion functions* $\widetilde{\mathbf{s}}_0, \widetilde{\mathbf{s}}_1, \ldots, \widetilde{\mathbf{s}}_{N-1}$ such that

$$\langle \widetilde{\mathbf{s}}_k, \mathbf{s}_l \rangle = \delta_{kl} = \begin{cases} 0 & k \neq l \\ 1 & k = l \end{cases} \tag{7-46}$$

Neither the expansion functions nor their duals need be orthonormal themselves. Given a set of *biorthonormal expansion functions*, Eqs. (7-35) and (7-36) become

$$\mathbf{T} = \widetilde{\mathbf{A}} \mathbf{F} \widetilde{\mathbf{A}}^T \tag{7-47}$$

and

$$\mathbf{F} = \mathbf{A}^T \mathbf{T} \mathbf{A} \tag{7-48}$$

Transformation matrix $\mathbf{A}$ remains as defined in Eq. (7-24); *dual transformation matrix* $\widetilde{\mathbf{A}} = [\widetilde{\mathbf{s}}_0 \quad \widetilde{\mathbf{s}}_1 \quad \ldots \quad \widetilde{\mathbf{s}}_{N-1}]^T$ is an $N \times N$ matrix whose rows are transposed dual expansion functions. When the expansion functions and their duals are identical—that is, when $\widetilde{\mathbf{s}}_u = \mathbf{s}_u$—Eqs. (7-47) and (7-48) reduce to Eqs. (7-35) and (7-36), respectively. The 1-D counterparts of Eqs. (7-47) and (7-48) are:

$$\mathbf{t} = \widetilde{\mathbf{A}} \mathbf{f} \tag{7-49}$$

$$\mathbf{f} = \mathbf{A}^T \mathbf{t} \tag{7-50}$$

EXAMPLE 7.5:   A biorthonormal transform.

Consider the real biorthonormal transformation matrices

$$\mathbf{A} = \begin{bmatrix} 0.5 & 0.5 & 0.5 & 0.5 \\ -1 & -1 & 1 & 1 \\ -0.5303 & 0.5303 & -0.1768 & 0.1768 \\ -0.1768 & 0.1768 & -0.5303 & 0.5303 \end{bmatrix} \quad \text{and} \quad \widetilde{\mathbf{A}} = \begin{bmatrix} 0.5 & 0.5 & 0.5 & 0.5 \\ -0.25 & -0.25 & 0.25 & 0.25 \\ -1.0607 & 1.0607 & 0.3536 & -0.3536 \\ 0.3536 & -0.3536 & -1.0607 & 1.0607 \end{bmatrix}$$

It is left as an exercise for the reader (see Problem 7.16) to show that $\mathbf{A}$ and $\widetilde{\mathbf{A}}$ are biorthonormal. The transform of 1-D column vector $\mathbf{f} = [30 \quad 11 \quad 210 \quad 6]^T$ is

$$\mathbf{t} = \widetilde{\mathbf{A}} \mathbf{f} = \begin{bmatrix} 0.5 & 0.5 & 0.5 & 0.5 \\ -0.25 & -0.25 & 0.25 & 0.25 \\ -1.0607 & 1.0607 & 0.3536 & -0.3536 \\ 0.3536 & -0.3536 & -1.0607 & 1.0607 \end{bmatrix} \begin{bmatrix} 30 \\ 11 \\ 210 \\ 6 \end{bmatrix} = \begin{bmatrix} 128.5 \\ 43.75 \\ 51.9723 \\ -209.6572 \end{bmatrix}$$

Since

$$\langle \mathbf{f}, \mathbf{f} \rangle = \mathbf{f}^T \mathbf{f} = \begin{bmatrix} 30 & 11 & 210 & 6 \end{bmatrix} \begin{bmatrix} 30 \\ 11 \\ 210 \\ 6 \end{bmatrix} = 45,157$$

and $\langle \mathbf{t}, \mathbf{t} \rangle = \mathbf{t}^T \mathbf{t} = 65,084$, which is not equal to $\langle \mathbf{f}, \mathbf{f} \rangle$, the transformation does *not* preserve inner products. It is, however, reversable:

$$\mathbf{f} = \mathbf{A}^T \mathbf{t} = \begin{bmatrix} 0.5 & 0.5 & 0.5 & 0.5 \\ -1 & -1 & 1 & 1 \\ -0.5303 & 0.5303 & -0.1768 & 0.1768 \\ -0.1768 & 0.1768 & -0.5303 & 0.5303 \end{bmatrix}^T \begin{bmatrix} 128.5 \\ 43.75 \\ 51.9723 \\ -209.6572 \end{bmatrix} = \begin{bmatrix} 30 \\ 11 \\ 210 \\ 6 \end{bmatrix}$$

Here, the forward and inverse transforms were computed using Eqs. (7-49) and (7-50), respectively.

Finally, we note the bulk of the concepts presented in this section can be generalized to continuous expansions of the form

$$f(x) = \sum_{u=-\infty}^{\infty} \alpha_u s_u(x) \tag{7-51}$$

where α_u and the $s_u(x)$ for $u = 0, \pm 1, \pm 2, \dots$ represent expansion coefficients and basis vectors of inner product space $C([a, b])$, respectively. For a given $f(x)$ and basis $s_u(x)$ for $u = 0, \pm 1, \pm 2, \dots$, the appropriate expansion coefficients can be computed from the definition of the integral inner product of $C([a, b])$ — i.e., Eq. (7-3) — and the general properties of all inner product spaces — i.e, Eqs. (7-10) through (7-15). Thus, for example, if $s_u(x)$ for $u = 0, \pm 1, \pm 2, \dots$ are orthonormal basis vectors of $C([a, b])$,

$$\alpha_u = \langle s_u(x), f(x) \rangle \tag{7-52}$$

Here, we have simply replaced i, z, and w_i in Eq. (7-13) with u, $f(x)$, and $s_u(x)$. In the next example, Eq. (7-52) will be used in the derivation of the continuous Fourier series.

EXAMPLE 7.6:   The Fourier series and discrete Fourier transform.

Consider the representation of a continuous periodic function of period T as a linear expansion of orthonormal basis vectors of the form

$$s_u(x) = \frac{1}{\sqrt{T}} e^{j2\pi ux/T} \quad \text{for } u = 0, \pm 1, \pm 2, \dots \tag{7-53}$$

In accordance with Eqs. (7-51) and (7-52),

$$f(x) = \sum_{u=-\infty}^{\infty} \alpha_u \left[\frac{1}{\sqrt{T}} e^{j2\pi ux/T} \right]$$

$$= \frac{1}{\sqrt{T}} \sum_{u=-\infty}^{\infty} \alpha_u e^{j2\pi ux/T} \tag{7-54}$$

and

$$\alpha_u = \langle s_u(x), f(x) \rangle$$

$$= \int_{-T/2}^{T/2} \left[\frac{1}{\sqrt{T}} e^{j2\pi ux/T} \right]^* f(x)\,dx$$

$$= \frac{1}{\sqrt{T}} \int_{-T/2}^{T/2} f(x) e^{-j2\pi ux/T}\,dx \tag{7-55}$$

With the exception of the variable names and normalization (i.e., the use of $1/\sqrt{T}$ in the above two equations as opposed to $1/T$ in only one of them), Eqs. (7-54) and (7-55) are the familiar Fourier series of Eqs. (4-8) and (4-9) in Chapter 4. An almost identical derivation, which is left as an exercise for the reader (see Problem 7.22), yields the following discrete counterparts of Eqs. (7-53) through (7-55):

$$s(x,u) = \frac{1}{\sqrt{N}} e^{j2\pi ux/N} \quad \text{for } u = 0, 1, \ldots, N-1 \tag{7-56}$$

$$f(x) = \frac{1}{\sqrt{N}} \sum_{u=0}^{N-1} T(u) e^{j2\pi ux/N} \tag{7-57}$$

and

$$T(u) = \frac{1}{\sqrt{N}} \sum_{x=0}^{N-1} f(x) e^{-j2\pi ux/N} \tag{7-58}$$

The discrete complex basis vectors of Eq. (7-56) are an orthonormal basis of inner product space $\mathbf{C}^N$. Equations (7-58) and (7-57), except for the variable names and normalization, are the familiar discrete Fourier transform of Eqs. (4-44) and (4-45) in Chapter 4.

Now consider the use of Eqs. (7-55) and (7-58) in the computation of both the Fourier series and discrete Fourier transform of $f(x) = \sin(2\pi x)$ of period $T = 1$. In accordance with Eq. (7-55),

$$\alpha_1 = \int_{-1/2}^{1/2} \left[\frac{1}{\sqrt{1}} e^{j2\pi(1)x/1} \right]^* \sin(2\pi x)\,dx$$

$$= \int_{-1/2}^{1/2} e^{-j2\pi x} \sin(2\pi x)\,dx = \int_{-1/2}^{1/2} [\cos(2\pi x) - j\sin(2\pi x)]\sin(2\pi x)\,dx$$

$$= \frac{1}{4\pi} \sin^2(2\pi x) - j\left[\frac{x}{2} - \frac{1}{8\pi} \sin(4\pi x) \right]\Bigg|_{-1/2}^{1/2} = -j0.5$$

and, in the same way, $\alpha_{-1} = j0.5$. Since all other coefficients are zero, the resulting Fourier series is

$$f(x) = j0.5e^{-j2\pi x} - j0.5e^{j2\pi x} \qquad (7\text{-}59)$$

Equation (7-58) with $N = 8$ and $f(x) = \sin(2\pi x)$ for $x = 0, 1, \ldots, 7$, on the other hand, yields

$$T(u) = \begin{cases} -j1.414 & u = 1 \\ +j1.414 & u = 7 \\ 0 & \text{otherwise} \end{cases} \qquad (7\text{-}60)$$

Figure 7.2 depicts both computations as "matrix multiplications" in which continuous or discrete basis vectors (the rows of matrix **A**) are multiplied by a continuous or discrete function (column vector **f**) and integrated or summed to produce a set of discrete expansion or transform coefficients (column vector **t**). For the Fourier series, the expansion coefficients are integral inner products of $\sin(2\pi x)$ and one of a potentially infinite set of continuous basis vectors. For the DFT, each transform coefficient is a discrete inner product of **f** and one of eight discrete basis vectors using Eq. (7-2). Note since the DFT is based on complex orthonormal basis vectors, the transform can be computed as a matrix multiplication [in accordance with Eq. (7-43)]. Thus, the inner products that generate the elements of transform **t** are embedded in matrix multiplication **Af**. That is, each element of **t** is formed by multiplying one row of **A**—i.e., one discrete expansion function—element by element by **f** and summing the resulting products.

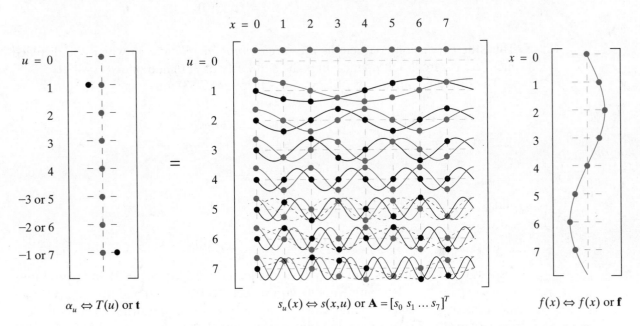

FIGURE 7.2 Depicting the continuous Fourier series and 8-point DFT of $f(x) = \sin(2\pi x)$ as "matrix multiplications." The real and imaginary parts of all complex quantities are shown in blue and black, respectively. Continuous and discrete functions are represented using lines and dots, respectively. Dashed lines are included to show that $\mathbf{s}_5 = \mathbf{s}_3^*$, $\mathbf{s}_6 = \mathbf{s}_2^*$, and $\mathbf{s}_7 = \mathbf{s}_1^*$, effectively cutting the maximum frequency of the DFT in half. The negative indices to the left of **t** are for the Fourier series computation alone.

7.3 CORRELATION

Example 7.6 highlights the role of inner products in the computation of orthogonal transform coefficients. In this section, we turn our attention to the relationship between those coefficients and correlation.

Given two continuous functions $f(x)$ and $g(x)$, the *correlation* of f and g, denoted $f \star g(\Delta x)$, is defined as

To be precise, we should use the term *cross-correlation* when $f(x) \neq g(x)$ and *auto-correlation* when $f(x) = g(x)$. Equation (7-61) is valid for both cases.

$$f \star g(\Delta x) = \int_{-\infty}^{\infty} f^*(x) g(x + \Delta x) dx$$

$$= \langle f(x), g(x + \Delta x) \rangle \tag{7-61}$$

where the final step follows from Eq. (7-3) with $a = -\infty$ and $b = \infty$. Sometimes called the *sliding inner product* of f and g, correlation measures the similarity of $f(x)$ and $g(x)$ as a function of their relative displacement Δx. If $\Delta x = 0$,

As the name *sliding inner product* suggests, visualize sliding one function over another, multiplying them together, and computing the area. As the area increases, the functions become increasingly similar.

$$f \star g(0) = \langle f(x), g(x) \rangle \tag{7-62}$$

and Eq. (7-52), which defines the coefficients of the continuous orthonormal expansion in Eq. (7-51), can be alternately written as

$$\alpha_u = \langle f, s_u \rangle = f \star s_u(0) \tag{7-63}$$

Thus, the expansion coefficients are *single-point correlations* in which the displacement Δx is zero. Each α_u measures the similarity of $f(x)$ and one $s_u(x)$.

The discrete equivalents of Eqs. (7-61) through (7-63) are

The equation for 2-D discrete correlation is given in Table 4.3. In Eq. (7-64), n and m are integers, f_n denotes the nth element of $\mathbf{f}$, and g_{n+m} denotes the $(n + m)$th element of $\mathbf{g}$. Equation (7-66) follows from Eqs. (7-65) and (7-23).

$$\mathbf{f} \star \mathbf{g}(m) = \sum_{x=-\infty}^{\infty} f_n^* g_{n+m} \tag{7-64}$$

$$\mathbf{f} \star \mathbf{g}(0) = \langle \mathbf{f}, \mathbf{g} \rangle \tag{7-65}$$

and

$$T(u) = \langle \mathbf{s}_u, \mathbf{f} \rangle = \mathbf{s}_u \star \mathbf{f}(0) \tag{7-66}$$

respectively. Comments similar to those made in regard to Eq. (7-63) and continuous series expansions also can be made with respect to Eq. (7-66) and discrete orthogonal transforms. Each element of an orthogonal transform [i.e., transform coefficient $T(u)$ of Eq. (7-23)] is a single-point correlation that measures the similarity of $\mathbf{f}$ and vector $\mathbf{s}_u$. This powerful property of orthogonal transforms is the basis upon which the sinusoidal interference in Fig. 2.45(a) of Example 2.11 in Chapter 2 and Fig. 4.65(a) of Example 4.25 in Chapter 4 was identified and eliminated.

EXAMPLE 7.7:   Correlation in the DFT of Example 7.6.

Consider again the 8-point DFT in Example 7.6 and note, in accordance with Eq. (7-56), the basis vectors are complex exponentials of the following harmonically related angular frequencies: $0, 2\pi, 4\pi, 6\pi, 8\pi, 6\pi, 4\pi$, and 2π (aliasing reduces the last three frequencies from $10\pi, 12\pi$, and 14π, respectively). Since discrete input $f(x) = \sin(2\pi x)$ is a single frequency sinusoid of angular frequency 2π, **f** should be highly correlated with basis vectors $\mathbf{s}_1$ and $\mathbf{s}_7$. As can be seen in Fig. 7.2, transform **t** does indeed reach its maximum at $u = 1$ and 7; it is nonzero at these two frequencies alone.

7.4 BASIS FUNCTIONS IN THE TIME-FREQUENCY PLANE

Because transforms measure the degree to which a function resembles a selected set of basis vectors, we now turn our attention to the basis vectors themselves. In the following discussions, the terms basis vector and basis function are synonomous.

As can be seen in Fig. 7.3, where the basis vectors of some commonly encountered transforms are depicted, most orthogonal bases are mathematically related sets of sinusoids, square waves, ramps, and other small waves called *wavelets*. If $h(t)$ is a basis vector and $g(t)$ is the function being transformed, transform coefficient $g \star h(0)$, as noted in the previous section, is a measure of the similarity of g and h. Large values of $g \star h(0)$ indicate that g and h share important characteristics in time and frequency (e.g., shape and bandwidth). Thus, if h is the ramp-shaped basis function at $u = 1$ in Fig. 7.3(d), transform coefficient $g \star h(0)$ can be used to detect linear brightness gradients across a row of an image. If h is a sinusoidal basis function like those of Fig. 7.3(a), on the other hand, $g \star h(0)$ can be used to spot sinusoidal interference patterns. Plots like those of Fig. 7.3, together with a similarity measure like $g \star h(0)$, can reveal a great deal about the time and frequency characteristics of the function being transformed.

In our introduction to the *time-frequency plane*, independent variables t and f, rather than spatial variables x and u, are employed. Continuous functions $g(t)$ and $h(f)$ take the place of $f(x)$ and $s_u(x)$ in the previous sections. Though the concepts are presented using continuous functions and variables, they are equally applicable to discrete functions and variables.

A purely objective descriptor of h, and thus of g for large values of $g \star h(0)$, is the location of h on the *time-frequency plane* of Fig. 7.4(a). Let $p_h(t) = |h(t)|^2 / \|h(t)\|^2$ be a probability density function with mean

In Eq. (7-67), each value of t is weighted by $p_h(t)$ to compute a weighted mean with respect to coordinate t.

$$\mu_t = \frac{1}{\|h(t)\|^2} \int_{-\infty}^{\infty} t |h(t)|^2 \, dt \tag{7-67}$$

and variance

$$\sigma_t^2 = \frac{1}{\|h(t)\|^2} \int_{-\infty}^{\infty} (t - \mu_t)^2 |h(t)|^2 \, dt \tag{7-68}$$

and let $p_H(f) = |H(f)|^2 / \|H(f)\|^2$ be a probability density function with mean

$$\mu_f = \frac{1}{\|H(f)\|^2} \int_{-\infty}^{\infty} f |H(f)|^2 \, df \tag{7-69}$$

and variance

$$\sigma_f^2 = \frac{1}{\|H(f)\|^2} \int_{-\infty}^{\infty} (f - \mu_f)^2 |H(f)|^2 \, df \tag{7-70}$$

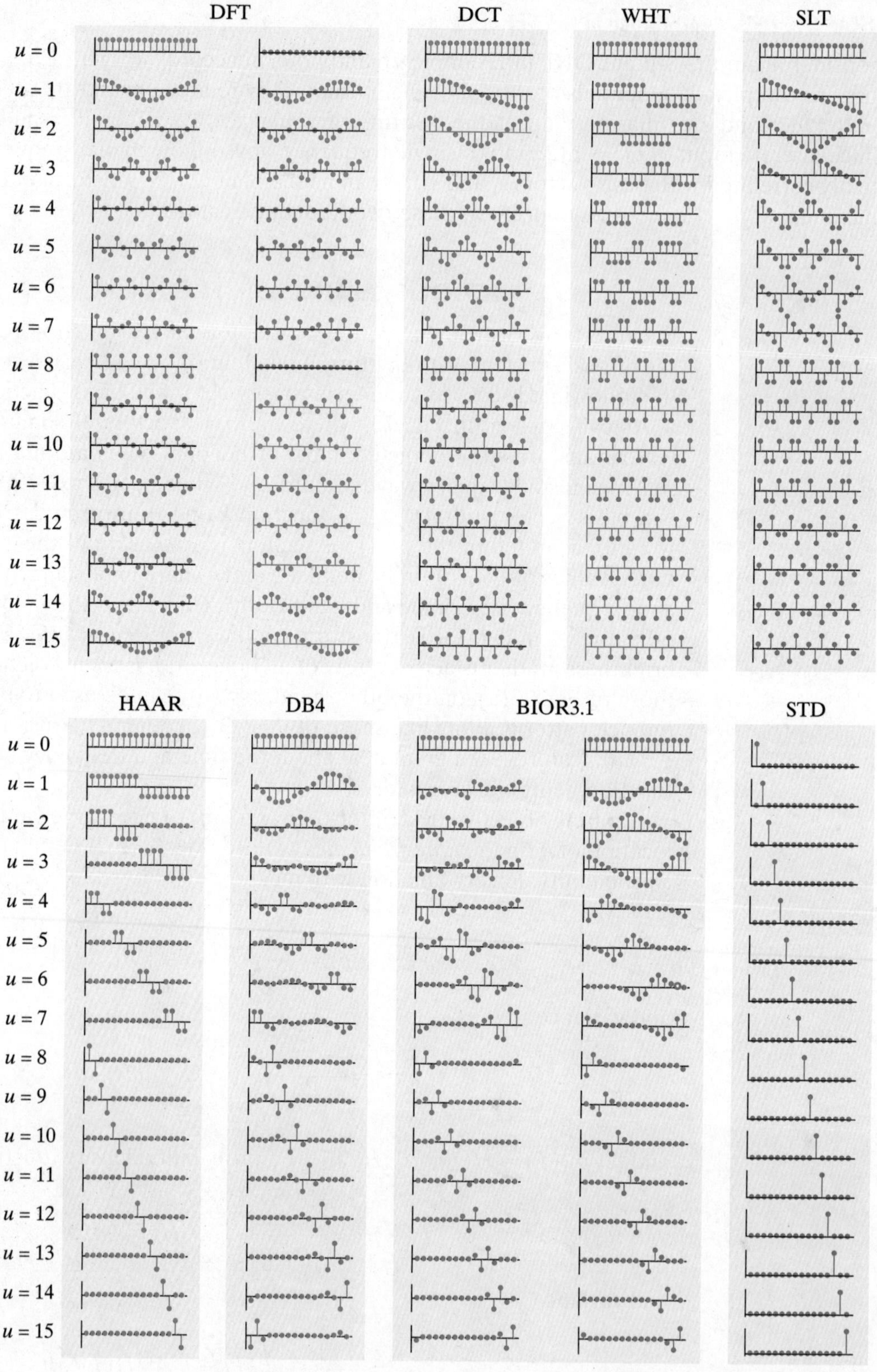

a	b	c	d
e	f	g	h

FIGURE 7.3
Basis vectors
(for $N = 16$) of
some commonly
encountered
transforms:
(a) Fourier basis
(real and imagi-
nary parts),
(b) discrete
Cosine basis,
(c) Walsh-Had-
amard basis,
(d) Slant basis,
(e) Haar basis,
(f) Daubechies
basis,
(g) Biorthogonal
B-spline basis and
its dual, and
(h) the standard
basis, which is
included for refer-
ence only (i.e., not
used as the basis
of a transform).

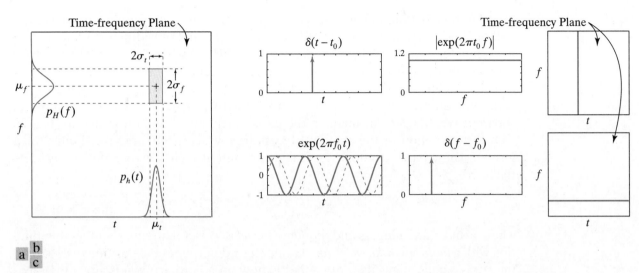

a
b
c

FIGURE 7.4 (a) Basis function localization in the time-frequency plane. (b) A standard basis function, its spectrum, and location in the time-frequency plane. (c) A complex sinusoidal basis function (with its real and imaginary parts shown as solid and dashed lines, respectively), its spectrum, and location in the time-frequency plane.

where f denotes frequency and $H(f)$ is the Fourier transform of $h(t)$. Then the energy[†] of basis function h, as illustrated in Fig. 7.4(a), is concentrated at (μ_t, μ_f) on the time-frequency plane. The majority of the energy falls in a rectangular region, called a *Heisenberg box* or *cell*, of area $4\sigma_t\sigma_f$ such that

The constant on the right side of Eq. (7-71) is ¼ if stated in terms of angular frequency ω. Equality is possible, but only with a Gaussian basis function, whose transform is also a Gaussian function.

$$\sigma_t^2\sigma_f^2 \geq \frac{1}{16\pi^2} \qquad (7\text{-}71)$$

Since the *support* of a function can be defined as the set of points where the function is nonzero, *Heisenberg's uncertainity principle* tells us that it is impossible for a function to have finite support in both time and frequency. Equation (7-71), called the *Heisenberg-Gabor inequaltiy*, places a lower bound on the area of the Heisenberg cell in Fig. 7.4(a), revealing that σ_t and σ_f cannot both be arbitrarily small. Thus, while basis function $\delta(t - t_0)$ in Fig. 7.4(b) is perfectly *localized* in time [that is, $\sigma_t = 0$ since the width of $\delta(t - t_0)$ is zero], its spectrum is nonzero on the entire f-axis. That is, since $\Im\{\delta(t - t_0)\} = \exp(-j2\pi f t_0)$ and $|\exp(-j2\pi f t_0)| = 1$ for all f, $\sigma_f = \infty$. The result is an infinitesimally narrow, infinitely high Heisenberg cell on the time-frequency plane. Basis function $\exp(2\pi f_0 t)$ of Fig. 7.4(c), on the other hand, is essentially nonzero on the entire time axis, but is perfectly localized in frequency. Because $\Im\{\exp(2\pi f_0 t)\} = \delta(f - f_0)$, spectrum $|\delta(f - f_0)|$ is zero at all frequencies other than $f = f_0$. The resulting Heisenberg cell is infinitely wide ($\sigma_t = \infty$) and infinitesimally small in height ($\sigma_f = 0$). As Figs. 7.4(b) and (c) illustrate, perfect localization in time is accompanied by a loss of localization in frequency and vice versa.

Returning again to Fig. 7.3, note the DFT basis in Fig. 7.3(a) and the standard basis in Fig. 7.3(h) are discrete examples (for $N = 16$) of the impulse and complex

[†]The energy of continuous function $h(t)$ is $\displaystyle\int_{-\infty}^{\infty} |h(t)|^2\, dt$.

The DFT basis functions do not appear to be frequency ordered because of aliasing. See Example. 7.6.

exponential functions in Figs. 7.4(c) and (b), respectively. Every other basis in the top half of Fig. 7.3 is both frequency ordered on index u and of width or support 16. For a given u, their locations in the time-frequency plane are similar. This is particularly evident when u is 8 and the basis functions are identical—as are their Heisenberg cells. For all other u, Heisenberg cell parameters μ_t, σ_t, μ_f, and σ_f are close in value, with small differences accounting for the distinctive shapes of the cosine, ramp, and square wave. In a similar manner, the basis functions in the bottom half of Fig. 7.3, with the exception of the standard basis already discussed, are also similar for a given u. These basis functions are scaled and shifted small waves, called *wavelets*, of the form

$$\psi_{s,\tau}(t) = 2^{s/2}\psi(2^s t - \tau) \tag{7-72}$$

where s and τ are integers and *mother wavelet* $\psi(t)$ is a real, square-integrable function with a *bandpass-like spectrum*. Parameter τ determines the position of $\psi_{s,\tau}(t)$ on the t-axis, s determines its width—that is, how broad or narrow it is along the t-axis, and $2^{s/2}$ controls its amplitude.

As will be seen in Section 7.10, the functions corresponding to $u = 0$ in Fig. 7.3 have lowpass spectra and are called *scaling functions*.

In conjunction with a properly designed mother wavelet, Eq. (7-72) generates a basis that is characterized by the Heisenberg cells on the right side of Fig. 7.5. Letting $\Psi(f)$ be the Fourier transform of $\psi(t)$, the transform of time-scaled wavelet $\psi(2^s t)$ is

The proof of Eq. (7-73) is left as an exercise for the reader (see Problem 7.24).

$$\Im\{\psi(2^s t)\} = \frac{1}{|2^s|}\Psi\left(\frac{f}{2^s}\right) \tag{7-73}$$

and for positive values of s, the spectrum is stretched—shifting each frequency component higher by a factor of 2^s. As was the case for the rectangular pulse in Example 4.1, compressing time expands the spectrum. This is illustrated graphically in Figs. 7.5(b)–(d). Note the width of the basis function in Fig. 7.5(c) is half of that in (d), while the width of its spectrum is double that of (d). It is shifted higher in frequency by a factor of two. The same can be said for the basis function and spectrum in Fig. 7.5(b) when compared to (c). This halving of support in time and doubling of support in frequency produces Heisenberg cells of differing widths and heights, but of equal area. Moreover, each row of cells on the right of Fig. 7.5 represents a unique scale s and range of frequencies. The cells within a row are shifted with respect to one another in time. In accordance with Eq. (4-71) and Table 4.4 of Chapter 4, if $\psi(t)$ is shifted in time by τ,

$$\Im\{\psi(t - \tau)\} = e^{-j2\pi\tau f}\Psi(f) \tag{7-74}$$

Thus, $|\Im\{\psi(t - \tau)\}| = |\Psi(f)|$ and the spectra of the time-shifted wavelets are identical. This is demonstrated by the basis functions in Figs. 7.5(a) and (b). Note their Heisenberg cells are identical in size and differ only in position.

A principle consequence of the preceding comments is that each wavelet basis function is characterized by a unique spectrum and location in time. Thus, the

a
b
c
d

FIGURE 7.5
Time and
frequency
localization
of 128-point
Daubechies basis
functions.

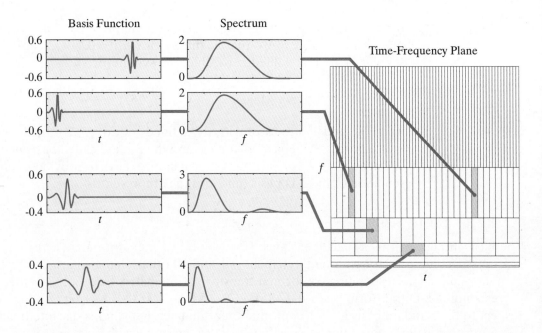

transform coefficients of a wavelet-based transform, as inner products measuring the similarity of the function being transformed and the associated wavelet basis functions, provide both frequency and temporal information. They furnish the equivalent of a musical score for the function being transformed, revealing not only what notes to play but also *when* to play them. This is true for all the wavelet bases depicted in the bottom half of Fig. 7.3. The bases in the top half of the figure provide only the notes; temporal information is lost in the transformation process or is difficult to extract from the transform coefficients (e.g., from the phase component of a Fourier transform).

7.5 BASIS IMAGES

Since inverse transformation kernel $s(x, y, u, v)$ in Eq. (7-32) of Section 7.2 depends only on indices x, y, u, v, and not on the values of $f(x, y)$ or $T(u, v)$, Eq. (7-32) can be alternately written as the matrix sum

$$\mathbf{F} = \sum_{u=0}^{N-1} \sum_{v=0}^{N-1} T(u, v) \mathbf{S}_{u,v} \tag{7-75}$$

where $\mathbf{F}$ is an $N \times N$ matrix containing the elements of $f(x, y)$ and

$$\mathbf{S}_{u,v} = \begin{bmatrix} s(0,0,u,v) & s(0,1,u,v) & \dots & s(0,N-1,u,v) \\ s(1,0,u,v) & \vdots & \dots & \vdots \\ \vdots & \vdots & \dots & \vdots \\ \vdots & \vdots & \dots & \vdots \\ \vdots & & & \\ s(N-1,0,u,v) & s(N-1,1,u,v) & \dots & s(N-1,N-1,u,v) \end{bmatrix} \tag{7-76}$$

for $u,v = 0,1, \ldots, N-1$. $\mathbf{F}$ is then explicitly defined as a linear combination of N^2 matrices of size $N \times N$—that is, the $\mathbf{S}_{u,v}$ for $u,v = 0,1, \ldots, N-1$. If the underlying $s(x,y,u,v)$ are real-valued, separable, and symmetric,

$$\mathbf{S}_{u,v} = \mathbf{s}_u \mathbf{s}_v^T \qquad (7\text{-}77)$$

where $\mathbf{s}_u$ and $\mathbf{s}_v$ are as previously defined by Eq. (7-22). In the context of digital image processing, $\mathbf{F}$ is a 2-D image and the $\mathbf{S}_{u,v}$ are called *basis images*. They can be arranged in an $N \times N$ array, as shown in Fig. 7.6(a), to provide a concise visual representation of the 2-D basis functions they represent.

EXAMPLE 7.8:   The basis images of the standard basis.

The basis in Fig. 7.3(h) is a specific instance (for $N = 16$) of *standard basis* $\{\mathbf{e}_0, \mathbf{e}_1, \ldots, \mathbf{e}_{N-1}\}$, where $\mathbf{e}_n$ is an $N \times 1$ column vector whose nth element is 1 and all other elements are 0. Because it is real and orthonormal, the corresponding orthogonal transformation matrix [see Eq. (7-24)] is $\mathbf{A} = \mathbf{I}$, while the corresponding 2-D transform [see Eq. (7-35)] is $\mathbf{T} = \mathbf{A}\mathbf{F}\mathbf{A}^T = \mathbf{I}\mathbf{F}\mathbf{I}^T = \mathbf{F}$. That is, the transform of $\mathbf{F}$ with respect to the standard basis is $\mathbf{F}$—a confirmation of the fact that when a discrete function is written in vector form, it is represented implicitly with respect to the standard basis.

Figure 7.6(b) shows the basis images of a 2-D standard basis of size 8×8. Like the 1-D basis vectors in Fig. 7.3(h), which are nonzero at only one instant of time (or value of x), the basis images in Fig. 7.6(b) are nonzero at only one point on the xy-plane. This follows from Eq. (7-77), since $\mathbf{S}_{u,v} = \mathbf{e}_u \mathbf{e}_v^T = \mathbf{E}_{u,v}$, where $\mathbf{E}_{u,v}$ is an $N \times N$ matrix of zeros with a 1 in the uth row and vth column. In the same way, the DFT basis images in Fig. 7.7 follow from Eq. (7-77), Eq. (7-22), and the defining equation of the 1-D DFT expansion functions [i.e., Eq. (7-56)]. Note the DFT basis image of maximum frequency occurs when u and v are 4, just as the 1-D DFT basis function of maximum frequency occurred at $u = 4$ in Fig. 7.2.

7.6 FOURIER-RELATED TRANSFORMS

As was noted in Chapter 4, the Fourier transform of a real function is complex-valued. In this section, we examine three Fourier-related transforms that are real rather

---

a b

FIGURE 7.6
(a) Basis image organization and
(b) a standard basis of size 8×8. For clarity, a gray border has been added around each basis image. The origin of each basis image (i.e., $x = y = 0$) is at its top left.

$\mathbf{S}_{0,0}$	$\mathbf{S}_{0,1}$	$\cdots$	$\cdots$	$\mathbf{S}_{0,N-1}$
$\mathbf{S}_{1,0}$	$\ddots$			$\vdots$
$\vdots$				
			$\ddots$	
				$\vdots$
$\mathbf{S}_{N-1,0}$	$\cdots$		$\cdots$	$\mathbf{S}_{N-1,N-1}$

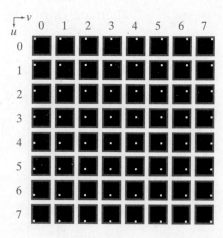

$$\frac{1}{\sqrt{8}}\begin{bmatrix} 1 & 1 & 1 & 1 & 1 & 1 & 1 & 1 \\ 1 & \omega & -j & -j\omega & -1 & -\omega & j & j\omega \\ 1 & -j & -1 & j & 1 & -j & -1 & j \\ 1 & -j\omega & j & \omega & -1 & j\omega & -j & -\omega \\ 1 & -1 & 1 & -1 & 1 & -1 & 1 & -1 \\ 1 & -\omega & -j & j\omega & -1 & \omega & j & -j\omega \\ 1 & j & -1 & -j & 1 & j & -1 & -j \\ 1 & j\omega & j & -\omega & -1 & -j\omega & -j & \omega \end{bmatrix}$$

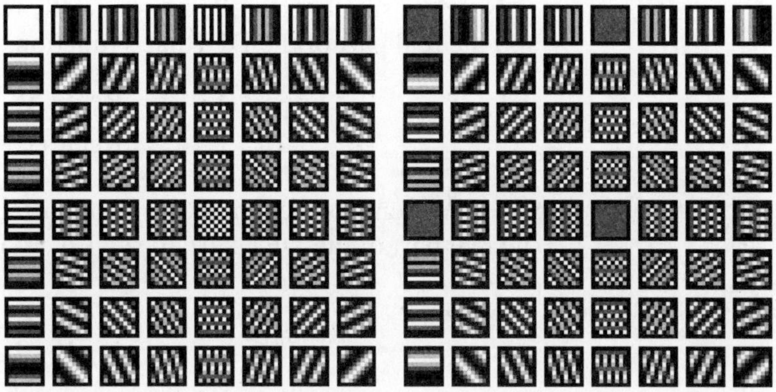

a b c

FIGURE 7.7 (a) Tranformation matrix $\mathbf{A}_F$ of the discrete Fourier transform for $N = 8$, where $\omega = e^{-j2\pi/8}$ or $(1-j)/\sqrt{2}$. (b) and (c) The real and imaginary parts of the DFT basis images of size 8×8. For clarity, a black border has been added around each basis image. For 1-D transforms, matrix $\mathbf{A}_F$ is used in conjunction with Eqs. (7-43) and (7-44); for 2-D transforms, it is used with Eqs. (7-41) and (7-42).

than complex-valued—the *discrete Hartley transform*, *discrete cosine transform*, and *discrete sine transform*. All three transforms avoid the computational complexity of complex numbers and can be implemented via fast FFT-like algorithms.

THE DISCRETE HARTLEY TRANSFORM

The transformation matrix of the *discrete Hartley transform* (DHT) is obtained by substituting the inverse transformation kernel

Function cas, an acronym for the *cosine-and-sin* function, is defined as $\mathrm{cas}(\theta) = \cos(\theta) + \sin(\theta)$.

$$\begin{aligned} s(x,u) &= \frac{1}{\sqrt{N}}\mathrm{cas}\left(\frac{2\pi ux}{N}\right) \\ &= \frac{1}{\sqrt{N}}\left[\cos\left(\frac{2\pi ux}{N}\right) + \sin\left(\frac{2\pi ux}{N}\right)\right] \end{aligned} \tag{7-78}$$

We will not consider the non-separable form

$s(x,y,u,v) =$
$\frac{1}{N}\mathrm{cas}\left(\frac{2\pi(ux+vy)}{N}\right)$.

whose separable 2-D counterpart is

$$s(x,y,u,v) = \left[\frac{1}{\sqrt{N}}\mathrm{cas}\left(\frac{2\pi ux}{N}\right)\right]\left[\frac{1}{\sqrt{N}}\mathrm{cas}\left(\frac{2\pi vy}{N}\right)\right] \tag{7-79}$$

into Eqs. (7-22) and (7-24). Since the resulting DHT transformation matrix—denoted $\mathbf{A}_{\mathrm{HY}}$ in Fig. 7.8—is real, orthogonal, and symmetric, $\mathbf{A}_{\mathrm{HY}} = \mathbf{A}_{\mathrm{HY}}^T = \mathbf{A}_{\mathrm{HY}}^{-1}$ and $\mathbf{A}_{\mathrm{HY}}$ can be used in the computation of both forward and inverse transforms. For 1-D transforms, $\mathbf{A}_{\mathrm{HY}}$ is used in conjunction with Eqs. (7-28) and (7-29) of Section 7.2; for 2-D transforms, Eqs. (7-35) and (7-36) are used. Since $\mathbf{A}_{\mathrm{HY}}$ is symmetric, the forward and inverse transforms are identical.

Note the similarity of the harmonically related DHT basis functions in Fig. 7.8(a) and the real part of the DFT basis functions in Fig. 7.2. It is easy to show that

$$
\begin{aligned}
\mathbf{A}_{HY} &= \mathrm{Real}\{\mathbf{A}_F\} - \mathrm{Imag}\{\mathbf{A}_F\} \\
&= \mathrm{Real}\{(1+j)\mathbf{A}_F\}
\end{aligned}
\tag{7-80}
$$

where $\mathbf{A}_F$ denotes the unitary transformation matrix of the DFT. Furthermore, since the real part of the DFT kernel [see Eq. (7-56)] is

In Eqs. (7-81) and (7-82), subscripts $_{HY}$ and $_F$ are used to denote the Hartley and Fourier kernels, respectively.

$$
\mathrm{Re}\{s_F(x,u)\} = \mathrm{Re}\left\{\frac{1}{\sqrt{N}}e^{j2\pi ux/N}\right\} = \frac{1}{\sqrt{N}}\cos\left(\frac{2\pi ux}{N}\right)
\tag{7-81}
$$

and triginometric identity $\mathrm{cas}(\theta) = \sqrt{2}\cos(\theta - \pi/4)$ can be used to rewrite the discrete Hartley kernel [see Eq. (7-78)] as

$$
s_H(x,u) = \sqrt{\frac{2}{N}}\cos\left(\frac{2\pi ux}{N} - \frac{\pi}{4}\right)
\tag{7-82}
$$

the basis functions of the discrete Fourier and Hartley transforms are scaled and shifted versions of one another—i.e., scaled by the $\sqrt{2}$ and shifted by $\pi/4$. The shift is clearly evident when comparing Figs. 7.2 and 7.8(a). Additionally, for a given value of N and sampling interal ΔT, the Fourier and Hartley transforms have the same frequency resolution $\Delta u = 1/(N\Delta T)$, same range of frequencies

Aliasing reduces the frequency range to $0.5R$, where R is as defined by Eq. (4.51).

$0.5R = 0.5(1/\Delta T) = 1/(2\Delta T)$, and are both undersampled when $u > N/2$. Compare Figs. 7.2 and 7.8(a) for $u = 5, 6, 7$. Finally, we note the 8×8 basis images of the two transforms are also similar. As can be seen in Figs. 7.8(c) and 7.7(b), for example, the basis images of maximum frequency occur when u and v are $N/2$ or 4.

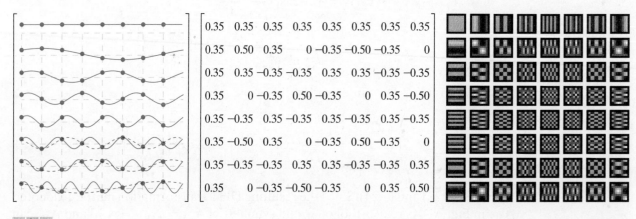

a b c

FIGURE 7.8 The transformation matrix and basis images of the discrete Hartley transform for $N = 8$: (a) Graphical representation of orthogonal transformation matrix $\mathbf{A}_{HY}$, (b) $\mathbf{A}_{HY}$ rounded to two decimal places, and (c) 2-D basis images. For 1-D transforms, matrix $\mathbf{A}_{HY}$ is used in conjunction with Eqs. (7-28) and (7-29); for 2-D transforms, it is used with Eqs. (7-35) and (7-36).

EXAMPLE 7.9:   **DHT and DFT reconstruction.**

Consider discrete function $\mathbf{f} = \begin{bmatrix} 1 & 1 & 0 & 0 & 0 & 0 & 0 & 0 \end{bmatrix}^T$ and its discrete Fourier transform

$$\mathbf{t}_F = \begin{bmatrix} 0.71 & 0.6 - j0.25 & 0.35 - j0.35 & 0.1 - j0.25 & 0 & 0.1 + j0.25 & 0.35 + j0.35 & 0.6 + j0.25 \end{bmatrix}^T$$

where $\mathbf{t}_F = \mathbf{A}_F\mathbf{f}$ and $\mathbf{A}_F = \mathbf{A}_{Fr} + j\mathbf{A}_{Fj}$ is the 8×8 unitary transformation matrix of Fig. 7.7(a). The real and imaginary parts of $\mathbf{t}_F$, denoted $\mathbf{t}_{Fr}$ and $\mathbf{t}_{Fj}$, are

$$\mathbf{t}_{Fr} = \begin{bmatrix} 0.71 & 0.60 & 0.35 & 0.10 & 0 & 0.10 & 0.35 & 0.60 \end{bmatrix}^T$$
$$\mathbf{t}_{Fj} = \begin{bmatrix} 0 & -0.25 & -0.35 & -0.25 & 0 & 0.25 & 0.35 & 0.25 \end{bmatrix}^T$$

and discrete Hartley transform $\mathbf{t}_{HY} = \mathbf{A}_{HY}\mathbf{f} = (\mathbf{A}_{Fr} - \mathbf{A}_{Fj})\mathbf{f} = \mathbf{A}_{Fr}\mathbf{f} - \mathbf{A}_{Fj}\mathbf{f} = \mathbf{t}_{Fr} - \mathbf{t}_{Fj}$ is

$$\mathbf{t}_{HY} = \begin{bmatrix} 0.71 & 0.85 & 0.71 & 0.35 & 0 & -0.15 & 0 & 0.35 \end{bmatrix}^T$$

In accordance with Eq. (7-17), $\mathbf{f}$ can be written as

$$f(x) = \sum_{u=0}^{7} T_{HY}(u)s_{HY}(x,u) \quad \text{for } x = 0,1,\ldots,7$$

where $\mathbf{f} = \begin{bmatrix} f(0) & f(1) & \ldots & f(7) \end{bmatrix}^T$ and $\mathbf{t}_{HY} = \begin{bmatrix} T_{HY}(0) & T_{HY}(1) & \ldots & T_{HY}(7) \end{bmatrix}^T$. Thus, $\mathbf{f}$ can be reconstructed from $\mathbf{t}_{HY}$ as a sum of products involving the computed transform coefficients and corresponding basis functions. In Fig. 6.9(a), such a reconstruction is done progressively, beginning with the average or DC value of $\mathbf{f}$ (for $u = 0$) at the top of the figure and converging to $\mathbf{f}$ (for $u = 0, 1, \ldots, 7$) at the bottom of the figure. As higher frequency basis functions are included in the sum, the reconstructed function becomes a better approximation of $\mathbf{f}$, with perfect reconstruction achieved when all eight weighted basis functions are summed to generate the equivalent of inverse discrete Hartley transform $\mathbf{f} = \mathbf{A}_{HY}^T\mathbf{t}_{HY}$. A similar progression is shown in Fig. 7.9(b) for the DFT.

THE DISCRETE COSINE TRANSFORM

The transformation matrix of the most commonly encountered form of the *discrete cosine transform* (DCT) is obtained by substituting the inverse transformation kernal

There are eight standard DCT variants and they assume different symmetry conditions. For example, the input could be assumed to be even about a sample or about a point halfway between two samples.

$$s(x,u) = \alpha(u)\cos\left(\frac{(2x+1)u\pi}{2N}\right) \tag{7-83}$$

where

$$\alpha(u) = \begin{cases} \sqrt{\dfrac{1}{N}} & \text{for } u = 0 \\ \sqrt{\dfrac{2}{N}} & \text{for } u = 1,2,\ldots,N-1 \end{cases} \tag{7-84}$$

FIGURE 7.9
Reconstructions
of a discrete
function by the
addition of pro-
gressively higher
frequency com-
ponents: (a) DHT
and (b) DFT.

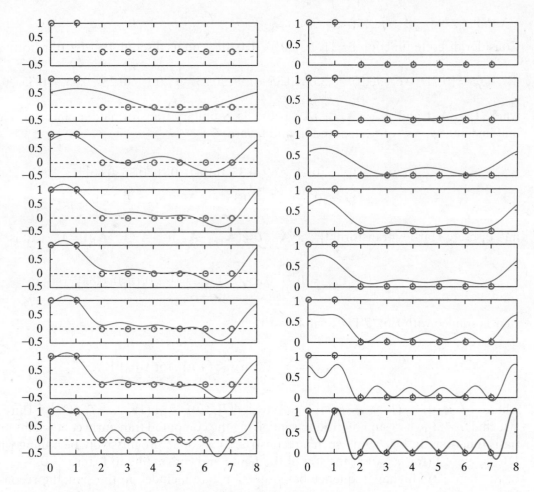

into Eqs. (7-22) and (7-24). The resulting transformation matrix, denoted as $\mathbf{A}_C$ in Fig. 7.10, is real and orthogonal, but not symmetric. The underlying basis functions are harmonically related cosines of frequency 0 to $R = [(N-1)/N][1/(2\Delta T)]$; the spacing between adjacent frequencies (i.e., the frequency resolution) is $\Delta u = 1/(2N\Delta T)$. A comparison of Fig. 7.10(a) to either Figs. 7.8(a) or 7.2 reveals that the spectrum of a discrete cosine transform has roughly the same frequency range as that of the Fourier and Hartley transforms, but twice the frequency resolution. If $N = 4$ and $\Delta T = 1$, for example, the resulting DCT coefficients are at frequencies $\{0, 0.5, 1, 1.5\}$, while the DFT spectral components correspond to frequencies $\{0, 1, 2, 1\}$. Figures 7.10(c) and 7.8(c) further illustrate the point. Note that the DCT basis image of maximum frequency occurs when u and v are 7, as opposed to 4 for the DFT. Since 2-D DCTs are based on the separable inverse transformation kernel

$$s(x, y, u, v) = \alpha(u)\alpha(v)\cos\left(\frac{(2x+1)u\pi}{2N}\right)\cos\left(\frac{(2y+1)v\pi}{2N}\right) \qquad (7\text{-}85)$$

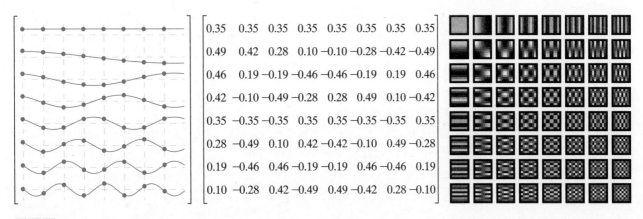

a b c

FIGURE 7.10 The transformation matrix and basis images of the discrete cosine transform for $N = 8$. (a) Graphical representation of orthogonal transformation matrix $\mathbf{A}_C$, (b) $\mathbf{A}_C$ rounded to two decimal places, and (c) basis images. For 1-D transforms, matrix $\mathbf{A}_C$ is used in conjunction with Eqs. (7-28) and (7-29); for 2-D transforms, it is used with Eqs. (7-35) and (7-36).

where $\alpha(u)$ and $\alpha(v)$ are defined in accordance with Eq. (7-84), transformation matrix $\mathbf{A}_C$ can be used in the computation of both 1- and 2-D transforms (see the caption of Fig. 7.10 for the appropriate transform equations).

While sharing several attributes of the discrete Fourier transform, the discrete cosine transform imposes a entirely different set of assumptions on the functions being processed. Rather than N-point periodicity, the underlying assumption of the DFT, the discrete cosine transform assumes $2N$-point periodicity *and* even symmetry. As can be seen in Fig. 7.11, while N-point periodicity can cause boundary discontinuities that introduce "artificial" high-frequency components into a transform, $2N$-point periodicity and even symmetry minimize discontinuity, as well as the accompanying high-frequency artifact. As will be seen in Chapter 8, this is an important advantage of the DCT in image compression. In light of the above comments, it should come as no surprise that the DCT of N-point function $f(x)$ can be obtained from the DFT of a $2N$-point symmetrically extended version of $f(x)$:

1. Symmetrically extend N-point discrete function $f(x)$ to obtain

$$g(x) = \begin{cases} f(x) & \text{for } 0 \le x < N \\ f(2N - x - 1) & \text{for } N \le x < 2N \end{cases} \tag{7-86}$$

where $\mathbf{f} = \begin{bmatrix} f(0) & f(1) & \dots & f(N-1) \end{bmatrix}^T$ and $\mathbf{g} = \begin{bmatrix} g(0) & g(1) & \dots & g(2N-1) \end{bmatrix}^T$.

2. Compute the $2N$-point discrete Fourier transform of $\mathbf{g}$:

$$\mathbf{t}_F = \mathbf{A}_F \mathbf{g} = \begin{bmatrix} \mathbf{t}_1 \\ \mathbf{t}_2 \end{bmatrix} \tag{7-87}$$

where $\mathbf{A}_F$ is the transformation matrix of the DFT and $2N$-element transform $\mathbf{t}_F$ is partitioned into two equal-length N-element column vectors, $\mathbf{t}_1$ and $\mathbf{t}_2$.

3. Let N-element column vector $\mathbf{h} = \begin{bmatrix} h(0) & h(1) & \dots & h(N-1) \end{bmatrix}^T$ where

$$h(u) = e^{-j\pi u/2N} \quad \text{for } u = 0, 1, \dots, N-1 \tag{7-88}$$

and let $\mathbf{s} = \begin{bmatrix} 1/\sqrt{2} & 1 & 1 & \dots & 1 \end{bmatrix}^T$.

4. The discrete cosine transform of $\mathbf{f}$ is then

$$\mathbf{t}_C = \text{Re}\{\mathbf{s} \circ \mathbf{h} \circ \mathbf{t}_1\} \tag{7-89}$$

where $\circ$ denotes the *Hadamard product*, a matrix multiplication in which the corresponding elements of two vectors or matrices are multiplied together—for example, $\begin{bmatrix} 3 & -0.5 \end{bmatrix} \circ \begin{bmatrix} 2 & 6 \end{bmatrix} = \begin{bmatrix} 6 & -3 \end{bmatrix}$.

EXAMPLE 7.10:　Computing a 4-point DCT from a 8-point DFT.

In this example, we use Eqs. (7-86) through (7-89) to compute the discrete cosine transform of 1-D function $f(x) = x^2$ for $x = 0, 1, 2, 3$.

1. Let $\mathbf{f} = \begin{bmatrix} 0 & 1 & 4 & 9 \end{bmatrix}^T$ and use Eq. (7-86) to create an 8-point extension of $\mathbf{f}$ with even symmetry. Extended function $\mathbf{g} = \begin{bmatrix} 0 & 1 & 4 & 9 & 9 & 4 & 1 & 0 \end{bmatrix}^T$ is one period of an even symmetric function like the one in Fig. 7.11(b).

2. Substituting the 8×8 unitary transformation matrix from Fig. 7.7(a) into Eq. (7-87), the discrete Fourier transform of $\mathbf{g}$ is

$$\mathbf{t}_F = \mathbf{A}_F\mathbf{g} = \begin{bmatrix} -9.9 \\ -6.18 - j2.56 \\ 1.41 + j1.41 \\ -0.18 - j0.44 \\ 0 \\ -0.18 + j0.44 \\ 1.41 - j1.41 \\ -6.18 + j2.56 \end{bmatrix} \text{ so } \mathbf{t}_1 = \begin{bmatrix} -9.9 \\ -6.18 - j2.56 \\ 1.41 + j1.41 \\ -0.18 - j0.44 \end{bmatrix} \text{ and } \mathbf{t}_2 = \begin{bmatrix} 0 \\ -0.18 + j0.44 \\ 1.41 - j1.41 \\ -6.18 + j2.56 \end{bmatrix}$$

3. In accordance with Eq. (7-88),

$$\mathbf{h} = \begin{bmatrix} 1 \\ e^{-j\pi/4} \\ e^{-j\pi/2} \\ e^{-j3\pi/4} \end{bmatrix} = \begin{bmatrix} 1 \\ 0.92 - j0.38 \\ 0.71 - j0.71 \\ 0.38 - j0.92 \end{bmatrix}$$

and $\mathbf{s} = \begin{bmatrix} 1/\sqrt{2} & 1 & 1 & 1 \end{bmatrix}^T = \begin{bmatrix} 0.71 & 1 & 1 & 1 \end{bmatrix}^T$.

4. The discrete cosine transform of $\mathbf{f}$ is then

$$\mathbf{t}_C = \text{Re}\{\mathbf{s} \circ \mathbf{h} \circ \mathbf{t}_1\} = \text{Re}\left\{ \begin{bmatrix} 0.71 \\ 1 \\ 1 \\ 1 \end{bmatrix} \circ \begin{bmatrix} 1 \\ 0.92 - j0.38 \\ 0.71 - j0.71 \\ 0.38 - j0.92 \end{bmatrix} \circ \begin{bmatrix} -9.9 \\ -6.18 - j2.56 \\ 1.41 + j1.41 \\ -0.18 - j0.44 \end{bmatrix} \right\} = \begin{bmatrix} 7 \\ -6.69 \\ 2 \\ -0.48 \end{bmatrix}$$

To validate the result, we substitute Eq. (7-83) into Eqs. (7-22) and (7-24) with $N = 4$ and use the resulting 4×4 DCT transformation matrix in Eq. (7-28) to obtain

$$\mathbf{t}_C = \mathbf{A}_C \mathbf{f} = \begin{bmatrix} 0.5 & 0.5 & 0.5 & 0.5 \\ 0.65 & 0.27 & -0.27 & -0.65 \\ 0.5 & -0.5 & -0.5 & 0.5 \\ 0.27 & -0.65 & 0.65 & -0.27 \end{bmatrix} \begin{bmatrix} 0 \\ 1 \\ 4 \\ 9 \end{bmatrix} = \begin{bmatrix} 7 \\ -6.69 \\ 2 \\ -0.48 \end{bmatrix}$$

Figure 7.12 illustrates the reconstruction of $\mathbf{f}$ by the inverse discrete cosine transform. Like the reconstructions in Fig. 7.9, the DC component at the top of the figure [i.e., Fig. 7.12(a)] is the average value of the discrete function—in this case, $(0 + 1 + 4 + 9)/4 = 3.5$. It is an initial but crude approximation of $\mathbf{f}$. As three additional cosines of increasing frequency are added in the (b), (c), and (d) parts of the figure, the accuracy of the approximation increases until a perfect reconstruction is achieved in (d). Note the x-axis has been extended to show that the resulting DCT expansion is indeed periodic with period $2N$ (in this case 8) and exhibits the even symmetry that is required of all discrete cosine transforms.

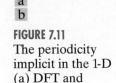

a
b

FIGURE 7.11
The periodicity
implicit in the 1-D
(a) DFT and
(b) DCT.

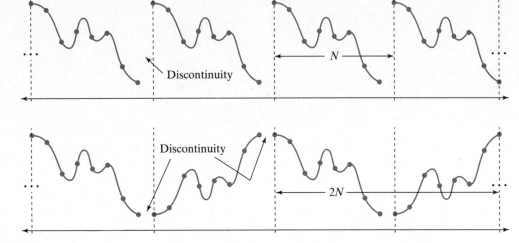

FIGURE 7.12
DCT recon-
struction of a
discrete function
by the addition
of progressively
higher frequency
components. Note
the 2N-point
periodicity and
even symmetry
imposed by the
DCT.

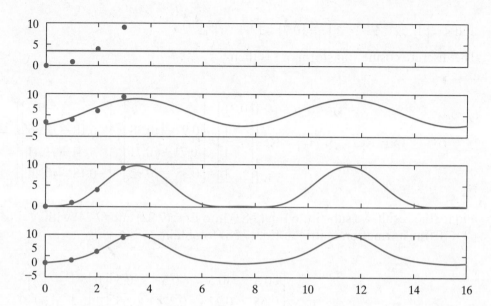

Like the DCT, there are
eight variants and they
assume different sym-
metry conditions—for
instance, is the input odd
about a sample or about
a point halfway between
two samples?

THE DISCRETE SINE TRANSFORM

The transformation matrix of the *discrete sine transform* (DST) is obtained by substituting the inverse transformation kernal

$$s(x,u) = \sqrt{\frac{2}{N+1}} \sin\left(\frac{(x+1)(u+1)\pi}{N+1}\right) \tag{7-90}$$

whose separable 2-D counterpart is

$$s(x,y,u,v) = \frac{2}{N+1} \sin\left(\frac{(x+1)(u+1)\pi}{N+1}\right)\sin\left(\frac{(y+1)(v+1)\pi}{N+1}\right) \tag{7-91}$$

into Eqs. (7-22) and (7-24). The resulting transformation matrix, denoted as $\mathbf{A}_S$ in
Fig. 7.13, is real, orthogonal, and symmetric. As can be seen in the (a) part of the
figure, the underlying basis functions are harmonically related sines of frequency
$1/[2(N+2)\Delta T]$ to $N/[2(N+2)\Delta T]$; the frequency resolution or the spacing
between adjacent frequencies is $\Delta u = 1/[2(N+2)\Delta T]$. Like the DCT, the DST has
roughly the same frequency range as the DFT, but twice the frequency resolution.
If $N = 4$ and $\Delta T = 1$, for example, the resulting DST coefficients are at frequencies
$\{0.4,\ 0.8,\ 1.2,\ 1.6\}$. Note unlike both the DCT and DFT, the DST has no DC (at
$u = 0$) component. This results from an underlying assumption that the function
being transformed is $2(N+1)$-point periodic and odd symmetric, making its average
value zero. In contrast to the DCT, where the function is assumed to be even, the
odd symmetry that is imposed by the DST does not reduce boundary discontinuity.
This is clear in Fig. 6.14, where the result of computing the forward and inverse
DCT of $f(x) = x^2$ for $x = 0, 1, 2, 3$ is shown. Note that the underlying continuous

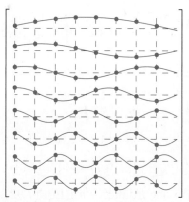
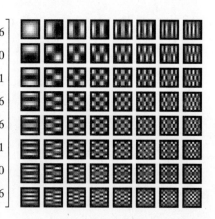

$$\begin{bmatrix} 0.16 & 0.30 & 0.41 & 0.46 & 0.46 & 0.41 & 0.30 & 0.16 \\ 0.30 & 0.46 & 0.41 & 0.16 & -0.16 & -0.41 & -0.46 & -0.30 \\ 0.41 & 0.41 & 0.00 & -0.41 & -0.41 & 0.00 & 0.41 & 0.41 \\ 0.46 & 0.16 & -0.41 & -0.30 & 0.30 & 0.41 & -0.16 & -0.46 \\ 0.46 & -0.16 & -0.41 & 0.30 & 0.30 & -0.41 & -0.16 & 0.46 \\ 0.41 & -0.41 & 0.00 & 0.41 & -0.41 & -0.00 & 0.41 & -0.41 \\ 0.30 & -0.46 & 0.41 & -0.16 & -0.16 & 0.41 & -0.46 & 0.30 \\ 0.16 & -0.30 & 0.41 & -0.46 & 0.46 & -0.41 & 0.30 & -0.16 \end{bmatrix}$$

a b c

FIGURE 7.13 The transformation matrix and basis images of the discrete sine transform for $N = 8$. (a) Graphical representation of orthogonal transformation matrix $\mathbf{A}_S$, (b) $\mathbf{A}_S$ rounded to two decimal places, and (c) basis images. For 1-D transforms, matrix $\mathbf{A}_S$ is used in conjunction with Eqs. (7-28) and (7-29); for 2-D transforms, it is used with Eqs. (7-35) and (7-36).

reconstruction, which was obtained by the same process that led to Fig. 6.12(d), exhibits the aforementioned periodicity, odd symmetry, and boundary discontinuity.

The discrete sine transform of an N-point function $f(x)$ can be obtained from the DFT of a $2(N + 1)$-point symmetrically extended version of $f(x)$ with odd symmetry:

1. Symmetrically extend N-point function f(x) to obtain

$$g(x) = \begin{cases} 0 & \text{for } x = 0 \\ f(x-1) & \text{for } 1 \le x \le N \\ 0 & \text{for } x = N + 1 \\ -f(2N - x + 1) & \text{for } N + 2 \le x \le 2N + 2 \end{cases} \tag{7-92}$$

where $\mathbf{f} = \begin{bmatrix} f(0) & f(1) & \dots & f(N-1) \end{bmatrix}^T$ and $\mathbf{g} = \begin{bmatrix} g(0) & g(1) & \dots & g(2N+2) \end{bmatrix}^T$.

2. Compute the $2(N + 1)$-point discrete Fourier transform of $\mathbf{g}$:

$$\mathbf{t}_F = \mathbf{A}_F \mathbf{g} = \begin{bmatrix} 0 \\ \mathbf{t}_1 \\ 0 \\ \mathbf{t}_2 \end{bmatrix} \tag{7-93}$$

FIGURE 7.14
A reconstruction of the DST of the function defined in Example 6.10.

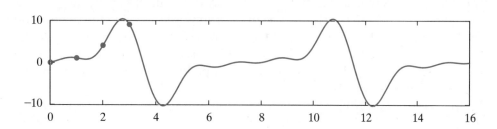

where $\mathbf{A_F}$ is the transformation matrix of the DFT and $2(N+1)$-element transform $\mathbf{t_F}$ is partitioned into two single-element zero vectors, $\mathbf{0} = [0]$, and two N-element column vectors $\mathbf{t}_1$ and $\mathbf{t}_2$.

3. The discrete sine transform of $\mathbf{f}$, denoted $\mathbf{t_S}$, is then

$$\mathbf{t_S} = -\text{Imag}\{\mathbf{t}_1\} \qquad (7\text{-}94)$$

EXAMPLE 7.11: Computing a 4-point DST from a 10-point DFT.

In this example, we use Eqs. (7-92) through (7-94) to find the DST of $\mathbf{f} = \begin{bmatrix} 0 & 1 & 4 & 9 \end{bmatrix}^T$ from Example 7.10:

1. Create a $2(N+1)$-point extended version of $\mathbf{f}$ with odd symmetry. In accordance with Eq. (7-92), $\mathbf{g} = \begin{bmatrix} 0 & 0 & 1 & 4 & 9 & 0 & -9 & -4 & -1 & 0 \end{bmatrix}^T$.

2. Compute the discrete Fourier transform of $\mathbf{g}$ using Eq. (7-93). Matrix $\mathbf{A_F}$ is a unitary DFT transformation matrix of size 10×10 and the resulting transform is

$$\mathbf{t_F} = \mathbf{A_F}\mathbf{g} = \begin{bmatrix} 0 & -j6.35 & j6.53 & -j3.56 & j1.54 & 0 & j6.35 & -j6.53 & j3.56 & -j1.54 \end{bmatrix}^T$$

Note the real part of $\mathbf{t_F}$ is zero and block $\mathbf{t}_1$ of $\mathbf{t_F}$ is $\begin{bmatrix} -j6.35 & j6.53 & -j3.56 & j1.54 \end{bmatrix}^T$.

3. In accordance with Eq. (7-94), the DST of $\mathbf{f}$ is then

$$\mathbf{t_S} = -\text{Imag}\{\mathbf{t}_1\} = \begin{bmatrix} 6.35 & -6.53 & 3.56 & -1.54 \end{bmatrix}^T$$

Alternately, the DST can be computed directly as

$$\mathbf{t_S} = \mathbf{A_S}\mathbf{f} = \begin{bmatrix} 0.37 & 0.60 & 0.60 & 0.37 \\ 0.60 & 0.37 & -0.37 & -0.60 \\ 0.60 & -0.37 & -0.37 & 0.60 \\ 0.37 & -0.60 & 0.60 & -0.37 \end{bmatrix} \begin{bmatrix} 0 \\ 1 \\ 4 \\ 9 \end{bmatrix} = \begin{bmatrix} 6.35 \\ -6.53 \\ 3.56 \\ -1.54 \end{bmatrix}$$

where $\mathbf{A_S}$ is obtained by substituting Eq. (7-90) into Eqs. (7-22) and (7-24) with $N = 4$.

EXAMPLE 7.12: Ideal lowpass filtering with Fourier-related transforms.

Figure 7.15 shows the results of applying an ideal lowpass filter to the test image that was used in Example 4.16 with all of the Fourier-related transforms that have been covered in this chapter. As in the Chapter 4 example, the test image shown in Fig. 7.15(a) is of size 688×688 and is padded to 1376×1376 before computing any transforms. For reference, the Fourier transform of the test image is shown in Fig. 7.15(b), where a blue overlay has been superimposed to show the lowpass filter function. Only the frequencies that are not shaded blue are passed by the filter. Since we are again using a cutoff frequency with a radius of 60, the filtered result in Fig. 7.15(c) is similar to that of Fig. 4.41(d), with any differences due to the use of zero padding rather than mirror padding. Note once more the blurring and ringing that was discussed in Example 4.16.

Figures 7.15(d)–(i) provide comparable results using the three Fourier-related transforms covered in this chapter. As was done for the Fourier transform in Fig. 6.15(b), Figs. 6.15(d)–(f) show the

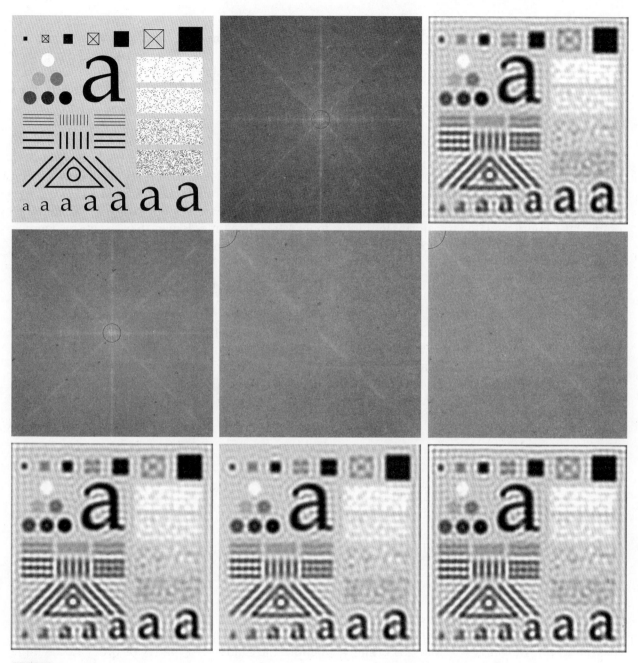

a b c
d e f
g h i

FIGURE 7.15 (a) Original image of the 688×688 test pattern from Fig. 4.41(a). (b) Discrete Fourier transform (DFT) of the test pattern in (a) after padding to size 1376×1376. The blue overlay is an ideal lowpass filter (ILPF) with a radius of 60. (c) Result of Fourier filtering. (d)–(f) Discrete Hartley transform, discrete cosine transform (DCT), and discrete sine transform (DST) of the test pattern in (a) after padding. The blue overlay is the same ILPF in (b), but appears bigger in (e) and (f) because of the higher frequency resolution of the DCT and DST. (g)–(i) Results of filtering for the Hartley, cosine, and sine transforms, respectively.

discrete Hartley, cosine, and sine transforms of the test image in Fig. 7.15(a) after zero-padding to size 1376×1376, respectively. Although the filter functions for the cosine and sine transforms, which are again superimposed in blue, appear to have twice the radii of the filters used with the Fourier and Hartley transforms, the same range of frequencies are passed by all filters. The apparent increase in size is due to the greater frequency resolution of the sine and cosine transforms, which has already been discussed. Note the spectra of these transforms do not need to be centered for easy interpretation, as is the case for the Fourier and Hartley spectra. Finally, we note for all practical purposes the filtered images in Figs. 7.15(g)–(i) are equivalent to the Fourier filtered result in Fig. 7.15(c).

To conclude the example, we note while Fourier-related transforms can be implemented in FFT-like algorithms or computed from the FFT itself, we used the matrix implementations that have been presented in this section to compute both the forward and inverse transforms. Using MATLAB®, Windows® 10, and a notebook PC with an Intel® i7-4600U processor at 2.1 GHz, the total times required to compute the Fourier-related transforms in this example were 2 to 5 times longer than the corresponding FFT computations. All computations, however, took less than a second.

7.7 WALSH-HADAMARD TRANSFORMS

Walsh-Hadamard transforms (WHTs) are non-sinusoidal transformations that decompose a function into a linear combination of rectangular basis functions, called *Walsh functions*, of value +1 and −1. The ordering of the basis functions within a Walsh-Hadamard transformation matrix determines the variant of the transform that is being computed. For *Hadamard ordering* (also called *natural ordering*), the transformation matrix is obtained by substituting the inverse transformation kernal

$$s(x,u) = \frac{1}{\sqrt{N}}(-1)^{\sum_{i=0}^{n-1} b_i(x)b_i(u)} \qquad (7\text{-}95)$$

into Eqs. (7-22) and (7-24), where the summation in the exponent of Eq. (7-95) is performed in modulo 2 arithmetic, $N = 2^n$, and $b_k(z)$ is the kth bit in the binary representation of z. For example, if $n = 3$ and $z = 6$ (110 in binary), $b_0(z) = 0$, $b_1(z) = 1$, and $b_2(z) = 1$. If $N = 2$, the resulting Hadamard-ordered transformation matrix is

A$_W$ is used to denote the transformation matrix of the Hadamard- or natural-ordered WHT. Although of size 2×2 here, it is more generally of size $N \times N$, where N is the dimension of the discrete function being transformed.

$$\mathbf{A}_W = \frac{1}{\sqrt{2}}\begin{bmatrix} 1 & 1 \\ 1 & -1 \end{bmatrix} \qquad (7\text{-}96)$$

where the matrix on the right (without the scalar multiplier) is called a *Hadamard matrix* of order 2. Letting $\mathbf{H}_N$ denote the Hadamard matrix of order N, a simple recursive relationship for generating Hadamard-ordered transfomation matrices is

$$\mathbf{A}_W = \frac{1}{\sqrt{N}}\mathbf{H}_N \qquad (7\text{-}97)$$

where

$$\mathbf{H}_{2N} = \begin{bmatrix} \mathbf{H}_N & \mathbf{H}_N \\ \mathbf{H}_N & -\mathbf{H}_N \end{bmatrix} \qquad (7\text{-}98)$$

and

$$\mathbf{H}_2 = \begin{bmatrix} 1 & 1 \\ 1 & -1 \end{bmatrix} \tag{7-99}$$

Thus, Eq. (7-96) follows from Eqs. (7-97) and (7-99). In the same way,

$$\mathbf{H}_4 = \begin{bmatrix} \mathbf{H}_2 & \mathbf{H}_2 \\ \mathbf{H}_2 & -\mathbf{H}_2 \end{bmatrix}$$

$$= \begin{bmatrix} 1 & 1 & 1 & 1 \\ 1 & -1 & 1 & -1 \\ 1 & 1 & -1 & -1 \\ 1 & -1 & -1 & 1 \end{bmatrix} \tag{7-100}$$

and

$$\mathbf{H}_8 = \begin{bmatrix} \mathbf{H}_4 & \mathbf{H}_4 \\ \mathbf{H}_4 & -\mathbf{H}_4 \end{bmatrix}$$

$$= \begin{bmatrix} 1 & 1 & 1 & 1 & 1 & 1 & 1 & 1 \\ 1 & -1 & 1 & -1 & 1 & -1 & 1 & -1 \\ 1 & 1 & -1 & -1 & 1 & 1 & -1 & -1 \\ 1 & -1 & -1 & 1 & 1 & -1 & -1 & 1 \\ 1 & 1 & 1 & 1 & -1 & -1 & -1 & -1 \\ 1 & -1 & 1 & -1 & -1 & 1 & -1 & 1 \\ 1 & 1 & -1 & -1 & -1 & -1 & 1 & 1 \\ 1 & -1 & -1 & 1 & -1 & 1 & 1 & -1 \end{bmatrix} \tag{7-101}$$

The corresponding Hadamard-ordered transformation matrices are obtained by substituting $\mathbf{H}_4$ and $\mathbf{H}_8$ into Eq. (7-97).

The number of sign changes along a row of a Hadamard matrix is known as the *sequency* of the row. Like frequency, sequency measures the rate of change of a function, and like the sinusoidal basis functions of the Fourier transform, every Walsh function has a unique sequency. Since the elements of a Hadamard matrix are derived from inverse kernal values, the sequency concept applies to basis functions $s(x,u)$ for $u = 0, 1, \ldots, N-1$ as well. For instance, the sequencies of the $\mathbf{H}_4$ basis vectors in Eq. (7-100) are 0, 3, 1, 2; the sequencies of the $\mathbf{H}_8$ basis vectors in Eq. (7-101) are 0, 7, 3, 4, 1, 6, 2, and 5. This arrangement of sequencies is the defining characteristic of a Hadamard-ordered Walsh-Hadamard transform.

Arranging the basis vectors of a Hadamard matrix so the sequency increases as a function of u is both desirable and common in signal and image processing applications. The transformation matrix of the resulting sequency-ordered Walsh-Hadamard transform is obtained by substituting the inverse transformation kernal

Recall that $N = 2^n$, so $n = \log_2 N$.

$$s(x,u) = \frac{1}{\sqrt{N}} (-1)^{\sum_{i=0}^{n-1} b_i(x)p_i(u)} \tag{7-102}$$

where

$$\begin{aligned}
p_0(u) &= b_{n-1}(u) \\
p_1(u) &= b_{n-1}(u) + b_{n-2}(u) \\
p_2(u) &= b_{n-2}(u) + b_{n-3}(u) \\
&\vdots \\
p_{n-1}(u) &= b_1(u) + b_0(u)
\end{aligned} \tag{7-103}$$

into Eqs. (7-22) and (7-24). As before, the summations in Eqs. (7-102) and (7-103) are performed in modulo 2 arithmetic. Thus, for example,

$$\mathbf{H}'_8 = \begin{bmatrix}
1 & 1 & 1 & 1 & 1 & 1 & 1 & 1 \\
1 & 1 & 1 & 1 & -1 & -1 & -1 & -1 \\
1 & 1 & -1 & -1 & -1 & -1 & 1 & 1 \\
1 & 1 & -1 & -1 & 1 & 1 & -1 & -1 \\
1 & -1 & -1 & 1 & 1 & -1 & -1 & 1 \\
1 & -1 & -1 & 1 & -1 & 1 & 1 & -1 \\
1 & -1 & 1 & -1 & -1 & 1 & -1 & 1 \\
1 & -1 & 1 & -1 & 1 & -1 & 1 & -1
\end{bmatrix} \tag{7-104}$$

where the apostrophe ($'$) has been added to indicate sequency ordering as opposed to Hadamard ordering. Note the sequencies of the rows of $\mathbf{H}'_8$ match their row numbers—i.e., 0, 1, 2, 3, 4, 5, 6, and 7. An alternate way to generate $\mathbf{H}'_8$ is to rearrange the rows of Hadamard-ordered $\mathbf{H}_8$, noting that row s of $\mathbf{H}'_8$ corresponds to the row of $\mathbf{H}_8$ that is the bit-reversed *gray code* of s. Since the n-bit gray code corresponding to $(s_{n-1} \ldots s_2 s_1 s_0)_2$ can be computed as

$$\begin{aligned}
g_i &= s_i \oplus s_{i+1} \quad \text{for } 0 \le i \le n-2 \\
g_{n-1} &= s_{n-1} \quad \text{for } i = n-1
\end{aligned} \tag{7-105}$$

where $\oplus$ denotes the exclusive OR operation, row s of $\mathbf{H}'_8$ is the same as row $(g_0 g_1 g_2 \ldots g_{n-1})_2$ of $\mathbf{H}_8$. For example, row 4 or $(100)_2$ of $\mathbf{H}'_8$, whose gray code is $(110)_2$, comes from row $(011)_2$ or 3 of $\mathbf{H}_8$. Note row 4 of $\mathbf{H}'_8$ in Eq. (7-104) is indeed identical to row 3 of $\mathbf{H}_8$ in Eq. (7-101).

Figures 7.16(a) and (b) depict graphically and numerically the sequency-ordered WHT transformation matrix for the case of $N = 8$. Note the sequency of the discrete

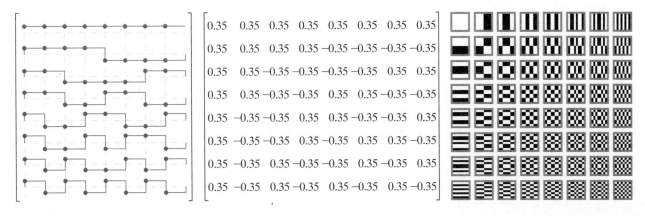

a b c

FIGURE 7.16 The transformation matrix and basis images of the sequency-ordered Walsh-Hadamard transform for $N = 8$. (a) Graphical representation of orthogonal transformation matrix $\mathbf{A}_{W'}$, (b) $\mathbf{A}_{W'}$ rounded to two decimal places, and (c) basis images. For 1-D transforms, matrix $\mathbf{A}_{W'}$ is used in conjunction with Eqs. (7-28) and (7-29); for 2-D transforms, it is used with Eqs. (7-35) and (7-36).

basis functions in Fig. 7.16(a) increase as u goes from 0 to 7, as does the sequency of the underlying square wave functions. Note also the transformation matrix in Fig. 7.16(b) is real, symmetric, and follows from Eqs. (7-105) and (7-97) as

$$\mathbf{A}_{W'} = \frac{1}{\sqrt{N}}\mathbf{H}'_8 \qquad (7\text{-}106)$$

It is left as an exercise for the reader to show that it is orthogonal and that $\mathbf{A}_{W'} = \mathbf{A}^T_{W'} = \mathbf{A}^{-1}_{W'}$. Finally, note the similarity of the sequency-ordered basis images in Fig. 7.16(c), which are based on the separable 2-D inverse transformation kernal

$$s(x, y, u, v) = \frac{1}{N}(-1)^{\sum_{i=0}^{n-1}[b_i(x)p_i(u)+b_i(y)p_i(v)]} \qquad (7\text{-}107)$$

to the basis images of the 2-D DCT in Fig. 7.10(c). Sequency increases as a function of both u and v, like frequency in the DCT basis images, but does not have as useful a physical interpretation.

EXAMPLE 7.13: A simple sequency-ordered Walsh-Hadamard transform.

To compute the sequency-ordered Walsh-Hadamard transform of the 1-D function $\mathbf{f} = [2 \quad 3 \quad 4 \quad 5]^T$, we begin with the Hadamard-ordered Hadamard matrix $\mathbf{H}_4$ of Eq. (7-100) and use the procedure described in conjunction with Eq. (7-105) to reorder the basis vectors. The mapping of the Hadamard-ordered basis vectors of $\mathbf{H}_4$ to the sequency-ordered basis vectors of $\mathbf{H}'_4$ is computed as follows:

Row of H_4'	Binary Code	Gray Code	Bit-Reversed Gray Code	Row of H_4
0	00	00	00	0
1	01	01	10	2
2	10	11	11	3
3	11	10	01	1

Thus, in accordance with Eqs. (7-106), the sequency-ordered Walsh-Hadamard transformation matrix of size 4×4 is

$$\mathbf{A}_{W'} = \frac{1}{\sqrt{4}}\mathbf{H}_{W'} = \frac{1}{2}\begin{bmatrix} 1 & 1 & 1 & 1 \\ 1 & 1 & -1 & -1 \\ 1 & -1 & -1 & 1 \\ 1 & -1 & 1 & -1 \end{bmatrix}$$

and the sequency-ordered transform is $\mathbf{t}_{W'} = \mathbf{A}_{W'}\mathbf{f} = [7 \;\; -2 \;\; 0 \;\; -1]^{T}$.

7.8 SLANT TRANSFORM

Many monochrome images have large areas of uniform intensity and areas of linearly increasing or decreasing brightness. With the exception of the discrete sine transform, all of the transforms that we have presented to this point include a basis vector (at frequency or sequency $u = 0$) for representing efficiently constant gray level areas, but none has a basis function that is targeted specifically at the representation of linearly increasing or decreasing intensity values. The transform considered in this section, called the *slant transform*, includes such a basis function. The transformation matrix of the slant transform of order $N \times N$ where $N = 2^n$ is generated recursively using

$$\mathbf{A}_{Sl} = \frac{1}{\sqrt{N}}\mathbf{S}_N \tag{7-108}$$

where *slant matrix*

$$\mathbf{S}_N = \begin{bmatrix} 1 & 0 & & 1 & 0 & \\ & & \mathbf{0} & & & \mathbf{0} \\ a_N & b_N & & -a_N & b_N & \\ \mathbf{0} & & \mathbf{I}_{(N/2)-2} & \mathbf{0} & & \mathbf{I}_{(N/2)-2} \\ 0 & 1 & & 0 & -1 & \\ & & \mathbf{0} & & & \mathbf{0} \\ -b_N & a_N & & b_N & a_N & \\ \mathbf{0} & & \mathbf{I}_{(N/2)-2} & \mathbf{0} & & -\mathbf{I}_{(N/2)-2} \end{bmatrix}\begin{bmatrix} \mathbf{S}_{N/2} & \mathbf{0} \\ \mathbf{0} & \mathbf{S}_{N/2} \end{bmatrix} \tag{7-109}$$

Note $\mathbf{I}_1$ is a 1×1 identity matrix $[1]$ and $\mathbf{I}_0$ is the empty matrix of size 0×0.

Here, $\mathbf{I}_N$ is the identity matrix of order $N \times N$,

$$\mathbf{S}_2 = \begin{bmatrix} 1 & 1 \\ 1 & -1 \end{bmatrix} \tag{7-110}$$

and coefficients a_N and b_N are

$$a_N = \left[\frac{3N^2}{4(N^2 - 1)} \right]^{1/2} \tag{7-111}$$

and

$$b_N = \left[\frac{N^2 - 4}{4(N^2 - 1)} \right]^{1/2} \tag{7-112}$$

for $N > 1$. When $N \geq 8$, matrix $\mathbf{S}_N$ is not sequency ordered, but can be made so using the procedure demonstrated in Example 6.13 for the WHT. An example of the use of Eqs. (7-108) through (7-112) is Slant transformation matrix

$$\mathbf{A}_{SI} = \frac{1}{\sqrt{4}} \mathbf{S}_4 = \frac{1}{2} \begin{bmatrix} 1 & 1 & 1 & 1 \\ \dfrac{3}{\sqrt{5}} & \dfrac{1}{\sqrt{5}} & \dfrac{-1}{\sqrt{5}} & \dfrac{-3}{\sqrt{5}} \\ 1 & -1 & -1 & 1 \\ \dfrac{1}{\sqrt{5}} & \dfrac{-3}{\sqrt{5}} & \dfrac{3}{\sqrt{5}} & \dfrac{-1}{\sqrt{5}} \end{bmatrix} \tag{7-113}$$

Since $N = 4$, the basis vectors of $\mathbf{A}_{SI}$ (and the rows of slant matrix of $\mathbf{S}_4$) are sequency ordered.

EXAMPLE 7.14: A simple 1-D slant transform.

Using Eqs. (7-28) and (7-113), the slant transform of function $\mathbf{f} = [2\ 3\ 4\ 5]^T$ from Example 7.13 is $\mathbf{t}_{SI} = \mathbf{A}_{SI}\mathbf{f} = [7\ -2.24\ 0\ 0]^T$. Note the transform contains only two nonzero terms, while the Walsh-Hadamard transform in the previous example had three nonzero terms. The slant transform represents $\mathbf{f}$ more efficiently because $\mathbf{f}$ is a linearly increasing function—that is, $\mathbf{f}$ is highly correlated with the slant basis vector of sequency one. Thus, there are fewer terms in a linear expansion using slant basis functions as opposed to Walsh basis functions.

Figures 7.17(a) and (b) depict graphically and numerically the sequency-ordered slant transformation matrix for the case of $N = 8$. Just as apostrophes ($'$) were used to denote sequency ordering in Walsh-Hadamard transforms, $\mathbf{S}_8'$ and $\mathbf{A}_{SI'}$ are used to denote sequency-ordered versions of Eqs. (7-108) and (7-109). Note the slant transformation matrix in Fig. 7.16(b) is real, but not symmetric. Thus, $\mathbf{A}_{SI'}^{-1} = \mathbf{A}_{SI'}^T$ but $\mathbf{A}_{SI'}^T \neq \mathbf{A}_{SI'}$. Matrix $\mathbf{A}_{SI'}$ is also orthogonal and can be used in conjunction with

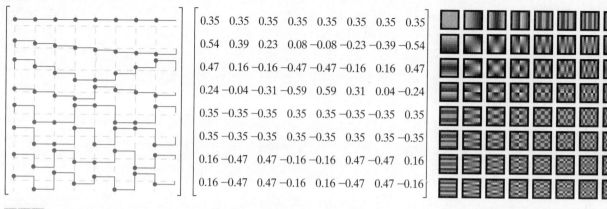

a b c

FIGURE 7.17 The transformation matrix and basis images of the slant transform for $N = 8$. (a) Graphical representation of orthogonal transformation matrix $\mathbf{A}_{Sl'}$, (b) $\mathbf{A}_{Sl'}$ rounded to two decimal places, and (c) basis images. For 1-D transforms, matrix $\mathbf{A}_{Sl'}$ is used in conjunction with Eqs. (7-28) and (7-29); for 2-D transforms, it is used with Eqs. (7-35) and (7-36).

Eqs. (7-35) and (7-36) to implement 2-D separable slant transforms. Figure 6.17(c) shows the 2-D slant basis images of size 8×8. Note for $4 \leq u \leq 5$ and $4 \leq v \leq 5$, they are identical to the corresponding basis images of the WHT in Fig. 7.16(c). This is also evident in Figs. 7.16(a) and 7.17(a) when $4 \leq u \leq 5$. In fact, all of the slant basis vectors bear a striking resemblance to the basis vectors of the Walsh-Hadamard transform. Finally, we note slant matrices have the necessary properties to allow implementation of a fast slant transform algorithm similar to the FFT.

7.9 HAAR TRANSFORM

Discovered in 1910, the basis functions of the *Haar transform* (Haar [1910]) were later recognized to be the oldest and simplest orthonormal wavelets. We will look at Haar's functions in the context of wavelets in the next section. In this section, we approach Haar's transform as another matrix-based transformation that employs a set of rectangular-shaped basis functions.

The Haar transform is based on *Haar functions*, $h_u(x)$, that are defined over the continuous, half-open interval $x \in [0,1)$. Variable u is an integer that for $u > 0$ can be decomposed uniquely as

$$u = 2^p + q \qquad (7\text{-}114)$$

where p is the largest power of 2 contained in u and q is the remainder—that is, $q = 2^p - u$. The Haar basis functions are then

$$h_u(x) = \begin{cases} 1 & u = 0 \text{ and } 0 \leq x < 1 \\ 2^{p/2} & u > 0 \text{ and } q/2^p \leq x < (q+0.5)/2^p \\ -2^{p/2} & u > 0 \text{ and } (q+0.5)/2^p \leq x < (q+1)/2^p \\ 0 & \text{otherwise} \end{cases} \qquad (7\text{-}115)$$

When u is 0, $h_0(x) = 1$ for all x; the first Haar function is independent of continuous variable x. For all other values of u, $h_u(x) = 0$ *except* in the half-open intervals $[q/2^p, (q+0.5)/2^p)$ and $[(q+0.5)/2^p, (q+1)/2^p)$, where it is a rectangular wave of magnitude $2^{p/2}$ and $-2^{p/2}$, respectively. Parameter p determines the amplitude and width of both rectangular waves, while q determines their position along x. As u increases, the rectangular waves become narrower and the number of functions that can be represented as linear combinations of the Haar functions increases. Figure 7.18(a) shows the first eight Haar functions (i.e., the curves depicted in blue).

Variables p and q are analogous to s and τ in Eq. (7-72).

The transformation matrix of the *discrete Haar transform* can be obtained by substituting the inverse transformation kernal

$$s(x,u) = \frac{1}{\sqrt{N}} h_u(x/N) \quad \text{for } x = 0,1,\ldots,N-1 \tag{7-116}$$

for $u = 0,1,\ldots,N-1$, where $N = 2^n$, into Eqs. (7-22) and (7-24). The resulting transformation matrix, denoted $\mathbf{A}_H$, can be written as a function of the $N \times N$ *Haar matrix*

Do not confuse the Haar matrix with the Hadamard matrix of Section 7.7. Since the same variable is used for both, the proper matrix must be determined from the context of the discussion.

$$\mathbf{H}_N = \begin{bmatrix} h_0(0/N) & h_0(1/N) & \cdots & h_0(N-1/N) \\ h_1(0/N) & h_1(1/N) & & \vdots \\ \vdots & & \ddots & \\ h_{N-1}(0/N) & \cdots & & h_{N-1}(N-1/N) \end{bmatrix} \tag{7-117}$$

as

$$\mathbf{A}_H = \frac{1}{\sqrt{N}} \mathbf{H}_N \tag{7-118}$$

For example, if $N = 2$,

$$\mathbf{A}_H = \frac{1}{\sqrt{2}} \begin{bmatrix} h_0(0) & h_0(1/2) \\ h_1(0) & h_1(1/2) \end{bmatrix} = \frac{1}{\sqrt{2}} \begin{bmatrix} 1 & 1 \\ 1 & -1 \end{bmatrix} \tag{7-119}$$

In the computation of $\mathbf{A}_H$, x and u of Eq. (7-116) are 0 and 1, so Eqs. (7-114), (7-115), and (7-116) give $s(0,0) = h_0(0)/\sqrt{2} = 1/\sqrt{2}$, $s(1,0) = h_0(0.5)/\sqrt{2} = 1/\sqrt{2}$, $s(0,1) = h_1(0)/\sqrt{2} = 1/\sqrt{2}$, and $s(1,1) = h_1(0.5)/\sqrt{2} = -1/\sqrt{2}$. For $N = 4$, u, q, and p of Eq. (7-114) assume the values

When u is 0, $h_u(x)$ is independent of p and q.

u	p	q
1	0	0
2	1	0
3	1	1

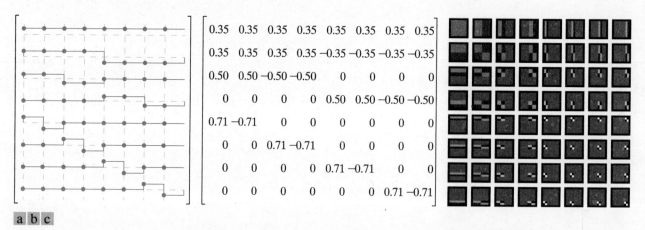

a b c

FIGURE 7.18 The transformation matrix and basis images of the discrete Haar transform for $N = 8$. (a) Graphical representation of orthogonal transformation matrix $\mathbf{A}_H$, (b) $\mathbf{A}_H$ rounded to two decimal places, and (c) basis images. For 1-D transforms, matrix $\mathbf{A}_H$ is used in conjunction with Eqs. (7-28) and (7-29); for 2-D transforms, it is used with Eqs. (7-35) and (7-36).

and the Haar transformation matrix of size 4×4 becomes

$$
\mathbf{A}_H = \frac{1}{2}
\begin{bmatrix}
1 & 1 & 1 & 1 \\
1 & 1 & -1 & -1 \\
\sqrt{2} & -\sqrt{2} & 0 & 0 \\
0 & 0 & \sqrt{2} & -\sqrt{2}
\end{bmatrix}
\tag{7-120}
$$

The transformation matrix for $N = 8$ is shown in Fig. 7.18(b). $\mathbf{A}_H$ is real, orthogonal, and sequency ordered. An important property of the Haar transformation matrix is that it can be decomposed into products of matrices with fewer nonzero entries than the original matrix. This is true of all of the transforms we have discussed to this point. They can be implemented in FFT-like alogrithms of complexity $O(N \log_2 N)$. The Haar transformation matrix, however, has fewer nonzero entries before the decomposition process begins, making less complex algorithms on the order of $O(N)$ possible. As can be seen in Fig. 7.18(c), the basis images of the separable 2-D Haar transform for images of size 8×8 also have few nonzero entries.

7.10 WAVELET TRANSFORMS

As was noted in Section 7.1, wavelets are small waves with bandpass spectra as defined in Eq. (7-72).

In 1987, *wavelets* were shown to be the foundation of a powerful new approach to signal processing and analysis called *multiresolution* theory (Mallat [1987]). Multiresolution theory incorporates and unifies techniques from a variety of disciplines, including subband coding from signal processing, quadrature mirror filtering from digital speech recognition, and pyramidal image processing. As its name implies, it is concerned with the representation and analysis of signals (or images) at more than one resolution. A *scaling function* is used to create a series of approximations of a function or image, each differing by a factor of 2 in resolution from its nearest neighboring approximations, and complementary functions, called *wavelets*, are used to encode the differences between adjacent approximations. The *discrete wavelet transform* (DWT) uses those wavelets, together with a single scaling function, to represent a function or image as a linear combination of the wavelets and scaling function. Thus, the wavelets and scaling function serve as an othonormal or biorthonormal basis of the DWT expansion. The Daubechies and Biorthogonal B-splines of Figs. 7.3(f) and (g) and the Haar basis functions of the previous section are but three of the many bases that can be used in DWTs.

In this section, we present a mathematical framework for the interpretation and application of discrete wavelet transforms. We use the discrete wavelet transform with respect to Haar basis functions to illustrate the concepts introduced. As you proceed through the material, remember that the discrete wavelet transform of a function with respect to Haar basis functions is *not* the Haar transform of the function (although the two are intimately related).

The discrete wavelet transform, like all transforms considered in this chapter, generates linear expansions of functions with respect to sets of orthonormal or biorthonormal expansion functions.

The coefficients of a 1-D full-scale DWT with respect to Haar wavelets and a 1-D Haar transform are the same.

SCALING FUNCTIONS

Consider the set of basis functions composed of all integer translations and binary scalings of the real, square-integrable *father scaling function* $\varphi(x)$ — that is, the set of scaled and translated functions $\{\varphi_{j,k}(x) \mid j,k \in \mathbf{Z}\}$ where

Z is the set of integers.

$$\varphi_{j,k}(x) = 2^{j/2} \varphi(2^j x - k) \tag{7-121}$$

In this equation, integer *translation* k determines the position of $\varphi_{j,k}(x)$ along the x-axis and *scale* j determines its shape — i.e., its width and amplitude. If we restrict j to some value, say $j = j_0$, then $\{\varphi_{j_0,k} \mid k \in \mathbf{Z}\}$ is the basis of the function space spanned by the $\varphi_{j,k}(x)$ for $j = j_0$ and $k = \ldots, -1, 0, 1, 2, \ldots$, denoted V_{j_0}. Increasing j_0 increases the number of representable functions in V_{j_0}, allowing functions with smaller variations and finer detail to be included in the space. As is demonstrated in Fig. 6.19 with Haar scaling functions, this is a consequence of the fact that as j_0 increases, the scaling functions used to represent the functions in V_{j_0} become narrower and separated by smaller changes in x.

Recall from Section 7.1 that the span of a basis is the set of functions that can be represented as linear combinations of the basis functions.

EXAMPLE 7.15: The Haar scaling function.

Consider the unit-height, unit-width scaling function

$$\varphi(x) = \begin{cases} 1 & 0 \leq x < 1 \\ 0 & \text{otherwise} \end{cases} \tag{7-122}$$

and note it is the Haar basis function $h_0(x)$ from Eq. (7-115). Figure 7.19 shows a few of the pulse-shaped scaling functions that can be generated by substituting Eq. (7-122) into Eq. (7-121). Note when the scale is 1 [i.e., when $j = 1$ as in Figs. 7.19(d) and (e)], the scaling functions are half as wide as when the scale is 0 (i.e., when $j = 0$ as in Figs. 7.19(a) and (b)). Moreover, for a given interval on x, there are

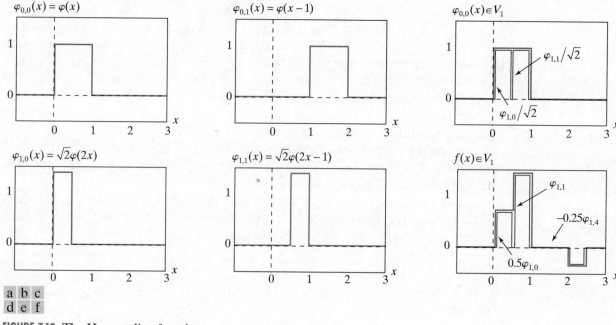

$\varphi_{0,0}(x) = \varphi(x)$

$\varphi_{0,1}(x) = \varphi(x-1)$

$\varphi_{0,0}(x) \in V_1$

$\varphi_{1,0}(x) = \sqrt{2}\varphi(2x)$

$\varphi_{1,1}(x) = \sqrt{2}\varphi(2x-1)$

$f(x) \in V_1$

a b c
d e f

FIGURE 7.19 The Haar scaling function.

twice as many scale 1 as scale 0 scaling functions. For example, two V_1 scaling functions, $\varphi_{1,0}$ and $\varphi_{1,1}$, are located in interval $0 \le x < 1$, while only one V_0 scaling function, $\varphi_{0,0}$, occupies the same interval.

Figure 7.19(f) shows a member of scaling space V_1 that does not belong in V_0. The scaling functions in Figs. 7.19(a) and (b) are too coarse to represent it. Higher-resolution functions, like those in Figs. 7.19(d) and (e), are required. They can be used, as is shown in Fig. 7.19(f), to represent the function as the three-term expansion $f(x) = 0.5\varphi_{1,0}(x) + \varphi_{1,1}(x) - 0.25\varphi_{1,4}(x)$. In a similar manner, scaling function $\varphi_{0,0}$, which is both a basis function and member of V_0, can be represented by a linear combination of V_1 scaling functions [see Fig. 7.19(c)] as follows:

$$\varphi_{0,k}(x) = \frac{1}{\sqrt{2}}\varphi_{1,2k}(x) + \frac{1}{\sqrt{2}}\varphi_{1,2k+1}(x)$$

The Haar scaling function of the preceding example, like the scaling functions of all discrete wavelet transforms, obeys the four fundamental requirements of *multi-resolution analysis* (Mallat [1989a]):

1. The scaling function is orthogonal to its integer tranlates.
2. The function spaces spanned by the scaling function at low scales are nested within those spanned at higher scales. That is,

$$V_{-\infty} \subset \ldots \subset V_{-1} \subset V_0 \subset V_1 \subset V_2 \subset \ldots \subset V_\infty \tag{7-123}$$

where $\subset$ is used to denote "a subspace of." The scaling functions satisfy the intuitive condition that if $f(x) \in V_j$, then $f(2x) \in V_{j+1}$.

3. The only function representable at every scale is $f(x) = 0$.

4. All measureable, square-integrable functions can be represented as a linear combination of the scaling function as $j \to \infty$. In other words,

$$V_\infty = L^2(\mathbf{R}) \tag{7-124}$$

where $L^2(\mathbf{R})$ is the set of measureable, square-integrable, 1-D functions.

Recall that **R** is the set of real numbers.

Under the above conditions, $\varphi(x)$ can be expressed as a linear combination of double-resolution copies of itself:

$$\varphi(x) = \sum_{k \in \mathbf{Z}} h_\varphi(k)\sqrt{2}\varphi(2x - k) \tag{7-125}$$

Called the *refinement* or *dilation equation,* Eq. (7-125) defines a series expansion in which the expansion functions, in accordance with Eq. (7-121), are scaling functions from one scale higher than $\varphi(x)$ and the $h_\varphi(k)$ are expansion coefficients. The expansion coefficients, which can be collected into an ordered set $\{h_\varphi(k)|k = 0, 1, 2, \ldots\} = \{h_\varphi(0), h_\varphi(1), \ldots\}$, are commonly called *scaling function coefficients.* For orthonormal scaling functions, it follows from Eqs. (7-51) and (7-52) that

Scaling function coefficients can also be combined in a *scaling vector.*

$$h_\varphi(k) = \langle \varphi(x), \sqrt{2}\varphi(2x - k) \rangle \tag{7-126}$$

EXAMPLE 7.16: Haar scaling function coefficients.

The coefficients of the Haar scaling function [i.e., Eq. (7-122)] are $\{h_\varphi(n)|n = 0, 1\} = \{1/\sqrt{2}, 1/\sqrt{2}\}$, the first row of Haar matrix $\mathbf{A}_H$ for $N = 2$ in Eq. (7-119). It is left as an exercise for the reader (see Problem 7.33) to compute these coefficients using Eq. (7-126). Equation (7-125) then yields

$$\varphi(x) = \frac{1}{\sqrt{2}}\left[\sqrt{2}\varphi(2x)\right] + \frac{1}{\sqrt{2}}\left[\sqrt{2}\varphi(2x - 1)\right]$$
$$= \varphi(2x) + \varphi(2x - 1)$$

This expansion is illustrated graphically in Fig. 7.19(c), where the bracketed terms of the preceding expression are seen to be $\varphi_{1,0}(x)$ and $\varphi_{1,1}(x)$.

WAVELET FUNCTIONS

Given a father scaling function that meets the MRA requirements of the previous section, there exists a *mother wavelet function* $\psi(x)$ whose integer translations and binary scalings,

$$\psi_{j,k}(x) = 2^{j/2}\psi(2^j x - k) \tag{7-127}$$

for all $j, k \in \mathbf{Z}$, span the difference between any two adjacent scaling spaces. If we let W_{j_0} denote the function space spanned by wavelet functions $\{\psi_{j_0,k} \mid k \in \mathbf{Z}\}$, then

$$V_{j_0+1} = V_{j_0} \oplus W_{j_0} \tag{7-128}$$

where $\oplus$ denotes the union of function spaces (like the union of sets). The *orthogonal complement* of V_{j_0} in V_{j_0+1} is W_{j_0}, and the scaling functions that are the basis of V_{j_0} are orthogonal to the wavelet functions that are the basis of W_{j_0}:

$$\left\langle \varphi_{j_0,k}(x), \psi_{j_0,l}(x) \right\rangle = 0 \quad \text{for } k \neq l \tag{7-129}$$

Figure 7.20 illustrates graphically the relationship between scaling and wavelet spaces. Each oval in the figure is a scaling space that, in accordance with Eq. (7-123), is nested or contained within the next higher resolution scaling space. The difference between adjacent scaling spaces is a wavelet space. Since wavelet space W_j resides within scaling space V_{j+1} and $\psi_{j,k}(x) \in W_j \subset V_{j+1}$, wavelet function $\psi(x)$ — like its scaling function counterpart in Eq. (7-125) — can be written as a weighted sum of shifted, double-resolution scaling functions. That is, we can write

$$\psi(x) = \sum_k h_\psi(k)\sqrt{2}\varphi(2x - k) \tag{7-130}$$

Wavelet function coefficients can also be combined in a *wavelet vector*.

where the $h_\psi(k)$ coefficients, called *wavelet function coefficients*, can be combined into the ordered set $\left\{ h_\psi(k) \middle| k = 0, 1, 2, \ldots \right\} = \left\{ h_\psi(0), h_\psi(1), \ldots \right\}$. Since integer wavelet translates are orthogonal to one another and to their complementary scaling functions, it can be shown (see, for example, Burrus, Gopinath, and Guo [1998]) that the $h_\psi(k)$ of Eq. (7-130) are related to the $h_\varphi(k)$ of Eq. (7-125) by

$$h_\psi(k) = (-1)^k h_\varphi(1 - k) \tag{7-131}$$

EXAMPLE 7.17: The Haar wavelet function and coefficients.

In the previous example, the Haar scaling coefficients were defined as $\left\{ h_\varphi(n) \middle| n = 0, 1 \right\} = \left\{ 1/\sqrt{2}, 1/\sqrt{2} \right\}$. Using Eq. (7-131), the corresponding wavelet function coefficients are

$$h_\psi(0) = (-1)^0 h_\varphi(1 - 0) = 1/\sqrt{2}$$
$$h_\psi(1) = (-1)^1 h_\varphi(1 - 1) = -1/\sqrt{2}$$

so $\left\{ h_\psi(n) \middle| n = 0, 1 \right\} = \left\{ 1/\sqrt{2}, -1/\sqrt{2} \right\}$. These coefficients correspond to the second row of matrix $\mathbf{A}_H$ for

FIGURE 7.20
The relationship between scaling and wavelet function spaces.

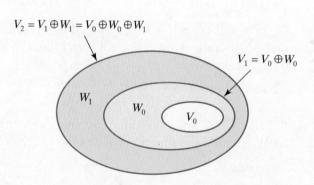

$$V_2 = V_1 \oplus W_1 = V_0 \oplus W_0 \oplus W_1$$

$$V_1 = V_0 \oplus W_0$$

W_1

W_0

V_0

$N = 2$ in Eq. (7-119). Substituting these values into Eq. (7-130), we get $\psi(x) = \varphi(2x) - \varphi(2x - 1)$, which is plotted in Fig. 7.21(a). Thus, the Haar *mother wavelet function* is

$$\psi(x) = \begin{cases} 1 & 0 \le x < 0.5 \\ -1 & 0.5 \le x < 1 \\ 0 & \text{elsewhere} \end{cases} \tag{7-132}$$

Note it is also the Haar basis function $h_1(x)$ of Eq. (7-115). Using Eq. (7-127), we can now generate the universe of scaled and translated Haar wavelets. Two such wavelets, $\psi_{0,2}(x)$ and $\psi_{1,0}(x)$, are plotted in Figs. 7.21(b) and (c), respectively. Note wavelet $\psi_{1,0}(x) \in W_1$ is narrower than $\psi_{0,2}(x) \in W_0$ and as such can be used to represent functions of finer detail.

Figure 7.21(d) shows a member of function space V_1 that is not in V_0. This function was considered in Example 7.15 [see Fig. 7.19(f)]. Although the function cannot be represented accurately in V_0, Eq. (7-128) indicates that it can be written as a function of V_0 and W_0 scaling and wavelet functions. The resulting expansion is

$$f(x) = f_a(x) + f_d(x)$$

where

$$f_a(x) = \frac{3\sqrt{2}}{4} \varphi_{0,0}(x) - \frac{\sqrt{2}}{8} \varphi_{0,2}(x)$$

and

$$f_d(x) = \frac{-\sqrt{2}}{4} \psi_{0,0}(x) - \frac{\sqrt{2}}{8} \psi_{0,2}(x)$$

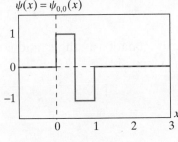

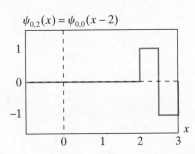

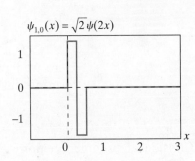

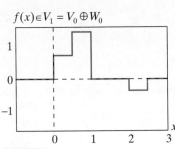

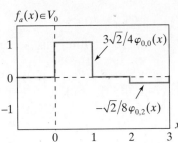

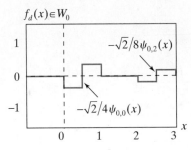

FIGURE 7.21 Haar wavelet functions.

Here, $f_a(x)$ is an approximation of $f(x)$ using V_0 scaling functions, while $f_d(x)$ is difference $f(x) - f_a(x)$ as a sum of W_0 wavelets. These approximations and differences, which are shown in Figs. 7.19(e) and (f), divide $f(x)$ in a manner similar to lowpass and highpass filtering. The low frequencies of $f(x)$ are captured in $f_a(x)$—it assumes the average value of $f(x)$ in each integer interval—while the higher-frequency details are encoded in $f_d(x)$.

WAVELET SERIES EXPANSION

Combining Eqs. (7-124) and (7-128), the space of all measureable, square-integrable functions can be defined as $L^2(\mathbf{R}) = V_{j_0} \oplus W_{j_0} \oplus W_{j_0+1} \oplus \ldots$, where j_0 is an arbitrary starting scale. We can then define the *wavelet series expansion* of function $f(x) \in L^2(\mathbf{R})$ with respect to wavelet $\psi(x)$ and scaling function $\varphi(x)$ as

$$f(x) = \sum_k c_{j_0}(k)\varphi_{j_0,k}(x) + \sum_{j=j_0}^{\infty}\sum_k d_j(k)\psi_{j,k}(x) \qquad (7\text{-}133)$$

where c_{j_0} and d_j for $j \geq j_0$ are called *approximation* and *detail coefficients*, respectively. Any measureable, square-integrable, 1-D function can be expressed as a weighted sum of V_{j_0} scaling functions and W_j wavelets for $j \geq j_0$. The first sum in Eq. (7-133) produces an approximation of $f(x)$ from scale j_0 scaling functions; each successive scale of the second sum provides increasing detail as a sum of higher-resolution wavelets. If the scaling and wavlet functions are orthonormal,

$$c_{j_0} = \langle f(x),\ \varphi_{j_0,k}(x) \rangle \qquad (7\text{-}134)$$

and

$$d_j = \langle f(x),\ \psi_{j,k}(x) \rangle \qquad (7\text{-}135)$$

Here, we have used Eq. (7-13). If they are part of a biorthogonal basis, the φ and ψ terms must be replaced by their dual functions, $\widetilde{\varphi}$ and $\widetilde{\psi}$, respectively.

EXAMPLE 7.18: The Haar wavelet series expansion of $y = x^2$.

Consider the simple function

$$y = \begin{cases} x^2 & 0 \leq x \leq 1 \\ 0 & \text{otherwise} \end{cases}$$

shown in Fig. 7.22(a). Using Haar wavelets—see Eqs. (7-122) and (7-132)—and starting scale $j_0 = 0$, Eqs. (7-134) and (7-135) can be used to compute the following expansion coefficients:

$$c_0(0) = \int_0^1 x^2 \varphi_{0,0}(x)\,dx = \int_0^1 x^2 dx = \left.\frac{x^3}{3}\right|_0^1 = \frac{1}{3}$$

$$d_0(0) = \int_0^1 x^2 \psi_{0,0}(x)\,dx = \int_0^{0.5} x^2 dx - \int_{0.5}^1 x^2 dx = -\frac{1}{4}$$

$$d_1(0) = \int_0^1 x^2 \psi_{1,0}(x)\,dx = \int_0^{0.25} x^2 \sqrt{2}\,dx - \int_{0.25}^{0.5} x^2 \sqrt{2}\,dx = -\frac{\sqrt{2}}{32}$$

$$d_1(1) = \int_0^1 x^2 \psi_{1,1}(x)\,dx = \int_{0.5}^{0.75} x^2 \sqrt{2}\,dx - \int_{0.75}^{1} x^2 \sqrt{2}\,dx = -\frac{3\sqrt{2}}{32}$$

Substituting these values into Eq. (7-133), we get the wavelet series expansion

$$y = \underbrace{\frac{1}{3}\varphi_{0,0}(x)}_{V_0} + \underbrace{\left[-\frac{1}{4}\psi_{0,0}(x)\right]}_{W_0} + \underbrace{\left[-\frac{\sqrt{2}}{32}\psi_{1,0}(x) - \frac{3\sqrt{2}}{32}\psi_{1,1}(x)\right]}_{W_1} + \cdots$$

$$\underbrace{\hphantom{\frac{1}{3}\varphi_{0,0}(x) + \left[-\frac{1}{4}\psi_{0,0}(x)\right]}}_{V_1 = V_0 \oplus W_0}$$

$$\underbrace{\hphantom{\frac{1}{3}\varphi_{0,0}(x) + \left[-\frac{1}{4}\psi_{0,0}(x)\right] + \left[-\frac{\sqrt{2}}{32}\psi_{1,0}(x) - \frac{3\sqrt{2}}{32}\psi_{1,1}(x)\right]}}_{V_2 = V_1 \oplus W_1 = V_0 \oplus W_0 \oplus W_1}$$

The first term in this expansion employs $c_0(0)$ to generate a V_0 approximation of the function being expanded. This approximation is shown in Fig. 7.22(b) and is the average value of the original function. The second term uses $d_0(0)$ to refine the approximation by adding a level of detail from wavelet space W_0. The added detail and resulting V_1 approximation are shown in Figs. 7.22(c) and (d), respectively. Another level of detail is formed from the products of $d_1(0)$ and $d_1(1)$ with the corresponding wavelets of W_1. This additional detail is shown in Fig. 7.22(e), and the resulting V_2 approximation is depicted in Fig. 7.22(f). Note the expansion is now beginning to resemble the original function. As higher scales (greater levels of detail) are added, the approximation becomes a more precise representation of the function, realizing it in the limit as $j \to \infty$.

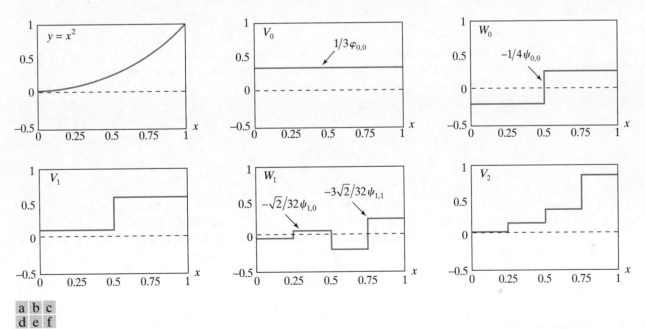

a b c
d e f

FIGURE 7.22 A wavelet series expansion of $y = x^2$ using Haar wavelets.

DISCRETE WAVELET TRANSFORM IN ONE DIMENSION

Like a Fourier series expansion, the wavelet series expansion of the previous section maps a function of a single continuous variable into a sequence of discrete coefficients. If the function being expanded is discrete, the coefficients of the expansion are its *discrete wavelet transform* (DWT) and the expansion itself is the function's *inverse discrete wavelet transform*. Letting $j_0 = 0$ in Eqs. (7-133) through (7-135) and restricting attention to N-point discrete functions in which N is a power of 2 (i.e., $N = 2^J$), we get

Remember that for discrete inputs, x is a discrete variable that takes on integer values between 0 and $N - 1$.

$$f(x) = \frac{1}{\sqrt{N}} \left[T_\varphi(0,0)\varphi(x) + \sum_{j=0}^{J-1} \sum_{k=0}^{2^j-1} T_\psi(j,k)\psi_{j,k}(x) \right] \qquad (7\text{-}136)$$

where

$$T_\varphi(0,0) = \left\langle f(x), \varphi_{0,0}(x) \right\rangle = \left\langle f(x), \varphi(x) \right\rangle = \frac{1}{\sqrt{N}} \sum_{x=0}^{N-1} f(x)\varphi^*(x) \qquad (7\text{-}137)$$

and

$$T_\psi(j,k) = \left\langle f(x), \psi_{j,k}(x) \right\rangle = \frac{1}{\sqrt{N}} \sum_{x=0}^{N-1} f(x)\psi_{j,k}^*(x) \qquad (7\text{-}138)$$

for $j = 0, 1, \ldots, J-1$ and $k = 0, 1, \ldots, 2^j - 1$. The transform coefficients defined by Eqs. (7-137) and (7-138) are called *approximation* and *detail coefficients*, respectively. They correspond to the $c_{j_0}(k)$ and $d_j(k)$ of the wavelet series expansion in the previous section. Note the integrations of the series expansion have been replaced by summations in Eqs. (7-137) through (7-138). In the discrete case, inner products like those of Eqs. (7-1) and (7-2), as opposed to Eq. (7-3), are used. In addition, a $1/\sqrt{N}$ normalizing factor, reminiscent of the DFT in Example 7.6, has been added to both the forward and inverse transforms. This factor alternately could be incorporated into the forward or inverse alone as $1/N$. Finally, it should be remembered that Eqs. (7-137) through (7-138) are valid for orthonormal bases. If the scaling and wavelet functions are real-valued, the conjugations can be dropped. If the basis is biorthogonal, the φ and ψ terms in Eqs. (7-137) and (7-138) must be replaced by their duals, $\widetilde{\varphi}$ and $\widetilde{\psi}$, respectively.

EXAMPLE 7.19: A 1-D discrete wavelet transform.

To illustrate the use of Eqs. (7-137) through (7-138), consider a discrete function of four points in which $f(0) = 1$, $f(1) = 4$, $f(2) = -3$, and $f(3) = 0$. Since $N = 4$, J is 2 and the summations in Eqs. (7-136) through (7-138) are performed for $x = 0, 1, 2, 3$. When j is 0, k is 0; when j is 1, k is 0 or 1. If we use Haar scaling and wavelet functions and assume the four samples of $f(x)$ are distributed over the support of the scaling function, which is 1, Eq. (7-137) gives

$$T_\varphi(0,0) = \frac{1}{2} \sum_{x=0}^{3} f(x)\varphi(x) = \frac{1}{2} \left[(1)(1) + (4)(1) + (-3)(1) + (0)(1) \right] = 1$$

Note we have employed uniformly spaced samples of the Haar scaling function for $j = k = 0$—i.e., $\varphi(x) = 1$ for $x = 0, 1, 2, 3$. The sampled values match the elements of the first row of Haar transformation matrix $\mathbf{A}_H$ in Eq. (7-120) of Section 7.9. Using Eq. (7-138) and similarly spaced samples of $\psi_{j,k}(x)$, which are the elements of rows 2, 3, and 4 of $\mathbf{A}_H$, we get

$$T_\psi(0,0) = \frac{1}{2}\left[(1)(1)+(4)(1)+(-3)(-1)+(0)(-1)\right] = 4$$

$$T_\psi(1,0) = \frac{1}{2}\left[(1)\left(\sqrt{2}\right)+(4)\left(-\sqrt{2}\right)+(-3)(0)+(0)(0)\right] = -1.5\sqrt{2}$$

$$T_\psi(1,1) = \frac{1}{2}\left[(1)(0)+(4)(0)+(-3)\left(\sqrt{2}\right)+(0)\left(-\sqrt{2}\right)\right] = -1.5\sqrt{2}$$

Thus, the discrete wavelet transform of our simple four-sample function relative to Haar scaling and wavelet functions is $\{1, 4, -1.5\sqrt{2}, -1.5\sqrt{2}\}$. Since the transform coefficents are a function of two variables—scale j and translation k—we combine them into an *ordered set*. The elements of this set turn out to be identical to the elements of the sequency-ordered Haar transform of the function:

$$\mathbf{t}_H = \mathbf{A}_H\mathbf{f} = \frac{1}{2}\begin{bmatrix} 1 & 1 & 1 & 1 \\ 1 & 1 & -1 & -1 \\ \sqrt{2} & -\sqrt{2} & 0 & 0 \\ 0 & 0 & \sqrt{2} & -\sqrt{2} \end{bmatrix}\begin{bmatrix} 1 \\ 4 \\ -3 \\ 0 \end{bmatrix} = \begin{bmatrix} 1 \\ 4 \\ -1.5\sqrt{2} \\ -1.5\sqrt{2} \end{bmatrix}$$

Recall from the previous section that Haar transforms are a function of a single transform domain variable, denoted u.

Equation (7-136) enables the reconstruction of the original function from its wavelet transform coefficients. Expanding the summation, we get

$$f(x) = \frac{1}{2}\left[T_\varphi(0,0)\varphi(x)+T_\psi(0,0)\psi_{0,0}(x)+T_\psi(1,0)\psi_{1,0}(x)+T_\psi(1,1)\psi_{1,1}(x)\right]$$

for $x = 0, 1, 2, 3$. If $x = 0$, for instance,

$$f(0) = \frac{1}{2}\left[(1)(1)+(4)(1)+\left(-1.5\sqrt{2}\right)\left(\sqrt{2}\right)+\left(-1.5\sqrt{2}\right)(0)\right] = 1$$

As in the forward case, uniformly spaced samples of the scaling and wavelet functions are used in the computation of the inverse.

The Fast Wavelet Transform

The multiresolution refinement equation and its wavelet counterpart, Eqs. (7-125) and (7-130), make it possible to define the scaling and wavelet functions at any scale as a function of shifted, double-resolution copies of the scaling functions at the next higher scale. In the same way, the expansion coefficients of the wavelet series expansion and discrete wavelet transform can be computed recursively (see Problem 7.35) using

$$c_j(k) = \sum_n h_\varphi(n-2k)c_{j+1}(n) \tag{7-139}$$

$$d_j(k) = \sum_n h_\psi(n-2k)c_{j+1}(n) \tag{7-140}$$

and

$$T_\varphi(j,k) = \sum_n h_\varphi(n-2k)T_\varphi(j+1,n) \tag{7-141}$$

$$T_\psi(j,k) = \sum_n h_\psi(n-2k)T_\varphi(j+1,n) \tag{7-142}$$

respectively. In contrast to Eqs. (7-133) and (7-136), where the only scaling coefficients that are needed in the computations are at scale j_0, Eqs. (7-139) through (7-142) require the computation of all scaling coefficients up to the highest scale of interest. Comparing these equations to the equation defining discrete convolution [i.e., Eq. (4-48)], we see that n is a dummy variable of convolution and the remaining minus signs and $2k$ terms reverse the order of the h_φ and h_ψ coefficients and sample the convolution results at $n = 0, 2, 4, ...$, respectively. Thus, for the discrete wavelet transform, we can rewrite Eqs. (7-141) and (7-142) as

$$T_\varphi(j,k) = T_\varphi(j+1,n) \star h_\varphi(-n) \tag{7-143}$$

$$T_\psi(j,k) = T_\varphi(j+1,n) \star h_\psi(-n) \tag{7-144}$$

where the convolutions are evaluated at instants $n = 0, 2, ..., 2^{j+1} - 2$. As indicated in Fig. 7.23, evaluating convolutions at nonnegative, even indices is equivalent to filtering and *downsampling* by 2 (i.e., discarding every other convolved value). For a 1-D sequence of samples $y(n)$ for $n = 0, 1, 2, ...$, downsampled sequence $y_{2\downarrow}(n)$ is defined as

$$y_{2\downarrow}(n) = y(2n) \quad \text{for } n = 0, 1, ... \tag{7-145}$$

Equations (7-143) and (7-144) are the defining equations of a computationally efficient form of the DWT called the *fast wavelet transform* (FWT). For an input sequence of length $N = 2^J$, the number of mathematical operations involved is on

FIGURE 7.23
A FWT analysis filter bank for orthonormal filters. The $\star$ and $2\downarrow$ denote convolution and downsampling by 2, respectively.

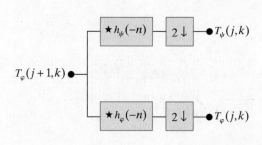

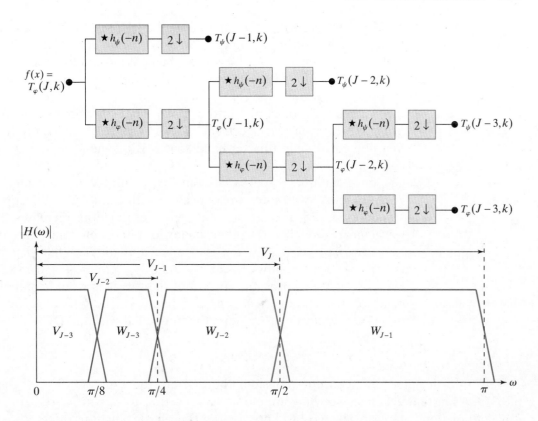

a
b

FIGURE 7.24
(a) A three-stage or three-scale FWT analysis filter bank and (b) its frequency-splitting characteristics. Because of symmetry in the DFT of the filter's impulse response, it is common to display only the $[0, \pi]$ region.

the order of $O(N)$. That is, the number of multiplications and additions is linear with respect to the length of the input sequence—because the number of multiplications and additions involved in the convolutions performed by the FWT filter bank in Fig. 7.23 is proportional to the length of the sequences being convolved. Thus, the FWT compares favorably with the FFT algorithm, which requires on the order of $O(N \log_2 N)$ operations.

A *P*-scale FWT employs *P* filter banks to generate a *P*-scale transform at scales $J - 1$, $J - 2$, ..., $J - P$, where $P \leq J$.

Figure 7.24(a) shows a three-scale filter bank in which the FWT *analysis filter* of Fig. 7.23 has been "iterated" three times to create a three-stage structure for computing transform coefficients at scales $J - 1$, $J - 2$, and $J - 3$. Note the highest scale coefficients are assumed to be samples of the function itself.[†] Otherwise, the approximation and detail coefficients at scale j are computed by convolving $T_\varphi(j + 1, k)$, the scale $j + 1$ approximation coefficients, with the order-reversed scaling and wavelet coefficients, $h_\varphi(-n)$ and $h_\psi(-n)$, and subsampling the results. If there are K scaling and wavelet function coefficients, the order reversed scaling and wavelet coefficients are $\{h_\varphi(K - 1 - m) \mid m = 0, 1, ..., K - 1\}$ and $\{h_\psi(K - 1 - m) \mid m = 0, 1, ..., K - 1\}$, respectively. For a discrete input of length $N = 2^J$, the filter bank in Fig. 7.23 can

---

[†]If function $f(x)$ is sampled above the Nyquist rate, as is usually the case, its samples are good approximations of the scaling coefficients at the sampling resolution and can be used as the starting high-resolution scaling coefficient inputs. In other words, no wavelet or detail coefficients are needed at the sampling scale. The highest-resolution scaling functions act as unit discrete impulse functions in Eqs. (7-141) and (7-142), allowing $f(x)$ to be used as the scaling (approximation) input to the first two-band filter bank (Odegard, Gopinath, and Burrus [1992]).

be iterated up to J times. In operation, the leftmost filter bank of Fig. 7.24(a) splits the input function into a lowpass *approximation* component that corresponds to scaling coefficients $T_\varphi(J-1,k)$ and a highpass *detail* component corresponding to coefficients $T_\psi(J-1,k)$. This is illustrated graphically in Fig. 7.24(b), where scaling space V_J is split into wavelet space W_{J-1} and scaling space V_{J-1}. The spectrum of the original function is split into two half-band components. The second filter bank in Fig. 7.24(a) splits the spectrum of scaling space V_{J-1}, the lower half-band of the first filter bank, into quarter-band spaces W_{J-2} and V_{J-2} and corresponding FWT coefficients $T_\psi(J-2,k)$ and $T_\varphi(J-2,k)$, respectively. Finally, the third filter bank generates eigth-band spaces W_{J-3} and V_{J-3} with FWT coefficients $T_\psi(J-3,k)$ and $T_\varphi(J-3,k)$. As was noted in connection with Eq. (7-73) of Section 7.4 and demonstrated in Fig. 7.5, as the scale of the wavelet functions increases, the spectra of the wavelets are stretched (i.e., their bandwidth is doubled and shifted higher by a factor of two). In Fig. 7.24(b), this is evidenced by the fact that the bandwidth of W_{J-1} is $\pi/2$, while the bandwidths of W_{J-2} and W_{J-3} are $\pi/4$ and $\pi/8$, respectively. For higher-scale transforms, the spectra of the wavelets would continue to decrease in bandwidth, but would never reach radian frequency $\omega = 0$. A lowpass scaling function is always needed to capture the frequencies around DC.

EXAMPLE 7.20: Computing a 1-D fast wavelet transform.

To illustrate the preceding concepts, consider the discrete function $f(x) = \{1, 4, -3, 0\}$ from Example 7.19. As in that example, we will compute its wavelet transform with respect to Haar scaling and wavelet functions. Here, however, we will not use the Haar basis functions directly. Instead, we will use the corresponding scaling and wavelet coefficients from Examples 7.16 and 7.17:

$$\{h_\varphi(n)|n = 0, 1\} = \{1/\sqrt{2}, 1/\sqrt{2}\} \tag{7-146}$$

and

$$\{h_\psi(n)|n = 0, 1\} = \{1/\sqrt{2}, -1/\sqrt{2}\} \tag{7-147}$$

Since the transform computed in Example 7.19 was the ordered set $\{T_\varphi(0,0), T_\psi(0,0), T_\psi(1,0), T_\psi(1,1)\}$, we will compute the corresponding two-scale FWT for scales $j = \{0,1\}$. Recall from the previous example that $k = 0$ when $j = 0$, while k is 0 and 1 when $j = 1$. The transform will be computed using a two-stage filter bank that parallels the three-stage filter bank of Fig. 7.24(a). Figure 7.25 shows the resulting filter bank and the sequences that follow from the required FWT convolutions and downsamplings. Note input function $f(x)$ serves as the scaling (or approximation) input to the left most filter bank. To compute the $T_\psi(1,n)$ coefficients that appear at the end of the upper branch of Fig. 7.25, we first convolve $f(x)$ with $h_\psi(-n)$. For Haar scaling and wavelet coefficients, $K = 2$ and the order reversed wavelet coefficients are $\{h_\psi(K-1-m)|m = 0, 1, ..., K-1\} = \{h_\psi(1-m)|m = 0, 1\} = \{-1/\sqrt{2}, 1/\sqrt{2}\}$. As explained in Section 3.4, convolution requires flipping one of the convolved functions about the origin, sliding it past the other, and computing the sum of the point-wise product of the two functions. Flipping order-reversed wavelet coefficients $\{-1/\sqrt{2}, 1/\sqrt{2}\}$ to get $\{1/\sqrt{2}, -1/\sqrt{2}\}$ and sliding them from left-to-right across input sequence $\{1, 4, -3, 0\}$, we get

$$\{-1/\sqrt{2}, -3/\sqrt{2}, 7/\sqrt{2}, -3/\sqrt{2}, 0\}$$

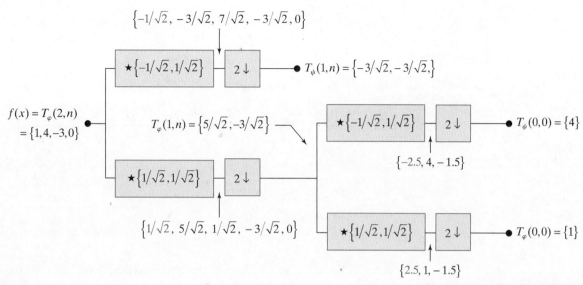

FIGURE 7.25 Computing a two-scale fast wavelet transform of sequence $\{1, 4, -3, 0\}$ using Haar scaling and wavelet coefficients.

where the first term corresponds to convolution index $n = -1$. In Fig. 7.25, convolution values that are associated with a negative dummy variable of convolution (i.e., $n < 0$) are denoted in blue. Since scale $j = 1$, the downsampled convolutions correspond to the even indices of n up to $2^{j+1} - 2$. Thus, $n = 0$ and 2 and $T_\psi(1,n) = \{-3/\sqrt{2}, -3/\sqrt{2}\}$. The remaining convolutions and downsamplings are performed in a similar manner.

The blocks containing a $\star$ in Figs. 7.23 through 7.25 are FIR filters. FIR filters are also discussed in Section 4.7.

Note we use $h(n)$ for analysis or decomposition filters, which include one scaling filter and one wavelet filter, and $g(n)$ for synthesis or reconstruction filters, which also include a scaling and wavelet filter. The scaling filters are sometimes called approximation or lowpass filters and have a subscript of 0 in Fig. 7.26, while the wavelet filters are called detail or highpass filters and have a subscript of 1.

In *digital signal processing* (DSP), filters like those in Figs. 7.23 through 7.25 are known as *finite impulse response* (FIR) filters. Their response to a unit impulse is a finite sequence of outputs that assumes the values of the filter coefficients. Figure 7.26(a) shows one well-known arrangement of real-coefficient, FIR filters that has been studied extensively in the literature. Called a two-band *subband coding* and *decoding* system, it is composed of two *analysis filters*, $h_0(n)$ and $h_1(n)$, and two *synthesis filters*, $g_0(n)$ and $g_1(n)$. The analysis filters decompose the input into two half-length sequences $f_0(n)$ and $f_1(n)$. As can be seen in Fig. 7.26(a), filter $h_0(n)$ is a lowpass filter whose output is an approximation of $f(x)$; filter $h_1(n)$ is a highpass filter whose output is the difference between the lowpass approximation and $f(x)$. As Fig. 7.26(b) shows, the spectrum of the input sequence is split into two halfbands, $H_0(\omega)$ and $H_1(\omega)$. Synthesis bank filters $g_0(n)$ and $g_1(n)$ are then used to reconstruct $\hat{f}(x)$ from *upsampled* versions of $f_0(n)$ and $f_1(n)$. For a 1-D sequence of samples $y(n)$, upsampled sequence $y_{2\uparrow}(n)$ can be defined as

$$y_{2\uparrow}(n) = \begin{cases} y(n/2) & \text{if } n \text{ is even} \\ 0 & \text{otherwise} \end{cases} \qquad (7\text{-}148)$$

where the upsampling is by a factor of 2. Upsampling by a factor of 2 can be thought of as inserting a 0 after every sample of $y(n)$.

FIGURE 7.26
(a) A two-band digital filtering system for sub-band coding and decoding and (b) its spectrum-splitting properties.

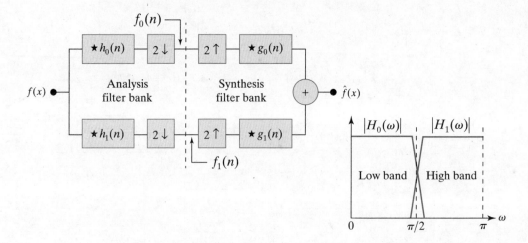

The goal in subband coding is to choose the analysis and synthesis filters so $\hat{f}(x) = f(x)$. When this is accomplished, the system is said to employ *perfect reconstruction filters* and the filters are, up to some constant factors, related as follows:

$$g_0(n) = (-1)^n h_1(n) \tag{7-149}$$

Equations (7-149) and (7-151) are described in detail in the filter bank literature (see, for example, Vetterli and Kovacevic [1995]). For many biorthogonal filters, g_0 and g_1 are different in length, requiring the shorter filter to be zero-padded. In *causal* filters, $n \geq 0$ and the ouput depends only on current and past inputs.

and

$$g_1(n) = (-1)^n h_0(n) \tag{7-150}$$

In these equations, $(-1)^n$ changes the signs of the odd-indexed analysis filter coefficients and is called *modulation*. Each synthesis filter is a modulated version of the analysis filter that opposes it diagonally in Fig. 7.26(a). Thus, the analysis and synthesis filters are said to be *cross-modulated*. Their impulse responses are biorthogonal. If they are also orthonormal and of length K, where K is divisible by 2, they satisfy the additional constraints that

$$
\begin{aligned}
g_1(n) &= (-1)^n g_0(K-1-n) \\
h_0(n) &= g_0(K-1-n) \\
h_1(n) &= g_1(K-1-n)
\end{aligned}
\tag{7-151}
$$

Noting the similarity between the FWT analysis filter bank in Fig. 7.23 and the subband analysis filter bank of Fig. 7.26(a), we can postulate the inverse FWT *synthesis filter bank* of Fig. 7.27. For the case of orthonormal filters, Eq. (7-151) constrains the synthesis filters to be order-reversed versions of the analysis filters. Comparing the filters in Figs. 7.23 and 7.27, we see this is indeed the case. It must be remembered, however, that perfect reconstruction is also possible with biorthogonal analysis and synthesis filters, which are not order-reversed versions of one another. Biorthogonal analysis and synthesis filters are cross-modulated in accordance with Eqs. (7-149) and (7-150). Finally, we note the inverse filter bank of Fig. 7.27, like the forward FWT

FIGURE 7.27
An inverse FWT
synthesis filter
bank for ortho-
normal filters.

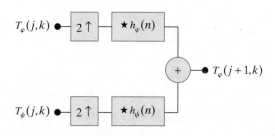

filter bank of Fig. 6.23, can be iterated for the computation of multiscale inverse FWTs. In the next example, a two-scale inverse FWT structure is considered. The coefficient combining process demonstrated there can be extended to any number of scales.

EXAMPLE 7.21: Computing a 1-D inverse fast wavelet transform.

Computation of the inverse fast wavelet transform mirrors its forward counterpart. Figure 7.28 illustrates the process for the sequence considered in Example 7.20. To begin the calculation, the level 0 approximation and detail coefficients are upsampled to yield $\{1,0\}$ and $\{4,0\}$, respectively. Convolution with filters $h_\varphi(n) = \{1/\sqrt{2}, 1/\sqrt{2}\}$ and $h_\psi(n) = \{1/\sqrt{2}, -1/\sqrt{2}\}$ produces $\{1/\sqrt{2}, 1/\sqrt{2}, 0\}$ and $\{4/\sqrt{2}, -4/\sqrt{2}, 0\}$, which when added give $T_\varphi(1,n) = \{5/\sqrt{2}, -3/\sqrt{2}\}$. Thus, the level 1 approximation of Fig. 7.28, which matches the computed approximation in Fig. 7.25, is reconstructed. Continuing in this manner, $f(x)$ is formed at the right of the second synthesis filter bank.

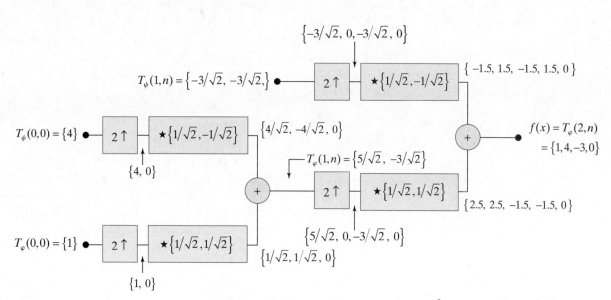

FIGURE 7.28 Computing a two-scale inverse fast wavelet transform of sequence $\{1, 4, -1.5\sqrt{2}, -1.5\sqrt{2}\}$ with Haar scaling and wavelet functions.

WAVELET TRANSFORMS IN TWO DIMENSIONS

The 1-D wavelet transform of the previous section is easily extended to 2-D functions such as images. In two dimensions, a two-dimensional scaling function, $\varphi(x, y)$, and three 2-D wavelets, $\psi^H(x, y)$, $\psi^V(x, y)$, and $\psi^D(x, y)$, are required. Each is the product of two 1-D functions. Excluding products that produce 1-D results, like $\varphi(x)\psi(x)$, the four remaining products produce the *separable* scaling function

$$\mu_f = \frac{1}{\|H(f)\|^2} \int_{-\infty}^{\infty} f|H(f)|^2 \, df \tag{7-152}$$

and separable, "directionally sensitive" wavelets

$$\psi^H(x, y) = \psi(x)\varphi(y) \tag{7-153}$$

$$\psi^V(x, y) = \varphi(x)\psi(y) \tag{7-154}$$

$$\psi^D(x, y) = \psi(x)\psi(y) \tag{7-155}$$

These wavelets measure functional variations—intensity changes in images—along different directions: ψ^H measures variations along columns (for example, horizontal edges), ψ^V responds to variations along rows (like vertical edges), and ψ^D corresponds to variations along diagonals. The directional sensitivity is a natural consequence of the separability in Eqs. (7-153) to (7-155); it does not increase the computational complexity of the 2-D transform discussed in this section.

Like the 1-D discrete wavelet transform, the 2-D DWT can be implemented using digital filters and downsamplers. With separable 2-D scaling and wavelet functions, we simply take the 1-D FWT of the rows of $f(x, y)$, followed by the 1-D FWT of the resulting columns. Figure 7.29(a) shows the process in block diagram form. Note, like its 1-D counterpart in Fig. 7.23, the 2-D FWT "filters" the scale $j+1$ approximation coefficients, denoted $T_\varphi(j+1, k, l)$ in the figure, to construct the scale j approximation and detail coefficients. In the 2-D case, however, we get three sets of detail coefficients—*horizontal details* $T_\psi^H(j, k, l)$, *vertical details* $T_\psi^V(j, k, l)$, and *diagonal details* $T_\psi^D(j, k, l)$.

The single-scale filter bank of Fig. 7.29(a) can be "iterated" (by tying the approximation output to the input of another filter bank) to produce a $P \le J$ scale transform in which scale j is equal to $J-1, J-2, \ldots, J-P$. As in the 1-D case, image $f(x, y)$ is used as the $T_\varphi(J, k, l)$ input. Convolving its rows with $h_\varphi(-n)$ and $h_\psi(-n)$ and downsampling its columns, we get two subimages whose horizontal resolutions are reduced by a factor of 2. The highpass or detail component characterizes the image's high-frequency information with vertical orientation; the lowpass, approximation component contains its low-frequency, vertical information. Both subimages are then filtered columnwise and downsampled to yield four quarter-size output subimages—T_φ, T_ψ^H, T_ψ^V, and T_ψ^D. These subimages, which are normally arranged as in Fig. 7.29(b), are the inner products of $f(x, y)$ and the two-dimensional scaling and

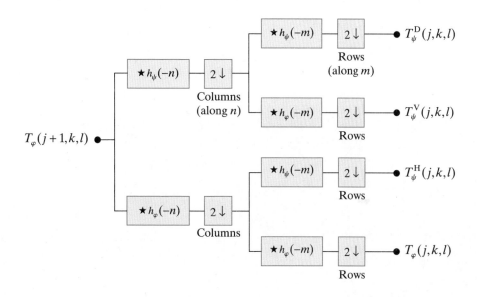

FIGURE 7.29
The 2-D fast wavelet transform:
(a) the analysis filter bank; (b) the resulting decomposition; and
(c) the synthesis filter bank.

Note m and n are dummy variables of convolution, while j, like in the 1-D case, is scale, and k and l are translations.

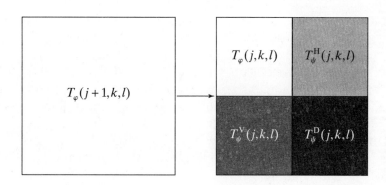

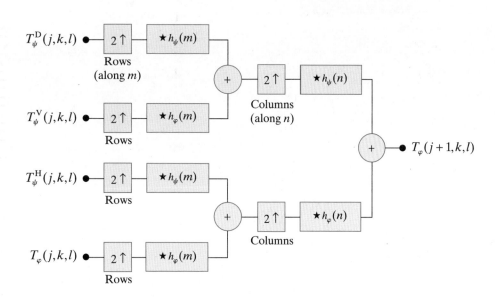

wavelet functions in Eqs. (7-152) through (7-155), followed by downsampling by two in each dimension.

Figure 7.29(c) shows the synthesis filter bank that reverses the process just described. As would be expected, the reconstruction algorithm is similar to the 1-D case. At each iteration, four-scale j approximation and detail subimages are upsampled and convolved with two 1-D filters—one operating on the subimages' columns and the other on its rows. Addition of the results yields the scale $j + 1$ approximation, and the process is repeated until the original image is reconstructed.

EXAMPLE 7.22: Computing 2-D fast wavelet transforms.

In this example, we compute a 2-D, multiscale FWT with respect to Haar basis functions and compare it to the traditional Haar transform of Section 7.9. Figures 7.30(a)–(d) show a 512×512 monochrome image of a vase on a windowsill, its one- and two-scale discrete wavelet transforms with respect to Haar basis functions, and its Haar transform, respectively. The computation of the wavelet transforms will be discussed shortly. The Haar transform in Fig. 7.30(d) is computed using a 512×512 Haar transformation matrix [see Eqs. (7-114) through (7-118)] and the matrix-based operations defined in Eq. (7-35). The detail coefficients in Figs. 7.30(b) and (c), as well as the Haar transform coefficients in Fig. 7.30(d), are scaled to make their underlying structure more visible. When the same area of any two transforms is shaded in blue, the corresponding pixels within those areas are identical in value.

To compute the one-scale FWT of Fig. 7.30(b), the image in Fig. 7.30(a) is used as the input to a filter bank like that of Fig. 7.29(a). Since $J = \log_2 512 = 9$ and $P = 1, T_\varphi(9,k,l) = f(x,y)$ and the four resulting quarter-size decomposition outputs [i.e., approximation $T_\varphi(8,k,l)$ and horizontal, vertical, and diagonal details $T_\psi^H(8,k,l)$, $T_\psi^V(8,k,l)$, and $T_\psi^D(8,k,l)$] are then arranged in accordance with Fig. 7.29(b) to produce Fig. 7.30(b). A similar process is used to generate the two-scale transform in Fig. 7.30(c), but the input to the filter bank is a quarter-size approximation subimage $T_\varphi(8,k,l)$, from the upper left-hand corner of Fig. 7.30(b). As can be seen in Fig. 7.30(c), the quarter-size approximation subimage is then replaced by the four quarter-size (now 1/16th of the size of the original image) decomposition results that were generated by the second filtering pass. Each pass through the filter bank produces four quarter-size output images which are substituted for the input from which they were derived. The process is repeatable until $P = J = 9$, which produces a nine-scale transform.

Note the directional nature of the subimages associated with T_ψ^H, T_ψ^V, and T_ψ^D in Figs. 7.30(b) and (c). The diagonal details in these images (i.e., the T_ψ^D areas shaded in blue) are identical to the correspondingly shaded areas of the Haar transform in Fig. 7.30(d). In the 1-D case, as was demonstrated in Example 7.19, a J-scale 1-D FWT with respect to Haar basis functions is the same as its 1-D Haar transform counterpart. This is due to the fact that the basis functions of the two transforms are identical; both contain one scaling function and a series of scaled and translated wavelet functions. In the 2-D case, however, the basis images differ. The 2-D separable scaling and wavelet functions defined in Eqs. (7-153) through (7-155) introduce horizontal and vertical directionality that is not present in a traditional Haar transform. Figures 7.31(a) and (b), for example, are the basis images of an 8×8 Haar transform and three-scale FWT with respect to Haar basis functions. Note the blue highlighted regions along the main diagonals in which the basis images match. The same pattern occurs in Fig. 7.30(b) through (d). If a nine-scale wavelet transform of the vase were computed, it would match the Haar transform in Fig. 7.30(d) in all of its shaded areas.

a b
c d

FIGURE 7.30
(a) A 512×512 image of a vase; (b) a one-scale FWT; (c) a two-scale FWT; and (d) the Haar transform of the original image. All transforms have been scaled to highlight their underlying structure. When corresponding areas of two transforms are shaded in blue, the correspondent pixels are identical.

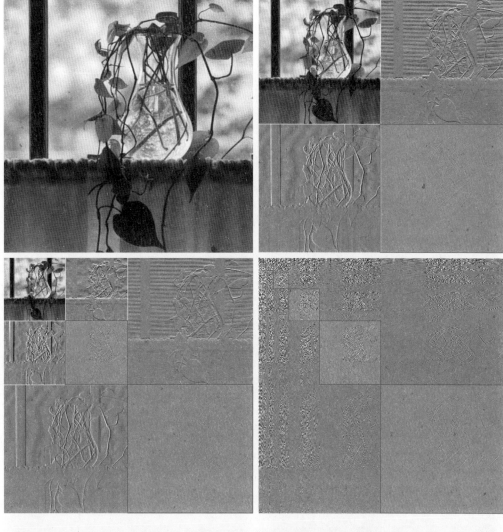

a b

FIGURE 7.31
(a) Haar basis images of size 8×8 [from Fig. 7.18(c)] and (b) the basis images of a three-scale 8×8 discrete wavelet transform with respect to Haar basis functions.

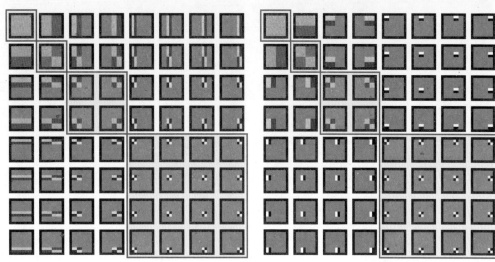

We conclude the section with a simple example that demonstrates the use of wavelets in image processing. As in the Fourier domain, the basic approach is to:

1. Compute the 2-D wavelet transform of an image with respect to a selected wavelet basis. Table 7.1 shows some representative bases, including their scaling and wavelet functions and corresponding filter coefficients. The filter coefficients are given in the context of Fig. 7.26. For orthonormal wavelets, lowpass synthesis coefficients are specified; the remaining filters must be computed using Eq. (7-151). For biorthonormal wavelets, two analysis filters are given and the synthesis filters must be computed using Eqs. (7-149) and (7-150).

2. Alter the computed transform to take advantage of the DWT's ability to (1) decorrelate image pixels, (2) reveal important frequency and temporal characteristics, and/or (3) measure the image's similarity to the transform's basis images. Modifications designed for image smoothing, sharpening, noise reduction, edge detection, and compression (to name only a few) are possible.

3. Compute the inverse wavelet transform.

Since the discrete wavelet transform decomposes an image into a weighted sum of spatially limited, bandlimited basis images, most Fourier-based imaging techniques have an equivalent "wavelet domain" counterpart.

EXAMPLE 7.23: Wavelet-based edge detection.

Figure 7.32 provides a simple illustration of the preceding three steps. Figure 7.32(a) shows a 128×128 computer-generated image of 2-D sine-shaped pulses on a black background. Figure 7.32(b) is the two-scale discrete wavelet transform of the image with respect to 4th-order *symlets*, short for "symmetrical wavelets." Although they are not perfectly symmetrical, they are designed to have the least asymmetry and highest number of *vanishing moments*[†] for a given compact support (Daubechies [1992]). Row 4 of Table 7.1 shows the wavelet and scaling functions of the symlets, as well as the coefficients of the corresponding lowpass synthesis filter. The remaining filter coefficients are obtained using Eq. (7-151) with K, the number of filter coefficients, set to 8:

$$g_1(n) = (-1)^n g_0(7-n) = \{-0.0758, 0.0296, 0.4976, -0.8037, 0.2979, 0.0992, -0.0126, -0.0322\}$$

$$h_0(n) = g_0(7-n) = \{-0.0758, -0.0296, 0.4976, 0.8037, 0.2979, -0.0992, -0.0126, 0.0322\}$$

$$h_1(n) = g_1(7-n) = \{-0.0322, -0.0126, 0.0992, 0.2979, -0.8037, 0.4976, 0.0296, -0.0758\}$$

In Fig. 7.32(c), the approximation component of the discrete wavelet transform has been eliminated by setting its values to zero. As Fig. 7.32(d) shows, the net effect of computing the inverse transform using these modified coefficients is edge enhancement, reminiscent of the Fourier-based image sharpening results discussed in Section 4.9. Note how well the transitions between signal and background are delineated, despite the fact that they are relatively soft, sinusoidal transitions. By zeroing the horizontal details as well—see Figs. 7.32(e) and (f)—we can isolate vertical edges.

[†]The kth moment of wavelet $\psi(x)$ is $m(k) = \int x^k \psi(x) dx$. Vanishing moments impact the smoothness of the scaling and wavelet functions and our ability to represent them as polynomials. An order-N symlet has N vanishing moments.

TABLE 7.1
Some representative wavelets.

Wavelet Name or Family	Scaling Function	Wavelet Function	Filter Coefficients
Haar The oldest and simplest wavelets. Orthogonal and discontinuous.			$g_0(n) = \left\{ 1/\sqrt{2},\ 1/\sqrt{2} \right\}$
Daubechies family Orthogonal with the most vanishing moments for a given support. Denoted db$N$, where N is the number of vanishing moments; db2 and db4 shown; db1 is the Haar of the previous row.			$g_0(n) = \{0.482963,$ $0.836516, 0.224144,$ $-0.129410\}$
			$g_0(n) = \{0.230372,$ $0.714847, 0.630881,$ $-0.027984,\ -0.187035,$ $0.030841, 0.032883,$ $-0.010597\}$
Symlet family Orthogonal with the least asymmetry and most vanishing moments for a given support (sym4 or 4th order shown).			$g_0(n) = \{0.032231,$ $-0.012604,\ -0.099220,$ $0.297858, 0.803739,$ $0.497619,\ -0.029636,$ $-0.075766\}$
Cohen-Daubechies-Feauveau 9/7 Biorthogonal B-spline used in the irreversible JPEG2000 compression standard (see Chapter 8).			$h_0(n) = \{0.026749,$ $-0.016864,\ -0.078223,$ $0.266864, 0.602949,$ $0.266864,\ -0.078223,$ $-0.016864, 0.026749\}$
			$h_1(n) = \{-0.091271,$ $-0.057544, 0.591272,$ $-1.115087, 0.591272,$ $0.057544,\ -0.091271, 0\}$

a b
c d
e f

FIGURE 7.32
Modifying a DWT for edge detection: (a) orginal image; (b) two-scale DWT with respect to 4th-order symlets; (c) modified DWT with the approximation set to zero; (d) the inverse DWT of (c); (e) modified DWT with the approximation and horizontal details set to zero; and (f) the inverse DWT of (e). (Note when the detail coefficients are zero, they are displayed as middle gray; when the approximation coefficients are zeroed, they display as black.)

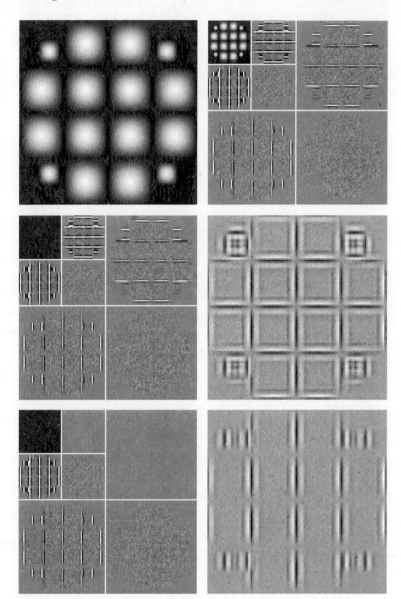

WAVELET PACKETS

A fast wavelet transform decomposes a function into a sum of scaling and wavelet functions whose bandwidths are logarithmically related. That is, the low-frequency content of the function is represented using scaling and wavelet functions with narrow bandwidths, while the high-frequency content is represented using functions with wider bandwidths. This is apparent in Fig. 6.5. Each horizontal strip of constant height tiles, which are the basis functions of a single FWT scale, increases logarithmically in height as you move up the frequency axis. To obtain greater control over the partitioning of the time-frequency plane (e.g., to get smaller bandwidths for higher frequencies), the FWT must be generalized to yield a more flexible decomposition called a *wavelet packet* (Coifman and Wickerhauser [1992]). The cost of this generalization is an increase in computational complexity from $O(N)$ for the FWT to $O(N \log_2 N)$ for a wavelet packet.

Consider again the three-scale filter bank of Fig. 7.24(a), but imagine the decomposition as a *binary tree*. Figure 7.33(a) details the structure of that tree, and links the appropriate FWT scaling and wavelet coefficients from Fig. 7.24(a) to the tree's *nodes*. The *root node* is assigned the highest-scale approximation coefficients, which are samples of the function itself, while the *leaves* inherit the transform's approximation and detail coefficient outputs. Two intermediate nodes, $T_\varphi(J-1,k)$ and $T_\varphi(J-2,k)$, are filter-bank approximations that are subsequently filtered to become four additional leaf nodes. Note the coefficients of each node are the weights of a linear expansion that produces a bandlimited "piece" of root node $f(x)$. Because any such piece is an element of a known scaling or wavelet subspace, we can replace the generating coefficients in Fig. 7.33(a) by the corresponding subspace. The result is the *subspace analysis tree* of Fig. 7.33(b).

Analysis trees provide a compact and informative way of representing multiscale wavelet transforms. They are simple to draw, take less space than their corresponding filter and subsampler-based block diagrams, and make it relatively easy to detect valid decompositions. The three-scale analysis tree of Fig. 7.33(b), for example, suggests three possible expansion options:

Recall that $\oplus$ denotes
the union of spaces (like
the union of sets). Equations (7-156) through
(7-158) can be derived by
the repeated application
of Eq. (7-128).

$$V_J = V_{J-1} \oplus W_{J-1} \qquad (7\text{-}156)$$

$$V_J = V_{J-2} \oplus W_{J-2} \oplus W_{J-1} \qquad (7\text{-}157)$$

$$V_J = V_{J-3} \oplus W_{J-3} \oplus W_{J-2} \oplus W_{J-1} \qquad (7\text{-}158)$$

They correspond to the one-, two-, and three-scale FWT decompositions of a 1-D function. A valid decomposition requires one approximation term (or scaling subspace) and enough detail components (or wavelet subspaces) to cover the spectrum of Fig. 7.24(b). In general, a P-scale FWT analysis tree supports P unique decompositions.

Analysis trees are also an efficient mechanism for representing wavelet packets, which are nothing more than conventional wavelet transforms with the details filtered iteratively. Thus, the three-scale FWT analysis tree of Fig. 7.33(b) becomes the

a b

FIGURE 7.33
An (a) coefficient tree and
(b) analysis tree
for the two-scale
FWT analysis
bank of Fig. 7.24.

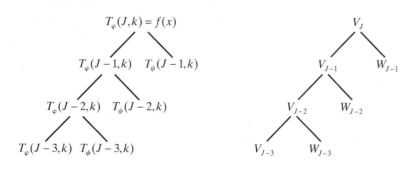

three-scale wavelet packet tree of Fig. 7.34. Note the additional subscripting that must be introduced. The first subscript of each double-subscripted node identifies the scale of the FWT parent node from which it is descended. The second, a variable length string of "A"s and "D"s, encodes the path from the parent node to the node being examined. An "A" designates approximation filtering, while a "D" indicates detail filtering. Subspace node $W_{J-1,\text{DA}}$, for example, is obtained by "filtering" the scale $J-1$ FWT coefficients (i.e., parent W_{J-1} in Fig. 7.34) through an additional detail filter (yielding $W_{J-1,\text{D}}$), followed by an approximation filter (giving $W_{J-1,\text{DA}}$). Figures 7.35(a) and (b) are the filter-bank and spectrum-splitting characteristics of the analysis tree in Fig. 7.34, respectively. Note the "naturally ordered" outputs of the filter bank in Fig. 7.35(a) have been reordered based on frequency content in Fig. 7.35(b) (see Problem 7.46 for more on "frequency ordered" wavelets).

The three-scale packet tree in Fig. 7.34 almost triples the number of decompositions (and associated time-frequency tilings) that are possible with the three-scale FWT tree. Recall that in a normal FWT, we split, filter, and downsample the lowpass bands alone. This creates a fixed logarithmic (base 2) relationship between the bandwidths of the scaling and wavelet spaces used in the representation of a function [see Figure 7.24(b)]. Thus, while the three-scale FWT analysis tree of Fig. 7.24(a) offers three possible decompositions—defined by Eqs. (7-156) to (7-158)—the wavelet packet tree of Fig. 7.34 supports 26 different decompositions. For instance, V_J and therefore function $f(x)$ can be expanded as

Recall that $\oplus$ denotes the union of spaces (like the union of sets). The 26 decompositions associated with Fig. 7.34 are determined by various combinations of nodes (spaces) that can be combined to represent the root node (space) at the top of the tree. Eqs. (7-159) and (7-160) define two of them.

$$V_J = V_{J-3} \oplus W_{J-3} \oplus W_{J-2,\text{A}} \oplus W_{J-2,\text{D}} \oplus W_{J-1,\text{AA}}$$
$$\oplus W_{J-1,\text{AD}} \oplus W_{J-1,\text{DA}} \oplus W_{J-1,\text{DD}} \tag{7-159}$$

whose spectrum is shown in Fig. 7.35(b), or as

$$V_J = V_{J-1} \oplus W_{J-1,\text{A}} \oplus W_{J-1,\text{DA}} \oplus W_{J-1,\text{DD}} \tag{7-160}$$

whose spectrum is depicted in Fig. 7.36. Note the difference between this last spectrum and the full packet spectrum of Fig. 7.35(b), or the three-scale FWT spectrum of

FIGURE 7.34
A three-scale wavelet packet analysis tree.

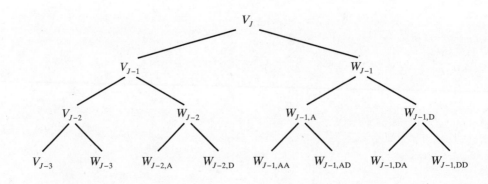

a
b

FIGURE 7.35
The (a) filter bank and (b) spectrum-splitting characteristics of a three-scale full wavelet packet analysis tree.

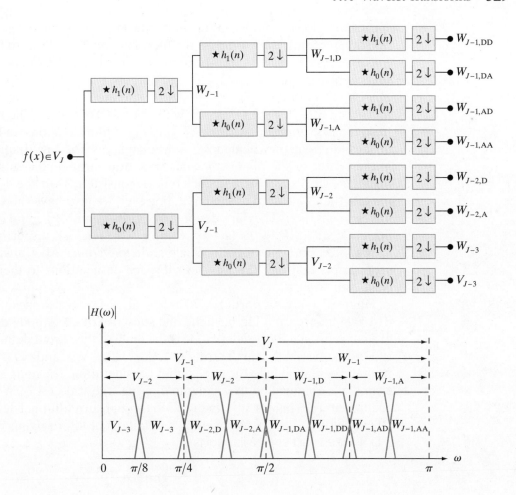

Fig. 7.24(b). In general, P-scale, 1-D wavelet packet transforms (and associated $P+1$-level analysis trees) support

$$D(P+1) = \left[D(P)\right]^2 + 1 \tag{7-161}$$

unique decompositions, where $D(1) = 1$. With such a large number of valid expansions, packet-based transforms provide improved control over the partitioning of the

FIGURE 7.36
The spectrum of the decomposition in Eq. (7-160).

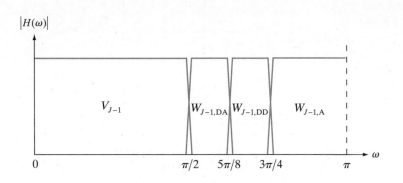

spectrum of the decomposed function. The cost of this control is an increase in computational complexity. Compare the filter bank in Fig. 7.35(a) to that of Fig. 7.24(a).

Now consider the 2-D, four-band filter bank of Fig. 7.29(a). As was noted earlier, it splits approximation $T_\varphi(j+1,k,l)$ into outputs $T_\varphi(j,k,l)$, $T_\psi^H(j,k,l)$, $T_\psi^V(j,k,l)$, and $T_\psi^D(j,k,l)$. As in the 1-D case, it can be "iterated" to generate P-scale transforms at scales $j = J-1, J-2, ..., J-P$, with $T_\varphi(J,k,l) = f(x,y)$. The spectrum resulting from the first iteration, with $j+1 = J$ in Fig. 7.29(a), is shown in Fig. 7.37(a). Note it divides the frequency plane into four equal areas. The low-frequency quarter-band in the center of the plane coincides with transform coefficients $T_\varphi(J-1,k,l)$ and scaling space V_{J-1}. This nomenclature is consistent with the 1-D case. To accommodate the 2-D nature of the input, however, we now have three (rather than one) wavelet subspaces. They are denoted W_{J-1}^H, W_{J-1}^V, and W_{J-1}^D and correspond to coefficients $T_\psi^H(J-1,k,l)$, $T_\psi^V(J-1,k,l)$, and $T_\psi^D(J-1,k,l)$, respectively. Figure 7.37(b) shows the resulting four-band, single-scale *quaternary FWT analysis tree*. Note the superscripts that link the wavelet subspace designations to their transform coefficient counterparts.

Figure 7.38 shows a portion of a three-scale, 2-D wavelet packet analysis tree. Like its 1-D counterpart in Fig. 6.34, the first subscript of every node that is a descendant of a conventional FWT detail node is the scale of the parent detail node. The second subscript, a variable length string of "A"s, "H"s, "V"s, and "D"s, encodes the path from the parent node to the node under consideration. The node labeled $W_{J-1,VD}^H$, for example, is obtained by "row/column filtering" the scale $J-1$ FWT horizontal detail coefficients (i.e., parent W_{J-1}^H in Fig. 7.38) through an additional detail/approximation filter (yielding $W_{J-1,V}^H$), followed by a detail/detail filter (giving $W_{J-1,VD}^H$). A P-scale, 2-D wavelet packet tree supports

$$D(P+1) = [D(P)]^4 + 1 \qquad (7\text{-}162)$$

unique expansions, where $D(1) = 1$. Thus, the three-scale tree of Fig. 7.38 offers 83,522 possible decompositions. The problem of selecting among them is the subject of the next example.

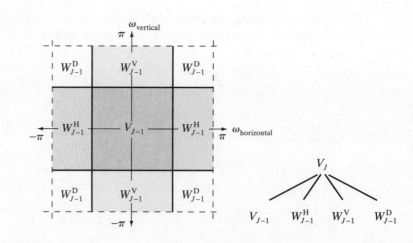

a b

FIGURE 7.37
The first decomposition of a 2-D FWT: (a) the spectrum and (b) the subspace analysis tree.

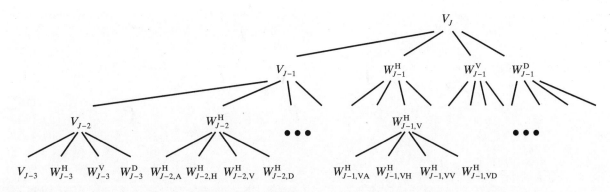

FIGURE 7.38 A three-scale, full wavelet packet decomposition tree. Only a portion of the tree is provided.

EXAMPLE 7.24: Two-dimensional wavelet packet decompositions.

As noted in the above discussion, a single wavelet packet tree presents numerous decomposition options. In fact, the number of possible decompositions is often so large that it is impractical, if not impossible, to enumerate or examine them individually. An efficient algorithm for finding optimal decompositions with respect to application specific criteria is highly desirable. As will be seen, classical *entropy-* and *energy-based cost functions* are applicable in many situations and are well-suited for use in binary and quaternary tree searching algorithms.

Consider the problem of reducing the amount of data needed to represent the 400×480 fingerprint image in Fig. 7.39(a). Image compression is discussed in detail in Chapter 8. In this example, we want to select the "best" three-scale wavelet packet decomposition as a starting point for the compression process. Using three-scale wavelet packet trees, there are 83,522 [per Eq. (7-162)] potential decompositions. Figure 7.39(b) shows one of them—a full wavelet packet, 64-leaf decomposition like the analysis tree of Fig. 7.38. Note the leaves of the tree correspond to the subbands of the 8×8 array of decomposed subimages in Fig. 7.39(b). The probability that this particular 64-leaf decomposition is in some way optimal for the purpose of compression, however, is relatively low. In the absence of a suitable optimality criterion, we can neither confirm nor deny it.

One reasonable criterion for selecting a decomposition for the compression of the image of Fig. 7.39(a) is the additive cost function

$$E(f) = \sum_{x,y} |f(x, y)| \tag{7-163}$$

This function provides one possible measure[†] of the energy content of 2-D function f. Under this measure, the energy of function $f(x, y) = 0$ for all x and y is 0. High values of E on the other hand, are indicative of functions with many nonzero values. Since most transform-based compression schemes work by truncating or thresholding the small coefficients to zero, a cost function that maximizes the number of near-zero values is a reasonable criterion for selecting a "good" decomposition from a compression point of view.

[†]Other possible energy measures include the sum of the squares of $f(x, y)$, the sum of the log of the squares, etc. Problem 7.48 defines one possible entropy-based cost function.

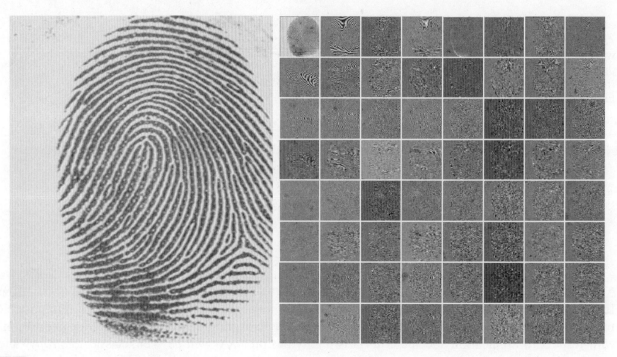

a b

FIGURE 7.39 (a) A scanned fingerprint and (b) its three-scale, full wavelet packet decomposition. Although the 64 subimages of the packet decomposition appear to be square (e.g., note the approximation subimage), this is merely an aberration of the program used to produce the result. (Original image courtesy of the National Institute of Standards and Technology.)

The cost function just described is both computationally simple and easily adapted to tree optimization routines. The optimization algorithm must use the function to minimize the "cost" of the leaf nodes in the decomposition tree. Minimal energy leaf nodes should be favored because they have more near-zero values, which leads to greater compression. Because the cost function of Eq. (7-163) is a local measure that uses only the information available at the node under consideration, an efficient algorithm for finding minimal energy solutions is easily constructed as follows:

For each node of the analysis tree, beginning with the root and proceeding level by level to the leaves:

1. Compute both the energy of the node, denoted E_P (for parent energy), and the energy of its four offspring—denoted as E_A, E_H, E_V, and E_D. For two-dimensional wavelet packet decompositions, the parent is a two-dimensional array of approximation or detail coefficients; the offspring are the filtered approximation, horizontal, vertical, and diagonal details.
2. If the combined energy of the offspring is less than the energy of the parent (that is, $E_A + E_H + E_V + E_D < E_P$), include the offspring in the analysis tree. If the combined energy of the offspring is greater than or equal to that of the parent, prune the offspring, keeping only the parent. It is a leaf of the optimized analysis tree.

The preceding algorithm can be used to (1) prune wavelet packet trees or (2) design procedures for computing optimal trees from scratch. In the latter case, nonessential siblings—descendants of nodes

FIGURE 7.40
An optimal
wavelet packet
decomposition for
the fingerprint of
Fig. 7.39(a).

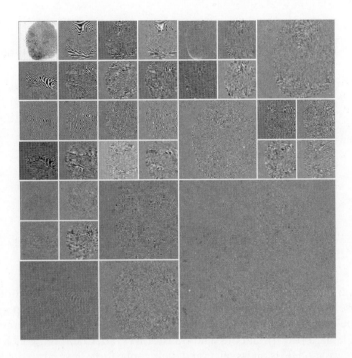

that would be eliminated in Step 2 of the algorithm—would not be computed. Figure 7.40 shows the optimized decomposition that results from applying the algorithm just described to the image of Fig. 7.39(a) with the cost function of Eq. (7-163). Note many of the original full packet decomposition's 64 subbands in Fig. 7.39(b) have been eliminated. In addition, the subimages that are not split (further decomposed) in Fig. 7.40 are relatively smooth and composed of pixels that are middle gray in value. Because all but the approximation subimage of this figure have been scaled so that gray level 128 indicates a zero-valued coefficient, these subimages contain little energy. There would be no overall decrease in energy realized by splitting them.

The preceding example is based on a real-world problem that was solved through the use of wavelets. The Federal Bureau of Investigation (FBI) currently maintains a large database of fingerprints, and has established a wavelet-based national standard for the digitization and compression of fingerprint images (FBI [1993]). Using Cohen-Daubechies-Feauveau (CDF) biorthogonal wavelets (Cohen, Daubechies, and Feauveau [1992]), the standard achieves a typical compression ratio of 15:1. Table 7.2 details the required analysis filter coefficients. Because the scaling and wavelet functions of the CDF family are symmetrical and have similar lengths, they are among the most widely used biorthogonal wavelets. The advantages of wavelet-based compression over the more traditional JPEG approach are examined in Chapter 8.

Summary, References, and Further Reading

The material in this chapter establishes a solid mathematical foundation for understanding and accessing the role of image transforms, including the discrete wavelet transform, in image processing. We approach transforms as series expansions in which the transform coefficients are inner products of a set of orthonormal or biorthonormal basis functions and the images being transformed. For many transforms, these inner products can be implemented

TABLE 7.2
Biorthogonal Cohen-Daubechies-Feauveau reconstruction and decomposition filter coefficients with 6 and 8 vanishing moments, respectively. (Cohen, Daubechies, and Feauveau [1992]).

n	$h_0(n)$	$h_1(n)$	n	$h_0(n)$	$h_1(n)$
0	0	0	9	0.825923	0.417849
1	0.001909	0	10	0.420796	0.040368
2	−0.001914	0	11	−0.094059	−0.078722
3	−0.016991	0.014427	12	−0.077263	−0.014468
4	0.011935	−0.014468	13	0.049733	0.0144263
5	0.049733	−0.078722	14	0.011935	0
6	−0.077263	0.040368	15	−0.016991	0
7	−0.094059	0.417849	16	−0.0019	0
8	0.420796	−0.758908	17	0.0019	0

as straightforward matrix operations. Further reading on the matrix formulation of image transforms is available in books like those of Andrews [1970] and Wang [2012], and in the original papers on the transforms themselves. See, for example, the original papers on the Haar transform (Haar [1910]), Walsh transform (Walsh [1923]), Hadamard transform (Hadamard [1893]), and the slant transform (Pratt, Chen, and Welch [1974]).

There are many good texts on wavelets and their application. Several complement our treatment and were relied upon during the development of the wavelet transform section of the chapter. Included among them are the books by Vetterli and Kovacevic [1995] and Burrus, Gopinath, and Guo [1998]. A partial listing of the imaging applications that have been approached from a wavelet point of view includes image matching, registration, segmentation, denoising, restoration, enhancement, compression (see Chapter 8), morphological filtering, and computed tomography. The history of wavelet analysis is recorded in a book by Hubbard [1998]. The early predecessors of wavelets were developed simultaneously in different fields and unified in a paper by Mallat [1987]. It brought a mathematical framework to the field. Much of the history of wavelets can be traced through the works of Meyer [1987] [1990] [1992a, 1992b] [1993], Mallat [1987] [1989a–c] [1998], and Daubechies [1988] [1990] [1992] [1993] [1996]. Finally, there have been a number of special issues devoted to wavelets, including a special issue on wavelet transforms and multiresolution signal anaysis in the *IEEE Transactions on Information Theory* [1992], a special issue on wavelets and signal processing in the *IEEE Transactions on Signal Processing* [1993], and a special section on multiresolution representation in the *IEEE Transactions on Pattern Analysis and Machine Intelligence* [1989]. All of the examples in the chapter were done using MATLAB (see Gonzalez et al. [2004]).

Problems

Solutions to the problems marked with an asterisk (*) are in the DIP4E Student Support Package (consult the book website: www.ImageProcessingPlace.com).

7.1   Given column vectors

$$s_0 = \begin{bmatrix} 1 \\ \sqrt{2} \\ 1 \end{bmatrix} \quad s_1 = \begin{bmatrix} 1 \\ 0 \\ -1 \end{bmatrix} \quad s_2 = \begin{bmatrix} 1 \\ -\sqrt{2} \\ 1 \end{bmatrix}$$

   (a) Prove that s_0, s_1, and s_2 are orthogonal.

   (b)*Are they orthonormal? If not, normalize them to create a transformation matrix of orthonormal vectors.

   (c) Using the result of (b), write an orthogonal transformation matrix for s_0, s_1, and s_2.

   (d) Compute the transform of column vector $\mathbf{f} = \begin{bmatrix} 1 & -\sqrt{2} & 2 \end{bmatrix}$.

   (e) Compute the inverse transform of the result in (d).

7.2   Prove that Eqs. (7-28) and (7-29) are a reversible transform pair.

7.3* Prove that $r(x,u) = s(x,u)$ in Eqs. (7-16) and (7-17) for real, orthonormal basis vectors.

7.4 Prove that if $\mathbf{A}^{*T}\mathbf{A} = \mathbf{I}$, the associated expansion functions are orthonormal.

7.5 Prove that matrix $\mathbf{A}_3$ in Example 7.3 is an orthogonal transformation matrix.

7.6 Describe an important property of an orthogonal transform.

7.7 Using Eqs. (7-4) and (7-5),

(a) Find the norm of $\mathbf{f} = \begin{bmatrix} 3+j2 & 1-j \end{bmatrix}^T$.

(b) Find the norm of $\mathbf{g} = \begin{bmatrix} 0.707 & -0.707 \end{bmatrix}^T$.

(c) Find the angle between $\mathbf{h} = \begin{bmatrix} 0.707 & 0.707 \end{bmatrix}^T$ and $\mathbf{g}$.

(d)* Find the norm of $f(x) = \cos x$.

(e) Find the angle between f from (d) and $g(x) = \sin x$.

(f) Are f and g orthogonal to one another?

(g) Are f and g orthonormal?

7.8 Using the results from Problem 7.1(c)–(e) and column vector $\mathbf{g} = \begin{bmatrix} 2 & \sqrt{2} & 1 \end{bmatrix}$:

(a) Compute the angle between $\mathbf{f}$ and $\mathbf{g}$.

(b) Compute the distance between f and g. *Hint:* The distance between vectors f and g is

$$d = \sqrt{\langle \mathbf{f} - \mathbf{g}, \mathbf{f} - \mathbf{g} \rangle}$$

(c)* Show that angles and distances are preserved by this orthogonal transform

7.9 Compute the inverse transform of $\mathbf{T}$ in Example 7.3.

7.10 Prove that the set of sinusoidal expansion functions $\{1, \cos x, \sin x, \cos 2x, \sin 2x, \ldots\}$ are orthogonal on the interval $[-\pi, \pi]$.

7.11 Compute the expansion coefficients of 2-tuple $[3\ 2]^T$ and write the corresponding expansions for the following bases:

(a)* $\mathbf{s}_0 = \begin{bmatrix} 0.707 & 0.707 \end{bmatrix}^T$, $\mathbf{s}_1 = \begin{bmatrix} 0.707 & -0.707 \end{bmatrix}^T$ on the set of real 2-tuples.

(b) $\mathbf{s}_0 = \begin{bmatrix} 1 & 0 \end{bmatrix}^T$, $\mathbf{s}_1 = \begin{bmatrix} 1 & 1 \end{bmatrix}^T$ and the dual vectors on the set of real 2-tuples.

7.12 Are expansion functions

$$\mathbf{s}_0 = \begin{bmatrix} 0 \\ 1 \\ 0 \\ 0 \end{bmatrix} \quad \mathbf{s}_1 = \begin{bmatrix} 0 \\ 0 \\ 0 \\ 1 \end{bmatrix} \quad \mathbf{s}_2 = \begin{bmatrix} 1 \\ 0 \\ 0 \\ 0 \end{bmatrix} \quad \mathbf{s}_3 = \begin{bmatrix} 0 \\ 0 \\ 1 \\ 0 \end{bmatrix}$$

orthonormal? If so, write the corresponding orthogonal transformation matrix.

7.13 If $\mathbf{f} = \begin{bmatrix} 1 & -3 & 2 & 4 \end{bmatrix}^T$, find the transform of $\mathbf{f}$ using the transformation matrix of Problem 7.12. Then compute the inverse and show that the transform is reversable.

7.14 Given the 2-D matrix

$$\mathbf{F} = \begin{bmatrix} 1 & -1 & 1 & 2 \\ -3 & 1 & 5 & -4 \\ 2 & -1 & 8 & 3 \\ 4 & -2 & 3 & -1 \end{bmatrix}$$

(a) Compute the transform of $\mathbf{F}$ with respect to the transformation matrix of Problem 7.12.

(b)* Explain how 2-D transform is broken into two 1-D transforms while computing the transform.

(c) Compute the 2-D inverse transform of the result from (a).

7.15 Prove that expansion functions

$$\mathbf{u}_0 = \begin{bmatrix} \sqrt{2}/2 \\ \sqrt{2}/2 \end{bmatrix} \quad \mathbf{u}_1 = \begin{bmatrix} -1 \\ 0.5 \end{bmatrix}$$

$$\tilde{\mathbf{u}}_0 = \begin{bmatrix} \sqrt{2}/3 \\ 2\sqrt{2}/3 \end{bmatrix} \quad \tilde{\mathbf{u}}_1 = \begin{bmatrix} -2/3 \\ 2/3 \end{bmatrix}$$

are biorthonormal. Then show by example whether inner products, angles, and distances are preserved by the transform.

7.16 Prove that $\mathbf{A}$ and $\tilde{\mathbf{A}}$ in Example 7.5 are biorthonormal.

(a) Using biorthonormal matrices $\mathbf{A}$ and $\tilde{\mathbf{A}}$ of Example 7.5, compute the transform of 4×4 array

$$\mathbf{F} = \begin{bmatrix} 16 & 5 & 9 & 4 \\ 2 & 11 & 7 & 14 \\ 3 & 10 & 6 & 15 \\ 13 & 8 & 12 & 1 \end{bmatrix}$$

(b) Compute the inverse transform of the result in (a).

7.17* Mention three Fourier-related transforms that are real rather than complex-valued.

7.18 Write a pair of 2-D transform matrix equations for complex biorthonormal expansion functions.

7.19 Using Eqs. (7-55) and (7-58) of Example 7.6, compute the Fourier series of $f(x) = \sin(2\pi x)$ of period $T = 1$.

7.20* Prove that the DFT expansion functions of Eq. (7-56) are orthonormal.

7.21 Prove Eq. (7-52).

7.22 Beginning with a series expansion of the expansion functions defined in Eq. (7-56), derive an expression for the discrete Fourier transform.

7.23 Given standard basis vectors $e_0 = \begin{bmatrix} 1 & 0 \end{bmatrix}^T$ and $e_1 = \begin{bmatrix} 0 & 1 \end{bmatrix}^T$ of inner product space $\mathbf{R}^2$ and an arbitrary vector r of length r and angle θ, compute the single-point cross-correlation of r with both e_0 and e_1. When does r resemble e_0 more than e_1 and vice versa?

7.24* Prove that the Fourier transform of time-scaled wavelet $\psi(2^s t)$ is given by Eq. (7-73).

7.25 Prove Eq. (7-80).

7.26 Compute the Haar transform of the 2×2 image

$$\begin{bmatrix} 2 & -3 \\ 5 & 4 \end{bmatrix}$$

7.27 Write a pair of discrete cosine transform equations of the form given in Eqs. (7-57) and (7-58) for the discrete Fouier transform.

7.28 Because the 2-D discrete cosine transform is separable, the 2-D DCT of an image can be computed by row and column passes with a 1-D DCT algorithm. In fact, an interesting property of the 1-D DCT is that it can be computed by using the FFT algorithm. Show in detail how this computation can be made.

7.29 Do the following:

(a) Compute the Fourier, sine, cosine and Hartley transformation matrices of size $N = 6$.

(b) Compute the Hartley transform of the discrete function $f(x) = \{-2, -5, -3, 1, 0, 3\}$ using Eq. (7-28).

(c) Compute the Hartley transform of the function in (b) from its discrete Fourier transform. Is it equal to the result in (b)?

(d) Use Eqs. (7-86) through (7-89) to compute the DCT of $f(x) = [3, -6, 1]$.

(e) Use Eq. (7-28) to compute the DST of the function in (b).

7.30 Compute the basis images of the Haar transform for $N = 2$.

7.31 Create a table mapping the rows of Hadamard-ordered transformation matrix $\mathbf{H}_{16}$ to sequency-ordered Hadamard transformation matrix $\mathbf{H}'_{16}$.

7.32 Obtain the Harr transformation matrix for $N = 8$.

7.33 Derive the Haar scaling coefficients from Eqs. (7-122) and (7-126).

7.34 Show that scaling function

$$\varphi(x) = \begin{cases} 1 & 0.25 \le x < 0.75 \\ 0 & \text{elsewhere} \end{cases}$$

does not satisfy the second requirement of a multiresolution analysis.

7.35* Derive Eq. (7-140).

7.36 Write an expression for scaling space V_3 as a function of scaling function $\varphi(x)$. Use the Haar scaling function definition of Eq. (7-122) to draw the Haar V_3 scaling functions at translations $k = \{0,1,2\}$.

7.37* Draw wavelet $\psi_{3,3}(x)$ for the Haar wavelet function. Write an expression for $\psi_{3,3}(x)$ in terms of Haar scaling functions.

7.38 Suppose function $f(x)$ is a member of Haar scaling space V_3—that is, $f(x) \in V_3$. Use Eq. (7-128) to express V_3 as a function of scaling space V_0 and any required wavelet spaces. If $f(x)$ is 0 outside the interval $[0, 1)$, sketch the scaling and wavelet functions required for a linear expansion of $f(x)$ based on your expression.

7.39 Compute the first four terms of the wavelet series expansion of the function used in Example 7.18 with starting scale $j_0 = 1$. Write the resulting expansion in terms of the scaling and wavelet functions involved. How does your result compare to the example, where the starting scale was $j_0 = 0$?

7.40 The DWT in Eqs. (7-137) and (7-138) is for a starting scale $j_0 = 0$.

    (a)* Rewrite these equations for any starting scale $j_0 \leq J$.

    (b) Recompute the 1-D DWT of function $f(x) = \{1, 4, -3, 0\}$ for $0 \leq x \leq 3$ in Example 7.19 with $j_0 = 1$ (rather than 0).

    (c) Use the result from (b) to compute $f(1)$ from the transform values.

7.41* Draw the FWT filter bank required to compute the transform in Problem 7.40. Label all inputs and outputs with the appropriate sequences.

7.42 What is the computational complexity of an N-point fast wavelet transform?

7.43 Answer the following:

    (a)* If the input to the three-scale FWT filter bank of Fig. 7.24(a) is the Haar scaling function $\varphi(x) = 1$ for $n = 0, 1, \ldots, 7$ and 0 elsewhere, what is the resulting transform with respect to Haar wavelets?

    (b) What is the transform if the input is the corresponding Haar wavelet function $\psi(x) = \{1, 1, 1, 1, -1, -1, -1, -1\}$ for $n = 0, 1, \ldots, 7$?

    (c) What input sequence produces transform $\{1, 0, 0, 0, 0, 0, B, 0\}$ with nonzero coefficient $T_\psi(2,2) = B$?

7.44 Compute the 2-D wavelet transform with respect to Haar wavelets of the 2×2 image

$$\begin{bmatrix} 3 & -1 \\ 6 & 2 \end{bmatrix}$$

Draw the required filter bank and label all inputs and outputs with the proper arrays.

7.45* In the Fourier domain

$$f(x - x_0, y - y_0) \Leftrightarrow F(u,v)e^{-2\pi(ux_0/M + vy_0/N)}$$

and translation does not affect the display of $|F(u,v)|$. Using the following sequence of images, explain the translation property of wavelet transforms. The top left image contains two 32×32 white squares centered on a 128×128 gray background. The top right image is its single-scale wavelet transform with respect to Haar wavelets. The bottom left image is the wavelet transform of the original image after shifting its 32 pixels to the right and downward, and the final (bottom right) image is the wavelet transform of the original image after it has been shifted one pixel to the right and downward.

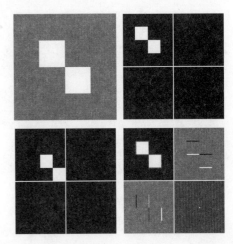

7.46 The following table shows the Haar wavelet and scaling functions for a four-scale fast wavelet transform. Sketch the additional basis functions needed for a full three-scale packet decomposition. Give the mathematical expression or expressions for determining them. Then order the basis functions according to frequency content and explain the results.

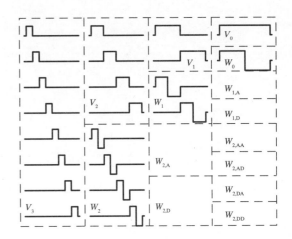

7.47 A wavelet packet decomposition of the vase from Fig. 7.30(a) is shown below.

(a) Draw the corresponding decomposition analysis tree, labeling all nodes with the names of the proper scaling and wavelet spaces.

(b) Draw and label the decomposition's frequency spectrum.

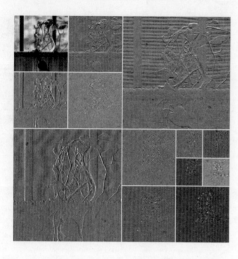

7.48 Using the Haar wavelet, determine the minimum entropy packet decomposition for the function for $f(x) = 0.25$ for $n = 0, 1, \ldots, 15$. Employ the nonnormalized Shannon entropy

$$E[f(x)] = \sum_x f^2(x)\ln\left[f^2(x)\right]$$

as the minimization criterion. Draw the optimal tree, labeling the nodes with the computed entropy values.

8 Image Compression and Watermarking

> But life is short and information endless ... Abbreviation is a
> necessary evil and the abbreviator's business is to make the best of
> a job which, although bad, is still better than nothing.
>
> *Aldous Huxley*
>
> The Titanic will protect itself.
>
> *Robert Ballard*

Preview

Image compression, the art and science of reducing the amount of data required to represent an image, is one of the most useful and commercially successful technologies in the field of digital image processing. The number of images that are compressed and decompressed daily is staggering, and the compressions and decompressions themselves are virtually invisible to the user. Everyone who owns a digital camera, surfs the web, or streams the latest Hollywood movies over the Internet benefits from the algorithms and standards that will be discussed in this chapter. The material, which is largely introductory in nature, is applicable to both still-image and video applications. We will introduce both theory and practice, examining the most frequently used compression techniques, and describing the industry standards that make them useful. The chapter concludes with an introduction to *digital image watermarking*, the process of inserting visible and invisible data (such as copyright information) into images.

Upon competion of this chapter, students should:

- Be able to measure the amount of information in a digital image.

- Understand the main sources of data redundancy in digital images.

- Know the difference between lossy and error-free compression, and the amount of compression that is possible with each.

- Be familiar with the popular image compression standards, such as JPEG and JPEG-2000, that are in use today.

- Understand the principal image compression methods, and how and why they work.

- Be able to compress and decompress grayscale, color, and video imagery.

- Know the differencc between visible, invisible, robust, fragile, public, private, restricted-key, and unrestricted-key watermarks.

- Understand the basics of watermark insertion and extraction in both the spatial and transform domain.

8.1 FUNDAMENTALS

The term *data compression* refers to the process of reducing the amount of data required to represent a given quantity of information. In this definition, *data* and *information* are not the same; data are the means by which information is conveyed. Because various amounts of data can be used to represent the same amount of information, representations that contain irrelevant or repeated information are said to contain *redundant data*. If we let b and b' denote the number of bits (or information-carrying units) in two representations of the same information, the *relative data redundancy*, R, of the representation with b bits is

$$R = 1 - \frac{1}{C} \tag{8-1}$$

where C, commonly called the *compression ratio*, is defined as

$$C = \frac{b}{b'} \tag{8-2}$$

If $C = 10$ (sometimes written 10:1), for instance, the larger representation has 10 bits of data for every 1 bit of data in the smaller representation. The corresponding relative data redundancy of the larger representation is 0.9 ($R = 0.9$), indicating that 90% of its data is redundant.

In the context of digital image compression, b in Eq. (8-2) usually is the number of bits needed to represent an image as a 2-D array of intensity values. The 2-D intensity arrays introduced in Section 2.4 are the preferred formats for human viewing and interpretation—and the standard by which all other representations are judged. When it comes to compact image representation, however, these formats are far from optimal. Two-dimensional intensity arrays suffer from three principal types of data redundancies that can be identified and exploited:

1. *Coding redundancy.* A code is a system of symbols (letters, numbers, bits, and the like) used to represent a body of information or set of events. Each piece of information or event is assigned a sequence of *code symbols*, called a *code word*. The number of symbols in each code word is its *length*. The 8-bit codes that are used to represent the intensities in most 2-D intensity arrays contain more bits than are needed to represent the intensities.

2. *Spatial* and *temporal redundancy.* Because the pixels of most 2-D intensity arrays are correlated spatially (i.e., each pixel is similar to or dependent upon neighboring pixels), information is unnecessarily replicated in the representations of the correlated pixels. In a video sequence, temporally correlated pixels (i.e., those similar to or dependent upon pixels in nearby frames) also duplicate information.

3. *Irrelevant information.* Most 2-D intensity arrays contain information that is ignored by the human visual system and/or extraneous to the intended use of the image. It is redundant in the sense that it is not used.

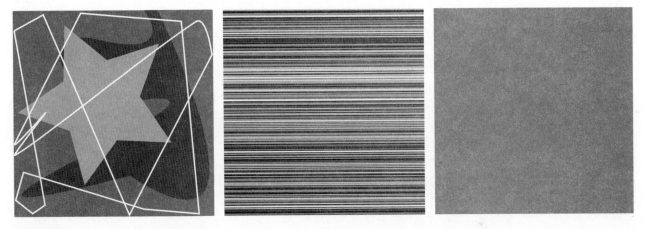

a b c

FIGURE 8.1 Computer generated $256 \times 256 \times 8$ bit images with (a) coding redundancy, (b) spatial redundancy, and (c) irrelevant information. (Each was designed to demonstrate one principal redundancy, but may exhibit others as well.)

The computer-generated images in Figs. 8.1(a) through (c) exhibit each of these fundamental redundancies. As will be seen in the next three sections, compression is achieved when one or more redundancy is reduced or eliminated.

CODING REDUNDANCY

In Chapter 3, we developed techniques for image enhancement by histogram processing, assuming that the intensity values of an image are random quantities. In this section, we will use a similar formulation to introduce optimal information coding.

Assume that a discrete random variable r_k in the interval $[0, L-1]$ is used to represent the intensities of an $M \times N$ image, and that each r_k occurs with probability $p_r(r_k)$. As in Section 3.3,

$$p_r(r_k) = \frac{n_k}{MN} \qquad k = 0, 1, 2, \ldots, L-1 \tag{8-3}$$

where L is the number of intensity values, and n_k is the number of times that the kth intensity appears in the image. If the number of bits used to represent each value of r_k is $l(r_k)$, then the average number of bits required to represent each pixel is

$$L_{\text{avg}} = \sum_{k=0}^{L-1} l(r_k) p_r(r_k) \tag{8-4}$$

That is, the average length of the code words assigned to the various intensity values is found by summing the products of the number of bits used to represent each intensity and the probability that the intensity occurs. The total number of bits required to represent an $M \times N$ image is MNL_{avg}. If the intensities are represented using a *natural m*-bit fixed-length code,[†] the right-hand side of Eq. (8-4) reduces to *m* bits. That is, $L_{avg} = m$ when *m* is substituted for $l(r_k)$. The constant *m* can be taken outside the summation, leaving only the sum of the $p_r(r_k)$ for $0 \leq k \leq L-1$, which, of course, equals 1.

The computer-generated image in Fig. 8.1(a) has the intensity distribution shown in the second column of Table 8.1. If a natural 8-bit binary code (denoted as code 1 in Table 8.1) is used to represent its four possible intensities, L_{avg} (the average number of bits for code 1) is 8 bits, because $l_1(r_k) = 8$ bits for all r_k. On the other hand, if the scheme designated as code 2 in Table 8.1 is used, the average length of the encoded pixels is, in accordance with Eq. (8-4),

$$L_{avg} = 0.25(2) + 0.47(1) + 0.03(3) = 1.81 \text{ bits}$$

The total number of bits needed to represent the entire image is $MNL_{avg} = 256 \times 56 \times 1.81$, or 118,621. From Eqs. (8-2) and (8-1), the resulting compression and corresponding relative redundancy are

$$C = \frac{256 \times 256 \times 8}{118,621} = \frac{8}{1.81} \approx 4.42$$

and

$$R = 1 - \frac{1}{4.42} = 0.774$$

respectively. Thus, 77.4% of the data in the original 8-bit 2-D intensity array is redundant.

The compression achieved by code 2 results from assigning fewer bits to the more probable intensity values than to the less probable ones. In the resulting *variable-length code*, r_{128} (the image's most probable intensity) is assigned the 1-bit code word 1 [of length $l_2(128) = 1$],while r_{255} (its least probable occurring intensity) is assigned the 3-bit code word 001 [of length $l_2(255) = 3$]. Note that the best *fixed-length code* that can be assigned to the intensities of the image in Fig. 8.1(a) is the natural 2-bit counting sequence $\{00,01,10,11\}$, but the resulting compression is only 8/2 or 4:1—about 10% less than the 4.42:1 compression of the variable-length code.

As the preceding example shows, *coding redundancy* is present when the codes assigned to a set of events (such as intensity values) do not take full advantage of the probabilities of the events. Coding redundancy is almost always present when the intensities of an image are represented using a natural binary code. The reason is that most images are composed of objects that have a regular and somewhat predictable morphology (shape) and reflectance, and are sampled so the objects being depicted are much larger than the picture elements. The natural consequence is that,

---

[†] A *natural* binary code is one in which each event or piece of information to be encoded (such as intensity value) is assigned one of 2^m codes from an *m*-bit binary counting sequence.

TABLE 8.1
Example of
variable-length
coding.

r_k	$p_r(r_k)$	Code 1	$l_1(r_k)$	Code 2	$l_2(r_k)$
$r_{87} = 87$	0.25	01010111	8	01	2
$r_{128} = 128$	0.47	01010111	8	1	1
$r_{186} = 186$	0.25	01010111	8	000	3
$r_{255} = 255$	0.03	01010111	8	001	3
r_k for $k = 87, 128, 186, 255$	0	—	8	—	0

for most images, certain intensities are more probable than others (that is, the histograms of most images are not uniform). A natural binary encoding assigns the same number of bits to both the most and least probable values, failing to minimize Eq. (8-4), and resulting in coding redundancy.

SPATIAL AND TEMPORAL REDUNDANCY

Consider the computer-generated collection of constant intensity lines in Fig. 8.1(b). In the corresponding 2-D intensity array:

1. All 256 intensities are equally probable. As Fig. 8.2 shows, the histogram of the image is uniform.
2. Because the intensity of each line was selected randomly, its pixels are independent of one another in the vertical direction.
3. Because the pixels along each line are identical, they are maximally correlated (completely dependent on one another) in the horizontal direction.

The first observation tells us that the image in Fig. 8.1(b) (when represented as a conventional 8-bit intensity array) cannot be compressed by variable-length coding alone. Unlike the image of Fig. 8.1(a) and Example 8.1, whose histogram was *not* uniform, a fixed-length 8-bit code in this case minimizes Eq. (8-4). Observations 2 and 3 reveal a significant spatial redundancy that can be eliminated by representing the image in Fig. 8.1(b) as a sequence of *run-length pairs*, where each run-length pair specifies the start of a new intensity and the number of consecutive pixels that have that intensity. A run-length based representation compresses the original 2-D, 8-bit

FIGURE 8.2
The intensity
histogram of the
image in
Fig. 8.1(b).

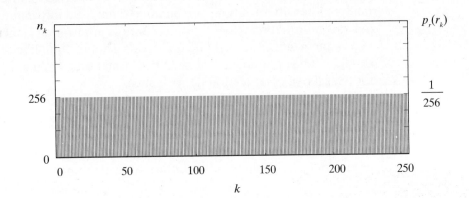

intensity array by $(256 \times 256 \times 8)/[(256 + 256) \times 8]$ or 128:1. Each 256-pixel line of the original representation is replaced by a single 8-bit intensity value and length 256 in the run-length representation.

In most images, pixels are correlated spatially (in both x and y) and in time (when the image is part of a video sequence). Because most pixel intensities can be predicted reasonably well from neighboring intensities, the information carried by a single pixel is small. Much of its visual contribution is redundant in the sense that it can be inferred from its neighbors. To reduce the redundancy associated with spatially and temporally correlated pixels, a 2-D intensity array must be transformed into a more efficient but usually "non-visual" representation. For example, run-lengths or the differences between adjacent pixels can be used. Transformations of this type are called *mappings*. A mapping is said to be *reversible* if the pixels of the original 2-D intensity array can be reconstructed without error from the transformed data set; otherwise, the mapping is said to be *irreversible*.

IRRELEVANT INFORMATION

One of the simplest ways to compress a set of data is to remove superfluous data from the set. In the context of digital image compression, information that is ignored by the human visual system, or is extraneous to the intended use of an image, are obvious candidates for omission. Thus, the computer-generated image in Fig. 8.1(c), because it appears to be a homogeneous field of gray, can be represented by its average intensity alone—a single 8-bit value. The original $256 \times 256 \times 8$ bit intensity array is reduced to a single byte, and the resulting compression is $(256 \times 256 \times 8)/8$ or 65,536:1. Of course, the original $256 \times 256 \times 8$ bit image must be recreated to view and/or analyze it, but there would be little or no perceived decrease in reconstructed image quality.

Figure 8.3(a) shows the histogram of the image in Fig. 8.1(c). Note that there are several intensity values (125 through 131) actually present. The human visual system averages these intensities, perceives only the average value, then ignores the small changes in intensity that are present in this case. Figure 8.3(b), a histogram-equalized version of the image in Fig. 8.1(c), makes the intensity changes visible *and* reveals two previously undetected regions of constant intensity—one oriented vertically, and the other horizontally. If the image in Fig. 8.1(c) is represented by its average value alone, this "invisible" structure (i.e., the constant intensity regions) and the random intensity variations surrounding them (real information) is lost. Whether or not this information should be preserved is application dependent. If the information is important, as it might be in a medical application like digital X-ray archival, it should not be omitted; otherwise, the information is redundant and can be excluded for the sake of compression performance.

We conclude this section by noting that the redundancy examined here is fundamentally different from the redundancies discussed in the previous two sections. Its elimination is possible because the information itself is not essential for normal visual processing and/or the intended use of the image. Because its omission results in a loss of quantitative information, its removal is commonly referred to as

a b

FIGURE 8.3
(a) Histogram
of the image in
Fig. 8.1(c) and
(b) a histogram
equalized version
of the image.

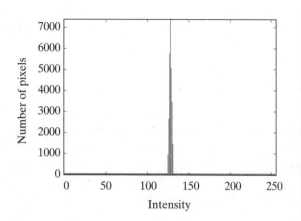

quantization. This terminology is consistent with normal use of the word, which generally means the mapping of a broad range of input values to a limited number of output values (see Section 2.4). Because information is lost, quantization is an irreversible operation.

MEASURING IMAGE INFORMATION

Consult the book website for a brief review of information and probability theory.

In the previous sections, we introduced several ways to reduce the amount of data used to represent an image. The question that naturally arises is: How few bits are actually needed to represent the information in an image? That is, is there a minimum amount of data that is sufficient to describe an image without losing information? *Information theory* provides the mathematical framework to answer this and related questions. Its fundamental premise is that the generation of information can be modeled as a probabilistic process which can be measured in a manner that agrees with intuition. In accordance with this supposition, a random event E with probability $P(E)$ is said to contain

$$I(E) = \log \frac{1}{P(E)} = -\log P(E) \tag{8-5}$$

units of information. If $P(E) = 1$ (that is, the event always occurs), $I(E) = 0$ and no information is attributed to it. Because no uncertainty is associated with the event, no information would be transferred by communicating that the event has occurred [it *always* occurs if $P(E) = 1$].

The base of the logarithm in Eq. (8-5) determines the unit used to measure information. If the base m logarithm is used, the measurement is said to be in m-ary units. If the base 2 is selected, the unit of information is the *bit*. Note that if $P(E) = \frac{1}{2}$, $I(E) = -\log_2 \frac{1}{2}$ or 1 bit. That is, 1 bit is the amount of information conveyed when one of two possible equally likely events occurs. A simple example is flipping a coin and communicating the result.

Given a source of statistically independent random events from a discrete set of possible events $\{a_1, a_1, \ldots, a_J\}$ with associated probabilities $\{P(a_1), P(a_1), \ldots, P(a_J)\}$, the average information per source output, called the *entropy* of the source, is

$$H = -\sum_{j=1}^{J} P(a_j) \log P(a_j) \tag{8-6}$$

The a_j in this equation are called *source symbols*. Because they are statistically independent, the source itself is called a *zero-memory source*.

If an image is considered to be the output of an imaginary zero-memory "intensity source," we can use the histogram of the observed image to estimate the symbol probabilities of the source. Then, the intensity source's entropy becomes

Equation (8-6) is for zero-memory sources with J source symbols. Equation (8-7) uses probablitiy estimates for the $L-1$ intensity values in an image.

$$\tilde{H} = -\sum_{k=0}^{L-1} p_r(r_k) \log_2 p_r(r_k) \tag{8-7}$$

where variables L, r_k, and $p_r(r_k)$ are as defined earlier and in Section 3.3. Because the base 2 logarithm is used, Eq. (8-7) is the average information per intensity output of the imaginary intensity source in bits. It is not possible to code the *intensity values* of the imaginary source (and thus the sample image) with fewer than $\tilde{H}$ bits/pixel.

EXAMPLE 8.2:   Image entropy estimates.

The entropy of the image in Fig. 8.1(a) can be estimated by substituting the intensity probabilities from Table 8.1 into Eq. (8-7):

$$\begin{aligned}
\tilde{H} &= -[0.25\log_2 0.25 + 0.47\log_2 0.47 + 0.25\log_2 0.25 + 0.03\log_2 0.03] \\
&= -[0.25(-2) + 0.47(-1.09) + 0.25(-2) + 0.03(-5.06)] \\
&\approx 1.6614 \text{ bits/pixel}
\end{aligned}$$

In a similar manner, the entropies of the images in Fig. 8.1(b) and (c) can be shown to be 8 bits/pixel and 1.566 bits/pixel, respectively. Note that the image in Fig. 8.1(a) appears to have the most visual information, but has almost the lowest computed entropy — 1.66 bits/pixel. The image in Fig. 8.1(b) has almost five times the entropy of the image in (a), but appears to have about the same (or less) visual information. The image in Fig. 8.1(c), which seems to have little or no information, has almost the same entropy as the image in (a). The obvious conclusion is that the amount of entropy, and thus information in an image, is far from intuitive.

Shannon's First Theorem

Recall that the variable-length code in Example 8.1 was able to represent the intensities of the image in Fig. 8.1(a) using only 1.81 bits/pixel. Although this is higher than the 1.6614 bits/pixel entropy estimate from Example 8.2, Shannon's first theorem, also called the *noiseless coding theorem* (Shannon [1948]), assures us that the image in Fig. 8.1(a) can be represented with as few as 1.6614 bits/pixel. To prove it in a general way, Shannon looked at representing groups of consecutive source symbols with a single code word (rather than one code word per source symbol), and showed that

$$\lim_{n \to \infty} \left[\frac{L_{avg,n}}{n} \right] = H \tag{8-8}$$

where $L_{avg,n}$ is the average number of code symbols required to represent all n-symbol groups. In the proof, he defined the *nth extension* of a zero-memory source to be the hypothetical source that produces n-symbol blocks[†] using the symbols of the original source, and computed $L_{avg,n}$ by applying Eq. (8-4) to the code words used to represent the n-symbol blocks. Equation (8-8) tells us that $L_{avg,n}/n$ can be made arbitrarily close to H by encoding infinitely long extensions of the single-symbol source. That is, it is possible to represent the output of a zero-memory source with an average of H information units per source symbol.

If we now return to the idea that an image is a "sample" of the intensity source that produced it, a block of n source symbols corresponds to a group of n adjacent pixels. To construct a variable-length code for n-pixel blocks, the relative frequencies of the blocks must be computed. But the nth extension of a hypothetical intensity source with 256 intensity values has 256^n possible n-pixel blocks. Even in the simple case of $n = 2$, a 65,536 element histogram and up to 65,536 variable-length code words must be generated. For $n = 3$, as many as 16,777,216 code words are needed. So even for small values of n, computational complexity limits the usefulness of the extension coding approach in practice.

Finally, we note that although Eq. (8-7) provides a lower bound on the compression that can be achieved when directly coding statistically independent pixels, it breaks down when the pixels of an image are correlated. Blocks of correlated pixels can be coded with fewer average bits per pixel than the equation predicts. Rather than using source extensions, less correlated descriptors (such as intensity run-lengths) are normally selected and coded without extension. This was the approach used to compress Fig. 8.1(b) in the section on spatial and temporal redundancy. When the output of a source of information depends on a finite number of preceding outputs, the source is called a *Markov source* or *finite memory source*.

FIDELITY CRITERIA

It was noted earlier that the removal of "irrelevant visual" information involves a loss of real or quantitative image information. Because information is lost, a means of quantifying the nature of the loss is needed. Two types of criteria can be used for such an assessment: (1) objective fidelity criteria, and (2) subjective fidelity criteria.

[†]The output of the nth extension is an n-tuple of symbols from the underlying *single-symbol source*. It was considered a *block random variable* in which the probability of each n-tuple is the product of the probabilities of its individual symbols. The entropy of the nth extension is then n times the entropy of the single-symbol source from which it is derived.

When information loss can be expressed as a mathematical function of the input and output of a compression process, it is said to be based on an *objective fidelity criterion*. An example is the root-mean-squared (rms) error between two images. Let $f(x,y)$ be an input image, and $\hat{f}(x,y)$ be an approximation of $f(x,y)$ that results from compressing and subsequently decompressing the input. For any value of x and y, the error $e(x,y)$ between $f(x,y)$ and $\hat{f}(x,y)$ is

$$e(x,y) = \hat{f}(x,y) - f(x,y) \tag{8-9}$$

so that the total error between the two images is

$$\sum_{x=0}^{M-1}\sum_{y=0}^{N-1}\left[\hat{f}(x,y) - f(x,y)\right]$$

where the images are of size $M \times N$. The *root-mean-squared error*, e_{rms}, between $f(x,y)$ and $\hat{f}(x,y)$ is then the square root of the squared error averaged over the $M \times N$ array, or

$$e_{\text{rms}} = \left[\frac{1}{MN}\sum_{x=0}^{M-1}\sum_{y=0}^{N-1}\left[\hat{f}(x,y) - f(x,y)\right]^2\right]^{1/2} \tag{8-10}$$

If $\hat{f}(x,y)$ is considered [by a simple rearrangement of the terms in Eq. (8-9)] to be the sum of the original image $f(x,y)$ and an error or "noise" signal $e(x,y)$, the *mean-squared signal-to-noise ratio* of the output image, denoted SNR_{ms}, can be defined as in Section 5.8:

$$\text{SNR}_{\text{ms}} = \frac{\displaystyle\sum_{x=0}^{M-1}\sum_{y=0}^{N-1}\hat{f}(x,y)^2}{\displaystyle\sum_{x=0}^{M-1}\sum_{y=0}^{N-1}\left[\hat{f}(x,y) - f(x,y)\right]^2} \tag{8-11}$$

The rms value of the signal-to-noise ratio, denoted SNR_{rms}, is obtained by taking the square root of Eq. (8-11).

While objective fidelity criteria offer a simple and convenient way to evaluate information loss, decompressed images are often ultimately viewed by humans. So, measuring image quality by the subjective evaluations of people is often more appropriate. This can be done by presenting a decompressed image to a cross section of viewers and averaging their evaluations. The evaluations may be made using an absolute rating scale, or by means of side-by-side comparisons of $f(x,y)$ and $\hat{f}(x,y)$. Table 8.2 shows one possible absolute rating scale. Side-by-side comparisons can be done with a scale such as $\{-3,-2,-1,0,1,2,3\}$ to represent the subjective evaluations $\{much\ worse,\ worse,\ slightly\ worse,\ the\ same,\ slightly\ better,\ better,\ much\ better\}$, respectively. In either case, the evaluations are based on *subjective fidelity criteria*.

TABLE 8.2
Rating scale of the Television Allocations Study Organization. (Frendendall and Behrend.)

Value	Rating	Description
1	Excellent	An image of extremely high quality, as good as you could desire.
2	Fine	An image of high quality, providing enjoyable viewing. Interference is not objectionable.
3	Passable	An image of acceptable quality. Interference is not objectionable.
4	Marginal	An image of poor quality; you wish you could improve it. Interference is somewhat objectionable.
5	Inferior	A very poor image, but you could watch it. Objectionable interference is definitely present.
6	Unusable	An image so bad that you could not watch it.

EXAMPLE 8.3: Image quality comparisons.

Figure 8.4 shows three different approximations of the image in Fig. 8.1(a). Using Eq. (8-10) with Fig. 8.1(a) as $f(x, y)$ and Figs. 8.4(a) through (c) as $\hat{f}(x, y)$, the computed rms errors are 5.17, 15.67, and 14.17 intensity levels, respectively. In terms of rms error (an objective fidelity criterion), the images are ranked in order of decreasing quality as $\{(a), (c), (b)\}$. A subjective evaluation of the images using Table 8.2, however, might yield an *excellent* rating for (a), a *marginal* rating for (b), and an *inferior* or *unusable* rating for (c). Thus, using a subjective fidelity criteria, (b) is ranked ahead of (c).

IMAGE COMPRESSION MODELS

As Fig. 8.5 shows, an image compression system is composed of two distinct functional components: an *encoder* and a *decoder*. The encoder performs compression, and the decoder performs the complementary operation of decompression. Both operations can be performed in software, as is the case in Web browsers and many commercial image-editing applications, or in a combination of hardware and firmware, as in commercial DVD players. A *codec* is a device or program that is capable of both encoding and decoding.

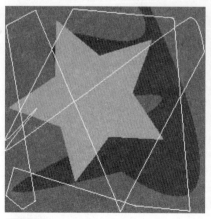 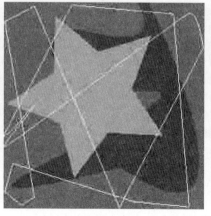 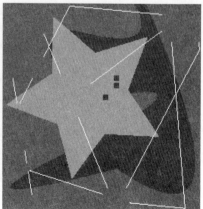

a b c

FIGURE 8.4 Three approximations of the image in Fig. 8.1(a).

FIGURE 8.5
Functional block
diagram of a
general image
compression
system.

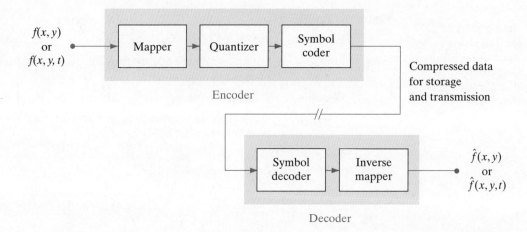

$f(x, y)$
or
$f(x, y, t)$

Mapper → Quantizer → Symbol coder

Compressed data
for storage
and transmission

Encoder

Symbol decoder → Inverse mapper

$\hat{f}(x, y)$
or
$\hat{f}(x, y, t)$

Decoder

Here, the notation
$f(x, \ldots)$ is used to denote
both $f(x, y)$ and $f(x, y, t)$.

Input image $f(x, \ldots)$ is fed into the encoder, which creates a compressed representation of the input. This representation is stored for later use, or transmitted for storage and use at a remote location. When the compressed representation is presented to its complementary decoder, a reconstructed output image $\hat{f}(x, \ldots)$ is generated. In still-image applications, the encoded input and decoder output are $f(x, y)$ and $\hat{f}(x, y)$, respectively. In video applications, they are $f(x, y, t)$ and $\hat{f}(x, y, t)$, where the discrete parameter t specifies time. In general, $\hat{f}(x, \ldots)$ may or may not be an exact replica of $f(x, \ldots)$. If it is, the compression system is called *error free*, *lossless*, or *information preserving*. If not, the reconstructed output image is distorted, and the compression system is referred to as *lossy*.

The Encoding or Compression Process

The encoder of Fig. 8.5 is designed to remove the redundancies described in the previous sections through a series of three independent operations. In the first stage of the encoding process, a *mapper* transforms $f(x, \ldots)$ into a (usually nonvisual) format designed to reduce spatial and temporal redundancy. This operation generally is reversible, and may or may not directly reduce the amount of data required to represent the image. Run-length coding is an example of a mapping that normally yields compression in the first step of the encoding process. The mapping of an image into a set of less correlated transform coefficients (see Section 8.9) is an example of the opposite case (the coefficients must be further processed to achieve compression). In video applications, the mapper uses previous (and, in some cases, future) video frames to facilitate the removal of temporal redundancy.

The *quantizer* in Fig. 8.5 reduces the accuracy of the mapper's output in accordance with a pre-established fidelity criterion. The goal is to keep irrelevant information out of the compressed representation. As noted earlier, this operation is irreversible. It must be omitted when error-free compression is desired. In video applications, the *bit rate* of the encoded output is often measured (in bits/second), and is used to adjust the operation of the quantizer so a predetermined average output rate is maintained. Thus, the visual quality of the output can vary from frame to frame as a function of image content.

In the third and final stage of the encoding process, the *symbol coder* of Fig. 8.5 generates a fixed-length or variable-length code to represent the quantizer output, and maps the output in accordance with the code. In many cases, a variable-length code is used. The shortest code words are assigned to the most frequently occurring quantizer output values, thus minimizing coding redundancy. This operation is reversible. Upon its completion, the input image has been processed for the removal of each of the three redundancies described in the previous sections.

The Decoding or Decompression Process

The decoder of Fig. 8.5 contains only two components: a *symbol decoder* and an *inverse mapper*. They perform, in reverse order, the inverse operations of the encoder's symbol encoder and mapper. Because quantization results in irreversible information loss, an inverse quantizer block is not included in the general decoder model. In video applications, decoded output frames are maintained in an internal frame store (not shown) and used to reinsert the temporal redundancy that was removed at the encoder.

IMAGE FORMATS, CONTAINERS, AND COMPRESSION STANDARDS

In the context of digital imaging, an *image file format* is a standard way to organize and store image data. It defines how the data is arranged and the type of compression (if any) that is used. An *image container* is similar to a file format, but handles multiple types of image data. Image *compression standards*, on the other hand, define procedures for compressing and decompressing images—that is, for reducing the amount of data needed to represent an image. These standards are the underpinning of the widespread acceptance of image compression technology.

Figure 8.6 lists the most important image compression standards, file formats, and containers in use today, grouped by the type of image handled. The entries in blue are international standards sanctioned by the *International Standards Organization* (ISO), the *International Electrotechnical Commission* (IEC), and/or the *International Telecommunications Union* (ITU-T)—a *United Nations* (UN) organization that was once called the *Consultative Committee of the International Telephone and Telegraph* (CCITT). Two video compression standards, VC-1 by the *Society of Motion Pictures and Television Engineers* (SMPTE) and AVS by the *Chinese Ministry of Information Industry* (MII), are also included. Note that they are shown in black, which is used in Fig. 8.6 to denote entries that are not sanctioned by an international standards organization.

Tables 8.3 through 8.5 summarize the standards, formats, and containers listed in Fig. 8.6. Responsible organizations, targeted applications, and key compression methods are identified. The compression methods themselves are the subject of Sections 8.2 through 8.11, where we will describe the principal lossy and error-free compression methods in use today. The focus of these sections is on methods that have proven useful in mainstream binary, continuous-tone still-image, and video compression standards. The standards themselves are used to demonstrate the methods presented. In Tables 8.3 through 8.5, forward references to the relevant sections in which the compression methods are described are enclosed in square brackets.

FIGURE 8.6
Some popular
image compres-
sion standards,
file formats,
and containers.
Internationally
sanctioned entries
are shown in blue;
all others are in
black.

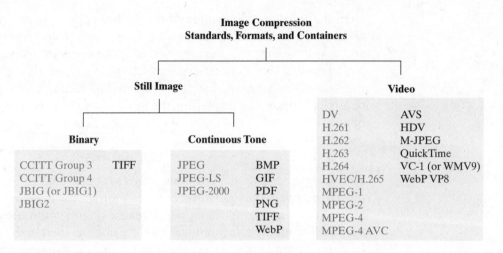

TABLE 8.3
Internationally sanctioned image compression standards. The numbers in brackets refer to sections in this chapter.

Name	Organization	Description
Bi-Level Still Images		
CCITT Group 3	ITU-T	Designed as a facsimile (FAX) method for transmitting binary documents over telephone lines. Supports 1-D and 2-D run-length [8.6] and Huffman [8.2] coding.
CCITT Group 4	ITU-T	A simplified and streamlined version of the CCITT Group 3 standard supporting 2-D run-length coding only.
JBIG or JBIG1	ISO/IEC/ ITU-T	A *Joint Bi-level Image Experts Group* standard for progressive, lossless compression of bi-level images. Continuous-tone images of up to 6 bits/pixel can be coded on a bit-plane basis [8.8]. Context-sensitive arithmetic coding [8.4] is used and an initial low-resolution version of the image can be gradually enhanced with additional compressed data.
JBIG2	ISO/IEC/ ITU-T	A follow-on to JBIG1 for bi-level images in desktop, Internet, and FAX applications. The compression method used is content based, with dictionary-based methods [8.7] for text and halftone regions, and Huffman [8.2] or arithmetic coding [8.4] for other image content. It can be lossy or lossless.
Continuous-Tone Still Images		
JPEG	ISO/IEC/ ITU-T	A *Joint Photographic Experts Group* standard for images of photographic quality. Its lossy baseline coding system (most commonly implemented) uses quantized discrete cosine transforms (DCT) on image blocks [8.9], Huffman [8.2], and run-length [8.6] coding. It is one of the most popular methods for compressing images on the Internet.
JPEG-LS	ISO/IEC/ ITU-T	A lossless to near-lossless standard for continuous-tone images based on adaptive prediction [8.10], context modeling [8.4], and Golomb coding [8.3].
JPEG-2000	ISO/IEC/ ITU-T	A follow-on to JPEG for increased compression of photographic quality images. Arithmetic coding [8.4] and quantized discrete wavelet transforms (DWT) [8.11] are used. The compression can be lossy or lossless.

TABLE 8.4
Internationally sanctioned video compresssion standards. The numbers in brackets refer to sections in this chapter.

Name	Organization	Description
DV	IEC	*Digital Video.* A video standard tailored to home and semiprofessional video production applications and equipment, such as electronic news gathering and camcorders. Frames are compressed independently for uncomplicated editing using a DCT-based approach [8.9] similar to JPEG.
H.261	ITU-T	A two-way videoconferencing standard for ISDN (*integrated services digital network*) lines. It supports non-interlaced 352×288 and 176×144 resolution images, called CIF (*Common Intermediate Format*) and QCIF (*Quarter CIF*), respectively. A DCT-based compression approach [8.9] similar to JPEG is used, with frame-to-frame prediction differencing [8.10] to reduce temporal redundancy. A block-based technique is used to compensate for motion between frames.
H.262	ITU-T	See MPEG-2 below.
H.263	ITU-T	An enhanced version of H.261 designed for ordinary telephone modems (i.e., 28.8 Kb/s) with additional resolutions: SQCIF (*Sub-Quarter* CIF 128×96), 4CIF (704×576) and 16CIF (1408×512).
H.264	ITU-T	An extension of H.261–H.263 for videoconferencing, streaming, and television. It supports prediction differences within frames [8.10], variable block size integer transforms (rather than the DCT), and context adaptive arithmetic coding [8.4].
H.265 MPEG-H HEVC	ISO/IEC ITU-T	*High Efficiency Video Coding* (HVEC). An extension of H.264 that includes support for macroblock sizes up to 64×64 and additional intraframe prediction modes, both useful in 4K video applications.
MPEG-1	ISO/IEC	A *Motion Pictures Expert Group* standard for CD-ROM applications with non-interlaced video at up to 1.5 Mb/s. It is similar to H.261 but frame predictions can be based on the previous frame, next frame, or an interpolation of both. It is supported by almost all computers and DVD players.
MPEG-2	ISO/IEC	An extension of MPEG-1 designed for DVDs with transfer rates at up to 15 Mb/s. Supports interlaced video and HDTV. It is the most successful video standard to date.
MPEG-4	ISO/IEC	An extension of MPEG-2 that supports variable block sizes and prediction differencing [8.10] within frames.
MPEG-4 AVC	ISO/IEC	MPEG-4 Part 10 *Advanced Video Coding* (AVC). Identical to H.264.

8.2 HUFFMAN CODING

With reference to Tables 8.3–8.5, Huffman codes are used in

- CCITT
- JBIG2
- JPEG
- MPEG-1, 2, 4
- H.261, H.262,
- H.263, H.264

and other compression standards.

One of the most popular techniques for removing coding redundancy is due to Huffman (Huffman [1952]). When coding the symbols of an information source individually, *Huffman coding* yields the smallest possible number of code symbols per source symbol. In terms of Shannon's first theorem (see Section 8.1), the resulting code is optimal for a fixed value of n, subject to the constraint that the source symbols be coded *one at a time*. In practice, the source symbols may be either the intensities of an image or the output of an intensity mapping operation (pixel differences, run lengths, and so on).

TABLE 8.5
Popular image and video compression standards, file formats, and containers not included in Tables 8.3 and 8.4. The numbers in brackets refer to sections in this chapter.·

Name	Organization	Description
Continuous-Tone Still Images		
BMP	Microsoft	*Windows Bitmap.* A file format used mainly for simple uncompressed images.
GIF	CompuServe	*Graphic Interchange Format.* A file format that uses lossless LZW coding [8.5] for 1- through 8-bit images. It is frequently used to make small animations and short low-resolution films for the Internet.
PDF	Adobe Systems	*Portable Document Format.* A format for representing 2-D documents in a device and resolution independent way. It can function as a container for JPEG, JPEG-2000, CCITT, and other compressed images. Some PDF versions have become ISO standards.
PNG	*World Wide Web Consortium* (W3C)	*Portable Network Graphics.* A file format that losslessly compresses full color images with transparency (up to 48 bits/pixel) by coding the difference between each pixel's value and a predicted value based on past pixels [8.10].
TIFF	Aldus	*Tagged Image File Format.* A flexible file format supporting a variety of image compression standards, including JPEG, JPEG-LS, JPEG-2000, JBIG2, and others.
WebP	Google	*WebP* supports lossy compression via WebP VP8 intraframe video compression (see below) and lossless compression using spatial prediction [8.10] and a variant of LZW backward referencing [8.5] and Huffman entropy coding [8.2]. Transparency is also supported.
Video		
AVS	MII	*Audio-Video Standard.* Similar to H.264 but uses exponential Golomb coding [8.3]. Developed in China.
HDV	Company consortium	*High Definition Video.* An extension of DV for HD television that uses compression similar to MPEG-2, including temporal redundancy removal by prediction differencing [8.10].
M-JPEG	Various companies	*Motion JPEG.* A compression format in which each frame is compressed independently using JPEG.
Quick-Time	Apple Computer	A media container supporting DV, H.261, H.262, H.264, MPEG-1, MPEG-2, MPEG-4, and other video compression formats.
VC-1 WMV9	SMPTE Microsoft	The most used video format on the Internet. Adopted for HD and *Blu-ray* high-definition DVDs. It is similar to H.264/AVC, using an integer DCT with varying block sizes [8.9 and 8.10] and context-dependent variable-length code tables [8.2], but no predictions within frames.
WebP VP8	Google	A file format based on block transform coding [8.9] prediction differences within frames and between frames [8.10]. The differences are entropy encoded using an adaptive arithmetic coder [8.4].

The first step in Huffman's approach is to create a series of source reductions by ordering the probabilities of the symbols under consideration, then combining the lowest probability symbols into a single symbol that replaces them in the next source reduction. Figure 8.7 illustrates this process for binary coding (*K*-ary Huffman codes also can be constructed). At the far left, a hypothetical set of source symbols and their probabilities are ordered from top to bottom in terms of decreasing probability values. To form the first source reduction, the bottom two probabilities, 0.06 and 0.04, are combined to form a "compound symbol" with probability 0.1. This compound symbol and its associated probability are placed in the first source reduction column so that the probabilities of the reduced source also are ordered from the most to the least probable. This process is then repeated until a reduced source with two symbols (at the far right) is reached.

The second step in Huffman's procedure is to code each reduced source, starting with the smallest source and working back to the original source. The minimal length binary code for a two-symbol source, of course, are the symbols 0 and 1. As Fig. 8.8 shows, these symbols are assigned to the two symbols on the right. (The assignment is arbitrary; reversing the order of the 0 and 1 would work just as well.) As the reduced source symbol with probability 0.6 was generated by combining two symbols in the reduced source to its left, the 0 used to code it is now assigned to both of these symbols, and a 0 and 1 are arbitrarily appended to each to distinguish them from each other. This operation is then repeated for each reduced source until the original source is reached. The final code appears at the far left in Fig. 8.8. The average length of this code is

$$L_{avg} = (0.4)(1) + (0.3)(2) + (0.1)(3) + (0.1)(4) + (0.06)(5) + (0.04)(5)$$
$$= 2.2 \text{ bits/pixel}$$

and the entropy of the source is 2.14 bits/symbol.

Huffman's procedure creates the optimal code for a set of symbols and probabilities *subject to the constraint* that the symbols be coded one at a time. After the code has been created, coding and/or error-free decoding is accomplished in a simple lookup table manner. The code itself is an instantaneous uniquely decodable block code. It is called a *block code* because each source symbol is mapped into a fixed sequence of code symbols. It is *instantaneous* because each code word in a string of

FIGURE 8.7
Huffman source reductions.

	Original source		Source reduction			
Symbol	Probability	1	2	3	4	
a_2	0.4	0.4	0.4	0.4	0.6	
a_6	0.3	0.3	0.3	0.3	0.4	
a_1	0.1	0.1	0.2	0.3		
a_4	0.1	0.1	0.1			
a_3	0.06	0.1				
a_5	0.04					

FIGURE 8.8
Huffman code
assignment
procedure.

	Original source			Source reduction			
Symbol	Probability	Code	1	2	3	4	
a_2	0.4	1	0.4 1	0.4 1	0.4 1	0.6 0	
a_6	0.3	00	0.3 00	0.3 00	0.3 00 ←	0.4 1	
a_1	0.1	011	0.1 011	0.2 010 ←	0.3 01 ←		
a_4	0.1	0100	0.1 0100 ←	0.1 011 ←			
a_3	0.06	01010 ←	0.1 0101 ←				
a_5	0.04	01011 ←					

code symbols can be decoded without referencing succeeding symbols. It is *uniquely decodable* because any string of code symbols can be decoded in only one way. Thus, any string of Huffman encoded symbols can be decoded by examining the individual symbols of the string in a left-to-right manner. For the binary code of Fig. 8.8, a left-to-right scan of the encoded string 010100111100 reveals that the first valid code word is 01010, which is the code for symbol a_3. The next valid code is 011, which corresponds to symbol a_1. Continuing in this manner reveals the completely decoded message to be $a_3 a_1 a_2 a_2 a_6$.

EXAMPLE 8.4:   Huffman Coding.

The 512×512 8-bit monochrome image in Fig. 8.9(a) has the intensity histogram shown in Fig. 8.9(b). Because the intensities are not equally probable, a MATLAB implementation of Huffman's procedure was used to encode them with 7.428 bits/pixel, including the Huffman code table that is required to reconstruct the original 8-bit image intensities. The compressed representation exceeds the estimated entropy of the image [7.3838 bits/pixel from Eq. (8-7)] by $512^2 \times (7.428 - 7.3838)$ or 11,587 bits—about 0.6%. The resulting compression ratio and corresponding relative redundancy are $C = 8/7.428 = 1.077$, and $R = 1 - (1/1.077) = 0.0715$, respectively. Thus 7.15% of the original 8-bit fixed-length intensity representation was removed as coding redundancy.

When a large number of symbols is to be coded, the construction of an optimal Huffman code is a nontrivial task. For the general case of J source symbols, J symbol probabilities, $J - 2$ source reductions, and $J - 2$ code assignments are required. When source symbol probabilities can be estimated in advance, "near optimal" coding can be achieved with pre-computed Huffman codes. Several popular image compression standards, including the JPEG and MPEG standards discussed in Sections 8.9 and 8.10, specify default Huffman coding tables that have been pre-computed based on experimental data.

8.3 GOLOMB CODING

With reference to
Tables 8.3–8.5, Golomb
codes are used in

• JPEG-LS
• AVS

compression.

In this section, we consider the coding of nonnegative integer inputs with exponentially decaying probability distributions. Inputs of this type can be optimally encoded (in the sense of Shannon's first theorem) using a family of codes that are computationally simpler than Huffman codes. The codes themselves were first proposed for the representation of nonnegative run lengths (Golomb [1966]). In the discussion

a b

FIGURE 8.9
(a) A 512×512
8-bit image and
(b) its histogram.

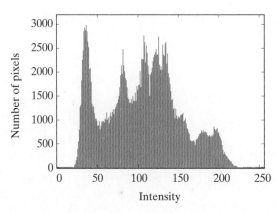

that follows, the notation $\lfloor x \rfloor$ denotes the largest integer less than or equal to x, $\lceil x \rceil$ means the smallest integer greater than or equal to x, and $x \bmod y$ is the remainder of x divided by y.

Given a nonnegative integer n and a positive integer *divisor* $m > 0$, the *Golomb code* of n with respect to m, denoted $G_m(n)$, is a combination of the unary code of *quotient* $\lfloor n/m \rfloor$ and the binary representation of *remainder* $n \bmod m$. $G_m(n)$ is constructed as follows:

1. Form the unary code of quotient $\lfloor n/m \rfloor$. (The *unary code* of an integer q is defined as q 1's followed by a 0.)
2. Let $k = \lceil \log_2 m \rceil$, $c = 2^k - m$, $r = n \bmod m$, and compute truncated remainder r' such that

$$r' = \begin{cases} r \text{ truncated to } k-1 \text{ bits} & 0 \le r < c \\ r + c \text{ truncated to } k \text{ bits} & \text{otherwise} \end{cases} \qquad (8\text{-}12)$$

3. Concatenate the results of Steps 1 and 2.

To compute $G_4(9)$, for example, begin by determining the unary code of the quotient $\lfloor 9/4 \rfloor = \lfloor 2.25 \rfloor = 2$, which is 110 (the result of Step 1). Then let $k = \lceil \log_2 4 \rceil = 2$, $c = 2^2 - 4 = 0$, and $r = 9 \bmod 4$, which in binary is $1001 \bmod 0100$ or 0001. In accordance with Eq. (8-12), r' is then r (i.e., 0001) truncated to 2 bits, which is 01 (the result of Step 2). Finally, concatenate 110 from Step 1 and 01 from Step 2 to get 11001, which is $G_4(9)$.

For the special case of $m = 2^k$, $c = 0$ and $r' = r = n \bmod m$ truncated to k bits in Eq. (8-12) for all n. The divisions required to generate the resulting Golomb codes become binary shift operations, and the computationally simpler codes are called *Golomb-Rice* or *Rice codes* (Rice [1975]). Columns 2, 3, and 4 of Table 8.6 list the G_1, G_2, and G_4 codes of the first ten nonnegative integers. Because m is a power of 2 in each case (i.e., $1 = 2^0$, $2 = 2^1$, and $4 = 2^2$), they are the first three Golomb-Rice codes as well. Moreover, G_1 is the unary code of the nonnegative integers because $\lfloor n/1 \rfloor = n$ and $n \bmod 1 = 0$ for all n.

TABLE 8.6
Several Golomb codes for the integers 0–9.

n	$G_1(n)$	$G_2(n)$	$G_4(n)$	$G_{exp}^0(n)$
0	0	00	000	0
1	10	01	001	100
2	110	100	010	101
3	1110	101	011	11000
4	11110	1100	1000	11001
5	111110	1101	1001	11010
6	1111110	11100	1010	11011
7	11111110	11101	1011	1110000
8	111111110	111100	11000	1110001
9	1111111110	111101	11001	1110010

Keeping in mind that Golomb codes only can be used to represent nonnegative integers, and that there are many Golomb codes to choose from, a key step in their effective application is the selection of divisor m. When the integers to be represented are *geometrically* distributed with a *probability mass function* (PMF)[†]

$$P(n) = (1-\rho)\rho^n \qquad (8\text{-}13)$$

for some $0 < \rho < 1$, Golomb codes can be shown to be optimal in the sense that $G_m(n)$ provides the shortest average code length of all uniquely decipherable codes (Gallager and Voorhis [1975]) when

$$m = \left\lceil \frac{\log_2(1+\rho)}{\log_2(1/\rho)} \right\rceil \qquad (8\text{-}14)$$

Figure 8.10(a) plots Eq. (8-13) for three values of ρ and graphically illustrates the symbol probabilities that Golomb codes handle well (that is, code efficiently). As is shown in the figure, small integers are much more probable than large ones.

Because the probabilities of the intensities in an image [see, for example, the histogram of Fig. 8.9(b)] are unlikely to match the probabilities specified in Eq. (8-13) and shown in Fig. 8.10(a), Golomb codes are seldom used for the coding of intensities. When intensity differences are to be coded, however, the probabilities of the resulting "difference values" (see Section 8.10) (with the notable exception of the negative differences) often resemble those of Eq. (8-13) and Fig. 8.10(a). To handle negative differences in Golomb coding, which can only represent nonnegative integers, a mapping like

---

[†]A *probability mass function* (PMF) is a function that defines the probability that a discrete random variable is exactly equal to some value. A PMF differs from a PDF in that a PDF's values are not probabilities; rather, the integral of a PDF over a specified interval is a probability.

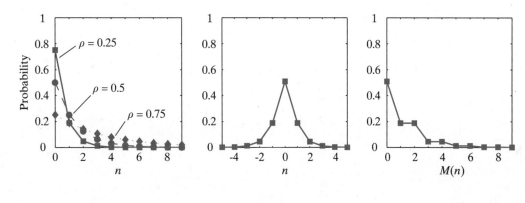

FIGURE 8.10
(a) Three one-sided geometric distributions from Eq. (8-13); (b) a two-sided exponentially decaying distribution; and (c) a reordered version of (b) using Eq. (8-15).

$$M(n) = \begin{cases} 2n & n \geq 0 \\ 2|n| - 1 & n < 0 \end{cases} \tag{8-15}$$

is typically used. Using this mapping, for example, the two-sided PMF shown in Fig. 8.10(b) can be transformed into the one-sided PMF in Fig. 8.10(c). Its integers are reordered, alternating the negative and positive integers so the negative integers are mapped into the odd positive integer positions. If $P(n)$ is two-sided and centered at zero, $P(M(n))$ will be one-sided. The mapped integers, $M(n)$, can then be efficiently encoded using an appropriate Golomb-Rice code (Weinberger et al. [1996]).

EXAMPLE 8.5:   Golomb-Rice coding.

Consider again the image from Fig. 8.1(c) and note that its histogram [see Fig. 8.3(a)] is similar to the two-sided distribution in Fig. 8.10(b) above. If we let n be some nonnegative integer intensity in the image, where $0 \leq n \leq 225$, and μ be the mean intensity, $P(n - \mu)$ is the two-sided distribution shown in Fig. 8.11(a). This plot was generated by normalizing the histogram in Fig. 8.3(a) by the total number of pixels in the image and shifting the normalized values to the left by 128 (which in effect subtracts the mean intensity from the image). In accordance with Eq. (8-15), $P(M(n - \mu))$ is then the one-sided distribution shown in Fig. 8.11(b). If the reordered intensity values are Golomb coded using a MATLAB implementation of code G_1 in column 2 of Table 8.6, the encoded representation is 4.5 times smaller than the original image (i.e., $C = 4.5$). The G_1 code realizes 4.5/5.1, or 88% of the theoretical compression possible with variable-length coding. [Based on the entropy calculated in Example (8-2), the maximum possible compression ratio through variable-length coding is $C = 8/1.566 \approx 5.1$.] Moreover, Golomb coding achieves 96% of the compression provided by a MATLAB implementation of Huffman's approach, and doesn't require the computation of a custom Huffman coding table.

Now consider the image in Fig. 8.9(a). If its intensities are Golomb coded using the same G_1 code as above, $C = 0.0922$. That is, there is *data expansion*. This is due to the fact that the probabilities of the intensities of the image in Fig. 8.9(a) are much different than the probabilities defined in Eq. (8-13). In a similar manner, Huffman codes can produce data expansion when used to encode symbols whose probabilities are different from those for which the code was computed. In practice, the further you depart from the input probability assumptions for which a code is designed, the greater the risk of poor compression performance and data expansion.

(a) The probability distribution of the image in Fig. 8.1(c) after subtracting the mean intensity from each pixel. (b) A mapped version of (a) using Eq. (8-15).

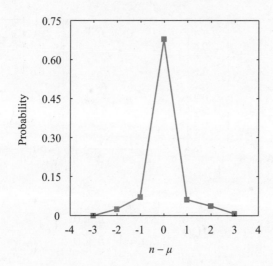
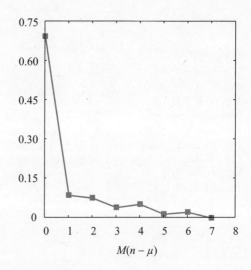

To conclude our coverage of Golomb codes, we note that Column 5 of Table 8.6 contains the first 10 codes of the zeroth-order *exponential Golomb code*, denoted $G_{exp}^0(n)$. Exponential-Golomb codes are useful for the encoding of run lengths, because both short and long runs are encoded efficiently. An order-k exponential-Golomb code $G_{exp}^k(n)$ is computed as follows:

1. Find an integer $i \geq 0$ such that

$$\sum_{j=0}^{i-1} 2^{j+k} \leq n < \sum_{j=0}^{i} 2^{j+k} \tag{8-16}$$

   and form the unary code of i. If $k = 0$, $i = \lfloor \log_2(n+1) \rfloor$ and the code is also known as the *Elias gamma code*.

2. Truncate the binary representation of

$$n - \sum_{j=0}^{i-1} 2^{j+k} \tag{8-17}$$

   to $k + i$ least significant bits.

3. Concatenate the results of Steps 1 and 2.

To find $G_{exp}^0(8)$, for example, we let $i = \lfloor \log_2 9 \rfloor$ or 3 in Step 1 because $k = 0$. Equation (8-16) is then satisfied because

$$\sum_{j=0}^{3-1} 2^{j+0} \leq 8 < \sum_{j=0}^{3} 2^{j+0}$$

$$\sum_{j=0}^{2} 2^j \leq 8 < \sum_{j=0}^{3} 2^j$$

$$2^0 + 2^1 + 2^2 \leq 8 < 2^0 + 2^1 + 2^2 + 2^3$$
$$7 \leq 8 < 15$$

The unary code of 3 is 1110 and Eq. (8-17) of Step 2 yields

$$8 - \sum_{j=0}^{3-1} 2^{j+0} = 8 - \sum_{j=0}^{2} 2^j = 8 - \left(2^0 + 2^1 + 2^2\right) = 8 - 7 = 1 = 0001$$

which when truncated to its $3 + 0$ least significant bits becomes 001. The concatenation of the results from Steps 1 and 2 then yields 1110001. Note that this is the entry in column 4 of Table 8.6 for $n = 8$. Finally, we note that like the Huffman codes of the last section, the Golomb codes of Table 8.6 are variable-length, instantaneous, and uniquely decodable block codes.

8.4 ARITHMETIC CODING

With reference to Tables 8.3–8.5, arithmetic coding is used in

- JBIG1
- JBIG2
- JPEG-2000
- H.264
- MPEG-4 AVC

and other compression standards.

Unlike the variable-length codes of the previous two sections, *arithmetic coding* generates nonblock codes. In arithmetic coding, which can be traced to the work of Elias (Abramson [1963]), a one-to-one correspondence between source symbols and code words does not exist. Instead, an entire sequence of source symbols (or message) is assigned a single arithmetic code word. The code word itself defines an interval of real numbers between 0 and 1. As the number of symbols in the message increases, the interval used to represent it becomes smaller, and the number of information units (say, bits) required to represent the interval becomes larger. Each symbol of the message reduces the size of the interval in accordance with its probability of occurrence. Because the technique does not require, as does Huffman's approach, that each source symbol translate into an integral number of code symbols (that is, that the symbols be coded one at a time), it achieves (but only in theory) the bound established by Shannon's first theorem of Section 8.1.

Figure 8.12 illustrates the basic arithmetic coding process. Here, a five-symbol sequence or message, $a_1 a_2 a_3 a_3 a_4$, from a four-symbol source is coded. At the start of the coding process, the message is assumed to occupy the entire half-open interval $[0, 1)$. As Table 8.7 shows, this interval is subdivided initially into four regions based on the probabilities of each source symbol. Symbol a_1, for example, is associated with subinterval $[0, 0.2)$. Because it is the first symbol of the message being coded, the message interval is initially narrowed to $[0, 0.2)$. Thus, in Fig. 8.12, $[0, 0.2)$ is expanded to the full height of the figure, and its end points labeled by the values of the narrowed range. The narrowed range is then subdivided in accordance with the original source

TABLE 8.7
Arithmetic coding example.

Source Symbol	Probability	Initial Subinterval
a_1	0.2	$[0.0, 0.2)$
a_2	0.2	$[0.2, 0.4)$
a_3	0.4	$[0.4, 0.8)$
a_4	0.2	$[0.8, 1.0)$

FIGURE 8.12
Arithmetic coding
procedure.

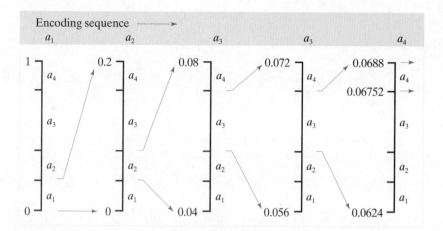

symbol probabilities, and the process continues with the next message symbol. In this manner, symbol a_2 narrows the subinterval to [0.04, 0.08), a_3 further narrows it to [0.056, 0.072), and so on. The final message symbol, which must be reserved as a special end-of-message indicator, narrows the range to [0.06752, 0.0688). Of course, any number within this subinterval, for example, 0.068, can be used to represent the message. In the arithmetically coded message of Fig. 8.12, three decimal digits are used to represent the five-symbol message. This translates into 0.6 decimal digits per source symbol and compares favorably with the entropy of the source, which, from Eq. 8.6, is 0.58 decimal digits per source symbol. As the length of the sequence being coded increases, the resulting arithmetic code approaches the bound established by Shannon's first theorem. In practice, two factors cause coding performance to fall short of the bound: (1) the addition of the end-of-message indicator that is needed to separate one message from another, and (2) the use of finite precision arithmetic. Practical implementations of arithmetic coding address the latter problem by introducing a scaling strategy and a rounding strategy (Langdon and Rissanen [1981]). The scaling strategy renormalizes each subinterval to the [0, 1) range before subdividing it in accordance with the symbol probabilities. The rounding strategy guarantees that the truncations associated with finite precision arithmetic do not prevent the coding subintervals from being accurately represented.

ADAPTIVE CONTEXT DEPENDENT PROBABILITY ESTIMATES

With accurate input symbol *probability models*, that is, models that provide the true probabilities of the symbols being coded, arithmetic coders are near optimal in the sense of minimizing the average number of code symbols required to represent the symbols being coded. As in both Huffman and Golomb coding, however, inaccurate probability models can lead to non-optimal results. A simple way to improve the accuracy of the probabilities employed is to use an adaptive, context dependent probability model. *Adaptive* probability models update symbol probabilities as symbols are coded or become known. Thus, the probabilities adapt to the local statistics of the symbols being coded. *Context-dependent* models provide probabilities that are based on a predefined neighborhood of pixels, called the *context*, around the symbols being coded. Normally, a *causal context* (one limited to symbols that have already been coded) is used. Both the Q-coder (Pennebaker et al. [1988]) and MQ-coder (ISO/IEC [2000]), two well-known arithmetic coding techniques that have been incorporated into the JBIG, JPEG-2000, and other important image compression standards, use probability models that are both adaptive and context dependent. The Q-coder dynamically updates symbol probabilities during the interval renormalizations that are part of the arithmetic coding process. Adaptive context dependent models also have been used in Golomb coding, for example, in the JPEG-LS compression standard.

Figure 8.13(a) diagrams the steps involved in adaptive, context-dependent arithmetic coding of *binary* source symbols. Arithmetic coding often is used when binary symbols are to be coded. As each symbol (or bit) begins the coding process, its context is formed in the *Context determination* block of Fig. 8.13(a). Figures 8.13(b) through (d) show three possible contexts that can be used: (1) the immediately preceding symbol, (2) a group of preceding symbols, and (3) some number of preceding symbols plus symbols on the previous scan line. For the three cases shown, the *Probability estimation* block must manage 2^1 (or 2), 2^8 (or 256), and 2^5 (or 32) contexts and their associated probabilities. For instance, if the context in Fig. 8.13(b) is used, conditional probabilities $P(0|a = 0)$ (the probability that the symbol being coded is a 0 given that the preceding symbol is a 0), $P(1|a = 0)$, $P(0|a = 1)$, and $P(1|a = 1)$ must be tracked. The appropriate probabilities are then passed to the *Arithmetic coding* block as a function of the current context, and drive the generation of the arithmetically coded output sequence in accordance with the process illustrated in Fig. 8.12. The probabilities associated with the context involved in the current coding step are then updated to reflect the fact that another symbol within that context has been processed.

Finally, we note that a variety of arithmetic coding techniques are protected by United States patents (and may be protected in other jurisdictions as well). Because

a		
b	c	d

FIGURE 8.13
(a) An adaptive, context-based arithmetic coding approach (often used for binary source symbols). (b)–(d) Three possible context models.

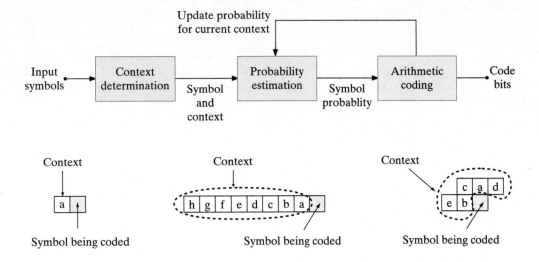

of these patents, and the possibility of unfavorable monetary judgments for their infringement, most implementations of the JPEG compression standard, which contains options for both Huffman and arithmetic coding, typically support Huffman coding alone.

8.5 LZW CODING

With reference to Tables 8.3–8.5, LZW coding is used in the
- GIF
- TIFF
- PDF

formats, but not in any of the internationally sanctioned compression standards.

The techniques covered in Sections 8.2 through 8.4 are focused on the removal of coding redundancy. In this section, we consider an error-free compression approach that also addresses spatial redundancies in an image. The technique, called *Lempel-Ziv-Welch* (LZW) *coding*, assigns fixed-length code words to variable length sequences of source symbols. Recall from the earlier section on measuring image information that Shannon used the idea of coding sequences of source symbols, rather than individual source symbols, in the proof of his first theorem. A key feature of LZW coding is that it requires no a priori knowledge of the probability of occurrence of the symbols to be encoded. Despite the fact that until recently it was protected under a United States patent, LZW compression has been integrated into a variety of mainstream imaging file formats, including GIF, TIFF, and PDF. The PNG format was created to get around LZW licensing requirements.

EXAMPLE 8.6: LZW coding Fig. 8.9(a).

Consider again the 512×512, 8-bit image from Fig. 8.9(a). Using Adobe Photoshop, an uncompressed TIFF version of this image requires 286,740 bytes of disk space—262,144 bytes for the 512×512 8-bit pixels plus 24,596 bytes of overhead. Using TIFF's LZW compression option, however, the resulting file is 224,420 bytes. The compression ratio is $C = 1.28$. Recall that for the Huffman encoded representation of Fig. 8.9(a) in Example 8.4, $C = 1.077$. The additional compression realized by the LZW approach is due the removal of some of the image's spatial redundancy.

LZW coding is conceptually very simple (Welch [1984]). At the onset of the coding process, a codebook or *dictionary* containing the source symbols to be coded is constructed. For 8-bit monochrome images, the first 256 words of the dictionary are assigned to intensities 0, 1, 2, ..., 255. As the encoder sequentially examines image pixels, intensity sequences that are not in the dictionary are placed in algorithmically determined (e.g., the next unused) locations. If the first two pixels of the image are white, for instance, sequence "255–255" might be assigned to location 256, the address following the locations reserved for intensity levels 0 through 255. The next time two consecutive white pixels are encountered, code word 256, the address of the location containing sequence 255–255, is used to represent them. If a 9-bit, 512-word dictionary is employed in the coding process, the original $(8 + 8)$ bits that were used to represent the two pixels are replaced by a single 9-bit code word. Clearly, the size of the dictionary is an important system parameter. If it is too small, the detection of matching intensity-level sequences will be less likely; if it is too large, the size of the code words will adversely affect compression performance.

EXAMPLE 8.7: LZW coding.

Consider the following 4×4, 8-bit image of a vertical edge:

$$
\begin{array}{cccc}
39 & 39 & 126 & 126 \\
39 & 39 & 126 & 126 \\
39 & 39 & 126 & 126 \\
39 & 39 & 126 & 126
\end{array}
$$

Table 8.8 details the steps involved in coding its 16 pixels. A 512-word dictionary with the following starting content is assumed:

Dictionary Location	Entry
0	0
1	1
⋮	⋮
255	255
256	—
⋮	⋮
511	—

Locations 256 through 511 initially are unused.

The image is encoded by processing its pixels in a left-to-right, top-to-bottom manner. Each successive intensity value is concatenated with a variable, column 1 of Table 8.8, called the "currently recognized sequence." As can be seen, this variable is initially null or empty. The dictionary is searched for each concatenated sequence and if found, as was the case in the first row of the table, is replaced by the newly concatenated and recognized (i.e., located in the dictionary) sequence. This was done in column 1 of row 2. No output codes are generated, nor is the dictionary altered. If the concatenated sequence is not found, however, the address of the currently recognized sequence is output as the next encoded value, the concatenated but unrecognized sequence is added to the dictionary, and the currently recognized sequence is initialized to the current pixel value. This occurred in row 2 of the table. The last two columns detail the intensity sequences that are added to the dictionary when scanning the entire 128-bit image. Nine additional code words are defined. At the conclusion of coding, the dictionary contains 265 code words and the LZW algorithm has successfully identified several repeating intensity sequences—leveraging them to reduce the original 128-bit image to 90 bits (i.e., 10 9-bit codes). The encoded output is obtained by reading the third column from top to bottom. The resulting compression ratio is 1.42:1.

A unique feature of the LZW coding just demonstrated is that the coding dictionary or code book is created while the data are being encoded. Remarkably, an LZW decoder builds an identical decompression dictionary as it simultaneously decodes the encoded data stream. It is left as an exercise to the reader (see Problem 8.20) to decode the output of the preceding example and reconstruct the code book. Although not needed in this example, most practical applications require a strategy

TABLE 8.8
LZW Coding
example.

Currently Recognized Sequence	Pixel Being Processed	Encoded Output	Dictionary Location (Code Word)	Dictionary Entry
	39			
39	39	39	256	39–39
39	126	39	257	39–126
126	126	126	258	126–126
126	39	126	259	126–39
39	39			
39–39	126	256	260	39–39–126
126	126			
126–126	39	258	261	126–126–39
39	39			
39-39	126			
39–39–126	126	260	262	39–39–126–126
126	39			
126-39	39	259	263	126–39–39
39	126			
39-126	126	257	264	39–126–126
126		126		

for handling dictionary overflow. A simple solution is to flush or reinitialize the dictionary when it becomes full and continue coding with a new initialized dictionary. A more complex option is to monitor compression performance and flush the dictionary when it becomes poor or unacceptable. Alternatively, the least used dictionary entries can be tracked and replaced when necessary.

8.6 RUN-LENGTH CODING

With reference to
Tables 8.3–8.5, the coding
of run-lengths is used in

- CCITT
- JBIG2
- JPEG
- M-JPEG
- MPEG-1,2,4
- BMP

and other compression standards and file formats.

As was noted earlier, images with repeating intensities along their rows (or columns) can often be compressed by representing runs of identical intensities as *run-length pairs*, where each run-length pair specifies the start of a new intensity and the number of consecutive pixels that have that intensity. The technique, referred to as *run-length encoding* (RLE), was developed in the 1950s and became, along with its 2-D extensions, the standard compression approach in facsimile (FAX) coding. Compression is achieved by eliminating a simple form of spatial redundancy—groups of identical intensities. When there are few (or no) runs of identical pixels, run-length encoding results in data expansion.

EXAMPLE 8.8:   RLE in the BMP file format.

The BMP file format uses a form of run-length encoding in which image data is represented in two different modes: encoded and absolute. Either mode can occur anywhere in the image. In *encoded* mode, a two byte RLE representation is used. The first byte specifies the number of consecutive pixels that have the color index contained in the second byte. The 8-bit color index selects the run's intensity (color or gray value) from a table of 256 possible intensities.

In *absolute* mode, the first byte is 0, and the second byte signals one of four possible conditions, as shown in Table 8.9. When the second byte is 0 or 1, the end of a line or the end of the image has been reached. If it is 2, the next two bytes contain unsigned horizontal and vertical offsets to a new spatial position (and pixel) in the image. If the second byte is between 3 and 255, it specifies the number of uncompressed pixels that follow with each subsequent byte containing the color index of one pixel. The total number of bytes must be aligned on a 16-bit word boundary.

An uncompressed BMP file (saved using Photoshop) of the $512 \times 512 \times 8$ bit image shown in Fig. 8.9(a) requires 263,244 bytes of memory. Compressed using BMP's RLE option, the file expands to 267,706 bytes, and the compression ratio is $C = 0.98$. There are not enough equal intensity runs to make run-length compression effective; a small amount of expansion occurs. For the image in Fig. 8.1(c), however, the BMP RLE option results in a compression ratio $C = 1.35$. (Note that due to differences in overhead, the uncompressed BMP file is smaller than the uncompressed TIFF file in Example 8.6.)

Run-length encoding is particularly effective when compressing binary images. Because there are only two possible intensities (black and white), adjacent pixels are more likely to be identical. In addition, each image row can be represented by a sequence of lengths only, rather than length-intensity pairs as was used in Example 8.8. The basic idea is to code each contiguous group (i.e., run) of 0's or 1's encountered in a left-to-right scan of a row by its length *and* to establish a convention for determining the value of the run. The most common conventions are (1) to specify the value of the first run of each row, or (2) to assume that each row begins with a white run, whose run length may in fact be zero.

Although run-length encoding is in itself an effective method of compressing binary images, additional compression can be achieved by variable-length coding the run lengths themselves. The black and white run lengths can be coded separately using variable-length codes that are specifically tailored to their own statistics. For example, letting symbol a_j represent a black run of length j, we can estimate the probability that symbol a_j was emitted by an imaginary black run-length source by dividing the number of black run lengths of length j in the entire image by the total number of black runs. An estimate of the entropy of this black run-length source, denoted as H_0, follows by substituting these probabilities into Eq. (8-6). A similar argument holds for the entropy of the white runs, denoted as H_1. The approximate run-length entropy of the image is then

$$H_{RL} = \frac{H_0 + H_1}{L_0 + L_1} \tag{8-18}$$

where the variables L_0 and L_1 denote the average values of black and white run lengths, respectively. Equation (8-18) provides an estimate of the average number of bits per pixel required to code the run lengths in a binary image using a variable-length code.

TABLE 8.9
BMP absolute coding mode options. In this mode, the first byte of the BMP pair is 0.

Second Byte Value	Condition
0	End of line
1	End of image
2	Move to a new position
3-255	Specify pixels individually

Two of the oldest and most widely used image compression standards are the CCITT Group 3 and 4 standards for binary image compression. Although they have been used in a variety of computer applications, they were originally designed as facsimile (FAX) coding methods for transmitting documents over telephone networks. The Group 3 standard uses a 1-D run-length coding technique in which the last $K - 1$ lines of each group of K lines (for $K = 2$ or 4) can be optionally coded in a 2-D manner. The Group 4 standard is a simplified or streamlined version of the Group 3 standard in which only 2-D coding is allowed. Both standards use the same 2-D coding approach, which is two-dimensional in the sense that information from the previous line is used to encode the current line. Both 1-D and 2-D coding will be discussed next.

ONE-DIMENSIONAL CCITT COMPRESSION

In the 1-D CCITT Group 3 compression standard, each line of an image[†] is encoded as a series of variable-length Huffman code words that represent the run lengths of alternating white and black runs in a left-to-right scan of the line. The compression method employed is commonly referred to as *Modified Huffman* (MH) coding. The code words themselves are of two types, which the standard refers to as *terminating codes* and *makeup codes*. If run length r is less than or equal to 63, a terminating code is used to represent it. The standard specifies different terminating codes for black and white runs. If $r > 63$, two codes are used; a makeup code for quotient $\lfloor r/64 \rfloor \times 64$, and terminating code for remainder $r \bmod 64$. Makeup codes may or may not depend on the intensity (black or white) of the run being coded. If $\lfloor r/64 \rfloor \times 64 \leq 1728$, separate black and white run makeup codes are specified; otherwise, makeup codes are independent of run intensity. The standard requires that each line begin with a white run-length code word, which may in fact be 00110101, the code for a white run of length zero. Finally, a unique end-of-line (EOL) code word 000000000001 is used to terminate each line, as well as to signal the first line of each new image. The end of a sequence of images is indicated by six consecutive EOLs.

Consult the book website for tables of the MH terminating and makeup codes.

Recall that the notation $\lfloor x \rfloor$ denotes the largest interger less than or equal to x.

TWO-DIMENSIONAL CCITT COMPRESSION

The 2-D compression approach adopted for both the CCITT Group 3 and 4 standards is a line-by-line method in which the position of each black-to-white or white-to-black run transition is coded with respect to the position of a *reference element* a_0 that is situated on the current *coding line*. The previously coded line is called the *reference line*; the reference line for the first line of each new image is an

---

[†] In the standard, images are referred to as *pages* and sequences of images are called *documents*.

imaginary white line. The 2-D coding technique that is used is called *Relative Element Address Designate* (READ) coding. In the Group 3 standard, one or three READ coded lines are allowed between successive MH coded lines; this technique is called *Modified READ* (MR) coding. In the Group 4 standard, a greater number of READ coded lines are allowed, and the method is called *Modified Modified READ* (MMR) coding. As was previously noted, the coding is two-dimensional in the sense that information from the previous line is used to encode the current line. Two-dimensional transforms are not involved.

Figure 8.14 shows the basic 2-D coding process for a single scan line. Note that the initial steps of the procedure are directed at locating several key *changing elements*: $a_0, a_1, a_2, b_1,$ and b_2. A changing element is defined by the standard as a pixel whose value is different from that of the previous pixel on the same line. The most important changing element is a_0 (the reference element), which is either set to the location of an imaginary white changing element to the left of the first pixel of each new coding line, or determined from the previous coding mode. Coding modes will be discussed in the following paragraph. After a_0 is located, a_1 is identified as the location of the next changing element to the right of a_0 on the current coding line, a_2 as the next changing element to the right of a_1 on the coding line, b_1 as the changing element of the opposite value (of a_0) and to the right of a_0 on the reference (or previous) line, and b_2 as the next changing element to the right of b_1 on the reference line. If any of these changing elements are not detected, they are set to the location of an imaginary pixel to the right of the last pixel on the appropriate line. Figure 8.15 provides two illustrations of the general relationships between the various changing elements.

After identification of the current reference element and associated changing elements, two simple tests are performed to select one of three possible coding modes: *pass mode*, *vertical mode*, or *horizontal mode*. The initial test, which corresponds to the first branch point in the flowchart in Fig. 8.14, compares the location of b_2 to that of a_1. The second test, which corresponds to the second branch point in Fig. 8.14, computes the distance (in pixels) between the locations of a_1 and b_1 and compares it against 3. Depending on the outcome of these tests, one of the three outlined coding blocks of Fig. 8.14 is entered and the appropriate coding procedure is executed. A new reference element is then established, as per the flowchart, in preparation for the next coding iteration.

Table 8.10 defines the specific codes utilized for each of the three possible coding modes. In pass mode, which specifically excludes the case in which b_2 is directly above a_1, only the pass mode code word 0001 is needed. As Fig. 8.15(a) shows, this mode identifies white or black reference line runs that do not overlap the current white or black coding line runs. In horizontal coding mode, the distances from a_0 to a_1 and a_1 to a_2 must be coded in accordance with the termination and makeup codes of 1-D CCITT Group 3 compression, then appended to the horizontal mode code word 001. This is indicated in Table 8.10 by the notation $001 + M(a_0a_1) + M(a_1a_2)$, where a_0a_1 and a_1a_2 denote the distances from a_0 to a_1 and a_1 to a_2, respectively. Finally, in vertical coding mode, one of six special variable-length codes is assigned to the distance between a_1 and b_1. Figure 8.15(b) illustrates the parameters involved in both

Consult the book website for the coding tables of the CCITT standard.

FIGURE 8.14
CCITT 2-D
READ coding
procedure. The
notation $|a_1b_1|$
denotes the abso-
lute value of the
distance between
changing
elements a_1
and b_1.

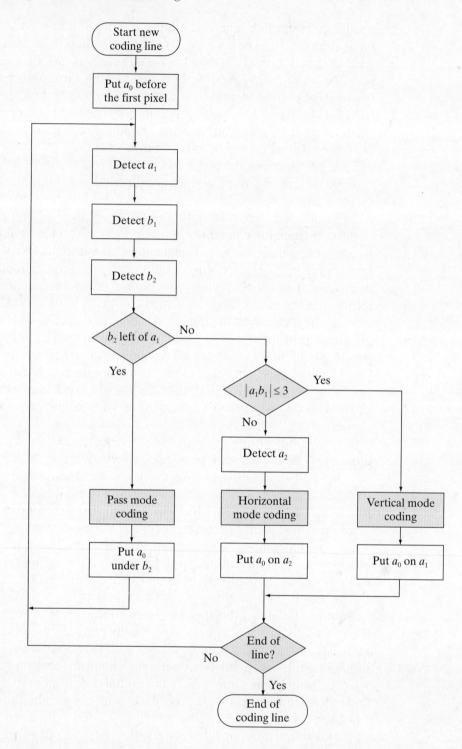

a
b

FIGURE 8.15
CCITT (a) pass mode and (b) horizontal and vertical mode coding parameters.

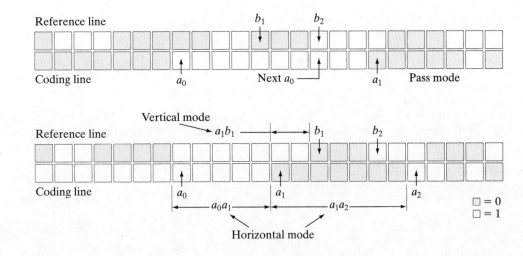

horizontal and vertical mode coding. The extension mode code word at the bottom of Table 8.10 is used to enter an optional facsimile coding mode. For example, the 0000001111 code is used to initiate an uncompressed mode of transmission.

EXAMPLE 8.9: CCITT vertical mode coding example.

Although Fig. 8.15(b) is annotated with the parameters for both horizontal and vertical mode coding (to facilitate the discussion above), the depicted pattern of black and white pixels is a case for vertical mode coding. That is, because b_2 is to the right of a_1, the first (or pass mode) test in Fig. 8.14 fails. The second test, which determines whether the vertical or horizontal coding mode is entered, indicates that vertical mode coding should be used, because the distance from a_1 to b_1 is less than 3. In accordance with Table 8.10, the appropriate code word is 000010, implying that a_1 is two pixels left of b_1. In preparation for the next coding iteration, a_0 is moved to the location of a_1.

TABLE 8.10
CCITT two-dimensional code table.

Mode	Code Word
Pass	0001
Horizontal	$001 + M(a_0a_1) + M(a_1a_2)$
Vertical	
$\quad a_1$ below b_1	1
$\quad a_1$ one to the right of b_1	011
$\quad a_1$ two to the right of b_1	000011
$\quad a_1$ three to the right of b_1	0000011
$\quad a_1$ one to the left of b_1	010
$\quad a_1$ two to the left of b_1	000010
$\quad a_1$ three to the left of b_1	0000010
Extension	0000001xxx

EXAMPLE 8.10: CCITT compression example.

Figure 8.16(a) is a 300 dpi scan of a 7×9.25 inch book page displayed at about 1/3 scale. Note that about half of the page contains text, around 9% is occupied by a halftone image, and the rest is white space. A section of the page is enlarged in Fig. 8.16(b). Keep in mind that we are dealing with a binary image; the illusion of gray tones is created, as was described in Section 4.5, by the halftoning process used in printing. If the binary pixels of the image in Fig. 8.16(a) are stored in groups of 8 pixels per byte, the 1952×2697 bit scanned image, commonly called a document, requires 658,068 bytes. An uncompressed PDF file of the document (created in Photoshop) requires 663,445 bytes. CCITT Group 3 compression reduces the file to 123,497 bytes, resulting in a compression ratio $C = 5.37$. CCITT Group 4 compression reduces the file to 110,456 bytes, increasing the compression ratio to about 6.

8.7 SYMBOL-BASED CODING

With reference to Tables 8.3–8.5, symbol-based coding is used in

- JBIG2

compression.

In *symbol-* or *token-based* coding, an image is represented as a collection of frequently occurring subimages, called *symbols*. Each such symbol is stored in a *symbol dictionary* and the image is coded as a set of triplets $\{(x_1, y_1, t_1), (x_2, y_2, t_2), \ldots\}$, where each (x_i, y_i) pair specifies the location of a symbol in the image and *token* t_i is the address of the symbol or subimage in the dictionary. That is, each triplet represents an instance of a dictionary symbol in the image. Storing repeated symbols only once can compress images significantly, particularly in document storage and retrieval applications where the symbols are often character bitmaps that are repeated many times.

a b

FIGURE 8.16
A binary scan of a book page: (a) scaled to show the general page content;
(b) scaled to show the binary pixels used in dithering.

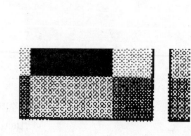

Consider the simple bilevel image in Fig. 8.17(a). It contains the single word, *banana*, which is composed of three unique symbols: a *b*, three *a*'s, and two *n*'s. Assuming that the *b* is the first symbol identified in the coding process, its 9×7 bitmap is stored in location 0 of the symbol dictionary. As Fig. 8.17(b) shows, the token identifying the *b* bitmap is 0. Thus, the first triplet in the encoded image's representation [see Fig. 8.17(c)] is $(0, 2, 0)$, indicating that the upper-left corner (an arbitrary convention) of the rectangular bitmap representing the *b* symbol is to be placed at location $(0, 2)$ in the decoded image. After the bitmaps for the *a* and *n* symbols have been identified and added to the dictionary, the remainder of the image can be encoded with five additional triplets. As long as the six triplets required to locate the symbols in the image, together with the three bitmaps required to define them, are smaller than the original image, compression occurs. In this case, the starting image has $9 \times 51 \times 1$ or 459 bits and, assuming that each triplet is composed of three bytes, the compressed representation has $(6 \times 3 \times 8) + [(9 \times 7) + (6 \times 7) + (6 \times 6)]$ or 285 bits; the resulting compression ratio $C = 1.61$. To decode the symbol-based representation in Fig. 8.17(c), you simply read the bitmaps of the symbols specified in the triplets from the symbol dictionary and place them at the spatial coordinates specified in each triplet.

Symbol-based compression was proposed in the early 1970s (Ascher and Nagy [1974]), but has become practical only recently. Advances in symbol-matching algorithms (see Chapter 12) and increased CPU computer processing speeds have made it possible to both select dictionary symbols and to find where they occur in an image in a timely manner. And like many other compression methods, symbol-based decoding is significantly faster than encoding. Finally, we note that both the symbol bitmaps that are stored in the dictionary and the triplets used to reference them themselves can be encoded to further improve compression performance. If, as in Fig. 8.17, only exact symbol matches are allowed, the resulting compression is lossless; if small differences are permitted, some level of reconstruction error will be present.

JBIG2 COMPRESSION

JBIG2 is an international standard for bilevel image compression. By segmenting an image into overlapping and/or non-overlapping regions of text, halftone, and generic content, compression techniques that are specifically optimized for each type of content are employed:

a b c

FIGURE 8.17
(a) A bi-level document, (b) symbol dictionary, and (c) the triplets used to locate the symbols in the document.

Token	Symbol		Triplet
0	b		$(0, 2, 0)$
			$(3, 10, 1)$
			$(3, 18, 2)$
1	a		$(3, 26, 1)$
			$(3, 34, 2)$
			$(3, 42, 1)$
2	n		

1. *Text regions* are composed of characters that are ideally suited for a symbol-based coding approach. Typically, each symbol will correspond to a character bitmap—a subimage representing a character of text. There is normally only one character bitmap (or subimage) in the symbol dictionary for each upper- and lowercase character of the font being used. For example, there would be one "a" bitmap in the dictionary, one "A" bitmap, one "b" bitmap, and so on.

   In lossy JBIG2 compression, often called *perceptually lossless* or *visually lossless*, we neglect differences between dictionary bitmaps (i.e., the reference character bitmaps or character templates) and specific instances of the corresponding characters in the image. In lossless compression, the differences are stored and used in conjunction with the triplets encoding each character (by the decoder) to produce the actual image bitmaps. All bitmaps are encoded either arithmetically or using MMR (see Section 8.6); the triplets used to access dictionary entries are either arithmetically or Huffman encoded.

2. *Halftone regions* are similar to text regions in that they are composed of patterns arranged in a regular grid. The symbols that are stored in the dictionary, however, are not character bitmaps but periodic patterns that represent intensities (e.g., of a photograph) that have been dithered to produce bilevel images for printing.

3. *Generic regions* contain non-text, non-halftone information, like line art and noise, and are compressed using either arithmetic or MMR coding.

As is true of many image compression standards, JBIG2 defines decoder behavior. It does not explicitly define a standard encoder, but is flexible enough to allow various encoder designs. Although the design of the encoder is left unspecified, it is important because it determines the level of compression that is achieved. After all, the encoder must segment the image into regions, choose the text and halftone symbols that are stored in the dictionaries, and decide when those symbols are essentially the same as, or different from, potential instances of the symbols in the image. The decoder simply uses that information to recreate the original image.

EXAMPLE 8.11: JBIG2 compression example.

Consider again the bilevel image in Fig. 8.16(a). Figure 8.18(a) shows a reconstructed section of the image after lossless JBIG2 encoding (by a commercially available document compression application). It is an exact replica of the original image. Note that the *d*s in the reconstructed text vary slightly, despite the fact that they were generated from the same *d* entry in the dictionary. The differences between that *d* and the *d*s in the image were used to refine the output of the dictionary. The standard defines an algorithm for accomplishing this during the decoding of the encoded dictionary bitmaps. For the purposes of our discussion, you can think of it as adding the difference between a dictionary bitmap and a specific instance of the corresponding character in the image to the bitmap read from the dictionary.

Figure 8.18(b) is another reconstruction of the area in Fig. 8.18(a) after perceptually lossless JBIG2 compression. Note that the *d*s in this figure are identical. They have been copied directly from the symbol dictionary. The reconstruction is called perceptually lossless because the text is readable and the font is even the same. The small differences shown in Fig. 8.18(c) between the *d*s in the original image and the *d* in the dictionary are considered unimportant because they do not affect readability. Remember that

FIGURE 8.18
JBIG2 compression comparison: (a) lossless compression and reconstruction; (b) perceptually lossless; and (c) the scaled difference between the two.

images of size images of size

just described   just described

esulting coeffic   esulting coeffic

nt arrays.   nt arrays.

retained coeffi   retained coeffi

:n we disregar   :n we disregar

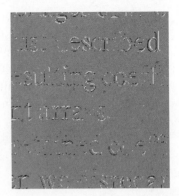

we are dealing with bilevel images, so there are only three intensities in Fig. 8.18(c). Intensity 128 indicates areas where there is no difference between the corresponding pixels of the images in Figs. 8.18(a) and (b); intensities 0 (black) and 255 (white) indicate pixels of opposite intensities in the two images—for example, a black pixel in one image that is white in the other, and vice versa.

The lossless JBIG2 compression that was used to generate Fig. 8.18(a) reduces the original 663,445 byte uncompressed PDF image to 32,705 bytes; the compression ratio is $C = 20.3$. Perceptually lossless JBIG2 compression reduces the image to 23,913 bytes, increasing the compression ratio to about 27.7. These compressions are 4 to 5 times greater than the CCITT Group 3 and 4 results from Example 8.10.

8.8 BIT-PLANE CODING

With reference to Tables 8.3–8.5, bit-plane coding is used in

- JBIG2
- JPEG-2000

compression standards.

The run-length and symbol-based techniques of the previous sections can be applied to images with more than two intensities by individually processing their bit planes. The technique, called *bit-plane coding*, is based on the concept of decomposing a multilevel (monochrome or color) image into a series of binary images (see Section 3.2) and compressing each binary image via one of several well-known binary compression methods. In this section, we describe the two most popular decomposition approaches.

The intensities of an m-bit monochrome image can be represented in the form of the base-2 polynomial

$$a_{m-1} 2^{m-1} + a_{m-2} 2^{m-2} + \ldots + a_1 2^1 + a_0 2^0 \tag{8-19}$$

Based on this property, a simple method of decomposing the image into a collection of binary images is to separate the m coefficients of the polynomial into m 1-bit bit planes. As noted in Section 3.2, the lowest-order bit plane (the plane corresponding to the least significant bit) is generated by collecting the a_0 bits of each pixel, while the highest-order bit plane contains the a_{m-1} bits or coefficients. In general, each bit plane is constructed by setting its pixels equal to the values of the appropriate bits or polynomial coefficients from each pixel in the original image. The inherent disadvantage of this decomposition approach is that small changes in intensity can have a significant impact on the complexity of the bit planes. If a pixel of intensity 127 (01111111) is adjacent to a pixel of intensity 128 (10000000), for instance, every bit plane will contain a corresponding 0 to 1 (or 1 to 0) transition. For example, because the most significant bits of the binary codes for 127 and 128 are different, the highest bit plane will contain a zero-valued pixel next to a pixel of value 1, creating a 0 to 1 (or 1 to 0) transition at that point.

An alternative decomposition approach (which reduces the effect of small intensity variations) is to first represent the image by an m-bit *Gray code*. The m-bit Gray code $g_{m-1} \cdots g_2 g_1 g_0$ that corresponds to the polynomial in Eq. (8-19) can be computed from

$$g_i = a_i \oplus a_{i+1} \quad 0 \le i \le m-2$$
$$g_{m-1} = a_{m-1}$$

(8-20)

Here, $\oplus$ denotes the exclusive OR operation. This code has the unique property that successive code words differ in only one bit position. Thus, small changes in intensity are less likely to affect all m bit planes. For instance, when intensity levels 127 and 128 are adjacent, only the highest-order bit plane will contain a 0 to 1 transition, because the Gray codes that correspond to 127 and 128 are 01000000 and 11000000, respectively.

EXAMPLE 8.12: Bit-plane coding.

Figures 8.19 and 8.20 show the eight binary and Gray-coded bit planes of the 8-bit monochrome image of the child in Fig. 8.19(a). Note that the high-order bit planes are far less complex than their low-order counterparts. That is, they contain large uniform areas of significantly less detail, busyness, or randomness. In addition, the Gray-coded bit planes are less complex than the corresponding binary bit planes. Both observations are reflected in the JBIG2 coding results of Table 8.11. Note, for instance, that the a_5 and g_5 results are significantly larger than the a_6 and g_6 compressions, and that both g_5 and g_6 are smaller than their a_5 and a_6 counterparts. This trend continues throughout the table, with the single exception of a_0. Gray-coding provides a compression advantage of about 1.06:1 on average. Combined together, the Gray-coded files compress the original monochrome image by $678,676/475,964$ or 1.43:1; the non-Gray-coded files compress the image by $678,676/503,916$ or 1.35:1.

Finally, we note that the two least significant bits in Fig. 8.20 have little apparent structure. Because this is typical of most 8-bit monochrome images, bit-plane coding is usually restricted to images of 6 bits/pixel or less. JBIG1, the predecessor to JBIG2, imposes such a limit.

8.9 BLOCK TRANSFORM CODING

With reference to Tables 8.3–8.5, block transform coding is used in

- JPEG
- M-JPEG
- MPEG-1,2,4
- H.261, H.262, H.263, and H.264
- DV and HDV
- VC-1

In this section, we consider a compression technique that divides an image into small non-overlapping blocks of equal size (e.g., 8×8) and processes the blocks independently using a 2-D transform. In *block transform coding*, a reversible, linear transform (such as the Fourier transform) is used to map each block or subimage into a set of transform coefficients, which are then quantized and coded. For most images, a significant number of the coefficients have small magnitudes and can be coarsely quantized (or discarded entirely) with little image distortion. A variety of

TABLE 8.11
JBIG2 lossless coding results for the binary and Gray-coded bit planes of Fig. 8.19(a). These results include the overhead of each bit plane's PDF representation.

Coefficient m	Binary Code (PDF bits)	Gray Code (PDF bits)	Compression Ratio
7	6,999	6,999	1.00
6	12,791	11,024	1.16
5	40,104	36,914	1.09
4	55,911	47,415	1.18
3	78,915	67,787	1.16
2	101,535	92,630	1.10
1	107,909	105,286	1.03
0	99,753	107,909	0.92

transformations, including the discrete Fourier transform (DFT) of Chapter 4, can be used to transform the image data.

Figure 8.21 shows a typical block transform coding system. The decoder implements the inverse sequence of steps (with the exception of the quantization function) of the encoder, which performs four relatively straightforward operations: subimage decomposition, transformation, quantization, and coding. An $M \times N$ input image is subdivided first into subimages of size $n \times n$, which are then transformed to generate MN/n^2 subimage transform arrays, each of size $n \times n$. The goal of the transformation process is to decorrelate the pixels of each subimage, or to pack as much information as possible into the smallest number of transform coefficients. The quantization stage then selectively eliminates or more coarsely quantizes the coefficients that carry the least amount of information in a predefined sense (several methods will be discussed later in the section). These coefficients have the smallest impact on reconstructed subimage quality. The encoding process terminates by coding (normally using a variable-length code) the quantized coefficients. Any or all of the transform encoding steps can be adapted to local image content, called *adaptive transform coding*, or fixed for all subimages, called *nonadaptive transform coding*.

In this section, we restrict our attention to square subimages (the most commonly used). It is assumed that the input image is padded, if necessary, so that both M and N are multiples of n.

TRANSFORM SELECTION

Block transform coding systems based on a variety of discrete 2-D transforms have been constructed and/or studied extensively. The choice of a particular transform in a given application depends on the amount of reconstruction error that can be tolerated and the computational resources available. Compression is achieved during the quantization of the transformed coefficients (not during the transformation step).

EXAMPLE 8.13: Block transform coding with the DFT, WHT, and DCT.

Figures 8.22(a) through (c) show three approximations of the 512×512 monochrome image in Fig. 8.9(a). These pictures were obtained by dividing the original image into subimages of size 8×8, representing each subimage using three of the transforms described in Chapter 7 (the DFT, WHT, and DCT transforms), truncating 50% of the resulting coefficients, and taking the inverse transform of the truncated coefficient arrays.

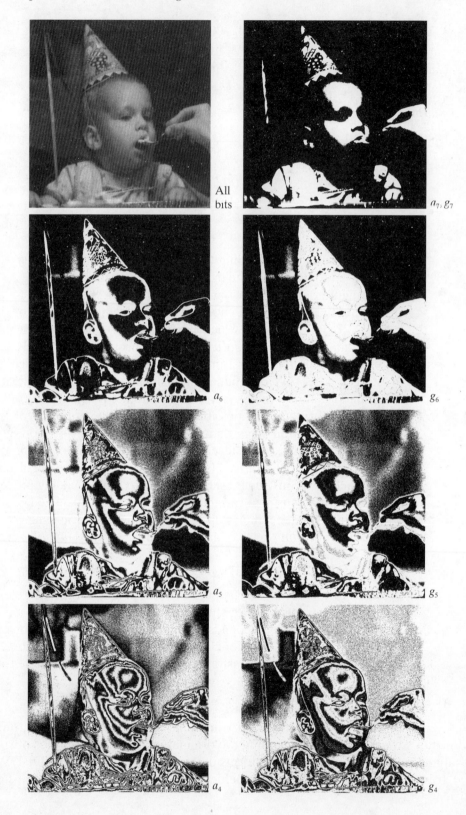

FIGURE 8.19
(a) A 256-bit
monochrome
image.
(b)–(h) The four
most significant
binary and
Gray-coded bit
planes of the
image in (a).

FIGURE 8.20
(a)–(h) The four
least significant
binary (left
column) and
Gray-coded
(right column)
bit planes of
the image in
Fig. 8.19(a).

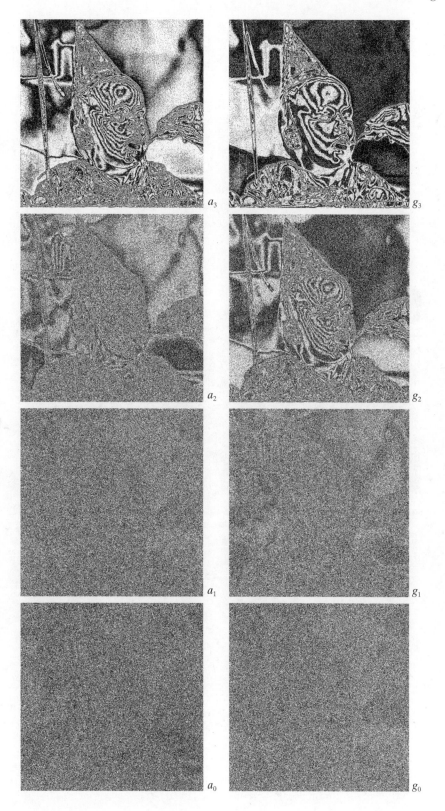

a
b

FIGURE 8.21
A block transform
coding system:
(a) encoder;
(b) decoder.

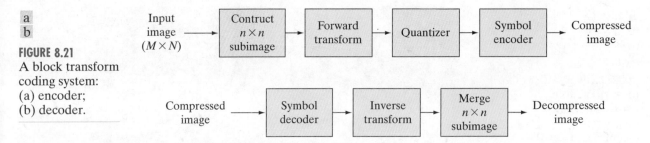

In each case, the 32 retained coefficients were selected on the basis of maximum magnitude. Note that in all cases, the 32 discarded coefficients had little visual impact on the quality of the reconstructed image. Their elimination, however, was accompanied by some mean-squared error, which can be seen in the scaled error images of Figs. 8.22(d) through (f). The actual rms errors were 2.32, 1.78, and 1.13 intensities, respectively.

a b c
d e f

FIGURE 8.22 Approximations of Fig. 8.9(a) using the (a) Fourier, (b) Walsh-Hadamard, and (c) cosine transforms, together with the corresponding scaled error images in (d)–(f).

The small differences in mean-squared reconstruction error noted in the preceding example are related directly to the energy or information packing properties of the transforms employed. In accordance with Eqs. (7-75) and (7-76) of Section 7.5, an $n \times n$ subimage $g(x, y)$ can be expressed as a function of its 2-D transform $T(u, v)$:

$$\mathbf{G} = \sum_{u=0}^{n-1} \sum_{v=0}^{n-1} T(u, v) \mathbf{S}_{uv} \tag{8-21}$$

for $x, y = 0, 1, 2, ..., n - 1$. $\mathbf{G}$, the matrix containing the pixels of the input subimage, is explicitly defined as a linear combination of n^2 basis images of size $n \times n$. Recall that the basis images of the DFT, DCT, and WHT transforms for $n = 8$ are shown in Figs. 7.7, 7.10, and 7.16. If we now define a transform coefficient *masking function*

$$\chi(u, v) = \begin{cases} 0 & \text{if } T(u, v) \text{ satisfies a specified truncation criterion} \\ 1 & \text{otherwise} \end{cases} \tag{8-22}$$

for $u, v = 0, 1, 2, ..., n - 1$, an approximation of $\mathbf{G}$ can be obtained from the truncated expansion

$$\hat{\mathbf{G}} = \sum_{u=0}^{n-1} \sum_{v=0}^{n-1} \chi(u, v) T(u, v) \mathbf{S}_{uv} \tag{8-23}$$

where $\chi(u, v)$ is constructed to eliminate the basis images that make the smallest contribution to the total sum in Eq. (8-21). The mean-squared error between subimage $\mathbf{G}$ and approximation $\hat{\mathbf{G}}$ then is

$$
\begin{aligned}
e_{ms} &= E\left\{\left\|\mathbf{G} - \hat{\mathbf{G}}\right\|^2\right\} \\
&= E\left\{\left\|\sum_{u=0}^{n-1} \sum_{v=0}^{n-1} T(u, v) \mathbf{S}_{uv} - \sum_{u=0}^{n-1} \sum_{v=0}^{n-1} \chi(u, v) T(u, v) \mathbf{S}_{uv}\right\|^2\right\} \\
&= E\left\{\left\|\sum_{u=0}^{n-1} \sum_{v=0}^{n-1} T(u, v) \mathbf{S}_{uv} \left[1 - \chi(u, v)\right]\right\|^2\right\} \\
&= \sum_{u=0}^{n-1} \sum_{v=0}^{n-1} \sigma_{T(u,v)}^2 \left[1 - \chi(u, v)\right]
\end{aligned}
\tag{8-24}
$$

where $\left\|\mathbf{G} - \hat{\mathbf{G}}\right\|$ is the norm of matrix $\left(\mathbf{G} - \hat{\mathbf{G}}\right)$ and $\sigma_{T(u,v)}^2$ is the variance of the coefficient at transform location (u, v). The final simplification is based on the orthonormal nature of the basis images and the assumption that the pixels of $\mathbf{G}$ are generated by a random process with zero mean and known covariance. The total mean-squared error of approximation thus is the sum of the variances of the discarded transform coefficients; that is, the coefficients for which $\chi(u, v) = 0$, so that $\left[1 - \chi(u, v)\right]$ in Eq. (8-24) is 1. Transformations that redistribute or pack the most information into the fewest coefficients provide the best subimage approximations and, consequently, the smallest reconstruction errors. Finally, under the assumptions that led to Eq. (8-24), the mean-squared error of the MN/n^2 subimages of an $M \times N$ image are identical. Thus the mean-squared error (being a measure of *average* error) of the $M \times N$ image equals the mean-squared error of a single subimage.

The earlier example showed that the information packing ability of the DCT is superior to that of the DFT and WHT. Although this condition usually holds for most images, the Karhunen-Loève transform (see Chapter 11), not the DCT, is the optimal transform in an information packing sense. This is due to the fact that the KLT minimizes the mean-squared error in Eq. (8-24) for any input image and any number of retained coefficients (Kramer and Mathews [1956]). However, because the KLT is data dependent, obtaining the KLT basis images for each subimage, in general, is a nontrivial computational task. For this reason, the KLT is used infrequently for image compression. Instead, a transform, such as the DFT, WHT, or DCT, whose basis images are fixed (input independent) is normally used. Of the possible input independent transforms, the nonsinusoidal transforms (such as the WHT transform) are the simplest to implement. The sinusoidal transforms (such as the DFT or DCT) more closely approximate the information packing ability of the optimal KLT.

Hence, most transform coding systems are based on the DCT, which provides a good compromise between information packing ability and computational complexity. In fact, the properties of the DCT have proved to be of such practical value that the DCT is an international standard for transform coding systems. Compared to the other input independent transforms, it has the advantages of having been implemented in a single integrated circuit, packing the most information into the fewest coefficients[†] (for most images), and minimizing the block-like appearance, called *blocking artifact*, that results when the boundaries between subimages become visible. This last property is particularly important in comparisons with the other sinusoidal transforms. As Fig. 7.11(a) of Section 7.6 shows, the implicit n-point periodicity of the DFT gives rise to boundary discontinuities that result in substantial high-frequency transform content. When the DFT transform coefficients are truncated or quantized, the Gibbs phenomenon[‡] causes the boundary points to take on erroneous values, which appear in an image as blocking artifact. That is, the boundaries between adjacent subimages become visible because the boundary pixels of the subimages assume the mean values of discontinuities formed at the boundary points [see Fig. 7.11(a)]. The DCT of Fig. 7.11(b) reduces this effect, because its implicit $2n$-point periodicity does not inherently produce boundary discontinuities.

An additional condition for optimality is that the masking function of Eq. (8-22) selects the KLT coefficients of maximum variance.

SUBIMAGE SIZE SELECTION

Another significant factor affecting transform coding error and computational complexity is subimage size. In most applications, images are subdivided so the correlation (redundancy) between adjacent subimages is reduced to some acceptable level

---

[†]Ahmed et al. [1974] first noticed that the KLT basis images of a first-order Markov image source closely resemble the DCT's basis images. As the correlation between adjacent pixels approaches one, the input-dependent KLT basis images become identical to the input-independent DCT basis images (Clarke [1985]).

[‡]This phenomenon, described in most electrical engineering texts on circuit analysis, occurs because the Fourier transform fails to converge uniformly at discontinuities. At discontinuities, Fourier expansions take the mean values of the points of discontinuity.

and so n is an integer power of 2 where, as before, n is the subimage dimension. The latter condition simplifies the computation of the subimage transforms (see the base-2 successive doubling method discussed in Section 4.11). In general, both the level of compression and computational complexity increase as the subimage size increases. The most popular subimage sizes are 8×8 and 16×16.

EXAMPLE 8.14: Effects of subimage size on transform coding.

Figure 8.23 illustrates graphically the impact of subimage size on transform coding reconstruction error. The data plotted were obtained by dividing the monochrome image of Fig. 8.9(a) into subimages of size $n \times n$, for $n = 2, 4, 8, 16, \ldots, 256, 512$, computing the transform of each subimage, truncating 75% of the resulting coefficients, and taking the inverse transform of the truncated arrays. Note that the Hadamard and cosine curves flatten as the size of the subimage becomes greater than 8×8, whereas the Fourier reconstruction error continues to decrease in this region. As n further increases, the Fourier reconstruction error crosses the Walsh-Hadamard curve and approaches the cosine result. This result is consistent with the theoretical and experimental findings reported by Netravali and Limb [1980] and by Pratt [2001] for a 2-D Markov image source.

All three curves intersect when 2×2 subimages are used. In this case, only one of the four coefficients (25%) of each transformed array was retained. The coefficient in all cases was the dc component, so the inverse transform simply replaced the four subimage pixels by their average value [see Eq. (4-92)]. This condition is evident in Fig. 8.24(b), which shows a zoomed portion of the 2×2 DCT result. Note that the blocking artifact that is prevalent in this result decreases as the subimage size increases to 4×4 and 8×8 in Figs. 8.24(c) and (d). Figure 8.24(a) shows a zoomed portion of the original image for reference.

BIT ALLOCATION

The reconstruction error associated with the truncated series expansion of Eq. (8-23) is a function of the number and relative importance of the transform coefficients that are discarded, as well as the precision that is used to represent the retained coefficients. In most transform coding systems, the retained coefficients are selected [that is, the masking function of Eq. (8-22) is constructed] on the basis of maximum vari-

FIGURE 8.23
Reconstruction error versus subimage size.

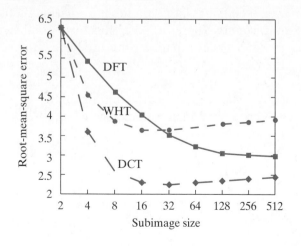

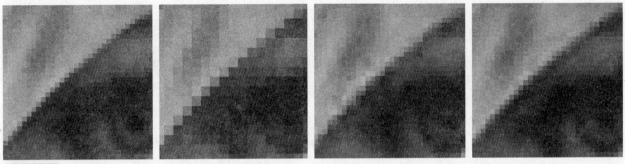

a b c d

FIGURE 8.24 Approximations of Fig. 8.24(a) using 25% of the DCT coefficients and (b) 2×2 subimages, (c) 4×4 subimages, and (d) 8×8 subimages. The original image in (a) is a zoomed section of Fig. 8.9(a).

ance, called *zonal coding*, or on the basis of maximum magnitude, called *threshold coding*. The overall process of truncating, quantizing, and coding the coefficients of a transformed subimage is commonly called *bit allocation*.

EXAMPLE 8.15: Bit allocation.

Figures 8.25(a) and (c) show two approximations of Fig. 8.9(a) in which 87.5% of the DCT coefficients of each 8×8 subimage were discarded. The first result was obtained via threshold coding by keeping the eight largest transform coefficients, and the second image was generated by using a zonal coding approach. In the latter case, each DCT coefficient was considered a random variable whose distribution could be computed over the ensemble of all transformed subimages. The eight distributions of largest variance (12.5% of the 64 coefficients in the transformed 8×8 subimage) were located and used to determine the coordinates [u and v of the coefficients, $T(u,v)$], that were retained for all subimages. Note that the threshold coding difference image of Fig. 8.25(b) contains less error than the zonal coding result in Fig. 8.25(d). Both images have been scaled to make the errors more visible. The corresponding rms errors are 4.5 and 6.5 intensities, respectively.

Zonal Coding Implementation

Zonal coding is based on the information theory concept of viewing information as uncertainty. Therefore, the transform coefficients of maximum variance carry the most image information, and should be retained in the coding process. The variances themselves can be calculated directly from the ensemble of MN/n^2 transformed subimage arrays (as in the preceding example) or based on an assumed image model (say, a Markov autocorrelation function). In either case, the zonal sampling process can be viewed, in accordance with Eq. (8-23), as multiplying each $T(u,v)$ by the corresponding element in a *zonal mask*, which is constructed by placing a 1 in the locations of maximum variance and a 0 in all other locations. Coefficients of maximum variance usually are located around the origin of an image transform, resulting in the typical zonal mask shown in Fig. 8.26(a).

The coefficients retained during the zonal sampling process must be quantized and coded, so zonal masks are sometimes depicted showing the number of bits used

a b
c d

FIGURE 8.25
Approximations
of Fig. 8.9(a) using
12.5% of the
DCT coefficients:
(a)–(b) threshold
coding results;
(c)–(d) zonal
coding results. The
difference images
are scaled by 4.

to code each coefficient [see Fig. 8.26(b)]. In most cases, the coefficients are allocated the same number of bits, or some fixed number of bits is distributed among them unequally. In the first case, the coefficients generally are normalized by their standard deviations and uniformly quantized. In the second case, a quantizer, such as an optimal Lloyd-Max quantizer (see Optimal quantizers in Section 8.10), is designed for each coefficient. To construct the required quantizers, the zeroth or DC coefficient normally is modeled by a Rayleigh density function, whereas the remaining coefficients are modeled by a Laplacian or Gaussian density.[†] The number of quantization levels (and thus the number of bits) allotted to each quantizer is made proportional to $\log_2 \sigma^2_{T(u,v)}$. Thus, the retained coefficients in Eq. (8-23)—which (in the context of the current discussion) are selected on the basis of maximum variance—are assigned bits in proportion to the logarithm of the coefficient variances.

Threshold Coding Implementation

Zonal coding usually is implemented by using a single fixed mask for all subimages. Threshold coding, however, is inherently adaptive in the sense that the location of the transform coefficients retained for each subimage vary from one subimage to another. In fact, threshold coding is the adaptive transform coding approach most

---

[†]As each coefficient is a linear combination of the pixels in its subimage [see Eq. (7-31)], the central-limit theorem suggests that, as subimage size increases, the coefficients tend to become Gaussian. This result does not apply to the dc coefficient, however, because nonnegative images always have positive dc coefficients.

1	1	1	1	1	0	0	0
1	1	1	1	0	0	0	0
1	1	1	0	0	0	0	0
1	1	0	0	0	0	0	0
1	0	0	0	0	0	0	0
0	0	0	0	0	0	0	0
0	0	0	0	0	0	0	0
0	0	0	0	0	0	0	0

8	7	6	4	3	2	1	0
7	6	5	4	3	2	1	0
6	5	4	3	3	1	1	0
4	4	3	3	2	1	0	0
3	3	3	2	1	1	0	0
2	2	1	1	1	0	0	0
1	1	1	0	0	0	0	0
0	0	0	0	0	0	0	0

1	1	0	1	1	0	0	0
1	1	1	0	0	0	0	0
1	1	0	0	0	0	0	0
1	0	0	0	0	0	0	0
0	0	0	0	0	0	0	0
0	0	0	0	0	0	0	0
0	0	0	0	0	0	0	0
0	0	0	0	0	0	0	0

0	1	5	6	14	15	27	28
2	4	7	13	16	26	29	42
3	8	12	17	25	30	41	43
9	11	18	24	31	40	44	53
10	19	23	32	39	45	52	54
20	22	33	38	46	51	55	60
21	34	37	47	50	56	59	61
35	36	48	49	57	58	62	63

often used in practice because of its computational simplicity. The underlying concept is that, for any subimage, the transform coefficients of largest magnitude make
the most significant contribution to reconstructed subimage quality, as demonstrated
in the last example. Because the locations of the maximum coefficients vary from
one subimage to another, the elements of $\chi(u,v)T(u,v)$ normally are reordered (in a
predefined manner) to form a 1-D, run-length coded sequence. Figure 8.26(c) shows
a typical *threshold mask* for one subimage of a hypothetical image. This mask provides a convenient way to visualize the threshold coding process for the corresponding subimage, as well as to mathematically describe the process using Eq. (8-23).
When the mask is applied [via Eq. (8-23)] to the subimage for which it was derived,
and the resulting $n \times n$ array is reordered to form an n^2-element coefficient sequence
in accordance with the zigzag ordering pattern of Fig. 8.26(d), the reordered 1-D
sequence contains several long runs of 0's. [The zigzag pattern becomes evident by
starting at 0 in Fig. 8.26(d) and following the numbers in sequence.] These runs
normally are run-length coded. The nonzero or retained coefficients, corresponding
to the mask locations that contain a 1, are represented using a variable-length code.

There are three basic ways to threshold a transformed subimage or, stated differently, to create a subimage threshold masking function of the form given in
Eq. (8-22): (1) A single global threshold can be applied to all subimages; (2) a different threshold can be used for each subimage, or; (3) the threshold can be varied as a
function of the location of each coefficient within the subimage. In the first approach,

The N in "N-largest coding" is not an image dimension, but refers to the number of coefficients that are kept.

the level of compression differs from image to image, depending on the number of coefficients that exceed the global threshold. In the second, called *N-largest coding*, the same number of coefficients is discarded for each subimage. As a result, the code rate is constant and known in advance. The third technique, like the first, results in a variable code rate, but offers the advantage that thresholding *and* quantization can be combined by replacing $\chi(u,v)T(u,v)$ in Eq. (8-23) with

$$\hat{T}(u,v) = \text{round}\left[\frac{T(u,v)}{Z(u,v)}\right] \tag{8-25}$$

where $\hat{T}(u,v)$ is a thresholded and quantized approximation of $T(u,v)$, and $Z(u,v)$ is an element of the following transform normalization array:

$$\mathbf{Z} = \begin{bmatrix} Z(0,0) & Z(0,1) & \dots & Z(0,n-1) \\ Z(1,0) & \vdots & \dots & \vdots \\ \vdots & \vdots & \dots & \vdots \\ \vdots & \vdots & \dots & \vdots \\ \vdots & \vdots & \dots & \vdots \\ Z(n-1,0) & Z(n-1,1) & \dots & Z(n-1,n-1) \end{bmatrix} \tag{8-26}$$

Before a normalized (thresholded and quantized) subimage transform, $\hat{T}(u,v)$, can be inverse transformed to obtain an approximation of subimage $g(x,y)$, it must be multiplied by $Z(u,v)$. The resulting denormalized array, denoted $\dot{T}(u,v)$ is an approximation of $\hat{T}(u,v)$:

$$\dot{T}(u,v) = \hat{T}(u,v)Z(u,v) \tag{8-27}$$

The inverse transform of $\dot{T}(u,v)$ yields the decompressed subimage approximation.

   Figure 8.27(a) graphically depicts Eq. (8-25) for the case in which $Z(u,v)$ is assigned a particular value c. Note that $\hat{T}(u,v)$ assumes integer value k if and only if

$$kc - \frac{c}{2} \le T(u,v) < kc + \frac{c}{2} \tag{8-28}$$

If $Z(u,v) > 2T(u,v)$, then $\hat{T}(u,v) = 0$ and the transform coefficient is completely truncated or discarded. When $\hat{T}(u,v)$ is represented with a variable-length code that increases in length as the magnitude of k increases, the number of bits used to represent $T(u,v)$ is controlled by the value of c. Thus, the elements of $\mathbf{Z}$ can be scaled to achieve a variety of compression levels. Figure 8.27(b) shows a typical normalization array. This array, which has been used extensively in the JPEG standardization efforts (see the next section), weighs each coefficient of a transformed subimage according to heuristically determined perceptual or psychovisual importance.

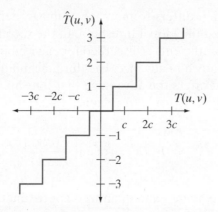

a b

FIGURE 8.27
(a) A threshold coding quantization curve [see Eq. (8-28)]. (b) A typical normalization matrix.

16	11	10	16	24	40	51	61
12	12	14	19	26	58	60	55
14	13	16	24	40	57	69	56
14	17	22	29	51	87	80	62
18	22	37	56	68	109	103	77
24	35	55	64	81	104	113	92
49	64	78	87	103	121	120	101
72	92	95	98	112	100	103	99

EXAMPLE 8.16: Illustration of threshold coding.

Figures 8.28(a) through (f) show six threshold-coded approximations of the monochrome image in Fig. 8.9(a). All images were generated using an 8×8 DCT and the normalization array of Fig. 8.27(b). The first result, which provides a compression ratio of about 12 to 1 (i.e., C = 12), was obtained by direct application of that normalization array. The remaining results, which compress the original image by 19, 30, 49, 85, and 182 to 1, were generated after multiplying (scaling) the normalization arrays by 2, 4, 8, 16, and 32, respectively. The corresponding rms errors are 3.83, 4.93, 6.62, 9.35, 13.94, and 22.46 intensity levels.

JPEG

One of the most popular and comprehensive continuous tone, still-frame compression standards is the JPEG standard. It defines three different coding systems: (1) a lossy baseline coding system, which is based on the DCT and is adequate for most compression applications; (2) an extended coding system for greater compression, higher precision, or progressive reconstruction applications; and (3) a lossless independent coding system for reversible compression. To be JPEG compatible, a product or system must include support for the baseline system. No particular file format, spatial resolution, or color space model is specified.

In the baseline system, often called the *sequential baseline system*, the input and output data precision is limited to 8 bits, whereas the quantized DCT values are restricted to 11 bits. The compression itself is performed in three sequential steps: DCT computation, quantization, and variable-length code assignment. The image is first subdivided into pixel blocks of size 8×8, which are processed left-to-right, top-to-bottom. As each 8×8 block or subimage is encountered, its 64 pixels are level-shifted by subtracting the quantity 2^{k-1}, where 2^k is the maximum number of intensity levels. The 2-D discrete cosine transform of the block is then computed, quantized in accordance with Eq. (8-25), and reordered, using the zigzag pattern of Fig. 8.26(d), to form a 1-D sequence of quantized coefficients.

Because the one-dimensionally reordered array generated under the zigzag pattern of Fig. 8.26(d) is arranged qualitatively according to increasing spatial frequency, the JPEG coding procedure is designed to take advantage of the long runs

a b c
d e f

FIGURE 8.28 Approximations of Fig. 8.9(a) using the DCT and normalization array of Fig. 8.27(b): (a) $\mathbf{Z}$, (b) $2\mathbf{Z}$, (c) $4\mathbf{Z}$, (d) $8\mathbf{Z}$, (e) $16\mathbf{Z}$, and (f) $32\mathbf{Z}$.

Consult the book website for the JPEG default Huffman code tables: (1) a JPEG coefficient category table, (2) a default DC code table, and (3) a default AC code table.

of zeros that normally result from the reordering. In particular, the nonzero AC[†] coefficients are coded using a variable-length code that defines the coefficient values and number of preceding zeros. The DC coefficient is difference coded relative to the DC coefficient of the previous subimage. The default JPEG Huffman codes for the luminance component of a color image, or intensity of a monochrome image, are available on the book website. The JPEG recommended luminance quantization array is given in Fig. 8.27(b) and can be scaled to provide a variety of compression levels. The scaling of this array allows users to select the "quality" of JPEG compressions. Although default coding tables and quantization arrays are provided for both color and monochrome processing, the user is free to construct custom tables and/or arrays, which may be adapted to the characteristics of the image being compressed.

[†]In the standard, the term AC denotes all transform coefficients with the exception of the zeroth or DC coefficient.

EXAMPLE 8.17: JPEG baseline coding and decoding.

Consider compression and reconstruction of the following 8×8 subimage with the JPEG baseline standard:

52	55	61	66	70	61	64	73
63	59	66	90	109	85	69	72
62	59	68	113	144	104	66	73
63	58	71	122	154	106	70	69
67	61	68	104	126	88	68	70
79	65	60	70	77	63	58	75
85	71	64	59	55	61	65	83
87	79	69	68	65	76	78	94

The original image consists of 256 or 2^8 possible intensities, so the coding process begins by level shifting the pixels of the original subimage by -2^7 or -128 intensity levels. The resulting shifted array is

−76	−73	−67	−62	−58	−67	−64	−55
−65	−69	−62	−38	−19	−43	−59	−56
−66	−69	−60	−15	16	−24	−62	−55
−65	−70	−57	−6	26	−22	−58	−59
−61	−67	−60	−24	−2	−40	−60	−58
−49	−63	−68	−58	−51	−65	−70	−53
−43	−57	−64	−69	−73	−67	−63	−45
−41	−49	−59	−60	−63	−52	−50	−34

which, when transformed in accordance with the forward DCT of Eq. (7-31) with $r(x, y, u, v) = s(x, y, u, v)$ of Eq. (7-85) for $n = 8$ becomes

−415	−29	−62	25	55	−20	−1	3
7	−21	−62	9	11	−7	−6	6
−46	8	77	−25	−30	10	7	−5
−50	13	35	−15	−9	6	0	3
11	−8	−13	−2	−1	1	−4	1
−10	1	3	−3	−1	0	2	−1
−4	−1	2	−1	2	−3	1	−2
−1	−1	−1	−2	−1	−1	0	−1

If the JPEG recommended normalization array of Fig. 8.27(b) is used to quantize the transformed array, the scaled and truncated [that is, normalized in accordance with Eq. (8-25)] coefficients are

−26	−3	−6	2	2	0	0	0
1	−2	−4	0	0	0	0	0
−3	1	5	−1	−1	0	0	0
−4	1	2	−1	0	0	0	0
1	0	0	0	0	0	0	0
0	0	0	0	0	0	0	0
0	0	0	0	0	0	0	0
0	0	0	0	0	0	0	0

where, for instance, the DC coefficient is computed as

$$\hat{T}(0,0) = \text{round}\left[\frac{T(0,0)}{Z(0,0)}\right]$$

$$= \text{round}\left[\frac{-415}{16}\right] = -26$$

Note that the transformation and normalization process produces a large number of zero-valued coefficients. When the coefficients are reordered in accordance with the zigzag ordering pattern of Fig. 8.26(d), the resulting 1-D coefficient sequence is

$$\left[-26 \ -3 \ 1 \ -3 \ -2 \ -6 \ 2 \ -4 \ 1 \ -4 \ 1 \ 1 \ 5 \ 0 \ 2 \ 0 \ 0 \ -1 \ 2 \ 0 \ 0 \ 0 \ 0 \ 0 \ -1 \ -1 \ \text{EOB}\right]$$

where the EOB symbol denotes the end-of-block condition. A special EOB Huffman code word (see category 0 and run-length 0 of the JPEG default AC code table on the book website) is provided to indicate that the remainder of the coefficients in a reordered sequence are zeros.

The construction of the default JPEG code for the reordered coefficient sequence begins with the computation of the difference between the current DC coefficient and that of the previously encoded subimage. Assuming the DC coefficient of the transformed and quantized subimage to its immediate left was −17, the resulting DPCM difference is $\left[-26 - (-17)\right]$ or −9, which lies in DC difference category 4 of the JPEG coefficient category table (see the book website). In accordance with the default Huffman difference code, the proper base code for a category 4 difference is 101 (a 3-bit code), while the total length of a completely encoded category 4 coefficient is 7 bits. The remaining 4 bits must be generated from the least significant bits (LSBs) of the difference value. For a general DC difference category (say, category K), an additional K bits are needed and computed as either the K LSBs of the positive difference or the K LSBs of the negative difference minus 1. For a difference of −9, the appropriate LSBs are $(0111) - 1$ or 0110, and the complete DPCM coded DC code word is 1010110.

The nonzero AC coefficients of the reordered array are coded similarly. The principal difference is that each default AC Huffman code word depends on the number of zero-valued coefficients preceding the nonzero coefficient to be coded, as well as the magnitude category of the nonzero coefficient. (See the column labeled Run/Category in the JPEG AC code table on the book website.) Thus, the first nonzero AC coefficient of the reordered array (−3) is coded as 0100. The first 2 bits of this code indicate that the coefficient was in magnitude category 2 and preceded by no zero-valued coefficients; the last 2 bits are generated by the same process used to arrive at the LSBs of the DC difference code. Continuing in this manner, the completely coded (reordered) array is

1010110 0100 001 0100 0101 100001 0110 100011 001 100011 001
001 100101 11100110 110110 0110 11110100 000 1010

where the spaces have been inserted solely for readability. Although it was not needed in this example, the default JPEG code contains a special code word for a run of 15 zeros followed by a zero. The total number of bits in the completely coded reordered array (and thus the number of bits required to represent the entire 8×8, 8-bit subimage of this example) is 92. The resulting compression ratio is 512/92, or about 5.6:1.

To decompress a JPEG compressed subimage, the decoder must first recreate the normalized transform coefficients that led to the compressed bit stream. Because a Huffman-coded binary sequence is instantaneous and uniquely decodable, this step is easily accomplished in a simple lookup table manner. Here, the regenerated array of quantized coefficients is

−26	−3	−6	2	2	0	0	0
1	−2	−4	0	0	0	0	0
−3	1	5	−1	−1	0	0	0
−4	1	2	−1	0	0	0	0
1	0	0	0	0	0	0	0
0	0	0	0	0	0	0	0
0	0	0	0	0	0	0	0
0	0	0	0	0	0	0	0

After denormalization in accordance with Eq. (8-27), the array becomes

−416	−33	−60	32	48	0	0	0
12	−24	−56	0	0	0	0	0
−42	13	80	−24	−40	0	0	0
−56	17	44	−29	0	0	0	0
18	0	0	0	0	0	0	0
0	0	0	0	0	0	0	0
0	0	0	0	0	0	0	0
0	0	0	0	0	0	0	0

where, for example, the DC coefficient is computed as

$$\dot{T}(0,0) = \hat{T}(0,0)Z(0,0) = (-26)(16) = -416$$

The completely reconstructed subimage is obtained by taking the inverse DCT of the denormalized array in accordance with Eqs. (7-32) and (7-85) to obtain

−70	−64	−61	−64	−69	−66	−58	−50
−72	−73	−61	−39	−30	−40	−54	−59
−68	−78	−58	−9	13	−12	−48	−64
−59	−77	−57	0	22	−13	−51	−60
−54	−75	−64	−23	−13	−44	−63	−56
−52	−71	−72	−54	−54	−71	−71	−54
−45	−59	−70	−68	−67	−67	−61	−50
−35	−47	−61	−66	−60	−48	−44	−44

and level shifting each inverse transformed pixel by 2^7 (or +128) to yield

58	64	67	64	59	62	70	78
56	55	67	89	98	88	74	69
60	50	70	119	141	116	80	64
69	51	71	128	149	115	77	68
74	53	64	105	115	84	65	72
76	57	56	74	75	57	57	74
83	69	59	60	61	61	67	78
93	81	67	62	69	80	84	84

Any differences between the original and reconstructed subimage are a result of the lossy nature of the JPEG compression and decompression process. In this example, the errors range from −14 to +11 and are distributed as follows:

−6	−9	−6	2	11	−1	−6	−5
7	4	−1	1	11	−3	−5	3
2	9	−2	−6	−3	−12	−14	9
−6	7	0	−4	−5	−9	−7	1
−7	8	4	−1	6	4	3	−2
3	8	4	−4	2	6	1	1
2	2	5	−1	−6	0	−2	5
−6	−2	2	6	−4	−4	−6	10

The root-mean-squared error of the overall compression and reconstruction process is approximately 5.8 intensity levels.

EXAMPLE 8.18: Illustration of JPEG coding.

Figures 8.29(a) and (d) show two JPEG approximations of the monochrome image in Fig. 8.9(a). The first result provides a compression of 25:1; the second compresses the original image by 52:1. The differences between the original image and the reconstructed images in Figs. 8.29(a) and (d) are shown in Figs. 8.29(b) and (e), respectively. The corresponding rms errors are 5.4 and 10.7 intensities. The errors are clearly visible in the zoomed images in Figs. 8.29(c) and (f). These images show a magnified section of Figs. 8.29(a) and (d), respectively. Note that the JPEG blocking artifact increases with compression.

8.10 PREDICTIVE CODING

With reference to Tables 8.3–8.5, predictive coding is used in

- JBIG2
- JPEG
- JPEG-LS
- MPEG-1,2,4
- H.261, H.262, H.263, and H.264
- HDV
- VC-1

and other compression standards and file formats.

We now turn to a simpler approach that achieves good compression without significant computational overhead *and* can be either error-free or lossy. The approach, commonly referred to as *predictive coding*, is based on eliminating the redundancies of closely spaced pixels—in space and/or time—by extracting and coding only the *new information* in each pixel. The new information of a pixel is defined as the difference between the actual and predicted value of the pixel.

LOSSLESS PREDICTIVE CODING

Figure 8.30 shows the basic components of a *lossless predictive coding* system. The system consists of an encoder and a decoder, each containing an identical *predictor*. As successive samples of discrete time input signal, $f(n)$, are introduced to the encoder, the predictor generates the anticipated value of each sample based on a specified number of past samples. The output of the predictor is then rounded to the nearest integer, denoted $\hat{f}(n)$, and used to form the difference or *prediction error*

$$e(n) = f(n) - \hat{f}(n) \tag{8-29}$$

which is encoded using a variable-length code (by the symbol encoder) to generate the next element of the compressed data stream. The decoder in Fig. 8.30(b) reconstructs $e(n)$ from the received variable-length code words and performs the inverse operation

$$f(n) = e(n) + \hat{f}(n) \tag{8-30}$$

to decompress or recreate the original input sequence.

Various local, global, and adaptive methods (see the later subsection entitled Lossy predictive coding) can be used to generate $\hat{f}(n)$. In many cases, the prediction is formed as a linear combination of m previous samples. That is,

$$\hat{f}(n) = \text{round}\left[\sum_{i=1}^{m} \alpha_i f(n-i)\right] \tag{8-31}$$

where m is the *order* of the linear predictor, round is a function used to denote the rounding or nearest integer operation, and the α_i for $i = 1, 2, \dots, m$ are prediction

a b c
d e f

FIGURE 8.29 Two JPEG approximations of Fig. 8.9(a). Each row contains a result after compression and reconstruction, the scaled difference between the result and the original image, and a zoomed portion of the reconstructed image.

coefficients. If the input sequence in Fig. 8.30(a) is considered to be samples of an image, the $f(n)$ in Eqs. (8-29) through (8-31) are pixels—and the m samples used to predict the value of each pixel come from the current scan line (called 1-D linear predictive coding), from the current and previous scan lines (called 2-D linear predictive coding), or from the current image and previous images in a sequence of images (called 3-D linear predictive coding). Thus, for 1-D linear predictive image coding, Eq. (8-31) can be written as

$$\hat{f}(x,y) = \text{round}\left[\sum_{i=1}^{m} \alpha_i f(x, y-i)\right] \tag{8-32}$$

where each sample is now expressed explicitly as a function of the input image's spatial coordinates, x and y. Note that Eq. (8-32) indicates that the 1-D linear prediction is a function of the previous pixels on the current line alone. In 2-D predictive coding,

a
b

FIGURE 8.30
A lossless predictive coding model:
(a) encoder;
(b) decoder.

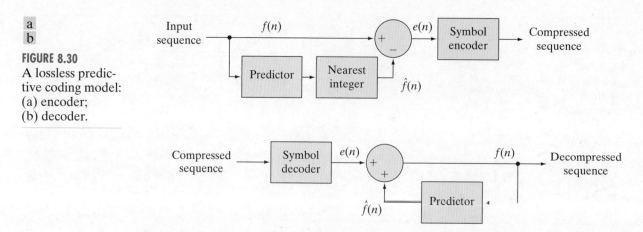

the prediction is a function of the previous pixels in a left-to-right, top-to-bottom scan of an image. In the 3-D case, it is based on these pixels and the previous pixels of preceding frames. Equation (8-32) cannot be evaluated for the first m pixels of each line, so those pixels must be coded by using other means (such as a Huffman code) and considered as an overhead of the predictive coding process. Similar comments apply to the higher-dimensional cases.

EXAMPLE 8.19: Predictive coding and spatial redundancy.

Consider encoding the monochrome image of Fig. 8.31(a) using the simple first-order (i.e., $m = 1$) linear predictor from Eq. (8-32)

$$\hat{f}(x,y) = \text{round}\left[\alpha f(x, y-1)\right] \tag{8-33}$$

This equation is a simplification of Eq. (8-32), with $m = 1$ and the subscript of lone prediction coefficient α_1 removed as unnecessary. A predictor of this general form is called a *previous pixel* predictor, and the corresponding predictive coding procedure is known as *differential coding* or *previous pixel coding*. Figure 8.31(c) shows the prediction error image, $e(x, y) = f(x, y) - \hat{f}(x, y)$ that results from Eq. (8-33) with $\alpha = 1$. The scaling of this image is such that intensity 128 represents a prediction error of zero, while all nonzero positive and negative prediction errors (under and over estimates) are displayed as lighter and darker shades of gray, respectively. The mean value of the prediction image is 128.26. Because intensity 128 corresponds to a prediction error of 0, the average prediction error is only 0.26 bits.

Figures 8.31(b) and (d) show the intensity histogram of the image in Fig. 8.31(a) and the histogram of prediction error $e(x, y)$, respectively. Note that the standard deviation of the prediction error in Fig. 8.31(d) is much smaller than the standard deviation of the intensities in the original image. Moreover, the entropy of the prediction error, as estimated using Eq. (8-7), is significantly less than the estimated entropy of the original image (3.99 bits/pixel as opposed to 7.25 bits/pixel). This decrease in entropy reflects removal of a great deal of spatial redundancy, despite the fact that for k-bit images, $(k + 1)$-bit numbers are needed to represent accurately the prediction error sequence $e(x, y)$. (Note that the variable-length encoded prediction error is the compressed image.) In general, the maximum compression of a predictive coding approach can be estimated by dividing the average number of bits used

a b
c d

FIGURE 8.31
(a) A view of the
Earth from an
orbiting space
shuttle. (b) The
intensity histo-
gram of (a).
(c) The predic-
tion error image
resulting from
Eq. (8-33).
(d) A histogram
of the prediction
error.
(Original image
courtesy of
NASA.)

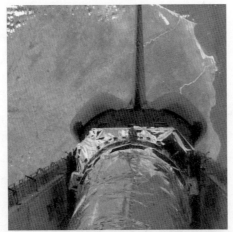

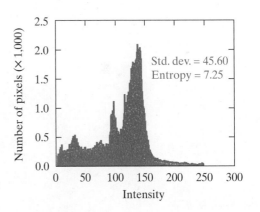

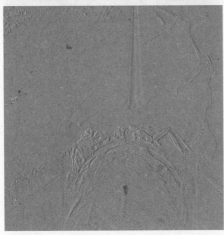

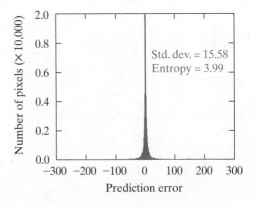

to represent each pixel in the original image by an estimate of the entropy of the prediction error. In this example, any variable-length coding procedure can be used to code $e(x, y)$, but the resulting compression will be limited to about 8/3.99, or 2:1.

The preceding example illustrates that the compression achieved in predictive coding is related directly to the entropy reduction that results from mapping an input image into a prediction error sequence, often called a *prediction residual*. Because spatial redundancy is removed by the prediction and differencing process, the probability density function of the prediction residual is, in general, highly peaked at zero, and characterized by a relatively small (in comparison to the input intensity distribution) variance. In fact, it is often modeled by a zero mean uncorrelated Laplacian PDF

$$p_e(e) = \frac{1}{\sqrt{2}\sigma_e} e^{\frac{-\sqrt{2}|e|}{\sigma_e}} \tag{8-34}$$

where σ_e is the standard deviation of e.

FIGURE 8.32
(a) and (b) Two
views of Earth
from an orbit-
ing space shuttle
video. (c) The
prediction error
image resulting
from Eq. (8-35).
(d) A histogram
of the prediction
error.
(Original images
courtesy of
NASA.)

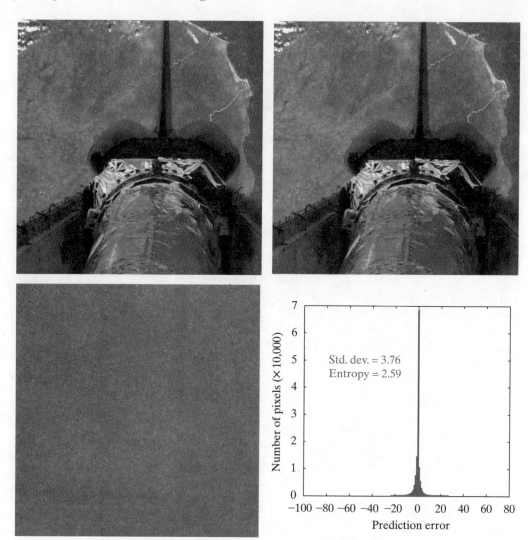

EXAMPLE 8.20: Predictive coding and temporal redundancy.

The image in Fig. 8.31(a) is a portion of a frame of NASA video in which the Earth is moving from left to right with respect to a stationary camera attached to the space shuttle. It is repeated in Fig. 8.32(b), along with its immediately preceding frame in Fig. 8.32(a). Using the first-order linear predictor

$$\hat{f}(x, y, t) = \text{round}\left[\alpha f(x, y, t-1)\right] \tag{8-35}$$

with $\alpha = 1$, the intensities of the pixels in Fig. 8.32(b) can be predicted from the corresponding pixels in (a). Figure 8.34(c) is the resulting prediction residual image, $e(x, y, t) = f(x, y, t) - \hat{f}(x, y, t)$. Figure 8.31(d) is the histogram of $e(x, y, t)$. Note there is very little prediction error. The standard deviation of the error is much smaller than in the previous example: 3.76 bits/pixel as opposed to 15.58 bits/pixel. In addition, the entropy of the prediction error [computed using Eq. (8-7)] has decreased from 3.99 to 2.59 bits/pixel. (Recall again that the variable-length encoded prediction error is the compressed image.) By variable-length coding the resulting prediction residual, the original image is compressed by approximately 8/2.59 or 3.1:1, a 50% improvement over the 2:1 compression obtained using the spatially oriented previous pixel predictor in Example 8.19.

MOTION COMPENSATED PREDICTION RESIDUALS

As you saw in Example 8.20, successive frames in a video sequence often are very similar. Coding their differences can reduce temporal redundancy and provide significant compression. However, when a sequence of frames contains rapidly moving objects—or involves camera zoom and pan, sudden scene changes, or fade-ins and fade-outs—the similarity between neighboring frames is reduced, and compression is affected negatively. That is, like most compression techniques (see Example 8.5), temporally based predictive coding works best with certain kinds of inputs, namely, a sequence of images with significant temporal redundancy. When used on images with little temporal redundancy, data expansion can occur. Video compression systems avoid the problem of data expansion in two ways:

1. By tracking object movement and compensating for it during the prediction and differencing process.
2. By switching to an alternate coding method when there is insufficient *interframe* correlation (similarity between frames) to make predictive coding advantageous.

The first of these, called *motion compensation*, is the subject of the remainder of this section. Before proceeding, however, we should note that when there is insufficient interframe correlation to make predictive coding effective, the second problem is typically addressed using a block-oriented 2-D transform, like JPEG's DCT-based coding (see the previous section). Frames compressed in this way (i.e., without a prediction residual) are called *intraframes* or *Independent frames* (*I-frames*). They can be decoded without access to other frames in the video to which they belong. I-frames usually resemble JPEG encoded images, and are ideal starting points for the generation of prediction residuals. Moreover, they provide a high degree of random access, ease of editing, and resistance to the propagation of transmission error. As a result, all standards require the periodic insertion of I-frames into the compressed video codestream.

Figure 8.33 illustrates the basics of motion-compensated predictive coding. Each video frame is divided into non-overlapping rectangular regions (typically of size 4×4 to 16×16) called *macroblocks*. (Only one macroblock is shown in Fig. 8.33.) The "movement" of each macroblock with respect to its "most likely" position in the previous (or subsequent) video frame, called the *reference frame*, is encoded in a *motion vector*. The vector describes the motion by defining the horizontal and vertical *displacement* from the "most likely" position. The displacements typically are specified to the nearest pixel, ½ pixel, or ¼ pixel precision. If subpixel precision is used, the predictions must be interpolated [e.g., using bilinear interpolation (see Section 2.4)] from a combination of pixels in the reference frame. An encoded frame that is based on the previous frame (a *forward prediction* in Fig. 8.33) is called a *Pre-*

The "most likely" position is the one that minimizes an error measure between the reference macroblock and the macroblock being encoded. The two blocks do not have to be representations of the same object, but they must minimize the error measure.

FIGURE 8.33
Macroblock
motion specifica-
tion.

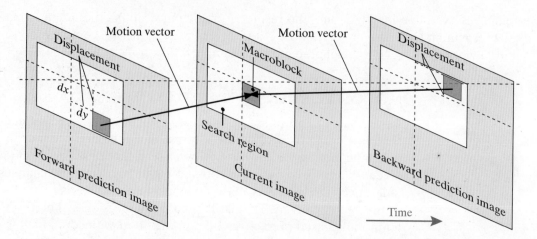

dictive frame (*P-frame*); one that is based on the subsequent frame (a *backward pre-diction* in Fig. 8.33) is called a *Bidirectional frame* (*B-frame*). B-frames require the compressed codestream to be reordered so that frames are presented to the decoder in the proper decoding sequence, rather than the natural display order.

As you might expect, *motion estimation* is the key component of motion compen-sation. During motion estimation, the motion of objects is measured and encoded into motion vectors. The search for the "best" motion vector requires that a criterion of optimality be defined. For example, motion vectors may be selected on the basis of maximum correlation or minimum error between macroblock pixels and the pre-dicted pixels (or interpolated pixels for sub-pixel motion vectors) from the chosen reference frame. One of the most commonly used error measures is *mean absolute distortion* (*MAD*)

$$MAD(x,y) = \frac{1}{mn} \sum_{i=0}^{m-1} \sum_{j=0}^{n-1} \left| f(x+i,\, y+j) - p(x+i+dx,\, y+j+dy) \right| \quad \text{(8-36)}$$

where x and y are the coordinates of the upper-left pixel of the $m \times n$ macroblock being coded, dx and dy are displacements from the reference frame as shown in Fig. 8.33, and p is an array of predicted macroblock pixel values. For sub-pixel motion vector estimation, p is interpolated from pixels in the reference frame. Typi-cally, dx and dy must fall within a limited search region (see Fig. 8.33) around each macroblock. Values from ±8 to ±64 pixels are common, and the horizontal search area is often slightly larger than the vertical area. A more computationally efficient error measure, called the *sum of absolute distortions* (*SAD*), omits the $1/mn$ factor in Eq. (8-36).

Given a selection criterion like that of Eq. (8-36), motion estimation is performed by searching for the dx and dy that minimize $MAD(x,y)$ over the allowed range of motion vector displacements, including subpixel displacements. This process often is called *block matching*. An exhaustive search guarantees the best possible result, but is computationally expensive because every possible motion must be tested over the entire displacement range. For 16×16 macroblocks and a ±32 pixel displacement range (not out of the question for action films and sporting events), 4225 16×16 *MAD* calculations must be performed for each macroblock in a frame when integer displacement precision is used. If ½ or ¼ pixel precision is desired, the number of calculations is multiplied by a factor of 4 or 16, respectively. Fast search algorithms can reduce the computational burden, but may or may not yield optimal motion vectors. A number of fast block-based motion estimation algorithms have been proposed and studied in the literature (see Furht et al. [1997] or Mitchell et al. [1997]).

EXAMPLE 8.21: Motion compensated prediction.

Figures 8.34(a) and (b) were taken from the same NASA video sequence used in Examples 8.19 and 8.20. Figure 8.34(b) is identical to Figs. 8.31(a) and 8.32(b); Fig. 8.34(a) is the corresponding section of a frame occurring thirteen frames earlier. Figure 8.34(c) is the difference between the two frames, scaled to the full intensity range. Note that the difference is 0 in the area of the stationary (with respect to the camera) space shuttle, but there are significant differences in the remainder of the image due to the relative motion of the Earth. The standard deviation of the prediction residual in Fig. 8.34(c) is 12.73 intensity levels; its entropy [using Eq. (8-7)] is 4.17 bits/pixel. The maximum compression achievable, when variable-length coding the prediction residual, is $C = 8/4.17 = 1.92$.

Figure 8.34(d) shows a motion compensated prediction residual with a much lower standard deviation (5.62 as opposed to 12.73 intensity levels) and slightly lower entropy (3.04 vs. 4.17 bits/pixel). The entropy was computed using Eq. (8-7). If the prediction residual in Fig. 8.34(d) is variable-length coded, the resulting compression ratio is $C = 8/3.04 = 2.63$. To generate this prediction residual, we divided Fig. 8.34(b) into non-overlapping 16×16 macroblocks and compared each macroblock against every 16×16 region in Fig. 8.34(a)—the reference frame—that fell within ±16 pixels of the macroblock's position in (b). We then used Eq. (8-36) to determine the best match by selecting displacement (dx, dy) with the lowest *MAD*. The resulting displacements are the x and y components of the motion vectors shown in Fig. 8.34(e). The white dots in the figure are the heads of the motion vectors; they indicate the upper-left-hand corner of the coded macroblocks. As you can see from the pattern of the vectors, the predominant motion in the image is from left to right. In the lower portion of the image, which corresponds to the area of the space shuttle in the original image, there is no motion, and therefore no motion vectors displayed. Macroblocks in this area are predicted from similarly located (i.e., the corresponding) macroblocks in the reference frame. Because the motion vectors in Fig. 8.34(e) are highly correlated, they can be variable-length coded to reduce their storage and transmission requirements

---

The visual difference between Figs. 8.34(c) and 8.35(a) is due to scaling. The image in Fig. 8.35(a) has been scaled to match Figs. 8.35(b)–(d).

Figure 8.35 illustrates the increased prediction accuracy that is possible with sub-pixel motion compensation. Figure 8.35(a) is repeated from Fig. 8.34(c) and included as a point of reference; it shows the prediction error that results without motion compensation. The images in Figs. 8.35(b), (c), and (d) are motion compensated prediction residuals. They are based on the same two frames that were used in Example 8.21 and computed with macroblock displacements to 1, ½, and ¼ pixel resolution (i.e., precision), respectively. Macroblocks of size 8×8 were used; displacements were limited to ±8 pixels.

The most significant visual difference between the prediction residuals in Fig. 8.35 is the number and size of intensity peaks and valleys—their darkest and lightest areas of intensity. The ¼ pixel residual in Fig. 8.35(d) is the "flattest" of the four

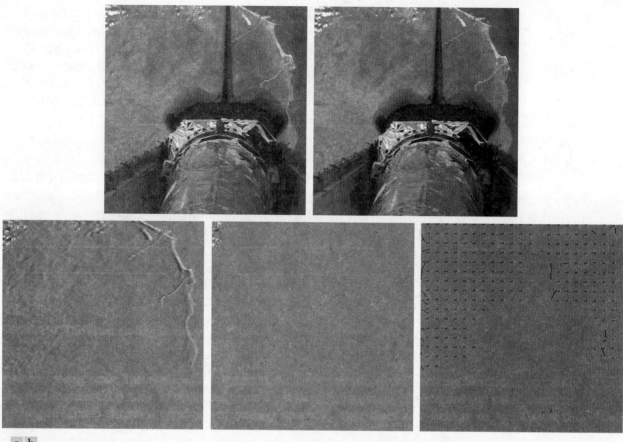

FIGURE 8.34 (a) and (b) Two views of Earth that are thirteen frames apart in an orbiting space shuttle video. (c) A prediction error image without motion compensation. (d) The prediction residual with motion compensation. (e) The motion vectors associated with (d). The white dots in (e) represent the arrow heads of the motion vectors that are depicted. (Original images courtesy of NASA.)

images, with the fewest excursions to black or white. As would be expected, it has the narrowest histogram. The standard deviations of the prediction residuals in Figs. 8.35(a) through (d) decrease as motion vector precision increases from 12.7 to 4.4, 4, and 3.8 pixels, respectively. The entropies of the residuals, as determined using Eq. (8-7), are 4.17, 3.34, 3.35, and 3.34 bits/pixel, respectively. Thus, the motion compensated residuals contain about the same amount of information, despite the fact that the residuals in Figs. 8.35(c) and (d) use additional bits to accommodate ½ and ¼ pixel interpolation. Finally, we note that there is an obvious strip of increased prediction error on the left side of each motion compensated residual. This is due to the left-to-right motion of the Earth, which introduces new or previously unseen areas of the Earth's terrain into the left side of each image. Because these areas are absent from the previous frames, they cannot be accurately predicted, regardless of the precision used to compute motion vectors.

a b
c d

FIGURE 8.35
Sub-pixel motion compensated prediction residuals: (a) without motion compensation; (b) single pixel precision; (c) ½ pixel precision; and (d) ¼ pixel precision. (All prediction errors have been scaled to the full intensity range and then multiplied by 2 to increase their visibility.)

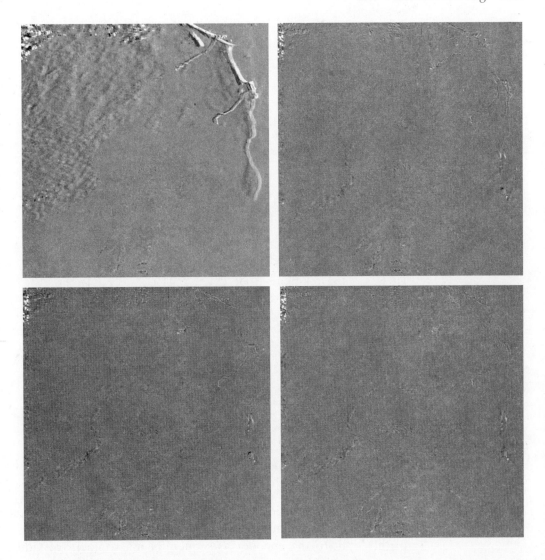

Motion estimation is a computationally demanding task. Fortunately, only the encoder must estimate macroblock motion. Given the motion vectors of the macroblocks, the decoder simply accesses the areas of the reference frames that were used in the encoder to form the prediction residuals. Because of this, motion estimation is not included in most video compression standards. Compression standards focus on the decoder, placing constraints on macroblock dimensions, motion vector precision, horizontal and vertical displacement ranges, and the like. Table 8.12 gives the key predictive coding parameters of some the most important video compression standards. Note that most of the standards use an 8×8 DCT for I-frame encoding, but specify a larger area (i.e., 16×16 macroblock) for motion compensation. In addition, even the P- and B-frame prediction residuals are transform coded due to the effectiveness of DCT coefficient quantization. Finally, we note that the H.264 and MPEG-4 AVC standards support intraframe predictive coding (in I-frames) to reduce spatial redundancy.

TABLE 8.12
Predictive coding in video compression standards.

Parameter	H.261	MPEG-1	H.262 MPEG-2	H.263	MPEG-4	VC-1 WMV-9	H.264 MPEG-4 AVC
Motion vector precision	1	½	½	½	¼	¼	¼
Macroblock sizes	16×16	16×16	16×16 16×8	16×16 8×8	16×16 8×8	16×16 8×8	16×16 16×8 8×8 8×4 4×8 4×4
Transform	8×8 DCT	8×8 DCT	8×8 DCT	8×8 DCT	8×8 DCT	8×8 8×4 4×8 4×4 Integer DCT	4×4 8×8 Integer
Interframe predictions	P	P, B	P, B	P, B	P, B	P, B	P, B
I-frame intra-predictions	No	No	No	No	No	No	Yes

Quantization as defined earlier in the chapter is irreversible. The "inverse quantizer" in Fig. 8.36 does not prevent information loss.

Figure 8.36 shows a typical motion compensated video encoder. It exploits redundancies within and between adjacent video frames, motion uniformity between frames, and the psychovisual properties of the human visual system. We can think of the input to the encoder as sequential macroblocks of video. For color video, each macroblock is composed of a luminance block and two chrominance blocks. Because the eye has far less spatial acuity for color than for luminance, the chrominance blocks often are sampled at half the horizontal and vertical resolution of the luminance block. The dark blue elements in the figure parallel the transformation, quantization, and variable-length coding operations of a JPEG encoder. The principal difference is the input, which may be a conventional macroblock of image data (for I-frames), or the difference between a conventional macroblock and a prediction of it based on previous and/or subsequent video frames (for P- and B-frames). The encoder includes an *inverse quantizer* and *inverse mapper* (e.g., inverse DCT) so that its predictions match those of the complementary decoder. Also, it is designed to produce compressed bit streams that match the capacity of the intended video channel. To accomplish this, the quantization parameters are adjusted by a *rate controller* as a function of the occupancy of an output *buffer*. As the buffer becomes fuller, the quantization is made coarser, so fewer bits stream into the buffer.

FIGURE 8.36
A typical motion compensated video encoder.

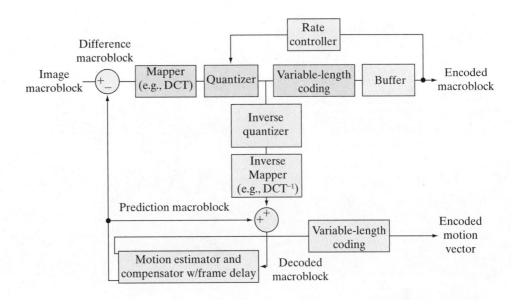

We conclude our discussion of motion compensated predictive coding with an example illustrating the kind of compression that is possible with modern video compression methods. Figure 8.37 shows fifteen frames of a 1 minute HD $\mathbf{x}(3) \in c_1$.   full-color NASA video, parts of which have been used throughout this section. Although the images shown are monochrome, the video is a sequence of 1,829 full-color frames. Note that there are a variety of scenes, a great deal of motion, and multiple fade effects. For example, the video opens with a 150 frame fade-in from black, which includes frames 21 and 44 in Fig. 8.37, and concludes with a fade sequence containing frames 1595, 1609, and 1652 in Fig. 8.37, followed by a final fade to black. There are also several abrupt scene changes, like the change involving frames 1303 and 1304 in Fig. 8.37.

An H.264 compressed version of the NASA video stored as a Quicktime file (see Table 8.5) requires 44.56 MB of storage, plus another 1.39 MB for the associated audio. The video quality is excellent. About 5 GB of data would be needed to store the video frames as uncompressed full-color images. It should be noted that the video contains sequences involving both rotation and scale change (e.g., the sequence including frames 959, 1023, and 1088 in Fig. 8.37). The discussion in this section, however, has been limited to translation alone. (See the book website for the NASA video segment used in this example.)

LOSSY PREDICTIVE CODING

In this section, we add a quantizer to the lossless predictive coding model introduced earlier, and examine the trade-off between reconstruction accuracy and compression performance within the context of spatial predictors. As Fig. 8.38 shows, the quantizer, which replaces the nearest integer function of the error-free encoder, is inserted between the symbol encoder and the point at which the prediction error is formed. It maps the prediction error into a limited range of outputs, denoted $\dot{e}(n)$, which establish the amount of compression and distortion that occurs.

Frame 0021   Frame 0044   Frame 0201

Frame 0266   Frame 0424   Frame 0801

Frame 0959   Frame 1023   Frame 1088

Frame 1224   Frame 1303   Frame 1304

Frame 1595   Frame 1609   Frame 1652

FIGURE 8.37 Fifteen frames from an 1829-frame, 1-minute NASA video. The original video is in HD full color. (Courtesy of NASA.)

In order to accommodate the insertion of the quantization step, the error-free encoder of Fig. 8.30(a) must be altered so the predictions generated by the encoder and decoder are equivalent. As Fig. 8.38(a) shows, this is accomplished by placing the lossy encoder's predictor within a feedback loop, where its input, denoted as $\dot{f}(n)$, is generated as a function of past predictions and the corresponding quantized errors. That is,

$$\dot{f}(n) = \dot{e}(n) + \hat{f}(n) \tag{8-37}$$

where $\hat{f}(n)$ is as defined earlier. This closed loop configuration prevents error buildup at the decoder's output. Note in Fig. 8.38(b) that the output of the decoder is given also by Eq. (8-37).

EXAMPLE 8.23: Delta modulation.

Delta modulation (DM) is a simple but well-known form of lossy predictive coding in which the predictor and quantizer are defined as

$$\hat{f}(n) = \alpha \dot{f}(n-1) \tag{8-38}$$

and

$$\dot{e}(n) = \begin{cases} +\zeta & \text{for } e(n) > 0 \\ -\zeta & \text{otherwise} \end{cases} \tag{8-39}$$

where α is a prediction coefficient (normally less than 1), and ζ is a positive constant. The output of the quantizer, $\dot{e}(n)$, can be represented by a single bit [see Fig. 8.39(a)], so the symbol encoder of Fig. 8.38(a) can utilize a 1-bit fixed-length code. The resulting DM code rate is 1 bit/pixel.

Figure 8.39(c) illustrates the mechanics of the delta modulation process, where the calculations needed to compress and reconstruct input sequence {14, 15, 14, 15, 13, 15, 15, 14, 20, 26, 27, 28, 27, 27, 29, 37, 47, 62, 75, 77, 78, 79, 80, 81, 81, 82, 82} with $\alpha = 1$ and $\zeta = 6.5$ are tabulated. The process begins with the

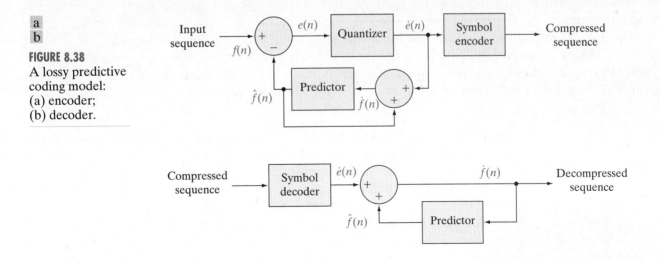

a
b

FIGURE 8.38
A lossy predictive coding model:
(a) encoder;
(b) decoder.

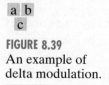

FIGURE 8.39
An example of
delta modulation.

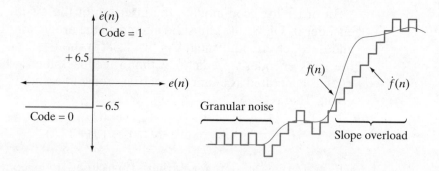

Input		Encoder				Decoder		Error
n	$f(n)$	$\hat{f}(n)$	$e(n)$	$\dot{e}(n)$	$\dot{f}(n)$	$\hat{f}(n)$	$\dot{f}(n)$	$f(n) - \dot{f}(n)$
0	14	–	–	–	14.0	–	14.0	0.0
1	15	14.0	1.0	6.5	20.5	14.0	20.5	– 5.5
2	14	20.5	– 6.5	– 6.5	14.0	20.5	14.0	0.0
3	15	14.0	1.0	6.5	20.5	14.0	20.5	– 5.5
.	.	.	.	.	.	.	.	.
.	.	.	.	.	.	.	.	.
14	29	20.5	8.5	6.5	27.0	20.5	27.0	2.0
15	37	27.0	10.0	6.5	33.5	27.0	33.5	3.5
16	47	33.5	13.5	6.5	40.0	33.5	40.0	7.0
17	62	40.0	22.0	6.5	46.5	40.0	46.5	15.5
18	75	46.5	28.5	6.5	53.0	46.5	53.0	22.0
19	77	53.0	24.0	6.5	59.6	53.0	59.5	17.5
.	.	.	.	.	.	.	.	.
.	.	.	.	.	.	.	.	.

error-free transfer of the first input sample to the decoder. With the initial condition $\dot{f}(0) = f(0) = 14$ established at both the encoder and decoder, the remaining outputs can be computed by repeatedly evaluating Eqs. (8-38), (8-29), (8-39), and (8-37). Thus, when $n = 1$, for example, $\hat{f}(1) = (1)(14) = 14$, $e(1) = 15 - 14 = 1$, $\dot{e}(1) = +6.5$ (because $e(1) > 0$), $\dot{f}(1) = 6.4 + 14 = 20.5$, and the resulting reconstruction error is $(15 - 20.5)$, or -5.5.

Figure 8.39(b) graphically shows the tabulated data in Fig. 8.39(c). Both the input and completely decoded output $\left[f(n) \text{ and } \dot{f}(n) \right]$ are shown. Note that in the rapidly changing area from $n = 14$ to 19, where ζ was too small to represent the input's largest changes, a distortion known as *slope overload* occurs. Moreover, when ζ was too large to represent the input's smallest changes, as in the relatively smooth region from $n = 0$ to $n = 7$, *granular noise* appears. In images, these two phenomena lead to blurred object edges and grainy or noisy surfaces (that is, distorted smooth areas).

The distortions noted in the preceding example are common to all forms of lossy predictive coding. The severity of these distortions depends on a complex set of interactions between the quantization and prediction methods employed. Despite these interactions, the predictor normally is designed with the assumption of no quantization error, and the quantizer is designed to minimize its own error. That is, the predictor and quantizer are designed independently of each other.

OPTIMAL PREDICTORS

In many predictive coding applications, the predictor is chosen to minimize the encoder's mean-squared prediction error

The notation $E\{\cdot\}$ denotes the statistical expectation operator.

$$E\{e^2(n)\} = E\left\{\left[f(n) - \hat{f}(n)\right]^2\right\} \tag{8-40}$$

subject to the constraint that

$$\dot{f}(n) = \dot{e}(n) + \hat{f}(n) \approx e(n) + \hat{f}(n) = f(n) \tag{8-41}$$

and

$$\hat{f}(n) = \sum_{i=1}^{m} \alpha_i f(n-i) \tag{8-42}$$

That is, the optimization criterion is minimal mean-squared prediction error, the quantization error is assumed to be negligible $[\dot{e}(n) \approx e(n)]$, and the prediction is constrained to a linear combination of m previous samples. These restrictions are not essential, but they considerably simplify the analysis and, at the same time, decrease the computational complexity of the predictor. The resulting predictive coding approach is referred to as *differential pulse code modulation* (DPCM).

In general, the optimal predictor for a non-Gaussian sequence is a nonlinear function of the samples used to form the estimate.

Under these conditions, the optimal predictor design problem is reduced to the relatively straightforward exercise of selecting the m prediction coefficients that minimize the expression

$$E\{e^2(n)\} = E\left\{\left[f(n) - \sum_{i=1}^{m} \alpha_i f(n-i)\right]^2\right\} \tag{8-43}$$

Differentiating Eq. (8-43) with respect to each coefficient, equating the derivatives to zero, and solving the resulting set of simultaneous equations under the assumption that $f(n)$ has mean zero and variance σ^2 yields

$$\boldsymbol{\alpha} = \mathbf{R}^{-1}\mathbf{r} \tag{8-44}$$

where $\mathbf{R}^{-1}$ is the inverse of the $m \times m$ autocorrelation matrix

$$\mathbf{R} = \begin{bmatrix} E\{f(n-1)\,f(n-1)\} & E\{f(n-1)f(n-2)\} & \cdots & E\{f(n-1)f(n-m)\} \\ E\{f(n-2)\,f(n-1)\} & \vdots & \cdots & \vdots \\ \vdots & \vdots & \cdots & \vdots \\ \vdots & \vdots & \cdots & \vdots \\ \vdots & \vdots & \cdots & \vdots \\ E\{f(n-m)\,f(n-1)\} & E\{f(n-m)f(n-2)\} & \cdots & E\{f(n-m)f(n-m)\} \end{bmatrix}$$

$$\tag{8-45}$$

and **r** and $\boldsymbol{\alpha}$ are the m-element vectors

$$\mathbf{r} = \begin{bmatrix} E\{f(n)f(n-1)\} \\ E\{f(n)f(n-2)\} \\ \vdots \\ E\{f(n)f(n-m)\} \end{bmatrix} \qquad \boldsymbol{\alpha} = \begin{bmatrix} \alpha_1 \\ \alpha_2 \\ \vdots \\ \alpha_m \end{bmatrix} \tag{8-46}$$

Thus for any input sequence, the coefficients that minimize Eq. (8-43) can be determined via a series of elementary matrix operations. Moreover, the coefficients depend only on the autocorrelations of the samples in the original sequence. The variance of the prediction error that results from the use of these optimal coefficients is

$$\sigma_e^2 = \sigma^2 - \boldsymbol{\alpha}^T \mathbf{r} = \sigma^2 - \sum_{i=1}^{m} E\{f(n)f(n-i)\}\alpha_i \tag{8-47}$$

Although the mechanics of evaluating Eq. (8-44) are quite simple, computation of the autocorrelations needed to form **R** and **r** is so difficult in practice that *local* predictions (those in which the prediction coefficients are computed for each input sequence) are almost never used. In most cases, a set of *global* coefficients is computed by assuming a simple input model and substituting the corresponding autocorrelations into Eqs. (8-45) and (8-46). For instance, when a 2-D Markov image source (see Section 8.1) with separable autocorrelation function

$$E\{f(x,y)f(x-i,y-j)\} = \sigma^2 \rho_v^i \rho_h^j \tag{8-48}$$

and generalized fourth-order linear predictor

$$\begin{aligned} \hat{f}(x,y) = &\,\alpha_1 f(x,y-1) + \alpha_2 f(x-1,y-1) \\ &+ \alpha_3 f(x-1,y) + \alpha_4 f(x-1,y+1) \end{aligned} \tag{8-49}$$

are assumed, the resulting optimal coefficients (Jain [1989]) are

$$\alpha_1 = \rho_h \quad \alpha_2 = -\rho_v \rho_h \quad \alpha_3 = \rho_v \quad \alpha_4 = 0 \tag{8-50}$$

where ρ_h and ρ_h are the horizontal and vertical correlation coefficients, respectively, of the image under consideration.

Finally, the sum of the prediction coefficients in Eq. (8-42) is normally required to be less than or equal to one. That is,

$$\sum_{i=1}^{m} \alpha_i \leq 1 \tag{8-51}$$

This restriction is made to ensure that the output of the predictor falls within the allowed range of the input, and to reduce the impact of transmission noise [which generally is seen as horizontal streaks in reconstructed images when the input to Fig. 8.38(a) is an image]. Reducing the DPCM decoder's susceptibility to input noise is important, because a single error (under the right circumstances) can propagate to all future outputs. That is, the decoder's output may become unstable. Further restricting Eq. (8-51) to be strictly less than 1 confines the impact of an input error to a small number of outputs.

EXAMPLE 8.24: Comparison of prediction techniques.

Consider the prediction error that results from DPCM coding the monochrome image of Fig. 8.9(a) under the assumption of zero quantization error and with each of four predictors:

$$\hat{f}(x,y) = 0.97f(x,y-1) \tag{8-52}$$

$$\hat{f}(x,y) = 0.5f(x,y-1) + 0.5f(x-1,y) \tag{8-53}$$

$$\hat{f}(x,y) = 0.75f(x,y-1) + 0.75f(x-1,y) - 0.5f(x-1,y-1) \tag{8-54}$$

$$\hat{f}(x,y) = \begin{cases} 0.97f(x,y-1) & \text{if } \Delta h \leq \Delta v \\ 0.97f(x-1,y) & \text{otherwise} \end{cases} \tag{8-55}$$

where $\Delta h = |f(x-1,y) - f(x-1,y-1)|$ and $\Delta v = |f(x,y-1) - f(x-1,y-1)|$ denote the horizontal and vertical gradients at point (x,y). Equations (8-52) through (8-55) define a relatively robust set of α_i that provide satisfactory performance over a wide range of images. The adaptive predictor of Eq. (8-55) is designed to improve edge rendition by computing a local measure of the directional properties of an image (Δh and Δv), and selecting a predictor specifically tailored to the measured behavior.

Figures 8.40(a) through (d) show the prediction error images that result from using the predictors of Eqs. (8-52) through (8-55). Note that the visually perceptible error decreases as the order of the predictor increases.[†] The standard deviations of the prediction errors follow a similar pattern. They are 11.1, 9.8, 9.1, and 9.7 intensity levels, respectively.

OPTIMAL QUANTIZATION

The staircase quantization function $t = q(s)$ in Fig. 8.41 is an odd function of s [that is, $q(-s) = -q(s)$] that can be described completely by the $L/2$ values of s_i and t_i shown in the first quadrant of the graph. These break points define function discontinuities, and are called the *decision* and *reconstruction levels* of the quantizer. As a matter of convention, s is considered to be mapped to t_i if it lies in the half-open interval $(s_i, s_{i+1}]$.

The quantizer design problem is to select the best s_i and t_i for a particular optimization criterion and input probability density function $p(s)$. If the optimization

---

[†] Predictors that use more than three or four previous pixels provide little compression gain for the added predictor complexity (Habibi [1971]).

FIGURE 8.40
A comparison of
four linear
prediction
techniques.

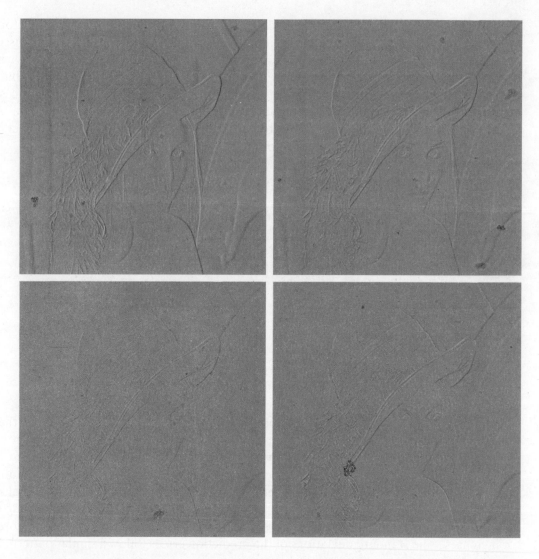

criterion, which could be either a statistical or psychovisual measure,[†] is the mini-mization of the mean-squared quantization error (that is $E\{(s_i - t_i)^2\}$) and $p(s)$ is an even function, the conditions for minimal error (Max [1960]) are

$$\int_{s_{i-1}}^{s_i} (s - t_i)p(s)ds = 0 \qquad i = 1, 2, \ldots, \frac{L}{2} \tag{8-56}$$

$$s_i = \begin{cases} 0 & i = 0 \\ \dfrac{t_i + t_{i+1}}{2} & i = 1, 2, \ldots, \dfrac{L}{2} - 1 \\ \infty & i = \dfrac{L}{2} \end{cases} \tag{8-57}$$

[†]See Netravali [1977] and Limb for more on psychovisual measures.

FIGURE 8.41
A typical quantization function.

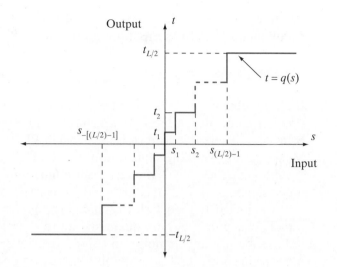

and

$$s_{-i} = -s_i \qquad t_{-i} = -t_i \tag{8-58}$$

Equation (8-56) indicates that the reconstruction levels are the centroids of the areas under $p(s)$ over the specified decision intervals, whereas Eq. (8-57) indicates that the decision levels are halfway between the reconstruction levels. Equation (8-58) is a consequence of the fact that q is an odd function. For any L, the s_i and t_i that satisfy Eqs. (8-56) through (8-58) are optimal in the mean-squared error sense; the corresponding quantizer is called an L-level *Lloyd-Max* quantizer.

Table 8.13 lists the 2-, 4-, and 8-level Lloyd-Max decision and reconstruction levels for a unit variance Laplacian probability density function [see Eq. (8-34)]. Because obtaining an explicit or closed-form solution to Eqs. (8-56) through (8-58) for most nontrivial $p(s)$ is difficult, these values were generated numerically (Paez and Glisson [1972]). The three quantizers shown provide fixed output rates of 1, 2, and 3 bits/pixel, respectively. As Table 8.13 was constructed for a unit variance distribution, the reconstruction and decision levels for the case of $\sigma \neq 1$ are obtained by multiplying the tabulated values by the standard deviation of the probability density

TABLE 8.13
Lloyd-Max quantizers for a Laplacian probability density function of unit variance.

Levels	2		4		8	
	s_i	t_i	s_i	t_i	s_i	t_i
1	∞	0.707	1.102	0.395	0.504	0.222
2			∞	1.810	1.181	0.785
3					2.285	1.576
4					∞	2.994
θ		1.414		1.087		0.731

function under consideration. The final row of the table lists the step size, θ, that simultaneously satisfies Eqs. (8-56) through (8-58) and the additional constraint that

$$t_i - t_{i-1} = s_i - s_{i-1} = \theta \qquad (8-59)$$

If a symbol encoder that utilizes a variable-length code is used in the general lossy predictive encoder of Fig. 8.38(a), an *optimum uniform quantizer* of step size θ will provide a lower code rate (for a Laplacian PDF) than a fixed-length coded Lloyd-Max quantizer with the same output fidelity (O'Neil [1971]).

Although the Lloyd-Max and optimum uniform quantizers are not adaptive, much can be gained from adjusting the quantization levels based on the local behavior of an image. In theory, slowly changing regions can be finely quantized, while the rapidly changing areas are quantized more coarsely. This approach simultaneously reduces both granular noise and slope overload, while requiring only a minimal increase in code rate. The trade-off is increased quantizer complexity.

8.11 WAVELET CODING

With reference to Tables 8.3–8.5, wavelet coding is used in the

• JPEG-2000

compression standard.

As with the block transform coding techniques presented earlier, wavelet coding is based on the idea that the coefficients of a transform that decorrelates the pixels of an image can be coded more efficiently than the original pixels themselves. If the basis functions of the transform (in this case wavelets) pack most of the important visual information into a small number of coefficients, the remaining coefficients can be quantized coarsely or truncated to zero with little image distortion.

Figure 8.42 shows a typical wavelet coding system. To encode a $2^J \times 2^J$ image, an analyzing wavelet, ψ, and minimum decomposition level, $J - P$, are selected and used to compute the discrete wavelet transform of the image. If the wavelet has a complementary scaling function φ, the fast wavelet transform (see Section 7.10) can be used. In either case, the computed transform converts a large portion of the original image to horizontal, vertical, and diagonal decomposition coefficients with zero mean and Laplacian-like probabilities. Because many of the computed coefficients carry little visual information, they can be quantized and coded to minimize intercoefficient and coding redundancy. Moreover, the quantization can be adapted to exploit any positional correlation across the P decomposition levels. One or more lossless coding methods, such as run-length, Huffman, arithmetic, and bit-plane coding, can be incorporated into the final symbol coding step. Decoding is accomplished by inverting the encoding operations, with the exception of quantization, which cannot be reversed exactly.

The principal difference between the wavelet-based system of Fig. 8.42 and the transform coding system of Fig. 8.21 is the omission of the subimage processing stages of the transform coder. Because wavelet transforms are both computationally efficient and inherently local (i.e., their basis functions are limited in duration), subdivision of the original image is unnecessary. As you will see later in this section, the removal of the subdivision step eliminates the blocking artifact that characterizes DCT-based approximations at high compression ratios.

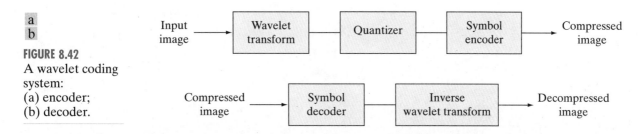

a
b

FIGURE 8.42
A wavelet coding
system:
(a) encoder;
(b) decoder.

WAVELET SELECTION

The wavelets chosen as the basis of the forward and inverse transforms in Fig. 8.42 affect all aspects of wavelet coding system design and performance. They impact directly the computational complexity of the transforms and, less directly, the system's ability to compress and reconstruct images of acceptable error. When the transforming wavelet has a companion scaling function, the transformation can be implemented as a sequence of digital filtering operations, with the number of filter taps equal to the number of nonzero wavelet and scaling vector coefficients. The ability of the wavelet to pack information into a small number of transform coefficients determines its compression and reconstruction performance.

The most widely used expansion functions for wavelet-based compression are the Daubechies wavelets and biorthogonal wavelets. The latter allow useful analysis properties, like the number of vanishing moments (see Section 7.10), to be incorporated into the decomposition filters, while important synthesis properties, like smoothness of reconstruction, are built into the reconstruction filters.

EXAMPLE 8.25: Wavelet bases in wavelet coding.

Figure 8.43 contains four discrete wavelet transforms of Fig. 8.9(a). Haar wavelets, the simplest and only discontinuous wavelets considered in this example, were used as the expansion or basis functions in Fig. 8.43(a). Daubechies wavelets, among the most popular imaging wavelets, were used in Fig. 8.43(b), and symlets, which are an extension of the Daubechies wavelets with increased symmetry, were used in Fig. 8.43(c). The Cohen-Daubechies-Feauveau wavelets employed in Fig. 8.43(d) are included to illustrate the capabilities of biorthogonal wavelets. As in previous results of this type, all detail coefficients were scaled to make the underlying structure more visible, with intensity 128 corresponding to coefficient value 0.

As you can see in Table 8.14, the number of operations involved in the computation of the transforms in Fig. 8.43 increases from 4 to 28 multiplications and additions per coefficient (for each decomposition

TABLE 8.14
Wavelet transform filter taps and zeroed coefficients when truncating the transforms in Fig. 8.43 below 1.5.

Wavelet	Filter Taps (Scaling + Wavelet)	Zeroed Coefficients
Haar	2 + 2	33.3%
Daubechies	8 + 8	40.9%
Symlet	8 + 8	41.2%
Biorthogonal	17 + 11	42.1%

FIGURE 8.43
Three-scale wavelet transforms of Fig. 8.9(a) with respect to (a) Haar wavelets, (b) Daubechies wavelets, (c) symlets, and (d) Cohen-Daubechies-Feauveau biorthogonal wavelets.

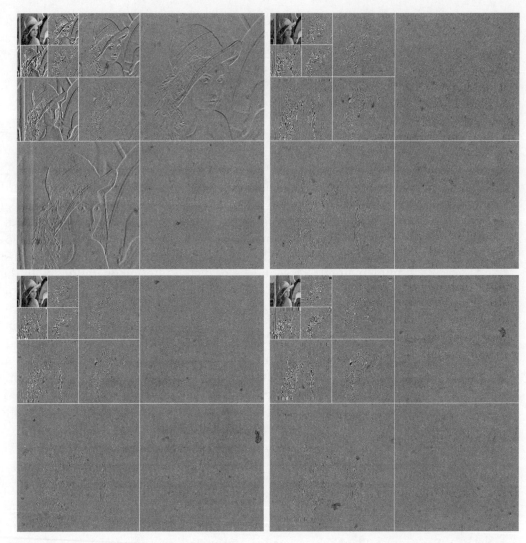

level) as you move from Fig. 8.43(a) to (d). All four transforms were computed using a fast wavelet transform (i.e., filter bank) formulation. Note that as the computational complexity (i.e., the number of filter taps) increases, the information packing performance does as well. When Haar wavelets are employed and the detail coefficients below 1.5 are truncated to zero, 33.8% of the total transform is zeroed. With the more complex biorthogonal wavelets, the number of zeroed coefficients rises to 42.1%, increasing the potential compression by almost 10%.

DECOMPOSITION LEVEL SELECTION

Another factor affecting wavelet coding computational complexity and reconstruction error is the number of transform decomposition levels. Because a P-scale fast wavelet transform involves P filter bank iterations, the number of operations in the computation of the forward and inverse transforms increases with the number of decomposition levels. Moreover, quantizing the increasingly lower-scale coefficients that result with more decomposition levels affects increasingly larger areas of the reconstructed image. In many applications, like searching image databases or transmitting images for progressive reconstruction, the resolution of the stored or transmitted images, and the scale of the lowest useful approximations, normally determine the number of transform levels.

EXAMPLE 8.26: Decomposition levels in wavelet coding.

Table 8.15 illustrates the effect of decomposition level selection on the coding of Fig. 8.9(a) using biorthogonal wavelets and a fixed global threshold of 25. As in the previous wavelet coding example, only detail coefficients are truncated. The table lists both the percentage of zeroed coefficients and the resulting rms reconstruction errors from Eq. (8-10). Note that the initial decompositions are responsible for the majority of the data compression. There is little change in the number of truncated coefficients above three decomposition levels.

QUANTIZER DESIGN

The most important factor affecting wavelet coding compression and reconstruction error is coefficient quantization. Although the most widely used quantizers are uniform, the effectiveness of the quantization can be improved significantly by (1) introducing a larger quantization interval around zero, called a *dead zone*, or (2) adapting the size of the quantization interval from scale to scale. In either case, the selected quantization intervals must be transmitted to the decoder with the encoded image bit stream. The intervals themselves may be determined heuristically, or computed automatically based on the image being compressed. For example, a global coefficient threshold could be computed as the median of the absolute values of the first-level detail coefficients or as a function of the number of zeroes that are truncated and the amount of energy that is retained in the reconstructed image.

One measure of the energy of a digital signal is the sum of the squared samples.

EXAMPLE 8.27: Dead zone interval selection in wavelet coding.

Figure 8.44 illustrates the impact of dead zone interval size on the percentage of truncated detail coefficients for a three-scale biorthogonal wavelet-based encoding of Fig. 8.9(a). As the size of the dead zone increases, the number of truncated coefficients does as well. Above the knee of the curve (i.e., beyond 5),

TABLE 8.15
Decomposition level impact on wavelet coding the 512×512 image of Fig. 8.9(a).

Decomposition Level (Scales or Filter Bank Iterations)	Approximation Coefficient Image	Truncated Coefficients (%)	Reconstruction Error (rms)
1	256×256	74.7%	3.27
2	128×128	91.7%	4.23
3	64×64	95.1%	4.54
4	32×32	95.6%	4.61
5	16×16	95.5%	4.63

FIGURE 8.44
The impact of
dead zone interval
selection on
wavelet coding.

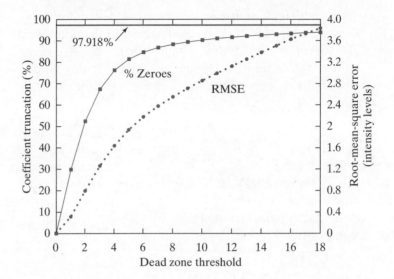

there is little gain. This is due to the fact that the histogram of the detail coefficients is highly peaked around zero.

The rms reconstruction errors corresponding to the dead zone thresholds in Fig. 8.44 increase from 0 to 1.94 intensity levels at a threshold of 5, and to 3.83 intensity levels for a threshold of 18, where the number of zeroes reaches 93.85%. If every detail coefficient were eliminated, that percentage would increase to about 97.92% (by about 4%), but the reconstruction error would grow to 12.3 intensity levels.

JPEG-2000

JPEG-2000 extends the popular JPEG standard to provide increased flexibility in both the compression of continuous-tone still images and access to the compressed data. For example, portions of a JPEG-2000 compressed image can be extracted for retransmission, storage, display, and/or editing. The standard is based on the wavelet coding techniques just described. Coefficient quantization is adapted to individual scales and subbands, and the quantized coefficients are arithmetically coded on a bit-plane basis (see Sections 8.4 and 8.8). Using the notation of the standard, an image is encoded as follows (ISO/IEC [2000]).

Ssiz is used in the standard to denote intensity resolution.

The first step of the encoding process is to DC level shift the samples of the *Ssiz*-bit unsigned image to be coded by subtracting 2^{Ssiz-1}. If the image has more than one component, such as the red, green, and blue planes of a color image, each component is shifted individually. If there are exactly three components, they may be optionally decorrelated using a reversible or nonreversible linear combination of the components. The *irreversible component transform* of the standard, for example, is

The irreversible component transform is the component transform used for lossy compression. The component transform itself is not irreversible. A different component transform is used for reversible compression.

$$Y_0(x,y) = 0.299 I_0(x,y) + 0.587 I_1(x,y) + 0.114 I_2(x,y)$$
$$Y_1(x,y) = -0.16875 I_0(x,y) - 0.33126 I_1(x,y) + 0.5 I_2(x,y) \qquad (8\text{-}60)$$
$$Y_2(x,y) = 0.5 I_0(x,y) - 0.41869 I_1(x,y) - 0.08131 I_2(x,y)$$

where I_0, I_1, and I_2 are the level-shifted input components, and Y_0, Y_1, and Y_2 are the corresponding decorrelated components. If the input components are the red, green, and blue planes of a color image, Eq. (8-60) approximates the $R'G'B'$ to $Y'C_bC_r$ color video transform (Poynton [1996]).[†] The goal of the transformation is to improve compression efficiency; transformed components Y_1 and Y_2 are difference images whose histograms are highly peaked around zero.

After the image has been level-shifted and optionally decorrelated, its components can be divided into *tiles*. Tiles are rectangular arrays of pixels that are processed independently. Because an image can have more than one component (e.g., it could be made up of three color components), the tiling process creates *tile components*. Each tile component can be reconstructed independently, providing a simple mechanism for accessing and/or manipulating a limited region of a coded image. For example, an image having a 16:9 aspect ratio could be subdivided into tiles so one of its tiles is a subimage with a 4:3 aspect ratio. That tile then could be reconstructed without accessing the other tiles in the compressed image. If the image is not subdivided into tiles, it is a single tile.

The 1-D discrete wavelet transform of the rows and columns of each tile component is then computed. For error-free compression, the transform is based on a biorthogonal, 5/3 coefficient scaling and wavelet vector (Le Gall and Tabatabai [1988]). A rounding procedure is defined for non-integer-valued transform coefficients. In lossy applications, a 9/7 coefficient scaling-wavelet vector is employed (Antonini, Barlaud, Mathieu, and Daubechies [1992]). In either case, the transform is computed using the fast wavelet transform of Section 7.10 or via a complementary *lifting-based* approach (Mallat [1999]). For example, in lossy applications, the coefficients used to construct the 9/7 FWT analysis filter bank are given in Table 7.1. The complementary lifting-based implementation involves six sequential "lifting" and "scaling" operations:

> Lifting-based implementations are another way to compute wavelet transforms. The coefficients used in the approach are directly related to the FWT filter bank coefficients.

$$Y(2n+1) = X(2n+1) + \alpha\left[X(2n) + X(2n+2)\right] \qquad i_0 - 3 \le 2n+1 < i_1 + 3$$
$$Y(2n) = X(2n) + \beta\left[Y(2n-1) + Y(2n+1)\right] \qquad i_0 - 2 \le 2n < i_1 + 2$$
$$Y(2n+1) = Y(2n+1) + \gamma\left[Y(2n) + Y(2n+2)\right] \qquad i_0 - 1 \le 2n+1 < i_1 + 1$$
$$Y(2n) = Y(2n) + \delta\left[Y(2n-1) + Y(2n+1)\right] \qquad i_0 \le 2n < i_1$$
$$Y(2n+1) = -KY(2n+1) \qquad i_0 \le 2n+1 < i_1$$
$$Y(2n) = Y(2n)/K \qquad i_0 \le 2n < i_1$$

$$(8\text{-}61)$$

Here, X is the tile component being transformed, Y is the resulting transform, and i_0 and i_1 define the position of the tile component within a component. That is, they are the indices of the first sample of the tile-component row or column being transformed and the one immediately following the last sample. Variable

---

[†] $R'G'B'$ is a gamma-corrected, nonlinear version of a linear CIE (International Commission on Illumination) RGB colorimetry value. Y' is luminance and C_b and C_r are color differences (i.e., scaled $B' - Y'$ and $R' - Y'$ values).

n assumes values based on i_0, i_1, and determines which of the six operations is being performed. If $n < i_0$ or $n > i_1$, $X(n)$ is obtained by symmetrically extending X. For example, $X(i_0 - 1) = X(i_0 + 1)$, $X(i_0 - 2) = X(i_0 + 2)$, $X(i_1) = X(i_1 - 2)$, and $X(i_1 + 1) = X(i_1 - 3)$. At the conclusion of the lifting and scaling operations, the even-indexed values of Y are equivalent to the FWT lowpass filtered output; the odd-indexed values of Y correspond to the highpass FWT filtered result. Lifting parameters α, β, γ, and δ are -1.586134342, -0.052980118, 0.882911075, and 0.433506852, respectively, and scaling factor K is 1.230174105.

These lifting-based coefficients are specified in the standard.

Recall from Chapter 7 that the DWT decomposes an image into a set of band-limited components called subbands.

The transformation just described produces four subbands; a low-resolution approximation of the tile component and the component's horizontal, vertical, and diagonal frequency characteristics. Repeating the transformation N_L times, with subsequent iterations restricted to the previous decomposition's approximation coefficients, produces an N_L-scale wavelet transform. Adjacent scales are related spatially by powers of 2, and the lowest scale contains the only explicitly defined approximation of the original tile component. As can be surmised from Fig. 8.45, where the notation of the JPEG-2000 standard is summarized for the case of $N_L = 2$, a general N_L-scale transform contains $3N_L + 1$ subbands whose coefficients are denoted a_b for $b = N_L HL, \dots, 1HL, 1LH, 1HH$. The standard does not specify the number of scales to be computed.

When each of the tile components has been processed, the total number of transform coefficients is equal to the number of samples in the original image, but the important visual information is concentrated in a few coefficients. To reduce the number of bits needed to represent the transform, coefficient $a_b(u,v)$ of subband b is quantized to value $q_b(u,v)$ using

$$q_b(u,v) = \text{sign}[a_b(u,v)] \cdot \text{floor}\left[\frac{|a_b(u,v)|}{\Delta_b}\right] \tag{8-62}$$

where the *quantiztion step size* Δ_b is

$$\Delta_b = 2^{R_b - \varepsilon_b}\left(1 + \frac{\mu_b}{2^{11}}\right) \tag{8-63}$$

Do not confuse the standard's definition of nominal dynamic range with the closely related definition in Chapter 2.

R_b is the *nominal dynamic range* of subband b, while ε_b and μ_b are the number of bits allotted to the *exponent* and *mantissa* of the subband's coefficients. The nominal dynamic range of subband b is the sum of the number of bits used to represent the original image and the *analysis gain* bits for subband b. Subband analysis gain bits follow the simple pattern shown in Fig. 8.45. For example, there are two analysis gain bits for subband $b = 1HH$.

For error-free compression, $\mu_b = 0$, $R_b = \varepsilon_b$, and $\Delta_b = 1$. For irreversible compression, no particular quantization step size is specified in the standard. Instead, the number of exponent and mantissa bits must be provided to the decoder on a subband basis, called *expounded quantization*, or for the $N_L LL$ subband only, called *derived quantization*. In the latter case, the remaining subbands are quantized using extrapolated $N_L LL$ subband parameters. Letting ε_0 and μ_0 be the number of bits allocated to the $N_L LL$ subband, the extrapolated parameters for subband b are

$$\mu_b = \mu_0$$
$$\varepsilon_b = \varepsilon_0 + n_b - N_L$$

(8-64)

where n_b denotes the number of subband decomposition levels from the original image tile component to subband b.

In the final steps of the encoding process, the coefficients of each transformed tile-component's subbands are arranged into rectangular blocks called *code blocks*, which are coded individually, one bit plane at a time. Starting from the most significant bit plane with a nonzero element, each bit plane is processed in three passes. Each bit (in a bit plane) is coded in only one of the three passes, which are called *significance propagation*, *magnitude refinement*, and *cleanup*. The outputs are then arithmetically coded and grouped with similar passes from other code blocks to form *layers*. A layer is an arbitrary number of groupings of coding passes from each code block. The resulting layers finally are partitioned into *packets*, providing an additional method of extracting a spatial region of interest from the total code stream. Packets are the fundamental unit of the encoded code stream.

JPEG-2000 decoders simply invert the operations previously described. After reconstructing the subbands of the tile-components from the arithmetically coded JPEG-2000 packets, a user-selected number of the subbands is decoded. Although the encoder may have encoded M_b bit planes for a particular subband, the user, due to the embedded nature of the code stream, may choose to decode only N_b bit planes. This amounts to quantizing the coefficients of the code block using a step

FIGURE 8.45
JPEG 2000 two-scale wavelet transform tile-component coefficient notation and analysis gain.

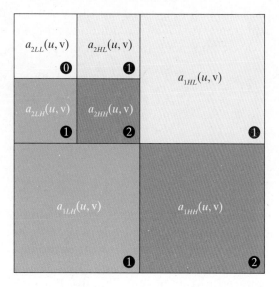

Quantization as defined earlier in the chapter is irreversible. The term "inverse quantized" does not mean that there is no information loss. This process is lossy except for the case of reversible JPEG-2000 compression, where $\mu_b = 0$, $R_b = \varepsilon_b$, and $\Delta_b = 1$.

size of $2^{M_b - N_b} \cdot \Delta_b$. Any nondecoded bits are set to zero and the resulting coefficients, denoted $\bar{q}_b(u,v)$, are inverse quantized using

$$R_{q_b}(u,v) = \begin{cases} \left(\bar{q}_b(u,v) + r \cdot 2^{M_b - N_b(u,v)}\right) \cdot \Delta_b & \bar{q}_b(u,v) > 0 \\ \left(\bar{q}_b(u,v) - r \cdot 2^{M_b - N_b(u,v)}\right) \cdot \Delta_b & \bar{q}_b(u,v) < 0 \\ 0 & \bar{q}_b(u,v) = 0 \end{cases} \quad (8\text{-}65)$$

where $R_{q_b}(u,v)$ denotes an inverse-quantized transform coefficient, and $N_b(u,v)$ is the number of decoded bit planes for $\bar{q}_b(u,v)$. *Reconstruction parameter r* is chosen by the decoder to produce the best visual or objective quality of reconstruction. Generally, $0 \leq r < 1$, with a common value being $r = 1/2$. The inverse-quantized coefficients then are inverse-transformed by column and by row using an FWT^{-1} filter bank whose coefficients are obtained from Table 7.1, or via the following lifting-based operations:

$$
\begin{aligned}
X(2n) &= K \cdot Y(2n) & i_0 - 3 \leq 2n < i_1 + 3 \\
X(2n+1) &= (-1/K)Y(2n+1) & i_0 - 2 \leq 2n - 1 < i_1 + 2 \\
X(2n) &= X(2n) - \delta\left[X(2n-1) + X(2n+1)\right] & i_0 - 3 \leq 2n < i_1 + 3 \\
X(2n+1) &= X(2n+1) - \gamma\left[X(2n) + X(2n+2)\right] & i_0 - 2 \leq 2n + 1 < i_1 + 2 \\
X(2n) &= X(2n) - \beta\left[X(2n-1) + X(2n+1)\right] & i_0 - 1 \leq 2n < i_1 + 1 \\
X(2n+1) &= X(2n+1) - \alpha\left[X(2n) + X(2n+2)\right] & i_0 \leq 2n + 1 < i_1
\end{aligned}
\quad (8\text{-}66)
$$

where parameters α, β, γ, δ, and K are as defined for Eq. (8-61). Inverse-quantized coefficient row or column element $Y(n)$ is symmetrically extended when necessary. The final decoding steps are the assembly of the component tiles, inverse component transformation (if required), and DC level shifting. For irreversible coding, the inverse component transformation is

$$
\begin{aligned}
I_0(x,y) &= Y_0(x,y) + 1.402 Y_2(x,y) \\
I_1(x,y) &= Y_0(x,y) - 0.34413 Y_1(x,y) - 0.71414 Y_2(x,y) \\
I_2(x,y) &= Y_0(x,y) + 1.772 Y_1(x,y)
\end{aligned}
\quad (8\text{-}67)
$$

and the transformed pixels are shifted by $+2^{Ssiz-1}$.

EXAMPLE 8.28: A comparison of JPEG-2000 wavelet-based coding and JPEG DCT-based compression.

Figure 8.46 shows four JPEG-2000 approximations of the monochrome image in Figure 8.9(a). Successive rows of the figure illustrate increasing levels of compression, including $C = 25, 52, 75$, and 105. The images in column 1 are decompressed JPEG-2000 encodings. The differences between these images and the original image [see Fig. 8.9(a)] are shown in the second column, and the third column contains a zoomed portion of the reconstructions in column 1. Because the compression ratios for the first two rows are virtually identical to the compression ratios in Example 8.18, these results can be compared (both qualitatively and quantitatively) to the JPEG transform-based results in Figs. 8.29(a) through (f).

FIGURE 8.46 Four JPEG-2000 approximations of Fig. 8.9(a). Each row contains a result after compression and reconstruction, the scaled difference between the result and the original image, and a zoomed portion of the reconstructed image. (Compare the results in rows 1 and 2 with the JPEG results in Fig. 8.29.).

A visual comparison of the error images in rows 1 and 2 of Fig. 8.46 with the corresponding images in Figs. 8.29(b) and (e) reveals a noticeable decrease of error in the JPEG-2000 results—3.86 and 5.77 intensity levels, as opposed to 5.4 and 10.7 intensity levels for the JPEG results. The computed errors favor the wavelet-based results at both compression levels. Besides decreasing reconstruction error, wavelet coding dramatically increases (in a subjective sense) image quality. Note that the blocking artifact that dominated the JPEG results [see Figs. 8.29(c) and (f)] is not present in Fig. 8.46. Finally, we note that the compression achieved in rows 3 and 4 of Fig. 8.46 is not practical with JPEG. JPEG-2000 provides useable images that are compressed by more than 100:1, with the most objectionable degradation being increased image blur.

8.12 DIGITAL IMAGE WATERMARKING

The methods and standards of Sections 8.2 through 8.11 make the distribution of images (in photographs or videos) on digital media and over the Internet practical. Unfortunately, the images so distributed can be copied repeatedly and without error, putting the rights of their owners at risk. Even when encrypted for distribution, images are unprotected after decryption. One way to discourage illegal duplication is to insert one or more items of information, collectively called a *watermark*, into potentially vulnerable images in such a way that the watermarks are inseparable from the images themselves. As integral parts of the watermarked images, they protect the rights of their owners in a variety of ways, including:

1. *Copyright identification.* Watermarks can provide information that serves as proof of ownership when the rights of the owner have been infringed.

2. *User identification* or *fingerprinting.* The identity of legal users can be encoded in watermarks and used to identify sources of illegal copies.

3. *Authenticity determination.* The presence of a watermark can guarantee that an image has not been altered, assuming the watermark is designed to be destroyed by any modification of the image.

4. *Automated monitoring.* Watermarks can be monitored by systems that track when and where images are used (e.g., programs that search the Web for images placed on Web pages). Monitoring is useful for royalty collection and/or the location of illegal users.

5. *Copy protection.* Watermarks can specify rules of image usage and copying (e.g., to DVD players).

In this section, we provide a brief overview of *digital image watermarking*, which is the process of inserting data into an image in such a way that it can be used to make an assertion about the image. The methods described have little in common with the compression techniques presented in the previous sections (although they do involve the coding of information). In fact, watermarking and compression are in some ways opposites. While the objective in compression is to reduce the amount of data used to represent images, the goal in watermarking is to add information and data (i.e., watermarks) to them. As will be seen in the remainder of the section, the watermarks themselves can be either visible or invisible.

A *visible watermark* is an opaque or semi-transparent subimage or image that is placed on top of another image (i.e., the image being watermarked) so that it is obvious to the viewer. Television networks often place visible watermarks (fashioned after their logos) in the upper or lower right-hand corner of the television screen. As the following example illustrates, visible watermarking typically is performed in the spatial domain.

EXAMPLE 8.29: A simple visible watermark.

The image in Fig. 8.47(b) is the lower right-hand quadrant of the image in Fig. 8.9(a) with a scaled version of the watermark in Fig. 8.47(a) overlaid on top of it. Letting f_w denote the watermarked image, we can express it as a linear combination of the unmarked image f and watermark w using

$$f_w = (1 - \alpha)f + \alpha w \qquad (8\text{-}68)$$

where constant α controls the relative visibility of the watermark and the underlying image. If α is 1, the watermark is opaque and the underlying image is completely obscured. As α approaches 0, more of the underlying image and less of the watermark is seen. In general, $0 < \alpha \leq 1$; in Fig. 8.47(b), $\alpha = 0.3$. Figure 8.47(c) is the computed difference (scaled in intensity) between the watermarked image in (b) and the unmarked image in Fig. 8.9(a). Intensity 128 represents a difference of 0. Note that the underlying image is clearly visible through the "semi-transparent" watermark. This is evident in both Fig. 8.47(b) and the difference image in Fig. 8.47(c).

Unlike the visible watermark of the previous example, *invisible watermarks* cannot be seen with the naked eye. They are imperceptible but can be recovered with an appropriate decoding algorithm. Invisibility is assured by inserting them as visually redundant information [information that the human visual system ignores or cannot

a
b c

FIGURE 8.47
A simple visible watermark:
(a) watermark;
(b) the water-marked image; and
(c) the difference between the watermarked image and the original (non-watermarked) image.

perceive (see Section 8.1)]. Figure 8.48(a) provides a simple example. Because the least significant bits of an 8-bit image have virtually no effect on our perception of the image, the watermark from Fig. 8.47(a) was inserted or "hidden" in its two least significant bits. Using the notation introduced above, we let

$$f_w = 4\left(\frac{f}{4}\right) + \frac{w}{64} \tag{8-69}$$

and use unsigned integer arithmetic to perform the calculations. Dividing and multiplying by 4 sets the two least significant bits of f to 0, dividing w by 64 shifts its two most significant bits into the two least significant bit positions, and adding the two results generates the *LSB watermarked image*. Note that the embedded watermark is not visible in Fig. 8.48(a). By zeroing the most significant 6 bits of this image and scaling the remaining values to the full intensity range, however, the watermark can be extracted as in Fig. 8.48(b).

An important property of invisible watermarks is their resistance to both accidental and intentional attempts to remove them. *Fragile invisible watermarks* are destroyed by any modification of the images in which they are embedded. In some applications, like image authentication, this is a desirable characteristic. As Figs. 8.48(c) and (d) show, the LSB watermarked image in Fig. 8.48(a) contains a fragile invisible watermark. If the image in (a) is compressed and decompressed using lossy JPEG, the watermark is destroyed. Figure 8.48(c) is the result after com-

a b
c d

FIGURE 8.48
A simple invisible watermark:
(a) watermarked image;
(b) the extracted watermark;
(c) the watermarked image after high quality JPEG compression and decompression; and
(d) the extracted watermark from (c).

pressing and decompressing Fig. 8.48(a); the rms error is 2.1 bits. If we try to extract the watermark from this image using the same method as in (b), the result is unintelligible [see Fig. 8.48(d)]. Although lossy compression and decompression preserved the important visual information in the image, the fragile watermark was destroyed.

Robust invisible watermarks are designed to survive image modification, whether the so-called *attacks* are inadvertent or intentional. Common inadvertent attacks include lossy compression, linear and nonlinear filtering, cropping, rotation, resampling, and the like. Intentional attacks range from printing and rescanning to adding additional watermarks and/or noise. Of course, it is unnecessary to withstand attacks that leave the image itself unusable.

Figure 8.49 shows the basic components of a typical image watermarking system. The encoder in Fig. 8.49(a) inserts watermark w_i into image f_i producing watermarked image f_{w_i}; the complementary decoder in (b) extracts and validates the presence of w_i in watermarked input f_{w_i} or unmarked input f_j. If w_i is visible, the decoder is not needed. If it is invisible, the decoder may or may not require a copy of f_i and w_i [shown in blue in Fig. 8.49(b)] to do its job. If f_i and/or w_i are used, the watermarking system is known as a *private* or *restricted-key* system; if not, it is a *public* or *unrestricted-key* system. Because the decoder must process both marked and unmarked images, $w_\emptyset$ is used in Fig. 8.49(b) to denote the absence of a mark. Finally, we note that to determine the presence of w_i in an image, the decoder must correlate extracted watermark w_j with w_i and compare the result to a predefined threshold. The threshold sets the degree of similarity that is acceptable for a "match."

EXAMPLE 8.30: A DCT-based invisible robust watermark.

Mark insertion and *extraction* can be performed in the spatial domain, as in the previous examples, or in the transform domain. Figures 8.50(a) and (c) show two watermarked versions of the image in Fig. 8.9(a) using the DCT-based watermarking approach outlined here (Cox et al. [1997]):

1. Compute the 2-D DCT of the image to be watermarked.
2. Locate its K largest coefficients, $c_1, c_2, ..., c_K$, by magnitude.
3. Create a watermark by generating a K-element pseudo-random sequence of numbers, $\omega_1, \omega_2, ..., \omega_K$, taken from a Gaussian distribution with mean $\mu = 0$ and variance $\sigma^2 = 1$. (Note: A pseudo-random number sequence approximates the properties of random numbers. It is not truly random because it depends on a predetermined initial value.)
4. Embed the watermark from Step 3 into the K largest DCT coefficients from Step 2 using the following equation

$$c_i' = c_i \cdot (1 + \alpha \omega_i) \qquad 1 \leq i \leq K \tag{8-70}$$

   for a specified constant $\alpha > 0$ (that controls the extent to which ω_i alters c_i). Replace the original c_i with the computed c_i' from Eq. (8-70). (For the images in Fig. 8.50, $\alpha = 0.1$ and $K = 1000$.)
5. Compute the inverse DCT of the result from Step 4.

By employing watermarks made from pseudo-random numbers and spreading them across an image's perceptually significant frequency components, α can be made small, reducing watermark visibility. At

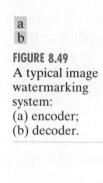

FIGURE 8.49
A typical image
watermarking
system:
(a) encoder;
(b) decoder.

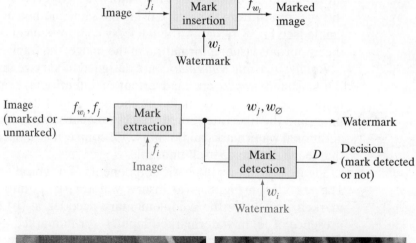

a b
c d

FIGURE 8.50
(a) and (c) Two
watermarked
versions of
Fig. 8.9(a);
(b) and (d)
the differences
(scaled in inten-
sity) between
the watermarked
versions and the
unmarked image.
These two images
show the inten-
sity contribution
(although scaled
dramatically) of
the pseudo-
random water-
marks on the
original image.

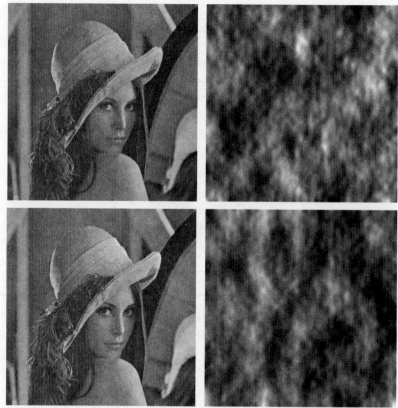

the same time, watermark security is kept high because (1) the watermarks are composed of pseudo-random numbers with no obvious structure, (2) the watermarks are embedded in multiple frequency components with spatial impact over the entire 2-D image (so their location is not obvious) and (3) attacks against them tend to degrade the image as well (i.e., the image's most important frequency components must be altered to affect the watermarks).

Figures 8.50(b) and (d) make the changes in image intensity that result from the pseudo-random numbers that are embedded in the DCT coefficients of the watermarked images in Figs. 8.50(a) and (c) visible. Obviously, the pseudo-random numbers must have an effect (even if too small to see) on the watermarked images. To display the effect, the images in Figs. 8.50(a) and (c) were subtracted from the unmarked image in Fig. 8.9(a) and scaled in intensity to the range [0, 255]. Figures 8.50(b) and (d) are the resulting images; they show the 2-D spatial contributions of the pseudo-random numbers. Because they have been scaled, however, you cannot simply add these images to the image in Fig. 8.9(a) and get the watermarked images in Figs. 8.50(a) and (c). As can be seen in Figs. 8.50(a) and (c), their actual intensity perturbations are small to negligible.

To determine whether a particular image is a copy of a previously watermarked image with watermark $\omega_1, \omega_2, \ldots, \omega_K$ and DCT coefficients $c_1, c_2, \ldots, c_K$, we use the following procedure:

1. Compute the 2-D DCT of the image in question.

2. Extract the K DCT coefficients (in the positions corresponding to $c_1, c_2, \ldots, c_K$ of Step 2 in the watermarking procedure) and denote the coefficients as $\hat{c}_1, \hat{c}_2, \ldots, \hat{c}_K$. If the image in question is the previously watermarked image (without modification), $\hat{c}_i = c_i'$ for $1 \le i \le K$. If it is a modified copy of the watermarked image (i.e., it has undergone some sort of attack), $\hat{c}_i \approx c_i'$ for $1 \le i \le K$ (the $\hat{c}_i$ will be approximations of the c_i'). Otherwise, the image in question will be an unmarked image or an image with a completely different watermark, and the $\hat{c}_i$ will bear no resemblance to the original $\hat{c}_i$.

3. Compute watermark $\hat{\omega}_1, \hat{\omega}_2, \ldots, \hat{\omega}_K$ using

$$\hat{\omega}_i = \frac{\hat{c}_i - c_i}{\alpha c_i} \quad \text{for } 1 \le i \le k \tag{8-71}$$

Recall that watermarks are sequences of pseudo-random numbers.

4. Measure the similarity of $\hat{\omega}_1, \hat{\omega}_2, \ldots, \hat{\omega}_K$ (from Step 3) and $\omega_1, \omega_2, \ldots, \omega_K$ (from Step 3 of the watermarking procedure) using a metric such as the correlation coefficient

$$\gamma = \frac{\sum_{i=1}^{K} (\hat{\omega}_i - \bar{\hat{\omega}})(\omega_i - \bar{\omega})}{\sqrt{\sum_{i=1}^{K} (\hat{\omega}_i - \bar{\hat{\omega}})^2 \cdot \sum_{i=1}^{K} (\omega_i - \bar{\omega})^2}} \quad 1 \le i \le K \tag{8-72}$$

where $\bar{\omega}$ and $\bar{\hat{\omega}}$ are the means of the two K-element watermarks. (Note: Correlation coefficients are discussed in detail in Section 12.3.)

5. Compare the measured similarity, γ, to a predefined threshold, T, and make a binary detection decision:

$$D = \begin{cases} 1 & \text{if } \gamma \ge T \\ 0 & \text{otherwise} \end{cases} \tag{8-73}$$

In other words, $D = 1$ indicates that watermark $\omega_1, \omega_2, \ldots, \omega_K$ is present (with respect to the specified threshold, T); $D = 0$ indicates that it was not.

Using this procedure, the original watermarked image in Fig. 8.50(a), measured against itself, yields a correlation coefficient of 0.9999, i.e., $\gamma = 0.9999$. It is an unmistakable match. In a similar manner, the image in Fig. 8.50(b), when measured against the image in Fig. 8.50(a), results in a γ of 0.0417. It could not be mistaken for the watermarked image in Fig. 8.50(a) because the correlation coefficient is so low.

To conclude the section, we note that the DCT-based watermarking approach of the previous example is fairly resistant to watermark attacks, partly because it is a private or restricted-key method. Restricted-key methods are always more resilient than their unrestricted-key counterparts. Using the watermarked image in Fig. 8.50(a), Fig. 8.51 illustrates the ability of the method to withstand a variety of common attacks. As can be seen in the figure, watermark detection is quite good over the range of attacks that were implemented; the resulting correlation coefficients (shown under each image in the figure) vary from 0.3113 to 0.9945. When subjected to a high quality but lossy (resulting in an rms error of 7 intensities) JPEG compression and decompression, $\gamma = 0.9945$. Even when the compression and reconstruction yields an rms error of 10 intensity levels, $\gamma = 0.7395$; and the usability of this image has been significantly degraded. Significant smoothing by spatial filtering and the addition of Gaussian noise do not reduce the correlation coefficient below 0.8230. However, histogram equalization reduces γ to 0.5210; and rotation has the largest effect; reducing γ to 0.3313. All attacks, except for the lossy JPEG compression and reconstruction in Fig. 8.51(a), have significantly reduced the usability of the original watermarked image.

Summary, References, and Further Reading

The principal objectives of this chapter were to present the theoretic foundation of digital image compression, to describe the most commonly used compression methods, and to introduce the related area of digital image watermarking. Although the level of the presentation is introductory in nature, the references provide an entry into the extensive body of literature dealing with the topics discussed. As evidenced by the international standards listed in Tables 8.3 through 8.5, compression plays a key role in document image storage and transmission, the Internet, and commercial video distribution (e.g., DVDs). It is one of the few areas of image processing that has received a sufficiently broad commercial appeal to warrant the adoption of widely accepted standards. Image watermarking is becoming increasingly important as more and more images are distributed in compressed digital form.

The introductory material of the chapter, which is generally confined to Section 8.1, is basic to image compression, and may be found in one form or another in most of the general image processing books cited at the end of Chapter 1. For additional information on the human visual system, see Netravali and Limb [1980], as well as Huang [1966], Schreiber and Knapp [1958], and the references cited at the end of Chapter 2. For more on information theory, see the book website or Abramson [1963], Blahut [1987], and Berger [1971]. Shannon's classic paper, "A Mathematical Theory of Communication" [1948], lays the foundation for the area and is another excellent reference. Subjective fidelity criteria are discussed in Frendendall and Behrend [1960]. Throughout the chapter, a variety of compression standards are used in examples. Most of them were implemented using Adobe Photoshop (with freely available compression plug-ins) and/or MATLAB, which is described in Gonzalez et al. [2004]. Compression standards, as a rule, are lengthy and complex; we have not attempted to cover any of them in their entirety. For more information on a particular standard, see the published documents of the appropriate standards organization—the International Standards Organization, International Electrotechnical Commission, and/or the International Telecommunications Union.

The lossy and error-free compression techniques described in Sections 8.2 through 8.11 and watermarking techniques in Section 8.12 are, for the most part, based on the original papers cited in the text. The algorithms covered are representative of the work in this area, but are by no means exhaustive. The material on LZW coding has its origins in the work of Ziv and Lempel [1977, 1978]. The material on arithmetic coding follows the development in Witten, Neal, and Cleary [1987]. One of the more important implementations of arithmetic coding is summarized in Pennebaker et al. [1988]. For a good discussion of lossless predictive coding, see the tutorial by Rabbani and Jones [1991]. The adaptive predictor of Eq. (8-55) is from Graham [1958]. For more on motion compensation, see S. Solari [1997], which also contains an introduction to general video compression and compression standards, and Mitchell et al. [1997]. The DCT-based watermarking technique in Section 8.12 is based on the paper by Cox et al. [1997]. For more on watermarking, see the books by Cox et al. [2001] and Parhi and Nishitani [1999]. See also the paper by S. Mohanty [1999].

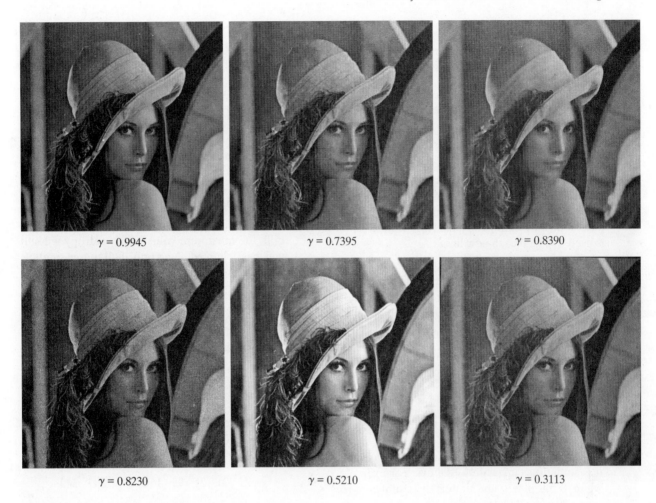

$\gamma = 0.9945$ $\gamma = 0.7395$ $\gamma = 0.8390$

$\gamma = 0.8230$ $\gamma = 0.5210$ $\gamma = 0.3113$

a b c
d e f

FIGURE 8.51 Attacks on the watermarked image in Fig. 8.50(a): (a) lossy JPEG compression and decompression with an rms error of seven intensity levels; (b) lossy JPEG compression and decompression with an rms error of 10 intensity levels (note the blocking artifact); (c) smoothing by spatial filtering; (d) the addition of Gaussian noise; (e) histogram equalization; and (f) rotation. Each image is a modified version of the watermarked image in Fig. 8.50(a). After modification, they retain their watermarks to varying degrees, as indicated by the correlation coefficients below each image.

Many survey articles have been devoted to the field of image compression. Noteworthy are Netravali and Limb [1980], A. K. Jain [1981], a special issue on picture communication systems in the *IEEE Transactions on Communications* [1981], a special issue on the encoding of graphics in the *Proceedings of IEEE* [1980], a special issue on visual communication systems in the *Proceedings of the IEEE* [1985], a special issue on image sequence compression in the *IEEE Transactions on Image Processing* [1994], and a special issue on vector quantization in the *IEEE Transactions on Image Processing* [1996]. In addition, most issues of the *IEEE Transactions on Image Processing*, *IEEE Transactions on Circuits and Systems for Video Technology*, and *IEEE Transactions on Multimedia* include articles on video and still image compression, motion compensation, and watermarking.

Problems

Solutions to the problems marked with an asterisk (*) are in the DIP4E Student Support Package (consult the book website: www.ImageProcessingPlace.com).

8.1 Explain the image compression system with a suitable diagram.

8.2 One variation of run-length coding involves (1) coding only the runs of 0's or 1's (not both) and (2) assigning a special code to the start of each line to reduce the effect of transmission errors. One possible code pair is (x_k, r_k), where x_k and r_k represent the kth run's starting coordinate and run length, respectively. The code $(0, 0)$ is used to signal each new line.

    (a) Derive a general expression for the maximum average runs per scan line required to guarantee data compression when run-length coding a $2^n \times 2^n$ binary image.

    (b) Compute the maximum allowable value for $n = 10$.

8.3 Consider an 8-pixel line of intensity data, {255, 118, 127, 182, 18, 178, 82, 55}. If it is uniformly quantized with 4-bit accuracy, compute the rms error and rms signal-to-noise ratios for the quantized data.

8.4* Although quantization results in information loss, it is sometimes invisible to the eye. For example, when 8-bit pixels are uniformly quantized to fewer bits/pixel, false contouring often occurs. It can be reduced or eliminated using *improved gray-scale* (IGS) *quantization*. A sum—initially set to zero—is formed from the current 8-bit intensity value and the four least significant bits of the previously generated sum. If the four most significant bits of the intensity value are 1111_2, however, 0000_2 is added instead. The four most significant bits of the resulting sum are used as the coded pixel value.

    (a) Construct the IGS code for the intensity data in Problem 8.3.

    (b) Compute the rms error and rms signal-to-noise ratios for the decoded IGS data.

8.5 Determine the following

s_0	s_1	s_2	s_3	s_4
0.55	0.15	0.15	0.10	0.05

    (a) Huffmann code

    (b) Average length of the code.

8.6* The base e unit of information is commonly called a *nat*, and the base-10 information unit is called a *Hartley*. Compute the conversion factors needed to relate these units to the base-2 unit of information (the bit).

8.7* Prove that, for a zero-memory source with q symbols, the maximum value of the entropy is $\log q$, which is achieved if and only if all source symbols are equiprobable. [*Hint:* Consider the quantity $\log q - H(z)$ and note the inequality $\ln x \leq x - 1$.]

8.8 Answer the following.

    (a) How many unique Huffman codes are there for a three-symbol source?

    (b) Construct them.

8.9 Consider the simple 4×8, 8-bit image:

$$
\begin{array}{cccccccc}
21 & 21 & 21 & 95 & 169 & 243 & 243 & 243 \\
21 & 21 & 21 & 95 & 169 & 243 & 243 & 243 \\
21 & 21 & 21 & 95 & 169 & 243 & 243 & 243 \\
21 & 21 & 21 & 95 & 169 & 243 & 243 & 243
\end{array}
$$

    (a) Compute the entropy of the image.

    (b) Compress the image using Huffman coding.

    (c) Compute the compression achieved and the effectiveness of the Huffman coding.

    (d)* Consider Huffman encoding pairs of pixels rather than individual pixels. That is, consider the image to be produced by the second extension of the zero-memory source that produced the original image. What is the entropy of the image when looked at as pairs of pixels?

    (e) Consider coding the differences between adjacent pixels. What is the entropy of the new difference image? What does this tell us about compressing the image?

    (f) Explain the entropy differences in (a), (d) and (e).

8.10 Using the Huffman code in Fig. 8.8, decode the encoded string 0101101010010000011000100.

8.11 Compute Golomb code $G_4(n)$ for $0 \le n \le 15$.

8.12 How can one restrict illegal duplication of photographs or videos on digital media? What are the ways in which they protect the rights of their owners?

8.13 The code created using Huffman's procedure is itself an instantaneous uniquely decodable block code. Explain this statement.

8.14 Compute exponential Golomb code $G_{\exp}^2(n)$ for $0 \le n \le 15$.

8.15* Write a general procedure for decoding exponential Golomb code $G_{\exp}^k(n)$.

8.16 Plot the optimal Golomb coding parameter m as a function of ρ for $0 < \rho < 1$ in Eq. (8-14).

8.17 Explain the basic components of watermarking system with a suitable diagram.

8.18* The arithmetic decoding process is the reverse of the encoding procedure. Decode the message 0.23355 given the coding model

Symbol	Probability
a	0.2
e	0.3
i	0.1
o	0.2
u	0.1
!	0.1

8.19 Use the LZW coding algorithm to encode the 7-bit ASCII string "aaaaaaaaaaa".

8.20* Devise an algorithm for decoding the LZW encoded output of Example 8.7. Since the dictionary that was used during the encoding is not available, the code book must be reproduced as the output is decoded.

8.21 Decode the BMP encoded sequence $\{3, 4, 5, 6, 0, 3, 103, 125, 67, 0, 2, 47\}$.

8.22 Do the following:

(a) Construct the entire 3-bit Gray code.

(b) Create a general procedure for converting a Gray-coded number to its binary equivalent and use it to decode 0101010101100100.

8.23 Use the CCITT Group 4 compression algorithm to code the second line of the following two-line segment:

$$01100111001111111100001$$

$$11111110001110000111111$$

Assume that the initial reference element a_0 is located on the first pixel of the second line segment. (*Note:* Employ the CCITT 2-D code table from the book website.)

8.24* Do the following.

(a) List all the members of JPEG DC coefficient difference category 3.

(b) Compute their default Huffman codes using using the appropriate Huffamn code table from the book website.

8.25 How many computations are required to find the optimal motion vector of a macroblock of size 8×8 using the MAD optimality criterion, single pixel precision, and a maximum allowable displacement of 8 pixels? What would it become for ¼ pixel precision?

8.26 What is the difference between P-frame and B-frame?

8.27* Draw the block diagram of the companion motion compensated video decoder for the encoder in Fig. 8.36.

8.28 An image whose autocorrelation function is of the form of Eq. (8-48) with $\rho_h = 0$ is to be DPCM coded using a second-order predictor.

(a) Form the autocorrelation matrix **R** and vector **r**.

(b) Find the optimal prediction coefficients.

(c) Compute the variance of the prediction error that would result from using the optimal coefficients.

8.29* Derive the Lloyd-Max decision and reconstruction levels for $L = 4$ and the uniform probability density function

$$p(s) = \begin{cases} \dfrac{1}{2A} & -A \le s \le A \\ 0 & \text{otherwise} \end{cases}$$

8.30 A radiologist from a well-known research hospital recently attended a medical conference at which a system that could transmit 4096×4096 12-bit digitized X-ray images over standard T1 (1.544 Mb/s) phone lines was exhibited. The system transmitted the images in a compressed format using a progressive technique in which a reasonably good approximation of the X-ray was first reconstructed at the viewing station, then refined gradually to produce an error-free display. The transmission of the data needed to generate the first approximation took approximately 5 or 6 s. Refinements were made every 5 or 6 s (on the average) for the next 1 min, with the first and last refinements having the most and least significant impact on the reconstructed X-ray, respectively. The physician was favorably impressed with the system, because she could begin her diagnosis by using the first approximation of the X-ray and complete it as the error-free reconstruction of the X-ray was being generated. Upon returning to her office, she submitted a purchase request to the hospital administrator. Unfortunately, the hospital was on a relatively tight budget, which recently had been stretched by the hiring of an aspiring young electrical engineering graduate. To appease the radiologist, the administrator gave the young engineer the task of designing such a system. (He thought it might be cheaper to design and build a similar system in-house. The hospital currently owned some of the elements of such a system, but the transmission of the raw X-ray data took more than 2 min.) The administrator asked the engineer to have an initial block diagram by the afternoon staff meeting. With little time and only a copy of *Digital Image Processing* from his recent school days in hand, the engineer was able to devise a system conceptually to satisfy the transmission and associated compression requirements. Construct a conceptual block diagram of such a system, specifying the compression techniques you would recommend.

8.31 Show that the lifting-based wavelet transform defined by Eq. (8-61) is equivalent to the traditional FWT filter bank implementation using the coefficients in Table 7.1. Define the filter coefficients in terms of α, β, γ, δ, and K.

8.32 Compute the quantization step sizes of the subbands for a JPEG-2000 encoded image in which derived quantization is used and 8 bits are allotted to the mantissa and exponent of the $2LL$ subband.

8.33 How would you add a visible watermark to an image in the frequency domain?

8.34* Design an invisible watermarking system based on the discrete Fourier transform.

8.35 Design an invisible watermarking system based on the discrete wavelet transform.

9 Morphological Image Processing

In form and feature, face and limb,
I grew so like my brother
That folks got taking me for him
And each for one another.

Henry Sambrook Leigh, Carols of Cockayne, The Twins

Preview

The word *morphology* commonly denotes a branch of biology that deals with the form and structure of animals and plants. We use the same word here in the context of *mathematical morphology* as a tool for extracting image components that are useful in the representation and description of region shape, such as boundaries, skeletons, and the convex hull. We are interested also in morphological techniques for pre- or postprocessing, such as morphological filtering, thinning, and pruning.

In the following sections, we will develop a number of fundamental concepts in mathematical morphology, and illustrate how they are applied in image processing. The material in this chapter begins a transition from methods whose inputs and outputs are images, to methods whose outputs are image attributes, for tasks such as object extraction and description. Morphology is one of several tools developed in the remainder of the book—such as segmentation, feature extraction, and object recognition—that form the foundation of techniques for extracting "meaning" from an image. The material in the following sections of this chapter deals with methods for processing both binary and grayscale images.

Upon completion of this chapter, readers should:

- Understand basic concepts of mathematical morphology, and how to apply them to digital image processing.

- Be familiar with the tools used for binary image morphology, including erosion, dilation, opening, closing, and how to combine them to generate more complex tools.

- Be able to develop algorithms based on binary image morphology for performing tasks such as morphological smoothing, edge detection, extracting connected components, and skeletonizing.

- Be familiar with how binary image morphology can be extended to grayscale images.

- Be able to develop algorithms for grayscale image processing for tasks such as textural segmentation, granulometry, computing grayscale image gradients, and others.

635

9.1 PRELIMINARIES

Before proceeding, you will find it helpful to review the discussion in Section 2.4 dealing with representing images, the discussion on connectivity in Section 2.5, and the discussion on sets in Section 2.6.

The language of mathematical morphology is set theory. As such, morphology offers a unified and powerful approach to numerous image processing problems. When working with images, sets in mathematical morphology represent objects in those images. In binary images, the sets in question are members of the 2-D integer space Z^2, where each element of a set is a tuple (2-D vector) whose coordinates are the coordinates of an object (typically foreground) pixel in the image. Grayscale digital images can be represented as sets whose components are in Z^3. In this case, two components of each element of the set refer to the coordinates of a pixel, and the third corresponds to its discrete intensity value. Sets in higher dimensional spaces can contain other image attributes, such as color and time-varying components.

Morphological operations are defined in terms of sets. In image processing, we use morphology with two types of sets of pixels: *objects* and *structuring elements* (SE's). Typically, objects are defined as sets of foreground pixels. Structuring elements can be specified in terms of both foreground and background pixels. In addition, structuring elements sometimes contain so-called "don't care" elements, denoted by ×, signifying that the value of that particular element in the SE does not matter. In this sense, the value can be ignored, or it can be made to fit a desired value in the evaluation of an expression; for example, it might take on the value of a pixel in an image in applications in which value matching is the objective.

Because the images with which we work are rectangular arrays, and sets in general are of arbitrary shape, applications of morphology in image processing require that sets be embedded in rectangular arrays. In forming such arrays, we assign a background value to all pixels that are not members of object sets. The top row in Fig. 9.1 shows an example. On the left are sets in the graphical format you are accustomed to seeing in book figures. In the center, the sets have been embedded in a rectangular background (white) to form a graphical image.[†] On the right, we show a digital image (notice the grid) which is the format we use for digital image processing.

Structuring elements are defined in the same manner, and the second row in Fig. 9.1 shows an example. There is an important difference between the way we represent digital images and digital structuring elements. Observe on the top right that there is a border of background pixels surrounding the objects, while there is none in the SE. As you will learn shortly, structuring elements are used in a form similar to spatial convolution kernels (see Fig. 3.28), and the image border just described is similar to the padding we discussed in Section 3.4 and 3.5. The operations are different in morphology, but the padding and sliding operations are the same as in convolution.

In addition to the set definitions given in Section 2.6, the concept of set reflection and translation are used extensively in morphology in connection with structuring elements. The *reflection* of a set (structuring element) B about its origin, denoted by $\hat{B}$, is defined as

---

[†] Sets are shown as drawings of objects (e.g. squares and triangles) of arbitrary shape. A graphical image contains sets that have been embedded into a background to form a rectangular array. When we intend for a drawing to be interpreted as a *digital* image (or structuring element), we include a grid in illustrations that might otherwise be ambiguous. Objects in all drawings are shaded, and the background is shown in white. When working with actual binary images, we say that objects are *foreground* pixels. All other pixels are *background*.

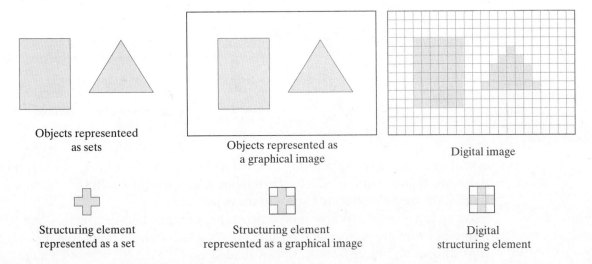

Objects represented
as sets

Objects represented as
a graphical image

Digital image

Structuring element
represented as a set

Structuring element
represented as a graphical image

Digital
structuring element

FIGURE 9.1 Top row. *Left:* Objects represented as graphical sets. *Center:* Objects embedded in a background to form a graphical image. *Right:* Object and background are digitized to form a digital image (note the grid). Second row: Example of a structuring element represented as a set, a graphical image, and finally as a digital SE.

$$\hat{B} = \left\{ w \mid w = -b, \text{ for } b \in B \right\} \tag{9-1}$$

That is, if B is a set of points in 2-D, then $\hat{B}$ is the set of points in B whose (x, y) coordinates have been replaced by $(-x, -y)$. Figure 9.2 shows several examples of digital sets (structuring elements) and their reflection. The dot denotes the origin of the SE. Note that reflection consists simply of rotating an SE by 180° about its origin, and that all elements, including the background and don't care elements, are rotated.

Reflection is the same operation we performed with kernels prior to spatial convolution, as explained in Section 3.4.

The *translation* of a set B by point $z = (z_1, z_2)$, denoted $(B)_z$, is defined as

$$(B)_z = \left\{ c \mid c = b + z, \text{ for } b \in B \right\} \tag{9-2}$$

That is, if B is a set of pixels in 2-D, then $(B)_z$ is the set of pixels in B whose (x, y) coordinates have been replaced by $(x + z_1, y + z_2)$. This construct is used to translate (slide) a structuring element over an image, and each location perform a set

FIGURE 9.2
Structuring elements and their reflections about the origin (the ×'s are don't care elements, and the dots denote the origin). Reflection is rotation by 180° of an SE about its origin.

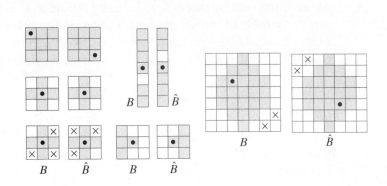

a b c

FIGURE 9.3
(a) A binary image containing one object (set), *A*. (b) A structuring element, *B*. (c) Image resulting from a morphological operation (see text).

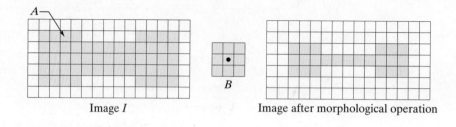

Image *I*   Image after morphological operation

operation between the structuring element and the area of the image directly under it, as we explained in Fig. 3.28 for correlation and convolution. Both reflection and translation are defined with respect to the *origin* of *B*.

As an introduction to how morphological operations between images and structuring elements are performed, consider Fig 9.3, which shows a simple binary image, *I*, consisting of an object (set) *A*, shown shaded, and a 3×3 SE whose elements are all 1's (foreground pixels). The background pixels (0's) are shown in white. We are interested in performing the following morphological operations: (1) form a new image, of the same size as *I*, consisting only of background values initially, (2) translate (slide) *B* over image *I*, and (3) at each increment of translation, if *B* is *completely* contained in *A*, mark the *location* of the origin of *B* as a *foreground* pixel in the new image; otherwise, leave it as a *background* point. Figure 9.3(c) is the result after the origin of *B* has visited every element of *I*. We see that, when the origin of *B* is on a border element of *A*, part of *B* ceases to be contained in *A*, thus eliminating that location of the origin of *B* as a possible foreground point of the new image. The net result is that the boundary of set *A* is *eroded*, as Fig. 9.3(e) shows. Because of the way in which we defined the operation, the maximum excursion needed for *B* in *I* is when the origin of *B* (which is at its center) is contained in *A*. With *B* being of size 3×3, the narrowest background padding we needed was one pixel wide, as shown in Fig. 9.3(a). By using the smallest border needed for an operation, we keep the drawings smaller. In practice, we specify the width of padding based on the maximum dimensions of the structuring elements used, regardless of the operations being performed.

The reason we generally specify the padding border to be of the same dimensions as *B*, is that some morphological operations are defined for an entire structuring element, and cannot be interpreted with respect to the location of its origin.

When we use terminology such as "the structuring element *B* is contained in set *A*," we mean *specifically* that the *foreground* elements of *B* overlap *only* elements of *A*. This becomes an important issue when *B* also contains background and, possibly, don't care elements. Also, we use set *A* to denote *all* foreground pixels of *I*. Those foreground elements can be a *single* object, as in Fig. 9.3, or they can represent *disjoint* subsets of foreground elements, as in the first row of Fig. 9.1. We will discuss binary images and structuring elements from Sections 9.2 through 9.7. Then, in Section 9.8, we will extend the binary ideas to grayscale images and structuring elements.

9.2 EROSION AND DILATION

We begin the discussion of morphology by studying two operations: *erosion* and *dilation*. These operations are fundamental to morphological processing. In fact, many of the morphological algorithms discussed in this chapter are based on these two primitive operations.

EROSION

Remember, set *A* can represent (be the union of) multiple disjoint sets of foreground pixels (i.e., objects).

Morphological expressions are written in terms of structuring elements and a set, *A*, of foreground pixels, or in terms of structuring elements and an image, *I*, that contains *A*. We consider the former approach first. With *A* and *B* as sets in Z^2, the *erosion* of *A* by *B*, denoted $A \ominus B$, is defined as

$$A \ominus B = \left\{ z \,\middle|\, (B)_z \subseteq A \right\} \tag{9-3}$$

where *A* is a set of foreground pixels, *B* is a structuring element, and the *z*'s are foreground values (1's). In words, this equation indicates that the erosion of *A* by *B* is the set of all points *z* such that *B*, translated by *z*, is contained in *A*. (Remember, displacement is defined with respect to the *origin* of *B*.) Equation (9-3) is the formulation that resulted in the *foreground* pixels of the image in Fig. 9.3(c).

As noted, we work with sets of foreground pixels embedded in a set of background pixels to form a complete image, *I*. Thus, inputs and outputs of our morphological procedures are images, not individual sets. We *could* make this fact explicit by writing Eq. (9-3) as

$$I \ominus B = \left\{ z \,\middle|\, (B)_z \subseteq A \text{ and } A \subseteq I \right\} \cup \left\{ A^c \,\middle|\, A^c \subseteq I \right\} \tag{9-4}$$

where *I* is a rectangular array of foreground and background pixels. The contents of the first braces say the same thing as Eq. (9-3), with the added clarification that *A* is a subset of (i.e., is contained in) *I*. The union with the operation inside the second set of braces "adds" the pixels that are not in subset *A* (i.e., A^c, which is the set of background pixels) to the result from the first braces, requiring also that the background pixels be part of the rectangle defined by *I*. In words, all this equation says is that erosion of *I* by *B* is the set of all points, *z*, such that *B*, translated by *z*, is contained in *A*. The equation also makes explicit that *A* is contained in *I*, that the result is embedded in a set of background pixels, and that the entire process is of the same size as *I*.

Of course, we do not use the cumbersome notation of Eq. (9-4), which we show only to emphasize an important point. Instead, we use the notation $A \ominus B$ when a morphological operation uses *only* foreground elements, and $I \ominus B$ when the operation uses foreground *and* background elements. This distinction may seem trivial, but suppose that we want to perform erosion with Eq. (9-3), using the foreground elements of the structuring element in the last column in Fig. 9.2. This structuring element also has background elements, but Eq. (9-3) assumes that *B* only has foreground elements. In fact, erosion is *defined* only for operations between foreground elements, so writing $I \ominus B$ would be meaningless without the "explanation" embedded in Eq. (9-4). To avoid confusion, we use *A* in morphological expressions when the operation involves only foreground elements, and *I* when the operation also involves background and/or "don't-care" elements. We also avoid using standard morphological symbols like $\ominus$ when working with "mixed" SEs. For example, later in Eq. (9-17) we use the symbol $\circledast$ in the expression $I \circledast B = \{ z \,|\, (B)_z \subseteq I \}$, which has the same *form* as Eq. (9-3), but instead involves an entire image and the mixed-value SE in the last column of Fig. 9.2. As you will see, using SE's with mixed values adds considerable power to morphological operations.

Returning to our discussion of Eq. (9-3), because the statement that B has to be contained in A is equivalent to B not sharing any common elements with the background (i.e., the set complement of A), we can express erosion equivalently as

$$A \ominus B = \left\{ z \mid (B)_z \cap A^c = \varnothing \right\} \tag{9-5}$$

where, as defined in Section 2.6, $\varnothing$ is the empty set.

Figure 9.4 shows an example of erosion. The elements of set A (shaded) are the foreground pixels of image I, and, as before, the background is shown in white. The solid boundary inside the dashed boundary in Fig. 9.4(c) is the limit beyond which further displacements of the origin of B would cause some elements of the structuring element to cease being completely contained in A. Thus, the locus of points (locations of the origin of B) within (and including) this boundary constitutes the foreground elements of the erosion of A by B. We show the resulting erosion shaded in Fig. 9.4(c), and the background as white. Erosion is the *set* of values of z that satisfy Eqs. (9-3) or (9-5). The boundary of A is shown dashed in Figs. 9.4(c) and (e) as a reference; it is not part of the erosion. Figure 9.4(d) shows an elongated structuring element, and Fig. 9.4(e) shows the erosion of A by this element. Note that the original object was eroded to a line. As you can see, the result of erosion is controlled by the shape of the structuring element. In both cases, the assumption is that the image was padded to accommodate all excursions of B, and that the result was cropped to the same size as the original image, just as we did with images processed by spatial convolution in Chapter 3.

Equations (9-3) and (9-5) are not the only definitions of erosion (see Problems 9.12 and 9.13 for two additional, equivalent definitions). However, the former equations have the advantage of being more intuitive when the structuring element B is viewed as if it were a spatial kernel that slides over a set, as in convolution.

a	b	c
d	e	

FIGURE 9.4
(a) Image I, consisting of a set (object) A, and background.
(b) Square SE, B (the dot is the origin).
(c) Erosion of A by B (shown shaded in the resulting image).
(d) Elongated SE.
(e) Erosion of A by B. (The erosion is a line.) The dotted border in (c) and (e) is the boundary of A, shown for reference.

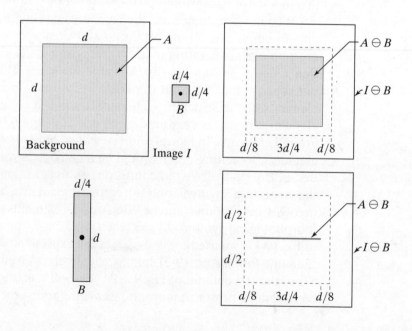

EXAMPLE 9.1: Using erosion to remove image components.

Figure 9.5(a) is a binary image depicting a simple wire-bond mask. As mentioned previously, we generally show the foreground pixels in binary images in white and the background in black. Suppose that we want to remove the lines connecting the center region to the border pads in Fig. 9.5(a). Eroding the image (i.e., eroding the *foreground* pixels of the image) with a square structuring element of size 11×11 whose components are all 1's removed most of the lines, as Fig. 9.5(b) shows. The reason that the two vertical lines in the center were thinned but not removed completely is that their width is greater than 11 pixels. Changing the SE size to 15×15 elements and eroding the original image again did remove all the connecting lines, as Fig. 9.5(c) shows. An alternate approach would have been to erode the image in Fig. 9.5(b) again, using the same 11×11, or smaller, SE. Increasing the size of the structuring element even more would eliminate larger components. For example, the connecting lines and the border pads can be removed with a structuring element of size 45×45 elements applied to the original image, as Fig. 9.5(d) shows.

We see from this example that erosion shrinks or thins objects in a binary image. In fact, we can view erosion as a *morphological filtering* operation in which image details smaller than the structuring element are filtered (removed) from the image. In Fig. 9.5, erosion performed the function of a "line filter." We will return to the concept of morphological filters in Sections 9.4 and 9.8.

DILATION

With A and B as sets in Z^2, the dilation of A by B, denoted as $A \oplus B$, is defined as

$$A \oplus B = \left\{ z \,\middle|\, (\hat{B})_z \cap A \neq \varnothing \right\} \tag{9-6}$$

a b
c d

FIGURE 9.5
Using erosion to remove image components.
(a) A 486×486 binary image of a wire-bond mask in which foreground pixels are shown in white.
(b)–(d) Image eroded using square structuring elements of sizes 11×11, 15×15, and 45×45 elements, respectively, all valued 1.

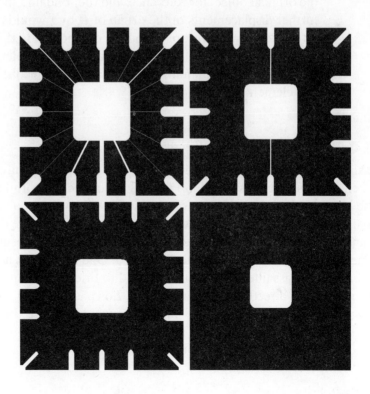

This equation is based on reflecting B about its origin and translating the reflection by z, as in erosion. The dilation of A by B then is the set of all displacements, z, such that the foreground elements of $\hat{B}$ overlap at least one element of A. (Remember, z is the displacement of the origin of $\hat{B}$.) Based on this interpretation, Eq. (9-6) can be written equivalently as

$$A \oplus B = \left\{ z \,\middle|\, [(\hat{B})_z \cap A] \subseteq A \right\} \tag{9-7}$$

Equations (9-6) and (9-7) are not the only definitions of dilation currently in use (see Problems 9.14 and 9.15 for two different, yet equivalent, definitions). As with erosion, the preceding definitions have the advantage of being more intuitive when structuring element B is viewed as a convolution kernel. As noted earlier, the basic process of flipping (rotating) B about its origin and then successively displacing it so that it slides over set A is analogous to spatial convolution. However, keep in mind that dilation is based on set operations and therefore is a nonlinear operation, whereas convolution is a sum of products, which is a linear operation.

Unlike erosion, which is a shrinking or thinning operation, dilation "grows" or "thickens" objects in a binary image. The manner and extent of this thickening is controlled by the shape and size of the structuring element used. Figure 9.6(a) shows the same object used in Fig. 9.4 (the background area is larger to accommodate the dilation), and Fig. 9.6(b) shows a structuring element (in this case $\hat{B} = B$ because the SE is symmetric about its origin). The dashed line in Fig. 9.6(c) shows the boundary of the original object for reference, and the solid line shows the limit beyond which any further displacements of the origin of $\hat{B}$ by z would cause the intersection of $\hat{B}$ and A to be empty. Therefore, all points on and inside this boundary constitute the dilation of A by B. Figure 9.6(d) shows a structuring element designed to achieve more dilation vertically than horizontally, and Fig. 9.6(e) shows the dilation achieved with this element.

EXAMPLE 9.2: Using dilation to repair broken characters in an image.

One of the simplest applications of dilation is for bridging gaps. Figure 9.7(a) shows the same image with broken characters that we studied in Fig. 4.48 in connection with lowpass filtering. The maximum length of the breaks is known to be two pixels. Figure 9.7(b) shows a structuring element that can be used for repairing the gaps. As noted earlier, we use white (1) to denote the foreground and black (0) for the background when working with images. Figure 9.7(c) shows the result of dilating the original image with the structuring element. The gaps were bridged. One important advantage of the morphological approach over the lowpass filtering method we used to bridge the gaps in Fig. 4.48 is that the morphological method resulted directly in a binary image. Lowpass filtering, on the other hand, started with a binary image and produced a grayscale image that would require thresholding to convert it back to binary form (we will discuss thresholding in Chapter 10). Observe that set A in this application consists of numerous disjointed objects of foreground pixels.

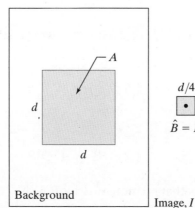

a b c
d e

FIGURE 9.6
(a) Image I, composed of set (object) A and background.
(b) Square SE (the dot is the origin).
(c) Dilation of A by B (shown shaded).
(d) Elongated SE.
(e) Dilation of A by this element. The dotted line in (c) and (e) is the boundary of A, shown for reference.

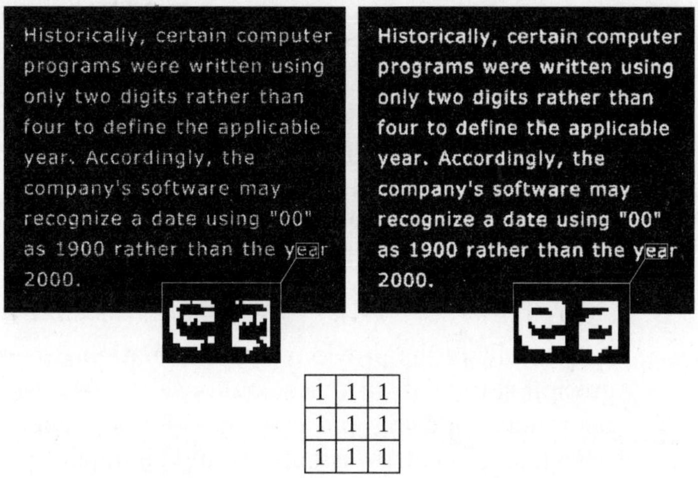

Background

Image, I

$d/4$

$d/4$

$\hat{B} = B$

$A \oplus B$

$d/8$ d $d/8$

$I \oplus B$

$d/4$

d

$\hat{B} = B$

$A \oplus B$

$d/2$

d

$d/2$

$d/8$ d $d/8$

$I \oplus B$

a   c
  b

FIGURE 9.7
(a) Low-resolution text showing broken characters (see magnified view).
(b) Structuring element.
(c) Dilation of (a) by (b). Broken segments were joined.

1	1	1
1	1	1
1	1	1

DUALITY

Erosion and dilation are *duals* of each other with respect to set complementation and reflection. That is,

$$(A \ominus B)^c = A^c \oplus \hat{B} \tag{9-8}$$

and

$$(A \oplus B)^c = A^c \ominus \hat{B} \tag{9-9}$$

Equation (9-8) indicates that erosion of A by B is the complement of the dilation of A^c by $\hat{B}$, and vice versa. The duality property is useful when the structuring element values are symmetric with respect to its origin (as often is the case), so that $\hat{B} = B$. Then, we can obtain the erosion of A simply by dilating its background (i.e., dilating A^c) with the same structuring element and complementing the result. Similar comments apply to Eq. (9-9).

We proceed to prove formally the validity of Eq. (9-8) in order to illustrate a typical approach for establishing the validity of morphological expressions. Starting with the definition of erosion, it follows that

$$(A \ominus B)^c = \left\{ z \,\middle|\, (B)_z \subseteq A \right\}^c$$

If set $(B)_z$ is contained in A, then it follows that $(B)_z \cap A^c = \varnothing$, in which case the preceding expression becomes

$$(A \ominus B)^c = \left\{ z \,\middle|\, (B)_z \cap A^c = \varnothing \right\}^c$$

But the *complement* of the set of z's that satisfy $(B)_z \cap A^c = \varnothing$ is the set of z's such that $(B)_z \cap A^c \neq \varnothing$. Therefore,

$$(A \ominus B)^c = \left\{ z \,\middle|\, (B)_z \cap A^c \neq \varnothing \right\}$$
$$= A^c \oplus \hat{B}$$

where the last step follows from the definition of dilation in Eq. (9-6) and its equivalent form in Eq. (9-7). This concludes the proof. A similar line of reasoning can be used to prove Eq. (9-9) (see Problem 9.16).

9.3 OPENING AND CLOSING

As you saw in the previous section, dilation expands the components of a set and erosion shrinks it. In this section, we discuss two other important morphological operations: opening and closing. Opening generally smoothes the contour of an object, breaks narrow isthmuses, and eliminates thin protrusions. Closing also tends to smooth sections of contours, but, as opposed to opening, it generally fuses narrow breaks and long thin gulfs, eliminates small holes, and fills gaps in the contour.

The *opening* of set A by structuring element B, denoted by $A \circ B$, is defined as

$$A \circ B = (A \ominus B) \oplus B \tag{9-10}$$

Thus, the opening A by B is the erosion of A by B, followed by a dilation of the result by B.

Similarly, the *closing* of set A by structuring element B, denoted $A \bullet B$, is defined as

$$A \bullet B = (A \oplus B) \ominus B \tag{9-11}$$

which says that the closing of A by B is simply the dilation of A by B, followed by erosion of the result by B.

Equation (9-10) has a simple geometrical interpretation: The opening of A by B is the union of all the translations of B so that B fits entirely in A. Figure 9.8(a) shows an image containing a set (object) A and Fig. 9.8(b) is a solid, circular structuring element, B. Figure 9.8(c) shows some of the translations of B such that it is contained within A, and the set shown shaded in Fig. 9.8(d) is the union of all such possible translations. Observe that, in this case, the opening is a set composed of two disjoint subsets, resulting from the fact that B could not fit in the narrow segment in the center of A. As you will see shortly, the ability to eliminate regions narrower than the structuring element is one of the key features of morphological opening.

The interpretation that the opening of A by B is the union of all the translations of B such that B fits entirely within A can be written in equation form as

$$A \circ B = \bigcup \left\{ (B)_z \,\middle|\, (B)_z \subseteq A \right\} \tag{9-12}$$

where $\cup$ denotes the union of the sets inside the braces.

When a circular structuring element is used for opening, the analogy is often made of the shape of the opening being determined by a "rolling ball" reaching as far as it can on the inner boundary of a set. For morphological closing the ball rolls outside, and the shape of the closing is determined by how far the ball can reach into the boundary.

a b
c d

FIGURE 9.8
(a) Image I, composed of set (object) A and background.
(b) Structuring element, B.
(c) Translations of B while being contained in A. (A is shown dark for clarity.)
(d) Opening of A by B.

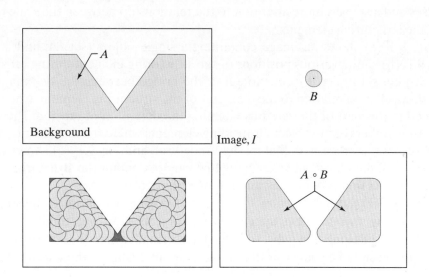

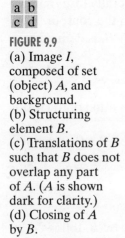

FIGURE 9.9
(a) Image I, composed of set (object) A, and background.
(b) Structuring element B.
(c) Translations of B such that B does not overlap any part of A. (A is shown dark for clarity.)
(d) Closing of A by B.

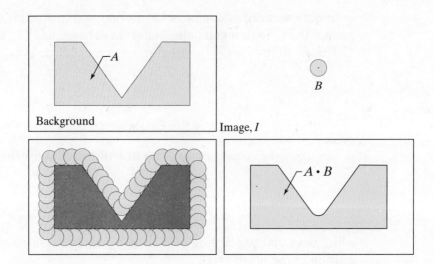

Closing has a similar geometric interpretation, except that now we translate B *outside* A. The closing is then the *complement* of the union of all translations of B that *do not* overlap A. Figure 9.9 illustrates this concept. Note that the boundary of the closing is determined by the furthest points B could reach without going inside any part of A. Based on this interpretation, we can write the closing of A by B as

$$A \bullet B = \left[\bigcup \left\{ (B)_z \,\middle|\, (B)_z \cap A = \varnothing \right\} \right]^c \tag{9-13}$$

EXAMPLE 9.3: Morphological opening and closing.

Figure 9.10 shows in more detail the process and properties of opening and closing. Unlike Figs. 9.8 and 9.9, whose main objectives are overall geometrical interpretations, this figure shows the individual processes and also pays more attention to the relationship between the scale of the final results and the size of the structuring elements.

Figure 9.10(a) shows an image containing a single object (set) A, and a disk structuring element. Figure 9.10(b) shows various positions of the structuring element during erosion. This process resulted in the disjoint set in Fig. 9.10(c). Note how the bridge between the two main sections was eliminated. Its width was thin in relation to the diameter of the structuring element, which could not be completely contained in this part of the set, thus violating the definition of erosion. The same was true of the two rightmost members of the object. Protruding elements where the disk did not fit were eliminated. Figure 9.10(d) shows the process of dilating the eroded set, and Fig. 9.10(e) shows the final result of opening. Morphological opening removes regions that cannot contain the structuring element, smoothes object contours, breaks thin connections, and removes thin protrusions.

Figures 9.10(f) through (i) show the results of closing A with the same structuring element. As with opening, closing also smoothes the contours of objects. However, unlike opening, closing tends to join narrow breaks, fills long thin gulfs, and fills objects smaller than the structuring element. In this example, the principal result of closing was that it filled the small gulf on the left of set A.

As with erosion and dilation, opening and closing are duals of each other with respect to set complementation and reflection:

$$(A \circ B)^c = \left(A^c \bullet \hat{B}\right) \tag{9-14}$$

and

$$(A \bullet B)^c = \left(A^c \circ \hat{B}\right) \tag{9-15}$$

We leave the proof of these equations as an exercise (see Problem 9.20).

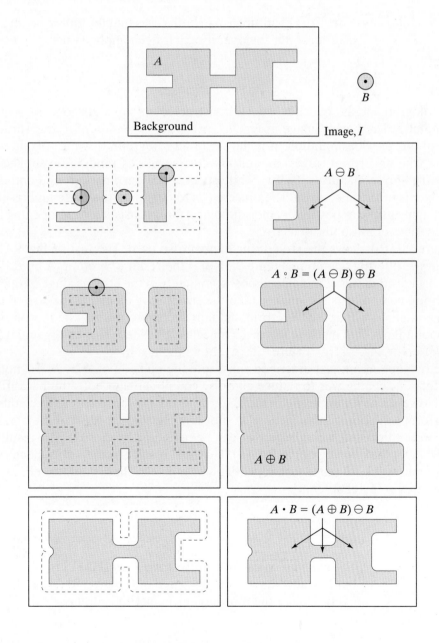

a
b c
d e
f g
h i

FIGURE 9.10
Morphological opening and closing.
(a) Image I, composed of a set (object) A and background; a solid, circular structuring element is shown also. (The dot is the origin.)
(b) Structuring element in various positions.
(c)-(i) The morphological operations used to obtain the opening and closing.

Morphological opening has the following properties:

(a) $A \circ B$ is a subset of A.

(b) If C is a subset of D, then $C \circ B$ is a subset of $D \circ B$.

(c) $(A \circ B) \circ B = A \circ B$.

Similarly, closing satisfies the following properties:

(a) A is a subset of $A \bullet B$.

(b) If C is a subset of D, then $C \bullet B$ is a subset of $D \bullet B$.

(c) $(A \bullet B) \bullet B = A \bullet B$.

Note from condition (c) in both cases that multiple openings or closings of a set have no effect after the operation has been applied once.

EXAMPLE 9.4: Using opening and closing for morphological filtering.

Morphological operations can be used to construct filters similar in concept to the spatial filters discussed in Chapter 3. The binary image in Fig. 9.11(a) shows a section of a fingerprint corrupted by noise. In terms of our previous notation, A is the set of all foreground (white) pixels, which includes objects of interest (the fingerprint ridges) as well as white specks of random noise. The background is black, as before. The noise manifests itself as white specks on a dark background and dark specks on the white components of the fingerprint. The objective is to eliminate the noise and its effects on the print, while distorting it as little as possible. A morphological filter consisting of an opening followed by a closing can be used to accomplish this objective.

Figure 9.11(b) shows the structuring element we used. The rest of Fig. 9.11 shows the sequence of steps in the filtering operation. Figure 9.11(c) is the result of eroding A by B. The white speckled noise in the background was eliminated almost completely in the erosion stage of opening because in this case most noise components are smaller than the structuring element. The size of the noise elements (dark spots) contained within the fingerprint actually increased in size. The reason is that these elements are inner boundaries that increase in size as objects are eroded. This enlargement is countered by performing dilation on Fig. 9.11(c). Figure 9.11(d) shows the result.

The two operations just described constitute the opening of A by B. We note in Fig. 9.11(d) that the net effect of opening was to reduce all noise components in both the background and the fingerprint itself. However, new gaps between the fingerprint ridges were created. To counter this undesirable effect, we perform a dilation on the opening, as shown in Fig. 9.11(e). Most of the breaks were restored, but the ridges were thickened, a condition that can be remedied by erosion. The result, shown in Fig. 9.11(f), is the closing of the opening of Fig. 9.11(d). This final result is remarkably clean of noise specks, but it still shows some specks of noise that appear as single pixels. These could be eliminated by methods we will discuss later in this chapter.

9.4 THE HIT-OR-MISS TRANSFORM

The morphological *hit-or-miss transform* (HMT) is a basic tool for shape detection. Let I be a binary image composed of foreground (A) and background pixels, respectively. Unlike the morphological methods discussed thus far, the HMT utilizes *two*

FIGURE 9.11
(a) Noisy image.
(b) Structuring
element.
(c) Eroded image.
(d) Dilation of the
erosion (opening
of A). (e) Dilation
of the opening.
(f) Closing of the
opening.
(Original image
courtesy of the
National Institute
of Standards and
Technology.)

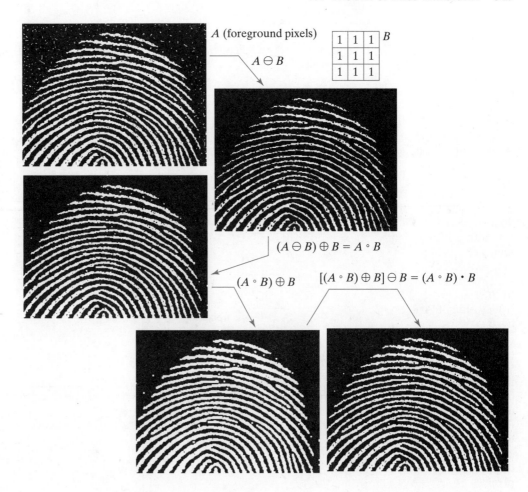

With reference to the
explanation of Eq. (9-4),
we show the
morphological HMT
operation working
directly on image I, to
make it explicit that the
structuring elements
work on sets of
foreground *and* back-
ground pixels
simultaneously.

structuring elements: B_1, for detecting shapes in the foreground, and B_2, for detecting shapes in the background. The HMT of image I is defined as

$$I \circledast B_{1,2} = \left\{ z \big| (B_1)_z \subseteq A \text{ and } (B_2)_z \subseteq A^c \right\}$$
$$= (A \ominus B_1) \cap (A^c \ominus B_2)$$

(9-16)

where the second line follows from the definition of erosion in Eq. (9-3). In words, this equation says that the morphological HMT is the set of translations, z, of structuring elements B_1 and B_2 such that, *simultaneously*, B_1 found a match in the foreground (i.e., B_1 is contained in A) *and* B_2 found a match in the background (i.e., B_2 is contained in A^c). The word "simultaneous" implies that z is the *same* translation of both structuring elements. The word "miss" in the HMT arises from the fact that B_2 finding a match in A^c is the same as B_2 not finding (missing) a match in A.

Figure 9.12 illustrates the concepts just introduced. Suppose that we want to find the location of the origin of object (set) D in image I. Here, A is the union of all object sets, so D is a subset of A. The need for two structuring elements capable

FIGURE 9.12
(a) Image consisting of a foreground (1's) equal to the union, A, of set of objects, and a background of 0's.
(b) Image with its foreground defined as A^c.
(c) Structuring elements designed to detect object D.
(d) Erosion of A by B_1.
(e) Erosion of A^c by B_2.
(f) Intersection of (d) and (e), showing the location of the origin of D, as desired. The dots indicate the origin of their respective components. Each dot is a single pixel.

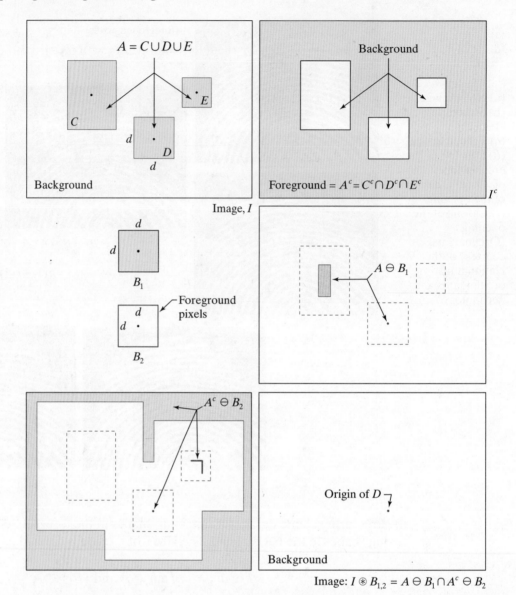

of detecting properties of both the foreground and background becomes immediately obvious. All three objects are composed of foreground pixels, and one way of explaining why they appear as different shapes is because each occupies a different area of the background. In other words, the nature of a shape is determined by the geometrical arrangement of both foreground and background pixels.

Figure 9.12(a) shows that I is composed of foreground (A) and background pixels. Figure 9.12(b) is I^c, the complement of I. The foreground of I^c is defined as the set of pixels in A^c, and the background is the union of the complement of the three objects. Figure 9.12(c) shows the two structuring elements needed to detect D. Element B_1 is equal to D itself. As Fig. 9.12(d) shows, the erosion of A by B_1 contains a single point: the origin of D, as desired, but it also contains parts of object C.

Structuring element B_2 is designed to detect D in I^c. Because D is composed of background elements in I^c, and erosion works with foreground elements, B_2 has to be designed to detect the *border* of D, which is composed of foreground pixels in I^c. The SE in Fig. 9.12(c) does precisely this. It consists of a rectangle of foreground elements one pixel thick. The size of the rectangle is such that is encloses the size of D. Figure 9.12(e) shows (shaded) the erosion of the foreground of I^c by B_2. It contains the origin of D, but is also contains parts of sets A^c and C. (The outer shaded area in Fig. 9.12(e) is larger than shown (see Problem 9.25); the result was cropped to the same size as image I for consistency.) The only elements that are common in Figs. 9.12(d) and (e) is the origin of D, so the intersection of these two sets of elements gives the location of that point, as desired. Figure 9.12(f) shows the final result.

The preceding explanation is the classic way of presenting the HMT using erosion, which is defined only for foreground pixels. A good question at this point is: Why not try to detect D directly in image I using a single structuring element, instead of going thorough such a laborious process? The answer is that it is possible to do so, but not in the "traditional" context of erosion the way we defined it in Eqs. (9-3) and (9-5). In order to detect D directly in image I, we would have to be able to process foreground and background pixels *simultaneously*, rather than processing just foreground pixels, as required by the definition of erosion.

To show how this can be done for the example in Fig. 9.12, we define a structuring element, B, identical to D, but having in addition a border of *background* elements with a width of one pixel. We can use a structuring element formed in such a way to restate the HMT as

$$I \circledast B = \left\{ z \,\middle|\, (B)_z \subseteq I \right\} \tag{9-17}$$

The *form* is the same as Eq. (9-3), but now we test to see if $(B)_z$ is a subset of *image I*, which is composed of *both* foreground and background pixels. This formulation is general, in the sense that B can be structured to detect any arrangement of pixels in image I, as Figs. 9.13 and 9.14 will illustrate.

Figure 9.13 shows graphically the same solution as Fig. 9.12(f), but using the single structuring element discussed in the previous paragraph. Figure 9.14 shows several examples based on using Eq. (9-17). The first row shows the result of using a small SE composed of both foreground (shaded) and background elements. This SE is designed to detect one-pixel holes (i.e., one background pixel surrounded by a connected border of foreground pixels) contained in image I. The SE in the second row is capable of detecting the foreground corner pixel of the top, right corner of the object in I. Using this SE in Eq. (9-17) yielded the image on the right. As you can see, the correct pixel was identified. The last row of Fig. 9.14 is more interesting, as it shows a structuring element composed of foreground, background, and "don't care" elements which, as mentioned earlier, we denote by ×'s. You can think of the value of a don't care element as always matching its corresponding pixel in an image. In this example, when the SE is centered on the top, right corner pixel, the don't care elements in the top of the SE can be considered to be background, and the don't care elements on the bottom row as foreground, producing a correct

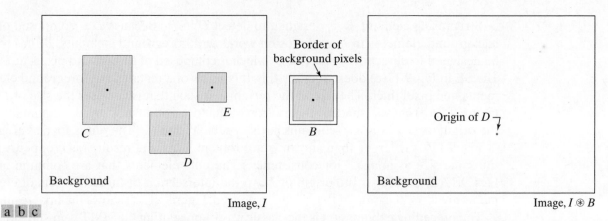

a b c

FIGURE 9.13 Same solution as in Fig. 9.12, but using Eq. (9-17) with a single structuring element.

match. When the SE is centered on the bottom, right corner pixel, the role of the don't care elements is reversed, again resulting in a correct match. The other border pixels between the two corners were similarly detected by considering all don't care elements as foreground. Thus, using don't care elements increases the flexibility of structuring elements to perform multiple roles.

9.5 SOME BASIC MORPHOLOGICAL ALGORITHMS

With the preceding discussion as a foundation, we are now ready to consider some practical uses of morphology. When dealing with binary images, one of the principal applications of morphology is in extracting image components that are useful in the

a b c
d e f
g h i

FIGURE 9.14
Three examples of using a single structuring element and Eq. (9-17) to detect specific features. First row: detection of single-pixel holes. Second row: detection of an upper-right corner. Third row: detection of multiple features.

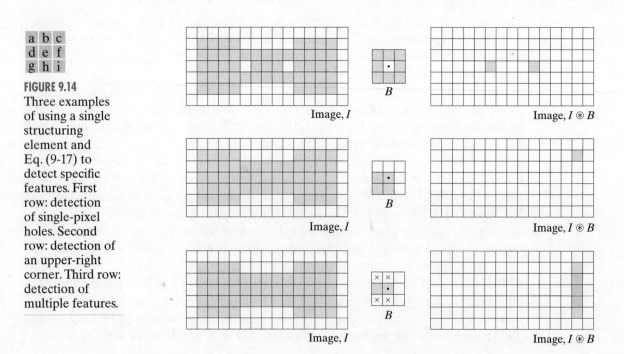

representation and description of shape. In particular, we consider morphological algorithms for extracting boundaries, connected components, the convex hull, and the skeleton of a region. We also develop several methods (for region filling, thinning, thickening, and pruning) that are used frequently for pre- or post-processing. We make extensive use in this section of "mini-images," designed to clarify the mechanics of each morphological method as we introduce it. These binary images are shown graphically with foreground (1's) shaded and background (0's) in white, as before.

BOUNDARY EXTRACTION

The boundary of a set A of foreground pixels, denoted by $\beta(A)$, can be obtained by first eroding A by a suitable structuring element B, and then performing the set difference between A and its erosion. That is,

$$\beta(A) = A - (A \ominus B) \tag{9-18}$$

Figure 9.15 illustrates the mechanics of boundary extraction. It shows a simple binary object, a structuring element B, and the result of using Eq. (9-18). The structuring element in Fig. 9.15(b) is among the most frequently used, but it is not unique. For example, using a 5×5 structuring element of 1's would result in a boundary between 2 and 3 pixels thick. It is understood that the image in Fig. 9.15(a) was padded with a border of background elements, and that the results were cropped back to the original size after the morphological operations were completed.

EXAMPLE 9.5: Boundary extraction.

Figure 9.16 further illustrates the use of Eq. (9-18) using a 3×3 structuring element of 1's. As before when working with images, we show foreground pixels (1's) in white and background pixels (0's) in black. The elements of the SE, which are 1's, also are treated as white. Because of the size of the structuring element used, the boundary in Fig. 9.16(b) is one pixel thick.

HOLE FILLING

As mentioned in the discussion of Fig. 9.14, a *hole* may be defined as a background region surrounded by a connected border of foreground pixels. In this section, we develop an algorithm based on set dilation, complementation, and intersection for

a b
c d

FIGURE 9.15
(a) Set, A, of foreground pixels.
(b) Structuring element.
(c) A eroded by B.
(d) Boundary of A.

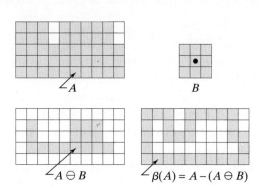

A B $A \ominus B$ $\beta(A) = A - (A \ominus B)$

a b

FIGURE 9.16
(a) A binary image.
(b) Result of using Eq. (9-18) with the structuring element in Fig. 9.15(b).

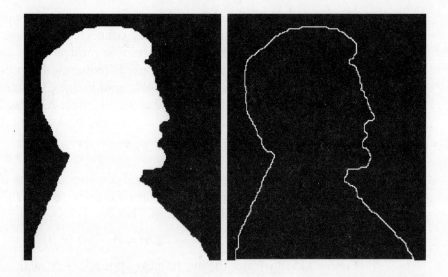

filling holes in an image. Let A denote a set whose elements are 8-connected boundaries, with each boundary enclosing a background region (i.e., a hole). Given a point in each hole, the objective is to fill all the holes with foreground elements (1's).

We begin by forming an array, X_0, of 0's (the same size as I, the image containing A), except at locations in X_0 that correspond to pixels that are known to be holes, which we set to 1. Then, the following procedure fills all the holes with 1's:

> Remember, the dilation of image X by B is the dilation of the *foreground* elements of X by B.

$$X_k = (X_{k-1} \oplus B) \cap I^c \qquad k = 1, 2, 3, \ldots \qquad (9\text{-}19)$$

where B is the symmetric structuring element in Fig. 9.17(c). The algorithm terminates at iteration step k if $X_k = X_{k-1}$. Then, X_k contains all the filled holes. The set union of X_k and I contains all the filled holes and their boundaries.

The dilation in Eq. (9-19) would fill the entire area if left unchecked, but the intersection at each step with I^c limits the result to inside the region of interest. This is our first example of how a morphological process can be *conditioned* to meet a desired property. In the current application, the process is appropriately called *conditional dilation*. The rest of Fig. 9.17 illustrates further the mechanics of Eq. (9-19). This example only has one hole, but the concept applies to any finite number of holes, assuming that a point inside each hole is given (we remove this requirement in Section 9.6).

EXAMPLE 9.6: Morphological hole filling.

Figure 9.18(a) shows an image of white circles with black holes. An image such as this might result from thresholding into two levels a scene containing polished spheres (e.g., ball bearings). The dark circular areas inside the spheres would result from reflections. The objective is to eliminate the reflections by filling the holes in the image. Figure 9.18(b) shows the result of filling all the spheres. Because it must be known whether black points are background points or sphere inner points (i.e., holes), fully automating this procedure requires that additional "intelligence" be built into the algorithm. We will give a fully automatic approach in Section 9.6 based on morphological reconstruction (see Problem 9.36 also).

a b c
d e f
g h i

FIGURE 9.17
Hole filling.
(a) Set A (shown shaded) contained in image I.
(b) Complement of I.
(c) Structuring element B. *Only* the foreground elements are used in computations
(d) Initial point inside hole, set to 1.
(e)–(h) Various steps of Eq. (9-19).
(i) Final result [union of (a) and (h)].

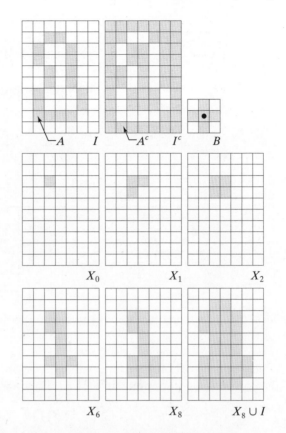

EXTRACTION OF CONNECTED COMPONENTS

Connectivity and connected components are discussed in Section 2.5.

Being able to extract connected components from a binary image is central to many automated image analysis applications. Let A be a set of foreground pixels consisting of one or more connected components, and form an image X_0 (of the same size as I, the image containing A) whose elements are 0's (background values), except at each location known to correspond to a point in each connected component in A,

a b

FIGURE 9.18
(a) Binary image. The white dots inside the regions (shown enlarged for clarity) are the starting points for the hole-filling algorithm.
(b) Result of filling all holes.

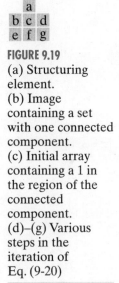

FIGURE 9.19
(a) Structuring element.
(b) Image containing a set with one connected component.
(c) Initial array containing a 1 in the region of the connected component.
(d)–(g) Various steps in the iteration of Eq. (9-20)

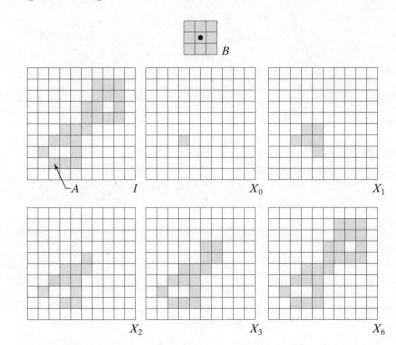

which we set to 1 (foreground value). The objective is to start with X_0 and find all the connected components in I. The following iterative procedure accomplishes this:

$$X_k = (X_{k-1} \oplus B) \cap I \qquad k = 1, 2, 3, \ldots \qquad (9\text{-}20)$$

where B is the SE in Fig. 9.19(a). The procedure terminates when $X_k = X_{k-1}$, with X_k containing all the connected components of foreground pixels in the image. Both Eqs. (9-19) and (9-20) use conditional dilation to limit the growth of set dilation, but Eq. (9-20) uses I instead of I^c. This is because here we are looking for foreground points, while the objective of (9-19) is to find background points. Figure 9.19 illustrates the mechanics of Eq. (9-20), with convergence being achieved for $k = 6$. Note that the shape of the structuring element used is based on 8-connectivity between pixels. As in the hole-filling algorithm, Eq. (9-20) is applicable to any finite number of connected components contained in I, assuming that a point is known in each. See Problem 9.37 for a completely automated procedure that removes this requirement.

EXAMPLE 9.7: Using connected components to detect foreign objects in packaged food.

Connected components are used frequently for automated inspection. Figure 9.20(a) shows an X-ray image of a chicken breast that contains bone fragments. It is important to be able to detect such foreign objects in processed foods before shipping. In this application, the density of the bones is such that their nominal intensity values are significantly different from the background. This makes extraction of the bones from the background a simple matter by using a single threshold (thresholding was introduced in Section 3.1 and we will discuss in more detail in Section 10.3). The result is the binary image in Fig. 9.20(b).

The most significant feature in this figure is the fact that the points that remain after thresholding are clustered into objects (bones), rather than being scattered. We can make sure that only objects of

a
b
c d

FIGURE 9.20
(a) X-ray image of a chicken filet with bone fragments.
(b) Thresholded image (shown as the negative for clarity).
(c) Image eroded with a 5×5 SE of 1's.
(d) Number of pixels in the connected components of (c). (Image (a) courtesy of NTB Elektronische Geraete GmbH, Diepholz, Germany, www.ntbxray.com.)

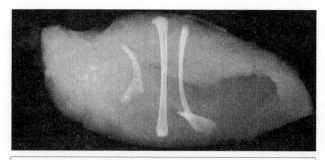

Connected component	No. of pixels in connected comp
01	11
02	9
03	9
04	39
05	133
06	1
07	1
08	743
09	7
10	11
11	11
12	9
13	9
14	674
15	85

"significant" size are contained in the binary image by eroding its foreground. In this example, we define as significant any object that remains after erosion with a 5×5 SE of 1's. Figure 9.20(c) shows the result of erosion. The next step is to analyze the size of the objects that remain. We label (identify) these objects by extracting the connected components in the image. The table in Fig. 9.20(d) lists the results of the extraction. There are 15 connected components, with four of them being dominant in size. This is enough evidence to conclude that significant, undesirable objects are contained in the original image. If needed, further characterization (such as shape) is possible using the techniques discussed in Chapter 11.

CONVEX HULL

A set, S, of points in the Euclidean plane is said to be *convex* if and only if a straight line segment joining any two points in S lies entirely within S. The *convex hull*, H, of S is the smallest convex set containing S. The *convex deficiency* of S is defined as the set difference $H - S$. Unlike the Euclidean plane, the digital image plane (see Fig. 2.19) only allows points at discrete coordinates. Thus, the sets with which we work are *digital sets*. The same concepts of convexity are applicable to digital sets, but the definition of a convex digital set is slightly different. A *digital set*, A, is said to be *convex* if and only if its Euclidean convex hull only contains digital points belonging to A. A simple way to visualize if a digital set of foreground points is convex is to join its boundary points by straight (continuous) Euclidean line segments. If only foreground points are contained within the set formed by the line segments, then the set is convex; otherwise it is not. The definitions of convex hull and convex deficiency given above for S, extend directly to digital sets. The following morphological algorithm can be used to obtain an approximation of the convex hull of a set A of foreground pixels, embedded in a binary image, I.

Let B^i, $i = 1, 2, 3, 4$, denote the four structuring elements in Fig. 9.21(a). The procedure consists of implementing the morphological equation

$$X_k^i = \left(X_{k-1}^i \circledast B^i\right) \cup X_{k-1}^i \quad i = 1, 2, 3, 4 \quad \text{and} \quad k = 1, 2, 3, \ldots \quad (9\text{-}21)$$

with $X_0^i = I$. When the procedure converges using the ith structuring element (i.e., when $X_k^i = X_{k-1}^i$), we let $D^i = X_k^i$. Then, the convex hull of A is the union of the four results:

$$C(A) = \bigcup_{i=1}^{4} D^i \quad (9\text{-}22)$$

Thus, the method consists of iteratively applying the hit-or-miss transform to I with B^1 until convergence, then letting $D^1 = X_k^1$, where k is the step at which convergence occurred. The procedure is repeated with B^2 (applied to I) until no further changes occur, and so on. The union of the four resulting D^i constitutes the convex hull of A. The algorithm is initialized with $k = 0$ and $X_0^i = I$ every time that i (i.e., the structuring element) changes.

Figure 9.21 illustrates the use of Eqs. (9-21) and (9-22). Figure 9.21(a) shows the structuring elements used to extract the convex hull. The origin of each element is at its center. As before, the × entries indicate "don't care" elements. Recall that the HMT is said to have found a match of structuring element B^i in a 3×3 region of I, if all the elements of B^i find corresponding matches in that region. As noted earlier, when computing a match, a "don't care" element can be interpreted as always matching the value of its corresponding element in the image. Note in Fig. 9.21(a) that B^i is a clockwise rotation of B^{i-1} by 90°.

Figure 9.21(b) shows a set A for which the convex hull is sought. As before, the set is embedded in an array of background elements to form an image, I. Starting with $X_0^1 = I$ resulted in the set in Fig. 9.21(c) after five iterations of Eq. (9-21). Then, letting $X_0^2 = I$ and again using Eq. (9-21) resulted in the set in Fig. 9.21(d) (convergence was achieved in only two steps in this case). The next two results were obtained in the same manner. Finally, forming the union of the sets in Figs. 9.21(c), (d), (e), and (f) resulted in the convex hull in Fig. 9.21(g). The contribution of each structuring element is highlighted in the composite set shown in Fig. 9.21(h).

One obvious shortcoming of the procedure just discussed is that the convex hull can grow beyond the minimum dimensions required to guarantee convexity, thus violating the definition of the convex hull. This, in fact, is what happened in this case. One simple approach to reduce this growth is to place limits so that it does not extend beyond the vertical and horizontal dimensions of set A. Imposing this

FIGURE 9.21
(a) Structuring elements.
(b) Set A.
(c)–(f) Results of convergence with the structuring elements shown in (a).
(g) Convex hull.
(h) Convex hull showing the contribution of each structuring element.

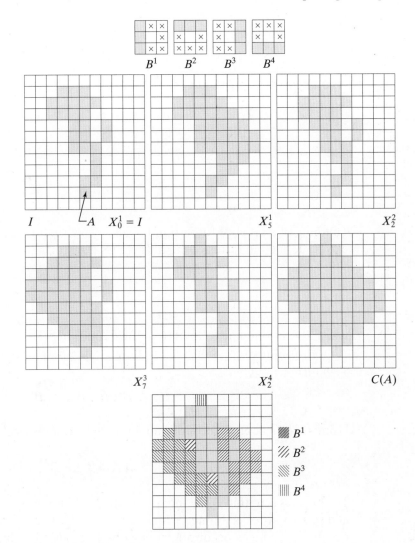

limitation on the example in Fig. 9.21 resulted in Fig. 9.22(a). Joining the boundary pixels of the reduced set (remember, the pixels are the center points of the squares) show that no set points lie outside these lines, indicating that the set is convex. By inspection, you can see that no points can be deleted from this set without losing convexity, so the reduced set is the convex hull of A.

Of course, the limits we used to produce Fig. 9.22 do not constitute a general approach for obtaining the minimum convex set enclosing a set in question; it is simply an easy-to-implement heuristic. The reason why the convex hull algorithm did not yield a closer approximation of the actual convex hull is because of the structuring elements used. The SEs in Fig. 9.21(a) "look" only in four orthogonal directions. We could achieve greater accuracy by looking in additional directions, such as the diagonals, for example. The price paid is increased algorithm complexity and a higher computational load.

a b

FIGURE 9.22
(a) Result of limiting growth of the convex hull algorithm.
(b) Straight lines connecting the boundary points show that the new set is convex also.

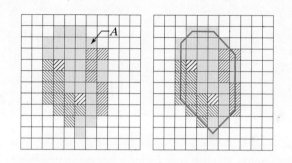

THINNING

Thinning of a set A of foreground pixels by a structuring element B, denoted $A \otimes B$, can be defined in terms of the hit-or-miss transform:

$$A \otimes B = A - (A \circledast B)$$
$$= A \cap (A \circledast B)^c \tag{9-23}$$

where the second line follows from the definition of set difference given in Eq. (2-40). A more useful expression for thinning A symmetrically is based on a *sequence* of structuring elements:

$$\{B\} = \{B^1, B^2, B^3, \ldots, B^n\} \tag{9-24}$$

Using this concept, we now define thinning by a sequence of structuring elements as

$$A \otimes \{B\} = \left(\ldots \left(\left(A \otimes B^1 \right) \otimes B^2 \right) \ldots \right) \otimes B^n \right) \tag{9-25}$$

The process is to thin A by one pass with B^1, then thin the result with one pass of B^2, and so on, until A is thinned with one pass of B^n. The entire process is repeated until no further changes occur after one complete pass through all structuring elements. Each individual thinning pass is performed using Eq. (9-23).

As before, we assume that the image containing A was padded to accommodate all excursions of B, and that the result was cropped. We show only A for simplicity.

Figure 9.23(a) shows a set of structuring elements used routinely for thinning (note that B^i is equal to B^{i-1} rotated clockwise by 45°), and Fig. 9.23(b) shows a set A to be thinned, using the procedure just discussed. Figure 9.23(c) shows the result of thinning A with one pass of B^1 to obtain A_1. Figure 9.23(c) is the result of thinning A_1 with B^2, and Figs. 9.21(e) through (k) show the results of passes with the remaining structuring elements (there were no changes from A_7 to A_8 or from A_9 to A_{11}.) Convergence was achieved after the second pass of B^6. Figure 9.23(l) shows the thinned result. Finally, Fig. 9.23(m) shows the thinned set converted to m-connectivity (see Section 2.5 and Problem 9.29) to eliminate multiple paths.

THICKENING

Thickening is the morphological dual of thinning and is defined by the expression

$$A \odot B = A \cup (A \circledast B) \tag{9-26}$$

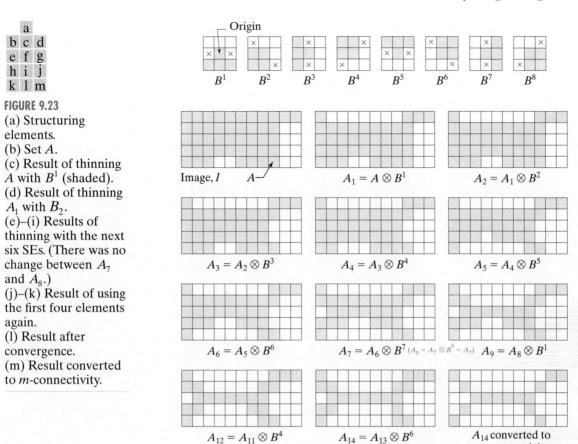

a		
b	c	d
e	f	g
h	i	j
k	l	m

FIGURE 9.23
(a) Structuring elements.
(b) Set A.
(c) Result of thinning A with B^1 (shaded).
(d) Result of thinning A_1 with B_2.
(e)–(i) Results of thinning with the next six SEs. (There was no change between A_7 and A_8.)
(j)–(k) Result of using the first four elements again.
(l) Result after convergence.
(m) Result converted to m-connectivity.

where B is a structuring element suitable for thickening. As in thinning, thickening can be defined as a sequential operation:

$$A \odot \{B\} = \left(\ldots \left(\left(A \odot B^1 \right) \odot B^2 \right) \ldots \right) \odot B^n \right) \qquad (9\text{-}27)$$

The structuring elements used for thickening have the same form as those shown in Fig. 9.23(a), but with all 1's and 0's interchanged. However, a separate algorithm for thickening is seldom used in practice. Instead, the usual procedure is to thin the background of the set in question, then complement the result. In other words, to thicken a set A we form A^c, thin A^c, and then complement the thinned set to obtain the thickening of A. Figure 9.24 illustrates this procedure. As before, we show only set A and image I, and not the padded version of I.

Depending on the structure of A, this procedure can result in disconnected points, as Fig. 9.24(d) shows. Hence thickening by this method usually is followed by post-processing to remove disconnected points. Note from Fig. 9.24(c) that the thinned background forms a boundary for the thickening process. This useful feature is not present in the direct implementation of thickening using Eq. (9-27), and it is one of the principal reasons for using background thinning to accomplish thickening.

FIGURE 9.24
(a) Set A.
(b) Complement of A.
(c) Result of
thinning the
complement.
(d) Thickened set
obtained by
complementing (c).
(e) Final result, with
no disconnected
points.

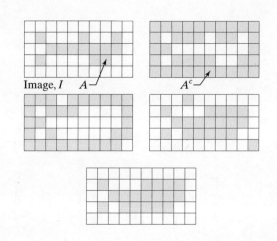

Image, I A A^c

SKELETONS

We will discuss skeletons
in more detail in Section
11.2.

As Fig. 9.25 shows, the notion of a *skeleton* $S(A)$ of a set A is intuitively simple. We deduce from this figure that

(a) If z is a point of $S(A)$, and $(D)_z$ is the largest disk centered at z and contained in A, one cannot find a larger disk (not necessarily centered at z) containing $(D)_z$ and simultaneously included in A. A disk $(D)_z$ satisfying these conditions is called a *maximum disk*.

(b) If $(D)_z$ is a maximum disk, it touches the boundary of A at two or more different places.

The skeleton of A can be expressed in terms of erosions and openings. That is, it can be shown (Serra [1982]) that

$$S(A) = \bigcup_{k=0}^{K} S_k(A) \tag{9-28}$$

with

$$S_k(A) = (A \ominus kB) - (A \ominus kB) \circ B \tag{9-29}$$

where B is a structuring element, and $(A \ominus kB)$ indicates k successive erosions starting with A; that is, A is first eroded by B, the result is eroded by B, and so on:

$$(A \ominus kB) = \Big((...((A \ominus B) \ominus B) \ominus ...\Big) \ominus B\Big) \tag{9-30}$$

k times. K in Eq. (9-28) is the last iterative step before A erodes to an empty set. In other words,

$$K = \max\Big\{k \,\big|\, (A \ominus kB) \neq \varnothing\Big\} \tag{9-31}$$

The formulation in Eqs. (9-28) and (9-29) indicate that $S(A)$ can be obtained as the union of the skeleton subsets $S_k(A)$, $k = 0, 1, 2, ..., K$.

a b
c d

FIGURE 9.25
(a) Set A.
(b) Various positions of maximum disks whose centers partially define the skeleton of A.
(c) Another maximum disk, whose center defines a different segment of the skeleton of A.
(d) Complete skeleton (dashed).

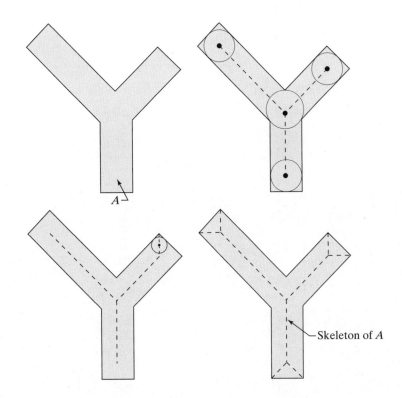

It can be shown (Serra [1982]) that A can be reconstructed from these subsets:

$$A = \bigcup_{k=0}^{K} \left(S_k(A) \oplus kB \right) \tag{9-32}$$

where $\left(S_k(A) \oplus kB \right)$ denotes k successive dilations, starting with $S_k(A)$; that is,

$$\left(S_k(A) \oplus kB \right) = \left(\left(\ldots \left(\left(S_k(A) \oplus B \right) \oplus B \right) \oplus \ldots \right) \oplus B \right) \tag{9-33}$$

EXAMPLE 9.8: Computing the skeleton of a simple set.

Figure 9.26 illustrates the concepts just discussed. The first column shows the original set (at the top) and two erosions by the structuring element B shown in the figure. Note that one more erosion would yield the empty set, so $K = 2$ in this case. The second column shows the opening by B of the sets in the first column. These results are easily explained by the fitting characterization of the opening operation discussed in connection with Fig. 9.8. The third column contains the set differences between the first and second columns. Thus, the three entries in the third column are $S_0(A)$, $S_1(A)$, and $S_2(A)$, respectively.

The fourth column contains two partial skeletons, and the final result at the bottom of the column. The final skeleton not only is thicker than it needs to be but, more important, it is not connected. This result is not unexpected, as nothing in the preceding formulation of the morphological skeleton guarantees connectivity. Morphology produces an elegant formulation in terms of erosions and openings of the given set. However, heuristic formulations (see Section 11.2) are needed if, as is usually the case, the skeleton must be maximally thin, connected, and minimally eroded.

FIGURE 9.26
Implementation
of Eqs. (9-28)
through (9-33).
The original set is
at the top left, and
its morphologi-
cal skeleton is at
the bottom of the
fourth column.
The reconstructed
set is at the
bottom of the
sixth column.

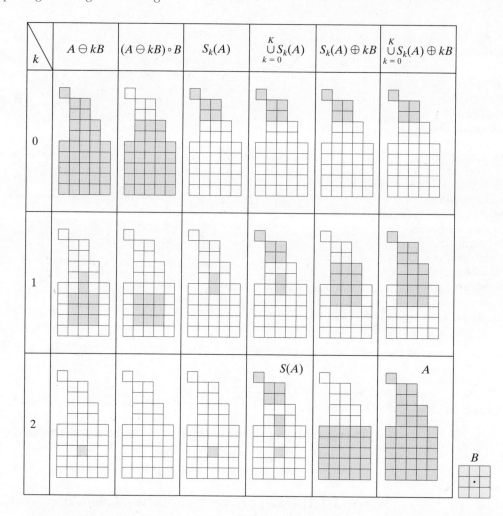

The entries in the fifth and sixth columns deal with reconstructing the original set from its skeleton subsets. The fifth column are the dilations of $S_k(A)$; that is, $S_0(A)$, $S_1(k) \oplus B$, and $S_2(A) \oplus 2B = (S_2(A) \oplus B) \oplus B$. Finally, the last column shows reconstruction of set A which, according to Eq. (9-32), is the union of the dilated skeleton subsets shown in the fifth column.

PRUNING

Pruning methods are an essential complement to thinning and skeletonizing algorithms, because these procedures tend to leave *spurs* ("parasitic" components) that need to be "cleaned up" by postprocessing. We begin the discussion with a pruning problem, then develop a solution based on the material introduced in the preceding sections. Thus, we take this opportunity to illustrate how to solve a problem by combining several of the morphological techniques discussed up to this point.

A common approach in the automated recognition of hand-printed characters is to analyze the shape of the skeleton of a character. These skeletons often contain spurs, caused during erosion by noise and non-uniformities in the character strokes.

In this section we develop a morphological technique for handling this problem, starting with the assumption that the length of a parasitic component does not exceed a specified number of pixels.

Figure 9.27(a) shows the skeleton of a hand-printed letter "a." The spur on the leftmost part of the character exemplifies what we are interested in removing. The solution is based on suppressing a spur branch by successively eliminating its end point. Of course, this also shortens (or eliminates) other branches in the character but, in the absence of other structural information, the assumption in this example is that any branch with three or less pixels is to be eliminated. Thinning of a set A, with a sequence of structuring elements designed to detect only end points, achieves the desired result. That is, let

$$X_1 = A \otimes \{B\} \tag{9-34}$$

where $\{B\}$ denotes the structuring element sequence in Fig. 9.27(b) [see Eq. (9-24) regarding structuring-element sequences]. The sequence of structuring elements consists of two different structures, each of which is rotated 90° for a total of eight elements. The × in Fig. 9.27(b) signifies a "don't care" condition, as defined earlier. (Note that each SE is a detector for an end point in a particular orientation.)

We may define an end point *as the center point of a 3×3 region that satisfies any of the arrangements in Fig. 9.27(b).*

a	b
c	d
e	f

FIGURE 9.27
(a) Set A of foreground pixels (shaded).
(b) SEs used for deleting end points.
(c) Result of three cycles of thinning.
(d) End points of (c).
(e) Dilation of end points conditioned on (a).
(f) Pruned image.

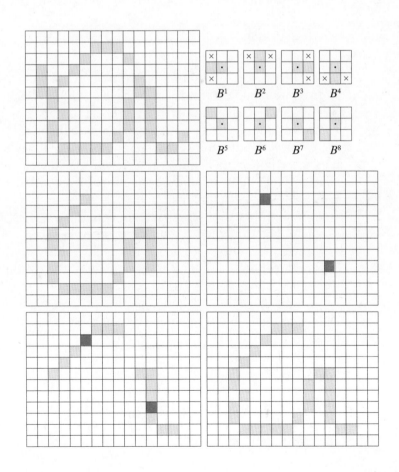

Applying Eq. (9-34) to A three times yielded the set X_1 in Fig. 9.27(c). The next step is to "restore" the character to its original form, but with the parasitic branches removed. This requires that we first form a set X_2 containing all end points in X_1 [Fig. 9.27(e)]:

$$X_2 = \bigcup_{k=1}^{8} \left(X_1 \circledast B^k \right) \tag{9-35}$$

where the B^k are the end-point detectors in Fig. 9.27(b). The next step is dilation of the end points. Typically, the number of dilations is less than the number of end-point removals to reduce the probability of "growing" back some of the spurs. In this case, we know by inspection that no new spurs are created, so we dilate the end points three times using A as a delimiter. This is the same number of thinning passes:

$$X_3 = \left(X_2 \oplus H \right) \cap A \tag{9-36}$$

where H is a 3×3 structuring element of 1's, and the intersection with A is applied after each step. As in the case of region filling, this type of conditional dilation prevents the creation of 1-valued elements outside the region of interest, as illustrated by the result in Fig. 9.27(e). Finally, the union of X_1 and X_3,

$$X_4 = X_1 \cup X_3 \tag{9-37}$$

yields the desired result in Fig. 9.27(f).

In more complex scenarios, using Eq. (9-36) sometimes picks up the "tips" of some branches. This can occur when the end points of these branches are near the skeleton. Although Eq. (9-36) may eliminate them, they can be picked up again during dilation because they are valid points in A. However, unless entire parasitic elements are picked up again (a rare case if these elements are short with respect to valid strokes), detecting and eliminating the reconstructed elements is easy because they are disconnected regions.

A natural thought at this juncture is that there must be easier ways to solve this problem. For example, we could just keep track of all deleted points and simply reconnect the appropriate points to all end points left after application of Eq. (9-34). This argument is valid, but the advantage of the formulation just presented is that we used existing morphological constructs to solve the problem. When a set of such tools is available, the advantage is that no new algorithms have to be written. We simply combine the necessary morphological functions into a sequence of operations.

Sometimes you will encounter end point detectors based on a single structuring element, similar to the first SE in Fig. 9.27(b), but having "don't care" conditions along the entire first column instead having a foreground element separating the corner $\times$'s. This is incorrect. For example, the former element would identify the point located in the eighth row, fourth column of Fig. 9.27(a) as an end point, thus eliminating it and breaking the connectivity of that part of the stroke.

9.6 MORPHOLOGICAL RECONSTRUCTION

The morphological concepts discussed thus far involve a single image and one or more structuring elements. In this section, we discuss a powerful morphological transformation called *morphological reconstruction* that involves two images and a structuring element. One image, the *marker*, which we denote by F, contains the starting points for reconstruction. The other image, the *mask*, denoted by G, constrains (conditions) the reconstruction. The structuring element is used to define connectivity.[†] For 2-D applications, connectivity typically is defined as 8-connectivity, which is implied by a structuring element of size 3×3 whose elements are all 1's.

See Section 2.5 regarding connectivity.

GEODESIC DILATION AND EROSION

Central to morphological reconstruction are the concepts of geodesic dilation and geodesic erosion. Let F denote the marker image and G the mask image. We assume in this discussion that both are binary images and that $F \subseteq G$. The *geodesic dilation of size* 1 of the marker image with respect to the mask, denoted by $D_G^{(1)}(F)$, is defined as

$$D_G^{(1)}(F) = (F \oplus B) \cap G \tag{9-38}$$

where, as usual, $\cap$ denotes the set intersection (here $\cap$ may be interpreted as a logical AND because we are dealing with binary quantities). The *geodesic dilation of size n* of F with respect to G is defined as

$$D_G^{(n)}(F) = D_G^{(1)}\left(D_G^{(n-1)}(F)\right) \tag{9-39}$$

where $n \geq 1$ is an integer, and $D_G^{(0)}(F) = F$. In this recursive expression, the set intersection indicated in Eq. (9-38) is performed at each step.[‡] Note that the intersection operation guarantees that mask G will limit the growth (dilation) of marker F. Figure 9.28 shows a simple example of a geodesic dilation of size 1. The steps in the figure are a direct implementation of Eq. (9-38). Note that the marker F consists of just one point from the object in G. The idea is to grow (dilate) this point successively, masking of the result at each step by G. Continuing with this process would yield a result whose shape is influenced by the structure of G. In this simple case, the reconstruction would eventually result in an image identical to G (see Fig. 9.30).

The *geodesic erosion of size* 1 of marker F with respect to mask G is defined as

$$E_G^{(1)}(F) = (F \ominus B) \cup G \tag{9-40}$$

[†] In much of the literature on morphological reconstruction, the structuring element is tacitly assumed to be isotropic and typically is called an *elementary isotropic structuring element*. In the context of this chapter, an example of such an SE is a 3×3 array of 1's with the origin at the center.

[‡] Although it is more intuitive to develop morphological reconstruction methods using recursive formulations (as we do here), their practical implementation typically is based on more computationally efficient algorithms (see, for example, Vincent [1993] and Soille [2003]).

FIGURE 9.28
Illustration of a
geodesic
dilation of
size 1. Note that
the marker image
contains a point
from the object
in *G*. If continued,
subsequent dila-
tions and maskings
would eventually
result in the object
contained in *G*.

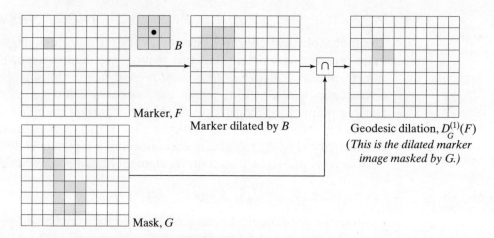

Marker, *F*

Marker dilated by *B*

Geodesic dilation, $D_G^{(1)}(F)$
(*This is the dilated marker
image masked by G.*)

Mask, *G*

where $\cup$ denotes set union (or logical OR operation). The geodesic erosion of size *n* of *F* with respect to *G* is defined as

$$E_G^{(n)}(F) = E_G^{(1)}\left(E_G^{(n-1)}(F)\right) \qquad (9\text{-}41)$$

where $n \geq 1$ is an integer and $E_G^{(0)}(F) = F$. The set union in Eq. (9-40) is performed at each step, and guarantees that geodesic erosion of an image remains greater than or equal to its mask image. As you might have expected from the forms in Eqs. (9-38) and (9-40), geodesic dilation and erosion are duals with respect to set complementation (see Problem 9.41). Figure 9.29 shows an example of a geodesic erosion of size 1. The steps in the figure are a direct implementation of Eq. (9-40).

Geodesic dilation and erosion converge after a finite number of iterative steps, because propagation or shrinking of the marker image is constrained by the mask.

MORPHOLOGICAL RECONSTRUCTION BY DILATION AND BY EROSION

Based on the preceding concepts, *morphological reconstruction by dilation* of a marker image *F* with respect to a mask image *G*, denoted $R_G^D(F)$, is defined as the geodesic dilation of *F* with respect to *G*, iterated until stability is achieved; that is,

$$R_G^D(F) = D_G^{(k)}(F) \qquad (9\text{-}42)$$

with *k* such that $D_G^{(k)}(F) = D_G^{(k+1)}(F)$.

Figure 9.30 illustrates reconstruction by dilation. Figure 9.30(a) continues the process begun in Fig. 9.28. The next step in reconstruction after obtaining $D_G^{(1)}(F)$ is to dilate this result, then AND it with mask *G* to yield $D_G^{(2)}(F)$, as Fig. 9.30(b) shows. Dilation of $D_G^{(2)}(F)$ and masking with *G* then yields $D_G^{(3)}(F)$, and so on. This procedure is repeated until stability is reached. Carrying out this example one more step would give $D_G^{(5)}(F) = D_G^{(6)}(F)$, so the image, morphologically reconstructed by dilation, is given by $R_G^D(F) = D_G^{(5)}(F)$, as indicated in Eq. (9-42). The reconstructed image is identical to the mask, as expected.

FIGURE 9.29
Illustration of a geodesic erosion of size 1.

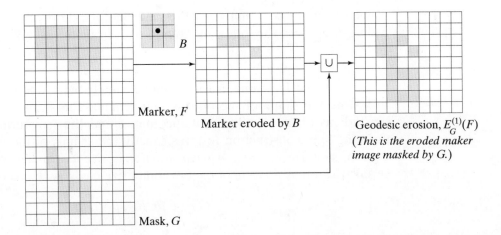

Marker, F

Marker eroded by B

Geodesic erosion, $E_G^{(1)}(F)$
(*This is the eroded maker image masked by G.*)

Mask, G

In a similar manner, the *morphological reconstruction by erosion* of a marker image F with respect to a mask image G, denoted $R_G^E(F)$, is defined as the geodesic erosion of F with respect to G, iterated until stability; that is,

$$R_G^E(F) = E_G^{(k)}(F) \tag{9-43}$$

with k such that $E_G^{(k)}(F) = E_G^{(k+1)}(F)$. As an exercise, generate a figure similar to Fig. 9.30 for morphological reconstruction by erosion. Reconstruction by dilation and erosion are duals with respect to set complementation (see Problem 9.42).

SAMPLE APPLICATIONS

Morphological reconstruction has a broad spectrum of practical applications, each determined by the selection of the marker and mask images, by the structuring

a	b	c	d
e	f	g	h

FIGURE 9.30
Illustration of morphological reconstruction by dilation. Sets $D_G^{(1)}(F), G, B$ and F are from Fig. 9.28. The mask (G) is shown dotted for reference.

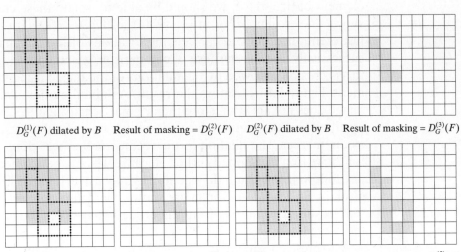

$D_G^{(1)}(F)$ dilated by B Result of masking $= D_G^{(2)}(F)$ $D_G^{(2)}(F)$ dilated by B Result of masking $= D_G^{(3)}(F)$

$D_G^{(3)}(F)$ dilated by B Result of masking $= D_G^{(4)}(F)$ $D_G^{(4)}(F)$ dilated by B Result of masking $= D_G^{(5)}(F)$
No changes after this point, so $R_G^D(F) = D_G^{(5)}(F)$

elements, and by combinations of the morphological operations defined in the preceding discussion. The following examples illustrate the usefulness of these concepts.

Opening by Reconstruction

In morphological opening, erosion removes small objects and then dilation attempts to restore the shape of the objects that remain. The accuracy of this restoration dependents on the similarity of the shapes and the structuring element(s) used. Opening by reconstruction restores exactly the shapes of the objects that remain after erosion. The *opening by reconstruction* of size n of an image F is defined as the reconstruction by dilation of the erosion of size n of F with respect to F; that is,

A expression similar to this equation can be written for closing by reconstruction (see Table 9.1 and Problem 9.44).

$$O_R^{(n)}(F) = R_F^D(F \ominus nB) \tag{9-44}$$

where $F \ominus nB$ indicates n erosions by B starting with F, as defined in Eq. (9-30). Note that F itself is used as the mask. By comparing this equation with Eq. (9-42), we see that Eq. (9-44) indicates that the opening by reconstruction uses an eroded version of F as the marker in reconstruction by dilation.

As you will see in Fig. 9.31, Eq. (9-44) can lead to some interesting results. Typically, the structuring element, B, used in Eq. (9-44) is designed to extract some feature of interest, based on erosion. However, as mentioned at the beginning of this section, the structuring element used in reconstruction (i.e., in the dilation that is performed to obtain R_F^D) is designed to define connectivity and, for 2-D, that structuring element typically is a 3×3 array of 1's. It is important that you do not confuse this SE with the structuring element, B, used for erosion in Eq. (9-44). Finally, we point out that this equation is most commonly used with $n = 1$.

Figure 9.31 shows an example of opening by reconstruction. We are interested in extracting from Fig. 9.31(a) the characters that contain long, vertical strokes. This objective determines the nature of B in Eq. (9-44). The average height of the tall characters in the figure is 51 pixels. By eroding the image with a thin structuring element of size 51×1, we should be able to isolate these characters. Figure 9.31(b) shows one erosion [$n = 1$ in Eq. (9-44)] of Fig. 9.31(a) with the structuring element just mentioned. As you can see, the locations of the tall characters were extracted successively. For the purpose of comparison, we computed the opening (remember this is erosion followed by the dilation) of the image using the same structuring element. Figure 9.31(c) shows the result. As noted earlier, simply dilating an eroded image does not always restore the original. Finally, Fig. 9.31(d) is the reconstruction by dilation of the original image using that image as the mask and the eroded image as the marker. The dilation in the reconstruction was done using a 3×3 SE of 1's, for the reason mentioned earlier. Because we only performed one erosion, the steps just followed constitute the opening by reconstruction (of size 1) of F [i.e., $O_R^{(1)}(F)$] given in Eq. (9-44). As the figure shows, characters containing long vertical strokes were restored accurately from the eroded image (i.e., the marker); all other characters were removed.

A expression similar to Eq. (9-44) can be written for *closing by reconstruction* (see Table 9.1 and Problem 9.44). The difference is that the marker used for closing by reconstruction is the dilation of F and, instead of R_F^D, we use R_F^E. As you saw,

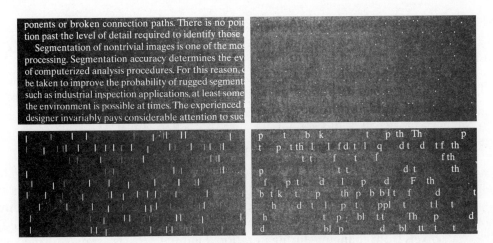

a b
c d

FIGURE 9.31 (a) Text image of size 918×2018 pixels. The approximate average height of the tall characters is 51 pixels. (b) Erosion of (a) with a structuring element of size 51×1 elements (all 1's). (c) Opening of (a) with the same structuring element, shown for comparison. (d) Result of opening by reconstruction.

opening by reconstruction works with images in which the background is black (0) and the foreground is white (1). Closing by reconstruction works with the opposite scenario. For example, if we were working with the complement of Fig. 9.31(a), the background would be white and the foreground black. To solve the same problem of extracting the tall characters, we would use opening by reconstruction. All the other images in Fig. 9.31 would be identical, except that they would be black on white. The structuring element used would be the *same* in both cases, so the operations of closing by reconstruction would be performed on background pixels.

Automatic Algorithm for Filling Holes

In Section 9.5, we developed an algorithm for filling holes based on knowing a starting point in each hole. Here, we develop a fully automated procedure based on morphological reconstruction. Let $I(x, y)$ denote a binary image, and suppose that we form a marker image F that is 0 everywhere, except at the image border, where it is set to $1 - I$, that is,

$$F(x, y) = \begin{cases} 1 - I(x, y) & \text{if } (x, y) \text{ is on the border of } I \\ 0 & \text{otherwise} \end{cases} \tag{9-45}$$

Then,

$$H = \left[R_{I^c}^D (F) \right]^c \tag{9-46}$$

is a binary image equal to I with all holes filled.

To see how Eqs. (9-45) and (9-46) cause holes in an image to be filled, consider Figs. 9.32(a) and (b), which show an image, I, containing one hole, and the image a b c d e f g

FIGURE 9.32
Hole filling using morphological reconstruction.

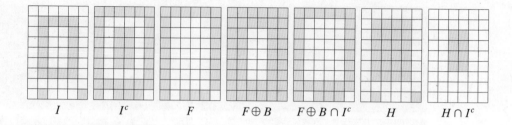

$$I \qquad I^c \qquad F \qquad F \oplus B \qquad F \oplus B \cap I^c \qquad H \qquad H \cap I^c$$

complement, respectively. The complement of I sets all foreground (1-valued) pixels to background (0-valued) pixels, and vice versa. By definition, a hole is surrounded by foreground pixels. Therefore, this operation builds a "wall" of 0's around the hole. Because I^c is used as an AND mask, what we are doing is protecting all foreground pixels from changing during iteration. Figure 9.32(c) is array F, formed according to Eq. (9-45), and Fig. 9.32(d), using a 3×3 SE of 1's. The marker F has a border of 1's (except at locations where I is 1), so the dilation of the marker points starts at the border and proceeds inward. Figure 9.32(e) shows the geodesic dilation of F using I^c as the mask. We see that all locations in this result that correspond to foreground pixels of I are now 0, and that this is true for the hole pixels as well. Another iteration will yield the same result which, when complemented as required by Eq. (9-46), gives the result in Fig. 9.32(f). The hole is now filled and the rest of image I was unchanged. The operation $H \cap I^c$ yields an image containing 1-valued pixels in the locations corresponding to the holes in I and 0's elsewhere, as Fig. 9.32(g) shows.

Figure 9.33 shows a more practical example. Figure 9.33(b) shows the complement of the text image in Fig. 9.33(a), and Fig. 9.33(c) is the marker image, F, generated using Eq. (9-45). This image is all black with a white (1's) border, except at locations corresponding to 1's in the border of the original image (the border values are not easily discernible by eye at the magnification shown, and also because the page is nearly white). Finally, Fig. 9.33(d) shows the image with all the holes filled.

Border Clearing

Extracting objects from an image for subsequent shape analysis is a fundamental task in automated image processing. An algorithm for detecting objects that touch (i.e., are connected to) the border is a useful tool because (1) it can be used to screen images so that only complete objects remain for further processing, or (2) it can be used as a signal that partial objects are present in the field of view. As a final illustration of the concepts introduced in this section, we develop a border-clearing procedure based on morphological reconstruction. In this application, we use the original image as the mask and the following marker image:

$$F(x,y) = \begin{cases} I(x,y) & \text{if } (x,y) \text{ is on the border of } I \\ 0 & \text{otherwise} \end{cases} \tag{9-47}$$

The border-clearing algorithm first computes the morphological reconstruction $R_I^D(F)$ (which extracts the objects touching the border), and then computes the following difference:

a b
c d

FIGURE 9.33
(a) Text image of size 918×2018 pixels.
(b) Complement of (a) for use as a mask image.
(c) Marker image.
(d) Result of hole-filling using Eqs. (9-45) and (9-46).

$$X = I - R_I^D(F) \qquad (9\text{-}48)$$

to obtain an image, X, with no objects touching the border.

As an example, consider the original text image from Fig. 9.31(a) again. Figure 9.34(a) shows the reconstruction $R_I^D(F)$ obtained using a 3×3 structuring element of 1's. The objects touching the border of the original image are visible in the right side of Fig. 9.34(a). Figure 9.34(b) shows image X, computed using Eq. (9-48). If the task at hand were automated character recognition, having an image in which no characters touch the border is most useful because the problem of having to recognize partial characters (a difficult task at best) is avoided.

9.7 SUMMARY OF MORPHOLOGICAL OPERATIONS ON BINARY IMAGES

Figure 9.35 summarizes the types of structuring elements used in the various binary morphological methods discussed thus far. The shaded elements are foreground values (typically denoted by 1's in numerical arrays), the elements in white are background values (typically denoted by 0's), and the ×'s are "don't care" elements. Table 9.1 summarizes the binary morphological results developed in the preceding sections. The Roman numerals in the third column of Table 9.1 refer to the structuring elements in Fig. 9.35.

a b

FIGURE 9.34
(a) Reconstruction by dilation of marker image. (b) Image with no objects touching the border. The original image is Fig. 9.31(a).

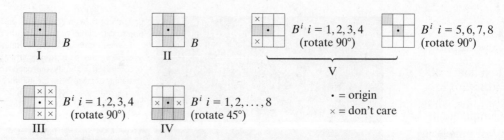

9.8 GRAYSCALE MORPHOLOGY

In this section, we extend to grayscale images the basic operations of dilation, erosion, opening, and closing. We then use these operations to develop several basic grayscale morphological algorithms. Throughout the discussion that follows, we deal with digital functions of the form $f(x, y)$ and $b(x, y)$, where $f(x, y)$ is a grayscale image and $b(x, y)$ is a structuring element. The assumption is that these functions are discrete in the sense defined in Section 2.4. That is, if Z denotes the set of real integers, then the coordinates (x, y) are integers from the Cartesian product Z^2, and $f(x, y)$ and $b(x, y)$ are functions that assign an intensity value (a real number from the set of real numbers, R) to each distinct pair of coordinates (x, y). If the intensity levels are integers also, then Z replaces R.

Structuring elements in grayscale morphology perform the same basic functions as their binary counterparts: They are used as "probes" to examine a given image for specific properties. Structuring elements in grayscale morphology belong to one of two categories: *nonflat* and *flat*. Figure 9.36 shows an example of each. Figure 9.36(a) is a hemispherical grayscale SE shown as an image, and Fig. 9.36(c) is a horizontal intensity profile through its center. Figure 9.34(b) shows a flat structuring element in the shape of a disk, and Fig. 9.36(d) is its corresponding intensity profile. (The shape of this profile explains the origin of the word "flat.") The elements in Fig. 9.36 are shown as continuous quantities for clarity; their computer implementation is based on digital approximations. Because of a number of difficulties discussed later in this section, grayscale nonflat SEs are not used frequently in practice. Finally, we mention that, as in the binary case, the origin of grayscale structuring elements must be clearly identified. Unless mentioned otherwise, all the examples in this section are based on symmetrical, flat structuring elements of unit height whose origins are at the center. The reflection of an SE in grayscale morphology is as defined in Section 9.1; we denote it in the following discussion by $\hat{b}(x, y) = b(-x, -y)$.

GRAYSCALE EROSION AND DILATION

The *grayscale erosion* of f by a flat structuring element b at location (x, y) is defined as the *minimum* value of the image in the region coincident with $b(x, y)$ when the origin of b is at (x, y). In equation form, the erosion at (x, y) of an image f by a structuring element b is given as

$$[f \ominus b](x, y) = \min_{(s, t) \in b} \{f(x + s, y + t)\} \tag{9-49}$$

TABLE 9.1
Summary of binary morphological operations and their properties. A is a set of foreground pixels contained in binary image I, and B is a structuring element. I is a binary image (containing A), with 1's corresponding to the elements of A and 0's elsewhere. The Roman numerals refer to the structuring elements in Fig. 9.35.

Operation	Equation	Comments
Translation	$(B)_z = \{c \mid c = b + z, \text{ for } b \in B\}$	Translates the origin of B to point z.
Reflection	$\hat{B} = \{w \mid w = -b, \text{ for } b \in B\}$	Reflects B about its origin.
Complement	$A^c = \{w \mid w \notin A\}$	Set of points not in A.
Difference	$A - B = \{w \mid w \in A, w \notin B\}$ $= A \cap B^c$	Set of points in A, but not in B.
Erosion	$A \ominus B = \{z \mid (B)_z \subseteq A\}$	Erodes the boundary of A. (I)
Dilation	$A \oplus B = \{z \mid (\hat{B})_z \cap A \neq \varnothing\}$	Dilates the boundary of A. (I)
Opening	$A \circ B = (A \ominus B) \oplus B$	Smoothes contours, breaks narrow isthmuses, and eliminates small islands and sharp peaks. (I)
Closing	$A \cdot B = (A \oplus B) \ominus B$	Smoothes contours, fuses narrow breaks and long thin gulfs, and eliminates small holes. (I)
Hit-or-miss transform	$I \circledast B = \{z \mid (B)_z \subseteq I\}$	Finds instances of B in image I. B contains *both* foreground and background elements.
Boundary extraction	$\beta(A) = A - (A \ominus B)$	Set of points on the boundary of set A. (I)
Hole filling	$X_k = (X_{k-1} \oplus B) \cap I^c$ $k = 1, 2, 3, \ldots$	Fills holes in A. X_0 is of same size as I, with a 1 in each hole and 0's elsewhere. (II)
Connected components	$X_k = (X_{k-1} \oplus B) \cap I$ $k = 1, 2, 3, \ldots$	Finds connected components in I. X_0 is a set, the same size as I, with a 1 in each connected component and 0's elsewhere. (I)
Convex hull	$X_k^i = (X_{k-1}^i \circledast B^i) \cup X_{k-1}^i;$ $i = 1, 2, 3, 4 \quad k = 1, 2, 3, \ldots$ $X_0^i = I; D^i = X_{conv}^i; C(A) = \bigcup_{i=1}^{4} D^i$	Finds the convex hull, $C(A)$, of a set, A, of foreground pixels contained in image I. X_{conv}^i means that $X_k^i = X_{k-1}^i$. (III)

TABLE 9.1
(*Continued*)

Operation	Equation	Comments
Thinning	$A \otimes B = A - (A \circledast B)$ $= A \cap (A \circledast B)^c$ $A \otimes \{B\} =$ $\left(\left(\ldots \left(\left(A \otimes B^1 \right) \otimes B^2 \right) \ldots \right) \otimes B^n \right)$ $\{B\} = \{B^1, B^2, B^3, \ldots, B^n\}$	Thins set A. The first two equations give the basic definition of thinning. The last two equations denote thinning by a sequence of structuring elements. This method is normally used in practice. (IV)
Thickening	$A \odot B = A \cup (A \circledast B)$ $A \odot \{B\} =$ $\left(\left(\ldots \left(\left(A \odot B^1 \right) \odot B^2 \right) \ldots \right) \odot B^n \right)$	Thickens set A using a sequence of structuring elements, as above. Uses (IV) with 0's and 1's reversed.
Skeletons	$S(A) = \bigcup_{k=0}^{K} S_k(A)$ $S_k(A) = (A \ominus kB)$ $\qquad - (A \ominus kB) \circ B$ Reconstruction of A: $A = \bigcup_{k=0}^{K} \left(S_k(A) \oplus kB \right)$	Finds the skeleton $S(A)$ of set A. The last equation indicates that A can be reconstructed from its skeleton subsets $S_k(A)$. K is the value of the iterative step after which the set A erodes to the empty set. The notation $(A \ominus kB)$ denotes the kth iteration of successive erosions of A by B. (I)
Pruning	$X_1 = A \otimes \{B\}$ $X_2 = \bigcup_{k=1}^{8} \left(X_1 \circledast B^k \right)$ $X_3 = (X_2 \oplus H) \cap A$ $X_4 = X_1 \cup X_3$	X_4 is the result of pruning set A. The number of times that the first equation is applied to obtain X_1 must be specified. Structuring elements (V) are used for the first two equations. In the third equation H denotes structuring element. (I)
Geodesic dilation–size 1	$D_G^{(1)}(F) = (F \oplus B) \cap G$	F and G are called the *marker* and the *mask* images, respectively. (I)
Geodesic dilation–size n	$D_G^{(n)}(F) = D_G^{(1)}\left(D_G^{(n-1)}(F) \right)$	Same comment as above.
Geodesic erosion–size 1	$E_G^{(1)}(F) = (F \ominus B) \cup G$	Same comment as above.
Geodesic erosion–size n	$E_G^{(n)}(F) = E_G^{(1)}\left(E_G^{(n-1)}(F) \right)$	Same comment as above.
Morphological reconstruction by dilation	$R_G^D(F) = D_G^{(k)}(F)$	With k is such that $D_G^{(k)}(F) = D_G^{(k+1)}(F)$.

TABLE 9.1
(*Continued*)

Operation	Equation	Comments
Morphological reconstruction by erosion	$R_G^E(F) = E_G^{(k)}(F)$	With k such that $E_G^{(k)}(F) = E_G^{(k+1)}(F)$.
Opening by reconstruction	$O_R^{(n)}(F) = R_F^D(F \ominus nB)$	$F \ominus nB$ indicates n successive erosions by B, starting with F. The form of B is application-dependent.
Closing by reconstruction	$C_R^{(n)}(F) = R_F^E(F \oplus nB)$	$F \oplus nB$ indicates n successive dilations by B, starting with F. The form of B is application-dependent.
Hole filling	$H = \left[R_{I^c}^D(F) \right]^c$	H is equal to the input image I, but with all holes filled. See Eq. (9-45) for the definition of marker image F.
Border clearing	$X = I - R_I^D(F)$	X is equal to the input image I, but with all objects that touch (are connected to) the boundary removed. See Eq. (9-47) for the definition of marker image F.

FIGURE 9.36
Nonflat and flat structuring elements, and corresponding horizontal intensity profiles through their centers. All examples in this section are based on flat SEs.

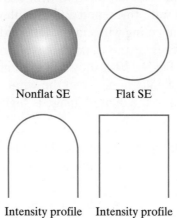

Nonflat SE   Flat SE

Intensity profile   Intensity profile

where, in a manner similar to spatial correlation (see Section 3.4), x and y are incremented through all values required so that the origin of b visits every pixel in f. That is, to find the erosion of f by b, we place the origin of the structuring element at every pixel location in the image. The erosion at any location is determined by selecting the minimum value of f in the region coincident with b. For example, if b is a square structuring element of size 3×3, obtaining the erosion at a point requires finding the minimum of the nine values of f contained in the 3×3 region spanned by b when its origin is at that point.

Similarly, the *grayscale dilation* of f by a flat structuring element b at any location (x, y) is defined as the *maximum* value of the image in the window spanned by $\hat{b}$ when the origin of $\hat{b}$ is at (x, y). That is,

$$[f \oplus b](x, y) = \max_{(s,t) \in \hat{b}} \{f(x - s, y - t)\} \tag{9-50}$$

where we used the fact stated earlier that $\hat{b}(c, d) = b(-c, -d)$. The explanation of this equation is identical to the explanation in the previous paragraph, but using the maximum, rather than the minimum operation, and keeping in mind that the structuring element is reflected about its origin, which we take into account by using $(-s, -t)$ in the argument of the function. This is analogous to spatial convolution, as explained in Section 3.4.

EXAMPLE 9.9: Grayscale erosion and dilation.

Because grayscale erosion with a flat SE computes the minimum intensity value of f in every neighborhood of (x, y) coincident with b, we expect in general that an eroded grayscale image will be darker than the original, that the sizes (with respect to the size of the SE) of bright features will be reduced, and that the sizes of dark features will be increased. Figure 9.37(b) shows the erosion of Fig. 9.37(a) using a disk SE of unit height and a radius of 2 pixels. The effects just mentioned are clearly visible in the eroded image. For instance, note how the intensities of the small bright dots were reduced, making them barely visible in Fig. 9.37(b), while the dark features grew in thickness. The general background of the eroded image is slightly darker than the background of the original image.

Similarly, Fig. 9.37(c) is the result of dilation with the same SE. The effects are the opposite of using erosion. The bright features were thickened and the intensities of the darker features were reduced. In particular, the thin black connecting wires in the left, middle, and right bottom of Fig. 9.37(a) are barely visible in Fig. 9.37(c). The sizes of the dark dots were reduced as a result of dilation, but, unlike the eroded small white dots in Fig. 9.37(b), they still are easily visible in the dilated image. The reason is that the black dots were originally larger than the white dots with respect to the size of the SE. Finally, observe that the background of the dilated image is slightly lighter than that of Fig. 9.37(a).

Nonflat SEs have grayscale values that vary over their domain of definition. The erosion of image f by nonflat structuring element, b_N, is defined as

$$[f \ominus b_N](x, y) = \min_{(s,t) \in b_N} \{f(x + s, y + t) - b_N(s, t)\} \tag{9-51}$$

a b c

FIGURE 9.37
(a) Gray-scale
X-ray image of
size 448×425
pixels. (b) Erosion
using a flat disk SE
with a radius of 2
pixels. (c) Dilation
using the same SE.
(Original image
courtesy of Lixi,
Inc.)

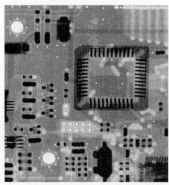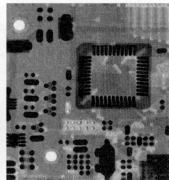

Here, we subtract values from f to determine the erosion at any point. Unlike Eq. (9-49), erosion using a nonflat SE is not bounded in general by the values of f, which can be problematic in interpreting results. Grayscale SEs are seldom used in practice because of this, the potential difficulties in selecting meaningful elements for b_N, and the added computational burden when compared with Eq. (9-49).

In a similar manner, dilation using a nonflat SE is defined as

$$[f \oplus b_N](x, y) = \max_{(s, t) \in \hat{b}_N} \left\{ f(x - s, y - t) + \hat{b}_N(s, t) \right\} \qquad (9\text{-}52)$$

The same comments made in the previous paragraph are applicable to dilation with nonflat SEs. When all the elements of b_N are constant (i.e., the SE is flat), Eqs. (9-51) and (9-52) reduce to Eqs. (9-49) and (9-50), respectively, within a scalar constant equal to the amplitude of the SE.

As in the binary case, grayscale erosion and dilation are duals with respect complementation and reflection; that is,

$$[f \ominus b]^c(x, y) = \left[f^c \oplus \hat{b} \right](x, y) \qquad (9\text{-}53)$$

where $f^c(x, y) = -f(x, y)$ and $\hat{b}(x, y) = b(-x, -y)$. The same expression holds for nonflat structuring elements. Except as needed for clarity, we simplify the notation in the following discussion by suppressing the arguments of all functions, in which case the preceding equation is written as

$$(f \ominus b)^c = f^c \oplus \hat{b} \qquad (9\text{-}54)$$

Similarly,

$$(f \oplus b)^c = f^c \ominus \hat{b} \qquad (9\text{-}55)$$

Erosion and dilation by themselves are not particularly useful in grayscale image processing. As with their binary counterparts, these operations become powerful when used in combination to derive higher-level algorithms.

GRAYSCALE OPENING AND CLOSING

Although we deal with flat SEs in the following discussion, the concepts discussed are applicable also to nonflat structuring elements.

The expressions for opening and closing grayscale images have the same form as their binary counterparts. The *grayscale opening* of image f by structuring element b, denoted $f \circ b$, is

$$f \circ b = (f \ominus b) \oplus b \tag{9-56}$$

As before, opening is simply the erosion of f by b, followed by a dilation of the result by b. Similarly, the *grayscale closing* of f by b, denoted $f \bullet b$, is

$$f \bullet b = (f \oplus b) \ominus b \tag{9-57}$$

The opening and closing for grayscale images are duals with respect to complementation and SE reflection:

$$(f \bullet b)^c = f^c \circ \hat{b} \tag{9-58}$$

and

$$(f \circ b)^c = f^c \bullet \hat{b} \tag{9-59}$$

Because $f^c = -f$, we can write Eq. (9-58) as $-(f \bullet b) = (-f \circ b)$, and similarly for Eq. (9-59).

Opening and closing of grayscale images have a simple geometric interpretation. Suppose that an image function $f(x, y)$ is viewed as a 3-D surface; that is, its intensity values are interpreted as height values over the xy-plane, as in Fig. 2.18(a). Then the opening of f by b can be interpreted geometrically as pushing the structuring element up from below against the undersurface of f. At each location of the origin of b, the opening is the highest value reached by any part of b as it pushes up against the undersurface of f. The complete opening is then the set of all such values obtained by the origin of b visiting every (x, y) coordinate of f.

Figure 9.38 illustrates the concept in one dimension. Suppose the curve in Fig. 9.38(a) is the intensity profile along a single row of an image. Figure 9.38(b) shows a flat structuring element in several positions, pushed up against the bottom of the curve. The heavy curve in Fig. 9.38(c) is the complete opening. Because the structuring element is too large to fit completely inside the upward peaks of the curve, the tops of the peaks are clipped by the opening, with the amount removed being proportional to how far the structuring element was able to reach into the peak. In general, openings are used to remove small, bright details, while leaving the overall intensity levels and larger bright features relatively undisturbed.

Figure 9.38(d) is a graphical illustration of closing. Observe that the structuring element is pushed down on top of the curve while being translated to all locations. The closing, shown in Fig. 9.38(e), is constructed by finding the lowest points reached by any part of the structuring element as it slides against the upper side of the curve. The grayscale opening satisfies the following properties:

a
b
c
d
e

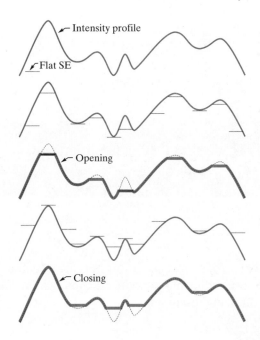

FIGURE 9.38
Grayscale opening and closing in one dimension.
(a) Original 1-D signal.
(b) Flat structuring element pushed up underneath the signal.
(c) Opening.
(d) Flat structuring element pushed down along the top of the signal.
(e) Closing.

(a) $f \circ b \lrcorner f$

(b) If $f_1 \lrcorner f_2$, then $(f_1 \circ b) \lrcorner (f_2 \circ b)$

(c) $(f \circ b) \circ b = f \circ b$

The notation $q \lrcorner r$ is used to indicate that the domain of q is a subset of the domain of r, and also that $q(x, y) \leq r(x, y)$ for any (x, y) in the domain of q.

Similarly, the closing operation satisfies the following properties:

(a) $f \lrcorner f \bullet b$

(b) If $f_1 \lrcorner f_2$, then $(f_1 \bullet b) \lrcorner (f_2 \bullet b)$

(c) $(f \bullet b) \bullet b = f \bullet b$

The usefulness of these properties is similar to that of their binary counterparts.

EXAMPLE 9.10: Grayscale opening and closing.

Figure 9.39 extends to 2-D the 1-D concepts illustrated in Fig. 9.38. Figure 9.39(a) is the same image we used in Example 9.9, and Fig. 9.39(b) is the opening obtained using a disk structuring element of unit height and radius of 3 pixels. As expected, the intensity of all bright features decreased, depending on the sizes of the features relative to the size of the SE. Comparing this figure with Fig. 9.37(b), we see that, unlike the result of erosion, opening had negligible effect on the dark features of the image, and the effect on the background was negligible. Similarly, Fig. 9.39(c) shows the closing of the image with a disk of radius 5 (the small round black dots are larger than the small white dots, so a larger disk was needed to achieve results comparable to the opening). In this image, the bright details and background were relatively unaffected, but the dark features were attenuated, with the degree of attenuation being dependent on the relative sizes of the features with respect to the SE.

FIGURE 9.39
(a) A grayscale
X-ray image of
size 448×425
pixels.
(b) Opening using
a disk SE with a
radius of 3 pixels.
(c) Closing using
an SE of radius 5.

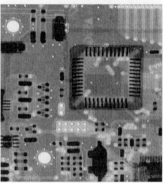
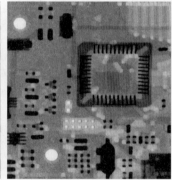

SOME BASIC GRAYSCALE MORPHOLOGICAL ALGORITHMS

Numerous grayscale morphological techniques are based on the grayscale morphological concepts introduced thus far. We illustrate some of these algorithms in the following discussion.

Morphological Smoothing

Because opening suppresses bright details smaller than the specified SE while leaving dark details relatively unaffected, and closing generally has the opposite effect, these two operations are used often in combination as *morphological filters* for image smoothing and noise removal. Consider Fig. 9.40(a), which shows an image of the Cygnus Loop supernova taken in the X-ray band (see Fig. 1.7 for details about this image). For purposes of the present discussion, suppose that the central light region is the object of interest, and that the smaller components are noise. Our objective is to remove the noise. Figure 9.40(b) shows the result of opening the original image with a flat disk of radius 1, then closing the opening with an SE of the same size. Figures 9.40(c) and (d) show the results of the same operation using SEs of radii 3 and 5, respectively. As expected, this sequence shows progressive removal of small components as a function of SE size. In the last result, we see that the noise has been almost eliminated. The noise components on the lower right side of the image could not be removed completely because their sizes are larger than the other image elements that were successfully removed.

The results in Fig. 9.40 are based on opening the original image, then closing the opening. A procedure used sometimes is to perform *alternating sequential filtering*, in which the opening–closing sequence starts with the original image, but subsequent steps perform the opening and closing on the results of the previous step. This type of filtering is useful in automated image analysis, in which results at each step are compared against a specified metric. This approach generally results in more blurring for the same size SE than the method illustrated in Fig. 9.40.

See Section 3.6 for a definition of the image gradient.

Morphological Gradient

Dilation and erosion can be used in combination with image subtraction to obtain the morphological gradient, g, of a grayscale image f, as follows:

a b
c d

FIGURE 9.40
(a) 566×566 image of the Cygnus Loop supernova, taken in the X-ray band by NASA's Hubble Telescope.
(b)–(d) Results of performing opening and closing sequences on the original image with disk structuring elements of radii, 1, 3, and 5, respectively. (Original image courtesy of NASA.)

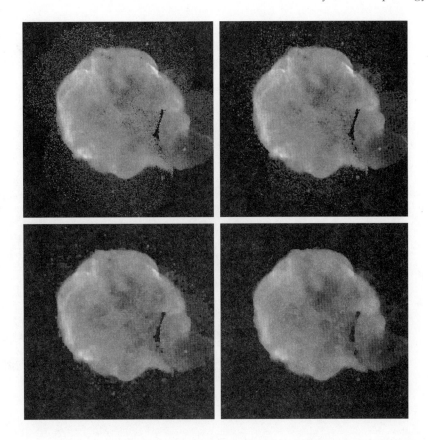

$$g = (f \oplus b) - (f \ominus b) \qquad (9\text{-}60)$$

where b is a suitable structuring element. The overall effect achieved by using this equation is that dilation thickens regions in an image, and erosion shrinks them. Their difference emphasizes the boundaries between regions. Homogenous areas are not affected (provided that the SE is not too large relative to the resolution of the image) so the subtraction operation tends to eliminate them. The net result is an image in which the edges are enhanced and the contribution of the homogeneous areas is suppressed, thus producing a "derivative-like" (gradient) effect.

Figure 9.41 shows an example. Figure 9.41(a) is a head CT scan, and the next two figures are the opening and closing with a 3×3 flat SE of 1's. Note the thickening and shrinking just mentioned. Figure 9.41(d) is the morphological gradient obtained using Eq. (9-60). As you can see, the boundaries between regions were clearly delineated, as expected of a 2-D derivative image.

Top-Hat and Bottom-Hat Transformations

Combining image subtraction with openings and closings results in so-called top-hat and bottom-hat transformations. The *top-hat transformation* of a grayscale image f is defined as f minus its opening:

a b
c d

FIGURE 9.41
(a) 512×512 image of a head CT scan.
(b) Dilation.
(c) Erosion.
(d) Morphological gradient, computed as the difference between (b) and (c). (Original image courtesy of Dr. David R. Pickens, Vanderbilt University.)

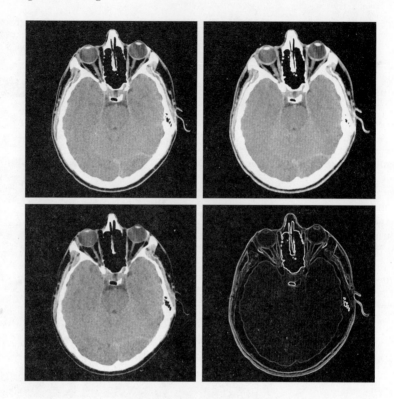

$$T_{\text{hat}}(f) = f - (f \circ b) \tag{9-61}$$

Similarly, the *bottom-hat transformation* of f is defined as the closing of f minus f:

$$B_{\text{hat}}(f) = (f \bullet b) - f \tag{9-62}$$

One of the principal applications of these transformations is in removing objects from an image by using a structuring element in the opening or closing operation that does not fit the objects to be removed. The difference operation then yields an image in which only the removed components remain. The top-hat transformation is used for light objects on a dark background, and the bottom-hat transformation is used for the opposite situation. For this reason, the names *white top-hat* and *black top-hat*, respectively, are used frequently when referring to these two transformations.

An important use of top-hat transformations is for correcting the effects of non-uniform illumination. As you will learn in Chapter 10, proper (uniform) illumination plays a central role in being able to extract objects from the background in an image. This process is fundamental in automated image analysis, and is often used in conjunction with thresholding, as you will learn in Chapter 10.

To illustrate, consider Fig. 9.42(a), which shows an image of grains of rice. This image was obtained under nonuniform lighting, as evidenced by the darker area in the bottom rightmost part of the image. Figure 9.42(b) shows the result of thresholding using Otsu's method, an optimal thresholding method to be discussed in Section 10.3. The net result of nonuniform illumination was to cause segmentation

a b
c d e

FIGURE 9.42 Using the top-hat transformation for *shading correction.* (a) Original image of size 600×600 pixels. (b) Thresholded image. (c) Image opened using a disk SE of radius 40. (d) Top-hat transformation (the image minus its opening). (e) Thresholded top-hat image.

errors in the dark area (several grains of rice were not extracted from the background), as well as in the top left part of the image, where parts of the background were interpreted as rice. Figure 9.42(c) shows the opening of the image with a disk of radius 40. This SE was large enough so that it would not fit in any of the objects. As a result, the objects were eliminated, leaving only an approximation of the background. The shading pattern is clear in this image. By subtracting this image from the original (i.e., by applying a top-hat transformation), the background should become more uniform. This is indeed the case, as Fig. 9.42(d) shows. The background is not perfectly uniform, but the differences between light and dark extremes are less, and this was enough to yield a correct thresholding result, in which all the rice grains were properly extracted using Otsu's method, as Fig. 9.42(e) shows.

Granulometry

In the context of this discussion, *granulometry* is a field that deals with determining the size distribution of particles in an image. Particles seldom are neatly separated, which makes counting based on identifying individual particles a difficult task. Morphology can be used to estimate particle size distribution indirectly, without having to identify and measure individual particles.

The approach is simple. With particles having regular shapes that are lighter than the background, the method consists of applying openings with SEs of increasing sizes. The basic idea is that opening operations of a particular size should have the most effect on regions of the input image that contain particles of similar size. For each image resulting from an opening, we compute the sum of the pixel values. This sum, called the *surface area*, decreases as a function of increasing SE size because, as we discussed earlier, openings decrease the intensity of light features in an image. This procedure yields a 1-D array each element of which is the sum of the pixels in the opening for the size SE corresponding to that location in the array. To emphasize changes between successive openings, we compute the difference between adjacent elements of the 1-D array. If the differences are plotted, the peaks in the plot are an indication of the predominant size distributions of the particles in the image.

As an example, consider the image of wood dowel plugs of two dominant sizes in Fig. 9.43(a). The wood grain in the dowels is likely to introduce variations in the openings, so smoothing is a sensible preprocessing step. Figure Fig. 9.43(b) shows the image smoothed using the morphological smoothing filter discussed earlier, with a disk of radius 5. Figures 9.43(c) through (f) show image openings with disks of radii 10, 20, 25, and 30, respectively. Note in Fig. 9.43(d) that the intensity contribution due to the small dowels has been almost eliminated. In Fig. 9.43(e) the contribution of the large dowels has been reduced significantly, and in Fig. 9.43(f) even more so. Observe in Fig. 9.43(e) that the large dowel near the top right of the image is much darker than the others because its size is smaller than other lager dowels. This would be useful information if we had been attempting to detect defective dowels.

Figure 9.44 shows a plot of the difference array. As mentioned previously, we expect significant differences (peaks in the plot) around radii at which the SE is

a b c
d e f

FIGURE 9.43
(a) 531×675 image of wood dowels.
(b) Smoothed image.
(c)–(f) Openings of (b) with disks of radii equal to 10, 20, 25, and 30 pixels, respectively.
(Original image courtesy of Dr. Steve Eddins, MathWorks, Inc.)

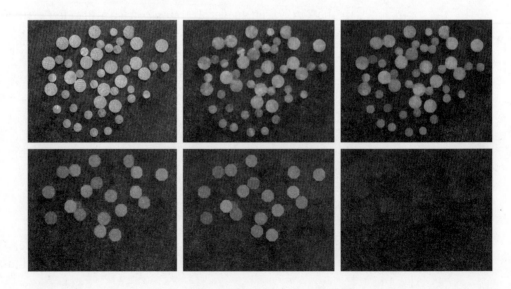

FIGURE 9.44
Differences in
surface area as
a function of SE
disk radius, r.
The two peaks
indicate that there
are two dominant
particle sizes in
the image.

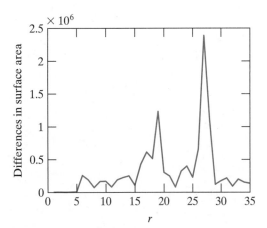

large enough to encompass a set of particles of approximately the same diameter. The result in Fig. 9.44 has two distinct peaks, clearly indicating the presence of two dominant object sizes in the image.

Textural Segmentation

Figure 9.45(a) shows a noisy image of dark blobs superimposed on a light background. The image has two textural regions: a region composed of large blobs on the right and a region on the left composed of smaller blobs. The objective is to find a boundary between the two regions based on their textural content, which in this case is determined by the sizes and spatial distribution of the blobs (we discuss texture in Chapter 11). The process of partitioning an image into regions is called *segmentation*, which is the topic of Chapter 10.

The objects of interest are darker than the background, and we know that if we close the image with a structuring element larger than the small blobs, these blobs will be removed. The result in Fig. 9.45(b), obtained by closing the input image using a disk with a radius of 30 pixels, shows that indeed this is the case. (The radius of the smaller blobs is approximately 25 pixels.) So, at this point, we have an image with large, dark blobs on a light background. If we open this image with a structuring element that is large relative to the separation between these blobs, the net result should be an image in which the light patches between the blobs are removed, leaving the dark blobs, and also the now dark patches between these blobs. Figure 9.45(c) shows the result, obtained using a disk of radius 60.

Performing a morphological gradient on this image with, say, a 3×3 SE of 1's, will give us the boundary between the two regions. Figure 9.45(d) shows the boundary obtained from the morphological gradient operation, superimposed on the original image. All pixels to the right of this boundary are said to belong to the texture region characterized by large blobs, and conversely for the pixels on the left of the boundary. You will find it instructive to work through this example in more detail using the graphical analogy for opening and closing illustrated in Fig. 9.38.

FIGURE 9.45
Textural
segmentation.
(a) A 600×600
image consisting
of two types of
blobs.
(b) Image with
small blobs
removed by
closing (a).
(c) Image with
light patches
between large
blobs removed by
opening (b).
(d) Original
image with
boundary
between the two
regions in (c)
superimposed.
The boundary was
obtained using
a morphological
gradient.

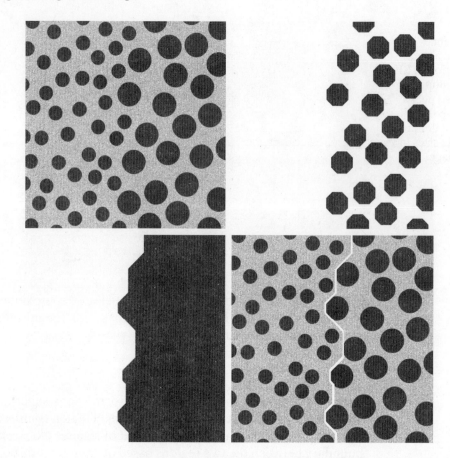

GRAYSCALE MORPHOLOGICAL RECONSTRUCTION

As mentioned earlier, it is understood that f and g are functions of x and y. We omit the coordinates to simplify the notation.

Grayscale morphological reconstruction is defined in the same manner introduced in Section 9.6 for binary images. Let f and g denote the *marker* and *mask* images, respectively. We assume that both are grayscale images of the same size and that $f \leq g$, meaning that the intensity of f at any point in the image is less than the intensity of g at that point. The *geodesic dilation of size* 1 of f with respect to g is defined as

$$D_g^{(1)}(f) = (f \oplus b) \wedge g \tag{9-63}$$

where $\wedge$ denotes the *point-wise minimum operator*, and b is a suitable structuring element. We see that the geodesic dilation of size 1 is obtained by first computing the dilation of f by b, then selecting the minimum between the result and g at every point (x, y). The dilation is given by Eq. (9-50) if b is a flat SE, or by Eq. (9-52) if it is not.

The *geodesic dilation of size* n of f with respect to g is defined as

$$D_g^{(n)}(f) = D_g^{(1)}\left(D_g^{(n-1)}(f)\right) \tag{9-64}$$

with $D_g^{(0)}(f) = f$.

See Problem 9.33 for a list of dual relationships between expressions in this section.

Similarly, the *geodesic erosion of size* 1 of f with respect to g is defined as

$$E_g^{(1)}(f) = (f \ominus b) \vee g \tag{9-65}$$

where $\vee$ denotes the *point-wise maximum operator*. The *geodesic erosion of size n* is defined as

$$E_g^{(n)}(f) = E_g^{(1)}\left(E_g^{(n-1)}(f)\right) \tag{9-66}$$

with $E_g^{(0)}(f) = f$.

The *morphological reconstruction by dilation* of a *grayscale mask image*, g, by a *grayscale marker image*, f, denoted by $R_g^{(D)}(f)$, is defined as the geodesic dilation of f with respect to g, iterated until stability is reached; that is,

$$R_g^D(f) = D_g^{(k)}(f) \tag{9-67}$$

with k such that $D_g^{(k)}(f) = D_g^{(k+1)}(f)$. The *morphological reconstruction by erosion* of g by f, denoted by $R_g^E(f)$, is similarly defined as

$$R_g^E(f) = E_g^{(k)}(f) \tag{9-68}$$

with k such that $E_g^{(k)}(f) = E_g^{(k+1)}(f)$.

As in the binary case, opening by reconstruction of grayscale images first erodes the input image and uses it as a marker, and uses the image itself as the mask. The *opening by reconstruction of size n* of an image f is defined as the reconstruction by dilation of the erosion of size n of f with respect to f; that is,

$$O_R^{(n)}(f) = R_f^D(f \ominus nb) \tag{9-69}$$

where $f \ominus nb$ denotes n successive erosions by b, starting with f, as explained in connection with Eq. (9-30) (note that f itself is used as the mask). Recall also from the discussion of Eq. (9-44) for binary images that the objective of opening by reconstruction is to preserve the shape of the image components that remain after erosion.

Similarly, the *closing by reconstruction of size n* of an image f is defined as the reconstruction by erosion of the dilation of size n of f with respect to f; that is,

$$C_R^{(n)}(f) = R_f^E(f \oplus nb) \tag{9-70}$$

where $f \oplus nb$ denotes n successive dilations by b, starting with f. Because of duality, the closing by reconstruction of an image can be obtained by complementing the image, obtaining the opening by reconstruction, and complementing the result. Finally, as the following example shows, a useful technique called *top-hat by reconstruction* consists of subtracting from an image its opening by reconstruction.

EXAMPLE 9.11: Using grayscale morphological reconstruction to flatten a complex background.

In this example, we illustrate the use of grayscale reconstruction in several steps. The objective is to normalize the irregular background of the image in Fig. 9.46(a), leaving only text on a background of con-

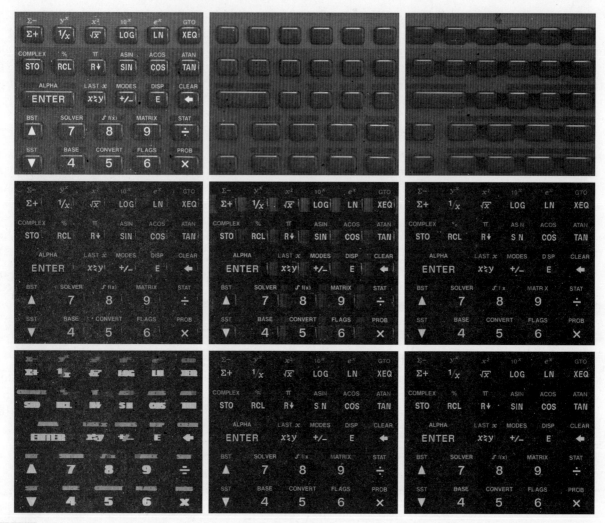

a b c
d e f
g h i

FIGURE 9.46 (a) Original image of size 1134×1360 pixels. (b) Opening by reconstruction of (a), using a structuring element consisting of a horizontal line 71 pixels long in the erosion. (c) Opening of (a) using the same SE. (d) Top-hat by reconstruction. (e) Result of applying just a top-hat transformation. (f) Opening by reconstruction of (d), using a horizontal line 11 pixels long. (g) Dilation of (f) using a horizontal line 21 pixels long. (h) Minimum of (d) and (g). (i) Final reconstruction result. (Images courtesy of Dr. Steve Eddins, MathWorks, Inc.)

stant intensity. The solution of this problem is a good illustration of the power of grayscale morphology. We begin by suppressing the horizontal reflection on the top of the keys. The reflections are wider than any single character in the image, so we should be able to suppress them by performing an opening by reconstruction using a long horizontal line in the erosion operation. This operation will yield the background containing the keys and their reflections. Subtracting this from the original image (i.e., performing a top-hat by reconstruction) will eliminate the horizontal reflections and variations in background from the original image.

Figure 9.46(b) shows the result of opening by reconstruction of the original image using a horizontal line of size 1×71 pixels for the SE in the erosion operation. We could have used an opening to remove the characters, but the resulting background would not have been as uniform, as Fig. 9.46(c) shows (compare the regions between the keys in the two images). Figure 9.46(d) shows the result of subtracting Fig. 9.46(b) from Fig. 9.46(a). As expected, the horizontal reflections and variations in background were suppressed. For comparison, Fig. 9.46(e) shows the result of performing just a top-hat transformation (i.e., subtracting the "standard" opening from the image). As expected from the characteristics of the background in Fig. 9.46(c), the background in Fig. 9.46(e) is not nearly as uniform as in Fig. 9.46(d).

The next step is to remove the vertical reflections from the edges of the keys, visible in Fig. 9.46(d). We can do this by performing an opening by reconstruction with a line SE whose width is approximately equal to the reflections (about 11 pixels in this case). Figure 9.46(f) shows the result of performing this operation on Fig. 9.46(d). The vertical reflections were suppressed, but so were thin, vertical strokes that are valid characters (for example, the I in SIN), so we have to find a way to restore the latter. The suppressed characters are very close to the other characters so, if we dilate the remaining characters horizontally, the dilated characters will overlap the area previously occupied by the suppressed characters. Figure 9.46(g), obtained by dilating Fig. 9.46(f) with a line SE of size 1×21 elements, shows that indeed this is case.

All that remains at this point is to restore the suppressed characters. Consider an image formed as the point-wise minimum between the dilated image in Fig. 9.46(g) and the top-hat by reconstruction in Fig. 9.46(d). Figure 9.46(h) shows the minimum image (although this result appears to be close to our objective, note that the I in SIN is still missing). By using this image as a marker and the dilated image as the mask in grayscale reconstruction [Eq. (9-67)], we obtained the final result in Fig. 9.46(i). This image shows that all characters were properly extracted from the original, irregular background, including the background of the keys. The background in Fig. 9.46(i) is uniform throughout.

Summary, References, and Further Reading

The morphological concepts and techniques introduced in this chapter constitute a powerful set of tools for extracting features of interest in an image. One of the most appealing aspects of morphological image processing is the extensive set-theoretic foundation from which morphological techniques have evolved. A significant advantage in terms of implementation is that dilation and erosion are primitive operations, which are the basis for a broad class of morphological algorithms. As will be shown in the following chapter, morphology can be used as the basis for developing image segmentation procedures with numerous applications. As we will discuss in Chapter 11, morphological techniques also play a major role in procedures for image feature extraction.

The book by Serra [1982] is a fundamental reference on morphological image processing. See also Serra [1988], Giardina and Dougherty [1988], and Haralick and Shapiro [1992]. For an overview of both binary and gray-scale morphology, see Basart and Gonzalez [1992] and Basart et al. [1992]. This set of references provides ample basic background for the material covered in Sections 9.1 through 9.4. For a good overview of the material in Sections 9.5 and 9.6, see the book by Soille [2003].

Important issues of implementing morphological algorithms such as the ones given in Section 9.5 and 9.6 are exemplified in the papers by Jones and Svalbe [1994], Sussner and Ritter [1997], and Shaked and Bruckstein [1998]. A paper by Vincent [1993] is especially important in terms of practical details for implementing gray-scale morphological algorithms. For additional reading on the theory and applications of morphological image processing, see the books by Goutsias and Bloomberg [2000], and by Beyerer et al. [2016]. To get an idea of the state of the art in fast computer implementation of morphological algorithms, see Thurley and Danell [2012]. For details on the software aspects of many of the examples in this chapter, see Gonzalez, Woods, and Eddins [2009].

Problems

Solutions to the problems marked with an asterisk (*) are in the DIP4E Student Support Package (consult the book website: www.ImageProcessingPlace.com).

9.1 Find the reflection, $\hat{B}$, of each of the following structuring elements. The dot indicates the origin of the SE.

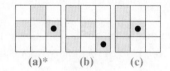

(a)*   **(b)**   **(c)**

9.2 Sketch the result of eroding Fig. 9.3(a) with each of the following structuring elements.

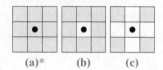

(a)*   **(b)**   **(c)**

9.3* Eq. (9-3) expresses the erosion of a set A of foreground pixels by structuring element B. Write an equivalent expression that represents erosion in terms of background of A.

9.4 Let f be a grayscale image, and let b be a flat structuring element.

    (a)* What do you think would happen if we erode f by b?

    (b) What do you think would happen if we dilate f by b?

9.5 You are given a "black-box" function that computes erosion. You are told that this function automatically pads the input image with a border whose width is the thinnest border possible, as determined by the dimensions of the structuring element (e.g., for a 3×3 structuring element the border would be one pixel wide). However, you are not told whether the padding is composed of background (0) or foreground (1) values. Propose an experiment for answering this question.

9.6 Do the following:

    (a)* Dilate Fig. 9.3(a) using the structuring element in figure (a) of Problem 9.2.

    (b) Repeat (a) using the structuring element in figure (b).

    (c) Repeat (a) using the structuring element in figure (c).

9.7 In context of erosion and dilation, how is duality property useful when the values of structuring element are symmetric with respect to its origin?

9.8 With reference to the image at the top of the figure shown below, answer the following:

    (a)* Give the structuring element and morphological operation(s) that produced image (a). Show the origin of the structuring element. The dashed lines denote the boundary of the original object and are shown for reference; they are not part of the result. (The white elements are foreground pixels.)

    (b) Repeat part (a) for the output shown in image (b).

    (c)* Repeat part (a) for the output shown in image (c).

    (d) Repeat part (a) for the solution shown in figure (d). Note that in image (d) all corners are rounded.

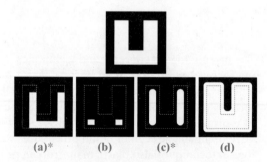

(a)*   **(b)**   **(c)***   **(d)**

9.9 Let A denote the set shown shaded in the following figure, and refer to the structuring elements shown (the black dots denote the origin). Sketch the result of the following operations:

    (a)* $\left(A \ominus B^4 \right) \oplus B^2$.

    (b) $\left(A \ominus B^1 \right) \oplus B^3$.

    (c) $\left(A \oplus B^3 \right) \ominus B^2$

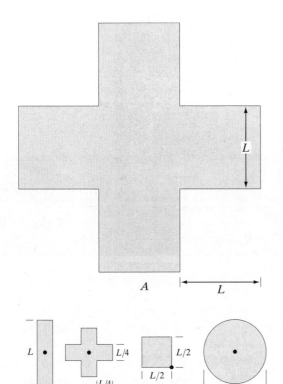

A L

L $\bullet$ $|L/4|$ B^1

$\bullet$ $L/4$ $|L/4|$ B^2

$\bullet$ $L/2$ $|L/2|$ B^3

$\bullet$ L B^4

9.10 Be specific in answering the following:

(a)* What is the difference between dilation and convolution?

(b) How is dilation different from erosion?

9.11 Be specific in answering the following:

(a) Assuming that a trivial (one point) structuring element is not used, how can you erode an image to one element?

(b) What should be the size of the starting image to erode the image to one element?

9.12* An alternative definition of erosion is

$$A \ominus B = \left\{ w \in Z^2 \,|\, w + b \in A \text{ for every } b \in B \right\}$$

Show that this definition is equivalent to the definition in Eq. (9-3).

9.13 Do the following:

(a) Show that the definition of erosion given in Problem 9.12 is equivalent to yet another definition of erosion:

$$A \ominus B = \bigcap_{b \in B} (A)_{-b}$$

(If $-b$ is replaced with b, this expression is called the *Minkowsky subtraction* of two sets.)

(b)* Show that the expression in (a) is equivalent to the definition in Eq. (9-3).

9.14* An alternative definition of dilation is

$$A \oplus B = \left\{ w \in Z^2 \,|\, w = a + b, \text{ for some } a \in A \text{ and } b \in B \right\}$$

Show that this definition and the definition in Eq. (9-6) are equivalent.

9.15 Do the following:

(a) Show that the definition of dilation given in Problem 9.14 is equivalent to yet another definition of dilation:

$$A \oplus B = \bigcup_{b \in B} (A)_b$$

(This expression is called the *Minkowsky addition* of two sets.)

(b)* Show that the expression in (a) is equivalent also to the definition in Eq. (9-6).

9.16 Prove the validity of the duality expression given in Eq. (9-9).

9.17 Answer the following:

(a)* The curved portions the black border of Fig. 9.8(d) delineate the opening of set A in Fig. 9.8(a), but those curved segments are not part of the boundary of A. Are the black straight-line portions in (d) part of the boundary of A? Explain.

(b) The curved portions the black border of Fig. 9.9(d) delineate the closing of set A in Fig. 9.9(a), but those curved segments are not part of the boundary of A. Are the black straight line portions of the boundary in (d) part of the boundary of A? Explain.

9.18 Show all intermediate steps of your computations for the following:

(a)* Obtain the opening of the figure below using a 3×3 SE of 1's. Do all operations manually.

(b) Repeat (a) for the closing operation.

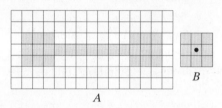

A

B

9.19 A is a solid rectangle of 1's of size $M \times N$ with a 1-pixel border of 0's, and m and n below are odd integers. Discuss what the result will be in each case.

(a)*A is opened with a structuring element of 1's of size $m \times n$.

(b) A is closed with a structuring element of 1's of size $m \times n$.

9.20 Show the validity of the following duality expressions [these are Eqs. (9-14) and (9-15)]:

(a)* $(A \circ B)^c = A^c \bullet \hat{B}$.

(b) $(A \bullet B)^c = A^c \circ \hat{B}$.

9.21 Answer the following:

(a)* Define the opening morphological operation.

(b)* List its three properties.

(c) Prove the validity of its properties.

9.22 Answer the following:

(a) Define the closing morphological operation.

(b) List its three properties.

(c) Prove the validity of its properties.

9.23 Consider the three binary images shown in the following figure. The image on the left is composed of squares of sizes 1, 3, 5, 7, 9, and 15 pixels on the side. The image in the middle was generated by eroding the image on the left with a square structuring element of 1s, of size 13×13 pixels, with the objective of eliminating all the squares, except the largest ones. Finally, the image on the right is

the result of dilating the image in the center with the same structuring, with the objective of restoring the largest squares. You know that erosion followed by dilation is the opening of an image, and you know also that opening generally does not restore objects to their original form. Explain why full reconstruction of the large squares was possible in this case.

9.24* Assume that SE B_2 in Fig. 9.12 has a border of foreground pixels that is more than one pixel wide. Assuming that all four sides of the border are the same, what is the maximum width of a border we can use around B_2 before the solution shown in Fig. 9.12(f) fails?

9.25 We mentioned when discussing Fig. 9.12(e) that the image had been cropped for consistency. Assume that Fig. 9.12(b) was padded with the minimum border required to encompass the maximum excursions of B_2 after which no further changes would occur in the erosion. What did Fig. 9.12(e) look like before it was cropped?

9.26 Sketch the result of applying the hit-or-miss transform to the image below, using the SE shown. Indicate clearly the origin and border you select for the structuring element.

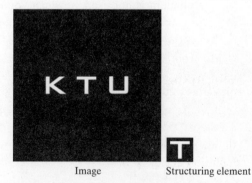

Image   Structuring element

9.27* Give the foundation of an algorithm for converting an 8-connected, closed curve to a 4-connected curve (see Section 2.5 regarding connectivity). The input is a binary image, I, in which the curve consists of 1-valued pixels embedded in a background of 0's. The output should be a binary image also, containing the new curve. You may assume that the curve is fully connected, is one pixel thick, and has no branches. You do not need to (but you may) state the algorithm in a step-by-step manner. An overall plan containing all the information needed to implement a working algorithm is sufficient.

9.28 Give the foundation of an algorithm for converting a 4-connected closed curve to a curve containing *only* 8-connected pixels (see Section 2.5 regarding connectivity). The input is a binary image, I, in which the curve consists of 1-valued pixels embedded in a background of 0's. The output should be a binary image also, containing the new curve. You may assume that the curve is fully connected, it is one-pixel-wide, and has no branches. You do not need to (but you may) state the algorithm in a step-by-step manner. An overall plan containing all the information needed to implement a working algorithm is sufficient.

9.29 Give the foundation of an algorithm for converting an 8-connected closed curve to an *m*-connected curve (see Section 2.5 regarding connectivity). The input is a binary image, I, in which the curve consists of 1-valued pixels embedded in a background of 0's. The output should be a binary image also, containing the new curve. You may assume that the curve is fully connected, it is one-pixel-wide, and has no branches. You do not need to (but you may) state the algorithm in a step-by-step manner. An overall plan containing all the information needed to implement a working algorithm is sufficient.

9.30* Three curve types (lake, bay, and line segment) useful for differentiating thinned objects in an image are shown in the following figure. Develop a morphological/logical algorithm for differentiating between these shapes. The input to your algorithm would be one of these three curves. The output must be the type of the input. You may assume that the curves are 1 pixel thick and are fully connected. They can appear in any orientation.

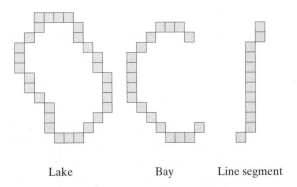

Lake   Bay   Line segment

9.31 How can you extract the boundary of a set A of foreground pixels? Give an expression for the same.

9.32 Answer the following:

(a)* Discuss the effect of using the structuring element in Fig. 9.17(c) for boundary extraction, instead of the element in Fig. 9.15(b).

(b) What would be the effect of using a 3×3 structuring element composed of all 1's in the hole filling algorithm of Eq. (9-19), instead of the structuring element in Fig. 9.17(c)?

9.33 Discuss what you would expect the result to be in each of the following cases:

(a)* The starting point of the hole filling algorithm of Eq. (9-19) is a point *on* the outer boundary of the object containing the hole.

(b) The starting point in the hole filling algorithm is *outside* of the boundary (i.e., the starting point is a background pixel).

9.34 Sketch the convex hull of the large figure in Problem 9.9. Assume that $L = 3$ pixels.

9.35 Obtain the convex deficiency of set A shown in Fig. 9.21(b). Use the convex hull in Fig. 9.22(a).

9.36 Do the following:

(a)* Propose a method using any of the methods developed in this chapter for automating the example in Fig. 9.18. You may assume that the spheres do not touch each other and that none touch the border of the image.

(b) Repeat (a), but allowing the spheres to touch in arbitrary ways, including the border.

9.37* The algorithm for extracting connected components discussed in Section 9.5 requires that a point be known in each connected component in order to extract them all. Suppose that you are given a binary image containing an arbitrary (unknown) number of connected components. Propose a completely automated procedure for extracting all connected components. Assume that points belonging to connected components are labeled 1 and background points are labeled 0.

9.38 How does the morphological transformation called morphological reconstruction function?

9.39 With reference to the hole-filling algorithm in Eqs. (9-45) and (9-46):

(a)* Explain what would happen if all border points of I are 1 (foreground).

(b) If the result in (a) gives the result that you would expect, explain why. If it does not, explain how you would modify the algorithm so that it works as expected.

9.40* What do opening by reconstruction and closing by reconstruction in morphological reconstruction by erosion?

9.41 Show that geodesic erosion and dilation (Section 9.6) are duals with respect to set complementation. That is, assuming that the structuring element is symmetric about its origin, show that:

(a)* $E_G^{(n)}(F) = \left[D_{G^c}^{(1)} \left[D_{G^c}^{(n-1)}(F^c) \right] \right]^c$ and, conversely, that

(b) $D_G^{(n)}(F) = \left[E_{G^c}^{(1)} \left[E_{G^c}^{(n-1)}(F^c) \right] \right]^c$.

(*Hint:* Use proof by induction.)

9.42 Show that reconstruction by dilation and reconstruction by erosion (Section 9.6) are duals with respect to set complementation. That is, assuming that the structuring element is symmetric about its origin, show that $R_G^D(F) = \left[R_{G^c}^E(F^c) \right]^c$ and, conversely, that $R_G^E(F) = \left[R_{G^c}^D(F^c) \right]^c$. (*Hint:* Consider using the results from Problem 9.41.)

9.43 Show that:

(a)* $(F \ominus nB)^c = F^c \oplus n\hat{B}$, where $F \ominus nB$ indicates n successive erosions, starting with B; and similarly, that

(b) $(F \oplus nB)^c = F^c \ominus n\hat{B}$.

9.44 Show the validity of the following binary morphological expressions. You may assume that the structuring element is symmetric about its origin.

(a)* $O_R^{(n)}(F) = \left[C_R^{(n)}(F^c) \right]^c$.

(b) $C_R^{(n)}(F) = \left[O_R^{(n)}(F^c) \right]^c$.

9.45 Prove the validity of the following grayscale morphological expressions. Recall from the discussion in Section 9.8 that $f^c(x, y) = -f(x, y)$ and that $\hat{b}(x, y) = b(-x, -y)$.

(a)* $(f \ominus b) = f^c \oplus \hat{b}$.

(b) $(f \oplus b)^c = f^c \ominus \hat{b}$.

(c) $(f \cdot b)^c = f^c \circ \hat{b}$.

(d)* $(f \circ b)^c = f^c \cdot \hat{b}$.

9.46 Prove the validity of the following grayscale morphological expressions. Recall that $f^c(x, y) = -f(x, y)$ and that $\hat{b}(x, y) = b(-x, -y)$. (*Hint:* Use proof by induction.)

(a)* $D_g^{(n)}(f) = \left[E_{g^c}^{(1)} [E_{g^c}^{(n-1)}(f^c)] \right]^c$. Assume a symmetric structuring element.

(b) $E_g^{(n)}(f) = \left[D_{g^c}^{(1)} [D_{g^c}^{(n-1)}(f^c)] \right]^c$. Assume a symmetric structuring element.

9.47 Prove the validity of the following grayscale morphological expressions.

(a)* $R_g^D(f) = \left[R_{g^c}^E(f^c) \right]^c$.

(b) $R_g^E(f) = \left[R_{g^c}^D(f^c) \right]^c$.

9.48 Prove the validity of the following grayscale morphological expressions.

(a)* $(f \ominus nb)^c = \left(f^c \oplus n\hat{b} \right)$, where $(f \ominus nb)$ indicates n successive erosions, starting with b.

(b) $(f \oplus nb)^c = \left(f^c \ominus n\hat{b} \right)$.

9.49 Prove the validity of the following grayscale morphological expressions. Recall that $f^c(x, y) = -f(x, y)$ and that $\hat{b}(x, y) = b(-x, -y)$. Assume a symmetric structuring element.

(a)* $O_R^{(n)}(f) = \left[C_R^{(n)}(f^c) \right]^c$.

(b) $C_R^{(n)}(f) = \left[O_R^{(n)}(f^c) \right]^c$.

9.50 Consider the image below, which shows a region of small circles enclosed by a region of larger circles.

(a) Would you expect the method used to generate Fig. 9.45(d) to work with this image also? Explain your reasoning, including any assumptions that you need to make for the method to work.

(b)* If your answer to (a) is yes, sketch what the boundary will look like.

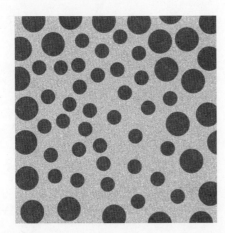

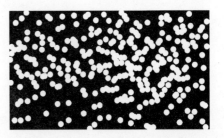

9.51 A preprocessing step in an application of microscopy is concerned with the issue of isolating individual round particles from similar particles that overlap in groups of two or more particles (see the following image). Assuming that all particles are of the same size, propose a morphological algorithm that produces three images consisting respectively of:

(a)* Only particles that have merged with the boundary of the image.

(b) Only overlapping particles.

(c) Only nonoverlapping particles.

9.52 A high-technology manufacturing plant is awarded a government contract to manufacture high-precision washers of the form shown. The terms of the contract require that the shape of all washers be inspected by an imaging system. In this context, shape inspection refers to deviations from round on the inner and outer edges of the washers. You may assume the following: (1) A "golden" (perfect with respect to the problem) image of an acceptable washer is available; and (2) the imaging and positioning components ultimately used in the system will have an accuracy high enough to allow you to ignore errors due to digitalization and positioning. You are hired as a consultant to help specify the visual inspection part of the system. Propose a solution based on morphological/logical operations.

10

Image Segmentation

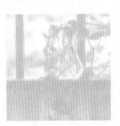

The whole is equal to the sum of its parts.

Euclid

The whole is greater than the sum of its parts.

Max Wertheimer

Preview

The material in the previous chapter began a transition from image processing methods whose inputs and outputs are images, to methods in which the inputs are images but the outputs are attributes extracted from those images. Most of the segmentation algorithms in this chapter are based on one of two basic properties of image intensity values: *discontinuity* and *similarity*. In the first category, the approach is to partition an image into regions based on abrupt changes in intensity, such as edges. Approaches in the second category are based on partitioning an image into regions that are similar according to a set of predefined criteria. Thresholding, region growing, and region splitting and merging are examples of methods in this category. We show that improvements in segmentation performance can be achieved by combining methods from distinct categories, such as techniques in which edge detection is combined with thresholding. We discuss also image segmentation using clustering and superpixels, and give an introduction to graph cuts, an approach ideally suited for extracting the principal regions of an image. This is followed by a discussion of image segmentation based on morphology, an approach that combines several of the attributes of segmentation based on the techniques presented in the first part of the chapter. We conclude the chapter with a brief discussion on the use of motion cues for segmentation.

Upon completion of this chapter, readers should:

■ Understand the characteristics of various types of edges found in practice.

■ Understand how to use spatial filtering for edge detection.

■ Be familiar with other types of edge detection methods that go beyond spatial filtering.

■ Understand image thresholding using several different approaches.

■ Know how to combine thresholding and spatial filtering to improve segmentation.

■ Be familiar with region-based segmentation, including clustering and superpixels.

■ Understand how graph cuts and morphological watersheds are used for segmentation.

■ Be familiar with basic techniques for utilizing motion in image segmentation.

10.1 FUNDAMENTALS

Let R represent the entire spatial region occupied by an image. We may view image segmentation as a process that partitions R into n subregions, $R_1, R_2, \ldots, R_n$, such that

(a) $\displaystyle\bigcup_{i=1}^{n} R_i = R.$

(b) R_i is a connected set, for $i = 0, 1, 2, \ldots, n.$

(c) $R_i \cap R_j = \varnothing$ for all i and j, $i \neq j.$

(d) $Q(R_i) = \text{TRUE}$ for $i = 0, 1, 2, \ldots, n.$

(e) $Q(R_i \cup R_j) = \text{FALSE}$ for any adjacent regions R_i and R_j.

where $Q(R_k)$ is a logical predicate defined over the points in set R_k, and $\varnothing$ is the null set. The symbols $\cup$ and $\cap$ represent set union and intersection, respectively, as defined in Section 2.6. Two regions R_i and R_j are said to be *adjacent* if their union forms a connected set, as defined in Section 2.5. If the set formed by the union of two regions is not connected, the regions are said to *disjoint*.

Condition (a) indicates that the segmentation must be *complete*, in the sense that every pixel must be in a region. Condition (b) requires that points in a region be connected in some predefined sense (e.g., the points must be 8-connected). Condition (c) says that the regions must be disjoint. Condition (d) deals with the properties that must be satisfied by the pixels in a segmented region—for example, $Q(R_i) = \text{TRUE}$ if all pixels in R_i have the same intensity. Finally, condition (e) indicates that two adjacent regions R_i and R_j must be different in the sense of predicate Q.[†]

Thus, we see that the fundamental problem in segmentation is to partition an image into regions that satisfy the preceding conditions. Segmentation algorithms for monochrome images generally are based on one of two basic categories dealing with properties of intensity values: *discontinuity* and *similarity*. In the first category, we assume that boundaries of regions are sufficiently different from each other, and from the background, to allow boundary detection based on local discontinuities in intensity. *Edge-based* segmentation is the principal approach used in this category. *Region-based* segmentation approaches in the second category are based on partitioning an image into regions that are similar according to a set of predefined criteria.

Figure 10.1 illustrates the preceding concepts. Figure 10.1(a) shows an image of a region of constant intensity superimposed on a darker background, also of constant intensity. These two regions comprise the overall image. Figure 10.1(b) shows the result of computing the boundary of the inner region based on intensity discontinuities. Points on the inside and outside of the boundary are black (zero) because there are no discontinuities in intensity in those regions. To segment the image, we assign one level (say, white) to the pixels on or inside the boundary, and another level (e.g., black) to all points exterior to the boundary. Figure 10.1(c) shows the result of such a procedure. We see that conditions (a) through (c) stated at the beginning of this

---

[†] In general, Q can be a compound expression such as, "$Q(R_i) = \text{TRUE}$ if the average intensity of the pixels in region R_i is less than m_i AND if the standard deviation of their intensity is greater than σ_i," where m_i and σ_i are specified constants.

a b c
d e f

FIGURE 10.1
(a) Image of a constant intensity region.
(b) Boundary based on intensity discontinuities.
(c) Result of segmentation.
(d) Image of a texture region.
(e) Result of intensity discontinuity computations (note the large number of small edges).
(f) Result of segmentation based on region properties.

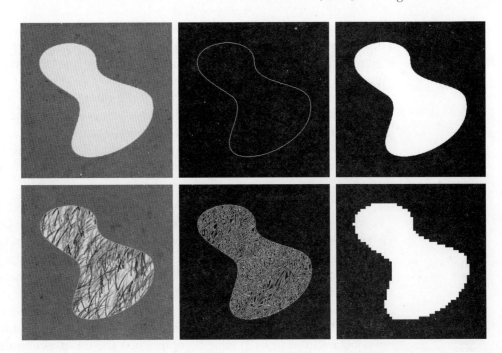

section are satisfied by this result. The predicate of condition (d) is: If a pixel is on, or inside the boundary, label it white; otherwise, label it black. We see that this predicate is TRUE for the points labeled black or white in Fig. 10.1(c). Similarly, the two segmented regions (object and background) satisfy condition (e).

The next three images illustrate region-based segmentation. Figure 10.1(d) is similar to Fig. 10.1(a), but the intensities of the inner region form a textured pattern. Figure 10.1(e) shows the result of computing intensity discontinuities in this image. The numerous spurious changes in intensity make it difficult to identify a unique boundary for the original image because many of the nonzero intensity changes are connected to the boundary, so edge-based segmentation is not a suitable approach. However, we note that the outer region is constant, so all we need to solve this segmentation problem is a predicate that differentiates between textured and constant regions. The standard deviation of pixel values is a measure that accomplishes this because it is nonzero in areas of the texture region, and zero otherwise. Figure 10.1(f) shows the result of dividing the original image into subregions of size 8×8. Each subregion was then labeled white if the standard deviation of its pixels was positive (i.e., if the predicate was TRUE), and zero otherwise. The result has a "blocky" appearance around the edge of the region because groups of 8×8 squares were labeled with the same intensity (smaller squares would have given a smoother region boundary). Finally, note that these results also satisfy the five segmentation conditions stated at the beginning of this section.

10.2 POINT, LINE, AND EDGE DETECTION

The focus of this section is on segmentation methods that are based on detecting sharp, *local* changes in intensity. The three types of image characteristics in which

When we refer to lines, we are referring to thin structures, typically just a few pixels thick. Such lines may correspond, for example, to elements of a digitized architectural drawing, or roads in a satellite image.

we are interested are isolated points, lines, and edges. *Edge pixels* are pixels at which the intensity of an image changes abruptly, and *edges* (or *edge segments*) are sets of connected edge pixels (see Section 2.5 regarding connectivity). *Edge detectors* are local image processing tools designed to detect edge pixels. A *line* may be viewed as a (typically) thin edge segment in which the intensity of the background on either side of the line is either much higher or much lower than the intensity of the line pixels. In fact, as we will discuss later, lines give rise to so-called "roof edges." Finally, an *isolated point* may be viewed as a foreground (background) pixel surrounded by background (foreground) pixels.

BACKGROUND

As we saw in Section 3.5, local averaging smoothes an image. Given that averaging is analogous to integration, it is intuitive that abrupt, local changes in intensity can be detected using derivatives. For reasons that will become evident shortly, first- and second-order derivatives are particularly well suited for this purpose.

Derivatives of a digital function are defined in terms of *finite differences*. There are various ways to compute these differences but, as explained in Section 3.6, we require that any approximation used for first derivatives (1) must be zero in areas of constant intensity; (2) must be nonzero at the onset of an intensity step or ramp; and (3) must be nonzero at points along an intensity ramp. Similarly, we require that an approximation used for second derivatives (1) must be zero in areas of constant intensity; (2) must be nonzero at the onset and end of an intensity step or ramp; and (3) must be zero along intensity ramps. Because we are dealing with digital quantities whose values are finite, the maximum possible intensity change is also finite, and the shortest distance over which a change can occur is between adjacent pixels.

We obtain an approximation to the first-order derivative at an arbitrary point x of a one-dimensional function $f(x)$ by expanding the function $f(x + \Delta x)$ into a Taylor series about x

Remember, the notation $n!$ means "n factorial": $n! = 1 \times 2 \times \cdots \times n$.

$$f(x + \Delta x) = f(x) + \Delta x \frac{\partial f(x)}{\partial x} + \frac{(\Delta x)^2}{2!} \frac{\partial^2 f(x)}{\partial x^2} + \frac{(\Delta x)^3}{3!} \frac{\partial^3 f(x)}{\partial x^3} + \cdots \cdots$$

$$= \sum_{n=0}^{\infty} \frac{(\Delta x)^n}{n!} \frac{\partial^n f(x)}{\partial x^n}$$

(10-1)

where Δx is the separation between samples of f. For our purposes, this separation is measured in pixel units. Thus, following the convention in the book, $\Delta x = 1$ for the sample preceding x and $\Delta x = -1$ for the sample following x. When $\Delta x = 1$, Eq. (10-1) becomes

Although this is an expression of only one variable, we used partial derivatives notation for consistency when we discuss functions of two variables later in this section.

$$f(x + 1) = f(x) + \frac{\partial f(x)}{\partial x} + \frac{1}{2!} \frac{\partial^2 f(x)}{\partial x^2} + \frac{1}{3!} \frac{\partial^3 f(x)}{\partial x^3} + \cdots \cdots$$

$$= \sum_{n=0}^{\infty} \frac{1}{n!} \frac{\partial^n f(x)}{\partial x^n}$$

(10-2)

Similarly, when $\Delta x = -1$,

$$f(x-1) = f(x) - \frac{\partial f(x)}{\partial x} + \frac{1}{2!}\frac{\partial^2 f(x)}{\partial x^2} - \frac{1}{3!}\frac{\partial^3 f(x)}{\partial x^3} + \cdots\cdots$$
$$= \sum_{n=0}^{\infty} \frac{(-1)^n}{n!}\frac{\partial^n f(x)}{\partial x^n} \tag{10-3}$$

In what follows, we compute *intensity differences* using just a few terms of the Taylor series. For first-order derivatives we use only the linear terms, and we can form differences in one of three ways.

The *forward difference* is obtained from Eq. (10-2):

$$\frac{\partial f(x)}{\partial x} = f'(x) = f(x+1) - f(x) \tag{10-4}$$

where, as you can see, we kept only the linear terms. The *backward difference* is similarly obtained by keeping only the linear terms in Eq. (10-3):

$$\frac{\partial f(x)}{\partial x} = f'(x) = f(x) - f(x-1) \tag{10-5}$$

and the *central difference* is obtained by subtracting Eq. (10-3) from Eq. (10-2):

$$\frac{\partial f(x)}{\partial x} = f'(x) = \frac{f(x+1) - f(x-1)}{2} \tag{10-6}$$

The higher terms of the series that we did not use represent the error between an exact and an approximate derivative expansion. In general, the more terms we use from the Taylor series to represent a derivative, the more accurate the approximation will be. To include more terms implies that more points are used in the approximation, yielding a lower error. However, it turns out that central differences have a lower error for the same number of points (see Problem 10.1). For this reason, derivatives are usually expressed as central differences.

The *second order* derivative based on a central difference, $\partial^2 f(x)/\partial x^2$, is obtained by adding Eqs. (10-2) and (10-3):

$$\frac{\partial^2 f(x)}{\partial x^2} = f''(x) = f(x+1) - 2f(x) + f(x-1) \tag{10-7}$$

To obtain the *third order, central derivative* we need one more point on either side of x. That is, we need the Taylor expansions for $f(x+2)$ and $f(x-2)$, which we obtain from Eqs. (10-2) and (10-3) with $\Delta x = 2$ and $\Delta x = -2$, respectively. The strategy is to combine the two Taylor expansions to eliminate all derivatives lower than the third. The result after ignoring all higher-order terms [see Problem 10.2(a)] is

$$\frac{\partial^3 f(x)}{\partial x^3} = f'''(x) = \frac{f(x+2) - 2f(x+1) + 0f(x) + 2f(x-1) - f(x-2)}{2} \quad (10\text{-}8)$$

Similarly [see Problem 10.2(b)], the *fourth* finite difference (the highest we use in the book) after ignoring all higher order terms is given by

$$\frac{\partial^4 f(x)}{\partial x^4} = f''''(x) = f(x+2) - 4f(x+1) + 6f(x) - 4f(x-1) + f(x-2) \quad (10\text{-}9)$$

Table 10.1 summarizes the first four central derivatives just discussed. Note the symmetry of the coefficients about the center point. This symmetry is at the root of why central differences have a lower approximation error for the same number of points than the other two differences. For two variables, we apply the results in Table 10.1 to each variable independently. For example,

$$\frac{\partial^2 f(x,y)}{\partial x^2} = f(x+1,y) - 2f(x,y) + f(x-1,y) \quad (10\text{-}10)$$

and

$$\frac{\partial^2 f(x,y)}{\partial y^2} = f(x,y+1) - 2f(x,y) + f(x,y-1) \quad (10\text{-}11)$$

It is easily verified that the first and second-order derivatives in Eqs. (10-4) through (10-7) satisfy the conditions stated at the beginning of this section regarding derivatives of the first and second order. To illustrate this, consider Fig. 10.2. Part (a) shows an image of various objects, a line, and an isolated point. Figure 10.2(b) shows a horizontal intensity profile (scan line) through the center of the image, including the isolated point. Transitions in intensity between the solid objects and the background along the scan line show two types of edges: *ramp edges* (on the left) and *step edges* (on the right). As we will discuss later, intensity transitions involving thin objects such as lines often are referred to as *roof edges*.

Figure 10.2(c) shows a simplified profile, with just enough points to make it possible for us to analyze manually how the first- and second-order derivatives behave as they encounter a point, a line, and the edges of objects. In this diagram the transition

TABLE 10.1

First four central digital derivatives (finite differences) for samples taken uniformly, $\Delta x = 1$ units apart.

	$f(x+2)$	$f(x+1)$	$f(x)$	$f(x-1)$	$f(x-2)$
$2f'(x)$		1	0	-1	
$f''(x)$		1	-2	1	
$2f'''(x)$	1	-2	0	2	-1
$f''''(x)$	1	-4	6	-4	1

a b
c

FIGURE 10.2
(a) Image.
(b) Horizontal
intensity profile
that includes the
isolated point
indicated by the
arrow.
(c) Subsampled
profile; the dashes
were added
for clarity. The
numbers in the
boxes are the
intensity values
of the dots shown
in the profile. The
derivatives were
obtained using
Eqs. (10-4) for the
first derivative
and Eq. (10-7) for
the second.

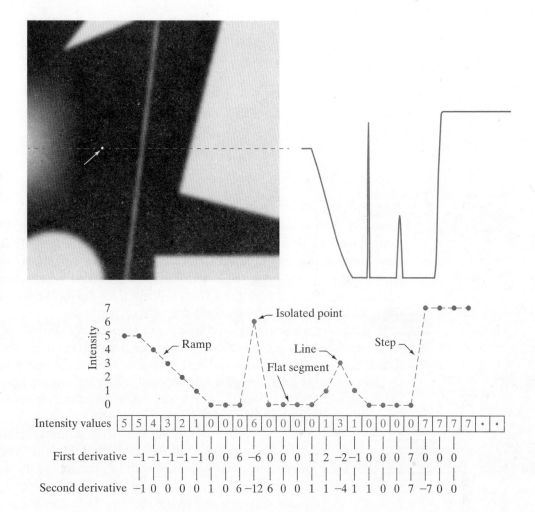

in the ramp spans four pixels, the noise point is a single pixel, the line is three pixels thick, and the transition of the step edge takes place between adjacent pixels. The number of intensity levels was limited to eight for simplicity.

Consider the properties of the first and second derivatives as we traverse the profile from left to right. Initially, the first-order derivative is nonzero at the onset and along the entire intensity ramp, while the second-order derivative is nonzero only at the onset and end of the ramp. Because the edges of digital images resemble this type of transition, we conclude that first-order derivatives produce "thick" edges, and second-order derivatives much thinner ones. Next we encounter the isolated noise point. Here, the magnitude of the response at the point is much stronger for the second- than for the first-order derivative. This is not unexpected, because a second-order derivative is much more aggressive than a first-order derivative in enhancing sharp changes. Thus, we can expect second-order derivatives to enhance fine detail (including noise) much more than first-order derivatives. The line in this example is rather thin, so it too is fine detail, and we see again that the second derivative has a larger magnitude. Finally, note in both the ramp and step edges that the

FIGURE 10.3
A general 3×3
spatial filter
kernel. The w's
are the kernel
coefficients
(weights).

w_1	w_2	w_3
w_4	w_5	w_6
w_7	w_8	w_9

second derivative has opposite signs (negative to positive or positive to negative) as it transitions into and out of an edge. This "double-edge" effect is an important characteristic that can be used to locate edges, as we will show later in this section. As we move into the edge, the sign of the second derivative is used also to determine whether an edge is a transition from light to dark (negative second derivative), or from dark to light (positive second derivative)

In summary, we arrive at the following conclusions: (1) First-order derivatives generally produce thicker edges. (2) Second-order derivatives have a stronger response to fine detail, such as thin lines, isolated points, and noise. (3) Second-order derivatives produce a double-edge response at ramp and step transitions in intensity. (4) The sign of the second derivative can be used to determine whether a transition into an edge is from light to dark or dark to light.

The approach of choice for computing first and second derivatives at every pixel location in an image is to use spatial convolution. For the 3×3 filter kernel in Fig. 10.3, the procedure is to compute the sum of products of the kernel coefficients with the intensity values in the region encompassed by the kernel, as we explained in Section 3.4. That is, the response of the filter at the center point of the kernel is

This equation is an expansion of Eq. (3-35) for a 3×3 kernel, valid at one point, and using simplified subscript notation for the kernel coefficients.

$$Z = w_1 z_1 + w_2 z_2 + \ldots + w_9 z_9$$
$$= \sum_{k=1}^{9} w_k z_k \tag{10-12}$$

where z_k is the intensity of the pixel whose spatial location corresponds to the location of the kth kernel coefficient.

DETECTION OF ISOLATED POINTS

Based on the conclusions reached in the preceding section, we know that point detection should be based on the second derivative which, from the discussion in Section 3.6, means using the Laplacian:

$$\nabla^2 f(x, y) = \frac{\partial^2 f}{\partial x^2} + \frac{\partial^2 f}{\partial y^2} \tag{10-13}$$

where the partial derivatives are computed using the second-order finite differences in Eqs. (10-10) and (10-11). The Laplacian is then

$$\nabla^2 f(x,y) = f(x+1,y) + f(x-1,y) + f(x,y+1) + f(x,y-1) - 4f(x,y) \quad (10\text{-}14)$$

As explained in Section 3.6, this expression can be implemented using the Laplacian kernel in Fig. 10.4(a) in Example 10.1. We then we say that a point has been detected at a location (x,y) on which the kernel is centered if the absolute value of the response of the filter at that point exceeds a specified threshold. Such points are labeled 1 and all others are labeled 0 in the output image, thus producing a binary image. In other words, we use the expression:

$$g(x,y) = \begin{cases} 1 & \text{if } |Z(x,y)| > T \\ 0 & \text{otherwise} \end{cases} \quad (10\text{-}15)$$

where $g(x,y)$ is the output image, T is a nonnegative threshold, and Z is given by Eq. (10-12). This formulation simply measures the weighted differences between a pixel and its 8-neighbors. Intuitively, the idea is that the intensity of an isolated point will be quite different from its surroundings, and thus will be easily detectable by this type of kernel. Differences in intensity that are considered of interest are those large enough (as determined by T) to be considered isolated points. Note that, as usual for a derivative kernel, the coefficients sum to zero, indicating that the filter response will be zero in areas of constant intensity.

EXAMPLE 10.1: Detection of isolated points in an image.

Figure 10.4(b) is an X-ray image of a turbine blade from a jet engine. The blade has a porosity manifested by a single black pixel in the upper-right quadrant of the image. Figure 10.4(c) is the result of filtering the image with the Laplacian kernel, and Fig. 10.4(d) shows the result of Eq. (10-15) with T equal to 90% of the highest absolute pixel value of the image in Fig. 10.4(c). The single pixel is clearly visible in this image at the tip of the arrow (the pixel was enlarged to enhance its visibility). This type of detection process is specialized because it is based on abrupt intensity changes at single-pixel locations that are surrounded by a homogeneous background in the area of the detector kernel. When this condition is not satisfied, other methods discussed in this chapter are more suitable for detecting intensity changes.

LINE DETECTION

The next level of complexity is line detection. Based on the discussion earlier in this section, we know that for line detection we can expect second derivatives to result in a stronger filter response, and to produce thinner lines than first derivatives. Thus, we can use the Laplacian kernel in Fig. 10.4(a) for line detection also, keeping in mind that the double-line effect of the second derivative must be handled properly. The following example illustrates the procedure.

FIGURE 10.4
(a) Laplacian kernel used for point detection.
(b) X-ray image of a turbine blade with a porosity manifested by a single black pixel.
(c) Result of convolving the kernel with the image.
(d) Result of using Eq. (10-15) was a single point (shown enlarged at the tip of the arrow). (Original image courtesy of X-TEK Systems, Ltd.)

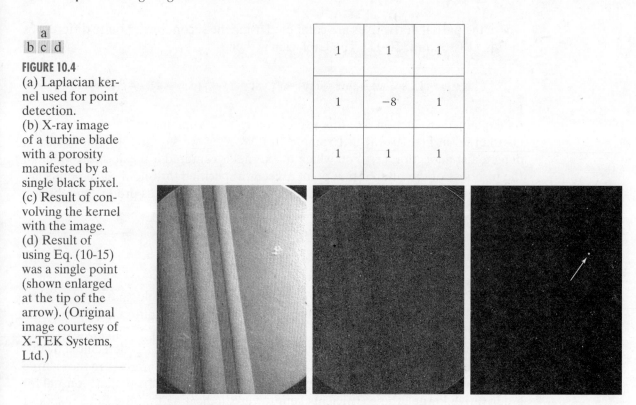

EXAMPLE 10.2: Using the Laplacian for line detection.

Figure 10.5(a) shows a 486×486 (binary) portion of a wire-bond mask for an electronic circuit, and Fig. 10.5(b) shows its Laplacian image. Because the Laplacian image contains negative values (see the discussion after Example 3.18), scaling is necessary for display. As the magnified section shows, mid gray represents zero, darker shades of gray represent negative values, and lighter shades are positive. The double-line effect is clearly visible in the magnified region.

At first, it might appear that the negative values can be handled simply by taking the absolute value of the Laplacian image. However, as Fig. 10.5(c) shows, this approach doubles the thickness of the lines. A more suitable approach is to use only the positive values of the Laplacian (in noisy situations we use the values that exceed a positive threshold to eliminate random variations about zero caused by the noise). As Fig. 10.5(d) shows, this approach results in thinner lines that generally are more useful. Note in Figs. 10.5(b) through (d) that when the lines are wide with respect to the size of the Laplacian kernel, the lines are separated by a zero "valley." This is not unexpected. For example, when the 3×3 kernel is centered on a line of constant intensity 5 pixels wide, the response will be zero, thus producing the effect just mentioned. When we talk about line detection, the assumption is that lines are thin with respect to the size of the detector. Lines that do not satisfy this assumption are best treated as regions and handled by the edge detection methods discussed in the following section.

The Laplacian detector kernel in Fig. 10.4(a) is isotropic, so its response is independent of direction (with respect to the four directions of the 3×3 kernel: vertical, horizontal, and two diagonals). Often, interest lies in detecting lines in *specified*

a b
c d

FIGURE 10.5
(a) Original image.
(b) Laplacian image; the magnified section shows the positive/negative double-line effect characteristic of the Laplacian.
(c) Absolute value of the Laplacian.
(d) Positive values of the Laplacian.

directions. Consider the kernels in Fig. 10.6. Suppose that an image with a constant background and containing various lines (oriented at $0°$, $\pm 45°$, and $90°$) is filtered with the first kernel. The maximum responses would occur at image locations in which a horizontal line passes through the middle row of the kernel. This is easily verified by sketching a simple array of 1's with a line of a different intensity (say, 5s) running horizontally through the array. A similar experiment would reveal that the second kernel in Fig. 10.6 responds best to lines oriented at $+45°$; the third kernel to vertical lines; and the fourth kernel to lines in the $-45°$ direction. The preferred direction of each kernel is weighted with a larger coefficient (i.e., 2) than other possible directions. The coefficients in each kernel sum to zero, indicating a zero response in areas of constant intensity.

Let Z_1, Z_2, Z_3, and Z_4 denote the responses of the kernels in Fig. 10.6, from left to right, where the Zs are given by Eq. (10-12). Suppose that an image is filtered with these four kernels, one at a time. If, at a given point in the image, $|Z_k| > |Z_j|$, for all $j \neq k$, that point is said to be more likely associated with a line in the direction of kernel k. For example, if at a point in the image, $|Z_1| > |Z_j|$ for $j = 2, 3, 4$, that

-1	-1	-1
2	2	2
-1	-1	-1

2	-1	-1
-1	2	-1
-1	-1	2

-1	2	-1
-1	2	-1
-1	2	-1

-1	-1	2
-1	2	-1
2	-1	-1

| Horizontal | +45° | Vertical | -45° |

a b c d

FIGURE 10.6 Line detection kernels. Detection angles are with respect to the axis system in Fig. 2.19, with positive angles measured counterclockwise with respect to the (vertical) x-axis.

point is said to be more likely associated with a horizontal line. If we are interested in detecting all the lines in an image in the direction defined by a given kernel, we simply run the kernel through the image and threshold the absolute value of the result, as in Eq. (10-15). The nonzero points remaining after thresholding are the strongest responses which, for lines one pixel thick, correspond closest to the direction defined by the kernel. The following example illustrates this procedure.

EXAMPLE 10.3: Detecting lines in specified directions.

Figure 10.7(a) shows the image used in the previous example. Suppose that we are interested in finding all the lines that are one pixel thick and oriented at +45°. For this purpose, we use the kernel in Fig. 10.6(b). Figure 10.7(b) is the result of filtering the image with that kernel. As before, the shades darker than the gray background in Fig. 10.7(b) correspond to negative values. There are two principal segments in the image oriented in the +45° direction, one in the top left and one at the bottom right. Figures 10.7(c) and (d) show zoomed sections of Fig. 10.7(b) corresponding to these two areas. The straight line segment in Fig. 10.7(d) is brighter than the segment in Fig. 10.7(c) because the line segment in the bottom right of Fig. 10.7(a) is one pixel thick, while the one at the top left is not. The kernel is "tuned" to detect one-pixel-thick lines in the +45° direction, so we expect its response to be stronger when such lines are detected. Figure 10.7(e) shows the positive values of Fig. 10.7(b). Because we are interested in the strongest response, we let T equal 254 (the maximum value in Fig. 10.7(e) minus one). Figure 10.7(f) shows in white the points whose values satisfied the condition $g > T$, where g is the image in Fig. 10.7(e). The isolated points in the figure are points that also had similarly strong responses to the kernel. In the original image, these points and their immediate neighbors are oriented in such a way that the kernel produced a maximum response at those locations. These isolated points can be detected using the kernel in Fig. 10.4(a) and then deleted, or they can be deleted using morphological operators, as discussed in the last chapter.

EDGE MODELS

Edge detection is an approach used frequently for segmenting images based on abrupt (local) changes in intensity. We begin by introducing several ways to model edges and then discuss a number of approaches for edge detection.

a b c
d e f

FIGURE 10.7 (a) Image of a wire-bond template. (b) Result of processing with the +45° line detector kernel in Fig. 10.6. (c) Zoomed view of the top left region of (b). (d) Zoomed view of the bottom right region of (b). (e) The image in (b) with all negative values set to zero. (f) All points (in white) whose values satisfied the condition $g > T$, where g is the image in (e) and $T = 254$ (the maximum pixel value in the image minus 1). (The points in (f) were enlarged to make them easier to see.)

Edge models are classified according to their intensity profiles. A *step edge* is characterized by a transition between two intensity levels occurring ideally over the distance of one pixel. Figure 10.8(a) shows a section of a vertical step edge and a horizontal intensity profile through the edge. Step edges occur, for example, in images generated by a computer for use in areas such as solid modeling and animation. These clean, *ideal* edges can occur over the distance of one pixel, provided that no additional processing (such as smoothing) is used to make them look "real." Digital step edges are used frequently as edge models in algorithm development. For example, the Canny edge detection algorithm discussed later in this section was derived originally using a step-edge model.

In practice, digital images have edges that are blurred and noisy, with the degree of blurring determined principally by limitations in the focusing mechanism (e.g., lenses in the case of optical images), and the noise level determined principally by the electronic components of the imaging system. In such situations, edges are more

a b c

FIGURE 10.8
From left to right, models (ideal representations) of a step, a ramp, and a roof edge, and their corresponding intensity profiles.

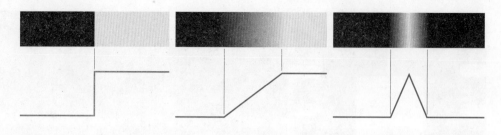

closely modeled as having an intensity *ramp* profile, such as the edge in Fig. 10.8(b). The slope of the ramp is inversely proportional to the degree to which the edge is blurred. In this model, we no longer have a single "edge point" along the profile. Instead, an edge point now is any point contained in the ramp, and an edge segment would then be a set of such points that are connected.

A third type of edge is the so-called *roof edge*, having the characteristics illustrated in Fig. 10.8(c). Roof edges are models of lines through a region, with the base (width) of the edge being determined by the thickness and sharpness of the line. In the limit, when its base is one pixel wide, a roof edge is nothing more than a one-pixel-thick line running through a region in an image. Roof edges arise, for example, in range imaging, when thin objects (such as pipes) are closer to the sensor than the background (such as walls). The pipes appear brighter and thus create an image similar to the model in Fig. 10.8(c). Other areas in which roof edges appear routinely are in the digitization of line drawings and also in satellite images, where thin features, such as roads, can be modeled by this type of edge.

It is not unusual to find images that contain all three types of edges. Although blurring and noise result in deviations from the ideal shapes, edges in images that are reasonably sharp and have a moderate amount of noise do resemble the characteristics of the edge models in Fig. 10.8, as the profiles in Fig. 10.9 illustrate. What the models in Fig. 10.8 allow us to do is write mathematical expressions for edges in the development of image processing algorithms. The performance of these algorithms will depend on the differences between actual edges and the models used in developing the algorithms.

Figure 10.10(a) shows the image from which the segment in Fig. 10.8(b) was extracted. Figure 10.10(b) shows a horizontal intensity profile. This figure shows also the first and second derivatives of the intensity profile. Moving from left to right along the intensity profile, we note that the first derivative is positive at the onset of the ramp and at points on the ramp, and it is zero in areas of constant intensity. The second derivative is positive at the beginning of the ramp, negative at the end of the ramp, zero at points on the ramp, and zero at points of constant intensity. The signs of the derivatives just discussed would be reversed for an edge that transitions from light to dark. The intersection between the zero intensity axis and a line extending between the extrema of the second derivative marks a point called the *zero crossing* of the second derivative.

We conclude from these observations that the *magnitude* of the first derivative can be used to detect the presence of an edge at a point in an image. Similarly, the *sign* of the second derivative can be used to determine whether an edge pixel lies on

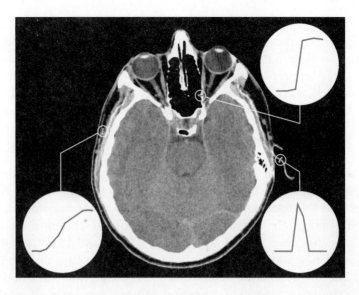

FIGURE 10.9 A 1508×1970 image showing (zoomed) actual ramp (bottom, left), step (top, right), and roof edge profiles. The profiles are from dark to light, in the areas enclosed by the small circles. The ramp and step profiles span 9 pixels and 2 pixels, respectively. The base of the roof edge is 3 pixels. (Original image courtesy of Dr. David R. Pickens, Vanderbilt University.)

the dark or light side of an edge. Two additional properties of the second derivative around an edge are: (1) it produces two values for every edge in an image; and (2) its zero crossings can be used for locating the centers of thick edges, as we will show later in this section. Some edge models utilize a smooth transition into and out of

a b

FIGURE 10.10
(a) Two regions of constant intensity separated by an ideal ramp edge. (b) Detail near the edge, showing a horizontal intensity profile, and its first and second derivatives.

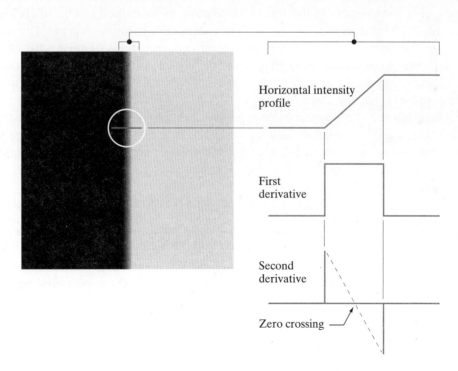

the ramp (see Problem 10.9). However, the conclusions reached using those models are the same as with an ideal ramp, and working with the latter simplifies theoretical formulations. Finally, although attention thus far has been limited to a 1-D horizontal profile, a similar argument applies to an edge of any orientation in an image. We simply define a profile perpendicular to the edge direction at any desired point, and interpret the results in the same manner as for the vertical edge just discussed.

EXAMPLE 10.4:   Behavior of the first and second derivatives in the region of a noisy edge.

The edge models in Fig. 10.8 are free of noise. The image segments in the first column in Fig. 10.11 show close-ups of four ramp edges that transition from a black region on the left to a white region on the right (keep in mind that the entire transition from black to white is a single edge). The image segment at the top left is free of noise. The other three images in the first column are corrupted by additive Gaussian noise with zero mean and standard deviation of 0.1, 1.0, and 10.0 intensity levels, respectively. The graph below each image is a horizontal intensity profile passing through the center of the image. All images have 8 bits of intensity resolution, with 0 and 255 representing black and white, respectively.

Consider the image at the top of the center column. As discussed in connection with Fig. 10.10(b), the derivative of the scan line on the left is zero in the constant areas. These are the two black bands shown in the derivative image. The derivatives at points on the ramp are constant and equal to the slope of the ramp. These constant values in the derivative image are shown in gray. As we move down the center column, the derivatives become increasingly different from the noiseless case. In fact, it would be difficult to associate the last profile in the center column with the first derivative of a ramp edge. What makes these results interesting is that the noise is almost visually undetectable in the images on the left column. These examples are good illustrations of the sensitivity of derivatives to noise.

As expected, the second derivative is even more sensitive to noise. The second derivative of the noiseless image is shown at the top of the right column. The thin white and black vertical lines are the positive and negative components of the second derivative, as explained in Fig. 10.10. The gray in these images represents zero (as discussed earlier, scaling causes zero to show as gray). The only noisy second derivative image that barely resembles the noiseless case corresponds to noise with a standard deviation of 0.1. The remaining second-derivative images and profiles clearly illustrate that it would be difficult indeed to detect their positive and negative components, which are the truly useful features of the second derivative in terms of edge detection.

The fact that such little visual noise can have such a significant impact on the two key derivatives used for detecting edges is an important issue to keep in mind. In particular, image smoothing should be a serious consideration prior to the use of derivatives in applications where noise with levels similar to those we have just discussed is likely to be present.

In summary, the three steps performed typically for edge detection are:

1. *Image smoothing for noise reduction.* The need for this step is illustrated by the results in the second and third columns of Fig. 10.11.
2. *Detection of edge points.* As mentioned earlier, this is a local operation that extracts from an image all points that are potential edge-point candidates.
3. *Edge localization.* The objective of this step is to select from the candidate points only the points that are members of the set of points comprising an edge.

The remainder of this section deals with techniques for achieving these objectives.

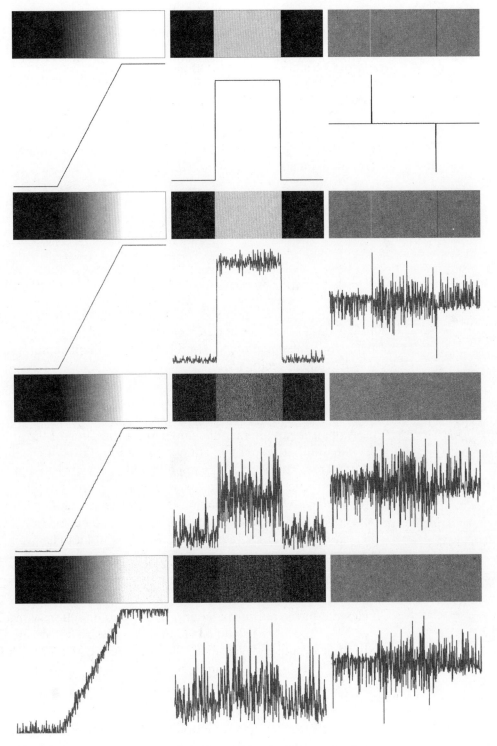

FIGURE 10.11 First column: 8-bit images with values in the range [0, 255], and intensity profiles of a ramp edge corrupted by Gaussian noise of zero mean and standard deviations of 0.0, 0.1, 1.0, and 10.0 intensity levels, respectively. Second column: First-derivative images and intensity profiles. Third column: Second-derivative images and intensity profiles.

BASIC EDGE DETECTION

As illustrated in the preceding discussion, detecting changes in intensity for the purpose of finding edges can be accomplished using first- or second-order derivatives. We begin with first-order derivatives, and work with second-order derivatives in the following subsection.

The Image Gradient and Its Properties

The tool of choice for finding edge strength *and* direction at an arbitrary location (x, y) of an image, f, is the *gradient*, denoted by ∇f and defined as the *vector*

For convenience, we repeat here some of the gradient concepts and equations introduced in Chapter 3.

$$\nabla f(x,y) \equiv \mathrm{grad}[f(x,y)] \equiv \begin{bmatrix} g_x(x,y) \\ g_y(x,y) \end{bmatrix} = \begin{bmatrix} \dfrac{\partial f(x,y)}{\partial x} \\ \dfrac{\partial f(x,y)}{\partial y} \end{bmatrix} \tag{10-16}$$

This vector has the well-known property that it points in the direction of maximum rate of change of f at (x, y) (see Problem 10.10). Equation (10-16) is valid at an arbitrary (but *single*) point (x, y). When evaluated for all applicable values of x and y, $\nabla f(x, y)$ becomes a *vector image*, each element of which is a vector given by Eq. (10-16). The *magnitude*, $M(x, y)$, of this gradient vector at a point (x, y) is given by its Euclidean vector norm:

$$M(x,y) = \|\nabla f(x,y)\| = \sqrt{g_x^2(x,y) + g_y^2(x,y)} \tag{10-17}$$

This is the *value* of the rate of change in the direction of the gradient vector at point (x, y). Note that $M(x, y)$, $\|\nabla f(x, y)\|$, $g_x(x, y)$, and $g_y(x, y)$ are arrays of the same size as f, created when x and y are allowed to vary over all pixel locations in f. It is common practice to refer to $M(x, y)$ and $\|\nabla f(x, y)\|$ as the *gradient image*, or simply as the *gradient* when the meaning is clear. The summation, square, and square root operations are elementwise operations, as defined in Section 2.6.

The *direction* of the gradient vector at a point (x, y) is given by

$$\alpha(x, y) = \tan^{-1}\left[\frac{g_y(x,y)}{g_x(x,y)}\right] \tag{10-18}$$

Angles are measured in the counterclockwise direction with respect to the x-axis (see Fig. 2.19). This is also an image of the same size as f, created by the elementwise division of g_x and g_y over all applicable values of x and y. The following example illustrates, the direction of an edge at a point (x, y) is orthogonal to the direction, $\alpha(x, y)$, of the gradient vector at the point.

EXAMPLE 10.5: Computing the gradient.

Figure 10.12(a) shows a zoomed section of an image containing a straight edge segment. Each square corresponds to a pixel, and we are interested in obtaining the strength and direction of the edge at the point highlighted with a box. The shaded pixels in this figure are assumed to have value 0, and the white

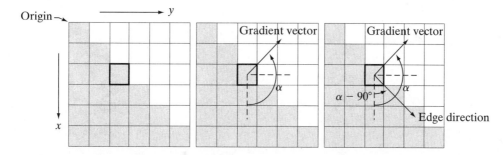

a b c

FIGURE 10.12 Using the gradient to determine edge strength and direction at a point. Note that the edge direction is perpendicular to the direction of the gradient vector at the point where the gradient is computed. Each square represents one pixel. (Recall from Fig. 2.19 that the origin of our coordinate system is at the top, left.)

pixels have value 1. We discuss after this example an approach for computing the derivatives in the x- and y-directions using a 3×3 neighborhood centered at a point. The method consists of subtracting the pixels in the top row of the neighborhood from the pixels in the bottom row to obtain the partial derivative in the x-direction. Similarly, we subtract the pixels in the left column from the pixels in the right column of the neighborhood to obtain the partial derivative in the y-direction. It then follows, using these differences as our estimates of the partials, that $\partial f / \partial x = -2$ and $\partial f / \partial y = 2$ at the point in question. Then,

$$
\nabla f = \begin{bmatrix} g_x \\ g_y \end{bmatrix} = \begin{bmatrix} \dfrac{\partial f}{\partial x} \\ \dfrac{\partial f}{\partial y} \end{bmatrix} = \begin{bmatrix} -2 \\ 2 \end{bmatrix}
$$

from which we obtain $\|\nabla f\| = 2\sqrt{2}$ at that point. Similarly, the direction of the gradient vector at the same point follows from Eq. (10-18): $\alpha = \tan^{-1}\left(g_y / g_x\right) = -45°$, which is the same as $135°$ measured in the positive (counterclockwise) direction with respect to the x-axis in our image coordinate system (see Fig. 2.19). Figure 10.12(b) shows the gradient vector and its direction angle.

As mentioned earlier, the direction of an edge at a point is orthogonal to the gradient vector at that point. So the direction angle of the edge in this example is $\alpha - 90° = 135° - 90° = 45°$, as Fig. 10.12(c) shows. All edge points in Fig. 10.12(a) have the same gradient, so the entire edge segment is in the same direction. The gradient vector sometimes is called the *edge normal*. When the vector is normalized to unit length by dividing it by its magnitude, the resulting vector is referred to as the *edge unit normal*.

Gradient Operators

Obtaining the gradient of an image requires computing the partial derivatives $\partial f / \partial x$ and $\partial f / \partial y$ at every pixel location in the image. For the gradient, we typically use a forward or centered finite difference (see Table 10.1). Using forward differences we obtain

$$
g_x(x, y) = \frac{\partial f(x, y)}{\partial x} = f(x + 1, y) - f(x, y) \tag{10-19}
$$

a b

FIGURE 10.13
1-D kernels used to
implement Eqs.
(10-19) and (10-20).

and

$$g_y(x,y) = \frac{\partial f(x,y)}{\partial y} = f(x, y+1) - f(x, y) \qquad (10\text{-}20)$$

These two equations can be implemented for all values of x and y by filtering $f(x,y)$ with the 1-D kernels in Fig. 10.13.

When diagonal edge direction is of interest, we need 2-D kernels. The *Roberts cross-gradient operators* (Roberts [1965]) are one of the earliest attempts to use 2-D kernels with a diagonal preference. Consider the 3×3 region in Fig. 10.14(a). The Roberts operators are based on implementing the diagonal differences

Filter kernels used to compute the derivatives needed for the gradient are often called gradient operators, difference operators, edge operators, or edge detectors.

$$g_x = \frac{\partial f}{\partial x} = (z_9 - z_5) \qquad (10\text{-}21)$$

and

$$g_y = \frac{\partial f}{\partial y} = (z_8 - z_6) \qquad (10\text{-}22)$$

These derivatives can be implemented by filtering an image with the kernels shown in Figs. 10.14(b) and (c).

Kernels of size 2×2 are simple conceptually, but they are not as useful for computing edge direction as kernels that are symmetric about their centers, the smallest of which are of size 3×3. These kernels take into account the nature of the data on opposite sides of the center point, and thus carry more information regarding the direction of an edge. The simplest digital approximations to the partial derivatives using kernels of size 3×3 are given by

Observe that these two equations are first-order central differences as given in Eq. (10-6), but multiplied by 2.

$$g_x = \frac{\partial f}{\partial x} = (z_7 + z_8 + z_9) - (z_1 + z_2 + z_3)$$

and $\qquad\qquad\qquad\qquad\qquad\qquad\qquad\qquad\qquad\qquad (10\text{-}23)$

$$g_y = \frac{\partial f}{\partial y} = (z_3 + z_6 + z_9) - (z_1 + z_4 + z_7)$$

In this formulation, the difference between the third and first rows of the 3×3 region approximates the derivative in the x-direction, and the difference between the third and first columns approximate the derivative in the y-direction. Intuitively, we would expect these approximations to be more accurate than the approximations obtained using the Roberts operators. Equations (10-22) and (10-23) can be implemented over an entire image by filtering it with the two kernels in Figs. 10.14(d) and (e). These kernels are called the *Prewitt operators* (Prewitt [1970]).

A slight variation of the preceding two equations uses a weight of 2 in the center coefficient:

a
b c
d e
f g

FIGURE 10.14
A 3×3 region
of an image (the
z's are intensity
values), and
various kernels
used to compute
the gradient at the
point labeled z_5.

z_1	z_2	z_3
z_4	z_5	z_6
z_7	z_8	z_9

-1	0
0	1

0	-1
1	0

Roberts

-1	-1	-1
0	0	0
1	1	1

-1	0	1
-1	0	1
-1	0	1

Prewitt

-1	-2	-1
0	0	0
1	2	1

-1	0	1
-2	0	2
-1	0	1

Sobel

$$g_x = \frac{\partial f}{\partial x} = (z_7 + 2z_8 + z_9) - (z_1 + 2z_2 + z_3) \tag{10-24}$$

and

$$g_y = \frac{\partial f}{\partial y} = (z_3 + 2z_6 + z_9) - (z_1 + 2z_4 + z_7) \tag{10-25}$$

It can be demonstrated (see Problem 10.12) that using a 2 in the center location provides image smoothing. Figures 10.14(f) and (g) show the kernels used to implement Eqs. (10-24) and (10-25). These kernels are called the *Sobel operators* (Sobel [1970]).

The Prewitt kernels are simpler to implement than the Sobel kernels, but the slight computational difference between them typically is not an issue. The fact that the Sobel kernels have better noise-suppression (smoothing) characteristics makes them preferable because, as mentioned earlier in the discussion of Fig. 10.11, noise suppression is an important issue when dealing with derivatives. Note that the

Recall the important result in Problem 3.32 that using a kernel whose coefficients sum to zero produces a filtered image whose pixels also sum to zero. This implies in general that some pixels will be negative. Similarly, if the kernel coefficients sum to 1, the sum of pixels in the original and filtered images will be the same (see Problem 3.31).

coefficients of all the kernels in Fig. 10.14 sum to zero, thus giving a response of zero in areas of constant intensity, as expected of derivative operators.

Any of the pairs of kernels from Fig. 10.14 are convolved with an image to obtain the gradient components g_x and g_y at every pixel location. These two partial derivative arrays are then used to estimate edge strength and direction. Obtaining the magnitude of the gradient requires the computations in Eq. (10-17). This implementation is not always desirable because of the computational burden required by squares and square roots, and an approach used frequently is to approximate the magnitude of the gradient by absolute values:

$$M(x, y) \approx |g_x| + |g_y| \qquad (10\text{-}26)$$

This equation is more attractive computationally, and it still preserves relative changes in intensity levels. The price paid for this advantage is that the resulting filters will not be isotropic (invariant to rotation) in general. However, this is not an issue when kernels such as the Prewitt and Sobel kernels are used to compute g_x and g_y because these kernels give isotropic results only for vertical and horizontal edges. This means that results would be isotropic only for edges in those two directions anyway, regardless of which of the two equations is used. That is, Eqs. (10-17) and (10-26) give identical results for vertical and horizontal edges when either the Sobel or Prewitt kernels are used (see Problem 10.11).

The 3×3 kernels in Fig. 10.14 exhibit their strongest response predominantly for vertical and horizontal edges. The *Kirsch compass kernels* (Kirsch [1971]) in Fig. 10.15, are designed to detect edge magnitude *and* direction (angle) in all eight compass directions. Instead of computing the magnitude using Eq. (10-17) and angle using Eq. (10-18), Kirsch's approach was to determine the edge magnitude by convolving an image with all eight kernels and assign the edge magnitude at a point as the response of the kernel that gave strongest convolution value at that point. The edge angle at that point is then the direction associated with that kernel. For example, if the strongest value at a point in the image resulted from using the north (N) kernel, the edge magnitude at that point would be assigned the response of that kernel, and the direction would be 0° (because compass kernel pairs differ by a rotation of 180°; choosing the maximum response will always result in a positive number). Although when working with, say, the Sobel kernels, we think of a north or south edge as being vertical, the N and S compass kernels differentiate between the two, the difference being the direction of the intensity transitions defining the edge. For example, assuming that intensity values are in the range [0, 1], the binary edge in Fig. 10.8(a) is defined by black (0) on the left and white (1) on the right. When all Kirsch kernels are applied to this edge, the N kernel will yield the highest value, thus indicating an edge oriented in the north direction (at the point of the computation).

EXAMPLE 10.6: Illustration of the 2-D gradient magnitude and angle.

Figure 10.16 illustrates the Sobel absolute value response of the two components of the gradient, $|g_x|$ and $|g_y|$, as well as the gradient image formed from the sum of these two components. The directionality of the horizontal and vertical components of the gradient is evident in Figs. 10.16(b) and (c). Note, for

a b c d
e f g h

FIGURE 10.15
Kirsch compass kernels. The edge direction of strongest response of each kernel is labeled below it.

−3	−3	5	−3	5	5	5	5	5	5	5	−3
−3	0	5	−3	0	5	−3	0	−3	5	0	−3
−3	−3	5	−3	−3	−3	−3	−3	−3	−3	−3	−3

N   NW   W   SW

5	−3	−3	−3	−3	−3	−3	−3	−3	−3	−3	−3
5	0	−3	5	0	−3	−3	0	−3	−3	0	5
5	−3	−3	5	5	−3	5	5	5	−3	5	5

S   SE   E   NE

example, how strong the roof tile, horizontal brick joints, and horizontal segments of the windows are in Fig. 10.16(b) compared to other edges. In contrast, Fig. 10.16(c) favors features such as the vertical components of the façade and windows. It is common terminology to use the term *edge map* when referring to an image whose principal features are edges, such as gradient magnitude images. The intensities of the image in Fig. 10.16(a) were scaled to the range [0, 1]. We use values in this range to simplify parameter selection in the various methods for edge detection discussed in this section.

a b
c d

FIGURE 10.16
(a) Image of size 834×1114 pixels, with intensity values scaled to the range [0,1].
(b) $|g_x|$, the component of the gradient in the x-direction, obtained using the Sobel kernel in Fig. 10.14(f) to filter the image.
(c) $|g_y|$, obtained using the kernel in Fig. 10.14(g).
(d) The gradient image, $|g_x| + |g_y|$.

FIGURE 10.17
Gradient angle
image computed
using Eq. (10-18).
Areas of constant
intensity in this
image indicate
that the direction
of the gradient
vector is the same
at all the pixel
locations in those
regions.

Figure 10.17 shows the gradient angle image computed using Eq. (10-18). In general, angle images are not as useful as gradient magnitude images for edge detection, but they do complement the information extracted from an image using the magnitude of the gradient. For instance, the constant intensity areas in Fig. 10.16(a), such as the front edge of the sloping roof and top horizontal bands of the front wall, are constant in Fig. 10.17, indicating that the gradient vector direction at all the pixel locations in those regions is the same. As we will show later in this section, angle information plays a key supporting role in the implementation of the Canny edge detection algorithm, a widely used edge detection scheme.

The original image in Fig. 10.16(a) is of reasonably high resolution, and at the distance the image was acquired, the contribution made to image detail by the wall bricks is significant. This level of fine detail often is undesirable in edge detection because it tends to act as noise, which is enhanced by derivative computations and thus complicates detection of the principal edges. One way to reduce fine detail is to smooth the image prior to computing the edges. Figure 10.18 shows the same sequence of images as in Fig. 10.16, but with the original image smoothed first using a 5×5 averaging filter (see Section 3.5 regarding smoothing filters). The response of each kernel now shows almost no contribution due to the bricks, with the results being dominated mostly by the principal edges in the image.

Figures 10.16 and 10.18 show that the horizontal and vertical Sobel kernels do not differentiate between edges in the ±45° directions. If it is important to emphasize edges oriented in particular diagonal directions, then one of the Kirsch kernels in Fig. 10.15 should be used. Figures 10.19(a) and (b) show the responses of the 45° (NW) and −45° (SW) Kirsch kernels, respectively. The stronger diagonal selectivity of these kernels is evident in these figures. Both kernels have similar responses to horizontal and vertical edges, but the response in these directions is weaker.

Combining the Gradient with Thresholding

The threshold used to generate Fig. 10.20(a) was selected so that most of the small edges caused by the bricks were eliminated. This was the same objective as when the image in Fig. 10.16(a) was smoothed prior to computing the gradient.

The results in Fig. 10.18 show that edge detection can be made more selective by smoothing the image prior to computing the gradient. Another approach aimed at achieving the same objective is to threshold the gradient image. For example, Fig. 10.20(a) shows the gradient image from Fig. 10.16(d), thresholded so that pixels with values greater than or equal to 33% of the maximum value of the gradient image are shown in white, while pixels below the threshold value are shown in

FIGURE 10.18
Same sequence as
in Fig. 10.16, but
with the original
image smoothed
using a 5×5 averaging kernel prior
to edge detection.

black. Comparing this image with Fig. 10.16(d), we see that there are fewer edges in
the thresholded image, and that the edges in this image are much sharper (see, for
example, the edges in the roof tile). On the other hand, numerous edges, such as the
sloping line defining the far edge of the roof (see arrow), are broken in the thresholded image.

When interest lies both in highlighting the principal edges and on maintaining
as much connectivity as possible, it is common practice to use both smoothing and
thresholding. Figure 10.20(b) shows the result of thresholding Fig. 10.18(d), which is
the gradient of the smoothed image. This result shows a reduced number of broken
edges; for instance, compare the corresponding edges identified by the arrows in Figs.
10.20(a) and (b).

a b

FIGURE 10.19
Diagonal edge
detection.
(a) Result of using
the Kirsch kernel in
Fig. 10.15(c).
(b) Result of using
the kernel in Fig.
10.15(d). The input
image in both cases
was Fig. 10.18(a).

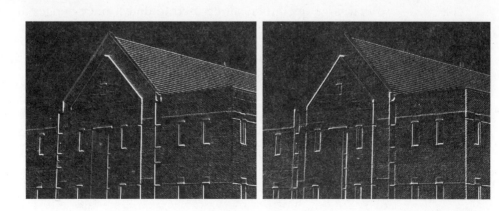

FIGURE 10.20
(a) Result of thresholding Fig. 10.16(d), the gradient of the original image. (b) Result of thresholding Fig. 10.18(d), the gradient of the smoothed image.

MORE ADVANCED TECHNIQUES FOR EDGE DETECTION

The edge-detection methods discussed in the previous subsections are based on filtering an image with one or more kernels, with no provisions made for edge characteristics and noise content. In this section, we discuss more advanced techniques that attempt to improve on simple edge-detection methods by taking into account factors such as image noise and the nature of edges themselves.

The Marr-Hildreth Edge Detector

One of the earliest successful attempts at incorporating more sophisticated analysis into the edge-finding process is attributed to Marr and Hildreth [1980]. Edge-detection methods in use at the time were based on small operators, such as the Sobel kernels discussed earlier. Marr and Hildreth argued (1) that intensity changes are not independent of image scale, implying that their detection requires using operators of different sizes; and (2) that a sudden intensity change will give rise to a peak or trough in the first derivative or, equivalently, to a zero crossing in the second derivative (as we saw in Fig. 10.10).

These ideas suggest that an operator used for edge detection should have two salient features. First and foremost, it should be a differential operator capable of computing a digital approximation of the first or second derivative at every point in the image. Second, it should be capable of being "tuned" to act at any desired scale, so that large operators can be used to detect blurry edges and small operators to detect sharply focused fine detail.

Marr and Hildreth suggested that the most satisfactory operator fulfilling these conditions is the filter $\nabla^2 G$ where, as defined in Section 3.6, ∇^2 is the Laplacian, and G is the 2-D Gaussian function

Equation (10-27) differs from the definition of a Gaussian function by a multiplicative constant [see Eq. (3-45)]. Here, we are interested only in the general shape of the Gaussian function.

$$G(x,y) = e^{-\frac{x^2+y^2}{2\sigma^2}} \tag{10-27}$$

with standard deviation σ (sometimes σ is called the *space constant* in this context). We find an expression for $\nabla^2 G$ by applying the Laplacian to Eq. (10-27):

$$\nabla^2 G(x,y) = \frac{\partial^2 G(x,y)}{\partial x^2} + \frac{\partial^2 G(x,y)}{\partial y^2}$$

$$= \frac{\partial}{\partial x}\left(\frac{-x}{\sigma^2}e^{-\frac{x^2+y^2}{2\sigma^2}}\right) + \frac{\partial}{\partial y}\left(\frac{-y}{\sigma^2}e^{-\frac{x^2+y^2}{2\sigma^2}}\right) \qquad (10\text{-}28)$$

$$= \left(\frac{x^2}{\sigma^4} - \frac{1}{\sigma^2}\right)e^{-\frac{x^2+y^2}{2\sigma^2}} + \left(\frac{y^2}{\sigma^4} - \frac{1}{\sigma^2}\right)e^{-\frac{x^2+y^2}{2\sigma^2}}$$

Collecting terms, we obtain

$$\nabla^2 G(x,y) = \left(\frac{x^2+y^2-2\sigma^2}{\sigma^4}\right)e^{-\frac{x^2+y^2}{2\sigma^2}} \qquad (10\text{-}29)$$

This expression is called the *Laplacian of a Gaussian* (LoG).

Figures 10.21(a) through (c) show a 3-D plot, image, and cross-section of the negative of the LoG function (note that the zero crossings of the LoG occur at $x^2 + y^2 = 2\sigma^2$, which defines a circle of radius $\sqrt{2}\sigma$ centered on the peak of the Gaussian function). Because of the shape illustrated in Fig. 10.21(a), the LoG function sometimes is called the *Mexican hat operator*. Figure 10.21(d) shows a 5×5 kernel that approximates the shape in Fig. 10.21(a) (normally, we would use the negative of this kernel). This approximation is not unique. Its purpose is to capture the essential shape of the LoG function; in terms of Fig. 10.21(a), this means a positive, central term surrounded by an adjacent, negative region whose values decrease as a function of distance from the origin, and a zero outer region. The coefficients must sum to zero so that the response of the kernel is zero in areas of constant intensity.

Filter kernels of arbitrary size (but fixed σ) can be generated by sampling Eq. (10-29), and scaling the coefficients so that they sum to zero. A more effective approach for generating a LoG kernel is sampling Eq. (10-27) to the desired size, then convolving the resulting array with a Laplacian kernel, such as the kernel in Fig. 10.4(a). Because convolving an image with a kernel whose coefficients sum to zero yields an image whose elements also sum to zero (see Problems 3.32 and 10.16), this approach automatically satisfies the requirement that the sum of the LoG kernel coefficients be zero. We will discuss size selection for LoG filter later in this section.

There are two fundamental ideas behind the selection of the operator $\nabla^2 G$. First, the Gaussian part of the operator blurs the image, thus reducing the intensity of structures (including noise) at scales much smaller than σ. Unlike the averaging filter used in Fig. 10.18, the Gaussian function is smooth in both the spatial and frequency domains (see Section 4.8), and is thus less likely to introduce artifacts (e.g., ringing) not present in the original image. The other idea concerns the second-derivative properties of the Laplacian operator, ∇^2. Although first derivatives can be used for detecting abrupt changes in intensity, they are directional operators. The Laplacian, on the other hand, has the important advantage of being isotropic (invariant to rotation), which not only corresponds to characteristics of the human visual system (Marr [1982]) but also responds equally to changes in intensity in any kernel

a b
c d

FIGURE 10.21
(a) 3-D plot of
the *negative* of the
LoG.
(b) Negative of
the LoG
displayed as an
image.
(c) Cross section
of (a) showing
zero crossings.
(d) 5 × 5 kernel
approximation to
the shape in (a).
The negative
of this kernel
would be used in
practice.

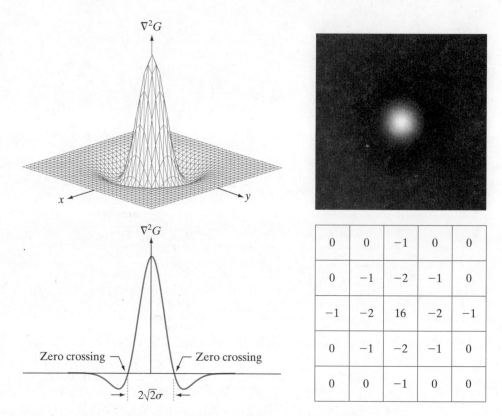

direction, thus avoiding having to use multiple kernels to calculate the strongest response at any point in the image.

The Marr-Hildreth algorithm consists of convolving the LoG kernel with an input image,

$$g(x, y) = \left[\nabla^2 G(x, y)\right] \star f(x, y) \tag{10-30}$$

and then finding the zero crossings of $g(x, y)$ to determine the locations of edges in $f(x, y)$. Because the Laplacian and convolution are linear processes, we can write Eq. (10-30) as

This expression is
implemented in the
spatial domain using
Eq. (3-35). It can be
implemented also in the
frequency domain using
Eq. (4-104).

$$g(x, y) = \nabla^2 \left[G(x, y) \star f(x, y)\right] \tag{10-31}$$

indicating that we can smooth the image first with a Gaussian filter and then compute the Laplacian of the result. These two equations give identical results.

The Marr-Hildreth edge-detection algorithm may be summarized as follows:

1. Filter the input image with an $n \times n$ Gaussian lowpass kernel obtained by sampling Eq. (10-27).
2. Compute the Laplacian of the image resulting from Step 1 using, for example, the 3×3 kernel in Fig. 10.4(a). [Steps 1 and 2 implement Eq. (10-31).]
3. Find the zero crossings of the image from Step 2.

To specify the size of the Gaussian kernel, recall from our discussion of Fig. 3.35 that the values of a Gaussian function at a distance larger than 3σ from the mean are small enough so that they can be ignored. As discussed in Section 3.5, this implies using a Gaussian kernel of size $\lceil 6\sigma \rceil \times \lceil 6\sigma \rceil$, where $\lceil 6\sigma \rceil$ denotes the ceiling of 6σ; that is, smallest integer not less than 6σ. Because we work with kernels of odd dimensions, we would use the smallest *odd* integer satisfying this condition. Using a kernel smaller than this will "truncate" the LoG function, with the degree of truncation being inversely proportional to the size of the kernel. Using a larger kernel would make little difference in the result.

As explained in Section 3.5, $\lceil \cdot \rceil$ and $\lfloor \cdot \rfloor$ denote the *ceiling* and *floor* functions. That is, the ceiling and floor functions map a real number to the smallest following, or the largest previous, integer, respectively.

One approach for finding the zero crossings at any pixel, p, of the filtered image, $g(x, y)$, is to use a 3×3 neighborhood centered at p. A zero crossing at p implies that the signs of at least two of its opposing neighboring pixels must differ. There are four cases to test: left/right, up/down, and the two diagonals. If the values of $g(x, y)$ are being compared against a threshold (a common approach), then not only must the signs of opposing neighbors be different, but the absolute value of their numerical difference must also exceed the threshold before we can call p a zero-crossing pixel. We illustrate this approach in Example 10.7.

Attempts to find zero crossings by finding the coordinates (x, y) where $g(x, y) = 0$ are impractical because of noise and other computational inaccuracies.

Computing zero crossings is the key feature of the Marr-Hildreth edge-detection method. The approach discussed in the previous paragraph is attractive because of its simplicity of implementation and because it generally gives good results. If the accuracy of the zero-crossing locations found using this method is inadequate in a particular application, then a technique proposed by Huertas and Medioni [1986] for finding zero crossings with *subpixel accuracy* can be employed.

EXAMPLE 10.7: **Illustration of the Marr-Hildreth edge-detection method.**

Figure 10.22(a) shows the building image used earlier and Fig. 10.22(b) is the result of Steps 1 and 2 of the Marr-Hildreth algorithm, using $\sigma = 4$ (approximately 0.5% of the short dimension of the image) and $n = 25$ to satisfy the size condition stated above. As in Fig. 10.5, the gray tones in this image are due to scaling. Figure 10.22(c) shows the zero crossings obtained using the 3×3 neighborhood approach just discussed, with a threshold of zero. Note that all the edges form closed loops. This so-called "spaghetti effect" is a serious drawback of this method when a threshold value of zero is used (see Problem 10.17). We avoid closed-loop edges by using a positive threshold.

Figure 10.22(d) shows the result of using a threshold approximately equal to 4% of the maximum value of the LoG image. The majority of the principal edges were readily detected, and "irrelevant" features, such as the edges due to the bricks and the tile roof, were filtered out. This type of performance is virtually impossible to obtain using the gradient-based edge-detection techniques discussed earlier. Another important consequence of using zero crossings for edge detection is that the resulting edges are 1 pixel thick. This property simplifies subsequent stages of processing, such as edge linking.

It is possible to approximate the LoG function in Eq. (10-29) by a *difference of Gaussians* (DoG):

$$D_G(x, y) = \frac{1}{2\pi\sigma_1^2} e^{-\frac{x^2 + y^2}{2\sigma_1^2}} - \frac{1}{2\pi\sigma_2^2} e^{-\frac{x^2 + y^2}{2\sigma_2^2}} \tag{10-32}$$

a b
c d

FIGURE 10.22
(a) Image of size
834 × 1114 pixels,
with intensity
values scaled to the
range [0, 1].
(b) Result of
Steps 1 and 2 of
the Marr-Hildreth
algorithm using
$\sigma = 4$ and $n = 25$.
(c) Zero cross-
ings of (b) using
a threshold of 0
(note the closed-
loop edges).
(d) Zero cross-
ings found using a
threshold equal to
4% of the maxi-
mum value of the
image in (b). Note
the thin edges.

with $\sigma_1 > \sigma_2$. Experimental results suggest that certain "channels" in the human vision system are selective with respect to orientation and frequency, and can be modeled using Eq. (10-32) with a ratio of standard deviations of 1.75:1. Using the ratio 1.6:1 preserves the basic characteristics of these observations and also provides a closer "engineering" approximation to the LoG function (Marr and Hildreth [1980]). In order for the LoG and DoG to have the same zero crossings, the value of σ for the LoG must be selected based on the following equation (see Problem 10.19):

$$\sigma^2 = \frac{\sigma_1^2 \sigma_2^2}{\sigma_1^2 - \sigma_2^2} \ln\left[\frac{\sigma_1^2}{\sigma_2^2}\right] \tag{10-33}$$

Although the zero crossings of the LoG and DoG will be the same when this value of σ is used, their amplitude scales will be different. We can make them compatible by scaling both functions so that they have the same value at the origin.

The profiles in Figs. 10.23(a) and (b) were generated with standard deviation ratios of 1:1.75 and 1:1.6, respectively (by convention, the curves shown are inverted, as in Fig. 10.21). The LoG profiles are the solid lines, and the DoG profiles are dotted. The curves shown are intensity profiles through the center of the LoG and DoG arrays, generated by sampling Eqs. (10-29) and (10-32), respectively. The amplitude of all curves at the origin were normalized to 1. As Fig. 10.23(b) shows, the ratio 1:1.6 yielded a slightly closer approximation of the LoG and DoG functions (for example, compare the bottom lobes of the two figures).

a b

FIGURE 10.23
(a) Negatives of the LoG (solid) and DoG (dotted) profiles using a σ ratio of 1.75:1. (b) Profiles obtained using a ratio of 1.6:1.

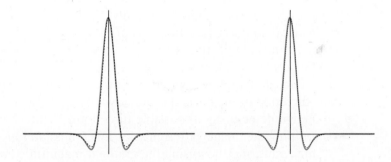

Gaussian kernels are separable (see Section 3.4). Therefore, both the LoG and the DoG filtering operations can be implemented with 1-D convolutions instead of using 2-D convolutions directly (see Problem 10.19). For an image of size $M \times N$ and a kernel of size $n \times n$, doing so reduces the number of multiplications and additions for each convolution from being proportional to $n^2 MN$ for 2-D convolutions to being proportional to nMN for 1-D convolutions. This implementation difference is significant. For example, if $n = 25$, a 1-D implementation will require on the order of 12 times fewer multiplication and addition operations than using 2-D convolution.

The Canny Edge Detector

Although the algorithm is more complex, the performance of the Canny edge detector (Canny [1986]) discussed in this section is superior in general to the edge detectors discussed thus far. Canny's approach is based on three basic objectives:

1. *Low error rate.* All edges should be found, and there should be no spurious responses.

2. *Edge points should be well localized.* The edges located must be as close as possible to the true edges. That is, the distance between a point marked as an edge by the detector and the center of the true edge should be minimum.

3. *Single edge point response.* The detector should return only one point for each true edge point. That is, the number of local maxima around the true edge should be minimum. This means that the detector should not identify multiple edge pixels where only a single edge point exists.

The essence of Canny's work was in expressing the preceding three criteria mathematically, and then attempting to find optimal solutions to these formulations. In general, it is difficult (or impossible) to find a closed-form solution that satisfies all the preceding objectives. However, using numerical optimization with 1-D step edges corrupted by additive white Gaussian noise[†] led to the conclusion that a good approximation to the optimal step edge detector is the *first derivative of a Gaussian*,

$$\frac{d}{dx} e^{-\frac{x^2}{2\sigma^2}} = \frac{-x}{\sigma^2} e^{-\frac{x^2}{2\sigma^2}} \tag{10-34}$$

[†]Recall that *white noise* is noise having a frequency spectrum that is continuous and uniform over a specified frequency band. *White Gaussian noise* is white noise in which the distribution of amplitude values is Gaussian. Gaussian white noise is a good approximation of many real-world situations and generates mathematically tractable models. It has the useful property that its values are statistically independent.

where the approximation was only about 20% worse that using the optimized numerical solution (a difference of this magnitude generally is visually imperceptible in most applications).

Generalizing the preceding result to 2-D involves recognizing that the 1-D approach still applies in the direction of the edge normal (see Fig. 10.12). Because the direction of the normal is unknown beforehand, this would require applying the 1-D edge detector in all possible directions. This task can be approximated by first smoothing the image with a circular 2-D Gaussian function, computing the gradient of the result, and then using the gradient magnitude and direction to estimate edge strength and direction at every point.

Let $f(x,y)$ denote the input image and $G(x,y)$ denote the Gaussian function:

$$G(x,y) = e^{-\frac{x^2+y^2}{2\sigma^2}} \qquad (10\text{-}35)$$

We form a smoothed image, $f_s(x,y)$, by convolving f and G:

$$f_s(x,y) = G(x,y) \star f(x,y) \qquad (10\text{-}36)$$

This operation is followed by computing the gradient magnitude and direction (angle), as discussed earlier:

$$M_s(x,y) = \left\| \nabla f_s(x,y) \right\| = \sqrt{g_x^2(x,y) + g_y^2(x,y)} \qquad (10\text{-}37)$$

and

$$\alpha(x,y) = \tan^{-1}\left[\frac{g_y(x,y)}{g_x(x,y)} \right] \qquad (10\text{-}38)$$

with $g_x(x,y) = \partial f_s(x,y)/\partial x$ and $g_y(x,y) = \partial f_s(x,y)/\partial y$. Any of the derivative filter kernel pairs in Fig. 10.14 can be used to obtain $g_x(x,y)$ and $g_y(x,y)$. Equation (10-36) is implemented using an $n \times n$ Gaussian kernel whose size is discussed below. Keep in mind that $\left\| \nabla f_s(x,y) \right\|$ and $\alpha(x,y)$ are arrays of the same size as the image from which they are computed.

Gradient image $\left\| \nabla f_s(x,y) \right\|$ typically contains wide ridges around local maxima. The next step is to thin those ridges. One approach is to use *nonmaxima suppression*. The essence of this approach is to specify a number of discrete orientations of the edge normal (gradient vector). For example, in a 3×3 region we can define four orientations[†] for an edge passing through the center point of the region: horizontal, vertical, +45°, and −45°. Figure 10.24(a) shows the situation for the two possible orientations of a horizontal edge. Because we have to quantize all possible edge directions into four ranges, we have to define a range of directions over which we consider an edge to be horizontal. We determine edge direction from the direction of the edge normal, which we obtain directly from the image data using Eq. (10-38). As Fig. 10.24(b) shows, if the edge normal is in the range of directions from −22.5° to

---

[†]Every edge has two possible orientations. For example, an edge whose normal is oriented at 0° and an edge whose normal is oriented at 180° are the same *horizontal* edge.

FIGURE 10.24
(a) Two possible
orientations of a
horizontal edge
(shaded) in a 3×3
neighborhood.
(b) Range of values
(shaded) of α, the
direction angle of
the edge normal
for a horizontal
edge. (c) The angle
ranges of the edge
normals for the
four types of edge
directions in a 3×3
neighborhood.
Each edge direc-
tion has two ranges,
shown in corre-
sponding shades.

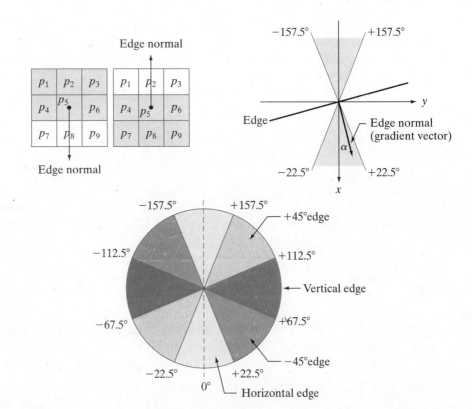

22.5° or from −157.5° to 157.5°, we call the edge a horizontal edge. Figure 10.24(c) shows the angle ranges corresponding to the four directions under consideration.

Let d_1, d_2, d_3, and d_4 denote the four basic edge directions just discussed for a 3×3 region: horizontal, −45°, vertical, and +45°, respectively. We can formulate the following nonmaxima suppression scheme for a 3×3 region centered at an arbitrary point (x, y) in α:

1. Find the direction d_k that is closest to $\alpha(x, y)$.
2. Let K denote the value of $\|\nabla f_s\|$ at (x, y). If K is less than the value of $\|\nabla f_s\|$ at one or both of the neighbors of point (x, y) along d_k, let $g_N(x, y) = 0$ (suppression); otherwise, let $g_N(x, y) = K$.

When repeated for all values of x and y, this procedure yields a nonmaxima sup-pressed image $g_N(x, y)$ that is of the same size as $f_s(x, y)$. For example, with reference to Fig. 10.24(a), letting (x, y) be at p_5, and assuming a horizontal edge through p_5, the pixels of interest in Step 2 would be p_2 and p_8. Image $g_N(x, y)$ contains only the thinned edges; it is equal to image $\|\nabla f_s(x, y)\|$ with the nonmaxima edge points sup-pressed.

The final operation is to threshold $g_N(x, y)$ to reduce false edge points. In the Marr-Hildreth algorithm we did this using a single threshold, in which all values below the threshold were set to 0. If we set the threshold too low, there will still be some false edges (called *false positives*). If the threshold is set too high, then valid edge points will be eliminated (*false negatives*). Canny's algorithm attempts to improve on this situation by using *hysteresis thresholding* which, as we will discuss in Section 10.3, uses two thresholds: a low threshold, T_L and a high threshold, T_H. Experimental evidence (Canny [1986]) suggests that the ratio of the high to low threshold should be in the range of 2:1 to 3:1.

We can visualize the thresholding operation as creating two additional images:

$$g_{NH}(x,y) = g_N(x,y) \geq T_H \tag{10-39}$$

and

$$g_{NL}(x,y) = g_N(x,y) \geq T_L \tag{10-40}$$

Initially, $g_{NH}(x,y)$ and $g_{NL}(x,y)$ are set to 0. After thresholding, $g_{NH}(x,y)$ will usually have fewer nonzero pixels than $g_{NL}(x,y)$, but all the nonzero pixels in $g_{NH}(x,y)$ will be contained in $g_{NL}(x,y)$ because the latter image is formed with a lower threshold. We eliminate from $g_{NL}(x,y)$ all the nonzero pixels from $g_{NH}(x,y)$ by letting

$$g_{NL}(x,y) = g_{NL}(x,y) - g_{NH}(x,y) \tag{10-41}$$

The nonzero pixels in $g_{NH}(x,y)$ and $g_{NL}(x,y)$ may be viewed as being "strong" and "weak" edge pixels, respectively. After the thresholding operations, all strong pixels in $g_{NH}(x,y)$ are assumed to be valid edge pixels, and are so marked immediately. Depending on the value of T_H, the edges in $g_{NH}(x,y)$ typically have gaps. Longer edges are formed using the following procedure:

(a) Locate the next unvisited edge pixel, p, in $g_{NH}(x,y)$.

(b) Mark as valid edge pixels all the weak pixels in $g_{NL}(x,y)$ that are connected to p using, say, 8-connectivity.

(c) If all nonzero pixels in $g_{NH}(x,y)$ have been visited go to Step (d). Else, return to Step (a).

(d) Set to zero all pixels in $g_{NL}(x,y)$ that were not marked as valid edge pixels.

At the end of this procedure, the final image output by the Canny algorithm is formed by appending to $g_{NH}(x,y)$ all the nonzero pixels from $g_{NL}(x,y)$.

We used two additional images, $g_{NH}(x,y)$ and $g_{NL}(x,y)$ to simplify the discussion. In practice, hysteresis thresholding can be implemented directly during nonmaxima suppression, and thresholding can be implemented directly on $g_N(x,y)$ by forming a list of strong pixels and the weak pixels connected to them.

Summarizing, the Canny edge detection algorithm consists of the following steps:

1. Smooth the input image with a Gaussian filter.

2. Compute the gradient magnitude and angle images.

3. Apply nonmaxima suppression to the gradient magnitude image.

4. Use double thresholding and connectivity analysis to detect and link edges.

Although the edges after nonmaxima suppression are thinner than raw gradient edges, the former can still be thicker than one pixel. To obtain edges one pixel thick, it is typical to follow Step 4 with one pass of an edge-thinning algorithm (see Section 9.5).

As mentioned earlier, smoothing is accomplished by convolving the input image with a Gaussian kernel whose size, $n \times n$, must be chosen. Once a value of σ has been specified, we can use the approach discussed in connection with the Marr-Hildreth algorithm to determine an odd value of n that provides the "full" smoothing capability of the Gaussian filter for the specified value of σ.

Usually, selecting a suitable value of σ for the first time in an application requires experimentation.

Some final comments on implementation: As noted earlier in the discussion of the Marr-Hildreth edge detector, the 2-D Gaussian function in Eq. (10-35) is separable into a product of two 1-D Gaussians. Thus, Step 1 of the Canny algorithm can be formulated as 1-D convolutions that operate on the rows (columns) of the image one at a time, and then work on the columns (rows) of the result. Furthermore, if we use the approximations in Eqs. (10-19) and (10-20), we can also implement the gradient computations required for Step 2 as 1-D convolutions (see Problem 10.22).

EXAMPLE 10.8: Illustration and comparison of the Canny edge-detection method.

Figure 10.25(a) shows the familiar building image. For comparison, Figs. 10.25(b) and (c) show, respectively, the result in Fig. 10.20(b) obtained using the thresholded gradient, and Fig. 10.22(d) using the Marr-Hildreth detector. Recall that the parameters used in generating those two images were selected to detect the principal edges, while attempting to reduce "irrelevant" features, such as the edges of the bricks and the roof tiles.

Figure 10.25(d) shows the result obtained with the Canny algorithm using the parameters $T_L = 0.04$, $T_H = 0.10$ (2.5 times the value of the low threshold), $\sigma = 4$, and a kernel of size 25×25, which corresponds to the smallest odd integer not less than 6σ. These parameters were chosen experimentally

a b
c d

FIGURE 10.25
(a) Original image of size 834×1114 pixels, with intensity values scaled to the range [0, 1].
(b) Thresholded gradient of the smoothed image.
(c) Image obtained using the Marr-Hildreth algorithm.
(d) Image obtained using the Canny algorithm. Note the significant improvement of the Canny image compared to the other two.

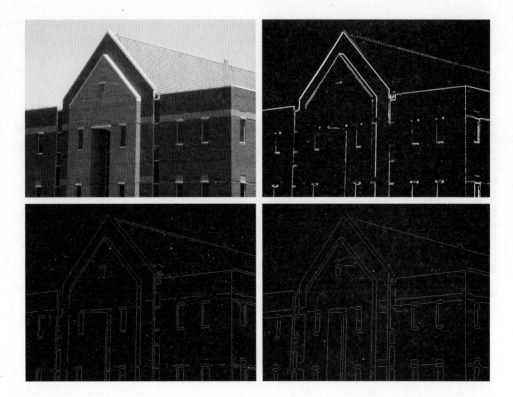

to achieve the objectives stated in the previous paragraph for the gradient and Marr-Hildreth images. Comparing the Canny image with the other two images, we see in the Canny result significant improvements in detail of the principal edges and, at the same time, more rejection of irrelevant features. For example, note that both edges of the concrete band lining the bricks in the upper section of the image were detected by the Canny algorithm, whereas the thresholded gradient lost both of these edges, and the Marr-Hildreth method detected only the upper one. In terms of filtering out irrelevant detail, the Canny image does not contain a single edge due to the roof tiles; this is not true in the other two images. The quality of the lines with regard to continuity, thinness, and straightness is also superior in the Canny image. Results such as these have made the Canny algorithm a tool of choice for edge detection.

EXAMPLE 10.9: Another illustration of the three principal edge-detection methods discussed in this section.

As another comparison of the three principal edge-detection methods discussed in this section, consider Fig. 10.26(a), which shows a 512×512 head CT image. Our objective is to extract the edges of the outer contour of the brain (the gray region in the image), the contour of the spinal region (shown directly behind the nose, toward the front of the brain), and the outer contour of the head. We wish to generate the thinnest, continuous contours possible, while eliminating edge details related to the gray content in the eyes and brain areas.

Figure 10.26(b) shows a thresholded gradient image that was first smoothed using a 5×5 averaging kernel. The threshold required to achieve the result shown was 15% of the maximum value of the gradient image. Figure 10.26(c) shows the result obtained with the Marr-Hildreth edge-detection algorithm with a threshold of 0.002, $\sigma = 3$, and a kernel of size 19×19. Figure 10.26(d) was obtained using the Canny algorithm with $T_L = 0.05, T_H = 0.15$ (3 times the value of the low threshold), $\sigma = 2$, and a kernel of size 13×13.

a b
c d

FIGURE 10.26
(a) Head CT image of size 512×512 pixels, with intensity values scaled to the range $[0, 1]$.
(b) Thresholded gradient of the smoothed image.
(c) Image obtained using the Marr-Hildreth algorithm.
(d) Image obtained using the Canny algorithm.
(Original image courtesy of Dr. David R. Pickens, Vanderbilt University.)

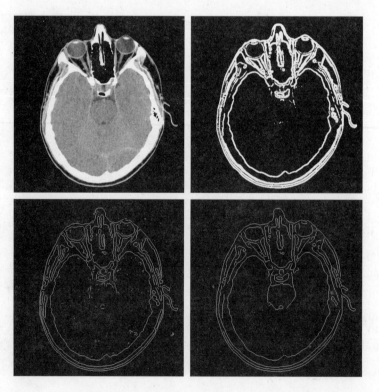

In terms of edge quality and the ability to eliminate irrelevant detail, the results in Fig. 10.26 correspond closely to the results and conclusions in the previous example. Note also that the Canny algorithm was the only procedure capable of yielding a totally unbroken edge for the posterior boundary of the brain, and the closest boundary of the spinal cord. It was also the only procedure capable of finding the cleanest contours, while eliminating all the edges associated with the gray brain matter in the original image.

The price paid for the improved performance of the Canny algorithm is a significantly more complex implementation than the two approaches discussed earlier. In some applications, such as real-time industrial image processing, cost and speed requirements usually dictate the use of simpler techniques, principally the thresholded gradient approach. When edge quality is the driving force, the Marr-Hildreth and Canny algorithms, especially the latter, offer superior alternatives.

LINKING EDGE POINTS

Ideally, edge detection should yield sets of pixels lying only on edges. In practice, these pixels seldom characterize edges completely because of noise, breaks in the edges caused by nonuniform illumination, and other effects that introduce discontinuities in intensity values. Therefore, edge detection typically is followed by linking algorithms designed to assemble edge pixels into meaningful edges and/or region boundaries. In this section, we discuss two fundamental approaches to edge linking that are representative of techniques used in practice. The first requires knowledge about edge points in a local region (e.g., a 3×3 neighborhood), and the second is a global approach that works with an entire edge map. As it turns out, linking points along the boundary of a region is also an important aspect of some of the segmentation methods discussed in the next chapter, and in extracting features from a segmented image, as we will do in Chapter 11. Thus, you will encounter additional edge-point linking methods in the next two chapters.

Local Processing

A simple approach for linking edge points is to analyze the characteristics of pixels in a small neighborhood about every point (x, y) that has been declared an edge point by one of the techniques discussed in the preceding sections. All points that are similar according to predefined criteria are linked, forming an edge of pixels that share common properties according to the specified criteria.

The two principal properties used for establishing similarity of edge pixels in this kind of local analysis are (1) the strength (magnitude) and (2) the direction of the gradient vector. The first property is based on Eq. (10-17). Let S_{xy} denote the set of coordinates of a neighborhood centered at point (x, y) in an image. An edge pixel with coordinates (s, t) in S_{xy} is similar in *magnitude* to the pixel at (x, y) if

$$|M(s,t) - M(x,y)| \le E \tag{10-42}$$

where E is a positive threshold.

The direction angle of the gradient vector is given by Eq. (10-18). An edge pixel with coordinates (s,t) in S_{xy} has an *angle* similar to the pixel at (x,y) if

$$|\alpha(s,t) - \alpha(x,y)| \le A \qquad (10\text{-}43)$$

where A is a positive angle threshold. As noted earlier, the direction of the edge at (x,y) is perpendicular to the direction of the gradient vector at that point.

A pixel with coordinates (s,t) in S_{xy} is considered to be linked to the pixel at (x,y) if both magnitude and direction criteria are satisfied. This process is repeated for every edge pixel. As the center of the neighborhood is moved from pixel to pixel, a record of linked points is kept. A simple bookkeeping procedure is to assign a different intensity value to each set of linked edge pixels.

The preceding formulation is computationally expensive because all neighbors of every point have to be examined. A simplification particularly well suited for real time applications consists of the following steps:

1. Compute the gradient magnitude and angle arrays, $M(x,y)$ and $\alpha(x,y)$, of the input image, $f(x,y)$.

2. Form a binary image, $g(x,y)$, whose value at any point (x,y) is given by:

$$g(x,y) = \begin{cases} 1 & \text{if } M(x,y) > T_M \text{ AND } \alpha(x,y) = A \pm T_A \\ 0 & \text{otherwise} \end{cases}$$

   where T_M is a threshold, A is a specified angle direction, and $\pm T_A$ defines a "band" of acceptable directions about A.

3. Scan the rows of g and fill (set to 1) all gaps (sets of 0's) in each row that do not exceed a specified length, L. Note that, by definition, a gap is bounded at both ends by one or more 1's. The rows are processed individually, with no "memory" kept between them.

4. To detect gaps in any other direction, θ, rotate g by this angle and apply the horizontal scanning procedure in Step 3. Rotate the result back by $-\theta$.

When interest lies in horizontal and vertical edge linking, Step 4 becomes a simple procedure in which g is rotated ninety degrees, the rows are scanned, and the result is rotated back. This is the application found most frequently in practice and, as the following example shows, this approach can yield good results. In general, image rotation is an expensive computational process so, when linking in numerous angle directions is required, it is more practical to combine Steps 3 and 4 into a single, radial scanning procedure.

EXAMPLE 10.10: Edge linking using local processing.

Figure 10.27(a) shows a 534×566 image of the rear of a vehicle. The objective of this example is to illustrate the use of the preceding algorithm for finding rectangles whose sizes makes them suitable candidates for license plates. The formation of these rectangles can be accomplished by detecting

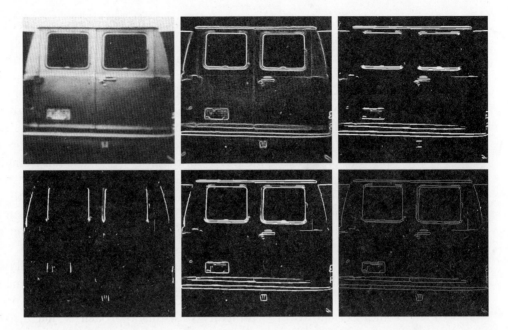

a b c
d e f

FIGURE 10.27
(a) Image of the rear of a vehicle.
(b) Gradient magnitude image.
(c) Horizontally connected edge pixels.
(d) Vertically connected edge pixels.
(e) The logical OR of (c) and (d).
(f) Final result, using morphological thinning. (Original image courtesy of Perceptics Corporation.)

strong horizontal and vertical edges. Figure 10.27(b) shows the gradient magnitude image, $M(x, y)$, and Figs. 10.27(c) and (d) show the result of Steps 3 and 4 of the algorithm, obtained by letting T_M equal to 30% of the maximum gradient value, $A = 90°$, $T_A = 45°$, and filling all gaps of 25 or fewer pixels (approximately 5% of the image width). A large range of allowable angle directions was required to detect the rounded corners of the license plate enclosure, as well as the rear windows of the vehicle. Figure 10.27(e) is the result of forming the logical OR of the two preceding images, and Fig. 10.27(f) was obtained by thinning 10.27(e) with the thinning procedure discussed in Section 9.5. As Fig. 10.27(f) shows, the rectangle corresponding to the license plate was clearly detected in the image. It would be a simple matter to isolate the license plate from all the rectangles in the image, using the fact that the width-to-height ratio of license plates have distinctive proportions (e.g., a 2:1 ratio in U.S. plates).

Global Processing Using the Hough Transform

The method discussed in the previous section is applicable in situations in which knowledge about pixels belonging to individual objects is available. Often, we have to work in unstructured environments in which all we have is an edge map and no knowledge about where objects of interest might be. In such situations, all pixels are candidates for linking, and thus have to be accepted or eliminated based on predefined *global* properties. In this section, we develop an approach based on whether sets of pixels lie on curves of a specified shape. Once detected, these curves form the edges or region boundaries of interest.

Given n points in an image, suppose that we want to find subsets of these points that lie on straight lines. One possible solution is to find all lines determined by every pair of points, then find all subsets of points that are close to particular lines. This approach involves finding $n(n-1)/2 \sim n^2$ lines, then performing $(n)(n(n-1))/2 \sim n^3$

comparisons of every point to all lines. This is a computationally prohibitive task in most applications.

The original formulation of the Hough transform presented here works with straight lines. For a generalization to arbitrary shapes, see Ballard [1981].

Hough [1962] proposed an alternative approach, commonly referred to as the *Hough transform*. Let (x_i, y_i) denote a point in the xy-plane and consider the general equation of a straight line in slope-intercept form: $y_i = ax_i + b$. Infinitely many lines pass through (x_i, y_i), but they all satisfy the equation $y_i = ax_i + b$ for varying values of a and b. However, writing this equation as $b = -x_i a + y_i$ and considering the ab-plane (also called *parameter space*) yields the equation of a *single* line for a fixed point (x_i, y_i). Furthermore, a second point (x_j, y_j) also has a single line in parameter space associated with it, which intersects the line associated with (x_i, y_i) at some point (a', b') in parameter space, where a' is the slope and b' the intercept of the line containing both (x_i, y_i) and (x_j, y_j) in the xy-plane (we are assuming, of course, that the lines are not parallel). In fact, *all* points on this line have lines in parameter space that intersect at (a', b'). Figure 10.28 illustrates these concepts.

In principle, the parameter space lines corresponding to all points (x_k, y_k) in the xy-plane could be plotted, and the principal lines in that plane could be found by identifying points in parameter space where large numbers of parameter-space lines intersect. However, a difficulty with this approach is that a, (the slope of a line) approaches infinity as the line approaches the vertical direction. One way around this difficulty is to use *the normal representation* of a line:

$$x \cos\theta + y \sin\theta = \rho \qquad (10\text{-}44)$$

Figure 10.29(a) illustrates the geometrical interpretation of the parameters ρ and θ. A horizontal line has $\theta = 0°$, with ρ being equal to the positive x-intercept. Similarly, a vertical line has $\theta = 90°$, with ρ being equal to the positive y-intercept, or $\theta = -90°$, with ρ being equal to the negative y-intercept (we limit the angle to the range $-90° \leq \theta \leq 90°$). Each sinusoidal curve in Figure 10.29(b) represents the family of lines that pass through a particular point (x_k, y_k) in the xy-plane. The intersection point (ρ', θ') in Fig. 10.29(b) corresponds to the line that passes through both (x_i, y_i) and (x_j, y_j) in Fig. 10.29(a).

The computational attractiveness of the Hough transform arises from subdividing the $\rho\theta$ parameter space into so-called *accumulator cells*, as Fig. 10.29(c) illustrates, where $(\rho_{\min}, \rho_{\max})$ and $(\theta_{\min}, \theta_{\max})$ are the expected ranges of the parameter values:

a b

FIGURE 10.28
(a) *xy*-plane.
(b) Parameter space.

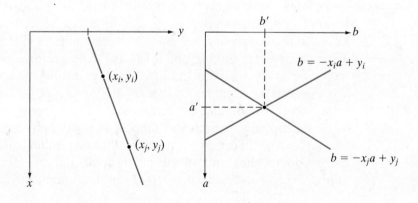

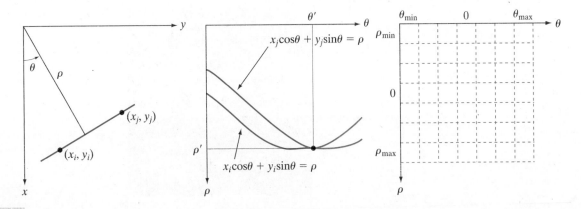

a b c

FIGURE 10.29 (a) (ρ,θ) parameterization of a line in the xy-plane. (b) Sinusoidal curves in the $\rho\theta$-plane; the point of intersection (ρ',θ') corresponds to the line passing through points (x_i,y_i) and (x_j,y_j) in the xy-plane. (c) Division of the $\rho\theta$-plane into accumulator cells.

$-90° \leq \theta \leq 90°$ and $-D \leq \rho \leq D$, where D is the maximum distance between opposite corners in an image. The cell at coordinates (i,j) with accumulator value $A(i,j)$ corresponds to the square associated with parameter-space coordinates (ρ_i, θ_j). Initially, these cells are set to zero. Then, for every non-background point (x_k, y_k) in the xy-plane, we let θ equal each of the allowed subdivision values on the θ-axis and solve for the corresponding ρ using the equation $\rho = x_k \cos\theta + y_k \sin\theta$. The resulting ρ values are then rounded off to the nearest allowed cell value along the ρ axis. If a choice of θ_q results in the solution ρ_p, then we let $A(p,q) = A(p,q)+1$. At the end of the procedure, a value of K in a cell $A(i,j)$ means that K points in the xy-plane lie on the line $x\cos\theta_j + y\sin\theta_j = \rho_i$. The number of subdivisions in the $\rho\theta$-plane determines the accuracy of the colinearity of these points. It can be shown (see Problem 10.27) that the number of computations in the method just discussed is linear with respect to n, the number of non-background points in the xy-plane.

EXAMPLE 10.11: Some basic properties of the Hough transform.

Figure 10.30 illustrates the Hough transform based on Eq. (10-44). Figure 10.30(a) shows an image of size $M \times M$ ($M = 101$) with five labeled white points, and Fig. 10.30(b) shows each of these points mapped onto the $\rho\theta$-plane using subdivisions of one unit for the ρ and θ axes. The range of θ values is $\pm 90°$, and the range of ρ values is $\pm\sqrt{2}M$. As Fig. 10.30(b) shows, each curve has a different sinusoidal shape. The horizontal line resulting from the mapping of point 1 is a sinusoid of zero amplitude.

The points labeled A (not to be confused with accumulator values) and B in Fig. 10.30(b) illustrate the colinearity detection property of the Hough transform. For example, point B, marks the intersection of the curves corresponding to points 2, 3, and 4 in the xy image plane. The location of point A indicates that these three points lie on a straight line passing through the origin ($\rho = 0$) and oriented at $-45°$ [see Fig. 10.29(a)]. Similarly, the curves intersecting at point B in parameter space indicate that points 2, 3, and 4 lie on a straight line oriented at $45°$, and whose distance from the origin is $\rho = 71$ (one-half the diagonal distance from the origin of the image to the opposite corner, rounded to the nearest integer

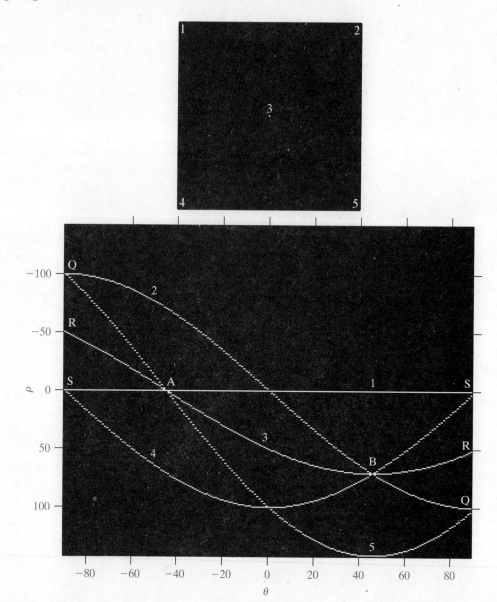

a
b

FIGURE 10.30
(a) Image of size
101×101 pixels,
containing five
white points (four
in the corners and
one in the center).
(b) Corresponding
parameter space.

value). Finally, the points labeled Q, R, and S in Fig. 10.30(b) illustrate the fact that the Hough transform exhibits a reflective adjacency relationship at the right and left edges of the parameter space. This property is the result of the manner in which ρ and θ change sign at the $\pm 90°$ boundaries.

Although the focus thus far has been on straight lines, the Hough transform is applicable to any function of the form $g(\mathbf{v}, \mathbf{c}) = 0$, where $\mathbf{v}$ is a vector of coordinates and $\mathbf{c}$ is a vector of coefficients. For example, points lying on the circle

$$(x - c_1)^2 + (y - c_2)^2 = c_3^2 \tag{10-45}$$

can be detected by using the basic approach just discussed. The difference is the presence of three parameters c_1, c_2, and c_3 that result in a 3-D parameter space with cube-like cells, and accumulators of the form $A(i,j,k)$. The procedure is to increment c_1 and c_2, solve for the value of c_3 that satisfies Eq. (10-45), and update the accumulator cell associated with the triplet (c_1, c_2, c_3). Clearly, the complexity of the Hough transform depends on the number of coordinates and coefficients in a given functional representation. As noted earlier, generalizations of the Hough transform to detect curves with no simple analytic representations are possible, as is the application of the transform to grayscale images.

Returning to the edge-linking problem, an approach based on the Hough transform is as follows:

1. Obtain a binary edge map using any of the methods discussed earlier in this section.
2. Specify subdivisions in the $\rho\theta$-plane.
3. Examine the counts of the accumulator cells for high pixel concentrations.
4. Examine the relationship (principally for continuity) between pixels in a chosen cell.

Continuity in this case usually is based on computing the distance between disconnected pixels corresponding to a given accumulator cell. A gap in a line associated with a given cell is bridged if the length of the gap is less than a specified threshold. Being able to group lines based on direction is a global concept applicable over the entire image, requiring only that we examine pixels associated with specific accumulator cells. The following example illustrates these concepts.

EXAMPLE 10.12: Using the Hough transform for edge linking.

Figure 10.31(a) shows an aerial image of an airport. The objective of this example is to use the Hough transform to extract the two edges defining the principal runway. A solution to such a problem might be of interest, for instance, in applications involving autonomous air navigation.

The first step is to obtain an edge map. Figure 10.31(b) shows the edge map obtained using Canny's algorithm with the same parameters and procedure used in Example 10.9. For the purpose of computing the Hough transform, similar results can be obtained using any of the other edge-detection techniques discussed earlier. Figure 10.31(c) shows the Hough parameter space obtained using $1°$ increments for θ, and one-pixel increments for ρ.

The runway of interest is oriented approximately $1°$ off the north direction, so we select the cells corresponding to $\pm 90°$ and containing the highest count because the runways are the longest lines oriented in these directions. The small boxes on the edges of Fig. 10.31(c) highlight these cells. As mentioned earlier in connection with Fig. 10.30(b), the Hough transform exhibits adjacency at the edges. Another way of interpreting this property is that a line oriented at $+90°$ and a line oriented at $-90°$ are equivalent (i.e., they are both vertical). Figure 10.31(d) shows the lines corresponding to the two accumulator cells just discussed, and Fig. 10.31(e) shows the lines superimposed on the original image. The lines were obtained by joining all gaps not exceeding 20% (approximately 100 pixels) of the image height. These lines clearly correspond to the edges of the runway of interest.

Note that the only information needed to solve this problem was the orientation of the runway and the observer's position relative to it. In other words, a vehicle navigating autonomously would know that if the runway of interest faces north, and the vehicle's direction of travel also is north, the runway should appear vertically in the image. Other relative orientations are handled in a similar manner. The

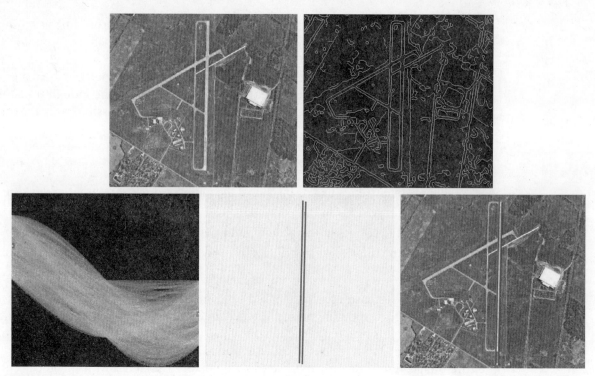

a b
c d e

FIGURE 10.31 (a) A 502×564 aerial image of an airport. (b) Edge map obtained using Canny's algorithm. (c) Hough parameter space (the boxes highlight the points associated with long vertical lines). (d) Lines in the image plane corresponding to the points highlighted by the boxes. (e) Lines superimposed on the original image.

orientations of runways throughout the world are available in flight charts, and the direction of travel is easily obtainable using GPS (Global Positioning System) information. This information also could be used to compute the distance between the vehicle and the runway, thus allowing estimates of parameters such as expected length of lines relative to image size, as we did in this example.

10.3 THRESHOLDING

Because of its intuitive properties, simplicity of implementation, and computational speed, image thresholding enjoys a central position in applications of image segmentation. Thresholding was introduced in Section 3.1, and we have used it in various discussions since then. In this section, we discuss thresholding in a more formal way, and develop techniques that are considerably more general than what has been presented thus far.

FOUNDATION

In the previous section, regions were identified by first finding edge segments, then attempting to link the segments into boundaries. In this section, we discuss techniques for partitioning images directly into regions based on intensity values and/or properties of these values.

The Basics of Intensity Thresholding

Suppose that the intensity histogram in Fig. 10.32(a) corresponds to an image, $f(x, y)$, composed of light objects on a dark background, in such a way that object and background pixels have intensity values grouped into two dominant modes. One obvious way to extract the objects from the background is to select a threshold, T, that separates these modes. Then, any point (x, y) in the image at which $f(x, y) > T$ is called an *object point*. Otherwise, the point is called a *background* point. In other words, the segmented image, denoted by $g(x, y)$, is given by

Remember, $f(x, y)$ denotes the intensity of f at coordinates (x, y).

Although we follow convention in using 0 intensity for the background and 1 for object pixels, any two distinct values can be used in Eq. (10-46).

$$g(x, y) = \begin{cases} 1 & \text{if } f(x, y) > T \\ 0 & \text{if } f(x, y) \le T \end{cases} \tag{10-46}$$

When T is a constant applicable over an entire image, the process given in this equation is referred to as *global thresholding*. When the value of T changes over an image, we use the term *variable thresholding*. The terms *local* or *regional* thresholding are used sometimes to denote variable thresholding in which the value of T at any point (x, y) in an image depends on properties of a neighborhood of (x, y) (for example, the average intensity of the pixels in the neighborhood). If T depends on the spatial coordinates (x, y) themselves, then variable thresholding is often referred to as *dynamic* or *adaptive* thresholding. Use of these terms is not universal.

Figure 10.32(b) shows a more difficult thresholding problem involving a histogram with three dominant modes corresponding, for example, to two types of light objects on a dark background. Here, *multiple thresholding* classifies a point (x, y) as belonging to the background if $f(x, y) \le T_1$, to one object class if $T_1 < f(x, y) \le T_2$, and to the other object class if $f(x, y) > T_2$. That is, the segmented image is given by

$$g(x, y) = \begin{cases} a & \text{if } f(x, y) > T_2 \\ b & \text{if } T_1 < f(x, y) \le T_2 \\ c & \text{if } f(x, y) \le T_1 \end{cases} \tag{10-47}$$

a b

FIGURE 10.32
Intensity histograms that can be partitioned (a) by a single threshold, and (b) by dual thresholds.

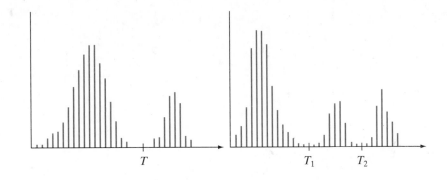

where *a, b,* and *c* are any three distinct intensity values. We will discuss dual threshold-ing later in this section. Segmentation problems requiring more than two thresholds are difficult (or often impossible) to solve, and better results usually are obtained using other methods, such as variable thresholding, as will be discussed later in this section, or region growing, as we will discuss in Section 10.4.

Based on the preceding discussion, we may infer intuitively that the success of intensity thresholding is related directly to the width and depth of the valley(s) sepa-rating the histogram modes. In turn, the key factors affecting the properties of the valley(s) are: (1) the separation between peaks (the further apart the peaks are, the better the chances of separating the modes); (2) the noise content in the image (the modes broaden as noise increases); (3) the relative sizes of objects and background; (4) the uniformity of the illumination source; and (5) the uniformity of the reflectance properties of the image.

The Role of Noise in Image Thresholding

The simple synthetic image in Fig. 10.33(a) is free of noise, so its histogram con-sists of two "spike" modes, as Fig. 10.33(d) shows. Segmenting this image into two regions is a trivial task: we just select a threshold anywhere between the two modes. Figure 10.33(b) shows the original image corrupted by Gaussian noise of zero mean and a standard deviation of 10 intensity levels. The modes are broader now

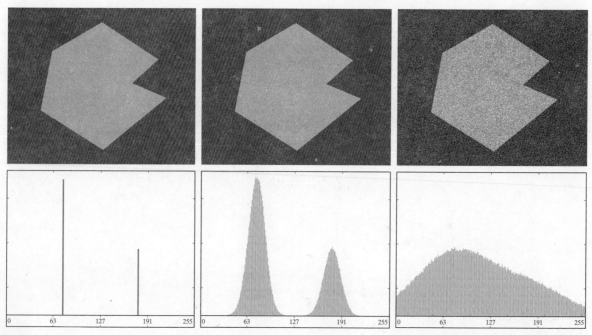

a b c
d e f

FIGURE 10.33 (a) Noiseless 8-bit image. (b) Image with additive Gaussian noise of mean 0 and standard deviation of 10 intensity levels. (c) Image with additive Gaussian noise of mean 0 and standard deviation of 50 intensity levels. (d) through (f) Corresponding histograms.

[see Fig. 10.33(e)], but their separation is enough so that the depth of the valley between them is sufficient to make the modes easy to separate. A threshold placed midway between the two peaks would do the job. Figure 10.33(c) shows the result of corrupting the image with Gaussian noise of zero mean and a standard deviation of 50 intensity levels. As the histogram in Fig. 10.33(f) shows, the situation is much more serious now, as there is no way to differentiate between the two modes. Without additional processing (such as the methods discussed later in this section) we have little hope of finding a suitable threshold for segmenting this image.

The Role of Illumination and Reflectance in Image Thresholding

Figure 10.34 illustrates the effect that illumination can have on the histogram of an image. Figure 10.34(a) is the noisy image from Fig. 10.33(b), and Fig. 10.34(d) shows its histogram. As before, this image is easily segmentable with a single threshold. With reference to the image formation model discussed in Section 2.3, suppose that we multiply the image in Fig. 10.34(a) by a nonuniform intensity function, such as the intensity ramp in Fig. 10.37(b), whose histogram is shown in Fig. 10.34(e). Figure 10.34(c) shows the product of these two images, and Fig. 10.34(f) is the resulting histogram. The deep valley between peaks was corrupted to the point where separation of the modes without additional processing (to be discussed later in this section) is no longer possible. Similar results would be obtained if the illumination was

In theory, the histogram of a ramp image is uniform. In practice, the degree of uniformity depends on the size of the image and number of intensity levels.

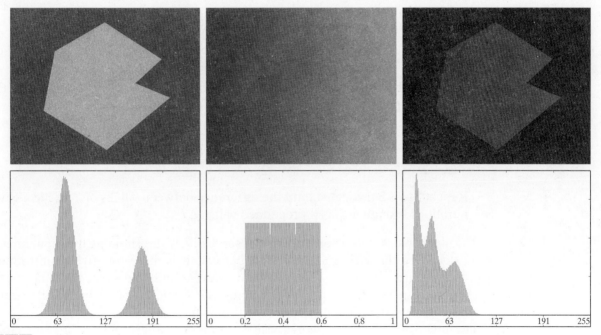

a b c
d e f

FIGURE 10.34 (a) Noisy image. (b) Intensity ramp in the range [0.2, 0.6]. (c) Product of (a) and (b). (d) through (f) Corresponding histograms.

perfectly uniform, but the reflectance of the image was not, as a results, for example, of natural reflectivity variations in the surface of objects and/or background.

The important point is that illumination and reflectance play a central role in the success of image segmentation using thresholding or other segmentation techniques. Therefore, controlling these factors when possible should be the first step considered in the solution of a segmentation problem. There are three basic approaches to the problem when control over these factors is not possible. The first is to correct the shading pattern directly. For example, nonuniform (but fixed) illumination can be corrected by multiplying the image by the inverse of the pattern, which can be obtained by imaging a flat surface of constant intensity. The second is to attempt to correct the global shading pattern via processing using, for example, the top-hat transformation introduced in Section 9.8. The third approach is to "work around" nonuniformities using variable thresholding, as discussed later in this section.

BASIC GLOBAL THRESHOLDING

When the intensity distributions of objects and background pixels are sufficiently distinct, it is possible to use a single (*global*) threshold applicable over the entire image. In most applications, there is usually enough variability between images that, even if global thresholding is a suitable approach, an algorithm capable of estimating the threshold value for each image is required. The following iterative algorithm can be used for this purpose:

1. Select an initial estimate for the global threshold, T.
2. Segment the image using T in Eq. (10-46). This will produce two groups of pixels: G_1, consisting of pixels with intensity values $> T$; and G_2, consisting of pixels with values $\leq T$.
3. Compute the average (mean) intensity values m_1 and m_2 for the pixels in G_1 and G_2, respectively.
4. Compute a new threshold value midway between m_1 and m_2:

$$T = \frac{1}{2}(m_1 + m_2)$$

5. Repeat Steps 2 through 4 until the difference between values of T in successive iterations is smaller than a predefined value, ΔT.

The algorithm is stated here in terms of successively thresholding the input image and calculating the means at each step, because it is more intuitive to introduce it in this manner. However, it is possible to develop an equivalent (and more efficient) procedure by expressing all computations in the terms of the image histogram, which has to be computed only once (see Problem 10.29).

The preceding algorithm works well in situations where there is a reasonably clear valley between the modes of the histogram related to objects and background. Parameter ΔT is used to stop iterating when the changes in threshold values is small. The initial threshold must be chosen greater than the minimum and less than the maximum intensity level in the image (the average intensity of the image is a good

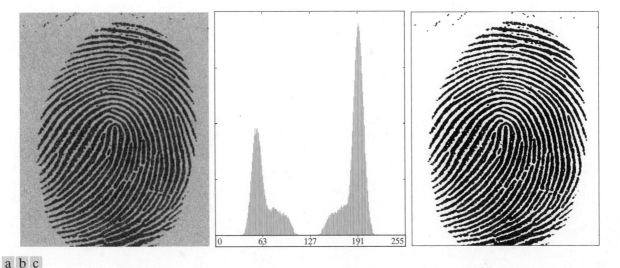

a b c

FIGURE 10.35 (a) Noisy fingerprint. (b) Histogram. (c) Segmented result using a global threshold (thin image border added for clarity). (Original image courtesy of the National Institute of Standards and Technology.).

initial choice for T). If this condition is met, the algorithm converges in a finite number of steps, whether or not the modes are separable (see Problem 10.30).

EXAMPLE 10.13: Global thresholding.

Figure 10.35 shows an example of segmentation using the preceding iterative algorithm. Figure 10.35(a) is the original image and Fig. 10.35(b) is the image histogram, showing a distinct valley. Application of the basic global algorithm resulted in the threshold $T = 125.4$ after three iterations, starting with T equal to the average intensity of the image, and using $\Delta T = 0$. Figure 10.35(c) shows the result obtained using $T = 125$ to segment the original image. As expected from the clear separation of modes in the histogram, the segmentation between object and background was perfect.

OPTIMUM GLOBAL THRESHOLDING USING OTSU'S METHOD

Thresholding may be viewed as a statistical-decision theory problem whose objective is to minimize the average error incurred in assigning pixels to two or more groups (also called *classes*). This problem is known to have an elegant closed-form solution known as the *Bayes decision function* (see Section 12.4). The solution is based on only two parameters: the probability density function (PDF) of the intensity levels of each class, and the probability that each class occurs in a given application. Unfortunately, estimating PDFs is not a trivial matter, so the problem usually is simplified by making workable assumptions about the form of the PDFs, such as assuming that they are Gaussian functions. Even with simplifications, the process of implementing solutions using these assumptions can be complex and not always well-suited for real-time applications.

The approach in the following discussion, called *Otsu's method* (Otsu [1979]), is an attractive alternative. The method is optimum in the sense that it maximizes the *between-class variance*, a well-known measure used in statistical discriminant analysis. The basic idea is that properly thresholded classes should be distinct with respect to the intensity values of their pixels and, conversely, that a threshold giving the best separation between classes in terms of their intensity values would be the best (optimum) threshold. In addition to its optimality, Otsu's method has the important property that it is based entirely on computations performed on the histogram of an image, an easily obtainable 1-D array (see Section 3.3).

Let $\{0, 1, 2, \ldots, L-1\}$ denote the set of L distinct integer intensity levels in a digital image of size $M \times N$ pixels, and let n_i denote the number of pixels with intensity i. The total number, MN, of pixels in the image is $MN = n_0 + n_1 + n_2 + \cdots + n_{L-1}$. The normalized histogram (see Section 3.3) has components $p_i = n_i/MN$, from which it follows that

$$\sum_{i=0}^{L-1} p_i = 1 \qquad p_i \geq 0 \tag{10-48}$$

Now, suppose that we select a threshold $T(k) = k$, $0 < k < L-1$, and use it to threshold the input image into two classes, c_1 and c_2, where c_1 consists of all the pixels in the image with intensity values in the range $[0, k]$ and c_2 consists of the pixels with values in the range $[k+1, L-1]$. Using this threshold, the probability, $P_1(k)$, that a pixel is assigned to (i.e., thresholded into) class c_1 is given by the cumulative sum

$$P_1(k) = \sum_{i=0}^{k} p_i \tag{10-49}$$

Viewed another way, this is the probability of class c_1 occurring. For example, if we set $k = 0$, the probability of class c_1 having any pixels assigned to it is zero. Similarly, the probability of class c_2 occurring is

$$P_2(k) = \sum_{i=k+1}^{L-1} p_i = 1 - P_1(k) \tag{10-50}$$

From Eq. (3-25), the *mean intensity* value of the pixels in c_1 is

$$m_1(k) = \sum_{i=0}^{k} iP(i/c_1) = \sum_{i=0}^{k} iP(c_1/i)P(i)/P(c_1)$$

$$= \frac{1}{P_1(k)} \sum_{i=0}^{k} ip_i \tag{10-51}$$

where $P_1(k)$ is given by Eq. (10-49). The term $P(i/c_1)$ in Eq. (10-51) is the probability of intensity value i, given that i comes from class c_1. The rightmost term in the first line of the equation follows from Bayes' formula:

$$P(A/B) = P(B/A)P(A)/P(B)$$

The second line follows from the fact that $P(c_1/i)$, the probability of c_1 given i, is 1 because we are dealing only with values of i from class c_1. Also, $P(i)$ is the probability of the ith value, which is the ith component of the histogram, p_i. Finally, $P(c_1)$ is the probability of class c_1 which, from Eq. (10-49), is equal to $P_1(k)$.

Similarly, the *mean intensity* value of the pixels assigned to class c_2 is

$$m_2(k) = \sum_{i=k+1}^{L-1} iP(i/c_2)$$

$$= \frac{1}{P_2(k)} \sum_{i=k+1}^{L-1} ip_i$$

(10-52)

The *cumulative mean* (average intensity) up to level k is given by

$$m(k) = \sum_{i=0}^{k} ip_i$$

(10-53)

and the average intensity of the entire image (i.e., the *global* mean) is given by

$$m_G = \sum_{i=0}^{L-1} ip_i$$

(10-54)

The validity of the following two equations can be verified by direct substitution of the preceding results:

$$P_1 m_1 + P_2 m_2 = m_G$$

(10-55)

and

$$P_1 + P_2 = 1$$

(10-56)

where we have omitted the ks temporarily in favor of notational clarity.

In order to evaluate the effectiveness of the threshold at level k, we use the normalized, dimensionless measure

$$\eta = \frac{\sigma_B^2}{\sigma_G^2}$$

(10-57)

where σ_G^2 is the *global variance* [i.e., the intensity variance of all the pixels in the image, as given in Eq. (3-26)],

$$\sigma_G^2 = \sum_{i=0}^{L-1} (i - m_G)^2 p_i$$

(10-58)

and σ_B^2 is the *between-class variance*, defined as

$$\sigma_B^2 = P_1 (m_1 - m_G)^2 + P_2 (m_2 - m_G)^2$$

(10-59)

This expression can also be written as

$$\sigma_B^2 = P_1 P_2 (m_1 - m_2)^2$$

$$= \frac{(m_G P_1 - m)^2}{P_1 (1 - P_1)}$$

(10-60)

The second step in this equation makes sense only if P_1 is greater than 0 and less than 1, which, in view of Eq. (10-56), implies that P_2 must satisfy the same condition.

The first line of this equation follows from Eqs. (10-55), (10-56), and (10-59). The second line follows from Eqs. (10-50) through (10-54). This form is slightly more efficient computationally because the global mean, m_G, is computed only once, so only two parameters, m_1 and P_1, need to be computed for any value of k.

The first line in Eq. (10-60) indicates that the farther the two means m_1 and m_2 are from each other, the larger σ_B^2 will be, implying that the between-class variance is a measure of separability between classes. Because σ_G^2 is a constant, it follows that η also is a measure of separability, and maximizing this metric is equivalent to maximizing σ_B^2. The objective, then, is to determine the threshold value, k, that maximizes the between-class variance, as stated earlier. Note that Eq. (10-57) assumes implicitly that $\sigma_G^2 > 0$. This variance can be zero only when all the intensity levels in the image are the same, which implies the existence of only one class of pixels. This in turn means that $\eta = 0$ for a constant image because the separability of a single class from itself is zero.

Reintroducing k, we have the final results:

$$\eta(k) = \frac{\sigma_B^2(k)}{\sigma_G^2} \tag{10-61}$$

and

$$\sigma_B^2(k) = \frac{[m_G P_1(k) - m(k)]^2}{P_1(k)[1 - P_1(k)]} \tag{10-62}$$

Then, the optimum threshold is the value, k^*, that maximizes $\sigma_B^2(k)$:

$$\sigma_B^2(k^*) = \max_{0 \le k \le L-1} \sigma_B^2(k) \tag{10-63}$$

To find k^* we simply evaluate this equation for all *integer* values of k (subject to the condition $0 < P_1(k) < 1$) and select the value of k that yielded the maximum $\sigma_B^2(k)$. If the maximum exists for more than one value of k, it is customary to average the various values of k for which $\sigma_B^2(k)$ is maximum. It can be shown (see Problem 10.36) that a maximum always exists, subject to the condition $0 < P_1(k) < 1$. Evaluating Eqs. (10-62) and (10-63) for all values of k is a relatively inexpensive computational procedure, because the maximum number of integer values that k can have is L, which is only 256 for 8-bit images.

Once k^* has been obtained, input image $f(x, y)$ is segmented as before:

$$g(x, y) = \begin{cases} 1 & \text{if } f(x, y) > k^* \\ 0 & \text{if } f(x, y) \le k^* \end{cases} \tag{10-64}$$

for $x = 0, 1, 2, \ldots, M-1$ and $y = 0, 1, 2, \ldots, N-1$. Note that all the quantities needed to evaluate Eq. (10-62) are obtained using only the histogram of $f(x, y)$. In addition to the optimum threshold, other information regarding the segmented image can be extracted from the histogram. For example, $P_1(k^*)$ and $P_2(k^*)$, the class probabilities evaluated at the optimum threshold, indicate the portions of the areas occupied by the classes (groups of pixels) in the thresholded image. Similarly, the means $m_1(k^*)$ and $m_2(k^*)$ are estimates of the average intensity of the classes in the original image.

In general, the measure in Eq.(10-61) has values in the range

$$0 \leq \eta(k) \leq 1 \tag{10-65}$$

for values of k in the range $[0, L-1]$. When evaluated at the optimum threshold k^*, this measure is a quantitative estimate of the separability of classes, which in turn gives us an idea of the accuracy of thresholding a given image with k^*. The lower bound in Eq. (10-65) is attainable only by images with a single, constant intensity level. The upper bound is attainable only by two-valued images with intensities equal to 0 and $L-1$ (see Problem 10.37).

Otsu's algorithm may be summarized as follows:

1. Compute the normalized histogram of the input image. Denote the components of the histogram by p_i, $i = 0, 1, 2, \ldots, L-1$.
2. Compute the cumulative sums, $P_1(k)$, for $k = 0, 1, 2, \ldots, L-1$, using Eq. (10-49).
3. Compute the cumulative means, $m(k)$, for $k = 0, 1, 2, \ldots, L-1$, using Eq. (10-53).
4. Compute the global mean, m_G, using Eq. (10-54).
5. Compute the between-class variance term, $\sigma_B^2(k)$, for $k = 0, 1, 2, \ldots, L-1$, using Eq. (10-62).
6. Obtain the Otsu threshold, k^*, as the value of k for which $\sigma_B^2(k)$ is maximum. If the maximum is not unique, obtain k^* by averaging the values of k corresponding to the various maxima detected.
7. Compute the global variance, σ_G^2, using Eq. (10-58), and then obtain the separability measure, η^*, by evaluating Eq. (10-61) with $k = k^*$.

The following example illustrates the use of this algorithm.

EXAMPLE 10.14: Optimum global thresholding using Otsu's method.

Figure 10.36(a) shows an optical microscope image of polymersome cells. These are cells artificially engineered using polymers. They are invisible to the human immune system and can be used, for example, to deliver medication to targeted regions of the body. Figure 10.36(b) shows the image histogram. The objective of this example is to segment the molecules from the background. Figure 10.36(c) is the result of using the basic global thresholding algorithm discussed earlier. Because the histogram has no distinct valleys and the intensity difference between the background and objects is small, the algorithm failed to achieve the desired segmentation. Figure 10.36(d) shows the result obtained using Otsu's method. This result obviously is superior to Fig. 10.36(c). The threshold value computed by the basic algorithm was 169, while the threshold computed by Otsu's method was 182, which is closer to the lighter areas in the image defining the cells. The separability measure η^* was 0.467.

As a point of interest, applying Otsu's method to the fingerprint image in Example 10.13 yielded a threshold of 125 and a separability measure of 0.944. The threshold is identical to the value (rounded to the nearest integer) obtained with the basic algorithm. This is not unexpected, given the nature of the histogram. In fact, the separability measure is high because of the relatively large separation between modes and the deep valley between them.

a b
c d

FIGURE 10.36
(a) Original
image.
(b) Histogram
(high peaks
were clipped to
highlight details in
the lower values).
(c) Segmenta-
tion result using
the basic global
algorithm from
Section 10.3.
(d) Result using
Otsu's method.
(Original image
courtesy of
Professor Daniel
A. Hammer, the
University of
Pennsylvania.)

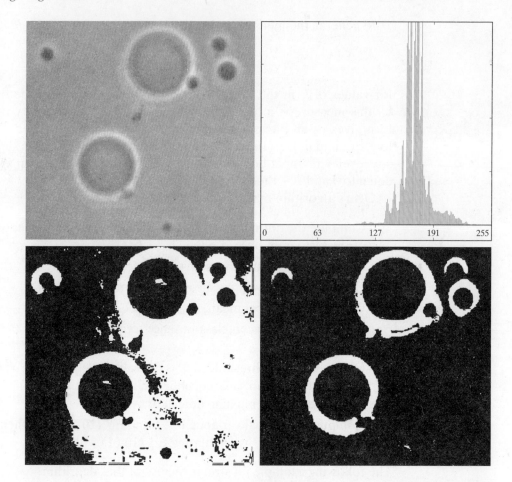

USING IMAGE SMOOTHING TO IMPROVE GLOBAL THRESHOLDING

As illustrated in Fig. 10.33, noise can turn a simple thresholding problem into an unsolvable one. When noise cannot be reduced at the source, and thresholding is the preferred segmentation method, a technique that often enhances performance is to smooth the image prior to thresholding. We illustrate this approach with an example.

Figure 10.37(a) is the image from Fig. 10.33(c), Fig. 10.37(b) shows its histogram, and Fig. 10.37(c) is the image thresholded using Otsu's method. Every black point in the white region and every white point in the black region is a thresholding error, so the segmentation was highly unsuccessful. Figure 10.37(d) shows the result of smoothing the noisy image with an averaging kernel of size 5×5 (the image is of size 651×814 pixels), and Fig. 10.37(e) is its histogram. The improvement in the shape of the histogram as a result of smoothing is evident, and we would expect thresholding of the smoothed image to be nearly perfect. Figure 10.37(f) shows this to be the case. The slight distortion of the boundary between object and background in the segmented, smoothed image was caused by the blurring of the boundary. In fact, the more aggressively we smooth an image, the more boundary errors we should antici-pate in the segmented result.

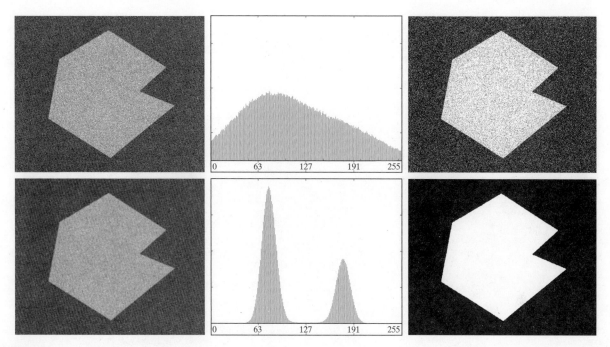

a b c
d e f

FIGURE 10.37 (a) Noisy image from Fig. 10.33(c) and (b) its histogram. (c) Result obtained using Otsu's method. (d) Noisy image smoothed using a 5×5 averaging kernel and (e) its histogram. (f) Result of thresholding using Otsu's method.

Next, we investigate the effect of severely reducing the size of the foreground region with respect to the background. Figure 10.38(a) shows the result. The noise in this image is additive Gaussian noise with zero mean and a standard deviation of 10 intensity levels (as opposed to 50 in the previous example). As Fig. 10.38(b) shows, the histogram has no clear valley, so we would expect segmentation to fail, a fact that is confirmed by the result in Fig. 10.38(c). Figure 10.38(d) shows the image smoothed with an averaging kernel of size 5×5, and Fig. 10.38(e) is the corresponding histogram. As expected, the net effect was to reduce the spread of the histogram, but the distribution still is unimodal. As Fig. 10.38(f) shows, segmentation failed again. The reason for the failure can be traced to the fact that the region is so small that its contribution to the histogram is insignificant compared to the intensity spread caused by noise. In situations such as this, the approach discussed in the following section is more likely to succeed.

USING EDGES TO IMPROVE GLOBAL THRESHOLDING

Based on the discussion thus far, we conclude that the chances of finding a "good" threshold are enhanced considerably if the histogram peaks are tall, narrow, symmetric, and separated by deep valleys. One approach for improving the shape of histograms is to consider only those pixels that lie on or near the edges between

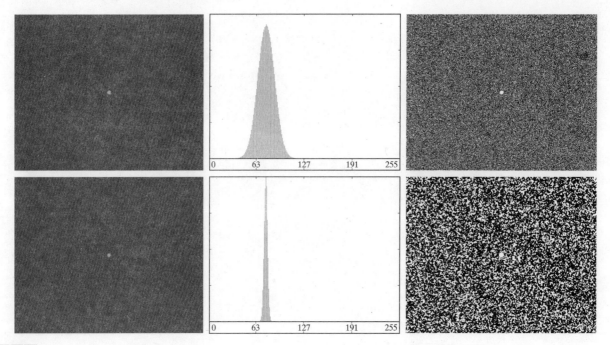

a b c
d e f

FIGURE 10.38 (a) Noisy image and (b) its histogram. (c) Result obtained using Otsu's method. (d) Noisy image smoothed using a 5 × 5 averaging kernel and (e) its histogram. (f) Result of thresholding using Otsu's method. Thresholding failed in both cases to extract the object of interest. (See Fig. 10.39 for a better solution.)

objects and the background. An immediate and obvious improvement is that histograms should be less dependent on the relative sizes of objects and background. For instance, the histogram of an image composed of a small object on a large background area (or vice versa) would be dominated by a large peak because of the high concentration of one type of pixels. We saw in Fig. 10.38 that this can lead to failure in thresholding.

If only the pixels on or near the edges between objects and background were used, the resulting histogram would have peaks of approximately the same height. In addition, the probability that any of those pixels lies on an object would be approximately equal to the probability that it lies on the background, thus improving the symmetry of the histogram modes. Finally, as indicated in the following paragraph, using pixels that satisfy some simple measures based on gradient and Laplacian operators has a tendency to deepen the valley between histogram peaks.

The approach just discussed assumes that the edges between objects and background are known. This information clearly is not available during segmentation, as finding a division between objects and background is precisely what segmentation aims to do. However, an indication of whether a pixel is on an edge may be obtained by computing its gradient or Laplacian. For example, the average value of the Laplacian is 0 at the transition of an edge (see Fig. 10.10), so the valleys of histograms formed from the pixels selected by a Laplacian criterion can be expected to be sparsely populated. This property tends to produce the desirable deep valleys discussed above. In practice, comparable results typically are obtained using either the gradient or Laplacian images, with the latter being favored because it is computationally more attractive and is also created using an isotropic edge detector.

The preceding discussion is summarized in the following algorithm, where $f(x,y)$ is the input image:

It is possible to modify this algorithm so that both the magnitude of the gradient and the absolute value of the Laplacian images are used. In this case, we would specify a threshold for each image and form the logical OR of the two results to obtain the marker image. This approach is useful when more control is desired over the points deemed to be valid edge points.

1. Compute an edge image as either the magnitude of the gradient, or absolute value of the Laplacian, of $f(x,y)$ using any of the methods in Section 10.2.

2. Specify a threshold value, T.

3. Threshold the image from Step 1 using T from Step 2 to produce a binary image, $g_T(x,y)$. This image is used as a mask image in the following step to select pixels from $f(x,y)$ corresponding to "strong" edge pixels in the mask.

4. Compute a histogram using only the pixels in $f(x,y)$ that correspond to the locations of the 1-valued pixels in $g_T(x,y)$.

5. Use the histogram from Step 4 to segment $f(x,y)$ globally using, for example, Otsu's method.

The nth percentile is the smallest number that is greater than $n\%$ of the numbers in a given set. For example, if you received a 95 in a test and this score was greater than 85% of all the students taking the test, then you would be in the 85th percentile with respect to the test scores.

If T is set to any value less than the minimum value of the edge image then, according to Eq. (10-46), $g_T(x,y)$ will consist of all 1's, implying that all pixels of $f(x,y)$ will be used to compute the image histogram. In this case, the preceding algorithm becomes global thresholding using the histogram of the original image. It is customary to specify the value of T to correspond to a percentile, which typically is set high (e.g., in the high 90's) so that few pixels in the gradient/Laplacian image will be used in the computation. The following examples illustrate the concepts just discussed. The first example uses the gradient, and the second uses the Laplacian. Similar results can be obtained in both examples using either approach. The important issue is to generate a suitable derivative image.

EXAMPLE 10.15: Using edge information based on the gradient to improve global thresholding.

Figures 10.39(a) and (b) show the image and histogram from Fig. 10.38. You saw that this image could not be segmented by smoothing followed by thresholding. The objective of this example is to solve the problem using edge information. Figure 10.39(c) is the mask image, $g_T(x,y)$, formed as gradient magnitude image thresholded at the 99.7 percentile. Figure 10.39(d) is the image formed by multiplying the mask by the input image. Figure 10.39(e) is the histogram of the nonzero elements in Fig. 10.39(d). Note that this histogram has the important features discussed earlier; that is, it has reasonably symmetrical modes separated by a deep valley. Thus, while the histogram of the original noisy image offered no hope for successful thresholding, the histogram in Fig. 10.39(e) indicates that thresholding of the small object from the background is indeed possible. The result in Fig. 10.39(f) shows that this is the case. This image was generated using Otsu's method [to obtain a threshold based on the histogram in Fig. 10.42(e)], and then applying the Otsu threshold globally to the noisy image in Fig. 10.39(a). The result is nearly perfect.

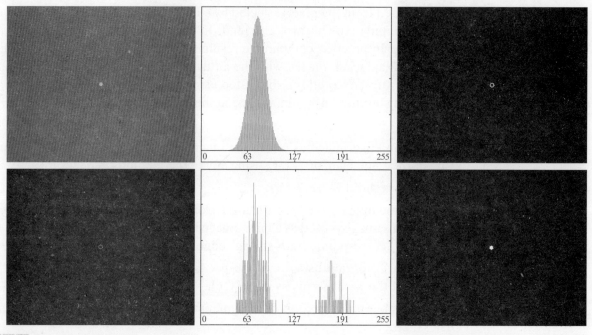

<table>
<tr><td>a</td><td>b</td><td>c</td></tr>
<tr><td>d</td><td>e</td><td>f</td></tr>
</table>

FIGURE 10.39 (a) Noisy image from Fig. 10.38(a) and (b) its histogram. (c) Mask image formed as the gradient magnitude image thresholded at the 99.7 percentile. (d) Image formed as the product of (a) and (c). (e) Histogram of the nonzero pixels in the image in (d). (f) Result of segmenting image (a) with the Otsu threshold based on the histogram in (e). The threshold was 134, which is approximately midway between the peaks in this histogram.

EXAMPLE 10.16: Using edge information based on the Laplacian to improve global thresholding.

In this example, we consider a more complex thresholding problem. Figure 10.40(a) shows an 8-bit image of yeast cells for which we want to use global thresholding to obtain the regions corresponding to the bright spots. As a starting point, Fig. 10.40(b) shows the image histogram, and Fig. 10.40(c) is the result obtained using Otsu's method directly on the image, based on the histogram shown. We see that Otsu's method failed to achieve the original objective of detecting the bright spots. Although the method was able to isolate some of the cell regions themselves, several of the segmented regions on the right were actually joined. The threshold computed by the Otsu method was 42, and the separability measure was 0.636.

Figure 10.40(d) shows the mask image $g_T(x, y)$ obtained by computing the absolute value of the Laplacian image, then thresholding it with T set to 115 on an intensity scale in the range [0, 255]. This value of T corresponds approximately to the 99.5 percentile of the values in the absolute Laplacian image, so thresholding at this level results in a sparse set of pixels, as Fig. 10.40(d) shows. Note in this image how the points cluster near the edges of the bright spots, as expected from the preceding discussion. Figure 10.40(e) is the histogram of the nonzero pixels in the product of (a) and (d). Finally, Fig. 10.40(f) shows the result of globally segmenting the original image using Otsu's method based on the histogram in Fig. 10.40(e). This result agrees with the locations of the bright spots in the image. The threshold computed by the Otsu method was 115, and the separability measure was 0.762, both of which are higher than the values obtained by using the original histogram.

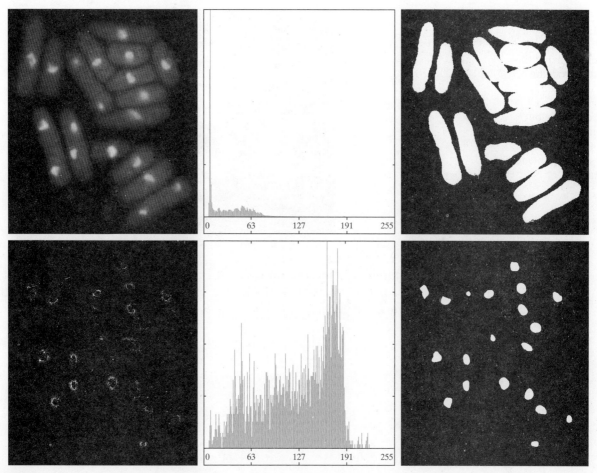

a b c
d e f

FIGURE 10.40 (a) Image of yeast cells. (b) Histogram of (a). (c) Segmentation of (a) with Otsu's method using the histogram in (b). (d) Mask image formed by thresholding the absolute Laplacian image. (e) Histogram of the non-zero pixels in the product of (a) and (d). (f) Original image thresholded using Otsu's method based on the histogram in (e). (Original image courtesy of Professor Susan L. Forsburg, University of Southern California.)

By varying the percentile at which the threshold is set, we can even improve the segmentation of the complete cell regions. For example, Fig. 10.41 shows the result obtained using the same procedure as in the previous paragraph, but with the threshold set at 55, which is approximately 5% of the maximum value of the absolute Laplacian image. This value is at the 53.9 percentile of the values in that image. This result clearly is superior to the result in Fig. 10.40(c) obtained using Otsu's method with the histogram of the original image.

MULTIPLE THRESHOLDS

Thus far, we have focused attention on image segmentation using a single global threshold. Otsu's method can be extended to an arbitrary number of thresholds

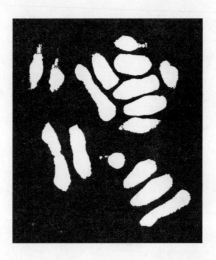

In applications involving
more than one variable
(for example the RGB
components of a color
image), thresholding can
be implemented using a
distance measure, such
as the *Euclidean distance*,
or *Mahalanobis distance*
discussed in Section 6.7
(see Eqs. (6-48), (6-49),
and Example 6.15).

because the separability measure on which it is based also extends to an arbitrary number of classes (Fukunaga [1972]). In the case of K classes, $c_1, c_2, \ldots, c_K$, the between-class variance generalizes to the expression

$$\sigma_B^2 = \sum_{k=1}^{K} P_k \left(m_k - m_G \right)^2 \tag{10-66}$$

where

$$P_k = \sum_{i \in c_k} p_i \tag{10-67}$$

and

$$m_k = \frac{1}{P_k} \sum_{i \in c_k} i p_i \tag{10-68}$$

As before, m_G is the global mean given in Eq. (10-54). The K classes are separated by $K-1$ thresholds whose values, $k_1^*, k_2^*, \ldots, k_{K-1}^*$, are the values that maximize Eq. (10-66):

$$\sigma_B^2 \left(k_1^*, k_2^*, \ldots, k_{K-1}^* \right) \;=\; \max_{0 < k_1 < k_2 < \ldots k_K < L-1} \sigma_B^2 \left(k_1, k_2, \ldots k_{K-1} \right) \tag{10-69}$$

Although this result is applicable to an arbitrary number of classes, it begins to lose meaning as the number of classes increases because we are dealing with only one variable (intensity). In fact, the between-class variance usually is cast in terms of multiple variables expressed as vectors (Fukunaga [1972]). In practice, using multiple global thresholding is considered a viable approach when there is reason to believe that the problem can be solved effectively with two thresholds. Applications that require more than two thresholds generally are solved using more than just intensity values. Instead, the approach is to use additional descriptors (e.g., color) and the application is cast as a pattern recognition problem, as you will learn shortly in the discussion on multivariable thresholding.

Recall from the discussion of the Canny edge detector that thresholding with two thresholds is referred to as *hysteresis thresholding*.

For three classes consisting of three intensity intervals (which are separated by two thresholds), the between-class variance is given by:

$$\sigma_B^2 = P_1\left(m_1 - m_G\right)^2 + P_2\left(m_2 - m_G\right)^2 + P_3\left(m_3 - m_G\right)^2 \tag{10-70}$$

where

$$P_1 = \sum_{i=0}^{k_1} p_i$$

$$P_2 = \sum_{i=k_1+1}^{k_2} p_i \tag{10-71}$$

$$P_3 = \sum_{i=k_2+1}^{L-1} p_i$$

and

$$m_1 = \frac{1}{P_1} \sum_{i=0}^{k_1} i p_i$$

$$m_2 = \frac{1}{P_2} \sum_{i=k_1+1}^{k_2} i p_i \tag{10-72}$$

$$m_3 = \frac{1}{P_3} \sum_{i=k_2+1}^{L-1} i p_i$$

As in Eqs. (10-55) and (10-56), the following relationships hold:

$$P_1 m_1 + P_2 m_2 + P_3 m_3 = m_G \tag{10-73}$$

and

$$P_1 + P_2 + P_3 = 1 \tag{10-74}$$

We see from Eqs. (10-71) and (10-72) that P and m, and therefore σ_B^2, are functions of k_1 and k_2. The two optimum threshold values, k_1^* and k_2^*, are the values that maximize $\sigma_B^2(k_1, k_2)$. That is, as indicated in Eq. (10-69), we find the optimum thresholds by finding

$$\sigma_B^2\left(k_1^*, k_2^*\right) = \max_{0 < k_1 < k_2 < L-1} \sigma_B^2\left(k_1, k_2\right) \tag{10-75}$$

The procedure starts by selecting the first value of k_1 (that value is 1 because looking for a threshold at 0 intensity makes no sense; also, keep in mind that the increment values are integers because we are dealing with integer intensity values). Next, k_2 is incremented through all its values greater than k_1 and less than $L-1$ (i.e., $k_2 = k_1 + 1, \ldots, L-2$). Then, k_1 is incremented to its next value and k_2 is incremented again through all its values greater than k_1. This procedure is repeated until $k_1 = L-3$. The result of this procedure is a 2-D array, $\sigma_B^2(k_1, k_2)$, and the last step is to look for the maximum value in this array. The values of k_1 and k_2 corresponding to that maximum in the array are the optimum thresholds, k_1^* and k_2^*.

If there are several maxima, the corresponding values of k_1 and k_2 are averaged to obtain the final thresholds. The thresholded image is then given by

$$g(x,y) = \begin{cases} a & \text{if } f(x,y) \leq k_1^* \\ b & \text{if } k_1^* < f(x,y) \leq k_2^* \\ c & \text{if } f(x,y) > k_2^* \end{cases} \tag{10-76}$$

where $a, b,$ and c are any three distinct intensity values.

Finally, the separability measure defined earlier for one threshold extends directly to multiple thresholds:

$$\eta\left(k_1^*, k_2^*\right) = \frac{\sigma_B^2\left(k_1^*, k_2^*\right)}{\sigma_G^2} \tag{10-77}$$

where σ_G^2 is the total image variance from Eq. (10-58).

EXAMPLE 10.17: Multiple global thresholding.

Figure 10.42(a) shows an image of an iceberg. The objective of this example is to segment the image into three regions: the dark background, the illuminated area of the iceberg, and the area in shadows. It is evident from the image histogram in Fig. 10.42(b) that two thresholds are required to solve this problem. The procedure discussed above resulted in the thresholds $k_1^* = 80$ and $k_2^* = 177$, which we note from Fig. 10.45(b) are near the centers of the two histogram valleys. Figure 10.42(c) is the segmentation that resulted using these two thresholds in Eq. (10-76). The separability measure was 0.954. The principal reason this example worked out so well can be traced to the histogram having three distinct modes separated by reasonably wide, deep valleys. But we can do even better using superpixels, as you will see in Section 10.5.

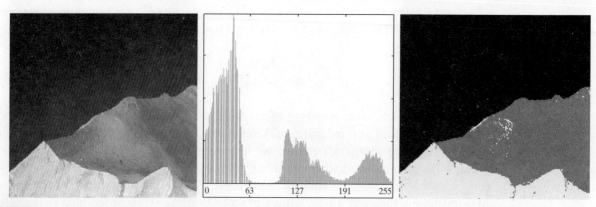

a b c

FIGURE 10.42 (a) Image of an iceberg. (b) Histogram. (c) Image segmented into three regions using dual Otsu thresholds. (Original image courtesy of NOAA.)

VARIABLE THRESHOLDING

As discussed earlier in this section, factors such as noise and nonuniform illumination play a major role in the performance of a thresholding algorithm. We showed that image smoothing and the use of edge information can help significantly. However, sometimes this type of preprocessing is either impractical or ineffective in improving the situation, to the point where the problem cannot be solved by any of the thresholding methods discussed thus far. In such situations, the next level of thresholding complexity involves variable thresholding, as we will illustrate in the following discussion.

Variable Thresholding Based on Local Image Properties

A basic approach to variable thresholding is to compute a threshold at every point, (x, y), in the image based on one or more specified properties in a neighborhood of (x, y). Although this may seem like a laborious process, modern algorithms and hardware allow for fast neighborhood processing, especially for common functions such as logical and arithmetic operations.

We illustrate the approach using the mean and standard deviation of the pixel values in a neighborhood of every point in an image. These two quantities are useful for determining local thresholds because, as you know from Chapter 3, they are descriptors of average intensity and contrast. Let m_{xy} and σ_{xy} denote the mean and standard deviation of the set of pixel values in a neighborhood, S_{xy}, centered at coordinates (x, y) in an image (see Section 3.3 regarding computation of the local mean and standard deviation). The following are common forms of variable thresholds based on the local image properties:

We simplified the notation slightly from the form we used in Eqs. (3-27) and (3-28) by letting xy imply a neighborhood S, centered at coordinates (x, y).

$$T_{xy} = a\sigma_{xy} + bm_{xy} \tag{10-78}$$

where a and b are nonnegative constants, and

$$T_{xy} = a\sigma_{xy} + bm_G \tag{10-79}$$

where m_G is the global image mean. The segmented image is computed as

Note that T_{xy} is a threshold *array* of the same size as the image from which it was obtained. The threshold at a location (x,y) in the array is used to segment the value of an image at that location.

$$g(x, y) = \begin{cases} 1 & \text{if } f(x,y) > T_{xy} \\ 0 & \text{if } f(x,y) \leq T_{xy} \end{cases} \tag{10-80}$$

where $f(x, y)$ is the input image. This equation is evaluated for all pixel locations in the image, and a different threshold is computed at each location (x, y) using the pixels in the neighborhood S_{xy}.

Significant power (with a modest increase in computation) can be added to variable thresholding by using predicates based on the parameters computed in the neighborhood of a point (x, y):

$$g(x, y) = \begin{cases} 1 & \text{if } Q(\text{local parameters}) \text{ is TRUE} \\ 0 & \text{if } Q(\text{local parameters}) \text{ is FALSE} \end{cases} \tag{10-81}$$

where Q is a *predicate* based on parameters computed using the pixels in neighborhood S_{xy}. For example, consider the following predicate, $Q(\sigma_{xy}, m_{xy})$, based on the local mean and standard deviation:

$$Q(\sigma_{xy}, m_{xy}) = \begin{cases} \text{TRUE} & \text{if } f(x,y) > a\sigma_{xy} \text{ AND } f(x,y) > bm_{xy} \\ \text{FALSE} & \text{otherwise} \end{cases} \quad (10\text{-}82)$$

Note that Eq. (10-80) is a special case of Eq. (10-81), obtained by letting Q be TRUE if $f(x,y) > T_{xy}$ and FALSE otherwise. In this case, the predicate is based simply on the intensity at a point.

EXAMPLE 10.18: Variable thresholding based on local image properties.

Figure 10.43(a) shows the yeast image from Example 10.16. This image has three predominant intensity levels, so it is reasonable to assume that perhaps dual thresholding could be a good segmentation approach. Figure 10.43(b) is the result of using the dual thresholding method summarized in Eq. (10-76). As the figure shows, it was possible to isolate the bright areas from the background, but the mid-gray regions on the right side of the image were not segmented (i.e., separated) properly. To illustrate the use

a b
c d

FIGURE 10.43
(a) Image from Fig. 10.40.
(b) Image segmented using the dual thresholding approach given by Eq. (10-76).
(c) Image of local standard deviations.
(d) Result obtained using local thresholding.

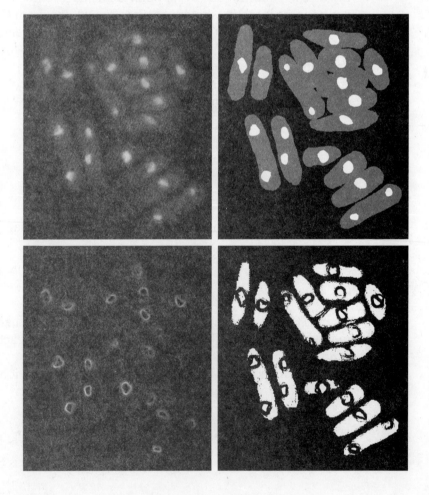

of local thresholding, we computed the local standard deviation σ_{xy} for all (x, y) in the input image using a neighborhood of size 3×3. Figure 10.43(c) shows the result. Note how the faint outer lines correctly delineate the boundaries of the cells. Next, we formed a predicate of the form shown in Eq. (10-82), but using the global mean instead of m_{xy}. Choosing the global mean generally gives better results when the background is nearly constant and all the object intensities are above or below the background intensity. The values $a = 30$ and $b = 1.5$ were used to complete the specification of the predicate (these values were determined experimentally, as is usually the case in applications such as this). The image was then segmented using Eq. (10-82). As Fig. 10.43(d) shows, the segmentation was quite successful. Note in particular that all the outer regions were segmented properly, and that most of the inner, brighter regions were isolated correctly.

Variable Thresholding Based on Moving Averages

A special case of the variable thresholding method discussed in the previous section is based on computing a moving average along scan lines of an image. This implementation is useful in applications such as document processing, where speed is a fundamental requirement. The scanning typically is carried out line by line in a zigzag pattern to reduce illumination bias. Let z_{k+1} denote the intensity of the point encountered in the scanning sequence at step $k + 1$. The moving average (mean intensity) at this new point is given by

$$m(k + 1) = \frac{1}{n} \sum_{i=k+2-n}^{k+1} z_i \qquad \text{for } k \geq n - 1$$

$$= m(k) + \frac{1}{n}\left(z_{k+1} - z_{k-n}\right) \qquad \text{for } k \geq n + 1 \tag{10-83}$$

where n is the number of points used in computing the average, and $m(1) = z_1$. The conditions imposed on k are so that all subscripts on z_k are positive. All this means is that n points must be available for computing the average. When k is less than the limits shown (this happens near the image borders) the averages are formed with the available image points. Because a moving average is computed for every point in the image, segmentation is implemented using Eq. (10-80) with $T_{xy} = cm_{xy}$, where c is positive scalar, and m_{xy} is the moving average from Eq. (10-83) at point (x, y) in the input image.

EXAMPLE 10.19: Document thresholding using moving averages.

Figure 10.44(a) shows an image of handwritten text shaded by a spot intensity pattern. This form of intensity shading is typical of images obtained using spot illumination (such as a photographic flash). Figure 10.44(b) is the result of segmentation using the Otsu global thresholding method. It is not unexpected that global thresholding could not overcome the intensity variation because the method generally performs poorly when the areas of interest are embedded in a nonuniform illumination field. Figure 10.44(c) shows successful segmentation with local thresholding using moving averages. For images of written material, a rule of thumb is to let n equal five times the average stroke width. In this case, the average width was 4 pixels, so we let $n = 20$ in Eq. (10-83) and used $c = 0.5$.

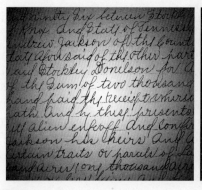 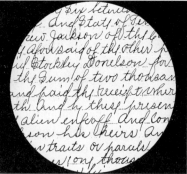

a b c

FIGURE 10.44 (a) Text image corrupted by spot shading. (b) Result of global thresholding using Otsu's method. (c) Result of local thresholding using moving averages.

As another illustration of the effectiveness of this segmentation approach, we used the same parameters as in the previous paragraph to segment the image in Fig. 10.45(a), which is corrupted by a sinusoidal intensity variation typical of the variations that may occur when the power supply in a document scanner is not properly grounded. As Figs. 10.45(b) and (c) show, the segmentation results are comparable to those in Fig. 10.44.

Note that successful segmentation results were obtained in both cases using the same values for n and c, which shows the relative ruggedness of the approach. In general, thresholding based on moving averages works well when the objects of interest are small (or thin) with respect to the image size, a condition satisfied by images of typed or handwritten text.

10.4 SEGMENTATION BY REGION GROWING AND BY REGION SPLITTING AND MERGING

You should review the terminology introduced in Section 10.1 before proceeding.

As we discussed in Section 10.1, the objective of segmentation is to partition an image into regions. In Section 10.2, we approached this problem by attempting to find boundaries between regions based on discontinuities in intensity levels, whereas in Section 10.3, segmentation was accomplished via thresholds based on the distribution of pixel properties, such as intensity values or color. In this section and in Sections 10.5 and 10.6, we discuss segmentation techniques that find the regions directly. In Section 10.7, we will discuss a method that finds the regions and their boundaries simultaneously.

REGION GROWING

As its name implies, *region growing* is a procedure that groups pixels or subregions into larger regions based on predefined criteria for growth. The basic approach is to start with a set of "seed" points, and from these grow regions by appending to each seed those neighboring pixels that have predefined properties similar to the seed (such as ranges of intensity or color).

Selecting a set of one or more starting points can often be based on the nature of the problem, as we show later in Example 10.20. When a priori information is not

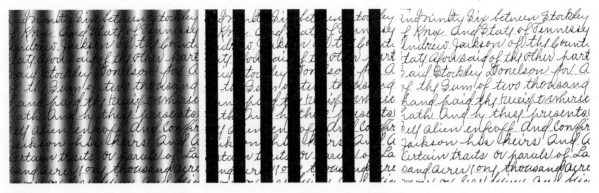

a b c

FIGURE 10.45 (a) Text image corrupted by sinusoidal shading. (b) Result of global thresholding using Otsu's method. (c) Result of local thresholding using moving averages..

available, the procedure is to compute at every pixel the same set of properties that ultimately will be used to assign pixels to regions during the growing process. If the result of these computations shows clusters of values, the pixels whose properties place them near the centroid of these clusters can be used as seeds.

The selection of similarity criteria depends not only on the problem under consideration, but also on the type of image data available. For example, the analysis of land-use satellite imagery depends heavily on the use of color. This problem would be significantly more difficult, or even impossible, to solve without the inherent information available in color images. When the images are monochrome, region analysis must be carried out with a set of descriptors based on intensity levels and spatial properties (such as moments or texture). We will discuss descriptors useful for region characterization in Chapter 11.

Descriptors alone can yield misleading results if connectivity properties are not used in the region-growing process. For example, visualize a random arrangement of pixels that have three distinct intensity values. Grouping pixels with the same intensity value to form a "region," without paying attention to connectivity, would yield a segmentation result that is meaningless in the context of this discussion.

Another problem in region growing is the formulation of a stopping rule. Region growth should stop when no more pixels satisfy the criteria for inclusion in that region. Criteria such as intensity values, texture, and color are local in nature and do not take into account the "history" of region growth. Additional criteria that can increase the power of a region-growing algorithm utilize the concept of size, likeness between a candidate pixel and the pixels grown so far (such as a comparison of the intensity of a candidate and the average intensity of the grown region), and the shape of the region being grown. The use of these types of descriptors is based on the assumption that a model of expected results is at least partially available.

Let: $f(x, y)$ denote an input image; $S(x, y)$ denote a *seed* array containing 1's at the locations of seed points and 0's elsewhere; and Q denote a *predicate* to be applied at each location (x, y). Arrays f and S are assumed to be of the same size. A basic region-growing algorithm based on 8-connectivity may be stated as follows.

See Sections 2.5 and 9.5 regarding connected components, and Section 9.2 regarding erosion.

1. Find all connected components in $S(x, y)$ and reduce each connected component to one pixel; label all such pixels found as 1. All other pixels in S are labeled 0.

2. Form an image f_Q such that, at each point (x, y), $f_Q(x, y) = 1$ if the input image satisfies a given predicate, Q, at those coordinates, and $f_Q(x, y) = 0$ otherwise.

3. Let g be an image formed by appending to each seed point in S all the 1-valued points in f_Q that are 8-connected to that seed point.

4. Label each connected component in g with a different region label (e.g., integers or letters). This is the segmented image obtained by region growing.

The following example illustrates the mechanics of this algorithm.

EXAMPLE 10.20: Segmentation by region growing.

Figure 10.46(a) shows an 8-bit X-ray image of a weld (the horizontal dark region) containing several cracks and porosities (the bright regions running horizontally through the center of the image). We illustrate the use of region growing by segmenting the defective weld regions. These regions could be used in applications such as weld inspection, for inclusion in a database of historical studies, or for controlling an automated welding system.

The first thing we do is determine the seed points. From the physics of the problem, we know that cracks and porosities will attenuate X-rays considerably less than solid welds, so we expect the regions containing these types of defects to be significantly brighter than other parts of the X-ray image. We can extract the seed points by thresholding the original image, using a threshold set at a high percentile. Figure 10.46(b) shows the histogram of the image, and Fig. 10.46(c) shows the thresholded result obtained with a threshold equal to the 99.9 percentile of intensity values in the image, which in this case was 254 (see Section 10.3 regarding percentiles). Figure 10.46(d) shows the result of morphologically eroding each connected component in Fig. 10.46(c) to a single point.

Next, we have to specify a predicate. In this example, we are interested in appending to each seed all the pixels that (a) are 8-connected to that seed, and (b) are "similar" to it. Using absolute intensity differences as a measure of similarity, our predicate applied at each location (x, y) is

$$Q = \begin{cases} \text{TRUE} & \text{if the absolute difference of intensities} \\ & \text{between the seed and the pixel at } (x, y) \text{ is } \leq T \\ \text{FALSE} & \text{otherwise} \end{cases}$$

where T is a specified threshold. Although this predicate is based on intensity differences and uses a single threshold, we could specify more complex schemes in which a different threshold is applied to each pixel, and properties other than differences are used. In this case, the preceding predicate is sufficient to solve the problem, as the rest of this example shows.

From the previous paragraph, we know that all seed values are 255 because the image was thresholded with a threshold of 254. Figure 10.46(e) shows the difference between the seed value (255) and Fig. 10.46(a). The image in Fig. 10.46(e) contains all the differences needed to compute the predicate at each location (x, y). Figure 10.46(f) shows the corresponding histogram. We need a threshold to use in the predicate to establish similarity. The histogram has three principal modes, so we can start by applying to the difference image the dual thresholding technique discussed in Section 10.3. The resulting two thresholds in this case were $T_1 = 68$ and $T_2 = 126$, which we see correspond closely to the valleys of the histogram. (As a brief digression, we segmented the image using these two thresholds. The result in

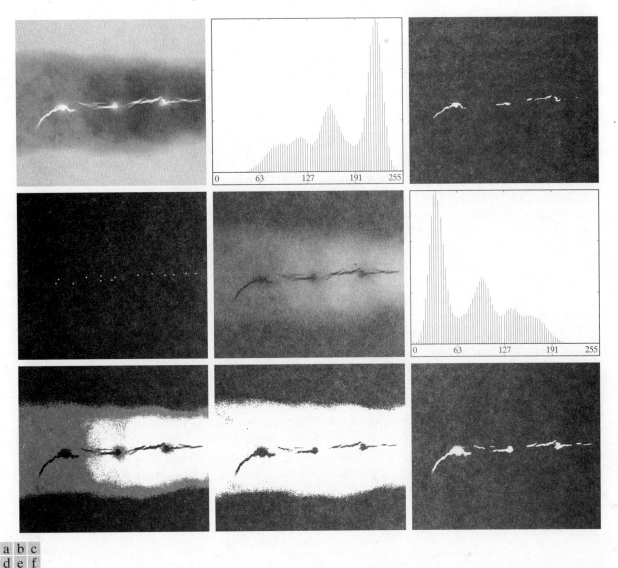

a b c
d e f
g h i

Figure **10.46** (a) X-ray image of a defective weld. (b) Histogram. (c) Initial seed image. (d) Final seed image (the points were enlarged for clarity). (e) Absolute value of the difference between the seed value (255) and (a). (f) Histogram of (e). (g) Difference image thresholded using dual thresholds. (h) Difference image thresholded with the smallest of the dual thresholds. (i) Segmentation result obtained by region growing. (Original image courtesy of X-TEK Systems, Ltd.)

Fig. 10.46(g) shows that segmenting the defects cannot be accomplished using dual thresholds, despite the fact that the thresholds are in the deep valleys of the histogram.)

Figure 10.46(h) shows the result of thresholding the difference image with only T_1. The black points are the pixels for which the predicate was TRUE; the others failed the predicate. The important result here is that the points in the good regions of the weld failed the predicate, so they will not be included in the final result. The points in the outer region will be considered by the region-growing algorithm as candidates. However, Step 3 will reject the outer points because they are not 8-connected to the seeds. In fact, as Fig. 10.46(i) shows, this step resulted in the correct segmentation, indicating that the use of connectivity was a fundamental requirement in this case. Finally, note that in Step 4 we used the same value for all the regions found by the algorithm. In this case, it was visually preferable to do so because all those regions have the same physical meaning in this application—they all represent porosities.

REGION SPLITTING AND MERGING

The procedure just discussed grows regions from seed points. An alternative is to subdivide an image initially into a set of disjoint regions and then merge and/or split the regions in an attempt to satisfy the conditions of segmentation stated in Section 10.1. The basics of region splitting and merging are discussed next.

Let R represent the entire image region and select a predicate Q. One approach for segmenting R is to subdivide it successively into smaller and smaller quadrant regions so that, for any region $R_i, Q(R_i) =$ TRUE. We start with the entire region, R. If $Q(R) =$ FALSE, we divide the image into quadrants. If Q is FALSE for any quadrant, we subdivide that quadrant into sub-quadrants, and so on. This splitting technique has a convenient representation in the form of so-called *quadtrees*; that is, trees in which each node has exactly four descendants, as Fig. 10.47 shows (the images corresponding to the nodes of a quadtree sometimes are called *quadregions* or *quadimages*). Note that the root of the tree corresponds to the entire image, and that each node corresponds to the subdivision of a node into four descendant nodes. In this case, only R_4 was subdivided further.

If only splitting is used, the final partition normally contains adjacent regions with identical properties. This drawback can be remedied by allowing *merging* as well as splitting. Satisfying the constraints of segmentation outlined in Section 10.1 requires merging only adjacent regions whose combined pixels satisfy the predicate Q. That is, two adjacent regions R_j and R_k are merged only if $Q(R_j \cup R_k) =$ TRUE.

The preceding discussion can be summarized by the following procedure in which, at any step, we

See Section 2.5 regarding region adjacency.

1. Split into four disjoint quadrants any region R_i for which $Q(R_i) =$ FALSE.

2. When no further splitting is possible, merge any adjacent regions R_j and R_k for which $Q(R_j \cup R_k) =$ TRUE.

a b

FIGURE 10.47
(a) Partitioned image.
(b) Corresponding quadtree.
R represents the entire image region.

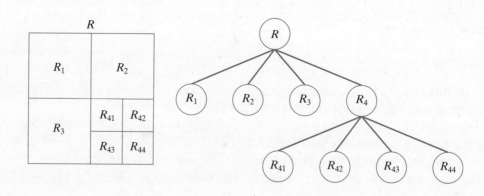

3. Stop when no further merging is possible.

Numerous variations of this basic theme are possible. For example, a significant simplification results if in Step 2 we allow merging of any two adjacent regions R_j and R_k if each one satisfies the predicate individually. This results in a much simpler (and faster) algorithm, because testing of the predicate is limited to individual quadregions. As the following example shows, this simplification is still capable of yielding good segmentation results.

EXAMPLE 10.21: Segmentation by region splitting and merging.

Figure 10.48(a) shows a 566×566 X-ray image of the Cygnus Loop supernova. The objective of this example is to segment (extract from the image) the "ring" of less dense matter surrounding the dense inner region. The region of interest has some obvious characteristics that should help in its segmentation. First, we note that the data in this region has a random nature, indicating that its standard deviation should be greater than the standard deviation of the background (which is near 0) and of the large central region, which is smooth. Similarly, the mean value (average intensity) of a region containing data from the outer ring should be greater than the mean of the darker background and less than the mean of the lighter central region. Thus, we should be able to segment the region of interest using the following predicate:

a b
c d

FIGURE 10.48
(a) Image of the Cygnus Loop supernova, taken in the X-ray band by NASA's Hubble Telescope. (b) through (d) Results of limiting the smallest allowed quadregion to be of sizes of 32×32, 16×16, and 8×8 pixels, respectively. (Original image courtesy of NASA.)

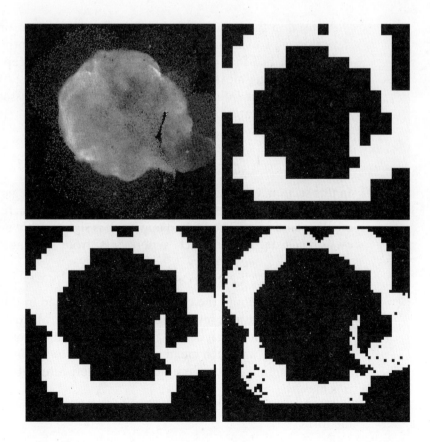

$$Q(R) = \begin{cases} \text{TRUE} & \text{if } \sigma_R > a \ \text{AND} \ 0 < m_R < b \\ \text{FALSE} & \text{otherwise} \end{cases}$$

where σ_R and m_R are the standard deviation and mean of the region being processed, and a and b are nonnegative constants.

Analysis of several regions in the outer area of interest revealed that the mean intensity of pixels in those regions did not exceed 125, and the standard deviation was always greater than 10. Figures 10.48(b) through (d) show the results obtained using these values for a and b, and varying the minimum size allowed for the quadregions from 32 to 8. The pixels in a quadregion that satisfied the predicate were set to white; all others in that region were set to black. The best result in terms of capturing the shape of the outer region was obtained using quadregions of size 16×16. The small black squares in Fig. 10.48(d) are quadregions of size 8×8 whose pixels did not satisfy the predicate. Using smaller quadregions would result in increasing numbers of such black regions. Using regions larger than the one illustrated here would result in a more "block-like" segmentation. Note that in all cases the segmented region (white pixels) was a connected region that completely separates the inner, smoother region from the background. Thus, the segmentation effectively partitioned the image into three distinct areas that correspond to the three principal features in the image: background, a dense region, and a sparse region. Using any of the white regions in Fig. 10.48 as a mask would make it a relatively simple task to extract these regions from the original image (see Problem 10.43). As in Example 10.20, these results could not have been obtained using edge- or threshold-based segmentation.

As used in the preceding example, properties based on the mean and standard deviation of pixel intensities in a region attempt to quantify the texture of the region (see Section 11.3 for a discussion on texture). The concept of texture segmentation is based on using measures of texture in the predicates. In other words, we can perform texture segmentation by any of the methods discussed in this section simply by specifying predicates based on texture content.

10.5 REGION SEGMENTATION USING CLUSTERING AND SUPERPIXELS

In this section, we discuss two related approaches to region segmentation. The first is a classical approach based on seeking clusters in data, related to such variables as intensity and color. The second approach is significantly more modern, and is based on using clustering to extract "superpixels" from an image.

REGION SEGMENTATION USING K-MEANS CLUSTERING

A more general form of clustering is *unsupervised clustering*, in which a clustering algorithm attempts to find a meaningful set of clusters in a given set of samples. We do not address this topic, as our focus in this brief introduction is only to illustrate how *supervised clustering* is used for image segmentation.

The basic idea behind the clustering approach used in this chapter is to partition a set, Q, of observations into a specified number, k, of clusters. In k-means clustering, each observation is assigned to the cluster with the nearest mean (hence the name of the method), and each mean is called the *prototype* of its cluster. A *k-means algorithm* is an iterative procedure that successively refines the means until convergence is achieved.

Let $\{\mathbf{z}_1, \mathbf{z}_2, \ldots, \mathbf{z}_Q\}$ be set of vector observations (samples). These vectors have the form

$$\mathbf{z} = \begin{bmatrix} z_1 \\ z_2 \\ \vdots \\ z_n \end{bmatrix} \tag{10-84}$$

In image segmentation, each component of a vector $\mathbf{z}$ represents a numerical pixel attribute. For example, if segmentation is based on just grayscale intensity, then $\mathbf{z} = z$ is a scalar representing the intensity of a pixel. If we are segmenting RGB color images, $\mathbf{z}$ typically is a 3-D vector, each component of which is the intensity of a pixel in one of the three primary color images, as we discussed in Chapter 6. The objective of k-means clustering is to partition the set Q of observations into k ($k \le Q$) disjoint cluster sets $C = \{C_1, C_2, \ldots, C_k\}$, so that the following criterion of optimality is satisfied:[†]

$$\arg\min_{C} \left(\sum_{i=1}^{k} \sum_{\mathbf{z} \in C_i} \|\mathbf{z} - \mathbf{m}_i\|^2 \right) \tag{10-85}$$

where $\mathbf{m}_i$ is the *mean vector* (or *centroid*) of the samples in set C_i and $\|\text{arg}\|$ is the vector norm of the argument. Typically, the Euclidean norm is used, so the term $\|\mathbf{z} - \mathbf{m}_i\|$ is the familiar *Euclidean distance* from a sample in C_i to mean $\mathbf{m}_i$. In words, this equation says that we are interested in finding the sets $C = \{C_1, C_2, \ldots, C_k\}$ such that the *sum of the distances* from each point in a set to the mean of that set is minimum.

Unfortunately, finding this minimum is an NP-hard problem for which no practical solution is known. As a result, a number of heuristic methods that attempt to find approximations to the minimum have been proposed over the years. In this section, we discuss what is generally considered to be the "standard" k-means algorithm, which is based on the Euclidean distance (see Section 2.6). Given a set $\{\mathbf{z}_1, \mathbf{z}_2, \ldots, \mathbf{z}_Q\}$ of vector observation and a specified value of k, the algorithm is as follows:

These initial means are the initial cluster centers. They are also called seeds.

1. ***Initialize the algorithm:*** Specify an initial set of means, $\mathbf{m}_i(1)$, $i = 1, 2, \ldots, k$.

2. ***Assign samples to clusters:*** Assign each sample to the cluster set whose mean is the closest (ties are resolved arbitrarily, but samples are assigned to only *one* cluster):

$$\mathbf{z}_q \to C_i \ \text{ if } \ \|\mathbf{z}_q - \mathbf{m}_i\|^2 < \|\mathbf{z}_q - \mathbf{m}_j\|^2 \quad j = 1, 2, \ldots, k \ (j \ne i); \ \ q = 1, 2, \ldots, Q$$

3. ***Update the cluster centers (means):***

$$\mathbf{m}_i = \frac{1}{|C_i|} \sum_{\mathbf{z} \in C_i} \mathbf{z} \quad i = 1, 2, \ldots, k$$

where $|C_i|$ is the number of samples in cluster set C_i.

4. ***Test for completion:*** Compute the Euclidean norms of the differences between the mean vectors in the current and previous steps. Compute the residual error, E, as the sum of the k norms. Stop if $E \le T$, where T a specified, nonnegative threshold. Else, go back to Step 2.

[†] Remember, $\min_{x}(h(x))$ is the minimum of h with respected to x, whereas $\arg\min_{x}(h(x))$ is the value (or values) of x at which h is minimum.

a b

FIGURE 10.49
(a) Image of size
688×688 pixels.
(b) Image
segmented using
the k-means
algorithm with
$k = 3$.

When $T = 0$, this algorithm is known to converge in a finite number of iterations to a local minimum. It is not guaranteed to yield the global minimum required to minimize Eq. (10-85). The result at convergence does depend on the initial values chosen for $\mathbf{m}_i$. An approach used frequently in data analysis is to specify the initial means as k randomly chosen samples from the given sample set, and to run the algorithm several times, with a new random set of initial samples each time. This is to test the "stability" of the solution. In image segmentation, the important issue is the value selected for k because this determines the number of segmented regions; thus, multiple passes are rarely used.

EXAMPLE 10.22: Using k-means clustering for segmentation.

Figure 10.49(a) shows an image of size 688×688 pixels, and Fig. 10.49(b) is the segmentation obtained using the k-means algorithm with $k = 3$. As you can see, the algorithm was able to extract all the meaningful regions of this image with high accuracy. For example, compare the quality of the characters in both images. It is important to realize that the entire segmentation was done by clustering of a single variable (intensity). Because k-means works with vector observations in general, its power to discriminate between regions increases as the number of components of vector $\mathbf{z}$ in Eq. (10-84) increases.

REGION SEGMENTATION USING SUPERPIXELS

The idea behind *superpixels* is to replace the standard pixel grid by grouping pixels into primitive regions that are more perceptually meaningful than individual pixels. The objectives are to lessen computational load, and to improve the performance of segmentation algorithms by reducing irrelevant detail. A simple example will help explain the basic approach of superpixel representations.

Figure 10.50(a) shows an image of size 600×800 (480,000) pixels containing various levels of detail that could be described verbally as: "This is an image of two large carved figures in the foreground, and at least three, much smaller, carved figures resting on a fence behind the large figures. The figures are on a beach, with the

a b c

FIGURE 10.50 (a) Image of size 600×480 (480,000) pixels. (b) Image composed of 4,000 superpixels (the boundaries between superpixels (in white) are superimposed on the superpixel image for reference—the boundaries are not part of the data). (c) Superpixel image. (Original image courtesy of the U.S. National Park Services.).

Figures 10.50(b) and (c) were obtained using a method to be discussed later in this section.

ocean and sky in the background." Figure 10.50(b) shows the same image represented by 4,000 superpixels and their boundaries (the boundaries are shown for reference—they are not part of the data), and Fig. 10.50(c) shows the superpixel image. One could argue that the level of detail in the superpixel image would lead to the same description as the original, but the former contains only 4,000 primitive units, as opposed to 480,000 in the original. Whether the superpixel representation is "adequate" depends on the application. If the objective is to describe the image at the level of detail mentioned above, then the answer is yes. On the other hand, if the objective is to detect imperfections at pixel-level resolutions, then the answer obviously is no. And there are application, such as computerized medical diagnosis, in which approximate representations of any kind are not acceptable. Nevertheless, numerous application areas, such as image-database queries, autonomous navigation, and certain branches of robotics, in which economy of implementation and potential improvements in segmentation performance far outweigh any appreciable loss of image detail.

One important requirement of any superpixel representation is *adherence to boundaries*. This means that boundaries between regions of interest must be preserved in a superpixel image. We can see that this indeed is the case with the image in Fig. 10.50(c). Note, for example, how clear the boundaries between the figures and the background are. The same is true of the boundaries between the beach and the ocean, and between the ocean and the sky. Other important characteristics are the preservations of topological properties and, of course, computational efficiency. The superpixel algorithm discussed in this section meets these requirements.

As another illustration, we show the results of severely decreasing the number of superpixels to 1,000, 500, and 250. The results in Fig. 10.51, show a significant loss of detail compared to Fig. 10.50(a), but the first two images contain most of the detail relevant to the image description discussed earlier. A notable difference is that two of the three small carvings on the fence in the back were eliminated. The 250-element superpixel image even lost the third. However, the boundaries between the principal regions, as well as the basic topology of the images, were preserved.

FIGURE 10.51 Top row: Results of using 1,000, 500, and 250 superpixels in the representation of Fig. 10.50(a). As before, the boundaries between superpixels are superimposed on the images for reference. Bottom row: Superpixel images.

SLIC Superpixel Algorithm

In this section we discuss an algorithm for generating superpixels, called *simple linear iterative clustering* (SLIC). This algorithm, developed by Achanta et al. [2012], is conceptually simple, and has computational and other performance advantages over other superpixels techniques. SLIC is a modification of the *k*-means algorithm discussed in the previous section. SLIC observations typically use (but are not limited to) 5-dimensional vectors containing three color components and two spatial coordinates. For example, if we are using the RGB color system, the 5-dimensional vector associated with an image pixel has the form

As you will learn in Chapter 11, vectors containing image attributes are called *feature vectors*.

$$\mathbf{z} = \begin{bmatrix} r \\ g \\ b \\ x \\ y \end{bmatrix} \tag{10-86}$$

where (r, g, b) are the three color components of a pixel, and (x, y) are its two spatial coordinates. Let n_{sp} denote the desired number of superpixels and let n_{tp} denote the total number of pixels in the image. The initial superpixel centers, $\mathbf{m}_i = \begin{bmatrix} r_i & g_i & b_i & x_i & y_i \end{bmatrix}^T$, $i = 1, 2, \ldots, n_{sp}$, are obtained by sampling the image on a regular grid spaced s units apart. To generate superpixels approximately equal in size (i.e., area), the grid spacing interval is selected as $s = [n_{tp}/n_{sp}]^{1/2}$. To prevent centering a superpixel on the edge of the image, and to reduce the chances of starting at a noisy point, the initial cluster centers are moved to the lowest gradient position in the 3×3 neighborhood about each center.

The SLIC superpixel algorithm consists of the following steps. Keep in mind that superpixels are vectors in general. When we refer to a "pixel" in the algorithm, we are referring to the (x, y) *location* of the superpixel relative to the image.

1. ***Initialize the algorithm:*** Compute the initial superpixel cluster centers,

$$\mathbf{m}_i = \begin{bmatrix} r_i & g_i & b_i & x_i & y_i \end{bmatrix}^T, \ i = 1, 2, \ldots, n_{sp}$$

by sampling the image at regular grid steps, s. Move the cluster centers to the lowest gradient position in a 3×3 neighborhood. For each pixel location, p, in the image, set a label $L(p) = -1$ and a distance $d(p) = \infty$.

2. ***Assign samples to cluster centers:*** For each cluster center $\mathbf{m}_i$, $i = 1, 2, \ldots, n_{sp}$, compute the distance, $D_i(p)$ between $\mathbf{m}_i$ and *each* pixel p in a $2s \times 2s$ neighborhood about $\mathbf{m}_i$. Then, for each p and $i = 1, 2, \ldots, n_{sp}$, if $D_i < d(p)$, let $d(p) = D_i$ and $L(p) = i$.

3. ***Update the cluster centers:*** Let C_i denote the set of pixels in the image with label $L(p) = i$. Update $\mathbf{m}_i$:

$$\mathbf{m}_i = \frac{1}{|C_i|} \sum_{\mathbf{z} \in C_i} \mathbf{z} \quad i = 1, 2, \ldots, n_{sp}$$

where $|C_i|$ is the number of pixels in set C_i, and the $\mathbf{z}$'s are given by Eq. (10-86).

4. ***Test for convergence:*** Compute the Euclidean norms of the differences between the mean vectors in the current and previous steps. Compute the residual error, E, as the sum of the n_{sp} norms. If $E < T$, where T a specified nonnegative threshold, go to Step 5. Else, go back to Step 2.

5. ***Post-process the superpixel regions:*** Replace all the superpixels in each region, C_i, by their average value, $\mathbf{m}_i$.

Note in Step 5 that superpixels end up as contiguous regions of constant value. The average value is not the only way to compute this constant, but it is the most widely used. For graylevel images, the average is just the average intensity of all the pixels in the region spanned by the superpixel. This algorithm is similar to the k-means algorithm in the previous section, with the exceptions that the distances, D_i, are not specified as Euclidean distances (see below), and that these distances are computed for regions of size $2s \times 2s$, rather than for all the pixels in the image, thus reducing computation time significantly. In practice, SLIC convergence with respect to E can be achieved with fairly large values of T. For example, all results reported by Achanta et al. [2012] were obtained using $T = 10$.

Specifying the Distance Measure

SLIC superpixels correspond to clusters in a space whose coordinates are colors and spatial variables. It would be senseless to use a single Euclidean distance in this case, because the scales in the axes of this coordinate system are different and unrelated. In other words, spatial and color distances must be treated separately. This is accomplished by normalizing the distance of the various components, then combining them into a single measure. Let d_c and d_s denote the color and spatial Euclidean distances between two points in a cluster, respectively:

$$d_c = \left[(r_j - r_i)^2 + (g_j - g_i)^2 + (b_j - b_i)^2 \right]^{1/2}$$ (10-87)

and

$$d_s = \left[(x_j - x_i)^2 + (y_j - y_i)^2 \right]^{1/2}$$ (10-88)

We then define D as the *composite* distance

$$D = \left[\left(\frac{d_c}{d_{cm}} \right)^2 + \left(\frac{d_s}{d_{sm}} \right)^2 \right]^{1/2}$$ (10-89)

where d_{cm} and d_{sm} are the maximum expected values of d_c and d_s. The maximum spatial distance should correspond to the sampling interval; that is, $d_{sm} = s = [n_{tp}/n_{sp}]^{1/2}$. Determining the maximum color distance is not as straightforward, because these distances can vary significantly from cluster to cluster, and from image to image. A solution is to set d_{cm} to a constant c so that Eq. (10-89) becomes

$$D = \left[\left(\frac{d_c}{c} \right)^2 + \left(\frac{d_s}{s} \right)^2 \right]^{1/2}$$ (10-90)

We can write this equation as

$$D = \left[d_c^2 + \left(\frac{d_s}{s} \right)^2 c^2 \right]^{1/2}$$ (10-91)

This is the distance measure used for each cluster in the algorithm. Constant c can be used to weigh the relative importance between color similarity and spatial proximity. When c is large, spatial proximity is more important, and the resulting superpixels are more compact. When c is small, the resulting superpixels adhere more tightly to image boundaries, but have less regular size and shape.

For grayscale images, as in Example 10.23 below, we use

$$d_c = \left[(l_j - l_i)^2 \right]^{1/2}$$ (10-92)

in Eq. (10-91), where the l's are intensity levels of the points for which the distance is being computed.

In 3-D, superpixels become *supervoxels*, which are handled by defining

$$d_s = \left[(x_j - x_i)^2 + (y_j - y_i)^2 + (z_j - z_i)^2 \right]^{1/2} \qquad (10\text{-}93)$$

where the z's are the coordinates of the third spatial dimension. We must also add the third spatial variable, z, to the vector in Eq. (10-86).

Because no provision is made in the algorithm to enforce connectivity, it is possible for isolated pixels to remain after convergence. These are assigned the label of the nearest cluster using a connected components algorithm (see Section 9.6). Although we explained the algorithm in the context of RGB color components, the method is equally applicable to other colors systems. In fact, other components of vector $\mathbf{z}$ in Eq. (10-86) (with the exception of the spatial variables) could be other real-valued feature values, provided that a meaningful distance measure can be defined for them.

EXAMPLE 10.23: Using superpixels for image segmentation.

Figure 10.52(a) shows an image of an iceberg, and Fig. 10.52(b) shows the result of segmenting this image using the k-means algorithm developed in the last section, with $k = 3$. Although the main regions of the image were segmented, there are numerous segmentation errors in both regions of the iceberg, and also on the boundary separating it from the background. Errors are visible as isolated pixels (and also as small groups of pixels) with the wrong shade (e.g., black pixels within a white region). Figure 10.52(c) shows a 100-superpixel representation of the image with the superpixel boundaries superimposed for reference, and Fig. 10.52(d) shows the same image without the boundaries. Figure 10.52(e) is the segmentation of (d) using the k-means algorithm with $k = 3$ as before. Note the significant improvement over the result in (b), indicating that the original image has considerably more (irrelevant) detail than is needed for a proper segmentation. In terms of computational advantage, consider that generating Fig. 10.52(b) required individual processing of over 300K pixels, while (e) required processing of 100 pixels with considerably fewer shades of gray.

10.6 REGION SEGMENTATION USING GRAPH CUTS

In this section, we discuss an approach for partitioning an image into regions by expressing the pixels of the image as nodes of a graph, and then finding an optimum partition (*cut*) of the graph into groups of nodes. Optimality is based on criteria whose values are high for members within a group (i.e., a region) and low across members of different groups. As you will see later in this section, graph-cut segmentation is capable in some cases of results that can be superior to the results achievable by any of the segmentation methods studied thus far. The price of this potential benefit is added complexity in implementation, which generally translates into slower execution.

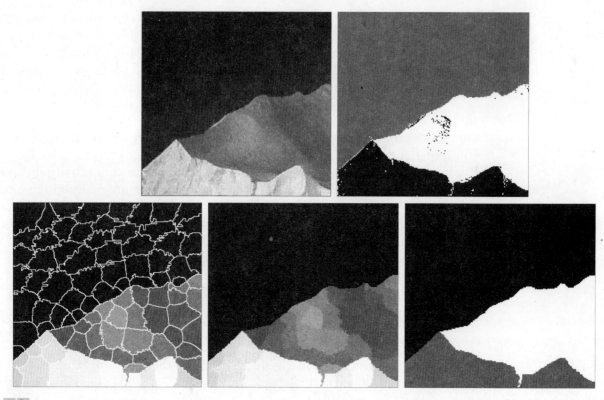

a b
c d e

FIGURE 10.52 (a) Image of size 533×566 (301,678) pixels. (b) Image segmented using the k-means algorithm. (c) 100-element superpixel image showing boundaries for reference. (d) Same image without boundaries. (e) Superpixel image (d) segmented using the k-means algorithm. (Original image courtesy of NOAA.)

IMAGES AS GRAPHS

Nodes and edges are also referred to as *vertices* and *links*, respectively.

A graph, G, is a mathematical structure consisting of a set V of *nodes* and a set E of *edges* connecting those vertices:

$$G = (V, E) \tag{10-94}$$

where V is a set and

See Section 2.5 for an explanation of the Cartesian product $V \times V$ and for a review of the set symbols used in this section.

$$E \subseteq V \times V \tag{10-95}$$

is a set of ordered pairs of elements from V. If $(u, v) \in E$ implies that $(v, u) \in E$, and vice versa, the graph is said to be *undirected*; otherwise the graph is *directed*. For example, we may consider a street map as a graph in which the nodes are street intersections, and the edges are the streets connecting those intersections. If all streets are bidirectional, the graph is undirected (meaning that we can travel both ways from any two intersections). Otherwise, if at least one street is a one-way street, the graph is directed.

The types of graphs in which we are interested are undirected graphs whose edges are further characterized by a matrix, $\mathbf{W}$, whose element $w(i,j)$ is a weight associated with the edge that connects nodes i and j. Because the graph is undirected, $w(i,j) = w(j,i)$, which means that $\mathbf{W}$ is a symmetric matrix. The weights are selected to be proportional to one or more similarity measures between all pairs of nodes. A graph whose edges are associated with weights is called a *weighted graph*.

The essence of the material in this section is to represent an image to be segmented as a weighted, undirected graph, where the nodes of the graph are the pixels in the image, and an edge is formed between every pair of nodes. The weight, $w(i,j)$, of each edge is a function of the similarity between nodes i and j. We then seek to partition the nodes of the graph into disjoint subsets $V_1, V_2, \ldots, V_K$ where, by some measure, the similarity among the nodes within a subset is high, and the similarity across the nodes of different subsets is low. The nodes of the partitioned subsets correspond to the regions in the segmented image.

Superpixels are also well suited for use as graph nodes. Thus, when we refer in this section to "pixels" in an image, we are, by implication, also referring to superpixels.

Set V is partitioned into subsets by cutting the graph. A *cut* of a graph is a partition of V into two subsets A and B such that

$$A \cup B = V \text{ and } A \cap B = \varnothing \qquad (10\text{-}96)$$

where the cut is implemented by removing the edges connecting subgraphs A and B. There are two key aspects of using graph cuts for image segmentation: (1) how to associate a graph with an image; and (2) how to cut the graph in a way that makes sense in terms of partitioning the image into background and foreground (object) pixels. We address these two questions next.

Figure 10.53 shows a simplified approach for generating a graph from an image. The nodes of the graph correspond to the pixels in the image and, to keep the explanation simple, we allow edges only between adjacent pixels using 4-connectivity, which means that there are no diagonal edges linking the pixels. But, keep in mind that, in general, edges are specified between every pair of pixels. The weights for the edges typically are formed from spatial relationships (for example, distance from the vertex pixel) and intensity measures (for example, texture and color), consistent with exhibiting similarity between pixels. In this simple example, we define the degree of similarity between two pixels as the inverse of the difference in their intensities. That is, for two nodes (pixels) n_i and n_j, the weight of the edge between them is $w(i,j) = 1/(|I(n_i) - I(n_j)| + c)$, where $I(n_i)$ and $I(n_j)$, are the intensities of the two nodes (pixels) and c is a constant included to prevent division by 0. Thus, the closer the values of intensity between adjacent pixels is, the larger the value of w will be.

For illustrative purposes, the thickness of each edge in Fig. 10.53 is shown proportional to the degree of similarity between the pixels that it connects (see Problem 10.44). As you can see in the figure, the edges between the dark pixels are stronger than the edges between dark and light pixels, and vice versa. Conceptually, segmentation is achieved by cutting the graph along its weak edges, as illustrated by the dashed line in Fig. 10.53(d). Figure 10.53(c) shows the segmented image.

Although the basic structure in Fig. 10.53 is the focus of the discussion in this section, we mention for completeness another common approach for constructing

FIGURE 10.53
(a) A 3×3 image.
(c) A corresponding
graph.
(d) Graph cut.
(c) Segmented
image.

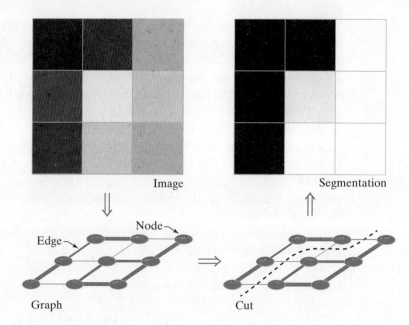

image graphs. Figure 10.54 shows the same graph as the one we just discussed, but here you see two additional nodes called the *source* and *sink terminal* nodes, respectively, each connected to all nodes in the graph via unidirectional links called *t-links*. The terminal nodes are not part of the image; their role, for example, is to associate with each pixel a probability that it is a background or foreground (object) pixel. The probabilities are the weights of the t-links. In Figs. 10.54(c) and (d), the thickness of each t-link is proportional to the value of the probability that the graph node to which it is connected is a foreground or background pixel (the thicknesses shown are so that the segmentation result would be the same as in Fig. 10.53). Which of the two nodes we call background or foreground is arbitrary.

MINIMUM GRAPH CUTS

Once an image has been expressed as a graph, the next step is to cut the graph into two or more subgraphs. The nodes (pixels) in each resulting subgraph correspond to a region in the segmented image. Approaches based on Fig. 10.54 rely on interpreting the graph as a flow network (of pipes, for example) and obtaining what is commonly referred to as a *minimum graph cut*. This formulation is based on the so-called *Max-Flow, Min-Cut Theorem*. This theorem states that, in a flow network, the maximum amount of flow passing from the source to the sink is equal to the *minimum cut*. This minimum cut is defined as the smallest *total* weight of the edges that, if removed, would disconnect the sink from the source:

$$cut(A,B) = \sum_{u \in A, v \in B} w(u,v) \qquad (10\text{-}97)$$

a b
c d

FIGURE 10.54
(a) Same image
as in Fig. 10.53(a).
(c) Corresponding
graph and terminal
nodes. (d) Graph
cut. (b) Segmented
image.

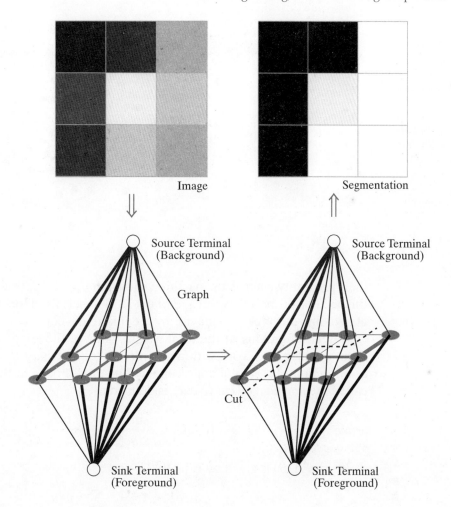

where A and B satisfy Eq. (10-96). The optimum partition of a graph is the one that minimizes this cut value. There is an exponential number of such partitions, which would present us with an intractable computational problem. However, efficient algorithms that run in polynomial time have been developed for solving max-flow problems. Therefore, based on the Max-Flow, Min-Cut Theorem, we can apply these algorithms to image segmentation, provided that we cast segmentation as a flow problem and select the weights for the edges and t-links such that minimum graph cuts will result in meaningful segmentations.

Although the min-cut approach offers an elegant solution, it can result in groupings that favor cutting small sets of isolated nodes in a graph, leading to improper segmentations. Figure 10.55 shows an example, in which the two regions of interest are characterized by the tightness of the pixel groupings. Meaningful edge weights that reflect this property would be inversely proportional to the distance between pairs of points. But this would lead to weights that would be smaller for isolated points, resulting in min cuts such as the example in Fig. 10.55. In fact, any cut that partitions out individual points on the left of the figure will have a smaller cut value in Eq. (10-4) than a cut that properly partitions the points into two groups based on

FIGURE 10.55
An example
showing how a
min cut can lead
to a meaningless
segmentation. In
this example, the
similarity between
pixels is defined
as their spatial
proximity, which
results in two
distinct regions.

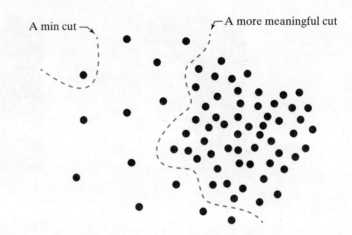

their proximity, such as the partition shown in Fig. 10.55. The approach presented in this section, proposed by Shi and Malik [2000] (see also Hochbaum [2010]), is aimed at avoiding this type of behavior by redefining the concept of a cut.

Instead of looking at the total weight value of the edges that connect two partitions, the idea is to work with a measure of "disassociation" that computes the cost as a fraction of the total edge connections to all nodes in the graph. This measure, called the *normalized cut* (*Ncut*), is defined as

$$Ncut(A,B) = \frac{cut(A,B)}{assoc(A,V)} + \frac{cut(A,B)}{assoc(B,V)} \qquad (10\text{-}98)$$

where $cut(A,B)$ is given by Eq. (10-97) and

$$assoc(A,V) = \sum_{u \in A, z \in V} w(u,z) \qquad (10\text{-}99)$$

is the sum of the weights of all the edges from the nodes of subgraph A to the nodes of the entire graph. Similarly,

$$assoc(B,V) = \sum_{v \in B, z \in V} w(v,z) \qquad (10\text{-}100)$$

is the sum of the weights of the edges from all the edges in B to the entire graph. As you can see, $assoc(A,V)$ is simply the cut of A from the rest of the graph, and similarly for $assoc(B,V)$.

By using $Ncut(A,B)$ instead of $cut(A,B)$, the cut that partitions isolated points will no longer have small values. You can see this, for example, by noting in Fig. 10.55 that if A is the single node shown, $cut(A,B)$ and $assoc(A,V)$ will have the same value. Thus, independently of how small $cut(A,B)$ is, $Ncut(A,B)$ will always be greater than or equal to 1, thus providing normalization for "pathological" cases such as this.

Based on similar concepts, we can define a measure for total *normalized association* within graph partitions as

$$Nassoc(A,B) = \frac{assoc(A,A)}{assoc(A,V)} + \frac{assoc(B,B)}{assoc(B,V)} \qquad (10\text{-}101)$$

where $assoc(A,A)$ and $assoc(B,B)$ are the total weights connecting the nodes within A and within B, respectively. It is not difficult to show (see Problem 10.46) that

$$Ncut(A,B) = 2 - Nassoc(A,B) \qquad (10\text{-}102)$$

which implies that minimizing $Ncut(A,B)$ simultaneously maximizes $Nassoc(A,B)$.

Based on the preceding discussion, image segmentation using graph cuts is now based on finding a partition that minimizes $Ncut(A,B)$. Unfortunately, minimizing this quantity exactly is an NP-complete computational task, and we can no longer rely on the solutions available for max flow because the approach being followed now is based on the concepts explained in connection with Fig. 10.53. However, Shi and Malik [2000] (see also Hochbaum [2010]) were able to find an approximate discrete solution to minimizing $Ncut(A,B)$ by formulating minimization as a generalized eigenvalue problem, for which numerous implementations exist.

COMPUTING MINIMAL GRAPH CUTS

As above, let V denote the nodes of a graph G, and let A and B be two subsets of V satisfying Eq. (10-96). Let K denote the number of nodes in V and define a K-dimensional *indicator* vector, $\mathbf{x}$, whose element x_i has the property $x_i = 1$ if node n_i of V is in A and $x_i = -1$ if it is in B. Let

If the nodes of graph G are the pixels in an image, then $K = M \times N$, where M and N are the number of rows and columns in the image.

$$d_i = \sum_j w(i,j) \qquad (10\text{-}103)$$

be the sum of the weights from node n_i to all other nodes in V. Using these definitions, we can write Eq. (10-98) as

$$Ncut(A,B) = \frac{cut(A,B)}{cut(A,V)} + \frac{cut(A,B)}{cut(B,V)}$$

$$= \frac{\sum\limits_{x_i>0,\, x_j<0} -w(i,j)x_i x_j}{\sum\limits_{x_i>0} d_i} + \frac{\sum\limits_{x_i<0,\, x_j>0} -w(i,j)x_i x_j}{\sum\limits_{x_i<0} d_i} \qquad (10\text{-}104)$$

The objective is to find a vector, $\mathbf{x}$, that minimizes $Ncut(A,B)$. A closed-form solution that minimizes Eq. (10-104) can be found, but only if the elements of $\mathbf{x}$ are allowed to be real, continuous numbers instead of being constrained to be ± 1. The solution derived by Shi and Malik [2000] is given by solving the generalized eigensystem expression

$$(\mathbf{D} - \mathbf{W})\mathbf{y} = \lambda \mathbf{D}\mathbf{y} \qquad (10\text{-}105)$$

where $\mathbf{D}$ is a $K \times K$ diagonal matrix with main-diagonal elements d_i, $i = 1, 2, \ldots, K$, and W is a $K \times K$ weight matrix with elements $w(i,j)$, as defined earlier. Solving

Eq. (10-105) gives K eigenvalues and K eigenvectors, each corresponding to one eigenvalue. The solution to our problem is the eigenvector corresponding the *second* smallest eigenvalue.

We can convert the preceding generalized eigenvalue formulation into a standard eigenvalue problem by writing Eq. (10-105) as (see Problem 10.45):

$$\mathbf{A}\mathbf{z} = \lambda\mathbf{z} \tag{10-106}$$

where

$$\mathbf{A} = \mathbf{D}^{-\frac{1}{2}}(\mathbf{D} - \mathbf{W})\mathbf{D}^{-\frac{1}{2}} \tag{10-107}$$

and

$$\mathbf{z} = \mathbf{D}^{\frac{1}{2}}\mathbf{y} \tag{10-108}$$

from which it follows that

$$\mathbf{y} = \mathbf{D}^{-\frac{1}{2}}\mathbf{z} \tag{10-109}$$

Thus, we can find the (continuous-valued) eigenvector corresponding to the second smallest eigenvalue using either a generalized or a standard eigenvalue solver. The desired (discrete) vector $\mathbf{x}$ can be generated from the resulting, continuous valued solution vector by finding a splitting point that divides the values of the continuous eigenvector elements into two parts. We do this by finding the splitting point that yields the smallest value of $Ncut(A, B)$, since this is the quantity we are trying to minimize. To simplify the search, we divide the range of values in the continuous vector into Q evenly spaced values, evaluate Eq. (10-104) for each value, and choose the splitting point that yields the smallest value of $Ncut(A, B)$. Then, all values of the eigenvector with values above the split point are assigned the value 1; all others are assigned the value −1. The result is the desired vector $\mathbf{x}$. Then, partition A is the set nodes in V corresponding to 1's in $\mathbf{x}$; the remaining nodes correspond to partition B. This partitioning is carried out only if the stability criterion discussed in the following paragraph is met.

Searching for a splitting point implies computing a total of Q values of $Ncut(A, B)$ and selecting the smallest one. A region that is not clearly segmentable into two subregions using the specified weights will usually result in many splitting points with similar values of $Ncut(A, B)$. Trying to segment such a region is likely to result in a meaningless partition. To avoid this behavior, a region (i.e., subgraph) is split only if it satisfies a *stability criterion*, obtained by first computing the histogram of the eigenvector values, then forming the ratio of the minimum to the maximum bin counts. In an "uncertain" eigenvector, the values in the histogram will stay relatively the same, and the ratio will be relatively high. Shi and Malik [2000] found experimentally that thresholding the ratio at 0.06 was a effective criterion for not splitting the region in question.

GRAPH CUT SEGMENTATION ALGORITHM

In the preceding discussion, we illustrated two ways in which edge weights can be generated from an image. In Figs. 10.53 and 10.54, we looked at weights generated using image intensity values, and in Fig. 10.55 we considered weights based on the distance between pixels. But these are just two examples of the many ways that we can generate a graph and corresponding weights from an image. For example, we could use color, texture, statistical moments about a region, and other types of features to be discussed in Chapter 11. In general, then, graphs can be constructed from image *features*, of which pixel intensities are a special case. With this concept as background, we can summarize the discussion thus far in this section as the following algorithm:

1. Given a set of features, specify a weighted graph, $G = (V, E)$ in which V contains the points in the feature space, and E contains the edges of the graph. Compute the edge weights and use them to construct matrices $\mathbf{W}$ and $\mathbf{D}$. Let K denote the desired number of partitions of the graph.
2. Solve the eigenvalue system $(\mathbf{D} - \mathbf{W})\mathbf{y} = \lambda \mathbf{D}\mathbf{y}$ to find the eigenvector with the second smallest eigenvalue.
3. Use the eigenvector from Step 2 to bipartition the graph by finding the splitting point such that $Ncut(A, B)$ is minimized.
4. If the number of cuts has not reached K, decide if the current partition should be subdivided by checking the stability of the cut.
5. Recursively repartition the segmented parts if necessary.

Note that the algorithm works by recursively generating two-way cuts. The number of groups (e.g., regions) in the segmented image is controlled by K. Other criteria, such as the maximum size allowed for each cut, can further refine the final segmentation. For example, when using pixels and their intensities as the basis for constructing the graph, we can specify the maximum and/or minimum size allowed for each region.

EXAMPLE 10.24: Specifying weights for graph cut segmentation.

In Fig. 10.53, we illustrated how to generate graph weights using intensity values, and in Fig. 10.55 we discussed briefly how to generate weights based on the distance between pixels. In this example, we give a more practical approach for generating weights that include both intensity and distance from a pixel, thus introducing the concept of a neighborhood in graph segmentation.

Let n_i and n_j denote two nodes (image pixels). As mentioned earlier in this section, weights are supposed to reflect the similarity between nodes in a graph. When considering segmentation, one of the principal ways to establish how likely two pixels in an image are to be a part of the same region or object is to determine the difference in their intensity values, and how close the pixels are to each other. The weight value of the edge between two pixels should be large when the pixels are very close in intensity and proximity (i.e., when the pixels are "similar), and should decrease as their intensity difference and distance from each other increases. That is, the weight value should be a function of how similar the pixels are in intensity and distance. These two concepts can be embedded into a single weight function using the following expression:

$$
w(i,j) = \begin{cases} e^{-\frac{[I(n_i)-I(n_j)]^2}{\sigma_I^2}} \; e^{-\frac{dist(n_i,\,n_j)}{\sigma_d^2}} & \text{if } \; dist(n_i, n_j) < r \\ 0 & \text{otherwise} \end{cases}
$$

where $I(n_i)$ is the intensity of node n_i, σ_I^2 and σ_d^2 are constants determining the spread of the two Gaussian-like functions, $dist(n_i, n_j)$ is the distance (e.g., the Euclidean distance) between the two nodes, and r is a radial constant that establishes how far away we are willing to consider similarity. The exponential terms decrease as a function of dissimilarity in intensity and as function of distance between the nodes, as required of our measure of similarity in this case.

EXAMPLE 10.25: Segmentation using graph cuts.

Graph cuts are ideally suited for obtaining a rough segmentation of the principal regions in an image. Figure 10.56 shows a typical result. Figure 10.56(a) is the familiar building image. Consistent with the idea of extracting the principal regions of an image, Fig. 10.56(b) shows the image smoothed with a simple 25×25 box kernel. Observe how the fine detail is smoothed out, leaving only major regional features such as the facade and sky. Figure 10.56(c) is the result of segmentation using the graph cut algorithm just developed, with weights of the form discussed in the previous example, and allowing only two partitions. Note how well the region corresponding to the building was extracted, with none of the details characteristic of the methods discussed earlier in this chapter. In fact, it would have been nearly impossible to obtain comparable results using any of the methods we have discussed thus far without significant additional processing. This type of result is ideal for tasks such as providing broad cues for autonomous navigation, for searching image databases, and for low-level image analysis.

10.7 SEGMENTATION USING MORPHOLOGICAL WATERSHEDS

Thus far, we have discussed segmentation based on three principal concepts: edge detection, thresholding, and region extraction. Each of these approaches was found to have advantages (for example, speed in the case of global thresholding) and disadvantages (for example, the need for post-processing, such as edge linking, in edge-based segmentation). In this section, we discuss an approach based on the concept of so-called *morphological watersheds*. Segmentation by watersheds embodies many of the concepts of the other three approaches and, as such, often produces more stable segmentation results, including connected segmentation boundaries. This approach also provides a simple framework for incorporating knowledge-based constraints (see Fig. 1.23) in the segmentation process, as we discuss at the end of this section.

BACKGROUND

The concept of a watershed is based on visualizing an image in three dimensions, two spatial coordinates versus intensity, as in Fig. 2.18(a). In such a "topographic" interpretation, we consider three types of points: (1) points belonging to a regional minimum; (2) points at which a drop of water, if placed at the location of any of those

a b c

FIGURE 10.56 (a) Image of size 600 × 600 pixels. (b) Image smoothed with a 25 × 25 box kernel. (c) Graph cut segmentation obtained by specifying two regions.

points, would fall with certainty to a single minimum; and (3) points at which water would be equally likely to fall to more than one such minimum. For a particular regional minimum, the set of points satisfying condition (2) is called the *catchment basin* or *watershed* of that minimum. The points satisfying condition (3) form crest lines on the topographic surface, and are referred to as *divide lines* or *watershed lines*.

The principal objective of segmentation algorithms based on these concepts is to find the watershed lines. The method for doing this can be explained with the aid of Fig. 10.57. Figure 10.57(a) shows a gray-scale image and Fig. 10.57(b) is a topographic view, in which the height of the "mountains" is proportional to intensity values in the input image. For ease of interpretation, the backsides of structures are shaded. This is not to be confused with intensity values; only the general topography of the three-dimensional representation is of interest. In order to prevent the rising water from spilling out through the edges of the image, we imagine the perimeter of the entire topography (image) being enclosed by dams that are higher than the highest possible mountain, whose value is determined by the highest possible intensity value in the input image.

Suppose that a hole is punched in each regional minimum [shown as dark areas in Fig. 10.57(b)] and that the entire topography is flooded from below by letting water rise through the holes at a uniform rate. Figure 10.57(c) shows the first stage of flooding, where the "water," shown in light gray, has covered only areas that correspond to the black *background* in the image. In Figs. 10.57(d) and (e) we see that the water now has risen into the first and second catchment basins, respectively. As the water continues to rise, it will eventually overflow from one catchment basin into another. The first indication of this is shown in 10.57(f). Here, water from the lower part of the left basin overflowed into the basin on the right, and a short "dam" (consisting of single pixels) was built to prevent water from merging at that level of flooding (the mathematical details of dam building are discussed in the following section). The

Because of neighboring contrast, the leftmost basin in Fig. 10.57(c) appears black, but it is a few shades lighter than the black background. The mid-gray in the second basin is a natural gray from the image in (a).

a c
b d

FIGURE 10.57
(a) Original image.
(b) Topographic view. Only the background is *black*. The basin on the left is slightly lighter than black.
(c) and (d) Two stages of flooding. All constant dark values of gray are intensities in the original image. Only constant *light gray* represents "water."
(Courtesy of Dr. S. Beucher, CMM/Ecole des Mines de Paris.)
(*Continued on next page.*)

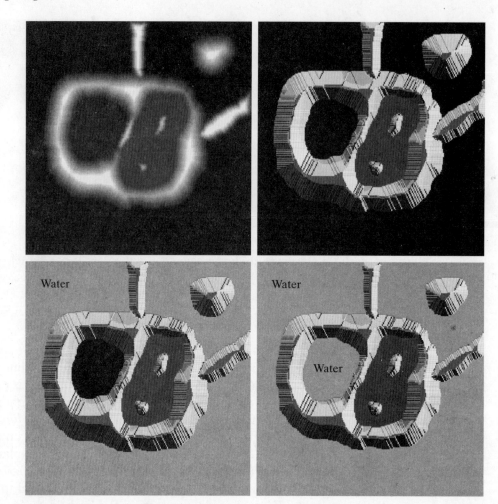

effect is more pronounced as water continues to rise, as shown in Fig. 10.57(g). This figure shows a longer dam between the two catchment basins and another dam in the top part of the right basin. The latter dam was built to prevent merging of water from that basin with water from areas corresponding to the background. This process is continued until the maximum level of flooding (corresponding to the highest intensity value in the image) is reached. The final dams correspond to the *watershed lines*, which are the desired segmentation boundaries. The result for this example is shown in Fig. 10.57(h) as dark, one-pixel-thick paths superimposed on the original image. Note the important property that the watershed lines form connected paths, thus giving continuous boundaries between regions.

One of the principal applications of watershed segmentation is in the extraction of nearly uniform (blob-like) objects from the background. Regions characterized by small variations in intensity have small gradient values. Thus, in practice, we often see watershed segmentation applied to the gradient of an image, rather than to the image itself. In this formulation, the regional minima of catchment basins correlate nicely with the small value of the gradient corresponding to the objects of interest.

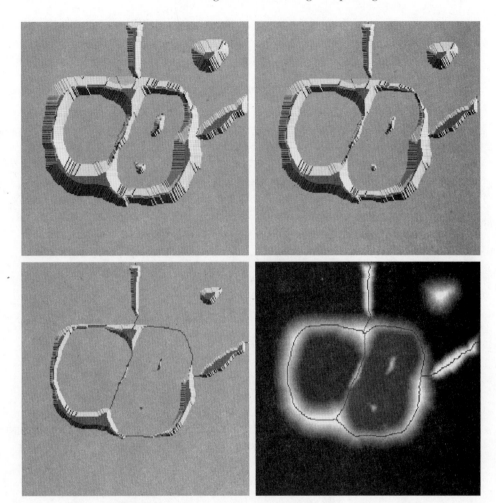

e f
g h

FIGURE 10.57
(Continued)
(e) Result of
further flooding.
(f) Beginning of
merging of water
from two
catchment basins
(a short dam was
built between
them).
(g) Longer dams.
(h) Final water-
shed (segmenta-
tion) lines super-
imposed on the
original image.
(Courtesy of Dr.
S. Beucher, CMM/
Ecole des Mines
de Paris.)

DAM CONSTRUCTION

Dam construction is based on binary images, which are members of 2-D integer space Z^2 (see Sections 2.4 and 2.6). The simplest way to construct dams separating sets of binary points is to use morphological dilation (see Section 9.2).

Figure 10.58 illustrates the basics of dam construction using dilation. Part (a) shows portions of two catchment basins at flooding step $n-1$, and Fig. 10.58(b) shows the result at the next flooding step, n. The water has spilled from one basin to the another and, therefore, a dam must be built to keep this from happening. In order to be consistent with notation to be introduced shortly, let M_1 and M_2 denote the sets of coordinates of points in two regional minima. Then let the set of coordinates of points *in the catchment basin* associated with these two minima at stage $n-1$ of flooding be denoted by $C_{n-1}(M_1)$ and $C_{n-1}(M_2)$, respectively. These are the two gray regions in Fig. 10.58(a).

Let $C[n-1]$ denote the union of these two sets. There are two connected components in Fig. 10.58(a), and only one component in Fig. 10.58(b). This connected

See Sections 2.5 and 9.5
regarding connected
components.

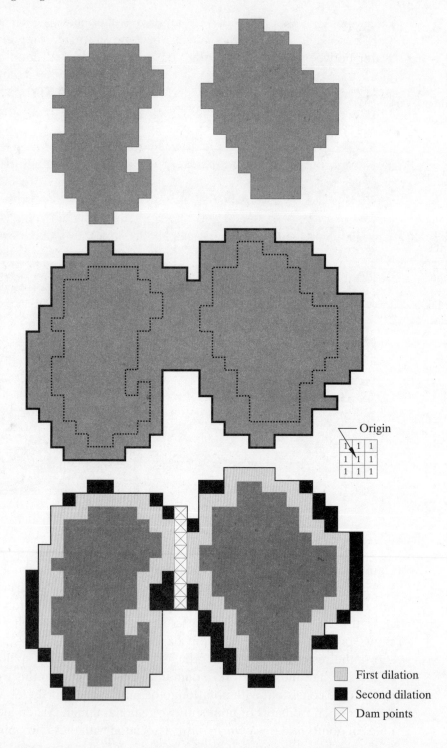

Origin

First dilation

Second dilation

Dam points

a
b
d c

FIGURE 10.58 (a) Two partially flooded catchment basins at stage $n-1$ of flooding. (b) Flooding at stage n, showing that water has spilled between basins. (c) Structuring element used for dilation. (d) Result of dilation and dam construction.

component encompasses the earlier two components, which are shown dashed. Two connected components having become a *single* component indicates that water between the two catchment basins has merged at flooding step n. Let this connected component be denoted by q. Note that the two components from step $n-1$ can be extracted from q by performing a logical AND operation, $q \cap C[n-1]$. Observe also that all points belonging to an individual catchment basin form a single connected component.

Suppose that each of the connected components in Fig. 10.58(a) is dilated by the structuring element in Fig. 10.58(c), subject to two conditions: (1) The dilation has to be constrained to q (this means that the center of the structuring element can be located only at points in q during dilation); and (2) the dilation cannot be performed on points that would cause the sets being dilated to merge (i.e., become a single connected component). Figure 10.58(d) shows that a first dilation pass (in light gray) expanded the boundary of each original connected component. Note that condition (1) was satisfied by every point during dilation, and that condition (2) did not apply to any point during the dilation process; thus, the boundary of each region was expanded uniformly.

In the second dilation, shown in black in 10.58(d), several points failed condition (1) while meeting condition (2), resulting in the broken perimeter shown in the figure. It is evident that the only points in q that satisfy the two conditions under consideration describe the one-pixel-thick connected path shown crossed-hatched in Fig. 10.58(d). This path is the desired separating dam at stage n of flooding. Construction of the dam at this level of flooding is completed by setting all the points in the path just determined to a value greater than the maximum possible intensity value of the image (e.g., greater than 255 for an 8-bit image). This will prevent water from crossing over the part of the completed dam as the level of flooding is increased. As noted earlier, dams built by this procedure, which are the desired segmentation boundaries, are connected components. In other words, this method eliminates the problems of broken segmentation lines.

Although the procedure just described is based on a simple example, the method used for more complex situations is exactly the same, including the use of the 3×3 symmetric structuring element in Fig. 10.58(c).

WATERSHED SEGMENTATION ALGORITHM

Let $M_1, M_2, \ldots, M_R$ be sets denoting the *coordinates* of the points in the regional minima of an image, $g(x, y)$. As mentioned earlier, this typically will be a gradient image. Let $C(M_i)$ be a set denoting the coordinates of the points in the catchment basin associated with regional minimum M_i (recall that the points in any catchment basin form a connected component). The notation min and max will be used to denote the minimum and maximum values of $g(x, y)$. Finally, let $T[n]$ represent the set of coordinates (s, t) for which $g(s, t) < n$. That is,

$$T[n] = \{(s,t) \mid g(s,t) < n\} \tag{10-110}$$

Geometrically, $T[n]$ is the set of coordinates of points in $g(x, y)$ lying below the plane $g(x, y) = n$.

The topography will be flooded in *integer* flood increments, from $n = \min + 1$ to $n = \max + 1$. At any step n of the flooding process, the algorithm needs to know the number of points below the flood depth. Conceptually, suppose that the coordinates in $T[n]$ that are below the plane $g(x, y) = n$ are "marked" black, and all other coordinates are marked white. Then when we look "down" on the xy-plane at any increment n of flooding, we will see a binary image in which black points correspond to points in the function that are below the plane $g(x, y) = n$. This interpretation is quite useful, and will make it easier to understand the following discussion.

Let $C_n(M_i)$ denote the set of coordinates of points in the catchment basin associated with minimum M_i that are flooded at stage n. With reference to the discussion in the previous paragraph, we may view $C_n(M_i)$ as a binary image given by

$$C_n(M_i) = C(M_i) \cap T[n] \tag{10-111}$$

In other words, $C_n(M_i) = 1$ at location (x, y) if $(x, y) \in C(M_i)$ AND $(x, y) \in T[n]$; otherwise $C_n(M_i) = 0$. The geometrical interpretation of this result is straightforward. We are simply using the AND operator to isolate at stage n of flooding the portion of the binary image in $T[n]$ that is associated with regional minimum M_i.

Next, let B denote the number of number of flooded catchment basins at stage n, and let $C[n]$ denote the union of these basins at stage n:

$$C[n] = \bigcup_{i=1}^{B} C_n(M_i) \tag{10-112}$$

Then $C[\max + 1]$ is the union of all catchment basins:

$$C[\max + 1] = \bigcup_{i=1}^{B} C(M_i) \tag{10-113}$$

It can be shown (see Problem 10.47) that the elements in both $C_n(M_i)$ and $T[n]$ are never replaced during execution of the algorithm, and that the number of elements in these two sets either increases or remains the same as n increases. Thus, it follows that $C[n-1]$ is a subset of $C[n]$. According to Eqs. (10-112) and (10-113), $C[n]$ is a subset of $T[n]$, so it follows that $C[n-1]$ is also a subset of $T[n]$. From this we have the important result that each connected component of $C[n-1]$ is contained in exactly one connected component of $T[n]$.

The algorithm for finding the watershed lines is initialized by letting $C[\min + 1] = T[\min + 1]$. The procedure then proceeds recursively, successively computing $C[n]$ from $C[n-1]$, using the following approach. Let Q denote the set of connected components in $T[n]$. Then, for each connected component $q \in Q[n]$, there are three possibilities:

1. $q \cap C[n-1]$ is empty.

2. $q \cap C[n-1]$ contains one connected component of $C[n-1]$.

3. $q \cap C[n-1]$ contains more than one connected component of $C[n-1]$.

The construction of $C[n]$ from $C[n-1]$ depends on which of these three conditions holds. Condition 1 occurs when a new minimum is encountered, in which case connected component q is incorporated into $C[n-1]$ to form $C[n]$. Condition 2 occurs when q lies within the catchment basin of some regional minimum, in which case q is incorporated into $C[n-1]$ to form $C[n]$. Condition 3 occurs when all (or part) of a ridge separating two or more catchment basins is encountered. Further flooding would cause the water level in these catchment basins to merge. Thus, a dam (or dams if more than two catchment basins are involved) must be built within q to prevent overflow between the catchment basins. As explained earlier, a one-pixel-thick dam can be constructed when needed by dilating $q \cap C[n-1]$ with a 3×3 structuring element of 1's, and constraining the dilation to q.

Algorithm efficiency is improved by using only values of n that correspond to existing intensity values in $g(x, y)$. We can determine these values, as well as the values of min and max, from the histogram of $g(x, y)$.

EXAMPLE 10.26: Illustration of the watershed segmentation algorithm.

Consider the image and its gradient in Figs. 10.59(a) and (b), respectively. Application of the watershed algorithm just described yielded the watershed lines (white paths) shown superimposed on the gradient image in Fig. 10.59(c). These segmentation boundaries are shown superimposed on the original image in Fig. 10.59(d). As noted at the beginning of this section, the segmentation boundaries have the important property of being connected paths.

THE USE OF MARKERS

Direct application of the watershed segmentation algorithm in the form discussed in the previous section generally leads to over-segmentation, caused by noise and other local irregularities of the gradient. As Fig. 10.60 illustrates, over-segmentation can be serious enough to render the result of the algorithm virtually useless. In this case, this means a large number of segmented regions. A practical solution to this problem is to limit the number of allowable regions by incorporating a preprocessing stage designed to bring additional knowledge into the segmentation procedure.

An approach used to control over-segmentation is based on the concept of markers. A *marker* is a connected component belonging to an image. We have *internal markers*, associated with objects of interest, and *external markers*, associated with the background. A procedure for marker selection typically will consist of two principal steps: (1) preprocessing; and (2) definition of a set of criteria that markers must satisfy. To illustrate, consider Fig. 10.60(a) again. Part of the problem that led to the over-segmented result in Fig. 10.60(b) is the large number of potential minima. Because of their size, many of these minima are irrelevant detail. As has been pointed out several times in earlier discussions, an effective method for minimizing the effect of small spatial detail is to filter the image with a smoothing filter. This is an appropriate preprocessing scheme in this case also.

a b
c d

FIGURE 10.59
(a) Image of blobs.
(b) Image gradient.
(c) Watershed lines, superimposed on the gradient image.
(d) Watershed lines superimposed on the original image.
(Courtesy of Dr. S. Beucher, CMM/ Ecole des Mines de Paris.)

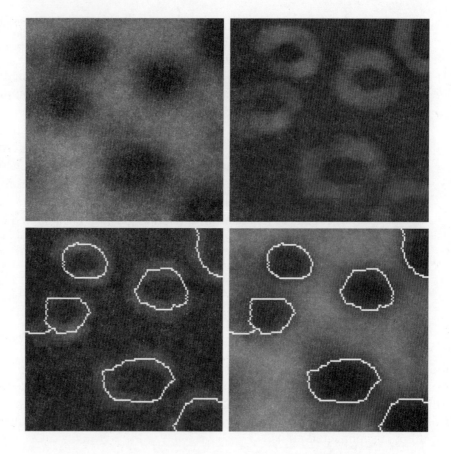

a b

FIGURE 10.60
(a) Electrophoresis image.
(b) Result of applying the watershed segmentation algorithm to the gradient image.
Over-segmentation is evident.
(Courtesy of Dr. S. Beucher, CMM/ Ecole des Mines de Paris.)

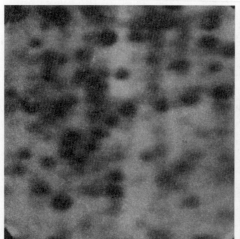 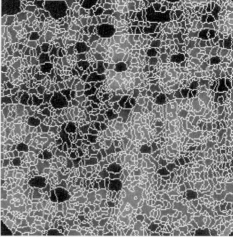

a b

FIGURE 10.61
(a) Image showing internal markers (light gray regions) and external markers (watershed lines).
(b) Result of segmentation. Note the improvement over Fig. 10.60(b). (Courtesy of Dr. S. Beucher, CMM/ Ecole des Mines de Paris.)

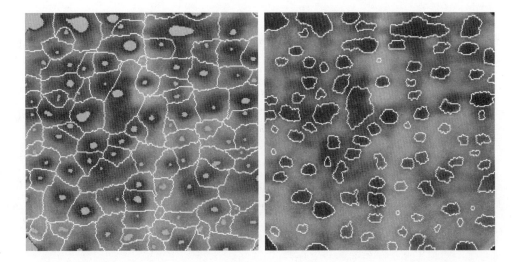

Suppose that we define an internal marker as (1) a region that is surrounded by points of higher "altitude"; (2) such that the points in the region form a connected component; and (3) in which all the points in the connected component have the same intensity value. After the image was smoothed, the internal markers resulting from this definition are shown as light gray, blob-like regions in Fig. 10.61(a). Next, the watershed algorithm was applied to the smoothed image, under the restriction that these internal markers be the only allowed regional minima. Figure 10.61(a) shows the resulting watershed lines. These watershed lines are defined as the external markers. Note that the points along the watershed line pass along the highest points between neighboring markers.

The external markers in Fig. 10.61(a) effectively partition the image into regions, with each region containing a single internal marker and part of the background. The problem is thus reduced to partitioning each of these regions into two: a single object, and its background. We can bring to bear on this simplified problem many of the segmentation techniques discussed earlier in this chapter. Another approach is simply to apply the watershed segmentation algorithm to each individual region. In other words, we simply take the gradient of the smoothed image [as in Fig. 10.59(b)] and restrict the algorithm to operate on a single watershed that contains the marker in that particular region. Figure 10.61(b) shows the result obtained using this approach. The improvement over the image in 10.60(b) is evident.

Marker selection can range from simple procedures based on intensity values and connectivity, as we just illustrated, to more complex descriptions involving size, shape, location, relative distances, texture content, and so on (see Chapter 11 regarding feature descriptors). The point is that using markers brings a priori knowledge to bear on the segmentation problem. Keep in mind that humans often aid segmentation and higher-level tasks in everyday vision by using a priori knowledge, one of the most familiar being the use of context. Thus, the fact that segmentation by watersheds offers a framework that can make effective use of this type of knowledge is a significant advantage of this method.

10.8 THE USE OF MOTION IN SEGMENTATION

Motion is a powerful cue used by humans and many animals to extract objects or regions of interest from a background of irrelevant detail. In imaging applications, motion arises from a relative displacement between the sensing system and the scene being viewed, such as in robotic applications, autonomous navigation, and dynamic scene analysis. In the following discussion we consider the use of motion in segmentation both spatially and in the frequency domain.

SPATIAL TECHNIQUES

In what follows, we will consider two approaches for detecting motion, working directly in the spatial domain. The key objective is to give you an idea how to measure changes in digital images using some straightforward techniques.

A Basic Approach

One of the simplest approaches for detecting changes between two image frames $f(x,y,t_i)$ and $f(x,y,t_j)$ taken at times t_i and t_j, respectively, is to compare the two images pixel by pixel. One procedure for doing this is to form a difference image. Suppose that we have a *reference image* containing only stationary components. Comparing this image against a subsequent image of the same scene, but including one or more moving objects, results in the difference of the two images canceling the stationary elements, leaving only nonzero entries that correspond to the nonstationary image components.

A *difference image* of two images (of the same size) taken at times t_i and t_j may be defined as

$$d_{ij}(x,y) = \begin{cases} 1 & \text{if } \left| f(x,y,t_i) - f(x,y,t_j) \right| > T \\ 0 & \text{otherwise} \end{cases} \tag{10-114}$$

where T is a nonnegative threshold. Note that $d_{ij}(x,y)$ has a value of 1 at spatial coordinates (x,y) only if the intensity difference between the two images is appreciably different at those coordinates, as determined by T. Note also that coordinates (x,y) in Eq. (10-114) span the dimensions of the two images, so the difference image is of the same size as the images in the sequence.

In the discussion that follows, all pixels in $d_{ij}(x,y)$ that have value 1 are considered the result of object motion. This approach is applicable only if the two images are registered spatially, and if the illumination is relatively constant within the bounds established by T. In practice, 1-valued entries in $d_{ij}(x,y)$ may arise as a result of noise also. Typically, these entries are isolated points in the difference image, and a simple approach to their removal is to form 4- or 8-connected regions of 1's in image $d_{ij}(x,y)$, then ignore any region that has less than a predetermined number of elements. Although it may result in ignoring small and/or slow-moving objects, this approach improves the chances that the remaining entries in the difference image actually are the result of motion, and not noise.

Although the method just described is simple, it is used frequently as the basis of imaging systems designed to detect changes in controlled environments, such as in surveillance of parking facilities, buildings, and similar fixed locales.

Accumulative Differences

Consider a sequence of image frames denoted by $f(x,y,t_1), f(x,y,t_2),\ldots,f(x,y,t_n)$, and let $f(x,y,t_1)$ be the reference image. An *accumulative difference image* (ADI) is formed by comparing this reference image with every subsequent image in the sequence. A counter for each pixel location in the accumulative image is incremented every time a difference occurs at that pixel location between the reference and an image in the sequence. Thus, when the kth frame is being compared with the reference, the entry in a given pixel of the accumulative image gives the number of times the intensity at that position was different [as determined by T in Eq. (10-114)] from the corresponding pixel value in the reference image.

Assuming that the intensity values of the moving objects are greater than the background, we consider three types of ADIs. Let $R(x,y)$ denote the reference image and, to simplify the notation, let k denote t_k so that $f(x,y,k) = f(x,y,t_k)$. We assume that $R(x,y) = f(x,y,1)$. Then, for any $k > 1$, and keeping in mind that the values of the ADIs are counts, we define the following accumulative differences for all relevant values of (x,y):

$$A_k(x,y) = \begin{cases} A_{k-1}(x,y) + 1 & \text{if } |R(x,y) - f(x,y,k)| > T \\ A_{k-1}(x,y) & \text{otherwise} \end{cases} \quad (10\text{-}115)$$

$$P_k(x,y) = \begin{cases} P_{k-1}(x,y) + 1 & \text{if } |R(x,y) - f(x,y,k)| > T \\ P_{k-1}(x,y) & \text{otherwise} \end{cases} \quad (10\text{-}116)$$

and

$$N_k(x,y) = \begin{cases} N_{k-1}(x,y) + 1 & \text{if } |R(x,y) - f(x,y,k)| < -T \\ N_{k-1}(x,y) & \text{otherwise} \end{cases} \quad (10\text{-}117)$$

where $A_k(x,y)$, $P_k(x,y)$, and $N_k(x,y)$ are the *absolute*, *positive*, and *negative* ADIs, respectively, computed using the kth image in the sequence. All three ADIs start out with zero counts and are of the same size as the images in the sequence. The order of the inequalities and signs of the thresholds in Eqs. (10-116) and (10-117) are reversed if the intensity values of the background pixels are greater than the values of the moving objects.

EXAMPLE 10.27: Computation of the absolute, positive, and negative accumulative difference images.

Figure 10.62 shows the three ADIs displayed as intensity images for a rectangular object of dimension 75×50 pixels that is moving in a southeasterly direction at a speed of $5\sqrt{2}$ pixels per frame. The images

a b c

FIGURE 10.62 ADIs of a rectangular object moving in a southeasterly direction. (a) Absolute ADI. (b) Positive ADI. (c) Negative ADI.

are of size 256×256 pixels. We note the following: (1) The nonzero area of the positive ADI is equal to the size of the moving object; (2) the location of the positive ADI corresponds to the location of the moving object in the reference frame; (3) the number of counts in the positive ADI stops increasing when the moving object is displaced completely with respect to the same object in the reference frame; (4) the absolute ADI contains the regions of the positive and negative ADI; and (5) the direction and speed of the moving object can be determined from the entries in the absolute and negative ADIs.

Establishing a Reference Image

A key to the success of the techniques just discussed is having a reference image against which subsequent comparisons can be made. The difference between two images in a dynamic imaging problem has the tendency to cancel all stationary components, leaving only image elements that correspond to noise and to the moving objects.

Obtaining a reference image with only stationary elements is not always possible, and building a reference from a set of images containing one or more moving objects becomes necessary. This applies particularly to situations describing busy scenes or in cases where frequent updating is required. One procedure for generating a reference image is as follows. Consider the first image in a sequence to be the reference image. When a nonstationary component has moved completely out of its position in the reference frame, the corresponding background in the present frame can be duplicated in the location originally occupied by the object in the reference frame. When all moving objects have moved completely out of their original positions, a reference image containing only stationary components will have been created. Object displacement can be established by monitoring the changes in the positive ADI, as indicated earlier. The following example illustrates how to build a reference frame using the approach just described.

EXAMPLE 10.28: Building a reference image.

Figures 10.63(a) and (b) show two image frames of a traffic intersection. The first image is considered the reference, and the second depicts the same scene some time later. The objective is to remove the principal moving objects in the reference image in order to create a static image. Although there are other smaller moving objects, the principal moving feature is the automobile at the intersection moving from left to right. For illustrative purposes we focus on this object. By monitoring the changes in the positive ADI, it is possible to determine the initial position of a moving object, as explained above. Once the area occupied by this object is identified, the object can be removed from the image by subtraction. By looking at the frame in the sequence at which the positive ADI stopped changing, we can copy from this image the area previously occupied by the moving object in the initial frame. This area then is pasted onto the image from which the object was cut out, thus restoring the background of that area. If this is done for all moving objects, the result is a reference image with only static components against which we can compare subsequent frames for motion detection. The reference image resulting from removing the east-bound moving vehicle and restoring the background is shown in Fig. 10.63(c).

FREQUENCY DOMAIN TECHNIQUES

In this section, we consider the problem of determining motion via a Fourier transform formulation. Consider a sequence $f(x, y, t)$, $t = 0, 1, 2, \dots, K - 1$, of K digital image frames of size $M \times N$ pixels, generated by a stationary camera. We begin the development by assuming that all frames have a homogeneous background of zero intensity. The exception is a single, 1-pixel object of unit intensity that is moving with constant velocity. Suppose that for frame one ($t = 0$), the object is at location (x', y') and the image plane is projected onto the x-axis; that is, the pixel intensities are summed (for each row) across the columns in the image. This operation yields a 1-D array with M entries that are zero, except at x', which is the x-coordinate of the single-point object. If we now multiply all the components of the 1-D array by the quantity $\exp[j2\pi a_1 x \Delta t]$ for $x = 0, 1, 2, \dots, M - 1$ and add the results, we obtain the single term $\exp[j2\pi a_1 x' \Delta t]$ because there is only one nonzero point in the array. In this notation, a_1 is a positive integer, and Δt is the time interval between frames.

a b c

FIGURE 10.63 Building a static reference image. (a) and (b) Two frames in a sequence. (c) Eastbound automobile subtracted from (a), and the background restored from the corresponding area in (b). (Jain and Jain.)

Suppose that in frame two ($t = 1$), the object has moved to coordinates $(x' + 1, y')$; that is, it has moved 1 pixel parallel to the x-axis. Then, repeating the projection procedure discussed in the previous paragraph yields the sum $\exp\left[j2\pi a_1 (x' + 1)\Delta t\right]$. If the object continues to move 1 pixel location per frame then, at any integer instant of time, t, the result will be $\exp\left[j2\pi a_1 (x' + t)\Delta t\right]$, which, using Euler's formula, may be expressed as

$$e^{j2\pi a_1(x'+t)\Delta t} = \cos\left[2\pi a_1 (x' + t)\Delta t\right] + j\sin\left[2\pi a_1 (x' + t)\Delta t\right] \qquad (10\text{-}118)$$

for $t = 0, 1, 2, \ldots, K - 1$. In other words, this procedure yields a complex sinusoid with frequency a_1. If the object were moving V_1 pixels (in the x-direction) between frames, the sinusoid would have frequency $V_1 a_1$. Because t varies between 0 and $K - 1$ in integer increments, restricting a_1 to have integer values causes the discrete Fourier transform of the complex sinusoid to have two peaks—one located at frequency $V_1 a_1$ and the other at $K - V_1 a_1$. This latter peak is the result of symmetry in the discrete Fourier transform, as discussed in Section 4.6, and may be ignored. Thus a peak search in the Fourier spectrum would yield one peak with value $V_1 a_1$. Dividing this quantity by a_1 yields V_1, which is the velocity component in the x-direction, as the frame rate is assumed to be known. A similar analysis would yield V_2, the component of velocity in the y-direction.

A sequence of frames in which no motion takes place produces identical exponential terms, whose Fourier transform would consist of a single peak at a frequency of 0 (a single dc term). Therefore, because the operations discussed so far are linear, the general case involving one or more moving objects in an arbitrary static background would have a Fourier transform with a peak at dc corresponding to static image components, and peaks at locations proportional to the velocities of the objects.

These concepts may be summarized as follows. For a sequence of k digital images of size $M \times N$ pixels, the sum of the weighted projections onto the x-axis at any integer instant of time is

$$g_x(t, a_1) = \sum_{x=0}^{M-1} \sum_{y=0}^{N-1} f(x, y, t) e^{j2\pi a_1 x \Delta t} \quad t = 0, 1, \ldots, K - 1 \qquad (10\text{-}119)$$

Similarly, the sum of the projections onto the y-axis is

$$g_y(t, a_2) = \sum_{y=0}^{N-1} \sum_{x=0}^{M-1} f(x, y, t) e^{j2\pi a_2 y \Delta t} \quad t = 0, 1, \ldots, K - 1 \qquad (10\text{-}120)$$

where, as noted earlier, a_1 and a_2 are positive integers.

The 1D Fourier transforms of Eqs. (10-119) and (10-120), respectively, are

$$G_x(u_1, a_1) = \sum_{t=0}^{K-1} g_x(t, a_1) e^{-j2\pi u_1 t / K} \quad u_1 = 0, 1, \ldots, K - 1 \qquad (10\text{-}121)$$

and

$$G_y(u_2,a_2) = \sum_{t=0}^{K-1} g_y(t,a_2)e^{-j2\pi u_2 t/K} \quad u_2 = 0,1,\ldots,K-1 \qquad (10\text{-}122)$$

These transforms are computed using an FFT algorithm, as discussed in Section 4.11. The frequency-velocity relationship is

$$u_1 = a_1 V_1 \qquad (10\text{-}123)$$

and

$$u_2 = a_2 V_2 \qquad (10\text{-}124)$$

In the preceding formulation, the unit of velocity is in pixels per total frame time. For example, $V_1 = 10$ indicates motion of 10 pixels in K frames. For frames that are taken uniformly, the actual physical speed depends on the frame rate and the distance between pixels. Thus, if $V_1 = 10$, and $K = 30$, the frame rate is two images per second, and the distance between pixels is 0.5 m, then the actual physical speed in the x-direction is

$$V_1 = (10\,\text{pixels})(0.5\,\text{m/pixel})(2\,\text{frames/s})(30\,\text{frames})$$

The sign of the x-component of the velocity is obtained by computing

$$S_{1x} = \frac{d^2\,\mathrm{Re}\big[g_x(t,a_1)\big]}{dt^2}\bigg|_{t=n} \qquad (10\text{-}125)$$

and

$$S_{2x} = \frac{d^2\,\mathrm{Im}\big[g_x(t,a_1)\big]}{dt^2}\bigg|_{t=n} \qquad (10\text{-}126)$$

Because g_x is sinusoidal, it can be shown (see Problem 10.53) that S_{1x} and S_{2x} will have the same sign at an arbitrary point in time, n, if the velocity component V_1 is positive. Conversely, opposite signs in S_{1x} and S_{2x} indicate a negative velocity component. If either S_{1x} or S_{2x} is zero, we consider the next closest point in time, $t = n \pm \Delta t$. Similar comments apply to computing the sign of V_2.

EXAMPLE 10.29: Detection of a small moving object via frequency-domain analysis.

Figures 10.64 through 10.66 illustrate the effectiveness of the approach just developed. Figure 10.64 shows one of a 32-frame sequence of LANDSAT images generated by adding white noise to a reference image. The sequence contains a superimposed target moving at 0.5 pixel per frame in the x-direction and 1 pixel per frame in the y-direction. The target, shown circled in Fig. 10.65, has a Gaussian intensity distribution spread over a small (9-pixel) area, and is not easily discernible by eye. Figure 10.66 shows

FIGURE 10.64
LANDSAT frame.
(Cowart, Snyder,
and Ruedger.)

the results of computing Eqs. (10-121) and (10-122) with $a_1 = 6$ and $a_2 = 4$, respectively. The peak at $u_1 = 3$ in Fig. 10.66(a) yields $V_1 = 0.5$ from Eq. (10-123). Similarly, the peak at $u_2 = 4$ in Fig. 10.66(b) yields $V_2 = 1.0$ from Eq. (10-124).

Guidelines for selecting a_1 and a_2 can be explained with the aid of Fig. 10.66. For instance, suppose that we had used $a_2 = 15$ instead of $a_2 = 4$. In that case, the peaks in Fig. 10.66(b) would now be at $u_2 = 15$ and 17 because $V_2 = 1.0$. This would be a seriously aliased result. As discussed in Section 4.5, aliasing is caused by under-sampling (too few frames in the present discussion, as the range of u is determined by K). Because $u = aV$, one possibility is to select a as the integer closest to $a = u_{max}/V_{max}$,

FIGURE 10.65
Intensity plot of
the image in
Fig. 10.64, with
the target circled.
(Rajala, Riddle,
and Snyder.)

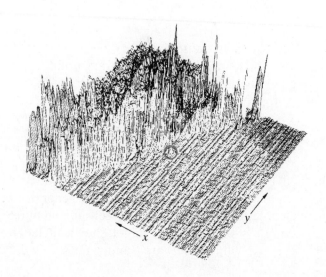

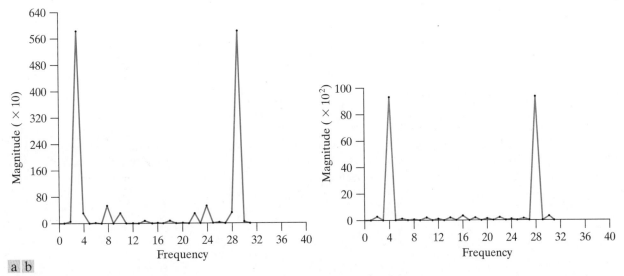

a b

FIGURE 10.66 (a) Spectrum of Eq. (10-121) showing a peak at $u_1 = 3$. (b) Spectrum of Eq. (10-122) showing a peak at $u_2 = 4$. (Rajala, Riddle, and Snyder.)

where u_{max} is the aliasing frequency limitation established by K, and V_{max} is the maximum expected object velocity.

Summary, References, and Further Reading

Because of its central role in autonomous image processing, segmentation is a topic covered in most books dealing with image processing, image analysis, and computer vision. The following books provide complementary and/or supplementary reading for our coverage of this topic: Umbaugh [2010]; Prince [2012]; Nixon and Aguado, A [2012]; Pratt [2014]; and Petrou and Petrou [2010].

Work dealing with the use of kernels to detect intensity discontinuities (see Section 10.2) has a long history. Numerous kernels have been proposed over the years: Roberts [1965]; Prewitt [1970]; and Kirsh [1971]. The Sobel operators are from [Sobel]; see also Danielsson and Seger [1990]. Our presentation of the zero-crossing properties of the Laplacian is based on Marr [1982]. The Canny edge detector discussed in Section 10.2 is due to Canny [1986]. The basic reference for the Hough transform is Hough [1962]. See Ballard [1981], for a generalization to arbitrary shapes.

Other approaches used to deal with the effects of illumination and reflectance on thresholding are illustrated by the work of Perez and Gonzalez [1987], Drew et al. [1999], and Toro and Funt [2007]. The optimum thresholding approach due to Otsu [1979] has gained considerable acceptance because it combines excellent performance with simplicity of implementation, requiring only estimation of image histograms. The basic idea of using preprocessing to improve thresholding dates back to an early paper by White and Rohrer [1983]), which combined thresholding, the gradient, and the Laplacian in the solution of a difficult segmentation problem.

See Fu and Mui [1981] for an early survey on the topic of region-oriented segmentation. The work of Haddon and Boyce [1990] and of Pavlidis and Liow [1990] are among the earliest efforts to integrate region and boundary information for the purpose of segmentation. Region growing is still an active area of research in image processing, as exemplified by Liangjia et al. [2013]. The basic reference on the k-means algorithm presented in Section 10.5 goes way back several decades to an obscure 1957 Bell Labs report by Lloyd, who subsequenty published in Lloyd [1982]. This algorithm was already being in used in areas such as pattern recognition in the 1960s and '70s (Tou and

Gonzalez [1974]). The superpixel algorithm presented in Section 10.5 is from Achanta et al. [2012]. See their paper for a listing and comparison of other superpixel approaches. The material on graph cuts is based on the paper by Shi and Malik [2000]. See Hochbaum [2010] for an example of faster implementations.

Segmentation by watersheds was shown in Section 10.7 to be a powerful concept. Early references dealing with segmentation by watersheds are Serra [1988], and Beucher and Meyer [1992]. As indicated in our discussion in Section 10.7, one of the key issues with watersheds is the problem of over-segmentation. The papers by Bleau and Leon [2000] and by Gaetano et al. [2015] are illustrative of approaches for dealing with this problem.

The material in Section 10.8 dealing with accumulative differences is from Jain, R. [1981]. See also Jain, Kasturi, and Schunck [1995]. The material dealing with motion via Fourier techniques is from Rajala, Riddle, and Snyder [1983]. The books by Snyder and Qi [2004], and by Chakrabarti et al. [2015], provide additional reading on motion estimation. For details on the software aspects of many of the examples in this chapter, see Gonzalez, Woods, and Eddins [2009].

Problems

Solutions to the problems marked with an asterisk (*) are in the DIP4E Student Support Package (consult the book website: www.ImageProcessingPlace.com)..

10.1* In a Taylor series approximation, the *remainder* (also called the *truncation error*) consists of all the terms not used in the approximation. The first term in the remainder of a finite difference approximation is indicative of the error in the approximation. The higher the derivative order of that term is, the lower the error will be in the approximation. All three approximations to the first derivative given in Eqs. (10-4)-(10-6) are computed using the same number of sample points. However, the error of the central difference approximation is less than the other two. Show that this is true.

10.2 State three fundamental steps performed in edge detection.

10.3 A binary image contains straight lines oriented horizontally, vertically, at 45°, and at –45°. Give a set of 5×5 masks that can be used to detect 1-pixel breaks in these lines. Assume that the intensities of the lines and background are 1 and 0, respectively.

10.4 Propose a technique for detecting gaps of length ranging between 1 and K pixels in line segments of a binary image. Assume that the lines are one pixel thick. Base your technique on 8-neighbor connectivity analysis, rather than attempting to construct kernels for detecting the gaps.

10.5* With reference to Fig. 10.6, what are the angles (measured with respect to the *x*-axis of the book axis convention in Fig. 2.19) of the horizontal and vertical lines to which the kernels in Figs. 10.6(a) and (c) are most responsive?

10.6 Refer to Fig. 10.7 in answering the following questions.

(a)* What is the assumption on which line detection is based?

(b) What happens if the lines do not satisfy that assumption?

10.7 With reference to the edge models in Fig. 10.8, answer the following without generating the gradient and angle images. Simply provide sketches of the profiles that show what you would expect the profiles of the magnitude and angle images to look like.

(a)* Suppose that we compute the gradient magnitude of each of these models using the Prewitt kernels in Fig. 10.14. Sketch what a horizontal profile through the center of each gradient image would look like.

(b) Sketch a horizontal profile for each corresponding angle image.

10.8 Consider a horizontal intensity profile through the middle of a binary image that contains a vertical step edge through the center of the image. Draw what the profile would look like after the image has been blurred by an averaging kernel of size $n \times n$ with coefficients equal to $1/n^2$. For simplicity, assume that the image was scaled so that its intensity levels are 0 on the left of the edge and 1 on its right. Also, assume that the size of the kernel is much smaller than the image, so that image border effects are not a concern near the center of the image.

10.9* Suppose that we had used the edge models in the following image, instead of the ramp in Fig. 10.10. Sketch the gradient and Laplacian of each profile.

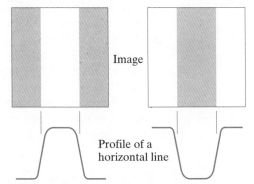

Image

Profile of a
horizontal line

10.10 What are the three objectives of Canny's approach in Canny edge detector.

10.11 Do the following.

(a) How would you modify the Sobel and Prewitt kernels in Fig. 10.14 so that they give their strongest gradient response for edges oriented at ±45°?

(b)* Show that the Sobel and Prewitt kernels in Fig. 10.14, and in (a) above, and give isotropic results only for horizontal and vertical edges, and for edges oriented at ±45°, respectively.

10.12 The results obtained by a single pass through an image of some 2-D kernels can be achieved also by two passes using 1-D kernels. For example, the same result of using a 3×3 smoothing kernel with coefficients 1/9 can be obtained by a pass of the kernel [1 1 1] through an image, followed by a pass of the result with the kernel $[1\ 1\ 1]^T$. The final result is then scaled by 1/9. Show that the response of Sobel kernels (Fig. 10.14) can be implemented similarly by one pass of the *differencing* kernel [−1 0 1] (or its vertical counterpart) followed by the smoothing kernel [1 2 1] (or its vertical counterpart).

10.13 A popular variation of the compass kernels shown in Fig. 10.15 is based on using coefficients with values 0, 1, and –1.

(a)* Give the form of the eight compass kernels using these coefficients. As in Fig. 10.15, let N, NW, ... denote the direction of the edge that gives the strongest response.

(b) Specify the gradient vector direction of the edges detected by each kernel in (a).

10.14 The rectangle in the following binary image is of size $m \times n$ pixels.

(a)* What would the magnitude of the gradient of this image look like based on using the approximation in Eq. (10-26)? Assume that g_x and g_y are obtained using the Sobel kernels. Show all relevant different pixel values in the gradient image.

(b) With reference to Eq. (10-18) and Fig. 10.12, sketch the histogram of edge *directions*. Be precise in labeling the height of each component of the histogram.

(c) What would the Laplacian of this image look like based on using Eq. (10-14)? Show all relevant different pixel values in the Laplacian image.

10.15 Suppose that an image $f(x,y)$ is convolved with a kernel of size $n \times n$ (with coefficients $1/n^2$) to produce a smoothed image $\bar{f}(x,y)$.

(a)* Derive an expression for edge strength (edge magnitude) as a function of n. Assume that n is odd and that the partial derivatives are computed using Eqs. (10-19) and (10-20).

(b) Show that the ratio of the maximum edge strength of the smoothed image to the maximum edge strength of the original image is $1/n$. In other words, edge strength is inversely proportional to the size of the smoothing kernel, as one would expect.

10.16 With reference to Eq. (10-29),

(a)* Show that the average value of the LoG operator, $\nabla^2 G(x, y)$, is zero.

(b) Show that the average value of any image convolved with this operator also is zero. (*Hint:* Consider solving this problem in the frequency domain, using the convolution theorem and the fact that the average value of a function is proportional to its Fourier transform evaluated at the origin.)

(c) Suppose that we: (1) used the kernel in Fig. 10.4(a) to approximate the Laplacian of a Gaussian, and (2) convolved this result with any image. What would be true in general of the values of the resulting image? Explain. (*Hint:* Take a look at Problem 3.32.)

10.17 Refer to Fig. 10.22(c).

(a) Explain why the edges form closed contours.

(b)* Does the zero-crossing method for finding edge location always result in closed contours? Explain.

10.18 One often finds in the literature a derivation of the Laplacian of a Gaussian (LoG) that starts with the expression

$$G(r) = e^{-r^2/2\sigma^2}$$

where $r^2 = x^2 + y^2$. The LoG is then derived by taking the second partial derivative with respect to r: $\nabla^2 G(r) = \partial^2 G(r)/\partial r^2$. Finally, $x^2 + y^2$ is substituted for r^2 to get the final (*incorrect*) result:

$$\nabla^2 G(x, y) = \left[\left(x^2 + y^2 - \sigma^2 \right)/\sigma^4 \right]$$
$$\exp\left[-\left(x^2 + y^2 \right)/2\sigma^2 \right]$$

Derive this result and explain the reason for the difference between this expression and Eq. (10-29).

10.19 Mention the steps of Marr-Hildreth edge-detection algorithm.

10.20 In the following, assume that G and f are discrete arrays of size $n \times n$ and $M \times N$, respectively.

(a) Show that the 2-D convolution of the Gaussian function $G(x, y)$ in Eq. (10-27) with an image $f(x, y)$ can be expressed as a 1-D convolution along the rows (columns) of $f(x, y)$, followed by a 1-D convolution along the columns (rows) of the result. (*Hints:* See Section 3.4 regarding discrete convolution and separability).

(b)* Derive an expression for the computational advantage using the 1-D convolution approach in (a) as opposed to implementing the 2-D convolution directly. Assume that $G(x, y)$ is sampled to produce an array of size $n \times n$ and that $f(x, y)$ is of size $M \times N$. The computational advantage is the ratio of the number of multiplications required for 2-D convolution to the number required for 1-D convolution. (*Hint:* Review the subsection on separable kernels in Section 3.4.)

10.21 Do the following.

(a) Show that Steps 1 and 2 of the Marr-Hildreth algorithm can be implemented using four 1-D convolutions. (*Hints:* Refer to Problem 10.20(a) and express the Laplacian operator as the sum of two partial derivatives, given by Eqs. (10-10) and (10-11), and implement each derivative using a 1-D kernel, as in Problem 10.12.)

(b) Derive an expression for the computational advantage of using the 1-D convolution approach in (a) as opposed to implementing the 2-D convolution directly. Assume that $G(x, y)$ is sampled to produce an array of size $n \times n$ and that $f(x, y)$ is of size $M \times N$. The computational advantage is the ratio of the number of multiplications required for 2-D convolution to the number required for 1-D convolution (see Problem 10.20).

10.22 Do the following.

(a)* Formulate Step 1 and the gradient magnitude image computation in Step 2 of the Canny algorithm using 1-D instead of 2-D convolutions.

(b) What is the computational advantage of using the 1-D convolution approach as opposed to implementing a 2-D convolution. Assume that the 2-D Gaussian filter in

Step 1 is sampled into an array of size $n \times n$ and that the input image is of size $M \times N$. Express the computational advantage as the ratio of the number of multiplications required by each method.

10.23 With reference to the three vertical edge models and corresponding profiles in Fig. 10.8 provide sketches of the profiles that would result from each of the following methods. You may sketch the profiles manually.

(a)* Suppose that we compute the gradient magnitude of each of the three edge model images using the Sobel kernels. Sketch the horizontal intensity profiles of the three resulting gradient images.

(b) Sketch the horizontal intensity profiles that would result from using the 3×3 Laplacian kernel in Fig. 10.10.4(a).

(c)* Repeat (b) using only the first two steps of the Marr-Hildreth edge detector.

(d) Repeat (b) using the first two steps of the Canny edge detector. You may ignore the angle images.

(e) Sketch the horizontal profiles of the angle images resulting from using the Canny edge detector.

10.24 In Example 10.9, we used a smoothing kernel of size 19×19 to generate Fig. 10.26(c) and a kernel of size 13×13 to generate Fig. 10.26(d). What was the rationale that led to choosing these values? (*Hint:* Observe that both are Gaussian kernels, and refer to the discussion of lowpass Gaussian kernels in Section 3.5.)

10.25 Refer to the Hough transform in Section 10.2.

(a) Propose a general procedure for obtaining the normal representation of a line from its slope-intercept form, $y = ax + b$.

(b)* Find the normal representation of the line $y = -2x + 1$.

10.26 Refer to Fig. 10.30 in answering the following questions:

(a)* What does the location of point A indicate in Fig. 10.30(b)?

(b)* What does the location of point B indicate in Fig. 10.30(b)?

(c) What does the location of points Q, R, and S indicate in Fig. 10.30(b)?

10.27 Show that the number of operations required to implement the accumulator-cell approach discussed in Section 10.2 is linear in n, the number of non-background points in the image plane (i.e., the xy-plane).

10.28 An important application of image segmentation is in processing images resulting from so-called *bubble chamber* events. These images arise from experiments in high-energy physics in which a beam of particles of known properties is directed onto a target of known nuclei. A typical event consists of incoming tracks, any one of which, upon a collision, branches out into secondary tracks of particles emanating from the point of collision. Propose a segmentation approach for detecting all tracks angled at any of the following six directions off the horizontal: $\pm 25°$, $\pm 50°$, and $\pm 75°$. The estimation error allowed in any of these six directions is $\pm 5°$. For a track to be valid it must be at least 100 pixels long and have no more than three gaps, each not exceeding 10 pixels. You may assume that the images have been preprocessed so that they are binary and that all tracks are 1 thick, except at the point of collision from which they emanate. Your procedure should be able to differentiate between tracks that have the same direction but different origins. (*Hint:* Base your solution on the Hough transform.)

10.29* Restate the basic global thresholding algorithm in Section 10.3 so that it uses the histogram of an image instead of the image itself.

10.30* Prove that the basic global thresholding algorithm in Section 10.3 converges in a finite number of steps. (*Hint:* Use the histogram formulation from Problem 10.29.)

10.31 Give an explanation why the initial threshold in the basic global thresholding algorithm in Section 10.3 must be between the minimum and maximum values in the image. (*Hint:* Construct an example that shows the algorithm failing for a threshold value selected outside this range.)

10.32* Assume that the initial threshold in the basic global thresholding algorithm in Section 10.3 is selected as a value between the minimum and maximum intensity values in an image. Do you think the final value of the threshold at convergence depends on the specific initial value used? Explain. (You can use a simple image example to support your conclusion.)

10.33 You may assume in both of the following cases that the initial threshold is in the open interval $(0, L-1)$.

(a)* Show that if the histogram of an image is uniform over all possible intensity levels, the basic global thresholding algorithm converges to the average intensity of the image.

(b) Show that if the histogram of an image is bimodal, with identical modes that are symmetric about their means, then the basic global thresholding algorithm will converge to the point halfway between the means of the modes.

10.34 Refer to the basic global thresholding algorithm in Section 10.3. Assume that in a given problem, the histogram is bimodal with modes that are Gaussian curves of the form $A_1 \exp[-(z-m_1)^2/2\sigma_1^2]$ and $A_2 \exp[-(z-m_2)^2/2\sigma_2^2]$. Assume that m_1 is greater than m_2, and that the initial T is between the max and min image intensities. Give conditions (in terms of the parameters of these curves) for the following to be true when the algorithm converges:

(a)* The threshold is equal to $(m_1 + m_2)/2$.

(b)* The threshold is to the left of m_2.

(c) The threshold is in the interval given by the equation $(m_1 + m_2/2) < T < m_1$.

10.35 Do the following:

(a)* Show how the first line in Eq. (10-60) follows from Eqs. (10-55), (10-56), and (10-59).

(b) Show how the second line in Eq. (10-60) follows from the first.

10.36 Show that a maximum value for Eq. (10-63) always exists for k in the range $0 \le k \le L-1$.

10.37* With reference to Eq. (10-65), advance an argument that establishes that $0 \le \eta(k) \le 1$ for k in the range $0 \le k \le L-1$, where the minimum is achievable only by images with constant intensity, and the maximum occurs only for 2-valued images with values 0 and $(L-1)$.

10.38 Do the following:

(a)* Suppose that the intensities of a digital image $f(x, y)$ are in the range $[0, 1]$ and that a threshold, T, successfully segmented the image into objects and background. Show that the threshold $T' = 1 - T$ will successfully segment the negative of $f(x, y)$ into the same regions. The term negative is used here in the sense defined in Section 3.2.

(b) The intensity transformation function in (a) that maps an image into its negative is a linear function with negative slope. State the conditions that an arbitrary intensity transformation function must satisfy for the segmentability of the original image with respect to a threshold, T, to be preserved. What would be the value of the threshold after the intensity transformation?

10.39 The objects and background in the image below have a mean intensity of 170 and 60, respectively, on a [0, 255] scale. The image is corrupted by Gaussian noise with 0 mean and a standard deviation of 10 intensity levels. Propose a thresholding method capable of a correct segmentation rate of 90% or higher. (Recall that 99.7% of the area of a Gaussian curve lies in a $\pm 3\sigma$ interval about the mean, where σ is the standard deviation.)

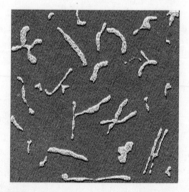

10.40 Refer to the intensity ramp image in Fig. 10.34(b) and the moving-average algorithm discussed in Section 10.3. Assume that the image is of size 500×700 pixels and that its minimum and maximum values are 0 and 1, where 0's are contained only in the first column.

(a)* What would be the result of segmenting this image with the moving-average algorithm using $b = 0$ and an arbitrary value for n. Explain what the segmented image would look like.

(b) Now reverse the direction of the ramp so that its leftmost value is 1 and the rightmost value is 0 and repeat (a).

(c) Repeat (a) but with $b = 1$ and $n = 2$.

(d) Repeat (a) but with $b = 1$ and $n = 100$.

10.41 Propose a region-growing algorithm to segment the image in Problem 10.39.

10.42* Segment the image shown by using the split and merge procedure discussed in Section 10.4. Let $Q(R_i) = $ TRUE if all pixels in R_i have the same intensity. Show the quadtree corresponding to your segmentation.

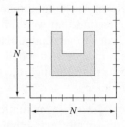

10.43 Consider the region of 1's resulting from the segmentation of the sparse regions in the image of the Cygnus Loop in Example 10.21. Propose a technique for using this region as a mask to isolate the three main components of the image: (1) background; (2) dense inner region; and (3) sparse outer region.

10.44 Let the pixels in the first row of a 3×3 image, like the one in Fig. 10.53(a), be labeled as 1, 2, 3, and the pixels in the second and third rows be labeled as 4, 5, 6 and 7, 8, 9, respectively. Let the intensity of these pixels be [90, 80, 30; 70, 5, 20; 80 20 30] where, for example, the intensity of pixel 2 is 80 and of pixel 4 it is 70. Compute the weights for the edges for the graph in Fig. 10.53(c), using the formula $w(i, j) = 30[1/(|I(n_i) - I(n_j)| + c)]$ explained in the text in connection with that figure (we scaled the formula by 30 to make the numerical results easier to interpret). Let $c = 0$ in this case.

10.45* Explain the steps of SLIC superpixel algorithm

10.46 Demonstrate the validity of Eq. (10-102).

10.47 Refer to the discussion in Section 10.7.

(a)* Show that the elements of $C_n(M_i)$ and $T[n]$ are never replaced during execution of the watershed segmentation algorithm.

(b) Show that the number of elements in sets $C_n(M_i)$ and $T[n]$ either increases or remains the same as n increases.

10.48 You saw in Section 10.7 that the boundaries obtained using the watershed segmentation algorithm form closed loops (for example, see Figs. 10.59 and 10.61). Advance an argument that establishes whether or not closed boundaries *always* result from application of this algorithm.

10.49* Give a step-by-step implementation of the dam-building procedure for the one-dimensional intensity cross section shown below. Show a drawing of the cross section at each step, showing "water" levels and dams constructed.

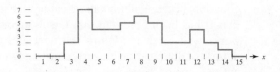

10.50 Calculate the distance measure for each cluster in the SLIC superpixel algorithm. Also, explain the significance of constant c in this.

10.51 Are the following statements true or false? Explain the reason for your answer in each.

(a)* The nonzero entries in the absolute ADI remain the same even if the object is moving.

(b) The nonzero entries in the positive ADI continue to change the area as the object is moving.

(c) The nonzero entries in the negative ADI do not grow in dimension even if the object is moving.

10.52 Suppose that in Example 10.31 motion along the x-axis is set to zero. The object now moves only along the y-axis at 1 pixel per frame for 28 frames and then (instantaneously) reverses direction and moves in exactly the opposite direction for another 28 frames. What would Figs. 10.63 and 10.64 look like under these conditions.

10.53* Mention the steps of Otsu's algorithm.

10.54 An automated pharmaceutical plant uses image processing to measure the shapes of medication tablets for the purpose of quality control. The segmentation stage of the system is based on Otsu's method. The speed of the inspection lines is so high that a very high rate flash illumination is required to "stop" motion. When new, the illumination lamps project a uniform pattern of light. However, as the lamps age, the illumination pattern deteriorates as a function of time and spatial coordinates according to the equation

$$i(x,y) = A(t) - t^2 e^{-[(x - M/2)^2 + (y - N/2)^2]}$$

where $(M/2, N/2)$ is the center of the viewing area and t is time measured in increments of months. The lamps are still experimental and the behavior of $A(t)$ is not fully understood by the manufacturer. All that is known is that, during the life of the lamps, $A(t)$ is always greater than the negative component in the preceding equation because illumination cannot be negative. It has been observed that Otsu's algorithm works well when the lamps are new, and their pattern of illumination is nearly constant over the entire image. However, segmentation performance deteriorates with time. Being experimental, the lamps are exceptionally expensive, so you are employed as a consultant to help solve the problem using digital image processing techniques to compensate for the changes in illumination, and

thus extend the useful life of the lamps. You are given flexibility to install any special markers or other visual cues in the viewing area of the imaging cameras. Propose a solution in sufficient detail that the engineering plant manager can understand your approach. (*Hint:* Review the image model discussed in Section 2.3 and consider using one or more targets of known reflectivity.)

10.55 The speed of a bullet in flight is to be estimated by using high-speed imaging techniques. The method of choice involves the use of a TV camera and flash that exposes the scene for K s. The bullet is 3 cm long, 1 cm wide, and its range of speed is 700 $\pm$ 200 m/s. The camera optics produce an image in which the bullet occupies 10% of the horizontal resolution of a 256×256 digital image.

(a)* Determine the maximum value of K that will guarantee that the blur from motion does not exceed 1 pixel.

(b) Determine the minimum number of frames per second that would have to be acquired in order to guarantee that at least two complete images of the bullet are obtained during its path through the field of view of the camera.

(c)* Propose a segmentation procedure for automatically extracting the bullet from a sequence of frames.

(d) Propose a method for automatically determining the speed of the bullet.

11 Feature Extraction

Well, but reflect; have we not several times
acknowledged that names rightly given are the
likenesses and images of the things which they name?

Socrates

Preview

After an image has been segmented into regions or their boundaries using methods such as those in Chapters 10 and 11, the resulting sets of segmented pixels usually have to be converted into a form suitable for further computer processing. Typically, the step after segmentation is *feature extraction*, which consists of feature detection and feature description. *Feature detection* refers to finding the features in an image, region, or boundary. *Feature description* assigns quantitative attributes to the detected features. For example, we might *detect* corners in a region boundary, and *describe* those corners by their orientation and location, both of which are quantitative attributes. Feature processing methods discussed in this chapter are subdivided into three principal categories, depending on whether they are applicable to boundaries, regions, or whole images. Some features are applicable to more than one category. Feature descriptors should be as insensitive as possible to variations in parameters such as scale, translation, rotation, illumination, and viewpoint. The descriptors discussed in this chapter are either insensitive to, or can be normalized to compensate for, variations in one or more of these parameters.

Upon completion of this chapter, readers should:

■ Understand the meaning and applicability of a broad class of features suitable for image processing.

■ Understand the concepts of feature vectors and feature space, and how to relate them to the various descriptors developed in this chapter.

■ Be skilled in the mathematical tools used in feature extraction algorithms.

■ Be familiar with the limitations of the various feature extraction methods discussed.

■ Understand the principal steps used in the solution of feature extraction problems.

■ Be able to formulate feature extraction algorithms.

■ Have a "feel" for the types of features that have a good chance of success in a given application.

811

11.1 BACKGROUND

Although there is no universally accepted, formal definition of what constitutes an *image feature*, there is little argument that, intuitively, we generally think of a feature as a distinctive attribute or description of "something" we want to label or differentiate. For our purposes, the key words here are *label* and *differentiate*. The "something" of interest in this chapter refers either to individual image objects, or even to entire images or sets of images. Thus, we think of features as attributes that are going to help us assign unique labels to objects in an image or, more generally, are going to be of value in differentiating between entire images or families of images.

There are two principal aspects of image *feature extraction*: *feature detection*, and *feature description*. That is, when we refer to feature extraction, we are referring to both detecting the features and then describing them. To be useful, the extraction process must encompass both. The terminology you are likely to encounter in image processing and analysis to describe feature detection and description varies, but a simple example will help clarify our use of these term. Suppose that we use object corners as features for some image processing task. In this chapter, detection refers to *finding* the corners in a region or image. Description, on the other hand, refers to *assigning quantitative* (or sometimes *qualitative*) *attributes* to the detected features, such as corner orientation, and location with respect to other corners. In other words, knowing that there are corners in an image has limited use without additional information that can help us differentiate between objects in an image, or between images, based on corners and their attributes.

Given that we want to use features for purposes of differentiation, the next question is: What are the important characteristics that these features must possess in the realm of digital image processing? You are already familiar with some of these characteristics. In general, features should be independent of location, rotation, and scale. Other factors, such as independence of illumination levels and changes caused by the viewpoint between the imaging sensor(s) and the scene, also are important. Whenever possible, preprocessing should be used to normalize input images before feature extraction. For example, in situations where changes in illumination are severe enough to cause difficulties in feature detection, it would make sense to preprocess an image to compensate for those changes. Histogram equalization or specification come to mind as automatic techniques that we know are helpful in this regard. The idea is to use as much a priori information as possible to preprocess images in order to improve the chances of accurate feature extraction.

When used in the context of a feature, the word "independent" usually has one of two meanings: invariant or covariant. A feature descriptor is *invariant* with respect to a set of transformations if its value remains unchanged after the application (to the entity being described) of any transformation from the family. A feature descriptor is *covariant* with respect to a set of transformations if applying to the entity any transformation from the set produces the same result in the descriptor. For example, consider this set of affine transformations: {*translation*, *reflection*, *rotation*}, and suppose that we have an elliptical region to which we assign the feature descriptor *area*. Clearly, applying any of these transformations to the region does not change its area.

See Table 2.3 regarding affine transformations.

Therefore, *area* is an invariant feature descriptor with respect to the given family of transformations. However, if we add the affine transformation *scaling* to the family, descriptor *area* ceases to be invariant with respect to the extended family. The descriptor is now covariant with respect to the family, because scaling the area of the region by any factor scales the value of the descriptor by the same factor. Similarly, the descriptor *direction* (of the principal axis of the region) is covariant because rotating the region by any angle has the same effect on the value of the descriptor. Most of the feature descriptors we use in this chapter are covariant in general, in the sense that they may be invariant to some transformations of interest, but not to others that may be equally as important. As you will see shortly, it is good practice to normalize as many relevant invariances as possible out of covariances. For instance, we can compensate for changes in direction of a region by computing its actual direction and rotating the region so that its principal axis points in a predefined direction. If we do this for every region detected in an image, *rotation* will cease to be covariant.

Another major classification of features is *local* vs. *global*. You are likely to see many different attempts to classify features as belonging to one of these two categories. What makes this difficult is that a feature may belong to both, depending on the application. For example, consider the descriptor *area* again, and suppose that we are applying it to the task of inspecting the degree to which bottles moving past an imaging sensor on a production line are full of liquid. The sensor and its accompanying software are capable of generating images of ten bottles at once, in which liquid in each bottle appears as a bright region, and the rest of the image appears as dark background. The area of a region in this fixed geometry is directly proportional to the amount of liquid in a bottle and, if detected and measured reliably, *area* is the only feature we need to solve the inspection problem. Each image has ten regions, so we consider area to be a local feature, in the sense that it is applicable to *individual* elements (regions) of an image. If the problem were to detect the *total* amount (area) of liquid in an image, we would now consider area to be a global descriptor. But the story does not end there. Suppose that the liquid inspection task is redefined so that it calculates the entire amount of liquid per day passing by the imaging station. We no longer care about the area of individual regions per se. Our units now are images. If we know the total area in an image, and we know the number of images, calculating the total amount of liquid in a day is trivial. Now the area of an entire image is a local feature, and the area of the total at the end of the day is global. Obviously, we could redefine the task so that the area at the end of a day becomes a local feature descriptor, and the area for all assembly lines becomes a global measure. And so on, endlessly. In this chapter, we call a feature *local* if it is applies to a member of a set, and *global* if it applies to the entire set, where "member" and "set" are determined by the application.

Features by themselves are seldom generated for human consumption, except in applications such as interactive image processing, topics that are not in the mainstream of this book. In fact, as you will see later, some feature extraction methods generate tens, hundreds, or even thousands of descriptor values that would appear meaningless if examined visually. Instead, feature description typically is used as a preprocessing step for higher-level tasks, such as image registration, object recognition for automated inspection, searching for patterns (e.g., individual faces and/or fingerprints) in image databases, and autonomous applications, such as robot and vehicle navigation. For these applications, numerical features usually are "packaged" in the form of a *feature vector*, (i.e., a $1 \times n$ or $n \times 1$ matrix) whose elements are the descriptors. An RGB image is one of the simplest examples. As you know from Chapter 6, each pixel of an RGB image can be expressed as 3-D vector,

$$\mathbf{x} = \begin{bmatrix} x_1 \\ x_2 \\ x_3 \end{bmatrix}$$

in which x_1 is the intensity value of the red image at a point, and the other components are the intensity values of the green and blue images at the same point. If color is used as a feature, then a region in an RGB image would be represented as a set of feature vectors (points) in 3-D space. When n descriptors are used, feature vectors become n-dimensional, and the space containing them is referred to as an *n-dimensional feature space*. You may "visualize" a set of n-dimensional feature vectors as a "hypercloud" of points in n-dimensional Euclidean space.

In this chapter, we group features into three principal categories: *boundary*, *region*, and *whole image* features. This subdivision is not based on the applicability of the methods we are about to discuss; rather, it is based on the fact that some categories make more sense than others when considered in the context of what is being described. For example, it is implied that when we refer to the "length of a boundary" we are referring to the "length of the boundary of a region," but it makes no sense to refer to the "length" of an image. It will become clear that many of the features we will be discussing are applicable to boundaries and regions, and some apply to whole images as well.

11.2 BOUNDARY PREPROCESSING

The segmentation techniques discussed in the previous two chapters yield raw data in the form of pixels along a boundary or pixels contained in a region. It is standard practice to use schemes that compact the segmented data into representations that facilitate the computation of descriptors. In this section, we discuss various boundary preprocessing approaches suitable for this purpose.

BOUNDARY FOLLOWING (TRACING)

You will find it helpful to review the discussion in Sections 2.5 on neighborhoods, adjacency and connectivity, and the discussion in Section 9.6 dealing with connected components.

Several of the algorithms discussed in this chapter require that the points in the boundary of a region be ordered in a clockwise or counterclockwise direction. Consequently, we begin our discussion by introducing a boundary-following algorithm whose output is an *ordered* sequence of points. We assume (1) that we are working with binary images in which object and background points are labeled 1 and 0, respectively; and (2) that images are padded with a border of 0's to eliminate the possibility of an object merging with the image border. For clarity, we limit the discussion to single regions. The approach is extended to multiple, disjoint regions by processing the regions individually.

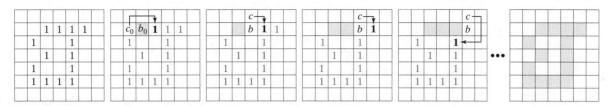

FIGURE 11.1 Illustration of the first few steps in the boundary-following algorithm. The point to be processed next is labeled in bold, black; the points yet to be processed are gray; and the points found by the algorithm are shaded. Squares without labels are considered background (0) values.

The following algorithm traces the boundary of a 1-valued region, R, in a binary image.

See Section 2.5 for the definition of 4-neighbors, 8-neighbors, and m-neighbors of a point,

1. Let the starting point, b_0, be the *uppermost-leftmost* point[†] in the image that is labeled 1. Denote by c_0 the *west* neighbor of b_0 [see Fig. 11.1(b)]. Clearly, c_0 is always a background point. Examine the 8-neighbors of b_0, starting at c_0 and proceeding in a clockwise direction. Let b_1 denote the *first* neighbor encountered whose value is 1, and let c_1 be the (background) point immediately preceding b_1 in the sequence. Store the locations of b_0 for use in Step 5.

2. Let $b = b_0$ and $c = c_0$.

3. Let the 8-neighbors of b, starting at c and proceeding in a clockwise direction, be denoted by $n_1, n_2, \ldots, n_8$. Find the first neighbor labeled 1 and denote it by n_k.

4. Let $b = n_k$ and $c = n_{k-1}$.

5. Repeat Steps 3 and 4 until $b = b_0$. The sequence of b points found when the algorithm stops is the set of ordered boundary points.

Note that c in Step 4 is always a background point because n_k is the first 1-valued point found in the clockwise scan. This algorithm is referred to as the *Moore boundary tracing algorithm* after Edward F. Moore, a pioneer in cellular automata theory.

Figure 11.1 illustrates the first few steps of the algorithm. It is easily verified (see Problem 11.1) that continuing with this procedure will yield the correct boundary, shown in Fig. 11.1(f), whose points are ordered in a clockwise sequence. The algorithm works equally well with more complex boundaries, such as the boundary with an attached branch in Fig. 11.2(a) or the self-intersecting boundary in Fig. 11.2(b). Multiple boundaries [Fig. 11.2(c)] are handled by processing one boundary at a time.

If we start with a binary region instead of a boundary, the algorithm extracts the *outer boundary* of the region. Typically, the resulting boundary will be one pixel thick, but not always [see Problem 11.1(b)]. If the objective is to find the boundaries of holes in a region (these are called the *inner* or *interior boundaries* of the region),

[†] As you will see later in this chapter and in Problem 11.8, the uppermost-leftmost point in a 1-valued boundary has the important property that a polygonal approximation to the boundary has a convex vertex at that location. Also, the left and north neighbors of the point are guaranteed to be background points. These properties make it a good "standard" point at which to start boundary-following algorithms.

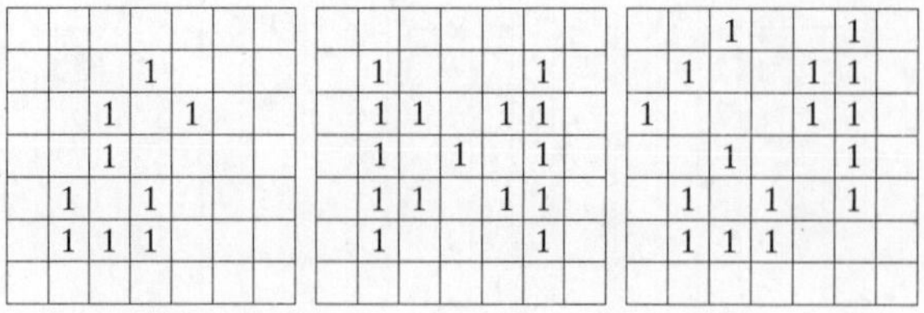

816 **Chapter 11** Feature Extraction

a b c

FIGURE 11.2 Examples of boundaries that can be processed by the boundary-following algorithm. (a) Closed boundary with a branch. (b) Self-intersecting boundary. (c) Multiple boundaries (processed one at a time).

a straightforward approach is to extract the holes (see Section 9.6) and treat them as 1-valued regions on a background of 0's. Applying the boundary-following algorithm to these regions will yield the inner boundaries of the original region.

We could have stated the algorithm just as easily based on following a boundary in the counterclockwise direction but you will find it easier to have just one algorithm and then reverse the order of the result to obtain a sequence in the opposite direction. We use both directions interchangeably (but consistently) in the following sections to help you become familiar with both approaches.

CHAIN CODES

Chain codes are used to represent a boundary by a connected sequence of straight-line segments of specified length and direction. We assume in this section that all curves are closed, simple curves (i.e., curves that are closed and not self intersecting).

Freeman Chain Codes

Typically, a chain code representation is based on 4- or 8-connectivity of the segments. The *direction* of each segment is coded by using a numbering scheme, as in Fig. 11.3. A boundary code formed as a sequence of such directional numbers is referred to as a *Freeman chain code*.

Digital images usually are acquired and processed in a grid format with equal spacing in the *x*- and *y*-directions, so a chain code could be generated by following a boundary in, say, a clockwise direction and assigning a direction to the segments connecting every pair of pixels. This level of detail generally is not used for two principal reasons: (1) The resulting chain would be quite long and (2) any small disturbances along the boundary due to noise or imperfect segmentation would cause changes in the code that may not be related to the principal shape features of the boundary.

An approach used to address these problems is to resample the boundary by selecting a larger grid spacing, as in Fig. 11.4(a). Then, as the boundary is traversed, a boundary point is assigned to a node of the coarser grid, depending on the proximity of the original boundary point to that node, as in Fig. 11.4(b). The resampled boundary obtained in this way can be represented by a 4- or 8-code. Figure 11.4(c) shows the coarser boundary points represented by an 8-directional chain code. It is a simple matter to convert from an 8-code to a 4-code and vice versa (see Problems 2.15, 9.27,

a b

FIGURE 11.3
Direction
numbers for
(a) 4-directional
chain code, and
(b) 8-directional
chain code.

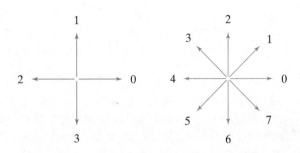

and 9.29). For the same reason mentioned when discussing boundary tracing earlier in this section, we chose the starting point in Fig. 11.4(c) as the uppermost-leftmost point of the boundary, which gives the chain code 0766…1212. As you might suspect, the spacing of the resampling grid is determined by the application in which the chain code is used.

If the sampling grid used to obtain a connected digital curve is a uniform quadrilateral (see Fig. 2.19) all points of a Freeman code based on Fig. 11.3 are guaranteed to coincide with the points of the curve. The same is true if a digital curve is subsampled using the same type of sampling grid, as in Fig. 11.4(b). This is because the samples of curves produced using such grids have the same arrangement as in Fig. 11.3, so all points are reachable as we traverse a curve from one point to the next to generate the code.

The numerical value of a chain code depends on the starting point. However, the code can be normalized with respect to the starting point by a straightforward procedure: We simply treat the chain code as a circular sequence of direction numbers and redefine the starting point so that the resulting sequence of numbers forms an integer of minimum magnitude. We can normalize also for rotation (in angles that are integer multiples of the directions in Fig. 11.3) by using the *first difference* of the chain code instead of the code itself. This difference is obtained by counting the number of direction changes (in a counterclockwise direction in Fig. 11.3) that separate two adjacent elements of the code. If we treat the code as a circular sequence to normalize it with respect to the starting point, then the first element of the difference is computed by using the transition between the last and first components of the chain.

a b c

FIGURE 11.4
(a) Digital
boundary with
resampling grid
superimposed.
(b) Result of
resampling.
(c) 8-directional
chain-coded
boundary.

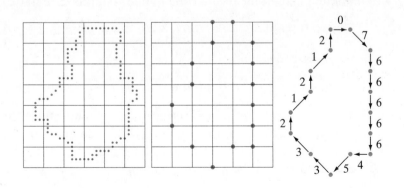

For instance, the first difference of the 4-directional chain code 10103322 is 3133030. Size normalization can be achieved by altering the spacing of the resampling grid.

The normalizations just discussed are exact only if the boundaries themselves are invariant to rotation (again, in angles that are integer multiples of the directions in Fig. 11.3) and scale change, which seldom is the case in practice. For instance, the same object digitized in two different orientations will have different boundary shapes in general, with the degree of dissimilarity being proportional to image resolution. This effect can be reduced by selecting chain elements that are long in proportion to the distance between pixels in the digitized image, and/or by orienting the resampling grid along the principal axes of the object to be coded, as discussed in Section 11.3, or along its eigen axes, as discussed in Section 11.5.

EXAMPLE 11.1: Freeman chain code and some of its variations.

Figure 11.5(a) shows a 570×570-pixel, 8-bit gray-scale image of a circular stroke embedded in small, randomly distributed specular fragments. The objective of this example is to obtain a Freeman chain code, the corresponding integer of minimum magnitude, and the first difference of the outer boundary of the stroke. Because the object of interest is embedded in small fragments, extracting its boundary would result in a noisy curve that would not be descriptive of the general shape of the object. As you know, smoothing is a routine process when working with noisy boundaries. Figure 11.5(b) shows the original image smoothed using a box kernel of size 9×9 pixels (see Section 3.5 for a discussion of spatial smoothing), and Fig. 11.5(c) is the result of thresholding this image with a global threshold obtained using Otsu's method. Note that the number of regions has been reduced to two (one of which is a dot), significantly simplifying the problem.

Figure 11.5(d) is the outer boundary of the region in Fig. 11.5(c). Obtaining the chain code of this boundary directly would result in a long sequence with small variations that are not representative of the global shape of the boundary, so we resample it before obtaining its chain code. This reduces insignificant variability. Figure 11.5(e) is the result of using a resampling grid with nodes 50 pixels apart (approximately 10% of the image width) and Fig. 11.5(f) is the result of joining the sample points by straight lines. This simpler approximation retained the principal features of the original boundary.

The 8-directional Freeman chain code of the simplified boundary is

$$0\ 0\ 0\ 0\ 6\ 0\ 6\ 6\ 6\ 6\ 6\ 6\ 6\ 6\ 4\ 4\ 4\ 4\ 4\ 2\ 4\ 2\ 2\ 2\ 2\ 2\ 0\ 2\ 2\ 0\ 2$$

The starting point of the boundary is at coordinates (2, 5) in the subsampled grid (remember from Fig. 2.19 that the origin of an image is at its top, left). This is the uppermost-leftmost point in Fig. 11.5(f). The integer of minimum magnitude of the code happens in this case to be the same as the chain code:

$$0\ 0\ 0\ 0\ 6\ 0\ 6\ 6\ 6\ 6\ 6\ 6\ 6\ 6\ 4\ 4\ 4\ 4\ 4\ 2\ 4\ 2\ 2\ 2\ 2\ 2\ 0\ 2\ 2\ 0\ 2$$

The first difference of the code is

$$0\ 0\ 0\ 6\ 2\ 6\ 0\ 0\ 0\ 0\ 0\ 0\ 6\ 0\ 0\ 0\ 0\ 6\ 2\ 6\ 0\ 0\ 0\ 0\ 6\ 2\ 0\ 6\ 2\ 6$$

Using this code to represent the boundary results in a significant reduction in the amount of data needed to store the boundary. In addition, working with code numbers offers a unified way to analyze the shape of a boundary, as we discuss in Section 11.3. Finally, keep in mind that the subsampled boundary can be recovered from any of the preceding codes.

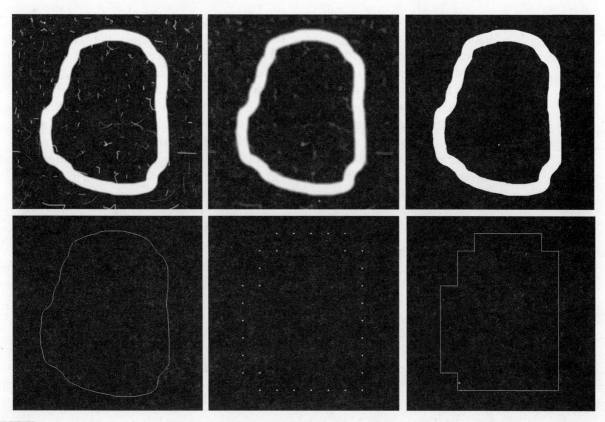

a b c
d e f

FIGURE 11.5 (a) Noisy image of size 570×570 pixels. (b) Image smoothed with a 9×9 box kernel. (c) Smoothed image, thresholded using Otsu's method. (d) Longest outer boundary of (c). (e) Subsampled boundary (the points are shown enlarged for clarity). (f) Connected points from (e).

Slope Chain Codes

Using Freeman chain codes generally requires resampling a boundary to smooth small variations, a process that implies defining a grid and subsequently assigning all boundary points to their closest neighbors in the grid. An alternative to this approach is to use *slope chain codes* (SCCs) (Bribiesca [1992, 2013]). The SCC of a 2-D curve is obtained by placing straight-line segments of equal length around the curve, with the end points of the segments touching the curve.

Obtaining an SSC requires calculating the *slope changes* between contiguous line segments, and normalizing the changes to the *continuou*s (open) interval $(-1, 1)$. This approach requires defining the length of the line segments, as opposed to Freeman codes, which require defining a grid and assigning curve points to it—a much more elaborate procedure. Like Freeman codes, SCCs are independent of rotation, but a larger range of possible slope changes provides a more accurate representation under rotation than the rotational independence of the Freeman codes, which is limited to the eight directions in Fig. 11.3(b). As with Freeman codes, SCCs are independent of translation, and can be normalized for scale changes (see Problem 11.8).

Figure 11.6 illustrates how an SCC is generated. The first step is to select the length of the line segment to use in generating the code [see Fig. 11.6(b)]. Next, a starting point (the origin) is specified (for an open curve, the logical starting point is one of its end points). As Fig. 11.6(c) shows, once the origin has been selected, one end of a line segment is placed at the origin and the other end of the segment is set to coincide with the curve. This point becomes the starting point of the next line segment, and we repeat this procedure until the starting point (or end point in the case of an open curve) is reached. As the figure illustrates, you can think of this process as a sequence of identical circles (with radius equal to the length of the line segment) traversing the curve. The intersections of the circles and the curve determine the nodes of the straight-line approximation to the curve.

Once the intersections of the circles are known, we determine the slope changes between contiguous line segments. Positive and zero slope changes are normalized to the open half interval $[0, 1)$, while negative slope changes are normalized to the open interval $(-1, 0)$. Not allowing slope changes of ± 1 eliminates the implementation issues that result from having to deal with the fact that such changes result in the same line segment with opposite directions.

The sequence of slope changes is the chain that defines the SCC approximation to the original curve. For example, the code for the curve in Fig. 11.6(e) is 0.12, 0.20, 0.21, 0.11, −0.11, −0.12, −0.21, −0.22, −0.24, −0.28, −0.28, −0.31, −0.30. The accuracy of the slope changes defined in Fig. 11.6(d) is 10^{-2}, resulting in an "alphabet" of 199 possible symbols (slope changes). The accuracy can be changed, of course. For instance, and accuracy of 10^{-1} produces an alphabet of 19 symbols (see Problem 11.6). Unlike a Freeman code, there is no guarantee that the last point of the coded curve will coincide with the last point of the curve itself. However, shortening the line

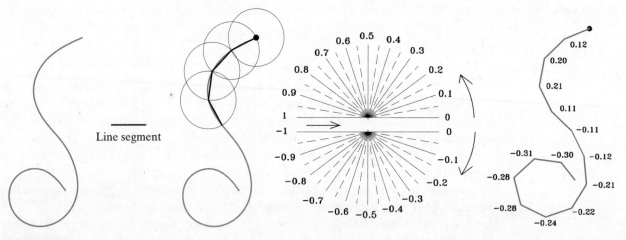

a b c d e

FIGURE 11.6 (a) An open curve. (b) A straight-line segment. (c) Traversing the curve using circumferences to determine slope changes; the dot is the origin (starting point). (d) Range of slope changes in the open interval $(-1, 1)$ (the arrow in the center of the chart indicates direction of travel). There can be ten subintervals between the slope numbers shown. (e) Resulting coded curve showing its corresponding numerical sequence of slope changes. (Courtesy of Professor Ernesto Bribiesca, IIMAS-UNAM, Mexico.)

length and/or increasing angle resolution often resolves the problem, because the results of computations are rounded to the nearest integer (remember we work with integer coordinates).

The *inverse* of an SCC is another chain of the same length, obtained by reversing the order of the symbols and their signs. The *mirror image* of a chain is obtained by starting at the origin and reversing the signs of the symbols. Finally, we point out that the preceding discussion is directly applicable to closed curves. Curve following would start at an arbitrary point (for example, the uppermost-leftmost point of the curve) and proceed in a clockwise or counterclockwise direction, stopping when the starting point is reached. We will illustrate an use of SSCs in Example 11.6.

BOUNDARY APPROXIMATIONS USING MINIMUM-PERIMETER POLYGONS

For an open curve, the number of segments of an exact polygonal approximation is equal to the number of points minus 1.

A digital boundary can be approximated with arbitrary accuracy by a polygon. For a closed curve, the approximation becomes exact when the number of segments of the polygon is equal to the number of points in the boundary, so each pair of adjacent points defines a segment of the polygon. The goal of a polygonal approximation is to capture the essence of the shape in a given boundary using the fewest possible number of segments. Generally, this problem is not trivial, and can turn into a time-consuming iterative search. However, approximation techniques of modest complexity are well suited for image-processing tasks. Among these, one of the most powerful is representing a boundary by a *minimum-perimeter polygon* (MPP), as defined in the following discussion.

Foundation

An intuitive approach for computing MPPs is to enclose a boundary [see Fig. 11.7(a)] by a set of concatenated cells, as in Fig. 11.7(b). Think of the boundary as a rubber band contained in the gray cells in Fig. 11.7(b). As it is allowed to shrink, the rubber band will be constrained by the vertices of the inner and outer walls of the region of the gray cells. Ultimately, this shrinking produces the shape of a polygon of minimum perimeter (with respect to this geometrical arrangement) that circumscribes the region enclosed by the cell strip, as in Fig. 11.7(c). Note in this figure that all the vertices of the MPP coincide with corners of either the inner or the outer wall.

The size of the cells determines the accuracy of the polygonal approximation. In the limit, if the size of each (square) cell corresponds to a pixel in the boundary, the maximum error in each cell between the boundary and the MPP approximation would be $\sqrt{2}d$, where d is the minimum possible distance between pixels (i.e., the distance between pixels established by the resolution of the original sampled boundary). This error can be reduced in half by forcing each cell in the polygonal approximation to be centered on its corresponding pixel in the original boundary. The objective is to use the largest possible cell size acceptable in a given application, thus producing MPPs with the fewest number of vertices. Our objective in this section is to formulate a procedure for finding these MPP vertices.

The cellular approach just described reduces the shape of the object enclosed by the original boundary, to the area circumscribed by the gray walls in Fig. 11.7(b).

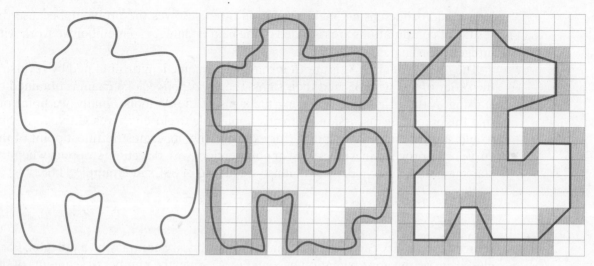

FIGURE 11.7 (a) An object boundary. (b) Boundary enclosed by cells (shaded). (c) Minimum-perimeter polygon obtained by allowing the boundary to shrink. The vertices of the polygon are created by the corners of the inner and outer walls of the gray region.

A convex vertex is the center point of a triplet of points that define an angle in the range $0° < \theta < 180°$. Similarly, angles of a concave vertex are in the range $180° < \theta < 360°$. An angle of $180°$ defines a *degenerate vertex* (i.e., segment of a straight line), which cannot be an MPP-vertex.

Figure 11.8(a) shows this shape in dark gray. Suppose that we traverse the boundary of the dark gray region in a *counterclockwise* direction. Every turn encountered in the traversal will be either a convex or a concave vertex (the angle of a vertex is defined as an *interior* angle of the boundary at that vertex). Convex and concave vertices are shown, respectively, as white and blue dots in Fig. 11.8(b). Note that these vertices are the vertices of the inner wall of the light-gray bounding region in Fig. 11.8(b), and that every concave (blue) vertex in the dark gray region has a corresponding concave "mirror" vertex in the light gray wall, located diagonally opposite the vertex. Figure 11.8(c) shows the mirrors of all the concave vertices, with the MPP from Fig. 11.7(c) superimposed for reference. We see that the vertices of the MPP coincide either with convex vertices in the inner wall (white dots) or with the mirrors of the concave vertices (blue dots) in the outer wall. Only convex vertices of the inner wall and concave vertices of the outer wall can be vertices of the MPP. Thus, our algorithm needs to focus attention only on those vertices.

MPP Algorithm

The set of cells enclosing a digital boundary [e.g., the gray cells in Fig. 11.7(b)] is called a *cellular complex*. We assume the cellular complexes to be *simply connected*, in the sense the boundaries they enclose are not self-intersecting. Based on this assumption, and letting *white* (*W*) denote convex vertices, and *blue* (*B*) denote mirrored concave vertices, we state the following observations:

1. The MPP bounded by a simply connected cellular complex is not self-intersecting.
2. Every *convex* vertex of the MPP is a *W* vertex, but not every *W* vertex of a boundary is a vertex of the MPP.

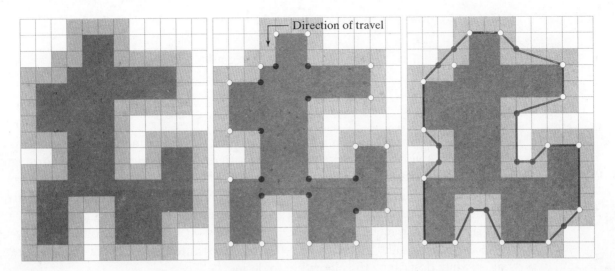

a b c

FIGURE 11.8 (a) Region (dark gray) resulting from enclosing the original boundary by cells (see Fig. 11.7). (b) Convex (white dots) and concave (blue dots) vertices obtained by following the boundary of the dark gray region in the counterclockwise direction. (c) Concave vertices (blue dots) displaced to their diagonal mirror locations in the outer wall of the bounding region; the convex vertices are not changed. The MPP (solid boundary) is superimposed for reference.

3. Every *mirrored concave* vertex of the MPP is a *B* vertex, but not every *B* vertex of a boundary is a vertex of the MPP.

4. All *B* vertices are on or outside the MPP, and all *W* vertices are on or inside the MPP.

5. The uppermost-leftmost vertex in a sequence of vertices contained in a cellular complex is always a *W* vertex of the MPP (see Problem 11.8).

These assertions can be proved formally (Sklansky et al. [1972], Sloboda et al. [1998], and Klette and Rosenfeld [2004]). However, their correctness is evident for our purposes (see Fig. 11.8), so we do not dwell on the proofs here. Unlike the angles of the vertices of the dark gray region in Fig. 11.8, the angles sustained by the vertices of the MPP are not necessarily multiples of 90°.

In the discussion that follows, we will need to calculate the orientation of triplets of points. Consider a triplet of points, (a, b, c), and let the coordinates of these points be $a = (a_x, a_y)$, $b = (b_x, b_y)$, and $c = (c_x, c_y)$. If we arrange these points as the rows of the matrix

$$\mathbf{A} = \begin{bmatrix} a_x & a_y & 1 \\ b_x & b_y & 1 \\ c_x & c_y & 1 \end{bmatrix} \tag{11-1}$$

Then, it follows from matrix analysis that

$$\det(\mathbf{A}) = \begin{cases} > 0 & \text{if } (a,b,c) \text{ is a counterclockwise sequence} \\ 0 & \text{if the points are colinear} \\ < 0 & \text{if } (a,b,c) \text{ is a clockwise sequence} \end{cases} \tag{11-2}$$

where $\det(\mathbf{A})$ is the determinant of $\mathbf{A}$. In terms of this equation, movement in a counterclockwise or clockwise direction is with respect to a right-handed coordinate system (see the footnote in the discussion of Fig. 2.19). For example, using the image coordinate system from Fig. 2.19 (in which the origin is at the top left, the positive x-axis extends vertically downward, and the positive y-axis extends horizontally to the right), the sequence $a = (3,4)$, $b = (2,3)$, and $c = (3,2)$ is in the counterclockwise direction. This would give $\det(\mathbf{A}) > 0$ when substituted into Eq. (11-2). It is convenient when describing the algorithm to define

$$\text{sgn}(a, b, c) \equiv \det(\mathbf{A}) \tag{11-3}$$

so that $\text{sgn}(a, b, c) > 0$ for a counterclockwise sequence, $\text{sgn}(a, b, c) < 0$ for a clockwise sequence, and $\text{sgn}(a, b, c) = 0$ when the points are collinear. Geometrically, $\text{sgn}(a, b, c) > 0$ indicates that point c lies on the positive side of pair (a, b) (i.e., c lies on the positive side of the line passing through points a and b). Similarly, if $\text{sgn}(a, b, c) < 0$, point c lies on the negative side of the line. Equations (11-2) and (11-3) give the same result if the sequence (c, a, b) or (b, c, a) is used because the direction of travel in the sequence is the same as for (a, b, c). However, the geometrical interpretation is different. For example, $\text{sgn}(c, a, b) > 0$ indicates that point b lies on the positive side of the line through points c and a.

To prepare the data for the MPP algorithm, we form a list of triplets consisting of a vertex label (e.g., V_0, V_1, etc.); the coordinates of each vertex; and an additional element denoting whether the vertex is W or B. It is important that the concave vertices be mirrored, as in Fig. 11.8(c), that the vertices be in sequential order,[†] and that the first vertex be the uppermost-leftmost vertex, which we know from property 5 is a W vertex of the MPP. Let V_0 denote this vertex. We assume that the vertices are arranged in the counterclockwise direction. The algorithm for finding MPPs uses two "crawler" points: a white crawler (W_C) and a blue crawler (B_C). W_C crawls along the convex (W) vertices, and B_C crawls along the concave (B) vertices. These two crawler points, the last MPP vertex found, and the vertex being examined are all that is necessary to implement the algorithm.

The algorithm starts by setting $W_C = B_C = V_0$ (recall that V_0 is an MPP-vertex). Then, at any step in the algorithm, let V_L denote the last MPP vertex found, and let V_k denote the current vertex being examined. One of the following three conditions can exist between V_L, V_k, and the two crawler points:

[†]Vertices of a boundary can be ordered by tracking the boundary using the boundary-following algorithm discussed earlier.

(a) V_k is on the positive side of the line through the pair of points (V_L, W_C), in which case $\text{sgn}(V_L, W_C, V_k) > 0$.

(b) V_k is on the negative side of the line though pair (V_L, W_C) or is collinear with it; that is $\text{sgn}(V_L, W_C, V_k) \leq 0$. Simultaneously, V_k lies to the positive side of the line through (V_L, B_C) or is collinear with it; that is, $\text{sgn}(V_L, B_C, V_k) \geq 0$.

(c) V_k is on the negative side of the line though pair (V_L, B_C), in which case $\text{sgn}(V_L, B_C, V_k) < 0$.

If condition (a) holds, the next MPP vertex is W_C, and we let $V_L = W_C$; then we reinitialize the algorithm by setting $W_C = B_C = V_L$, and start with the next vertex after the newly changed V_L.

If condition (b) holds, V_k becomes a *candidate* MPP vertex. In this case, we set $W_C = V_k$ if V_k is convex (i.e., it is a W vertex); otherwise we set $B_C = V_k$. We then continue with the next vertex in the list.

If condition (c) holds, the next MPP vertex is B_C and we let $V_L = B_C$; then we reinitialize the algorithm by setting $W_C = B_C = V_L$ and start with the next vertex after the newly changed V_L.

The algorithm stops when it reaches the first vertex again, and thus has processed all the vertices in the polygon. The V_L vertices found by the algorithm are the vertices of the MPP. Klette and Rosenfeld [2004] have proved that this algorithm finds all the MPP vertices of a polygon enclosed by a simply connected cellular complex.

EXAMPLE 11.2: A numerical example showing the details of how the MPP algorithm works.

A simple example in which we can follow the algorithm step-by-step will help clarify the preceding concepts. Consider the vertices in Fig. 11.8(c). In our image coordinate system, the top-left point of the grid is at coordinates $(0,0)$. Assuming unit grid spacing, the first few (counterclockwise) vertices are:

$$V_0 \, (1,4) \, W \mid V_1 \, (2,3) \, B \mid V_2 \, (3,3) \, W \mid V_3 \, (3,2) \, B \mid V_4 \, (4,1) \, W \mid V_5 \, (7,1) \, W \mid V_6 \, (8,2) \, B \mid V_7 \, (9,2) \, B$$

where the triplets are separated by vertical lines, and the B vertices are mirrored, as required by the algorithm.

The uppermost-leftmost vertex is always the first vertex of the MPP, so we start by letting V_L and V_0 be equal, $V_L = V_0 = (1,4)$, and initializing the other variables: $W_C = B_C = V_L = (1,4)$.

The next vertex is $V_1 = (2,3)$. In this case we have $\text{sgn}(V_L, W_C, V_1) = 0$ and $\text{sgn}(V_L, B_C, V_1) = 0$, so condition (b) holds. Because V_1 is a B (concave) vertex, we update the blue crawler: $B_C = V_1 = (2,3)$. At this stage, we have $V_L = (1,4)$, $W_C = (1,4)$, and $B_C = (2,3)$.

Next, we look at $V_2 = (3,3)$. In this case, $\text{sgn}(V_L, W_C, V_2) = 0$, and $\text{sgn}(V_L, B_C, V_2) = 1$, so condition (b) holds. Because V_2 is W, we update the white crawler: $W_C = (3,3)$.

The next vertex is $V_3 = (3,2)$. At this junction we have $V_L = (1,4)$, $W_C = (3,3)$, and $B_C = (2,3)$. Then, $\text{sgn}(V_L, W_C, V_3) = -2$ and $\text{sgn}(V_L, B_C, V_3) = 0$, so condition (b) holds again. Because V_3 is B, we let $B_C = V_3 = (4,3)$ and look at the next vertex.

The next vertex is $V_4 = (4,1)$. We are working with $V_L = (1,4)$, $W_C = (3,3)$, and $B_C = (3,2)$. The values of sgn are $\text{sgn}(V_L, W_C, V_4) = -3$ and $\text{sgn}(V_L, B_C, V_4) = 0$. So, condition (b) holds yet again, and we let $W_C = V_4 = (4,1)$ because V_4 is a W vertex.

The next vertex is $V_5 = (7,1)$. Using the values from the previous step we obtain $\text{sgn}(V_L, W_C, V_5) = 9$, so condition (a) is satisfied. Therefore, we let $V_L = W_C = (4,1)$ (this is V_4) and reinitialize: $B_C = W_C = V_L = (4,1)$. Note that once we knew that $\text{sgn}(V_L, W_C, V_5) > 0$ we did not bother to compute the other sgn expression. Also, reinitialization means that we start fresh again by examining the next vertex following the newly found MPP vertex. In this case, that next vertex is V_5, so we visit it again.

With $V_5 = (7,1)$, and using the new values of V_L, W_C, and B_C, it follows that $\text{sgn}(V_L, W_C, V_5) = 0$ and $\text{sgn}(V_L, B_C, V_5) = 0$, so condition (b) holds. Therefore, we let $W_C = V_5 = (7,1)$ because V_5 is a W vertex.

The next vertex is $V_6 = (8,2)$ and $\text{sgn}(V_L, W_C, V_6) = 3$, so condition (a) holds. Thus, we let $V_L = W_C = (7,1)$ and reinitialize the algorithm by setting $W_C = B_C = V_L$.

Because the algorithm was reinitialized at V_5, the next vertex is $V_6 = (8,2)$ again. Using the results from the previous step gives us $\text{sgn}(V_L, W_C, V_6) = 0$ and $\text{sgn}(V_L, B_C, V_6) = 0$, so condition (b) holds this time. Because V_6 is B we let $B_C = V_6 = (8,2)$.

Summarizing, we have found three vertices of the MPP up to this point: $V_1 = (1,4)$, $V_4 = (4,1)$, and $V_5 = (7,1)$. Continuing as above with the remaining vertices results in the MPP vertices in Fig. 11.8(c) (see Problem 11.9). The mirrored B vertices at $(2,3)$, $(3,2)$, and on the lower-right side at $(13,10)$, are on the boundary of the MPP. However, they are collinear and thus are not considered vertices of the MPP. Appropriately, the algorithm did not detect them as such.

EXAMPLE 11.3: Applying the MPP algorithm.

Figure 11.9(a) is a 566×566 binary image of a maple leaf, and Fig. 11.9(b) is its 8-connected boundary. The sequence in Figs. 11.9(c) through (h) shows MMP representations of this boundary using square cellular complex cells of sizes 2, 4, 6, 8, 16, and 32, respectively (the vertices in each figure were connected with straight lines to form a closed boundary). The leaf has two major features: a stem and three main lobes. The stem begins to be lost for cell sizes greater than 4×4, as Fig. 11.9(e) shows. The three main lobes are preserved reasonably well, even for a cell size of 16×16, as Fig. 11.9(g) shows. However, we see in Fig. 11.8(h) that by the time the cell size is increased to 32×32, this distinctive feature has been nearly lost.

The number of points in the original boundary [Fig. 11.9(b)] is 1900. The numbers of vertices in Figs. 11.9(c) through (h) are 206, 127, 92, 66, 32, and 13, respectively. Figure 11.9(e), which has 127 vertices, retained all the major features of the original boundary while achieving a data reduction of over 90%. So here we see a significant advantage of MMPs for representing a boundary. Another important advantage is that MPPs perform boundary smoothing. As explained in the previous section, this is a usual requirement when representing a boundary by a chain code.

SIGNATURES

A signature is a 1-D functional representation of a 2-D boundary and may be generated in various ways. One of the simplest is to plot the distance from the centroid to the boundary as a function of angle, as illustrated in Fig. 11.10. The basic idea of using signatures is to reduce the boundary representation to a 1-D function that presumably is easier to describe than the original 2-D boundary.

Based on the assumptions of uniformity in scaling with respect to both axes, and that sampling is taken at equal intervals of θ, changes in the size of a shape result in changes in the amplitude values of the corresponding signature. One way to

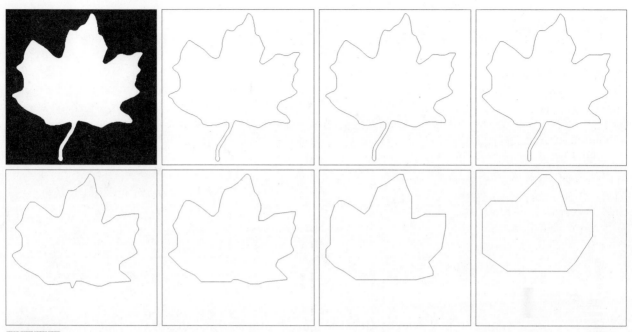

a b c d
e f g h

FIGURE 11.9 (a) 566 × 566 binary image. (b) 8-connected boundary. (c) through (h), MMPs obtained using square cells of sizes 2, 4, 6, 8, 16, and 32, respectively (the vertices were joined by straight-line segments for display). The number of boundary points in (b) is 1900. The numbers of vertices in (c) through (h) are 206, 127, 92, 66, 32, and 13, respectively. Images (b) through (h) are shown as negatives to make the boundaries easier to see.

normalize for this is to scale all functions so that they always span the same range of values, e.g., [0,1]. The main advantage of this method is simplicity, but it has the disadvantage that scaling of the entire function depends on only two values: the minimum and maximum. If the shapes are noisy, this can be a source of significant error from object to object. A more rugged (but also more computationally intensive) approach is to divide each sample by the variance of the signature, assuming that the variance is not zero—as in the case of Fig. 11.10(a)—or so small that it creates computational difficulties. Using the variance yields a variable scaling factor that is inversely proportional to changes in size and works much as automatic volume control does. Whatever the method used, the central idea is to remove dependency on size while preserving the fundamental shape of the waveforms.

Distance versus angle is not the only way to generate a signature. For example, another way is to traverse the boundary and, corresponding to each point on the boundary, plot the angle between a line tangent to the boundary at that point and a reference line. The resulting signature, although quite different from the $r(\theta)$ curves in Fig. 11.10, carries information about basic shape characteristics. For instance, horizontal segments in the curve correspond to straight lines along the boundary because the tangent angle is constant there. A variation of this approach is to use the so-called *slope density function* as a signature. This function is a histogram of

FIGURE 11.10
Distance-versus-angle signatures. In (a), $r(\theta)$ is constant. In (b), the signature consists of repetitions of the pattern $r(\theta) = A \sec\theta$ for $0 \leq \theta \leq \pi/4$, and $r(\theta) = A \csc\theta$ for $\pi/4 < \theta \leq \pi/2$.

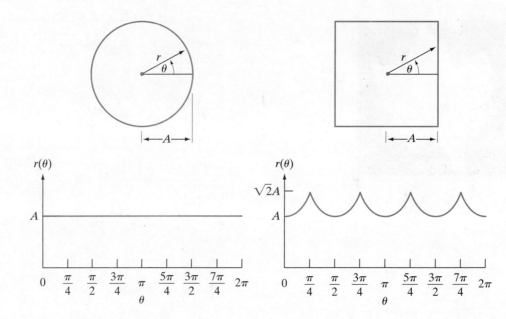

tangent-angle values. Because a histogram is a measure of the concentration of values, the slope density function responds strongly to sections of the boundary with constant tangent angles (straight or nearly straight segments) and has deep valleys in sections producing rapidly varying angles (corners or other sharp inflections).

EXAMPLE 11.4: Signatures of two regions.

Figures 11.11(a) and (d) show two binary objects, and Figs. 11.11(b) and (e) are their boundaries. The corresponding $r(\theta)$ signatures in Figs. 11.11(c) and (f) range from 0° to 360° in increments of 1°. The number of prominent peaks in the signatures is sufficient to differentiate between the shapes of the two objects.

SKELETONS, MEDIAL AXES, AND DISTANCE TRANSFORMS

Like boundaries, skeletons are related to the shape of a region. Skeletons can be computed from a boundary by filling the area enclosed by the boundary with foreground values, and treating the result as a binary region. In other words, a skeleton is computed using the coordinates of points in the entire region, including its boundary. The idea is to reduce a region to a tree or graph by computing its skeleton. As we explained in Section 9.5 (see Fig. 9.25), the *skeleton* of a region is the set of points in the region that are equidistant from the border of the region.

As is true of thinning, the MAT is highly susceptible to boundary and internal region irregularities, so smoothing and other preprocessing steps generally are required to obtain a clean a binary image.

The skeleton is obtained using one of two principal approaches: (1) by successively thinning the region (e.g., using morphological erosion) while preserving end points and line connectivity (this is called *topology-preserving* thinning); or (2) by computing the *medial axis* of the region via an efficient implementation of the *medial axis transform* (MAT) proposed by Blum [1967]. We discussed thinning in Section 9.5. The MAT of a region R with border B is as follows: For each point p in R, we find its closest neighbor in B. If p has more than one such neighbor, it is said

a b c
d e f

FIGURE 11.11
(a) and (d) Two binary regions, (b) and (e) their external boundaries, and (c) and (f) their corresponding $r(\theta)$ signatures. The horizontal axes in (c) and (f) correspond to angles from 0° to 360°, in increments of 1°.

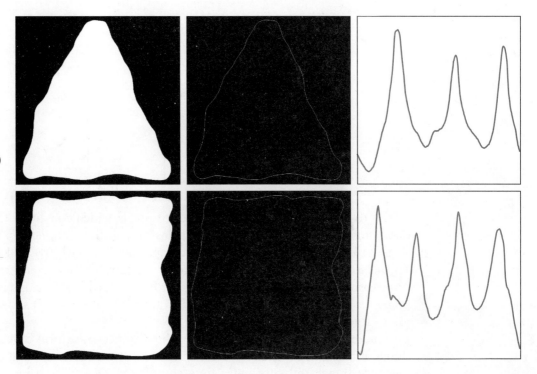

to belong to the medial axis of R. The concept of "closest" (and thus the resulting MAT) depends on the definition of a distance metric (see Section 2.5). Figure 11.12 shows some examples using the Euclidean distance. If the Euclidean distance is used, the resulting skeleton is the same as what would be obtained by using the maximum disks from Section 9.5. The skeleton of a region is *defined* as its medial axis.

The MAT of a region has an intuitive interpretation based on the "prairie fire" concept discussed in Section 11.3 (see Fig. 11.15). Consider an image region as a prairie of uniform, dry grass, and suppose that a fire is lit simultaneously along all the points on its border. All fire fronts will advance into the region at the same speed. The MAT of the region is the set of points reached by more than one fire front at the same time.

In general, the MAT comes considerably closer than thinning to producing skeletons that "make sense." However, computing the MAT of a region requires calculating the distance from every interior point to every point on the border of the region—an impractical endeavor in most applications. Instead, the approach is to obtain the skeleton equivalently from the *distance transform*, for which numerous efficient algorithms exist.

The distance transform of a region of foreground pixels in a background of zeros is the distance from every pixel to the *nearest* nonzero valued pixel. Figure 11.13(a) shows a small binary image, and Fig. 11.13(b) is its distance transform. Observe that every 1-valued pixel has a distance transform value of 0 because its closest nonzero valued pixel is itself. For the purpose of finding skeletons equivalent to the MAT, we are interested in the distance from the pixels of a region of foreground (white)

FIGURE 11.12
Medial axes (dashed) of three simple regions.

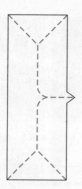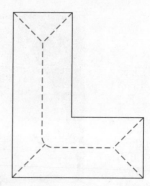

pixels to their nearest background (zero) pixels, which constitute the region boundary. Thus, we compute the distance transform of the *complement* of the image, as Figs. 11.13(c) and (d) illustrate. By comparing Figs. 11.13(d) and 11.12(a), we see in the former that the MAT (skeleton) is equivalent to the *ridge* of the distance transform [i.e., the ridge in the image in Fig. 11.13(d)]. This ridge is the set of *local maxima* [shown bold in Fig. 11.13(d)]. Figures 11.13(e) and (f) show the same effect on a larger (414×708) binary image.

Finding approaches for computing the distance transform efficiently has been a topic of research for many years. Numerous approaches exist that can compute the distance transform with linear time complexity, $O(K)$, for a binary image with K pixels. For example, the algorithm by Maurer et al. [2003] not only can compute the distance transform in $O(K)$, it can compute it in $O(K/P)$ using P processors.

a b
c d
e f

FIGURE 11.13
(a) A small image and (b) its distance transform. Note that all 1-valued pixels in (a) have corresponding 0's in (b). (c) A small image, and (d) the distance transform of its *complement*. (e) A larger image, and (f) the distance transform of its complement. The Euclidian distance was used throughout.

```
0   0   0   0   0                  1.41  1   1   1  1.41
0   1   1   1   0                   1    0   0   0   1
0   1   1   1   0                   1    0   0   0   1
0   0   0   0   0                  1.41  1   1   1  1.41
```

```
0   0   0   0   0   0   0   0   0        0   0   0   0   0   0   0   0   0
0   1   1   1   1   1   1   1   0        0   1   1   1   1   1   1   1   0
0   1   1   1   1   1   1   1   0        0   1   2   2   2   2   2   1   0
0   1   1   1   1   1   1   1   0        0   1   2   3   3   3   2   1   0
0   1   1   1   1   1   1   1   0        0   1   2   2   2   2   2   1   0
0   1   1   1   1   1   1   1   0        0   1   1   1   1   1   1   1   0
0   0   0   0   0   0   0   0   0        0   0   0   0   0   0   0   0   0
```

FIGURE 11.14
(a) Thresholded
image of blood
vessels.
(b) Skeleton
obtained by
thinning, shown
superimposed
on the image
(note the spurs).
(c) Result of 40
passes of spur
removal.
(d) Skeleton
obtained using the
distance
transform.

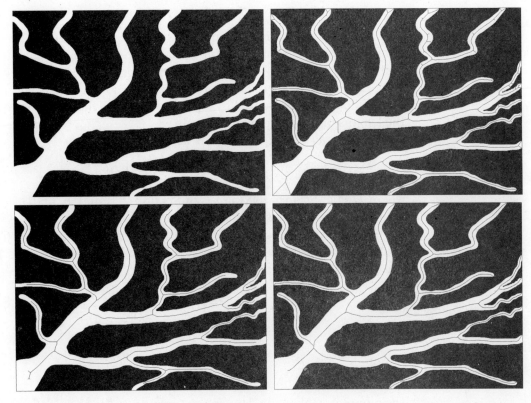

EXAMPLE 11.5: Skeletons obtained using thinning and pruning vs. the distance transform.

Figure 11.14(a) shows a segmented image of blood vessels, and Fig. 11.14(b) shows the skeleton obtained using morphological thinning. As we discussed in Chapter 9, thinning is characteristically accompanied by spurs, which certainly is the case here. Figure 11.14(c) shows the result of forty passes of spur removal. With the exception of the few small spurs visible on the bottom left of the image, pruning did a reasonable job of cleaning up the skeleton. One drawback of thinning is the loss of potentially important features. This was not the case here, except the pruned skeleton does not cover the full expanse of the image. Figure 11.14(c) shows the skeleton obtained using distance transform computations based on fast marching (see Lee et al. [2005] and Shi and Karl [2008]). The way the algorithm we used implements branch generation handles ambiguities such as spurs automatically.

The result in Fig. 11.14(d) is slightly superior to the result in Fig. 11.14(c), but both skeletons certainly capture the important features of the image in this case. A key advantage of the thinning approach is simplicity of implementation, which can be important in dedicated applications. Overall, distance-transform formulations tend to produce skeletons less prone to discontinuities, but overcoming the computational burden of the distance transform results in implementations that are considerably more complex than thinning.

11.3 BOUNDARY FEATURE DESCRIPTORS

We begin our discussion of feature descriptors by considering several fundamental approaches for describing region boundaries.

SOME BASIC BOUNDARY DESCRIPTORS

The *length* of a boundary is one of its simplest descriptors. The number of pixels along a boundary is an approximation of its length. For a chain-coded curve with unit spacing in both directions, the number of vertical and horizontal components plus $\sqrt{2}$ multiplied by the number of diagonal components gives its exact length. If the boundary is represented by a polygonal curve, the length is equal to the sum of the lengths of the polygonal segments.

The *diameter* of a boundary B is defined as

$$diameter(B) = \max_{i,j}\left[D\left(p_i, p_j\right)\right] \tag{11-4}$$

where D is a distance measure (see Section 2.5) and p_i and p_j are points on the boundary. The value of the diameter and the orientation of a line segment connecting the two extreme points that comprise the diameter is called the *major axis* (or *longest chord*) of the boundary. That is, if the major axis is defined by points (x_1, y_1) and (x_2, y_2), then the length and orientation of the major axis are given by

The major and minor axes are used also as regional descriptors.

$$length_m = \left[(x_2 - x_1)^2 + (y_2 - y_1)^2\right]^{1/2} \tag{11-5}$$

and

$$angle_m = \tan^{-1}\left[\frac{y_2 - y_1}{x_2 - x_1}\right]$$

The *minor axis* (also called the *longest perpendicular chord*) of a boundary is defined as the line perpendicular to the major axis, and of such length that a box passing through the outer four points of intersection of the boundary with the two axes completely encloses the boundary. The box just described is called the *basic rectangle* or *bounding box*, and the ratio of the major to the minor axis is called the *eccentricity* of the boundary. We give some examples of this descriptor in Section 11.4.

The *curvature* of a boundary is defined as the rate of change of slope. In general, obtaining reliable measures of curvature at a point of a raw digital boundary is difficult because these boundaries tend to be locally "ragged." Smoothing can help, but a more rugged measure of curvature is to use the difference between the slopes of adjacent boundary segments that have been represented as straight lines. Polygonal approximations are well-suited for this approach [see Fig. 11.8(c)], in which case we are concerned only with curvature at the vertices. As we traverse the polygon in the clockwise direction, a vertex point p is said to be *convex* if the change in slope at p is nonnegative; otherwise, p is said to be *concave*. The description can be refined further by using ranges for the changes of slope. For instance, p could be labeled as part of a nearly straight line segment if the absolute change of slope at that point is less than $10°$, or it could be labeled as "corner-like" point if the absolute change is in the range $90°$, $\pm 30°$.

We will discuss corners in detail later in this chapter.

Descriptors based on changes of slope can be formulated easily by expressing a boundary in the form of a slope chain code (SSC), as discussed earlier (see Fig. 11.6). A particularly useful boundary descriptor that is easily implemented using SSCs is *tortuosity*, a measure of the twists and turns of a curve. The tortuosity, τ, of a curve represented by an SCC is defined as the sum of the absolute values of the chain elements:

$$\tau = \sum_{i=1}^{n} |a_i| \tag{11-6}$$

where n is the number of elements in the SCC, and $|a_i|$ are the values (slope changes) of the elements in the code. The next example illustrates one use of this descriptor

EXAMPLE 11.6: Using slope chain codes to describe tortuosity.

An important measures of blood vessel morphology is its tortuosity. This metric can assist in the computer-aided diagnosis of Retinopathy of Prematurity (ROP), an eye disease that affects babies born prematurely (Bribiesca [2013]). ROP causes abnormal blood vessels to grow in the retina (see Section 2.1). This growth can cause the retina to detach from the back of the eye, potentially leading to blindness.

Figure 11.15(a) shows an image of the retina (called a *fundus* image) from a newborn baby. Ophthalmologists diagnose and make decisions about the initial treatment of ROP based on the appearance of retinal blood vessels. Dilatation and increased tortuosity of the retinal vessels are signs of highly probable ROP. Blood vessels denoted A, B, and C in Fig. 11.15 were selected to demonstrate the discriminative potential of SCCs for quantifying tortuosity (each vessel shown is a long, thin *region*, not a line segment).

The border of each vessel was extracted and its length (number of pixels), P, was calculated. To make SCC comparisons meaningful, the three boundaries were normalized so that each would have the same number, m, of straight-line segments. The length, L, of the line segment was then computed as $L = m/P$. It follows that the number of elements of each SCC is $m - 1$. The tortuosity, τ, of a curve represented by an SCC is defined as the sum of the absolute values of the chain elements, as noted in Eq. (11-6).

The table in Fig. 11.15(b) shows values of τ for vessels A, B, and C based on 51 straight-line segments (as noted above, $n = m - 1$). The values of tortuosity are in agreement with our visual analysis of the three vessels, showing B as being slightly "busier" than A, and C as having the fewest twists and turns.

a b

FIGURE 11.15
(a) Fundus image from a prematurely born baby with ROP. (b) Tortuosity of vessels A, B, and C. (Courtesy of Professor Ernesto Bribiesca, IIMAS-UNAM, Mexico.)

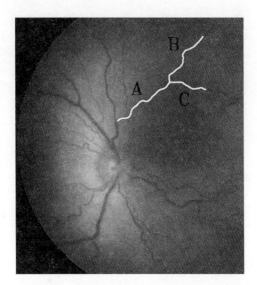

Curve	n	τ
A	50	2.3770
B	50	2.5132
C	50	1.6285

SHAPE NUMBERS

As explained Section 11.2, the first difference of smallest magnitude makes a Freeman chain code independent of the starting point, and is insensitive to rotation in increments of 90° if a 4-directional code is used.

The shape number of a Freeman chain-coded boundary, based on the 4-directional code of Fig. 11.3(a), is defined as the first difference of smallest magnitude. The *order*, n, of a shape number is defined as the number of digits in its representation. Moreover, n is even for a closed boundary, and its value limits the number of possible different shapes. Figure 11.16 shows all the shapes of order 4, 6, and 8, along with their chain-code representations, first differences, and corresponding shape numbers. Although the first difference of a 4-directional chain code is independent of rotation (in increments of 90°), the coded boundary in general depends on the orientation of the grid. One way to normalize the grid orientation is by aligning the chain-code grid with the sides of the basic rectangle defined in the previous section.

In practice, for a desired shape order, we find the rectangle of order n whose eccentricity (defined in Section 11.4) best approximates that of the basic rectangle, and use this new rectangle to establish the grid size. For example, if $n = 12$, all the rectangles of order 12 (that is, those whose perimeter length is 12) are of sizes 2×4, 3×3, and 1×5. If the eccentricity of the 2×4 rectangle best matches the eccentricity of the basic rectangle for a given boundary, we establish a 2×4 grid centered on the basic rectangle and use the procedure outlined in Section 11.2 to obtain the Freeman chain code. The shape number follows from the first difference of this code. Although the order of the resulting shape number usually equals n because of the way the grid spacing was selected, boundaries with depressions comparable to this spacing sometimes yield shape numbers of order greater than n. In this case, we specify a rectangle of order lower than n, and repeat the procedure until the resulting shape number is of order n. The order of a shape number starts at 4 and is always even because we are working with 4-connectivity and require that boundaries be closed.

FIGURE 11.16
All shapes of order 4, 6, and 8. The directions are from Fig. 11.3(a), and the dot indicates the starting point.

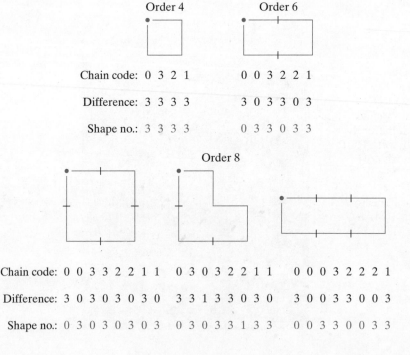

	Order 4	Order 6
Chain code:	0 3 2 1	0 0 3 2 2 1
Difference:	3 3 3 3	3 0 3 3 0 3
Shape no.:	3 3 3 3	0 3 3 0 3 3

Order 8

Chain code:	0 0 3 3 2 2 1 1	0 3 0 3 2 2 1 1	0 0 0 3 2 2 2 1
Difference:	3 0 3 0 3 0 3 0	3 3 1 3 3 0 3 0	3 0 0 3 3 0 0 3
Shape no.:	0 3 0 3 0 3 0 3	0 3 0 3 3 1 3 3	0 0 3 3 0 0 3 3

FIGURE 11.17
Steps in the generation of a shape number.

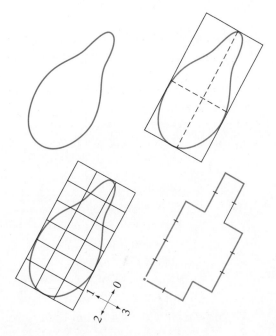

Chain code: 0 0 0 0 3 0 0 3 2 2 3 2 2 2 1 2 1 1

Difference: 3 0 0 0 3 1 0 3 3 0 1 3 0 0 3 1 3 0

Shape no.: 0 0 0 3 1 0 3 3 0 1 3 0 0 3 1 3 0 3

EXAMPLE 11.7: Computing shape numbers.

Suppose that $n = 18$ is specified for the boundary in Fig. 11.17(a). To obtain a shape number of this order we follow the steps just discussed. First, we find the basic rectangle, as shown in Fig. 11.17(b). Next we find the closest rectangle of order 18. It is a 3×6 rectangle, requiring the subdivision of the basic rectangle shown in Fig. 11.17(c). The chain-code directions are aligned with the resulting grid. The final step is to obtain the chain code and use its first difference to compute the shape number, as shown in Fig. 11.17(d).

FOURIER DESCRIPTORS

We use the "conventional" axis system here for consistency with the literature. However, the same result is obtained if we use the book image coordinate system whose origin is at the top left because both are right-handed coordinate systems (see Fig. 2.19). In the latter, the rows and columns represent the real and imaginary parts of the complex number.

Figure 11.18 shows a digital boundary in the xy-plane, consisting of K points. Starting at an arbitrary point (x_0, y_0), coordinate pairs $(x_0, y_0), (x_1, y_1), (x_2, y_2), \dots, (x_{K-1}, y_{K-1})$ are encountered in traversing the boundary, say, in the counterclockwise direction. These coordinates can be expressed in the form $x(k) = x_k$ and $y(k) = y_k$. Using this notation, the boundary itself can be represented as the sequence of coordinates $s(k) = [x(k), y(k)]$ for $k = 0, 1, 2, \dots, K - 1$. Moreover, each coordinate pair can be treated as a complex number so that

$$s(k) = x(k) + jy(k) \tag{11-7}$$

for $k = 0, 1, 2, \dots, K - 1$. That is, the x-axis is treated as the real axis and the y-axis as the imaginary axis of a sequence of complex numbers. Although the interpretation

FIGURE 11.18
A digital
boundary and its
representation
as sequence of
complex numbers.
The points (x_0, y_0)
and (x_1, y_1) are
(arbitrarily) the
first two points in
the sequence.

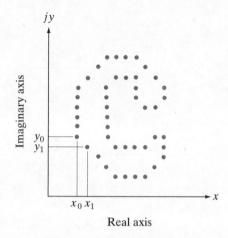

of the sequence was restated, the nature of the boundary itself was not changed. Of course, this representation has one great advantage: It reduces a 2-D to a 1-D description problem.

We know from Eq. (4-44) that the discrete Fourier transform (DFT) of $s(k)$ is

$$a(u) = \sum_{k=0}^{K-1} s(k)e^{-j2\pi uk/K} \qquad (11\text{-}8)$$

for $u = 0, 1, 2, \ldots, K - 1$. The complex coefficients $a(u)$ are called the *Fourier descriptors* of the boundary. The inverse Fourier transform of these coefficients restores $s(k)$. That is, from Eq. (4-45),

$$s(k) = \frac{1}{K} \sum_{u=0}^{K-1} a(u)e^{j2\pi uk/K} \qquad (11\text{-}9)$$

for $k = 0, 1, 2, \ldots, K - 1$. We know from Chapter 4 that the inverse is identical to the original input, provided that all the Fourier coefficients are used in Eq. (11-9). However, suppose that, instead of all the Fourier coefficients, only the first P coefficients are used. This is equivalent to setting $a(u) = 0$ for $u > P - 1$ in Eq. (11-9). The result is the following *approximation* to $s(k)$:

$$\hat{s}(k) = \frac{1}{K} \sum_{u=0}^{P-1} a(u)e^{j2\pi uk/K} \qquad (11\text{-}10)$$

for $k = 0, 1, 2, \ldots, K - 1$. Although only P terms are used to obtain each component of $\hat{s}(k)$, parameter k still ranges from 0 to $K - 1$. That is, the *same* number of points exists in the approximate boundary, but not as many terms are used in the reconstruction of each point.

Deleting the high-frequency coefficients is the same as filtering the transform with an ideal lowpass filter. You learned in Chapter 4 that the periodicity of the DFT requires that we center the transform prior to filtering it by multiplying it by $(-1)^x$. Thus, we use this procedure when implementing Eq. (11-8), and use it again to reverse the centering when computing the inverse in Eq. (11-10). Because of symmetry considerations in the DFT, the number of points in the boundary and its inverse must be even. This implies that the number of coefficients removed (set to 0) before the inverse is computed must be even. Because the transform is centered, we set to 0 half the number of coefficients on each end of the transform to preserve symmetry. Of course, the DFT and its inverse are computed using an FFT algorithm.

Recall from discussions of the Fourier transform in Chapter 4 that high-frequency components account for fine detail, and low-frequency components determine overall shape. Thus, the smaller we make P in Eq. (11-10), the more detail that will be lost on the boundary, as the following example illustrates.

EXAMPLE 11.8: Using Fourier descriptors.

Figure 11.19(a) shows the boundary of a human chromosome, consisting of 2868 points. The corresponding 2868 Fourier descriptors were obtained using Eq. (11-8). The objective of this example is to examine the effects of reconstructing the boundary using fewer Fourier descriptors. Figure 11.19(b) shows the boundary reconstructed using one-half of the 2868 descriptors in Eq. (11-10). Observe that there is no perceptible difference between this boundary and the original. Figures 11.19(c) through (h) show the boundaries reconstructed with the number of Fourier descriptors being 10%, 5%, 2.5%, 1.25%, 0.63% and 0.28% of 2868, respectively. When rounded to the nearest even integer, these percentages are equal to 286, 144, 72, 36, 18, and 8 descriptors, respectively. The important point is that 18 descriptors, a mere six-tenths of one percent of the original 2868 descriptors, were sufficient to retain the principal shape features of the original boundary: four long protrusions and two deep bays. Figure 11.19(h), obtained with 8 descriptors, is unacceptable because the principal features are lost. Further reductions to 4 and 2 descriptors would result in an ellipse and a circle, respectively (see Problem 11.18).

As the preceding example demonstrates, a few Fourier descriptors can be used to capture the essence of a boundary. This property is valuable, because these coefficients carry shape information. Thus, forming a feature vector from these coefficients can be used to differentiate between boundary shapes, as we will discuss in Chapter 12.

We have stated several times that descriptors should be as insensitive as possible to translation, rotation, and scale changes. In cases where results depend on the order in which points are processed, an additional constraint is that descriptors should be insensitive to the starting point. Fourier descriptors are not directly insensitive to these geometrical changes, but changes in these parameters can be related to simple transformations on the descriptors. For example, consider rotation and recall from basic mathematical analysis that rotation of a point by an angle θ about the origin of the complex plane is accomplished by multiplying the point by $e^{j\theta}$. Doing so to every point of $s(k)$ rotates the entire sequence about the origin. The rotated sequence is $s(k)e^{j\theta}$, whose Fourier descriptors are

$$a_r(u) = \sum_{k=0}^{K-1} s(k)e^{j\theta}e^{-j2\pi uk/K}$$

$$= a(u)e^{j\theta}$$

(11-11)

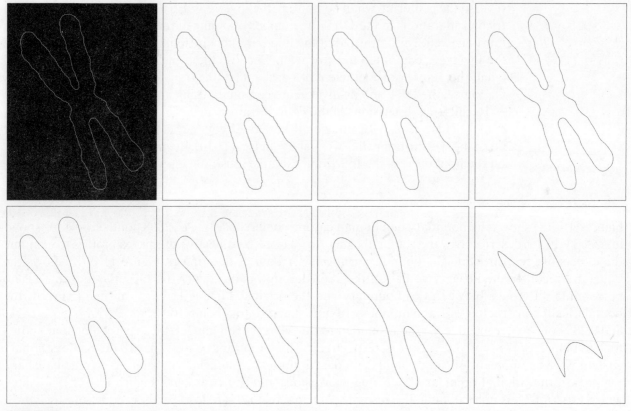

a b c d
e f g h

FIGURE 11.19 (a) Boundary of a human chromosome (2868 points). (b)–(h) Boundaries reconstructed using 1434, 286, 144, 72, 36, 18, and 8 Fourier descriptors, respectively. These numbers are approximately 50%, 10%, 5%, 2.5%, 1.25%, 0.63%, and 0.28% of 2868, respectively. Images (b)–(h) are shown as negatives to make the boundaries easier to see.

for $u = 0, 1, 2, \ldots, K - 1$. Thus, rotation simply affects all coefficients equally by a multiplicative *constant* term $e^{j\theta}$.

Table 11.1 summarizes the Fourier descriptors for a boundary sequence $s(k)$ that undergoes rotation, translation, scaling, and changes in the starting point. The symbol Δ_{xy} is defined as $\Delta_{xy} = \Delta x + j\Delta y$, so the notation $s_t(k) = s(k) + \Delta_{xy}$ indicates redefining (translating) the sequence as

$$s_t(k) = \left[x(k) + \Delta x \right] + j\left[y(k) + \Delta y \right] \tag{11-12}$$

Recall from Chapter 4 that the Fourier transform of a constant is an impulse located at the origin. Recall also that an impulse $\delta(u)$ is zero everywhere, except when $u = 0$.

Note that translation has no effect on the descriptors, except for $u = 0$, which has the value $\delta(0)$. Finally, the expression $s_p(k) = s(k - k_0)$ means redefining the sequence as

$$s_p(k) = x(k - k_0) + jy(k - k_0) \tag{11-13}$$

TABLE 11.1
Some basic
properties of
Fourier
descriptors.

Transformation	Boundary	Fourier Descriptor
Identity	$s(k)$	$a(u)$
Rotation	$s_r(k) = s(k)e^{j\theta}$	$a_r(u) = a(u)e^{j\theta}$
Translation	$s_t(k) = s(k) + \Delta_{xy}$	$a_t(u) = a(u) + \Delta_{xy}\delta(u)$
Scaling	$s_s(k) = \alpha s(k)$	$a_s(u) = \alpha a(u)$
Starting point	$s_p(k) = s(k - k_0)$	$a_p(u) = a(u)e^{-j2\pi k_0 u/K}$

which changes the starting point of the sequence from $k = 0$ to $k = k_0$. The last entry in Table 11.1 shows that a change in starting point affects all descriptors in a different (but known) way, in the sense that the term multiplying $a(u)$ depends on u.

STATISTICAL MOMENTS

We will discuss moments of two variable in Section 11.4.

Statistical moments of one variable are useful descriptors applicable to 1-D renditions of 2-D boundaries, such as signatures. To see how this can be accomplished, consider Fig. 11.20 which shows the signature from Fig. 11.10(b) sampled, and treated as an ordinary discrete function $g(r)$ of one variable, r.

Suppose that we treat the *amplitude* of g as a discrete random variable z and form an amplitude histogram $p(z_i)$, $i = 0, 1, 2, \ldots, A - 1$, where A is the number of discrete amplitude increments in which we divide the amplitude scale. If p is normalized so that the sum of its elements equals 1, then $p(z_i)$ is an estimate of the probability of intensity value z_i occurring. It then follows from Eq. (3-24) that the nth moment of z about its mean is

$$\mu_n(z) = \sum_{i=0}^{A-1} (z_i - m)^n p(z_i) \tag{11-14}$$

where

$$m = \sum_{i=0}^{A-1} z_i \, p(z_i) \tag{11-15}$$

As you know, m is the mean (average) value of z, and μ_2 is its variance. Generally, only the first few moments are required to differentiate between signatures of clearly distinct shapes.

FIGURE 11.20
Sampled
signature from
Fig. 11.10(b) treated as an ordinary, discrete function of one variable.

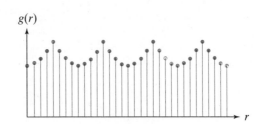

An alternative approach is to normalize the area of $g(r)$ in Fig. 11.20 to unity and treat it as a histogram. In other words, $g(r_i)$ is now treated as the probability of value r_i occurring. In this case, r is treated as the random variable and the moments are

$$\mu_n(r) = \sum_{i=0}^{K-1} (r_i - m)^n g(r_i) \tag{11-16}$$

where

$$m = \sum_{i=0}^{K-1} r_i g(r_i) \tag{11-17}$$

In these equations, K is the number of points on the boundary, and $\mu_n(r)$ is related directly to the shape of signature $g(r)$. For example, the second moment $\mu_2(r)$ measures the spread of the curve about the mean value of r, and the third moment $\mu_3(r)$ measures its symmetry with respect to the mean.

Although moments are used frequently for characterizing signatures, they are not the only descriptors used for this purpose. For instance, another approach is to compute the 1-D discrete Fourier transform of $g(r)$, obtain its spectrum, and use the first few components as descriptors. The advantage of moments over other techniques is that their implementation is straightforward and they also carry a "physical" interpretation of signature (and by implication boundary) shape. The insensitivity of this approach to rotation follows from the fact that signatures are independent of rotation, provided that the starting point is always the same along the boundary. Size normalization can be achieved by scaling the values of g and r.

11.4 REGION FEATURE DESCRIPTORS

As we did with boundaries, we begin the discussion of regional features with some basic region descriptors.

SOME BASIC DESCRIPTORS

The *major* and *minor* axes of a region, as well as the idea of a *bounding box*, are as defined earlier for boundaries. The *area* of a region is defined as the number of pixels in the region. The *perimeter* of a region is the length of its boundary. When area and perimeter are used as descriptors, they generally make sense only when they are normalized (Example 11.9 shows such a use). A more frequent use of these two descriptors is in measuring *compactness* of a region, defined as the perimeter squared over the area:

$$\text{compactness} = \frac{p^2}{A} \tag{11-18}$$

This is a dimensionless measure that is 4π for a circle (its minimum value) and 16 for a square.

A similar dimensionless measure is *circularity* (also called *roundness*), defined as

Sometimes compactness is defined as the inverse of the circularity. Obviously, these two measures are closely related.

$$\text{circularity} = \frac{4\pi A}{p^2} \tag{11-19}$$

The value of this descriptor is 1 for a circle (its maximum value) and $\pi/4$ for a square. Note that these two measures are independent of size, orientation, and translation. Another measure based on a circle is the *effective diameter*:

$$d_e = 2\sqrt{\frac{A}{\pi}} \qquad (11\text{-}20)$$

This is the diameter of a circle having the same area, A, as the region being processed. This measure is neither dimensionless nor independent of region size, but it is independent of orientation and translation. It can be normalized for size and made dimensionless by dividing it by the largest diameter expected in a given application.

In a manner analogous to the way we defined compactness and circularity relative to a circle, we define the *eccentricity* of a region relative to an ellipse as the eccentricity of an ellipse that has the same second central moments as the region. For 1-D, the second central moment is the variance. For 2-D discrete data, we have to consider the variance of each variable as well as the covariance between them. These are the components of the covariance matrix, which is estimated from samples using Eq. (11-21) below, with the samples in this case being 2-D vectors representing the coordinates of the data.

Figure 11.21(a) shows an ellipse in *standard form* (i.e., an ellipse whose major and minor axes are aligned with the coordinate axes). The eccentricity of such an ellipse is defined as the ratio of the distance between foci ($2c$ in Fig. 11.21), and the length of its major axis ($2a$), which gives the ratio $2c/2a = c/a$. That is,

$$\text{eccentricity} = \frac{c}{a} = \frac{\sqrt{a^2 - b^2}}{a} = \sqrt{1 - (b/a)^2} \quad a \geq b$$

However, we are interested in the eccentricity of an ellipse that has the same second central moments as a given 2-D region, which means that our ellipses can have arbitrary orientations. Intuitively, what we are trying to do is approximate our 2-D data by an elliptical region whose axes are aligned with the principal axes of the data, as Fig. 11.21(b) illustrates. As you will learn in Section 11.5 (see Example 11.17), the principal axes are the eigenvectors of the covariance matrix, $\mathbf{C}$, of the data, which is given by:

Often, you will the constant in Eq. (11-21) written as $1/K$ instead of $1/K{-}1$. The latter is used to obtain a statistically-unbiased estimate of $\mathbf{C}$. For our purposes, either formulation is acceptable.

$$\mathbf{C} = \frac{1}{K-1} \sum_{k=1}^{K} (\mathbf{z}_k - \bar{\mathbf{z}})(\mathbf{z}_k - \bar{\mathbf{z}})^T \qquad (11\text{-}21)$$

a b

FIGURE 11.21
(a) An ellipse in standard form.
(b) An ellipse approximating a region in arbitrary orientation.

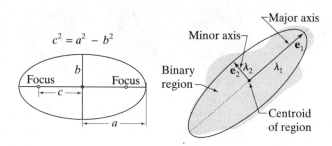

where $\mathbf{z}_k$ is a 2-D vector whose elements are the two spatial coordinates of a point in the region, K is the total number of points, and $\bar{\mathbf{z}}$ is the mean vector:

$$\bar{\mathbf{z}} = \frac{1}{K}\sum_{k=1}^{K}\mathbf{z}_k \tag{11-22}$$

The main diagonal elements of $\mathbf{C}$ are the variances of the coordinate values of the points in the region, and the off-diagonal elements are their covariances.

An ellipse oriented in the same direction as the principal axes of the region can be interpreted as the intersection of a 2-D Gaussian function with the xy-plane. The orientation of the axes of the ellipse are also in the direction of the eigenvectors of the covariance matrix, and the distances from the center of the ellipse to its intersection with its major and minor axes is equal to the largest and smallest eigenvalues of the covariance matrix, respectively, as Fig. 11.21(b) shows. With reference to Fig. 11.21, and the equation of its eccentricity given above, we see by analogy that the eccentricity of an ellipse with the same second moments as the region is given by

$$\text{eccentricity} = \frac{\sqrt{\lambda_2^2 - \lambda_1^2}}{\lambda_2} \tag{11-23}$$

$$= \sqrt{1 - (\lambda_1/\lambda_2)^2} \quad \lambda_2 \geq \lambda_1$$

For circular regions, $\lambda_1 = \lambda_2$ and the eccentricity is 0. For a line, $\lambda_1 = 0$ and the eccentricity is 1. Thus, values of this descriptor are in the range $[0,1]$.

EXAMPLE 11.9: Comparison of feature descriptors.

Figure 11.22 shows values of the preceding descriptors for several region shapes. None of the descriptors for the circle was exactly equal to its theoretical value because digitizing a circle introduces error into the computation, and because we approximated the length of a boundary as its number of elements. The eccentricity of the square did have an exact value of 0, because a square with no rotation aligns perfectly with the sampling grid. The other two descriptors for the square were close to their theoretical values also.

The values listed in the first two rows of Fig. 11.22 carry the same information. For example, we can tell that the star is less compact and less circular than the other shapes. Similarly, it is easy to tell from the numbers listed that the teardrop region has by far the largest eccentricity, but it is harder to differentiate from the other shapes using compactness or circularity.

As we discussed in Section 11.1, feature descriptors typically are arranged in the form of feature vectors for subsequent processing. Figure 11.23 shows the feature space for the descriptors in Fig. 11.22.

a b c d

FIGURE 11.22
Compactness,
circularity, and
eccentricity of
some simple
binary regions.

Descriptor				
Compactness	10.1701	42.2442	15.9836	13.2308
Circularity	1.2356	0.2975	0.7862	0.9478
Eccentricity	0.0411	0.0636	0	0.8117

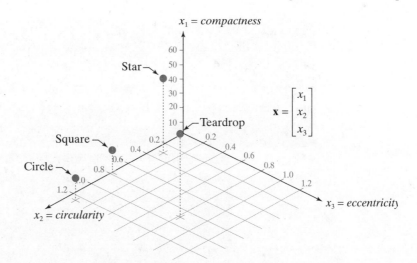

FIGURE 11.23
The descriptors from Fig. 11.22 in 3-D feature space. Each dot shown corresponds to a feature vector whose components are the three corresponding descriptors in Fig. 11.22.

Each point in feature space "encapsulates" the three descriptor values for each object. Although we can tell from looking at the values of the descriptors in the figure that the circle and square are much more similar than the other two objects, note how much clearer this fact is in feature space. You can imagine that if we had multiple samples of those objects corrupted by noise, it could become difficult to differentiate between vectors (points) corresponding to squares or circles. In contrast, the star and teardrop objects are far from each other, and from the circle and square, so they are less likely to be misclassified in the presence of noise. Feature space will play an important role in Chapter 12, when we discuss image pattern classification.

EXAMPLE 11.10: Using area features.

Even a simple descriptor such as normalized area can be quite useful for extracting information from images. For instance, Fig. 11.24 shows a night-time satellite infrared image of the Americas. As we discussed in Section 1.3, such images provide a global inventory of human settlements. The imaging sensors used to collect these images have the capability to detect visible and near infrared emissions, such as lights, fires, and flares. The table alongside the images shows (by region from top to bottom) the ratio of the area occupied by white (the lights) to the total light area in all four regions. A simple measurement like this can give, for example, a relative estimate by region of electrical energy consumption. The data can be refined by normalizing it with respect to land mass per region, with respect to population numbers, and so on.

TOPOLOGICAL DESCRIPTORS

Topology is the study of properties of a figure that are unaffected by any deformation, provided that there is no tearing or joining of the figure (sometimes these are called *rubber-sheet distortions*). For example, Fig. 11.25(a) shows a region with two holes. Obviously, a topological descriptor defined as the number of holes in the region will not be affected by a stretching or rotation transformation. However, the number of holes can change if the region is torn or folded. Because stretching

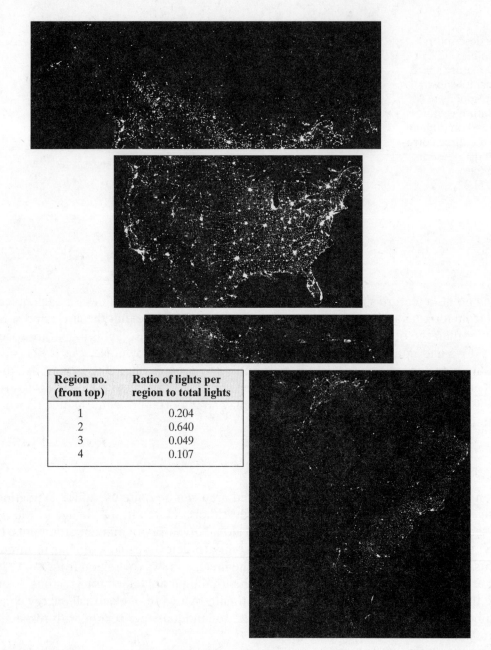

Region no. (from top)	Ratio of lights per region to total lights
1	0.204
2	0.640
3	0.049
4	0.107

affects distance, topological properties do not depend on the notion of distance or any properties implicitly based on the concept of a distance measure.

Another topological property useful for region description is the number of connected components of an image or region. Figure 11.25(b) shows a region with three connected components. The number of holes H and connected components C in a figure can be used to define the *Euler number*, E:

See Sections 2.5 and 9.5 regarding connected components.

$$E = C - H$$

(11-24)

a b

FIGURE 11.25
(a) A region with two holes.
(b) A region with three connected components.

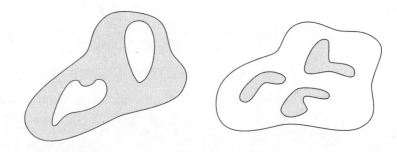

The Euler number is also a topological property. The regions shown in Fig. 11.26, for example, have Euler numbers equal to 0 and −1, respectively, because the "A" has one connected component and one hole, and the "B" has one connected component but two holes.

Regions represented by straight-line segments (referred to as *polygonal networks*) have a particularly simple interpretation in terms of the Euler number. Figure 11.27 shows a polygonal network. Classifying interior regions of such a network into faces and holes is often important. Denoting the number of vertices by V, the number of edges by Q, and the number of faces by F gives the following relationship, called the *Euler formula*:

$$V - Q + F = C - H \tag{11-25}$$

which, in view of Eq. (11-24), can be expressed as

$$V - Q + F = E \tag{11-26}$$

The network in Fig. 11.27 has seven vertices, eleven edges, two faces, one connected region, and three holes; thus the Euler number is −2 (i.e., $7 - 11 + 2 = 1 - 3 = -2$).

EXAMPLE 11.11: Extracting and characterizing the largest feature in a segmented image.

Figure 11.28(a) shows a 512 × 512, 8-bit image of Washington, D.C. taken by a NASA LANDSAT satellite. This image is in the near infrared band (see Fig. 1.10 for details). Suppose that we want to segment the river using only this image (as opposed to using several multispectral images, which would simplify the task, as you will see later in this chapter). Because the river is a dark, uniform region relative to the rest of the image, thresholding is an obvious approach to try. The result of thresholding the image with the highest possible threshold value before the river became a disconnected region is shown in Fig.

a b

FIGURE 11.26
Regions with Euler numbers equal to 0 and −1, respectively.

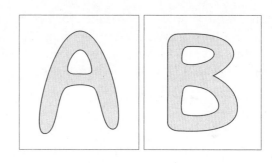

FIGURE 11.27
A region
containing a
polygonal
network.

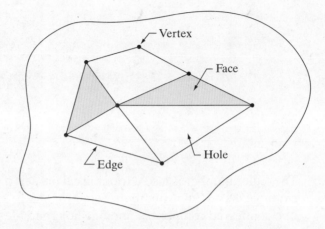

11.28(b). The threshold was selected manually to illustrate the point that it would be impossible in this case to segment the river by itself without other regions of the image also appearing in the thresholded result.

The image in Fig. 11.28(b) has 1591 connected components (obtained using 8-connectivity) and its Euler number is 1552, from which we deduce that the number of holes is 39. Figure 11.28(c) shows the connected component with the largest number of pixels (8479). This is the desired result, which we already know cannot be segmented by itself from the image using a threshold. Note how clean this result is. The number of holes in the region defined by the connected component just found would give us the number of land masses within the river. If we wanted to perform measurements, like the length of each branch of the river, we could use the skeleton of the connected component [Fig. 11.28(d)] to do so.

TEXTURE

An important approach to region description is to quantify its texture content. While no formal definition of texture exists, intuitively this descriptor provides measures of properties such as smoothness, coarseness, and regularity (Fig. 11.29 shows some examples). In this section, we discuss statistical and spectral approaches for describing the texture of a region. Statistical approaches yield characterizations of textures as smooth, coarse, grainy, and so on. Spectral techniques are based on properties of the Fourier spectrum and are used primarily to detect global periodicity in an image by identifying high-energy, narrow peaks in its spectrum.

Statistical Approaches

One of the simplest approaches for describing texture is to use statistical moments of the intensity histogram of an image or region. Let z be a random variable denoting intensity, and let $p(z_i)$, $i = 0, 1, 2, \ldots, L - 1$, be the corresponding normalized histogram, where L is the number of distinct intensity levels. From Eq. (3-24), the nth moment of z about the mean is

$$\mu_n(z) = \sum_{i=0}^{L-1} (z_i - m)^n p(z_i) \tag{11-27}$$

a b
c d

FIGURE 11.28
(a) Infrared image of the Washington, D.C. area.
(b) Thresholded image.
(c) The largest connected component of (b).
(d) Skeleton of (c). (Original image courtesy of NASA.)

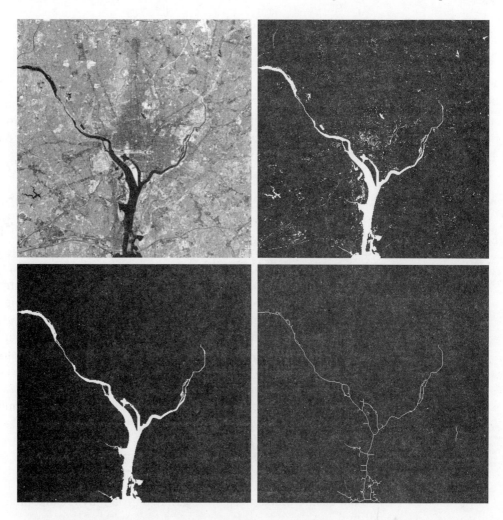

a b c

FIGURE 11.29
The white squares mark, from left to right, smooth, coarse, and regular textures. These are optical microscope images of a superconductor, human cholesterol, and a microprocessor. (Courtesy of Dr. Michael W. Davidson, Florida State University.)

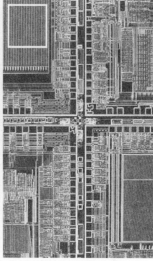

where m is the mean value of z (i.e., the average intensity of the image or region):

$$m = \sum_{i=0}^{L-1} z_i\, p(z_i) \tag{11-28}$$

Note from Eq. (11-27) that $\mu_0 = 1$ and $\mu_1 = 0$. The second moment [the variance $\sigma^2(z) = \mu_2(z)$] is particularly important in texture description. It is a measure of intensity contrast that can be used to establish descriptors of relative intensity smoothness. For example, the measure

$$R(z) = 1 - \frac{1}{1 + \sigma^2(z)} \tag{11-29}$$

is 0 for areas of constant intensity (the variance is zero there) and approaches 1 for large values of $\sigma^2(z)$. Because variance values tend to be large for grayscale images with values, for example, in the range 0 to 255, it is a good idea to normalize the variance to the interval $[0, 1]$ for use in Eq. (11-29). This is done simply by dividing $\sigma^2(z)$ by $(L-1)^2$ in Eq. (11-29). The standard deviation, $\sigma(z)$, also is used frequently as a measure of texture because its values are more intuitive.

For texture, typically we are interested in signs and relative magnitudes. If, in addition, normalization proves to be useful, we normalize the third and fourth moments.

As discussed in Section 2.6, the third moment, $\mu_3(z)$, is a measure of the skewness of the histogram while the fourth moment, $\mu_4(z)$, is a measure of its relative flatness. The fifth and higher moments are not so easily related to histogram shape, but they do provide further quantitative discrimination of texture content. Some useful additional texture measures based on histograms include a measure of *uniformity*, defined as

$$U(z) = \sum_{i=0}^{L-1} p^2(z_i) \tag{11-30}$$

and a measure of *average entropy* that, as you may recall from information theory, is defined as

$$e(z) = -\sum_{i=0}^{L-1} p(z_i) \log_2 p(z_i) \tag{11-31}$$

Because values of p are in the range $[0, 1]$ and their sum equals 1, the value of descriptor U is maximum for an image in which all intensity levels are equal (maximally uniform), and decreases from there. Entropy is a measure of variability, and is 0 for a constant image.

EXAMPLE 11.12: Texture descriptors based on histograms.

Table 11.2 lists the values of the preceding descriptors for the three types of textures highlighted in Fig. 11.29. The mean describes only the average intensity of each region and is useful only as a rough idea of intensity, not texture. The standard deviation is more informative; the numbers clearly show that the first texture has significantly less variability in intensity (it is smoother) than the other two textures. The coarse texture shows up clearly in this measure. As expected, the same comments hold for R, because it measures essentially the same thing as the standard deviation. The third moment is useful for

TABLE 11.2
Statistical texture measures for the subimages in Fig. 11.29.

Texture	Mean	Standard deviation	R (normalized)	3rd moment	Uniformity	Entropy
Smooth	82.64	11.79	0.002	−0.105	0.026	5.434
Coarse	143.56	74.63	0.079	−0.151	0.005	7.783
Regular	99.72	33.73	0.017	0.750	0.013	6.674

determining the symmetry of histograms and whether they are skewed to the left (negative value) or the right (positive value). This gives an indication of whether the intensity levels are biased toward the dark or light side of the mean. In terms of texture, the information derived from the third moment is useful only when variations between measurements are large. Looking at the measure of uniformity, we again conclude that the first subimage is smoother (more uniform than the rest) and that the most random (lowest uniformity) corresponds to the coarse texture. Finally, we see that the entropy values increase as uniformity decreases, leading us to the same conclusions regarding the texture of the regions as the uniformity measure did. The first subimage has the lowest variation in intensity levels, and the coarse image the most. The regular texture is in between the two extremes with respect to both of these measures.

Measures of texture computed using only histograms carry no information regarding spatial relationships between pixels, which is important when describing texture. One way to incorporate this type of information into the texture-analysis process is to consider not only the distribution of intensities, but also the *relative positions* of pixels in an image.

Let Q be an operator that defines the position of two pixels relative to each other, and consider an image, f, with L possible intensity levels. Let **G** be a matrix whose element g_{ij} is the number of times that pixel pairs with intensities z_i and z_j occur in image f in the position specified by Q, where $1 \le i, j \le L$. A matrix formed in this manner is referred to as a *graylevel* (or *intensity*) *co-occurrence matrix*. When the meaning is clear, **G** is referred to simply as a *co-occurrence matrix*.

Note that we are using the intensity range $[1, L]$ instead of the usual $[0, L-1]$. We do this so that intensity values will correspond with "traditional" matrix indexing (i.e., intensity value 1 corresponds to the first row and column indices of **G**).

Figure 11.30 shows an example of how to construct a co-occurrence matrix using $L = 8$ and a position operator Q defined as "one pixel immediately to the right" (i.e., the neighbor of a pixel is defined as the pixel immediately to its right). The array on the left is a small image and the array on the right is matrix **G**. We see that element $(1,1)$ of **G** is 1, because there is only one occurrence in f of a pixel valued 1 having a pixel valued 1 immediately to its right. Similarly, element $(6,2)$ of **G** is 3, because there are three occurrences in f of a pixel with a value of 6 having a pixel valued 2 immediately to its right. The other elements of **G** are similarly computed. If we had defined Q as, say, "one pixel to the right and one pixel above," then position $(1,1)$ in **G** would have been 0 because there are no instances in f of a 1 with another 1 in the position specified by Q. On the other hand, positions $(1,3)$, $(1,5)$, and $(1,7)$ in **G** would all be 1's, because intensity value 1 occurs in f with neighbors valued 3, 5, and 7 in the position specified by Q—one occurrence of each. As an exercise, you should compute all the elements of **G** using this definition of Q.

FIGURE 11.30
How to construct
a co-occurrence
matrix.

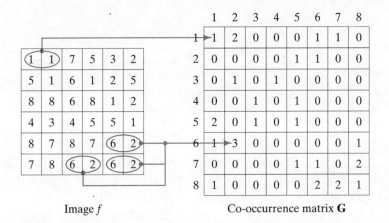

Image f Co-occurrence matrix **G**

The number of possible intensity levels in the image determines the size of matrix **G**. For an 8-bit image (256 possible intensity levels), **G** will be of size 256×256. This is not a problem when working with one matrix but, as you will see in as Example 11.13, co-occurrence matrices sometimes are used in sequences. One approach for reducing computations is to quantize the intensities into a few bands in order to keep the size of **G** manageable. For example, in the case of 256 intensities, we can do this by letting the first 32 intensity levels equal to 1, the next 32 equal to 2, and so on. This will result in a co-occurrence matrix of size 8×8.

The total number, n, of pixel pairs that satisfy Q is equal to the sum of the elements of **G** ($n = 30$ in the example of Fig. 11.30). Then, the quantity

$$p_{ij} = \frac{g_{ij}}{n}$$

is an estimate of the probability that a pair of points satisfying Q will have values (z_i, z_j). These probabilities are in the range $[0, 1]$ and their sum is 1:

$$\sum_{i=1}^{K} \sum_{j=1}^{K} p_{ij} = 1$$

where K is the row and column dimension of square matrix **G**.

Because **G** depends on Q, the presence of intensity texture patterns can be detected by choosing an appropriate position operator and analyzing the elements of **G**. A set of descriptors useful for characterizing the contents of **G** are listed in Table 11.3. The quantities used in the correlation descriptor (second row) are defined as follows:

$$m_r = \sum_{i=1}^{K} i \sum_{j=1}^{K} p_{ij}$$

$$m_c = \sum_{j=1}^{K} j \sum_{i=1}^{K} p_{ij}$$

and

TABLE 11.3
Descriptors used for characterizing co-occurrence matrices of size $K \times K$. The term p_{ij} is the ij-th term of **G** divided by the sum of the elements of **G**.

Descriptor	Explanation	Formula
Maximum probability	Measures the strongest response of **G**. The range of values is $[0, 1]$.	$\max\limits_{i,j}(p_{ij})$
Correlation	A measure of how correlated a pixel is to its neighbor over the entire image. The range of values is 1 to -1 corresponding to perfect positive and perfect negative correlations. This measure is not defined if either standard deviation is zero.	$\displaystyle\sum_{i=1}^{K}\sum_{j=1}^{K}\frac{(i-m_r)(j-m_c)\,p_{ij}}{\sigma_r\,\sigma_c}$ $\sigma_r \neq 0;\ \sigma_c \neq 0$
Contrast	A measure of intensity contrast between a pixel and its neighbor over the entire image. The range of values is 0 (when **G** is constant) to $(K-1)^2$.	$\displaystyle\sum_{i=1}^{K}\sum_{j=1}^{K}(i-j)^2\,p_{ij}$
Uniformity (also called Energy)	A measure of uniformity in the range $[0, 1]$. Uniformity is 1 for a constant image.	$\displaystyle\sum_{i=1}^{K}\sum_{j=1}^{K}p_{ij}^2$
Homogeneity	Measures the spatial closeness to the diagonal of the distribution of elements in **G**. The range of values is $[0, 1]$, with the maximum being achieved when **G** is a diagonal matrix.	$\displaystyle\sum_{i=1}^{K}\sum_{j=1}^{K}\frac{p_{ij}}{1+|i-j|}$
Entropy	Measures the randomness of the elements of **G**. The entropy is 0 when all p_{ij}'s are 0, and is maximum when the p_{ij}'s are uniformly distributed. The maximum value is thus $2\log_2 K$.	$-\displaystyle\sum_{i=1}^{K}\sum_{j=1}^{K}p_{ij}\log_2 p_{ij}$

$$\sigma_r^2 = \sum_{i=1}^{K}(i-m_r)^2 \sum_{j=1}^{K}p_{ij}$$

$$\sigma_c^2 = \sum_{j=1}^{K}(j-m_c)^2 \sum_{i=1}^{K}p_{ij}$$

If we let

$$P(i) = \sum_{j=1}^{K}p_{ij}$$

and

$$P(j) = \sum_{i=1}^{K}p_{ij}$$

then the preceding equations can be written as

$$m_r = \sum_{i=1}^{K}iP(i)$$

$$m_c = \sum_{j=1}^{K} j P(j)$$

$$\sigma_r^2 = \sum_{i=1}^{K} (i - m_r)^2 P(i)$$

and

$$\sigma_c^2 = \sum_{j=1}^{K} (j - m_c)^2 P(j)$$

With reference to Eqs. (11-27), (11-28), and to their explanation, we see that m_r is in the form of a mean computed along rows of the normalized $\mathbf{G}$, and m_c is a mean computed along the columns. Similarly, σ_r and σ_c are in the form of standard deviations (square roots of the variances) computed along rows and columns, respectively. Each of these terms is a scalar, independently of the size of $\mathbf{G}$.

Keep in mind when studying Table 11.3 that "neighbors" are with respect to the way in which Q is defined (i.e., neighbors do not necessarily have to be adjacent), and also that the p_{ij}'s are nothing more than normalized counts of the number of times that pixels having intensities z_i and z_j occur in f relative to the position specified in Q. Thus, all we are doing here is trying to find patterns (texture) in those counts.

EXAMPLE 11.13: Using descriptors to characterize co-occurrence matrices.

Figures 11.31(a) through (c) show images consisting of random, horizontally periodic (sine), and mixed pixel patterns, respectively. This example has two objectives: (1) to show values of the descriptors in Table 11.3 for the three co-occurrence matrices, $\mathbf{G}_1$, $\mathbf{G}_2$, and $\mathbf{G}_3$, corresponding (from top to bottom) to these images; and (2) to illustrate how sequences of co-occurrence matrices can be used to detect texture patterns in an image.

Figure 11.32 shows co-occurrence matrices $\mathbf{G}_1$, $\mathbf{G}_2$, and $\mathbf{G}_3$, displayed as images. These matrices were obtained using $L = 256$ and the position operator "one pixel immediately to the right." The value at coordinates (i, j) in these images is the number of times that pixel pairs with intensities z_i and z_j occur in f in the position specified by Q, so it is not surprising that Fig. 11.32(a) is a random image, given the nature of the image from which it was obtained.

Figure 11.32(b) is more interesting. The first obvious feature is the symmetry about the main diagonal. Because of the symmetry of the sine wave, the number of counts for a pair (z_i, z_j) is the same as for the pair (z_j, z_i), which produces a symmetric co-occurrence matrix. The nonzero elements of $\mathbf{G}_2$ are sparse because value differences between horizontally adjacent pixels in a horizontal sine wave are relatively small. It helps to remember in interpreting these concepts that a digitized sine wave is a staircase, with the height and width of each step depending on the frequency of the sine wave and the number of amplitude levels used in representing the function.

The structure of co-occurrence matrix $\mathbf{G}_3$ in Fig. 11.32(c) is more complex. High count values are grouped along the main diagonal also, but their distribution is more dense than for $\mathbf{G}_2$, a property that is indicative of an image with a rich variation in intensity values, but few large jumps in intensity between adjacent pixels. Examining Fig. 11.32(c), we see that there are large areas characterized by low variability

a
b
c

FIGURE 11.31
Images whose
pixels have
(a) random,
(b) periodic, and
(c) mixed texture
patterns. Each
image is of size
263×800 pixels.

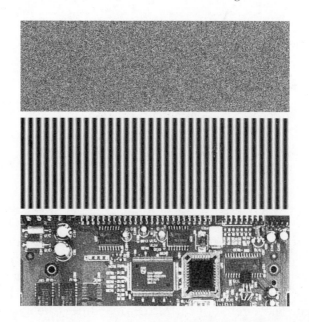

in intensities. The high transitions in intensity occur at object boundaries, but these counts are low with respect to the moderate intensity transitions over large areas, so they are obscured by the ability of an image display to show high and low values simultaneously, as we discussed in Chapter 3.

The preceding observations are qualitative. To quantify the "content" of co-occurrence matrices, we need descriptors such as those in Table 11.3. Table 11.4 shows values of these descriptors computed for the three co-occurrence matrices in Fig. 11.32. To use these descriptors, the co-occurrence matrices must be normalized by dividing them by the sum of their elements, as discussed earlier. The entries in Table 11.4 agree with what one would expect from the images in Fig. 11.31 and their corresponding co-occurrence matrices in Fig. 11.32. For example, consider the Maximum Probability column in Table 11.4. The highest probability corresponds to the third co-occurrence matrix, which tells us that this matrix has the highest number of counts (largest number of pixel pairs occurring in the image relative to the positions in Q) than the other two matrices. This agrees with our analysis of $\mathbf{G}_3$. The second column indicates that the highest correlation corresponds to $\mathbf{G}_2$, which in turn tells us that the intensities in the second image are highly correlated. The repetitiveness of the sinusoidal pattern in Fig. 11.31(b) indicates why this is so. Note that the correlation for $\mathbf{G}_1$ is essentially zero, indicating that there is virtually no correlation between adjacent pixels, a characteristic of random images such as the image in Fig. 11.31(a).

a b c

FIGURE 11.32
256×256
co-occurrence
matrices $\mathbf{G}_1, \mathbf{G}_2$,
and $\mathbf{G}_3$,
corresponding
from left to right
to the images in
Fig. 11.31.

TABLE 11.4
Descriptors evaluated using the co-occurrence matrices displayed as images in Fig. 11.32.

Normalized Co-occurrence Matrix	Maximum Probability	Correlation	Contrast	Uniformity	Homogeneity	Entropy
G_1/n_1	0.00006	−0.0005	10838	0.00002	0.0366	15.75
G_2/n_2	0.01500	0.9650	00570	0.01230	0.0824	06.43
G_3/n_3	0.06860	0.8798	01356	0.00480	0.2048	13.58

The contrast descriptor is highest for G_1 and lowest for G_2. Thus, we see that the less random an image is, the lower its contrast tends to be. We can see the reason by studying the matrix displayed in Fig. 11.32. The $(i - j)^2$ terms are differences of integers for $1 \leq i, j \leq L$, so they are the same for any G. Therefore, the probabilities of the elements of the normalized co-occurrence matrices are the factors that determine the value of contrast. Although G_1 has the lowest maximum probability, the other two matrices have many more zero or near-zero probabilities (the dark areas in Fig. 11.32). Because the sum of the values of G/n is 1, it is easy to see why the contrast descriptor tends to increase as a function of randomness.

The remaining three descriptors are explained in a similar manner. Uniformity increases as a function of the values of the probabilities squared. Thus, the less randomness there is in an image, the higher the uniformity descriptor will be, as the fifth column in Table 11.4 shows. Homogeneity measures the concentration of values of G with respect to the main diagonal. The values of the denominator term $(1 + |i - j|)$ are the same for all three co-occurrence matrices, and they decrease as i and j become closer in value (i.e., closer to the main diagonal). Thus, the matrix with the highest values of probabilities (numerator terms) near the main diagonal will have the highest value of homogeneity. As we discussed earlier, such a matrix will correspond to images with a "rich" gray-level content and areas of slowly varying intensity values. The entries in the sixth column of Table 11.4 are consistent with this interpretation.

The entries in the last column of the table are measures of randomness in co-occurrence matrices, which in turn translate into measures of randomness in the corresponding images. As expected, G_1 had the highest value because the image from which it was derived was totally random. The other two entries are self-explanatory. Note that the entropy measure for G_1 is near the theoretical maximum of 16 $(2 \log_2 256 = 16)$. The image in Fig. 11.31(a) is composed of uniform noise, so each intensity level has approximately an equal probability of occurrence, which is the condition stated in Table 11.3 for maximum entropy.

Thus far, we have dealt with single images and their co-occurrence matrices. Suppose that we want to "discover" (without looking at the images) if there are any sections in these images that contain repetitive components (i.e., periodic textures). One way to accomplish this goal is to examine the correlation descriptor for sequences of co-occurrence matrices, derived from these images by increasing the distance between neighbors. As mentioned earlier, it is customary when working with sequences of co-occurrence matrices to quantize the number of intensities in order to reduce matrix size and corresponding computational load. The following results were obtained using $L = 8$.

Figure 11.33 shows plots of the correlation descriptors as a function of horizontal "offset" (i.e., horizontal distance between neighbors) from 1 (for adjacent pixels) to 50. Figure 11.33(a) shows that all correlation values are near 0, indicating that no such patterns were found in the random image. The

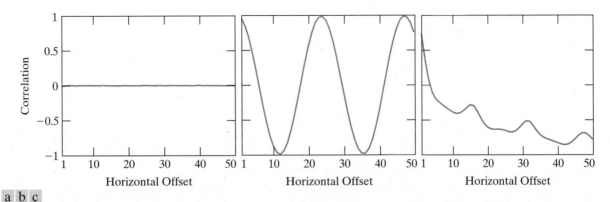

a b c

FIGURE 11.33 Values of the correlation descriptor as a function of offset (distance between "adjacent" pixels) corresponding to the (a) noisy, (b) sinusoidal, and (c) circuit board images in Fig. 11.31.

shape of the correlation in Fig. 11.33(b) is a clear indication that the input image is sinusoidal in the horizontal direction. Note that the correlation function starts at a high value, then decreases as the distance between neighbors increases, and then repeats itself.

Figure 11.33(c) shows that the correlation descriptor associated with the circuit board image decreases initially, but has a strong peak for an offset distance of 16 pixels. Analysis of the image in Fig. 11.31(c) shows that the upper solder joints form a repetitive pattern approximately 16 pixels apart (see Fig. 11.34). The next major peak is at 32, caused by the same pattern, but the amplitude of the peak is lower because the number of repetitions at this distance is less than at 16 pixels. A similar observation explains the even smaller peak at an offset of 48 pixels.

Spectral Approaches

As we discussed in Section 5.4, the Fourier spectrum is ideally suited for describing the directionality of periodic or semiperiodic 2-D patterns in an image. These global texture patterns are easily distinguishable as concentrations of high-energy bursts in the spectrum. Here, we consider three features of the Fourier spectrum that are useful for texture description: (1) prominent peaks in the spectrum give the principal direction of the texture patterns; (2) the location of the peaks in the frequency plane gives the fundamental spatial period of the patterns; and (3) eliminating any periodic components via filtering leaves nonperiodic image elements, which can then be described by statistical techniques. Recall that the spectrum is symmetric about the origin, so only half of the frequency plane needs to be considered. Thus, for the

FIGURE 11.34
A zoomed section of the circuit board image showing periodicity of components.

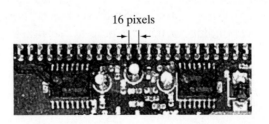

purpose of analysis, every periodic pattern is associated with only one peak in the spectrum, rather than two.

Detection and interpretation of the spectrum features just mentioned often are simplified by expressing the spectrum in polar coordinates to yield a function $S(r,\theta)$, where S is the spectrum function, and r and θ are the variables in this coordinate system. For each direction θ, $S(r,\theta)$ may be considered a 1-D function $S_\theta(r)$. Similarly, for each frequency r, $S_r(\theta)$ is a 1-D function. Analyzing $S_\theta(r)$ for a fixed value of θ yields the behavior of the spectrum (e.g., the presence of peaks) along a radial direction from the origin, whereas analyzing $S_r(\theta)$ for a fixed value of r yields the behavior along a circle centered on the origin.

A more global description is obtained by integrating (summing for discrete variables) these functions:

$$S(r) = \sum_{\theta=0}^{\pi} S_\theta(r) \tag{11-32}$$

and

$$S(\theta) = \sum_{r=1}^{R_0} S_r(\theta) \tag{11-33}$$

where R_0 is the radius of a circle centered at the origin.

The results of Eqs. (11-32) and (11-33) constitute a pair of values $\left[S(r), S(\theta)\right]$ for each pair of coordinates (r, θ). By varying these coordinates, we can generate two 1-D functions, $S(r)$ and $S(\theta)$, that constitute a spectral-energy description of texture for an entire image or region under consideration. Furthermore, descriptors of these functions themselves can be computed in order to characterize their behavior quantitatively. Descriptors useful for this purpose are the location of the highest value, the mean and variance of both the amplitude and axial variations, and the distance between the mean and the highest value of the function.

EXAMPLE 11.14: Spectral texture.

Figure 11.35(a) shows an image containing randomly distributed objects, and Fig. 11.35(b) shows an image in which these objects are arranged periodically. Figures 11.35(c) and (d) show the corresponding Fourier spectra. The periodic bursts of energy extending quadrilaterally in two dimensions in both Fourier spectra are due to the periodic texture of the coarse background material on which the objects rest. The other dominant components in the spectra in Fig. 11.35(c) are caused by the random orientation of the object edges in Fig. 11.35(a). On the other hand, the main energy in Fig. 11.35(d) not associated with the background is along the horizontal axis, corresponding to the strong vertical edges in Fig. 11.35(b).

Figures 11.36(a) and (b) are plots of $S(r)$ and $S(\theta)$ for the random objects, and similarly in (c) and (d) for the ordered objects. The plot of $S(r)$ for the random objects shows no strong periodic components (i.e., there are no dominant peaks in the spectrum besides the peak at the origin, which is the dc component). Conversely, the plot of $S(r)$ for the ordered objects shows a strong peak near $r = 15$ and a smaller one near $r = 25$, corresponding to the periodic horizontal repetition of the light (objects) and dark (background) regions in Fig. 11.35(b). Similarly, the random nature of the energy bursts in Fig. 11.35(c) is quite apparent in the plot of $S(\theta)$ in Fig. 11.36(b). By contrast, the plot in Fig. 11.36(d) shows strong energy components in the region near the origin and at $90°$ and $180°$. This is consistent with the energy distribution of the spectrum in Fig. 11.35(d).

a b
c d

FIGURE 11.35
(a) and (b) Images of random and ordered objects. (c) and (d) Corresponding Fourier spectra. All images are of size 600×600 pixels.

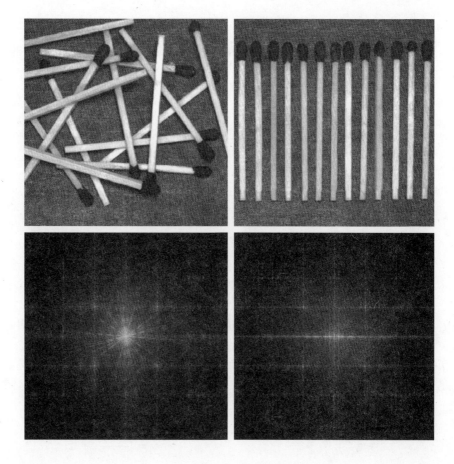

a b
c d

FIGURE 11.36
(a) and (b) Plots of $S(r)$ and $S(\theta)$ for Fig. 11.35(a). (c) and (d) Plots of $S(r)$ and $S(\theta)$ for Fig. 11.35(b). All vertical axes are $\times 10^5$.

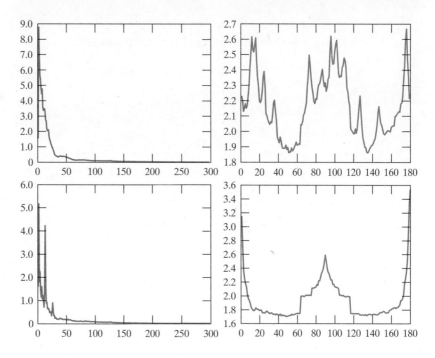

MOMENT INVARIANTS

The 2-D *moment* of order $(p+q)$ of an $M \times N$ digital image, $f(x, y)$, is defined as

$$m_{pq} = \sum_{x=0}^{M-1} \sum_{y=0}^{N-1} x^p y^q f(x, y) \qquad (11\text{-}34)$$

where $p = 0, 1, 2, \ldots$ and $q = 0, 1, 2, \ldots$ are integers. The corresponding *central moment* of order $(p+q)$ is defined as

$$\mu_{pq} = \sum_{x=0}^{M-1} \sum_{y=0}^{N-1} (x - \bar{x})^p (y - \bar{y})^q f(x, y) \qquad (11\text{-}35)$$

for $p = 0, 1, 2, \ldots$ and $q = 0, 1, 2, \ldots$, where

$$\bar{x} = \frac{m_{10}}{m_{00}} \text{ and } \bar{y} = \frac{m_{01}}{m_{00}} \qquad (11\text{-}36)$$

The *normalized central moment* of order $(p+q)$, denoted η_{pq}, is defined as

$$\eta_{pq} = \frac{\mu_{pq}}{\mu_{00}^{\gamma}} \qquad (11\text{-}37)$$

where

$$\gamma = \frac{p+q}{2} + 1 \qquad (11\text{-}38)$$

for $p + q = 2, 3, \ldots$. A set of seven, 2-D *moment invariants* can be derived from the second and third normalized central moments:[†]

$$\phi_1 = \eta_{20} + \eta_{02} \qquad (11\text{-}39)$$

$$\phi_2 = (\eta_{20} - \eta_{02})^2 + 4\eta_{11}^2 \qquad (11\text{-}40)$$

$$\phi_3 = (\eta_{30} - 3\eta_{12})^2 + (3\eta_{21} - \eta_{03})^2 \qquad (11\text{-}41)$$

$$\phi_4 = (\eta_{30} + \eta_{12})^2 + (\eta_{21} + \eta_{03})^2 \qquad (11\text{-}42)$$

[†]Derivation of these results requires concepts that are beyond the scope of this discussion. The book by Bell [1965] and the paper by Hu [1962] contain detailed discussions of these concepts. For generating moment invariants of an order higher than seven, see Flusser [2000]. Moment invariants can be generalized to n dimensions (see Mamistvalov [1998]).

$$\phi_5 = (\eta_{30} - 3\eta_{12})(\eta_{30} + \eta_{12})\left[(\eta_{30} + \eta_{12})^2 - 3(\eta_{21} + \eta_{03})^2\right]$$
$$+ (3\eta_{21} - \eta_{03})(\eta_{21} + \eta_{03})\left[3(\eta_{30} + \eta_{12})^2 - (\eta_{21} + \eta_{03})^2\right] \qquad (11\text{-}43)$$

$$\phi_6 = (\eta_{20} - \eta_{02})\left[(\eta_{30} + \eta_{12})^2 - (\eta_{21} + \eta_{03})^2\right]$$
$$+ 4\eta_{11}(\eta_{30} + \eta_{12})(\eta_{21} + \eta_{03}) \qquad (11\text{-}44)$$

$$\phi_7 = (3\eta_{21} - \eta_{03})(\eta_{30} + \eta_{12})\left[(\eta_{30} + \eta_{12})^2 - 3(\eta_{21} + \eta_{03})^2\right]$$
$$+ (3\eta_{12} - \eta_{30})(\eta_{21} + \eta_{03})\left[3(\eta_{30} + \eta_{12})^2 - (\eta_{21} + \eta_{03})^2\right] \qquad (11\text{-}45)$$

This set of moments is invariant to translation, scale change, mirroring (within a minus sign), and rotation. We can attach physical meaning to some of the low-order moment invariants. For example, ϕ_1 is the sum of two second moments with respect to the principal axes of data spread, so this moment can be interpreted as a measure of data spread. Similarly, ϕ_3 is the difference of second moments, and may be interpreted as a measure of "slenderness." However, as the order of the moment invariants increases, the complexity of their formulation causes physical meaning to be lost. The importance of Eqs. (11-39) through (11-45) is their invariance, not their physical meaning.

EXAMPLE 11.15: Moment invariants.

The objective of this example is to compute and compare the preceding moment invariants using the image in Fig. 11.37(a). The black (0) border was added to make all images in this example be of the same size; the zeros do not affect computation of the moment invariants. Figures 11.37(b) through (f) show the original image translated, scaled by 0.5 in both spatial dimensions, mirrored, rotated by 45°, and rotated by 90°, respectively. Table 11.5 summarizes the values of the seven moment invariants for these six images. To reduce dynamic range and thus simplify interpretation, the values shown are scaled using the expression $-\text{sgn}(\phi_i) \log_{10}(|\phi_i|)$. The absolute value is needed to handle any numbers that may be negative. The term $\text{sgn}(\phi_i)$ preserves the sign of ϕ_i, and the minus sign in front is there to handle fractions in the log computation. The idea is to make the numbers easier to interpret. Interest in this example is on the invariance and relative signs of the moments, not on their actual values. The two key points in Table 11.5 are: (1) the closeness of the values of the moments, independent of translation, scale change, mirroring and rotation; and (2) the fact that the *sign* of ϕ_7 is different for the mirrored image.

11.5 PRINCIPAL COMPONENTS AS FEATURE DESCRIPTORS

As we show in Example 11.17, principal components can be used also to normalize regions or boundaries for variations in size, translation, and rotation.

The material in this section is applicable to boundaries and regions. It is different from our discussion thus far, in the sense that features are based on more than one image. Suppose that we are given the three component images of a color image. The three images can be treated as a unit by expressing each group of three corresponding pixels as a vector, as discussed in Section 11.1. If we have a total of n registered

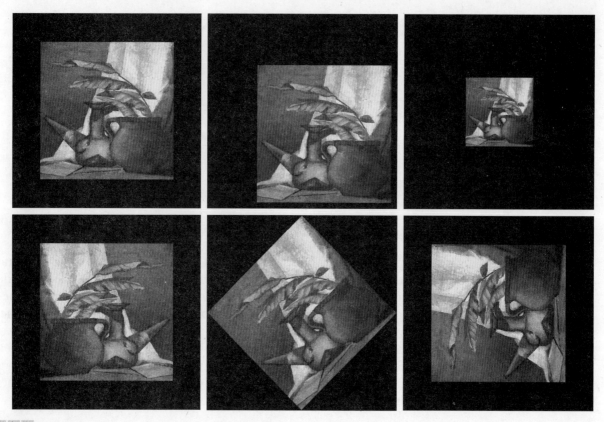

a b c
d e f

FIGURE 11.37 (a) Original image. (b)–(f) Images translated, scaled by one-half, mirrored, rotated by 45°, and rotated by 90°, respectively.

TABLE 11.5
Moment invariants for the images in Fig. 11.37.

Moment Invariant	Original Image	Translated	Half Size	Mirrored	Rotated 45°	Rotated 90°
ϕ_1	2.8662	2.8662	2.8664	2.8662	2.8661	2.8662
ϕ_2	7.1265	7.1265	7.1257	7.1265	7.1266	7.1265
ϕ_3	10.4109	10.4109	10.4047	10.4109	10.4115	10.4109
ϕ_4	10.3742	10.3742	10.3719	10.3742	10.3742	10.3742
ϕ_5	21.3674	21.3674	21.3924	21.3674	21.3663	21.3674
ϕ_6	13.9417	13.9417	13.9383	13.9417	13.9417	13.9417
ϕ_7	−20.7809	−20.7809	−20.7724	20.7809	−20.7813	−20.7809

images, then the corresponding pixels at the same spatial location in all images can be arranged as an n-dimensional vector:

$$\mathbf{x} = \begin{bmatrix} x_1 \\ x_2 \\ \vdots \\ x_n \end{bmatrix} \tag{11-46}$$

Throughout this section, the assumption is that all vectors are column vectors (i.e., matrices of order $n \times 1$). We can write them on a line of text simply by expressing them as $\mathbf{x} = (x_1, x_2, \ldots, x_n)^T$, where T indicates the transpose.

You may find it helpful to review the tutorials on probability and matrix theory available on the book website.

We can treat the vectors as random quantities, just like we did when constructing an intensity histogram. The only difference is that, instead of talking about quantities like the mean and variance of the random variables, we now talk about *mean vectors* and *covariance matrices*. The mean vector of the population is defined as

$$\mathbf{m_x} = E\{\mathbf{x}\} \tag{11-47}$$

where $E\{\mathbf{x}\}$ is the expected value of $\mathbf{x}$, and the subscript denotes that $\mathbf{m}$ is associated with the population of $\mathbf{x}$ vectors. Recall that the expected value of a vector or matrix is obtained by taking the expected value of each element.

The covariance matrix of the vector population is defined as

$$\mathbf{C_x} = E\left\{(\mathbf{x} - \mathbf{m_x})(\mathbf{x} - \mathbf{m_x})^T\right\} \tag{11-48}$$

Because $\mathbf{x}$ is n dimensional, $\mathbf{C_x}$ is an $n \times n$ matrix. Element c_{ii} of $\mathbf{C_x}$ is the variance of x_i, the ith component of the $\mathbf{x}$ vectors in the population, and element c_{ij} of $\mathbf{C_x}$ is the covariance between elements x_i and x_j of these vectors. Matrix $\mathbf{C_x}$ is real and symmetric. If elements x_i and x_j are uncorrelated, their covariance is zero and, therefore, $c_{ij} = 0$, resulting in a diagonal covariance matrix.

Because $\mathbf{C_x}$ is real and symmetric, finding a set of n orthonormal eigenvectors is always possible (Noble and Daniel [1988]). Let $\mathbf{e}_i$ and λ_i, $i = 1, 2, \ldots, n$, be the eigenvectors and corresponding eigenvalues of $\mathbf{C_x}$,[†] arranged (for convenience) in descending order so that $\lambda_j \geq \lambda_{j+1}$ for $j = 1, 2, \ldots, n-1$. Let $\mathbf{A}$ be a matrix whose *rows* are formed from the eigenvectors of $\mathbf{C_x}$, arranged in descending value of their eigenvalues, so that the first row of $\mathbf{A}$ is the eigenvector corresponding to the largest eigenvalue.

Suppose that we use $\mathbf{A}$ as a transformation matrix to map the $\mathbf{x}$'s into vectors denoted by $\mathbf{y}$'s, as follows:

$$\mathbf{y} = \mathbf{A}(\mathbf{x} - \mathbf{m_x}) \tag{11-49}$$

The Hotelling transform is the same as the discrete *Karhunen-Loève transform*, so the two names are used interchangeably in the literature.

This expression is called the *Hotelling transform*, which, as you will learn shortly, has some very interesting and useful properties.

[†] By definition, the eigenvector and eigenvalues of an $n \times n$ matrix $\mathbf{C}$ satisfy the equation $\mathbf{Ce}_i = \lambda_i \mathbf{e}_i$.

It is not difficult to show (see Problem 11.25) that the mean of the **y** vectors resulting from this transformation is zero; that is,

$$\mathbf{m_y} = E\{\mathbf{y}\} = \mathbf{0} \tag{11-50}$$

It follows from basic matrix theory that the covariance matrix of the **y**'s is given in terms of **A** and $\mathbf{C_x}$ by the expression

$$\mathbf{C_y} = \mathbf{A}\mathbf{C_x}\mathbf{A}^T \tag{11-51}$$

Furthermore, because of the way **A** was formed, $\mathbf{C_y}$ is a diagonal matrix whose elements along the main diagonal are the eigenvalues of $\mathbf{C_x}$; that is,

$$\mathbf{C_y} = \begin{bmatrix} \lambda_1 & & & 0 \\ & \lambda_2 & & \\ & & \ddots & \\ 0 & & & \lambda_n \end{bmatrix} \tag{11-52}$$

The off-diagonal elements of this covariance matrix are 0, so the elements of the **y** vectors are uncorrelated. Keep in mind that the λ_i are the eigenvalues of $\mathbf{C_x}$ and that the elements along the main diagonal of a diagonal matrix are its eigenvalues (Noble and Daniel [1988]). Thus, $\mathbf{C_x}$ and $\mathbf{C_y}$ have the same eigenvalues.

Another important property of the Hotelling transform deals with the reconstruction of **x** from **y**. Because the rows of **A** are orthonormal vectors, it follows that $\mathbf{A}^{-1} = \mathbf{A}^T$, and any vector **x** can be recovered from its corresponding **y** by using the expression

$$\mathbf{x} = \mathbf{A}^T\mathbf{y} + \mathbf{m_x} \tag{11-53}$$

But, suppose that, instead of using all the eigenvectors of $\mathbf{C_x}$, we form a matrix $\mathbf{A}_k$ from the k eigenvectors corresponding to the k largest eigenvalues, yielding a transformation matrix of order $k \times n$. The **y** vectors would then be k dimensional, and the reconstruction given in Eq. (11-53) would no longer be exact (this is somewhat analogous to the procedure we used in Section 11.3 to describe a boundary with a few Fourier coefficients).

The vector reconstructed by using $\mathbf{A}_k$ is

$$\hat{\mathbf{x}} = \mathbf{A}_k^T\mathbf{y} + \mathbf{m_x} \tag{11-54}$$

It can be shown that the mean squared error between **x** and $\hat{\mathbf{x}}$ is given by the expression

$$e_{ms} = \sum_{j=1}^{n} \lambda_j - \sum_{j=1}^{k} \lambda_j = \sum_{j=k+1}^{n} \lambda_j \tag{11-55}$$

Equation (11-55) indicates that the error is zero if $k = n$ (that is, if all the eigenvectors are used in the transformation). Because the λ_j's decrease monotonically,

Eq. (11-55) also shows that the error can be minimized by selecting the k eigenvectors associated with the largest eigenvalues. Thus, the Hotelling transform is optimal in the sense that it minimizes the mean squared error between the vectors $\mathbf{x}$ and their approximations $\hat{\mathbf{x}}$. Due to this idea of using the eigenvectors corresponding to the largest eigenvalues, the Hotelling transform also is known as the *principal components transform*.

EXAMPLE 11.16: Using principal components for image description.

Figure 11.38 shows six multispectral satellite images corresponding to six spectral bands: visible blue (450–520 nm), visible green (520–600 nm), visible red (630–690 nm), near infrared (760–900 nm), middle infrared (1550–1,750 nm), and thermal infrared (10,400–12,500 nm). The objective of this example is to illustrate how to use principal components as image features.

Organizing the images as in Fig. 11.39 leads to the formation of a six-element vector $\mathbf{x}$ from each set of corresponding pixels in the images, as discussed earlier in this section. The images in this example are of size 564×564 pixels, so the population consisted of $(564)^2 = 318,096$ vectors from which the mean vector, covariance matrix, and corresponding eigenvalues and eigenvectors were computed. The

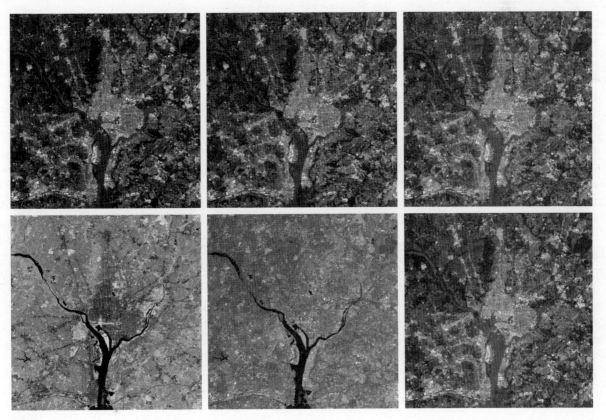

a b c
d e f

FIGURE 11.38 Multispectral images in the (a) visible blue, (b) visible green, (c) visible red, (d) near infrared, (e) middle infrared, and (f) thermal infrared bands. (Images courtesy of NASA.)

FIGURE 11.39
Forming of a
feature vector from
corresponding
pixels in six images.

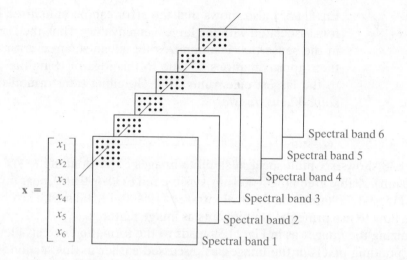

$$\mathbf{x} = \begin{bmatrix} x_1 \\ x_2 \\ x_3 \\ x_4 \\ x_5 \\ x_6 \end{bmatrix}$$

Spectral band 6
Spectral band 5
Spectral band 4
Spectral band 3
Spectral band 2
Spectral band 1

eigenvectors were then used as the rows of matrix $\mathbf{A}$, and a set of $\mathbf{y}$ vectors were obtained using Eq. (11-49). Similarly, we used Eq. (11-51) to obtain $\mathbf{C}_y$. Table 11.6 shows the eigenvalues of this matrix. Note the dominance of the first two eigenvalues.

A set of principal component images was generated using the $\mathbf{y}$ vectors mentioned in the previous paragraph (images are constructed from vectors by applying Fig. 11.39 in reverse). Figure 11.40 shows the results. Figure 11.40(a) was formed from the first component of the 318,096 $\mathbf{y}$ vectors, Fig. 11.40(b) from the second component of these vectors, and so on, so these images are of the same size as the original images in Fig. 11.38. The most obvious feature in the principal component images is that a significant portion of the contrast detail is contained in the first two images, and it decreases rapidly from there. The reason can be explained by looking at the eigenvalues. As Table 11.6 shows, the first two eigenvalues are much larger than the others. Because the eigenvalues are the variances of the elements of the $\mathbf{y}$ vectors, and variance is a measure of intensity contrast, it is not unexpected that the images formed from the vector components corresponding to the largest eigenvalues would exhibit the highest contrast. In fact, the first two images in Fig. 11.40 account for about 89% of the total variance. The other four images have low contrast detail because they account for only the remaining 11%.

According to Eqs. (11-54) and (11-55), if we used all the eigenvectors in matrix $\mathbf{A}$ we could reconstruct the original images from the principal component images with zero error between the original and reconstructed images (i.e., the images would be identical). If the objective is to store and/or transmit the principal component images and the transformation matrix for later reconstruction of the original images, it would make no sense to store and/or transmit all the principal component images because nothing would be gained. Suppose, however, that we keep and/or transmit only the two principal component images. Then there would be significant savings in storage and/or transmission (matrix $\mathbf{A}$ would be of size 2×6, so its impact would be negligible).

Figure 11.41 shows the results of reconstructing the six multispectral images from the two principal component images corresponding to the largest eigenvalues. The first five images are quite close in

TABLE 11.6
Eigenvalues of $\mathbf{C}_x$ obtained from the images in Fig. 11.38.

λ_1	λ_2	λ_3	λ_4	λ_5	λ_6
10344	2966	1401	203	94	31

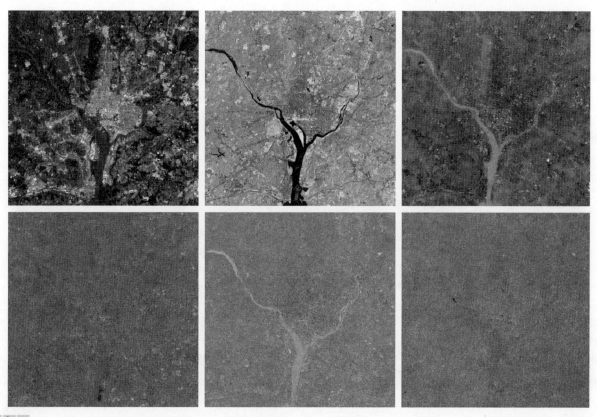

a b c
d e f

FIGURE 11.40 The six principal component images obtained from vectors computed using Eq. (11-49). Vectors are converted to images by applying Fig. 11.39 in reverse.

appearance to the originals in Fig. 11.38, but this is not true for the sixth image. The reason is that the original sixth image is actually blurry, but the two principal component images used in the reconstruction are sharp, therefore, the blurry "detail" is lost. Figure 11.42 shows the differences between the original and reconstructed images. The images in Fig. 11.42 were enhanced to highlight the differences between them. If they were shown without enhancement, the first five images would appear almost all black, with the sixth (difference) image showing the most variability.

EXAMPLE 11.17: Using principal components for normalizing for variations in size, translation, and rotation.

As we mentioned earlier in this chapter, feature descriptors should be as independent as possible of variations in size, translation, and rotation. Principal components provide a convenient way to normalize boundaries and/or regions for variations in these three variables. Consider the object in Fig. 11.43, and assume that its size, location, and orientation (rotation) are arbitrary. The points in the region (or its boundary) may be treated as 2-D vectors, $\mathbf{x} = (x_1, x_2)^T$, where x_1 and x_2 are the coordinates of any object point. All the points in the region or boundary constitute a 2-D vector population that can be used to compute the covariance matrix $\mathbf{C_x}$ and mean vector $\mathbf{m_x}$. One eigenvector of $\mathbf{C_x}$ points in the direction

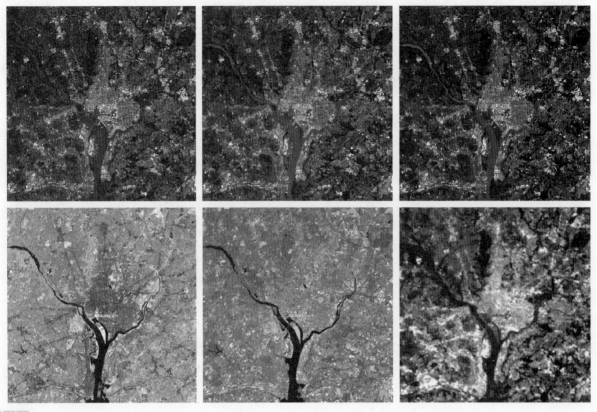

a b c
d e f

FIGURE 11.41 Multispectral images reconstructed using only the two principal component images corresponding to the two principal component vectors with the largest eigenvalues. Compare these images with the originals in Fig. 11.38.

of maximum variance (data spread) of the population, while the second eigenvector is perpendicular to the first, as Fig. 11.43(b) shows. In terms of the present discussion, the principal components transform in Eq. (11-49) accomplishes two things: (1) it establishes the center of the transformed coordinates system as the centroid (mean) of the population because $\mathbf{m_x}$ is subtracted from each $\mathbf{x}$; and (2) the $\mathbf{y}$ coordinates (vectors) it generates are rotated versions of the $\mathbf{x}$'s, so that the data align with the eigenvectors. If we define a (y_1, y_2) axis system so that y_1 is along the first eigenvector and y_2 is along the second, then the geometry that results is as illustrated in Fig. 11.43(c). That is, the dominant data directions are aligned with the new axis system. The same result will be obtained regardless of the size, translation, or rotation of the object, provided that all points in the region or boundary undergo the same transformation. If we wished to size-normalize the transformed data, we would divide the coordinates by the corresponding eigenvalues.

Observe in Fig. 11.43(c) that the points in the y-axes system can have both positive and negative values. To convert all coordinates to positive values, we simply subtract the vector $(y_{1\min}, y_{2\min})^T$ from all the $\mathbf{y}$ vectors. To displace the resulting points so that they are all greater than 0, as in Fig. 11.43(d), we add to them a vector $(a, b)^T$ where a and b are greater than 0.

Although the preceding discussion is straightforward in principle, the mechanics are a frequent source of confusion. Thus, we conclude this example with a simple manual illustration. Figure 11.44(a) shows

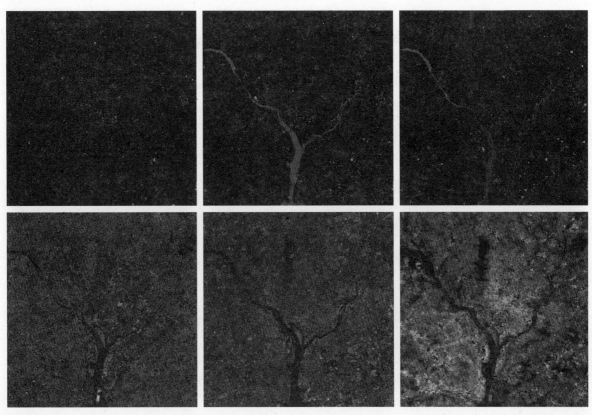

FIGURE 11.42 Differences between the original and reconstructed images. All images were enhanced by scaling them to the full $[0, 255]$ range to facilitate visual analysis.

---

four points with coordinates $(1, 1)$, $(2, 4)$, $(4, 2)$, and $(5, 5)$. The mean vector, covariance matrix, and normalized (unit length) eigenvectors of this population are:

$$\mathbf{m}_x = \begin{bmatrix} 3 \\ 3 \end{bmatrix}, \quad \mathbf{C}_x = \begin{bmatrix} 3.333 & 2.00 \\ 2.00 & 3.333 \end{bmatrix}$$

and

$$\mathbf{e}_1 = \begin{bmatrix} 0.707 \\ 0.707 \end{bmatrix}, \quad \mathbf{e}_2 = \begin{bmatrix} -0.707 \\ 0.707 \end{bmatrix}$$

The corresponding eigenvalues are $\lambda_1 = 5.333$ and $\lambda_2 = 1.333$. Figure 11.44(b) shows the eigenvectors superimposed on the data. From Eq. (11-49), the transformed points (the $\mathbf{y}$'s) are $(-2.828, 0)^T$, $(0, -1.414)^T$, $(0, 1.414)^T$, and $(2.828, 0)^T$. These points are plotted in Fig. 11.44(c). Note that they are aligned with the y-axes and that they have fractional values. When working with images, coordinate values are integers, making it necessary to round all values to their nearest integer value. Figure 11.44(d) shows the points rounded to the nearest integer and their location shifted so that all coordinate values are integers greater than 0, as in the original figure.

FIGURE 11.43
(a) An object.
(b) Object show-
ing eigenvectors
of its covariance
matrix.
(c) Transformed
object, obtained
using Eq. (11-49).
(d) Object
translated so that
all its coordinate
values are greater
than 0.

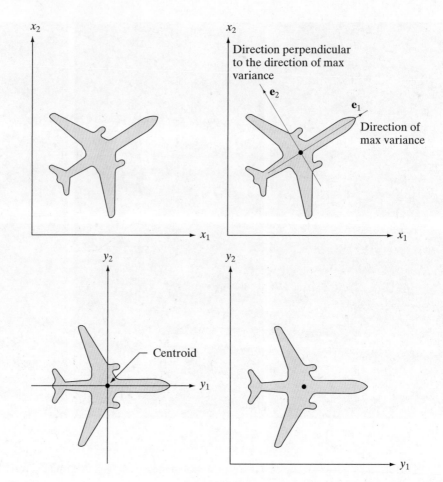

When transforming image pixels, keep in mind that image coordinates are the same as matrix coordi-nates; that is, (x, y) represents (r, c), and the origin is the top left. Axes of the principal components just illustrated are as shown in Figs. 11.43(a) and (d). You need to keep this in mind in interpreting the results of applying a principal components transformation to objects in an image.

11.6 WHOLE-IMAGE FEATURES

The descriptors introduced in Sections 11.2 through 11.4 are well suited for applica-tions (e.g., industrial inspection), in which *individual* regions can be segmented reli-ably using methods such as the ones discussed in Chapters 10 and 11. With the excep-tion of the application in Example 11.17, the principal components feature vectors in Section 11.5 are different from the earlier material, in the sense that they are based on multiple images. But even these descriptors are localized to sets of corresponding pixels. In some applications, such as searching image databases for matches (e.g., as in human face recognition), the variability between images is so extensive that the methods in Chapters 10 and 11 are not applicable.

a b
c d

FIGURE 11.44
A manual
example.
(a) Original points.
(b) Eigenvectors of
the covariance
matrix of the points
in (a).
(c) Transformed
points obtained
using Eq. (11-49).
(d) Points from (c),
rounded and trans-
lated so that all
coordinate values
are integers greater
than 0. The dashed
lines are included
to facilitate viewing.
They are not part of
the data.

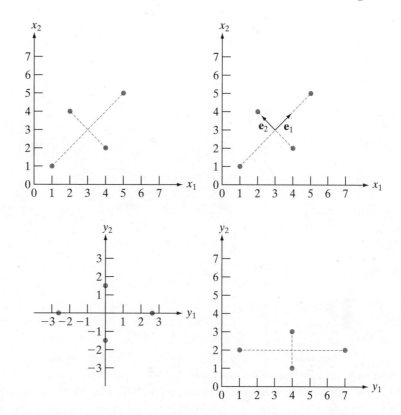

The state of the art in image processing is such that as the complexity of the task increases, the number of techniques suitable for addressing those tasks decreases. This is particularly true when dealing with feature descriptors applicable to entire images that are members of a large family of images. In this section, we discuss two of the principal feature detection methods currently being used for this purpose. One is based on detecting corners, and the other works with entire regions in an image. Then, in Section 11.7 we present a feature detection and description approach designed specifically to work with these types of features.

The discussion in
Sections 12.5 through
12.7 dealing with
neural networks is also
important in terms of
processing large numbers
of entire images for the
purpose of characterizing
their content.

Our use the term "corner"
is broader than just
90° corners; it refers to
features that are "corner-
like."

THE HARRIS-STEPHENS CORNER DETECTOR

Intuitively, we think of a corner as a rapid change of direction in a curve. Corners are highly effective features because they are distinctive and reasonably invariant to viewpoint. Because of these characteristics, corners are used routinely for matching image features in applications such as tracking for autonomous navigation, stereo machine vision algorithms, and image database queries.

In this section, we discuss an algorithm for corner detection formulated by Harris and Stephens [1988]. The idea behind the *Harris-Stephens (HS) corner detector* is illustrated in Fig. 11.45. The basic approach is this: Corners are detected by running a small window over an image, as we did in Chapter 3 for spatial filtering. The detector window is designed to compute intensity changes. We are interested in three scenarios: (1) Areas of zero (or small) intensity changes in all directions, which

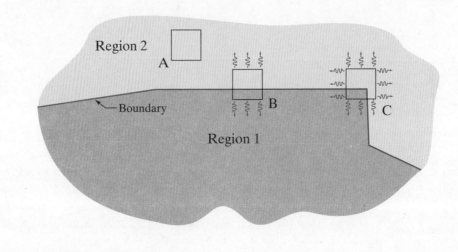

happens when the window is located in a constant (or nearly constant) region, as in location A in Fig. 11.45; (2) areas of changes in one direction but no (or small) changes in the orthogonal direction, which this happens when the window spans a boundary between two regions, as in location B; and (3) areas of significant changes in all directions, a condition that happens when the window contains a corner (or isolated points), as in location C. The HS corner detector is a mathematical formulation that attempts to differentiate between these three conditions.

Let f denote an image, and let $f(s,t)$ denote a patch of the image defined by the values of (s,t). A patch of the same size, but shifted by (x,y), is given by $f(s+x,t+y)$. Then, the weighted sum of squared differences between the two patches is given by

A patch is the image area spanned by the detector window at any given time.

$$C(x,y) = \sum_s \sum_t w(s,t)\big[f(s+x,t+y) - f(s,t)\big]^2 \qquad (11\text{-}56)$$

where $w(s,t)$ is a weighting function to be discussed shortly. The shifted patch can be approximated by the linear terms of a Taylor expansion

$$f(s+x,t+y) \approx f(s,t) + xf_x(s,t) + yf_y(s,t) \qquad (11\text{-}57)$$

where $f_x(s,t) = \partial f / \partial x$ and $f_y(s,t) = \partial f / \partial y$, both evaluated at (s,t). We can then write Eq. (11-56) as

$$C(x,y) = \sum_s \sum_t w(s,t)\big[xf_x(s,t) + yf_y(s,t)\big]^2 \qquad (11\text{-}58)$$

This equation can written in matrix form as

$$C(x,y) = [x \ \ y]\,\mathbf{M}\begin{bmatrix} x \\ y \end{bmatrix} \qquad (11\text{-}59)$$

where

$$\mathbf{M} = \sum_s \sum_t w(s,t)\mathbf{A} \tag{11-60}$$

and

$$\mathbf{A} = \begin{bmatrix} f_x^2 & f_x f_y \\ f_x f_y & f_y^2 \end{bmatrix} \tag{11-61}$$

Matrix **M** sometimes is called the *Harris matrix*. It is understood that its terms are evaluated at (s,t). If $w(s,t)$ is isotropic, then **M** is symmetric because **A** is. The weighting function $w(s,t)$ used in the HS detector generally has one of two forms: (1) it is 1 inside the patch and 0 elsewhere (i.e., it has the shape of a box lowpass filter kernel), or (2) it is an exponential function of the form

$$w(s,t) = e^{-(s^2+t^2)/2\sigma^2} \tag{11-62}$$

The box is used when computational speed is paramount and the noise level is low. The exponential form is used when data smoothing is important.

As illustrated in Fig. 11.45, a corner is characterized by large values in region C, in *both* spatial directions. However, when the patch spans a boundary there will also be a response in one direction. The question is: How can we tell the difference? As we discussed in Section 11.5 (see Example 11.17), the eigenvectors of a real, symmetric matrix (such as **M** above) point in the direction of maximum data spread, and the corresponding eigenvalues are proportional to the amount of data spread in the direction of the eigenvectors. In fact, the eigenvectors are the major axes of an ellipse fitting the data, and the magnitude of the eigenvalues are the distances from the center of the ellipse to the points where it intersects the major axes. Figure 11.46 illustrates how we can use these properties to differentiate between the three cases in which we are interested.

The small image patches in Figs. 11.46(a) through (c) are representative of regions A, B, and C in Fig. 11.45. In Fig. 11.46(d), we show values of (f_x, f_y) computed using the derivative kernels $w_y = [-1 \ 0 \ 1]$ and $w_x = w_y^T$ (remember, we use the coordinate system defined in Fig. 2.19). Because we compute the derivatives at each point in the patch, variations caused by noise result in scattered values, with the spread of the scatter being directly related to the noise level and its properties. As expected, the derivatives from the flat region form a nearly circular cluster, whose eigenvalues are almost identical, yielding a nearly circular fit to the points (we label these eigenvalues as "small" in relation to the other two plots). Figure 11.46(e) shows the derivatives of the patch containing the edge. Here, the spread is greater along the x-axis, and about nearly the same as Fig. 11.46 (a) in the y-axis. Thus, eigenvalue λ_x is "large" while λ_y is "small." Consequently, the ellipse fitting the data is elongated in the x-direction. Finally, Fig. 11.46(f) shows the derivatives of the patch containing the corner. Here, the data is spread along both directions, resulting in two large eigenvalues and a much larger and nearly circular fitting ellipse. From this we conclude that: (1) two small eigenvalues indicate nearly constant intensity; (2) one small and one large eigenvalue

As noted in Chapter 3, we do not use bold notation for vectors and matrices representing spatial kernels.

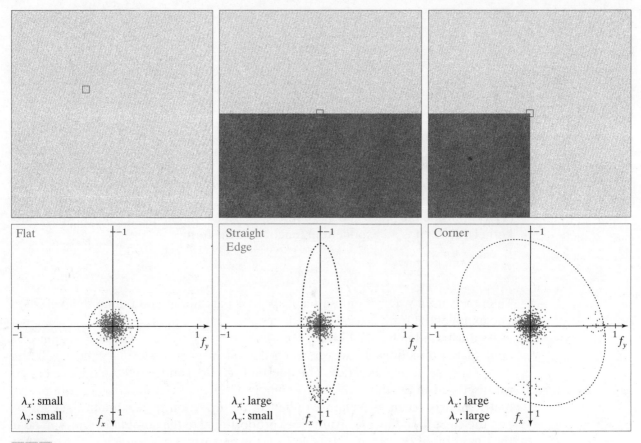

a b c
d e f

FIGURE 11.46 (a)–(c) Noisy images and image patches (small squares) encompassing image regions similar in content to those in Fig. 11.45. (d)–(f) Plots of value pairs (f_x, f_y) showing the characteristics of the eigenvalues of **M** that are useful for detecting the presence of a corner in an image patch.

The eigenvalues of the 2×2 matrix **M** can be expressed in a closed form (see Problem 11.31). However, their computation requires squares and square roots, which are expensive to process.

imply the presence of a vertical or horizontal boundary; and (3) two large eigenvalues imply the presence of a corner or (unfortunately) isolated bright points.

Thus, we see that the eigenvalues of the matrix formed from derivatives in the image patch can be used to differentiate between the three scenarios of interest. However, instead of using the eigenvalues (which are expensive to compute), the HS detector utilizes a measure of corner response based on the fact that the trace of a square matrix is equal to the sum of its eigenvalues, and its determinant is equal to the product of its eigenvalues. The measure is defined as

The advantage of this formulation is that the trace is the sum of the main diagonal terms of **M** (just two numbers). The determinant of a 2×2 matrix is the product of the main diagonal elements minus the product of the cross elements. These are trivial computations.

$$R = \lambda_x \lambda_y - k(\lambda_x + \lambda_y)^2$$
$$= \det(\mathbf{M}) - k\,\text{trace}^2(\mathbf{M})$$

(11-63)

where k is a constant to be explained shortly. Measure R has large positive values when both eigenvalues are large, indicating the presence of a corner; it has large negative values when one eigenvalue is large and the other small, indicating an edge;

and its absolute value is small when both eigenvalues are small, indicating that the image patch under consideration is flat.

Constant k is determined empirically, and its range of values depends on the implementation. For example, the MATLAB Image Processing Toolbox uses $0 < k < 0.25$. You can interpret k as a "sensitivity factor;" the smaller it is, the more likely the detector is to find corners. Typically, R is used with a threshold, T. We say that a corner at an image location has been detected only if $R > T$ for a patch at that location.

EXAMPLE 11.18: Applying the HS corner detector.

Figure 11.47(a) shows a noisy image, and Fig. 11.47(b) is the result of using the HS corner detector with $k = 0.04$ and $T = 0.01$ (the default values in our implementation). All corners of the squares were detected correctly, but the number of false detections is too high (note that all errors occurred on the right side of the image, where the difference in intensity between squares is less). Figure 11.47(c) shows

a b c
d e f

FIGURE 11.47 (a) A 600×600 image with values in the range [0,1], corrupted by additive Gaussian noise with 0 mean and variance of 0.006. (b) Result of applying the HS corner detector with $k = 0.04$ and $T = 0.01$ (the defaults). Several errors are visible. (c) Result using $k = 0.1$ and $T = 0.01$. (d) Result using $k = 0.1$ and $T = 0.1$. (e) Result using $k = 0.04$ and $T = 0.1$. (f) Result using $k = 0.04$ and $T = 0.3$ (only the strongest corners on the left were detected).

a b
c d

FIGURE 11.48
(a) Same as Fig.
11.47(a), but
corrupted with
Gaussian noise of
mean 0 and
variance 0.01.
(b) Result of using
the HS detector
with $k = 0.04$ and
$T = 0.01$ [compare
with Fig. 11.47(b)].
(c) Result with
$k = 0.249$, (near
the highest value
in our implementa-
tion), and $T = 0.01$.
(d) Result of using
$k = 0.04$ and
$T = 0.15$.

the result obtained by increasing k to 0.1 and leaving T at 0.01. This time, all corners were detected correctly. As Fig. 11.47(d) shows, increasing the threshold to $T = 0.1$ yielded the same result. In fact, using the default value of k and leaving T at 0.1 also produced the same result, as Fig. 11.47(e) shows. The point of all this is that there is considerable flexibility in the interplay between the values of k and T. Figure 11.47(f) shows the result obtained using the default value for k and using $T = 0.3$. As expected, increasing the value of the threshold eliminated some corners, yielding in this case only the corner of the squares with larger intensity differences. Increasing the value of k to 0.1 and setting T to its default value yielded the same result, as did using $k = 0.1$ and $T = 0.3$, demonstrating again the flexibility in the values chosen for these two parameters. However, as the level of noise increases, the range of possible values becomes narrower, as the results in the next paragraph illustrate.

Figure 11.48(a) shows the checkerboard corrupted by a much higher level of additive Gaussian noise (see the figure caption). Although this image does not appear much different than Fig. 11.47(a), the results using the default values of k and T are much worse than before. False corners were detected even on the left side of the image, where the intensity differences are much stronger. Figure 11.48(c) is the result of increasing k near the maximum value in our implementation (2.5) while keeping T at its default value. This time, k alone could not overcome the higher noise level. On the other hand, decreasing k to its default value and increasing T to 0.15 produced a perfect result, as Fig. 11.48(d) shows.

Figure 11.49(a) shows a more complex image with a significant number of corners embedded in various ranges of intensities. Figure 11.49(b) is the result obtained using the default values for k and T. As you can

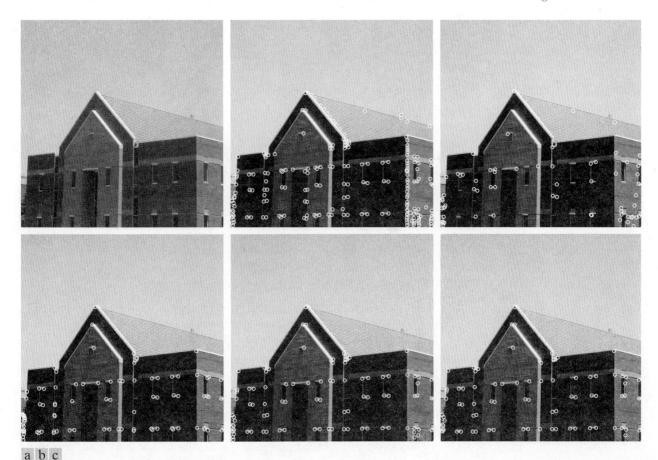

a b c
d e f

FIGURE 11.49 600×600 image of a building. (b) Result of applying the HS corner detector with $k = 0.04$ and $T = 0.01$ (the default values in our implementation). Numerous irrelevant corners were detected. (c) Result using $k = 0.249$ and the default value for T. (d) Result using $k = 0.17$ and $T = 0.05$. (e) Result using the default value for k and $T = 0.05$. (f) Result using the default value of k and $T = 0.07$.

see, numerous detection errors occurred (see, for example, the large number of wrong corner detections in the right edge of the building). Increasing k alone had little effect on the over-detection of corners until k was near its maximum value. Using the same values as in Fig. 11.48(c) resulted in the image in 11.49(c), which shows a reduced number of erroneous corners, at the expense of missing numerous important ones in the front of the building. Reducing k to 0.17 and increasing T to 0.05 did a much better job, as Fig. 11.49(d) show. Parameter k did not play a major role in corner detection for the building image. In fact, Figs. 11.49(e) and (f) show essentially the same level of performance obtained by reducing k to its default value of 0.04, and using $T = 0.05$ and $T = 0.07$, respectively.

Finally, Fig. 11.50 shows corner detection on a rotated image. The result in Fig. 11.50(b) was obtained using the same parameters we used in Fig. 11.49(f), showing the relative insensitivity of the method to rotation. Figures 11.49(f) and 11.50(b) show detection of at least one corner in every major structural feature of the image, such as the front door, all the windows, and the corners that define the apex of the facade. For matching purposes, these are excellent results.

FIGURE 11.50
(a) Image
rotated 5°.
(b) Corners
detected using the
parameters used
to obtain
Fig. 11.49(f).

MAXIMALLY STABLE EXTREMAL REGIONS (MSERs)

The Harris-Stephens corner detector discussed in the previous section is useful in applications characterized by sharp transitions of intensities, such as the intersection of straight edges, that result in corner-like features in an image. Conversely, the maximally stable extremal regions (MSERs) introduced by Matas et al. [2002] are more "blob" oriented. As with the HS corner detector, MSERs are intended to yield whole image features for the purpose of establishing correspondence between two or more images.

We know from Fig. 2.18 that a grayscale image can be viewed as a topographic map, with the xy-axes representing spatial coordinates, and the z-axis representing intensities. Imagine that we start thresholding an 8-bit grayscale image one intensity level at a time. The result of each thresholding is a binary image in which we show the pixels at or above the threshold in white, and the pixels below the threshold as black. When the threshold, T, is 0, the result is a white image (all pixel values are at or above 0). As we start increasing T in increments of one intensity level, we will begin to see black components in the resulting binary images. These correspond to local minima in the topographic map view of the image. These black regions may begin to grow and merge, but they never get smaller from image to image. Finally, when we reach $T = 255$, the resulting image will be black (there are no pixel values above this level). Because each stage of thresholding results in a binary image, there will be one or more connected components of white pixels in each image. The set of all such components resulting from all thresholdings is the set of *extremal regions*. Extremal regions that do not change size (number of pixels) appreciably over a range of threshold values are called *maximally stable extremal regions*.

As you will see shortly, the procedure just discussed can be cast in the form of a rooted, connected tree called a *component tree*, where each level of the tree corresponds to a value of the threshold discussed in the previous paragraph. Each node of this tree represents an extremal region, R, defined as

Remember, ∀
means "for any," ∈
means "belonging to,"
and a colon, :,
is used to
mean "it is true that."

$$\forall p \in R \text{ and } \forall q \in \text{boundary}(R) : I(p) > I(q) \tag{11-64}$$

where I is the image under consideration, and p and q are image points. This equation indicates that an extremal region R is a region of I, with the property that the intensity of any point in the region is higher than the intensity at any point in the boundary of the region. As usual, we assume that image intensities are integers, ordered from 0 (black) to the maximum intensity (e.g., 255 for 8-bit images), which are represented by white.

MSERs are found by analyzing the nodes of the component tree. For each connected region in the tree, we compute a stability measure, ψ, defined as

$$\psi(R_j^{T+n\Delta T}) = \frac{\left|R_i^{T+(n-1)\Delta T}\right| - \left|R_k^{T+(n+1)\Delta T}\right|}{\left|R_j^{T+n\Delta T}\right|} \tag{11-65}$$

where $|R|$ is the size of the area (number of pixels) of connected region R, T is a threshold value in the range $T \in [\min(I), \max(I)]$, and ΔT is a specified threshold increment. Regions $R_i^{T+(n-1)\Delta T}$, $R_j^{T+n\Delta T}$, and $R_k^{T+(n+1)\Delta T}$ are connected regions obtained at threshold levels $T + (n-1)\Delta T$, $T + n\Delta T$, and $T + (n+1)\Delta T$, respectively. In terms of the component tree, regions R_i and R_k are respectively the *parent* and *child* of region R_j. Because $T + (n-1)\Delta T < T + (n+1)\Delta T$, we are guaranteed that $|R_i^{T+(n-1)\Delta T}| \geq |R_k^{T+(n+1)\Delta T}|$. It then follows from Eq. (11-65) that $\psi \geq 0$. MSREs are the regions corresponding to the nodes in the tree that have a stability value that is a *local minimum* along the path of the tree containing that region. What this means in practice is that maximally stable regions are regions whose sizes do not change appreciably across two, $2\Delta T$ neighboring thresholded images.

Figure 11.51 illustrates the concepts just introduced. The grayscale image at the top consists of some simple regions of constant intensity, with values in the range $[0, 255]$. Based on the explanation of Eqs. (11-64) and (11-65), we used the threshold $T = 10$, which is in the range $\left[\min(I) = 5, \max(I) = 225\right]$. Choosing $\Delta T = 50$ segmented all the different regions of the image. The column of binary images on the left contains the results of thresholding the grayscale image with the threshold values shown. The resulting component tree is on the right. Note that the tree is shown "root up," which is the way you would normally program it.

All the squares in the grayscale image are of the same size (area); therefore, regardless of the image size, we can normalize the size of each square to 1. For example, if the image is of size 400×400 pixels, the size of each square is $100 \times 100 = 10^4$ pixels. Normalizing the size to 1 means that size 1 corresponds to 10^4 pixels (one square), size 2 corresponds to 2×10^4 pixels (two squares), and so forth. You can arrive at the same conclusion by noticing that the ratio in Eq. (11-65) eliminates the common 10^4 factor.

The component tree in Fig. 11.51 is a good summary of how the MSER algorithm works. The first level is the result of thresholding I with $T + \Delta T = 60$. There is only one connected component (white pixels) in the thresholded image on the left. The size of the connected component is 11 normalized units. As mentioned above, each node of a component tree, denoted by a subscripted R, contains *one* connected component consisting of white pixels. The next level in the tree is formed from the

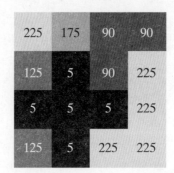

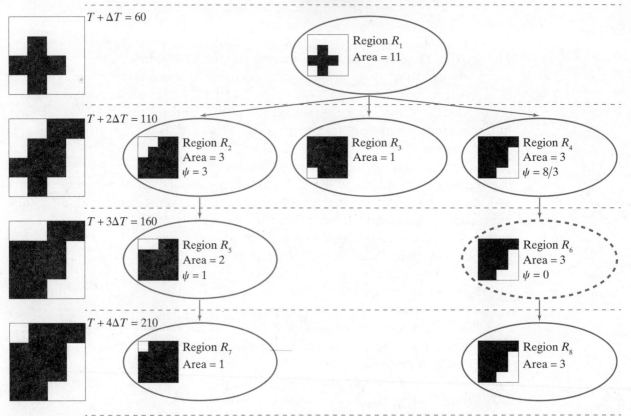

FIGURE 11.51 Detecting MSERs. Top: Grayscale image. Left: Thresholded images using $T = 10$ and $\Delta T = 50$. Right: Component tree, showing the individual regions. Only one MSER was detected (see dashed tree node on the rightmost branch of the tree). Each level of the tree is formed from the thresholded image on the left, at that same level. Each node of the tree contains one extremal region (connected component) shown in *white*, and denoted by a subscripted R.

regions in the binary image obtained by thresholding I using $T + 2\Delta T = 110$. As you can see on the left, this image has three connected components, so we create three nodes in the component tree at the level of the thresholded image. Similarly, the binary image obtained by thresholding I with $T + 3\Delta T = 160$ has two connected components, so we create two nodes in the tree at this level. These two connected components are children of the connected components in the previous level, so we place the new nodes in the same path as their respective parents. The next level of the tree is explained in the same manner. Note that the center node in the previous level had no children, so that path of the tree ends in the second level.

Because we need to check size variations between parent and child regions to determine stability, only the two middle regions (corresponding to threshold values of 110 and 160) are relevant in this example. As you can see in our component tree, only R_6 has a parent and child of similar size (the sizes are identical in this case). Therefore, region R_6 is the only MSER detected in this case. Observe that if we had used a single global threshold to detect the brightest regions, region R_7 would have been detected also (an undesirable result in this context). Thus, we see that although MSERs are based on intensity, they also depend on the nature of the background surrounding a region. In this case, R_6 was surrounded by a darker background than R_7, and the darker background was thresholded earlier in the tree, allowing the size of R_6 to remain constant over the two, $2\Delta T$ neighboring range required for detection as an MSER.

In our example, it was easy to detect an MSER as the only region that did not change size, which gave a stability factor 0. A value of zero automatically implies that an MSER has been found because the parent and child regions are of the same size. When working with more complex images, the values of stability factors seldom are zero because of variations in intensity caused by variables such as illumination, viewpoint, and noise. The concept of a local minimum mentioned earlier is simply a way of saying that MSERs are extremal regions that do change size significantly over a $2\Delta T$ thresholding range. What is considered a "significant" change depends on the application.

It is not unusual for numerous MSERs to be detected, many of which may not be meaningful because of their size. One way to control the number of regions detected is by the choice of ΔT. Another is to label as insignificant any region whose size is not in a specified size range. We illustrate this in Example 11.19.

Matas et al. [2002] indicate that MSERs are affine-covariant (see Section 11.1). This follows directly from the fact that area ratios are preserved under affine transformations, which in turn implies that for an affine transformation the original and transformed regions are related by that transformation. We illustrate this property in Figs. 11.54 and 11.55.

Finally, keep in mind that the preceding MSER formulation is designed to detect bright regions with darker surroundings. The same formulation applied to the negative (in the sense defined in Section 3.2) of an image will detect dark regions with lighter surroundings. If interest lies in detecting both types of regions simultaneously, we form the union of both sets of MSERs.

EXAMPLE 11.19: Extracting MSERs from grayscale images.

Figure 11.52(a) shows a slice image from a CT scan of a human head, and Fig. 11.52(b) shows the result of smoothing Fig. 11.52(a) with a box kernel of size 15×15 elements. Smoothing is used routinely as a

a b
c d

FIGURE 11.52
(a) 600×570 CT
slice of a human
head. (b) Image
smoothed with a
box kernel of size
15×15 elements. (c)
A extremal region
along the path of the
tree containing one
MSER.
(d) The MSER.
(All MSER regions
were limited to the
range 10,260–34,200
pixels, correspond-
ing to a range
between 3%
and 10% of image
size.)
(Original image
courtesy of Dr.
David R.
Pickens, Vanderbilt
University.)

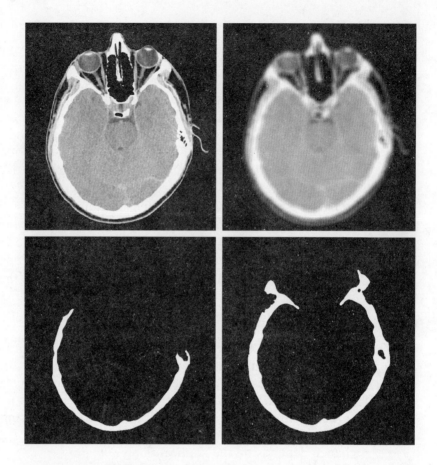

preprocessing step when ΔT is relatively small. In this case, we used $T = 0$ and $\Delta T = 10$. This increment was small enough to require smoothing for proper MSER detection. In addition, we used a "size filter," in the sense that the size (area) of an MSER had to be between 10,262 and 34,200 pixels; these size limits are 3% and 10% of the size of the image, respectively.

Figure 11.53 illustrates MSER detection on a more complex image. We used less blurring (a 5×5 box kernel) in this image because is has more fine detail. We used the same T and ΔT as in Fig. 11.52, and a valid MSER size in the range 10,000 to 30,000 pixels, corresponding approximately to 3% and 8% of image size, respectively. Two MSERs were detected using these parameters, as Figs. 11.53(c) and (d) show. The composite MSER, shown in Fig. 11.53(e), is a good representation of the front of the building.

Figure 11.54 shows the behavior under rotation of the MSERs detected in Fig. 11.53. Figure 11.54(a) is the building image rotated 5° in the conterclockwise direction. The image was cropped after rotation to eliminate the resulting black areas (see Fig. 2.41), which would change the nature of the image data and thus influence the results. Figure 11.54(b) is the result of performing the same smoothing as in Fig. 11.53, and Fig. 11.54(c) is the composite MSER detected using the same parameters as in Fig. 11.53(e). As you can see, the composite MSER of the rotated image corresponds quite closely to the MSER in Fig. 11.53(e).

Finally, Fig. 11.55 shows the behavior of the MSER detector under scale changes. Figure 11.55(a) is the building image scale to 0.5 of its original dimensions, and Fig. 11.55(b) shows the image smoothed with a correspondingly smaller box kernel of size 3×3. Because the image area is now one-fourth the size

a b
c d e

FIGURE 11.53 (a) Building image of size 600×600 pixels. (b) Image smoothed using a 5×5 box kernel. (c) and (d) MSERs detected using $T = 0$, $\Delta T = 10$, and MSER size range between 10,000 and 30,000 pixels, corresponding approximately to 3% and 8% of the area of the image. (e) Composite image.

of the original area, we reduced the valid MSER range by one-fourth to 2500–7500 pixels. Other than these changes, we used the same parameters as in Fig. 11.53. Figure 11.55(c) shows the resulting MSER. As you can see, this figure is quite close to the full-size result in Fig. 11.53(e).

11.7 SCALE-INVARIANT FEATURE TRANSFORM (SIFT)

SIFT is an algorithm developed by Lowe [2004] for extracting invariant features from an image. It is called a *transform* because it transforms image data into scale-invariant coordinates relative to local image features. SIFT is by far the most complex feature detection and description approach we discuss in this chapter.

As you progress though this section, you will notice the use of a significant number of experimentally determined parameters. Thus, unlike most of the formulations of individual approaches we have discussed thus far, SIFT is strongly heuristic. This is a consequence of the fact that our current knowledge is insufficient to tell us how

a b c

FIGURE 11.54 (a) Building image rotated 5° counterclockwise. (b) Smoothed image using the same kernel as in Fig. 11.53(b). (c) Composite MSER detected using the same parameters we used to obtain Fig. 11.53(e). The MSERs of the original and rotated images are almost identical.

to assemble a set of reasonably well-understood individual methods into a "system" capable of addressing problems that cannot be solved by any single known method acting alone. Thus, we are forced to determine experimentally the interplay between the various parameters controlling the performance of more complex systems.

When images are similar in nature (same scale, similar orientation, etc), corner detection and MSERs are suitable as whole image features. However, in the presence of variables such as scale changes, rotation, changes in illumination, and changes in viewpoint, we are forced to use methods like SIFT.

SIFT features (called *keypoints*) are invariant to image scale and rotation, and are robust across a range of affine distortions, changes in 3-D viewpoint, noise, and changes of illumination. The input to SIFT is an image. Its output is an n-dimensional feature vector whose elements are the invariant feature descriptors. We begin our discussion by analyzing how scale invariance is achieved by SIFT.

a b c

FIGURE 11.55 (a) Building image reduced to half-size. (b) Image smoothed with a 3×3 box kernel. (c) Composite MSER obtained with the same parameters as Fig. 11.53(e), but using a valid MSER region size range of 2,500–7,500 pixels.

SCALE SPACE

The first stage of the SIFT algorithm is to find image locations that are invariant to scale change. This is achieved by searching for stable features across all possible scales, using a function of scale known as *scale space*, which is a multi-scale representation suitable for handling image structures at different scales in a consistent manner. The idea is to have a formalism for handling the fact that objects in unconstrained scenes will appear in different ways, depending on the scale at which images are captured. Because these scales may not be known beforehand, a reasonable approach is to work with all relevant scales simultaneously. Scale space represents an image as a one-parameter *family* of smoothed images, with the objective of simulating the loss of detail that would occur as the scale of an image decreases. The parameter controlling the smoothing is referred to as the *scale parameter*.

In SIFT, Gaussian kernels are used to implement smoothing, so the scale parameter is the standard deviation. The reason for using Gaussian kernels in based on work performed by Lindberg [1994], who showed that the only smoothing kernel that meets a set of important constraints, such as linearity and shift-invariance, is the Gaussian lowpass kernel. Based on this, the scale space, $L(x,y,\sigma)$, of a grayscale image, $f(x,y)$,[†] is produced by convolving f with a variable-scale Gaussian kernel, $G(x,y,\sigma)$:

As in Chapter 3, "★" indicates spatial convolution.

$$L(x,y,\sigma) = G(x,y,\sigma) \star f(x,y) \tag{11-66}$$

where the scale is controlled by parameter σ, and G is of the form

$$G(x,y,\sigma) = \frac{1}{2\pi\sigma^2} e^{-(x^2+y^2)/2\sigma^2} \tag{11-67}$$

The input image $f(x,y)$ is successively convolved with Gaussian kernels having standard deviations $\sigma, k\sigma, k^2\sigma, k^3\sigma, \ldots$ to generate a "stack" of Gaussian-filtered (smoothed) images that are separated by a constant factor k, as shown in the lower left of Fig. 11.56.

SIFT subdivides scale space into *octaves*, with each octave corresponding to a doubling of σ, just as an octave in music theory corresponds to doubling the frequency of a sound signal. SIFT further subdivides each octave into an integer number, s, of intervals, so that an interval of 1 consists of two images, an interval of 2 consists of three images, and so forth. It then follows that the value used in the Gaussian kernel that generates the image corresponding to an octave is $k^s\sigma = 2\sigma$ which means that $k = 2^{1/s}$. For example, for $s = 2$, $k = \sqrt{2}$, and the input image is successively smoothed using standard deviations of $\sigma, (\sqrt{2})\sigma$, and $(\sqrt{2})^2\sigma$, so that the third image (i.e., the octave image for $s = 2$) in the sequence is filtered using a Gaussian kernel with standard deviation $(\sqrt{2})^2\sigma = 2\sigma$.

[†] Experimental results reported by Lowe [2004] suggest that smoothing the original image using a Gaussian kernel with $\sigma = 0.5$ and then doubling its size by linear (nearest-neighbor) interpolation improves the number of stable features detected by SIFT. This preprocessing step is an integral part of the algorithm. Images are assumed to have values in the range [0,1].

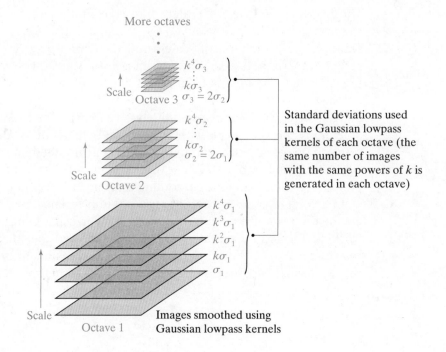

More octaves

Scale Octave 3 $\sigma_3 = 2\sigma_2$ $k\sigma_3$ $k^4\sigma_3$

Scale Octave 2 $\sigma_2 = 2\sigma_1$ $k\sigma_2$ $k^4\sigma_2$

Standard deviations used
in the Gaussian lowpass
kernels of each octave (the
same number of images
with the same powers of k is
generated in each octave)

$k^4\sigma_1$
$k^3\sigma_1$
$k^2\sigma_1$
$k\sigma_1$
σ_1

Scale Octave 1   Images smoothed using
                     Gaussian lowpass kernels

The preceding discussion indicates that the number of smoothed images gener-ated in an octave is $s + 1$. However, as you will see in the next section, the smoothed images in scale space are used to compute differences of Gaussians [see Eq. (10-32)] which, in order to cover a full octave, implies that an additional two images past the octave image are required, giving a total of $s + 3$ images. Because the octave image is always the $(s + 1)$th image in the stack (counting from the bottom), it follows that this image is the third image from the top in the expanded sequence of $s + 3$ images. Each octave in Fig. 11.56 contains five images, indicating that $s = 2$ was used in this case.

The *first* image in the *second* octave is formed by downsampling the original image (by skipping every other row and column), and then smoothing it using a kernel with twice the standard deviation used in the first octave (i.e., $\sigma_2 = 2\sigma_1$). Sub-sequent images in that octave are smoothed using σ_2, with the same sequence of values of k as in the first octave (this is denoted by dots in Fig. 11.56). The same basic procedure is then repeated for subsequent octaves. That is, the *first* image of the *new* octave is formed by: (1) downsampling the original image enough times to achieve half the size of the image in the previous octave, and (2) smoothing the downsam-pled image with a new standard deviation that is twice the standard deviation of the previous octave. The rest of the images in the new octave are obtained by smoothing the downsampled image with the new standard deviation multiplied by the same sequence of values of k as before.

When $k = \sqrt{2}$, we can obtain the first image of a new octave without having to smooth the downsampled image. This is because, for this value of k, the kernel used to smooth the first image of every octave is the same as the kernel used to smooth the *third* image from the top of the previous octave. Thus, the first image of a new octave can be obtained directly by downsampling that third image of the previous octave by 2. The result will be the same (see Problem 11.36). The third image from the top of any octave is called the *octave image* because the standard deviation used to smooth it is twice (i.e., $k^2 = 2$) the value of the standard deviation used to smooth the first image in the octave.

Figure 11.57 uses grayscale images to further illustrate how scale space is constructed in SIFT. Because each octave is composed of five images, it follows that we are again using $s = 2$. We chose $\sigma_1 = \sqrt{2}/2 = 0.707$ and $k = \sqrt{2} = 1.414$ for this example so that the numbers would result in familiar multiples. As in Fig. 11.56, the images going up scale space are blurred by using Gaussian kernels with progressively larger standard deviations, and the first image of the second and subsequent octaves is obtained by downsampling the octave image from the previous octave by 2. As you can see, the images become significantly more blurred (and consequently lose more fine detail) as they go up both in scale as well as in octave. The images in the third octave show significantly fewer details, but their gross appearance is unmistakably that of the same structure.

DETECTING LOCAL EXTREMA

SIFT initially finds the locations of keypoints using the Gaussian filtered images, then refines the locations and validity of those keypoints using two processing steps.

Finding the Initial Keypoints

Keypoint locations in scale space are found initially by SIFT by detecting extrema in the difference of Gaussians of two adjacent scale-space images in an octave, convolved with the input image that corresponds to that octave. For example, to find keypoint locations related to the first two levels of octave 1 in scale space, we look for extrema in the function

$$D(x,y,\sigma) = \left[G(x,y,k\sigma) - G(x,y,\sigma)\right] \star f(x,y) \tag{11-68}$$

It follows from Eq. (11-66) that

$$D(x,y,\sigma) = L(x,y,k\sigma) - L(x,y,\sigma) \tag{11-69}$$

In other words, all we have to do to form function $D(x,y,\sigma)$ is subtract the first two images of octave 1. Recall from the discussion of the Marr-Hildreth edge detector (Section 10.2) that the difference of Gaussians is an approximation to the Laplacian of a Gaussian (LoG). Therefore, Eq. (11-69) is nothing more than an approximation to Eq. (10-30). The key difference is that SIFT looks for extrema in $D(x,y,\sigma)$, whereas the Marr-Hildreth detector would look for the zero crossings of this function.

Lindberg [1994] showed that true scale invariance in scale space requires that the LoG be normalized by σ^2 (i.e., that $\sigma^2 \nabla^2 G$ be used). It can be shown (see Problem 11.34) that

FIGURE 11.57
Illustration using images of the first three octaves of scale space in SIFT. The entries in the table are values of standard deviation used at each scale of each octave. For example the standard deviation used in scale 2 of octave 1 is $k\sigma_1$, which is equal to 1.0. (The images of octave 1 are shown slightly overlapped to fit in the figure space.)

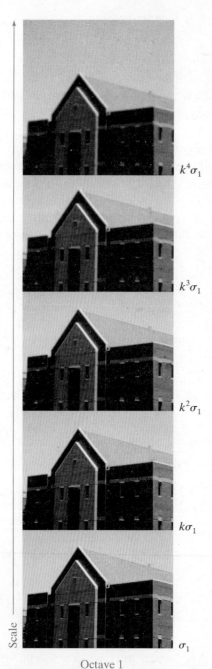

Octave 1

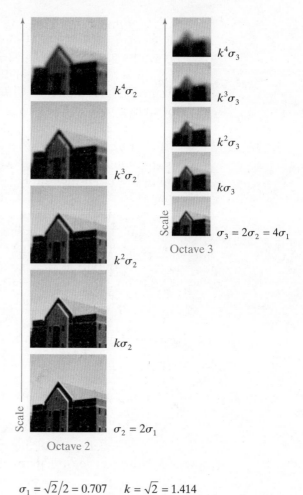

$$\sigma_1 = \sqrt{2}/2 = 0.707 \qquad k = \sqrt{2} = 1.414$$

Octave	Scale				
	1	**2**	**3**	**4**	**5**
1	0.707	1.000	1.414	2.000	2.828
2	1.414	2.000	2.828	4.000	5.657
3	2.828	4.000	5.657	8.000	11.314

$$G(x, y, k\sigma) - G(x, y, \sigma) \approx (k - 1)\sigma^2 \nabla^2 G \tag{11-70}$$

Therefore, DoGs already have the necessary scaling "built in." The factor $(k - 1)$ is constant over all scales, so it does not influence the process of locating extrema in scale space. Although Eqs. (11-68) and (11-69) are applicable to the first two images of octave 1, the same form of these equations is applicable to any two images from any octave, provided that the appropriate downsampled image is used, and the DoG is computed from two adjacent images in the octave.

Figure 11.58 illustrates the concepts just discussed, using the building image from Fig. 11.57. A total of $s + 2$ difference functions, $D(x, y, \sigma)$, are formed in each octave from all adjacent pairs of Gaussian-filtered images in that octave. These difference functions can be viewed as images, and one sample of such an image is shown for each of the three octaves in Fig. 11.58. As you might expect from the results in Fig. 11.57, the level of detail in these images decreases the further up we go in scale space.

Figure 11.59 shows the procedure used by SIFT to find extrema in a $D(x, y, \sigma)$ image. At each location (shown in black) in a $D(x, y, \sigma)$ image, the value of the pixel at that location is compared to the values of its eight neighbors in the current image and its nine neighbors in the images above and below. The point is selected as an extremum (maximum or minimum) point if its value is larger than the values of all its neighbors, or smaller than all of them. No extrema can be detected in the first (last) scale of an octave because it has no lower (upper) scale image of the same size.

Improving the Accuracy of Keypoint Locations

When a continuous function is sampled, its true maximum or minimum may actually be located between sample points. The usual approach used to get closer to the true

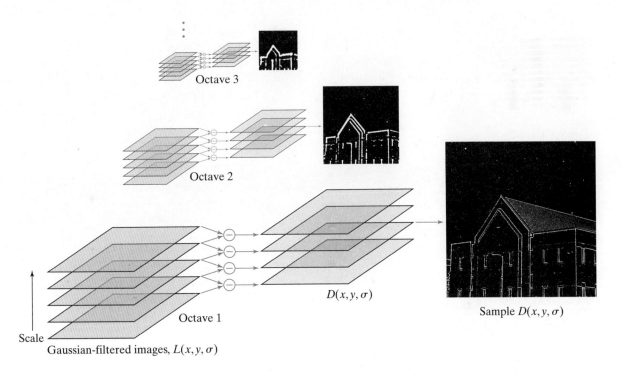

FIGURE 11.58 How Eq. (11-69) is implemented in scale space. There are $s + 3$ $L(x, y, \sigma)$ images and $s + 2$ corresponding $D(x, y, \sigma)$ images in each octave.

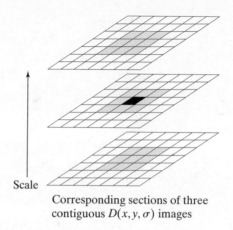

Scale

Corresponding sections of three
contiguous $D(x, y, \sigma)$ images

extremum (to achieve subpixel accuracy) is to fit an interpolating function at each
extremum point found in the digital function, then look for an improved extremum
location in the interpolated function. SIFT uses the linear and quadratic terms of
a Taylor series expansion of $D(x, y, \sigma)$, shifted so that the origin is located at the
sample point being examined. In vector form, the expression is

$$D(\mathbf{x}) = D + \left(\frac{\partial D}{\partial \mathbf{x}}\right)^T \mathbf{x} + \frac{1}{2}\mathbf{x}^T \frac{\partial}{\partial \mathbf{x}}\left(\frac{\partial D}{\partial \mathbf{x}}\right)\mathbf{x}$$
$$= D + (\nabla D)^T \mathbf{x} + \frac{1}{2}\mathbf{x}^T \mathbf{H} \mathbf{x} \tag{11-71}$$

where D and its derivatives are evaluated at the sample point, $\mathbf{x} = (x, y, \sigma)^T$ is the
offset from that point, ∇ is the familiar gradient operator,

$$\nabla D = \frac{\partial D}{\partial \mathbf{x}} = \begin{bmatrix} \partial D/\partial x \\ \partial D/\partial y \\ \partial D/\partial \sigma \end{bmatrix} \tag{11-72}$$

and $\mathbf{H}$ is the *Hessian matrix*

$$\mathbf{H} = \begin{bmatrix} \partial^2 D/\partial x^2 & \partial^2 D/\partial x \partial y & \partial^2 D/\partial x \partial \sigma \\ \partial^2 D/\partial y \partial x & \partial^2 D/\partial y^2 & \partial^2 D/\partial y \partial \sigma \\ \partial^2 D/\partial \sigma \partial x & \partial^2 D/\partial \sigma \partial y & \partial^2 D/\partial \sigma^2 \end{bmatrix} \tag{11-73}$$

The location of the extremum, $\hat{\mathbf{x}}$, is found by taking the derivative of Eq. (11-71) with
respect to $\mathbf{x}$ and setting it to zero, which gives us (see Problem 11.37):

Because D and its
derivatives are evalu-
ated at the sample point,
they are constants with
respect to $\mathbf{x}$.

$$\hat{\mathbf{x}} = -\mathbf{H}^{-1}(\nabla D) \tag{11-74}$$

The Hessian and gradient of D are approximated using differences of neighboring points, as we did in Section 10.2. The resulting 3×3 system of linear equations is easily solved computationally. If the offset $\hat{\mathbf{x}}$ is greater than 0.5 in any of its three dimensions, we conclude that the extremum lies closer to another sample point, in which case the sample point is changed and the interpolation is performed about that point instead. The final offset $\hat{\mathbf{x}}$ is added to the location of its sample point to obtain the interpolated estimate of the location of the extremum.

The function value at the extremum, $D(\hat{\mathbf{x}})$, is used by SIFT for rejecting unstable extrema with low contrast, where $D(\hat{\mathbf{x}})$ is obtained by substituting Eq. (11-74) into Eq. (11-71), giving (see Problem 11.37):

$$D(\hat{\mathbf{x}}) = D + \frac{1}{2}(\nabla D)^T \hat{\mathbf{x}} \tag{11-75}$$

In the experimental results reported by Lowe [2004], any extrema for which $D(\hat{\mathbf{x}})$ was less than 0.03 was rejected, based on all image values being in the range $[0, 1]$. This eliminates keypoints that have low contrast and/or are poorly localized.

Eliminating Edge Responses

If you display an image as a topographic map (see Fig. 2.18), edges will appear as ridges that have low curvature along the ridge and high curvature perpendicular to it.

Recall from Section 10.2 that using a difference of Gaussians yields edges in an image. But keypoints of interest in SIFT are "corner-like" features, which are significantly more localized. Thus, intensity transitions caused by edges are eliminated. To quantify the difference between edges and corners, we can look at local curvature. An edge is characterized by high curvature in one direction, and low curvature in the orthogonal direction. Curvature at a point in an image can be estimated from the 2×2 Hessian matrix evaluated at that point. Thus, to estimate local curvature of the DoG at any level in scalar space, we compute the Hessian matrix of D at that level:

$$\mathbf{H} = \begin{bmatrix} \partial^2 D/\partial x^2 & \partial^2 D/\partial x \partial y \\ \partial^2 D/\partial y \partial x & \partial^2 D/\partial y^2 \end{bmatrix} = \begin{bmatrix} D_{xx} & D_{xy} \\ D_{yx} & D_{yy} \end{bmatrix} \tag{11-76}$$

where the form on the right uses the same notation as the $\mathbf{A}$ term [Eq. (11-61)] of the Harris matrix (but note that the main diagonals are different). The eigenvalues of $\mathbf{H}$ are proportional to the curvatures of D. As we explained in connection with the Harris-Stephens corner detector, we can avoid direct computation of the eigenvalues by formulating tests based on the trace and determinant of $\mathbf{H}$, which are equal to the sum and product of the eigenvalues, respectively. To use notation different from the HS discussion, let α and β be the eigenvalues of $\mathbf{H}$ with the largest and smallest magnitude, respectively. Using the relationship between the eigenvalues of $\mathbf{H}$ and its trace and determinant we have (remember, $\mathbf{H}$ is is symmetric and of size 2×2) :

$$\text{Tr}(\mathbf{H}) = D_{xx} + D_{yy} = \alpha + \beta$$
$$\text{Det}(\mathbf{H}) = D_{xx}D_{yy} - (D_{xy})^2 = \alpha\beta \tag{11-77}$$

If the determinant is negative, the curvatures have different signs and the keypoint in question cannot be an extremum, so it is discarded.

Let r denote the ratio of the largest to the smallest eigenvalue. Then $\alpha = r\beta$ and

As with the HS corner detector, the advantage of this formulation is that the trace and determinants of 2×2 matrix **H** are easy to compute. See the margin note in Eq. (11-63).

$$\frac{[\text{Tr}(\mathbf{H})]^2}{\text{Det}(\mathbf{H})} = \frac{(\alpha + \beta)^2}{\alpha\beta} = \frac{(r\beta + \beta)^2}{r\beta^2} = \frac{(r + 1)^2}{r} \qquad (11\text{-}78)$$

which depends on the ratio of the eigenvalues, rather than their individual values. The minimum of $(r + 1)^2/r$ occurs when the eigenvalues are equal, and it increases with r. Therefore, to check that the ratio of principal curvatures is below some threshold, r, we only need to check

$$\frac{[\text{Tr}(\mathbf{H})]^2}{\text{Det}(\mathbf{H})} < \frac{(r + 1)^2}{r} \qquad (11\text{-}79)$$

which is a simple computation. In the experimental results reported by Lowe [2004], a value of $r = 10$ was used, meaning that keypoints with ratios of curvature greater than 10 were eliminated.

Figure 11.60 shows the SIFT keypoints detected in the building image using the approach discussed in this section. Keypoints for which $D(\hat{\mathbf{x}})$ in Eq. (11-75) was less than 0.03 were rejected, as were keypoints that failed to satisfy Eq. (11-79) with $r = 10$.

KEYPOINT ORIENTATION

At this point in the process, we have computed keypoints that SIFT considers stable. Because we know the location of each keypoint in scale space, we have achieved *scale independence*. The next step is to assign a consistent orientation to each keypoint based on local image properties. This allows us to represent a keypoint relative to its orientation and thus achieve *invariance to image rotation*. SIFT uses a

FIGURE 11.60
SIFT keypoints detected in the building image. The points were enlarged slightly to make them easier to see.

straightforward approach for this. The scale of the keypoint is used to select the Gaussian smoothed image, L, that is closest to that scale. In this way, all orientation computations are performed in a scale-invariant manner. Then, for each image sample, $L(x,y)$, at this scale, we compute the gradient magnitude, $M(x,y)$, and orientation angle, $\theta(x,y)$, using pixel differences:

See Section 10.2 regarding computation of the gradient magnitude and angle.

$$M(x,y) = \left[\left(L(x+1,y) - L(x-1,y) \right)^2 + \left(L(x,y+1) - L(x,y-1) \right)^2 \right]^{\frac{1}{2}} \quad (11\text{-}80)$$

and

$$\theta(x,y) = \tan^{-1}\left[\left(L(x,y+1) - L(x,y-1) \right) / \left(L(x+1,y) - L(x-1,y) \right) \right] \quad (11\text{-}81)$$

A histogram of orientations is formed from the gradient orientations of sample points in a neighborhood of each keypoint. The histogram has 36 bins covering the 360° range of orientations on the image plane. Each sample added to the histogram is weighed by its gradient magnitude, and by a circular Gaussian function with a standard deviation 1.5 times the scale of the keypoint.

Peaks in the histogram correspond to dominant local directions of local gradients. The highest peak in the histogram is detected and any other local peak that is within 80% of the highest peak is used also to create another keypoint with that orientation. Thus, for the locations with multiple peaks of similar magnitude, there will be multiple keypoints created at the same location and scale, but with *different* orientations. SIFT assigns multiple orientations to only about 15% of points with multiple orientations, but these contribute significant to image matching (to be discussed later and in Chapter 12). Finally, a parabola is fit to the three histogram values closest to each peak to interpolate the peak position for better accuracy.

Figure 11.61 shows the same keypoints as Fig. 11.60 superimposed on the image and showing keypoint orientations as arrows. Note the consistency of orientation

FIGURE 11.61
The keypoints from Fig. 11.60 superimposed on the original image. The arrows indicate keypoint orientations.

of similar sets of keypoints in the image. For example, observe the keypoints on the right, vertical corner of the building. The lengths of the arrows vary, depending on illumination and image content, but their direction is unmistakably consistent. Plots of keypoint orientations generally are quite cluttered and are not intended for general human interpretation. The value of keypoint orientation is in image matching, as we will illustrate later in our discussion.

KEYPOINT DESCRIPTORS

The procedures discussed up to this point are used for assigning an image location, scale, and orientation to each keypoint, thus providing invariance to these three variables. The next step is to compute a descriptor for a local region around each keypoint that is highly distinctive, but is at the same time as invariant as possible to changes in scale, orientation, illumination, and image viewpoint. The idea is to be able to use these descriptors to identify matches (similarities) between local regions in two or more images.

The approach used by SIFT to compute descriptors is based on experimental results suggesting that local image gradients appear to perform a function similar to what human vision does for matching and recognizing 3-D objects from different viewpoints (Lowe [2004]). Figure 11.62 summarizes the procedure used by SIFT to generate the descriptors associated with each keypoint. A region of size 16×16

FIGURE 11.62
Approach used to compute a keypoint descriptor.

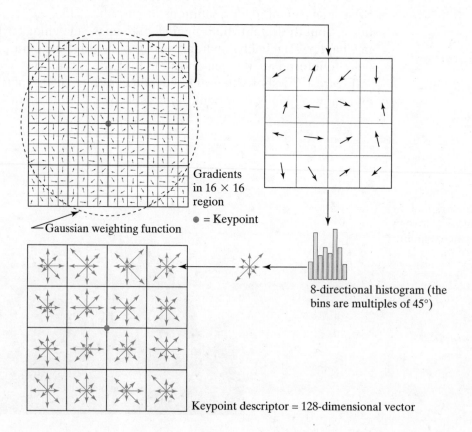

Gradients in 16×16 region

● = Keypoint

Gaussian weighting function

8-directional histogram (the bins are multiples of 45°)

Keypoint descriptor = 128-dimensional vector

pixels is centered on a keypoint, and the gradient magnitude and direction are computed at each point in the region using pixel differences. These are shown as randomly oriented arrows in the upper-left of the figure. A Gaussian weighting function with standard deviation equal to one-half the size of the region is then used to assign a weight that multiplies the magnitude of the gradient at each point. The Gaussian weighting function is shown as a circle in the figure, but it is understood that it is a bell-shaped surface whose values (weights) decrease as a function of distance from the center. The purpose of this function is to reduce sudden changes in the descriptor with small changes in the position of the function.

Because there is one gradient computation for each point in the region surrounding a keypoint, there are $(16)^2$ gradient directions to process for each keypoint. There are 16 directions in each 4×4 subregion. The top-rightmost subregion is shown zoomed in the figure to simplify the explanation of the next step, which consists of quantizing all gradient orientations in the 4×4 subregion into eight possible directions differing by $45°$. Rather than assigning a directional value as a full count to the bin to which it is closest, SIFT performs interpolation that *distributes* a histogram entry among *all* bins proportionally, depending on the distance from that value to the center of each bin. This is done by multiplying each entry into a bin by a weight of $1 - d$, where d is the shortest distance from the value to the center of a bin, measured in the units of the histogram spacing, so that the maximum possible distance is 1. For example, the center of the first bin is at $45°/2 = 22.5°$, the next center is at $22.5° + 45° = 67.5°$, and so on. Suppose that a particular directional value is $22.5°$. The distance from that value to the center of the first histogram bin is 0, so we would assign a full entry (i.e., a count of 1) to that bin in the histogram. The distance to the next center would be greater than 0, so we would assign a fraction of a full entry, that is $1 * (1 - d)$, to that bin, and so forth for all bins. In this way, every bin gets a proportional fraction of a count, thus avoiding "boundary" effects in which a descriptor changes abruptly as a small change in orientation causes it to be assigned from one bin to another.

Figure 11.62 shows the eight directions of a histogram as a small cluster of vectors, with the length of each vector being equal to the value of its corresponding bin. Sixteen histograms are computed, one for each 4×4 subregion of the 16×16 region surrounding a keypoint. A descriptor, shown on the lower left of the figure, then consists of a 4×4 array, each containing eight directional values. In SIFT, this descriptor data is organized as a 128-dimensional vector.

In order to achieve orientation invariance, the coordinates of the descriptor and the gradient orientations are rotated relative to the keypoint orientation. In order to reduce the effects of illumination, a feature vector is normalized in two stages. First, the vector is normalized to unit length by dividing each component by the vector norm. A change in image contrast resulting from each pixel value being multiplied by a constant will multiply the gradients by the same constant, so the change in contrast will be cancelled by the first normalization. A brightness change caused by a constant being added to each pixel will not affect the gradient values because they are computed from pixel differences. Therefore, the descriptor is invariant to affine changes in illumination. However, nonlinear illumination changes resulting, for example, from camera saturation, can also occur. These types of changes can cause large variations in the relative magnitudes of some of the gradients, but they are less likely to affect gradient orientation. SIFT reduces the influence of large gradient magnitudes by thresholding the values of the normalized feature vector so that all components are below the experimentally determined value of 0.2. After thresholding, the feature vector is renormalized to unit length.

SUMMARY OF THE SIFT ALGORITHM

As the material in the preceding sections shows, SIFT is a complex procedure consisting of many parts and empirically determined constants. The following is a step-by-step summary of the method.

As indicated at the beginning of this section, smoothing and doubling the size of the input image is assumed. Input images are assumed to have values in the range [0, 1].

1. *Construct the scale space.* This is done using the procedure outlined in Figs. 11.56 and 11.57. The parameters that need to be specified are σ, s, (k is computed from s), and the number of octaves. Suggested values are $\sigma = 1.6$, $s = 2$, and three octaves.

2. *Obtain the initial keypoints.* Compute the difference of Gaussians, $D(x, y, \sigma)$, from the smoothed images in scale space, as explained in Fig. 11.58 and Eq. (11-69). Find the extrema in each $D(x, y, \sigma)$ image using the method explained in Fig. 11.59. These are the initial keypoints.

3. *Improve the accuracy of the location of the keypoints.* Interpolate the values of $D(x, y, \sigma)$ via a Taylor expansion. The improved key point locations are given by Eq. (11-74).

4. *Delete unsuitable keypoints.* Eliminate keypoints that have low contrast and/or are poorly localized. This is done by evaluating D from Step 3 at the improved locations, using Eq. (11-75). All keypoints whose values of D are lower than a threshold are deleted. A suggested threshold value is 0.03. Keypoints associated with edges are deleted also, using Eq. (11-79). A value of 10 is suggested for r.

5. *Compute keypoint orientations.* Use Eqs. (11-80) and (11-81) to compute the magnitude and orientation of each keypoint using the histogram-based procedure discussed in connection with these equations.

6. *Compute keypoint descriptors.* Use the method summarized in Fig. 11.62 to compute a feature (descriptor) vector for each keypoint. If a region of size 16×16 around each keypoint is used, the result will be a 128-dimensional feature vector for each keypoint.

The following example illustrates the power of this algorithm.

EXAMPLE 11.20: Using SIFT for image matching.

We illustrate the performance of the SIFT algorithm by using it to find the number of matches between an image of a building and a subimage formed by extracting part of the right corner edge of the building. We also show results for rotated and scaled-down versions of the image and subimage. This type of process can be used in applications such as finding correspondences between two images for the purpose of image registration, and for finding instances of an image in a database of images.

Figure 11.63(a) shows the keypoints for the building image (this is the same as Fig. 11.61), and the keypoints for the subimage, which is a separate, much smaller image. The keypoints were computed

a b

FIGURE 11.63 (a) Keypoints and their directions (shown as gray arrows) for the building image and for a section of the right corner of the building. The subimage is a separate image and was processed as such. (b) Corresponding key points between the building and the subimage (the straight lines shown connect pairs of matching points). Only three of the 36 matches found are incorrect.

using SIFT *independently* for each image. The building shows 643 keypoints and the subimage 54 keypoints. Figure 11.63(b) shows the matches found by SIFT between the image and subimage; 36 keypoint matches were found and, as the figure shows, only three were incorrect. Considering the large number of initial keypoints, you can see that keypoint descriptors offer a high degree of accuracy for establishing correspondences between images.

Figure 11.64(a) shows keypoints for the building image after it was rotated by 5° counterclockwise, and for a subimage extracted from its right corner edge. The rotated image is smaller than the original because it was cropped to eliminate the constant areas created by rotation (see Fig. 2.41). Here, SIFT found 547 keypoints for the building and 49 for the subimage. A total of 26 matches were found and, as Fig. 11.64(b) shows, only two were incorrect.

Figure 11.65 shows the results obtained using SIFT on an image of the building reduced to half the size in both spatial directions. When SIFT was applied to the downsampled image and a corresponding subimage, no matches were found. This was remedied by brightening the reduced image slightly by manipulating the intensity gamma. The subimage was extracted from this image. Despite the fact that SIFT has the capability to handle some degree of changes in intensity, this example indicates that performance can be improved by enhancing the contrast of an image prior to processing. When working with a database of images, histogram specification (see Chapter 3) is an excellent tool for normalizing the intensity of all images using the characteristics of the image being queried. SIFT found 195 keypoints for the half-size image and 24 keypoints for the corresponding subimage. A total of seven matches were found between the two images, of which only one was incorrect.

The preceding two figures illustrate the insensitivity of SIFT to rotation and scale changes, but they are not ideal tests because the reason for seeking insensitivity to these variables in the first place is

a b

FIGURE 11.64 (a) Keypoints for the rotated (by 5°) building image and for a section of the right corner of the building. The subimage is a separate image and was processed as such. (b) Corresponding keypoints between the corner and the building. Of the 26 matches found, only two are in error.

that we do not always know a priori when images have been acquired under different conditions and geometrical arrangements. A more practical test is to compute features for a prototype image and test them against unknown samples. Figure 11.66 shows the results of such tests. Figure 11.66(a) is the original building image, for which SIFT features vectors were already computed (see Fig. 11.63). SIFT was used to compare the rotated subimage from Fig. 11.64(a) against the original, unrotated image. As Fig. 11.66(a) shows, 10 matches were found, of which two were incorrect. These are excellent results, considering the relatively small size of the subimage, and the fact that it was rotated. Figure 11.66(b) shows the results of matching the half-sized subimage against the original image. Eleven matches were found,

a b

FIGURE 11.65 (a) Keypoints for the half-sized building and a section of the right corner. (b) Corresponding keypoints between the corner and the building. Of the seven matches found, only one is in error.

a b

FIGURE 11.66 (a) Matches between the original building image and a rotated version of a segment of its right corner. Ten matches were found, of which two are incorrect. (b) Matches between the original image and a half-scaled version of a segment of its right corner. Here, 11 matches were found, of which four were incorrect.

of which four were incorrect. Again, these are good results, considering the fact that significant detail was lost in the subimage when it was rotated or reduced in size. If asked in both cases: Based solely on the matches found by SIFT, from which part of the building did the two subimages come? The obvious answer in both is that the subimages are from the right corner of the building. The preceding two tests illustrate the adaptability of SIFT to variations in rotation and scale.

Summary, References, and Further Reading

Feature extraction is a fundamental process in the operation of most automated image processing applications. As indicated by the range of feature detection and description techniques covered in this chapter, the choice of one method over another is determined by the problem under consideration. The objective is to choose feature descriptors that "capture" essential differences between objects, or classes of objects, while maintaining as much independence as possible to changes in variables such as location, scale, orientation, illumination, and viewing angle.

The Freeman chain code discussed in Section 11.2 was first proposed by Freeman [1961, 1974], while the slope chain code is due to Bribiesca [2013]. See Klette and Rosenfeld [2004] regarding the minimum-perimeter polygon algorithm. For additional reading on signatures see Ballard and Brown [1982]. The medial axis transform is generally credited to Blum [1967]. For efficient computation of the Euclidean distance transform used for skeletonizing see Maurer et al. [2003].

For additional reading on the basic boundary feature descriptors in Section 11.3, see Rosenfeld and Kak [1982]. The discussion on shape numbers is based on the work of Bribiesca and Guzman [1980]. For additional reading on Fourier descriptors, see the early paper by Zahn and Roskies [1972]. For an example of current uses of this technique, see Sikic and Konjicila [2016]. The discussion on statistical moments as boundary descriptors is from basic probability (for example, see Montgomery and Runger [2011]).

For additional reading on the basic region descriptors discussed in Section 11.4, see Rosenfeld and Kak [1982]. For further introductory reading on texture, see Haralick and Shapiro [1992] and Shapiro and Stockman [2001].

Our discussion of moment-invariants is based on Hu [1962]. For generating moments of arbitrary order, see Flusser [2000].

Hotelling [1933] was the first to derive and publish the approach that transforms discrete variables into uncorrelated coefficients (Section 11.5). He referred to this technique as the method of *principal components*. His paper gives considerable insight into the method and is worth reading. Principal components are still used widely in numerous fields, including image processing, as evidenced by Xiang et al. [2016]. The corner detector in Section 11.6 is from Harris and Stephens [1988], and our discussion of MSERs is based on Matas et al. [2002]. The SIFT material in Section 11.7 is from Lowe [2004]. For details on the software aspects of many of the examples in this chapter, see Gonzalez, Woods, and Eddins [2009].

Problems

Solutions to the problems marked with an asterisk (*) are in the DIP4E Student Support Package (consult the book website: www.ImageProcessingPlace.com).

11.1   What are the aspects of image feature extraction?

11.2   With reference to the Moore boundary-following algorithm explained in Section 11.2, answer the following, using the same grid as in Fig. 11.2 to identify boundary points in your explanation [remember, the origin is at (1,1), instead of our usual (0,0)]. Include the position of points *b* and *c* at each point you mention.

    (a)* Give the coordinates in Fig. 11.2(a) at which the algorithm starts and ends. What would it do when it arrived at the end point of the boundary?

    (b)   How would the algorithm behave when it arrived at the intersection point in Fig. 11.2(b) for the first time, and then for the second time?

11.3   Answer the following:

    (a)* Does normalizing the Freeman chain code of a closed curve so that the starting point is the smallest integer always give a unique starting point?

    (b)   Find the normalized starting point of the code 21031233322.

    (c)   Find the normalized starting point of the code 11076765543322.

11.4   Do the following:

    (a)* Show that the first difference of a chain code normalizes it to rotation, as explained in Section 11.2.

    (b)   Compute the first difference of the 4-directional chain code 0123332211

11.5   Answer the following:

    (a)* Given a one-pixel-thick, open or closed, 4-connected simple (does not intersect itself) digital curve, can a slope chain code be formulated so that it behaves exactly as a Freeman chain code? If your answer is no, explain why. If your answer is yes, explain how you would do it, detailing any assumptions you need to make for your answer to hold.

    (b)   Repeat (a) for an 8-connected curve.

    (c)   How would you normalize a slope chain code for scale changes?

11.6* How would you define the length of a boundary in the following curves?

    (a)   chain-coded curve

    (b)   polygonal curve

11.7   Let L be the length of the straight-line segments used in a slope chain code. Assume that L is such that an integral number of line segments fit the curve under consideration. Assume also that the angle accuracy is high enough so that it may be considered infinite for your purposes, answer the following:

    (a)* What is the tortuosity of a square boundary of size $d \times d$?

    (b)* What is the tortuosity of a circle of radius r?

(c) What is the tortuosity of a closed convex curve?

11.8* Advance an argument that explains why the uppermost-leftmost point of a digital closed curve has the property that a polygonal approximation to the curve has a convex vertex at that point.

11.9 With reference to Example 11.2, start with vertex V_7 and apply the MPP algorithm through, and including, V_{11}.

11.10 Do the following:

(a)* Explain why the rubber-band polygonal approximation approach discussed in Section 11.2 yields a polygon with minimum perimeter for a convex curve.

(b) Show that if each cell corresponds to a pixel on the boundary, the maximum possible error in that cell is $\sqrt{2}d$, where d is the minimum possible horizontal or vertical distance between adjacent pixels (i.e., the distance between lines in the sampling grid used to produce the digital image).

11.11 Explain how the MPP algorithm in Section 11.2 behaves under the following conditions:

(a)* One-pixel wide, one-pixel deep indentations.

(b)* One-pixel wide, two-or-more pixel deep indentations.

(c) One-pixel wide, n-pixel long protrusions.

11.12 Do the following.

(a)* Plot the signature of a square boundary using the tangent-angle method discussed in Section 11.2.

(b) Repeat (a) for the slope density function. Assume that the square is aligned with the x- and y-axes, and let the x-axis be the reference line. Start at the corner closest to the origin.

11.13 Find an expression for the signature of each of the following boundaries, and plot the signatures.

(a)* An equilateral triangle.

(b) A rectangle.

(c) An ellipse

11.14 Do the following:

(a)* With reference to Figs. 11.11(c) and (f), give a word description of an algorithm for counting the peaks in the two waveforms. Such an algorithm would allow us to differentiate between triangles and rectangles.

(b) How can you make your solution independent of scale changes? You may assume that the scale changes are the same in both directions.

11.15 Draw the medial axis of:

(a)* A circle.

(b)* A square.

(c) An equilateral triangle.

11.16 For the figure shown,

(a)* What is the order of the shape number for the figure shown?

(b) Obtain the shape number.

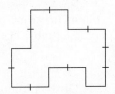

11.17* The procedure discussed in Section 11.3 for using Fourier descriptors consists of expressing the coordinates of a contour as complex numbers, taking the DFT of these numbers, and keeping only a few components of the DFT as descriptors of the boundary shape. The inverse DFT is then an approximation to the original contour. What class of contour shapes would have a DFT consisting of real numbers, and how would the axis system in Fig. 11.18 have to be set up to obtain those real numbers?

11.18 Show that if you use only two Fourier descriptors ($u = 0$ and $u = 1$) to reconstruct a boundary with Eq. (11-10), the result will always be a circle. (*Hint:* Use the parametric representation of a circle in the complex plane, and express the equation of a circle in polar coordinates.)

11.19 *Give the smallest number of statistical moment descriptors needed to differentiate between the signatures of the figures in Fig. 11.10.

11.20 Justify the following statement:

Two ellipses with different major axes have same mean and third statistical moment descriptors, but different second moment.

11.21 *Propose a set of descriptors capable of differentiating between the shapes of the characters 0, 1, 8, 9, and *X*. (*Hint:* Use topological descriptors in conjunction with the convex hull.)

11.22 Consider a binary image of size 100×100 pixels, with a vertical black band extending from columns 1 to 49 and a vertical white band extending from columns 50 to 100.

   (a) Obtain the co-occurrence matrix of this image using the position operator "one pixel to the right."

   (b) *Normalize the matrix so that its elements become probability estimates, as explained in Section 11.4.

   (c) Use your matrix from (b) to compute the six descriptors in Table 11.3.

11.23 Consider a checkerboard image composed of alternating black and white squares, each of size $m \times m$ pixels. Give a position operator that will yield a diagonal co-occurrence matrix.

11.24 Obtain the gray-level co-occurrence matrix of a 4×4 image composed of a checkerboard of alternating 1s and 0s if

   (a) *the position operator Q is defined as "one pixel to the right," and

   (b) the position operator Q is defined as "two pixels to the right."
   Assume that the top left pixel has value 1.

11.25 Do the following.

   (a) *Prove the validity of Eqs. (11-50) and (11-51).

   (b) Prove the validity of Eq. (11-52).

11.26 *We mentioned in Example 11.16 that a credible job could be done of reconstructing approximations to the six original images by using only the two principal-component images associated with the largest eigenvalues. What would be the mean squared error incurred in doing so? Express your answer as a percentage of the maximum possible error.

11.27 For a set of images of size 64×64, assume that the covariance matrix given in Eq. (11-52) is the identity matrix. What would be the mean squared error between the original images and images reconstructed using Eq. (11-54) with only half of the original eigenvectors?

11.28 Under what conditions would you expect the major axes of a boundary, defined in the discussion of Eq. (11-4), to be equal to the eigen axes of that boundary?

11.29 *You are contracted to design an image processing system for detecting imperfections on the inside of certain solid plastic wafers. The wafers are examined using an X-ray imaging system, which yields 8-bit images of size 512×512. In the absence of imperfections, the images appear uniform, having a mean intensity of 100 and variance of 400. The imperfections appear as blob-like regions in which about 70% of the pixels have excursions in intensity of 50 intensity levels or less about a mean of 100. A wafer is considered defective if such a region occupies an area exceeding 20×20 pixels in size. Propose a system based on texture analysis for solving this problem.

11.30 With reference to Fig. 11.46, answer the following:

   (a) *What is the cause of nearly identical clusters near the origin in Figs. 11.46(d)-(f).

   (b) Look carefully, and you will see a single point near coordinates (0.8, 0.8) in Fig. 11.46(f). What caused this point?

   (c) The results in Fig. 11.46(d)–(e) are for the small image patches shown in Figs. 11.46(a)–(b). What would the results look like if we performed the computations over the entire image, instead of limiting the computation to the patches?

11.31 When we discussed the Harris-Stephens corner detector, we mentioned that there is a closed-form formula for computing the eigenvalues of a 2×2 matrix.

(a)* Given matrix $\mathbf{M} = [a \ b; c \ d]$, give the general formula for finding its eigenvalues. Express your formula in terms of the trace and determinant of $\mathbf{M}$.

(b) Give the formula for *symmetric* matrices of size 2×2 in terms of its four elements, without using the trace nor the determinant.

11.32* With reference to the component tree in Fig. 11.51, assume that any pixels extending past the border of the small image are 0. Is region R_1 an extremal region? Explain.

11.33 Explain the concept of major axis of boundary with its length and orientation.

11.34* The well known heat-diffusion equation of a temperature function $g(x,y,z,t)$ of three spatial variables, (x,y,z), is given by $\partial g/\partial t - \alpha \nabla^2 g = 0$, where α is the thermal diffusivity and ∇^2 is the Laplacian operator. In terms of our discussion of SIFT, the form of this equation is used to establish a relationship between the difference of Gaussians and the scaled Laplacian, $\sigma^2 \nabla^2$. Show how this can be done to derive Eq. (11-70).

11.35 With reference to the SIFT algorithm discussed in Section 11.7, assume that the input image is square, of size $M \times M$ (with $M = 2^n$), and let the number of intervals per octave be $s = 2$.

(a) How many smoothed images will there be in each octave?

(b)* How many octaves could be generated before it is no longer possible to down-sample the image by 2?

(c) If the standard deviation used to smooth the first image in the first octave is σ, what are the values of standard deviation used to smooth the first image in each of the remaining octaves in (b)?

11.36 What is the purpose of using SIFT for an image? State the form of input and output to SIFT.

11.37 Do the following:

(a)* Show how to obtain Eq. (11-74) from Eq. (11-71).

(b) Show how Eq. (11-75) follows from Eqs. (11-74) and (11-71).

11.38 A company that bottles a variety of industrial chemicals employs you to design an approach for detecting when bottles of their product are not full. As they move along a conveyor line past an automatic filling and capping station, the bottles appear as shown in the following image. A bottle is considered imperfectly filled when the level of the liquid is below the midway point between the bottom of the neck and the shoulder of the bottle. The shoulder is defined as the intersection of the sides and slanted portions of the bottle. The bottles move at a high rate of speed, but the company has an imaging system equipped with an illumination flash front end that effectively stops motion, so you will be given images that look very close to the sample shown here. Based on the material you have learned up to this point, propose a solution for detecting bottles that are not filled properly. State clearly all assumptions that you make and that are likely to impact the solution you propose.

Why Gaussian kernels are used to implement smoothing in SIFT? Explain the scale space of grayscale image.

11.39 Why Gaussian kernels are used to implement smoothing in SIFT? Explain the scale space of grayscale image.

Image Pattern Classification

One of the most interesting aspects of the world is that it can be considered to be made up of patterns.

A pattern is essentially an arrangement. It is characterized by the order of the elements of which it is made, rather than by the intrinsic nature of these elements.

Norbert Wiener

Preview

We conclude our coverage of digital image processing with an introduction to techniques for image pattern classification. The approaches developed in this chapter are divided into three principal categories: classification by *prototype matching*, classification based on an *optimal statistical* formulation, and classification based on *neural networks*. The first two approaches are used extensively in applications in which the nature of the data is well understood, leading to an effective pairing of features and classifier design. These approaches often rely on a great deal of engineering to define features and elements of a classifier. Approaches based on neural networks rely less on such knowledge, and lend themselves well to applications in which pattern class characteristics (e.g., features) are learned by the system, rather than being specified a priori by a human designer. The focus of the material in this chapter is on principles, and on how they apply specifically in image pattern classification.

Upon completion of this chapter, readers should:

- Understand the meaning of patterns and pattern classes, and how they relate to digital image processing.
- Be familiar with the basics of minimum-distance classification.
- Know how to apply image correlation techniques for template matching.
- Understand the concept of string matching.
- Be familiar with Bayes classifiers.

- Understand perceptrons and their history.
- Be familiar with the concept of learning from training samples.
- Understand neural network architectures.
- Be familiar with the concept of deep learning in fully connected and deep convolutional neural networks. In particular, be familiar with the importance of the latter in digital image processing.

12.1 BACKGROUND

Humans possess the most sophisticated pattern recognition capabilities in the known biological world. By contrast, the capabilities of current recognition machines pale in comparison with tasks humans perform routinely, from being able to interpret the meaning of complex images, to our ability for generalizing knowledge stored in our brains. But recognition machines play an important, sometimes even crucial role in everyday life. Imagine what modern life would be like without machines that read barcodes, process bank checks, inspect the quality of manufactured products, read fingerprints, sort mail, and recognize speech.

In image pattern recognition, we think of a *pattern* as a spatial arrangement of features. A *pattern class* is a set of patterns that share some common properties. Pattern recognition by machine encompasses techniques for automatically assigning patterns to their respective classes. That is, given a pattern or sets of patterns whose class is unknown, the job of a pattern recognition system is to assign a class label to each of its input patterns.

There are four main stages involved in recognition: (1) sensing, (2) preprocessing, (3) feature extraction, and (4) classification. In terms of image processing, sensing is concerned with generating signals in a spatial (2-D) or higher-dimensional format. We covered numerous aspects of image sensing in Chapter 1. Preprocessing deals with techniques for tasks such as noise reduction, enhancement, restoration, and segmentation, as discussed in earlier chapters. You learned about feature extraction in Chapter 11. Classification, the focus of this chapter, deals with using a set of features as the basis for assigning class labels to unknown input image patterns.

In the following section, we will discuss three basic approaches used for image pattern classification: (1) classification based on matching unknown patterns against specified prototypes, (2) optimum statistical classifiers, and (3) neural networks. One way to characterize the differences between these approaches is in the level of "engineering" required to transform raw data into formats suitable for computer processing. Ultimately, recognition performance is determined by the discriminative power of the features used.

In classification based on prototypes, the objective is to make the features so unique and easily detectable that classification itself becomes a simple task. A good example of this are bank-check processors, which use stylized font styles to simplify machine processing (we will discuss this application in Section 12.3).

In the second category, classification is cast in decision-theoretic, statistical terms, and the classification approach is based on selecting parameters that can be shown to yield optimum classification performance in a statistical sense. Here, emphasis is placed on both the features used, and the design of the classifier. We will illustrate this approach in Section 12.4 by deriving the Bayes pattern classifier, starting from basic principles.

In the third category, classification is performed using neural networks. As you will learn in Sections 12.5 and 12.6, neural networks can operate using engineered features too, but they have the unique ability of being able to generate, on their own, representations (features) suitable for recognition. These systems can accomplish this using raw data, without the need for engineered features.

One characteristic shared by the preceding three approaches is that they are based on parameters that must be either specified or learned from patterns that represent the recognition problem we want to solve. The patterns can be *labeled*, meaning that we know the class of each pattern, or *unlabeled*, meaning that the data are known to be patterns, but the class of each pattern is unknown. A classic example of labeled data is the character recognition problem, in which a set of character samples is collected and the identity of each character is recorded as a label from the group 0 through 9 and *a* through *z*. An example of unlabeled data is when we are seeking clusters in a data set, with the aim of utilizing the resulting cluster centers as being prototypes of the pattern classes contained in the data.

When working with a labeled data, a given data set generally is subdivided into three subsets: a *training set*, a *validation set*, and a *test set* (a typical subdivision might be 50% training, and 25% each for the validation and test sets). The process by which a training set is used to generate classifier parameters is called *training*. In this mode, a classifier is given the class label of each pattern, the objective being to make adjustments in the parameters if the classifier makes a mistake in identifying the class of the given pattern. At this point, we might be working with several candidate designs. At the end of training, we use the validation set to compare the various designs against a performance objective. Typically, several iterations of training/validation are required to establish the design that comes closest to meeting the desired objective. Once a design has been selected, the final step is to determine how it will perform "in the field." For this, we use the test set, which consists of patterns that the system has never "seen" before. If the training and validation sets are truly representative of the data the system will encounter in practice, the results of training/validation should be close to the performance using the test set. If training/validation results are acceptable, but test results are not, we say that training/validation "over fit" the system parameters to the available data, in which case further work on the system architecture is required. Of course all this assumes that the given data are truly representative of the problem we want to solve, and that the problem in fact can be solved by available technology.

A system that is designed using training data is said to undergo *supervised learning*. If we are working with unlabeled data, the system learns the pattern classes themselves while in an *unsupervised* learning mode. In this chapter, we deal only with supervised learning. As you will see in this and the next chapter, supervised learning covers a broad range of approaches, from applications in which a system learns parameters of features whose form is fixed by a designer, to systems that utilize *deep learning* and large sets of raw data sets to learn, *on their own*, the features required for classification. These systems accomplish this task without a human designer having to specify the features, a priori.

After a brief discussion in the next section of how patterns are formed, and on the nature of patterns classes, we will discuss in Section 12.3 various approaches for prototype-based classification. In Section 12.4, we will start from basic principles and derive the equations of the Bayes classifier, an approach characterized by optimum classification performance on an average basis. We will also discuss supervised training of a Bayes classifier based on the assumption of multivariate Gaussian

Because the examples in this chapter are intended to demonstrate basic principles and are not large scale, we dispense with validation and subdivide the pattern data into training and test sets.

Generally, we associate the concept of deep learning with large sets of data. These ideas are discussed in more detail later in this section and next.

distributions. Starting with Section 12.5, we will spend the rest of the chapter discussing neural networks. We will begin Section 12.5 with a brief introduction to perceptrons and some historical facts about machine learning. Then, we will introduce the concept of deep neural networks and derive the equations of backpropagation, the method of choice for training deep neural nets. These networks are well-suited for applications in which input patterns are vectors. In Section 12.6, we will introduce deep convolutional neural networks, which currently are the preferred approach when the system inputs are digital images. After deriving the backpropagation equations used for training convolutional nets, we will give several examples of applications involving classes of images of various complexities. In addition to working directly with image inputs, deep convolutional nets are capable of learning, on their own, image features suitable for classification. This is accomplished starting with raw image data, as opposed to the other classification methods discussed in Sections 12.3 and 12.4, which rely on "engineered" features whose form, as noted earlier, is specified a priori by a human designer.

12.2 PATTERNS AND PATTERN CLASSES

In image pattern classification, the two principal pattern arrangements are quantitative and structural. *Quantitative patterns* are arranged in the form of *pattern vectors*. *Structural patterns* typically are composed of symbols, arranged in the form of *strings*, *trees*, or, less frequently, as *graphs*. Most of the work in this chapter is based on pattern vectors, but we will discuss structural patterns briefly at the end of this section, and give an example at the end of Section 12.3.

PATTERN VECTORS

Pattern vectors are represented by lowercase letters, such as $\mathbf{x}$, $\mathbf{y}$, and $\mathbf{z}$, and have the form

$$\mathbf{x} = \begin{bmatrix} x_1 \\ x_2 \\ \vdots \\ x_n \end{bmatrix} \tag{12-1}$$

where each component, x_i, represents the ith feature descriptor, and n is the total number of such descriptors. We can express a vector in the form of a column, as in Eq. (12-1), or in the equivalent row form $\mathbf{x} = (x_1, x_2, \ldots, x_n)^T$, where T indicates transposition. A pattern vector may be "viewed" as a point in n-dimensional Euclidean space, and a pattern class may be interpreted as a "hypercloud" of points in this *pattern space*. For the purpose of recognition, we like for our pattern classes to be grouped tightly, and as far away from each other as possible.

Pattern vectors can be formed directly from image pixel intensities by vectorizing the image using, for example, linear indexing, as in Fig. 12.1. A more common approach is for pattern elements to be features. An early example is the work of Fisher [1936] who, close to a century ago, reported the use of what then was a new

We discussed linear indexing in Section 2.4 (see Fig. 2.22).

a b

FIGURE 12.1
Using linear
indexing to
vectorize a
grayscale image.

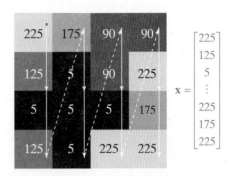

Sepals are the undergrowth
beneath the petals.

technique called *discriminant analysis* to recognize three types of iris flowers (*Iris setosa, virginica,* and *versicolor*). Fisher described each flower using four features: the length and width of the petals, and similarly for the sepals (see Fig. 12.2). This leads to the 4-D vectors shown in the figure. A set of these vectors, obtained for fifty samples of each flower gender, constitutes the three famous *Fisher iris pattern classes*. Had Fisher been working today, he probably would have added spectral colors and shape features to his measurements, yielding vectors of higher dimensionality. We will be working with the original iris data set later in this chapter.

A higher-level representation of patterns is based on feature descriptors of the types you learned in Chapter 11. For instance, pattern vectors formed from descriptors of boundary shape are well-suited for applications in controlled environments, such as industrial inspection. Figure 12.3 illustrates the concept. Here, we are interested in classifying different types of noisy shapes, a sample of which is shown in the figure. If we represent an object by its signature, we would obtain 1-D signals of the form shown in Fig. 12.3(b). We can express a signature as a vector by sampling its amplitude at increments of θ, then formimg a vector by letting $x_i = r(\theta_i)$, for $i = 0, 1, 2, \ldots, n$. Instead of using "raw" sampled signatures, a more common approach is to compute some function, $x_i = g(r(\theta_i))$, of the signature samples and use them to form vectors. You learned in Section 11.3 several approaches to do this, such as statistical moments.

FIGURE 12.2
Petal and sepal
width and length
measurements
(see arrows)
performed on iris
flowers for the
purpose of data
classification. The
image shown is of
the *Iris virginica*
gender. (Image
courtesy of
USDA.)

x_1 = Petal width
x_2 = Petal length
x_3 = Sepal width
x_4 = Sepal length

FIGURE 12.3
(a) A noisy object boundary, and (b) its corresponding signature.

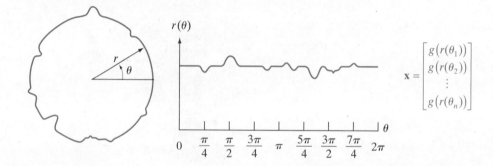

Vectors can be formed also from features of both boundary and regions. For example, the objects in Fig. 12.4 can be represented by 3-D vectors whose components capture shape information related to both boundary and region properties of single binary objects. Pattern vectors can be used also to represent properties of image regions. For example, the elements of the 6-D vector in Fig. 12.5 are texture measures based on the feature descriptors in Table 11.3. Figure 12.6 shows an example in which pattern vector elements are features that are invariant to transformations, such as image rotation and scaling (see Section 11.4).

When working with sequences of registered images, we have the option of using pattern vectors formed from corresponding pixels in those images (see Fig. 12.7). Forming pattern vectors in this way implies that recognition will be based on information extracted from the same spatial location across the images. Although this may seem like a very limiting approach, it is ideally suited for applications such as recognizing regions in multispectral images, as you will see in Section 12.4.

When working with entire images as units, we need the detail afforded by vectors of much-higher dimensionality, such as those we discussed in Section 11.7 in connection with the SIFT algorithm. However, a more powerful approach when working with entire images is to use deep convolutional neural networks. We will discuss neural nets in detail in Sections 12.5 and 12.6.

STRUCTURAL PATTERNS

Pattern vectors are not suitable for applications in which objects are represented by structural features, such as strings of symbols. Although they are used much less than vectors in image processing applications, patterns containing structural descriptions of objects are important in applications where shape is of interest. Figure 12.8 shows an example. The boundaries of the bottles were approximated by a polygon

FIGURE 12.4
Pattern vectors whose components capture both boundary and regional characteristics.

$$\mathbf{x} = \begin{bmatrix} x_1 \\ x_2 \\ x_3 \end{bmatrix} \qquad \begin{array}{l} x_1 = \text{compactness} \\ x_2 = \text{circularity} \\ x_3 = \text{eccentricity} \end{array}$$

FIGURE 12.5
An example of pattern vectors based on properties of subimages. See Table 11.3 for an explanation of the components of **x**.

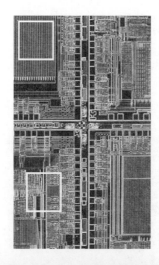

$$\mathbf{x} = \begin{bmatrix} x_1 \\ x_2 \\ x_3 \\ x_4 \\ x_5 \\ x_6 \end{bmatrix}$$

x_1 = max probability
x_2 = correlation
x_3 = contrast
x_4 = uniformity
x_5 = homogeneity
x_6 = entropy

FIGURE 12.6 Feature vectors with components that are invariant to transformations such as rotation, scaling, and translation. The vector components are moment invariants.

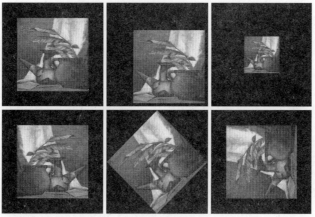

$$\mathbf{x} = \begin{bmatrix} x_1 \\ x_2 \\ x_3 \\ x_4 \\ x_5 \\ x_6 \\ x_7 \end{bmatrix} = \begin{bmatrix} \phi_1 \\ \phi_2 \\ \phi_3 \\ \phi_4 \\ \phi_5 \\ \phi_6 \\ \phi_7 \end{bmatrix}$$

The ϕ's are moment invariants

Images in spectral bands 1–3

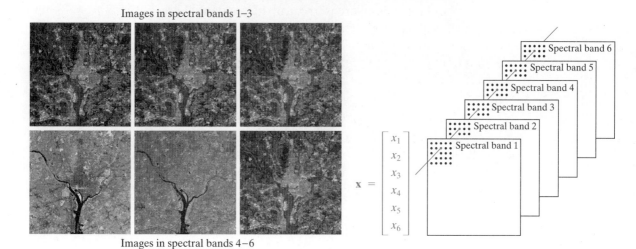

Images in spectral bands 4–6

$$\mathbf{x} = \begin{bmatrix} x_1 \\ x_2 \\ x_3 \\ x_4 \\ x_5 \\ x_6 \end{bmatrix}$$

Spectral band 1
Spectral band 2
Spectral band 3
Spectral band 4
Spectral band 5
Spectral band 6

FIGURE 12.7 Pattern (feature) vectors formed by concatenating corresponding pixels from a set of registered images. (Original images courtesy of NASA.)

FIGURE 12.8
Symbol string
generated from
a polygonal
approximation of
the boundaries of
medicine bottles.

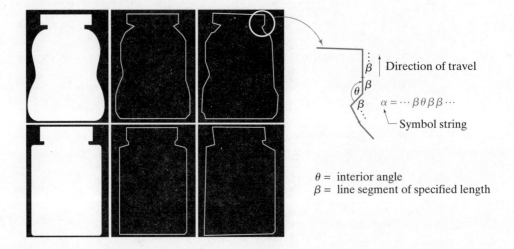

θ = interior angle
β = line segment of specified length

using the approach explained in Section 11.2. The boundary is subdivided into line segments (denoted by β in the figure), and the interior angle, θ, is computed at each intersection of two line segments. A string of sequential symbols is generated as the boundary is traversed in the counterclockwise direction, as the figure shows. *Strings* of this form are structural patterns, and the objective, as you will see in Section 12.3, is to match a given string against stored string prototypes.

A *tree* is another structural representation, suitable for higher-level descriptions of an entire image in terms of its component regions. Basically, most hierarchical ordering schemes lead to tree structures. For example, Fig. 12.9 shows a satellite image of a heavily built downtown area and surrounding residential areas. Let the symbol $ represent the root of a tree. The (upside down) tree shown in the figure was obtained using the structural relationship "composed of." Thus, the root of the tree represents the entire image. The next level indicates that the image is composed of a downtown and residential areas. In turn, the residential areas are composed of housing, highways, and shopping malls. The next level down in the tree further describes the housing and highways. We can continue this type of subdivision until we reach the limit of our ability to resolve different regions in the image.

12.3 PATTERN CLASSIFICATION BY PROTOTYPE MATCHING

Prototype matching involves comparing an unknown pattern against a set of prototypes, and assigning to the unknown pattern the class of the prototype that is the most "similar" to the unknown. Each prototype represents a unique pattern class, but there may be more than one prototype for each class. What distinguishes one matching method from another is the measure used to determine similarity.

MINIMUM-DISTANCE CLASSIFIER

The minimum-distance classifier is also referred to as the *nearest-neighbor classifier*.

One of the simplest and most widely used prototype matching methods is the *minimum-distance classifier* which, as its name implies, computes a distance-based measure between an unknown pattern vector and each of the class prototypes. It then assigns the unknown pattern to the class of its closest prototype. The prototype

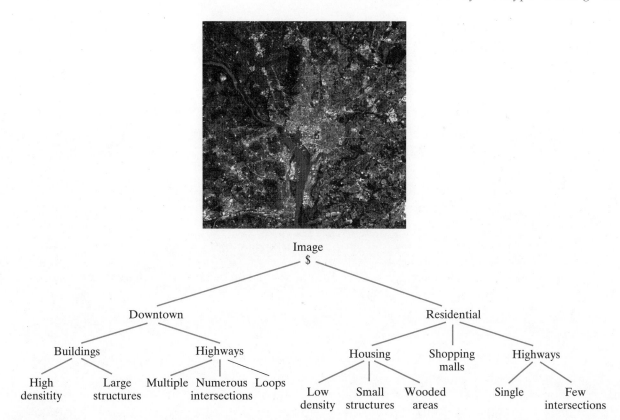

FIGURE 12.9 Tree representation of a satellite image showing a heavily built downtown area (Washington, D.C.) and surrounding residential areas. (Original image courtesy of NASA.)

vectors of the minimum-distance classifier usually are the mean vectors of the various pattern classes:

$$\mathbf{m}_j = \frac{1}{n_j} \sum_{\mathbf{x} \in c_j} \mathbf{x} \qquad j = 1, 2, \dots, N_c \qquad (12\text{-}2)$$

where n_j is the number of pattern vectors used to compute the jth mean vector, c_j is the jth pattern class, and N_c is the number of classes. If we use the Euclidean distance to determine similarity, the minimum-distance classifier computes the distances

$$D_j(\mathbf{x}) = \| \mathbf{x} - \mathbf{m}_j \| \qquad j = 1, 2, \dots, N_c \qquad (12\text{-}3)$$

where $\| \mathbf{a} \| = (\mathbf{a}^T \mathbf{a})^{1/2}$ is the Euclidean norm. The classifier then assigns an unknown pattern $\mathbf{x}$ to class c_i if $D_i(\mathbf{x}) < D_j(\mathbf{x})$ for $j = 1, 2, \dots, N_c$, $j \neq i$. Ties [i.e., $D_i(\mathbf{x}) = D_j(\mathbf{x})$] are resolved arbitrarily.

It is not difficult to show (see Problem 12.2) that selecting the smallest distance is equivalent to evaluating the functions

$$d_j(\mathbf{x}) = \mathbf{m}_j^T \mathbf{x} - \frac{1}{2} \mathbf{m}_j^T \mathbf{m}_j \qquad j = 1, 2, \dots, N_c \qquad (12\text{-}4)$$

and assigning an unknown pattern $\mathbf{x}$ to the class whose prototype yielded the *largest* value of d. That is, $\mathbf{x}$ is assigned to class c_i, if

$$d_i(\mathbf{x}) > d_j(\mathbf{x}) \qquad j = 1, 2, \ldots, N_c; \ \ j \neq i \tag{12-5}$$

When used for recognition, functions of this form are referred to as *decision* or *discriminant functions*.

The *decision boundary* separating class c_i from c_j is given by the values of $\mathbf{x}$ for which

$$d_i(\mathbf{x}) = d_j(\mathbf{x}) \tag{12-6}$$

or, equivalently, by values of $\mathbf{x}$ for which

$$d_i(\mathbf{x}) - d_j(\mathbf{x}) = 0 \tag{12-7}$$

The decision boundaries for a minimum-distance classifier follow directly from this equation and Eq. (12-4):

$$\begin{aligned} d_{ij}(\mathbf{x}) &= d_i(\mathbf{x}) - d_j(\mathbf{x}) \\ &= (\mathbf{m}_i - \mathbf{m}_j)^T \mathbf{x} - \frac{1}{2}(\mathbf{m}_i - \mathbf{m}_j)^T (\mathbf{m}_i + \mathbf{m}_j) = 0 \end{aligned} \tag{12-8}$$

The boundary given by Eq. (12-8) is the perpendicular bisector of the line segment joining $\mathbf{m}_i$ and $\mathbf{m}_j$ (see Problem 12.3). In 2-D (i.e., $n = 2$), the perpendicular bisector is a line, for $n = 3$ it is a plane, and for $n > 3$ it is called a *hyperplane*.

EXAMPLE 12.1: Illustration of the minimum-distance classifier for two classes in 2-D.

Figure 12.10 shows scatter plots of petal width and length values for the classes Iris versicolor and Iris setosa. As mentioned in the previous section, pattern vectors in the iris database consists of four measurements for each flower. We show only two here so that you can visualize the pattern classes and the decision boundary between them. We will work with the complete database later in this chapter.

We denote the Iris versicolor and setosa data as classes c_1 and c_2, respectively. The means of the two classes are $\mathbf{m}_1 = (4.3, 1.3)^T$ and $\mathbf{m}_2 = (1.5, 0.3)^T$. It then follows from Eq. (12-4) that

$$\begin{aligned} d_1(\mathbf{x}) &= \mathbf{m}_1^T \mathbf{x} - \frac{1}{2} \mathbf{m}_1^T \mathbf{m}_1 \\ &= 4.3 x_1 + 1.3 x_2 - 10.1 \end{aligned}$$

and

$$\begin{aligned} d_2(\mathbf{x}) &= \mathbf{m}_2^T \mathbf{x} - \frac{1}{2} \mathbf{m}_2^T \mathbf{m}_2 \\ &= 1.5 x_1 + 0.3 x_2 - 1.17 \end{aligned}$$

From Eq. (12-8), the equation of the boundary is

$$\begin{aligned} d_{12}(\mathbf{x}) &= d_1(\mathbf{x}) - d_2(\mathbf{x}) \\ &= 2.8 x_1 + 1.0 x_2 - 8.9 = 0 \end{aligned}$$

FIGURE 12.10
Decision boundary of a minimum distance classifier (based on two measurements) for the classes of Iris versicolor and Iris setosa. The dark dot and square are the means of the two classes.

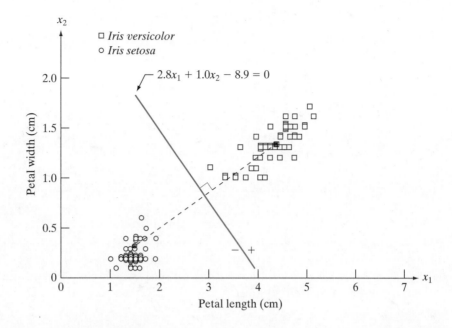

Figure 12.10 shows a plot of this boundary. Substituting any pattern vector from class c_1 into this equation would yield $d_{12}(\mathbf{x}) > 0$. Conversely, any pattern from class c_2 would give $d_{12}(\mathbf{x}) < 0$. Thus, given an unknown pattern $\mathbf{x}$ belonging to one of these two classes, the sign of $d_{12}(\mathbf{x})$ would be sufficient to determine the class to which that pattern belongs.

The minimum-distance classifier works well when the distance between means is large compared to the spread or randomness of each class with respect to its mean. In Section 12.4 we will show that the minimum-distance classifier yields optimum performance (in terms of minimizing the average loss of misclassification) when the distribution of each class about its mean is in the form of a spherical "hypercloud" in n-dimensional pattern space.

As noted earlier, one of the keys to accurate recognition performance is to specify features that are effective discriminators between classes. As a rule, the better the features are at meeting this objective, the better the recognition performance will be. In the case of the minimum-distance classifier this implies wide separation between means and tight grouping of the classes.

Systems based on the Banker's Association E-13B font character are a classic example of how highly engineered features can be used in conjunction with a simple classifier to achieve superior results. In the mid-1940s, bank checks were processed manually, which was a laborious, costly process prone to mistakes. As the volume of check writing increased in the early 1950s, banks became keenly interested in automating this task. In the middle 1950s, the E-13B font and the system that reads it became the standard solution to the problem. As Fig. 12.11 shows, this font set consists of 14 characters laid out on a 9×7 grid. The characters are stylized to maximize the difference between them. The font was designed to be compact and readable by humans, but the overriding purpose was that the characters should be readable by machine, quickly, and with very high accuracy.

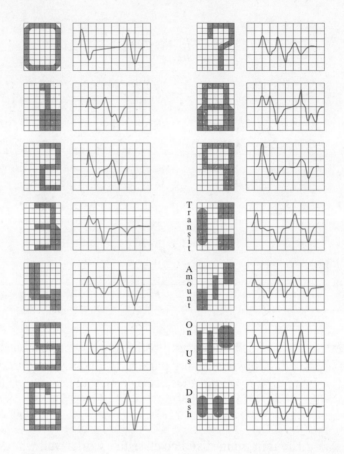

In addition to a stylized font design, the operation of the reading system is further enhanced by printing each character using an ink that contains finely ground magnetic material. To improve character detectability in a check being read, the ink is subjected to a magnetic field that accentuates each character against the background. The stylized design further enhances character detectability. The characters are scanned in a horizontal direction with a single-slit reading head that is narrower but taller than the characters. As a check passes through the head, the sensor produces a 1-D electrical signal (a signature) that is conditioned to be proportional to the rate of increase or decrease of the character area under the head. For example, consider the waveform of the number 0 in Fig. 12.11. As a check moves to the right past the head, the character area seen by the sensor begins to increase, producing a positive derivative (a positive rate of change). As the right leg of the character begins to pass under the head, the character area seen by the sensor begins to decrease, producing a negative derivative. When the head is in the middle zone of the character, the area remains nearly constant, producing a zero derivative. This waveform repeats itself as the other leg of the character enters the head. The design of the font ensures that the waveform of each character is distinct from all others. It also ensures that the peaks and zeros of each waveform occur approximately on the vertical lines of the background grid on which these waveforms are displayed, as the figure shows. The E-13B font has the property that sampling the waveforms only at these (nine) points yields enough information for their accurate classification. The effectiveness of these highly engineered features is further refined by the magnetized ink, which results in clean waveforms with almost no scatter.

Designing a minimum-distance classifier for this application is straightforward. We simply store the sample values of each waveform at the vertical lines of the grid, and let each set of the resulting samples be represented as a 9-D prototype vector, $\mathbf{m}_j$, $j = 1, 2, \ldots, 14$. When an unknown character is to be classified, the approach is to scan it in the manner just described, express the grid samples of the waveform as a 9-D vector, $\mathbf{x}$, and identify its class by selecting the class of the prototype vector that yields the highest value in Eq. (12-4). We do not even need a computer to do this. Very high classification speeds can be achieved with analog circuits composed of resistor banks (see Problem 12.4).

The most important lesson in this example is that a recognition problem often can be made trivial if we can control the environment in which the patterns are generated. The development and implementation of the E13-B font reading system is a striking example of this fact. On the other hand, this system would be inadequate if we added the requirement that it has to recognize the textual content and signature written on each check. For this, we need systems that are significantly more complex, such as the convolutional neural networks we will discuss in Section 12.6.

USING CORRELATION FOR 2-D PROTOTYPE MATCHING

We introduced the basic idea of spatial correlation and convolution in Section 3.4, and used these concepts extensively in Chapter 3 for spatial filtering. From Eq. (3-34), we know that correlation of a kernel w with an image $f(x, y)$ is given by

$$(w \star f)(x, y) = \sum_s \sum_t w(s, t) f(x + s, y + t) \tag{12-9}$$

where the limits of summation are taken over the region shared by w and f. This equation is evaluated for all values of the displacement variables x and y so all elements of w visit every pixel of f. As you know, correlation has its highest value(s) in the region(s) where f and w are equal or nearly equal. In other words, Eq. (12-9) finds locations where w *matches* a region of f. But this equation has the drawback that the result is sensitive to changes in the amplitude of either function. In order to normalize correlation to amplitude changes in one or both functions, we perform matching using the *correlation coefficient* instead:

To be formal, we should refer to correlation (and the correlation coefficient) as *cross-correlation* when the functions are different, and as *autocorrelation* when they are the same. However, it is customary to use the generic term *correlation* and *correlation coefficient,* except when the distinction is important (as in deriving equations, in which it makes a difference which is being applied).

$$\gamma(x, y) = \frac{\sum_s \sum_t \left[w(s, t) - \bar{w} \right] \left[f(x + s, y + t) - \bar{f}_{xy} \right]}{\left\{ \sum_s \sum_t \left[w(s, t) - \bar{w} \right]^2 \sum_s \sum_t \left[f(x + s, y + t) - \bar{f}_{xy} \right]^2 \right\}^{\frac{1}{2}}} \tag{12-10}$$

where the limits of summation are taken over the region shared by w and f, $\bar{w}$ is the average value of the kernel (computed only once), and $\bar{f}_{xy}$ is the average value of f in the region coincident with w. In image correlation work, w is often referred to as a *template* (i.e., a prototype subimage) and correlation is referred to as *template matching*.

FIGURE 12.12
The mechanics of
template
matching.

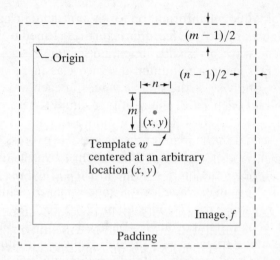

It can be shown (see Problem 12.5) that $\gamma(x, y)$ has values in the range $[-1, 1]$ and is thus normalized to changes in the amplitudes of w and f. The maximum value of γ occurs when the normalized w and the corresponding normalized region in f are identical. This indicates *maximum correlation* (the best possible match). The *minimum* occurs when the two normalized functions exhibit the least similarity in the sense of Eq. (12-10).

Figure 12.12 illustrates the mechanics of the procedure just described. The border around image f is padding, as explained in Section 3.4. In template matching, values of correlation when the center of the template is past the border of the image generally are of no interest, so the padding is limited to half the kernel width.

The template in Fig. 12.12 is of size $m \times n$, and it is shown with its center at an arbitrary location (x, y). The value of the correlation coefficient at that point is computed using Eq. (12-10). Then, the center of the template is incremented to an adjacent location and the procedure is repeated. Values of the correlation coefficient $\gamma(x, y)$ are obtained by moving the center of the template (i.e., by incrementing x and y) so the center of w visits every pixel in f. At the end of the procedure, we look for the maximum in $\gamma(x, y)$ to find where the best match occurred. It is possible to have multiple locations in $\gamma(x, y)$ with the same maximum value, indicating several matches between w and f.

EXAMPLE 12.2: Matching by correlation.

Figure 12.13(a) shows a 913×913 satellite image of 1992 Hurricane Andrew, in which the eye of the storm is clearly visible. We want to use correlation to find the location of the best match in Fig. 12.13(a) of the template in Fig. 12.13(b), which is a 31×31 subimage of the eye of the storm. Figure 12.13(c) shows the result of computing the correlation coefficient in Eq. (12-10) for all values of x and y in the original image. The size of this image was 943×943 pixels due to padding (see Fig. 12.12), but we cropped it to the size of the original image for display. The intensity in this image is proportional to the correlation values, and all negative correlations were clipped at 0 (black) to simplify the visual analysis of the image. The area of highest correlation values appears as a small white region in this image. The brightest point in this region matches with the center of the eye of the storm. Figure 12.13(d) shows as a

FIGURE 12.13
(a) 913×913
satellite image
of Hurricane
Andrew.
(b) 31×31
template of the
eye of the storm.
(c) Correlation
coefficient shown
as an image (note
the brightest
point, indicated
by an arrow).
(d) Location of
the best match
(identified by the
arrow). This point
is a single pixel,
but its size was
enlarged to make
it easier to see.
(Original image
courtesy of
NOAA.)

a b
c d

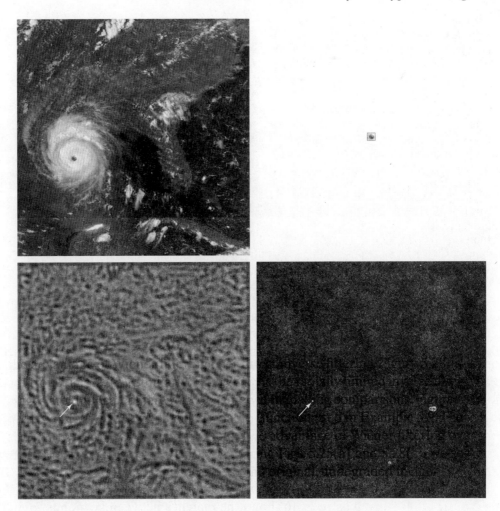

white dot the location of this maximum correlation value (in this case there was a unique match whose maximum value was 1), which we see corresponds closely with the location of the eye in Fig. 12.13(a).

MATCHING SIFT FEATURES

We discussed the scale-invariant feature transform (SIFT) in Section 11.7. SIFT computes a set of invariant features that can be used for matching between known (prototype) and unknown images. The SIFT implementation in Section 11.7 yields 128-dimensional feature vectors for each local region in an image. SIFT performs matching by looking for correspondences between sets of stored feature vector prototypes and feature vectors computed for an unknown image. Because of the large number of features involved, searching for exact matches is computationally intensive. Instead, the approach is to use a best-bin-first method that can identify the nearest neighbors with high probability using only a limited amount of computation (see Lowe [1999], [2004]). The search is further simplified by looking for clusters of potential solutions using the generalized Hough transform proposed by Ballard [1981]. We know from

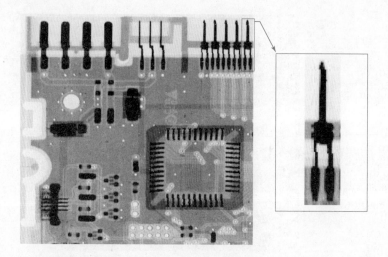

the discussion in Section 10.2 that the Hough transform simplifies looking for data patterns by utilizing bins that reduce the level of detail with which we look at a data set. We already discussed the SIFT algorithm in Section 11.7. The focus in this section is to further illustrate the capabilities of SIFT for prototype matching.

Figure 12.14 shows the circuit board image we have used several times before. The small rectangle enclosing the rightmost connector on the top of the large image identifies an area from which an image of the connector was extracted. The small image is shown zoomed for clarity. The sizes of the large and small images are shown in the figure caption. Figure 12.15 shows the keypoints found by SIFT, as explained in Section 11.7. They are visible as faint lines on both images. The zoomed view of the subimage shows them a little clearer. It is important to note that the keypoints for the image and subimage were found independently by SIFT. The large image had 2714 keypoints, and the small image had 35.

Figure 12.16 shows the matches between keypoints found by SIFT. A total of 41 matches were found between the two images. Because there are only 35 keypoints

FIGURE 12.15
Keypoints found
by SIFT. The
large image has
2714 keypoints
(visible as faint
gray lines). The
subimage has 35
keypoints. This is
a separate image,
and SIFT found
its keypoints inde-
pendently of the
large image. The
zoomed section is
shown for clarity.

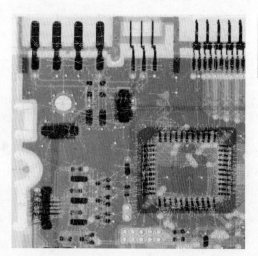
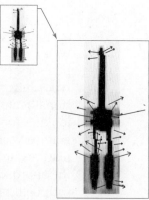

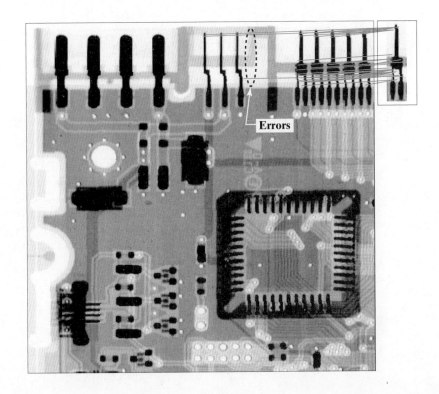

FIGURE 12.16
Matches found by SIFT between the large and small images. A total of 41 matching pairs were found. They are shown connected by straight lines. Only three of the matches were "real" errors (labeled "Errors" in the figure).

in the small image, obviously at least six matches are either incorrect, or there are multiple matches. Three of the errors are clearly visible as matches with connectors in the middle of the large image. However, if you compare the shape of the connectors in the middle of the large image, you can see that they are virtually identical to *parts* of the connectors on the right. Therefore, these errors can be explained on that basis. The other three extra matches are easier to explain. All connectors on the top right of the circuit board are identical, and we are comparing one of them against the rest. There is no way for a system to tell the difference between them. In fact, by looking at the connecting lines, we can see that the matches are between the subimage and all five connectors. These in fact are correct matches between the subimage and other connectors that are identical to it.

MATCHING STRUCTURAL PROTOTYPES

The techniques discussed up to this point deal with patterns quantitatively, and largely ignore any structural relationships inherent in pattern shapes. The methods discussed in this section seek to achieve pattern recognition by capitalizing precisely on these types of relationships. In this section, we introduce two basic approaches for the recognition of boundary shapes based on string representations, which are the most practical approach in structural pattern recognition.

Matching Shape Numbers

A procedure similar in concept to the minimum-distance classifier introduced earlier for pattern vectors can be formulated for comparing region boundaries that are described by shape numbers. With reference to the discussion in Section 11.3, the *degree of similarity*, k, between two region boundaries, is defined as the largest order for which their shape numbers still coincide. For example, let a and b denote shape numbers of closed boundaries represented by 4-directional chain codes. These two shapes have a degree of similarity k if

$$s_j(a) = s_j(b) \qquad \text{for } j = 4, 6, 8, \ldots, k; \text{ and}$$
$$s_j(a) \neq s_j(b) \qquad \text{for } j = k+2, k+4, \ldots \tag{12-11}$$

where s indicates shape number, and the subscript indicates shape order. The *distance* between two shapes a and b is defined as the inverse of their degree of similarity:

$$D(a,b) = \frac{1}{k} \tag{12-12}$$

This expression satisfies the following properties:

$$D(a,b) \geq 0$$
$$D(a,b) = 0 \quad \text{if and only if } a = b \tag{12-13}$$
$$D(a,c) \leq \max\big[D(a,b), D(b,c)\big]$$

Either k or D may be used to compare two shapes. If the degree of similarity is used, the larger k is, the more similar the shapes are (note that k is infinite for identical shapes). The reverse is true when Eq. (12-12) is used.

EXAMPLE 12.3: Matching shape numbers.

Suppose we have a shape, f, and want to find its closest match in a set of five shape prototypes, denoted by $a, b, c, d,$ and e, as shown in Fig. 12.17(a). The search may be visualized with the aid of the *similarity tree* in Fig. 12.17(b). The root of the tree corresponds to the lowest possible degree of similarity, which is 4. Suppose shapes are identical up to degree 8, with the exception of shape a, whose degree of similarity with respect to all other shapes is 6. Proceeding down the tree, we find that shape d has degree of similarity 8 with respect to all others, and so on. Shapes f and c match uniquely, having a higher degree of similarity than any other two shapes. Conversely, if a had been an unknown shape, all we could have said using this method is that a was similar to the other five shapes with degree of similarity 6. The same information can be summarized in the form of the *similarity matrix* in Fig. 12.17(c).

String Matching

Suppose two region boundaries, a and b, are coded into strings of symbols, denoted as $a_1 a_2 \ldots a_n$ and $b_1 b_2 \ldots b_m$, respectively. Let α represent the number of matches between the two strings, where a match occurs in the kth position if $a_k = b_k$. The number of symbols that do not match is

$$\beta = \max(|a|, |b|) - \alpha \tag{12-14}$$

FIGURE 12.17
(a) Shapes.
(b) Similarity
tree. (c) Similarity
matrix.
(Bribiesca and
Guzman.)

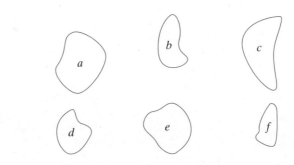

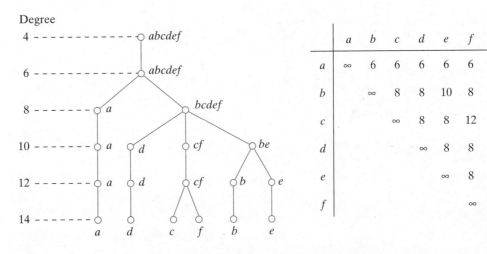

where |arg| is the length (number of symbols) of string in the argument. It can be shown that $\beta = 0$ if and only if a and b are identical (see Problem 12.7).

An effective measure of similarity is the ratio

$$R = \frac{\alpha}{\beta} = \frac{\alpha}{\max(|a|,|b|) - \alpha} \qquad (12\text{-}15)$$

We see that R is infinite for a perfect match and 0 when none of the corresponding symbols in a and b match ($\alpha = 0$ in this case). Because matching is done symbol by symbol, the starting point on each boundary is important in terms of reducing the amount of computation required to perform a match. Any method that normalizes to, or near, the same starting point is helpful if it provides a computational advantage over brute-force matching, which consists of starting at arbitrary points on each string, then shifting one of the strings (with wraparound) and computing Eq. (12-15) for each shift. The largest value of R gives the best match.

Refer to Section 11.2
for examples of how the
starting point of a curve
can be normalized.

EXAMPLE 12.4: String matching.

Figures 12.18(a) and (b) show sample boundaries from each of two object classes, which were approximated by a polygonal fit (see Section 11.2). Figures 12.18(c) and (d) show the polygonal approximations

FIGURE 12.18
(a) and (b) sample boundaries of two different object classes; (c) and (d) their corresponding polygonal approximations; (e)–(g) tabulations of R. (Sze and Yang.)

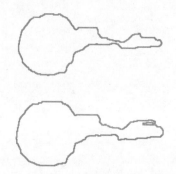

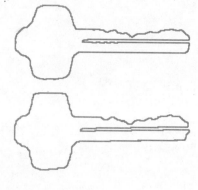

R	1.a	1.b	1.c	1.d	1.e	1.f
1.a	∞					
1.b	16.0	∞				
1.c	9.6	26.3	∞			
1.d	5.1	8.1	10.3	∞		
1.e	4.7	7.2	10.3	14.2	∞	
1.f	4.7	7.2	10.3	8.4	23.7	∞

R	2.a	2.b	2.c	2.d	2.e	2.f
2.a	∞					
2.b	33.5	∞				
2.c	4.8	5.8	∞			
2.d	3.6	4.2	19.3	∞		
2.e	2.8	3.3	9.2	18.3	∞	
2.f	2.6	3.0	7.7	13.5	27.0	∞

R	1.a	1.b	1.c	1.d	1.e	1.f
2.a	1.24	1.50	1.32	1.47	1.55	1.48
2.b	1.18	1.43	1.32	1.47	1.55	1.48
2.c	1.02	1.18	1.19	1.32	1.39	1.48
2.d	1.02	1.18	1.19	1.32	1.29	1.40
2.e	0.93	1.07	1.08	1.19	1.24	1.25
2.f	0.89	1.02	1.02	1.24	1.22	1.18

corresponding to the boundaries in Figs. 12.18(a) and (b), respectively. Strings were formed from the polygons by computing the interior angle, θ, between segments as each polygon was traversed clockwise. Angles were coded into one of eight possible symbols, corresponding to multiples of 45°; that is, $\alpha_1 : 0° < \theta \le 45°$; $\alpha_2 : 45° < \theta \le 90°$; ...; $\alpha_8 : 315° < \theta \le 360°$.

Figure 12.18(e) shows the results of computing the measure R for six samples of object 1 against themselves. The entries are values of R and, for example, the notation 1.c refers to the third string from object class 1. Figure 12.18(f) shows the results of comparing the strings of the second object class against themselves. Finally, Fig. 12.18(g) shows the R values obtained by comparing strings of one class against the other. These values of R are significantly smaller than any entry in the two preceding tabulations. This indicates that the R measure achieved a high degree of discrimination between the two classes of objects. For example, if the class of string 1.a had been unknown, the *smallest* value of R resulting from comparing this string against sample (prototype) strings of class 1 would have been 4.7 [see Fig. 12.18(e)]. By contrast, the *largest* value in comparing it against strings of class 2 would have been 1.24 [see Fig. 12.18(g)]. This result would have led to the conclusion that string 1.a is a member of object class 1. This approach to classification is analogous to the minimum-distance classifier introduced earlier.

12.4 OPTIMUM (BAYES) STATISTICAL CLASSIFIERS

In this section, we develop a probabilistic approach to pattern classification. As is true in most fields that deal with measuring and interpreting physical events, probability considerations become important in pattern recognition because of the randomness under which pattern classes normally are generated. As shown in the following discussion, it is possible to derive a classification approach that is optimal in the sense that, on average, it yields the lowest probability of committing classification errors (see Problem 12.12).

DERIVATION OF THE BAYES CLASSIFIER

The probability that a pattern vector $\mathbf{x}$ comes from class c_i is denoted by $p(c_i/\mathbf{x})$. If the pattern classifier decides that $\mathbf{x}$ came from class c_j when it actually came from c_i it incurs a *loss* (to be defined shortly), denoted by L_{ij}. Because pattern $\mathbf{x}$ may belong to any one of N_c possible classes, the average loss incurred in assigning $\mathbf{x}$ to class c_j is

$$r_j(\mathbf{x}) = \sum_{k=1}^{N_c} L_{kj} p(c_k/\mathbf{x}) \tag{12-16}$$

Quantity $r_j(\mathbf{x})$ is called the *conditional average risk* or *loss* in decision-theory terminology.

We know from Bayes' rule that $p(a/b) = [p(a)p(b/a)]/p(b)$, so we can write Eq. (12-16) as

$$r_j(\mathbf{x}) = \frac{1}{p(\mathbf{x})} \sum_{k=1}^{N_c} L_{kj} p(\mathbf{x}/c_k) P(c_k) \tag{12-17}$$

where $p(\mathbf{x}/c_k)$ is the probability density function (PDF) of the patterns from class c_k, and $P(c_k)$ is the probability of occurrence of class c_k (sometimes $P(c_k)$ is referred to as the *a priori*, or simply the *prior*, *probability*). Because $1/p(\mathbf{x})$ is positive and common to all the $r_j(\mathbf{x})$, $j = 1, 2, ..., N_c$, it can be dropped from Eq. (12-17) without affecting the relative order of these functions from the smallest to the largest value. The expression for the average loss then reduces to

$$r_j(\mathbf{x}) = \sum_{k=1}^{N_c} L_{kj} p(\mathbf{x}/c_k) P(c_k) \tag{12-18}$$

Given an unknown pattern, the classifier has N_c possible classes from which to choose. If the classifier computes $r_1(\mathbf{x}), r_2(\mathbf{x}), ..., r_{N_c}(\mathbf{x})$ for each pattern $\mathbf{x}$ and assigns the pattern to the class with the smallest loss, the total average loss with respect to all decisions will be minimum. The classifier that minimizes the total average loss is called the *Bayes classifier*. This classifier assigns an unknown pattern $\mathbf{x}$ to class c_i if $r_i(\mathbf{x}) < r_j(\mathbf{x})$ for $j = 1, 2, ..., N_c$; $j \neq i$. In other words, $\mathbf{x}$ is assigned to class c_i if

$$\sum_{k=1}^{N_c} L_{ki} p(\mathbf{x}/c_k) P(c_k) < \sum_{q=1}^{N_c} L_{qj} p(\mathbf{x}/c_q) P(c_q) \tag{12-19}$$

for all j; $j \neq i$. The loss for a correct decision generally is assigned a value of 0, and the loss for any incorrect decision usually is assigned a value of 1. Then, the loss function becomes

$$L_{ij} = 1 - \delta_{ij} \tag{12-20}$$

where $\delta_{ij} = 1$ if $i = j$, and $\delta_{ij} = 0$ if $i \neq j$. Equation (12-20) indicates a loss of unity for incorrect decisions and a loss of zero for correct decisions. Substituting Eq. (12-20) into Eq. (12-18) yields

$$
\begin{aligned}
r_j(\mathbf{x}) &= \sum_{k=1}^{N_c} \left(1 - \delta_{kj}\right) p\left(\mathbf{x}/c_k\right) P\left(c_k\right) \\
&= p(\mathbf{x}) - p\left(\mathbf{x}/c_j\right) P\left(c_j\right)
\end{aligned}
\tag{12-21}
$$

The Bayes classifier then assigns a pattern $\mathbf{x}$ to class c_i if, for all $j \neq i$,

$$p(\mathbf{x}) - p\left(\mathbf{x}/c_i\right) P\left(c_i\right) < p(\mathbf{x}) - p\left(\mathbf{x}/c_j\right) P\left(c_j\right) \tag{12-22}$$

or, equivalently, if

$$p\left(\mathbf{x}/c_i\right) P\left(c_i\right) > p\left(\mathbf{x}/c_j\right) P\left(c_j\right) \quad j = 1, 2, \ldots, N_c; \ j \neq i \tag{12-23}$$

Thus, the Bayes classifier for a 0-1 loss function computes *decision functions* of the form

$$d_j(\mathbf{x}) = p\left(\mathbf{x}/c_j\right) P\left(c_j\right) \quad j = 1, 2, \ldots, N_c \tag{12-24}$$

and assigns a pattern to class c_i if $d_i(x) > d_j(x)$ for all $j \neq i$. This is exactly the same process described in Eq. (12-5), but we are now dealing with decision functions that have been shown to be optimal in the sense that they minimize the average loss in misclassification.

For the optimality of Bayes decision functions to hold, the probability density functions of the patterns in each class, as well as the probability of occurrence of each class, must be known. The latter requirement usually is not a problem. For instance, if all classes are equally likely to occur, then $P(c_j) = 1/N_c$. Even if this condition is not true, these probabilities generally can be inferred from knowledge of the problem. Estimating the probability density functions $p(\mathbf{x}/c_j)$ is more difficult. If the pattern vectors are n-dimensional, then $p(\mathbf{x}/c_j)$ is a function of n variables. If the form of $p(\mathbf{x}/c_j)$ is not known, estimating it requires using multivariate estimation methods. These methods are difficult to apply in practice, especially if the number of representative patterns from each class is not large, or if the probability density functions are not well behaved. For these reasons, uses of the Bayes classifier often are based on assuming an analytic expression for the density functions. This in turn reduces the problem to one of estimating the necessary parameters from sample patterns from each class using training patterns. By far, the most prevalent form assumed for $p(\mathbf{x}/c_j)$ is the Gaussian probability density function. The closer this assumption is to reality, the closer the Bayes classifier approaches the minimum average loss in classification.

BAYES CLASSIFIER FOR GAUSSIAN PATTERN CLASSES

You may find it helpful to review the tutorial on probability available in the book website.

To begin, let us consider a 1-D problem ($n = 1$) involving two pattern classes ($N_c = 2$) governed by Gaussian densities, with means m_1 and m_2, and standard deviations σ_1 and σ_2, respectively. From Eq. (12-24) the Bayes decision functions have the form

$$d_j(x) = p(x/c_j)P(c_j)$$

$$= \frac{1}{\sqrt{2\pi}\sigma_j} e^{-\frac{(x - m_j)^2}{2\sigma_j^2}} P(c_j) \qquad j = 1, 2 \tag{12-25}$$

where the patterns are now scalars, denoted by x. Figure 12.19 shows a plot of the probability density functions for the two classes. The boundary between the two classes is a single point, x_0, such that $d_1(x_0) = d_2(x_0)$. If the two classes are equally likely to occur, then $P(c_1) = P(c_2) = 1/2$, and the decision boundary is the value of x_0 for which $p(x_0/c_1) = p(x_0/c_2)$. This point is the intersection of the two probability density functions, as shown in Fig. 12.19. Any pattern (point) to the right of x_0 is classified as belonging to class c_1. Similarly, any pattern to the left of x_0 is classified as belonging to class c_2. When the classes are not equally likely to occur, x_0 moves to the left if class c_1 is more likely to occur or, conversely, it moves to the right if class c_2 is more likely to occur. This result is to be expected, because the classifier is trying to minimize the loss of misclassification. For instance, in the extreme case, if class c_2 never occurs, the classifier would never make a mistake by always assigning all patterns to class c_1 (that is, x_0 would move to negative infinity).

In the n-dimensional case, the Gaussian density of the vectors in the jth pattern class has the form

$$p(\mathbf{x}/c_j) = \frac{1}{(2\pi)^{n/2}|\mathbf{C}_j|^{1/2}} e^{-\frac{1}{2}(\mathbf{x} - \mathbf{m}_j)^T \mathbf{C}_j^{-1}(\mathbf{x} - \mathbf{m}_j)} \tag{12-26}$$

where each density is specified completely by its mean vector $\mathbf{m}_j$ and covariance matrix $\mathbf{C}_j$, which are defined as

FIGURE 12.19
Probability density functions for two 1-D pattern classes. Point x_0 (at the intersection of the two curves) is the Bayes decision boundary if the two classes are equally likely to occur.

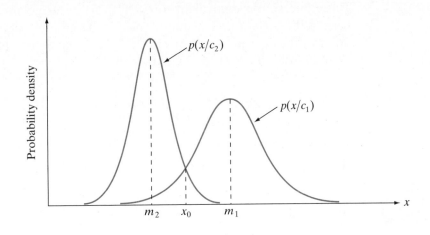

$$\mathbf{m}_j = E_j\{\mathbf{x}\} \tag{12-27}$$

and

$$\mathbf{C}_j = E_j\left\{\left(\mathbf{x} - \mathbf{m}_j\right)\left(\mathbf{x} - \mathbf{m}_j\right)^T\right\} \tag{12-28}$$

where $E_j\{\cdot\}$ is the expected value of the argument over the patterns of class c_j. In Eq. (12-26), n is the dimensionality of the pattern vectors, and $|\mathbf{C}_j|$ is the determinant of matrix $\mathbf{C}_j$. Approximating the expected value E_j by the sample average yields an estimate of the mean vector and covariance matrix:

$$\mathbf{m}_j = \frac{1}{n_j} \sum_{\mathbf{x} \in c_j} \mathbf{x} \tag{12-29}$$

and

$$\mathbf{C}_j = \frac{1}{n_j} \sum_{\mathbf{x} \in c_j} \mathbf{x}\mathbf{x}^T - \mathbf{m}_j\mathbf{m}_j^T \tag{12-30}$$

where n_j is the number of sample pattern vectors from class c_j and the summation is taken over these vectors. We will give an example later in this section of how to use these two expressions.

The covariance matrix is symmetric and positive semidefinite. Its kth diagonal element is the variance of the kth element of the pattern vectors. The kjth off-diagonal matrix element is the covariance of elements x_k and x_j in these vectors. The multivariate Gaussian density function reduces to the product of the univariate Gaussian density of each element of $\mathbf{x}$ when the off-diagonal elements of the covariance matrix are zero, which happens when the vector elements x_k and x_j are uncorrelated.

From Eq. (12-24), the Bayes decision function for class c_j is $d_j(\mathbf{x}) = p(\mathbf{x}/c_j)P(c_j)$. However, the exponential form of the Gaussian density allows us to work with the natural logarithm of this decision function, which is more convenient. In other words, we can use the form

$$\begin{aligned} d_j(\mathbf{x}) &= \ln\left[p\left(\mathbf{x}/c_j\right)P\left(c_j\right)\right] \\ &= \ln p\left(\mathbf{x}/c_j\right) + \ln P\left(c_j\right) \end{aligned} \tag{12-31}$$

This expression is equivalent to Eq. (12-24) in terms of classification performance because the logarithm is a monotonically increasing function. That is, the numerical order of the decision functions in Eqs. (12-24) and (12-31) is the same. Substituting Eq. (12-26) into Eq. (12-31) yields

As noted in Section 6.7 [see Eq. (6-49)], the square root of the rightmost term in this equation is called the *Mahalanobis distance*.

$$d_j(\mathbf{x}) = \ln P\left(c_j\right) - \frac{n}{2}\ln 2\pi - \frac{1}{2}\ln|\mathbf{C}_j| - \frac{1}{2}\left[\left(\mathbf{x} - \mathbf{m}_j\right)^T \mathbf{C}_j^{-1}\left(\mathbf{x} - \mathbf{m}_j\right)\right] \tag{12-32}$$

The term $(n/2)\ln 2\pi$ is the same for all classes, so it can be eliminated from Eq. (12-32), which then becomes

$$d_j(\mathbf{x}) = \ln P\left(c_j\right) - \frac{1}{2}\ln|\mathbf{C}_j| - \frac{1}{2}\left[\left(\mathbf{x} - \mathbf{m}_j\right)^T \mathbf{C}_j^{-1}\left(\mathbf{x} - \mathbf{m}_j\right)\right] \tag{12-33}$$

for $j = 1, 2, ..., N_c$. This equation gives the Bayes decision functions for Gaussian pattern classes under the condition of a 0-1 loss function.

The decision functions in Eq. (12-33) are hyperquadrics (quadratic functions in n-dimensional space), because no terms higher than the second degree in the components of $\mathbf{x}$ appear in the equation. Clearly, then, the best that a Bayes classifier for Gaussian patterns can do is to place a second-order decision boundary between each pair of pattern classes. If the pattern populations are truly Gaussian, no other boundary would yield a lesser average loss in classification.

If all covariance matrices are equal, then $\mathbf{C}_j = \mathbf{C}$ for $j = 1, 2, ..., N_c$. By expanding Eq. (12-33), and dropping all terms that do not depend on j, we obtain

$$d_j(\mathbf{x}) = \ln P(c_j) + \mathbf{x}^T \mathbf{C}^{-1} \mathbf{m}_j - \frac{1}{2} \mathbf{m}_j^T \mathbf{C}^{-1} \mathbf{m}_j \qquad (12\text{-}34)$$

which are linear decision functions (hyperplanes) for $j = 1, 2, ..., N_c$.

If, in addition, $\mathbf{C} = \mathbf{I}$, where $\mathbf{I}$ is the identity matrix, and also if the classes are equally likely (i.e., $P(c_j) = 1/N_c$ for all j), then we can drop the term $\ln P(c_j)$ because it would be the same for all values of j. Equation (12-34) then becomes

$$d_j(\mathbf{x}) = \mathbf{m}_j^T \mathbf{x} - \frac{1}{2} \mathbf{m}_j^T \mathbf{m}_j \qquad j = 1, 2, ..., N_c \qquad (12\text{-}35)$$

which we recognize as the decision functions for a minimum-distance classifier [see Eq. (12-4)]. Thus, as mentioned earlier, the minimum-distance classifier is optimum in the Bayes sense if (1) the pattern classes follow a Gaussian distribution, (2) all covariance matrices are equal to the identity matrix, and (3) all classes are equally likely to occur. Gaussian pattern classes satisfying these conditions are spherical clouds of identical shape in n dimensions (called *hyperspheres*). The minimum-distance classifier establishes a hyperplane between every pair of classes, with the property that the hyperplane is the perpendicular bisector of the line segment joining the center of the pair of hyperspheres. In 2-D, the patterns are distributed in circular regions, and the boundaries become lines that bisect the line segment joining the center of every pair of such circles.

EXAMPLE 12.5: A Bayes classifier for 3-D patterns.

We illustrate the mechanics of the preceding development using the simple patterns in Fig. 12.20. We assume that the patterns are samples from two Gaussian populations, and that the classes are equally likely to occur. Applying Eq. (12-29) to the patterns in the figure results in

$$\mathbf{m}_1 = \frac{1}{3}\begin{bmatrix} 3 \\ 1 \\ 1 \end{bmatrix} \quad \text{and} \quad \mathbf{m}_2 = \frac{1}{3}\begin{bmatrix} 1 \\ 3 \\ 3 \end{bmatrix}$$

And, from Eq. (12-30),

FIGURE 12.20
Two simple
pattern classes
and the portion
of their Bayes
decision bound-
ary (shaded) that
intersects the
cube.

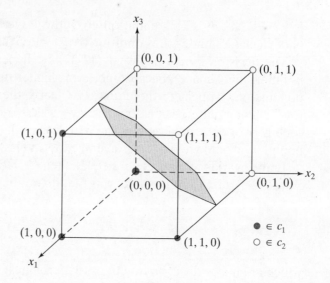

$$\mathbf{C}_1 = \mathbf{C}_2 = \frac{1}{16}\begin{bmatrix} 3 & 1 & 1 \\ 1 & 3 & -1 \\ 1 & -1 & 3 \end{bmatrix}$$

The inverse of this matrix is

$$\mathbf{C}_1^{-1} = \mathbf{C}_2^{-1} = \begin{bmatrix} 8 & -4 & -4 \\ -4 & 8 & 4 \\ -4 & 4 & 8 \end{bmatrix}$$

Next, we obtain the decision functions. Equation (12-34) applies because the covariance matrices are equal, and we are assuming that the classes are equally likely:

$$d_j(\mathbf{x}) = \mathbf{x}^T \mathbf{C}^{-1} \mathbf{m}_j - \frac{1}{2} \mathbf{m}_j^T \mathbf{C}^{-1} \mathbf{m}_j$$

Carrying out the vector-matrix expansion, we obtain the two decision functions:

$$d_1(\mathbf{x}) = 4x_1 - 1.5 \quad \text{and} \quad d_2(\mathbf{x}) = -4x_1 + 8x_2 + 8x_3 - 5.5$$

The decision boundary separating the two classes is then

$$d_1(\mathbf{x}) - d_2(\mathbf{x}) = 8x_1 - 8x_2 - 8x_3 + 4 = 0$$

Figure 12.20 shows a section of this planar surface. Note that the classes were separated effectively.

EXAMPLE 12.6: Classification of multispectral data using a Bayes classifier.

As discussed in Sections 1.3 and 11.5, a multispectral scanner responds to selected bands of the electromagnetic energy spectrum, such as the bands: 0.45–0.52, 0.53–0.61, 0.63–0.69, and 0.78–0.90 microns. These ranges are in the visible blue, visible green, visible red, and near infrared bands, respectively. A region on the ground scanned using these multispectral bands produces four digital images of the region, one for each band. If the images are registered spatially, they can be visualized as being stacked one behind the other, as illustrated in Fig. 12.7. As we explained in that figure, every point on the ground in this example can be represented by a 4-D pattern vector of the form $\mathbf{x} = (x_1, x_2, x_3, x_4)^T$, where x_1 is a shade of blue, x_2 a shade of green, and so on. If the images are of size 512×512 pixels, each stack of four multispectral images can be represented by 266,144 four-dimensional pattern vectors. As noted previously, the Bayes classifier for Gaussian patterns requires estimates of the mean vector and covariance matrix for each class. In remote sensing applications, these estimates are obtained using training multispectral data whose classes are known from each region of interest (this knowledge sometimes is referred to as *ground truth*). The resulting vectors are then used to estimate the required mean vectors and covariance matrices, as in Example 12.5.

Figures 12.21(a) through (d) show four 512×512 multispectral images of the Washington, D.C. area, taken in the bands mentioned in the previous paragraph. We are interested in classifying the pixels in these images into one of three pattern classes: *water*, *urban development*, or *vegetation*. The masks in Fig. 12.21(e) were superimposed on the images to extract samples representative of these three classes. Half of the samples were used for training (i.e., for estimating the mean vectors and covariance matrices), and the other half were used for independent testing to assess classifier performance. We assume that the a priori probabilities are equal, $P(c_j) = 1/3$; $j = 1, 2, 3$.

Table 12.1 summarizes the classification results we obtained with the training and test data sets. The percentage of training and test pattern vectors recognized correctly was about the same with both data sets, indicating that the learned parameters did not over-fit the parameters to the training data. The largest error in both cases was with patterns from the urban area. This is not unexpected, as vegetation is present there also (note that no patterns in the vegetation or urban areas were misclassified as water). Figure 12.21(f) shows as black dots the training and test patterns that were misclassified, and as white dots the patterns that were classified correctly. No black dots are visible in region 1, because the seven misclassified points are very close to the boundary of the white region. You can compute from the numbers in the table that the correct recognition rate was 96.4% for the training patterns, and 96.1% for the test patterns.

Figures 12.21(g) through (i) are more interesting. Here, we let the system classify *all* image pixels into one of the three categories. Figure 12.21(g) shows in white all pixels that were classified as water. Pixels not classified as water are shown in black. We see that the Bayes classifier did an excellent job of determining which parts of the image were water. Figure 12.21(h) shows in white all pixels classified as urban development; observe how well the system performed in recognizing urban features, such as the bridges and highways. Figure 12.21(i) shows the pixels classified as vegetation. The center area in Fig. 12.21(h) shows a high concentration of white pixels in the downtown area, with the density decreasing as a function of distance from the center of the image. Figure 12.21(i) shows the opposite effect, indicating the least vegetation toward the center of the image, where urban development is the densest.

We mentioned in Section 10.3 when discussing Otsu's method that thresholding may be viewed as a Bayes classification problem, which optimally assigns patterns to two or more classes. In fact, as the previous example shows, pixel-by-pixel classification may be viewed as a segmentation that partitions an image into two or more possible types of regions. If only one single variable (e.g., intensity) is used, then Eq. (12-24) becomes an optimum function that similarly partitions an image based on the intensity of its pixels, as we did in Section 10.3. Keep in mind that optimality requires that the PDF and a priori probability of each class be known. As we

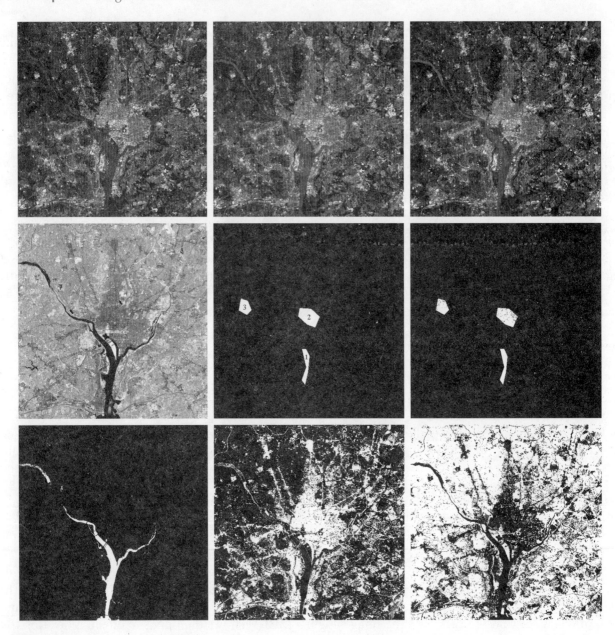

a b c
d e f
g h i

FIGURE 12.21 Bayes classification of multispectral data. (a)–(d) Images in the visible blue, visible green, visible red, and near infrared wavelength bands. (e) Masks for regions of water (labeled 1), urban development (labeled 2), and vegetation (labeled 3). (f) Results of classification; the black dots denote points classified incorrectly. The other (white) points were classified correctly. (g) All image pixels classified as water (in white). (h) All image pixels classified as urban development (in white). (i) All image pixels classified as vegetation (in white).

TABLE 12.1
Bayes classification of multispectral image data. Classes 1, 2, and 3 are water, urban, and vegetation, respectively.

	Training Patterns					Test Patterns				
Class	No. of Samples	Classified into Class			% Correct	Class	No. of Samples	Classified into Class			% Correct
		1	**2**	**3**				**1**	**2**	**3**	
1	484	482	2	0	99.6	1	483	478	3	2	98.9
2	933	0	885	48	94.9	2	932	0	880	52	94.4
3	483	0	19	464	96.1	3	482	0	16	466	96.7

have mentioned previously, estimating these densities is not a trivial task. If assumptions have to be made (e.g., as in assuming Gaussian densities), then the degree of optimality achieved in classification depends on how close the assumptions are to reality.

12.5 NEURAL NETWORKS AND DEEP LEARNING

The principal objectives of the material in this section and in Section 12.6 are to present an introduction to deep neural networks, and to derive the equations that are the foundation of deep learning. We will discuss two types of networks. In this section, we focus attention on multilayer, fully connected neural networks, whose inputs are pattern vectors of the form introduced in Section 12.2. In Section 12.6, we will discuss convolutional neural networks, which are capable of accepting images as inputs. We follow the same basic approach in presenting the material in these two sections. That is, we begin by developing the equations that describe how an input is mapped through the networks to generate the outputs that are used to classify that input. Then, we derive the equations of backpropagation, which are the tools used to train both types of networks. We give examples in both sections that illustrate the power of deep neural networks and deep learning for solving complex pattern classification problems.

BACKGROUND

The essence of the material that follows is the use of a multitude of elemental nonlinear computing elements (called *artificial neurons*), organized as networks whose interconnections are similar in some respects to the way in which neurons are interconnected in the visual cortex of mammals. The resulting models are referred to by various names, including *neural networks, neurocomputers, parallel distributed processing models, neuromorphic systems, layered self-adaptive networks*, and *connectionist models*. Here, we use the name *neural networks*, or *neural nets* for short. We use these networks as vehicles for adaptively learning the parameters of decision functions via successive presentations of training patterns.

Interest in neural networks dates back to the early 1940s, as exemplified by the work of McCulloch and Pitts [1943], who proposed neuron models in the form of binary thresholding devices, and stochastic algorithms involving sudden 0–1 and 1–0 changes of states, as the basis for modeling neural systems. Subsequent work by Hebb [1949] was based on mathematical models that attempted to capture the concept of learning by reinforcement or association.

During the mid-1950s and early 1960s, a class of so-called *learning machines* originated by Rosenblatt [1959, 1962] caused a great deal of excitement among researchers and practitioners of pattern recognition. The reason for the interest in these machines, called *perceptrons*, was the development of mathematical proofs showing that perceptrons, when trained with linearly separable training sets (i.e., training sets separable by a hyperplane), would converge to a solution in a finite number of iterative steps. The solution took the form of parameters (coefficients) of hyperplanes that were capable of correctly separating the classes represented by patterns of the training set.

Unfortunately, the expectations following discovery of what appeared to be a well-founded theoretical model of learning soon met with disappointment. The basic perceptron, and some of its generalizations, were inadequate for most pattern recognition tasks of practical significance. Subsequent attempts to extend the power of perceptron-like machines by considering multiple layers of these devices lacked effective training algorithms, such as those that had created interest in the perceptron itself. The state of the field of learning machines in the mid-1960s was summarized by Nilsson [1965]. A few years later, Minsky and Papert [1969] presented a discouraging analysis of the limitation of perceptron-like machines. This view was held as late as the mid-1980s, as evidenced by comments made by Simon [1986]. In this work, originally published in French in 1984, Simon dismisses the perceptron under the heading "Birth and Death of a Myth."

More recent results by Rumelhart, Hinton, and Williams [1986] dealing with the development of new training algorithms for multilayers of perceptron-like units have changed matters considerably. Their basic method, called *backpropagation* (*backprop* for short), provides an effective training method for multilayer networks. Although this training algorithm cannot be shown to converge to a solution in the sense of the proof for the single-layer perceptron, backpropagation is capable of generating results that have revolutionized the field of pattern recognition.

The approaches to pattern recognition we have studied up to this point rely on human-engineered techniques to transform raw data into formats suitable for computer processing. The methods of feature extraction we studied in Chapter 11 are examples of this. Unlike these approaches, neural networks can use backpropagation to automatically learn representations suitable for recognition, starting with raw data. Each layer in the network "refines" the representation into more abstract levels. This type of multilayered learning is commonly referred to as *deep learning*, and this capability is one of the underlying reasons why applications of neural networks have been so successful. As we noted at the beginning of this section, practical implementations of deep learning generally are associated with large data sets.

Of course, these are not "magical" systems that assemble themselves. Human intervention is still required for specifying parameters such as the number of layers, the number of artificial neurons per layer, and various coefficients that are problem dependent. Teaching proper recognition to a complex multilayer neural network is not a science; rather, it is an art that requires considerable knowledge and experimentation on the part of the designer. Countless applications of pattern recognition, especially in constrained environments, are best handled by more "traditional" methods. A good example of this is stylized font recognition. It would be senseless to develop a neural network to recognize the E-13B font we studied in Fig. 12.11. A minimum-distance classifier implemented on a hard-wired architecture is the ideal solution to this problem, provided that interest is limited to reading only the E-13B font printed on bank checks. On the other hand, neural networks have proved to be the ideal solution if the scope of application is expanded to require that all relevant text written on checks, including cursive script, be read with high accuracy.

Deep learning has shined in applications that defy other methods of solution. In the two decades following the introduction of backpropagation, neural networks have been used successfully in a broad range of applications. Some of them, such as speech recognition, have become an integral part of everyday life. When you speak into a smart phone, the nearly flawless recognition is performed by a neural network. This type of performance was unachievable just a few years ago. Other applications from which you benefit, perhaps without realizing it, are smart filters that learn user preferences for rerouting spam and other junk mail from email accounts, and the systems that read zip codes on postal mail. Often, you see television clips of vehicles navigating autonomously, and robots that are capable of interacting with their environment. Most are solutions based on neural networks. Less familiar applications include the automated discovery of new medicines, the prediction of gene mutations in DNA research, and advances in natural language understanding.

Although the list of practical uses of neural nets is long, applications of this technology in image pattern classification has been slower in gaining popularity. As you will learn shortly, using neural nets in image processing is based principally on neural network architectures called *convolutional neural nets* (denoted by *CNNs* or *ConvNets*). One of the earliest well-known applications of CNNs is the work of LeCun et al. [1989] for reading handwritten U.S. postal zip codes. A number of other applications followed shortly thereafter, but it was not until the results of the 2012 ImageNet Challenge were published (e.g., see Krizhevsky, Sutskever, and Hinton [2012]) that CNNs became widely used in image pattern recognition. Today, this is the approach of choice for addressing complex image recognition tasks.

The neural network literature is vast and rapidly evolving, so as usual, our approach is to focus on fundamentals. In this and the following sections, we will establish the foundation of how neural nets are trained, and how they operate after training. We will begin by briefly discussing perceptrons. Although these computing elements are not used per se in current neural network architectures, the operations they perform are almost identical to artificial neurons, which are the basic computing units of neural nets. In fact, an introduction to neural networks would be incomplete without a discussion of perceptrons. We will follow this discussion by developing in detail the theoretical foundation of backpropagation. After developing the basic backpropagation equations, we will recast them in matrix form, which reduces the training and operation of neural nets to a simple, straightforward cascade of matrix multiplications.

After studying several examples of fully connected neural nets, we will follow a similar approach in developing the foundation of CNNs, including how they differ from fully connected neural nets, and how their training is different. This is followed by several examples of how CNNs are used for image pattern classification.

THE PERCEPTRON

A single perceptron unit learns a linear boundary between two linearly separable pattern classes. Figure 12.22(a) shows the simplest possible example in two dimensions: two pattern classes, consisting of a single pattern each. A linear boundary in 2-D is a straight line with equation $y = ax + b$, where coefficient a is the *slope* and b is the *y-intercept*. Note that if $b = 0$, the line goes through the origin. Therefore, the function of parameter b is to displace the line from the origin without affecting its slope. For this reason, this "floating" coefficient that is not multiplied by a coordinate is often referred to as the *bias*, the *bias coefficient*, or the *bias weight*.

We are interested in a line that separates the two classes in Fig. 12.22. This is a line positioned in such a way that pattern (x_1, y_1) from class c_1 lies on one side of the line, and pattern (x_2, y_2) from class c_2 lies on the other. The locus of points (x, y) that are *on* the line, satisfy the equation $y - ax - b = 0$. It then follows that any point on one side of the line would yield a positive value when its coordinates are plugged into this equation, and conversely for a point on the other side.

Generally, we work with patterns in much higher dimensions than two, so we need more general notation. Points in n dimensions are vectors. The components of a vector, $x_1, x_2, \ldots, x_n$, are the coordinates of the point. For the coefficients of the boundary separating the two classes, we use the notation $w_1, w_2, \ldots, w_n, w_{n+1}$, where w_{n+1} is the bias. The general equation of our line using this notation is $w_1 x_1 + w_2 x_2 + w_3 = 0$ (we can express this equation in slope-intercept form as $x_2 + (w_1/w_2)x_1 + w_3/w_2 = 0$). Figure 12.22(b) is the same as (a), but using this notation. Comparing the two figures, we see that $y = x_2$, $x = x_1$, $a = w_1/w_2$, and $b = w_3/w_2$. Equipped with our more

FIGURE 12.22
(a) The simplest two-class example in 2-D, showing one possible decision boundary out of an infinite number of such boundaries.
(b) Same as (a), but with the decision boundary expressed using more general notation.

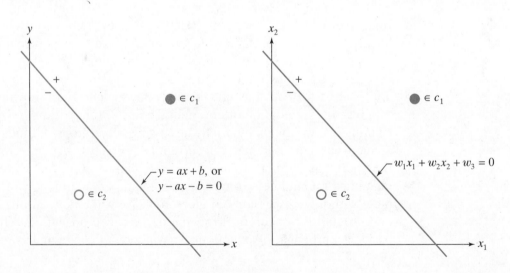

general notation, we say that an arbitrary point (x_1, x_2) is on the positive side of a line if $w_1 x_1 + w_2 x_2 + w_3 > 0$, and conversely for any point on the negative side. For points in 3-D, we work with the equation of a plane, $w_1 x_1 + w_2 x_2 + w_3 x_3 + w_4 = 0$, but would perform exactly the same test to see if a point lies on the positive or negative side of the plane. For a point in n dimensions, the test would be against a *hyperplane*, whose equation is

$$w_1 x_1 + w_2 x_2 + \cdots + w_n x_n + w_{n+1} = 0 \tag{12-36}$$

This equation is expressed in summation form as

$$\sum_{i=1}^{n} w_i x_i + w_{n+1} = 0 \tag{12-37}$$

or in vector form as

$$\boldsymbol{w}^T \mathbf{x} + w_{n+1} = 0 \tag{12-38}$$

where $\boldsymbol{w}$ and $\mathbf{x}$ are n-dimensional *column* vectors and $\boldsymbol{w}^T \mathbf{x}$ is the dot (inner) product of the two vectors. Because the inner product is commutative, we can express Eq. (12-38) in the equivalent form $\mathbf{x}^T \boldsymbol{w} + w_{n+1} = 0$. We refer to $\boldsymbol{w}$ as a *weight vector* and, as above, to w_{n+1} as a *bias*. Because the bias is a weight that is always multiplied by 1, sometimes we avoid repetition by using the term *weights, coefficients, or parameters* when referring to the bias and the elements of a weight vector collectively.

Stating the class separation problem in general form we say that, given any pattern vector $\mathbf{x}$ from a vector population, we want to find a set of weights with the property

It is customary to associate > with class c_1 and < with class c_2, but the sense of the inequality is arbitrary, provided that you are consistent. Note that this equation implements a *linear decision function*.

$$\boldsymbol{w}^T \mathbf{x} + w_{n+1} = \begin{cases} > 0 & \text{if } \mathbf{x} \in c_1 \\ < 0 & \text{if } \mathbf{x} \in c_2 \end{cases} \tag{12-39}$$

Linearly separable classes satisfy Eq. (12-39). That is, they are separable by single hyperplanes.

Finding a line that separates two *linearly separable* pattern classes in 2-D can be done by inspection. Finding a separating plane by visual inspection of 3-D data is more difficult, but it is doable. For $n > 3$, finding a separating hyperplane by inspection becomes impossible in general. We have to resort instead to an algorithm to find a solution. The perceptron is an implementation of such an algorithm. It attempts to find a solution by iteratively stepping through the patterns of each of two classes. It starts with an arbitrary weight vector and bias, and is guaranteed to converge in a finite number of iterations if the classes are linearly separable.

The perceptron algorithm is simple. Let $\alpha > 0$ denote a *correction increment* (also called the *learning increment* or the *learning rate*), let $\boldsymbol{w}(1)$ be a vector with arbitrary values, and let $w_{n+1}(1)$ be an arbitrary constant. Then, do the following for $k = 2, 3, \ldots$: For a pattern vector, $\mathbf{x}(k)$, at step k,

1) If $\mathbf{x}(k) \in c_1$ and $\boldsymbol{w}^T(k)\mathbf{x}(k) + w_{n+1}(k) \leq 0$, let

$$\boldsymbol{w}(k+1) = \boldsymbol{w}(k) + \alpha \mathbf{x}(k)$$
$$\omega_{n+1}(k+1) = \omega_{n+1}(k) + \alpha \tag{12-40}$$

2) If $\mathbf{x}(k) \in c_2$ and $\boldsymbol{w}^T(k)\mathbf{x}(k) + w_{n+1}(k) \geq 0$, let

$$
\begin{aligned}
\boldsymbol{w}(k+1) &= \boldsymbol{w}(k) - \alpha\mathbf{x}(k) \\
\omega_{n+1}(k+1) &= \omega_{n+1}(k) - \alpha
\end{aligned}
$$

(12-41)

3) Otherwise, let

$$
\begin{aligned}
\boldsymbol{w}(k+1) &= \boldsymbol{w}(k) \\
\omega_{n+1}(k+1) &= \omega_{n+1}(k)
\end{aligned}
$$

(12-42)

The correction in Eq. (12-40) is applied when the pattern is from class c_1 and Eq. (12-39) does not give a positive response. Similarly, the correction in Eq. (12-41) is applied when the pattern is from class c_2 and Eq. (12-39) does not give a negative response. As Eq. (12-42) shows, no change is made when Eq. (12-39) gives the correct response.

The notation in Eqs. (12-40) through (12-42) can be simplified if we add a 1 at the end of every pattern vector and include the bias in the weight vector. That is, we define $\mathbf{x} \triangleq [x_1, x_2, \dots, x_n, 1]^T$ and $\boldsymbol{w} \triangleq [w_1, w_2, \dots, w_n, w_{n+1}]^T$. Then, Eq. (12-39) becomes

$$
\boldsymbol{w}^T\mathbf{x} = \begin{cases} > 0 & \text{if } \mathbf{x} \in c_1 \\ < 0 & \text{if } \mathbf{x} \in c_2 \end{cases}
$$

(12-43)

where both vectors are now $(n+1)$-dimensional. In this formulation, $\mathbf{x}$ and $\boldsymbol{w}$ are referred to as *augmented* pattern and weight vectors, respectively. The algorithm in Eqs. (12-40) through (12-42) then becomes: For any pattern vector, $\mathbf{x}(k)$, at step k

1′) If $\mathbf{x}(k) \in c_1$ and $\boldsymbol{w}^T(k)\mathbf{x}(k) \leq 0$, let

$$
\boldsymbol{w}(k+1) = \boldsymbol{w}(k) + \alpha\mathbf{x}(k)
$$

(12-44)

2′) If $\mathbf{x}(k) \in c_2$ and $\boldsymbol{w}^T(k)\mathbf{x}(k) \geq 0$, let

$$
\boldsymbol{w}(k+1) = \boldsymbol{w}(k) - \alpha\mathbf{x}(k)
$$

(12-45)

3′) Otherwise, let

$$
\boldsymbol{w}(k+1) = \boldsymbol{w}(k)
$$

(12-46)

where the starting weight vector, $\boldsymbol{w}(1)$, is arbitrary and, as above, α is a positive constant. The procedure implemented by Eqs. (12-40)–(12-42) or (12-44)–(12-46) is called the *perceptron training algorithm*. The *perceptron convergence theorem* states that the algorithm is guaranteed to converge to a solution (i.e., a separating hyperplane) in a finite number of steps if the two pattern classes are linearly separable (see Problem 12.15). Normally, Eqs. (12-44)–(12-46) are the basis for implementing the perceptron training algorithm, and we will use it in the following paragraphs of this section. However, the notation in Eqs. (12-40)–(12-42), in which the bias is

FIGURE 12.23
Schematic of a perceptron, showing the operations it performs.

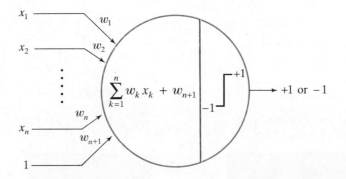

shown separately, is more prevalent in neural networks, so you need to be familiar with it as well.

Figure 12.23 shows a schematic diagram of the perceptron. As you can see, all this simple "machine" does is form a *sum of products* of an input pattern using the weights and bias found during training. The output of this operation is a scalar value that is then passed through an *activation function* to produce the unit's output. For the perceptron, the activation function is a thresholding function (we will consider other forms of activation when we discuss neural networks). If the thresholded output is a +1, we say that the pattern belongs to class c_1. Otherwise, a −1 indicates that the pattern belongs to class c_2. Values 1 and 0 sometimes are used to denote the two possible states of the output.

Note that the perceptron model implements Eq. (12-39), which is in the form of a decision function.

EXAMPLE 12.7: Using the perceptron algorithm to learn a decision boundary.

We illustrate the steps taken by a perceptron in learning the coefficients of a linear boundary by solving the mini problem in Fig. 12.22. To simplify manual computations, let the pattern vector furthest from the origin be $\mathbf{x} = [3\ 3\ 1]^T$, and the other be $\mathbf{x} = [1\ 1\ 1]^T$, where we augmented the vectors by appending a 1 at the end, as discussed earlier. To match the figure, let these two patterns belong to classes c_1 and c_2, respectively. Also, assume the patterns are "cycled" through the perceptron in that order during training (one complete iteration through all patterns of the training is called an *epoch*). To start, we let $\alpha = 1$ and $\boldsymbol{w}(1) = \mathbf{0} = [0\ 0\ 0]^T$; then,

For $k = 1$, $\mathbf{x}(1) = [3\ 3\ 1]^T \in c_1$, and $\boldsymbol{w}(1) = [0\ 0\ 0]^T$. Their inner product is zero,

$$\boldsymbol{w}^T(1)\mathbf{x}(1) = \begin{bmatrix} 0 & 0 & 0 \end{bmatrix} \begin{bmatrix} 3 \\ 3 \\ 1 \end{bmatrix} = 0$$

so Step 1′ of the second version of the training algorithm applies:

$$\boldsymbol{w}(2) = \boldsymbol{w}(1) + \alpha\mathbf{x}(1) = \begin{bmatrix} 0 \\ 0 \\ 0 \end{bmatrix} + (1)\begin{bmatrix} 3 \\ 3 \\ 1 \end{bmatrix} = \begin{bmatrix} 3 \\ 3 \\ 1 \end{bmatrix}$$

For $k = 2$, $\mathbf{x}(2) = [1\ 1\ 1]^T \in c_2$ and $\boldsymbol{w}(2) = [3\ 3\ 1]^T$. Their inner product is

$$w^T(2)\mathbf{x}(2) = \begin{bmatrix} 3 & 3 & 1 \end{bmatrix} \begin{bmatrix} 1 \\ 1 \\ 1 \end{bmatrix} = 7$$

The result is positive when it should have been negative, so Step 2' applies:

$$w(3) = w(2) - \alpha\mathbf{x}(2) = \begin{bmatrix} 3 \\ 3 \\ 1 \end{bmatrix} - (1)\begin{bmatrix} 1 \\ 1 \\ 1 \end{bmatrix} = \begin{bmatrix} 2 \\ 2 \\ 0 \end{bmatrix}$$

We have gone through a complete training epoch with at least one correction, so we cycle through the training set again.

For $k = 3$, $\mathbf{x}(3) = [3\ 3\ 1]^T \in c_1$, and $w(3) = [2\ 2\ 0]^T$. Their inner product is positive (i.e., 6) as it should be because $\mathbf{x}(3) \in c_1$. Therefore, Step 3' applies and the weight vector is not changed:

$$w(4) = w(3) = \begin{bmatrix} 2 \\ 2 \\ 0 \end{bmatrix}$$

For $k = 4$, $\mathbf{x}(4) = [1\ 1\ 1]^T \in c_2$, and $w(4) = [2\ 2\ 0]^T$. Their inner product is positive (i.e., 4) and it should have been negative, so Step 2' applies:

$$w(5) = w(4) - \alpha\mathbf{x}(4) = \begin{bmatrix} 2 \\ 2 \\ 0 \end{bmatrix} - (1)\begin{bmatrix} 1 \\ 1 \\ 1 \end{bmatrix} = \begin{bmatrix} 1 \\ 1 \\ -1 \end{bmatrix}$$

At least one correction was made, so we cycle through the training patterns again. For $k = 5$, we have $\mathbf{x}(5) = [3\ 3\ 1]^T \in c_1$, and, using $w(5)$, we compute their inner product to be 5. This is positive as it should be, so Step 3' applies and we let $w(6) = w(5) = [1\ 1\ -1]^T$. Following this procedure just discussed, you can show (see Problem 12.13) that the algorithm converges to the solution weight vector

$$w = w(12) = \begin{bmatrix} 1 \\ 1 \\ -3 \end{bmatrix}$$

which gives the decision boundary

$$x_1 + x_2 - 3 = 0$$

Figure 12.24(a) shows the boundary defined by this equation. As you can see, it clearly separates the patterns of the two classes. In terms of the terminology we used in the previous section, the *decision surface* learned by the perceptron is $d(\mathbf{x}) = d(x_1, x_2) = x_1 + x_2 - 3$, which is a plane. As before, the *decision boundary* is the locus of points such that $d(\mathbf{x}) = d(x_1, x_2) = 0$, which is a line. Another way to visualize this boundary is that it is the intersection of the decision surface (a plane) with the $x_1 x_2$-plane, as Fig. 12.24(b) shows. All points (x_1, x_2) such that $d(x_1, x_2) > 0$ are on the positive side of the boundary, and vice versa for $d(x_1, x_2) < 0$.

FIGURE 12.24
(a) Segment of the decision boundary learned by the perceptron algorithm.
(b) Section of the decision surface. The decision boundary is the intersection of the decision surface with the x_1x_2-plane.

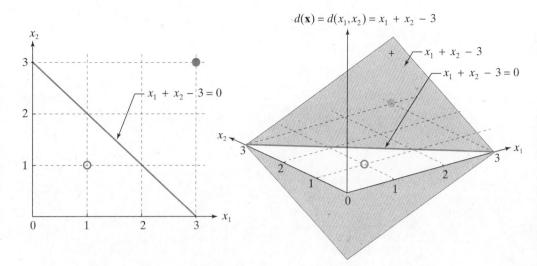

EXAMPLE 12.8: Using the perceptron to classify two sets of iris data measurements.

In Fig. 12.10 we showed a reduced set of the iris database in two dimensions, and mentioned that the only class that was separable from the others is the class of Iris setosa. As another illustration of the perceptron, we now find the full decision boundary between the Iris setosa and the Iris versicolor classes. As we mentioned when discussing Fig. 12.10, these are 4-D data sets. Letting $\alpha = 0.5$, and starting with all parameters equal to zero, the perceptron converged in only four epochs to the solution weight vector $\boldsymbol{w} = [0.65,\ 2.05,\ -2.60,\ -1.10,\ 0.50]^T$, where the last element is w_{n+1}.

In practice, linearly separable pattern classes are rare, and a significant amount of research effort during the 1960s and 1970s went into developing techniques for dealing with nonseparable pattern classes. With recent advances in neural networks, many of those methods have become items of mere historical interest, and we will not dwell on them here. However, we mention briefly one approach because it is relevant to the discussion of neural networks in the next section. The method is based on minimizing the error between the actual and desired response at any training step.

Let r denote the response we want the perceptron to have for any pattern during training. The output of our perceptron is either +1 or −1, so these are the two possible values that r can have. We want to find the augmented weight vector, $\boldsymbol{w}$, that minimizes the mean squared error (MSE) between the desired and actual responses of the perceptron. The function should be differentiable and have a unique minimum. The function of choice for this purpose is a quadratic of the form

The 1/2 is used to cancel out the 2 that will result from taking the derivative of this expression. Also, remember that $\boldsymbol{w}^T\mathbf{x}$ is a scalar.

$$E(\boldsymbol{w}) = \frac{1}{2}\left(r - \boldsymbol{w}^T\mathbf{x}\right)^2 \tag{12-47}$$

where E is our error measure, $\boldsymbol{w}$ is the weight vector we are seeking, $\mathbf{x}$ is any pattern from the training set, and r is the response we desire for that pattern. Both $\boldsymbol{w}$ and $\mathbf{x}$ are augmented vectors.

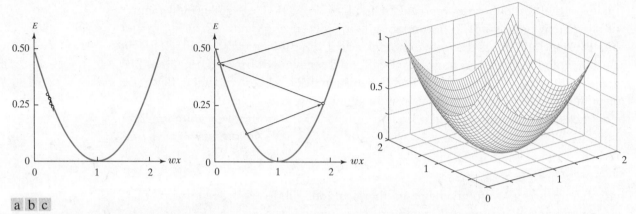

FIGURE 12.25 Plots of E as a function of wx for $r = 1$. (a) A value of α that is too small can slow down convergence. (b) If α is too large, large oscillations or divergence may occur. (c) Shape of the error function in 2-D.

We find the minimum of $E(\boldsymbol{w})$ using an iterative gradient descent algorithm, whose form is

Note that the right side of this equation is the gradient of $E(\boldsymbol{w})$.

$$\boldsymbol{w}(k+1) = \boldsymbol{w}(k) - \alpha \left[\frac{\partial E(\boldsymbol{w})}{\partial \boldsymbol{w}} \right]_{\boldsymbol{w}=\boldsymbol{w}(k)} \qquad (12\text{-}48)$$

where the starting weight vector is arbitrary, and $\alpha > 0$.

Figure 12.25(a) shows a plot of E for scalar values, w and x, of $\boldsymbol{w}$ and $\mathbf{x}$. We want to move w incrementally so $E(w)$ approaches a minimum, which implies that E should stop changing or, equivalently, that $\partial E(w)/\partial w = 0$. Equation (12-48) does precisely this. If $\partial E(w)/\partial w > 0$, a portion of this quantity (determined by the value of the learning increment α) is subtracted from $w(k)$ to create a new, updated value $w(k+1)$, of the weight. The opposite happens if $\partial E(w)/\partial w < 0$. If $\partial E(w)/\partial w = 0$, the weight is unchanged, meaning that we have arrived at a minimum, which is the solution we are seeking. The value of α determines the relative magnitude of the correction in weight value. If α is too small, the step changes will be correspondingly small and the weight would move slowly toward convergence, as Fig. 12.25(a) illustrates. On the other hand, choosing α too large could cause large oscillations on either side of the minimum, or even become unstable, as Fig. 12.25(b) illustrates. There is no general rule for choosing α. However, a logical approach is to start small and experiment by increasing α to determine its influence on a particular set of training patterns. Figure 12.25(c) shows the shape of the error function for two variables.

Because the error function is given analytically and it is differentiable, we can express Eq. (12-48) in a form that does not require computing the gradient explicitly at every step. The partial of $E(\boldsymbol{w})$ with respect to $\boldsymbol{w}$ is

$$\frac{\partial E(\boldsymbol{w})}{\partial \boldsymbol{w}} = -\left(r - \boldsymbol{w}^T \mathbf{x} \right) \mathbf{x} \qquad (12\text{-}49)$$

Substituting this result into Eq. (12-48) yields

$$\boldsymbol{w}(k+1) = \boldsymbol{w}(k) + \alpha\Big[r(k) - \boldsymbol{w}^{T}(k)\mathbf{x}(k)\Big]\mathbf{x}(k) \qquad (12\text{-}50)$$

which is in terms of known or easily computable terms. As before, $\boldsymbol{w}(1)$ is arbitrary.

Widrow and Stearns [1985] have shown that it is necessary (but not sufficient) for α to be in the range $0 < \alpha < 2$ for the algorithm in Eq. (12-50) to converge. A typical range for α is $0.1 < \alpha < 1.0$. Although the proof is not shown here, the algorithm converges to a solution that minimizes the mean squared error over the patterns of the training set. For this reason, the algorithm is often referred to as the *least-mean-squared-error* (LMSE) algorithm. In practice, we say that the algorithm has converged when the error decreases below a specified threshold. The solution at convergence may not be a hyperplane that fully partitions two linearly separable classes. That is, a mean-square-error solution does not imply a solution in the sense of the perceptron training theorem. This uncertainty is the price of using an algorithm whose convergence is independent of the linear separability of the pattern classes.

EXAMPLE 12.9: Using the LMSE algorithm.

It will be interesting to compare the performance of the LMSE algorithm using the same set of separable iris data as in Example 12.8. Figure 12.26(a) is a plot of the error [Eq. (12-47)] as a function of epoch for 50 epochs, using Eq. (12-50) (with $\alpha = 0.001$) to obtain the weights (we started with $\boldsymbol{w}(1) = \mathbf{0}$). Each epoch of training consisted of sequentially updating the weights, one pattern at a time, and computing Eq. (12-47) for each weight and the corresponding pattern. At the end of the epoch, the errors were added and divided by 100 (the total number of patterns) to obtain the mean squared error (MSE). This yielded one point of the curve of Fig. 12.26(a). After increasing and then decreasing rapidly, no appreciable difference in error occurred after about 20 epochs. For example, the error at the end of the 50th epoch was 0.02 and, at the end of 1,000 epochs, it was 0.0192. Getting smaller error values is possible by further decreasing α, but at the expense of slower decay in the error, as noted in Fig. 12.25. Keep in mind also that MSE is not directly proportional to correct recognition rate.

a b

FIGURE 12.26
MSE as a function of epoch for:
(a) the linearly separable Iris classes (setosa and versicolor); and (b) the linearly nonseparable Iris classes (versicolor and virginica).

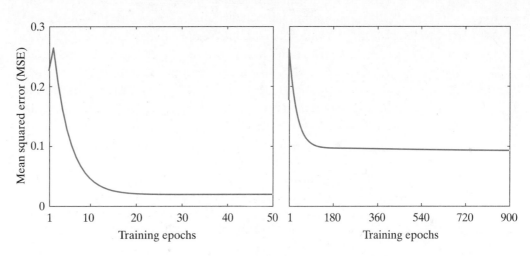

The weight vector at the end of 50 epochs of training was $\boldsymbol{w} = [0.098\ 0.357 - 0.548 - 0.255\ 0.075]^T$. All patterns were classified correctly into their two respective classes using this vector. That is, although the MSE did not become zero, the resulting weight vector was able to classify all the patterns correctly. But keep in mind that the LMSE algorithm does not always achieve 100% correct recognition of linearly separable classes.

As noted earlier, only the Iris setosa samples are linearly separable from the others. But the Iris versicolor and virginica samples are not. The perceptron algorithm would not converge when presented with these data, whereas the LMSE algorithm does. Figure 12.26(b) is the MSE as a function of training epoch for these two data sets, obtained using the same values for $\boldsymbol{w}(1)$ and α as in (a). This time, it took 900 epochs for the MSE to stabilize at 0.09, which is much higher than before. The resulting weight vector was $\boldsymbol{w} = [0.534\ 0.584 - 0.878 - 1.028\ 0.651]^T$. Using this vector resulted in seven misclassification errors out of 100 patterns, giving a recognition rate of 93%.

A classic example used to show the limitations of single linear decision boundaries (and hence single perceptron units) is the XOR classification problem. The table in Fig. 12.27(a) shows the definition of the XOR operator for two variables. As you can see, the XOR operation produces a logical true (1) value when either of the variables (but not both) is true; otherwise, the result is false (0). The XOR two-class pattern classification problem is set up by letting each pair of values A and B be a point in 2-D space, and letting the true (1) XOR values define one class, and the false (0) values define the other. In this case, we assigned the class c_1 label to patterns $\{(0,0),(1,1)\}$, and the c_2 label to patterns $\{(1,0),(0,1)\}$. A classifier capable of solving the XOR problem must respond with a value, say, 1, when a pattern from class c_1 is presented, and a different value, say, 0 or -1, when the input pattern is from class c_2. You can tell by inspection of Fig. 12.27(b) that a single linear decision boundary (a straight line) cannot separate the two classes correctly. This means that we cannot solve the problem with a single perceptron. The simplest linear boundary consists of two straight lines, as Fig. 12.27(b) shows. A more complex, nonlinear, boundary capable of solving the problem is a quadratic function, as in Fig. 12.27(c).

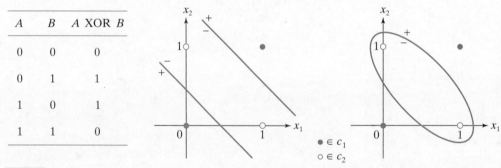

A	B	A XOR B
0	0	0
0	1	1
1	0	1
1	1	0

a b c

FIGURE 12.27 The XOR classification problem in 2-D. (a) Truth table definition of the XOR operator. (b) 2-D pattern classes formed by assigning the XOR truth values (1) to one pattern class, and false values (0) to another. The simplest decision boundary between the two classes consists of two straight lines. (c) Nonlinear (quadratic) boundary separating the two classes.

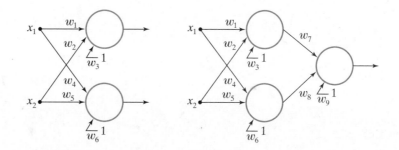

FIGURE 12.28
(a) Minimum perceptron solution to the XOR problem in 2-D. (b) A solution that implements the XOR truth table in Fig. 12.27(a).

Natural questions at this point are: Can more than one perceptron solve the XOR problem? If so, what is the minimum number of units required? We know that a single perceptron can implement one straight line, and we need to implement two lines, so the obvious answers are: yes to the first question, and two units to the second. Figure 12.28(a) shows the solution for two variables, which requires a total of six coefficients because we need two lines. The solution coefficients are such that, for either of the two patterns from class c_1, one output is true (1) and the other is false (0). The opposite condition must hold for either pattern from class c_2. This solution requires that we analyze two outputs. If we want to implement the truth table, meaning that a single output should give the same response as the XOR function [the third column in Fig. 12.27(a)], then we need one additional perceptron. Figure 12.28(b) shows the architecture for this solution. Here, one perceptron in the first layer maps any input from one class into a 1, and the other perceptron maps a pattern from the other class into a 0. This reduces the four possible inputs into two outputs, which is a two-point problem. As you know from Fig. 12.24, a single perceptron can solve this problem. Therefore, we need three perceptrons to implement the XOR table, as in Fig. 12.28(b).

With a little work, we could determine by inspection the coefficients needed to implement either solution in Fig. 12.28. However, rather than dwell on that, we focus attention in the following section on a more general, layered architecture, of which the XOR solution is a trivial, special case.

MULTILAYER FEEDFORWARD NEURAL NETWORKS

In this section, we discuss the architecture and operation of multilayer neural networks, and derive the equations of backpropagation used to train them. We then give several examples illustrating the capabilities of neural nets

Model of an Artificial Neuron

Neural networks are interconnected perceptron-like computing elements called *artificial neurons*. These neurons perform the same computations as the perceptron, but they differ from the latter in how they process the result of the computations. As illustrated in Fig. 12.23, the perceptron uses a "hard" thresholding function that outputs two values, such as +1 and −1, to perform classification. Suppose that in a network of perceptrons, the output before thresholding of one of the perceptrons is infinitesimally greater than zero. When thresholded, this very small signal will be turned into a +1. But a similarly small signal with the opposite sign would cause

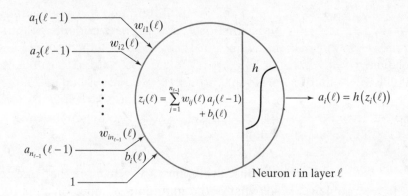

$$a_i(\ell) = h\big(z_i(\ell)\big)$$

a large swing in value from +1 to −1. Neural networks are formed from layers of computing units, in which the output of one unit affects the behavior of all units following it. The perceptron's sensitivity to the sign of small signals can cause serious stability problems in an interconnected system of such units, making perceptrons unsuitable for layered architectures.

The solution is to change the characteristic of the activation function from a hard-limiter to a smooth function. Figure 12.29 shows an example based on using the activation function

$$h(z) = \frac{1}{1 + e^{-z}} \tag{12-51}$$

where z is the result of the computation performed by the neuron, as shown in Fig. 12.29. Except for more complicated notation, and the use of a smooth function rather than a hard threshold, this model performs the same *sum-of-products* operations as in Eq. (12-36) for the perceptron. Note that the *bias* term is denoted by b instead

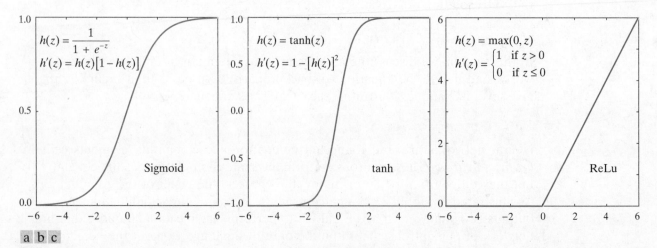

a b c

FIGURE 12.30 Various activation functions. (a) Sigmoid. (b) Hyperbolic tangent (also has a sigmoid shape, but it is centered about 0 in both dimensions). (c) Rectifier linear unit (ReLU).

of w_{n+1}, as we do the perceptron. It is customary to use different notation, typically b, in neural networks to denote the bias term, so we are following convention. The more complicated notation used in Fig. 12.29, which we will explain shortly, is needed because we will be dealing with multilayer arrangements with several neurons per layer. We use the symbol "ℓ" to denote layers.

As you can see by comparing Figs. 12.29 and 12.23, we use variable z to denote the sum-of-products computed by the neuron. The output of the unit, denoted by a, is obtained by passing z through h. We call h the *activation function*, and refer to its output, $a = h(z)$, as the *activation value* of the unit. Note in Fig. 12.29 that the inputs to a neuron are activation values from neurons in the previous layer. Figure 12.30(a) shows a plot of $h(z)$ from Eq. (12-51). Because this function has the shape of a sigmoid function, the unit in Fig. 12.29 is sometimes called an *artificial sigmoid neuron*, or simply a *sigmoid neuron*. Its derivative has a very nice form, expressible in terms of $h(z)$ [see Problem 12.16(a)]:

$$h'(z) = \frac{\partial h(z)}{\partial z} = h(z)\big[1 - h(z)\big] \qquad (12\text{-}52)$$

Figures 12.30(b) and (c) show two other forms of $h(z)$ used frequently. The hyperbolic tangent also has the shape of a sigmoid function, but it is symmetric about both axes. This property can help improve the convergence of the backpropagation algorithm to be discussed later. The function in Fig. 12.30(c) is called the *rectifier function*, and a unit using it is referred to a *rectifier linear unit* (ReLU). Often, you see the function itself referred to as the ReLU *activation function*. Experimental results suggest that this function tends to outperform the other two in deep neural networks.

Interconnecting Neurons to Form a Fully Connected Neural Network

Figure 12.31 shows a generic diagram of a multilayer neural network. A *layer* in the network is the set of nodes (neurons) in a column of the network. As indicated by the zoomed node in Fig. 12.31, all the nodes in the network are artificial neurons of the form shown in Fig. 12.29, except for the input layer, whose nodes are the components of an input pattern vector **x**. Therefore, the outputs (activation values) of the first layer are the values of the elements of **x**. The outputs of all other nodes are the activation values of neurons in a particular layer. Each layer in the network can have a different number of nodes, but each node has a *single* output. The multiple lines shown at the outputs of the neurons in Fig. 12.31 indicate that the output of every node is connected to the input of all nodes in the next layer, to form a *fully connected* network. We also require that there be no loops in the network. Such networks are called *feedforward networks*. Fully connected, feedforward neural nets are the only types of networks considered in this section.

We obviously know the values of the nodes in the first layer, and we can observe the values of the output neurons. All others are *hidden neurons,* and the layers that contain them are called *hidden layers*. Generally, we call a neural net with a single hidden layer a *shallow neural network*, and refer to network with two or more hidden layers as a *deep neural network*. However, this terminology is not universal, and

FIGURE 12.31
General model
of a feedforward,
fully connected
neural net. The
neuron is the
same as in
Fig. 12.29. Note
how the output of
each neuron goes
to the input of all
neurons in the
following layer,
hence the name
fully connected
for this type of
architecture.

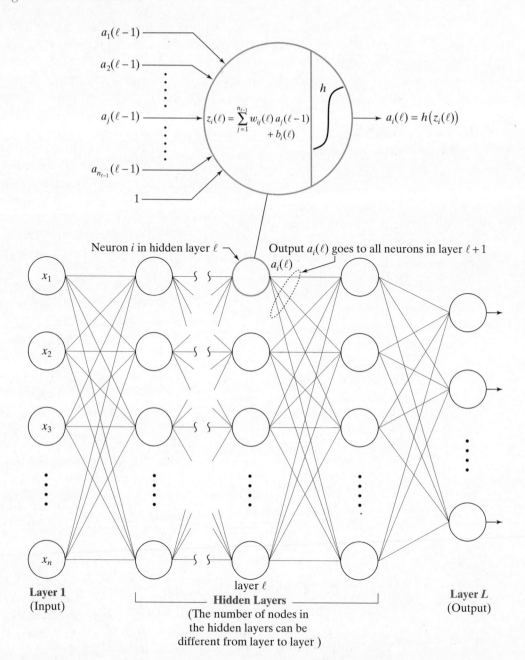

sometimes you will see the words "shallow" and "deep" used subjectively to denote
networks with a "few" and with "many" layers, respectively.

We used the notation in Eq. (12-37) to label all the inputs and weights of a perceptron. In a neural network, the notation is more complicated because we have to
account for neuron weights, inputs, and outputs within a layer, and also from layer
to layer. Ignoring layer notation for a moment, we denote by w_{ij} the weight that
associates the link connecting the *output* of neuron j to the input of neuron i. That is,

the first subscript denotes the neuron that *receives* the signal, and the second refers to the neuron that *sends* the signal. Because i precedes j alphabetically, it would seem to make more sense for i to send and for j to receive. The reason we use the notation as stated is to avoid a matrix transposition in the equation that describes propagation of signals through the network. This notation is convention, but there is no doubt that it is confusing, so special care is necessary to keep the notation straight.

Remember, a bias is a weight that is always multiplied by 1.

Because the biases depend only on the neuron containing it, a single subscript that associates a bias with a neuron is sufficient. For example, we use b_i to denote the bias value associated with the ith neuron in a given layer of the network. Our use of b instead of w_{n+1} (as we did for perceptrons) follows notational convention used in neural networks. The weights, biases, and activation function(s) completely define a neural network. Although the activation function of any neuron in a neural network could be different from the others, there is no convincing evidence to suggest that there is anything to be gained by doing so. We assume in all subsequent discussions that the same form of activation function is used in all neurons.

Let ℓ denote a layer in the network, for $\ell = 1, 2, \ldots, L$. With reference to Fig. 12.31, $\ell = 1$ denotes the input layer, $\ell = L$ is the output layer, and all other values of ℓ denote hidden layers. The number of neurons in layer ℓ is denoted n_ℓ. We have two options to include layer indexing in the parameters of a neural network. We can do it as a superscript, for example, w_{ij}^ℓ and b_i^ℓ; or we can use the notation $w_{ij}(\ell)$ and $b_i(\ell)$. The first option is more prevalent in the literature on neural network. We use the second option because it is more consistent with the way we describe iterative expressions in the book, and also because you may find it easier to follow. Using this notation, the output (activation value) of neuron k in layer ℓ is denoted $a_k(\ell)$.

Keep in mind that our objective in using neural networks is the same as for perceptrons: to determine the class membership of unknown input patterns. The most common way to perform pattern classification using a neural network is to assign a class label to each output neuron. Thus, a neural network with n_L outputs can classify an unknown pattern into one of n_L classes. The network assigns an unknown pattern vector $\mathbf{x}$ to class c_k if output neuron k has the largest activation value; that is, if $a_k(L) > a_j(L)$, $j = 1, 2, \ldots, n_L$; $j \neq k$.[†]

In this and the following section, the number of outputs of our neural networks will always equal the number of classes. But this is not a requirement. For instance, a network for classifying two pattern classes could be structured with a single output (Problem 12.17 illustrates such a case) because all we need for this task is two states, and a single neuron is capable of that. For three and four classes, we need three and four states, respectively, which can be achieved with two output neurons. Of course, the problem with this approach is that we would need additional logic to decipher the output combinations. It is simply more practical to have one neuron per output, and let the neuron with the highest output value determine the class of the input.

[†] Instead of a sigmoid or similar function in the final output layer, you will sometimes see a *softmax function* used instead. The concept is the same as we explained earlier, but the activation values in a softmax implementation are given by $a_i(L) = \exp[z_i(L)]/\sum_k \exp[z_i(L)]$, where the summation is over all outputs. In this formulation, the sum of all activations is 1, thus giving the outputs a probabilistic interpretation.

FORWARD PASS THROUGH A FEEDFORWARD NEURAL NETWORK

A *forward pass* through a neural network maps the input layer (i.e., values of **x**) to the output layer. The values in the output layer are used for determining the class of an input vector. The equations developed in this section explain how a feedforward neural network carries out the computations that result in its output. Implicit in the discussion in this section is that the network parameters (weights and biases) are known. The important results in this section will be summarized in Table 12.2 at the end of our discussion, but understanding the material that gets us there is important when we discuss training of neural nets in the next section.

The Equations of a Forward Pass

The outputs of the layer 1 are the components of input vector **x**:

$$a_j(1) = x_j \qquad j = 1, 2, \dots, n_1 \tag{12-53}$$

where $n_1 = n$ is the dimensionality of **x**. As illustrated in Figs. 12.29 and 12.31, the computation performed by neuron i in layer ℓ is given by

$$z_i(\ell) = \sum_{j=1}^{n_{\ell-1}} w_{ij}(\ell) a_j(\ell-1) + b_i(\ell) \tag{12-54}$$

for $i = 1, 2, \dots, n_\ell$ and $\ell = 2, \dots, L$. Quantity $z_i(\ell)$ is called the *net* (or *total*) *input* to neuron i in layer ℓ, and is sometimes denoted by net_i. The reason for this terminology is that $z_i(\ell)$ is formed using *all* outputs from layer $\ell - 1$. The output (activation value) of neuron i in layer ℓ is given by

$$a_i(\ell) = h\big(z_i(\ell)\big) \qquad i = 1, 2, \dots, n_\ell \tag{12-55}$$

where h is an activation function. The value of network *output* node i is

$$a_i(L) = h\big(z_i(L)\big) \qquad i = 1, 2, \dots, n_L \tag{12-56}$$

Equations (12-53) through (12-56) describe all the operations required to map the input of a fully connected feedforward network to its output.

EXAMPLE 12.10: Illustration of a forward pass through a fully connected neural network.

It will be helpful to consider a simple numerical example. Figure 12.32 shows a three-layer neural network consisting of the input layer, one hidden layer, and the output layer. The network accepts three inputs, and has two outputs. Thus, this network is capable of classifying 3-D patterns into one of two classes.

The numbers shown above the arrow heads on each input to a node are the weights of that node associated with the outputs from the nodes in the preceding layer. Similarly, the number shown in the output of each node is the activation value, a, of that node. As noted earlier, there is only one output value for each node, but it is routed to the input of every node in the next layer. The inputs associated with the 1's are bias values.

Let us look at the computations performed at each node, starting with the first (top) node in layer 2. We use Eq. (12-54) to compute the net input, $z_1(2)$, for that node:

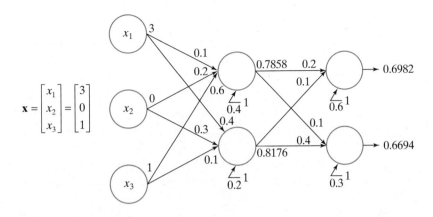

FIGURE 12.32
A small, fully connected, feedforward net with labeled weights, biases, and outputs. The activation function is a sigmoid.

$$z_1(2) = \sum_{j=1}^{3} w_{1j}(2)a_j(1) + b_1(2) = (0.1)(3) + (0.2)(0) + (0.6)(1) + 0.4 = 1.3$$

We obtain the output of this node using Eqs. (12-51) and (12-55):

$$a_1(2) = h(z_1(2)) = \frac{1}{1 + e^{-1.3}} = 0.7858$$

A similar computation gives the value for the output of the second node in the second layer,

$$z_2(2) = \sum_{j=1}^{3} w_{2j}(2)a_j(1) + b_2(2) = (0.4)(3) + (0.3)(0) + (0.1)(1) + 0.2 = 1.5$$

and

$$a_2(2) = h(z_2(2)) = \frac{1}{1 + e^{-1.5}} = 0.8176$$

We use the outputs of the nodes in layer 2 to obtain the net values of the neurons in layer 3:

$$z_1(3) = \sum_{j=1}^{2} w_{1j}(3)a_j(2) + b_1(3) = (0.2)(0.7858) + (0.1)(0.8176) + 0.6 = 0.8389$$

The output of this neuron is

$$a_1(3) = h(z_1(3)) = \frac{1}{1 + e^{-0.8389}} = 0.6982$$

Similarly,

$$z_2(3) = \sum_{j=1}^{2} w_{2j}(3)a_j(2) + b_2(3) = (0.1)(0.7858) + (0.4)(0.8176) + 0.3 = 0.7056$$

and

$$a_2(3) = h(z_2(2)) = \frac{1}{1 + e^{-0.7056}} = 0.6694$$

If we were using this network to classify the input, we would say that pattern $\mathbf{x}$ belongs to class c_1 because $a_1(L) > a_2(L)$, where $L = 3$ and $n_L = 2$ in this case.

Matrix Formulation

The details of the preceding example reveal that there are numerous individual computations involved in a pass through a neural network. If you wrote a computer program to automate the steps we just discussed, you would find the code to be very inefficient because of all the required loop computations, the numerous node and layer indexing you would need, and so forth. We can develop a more elegant (and computationally faster) implementation by using matrix operations. This means writing Eqs. (12-53) through (12-55) as follows.

First, note that the number of outputs in layer 1 is always of the same dimension as an input pattern, $\mathbf{x}$, so its matrix (vector) form is simple:

$$\mathbf{a}(1) = \mathbf{x} \tag{12-57}$$

Next, we look at Eq. (12-54). We know that the summation term is just the inner product of two vectors [see Eqs. (12-37) and (12-38)]. However, this equation has to be evaluated for all nodes in every layer past the first. This implies that a loop is required if we do the computations node by node. The solution is to form a matrix, $\mathbf{W}(\ell)$, that contains *all* the weights in layer ℓ. The structure of this matrix is simple — each of its *rows* contains the weights for one of the nodes in layer ℓ :

With reference to our earlier discussion on the order of the subscripts i and j, if we had let i be the sending node and j the receiver, this matrix would have to be transposed.

$$\mathbf{W}(\ell) = \begin{bmatrix} w_{11}(\ell) & w_{12}(\ell) & \cdots & w_{1n_{\ell-1}}(\ell) \\ w_{21}(\ell) & w_{22}(\ell) & \cdots & w_{2n_{\ell-1}}(\ell) \\ \vdots & \vdots & \cdots & \\ w_{n_\ell 1}(\ell) & w_{n_\ell 2}(\ell) & \cdots & w_{n_\ell n_{\ell-1}}(\ell) \end{bmatrix} \tag{12-58}$$

Then, we can obtain all the sum-of-products computations, $z_i(\ell)$, for layer ℓ simultaneously:

$$\mathbf{z}(\ell) = \mathbf{W}(\ell)\mathbf{a}(\ell - 1) + \mathbf{b}(\ell) \qquad \ell = 2, 3, \ldots, L \tag{12-59}$$

where $\mathbf{a}(\ell - 1)$ is a column vector of dimension $n_{\ell-1} \times 1$ containing the outputs of layer $\ell - 1$, $\mathbf{b}(\ell)$ is a column vector of dimension $n_\ell \times 1$ containing the bias values of all the neurons in layer ℓ, and $\mathbf{z}(\ell)$ is an $n_\ell \times 1$ column vector containing the net input values, $z_i(\ell), i = 1, 2, \ldots, n_\ell$, to all the nodes in layer ℓ. You can easily verify that Eq. (12-59) is dimensionally correct.

Because the activation function is applied to each net input independently of the others, the outputs of the network at any layer can be expressed in vector form as:

$$\mathbf{a}(\ell) = h[\mathbf{z}(\ell)] = \begin{bmatrix} h(z_1(\ell)) \\ h(z_2(\ell)) \\ \vdots \\ h(z_{n_\ell}(\ell)) \end{bmatrix} \tag{12-60}$$

Implementing Eqs. (12-57) through (12-60) requires just a series of matrix operations, with no loops.

FIGURE 12.33
Same as Fig. 12.32, but using matrix labeling.

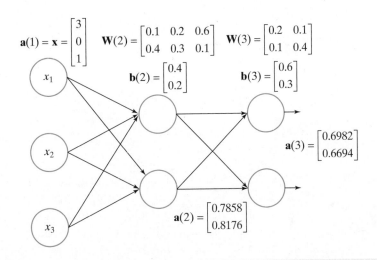

EXAMPLE 12.11: Redoing Example 12.10 using matrix operations.

Figure 12.33 shows the same neural network as in Fig. 12.32, but with all its parameters shown in matrix form. As you can see, the representation in Fig. 12.33 is more compact. Starting with

$$\mathbf{a}(1) = \begin{bmatrix} 3 \\ 0 \\ 1 \end{bmatrix}$$

it follows that

$$\mathbf{z}(2) = \mathbf{W}(2)\mathbf{a}(1) + \mathbf{b}(2) = \begin{bmatrix} 0.1 & 0.2 & 0.6 \\ 0.4 & 0.3 & 0.1 \end{bmatrix} \begin{bmatrix} 3 \\ 0 \\ 1 \end{bmatrix} + \begin{bmatrix} 0.4 \\ 0.2 \end{bmatrix} = \begin{bmatrix} 1.3 \\ 1.5 \end{bmatrix}$$

Then,

$$\mathbf{a}(2) = h[\mathbf{z}(2)] = \begin{bmatrix} h(z_1(2)) \\ h(z_2(2)) \end{bmatrix} = \begin{bmatrix} h(1.3) \\ h(1.5) \end{bmatrix} = \begin{bmatrix} 0.7858 \\ 0.8176 \end{bmatrix}$$

With $\mathbf{a}(2)$ as input to the next layer, we obtain

$$\mathbf{z}(3) = \mathbf{W}(3)\mathbf{a}(2) + \mathbf{b}(3) = \begin{bmatrix} 0.2 & 0.1 \\ 0.1 & 0.4 \end{bmatrix} \begin{bmatrix} 0.7858 \\ 0.8176 \end{bmatrix} + \begin{bmatrix} 0.6 \\ 0.3 \end{bmatrix} = \begin{bmatrix} 0.8389 \\ 0.7056 \end{bmatrix}$$

and, as before,

$$\mathbf{a}(3) = h[\mathbf{z}(3)] = \begin{bmatrix} h(z_1(3)) \\ h(z_2(3)) \end{bmatrix} = \begin{bmatrix} h(0.8389) \\ h(0.7056) \end{bmatrix} = \begin{bmatrix} 0.6982 \\ 0.6694 \end{bmatrix}$$

The clarity of the matrix formulation over the indexed notation used in Example 12.10 is evident.

Equations (12-57) through (12-60) are a significant improvement over node-by-node computations, but they apply only to one pattern. To classify multiple pattern vectors, we would have to loop through each pattern using the same set of matrix equations per loop iteration. What we are after is one set of matrix equations capable of processing *all* patterns in a single forward pass. Extending Eqs. (12-57) through (12-60) to this more general formulation is straightforward. We begin by arranging all our input pattern vectors as *columns* of a single matrix, $\mathbf{X}$, of dimension $n \times n_p$ where, as before, n is the dimensionality of the vectors and n_p is the number of pattern vectors. It follows from Eq. (12-57) that

$$\mathbf{A}(1) = \mathbf{X} \tag{12-61}$$

where each column of matrix $\mathbf{A}(1)$ contains the initial activation values (i.e., the vector values) for one pattern. This is a straightforward extension of Eq. (12-57), except that we are now dealing with an $n \times n_p$ matrix instead of an $n \times 1$ vector.

The parameters of a network do not change because we are processing more pattern vectors, so the weight matrix is as given in Eq. (12-58). This matrix is of size $n_\ell \times n_{\ell-1}$. When $\ell = 2$, we have that $\mathbf{W}(2)$ is of size $n_2 \times n$, because n_1 is always equal to n. Then, extending the product term of Eq. (12-59) to use $\mathbf{A}(2)$ instead of $\mathbf{a}(2)$, results in the matrix product $\mathbf{W}(2)\mathbf{A}(2)$, which is of size $(n_2 \times n)(n \times n_p) = n_2 \times n_p$. To this, we have to add the bias vector for the second layer, which is of size $n_2 \times 1$. Obviously, we cannot add a matrix of size $n_2 \times n_p$ and a vector of size $n_2 \times 1$. However, as is true of the weight matrices, the bias vectors do not change because we are processing more pattern vectors. We just have to account for one identical bias vector, $\mathbf{b}(2)$, per input vector. We do this by creating a matrix $\mathbf{B}(2)$ of size $n_2 \times n_p$, formed by concatenating column vector $\mathbf{b}(2)$ n_p times, horizontally. Then, Eq. (12-59) written in matrix becomes $\mathbf{Z}(2) = \mathbf{W}(2)\mathbf{A}(1) + \mathbf{B}(2)$. Matrix $\mathbf{Z}(2)$ is of size $n_2 \times n_p$; it contains the computation performed by Eq. (12-59), but for *all* input patterns. That is, each column of $\mathbf{Z}(2)$ is exactly the computation performed by Eq. (12-59) for one input pattern.

The concept just discussed applies to the transition from any layer to the next in the neural network, provided that we use the weights and bias appropriate for a particular location in the network. Therefore, the full matrix version of Eq. (12-59) is

$$\mathbf{Z}(\ell) = \mathbf{W}(\ell)\mathbf{A}(\ell - 1) + \mathbf{B}(\ell) \tag{12-62}$$

where $\mathbf{W}(\ell)$ is given by Eq. (12-58) and $\mathbf{B}(\ell)$ is an $n_\ell \times n_p$ matrix whose columns are duplicates of $\mathbf{b}(\ell)$, the bias vector containing the biases of the neurons in layer ℓ.

All that remains is the matrix formulation of the output of layer ℓ. As Eq. (12-60) shows, the activation function is applied independently to each element of the vector $\mathbf{z}(\ell)$. Because each column of $\mathbf{Z}(\ell)$ is simply the application of Eq. (12-60) corresponding to a particular input vector, it follows that

$$\mathbf{A}(\ell) = h\big[\mathbf{Z}(\ell)\big] \tag{12-63}$$

where activation function h is applied to each element of matrix $\mathbf{Z}(\ell)$.

Summarizing the dimensions in our matrix formulation, we have: $\mathbf{X}$ and $\mathbf{A}(1)$ are of size $n \times n_p$, $\mathbf{Z}(\ell)$ is of size $n_\ell \times n_p$, $\mathbf{W}(\ell)$ is of size $n_\ell \times n_{\ell-1}$, $\mathbf{A}(\ell-1)$ is of

TABLE 12.2

Steps in the matrix computation of a forward pass through a fully connected, feedforward multilayer neural net.

Step	Description	Equations
Step 1	Input patterns	$\mathbf{A}(1) = \mathbf{X}$
Step 2	Feedforward	For $\ell = 2, \ldots, L$, compute $\mathbf{Z}(\ell) = \mathbf{W}(\ell)\mathbf{A}(\ell - 1) + \mathbf{B}(\ell)$ and $\mathbf{A}(\ell) = h(\mathbf{Z}(\ell))$
Step 3	Output	$\mathbf{A}(L) = h(\mathbf{Z}(L))$

size $n_{\ell-1} \times n_p$, $\mathbf{B}(\ell)$ is of size $n_\ell \times n_p$, and $\mathbf{A}(\ell)$ is of size $n_\ell \times n_p$. Table 12.2 summarizes the matrix formulation for the forward pass through a fully connected, feedforward neural network for all pattern vectors. Implementing these operations in a matrix-oriented language like MATLAB is a trivial undertaking. Performance can be improved significantly by using dedicated hardware, such as one or more graphics processing units (GPUs).

The equations in Table 12.2 are used to classify each of a set of patterns into one of n_L pattern classes. Each column of output matrix $\mathbf{A}(L)$ contains the activation values of the n_L output neurons for a specific pattern vector. The class membership of that pattern is given by the location of the output neuron with the highest activation value. Of course, this assumes we know the weights and biases of the network. These are obtained during training using backpropagation, as we explain next.

USING BACKPROPAGATION TO TRAIN DEEP NEURAL NETWORKS

A neural network is defined completely by its weights, biases, and activation function. Training a neural network refers to using one or more sets of training patterns to estimate these parameters. During training, we know the desired response of every output neuron of a multilayer neural net. However, we have no way of knowing what the values of the outputs of hidden neurons should be. In this section, we develop the equations of *backpropagation*, the tool of choice for finding the value of the weights and biases in a multilayer network. This *training by backpropagation* involves four basic steps: (1) inputting the pattern vectors; (2) a forward pass through the network to classify all the patterns of the training set and determine the classification error; (3) a backward (backpropagation) pass that feeds the output error back through the network to compute the changes required to update the parameters; and (4) updating the weights and biases in the network. These steps are repeated until the error reaches an acceptable level. We will provide a summary of all principal results derived in this section at the end of the discussion (see Table 12.3). As you will see shortly, the principal mathematical tool needed to derive the equations of backpropagation is the chain rule from basic calculus.

The Equations of Backpropagation

Given a set of training patterns and a multilayer feedforward neural network architecture, the approach in the following discussion is to find the network parameters that minimize an *error* (also called *cost* or *objective*) *function*. Our interest is in classification performance, so we define the error function for a neural network as the average of the differences between desired and actual responses. Let **r** denote the desired response for a given pattern vector, **x**, and let **a**(L) denote the actual response of the network to that input. For example, in a ten-class recognition application, **r** and **a**(L) would be 10-D column vectors. The ten components of **a**(L) would be the ten outputs of the neural network, and the components of **r** would be zero, except for the element corresponding to the class of **x**, which would be 1. For example, if the input training pattern belongs to class 6, the 6th element of **r** would be 1 and the rest would be 0's.

The activation values of neuron j in the output layer is $a_j(L)$. We define the error of that neuron as

$$E_j = \frac{1}{2}\big(r_j - a_j(L)\big)^2 \tag{12-64}$$

for $j = 1, 2, \ldots, n_L$, where r_j is the desired response of output neuron $a_j(L)$ for a given pattern **x**. The output error with respect to a single **x** is the sum of the errors of all output neurons with respect to that vector:

$$E = \sum_{j=1}^{n_L} E_j = \frac{1}{2}\sum_{j=1}^{n_L}\big(r_j - a_j(L)\big)^2$$

$$= \frac{1}{2}\,\|\,\mathbf{r} - \mathbf{a}(L)\,\|^2 \tag{12-65}$$

See Eqs. (2-50) and (2-51) regarding the Euclidean vector norm.

where the second line follows from the definition of the Euclidean vector norm. The *total network output error* over all training patterns is defined as the sum of the errors of the individual patterns. We want to find the weights that minimize this total error. As we did for the LMSE perceptron, we find the solution using gradient descent. However, unlike the perceptron, we have no way for computing the gradients of the weights in the hidden nodes. The beauty of backpropagation is that we can achieve an equivalent result by propagating the output error back into the network.

When the meaning is clear, we sometimes include the bias term in the word "weights."

The key objective is to find a scheme to adjust all weights in a network using training patterns. In order to do this, we need to know how E changes with respect to the weights in the network. The weights are contained in the expression for the net input to each node [see Eq. (12-54)], so the quantity we are after is $\partial E/\partial z_j(\ell)$ where, as defined in Eq. (12-54), $z_j(\ell)$ is the net input to node j in layer ℓ. In order to simplify the notation later, we use the symbol $\delta_j(\ell)$ to denote $\partial E/\partial z_j(\ell)$. Because backpropagation starts with the output and works backward from there, we look first at

We use "j" generically to mean any node in the network. We are not concerned at the moment with inputs to, or outputs from, a node.

$$\delta_j(L) = \frac{\partial E}{\partial z_j(L)} \tag{12-66}$$

We can express this equation in terms of the output $a_j(L)$ using the chain rule:

$$\delta_j(L) = \frac{\partial E}{\partial z_j(L)} = \frac{\partial E}{\partial a_j(L)}\frac{\partial a_j(L)}{\partial z_j(L)} = \frac{\partial E}{\partial a_j(L)}\frac{\partial h\big(z_j(L)\big)}{\partial z_j(L)}$$

$$= \frac{\partial E}{\partial a_j(L)} h'\big(z_j(L)\big) \tag{12-67}$$

where we used Eq. (12-56) to obtain the last expression in the first line. This equation gives us the value of $\delta_j(L)$ in terms of quantities that can be observed or computed. For example, if we use Eq. (12-64) as our error measure, and Eq. (12-52) for $h'\big(z_j(x)\big)$, then

$$\delta_j(L) = h\big(z_j(L)\big)\Big[1 - h\big(z_j(L)\big)\Big]\Big[a_j(L) - r_j\Big] \tag{12-68}$$

where we interchanged the order of the terms. The $h\big(z_j(L)\big)$ are computed in the forward pass, $a_j(L)$ can be observed in the output of the network, and r_j is given along with $\mathbf{x}$ during training. Therefore, we can compute $\delta_j(L)$.

Because the relationship between the net input and the output of any neuron in any layer (except the first) is the same, the form of Eq. (12-66) is valid for any node j in any hidden layer:

$$\delta_j(\ell) = \frac{\partial E}{\partial z_j(\ell)} \tag{12-69}$$

This equation tells us how E changes with respect to a change in the net input to any neuron in the network. What we want to do next is express $\delta_j(\ell)$ in terms of $\delta_j(\ell+1)$. Because we will be proceeding backward in the network, this means that if we have this relationship, then we can start with $\delta_j(L)$ and find $\delta_j(L-1)$. We then use this result to find $\delta_j(L-2)$, and so on until we arrive at layer 2. We obtain the desired expression using the chain rule (see Problem 12.25):

$$\delta_j(\ell) = \frac{\partial E}{\partial z_j(\ell)} = \sum_i \frac{\partial E}{\partial z_i(\ell+1)}\frac{\partial z_i(\ell+1)}{\partial a_j(\ell)}\frac{\partial a_j(\ell)}{\partial z_j(\ell)}$$

$$= \sum_i \delta_i(\ell+1)\frac{\partial z_i(\ell+1)}{\partial a_j(\ell)} h'\big(z_j(\ell)\big) \tag{12-70}$$

$$= h'\big(z_j(\ell)\big)\sum_i w_{ij}(\ell+1)\delta_i(\ell+1)$$

for $\ell = L-1, L-2, \ldots 2$, where we used Eqs. (12-55) and (12-69) to obtain the middle line, and Eq. (12-54), plus some rearranging to obtain the last line.

The preceding development tells us how we can start with the error in the output (which we can compute) and obtain how that error changes as function of the net inputs to every node in the network. This is an intermediate step toward our final objective, which is to obtain expressions for $\partial E/\partial w_{ij}(\ell)$ and $\partial E/\partial b_i(\ell)$ in terms of $\delta_j(\ell) = \partial E/z_j(\ell)$. For this, we use the chain rule again:

$$\frac{\partial E}{\partial w_{ij}(\ell)} = \frac{\partial E}{\partial z_i(\ell)} \frac{\partial z_i(\ell)}{\partial w_{ij}(\ell)}$$

$$= \delta_i(\ell) \frac{\partial z_i(\ell)}{\partial w_{ij}(\ell)} \tag{12-71}$$

$$= a_j(\ell - 1)\delta_i(\ell)$$

where we used Eq. (12-54), Eq. (12-69), and interchanged the order of the results to clarify matrix formulations later in our discussion. Similarly (see Problem 12.26),

$$\frac{\partial E}{\partial b_i(\ell)} = \delta_i(\ell) \tag{12-72}$$

Now we have the rate of change of E with respect to the network weights and biases in terms of quantities we can compute. The last step is to use these results to update the network parameters using gradient descent:

$$w_{ij}(\ell) = w_{ij}(\ell) - \alpha \frac{\partial E(\ell)}{\partial w_{ij}(\ell)}$$

$$= w_{ij}(\ell) - \alpha \delta_i(\ell) a_j(\ell - 1) \tag{12-73}$$

and

$$b_i(\ell) = b_i(\ell) - \alpha \frac{\partial E}{\partial b_i(\ell)}$$

$$= b_i(\ell) - \alpha \delta_i(\ell) \tag{12-74}$$

for $\ell = L - 1, L - 2, \dots 2$, where the a's are computed in the forward pass, and the δ's are computed during backpropagation. As with the perceptron, α is the learning rate constant used in gradient descent. There are numerous approaches that attempt to find optimal learning rates, but ultimately this is a problem-dependent parameter that involves experimenting. A reasonable approach is to start with a small value of α (e.g., 0.01), then experiment with vectors from the training set to determine a suitable value in a given application. Remember, α is used only during training, so it has no effect on post-training operating performance.

Matrix Formulation

As with the equations that describe the forward pass through a neural network, the equations of backpropagation developed in the previous discussion are excellent for describing how the method works at a fundamental level, but they are clumsy when it comes to implementation. In this section, we follow a procedure similar to the one we used for the forward pass to develop the matrix equations for backpropagation.

As before, we arrange all the pattern vectors as columns of matrix $\mathbf{X}$, and package the weights of layer ℓ as matrix $\mathbf{W}(\ell)$. We use $\mathbf{D}(\ell)$ to denote the matrix equivalent of $\boldsymbol{\delta}(\ell)$, the vector containing the errors in layer ℓ. Our first step is to find an expression for $\mathbf{D}(L)$. We begin at the output and proceed backward, as before. From Eq. (12-67),

$$\boldsymbol{\delta}(L) = \begin{bmatrix} \delta_1(L) \\ \delta_2(L) \\ \vdots \\ \delta_{n_L}(L) \end{bmatrix} = \begin{bmatrix} \dfrac{\partial E}{\partial a_1(L)} h'(z_1(L)) \\ \dfrac{\partial E}{\partial a_2(L)} h'(z_2(L)) \\ \vdots \\ \dfrac{\partial E}{\partial a_{n_L}(L)} h'(z_{n_L}(L)) \end{bmatrix} = \begin{bmatrix} \dfrac{\partial E}{\partial a_1(L)} \\ \dfrac{\partial E}{\partial a_2(L)} \\ \vdots \\ \dfrac{\partial E}{\partial a_{n_L}(L)} \end{bmatrix} \odot \begin{bmatrix} h'(z_1(L)) \\ h'(z_2(L)) \\ \vdots \\ h'(z_{n_L}(L)) \end{bmatrix} \qquad (12\text{-}75)$$

where, as defined in Section 2.6, "$\odot$" denotes elementwise multiplication (of two vectors in this case). We can write the vector on the left of this symbol as $\partial E/\partial \mathbf{a}(L)$, and the vector on the right as $h'(\mathbf{z}(L))$. Then, we can write Eq. (12-75) as

$$\boldsymbol{\delta}(L) = \frac{\partial E}{\partial \mathbf{a}(L)} \odot h'(\mathbf{z}(L)) \qquad (12\text{-}76)$$

This $n_L \times 1$ column vector contains the activation values of all the output neurons for *one* pattern vector. The only error function we use in this chapter is a quadratic function, which is given in vector form in Eq. (12-65). The partial of that quadratic function with respect to $\mathbf{a}(L)$ is $(\mathbf{a}(L) - \mathbf{r})$ which, when substituted into Eq. (12-76), gives us

$$\boldsymbol{\delta}(L) = (\mathbf{a}(L) - \mathbf{r}) \odot h'(\mathbf{z}(L)) \qquad (12\text{-}77)$$

Column vector $\boldsymbol{\delta}(L)$ accounts for one pattern vector. To account for *all* n_p patterns simultaneously we form a matrix $\mathbf{D}(\ell)$, whose columns are the $\boldsymbol{\delta}(L)$ from Eq. (12-77), evaluated for a specific pattern vector. This is equivalent to writing Eq. (12-77) directly in matrix form as

$$\mathbf{D}(L) = (\mathbf{A}(L) - \mathbf{R}) \odot h'(\mathbf{Z}(L)) \qquad (12\text{-}78)$$

Each column of $\mathbf{A}(L)$ is the network output for one pattern. Similarly, each column of $\mathbf{R}$ is a binary vector with a 1 in the location corresponding to the class of a particular pattern vector, and 0's elsewhere, as explained earlier. Each column of the difference $(\mathbf{A}(L) - \mathbf{R})$ contains the components of $\|\mathbf{a} - \mathbf{r}\|$. Therefore, squaring the elements of a column, adding them, and dividing by 2 is the same as computing the error measure defined in Eq. (12-65), for one pattern. Adding all the column computations gives an average measure of error for all the patterns. Similarly, the columns of matrix $h'(\mathbf{Z}(L))$ are values of the net inputs to all output neurons, with each column corresponding to one pattern vector. All matrices in Eq. (12-78) are of size $n_L \times n_p$.

Following a similar line of reasoning, we can express Eq. (12-70) in matrix form as

$$\mathbf{D}(\ell) = \left(\mathbf{W}^T(\ell+1)\mathbf{D}(\ell+1)\right) \odot h'\left(\mathbf{Z}(\ell)\right) \qquad (12\text{-}79)$$

It is easily confirmed by dimensional analysis that the matrix $\mathbf{D}(\ell)$ is of size $n_\ell \times n_p$ (see Problem 12.27). Note that Eq. (12-79) uses the weight matrix transposed. This reflects the fact that the inputs to layer ℓ are coming from layer $\ell+1$, because in backpropagation we move in the direction opposite of a forward pass.

We complete the matrix formulation by expressing the weight and bias update equations in matrix form. Considering the weight matrix first, we can tell from Eqs. (12-70) and (12-73) that we are going to need matrices $\mathbf{W}(\ell)$, $\mathbf{D}(\ell)$, and $\mathbf{A}(\ell-1)$. We already know that $\mathbf{W}(\ell)$ is of size $n_\ell \times n_{\ell-1}$ and that $\mathbf{D}(\ell)$ is of size $n_\ell \times n_p$. Each column of matrix $\mathbf{A}(\ell-1)$ is the set of outputs of the neurons in layer $\ell-1$ for one pattern vector. There are n_p patterns, so $\mathbf{A}(\ell-1)$ is of size $n_{\ell-1} \times n_p$. From Eq. (12-73) we infer that $\mathbf{A}$ post-multiplies $\mathbf{D}$, so we are also going to need $\mathbf{A}^T(\ell-1)$, which is of size $n_p \times n_{\ell-1}$. Finally, recall that in a matrix formulation, we construct a matrix $\mathbf{B}(\ell)$ of size $n_\ell \times n_p$ whose columns are copies of vector $\mathbf{b}(\ell)$, which contains all the biases in layer ℓ.

Next, we look at updating the biases. We know from Eq. (12-74) that each element $b_i(\ell)$ of $\mathbf{b}(\ell)$ is updated as $b_i(\ell) = b_i(\ell) - \alpha\delta_i(\ell)$, for $i = 1, 2, \ldots, n_\ell$. Therefore, $\mathbf{b}(\ell) = \mathbf{b}(\ell) - \alpha\boldsymbol{\delta}(\ell)$. But this is for *one* pattern, and the columns of $\mathbf{D}(\ell)$ are the $\boldsymbol{\delta}(\ell)$'s for *all* patterns in the training set. This is handled in a matrix formulation by using the *average* of the columns of $\mathbf{D}(\ell)$ (this is the average error over all patterns) to update $\mathbf{b}(\ell)$.

Putting it all together results in the following two equations for updating the network parameters:

$$\mathbf{W}(\ell) = \mathbf{W}(\ell) - \alpha\mathbf{D}(\ell)\mathbf{A}^T(\ell-1) \qquad (12\text{-}80)$$

and

$$\mathbf{b}(\ell) = \mathbf{b}(\ell) - \alpha\sum_{k=1}^{n_p}\boldsymbol{\delta}_k(\ell) \qquad (12\text{-}81)$$

where $\boldsymbol{\delta}_k(\ell)$ is the kth column of matrix $\mathbf{D}(\ell)$. As before, we form matrix $\mathbf{B}(\ell)$ of size $n_\ell \times n_p$ by concatenating $\mathbf{b}(\ell)$ n_p times in the horizontal direction:

$$\mathbf{B}(\ell) = \underset{n_p \text{ times}}{\text{concatenate}}\{\mathbf{b}(\ell)\} \qquad (12\text{-}82)$$

As we mentioned earlier, backpropagation consists of four principal steps: (1) inputting the patterns, (2) a forward pass, (3) a backpropagation pass, and (4) a parameter update step. The process begins by specifying the initial weights and biases as (small) random numbers. Table 12.3 summarizes the matrix formulations of these four steps. During training, these steps are repeated for a number of specified epochs, or until a predefined measure of error is deemed to be small enough.

TABLE 12.3

Matrix formulation for training a feedforward, fully connected multilayer neural network using backpropagation. Steps 1–4 are for one epoch of training. $\mathbf{X}$, $\mathbf{R}$, and the learning rate parameter α, are provided to the network for training. The network is initialized by specifying weights, $\mathbf{W}(1)$, and biases, $\mathbf{B}(1)$, as small random numbers.

Step	Description	Equations
Step 1	Input patterns	$\mathbf{A}(1) = \mathbf{X}$
Step 2	Forward pass	For $\ell = 2, \dots, L$, compute: $\mathbf{Z}(\ell) = \mathbf{W}(\ell)\mathbf{A}(\ell-1) + \mathbf{B}(\ell)$; $\mathbf{A}(\ell) = h(\mathbf{Z}(\ell))$; $h'(\mathbf{Z}(\ell))$; and $\mathbf{D}(L) = (\mathbf{A}(L) - \mathbf{R}) \odot h'(\mathbf{Z}(L))$
Step 3	Backpropagation	For $\ell = L-1, L-2, \dots, 2$, compute $\mathbf{D}(\ell) = \left(\mathbf{W}^T(\ell+1)\mathbf{D}(\ell+1)\right) \odot h(\mathbf{Z}(\ell))$
Step 4	Update weights and biases	For $\ell = 2, \dots, L$, let $\mathbf{W}(\ell) = \mathbf{W}(\ell) - \alpha\mathbf{D}(\ell)\mathbf{A}^T(\ell-1)$, $\mathbf{b}(\ell) = \mathbf{b}(\ell) - \alpha\sum_{k=1}^{n_p}\boldsymbol{\delta}_k(\ell)$, and $\mathbf{B}(\ell) = \underset{n_p \text{ times}}{\text{concatenate}}\{\mathbf{b}(\ell)\}$, where the $\boldsymbol{\delta}_k(\ell)$ are the columns of $\mathbf{D}(\ell)$

There are two major types of errors in which we are interested. One is the *classification error*, which we compute by counting the number of patterns that were misclassified and dividing by the total number of patterns in the training set. Multiplying the result by 100 gives the percentage of patterns misclassified. Subtracting the result from 1 and multiplying by 100 gives the percent correct recognition. The other is the *mean squared error* (MSE), which is based on actual values of E. For the error defined in Eq. (12-65), this value is obtained (for one pattern) by squaring the elements of a column of the matrix $(\mathbf{A}(L) - \mathbf{R})$, adding them, and dividing by the result by 2 (see Problem 12.28). Repeating this operation for all columns and dividing the result by the number of patterns in $\mathbf{X}$ gives the MSE over the entire training set.

EXAMPLE 12.12: Using a fully connected neural net to solve the XOR problem.

Figure 12.34(a) shows the XOR classification problem discussed previously (the coordinates were chosen to center the patterns for convenience in indexing, but the spatial relationships are as before). Pattern matrix $\mathbf{X}$ and class membership matrix $\mathbf{R}$ are:

$$\mathbf{X} = \begin{bmatrix} 1 & -1 & -1 & 1 \\ 1 & -1 & 1 & -1 \end{bmatrix}; \quad \mathbf{R} = \begin{bmatrix} 1 & 1 & 0 & 0 \\ 0 & 0 & 1 & 1 \end{bmatrix}$$

We specified a neural network having three layers, with two nodes each (see Fig. 12.35). This is the smallest network consistent with our architecture in Fig. 12.31. Comparing it to the minimum perceptron arrangements in Fig. 12.28(a), we see that our neural network performs the same basic function, in the sense that it has two inputs and two outputs.

We used $\alpha = 1.0$, an initial set of Gaussian random weights of zero mean and standard deviation of 0.02, and the activation function in Eq. (12-51). We then trained the network for 10,000 epochs (we used a large number of epochs to get close to the values in the $\mathbf{R}$; we discuss below solutions with fewer epochs). The resulting weights and biases were:

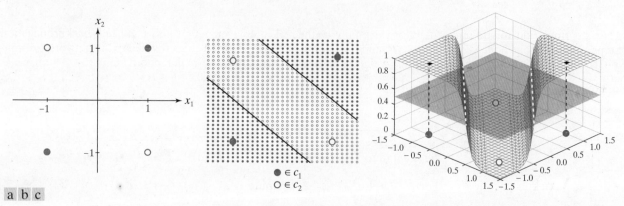

a b c

FIGURE 12.34 Neural net solution to the XOR problem. (a) Four patterns in an XOR arrangement. (b) Results of classifying additional points in the range −1.5 to 1.5 in increments of 0.1. All solid points were classified as belonging to class c_1 and all open circles were classified as belonging to class c_2. Together, the two lines separating the regions constitute the decision boundary [compare with Fig. 12.27(b)]. (c) Decision surface, shown as a mesh. The decision boundary is the pair of dashed, white lines in the intersection of the surface and a plane perpendicular to the vertical axis, intersecting that axis at 0.5. (Figure (c) is shown in a different perspective than (b) in order to make all four patterns visible.)

$$\mathbf{W}(2) = \begin{bmatrix} 4.792 & 4.792 \\ 4.486 & 4.486 \end{bmatrix}; \; \mathbf{b}(2) = \begin{bmatrix} 4.590 \\ -4.486 \end{bmatrix}; \; \mathbf{W}(3) = \begin{bmatrix} -9.180 & 9.429 \\ 9.178 & -9.427 \end{bmatrix}; \; \mathbf{b}(3) = \begin{bmatrix} 4.420 \\ -4.419 \end{bmatrix}$$

Figure 12.35 shows the neural net based on these values.

When presented with the four training patterns after training was completed, the results at the two outputs should have been equal to the values in **R**. Instead, the values were close:

$$\mathbf{A}(3) = \begin{bmatrix} 0.987 & 0.990 & 0.010 & 0.010 \\ 0.013 & 0.010 & 0.990 & 0.990 \end{bmatrix}$$

These weights and biases, along with the sigmoid activation function, completely specify our trained neural network. To test its performance with values other than the training patterns, which we know it classifies correctly, we created a set of 2-D test patterns by subdividing the pattern space into increments of 0.1, from −1.5 to 1.5 in both directions, and classified the resulting points using a forward pass through

FIGURE 12.35
Neural net used
to solve the XOR
problem, showing
the weights and
biases learned
via training using
the equations in
Table 12.3.

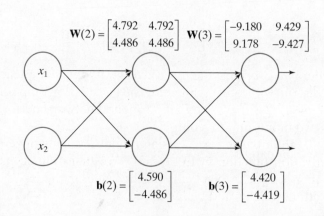

$$\mathbf{W}(2) = \begin{bmatrix} 4.792 & 4.792 \\ 4.486 & 4.486 \end{bmatrix} \quad \mathbf{W}(3) = \begin{bmatrix} -9.180 & 9.429 \\ 9.178 & -9.427 \end{bmatrix}$$

$$\mathbf{b}(2) = \begin{bmatrix} 4.590 \\ -4.486 \end{bmatrix} \quad \mathbf{b}(3) = \begin{bmatrix} 4.420 \\ -4.419 \end{bmatrix}$$

FIGURE 12.36
MSE as a function of training epochs for the XOR pattern arrangement.

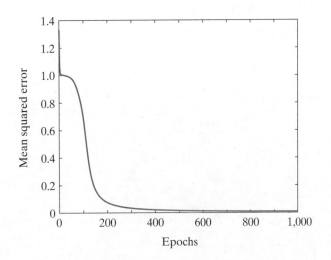

the network. If the activation value of output node 1 was greater than the activation value of output node 2, the pattern was assigned to class c_1; otherwise, it was assigned to class c_2. Fig. 12.34(b) is a plot of the results. Solid dots are points classified into to class c_1, and white dots were classified as belonging to class c_2. The boundaries between these two regions (shown as solid black lines) are precisely the boundaries in Fig. 12.27(b). Thus, our small neural network found the simplest boundary between the two classes, and thus performed the same function as the perceptron arrangement in Fig. 12.28(a).

Figure 12.34(c) shows the decision surface. This figure is analogous to Fig. 12.24(b), but it intersects the plane twice because the patterns are not linearly separable. Our decision boundary is the intersection of the decision surface with a plane perpendicular to the vertical axis, and intersecting that axis at 0.5. This is because the range of values in the output nodes is in the [0, 1] range, and we assign a pattern to the class for which one the two outputs had the largest value. The plane is shown shaded in the figure, and the decision boundary is shown as dashed white lines. We adjusted the viewing perspective of Fig. 12.34(c) so you can see all the XOR points.

Because classification in this case is based on selecting the largest output, we do not need the outputs to be so close to 1 and 0 as we showed above, provided they are greater for the patterns of class c_1 and conversely for the patterns of class c_2. This means that we can train the network using fewer epochs and still achieve correct recognition. For example, correct classification of the XOR patterns can be achieved using the parameters learned with as few as 150 epochs. Figure 12.36 shows the reason why this is possible. By the end of the 1000th epoch, the mean squared error has decreased almost to zero, so we would expect it to decrease very little from there for 10,000 epochs. We know from the preceding results that the neural net performed flawlessly using the weights learned with 10,000 epochs. Because the error for 1,000 and 10,000 epochs is close, we can expect the weights to be close as well. At 150 epochs, the error has decreased by close to 90% from its maximum, so the probability that the weights would perform well should be reasonably high, which was true in this case.

EXAMPLE 12.13: Using neural nets to classify multispectral image data.

In this example, we compare the recognition performance of the Bayes classifier we discussed in Section 12.4 and the multilayer neural nets discussed in this section. The objective here is the same as in Example 12.6: to classify the pixels of multispectral image data into three pattern classes: *water*, *urban*,

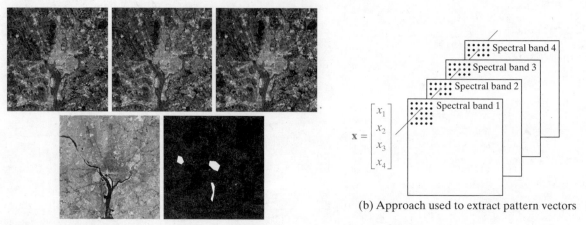

(a) Images in spectral bands 1–4 and binary mask used to extract training samples

(b) Approach used to extract pattern vectors

FIGURE 12.37 (a) Starting with the leftmost image: blue, green, red, near infrared, and binary mask images. In the mask, the lower region is for water, the center region is for the urban area, and the left mask corresponds to vegetation. All images are of size 512×512 pixels. (b) Approach used for generating 4-D pattern vectors from a stack of the four multispectral images. (Multispectral images courtesy of NASA.)

and *vegetation.* Figure 12.37 shows the four multispectral images used in the experiment, the masks used to extract the training and test samples, and the approach used to generate the 4-D pattern vectors.

As in Example 12.6, we extracted a total of 1900 training pattern vectors and 1887 test pattern vectors (see Table 12.1 for a listing of vectors by class). After preliminary runs with the training data to establish that the mean squared error was decreasing as a function of epoch, we determined that a neural net with one hidden layer of two nodes achieved stable learning with $\alpha = 0.001$ and 1,000 training epochs. Keeping those two parameters fixed, we varied the number of nodes in the internal layer, as listed in Table 12.4. The objective of these preliminary runs was to determine the smallest neural net that would give the best recognition rate. As you can see from the results in the table, [4 3 3] is clearly the architecture of choice in this case. Figure 12.38 shows this neural net, along with the parameters learned during training.

After the basic architecture was defined, we kept the learning rate constant at $\alpha = 0.001$ and varied the number of epochs to determine the best recognition rate with the architecture in Fig. 12.38. Table 12.5 shows the results. As you can see, the recognition rate improved slowly as a function of epoch, reaching a plateau at around 50,000 epochs. In fact, as Fig. 12.39 shows, the MSE decreased quickly up to about 800 training epochs and decreased slowly after that, explaining why the correct recognition rate changed so little after about 2,000 epochs. Similar results were obtained with $\alpha = 0.01$, but decreasing

TABLE 12.4
Recognition rate as a function of neural net architecture for $\alpha = 0.001$ and 1,000 training epochs. The network architecture is defined by the numbers in brackets. The first and last number inside each bracket refer to the number of input and output nodes, respectively. The inner entries give the number of nodes in each hidden layer.

Network Architecture	[4 2 3]	[4 3 3]	[4 4 3]	[4 5 3]	[4 2 2 3]	[4 4 3 3]	[4 4 4 3]	[4 10 3 3]	[4 10 10 3]
Recognition Rate	95.8%	96.2%	95.9%	96.1%	74.6%	90.8%	87.1%	84.9%	89.7%

FIGURE 12.38
Neural net
architecture used to
classify the
multispectral image
data in Fig. 12.37
into three classes:
water, urban, and
vegetation. The
parameters shown
were obtained
in 50,000 epochs
of training using
$\alpha = 0.001$.

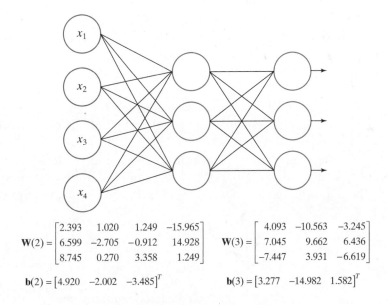

$$\mathbf{W}(2) = \begin{bmatrix} 2.393 & 1.020 & 1.249 & -15.965 \\ 6.599 & -2.705 & -0.912 & 14.928 \\ 8.745 & 0.270 & 3.358 & 1.249 \end{bmatrix} \quad \mathbf{W}(3) = \begin{bmatrix} 4.093 & -10.563 & -3.245 \\ 7.045 & 9.662 & 6.436 \\ -7.447 & 3.931 & -6.619 \end{bmatrix}$$

$$\mathbf{b}(2) = \begin{bmatrix} 4.920 & -2.002 & -3.485 \end{bmatrix}^T \quad \mathbf{b}(3) = \begin{bmatrix} 3.277 & -14.982 & 1.582 \end{bmatrix}^T$$

TABLE 12.5
Recognition performance on the training set as a function of training epochs. The learning rate constant was $\alpha = 0.001$ in all cases.

Training Epochs	1,000	10,000	20,000	30,000	40,000	50,000	60,000	70,000	80,000
Recognition Rate	95.3%	96.6%	96.7%	96.8%	96.9%	97.0%	97.0%	97.0%	97.0%

FIGURE 12.39
MSE for the
network
architecture in
Fig. 12.38 as a
function of the
number of
training epochs.
The learning rate
parameter was
$\alpha = 0.001$ in all
cases.

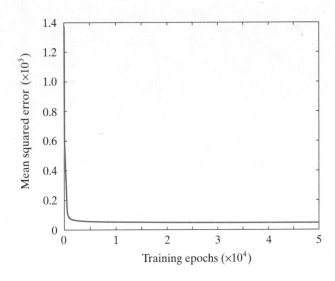

this parameter to $\alpha = 0.1$ resulted in a drop of the best correct recognition rate to 49.1%. Based on the preceding results, we used $\alpha = 0.001$ and 50,000 epochs to train the network.

The parameters in Fig. 12.38 were the result of training. The recognition rate for the training data using these parameters was 97%. We achieved a recognition rate of 95.6% on the test set using the same parameters. The difference between these two figures, and the 96.4% and 96.2%, respectively, obtained for the same data with the Bayes classifier (see Example 12.6), are statistically insignificant.

The fact that our neural networks achieved results comparable to those obtained with the Bayes classifier is not surprising. It can be shown (Duda, Hart, and Stork [2001]) that a three-layer neural net, trained by backpropagation using a sum of errors squared criterion, approximates the Bayes decision functions in the limit, as the number of training samples approaches infinity. Although our training sets were small, the data were well behaved enough to yield results that are close to what theory predicts.

12.6 DEEP CONVOLUTIONAL NEURAL NETWORKS

Up to this point, we have organized pattern features as vectors. Generally, this assumes that the form of those features has been specified (i.e., "engineered" by a human designer) and extracted from images prior to being input to a neural network (Example 12.13 is an illustration of this approach). But one of the strengths of neural networks is that they are capable of learning pattern features directly from training data. What we would like to do is input a set of training images directly into a neural network, and have the network learn the necessary features *on its own*. One way to do this would be to convert images to vectors directly by organizing the pixels based on a linear index (see Fig. 12.1), and then letting each element (pixel) of the linear index be an element of the vector. However, this approach does not utilize any spatial relationships that may exist between pixels in an image, such as pixel arrangements into corners, the presence of edge segments, and other features that may help to differentiate one image from another. In this section, we present a class of neural networks called *deep convolutional neural networks* (*CNNs* or *ConvNets* for short) that accept images as inputs and are ideally suited for automatic learning and image classification. In order to differentiate between CNNs and the neural nets we studied in Section 12.5, we will refer to the latter as "fully connected" neural networks.

A BASIC CNN ARCHITECTURE

In the following discussion, we use a *LeNet* architecture (see references at the end of this chapter) to introduce convolutional nets. We do this for two main reasons: First, the LeNet architecture is reasonably simple to understand. This makes it ideal for introducing basic CNN concepts. Second, our real interest is in deriving the equations of backpropagation for convolutional networks, a task that is simplified by the intuitiveness of LeNets.

To simplify the explanation of the CNN in Fig. 12.40, we focus attention initially on a single image input. Multiple input images are a trivial extension we will consider later in our discussion.

The CNN in Fig. 12.40 contains all the basic elements of a LeNet architecture, and we use it without loss of generality. A key difference between this architecture and the neural net architectures we studied in the previous section is that inputs to CNNs are 2-D arrays (images), while inputs to our fully connected neural networks are vectors. However, as you will see shortly, the computations performed by both networks are very similar: (1) a sum of products is formed, (2) a bias value is added,

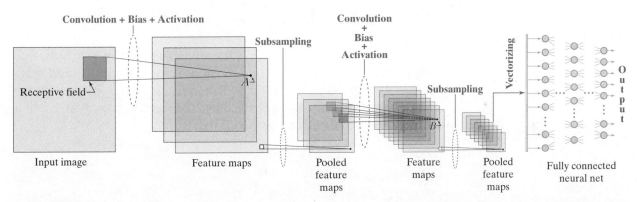

FIGURE 12.40 A CNN containing all the basic elements of a LeNet architecture. Points *A* and *B* are specific values to be addressed later in this section. The last pooled feature maps are vectorized and serve as the input to a fully connected neural network. The class to which the input image belongs is determined by the output neuron with the highest value.

(3) the result is passed through an activation function, and (4) the activation value becomes a single input to a following layer.

Despite the fact that the computations performed by CNNs and fully connected neural nets are similar, there are some basic differences between the two, beyond their input formats being 2-D versus vectors. An important difference is that CNNs are capable of learning 2-D features directly from raw image data, as mentioned earlier. Because the tools for systematically engineering comprehensive feature sets for complex image recognition tasks do not exist, having a system that can learn its own image features from raw image data is a crucial advantage of CNNs. Another major difference is in the way in which layers are connected. In a fully connected neural net, we feed the output of *every* neuron in a layer directly into the input of *every* neuron in the next layer. By contrast, in a CNN we feed into every input of a layer, a *single* value, determined by the convolution (hence the name *convolutional* neural net) over a spatial neighborhood in the output of the previous layer. Therefore, CNNs are not fully connected in the sense defined in the last section. Another difference is that the 2-D arrays from one layer to the next are subsampled to reduce sensitivity to translational variations in the input. These differences and their meaning will become clear as we look at various CNN configurations in the following discussion.

Basics of How a CNN Operates

As noted above, the type of neighborhood processing in CNNs is spatial convolution. We explained the mechanics of spatial convolution in Fig. 3.29, and expressed it mathematically in Eq. (3-35). As that equation shows, convolution computes a sum of products between pixels and a set of kernel weights. This operation is carried out at every spatial location in the input image. The result at each location (x, y) in the input is a scalar value. Think of this value as the output of a neuron in a layer of a fully connected neural net. If we add a bias and pass the result through an activation function (see Fig. 12.29), we have a complete analogy between the basic

We will discuss in the next subsection the exact form of neural computations in a CNN, and show they are equivalent in form to the computations performed by neurons in a fully connected neural net.

computations performed by a CNN and those performed by the neural nets discussed in the previous section.

These remarks are summarized in Fig. 12.40, the leftmost part of which shows a neighborhood at one location in the input image. In CNN terminology, these neighborhoods are called *receptive fields*. All a receptive field does is select a region of pixels in the input image. As the figure shows, the first operation performed by a CNN is convolution, whose values are generated by moving the receptive field over the image and, at each location, forming a sum of products of a set of weights and the pixels contained in the receptive field. The set of weights, arranged in the shape of the receptive field, is a *kernel*, as in Chapter 3. The number of spatial increments by which a receptive field is moved is called the *stride*. Our spatial convolutions in previous chapters had a stride of one, but that is not a requirement of the equations themselves. In CNNs, an important motivations for using strides greater than one is data reduction. For example, changing the stride from one to two reduces the image resolution by one-half in each spatial dimension, resulting in a three-fourths reduction in the amount of data per image. Another important motivation is as a substitute for subsampling which, as we discuss below, is used to reduce system sensitivity to spatial translation.

To each convolution value (sum of products) we add a bias, then pass the result through an activation function to generate a single value. Then, this value is fed to the corresponding (x, y) location in the input of the next layer. When repeated for all locations in the input image, the process just explained results in a 2-D set of values that we store in next layer as a 2-D array, called a *feature map*. This terminology is motivated by the fact that the role performed by convolution is to extract features such as edges, points, and blobs from the input (remember, convolution is the basis of spatial filtering, which we used in Chapter 3 for tasks such as smoothing, sharpening, and computing edges in an image). The same weights and a single bias are used to generate the convolution (feature map) values corresponding to all locations of the receptive field in the input image. This is done to cause the same feature to be detected at all points in the image. Using the same weights and bias for this purpose is called *weight* (or *parameter*) *sharing*.

In the terminology of Chapter 3, a feature map is a spatially filtered image.

Figure 12.40 shows three feature maps in the first layer of the network. The other two feature maps are generated in the manner just explained, but using a *different* set of weights and bias for each feature map. Because each set of weights and bias is different, each feature map generally will contain a different set of features, all extracted from the same input image. The feature maps are referred to collectively as a *convolutional layer*. Thus, the CNN in Fig. 12.40 has two convolutional layers.

The process after convolution and activation is *subsampling* (also called *pooling*), which is motivated by a model of the mammal visual cortex proposed by Hubel and Wiesel [1959]. Their findings suggest that parts of the visual cortex consist of *simple* and *complex* cells. The simple cells perform feature extraction, while the complex cells combine (aggregate) those features into a more meaningful whole. In this model, a reduction in spatial resolution appears to be responsible for achieving translational invariance. Pooling is a way of modeling this reduction in dimensionality. When training a CNN with large image databases, pooling has the additional advantage of reducing the volume of data being processed. You can think of the results of subsampling as producing *pooled feature maps*. In other words, a pooled feature map is a feature map of reduced spatial resolution. Pooling is done by subdividing a feature map into a set of small (typically 2×2) regions, called *pooling neighborhoods*, and replacing *all* elements in such a neighborhood by a *single* value. We assume that pooling neighborhoods are *adjacent* (i.e., they do not overlap). There are several ways to compute the pooled values; collectively, the different approaches are called *pooling methods*. Three common pooling methods are: (1) *average pooling*, in which the values in each neighborhood are replaced by the average of the values in the neighborhood; (2) *max-pooling*, which replaces the values in a neighborhood by the maximum value of its elements; and (3) L_2 pooling, in which the resulting pooled value is the square root of the sum of the neighborhood values squared. There is one pooled feature map for each feature map. The pooled feature maps are referred to collectively as a *pooling layer*. In Fig. 12.40 we used 2×2 pooling so each resulting pooled map is one-fourth the size of the preceding feature map. The use of receptive fields, convolution, parameter sharing, and pooling are characteristics unique to CNNs.

Adjacency is not a requirement of pooling per se. We assume it here for simplicity and because this is an approach that is used frequently.

Because feature maps are the result of spatial convolution, we know from Chapter 3 that they are simply filtered images. It then follows that pooled feature maps are filtered images of lower resolution. As Fig. 12.40 illustrates, the pooled feature maps in the first layer become the inputs to the next layer in the network. But, whereas we showed a single image as an input to the first layer, we now have multiple pooled feature maps (filtered images) that are inputs into the second layer.

To see how these multiple inputs to the second layer are handled, focus for a moment on one pooled feature map. To generate the values for the first feature map in the second convolutional layer, we perform convolution, add a bias, and use activation, as before. Then, we change the kernel and bias, and repeat the procedure for the second feature map, still using the same input. We do this for every remaining feature map, changing the kernel weights and bias for each. Then, we consider the next pooled feature map input and perform the same procedure (convolution, plus bias, plus activation) for every feature map in the second layer, using yet another set of different kernels and biases. When we are finished, we will have generated three values for the same location in every feature map, with one value coming from the corresponding location in each of the three inputs. The question now is: How do we combine these three individual values into one? The answer lies in the fact that convolution is a linear process, from which it follows that the three individual values are combined into one by superposition (that is, by adding them).

You could interpret the convolution with several input images as 3-D convolution, but with movement only in the spatial (x and y) directions. The result would be identical to summing individual convolutions with each image separately, as we do here.

In the first layer, we had one input image and three feature maps, so we needed three kernels to complete all required convolutions. In the second layer, we have three inputs and seven feature maps, so the total number of kernels (and biases) needed is $3 \times 7 = 21$. Each feature map is pooled to generate a corresponding pooled feature map, resulting in seven pooled feature maps. In Fig. 12.40, there are only two layers, so these seven pooled feature maps are the outputs of the last layer.

As usual, the ultimate objective is to use features for classification, so we need a classifier. As Fig. 12.40 shows, in a CNN we perform classification by feeding the value of the last pooled layer into a fully connected neural net, the details of which you learned in Section 12.5. But the outputs of a CNN are 2-D arrays (i.e., filtered images of reduced resolution), whereas the inputs to a fully connected net are vectors. Therefore, we have to *vectorize* the 2-D pooled feature maps in the last layer. We do this using linear indexing (see Fig. 12.1). Each 2-D array in the last layer of the CNN is converted into a vector, then all resulting vectors are concatenated (vertically for a column) to form a single vector. This vector propagates through the neural net, as explained in Section 12.5. In any given application, the number of outputs in the fully connected net is equal to the number of pattern classes being classified. As before, the output with the highest value determines the class of the input.

The parameters of the fully connected neural net are learned during training of the CNN, to be discussed shortly.

EXAMPLE 12.14:   Receptive fields, pooling neighborhoods, and their corresponding feature maps.

The top row of Fig. 12.41 shows a numerical example of the relative sizes of feature maps and pooled feature maps as a function of the sizes of receptive fields and pooling neighborhoods. The input image is of size 28×28 pixels, and the receptive field is of size 5×5. If we require that the receptive field be contained in the image during convolution, you know from Section 3.4 that the resulting convolution array (feature map) will be of size 24×24. If we use a pooling neighborhood of size 2×2, the resulting pooled feature maps will be of size 12×12, as the figure shows. As noted earlier, we assume that pooling neighborhoods do not overlap.

As an analogy with fully connected neural nets, think of each element of a 2-D array in the top row of Fig. 12.41 as a neuron. The outputs of the neurons in the input are pixel values. The neurons in the feature map of the first layer have output values generated by convolving with the input image a kernel whose size and shape are the same as the receptive field, and whose coefficients are learned during training. To each convolution value we add a bias and pass the result through an activation function to generate the output value of the corresponding neuron in the feature map. The output values of the neurons in the pooled feature maps are generated by pooling the output values of the neurons in the feature maps.

The second row in Fig. 12.41 illustrates visually how feature maps and pooled feature maps look based on the input image shown in the figure. The kernel shown is as described in the previous paragraph, and its weights (shown as intensity values) were learned from sample images using the training of the CNN described later in Example 12.17. Therefore, the nature of the learned features is determined by the learned kernel coefficients. Note that the contents of the feature maps are specific features detected by convolution. For example, some of the features emphasize edges in the the character. As mentioned earlier, the pooled features are lower-resolution versions of this effect.

EXAMPLE 12.15:   Graphical illustration of the functions performed by the components of a CNN.

Figure 12.42 shows the 28×28 image from Fig. 12.41, input into an expanded version of the CNN architecture from Fig. 12.40. The expanded CNN, which we will discuss in more detail in Example 12.17, has six feature maps in the first layer, and twelve in the second. It uses receptive fields of size 5×5, and pooling neighborhoods of size 2×2. Because the receptive fields are of size 5×5, the feature maps in the first layer are of size 24×24, as we explained in Example 12.14. Each feature map has its own set of weights and bias, so we will need a total of $(5 \times 5) \times 6 + 6 = 156$ parameters (six kernels with twenty-five weights each, and six biases) to generate the feature maps in the first layer. The top row of Fig. 12.43(a) shows the kernels with the weights learned during training of the CNN displayed as images, with intensity being proportional to kernel values.

FIGURE 12.41
Top row: How the sizes of receptive fields and pooling neighborhoods affect the sizes of feature maps and pooled feature maps.
Bottom row: An image example. This figure is explained in more detail in Example 12.17. (Image courtesy of NIST.)

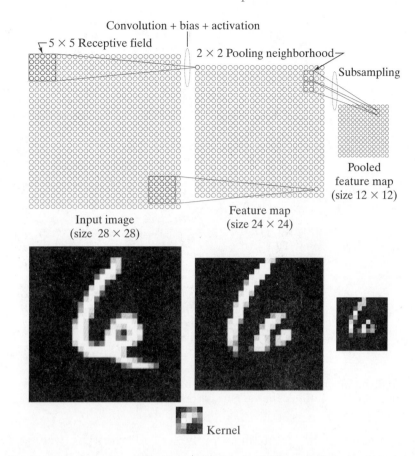

Convolution + bias + activation

5 × 5 Receptive field

2 × 2 Pooling neighborhood

Subsampling

Pooled feature map (size 12 × 12)

Input image (size 28 × 28)

Feature map (size 24 × 24)

Kernel

Because we used pooling neighborhoods of size 2×2, the pooled feature maps in the first layer of Fig. 12.42 are of size 12×12. As we discussed earlier, the number of feature maps and pooled feature maps is the same, so we will have six arrays of size 12×12 acting as inputs to the twelve feature maps in the second layer (the number of feature maps generally is different from layer to layer). Each feature map will have its own set of weights and bias, so will need a total of $6 \times (5 \times 5) \times 12 + 12 = 1812$

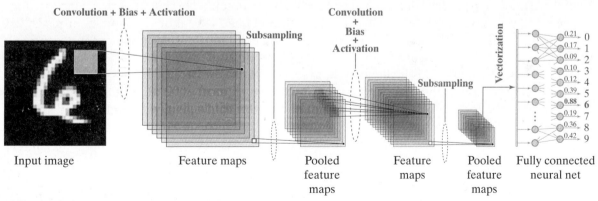

Convolution + Bias + Activation

Subsampling

Convolution + Bias + Activation

Subsampling

Vectorization

0.21 — 0
0.17 — 1
0.09 — 2
0.10 — 3
0.12 — 4
0.39 — 5
0.88 — **6**
0.19 — 7
0.36 — 8
0.42 — 9

Input image · Feature maps · Pooled feature maps · Feature maps · Pooled feature maps · Fully connected neural net

FIGURE 12.42 Numerical example illustrating the various functions of a CNN, including recognition of an input image. A sigmoid activation function was used throughout.

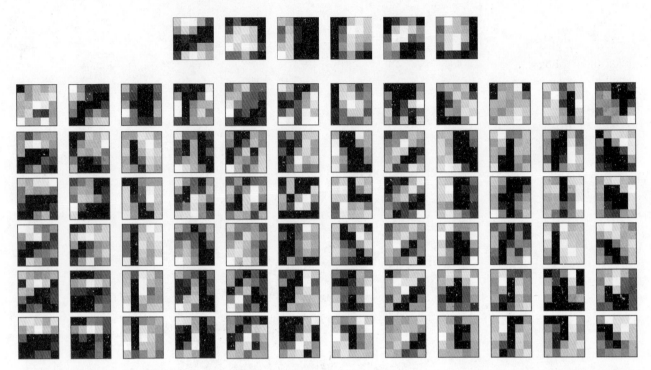

FIGURE 12.43 Top: The weights (shown as images of size 5×5) corresponding to the six feature maps in the first layer of the CNN in Fig. 12.42. Bottom: The weights corresponding to the twelve feature maps in the second layer.

parameters to generate the feature maps in the second layer (i.e., twelve sets of six kernels with twenty-five weights each, plus twelve biases). The bottom part of Fig. 12.43 shows the kernels as images. Because we are using receptive fields of size 5×5, the feature maps in the second layer are of size 8×8. Using 2×2 pooling neighborhoods resulted in pooled feature maps of size 4×4 in the second layer.

As we discussed earlier, the pooled feature maps in the last layer have to be vectorized to be able to input them into the fully connected neural net. Each pooled feature map resulted in a column vector of size 16×1. There are 12 of these vectors which, when concatenated vertically, resulted in a single vector of size 192×1. Therefore, our fully connected neural net has 192 input neurons. There are ten numeral classes, so there are 10 output neurons. As you will see later, we obtained excellent performance by using a neural net with no hidden layers, so our complete neural net had a total of 192 input neurons and 10 output neurons. For the input character shown in Fig. 12.42, the highest value in the output of the fully connected neural net was in the seventh neuron, which corresponds to the class of 6's. Therefore, the input was recognized properly. This is shown in bold text in the figure.

Figure 12.44 shows graphically what the feature maps look like as the input image propagates through the CNN. Consider the feature maps in the first layer. If you look at each map carefully, you will notice that it highlights a different characteristic of the input. For example, the map on the top of the first column highlights the two principal edges on the top of the character. The second map highlights the edges of the entire inner region, and the third highlights a "blob-like" nature of the digit, almost as if it had been blurred by a lowpass kernel. The other three images show other features. Although the pooled feature maps are lower-resolution versions of the original feature maps, they still retained the key characteristics of the features in the latter. If you look at the first two feature maps in the second layer, and compare them with the first two in the first layer, you can see that they could be interpreted as higher-

FIGURE 12.44
Visual summary
of an input image
propagating
through the CNN
in Fig. 12.42. Shown
as images are all the
results of
convolution
(feature maps) and
pooling (pooled
feature maps) for
both layers of the
network. (Example
12.17 contains more
details about this
figure.)

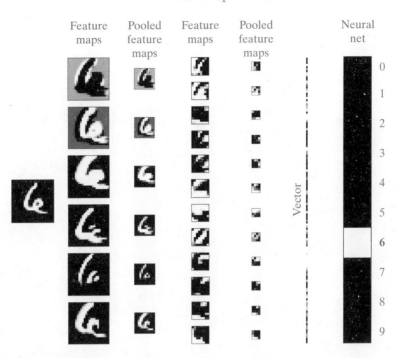

level abstractions of the top part of the character, in the sense that they show an area flanked on both sides by areas of opposite intensity. These abstractions are not always easy to analyze visually, but as you will see in later examples, they can be very effective. The vectorized version of the last pooled layer is self-explanatory. The output of the fully connected neural net shows dark for low values and white for the highest value, indicating that the input was properly recognized as a number 6. Later in this section, we will show that the simple CNN architecture in Fig. 12.42 is capable of recognizing the correct class of over 70,000 numerical samples with nearly perfect accuracy.

Neural Computations in a CNN

Recall from Fig. 12.29 that the basic computation performed by an artificial neuron is a sum of products between weights and values from a previous layer. To this we add a bias and call the result the *net* (*total*) *input* to the neuron, which we denoted by z_i. As we showed in Eq. (12-54), the sum involved in generating z_i is a single sum. The computations performed in a CNN to generate a single value in a feature map is 2-D convolution. As you learned in Chapter 3, this is a double sum of products between the coefficients of a kernel and the corresponding elements of the image array overlapped by the kernel. With reference to Fig. 12.40, let w denote a kernel formed by arranging the weights in the shape of the receptive field we discussed in connection with that figure. For notational consistency with Section 12.5, let $a_{x,y}$ denote image or pooled feature values, depending on the layer. The convolution value at any point (x, y) in the input is given by

$$w \star a_{x,y} = \sum_l \sum_k w_{l,k} a_{x-l,y-k} \tag{12-83}$$

where l and k span the dimensions of the kernel. Suppose that w is of size 3×3. Then, we can then expand this equation into the following sum of products:

$$
\begin{aligned}
w \star a_{x,y} = w \star a_{x,y} &= \sum_l \sum_k w_{l,k} a_{x-l,y-k} \\
&= w_{1,1} a_{x-1,y-1} + w_{1,2} a_{x-1,y-2} + \cdots + w_{3,3} a_{x-3,y-3}
\end{aligned}
$$

(12-84)

We could relabel the subscripts on w and a, and write instead

$$
\begin{aligned}
w \star a_{x,y} &= w_1 a_1 + w_2 a_2 + \cdots + w_9 a_9 \\
&= \sum_{i=1}^{9} w_i a_i
\end{aligned}
$$

(12-85)

The results of Eqs. (12-84) and (12-85) are identical. If we add a bias to the latter equation and call the result z we have

$$
\begin{aligned}
z &= \sum_{j=1}^{9} w_j a_j + b \\
&= w \star a_{x,y} + b
\end{aligned}
$$

(12-86)

The form of the first line of this equation is identical to Eq. (12-54). Therefore, we conclude that if we add a bias to the spatial convolution computation performed by a CNN at any fixed position (x, y) in the input, the result can be expressed in a form identical to the computation performed by an artificial neuron in a fully connected neural net. We need the x, y only to account for the fact that we are working in 2-D. If we think of z as the net input to a neuron, the analogy with the neurons discussed in Section 12.5 is completed by passing z through an activation function, h, to get the output of the neuron:

$$
a = h(z)
$$

(12-87)

This is exactly how the value of any point in a feature map (such as the point labeled A in Fig. 12.40) is computed.

Now consider point B in that figure. As mentioned earlier, its value is given by adding three convolution equations:

$$
\begin{aligned}
w_{l,k}^{(1)} \star a_{x,y}^{(1)} + w_{l,k}^{(2)} \star a_{x,y}^{(2)} + w_{l,k}^{(3)} \star a_{x,y}^{(3)} &= \sum_l \sum_k w_{l,k}^{(1)} a_{x-l,y-k}^{(1)} + \\
&\quad \sum_l \sum_k w_{l,k}^{(2)} a_{x-l,y-k}^{(2)} + \sum_l \sum_k w_{l,k}^{(2)} a_{x-l,y-k}^{(2)}
\end{aligned}
$$

(12-88)

where the superscripts refer to the three pooled feature maps in Fig. 12.40. The values of l, k, x, and y are the same in all three equations because all three kernels are of the same size and they move in unison. We could expand this equation and obtain a sum of products that is lengthier than for point A in Fig. 12.40, but we could still relabel all terms and obtain a sum of products that involves only one summation, *exactly* as before.

The preceding result tells us that the equations used to obtain the value of an element of any feature map in a CNN can be expressed in the form of the computation performed by an artificial neuron. This holds for any feature map, regardless of how many convolutions are involved in the computation of the elements of that feature map, in which case we would simply be dealing with the sum of more convolution equations. The implication is that we can use the basic form of Eqs. (12-86) and (12-87) to describe how the value of an element in any feature map of a CNN is obtained. This means we do not have to account explicitly for the number of different pooled feature maps (and hence the number of different kernels) used in a pooling layer. The result is a significant simplification of the equations that describe forward and backpropagation in a CNN.

Multiple Input Images

The values of $a_{x,y}$ just discussed are pixel values in the first layer but, in layers past the first, $a_{x,y}$ denotes values of pooled features. However, our equations do not differentiate based on what these variables actually represent. For example, suppose we replace the input to Fig. 12.40 with three images, such as the three components of an RGB image. The equations for the value of point A in the figure would now have the same form as those we stated for point B—only the weights and biases would be different. Thus, the results in the previous discussion for one input image are applicable directly to multiple input images. We will give an example of a CNN with three input images later in our discussion.

THE EQUATIONS OF A FORWARD PASS THROUGH A CNN

We concluded in the preceding discussion that we can express the result of convolving a kernel, w, and an input array with values $a_{x,y}$, as

As noted earlier, a kernel is formed by organizing the weights in the shape of a corresponding receptive field. Also keep in mind that w and $a_{x,y}$ represent *all* the weights and corresponding values in a set of input images or pooled features.

$$z_{x,y} = \sum_l \sum_k w_{l,k} a_{x-l,y-k} + b$$
$$= w \star a_{x,y} + b \qquad (12\text{-}89)$$

where l and k span the dimensions of the kernel, x and y span the dimensions of the input, and b is a bias. The corresponding value of $a_{x,y}$ is

$$a_{x,y} = h(z_{x,y}) \qquad (12\text{-}90)$$

But this $a_{x,y}$ is different from the one we used to compute Eq. (12-89), in which $a_{x,y}$ represents values from the previous layer. Thus, we are going to need additional notation to differentiate between layers. As in fully connected neural nets, we use ℓ for this purpose, and write Eqs. (12-89) and (12-90) as

$$z_{x,y}(\ell) = \sum_l \sum_k w_{l,k}(\ell) a_{x-l,y-k}(\ell-1) + b(\ell)$$
$$= w(\ell) \star a_{x,y}(\ell-1) + b(\ell) \qquad (12\text{-}91)$$

and

$$a_{x,y}(\ell) = h\left(z_{x,y}(\ell)\right) \tag{12-92}$$

for $\ell = 1, 2, \ldots, L_c$, where L_c is the number of convolutional layers, and $a_{x,y}(\ell)$ denotes the values of pooled features in convolutional layer ℓ. When $\ell = 1$,

$$a_{x,y}(0) = \left\{\text{values of pixels in the input image(s)}\right\} \tag{12-93}$$

When $\ell = L_c$,

$$a_{x,y}(L_c) = \left\{\text{values of pooled features in last layer of the CNN}\right\} \tag{12-94}$$

Note that ℓ starts at 1 instead of 2, as we did in Section 12.5. The reason is that we are naming layers, as in "convolutional layer ℓ." It would be confusing to start at convolutional layer 2. Finally, we note that the pooling does not require any convolutions. The only function of pooling is to reduce the spatial dimensions of the feature map preceding it, so we do not include explicit pooling equations here.

Equations (12-91) through (12-94) are all we need to compute all values in a forward pass through the convolutional section of a CNN. As described in Fig. 12.40, the values of the pooled features of the last layer are vectorized and fed into a fully connected feedforward neural network, whose forward propagation is explained in Eqs. (12-54) and (12-55) or, in matrix form, in Table 12.2.

THE EQUATIONS OF BACKPROPAGATION USED TO TRAIN CNNs

As you saw in the previous section, the feedforward equations of a CNN are similar to those of a fully connected neural net, but with multiplication replaced by convolution, and notation that reflects the fact that CNNs are not fully connected in the sense defined in Section 12.5. As you will see in this section, the equations of backpropagation also are similar in many respects to those in fully connected neural nets.

As in the derivation of backpropagation in Section 12.5, we start with the definition of how the output error of our CNN changes with respect to each neuron in the network. The form of the error is the same as for fully connected neural nets, but now it is a function of x and y instead of j:

$$\delta_{x,y}(\ell) = \frac{\partial E}{\partial z_{x,y}(\ell)} \tag{12-95}$$

As in Section 12.5, we want to relate this quantity to $\delta_{xy}(\ell+1)$, which we again do using the chain rule:

$$\delta_{x,y}(\ell) = \frac{\partial E}{\partial z_{x,y}(\ell)} = \sum_u \sum_v \frac{\partial E}{\partial z_{u,v}(\ell+1)} \frac{\partial z_{u,v}(\ell+1)}{\partial z_{x,y}(\ell)} \tag{12-96}$$

where u and v are any two variables of summation over the range of possible values of z. As noted in Section 12.5, these summations result from applying the chain rule.

By definition, the first term of the double summation of Eq. (12-96) is $\delta_{x,y}(\ell+1)$. So, we can write this equation as

$$\delta_{x,y}(\ell) = \frac{\partial E}{\partial z_{x,y}(\ell)} = \sum_u \sum_v \delta_{u,v}(\ell+1) \frac{\partial z_{u,v}(\ell+1)}{\partial z_{x,y}(\ell)} \tag{12-97}$$

Substituting Eq. (12-92) into Eq. (12-91), and using the resulting $z_{u,v}$ in Eq. (12-97), we obtain

$$\delta_{x,y}(\ell) = \sum_u \sum_v \delta_{u,v}(\ell+1) \frac{\partial}{\partial z_{x,y}(\ell)} \left[\sum_l \sum_k w_{l,k}(\ell+1) h\left(z_{u-l,v-k}(\ell)\right) + b(\ell+1) \right] \tag{12-98}$$

The derivative of the expression inside the brackets is zero unless $u - l = x$ and $v - k = y$, and because the derivative of $b(\ell+1)$ with respect to $z_{x,y}(\ell)$ is zero. But, if $u - l = x$ and $v - k = y$, then $l = u - x$ and $k = v - y$. Therefore, taking the indicated derivative of the expression in brackets, we can write Eq. (12-98) as

$$\delta_{x,y}(\ell) = \sum_u \sum_v \delta_{u,v}(\ell+1) \left[\sum_{u-x} \sum_{v-y} w_{u-x,v-y}(\ell+1) h'\left(z_{x,y}(\ell)\right) \right] \tag{12-99}$$

Values of x, y, u, and v are specified outside of the terms inside the brackets. Once the values of these variables are fixed, $u - x$ and $v - y$ inside the brackets are simply two *constants*. Therefore, the double summation evaluates to $w_{u-x,v-y}(\ell+1) h'\left(z_{x,y}(\ell)\right)$, and we can write Eq. (12-99) as

$$\begin{aligned}
\delta_{x,y}(\ell) &= \sum_u \sum_v \delta_{u,v}(\ell+1) w_{u-x,v-y}(\ell+1) h'\left(z_{x,y}(\ell)\right) \\
&= h'\left(z_{x,y}(\ell)\right) \sum_u \sum_v \delta_{u,v}(\ell+1) w_{u-x,v-y}(\ell+1)
\end{aligned} \tag{12-100}$$

The double sum expression in the second line of this equation is in the form of a convolution, but the displacements are the negatives of those in Eq. (12-91). Therefore, we can write Eq. (12-100) as

$$\delta_{x,y}(\ell) = h'\left(z_{x,y}(\ell)\right) \left[\delta_{x,y}(\ell+1) \star w_{-x,-y}(\ell+1) \right] \tag{12-101}$$

The negatives in the subscripts indicate that w is *reflected* about both spatial axes. This is the same as rotating w by 180°, as we explained in connection with Eq. (3-35). Using this fact, we finally arrive at an expression for the error at a layer ℓ by writing Eq. (12-101) equivalently as

The 180° rotation is for *each* 2-D kernel in a layer.

$$\delta_{x,y}(\ell) = h'\left(z_{x,y}(\ell)\right) \left[\delta_{x,y}(\ell+1) \star \text{rot}180\left(w_{x,y}(\ell+1)\right) \right] \tag{12-102}$$

But the kernels do not depend on x and y, so we can write this equation as

$$\delta_{x,y}(\ell) = h'\big(z_{x,y}(\ell)\big)\big[\delta_{x,y}(\ell+1) \star \mathrm{rot}180\big(w(\ell+1)\big)\big] \qquad (12\text{-}103)$$

As in Section 12.5, our final objective is to compute the change in E with respect to the weights and biases. Following a similar procedure as above, we obtain

$$\frac{\partial E}{\partial w_{l,k}} = \sum_x \sum_y \frac{\partial E}{\partial z_{x,y}(\ell)}\frac{\partial z_{x,y}(\ell)}{\partial w_{l,k}}$$

$$= \sum_x \sum_y \delta_{x,y}(\ell)\frac{\partial z_{x,y}(\ell)}{\partial w_{l,k}}$$

$$= \sum_x \sum_y \delta_{x,y}(\ell)\frac{\partial}{\partial w_{l,k}}\Big[\sum_l \sum_k w_{l,k}(\ell)h\big(z_{x-l,y-k}(\ell-1)\big) + b(\ell)\Big] \quad (12\text{-}104)$$

$$= \sum_x \sum_y \delta_{x,y}(\ell)h\big(z_{x-l,y-k}(\ell-1)\big)$$

$$= \sum_x \sum_y \delta_{x,y}(\ell)a_{x-l,y-k}(\ell-1)$$

where the last line follows from Eq. (12-92). This line is in the form of a convolution but, comparing it to Eq. (12-91), we see there is a sign reversal between the summation variables and their corresponding subscripts. To put it in the form of a convolution, we write the last line of Eq. (12-104) as

$$\frac{\partial E}{\partial w_{l,k}} = \sum_x \sum_y \delta_{x,y}(\ell)a_{-(l-x),-(k-y)}(\ell-1)$$

$$= \delta_{l,k}(\ell) \star a_{-l,-k}(\ell-1) \qquad (12\text{-}105)$$

$$= \delta_{l,k}(\ell) \star \mathrm{rot}180\big(a(\ell-1)\big)$$

Similarly (see Problem 12.32),

$$\frac{\partial E}{\partial b(\ell)} = \sum_x \sum_y \delta_{x,y}(\ell) \qquad (12\text{-}106)$$

Using the preceding two expressions in the gradient descent equations (see Section 12.5), it follows that

$$w_{l,k}(\ell) = w_{l,k}(\ell) - \alpha\frac{\partial E}{\partial w_{l,k}}$$

$$= w_{l,k}(\ell) - \alpha\delta_{l,k}(\ell) \star \mathrm{rot}180\big(a(\ell-1)\big) \qquad (12\text{-}107)$$

and

$$b(\ell) = b(\ell) \,-\, \alpha \frac{\partial E}{\partial b(\ell)}$$

$$= b(\ell) \,-\, \alpha \sum_x \sum_y \delta_{x,y}(\ell)$$

(12-108)

Equations (12-107) and (12-108) update the weights and bias of each convolution layer in a CNN. As we have mentioned before, it is understood that the $w_{l,k}$ represents *all* the weights of a layer. The variables l and k span the spatial dimensions of the 2-D kernels, all of which are of the same size.

In a forward pass, we went from a convolution layer to a pooled layer. In backpropagation, we are going in the opposite direction. But the pooled feature maps are smaller than their corresponding feature maps (see Fig. 12.40). Therefore, when going in the reverse direction, we *upsample* (e.g., by pixel replication) each pooled feature map to match the size of the feature map that generated it. Each pooled feature map corresponds to a unique feature map, so the path of backpropagation is clearly defined.

With reference to Fig. 12.40, backpropagation starts at the output of the fully connected neural net. We know from Section 12.5 how to update the weights of this network. When we get to the "interface" between the neural net and the CNN, we have to reverse the vectorization method used to generate input vectors. That is, before we can proceed with backpropagation using Eqs. (12-107) and (12-108), we have to *regenerate* the individual pooled feature maps from the single vector propagated back by the fully connected neural net.

We summarized in Table 12.3 the backpropagation steps for a fully connected neural net. Table 12.6 summarizes the steps for performing backpropagation in the CNN architecture in Fig. 12.40. The procedure is repeated for a specified number of

TABLE 12.6
The principal steps used to train a CNN. The network is initialized with a set of small random weights and biases. In backpropagation, a vector arriving (from the fully connected net) at the output pooling layer must be converted to 2-D arrays of the same size as the pooled feature maps in that layer. Each pooled feature map is upsampled to match the size of its corresponding feature map. The steps in the table are for one epoch of training.

Step	Description	Equations
Step 1	Input images	$a(0) =$ the set of image pixels in the input to layer 1
Step 2	Forward pass	For each neuron corresponding to location (x, y) in each feature map in layer ℓ compute: $z_{x,y}(\ell) = w(\ell) \star a_{x,y}(\ell-1) + b(\ell)$ and $a_{x,y}(\ell) = h\big(z_{x,y}(\ell)\big)$; $\ell = 1, 2, \dots, L_c$
Step 3	Backpropagation	For each neuron in each feature map in layer ℓ compute: $\delta_{x,y}(\ell) = h'\big(z_{x,y}(\ell)\big)\big[\delta_{x,y}(\ell+1) \star \mathrm{rot}180\big(w(\ell+1)\big)\big]$; $\ell = L_c - 1, L_c - 2, \dots, 1$
Step 4	Update parameters	Update the weights and bias for each feature map using $w_{l,k}(\ell) = w_{l,k}(\ell) - \alpha \delta_{l,k}(\ell) \star \mathrm{rot}180\big(a(\ell-1)\big)$ and $b(\ell) = b(\ell) - \alpha \sum_x \sum_y \delta_{x,y}(\ell)$; $\ell = 1, 2, \dots, L_c$

FIGURE 12.45
CNN with one
convolutional
layer used to
learn to recognize
the images in Fig.
12.46.

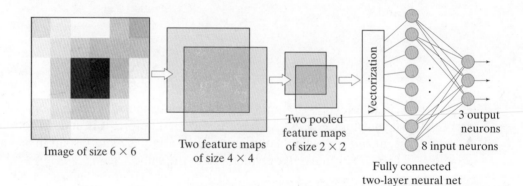

Image of size 6×6 — Two feature maps of size 4×4 — Two pooled feature maps of size 2×2 — Vectorization — 8 input neurons — 3 output neurons

Fully connected
two-layer neural net

epochs, or until the output error of the neural net reaches an acceptable value. The error is computed exactly as we did in Section 12.5. It can be the mean squared error, or the recognition error. Keep in mind that the weights in $w(\ell)$ and the bias value $b(\ell)$ are *different* for *each* feature map in layer ℓ.

EXAMPLE 12.16: Teaching a CNN to recognize some simple images.

We begin our illustrations of CNN performance by teaching the CNN in Fig. 12.45 to recognize the small 6×6 images in Fig. 12.46. As you can see on the left of this figure, there are three samples each of images of a horizontal stripe, a small centered square, and a vertical stripe. These images were used as the training set. On the right are noisy samples of images in these three categories. These were used as the test set.

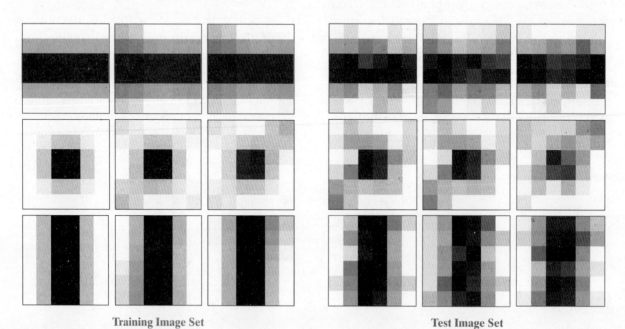

Training Image Set   **Test Image Set**

FIGURE 12.46 Left: Training images. Top row: Samples of a dark horizontal stripe. Center row: Samples of a centered dark square. Bottom row: Samples of a dark vertical stripe. Right: Noisy samples of the three categories on the left, created by adding Gaussian noise of zero mean and unit variance to the samples on the left. (All images are 8-bit grayscale images.)

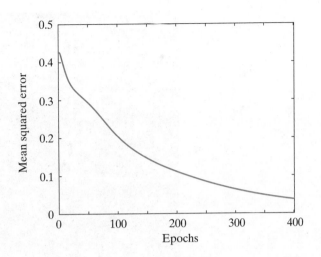

As Fig. 12.45 shows, the inputs to our system are single images. We used a receptor field of size 3×3, which resulted in feature maps of size 4×4. There are two feature maps, which means we need two kernels of size 3×3, and two biases. The pooled feature maps were generated using average pooling in neighborhoods of size 2×2. This resulted in two pooled feature maps of size 2×2, because the feature maps are of size 4×4. The two pooled maps contain eight total elements which were organized as an 8-D column vector to vectorize the output of the last layer. (We used linear indexing of each image, then concatenated the two resulting 4-D vectors into a single 8-D vector.) This vector was then fed into the fully connected neural net on the right, which consists of the input layer and a three-neuron output layer, one neuron per class. Because this network has no hidden layers, it implements linear decision functions (see Problem 12.18). To train the system, we used $\alpha = 1.0$ and ran the system for 400 epochs. Figure 12.47 is a plot of the MSE as a function of epoch. Perfect recognition of the training set was achieved after approximately 100 epochs of training, despite the fact that the MSE was relatively high there. Recognition of the test set was 100% as well. The kernel and bias values learned by the system were:

$$\boldsymbol{w}_1 = \begin{bmatrix} 3.0132 & 1.1808 & -0.0945 \\ 0.9718 & 0.7087 & -0.9093 \\ 0.7193 & 0.0230 & -0.8833 \end{bmatrix}, b_1 = -0.2990 \quad \boldsymbol{w}_2 = \begin{bmatrix} -0.7388 & 1.8832 & 4.1077 \\ -1.0027 & 0.3908 & 2.0357 \\ -1.2164 & -1.1853 & -0.1987 \end{bmatrix}, b_2 = -0.2834$$

It is important that the CNN learned these parameters automatically from the raw training images. No features in the sense discussed in Chapter 11 were employed.

EXAMPLE 12.17: Using a large training set to teach a CNN to recognize handwritten numerals.

In this example, we look at a more practical application using a database containing 60,000 training and 10,000 test images of handwritten numeric characters. The content of this database, called the *MNIST database*, is similar to a database from NIST (National Institute of Standards and Technology). The former is a "cleaned up" version of the latter, in which the characters have been centered and formatted into grayscale images of size 28×28 pixels. Both databases are freely available online. Figure 12.48 shows examples of typical numeric characters available in the databases. As you can see, there is

FIGURE 12.48
Samples
similar to those
available in the
NIST and MNIST
databases. Each
character
subimage is
of size 28×28
pixels.(Individual
images courtesy
of NIST.)

significant variability in the characters—and this is just a small sampling of the 70,000 characters available for experimentation.

Figure 12.49 shows the architecture of the CNN we trained to recognize the ten digits in the MNIST database. We trained the system for 200 epochs using $\alpha = 1.0$. Figure 12.50 shows the training MSE as a function of epoch for the 60,000 training images in the MNIST database.

Training was done using mini batches of 50 images at a time to improve the learning rate (see the discussion in Section 12.7). We also classified all images of the training set and all images of the test set after each epoch of training. The objective of doing this was to see how quickly the system was learning the characteristics of the data. Figure 12.51 shows the results. A high level of correct recognition performance was achieved after relatively few epochs for both data sets, with approximately 98% correct recognition achieved after about 40 epochs. This is consistent with the training MSE in Fig. 12.50, which dropped quickly, then began a slow descent after about 40 epochs. Another 160 epochs of training were required for the system to achieve recognition of about 99.9%. These are impressive results for such a small CNN.

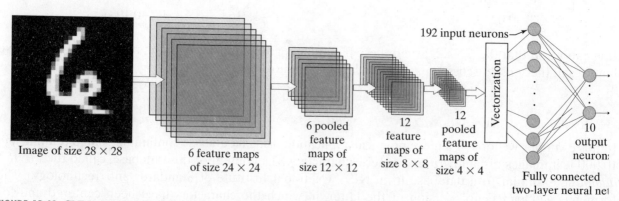

FIGURE 12.49 CNN used to recognize the ten digits in the MNIST database. The system was trained with 60,000 numerical character images of the same size as the image shown on the left. This architecture is the same as the architecture we used in Fig. 12.42. (Image courtesy of NIST.)

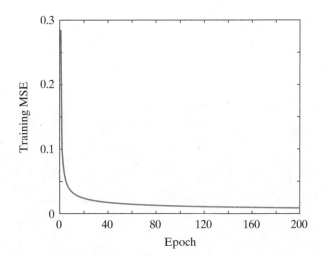

FIGURE 12.50
Training mean squared error as a function of epoch for the 60,000 training digit images in the MNIST database.

Figure 12.52 shows recognition performance on each digit class for both the training and test sets. The most revealing feature of these two graphs is that the CNN did equally as well on both sets of data. This is a good indication that the training was successful, and that it generalized well to digits it had not seen before. This is an example of the neural network not "over-fitting" the data in the training set.

Figure 12.53 shows the values of the kernels for the first feature map, displayed as intensities. There is one input image and six feature maps, so six kernels are required to generate the feature maps of the first layer. The dimensions of the kernels are the same as the receptive field, which we set at 5×5. Thus, the first image on the left in Fig. 12.53 is the 5×5 kernel corresponding to the first feature map. Figure 12.54 shows the kernels for the second layer. In this layer, we have six inputs (which are the pooled maps of the first layer) and twelve feature maps, so we need a total of $6 \times 12 = 72$ kernels and biases to generate the twelve feature maps in the second layer. Each column of Fig. 12.54 shows the six 5×5 kernels

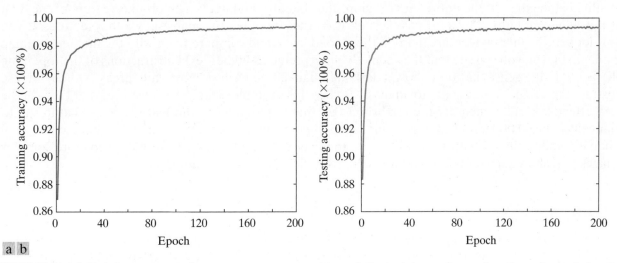

a b

FIGURE 12.51 (a) Training accuracy (percent correct recognition of the training set) as a function of epoch for the 60,000 training images in the MNIST database. The maximum achieved was 99.36% correct recognition. (b) Accuracy as a function of epoch for the 10,000 test images in the MNIST database. The maximum correct recognition rate was 99.13%.

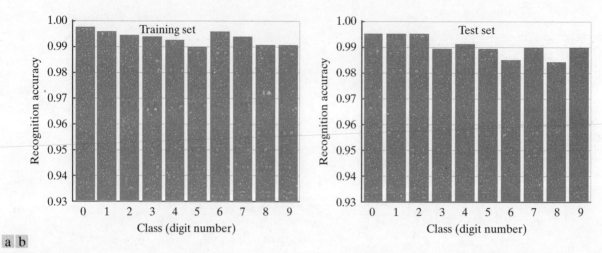

FIGURE 12.52 (a) Recognition accuracy of training set by image class. Each bar shows a number between 0 and 1. When multiplied by 100%, these numbers give the correct recognition percentage for that class. (b) Recognition results per class in the test set. In both graphs the recognition rate is above 98%.

corresponding to one of the feature maps in the second layer. We used 2×2 pooling in both layers, resulting in a 50% reduction of each of the two spatial dimensions of the feature maps.

Finally, it is of interest to visualize how one input image proceeds through the network, using the kernels learned during training. Figure 12.55 shows an input digit image from the test set, and the computations performed by the CNN at each layer. As before, we display numerical results as intensities.

Consider the results of convolution in the first layer. If you look at each resulting feature map carefully, you will notice that it highlights a different characteristic of the input. For example, the feature map on the top of the first column highlights the two vertical edges on the top of the character. The second highlights the edges of the entire inner region, and the third highlights a "blob-like" feature of the digit, as if it had been blurred by a lowpass kernel. The other three feature maps show other features. If you now look at the first two feature maps in the second layer, and compare them with the first feature map in the first layer, you can see that they could be interpreted as higher-level abstractions of the top of the character, in the sense that they show a dark area flanked on each side by white areas. Although these abstractions are not always easy to analyze visually, this example clearly demonstrates that they can be very effective. And, remember the important fact that our simple system learned these features automatically from 60,000 training images. This capability is what makes convolutional networks so powerful when it comes to image pattern classification. In the next example, we will consider even more complex images, and show some of the limitations of our simple CNN architecture.

EXAMPLE 12.18: Using a large image database to teach a CNN to recognize natural images.

In this example, we trained the same CNN architecture as in Fig. 12.49, but using the RGB color images in Fig. 12.56. These images are representative of those found in the CIFAR-10 database, a popular database used to test the performance of image classification systems. Our objective was to test the limitations of the CNN architecture in Fig. 12.49 by training it with data that is significantly more complex than the MNIST images in Example 12.17. The only difference between the architecture needed to

FIGURE 12.53
Kernels of the first layer after 200 epochs of training, shown as images.

FIGURE 12.54 Kernels of the second layer after 200 epochs of training, displayed as images of size 5×5. There are six inputs (pooled feature maps) into the second layer. Because there are twelve feature maps in the second layer, the CNN learned the weights of $6 \times 12 = 72$ kernels.

FIGURE 12.55
Results of a forward pass for one digit image through the CNN in Fig. 12.49 after training. The feature maps were generated using the kernels from Figs. 12.53 and 12.54, followed by pooling. The neural net is the two-layer neural network from Fig. 12.49. The output high value (in white) indicates that the CNN recognized the input properly. (This figure is the same as Fig. 12.44.)

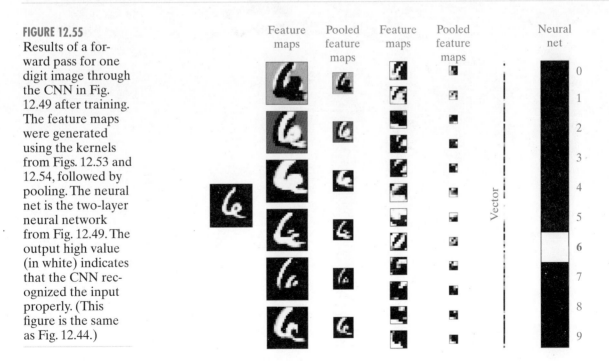

FIGURE 12.56
Mini images of size 32×32 pixels, representative of the 50,000 training and 10,000 test images in the CIFAR-10 database (the 10 stands for ten classes). The class names are shown on the right. (Images courtesy of Pearson Education.)

Airplane

Automobile

Bird

Cat

Deer

Dog

Frog

Horse

Ship

Truck

FIGURE 12.57
Training mean squared error as a function of the number of epochs for a training set of 50,000 CIFAR-10 images.

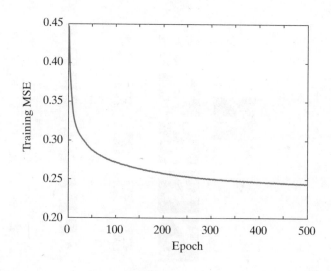

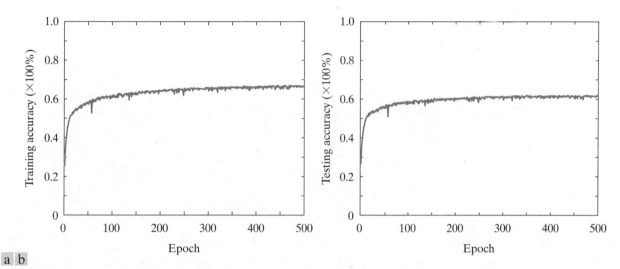

a b

FIGURE 12.58 (a) Training accuracy (percent correct recognition of the training set) as a function of epoch for the 50,000 training images in the CIFAR-10 database. (b) Accuracy as a function of epoch for the 10,000 CIFAR-10 test images.

process the CIFAR-10 images, and the architecture in Fig. 12.49, is that the CIFAR-10 images are RGB color images, and hence have three channels. We worked with these input images using the approach explained in the subsection entitled Multiple Input Images, on page 973.

We trained the modified CNN for 500 epochs using the 50,000 training images of the CIFAR-10 database. Figure 12.57 is a plot of the mean squared error as a function of epoch during the training phase. Observe that the MSE begins to plateau at a value of approximately 0.25. In contrast, the MSE plot in Fig. 12.50 for the MNIST data achieved a much lower final value. This is not unexpected, given that the CIFAR-10 images are significantly more complex, both in the objects of interest as well as their backgrounds. The lower expected recognition performance of the training set is confirmed by the training-accuracy plotted in Fig. 12.58(a) as a function of epoch. The recognition rate leveled-off around 68% for the training data and about 61% for the test data. Although these results are not nearly as good as those obtained for the MNIST data, they are consistent with what we would expect from a very basic network. It is possible to achieve over 96% accuracy on this database (see Graham [2015]), but that requires a more complex network and a different pooling strategy.

Figure 12.59 shows the recognition accuracy per class for the training and test image sets. With a few exceptions, the highest recognition rate in both the training and test sets was achieved for engineered objects, and the lowest was for small animals. Frogs were an exception, caused most likely by the fact that frog size and shape are more consistent than they are, for example, in dogs and birds. As you can see in Fig. 12.59, if the small animals were removed from the list, recognition performance on the rest of the images would have been considerably higher.

Figures 12.60 and Fig. 12.61 show the kernels of the first and second layers. Note that each column in Fig. 12.60 has three 5×5 kernels. This is because there are three input channels to the CNN in this example. If you look carefully at the columns in Fig. 12.60, you can detect a similarity in the arrangement and values of the coefficients. Although it is not obvious what the kernels are detecting, it is clear that they are consistent in each column, and that all columns are quite different from each other, indicating a capability to detect different features in the input images. We show Fig. 12.61 for completeness only, as

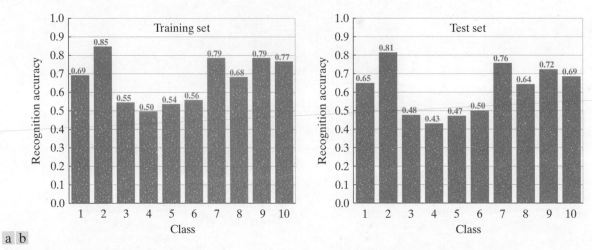

a b

FIGURE 12.59 (a) CIFAR-10 recognition rate of training set by image class. Each bar shows a number between 0 and 1. When multiplied by 100%, these numbers give the correct recognition percentage for that class. (b) Recognition results per class in the test set.

there is little we can infer that deep into the network, especially at this small scale, and considering the complexity of the images in the training set. Finally, Fig. 12.62 shows a complete recognition pass through the CNN using the weights in Figs. 12.60 and 12.61. The input shows the three color channels of the RGB image in the seventh column of the first row in Fig. 12.56. The feature maps in the first column, show the various features extracted from the input. The second column shows the pooling results, zoomed to the size of the features maps for clarity. The third and fourth columns show the results in the second layer, and the fifth column shows the vectorized output. Finally, the last column shows the result of recognition, with white representing a high output, and the others showing much smaller values. The input image was properly recognized as belonging to class 1.

FIGURE 12.60
Weights of the kernels of the first convolution layer after 500 epochs of training.

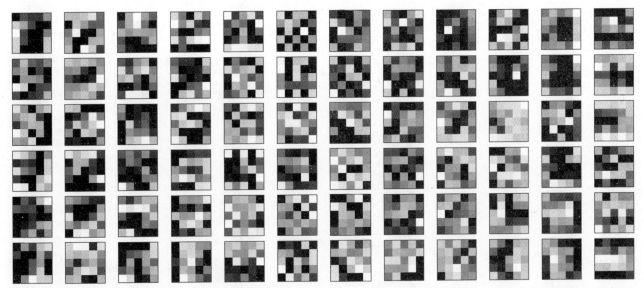

FIGURE 12.61 Weights of the kernels of the second convolution layer after 500 epochs of training. The interpretation of these kernels is the same as in Fig. 12.54.

12.7 SOME ADDITIONAL DETAILS OF IMPLEMENTATION

We mentioned in the previous section that neural (including convolutional) nets have the ability to learn features directly from training data, thus reducing the need for "engineered" features. While this is a significant advantage, it does not imply that the design of a neural network is free of human input. On the contrary, designing complex neural networks requires significant skill and experimentation.

In the last two sections, our focus was on the development of fundamental concepts in neural nets, with an emphasis on the derivation of backpropagation for both fully connected and convolutional nets. Backpropagation is the backbone of neural net design, but there are other important considerations that influence how well a neural net learns, and then generalizes to patterns it has not seen before. In this section, we discuss briefly some important aspects in the design of fully connected and convolutional neural networks.

One of the first questions when designing a neural net architecture is how many layers to specify for the network. Theoretically, the *universality approximation theorem* (Cybenco [1989]) tells us that, under mild conditions, arbitrarily complex decision functions can be *approximated* by a continuous feedforward neural network with a single hidden layer. Although the theorem does not tell us how to compute the parameters of that single hidden layer, it does indicate that structurally simple neural nets can be very powerful. You have seen this in some of the examples in the last two sections. Experimental evidence suggests that deep neural nets (i.e., networks with two or more hidden layers) are better than a single hidden layer network at learning abstract representations, which typically is the main point of learning. There is no such thing as an algorithm to determine the "optimum" number of layers to use in a neural network. Therefore, specifying the number of layers generally

FIGURE 12.62
Graphical
illustration of
a forward pass
through the
trained CNN.
The purpose
was to recognize
one input image
from the set in
Fig. 12.56. As the
output shows, the
image was
recognized
correctly as
belonging to class
1, the class of
airplanes.
(Original image
courtesy of
Pearson
Education.)

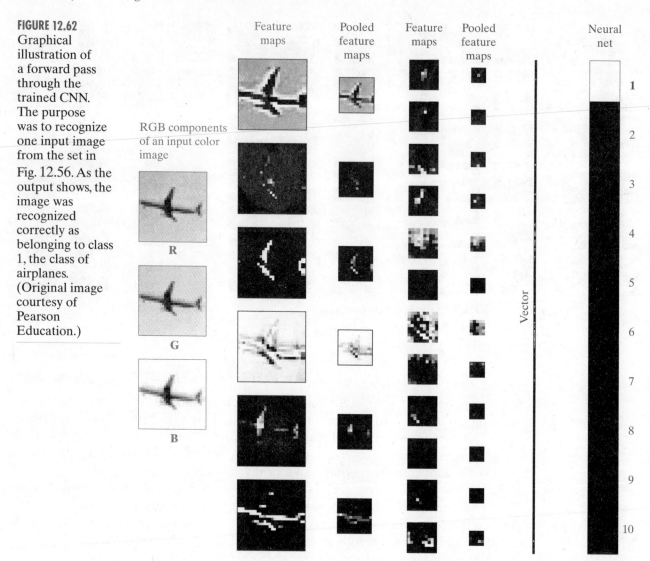

is determined by a combination of experience and experimentation. "Starting small"
is a logical approach to this problem. The more layers a network has, the higher the
probability that backpropagation will run into problems such as so-called *vanishing
gradients,* where gradient values are so small that gradient descent ceases to be effective. In convolutional networks, we have the added issue that the size of the inputs
decreases as the images propagate through the network. There are two causes for
this. The first is a natural size reduction caused by convolution itself, with the amount
of reduction being proportional to the size of the receptive fields. One solution is to
use *padding* prior to performing convolution operations, as we discussed in Section
3.4. The second (and most significant) cause of size reduction is pooling. The minimum pooling neighborhood is of size 2×2, which reduces the size of feature maps
by three-quarters at each layer. A solution that helps is to *upsample* the input images,

but this must done with care because the relative sizes of features of interest would increase proportionally, thus influencing the size selected for receptive fields.

After the number of layers has been specified, the next task is to specify the number of neurons per layer. We always know how many neurons are needed in the first and last layers, but the number of neurons for internal layer is also an open question with no theoretical "best" answer. If the objective is to keep the number of layers as small as possible, the power of the network is increased to some degree by increasing the number of neurons per layer.

The main aspects of specifying the architecture of a neural network are completed by specifying the activation function. In this chapter, we worked with sigmoid functions for consistency between examples, but there are applications in which hyperbolic tangent and ReLU activation functions are superior in terms of improving training performance.

Once a network architecture has been specified, training is the central aspect of making the architecture useful. Although the networks we discussed in this chapter are relatively simple, networks applied to very large-scale problems can have millions of nodes and require large blocks of time to train. When available, the parameters of a *pretrained* network are an ideal starting point for further training, or for validating recognition performance. Another central theme in training neural nets is the use of GPUs to accelerate matrix operations.

An issue often encountered in training is *over-fitting*, in which recognition of the training set is acceptable, but the recognition rate on samples not used for training is much lower. That is, the net is not able to *generalize* what it learned and apply it to inputs it has not encountered before. When additional training data is not available, the most common approach is to artificially enlarge the training set using transformations such as geometric distortions and intensity variations. The transformations are carried out while preserving the class membership of the transformed patterns. Another major approach is to use *dropout*, a technique that randomly drops nodes with their connections from a neural network during training. The idea is to change the architecture slightly to prevent the net from adapting too much to a fixed set of parameters (see Srivastava et al. [2014]).

In addition to computational speed, another important aspect of training is efficiency. Simple things, such as shuffling the input patterns at the beginning of each training epoch can reduce or eliminate the possibility of "cycling," in which parameter values repeat at regular intervals. *Stochastic gradient descent* is another important training refinement in which, instead of using the entire training set, samples are selected randomly and input into the network. You can think of this as dividing the training set into *mini-batches,* and then choosing a single sample from each mini-batch. This approach often results in speedier convergence during training.

In addition to the above topics, a paper by LeCun et al. [2012] is an excellent overview of the types of considerations introduced in the preceding discussion. In fact, the breath spanned by these topics is extensive enough to be the subject of an entire book (see Montavon et al. [2012]). The neural net architectures we discussed were by necessity limited in scope. You can get a good idea of the practical requirements of implementing practical networks by reading a paper by Krizhevsky, Sutskever, and Hinton [2012], which summarizes the design and implementation of a large-scale, deep convolutional neural network. There are a multitude of designs that have been implemented over the past decade, including commercial and free implementations. A quick internet search will reveal a multitude of available architectures.

Summary, References, and Further Reading

Background material for Sections 12.1 through 12.4 are the books by Theodoridis and Koutroumbas [2006], by Duda, Hart, and Stork [2001], and by Tou and Gonzalez [1974]. For additional reading on the material on matching shape numbers see Bribiesca and Guzman [1980]. On string matching, see Sze and Yang [1981]. A significant portion of this chapter was devoted to neural networks. This is a reflection of the fact that neural nets, and in particular convolutional neural nets, have made significant strides in the past decade in solving image pattern classifications problems. As in the rest of the book, our presentation of this topic focused on fundamentals, but the topics covered were thoroughly developed. What you have learned in this chapter is a solid foundation for much of the work being conducted in this area. As we mentioned earlier, the literature on neural nets is vast, and quickly growing. As a starting point, a basic book by Nielsen [2015] provides an excellent introduction to the topic. The more advanced book by Goodfellow, Bengio, and Courville [2016] provides more depth into the mathematical underpinning of neural nets. Two classic papers worth reading are by Rumelhart, Hinton, and Williams [1986], and by LeCun, Bengio, and Haffner [1998]. The LeNet architecture we discussed in Section 12.6 was introduced in the latter reference, and it is still a foundation for image pattern classification. A recent survey article by LeCun, Bengio, and Hinton [2015] gives an interesting perspective on the scope of applicability of neural nets in general. The paper by Krizhevsky, Sutskever, and Hinton [2012] was one of the most important catalysts leading to the significant increase in the present interest on convolutional networks, and on their applicability to image pattern classification. This paper is also a good overview of the details and techniques involved in implementing a large-scale convolutional neural network. For details on the software aspects of many of the examples in this chapter, see Gonzalez, Woods, and Eddins [2009].

Problems

Solutions to the problems marked with an asterisk (*) are in the DIP4E Student Support Package (consult the book website: www.ImageProcessingPlace.com).

12.1 Do the following:

  (a)* Compute the decision functions of a minimum distance classifier for the patterns in Fig. 12.10. You may obtain the required mean vectors by (careful) inspection.

  (b) Sketch the decision boundary implemented by the decision functions in (a).

12.2* Discuss in detail on pattern and pattern classes.

12.3 Show that the boundary given by Eq. (12-8) is the perpendicular bisector of the line joining the n-dimensional points $\mathbf{m}_i$ and $\mathbf{m}_j$.

12.4* Show how the minimum distance classifier discussed in connection with Fig. 12.11 could be implemented by using N_c resistor banks (N_c is the number of classes), a summing junction at each bank (for summing currents), and a maxi-

mum selector capable of selecting the maximum value of N_c decision functions in order to determine the class membership of a given input.

12.5* What do you mean by prototype matching? Explain the widely used method for prototype matching.

12.6 Show that the distance measure $D(a,b)$ in Eq. (12-12) satisfies the properties in Eq. (12-13).

12.7* Given two boundary regions, a and b, represented in the form of strings. If α represents the number of symbols that match and β represents the number of symbols that do not match. Now, state the condition when β will be zero. Also, prove the condition.

12.8 Explain the structural relationships inherent in pattern shapes by matching shape number. Also state the properties that satisfy the same.

12.9* The following pattern classes have Gaussian probability density functions:

$$\omega_1 : \{(0,0)^T, (-2,0)^T, (-2,-2)^T, (0,-2)^T\}$$
$$\omega_2 : \{(-4,-4)^T, (-6,-4)^T, (-6,-6)^T, (-4,-6)^T\}$$

(a) Assume that $P(\omega_1) = P(\omega_2) = 1/2$ and obtain the equation of the Bayes decision boundary between these two classes.

(b) Sketch the boundary.

12.10 Repeat Problem 12.9, but use the following pattern classes:

$$c_1 : \{(-1,0)^T, (0,-1)^T, (1,0)^T, (0,1)^T\}$$
$$c_2 : \{(-2,0)^T, (0,-2)^T, (2,0)^T, (0,2)^T\}$$

Note that the classes are not linearly separable.

12.11 In string matching, the largest value of R gives the best match. Justify the statement.

12.12* We derived the Bayes decision functions

$$d_j(\mathbf{x}) = p(\mathbf{x}/c_j) P(c_j), \ j = 1, 2, ..., N_c$$

using a 0-1 loss function. Prove that these decision functions minimize the probability of error. (*Hint:* The probability of error $p(e)$ is $1 - p(c)$, where $p(c)$ is the probability of being correct. For a pattern vector $\mathbf{x}$ belonging to class c_i, $p(c/\mathbf{x}) = p(c_i/\mathbf{x})$. Find $p(c)$ and show that $p(c)$ is maximum [$p(e)$ is minimum] when $p(\mathbf{x}/c_i)P(c_i)$ is maximum.)

12.13 Explain the probability density function for two 1-D pattern classes in Bayes classifier for Gaussian pattern classes.

12.14* The perceptron algorithm given in Eqs. (12-44) through (12-46) can be expressed in a more concise form by multiplying the patterns of class c_2 by -1, in which case the correction steps in the algorithm become $\mathbf{w}(k+1) = \mathbf{w}(k)$, if $\mathbf{w}^T(k)\mathbf{y}(k) > 0$, and $\mathbf{w}(k+1) = \mathbf{w}(k) + \alpha \mathbf{y}(k)$ otherwise, where we use $\mathbf{y}$ instead of $\mathbf{x}$ to make it clear that the patterns of class c_2 were multiplied by -1. This is one of several perceptron algorithm formulations that can be derived starting from the general gradient descent equation

$$\mathbf{w}(k+1) = \mathbf{w}(k) - \alpha \left[\frac{\partial J(\mathbf{w}, \mathbf{y})}{\partial \mathbf{w}} \right]_{\mathbf{w} = \mathbf{w}(k)}$$

where $\alpha > 0$, $J(\mathbf{w}, \mathbf{y})$ is a criterion function, and the partial derivative is evaluated at $\mathbf{w} = \mathbf{w}(k)$. Show that the perceptron algorithm in the problem statement can be obtained from this general gradient descent procedure by using the criterion function

$$J(\mathbf{w}, \mathbf{y}) = \frac{1}{2} \left(\left| \mathbf{w}^T \mathbf{y} \right| - \mathbf{w}^T \mathbf{y} \right)$$

(*Hint:* The partial derivative of $\mathbf{w}^T \mathbf{y}$ with respect to $\mathbf{w}$ is $\mathbf{y}$.)

12.15* Prove that the perceptron training algorithm given in Eqs. (12-44) through (12-46) converges in a finite number of steps if the training pattern sets are linearly separable. [*Hint:* Multiply the patterns of class c_2 by -1 and consider a non-negative threshold, T_0 so that the perceptron training algorithm (with $\alpha = 1$) is expressed in the form $\mathbf{w}(k+1) = \mathbf{w}(k)$, if $\mathbf{w}^T(k)\mathbf{y}(k) > T_0$, and $\mathbf{w}(k+1) = \mathbf{w}(k) + \alpha \mathbf{y}(k)$ otherwise. You may need to use the Cauchy-Schwartz inequality: $\|\mathbf{a}\|^2 \|\mathbf{b}\|^2 \geq (\mathbf{a}^T\mathbf{b})^2$.]

12.16 Derive equations of the derivatives of the following activation functions:

(a) The sigmoid activation function in Fig. 12.30(a).

(b) The hyperbolic tangent activation function in Fig. 12.30(b).

(c)* The ReLU activation function in Fig. 12.30(c).

12.17* Specify the structure, weights, and bias(es) of the smallest neural network capable of performing *exactly* the same function as a minimum distance classifier for two pattern classes in n-dimensional space. You may assume that the classes are tightly grouped and are linearly separable.

12.18 What is the decision boundary implemented by a neural network with n inputs, a single output neuron, and no hidden layers? Explain.

12.19 Specify the structure, weights, and bias of a neural network capable of performing exactly the same function as a Bayes classifier for two pattern classes in n-dimensional space. The classes are Gaussian with different means but equal covariance matrices.

12.20 Answer the following:

(a)* Under what conditions are the neural networks in Problems 12.17 and 12.19 identical?

(b) Suppose you specify a neural net architecture identical to the one in Problem 12.17. Would training by backpropagation yield the same weights and bias as that network if trained with a sufficiently large number of samples? Explain.

12.21 Two pattern classes in two dimensions are distributed in such a way that the patterns of class c_1 lie randomly along a circle of radius r_1. Similarly, the patterns of class c_2 lie randomly along a circle of radius r_2, where $r_2 = 2r_1$. Specify the structure of a neural network with the minimum number of layers and nodes needed to classify properly the patterns of these two classes.

12.22* If two classes are linearly separable, we can train a perceptron starting with weights and a bias that are all zero, and we would still get a solution. Can you do the same when training a neural network by backpropagation? Explain.

12.23 In feedforward neural network, calculate the output from the figure shown using matrix formulation.

$$a(1) = x = \begin{bmatrix} 5 \\ 0 \\ 1 \end{bmatrix} \quad W(2) = \begin{bmatrix} 0.2 & 0.5 & 0.1 \\ 0.3 & 0.4 & 0.2 \end{bmatrix} \quad W(3) = \begin{bmatrix} 0.1 & 0.3 \\ 0.5 & 0.1 \end{bmatrix}$$

$$b(2) = \begin{bmatrix} 0.3 \\ 0.1 \end{bmatrix} \qquad b(3) = \begin{bmatrix} 0.4 \\ 0.2 \end{bmatrix}$$

12.24 Answer the following:

(a) The last element of the input vector in Fig. 12.32 is 1. Is this vector augmented? Explain.

(b) Repeat the calculations in Fig. 12.32, but using weight matrices that are 100 times the values of those used in the figure.

(c)* What can you conclude in general from your results in (b)?

12.25 Answer the following:

(a)* The chain rule in Eq. (12-70) shows three terms. However, you are probably more

familiar with chain rule expressions that have two terms. Show that if you start with the expression

$$\delta_j(\ell) = \frac{\partial E}{\partial z_j(\ell)} = \sum_i \frac{\partial E}{\partial z_i(\ell+1)} \frac{\partial z_i(\ell+1)}{\partial z_j(\ell)}$$

you can arrive at the result in Eq. (12-70).

(b) Show how the middle term in the third line of Eq. (12-70) follows from the middle term in the second.

12.26 State all the values that are needed to compute in a forward pass through convolution section of a CNN.

12.27* Show that the dimensions of matrix $\mathbf{D}(\ell)$ in Eq. (12-79) are $n_\ell \times n_p$. (*Hint:* Some of the parameters in that equation are computed in forward propagation, so you already know their dimensions.)

12.28 With reference to the discussion following Eq. (12-82), explain why the error for one pattern is obtained by squaring the elements of one column of matrix $(\mathbf{A}(L) - \mathbf{R})$, adding them, and dividing the result by 2.

12.29* The matrix formulation in Table 12.3 contains all patterns as columns of a single matrix $\mathbf{X}$. This is ideal in terms of speed and economy of implementation. It is also well suited when training is done using mini-batches. However, there are applications in which the large number of training vectors is too large to hold in memory, and it becomes more practical to loop through each pattern using the vector formulation. Compose a table similar to Table 12.3, but using individual patterns, $\mathbf{x}$, instead of matrix $\mathbf{X}$.

12.30 Consider a CNN whose inputs are RGB color images of size 512×512 pixels. The network has two convolutional layers. Using this information, answer the following:

(a)* You are told that the spatial dimensions of the feature maps in the first layer are 504×504, and that there are 12 feature maps in the first layer. Assuming that no padding is used, and that the kernels used are square, and of an odd size, what are the spatial dimensions of these kernels?

(b) If subsampling is done using neighborhoods of size 2×2, what are the spatial dimensions of the pooled feature maps in the first layer?

(c) What is the depth (number) of the pooled feature maps in the first layer?

(d) The spatial dimensions of the convolution kernels in the second layer are 3×3. Assuming no padding, what are the sizes of the feature maps in the second layer?

(e) You are told that the number of feature maps in the second layer is 6, and that the size of the pooling neighborhoods is again 2×2. What are the dimensions of the vectors that result from vectorizing the last layer of the CNN? Assume that vectorization is done using linear indexing.

12.31 Suppose the input images to a CNN are padded to compensate for the size reduction caused by convolution and subsampling (pooling). Let P denote the thickness of the padding border, let V denote the width of the (square) input images, let S denote the stride, and let F denote the width of the (square) receptive field.

(a) Show that the number, N, of neurons in each row in the resulting feature map is

$$N = \frac{V + 2P - F}{S} + 1$$

(b) * How would you interpret a result using this equation that is not an integer?

12.32 * Show the validity of Eq. (12-106).

12.33 An experiment produces binary images of blobs that are nearly elliptical in shape, as the following example image shows. The blobs are of three sizes, with the average values of the principal axes of the ellipses being (1.3, 0.7), (1.0, 0.5), and (0.75, 0.25). The dimensions of these axes vary $\pm 10\%$ about their average values.

Develop an image processing system capable of rejecting incomplete or overlapping ellipses, then classifying the remaining single ellipses into one of the three given size classes. Show your solution in block diagram form, giving specific details regarding the operation of each block. Solve the classification problem using a minimum distance classifier, indicating clearly how you would go about obtaining training samples, and how you would use these samples to train the classifier.

12.34 A factory mass-produces small American flags for sporting events. The quality assurance team has observed that, during periods of peak production, some printing machines have a tendency to drop (randomly) between one and three stars and one or two entire stripes. Aside from these errors, the flags are perfect in every other way. Although the flags containing errors represent a small percentage of total production, the plant manager decides to solve the problem. After much investigation, she concludes that automatic inspection using image processing techniques is the most economical approach. The basic specifications are as follows: The flags are approximately 7.5 cm by 12.5 cm in size. They move lengthwise down the production line (individually, but with a $\pm 15\%$ variation in orientation) at approximately 50 cm/s, with a separation between flags of approximately 5 cm. In all cases, "approximately" means $\pm 5\%$. The plant manager employs you to design an image processing system for each production line. You are told that cost and simplicity are important parameters in determining the viability of your approach. Design a complete system based on the model of Fig. 1.23. Document your solution (including assumptions and specifications) in a brief (but clear) written report addressed to the plant manager. You can use any of the methods discussed in the book.

Bibliography

Abidi, M. A. and Gonzalez, R. C. (eds.) [1992]. *Data Fusion in Robotics and Machine Intelligence*, Academic Press, New York.

Abramson, N. [1963]. *Information Theory and Coding*, McGraw-Hill, New York.

Achanta, R., et al. [2012]. "SLIC Superpixels Compared to State-of-the-Art Superpixel Methods," *IEEE Trans. Pattern Anal. Mach. Intell.* vol. 34, no. 11, pp. 2274–2281.

Ahmed, N., Natarajan, T., and Rao, K. R. [1974]. "Discrete Cosine Transforms," *IEEE Trans. Comp.*, vol. C-23, pp. 90–93.

Andrews, H. C. [1970]. *Computer Techniques in Image Processing*, Academic Press, New York.

Andrews, H. C. and Hunt, B. R. [1977]. *Digital Image Restoration*, Prentice Hall, Englewood Cliffs, NJ.

Antonini, M., Barlaud, M., Mathieu, P., and Daubechies, I. [1992]. "Image Coding Using Wavelet Transform," *IEEE Trans. Image Process.*, vol. 1, no. 2, pp. 205–220.

Ascher, R.N. and Nagy, G. [1974]. "A Means for Achieving a High Degree of Compaction on Scan-Digitized Printed Text," *IEEE Transactions on Comp.*, C-23, pp. 1174–1179.

Ballard, D. H. [1981]. "Generalizing the Hough Transform to Detect Arbitrary Shapes," *Pattern Recognition*, vol. 13, no. 2, pp. 111–122.

Ballard, D. H. and Brown, C. M. [1982]. *Computer Vision*, Prentice Hall, Englewood Cliffs, NJ.

Basart, J. P., Chacklackal, M. S., and Gonzalez, R. C. [1992]. "Introduction to Gray-Scale Morphology," in *Advances in Image Analysis*, Y. Mahdavieh and R. C. Gonzalez (eds.), SPIE Press, Bellingham, WA, pp. 306–354.

Basart, J. P. and Gonzalez, R. C. [1992]. "Binary Morphology," in *Advances in Image Analysis*, Y. Mahdavieh and R. C. Gonzalez (eds.), SPIE Press, Bellingham, WA, pp. 277–305.

Bell, E.T. [1965]. *Men of Mathematics*, Simon & Schuster, New York.

Berger, T. [1971]. *Rate Distortion Theory*, Prentice Hall, Englewood Cliffs, N.J.

Beucher, S. and Meyer, F. [1992]. "The Morphological Approach of Segmentation: The Watershed Transformation," in *Mathematical Morphology in Image Processing*, E. Dougherty (ed.), Marcel Dekker, New York.

Beyerer, J., Puente Leon, F. and Frese, C. [2016]. *Machine Vision—Automated Visual Inspection: Theory, Practice, and Applications*, Springer-Verlag, Berlin, GermaNew York.

Blahut, R. E. [1987]. *Principles and Practice of Information Theory*, Addison-Wesley, Reading, MA.

Bleau, A. and Leon, L. J. [2000]. "Watershed-Based Segmentation and Region Merging," *Computer Vision and Image Understanding*, vol. 77, no. 3, pp. 317–370.

Blum, H. [1967]. "A Transformation for Extracting New Descriptors of Shape," in *Models for the Perception of Speech and Visual Form*, Wathen-Dunn, W. (ed.), MIT Press, Cambridge, MA.

Born, M. and Wolf, E. [1999]. *Principles of Optics: Electromagnetic Theory of Propagation, Interference and Diffraction of Light*, 7th ed., Cambridge University Press,Cambridge, UK.

Bracewell, R. N. [1995]. *Two-Dimensional Imaging*, Prentice Hall, Upper Saddle River, NJ.

Bracewell, R. N. [2003]. *Fourier Analysis and Imaging*, Springer, New York.

Bribiesca, E. [1992]. "A Geometric Structure for Two-Dimensional Shapes and Three Dimensional Surfaces," *Pattern Recognition*, vol. 25, pp. 483–496.

Bribiesca, E. [2013]. "A Measure of Tortuosity Based on Chain Coding," *Pattern Recognition*, vol. 46, pp. 716–724.

Bribiesca, E. and Guzman, A. [1980]. "How to Describe Pure Form and How to Measure Differences in Shape Using Shape Numbers," *Pattern Recognition*, vol. 12, no. 2, pp. 101–112.

Brigham, E. O. [1988]. *The Fast Fourier Transform and its Applications*, Prentice Hall, Upper Saddle River, NJ.

Bronson, R. and Costa, G. B. [2009]. *Matrix Methods: Applied Linear Algebra*, 3rd ed., Academic Press/Elsevier, Burlington, MA.

Burrus, C. S., Gopinath, R. A., and Guo, H. [1998]. *Introduction to Wavelets and Wavelet Transforms*, Prentice Hall, Upper Saddle River, NJ, pp.250–251.

Buzug, T. M. [2008]. *Computed Tomography: From Photon Statistics to Modern Cone-Beam CT*, Springer-Verlag, Berlin, Germany.

Cannon, T. M. [1974]. "Digital Image Deblurring by Non-Linear Homomorphic Filtering," Ph.D. thesis, University of Utah.

Canny, J. [1986]. "A Computational Approach for Edge Detection," *IEEE Trans. Pattern Anal. Machine Intell.*, vol. 8, no. 6, pp. 679–698.

Caselles, V., Kimmel, R., and Sapiro, G. [1997]. "Geodesic Active Contours," *Int'l J. Comp. Vision*, vol. 22, no. 1, pp. 61–79.

Castleman, K. R. [1996]. *Digital Image Processing*, 2nd ed., Prentice Hall, Upper Saddle River, NJ.

Chakrabarti, I., et al. [2015]. *Motion Estimation for Video Coding*, Springer Int'l Publishing, Cham, Switzerland.

Champeney, D. C. [1987]. *A Handbook of Fourier Theorems*, Cambridge University Press, London, UK.

Chan, T. F. and Vese, L. A. [2001]. "Active Contours Without Edges," *IEEE Trans. Image Process.*, vol. 10, no. 2, pp. 266–277.

Cheng, Y., Hu, X., Wang, J., Wang, Y., and Tamura, S. [2015]. "Accurate Vessel Segmentation with Constrained B-Snake," *IEEE Trans. Image Process.* vol. 24, no. 8, pp. 2440-2455.

Choromanska, A., et al. [2015]. "The Loss Surfaces of Multilayer Networks," *Proc. 18th Int'l Conference Artificial Intell. and Statistics* (AISTATS), vol. 38, pp. 192–204.

Clarke, R. J. [1985]. *Transform Coding of Images*, Academic Press, New York.

Cohen, A., Daubechies, I., and Feauveau, J.-C. [1992]. "Biorthogonal Bases of Compactly Supported Wavelets," *Commun. Pure and Appl. Math.*, vol. 45, pp. 485–560.

Coifman, R. R. and Wickerhauser, M. V. [1992]. "Entropy-Based Algorithms for Best Basis Selection," *IEEE Tran. Information Theory*, vol. 38, no. 2, pp. 713–718.

Coltuc, D., Bolon, P., and Chassery, J-M [2006]. "Exact Histogram Specification," *IEEE Trans. Image Process.*, vol. 15, no. 5, pp. 1143–1152.

Cornsweet, T. N. [1970]. *Visual Perception*, Academic Press, New York.

Cox, I., Kilian, J., Leighton, F., and Shamoon, T. [1997]. "Secure Spread Spectrum Watermarking for Multimedia," *IEEE Trans. Image Process.*, vol. 6, no. 12, pp. 1673–1687.

Cox, I., Miller, M., and Bloom, J. [2001]. *Digital Watermarking*, Morgan Kaufmann (Elsevier), New York.

Cybenco, G. [1989]. "Approximation by Superposition of a Sigmoidal Function," *Math. Control Signals Systems*, vol. 2, no. 4, pp. 303–314.

D. N. Joanes and C. A. Gill. [1998]. "Comparing Measures of Sample Skewness and Kurtosis". *The Statistician*, vol 47, no. 1, pp. 183–189.

Danielsson, P. E. and Seger, O. [1990]. "Generalized and Separable Sobel Operators," in *Machine Vision for Three-Dimensional Scenes*, Herbert Freeman (ed.), Academic Press, New York.

Daubechies, I. [1988]. "Orthonormal Bases of Compactly Supported Wavelets," *Commun. On Pure and Appl. Math.*, vol. 41, pp. 909–996.

Daubechies, I. [1990]. "The Wavelet Transform, Time-Frequency Localization and Signal Analysis," *IEEE Transactions on Information Theory*, vol. 36, no. 5, pp. 961–1005.

Daubechies, I. [1992]. *Ten Lectures on Wavelets*, Society for Industrial and Applied Mathematics, Philadelphia, PA.

Daubechies, I. [1993]. "Orthonormal Bases of Compactly Supported Wavelets II, Variations on a Theme," *SIAM J. Mathematical Analysis*, vol. 24, no. 2, pp. 499–519.

Daubechies, I. [1996]. "Where Do We Go from Here?—A Personal Point of View," *Proc. IEEE*, vol. 84, no. 4, pp. 510–513.

Delgado-Gonzalo, R., Uhlmann, V., and Unser, M. [2015]. "Snakes on a Plane: A Perfect Snap for Bioimage Analysis," *IEEE Signal Proc. Magazine*, vol. 32, no. 1, pp. 41–48.

de Moura, C. A. and Kubrusky, C. S. (eds.) [2013]. *The Courant-Friedrichs-Lewy (CLF) Condition*, Springer, New York.

Drew, M. S., Wei, J., and Li, Z.-N. [1999]. "Illumination Invariant Image Retrieval and Video Segmentation," *Pattern Recognition.*, vol. 32, no. 8, pp. 1369–1388.

Duda, R. O., Hart, P. E., and Stork, D. G. [2001]. *Pattern Classification*, John Wiley & Sons, New York.

Eng, H.-L. and Ma, K.-K. [2001]. "Noise Adaptive Soft-Switching Median Filter," *IEEE Trans. Image Process.*, vol. 10, no. 2, pp. 242–251.

Eng, H.-L. and Ma, K.-K. [2006]. "A Switching Median Filter With Boundary Discriminitative Noise Detection for Extremely Corrupted Images," *IEEE Trans. Image Process.*, vol. 15, no. 6, pp. 1506–1516.

Federal Bureau of Investigation [1993]. *WSQ Gray-Scale Fingerprint Image Compression Specification*, IAFIS-IC-0110v2, Washington, DC.

Feng, J., Cao, Z, and Pi, Y. [2013]. "Multiphase SAR Image Segmentation With Statistical-Model-Based Active Contours," *IEEE Trans. Geoscience and Remote Sensing*, vol. 51, no. 7, pp. 4190–4199.

Fisher, R. A. [1936]. "The Use of Multiple Measurements in Taxonomic Problems," *Ann. Eugenics*, vol. 7, Part 2, pp. 179–188. (Also in *Contributions to Mathematical Statistics*, John Wiley & Sons, New York, 1950.)

Flusser, J. [2000]. "On the Independence of Rotation Moment Invariants," *Pattern Recognition*, vol. 33, pp. 1405–1410.

Freeman, A. (translator) [1878]. *J. Fourier, The Analytical Theory of Heat*, Cambridge University Press, London, UK.

Freeman, H. [1961]. "On the Encoding of Arbitrary Geometric Configurations," *IEEE Trans. Elec. Computers*, vol. EC-10, pp. 260–268.

Freeman, H. [1974]. "Computer Processing of Line Drawings," *Comput. Surveys*, vol. 6, pp. 57–97.

Frendendall, G. L. and Behrend, W. L. [1960]. "Picture Quality—Procedures for Evaluating Subjective Effects of Interference," *Proc. IRE*, vol. 48, pp. 1030–1034.

Fukunaga, K. [1972]. *Introduction to Statistical Pattern Recognition*, Academic Press, New York.

Furht, B., Greenberg, J., and Westwater, R. [1997]. *Motion Estimation Algorithms for Video Compression*, Kluwer Academic Publishers, Boston.

Gaetano, R., Masi, G., Poggi, G., Verdoliva, L., and Scarpa, G. [2015]. "Marker-Controlled Watershed-Based Segmentation of Multiresolution Remote Sensing Images," *IEEE Trans. Geo Sci and Remote Sensing*, vol. 53, no. 6, pp. 2987–3004.

Gallager, R. and Voorhis, D. V. [1975]. "Optimal Source Codes for Geometrically Distributed Integer Alphabets," *IEEE Trans. Inform. Theory*, vol. IT-21, pp. 228–230.

Giardina, C. R. and Dougherty, E. R. [1988]. *Morphological Methods in Image and Signal Processing*, Prentice Hall, Upper Saddle River, NJ.

Golomb, S. W. [1966]. "Run-Length Encodings," *IEEE Trans. Inform. Theory*, vol. IT-12, pp. 399–401.

Gonzalez, R. C., Edwards, J. J., and Thomason, M. G. [1976]. "An Algorithm for the Inference of Tree Grammars," *Int. J. Comput. Info. Sci.*, vol. 5, no. 2, pp. 145–163.

Gonzalez, R. C., Woods, R. E., and Eddins, S. L. [2004]. *Digital Image Processing Using MATLAB*, Prentice Hall, Upper Saddle River, NJ.

Gonzalez, R. C., Woods, R. E., and Eddins, S. L. [2009]. *Digital Image Processing Using MATLAB*, 3rd ed., Gatesmark Publishing, Knoxville, TN.

Gonzalez, R. C. [1985]. "Industrial Computer Vision," in *Advances in Information Systems Science*, Tou, J. T. (ed.), Plenum, New York, pp. 345–385.

Gonzalez, R. C. [1986]. "Image Enhancement and Restoration," in *Handbook of Pattern Recognition and Image Processing*, Young, T. Y., and Fu, K. S. (eds.), Academic Press, New York, pp. 191–213.

Gonzalez, R. C. and Fittes, B. A. [1977]. "Gray-Level Transformations for Interactive Image Enhancement," *Mechanism and Machine Theory*, vol. 12, pp. 111–122

Gonzalez, R. C. and Safabakhsh, R. [1982]."Computer Vision Techniques for Industrial Applications," *IEEE Computer*, vol. 15, no. 12, pp. 17–32.

Gonzalez, R. C. and Thomason, M. G. [1978]. *Syntactic Pattern Recognition: An Introduction*, Addison-Wesley, Reading, MA.

Gonzalez, R. C. and Woods, R. E. [1992]. *Digital Image Processing*, Addison-Wesley, Reading, MA.

Gonzalez, R. C. and Woods, R. E. [2002]. *Digital Image Processing*, 2nd ed., Prentice Hall, Upper Saddle River, NJ.

Gonzalez, R. C. and Woods, R. E. [2008]. *Digital Image Processing*, 3rd ed., Prentice Hall, Upper Saddle River, NJ.

Goodfellow, I., Bengio, Y., and Courville, A. [2016]. *Deep Learning*, MIT Press, Boston, MA.

Goutsias, J., Vincent, L., and Bloomberg, D. S. (eds) [2000]. *Mathematical Morphology and Its Applications to Image and Signal Processing*, Kluwer Academic Publishers, Boston, MA.

Graham, B. [2015]. "Fractional Max-Pooling," *arXiv:1412.6071v4 [cs.CV], 12 May 2015*

Graham, R. E. [1958]. "Predictive Quantizing of Television Signals," *IRE Wescon Conv. Rec.*, vol. 2, pt. 2, pp. 147–157.

Gunturk, B. K. and Li, Xin (eds.) [2013]. *Image Restoration: Fundamentals and Advances*, CRC Press, Boca Raton, FL.

Haar, A. [1910]. "Zur Theorie der Orthogonalen Funktionensysteme," *Math. Annal.*, vol. 69, pp. 331–371.

Habibi, A. [1971]. "Comparison of Nth Order DPCM Encoder with Linear Transformations and Block Quantization Techniques," *IEEE Trans. Comm. Tech.*, vol. COM-19, no. 6, pp. 948–956.

Hadamard, J. [1893]. "Resolution d'une Question Relative aux Determinants," *Bull. Sci. Math.*, Ser. 2, vol. 17, part I, pp. 240–246.

Haralick, R. M. and Shapiro, L. G. [1992]. *Computer and Robot Vision*, vols 1 & 2, Addison-Wesley, Reading, MA.

Harris, C. and Stephens, M. [1988]. "A Combined Corner and Edge Detection," *Proc. 4th Alvey Vision Conference*, pp. 147-151.

Hebb, D. O. [1949]. *The Organization of Behavior: A Neuropsychological Theory*, John Wiley & Sons, New York.

Hensley, D. [2006]. *Continued Fractions*, World Scientific Publishing Co., River Edge, NJ.

Hespanha, J. P. [2009]. *Linear Systems Theory*, Princeton University Press, Princeton, NJ.

Hochbaum, D. [2010], "Polynomial Time Algorithms for Ratio Regions and a Variant of Normalized Cut" *IEEE Trans. Pattern Anal. and Machine Intell.* vol. 32, no. 5, pp. 889–898.

Hornik, K. [1991]. "Approximation Capabilities of Multilayer Feedforward Networks," *Neural Networks*, vol. 4, no. 2, pp. 251–257.

Hotelling, H. [1933]. "Analysis of a Complex of Statistical Variables into Principal Components," *J. Educ. Psychol.*, vol. 24, pp. 417–441, 498–520.

Hough, P. V. C. [1962]. "Methods and Means for Recognizing Complex Patterns," US Patent 3,069,654.

Hu, M. K. [1962]:"Visual Pattern Recognition by Moment Invariants," *IRE Trans. Info. Theory,* vol. IT-8, pp. 179–187.

Huang, T. S. [1965]:"PCM Picture Transmission," *IEEE Spectrum*, vol. 2, no. 12, pp. 57–63.

Huang, T. S. [1966]. "Digital Picture Coding," *Proc. Natl. Electron. Conf.*, pp. 793–797.

Hubbard, B. B. [1998]. *The World According to Wavelets—The Story of a Mathematical Technique in the Making*, 2nd ed., A. K. Peters, Ltd., Wellesley, MA.

Hubel, D. H. and Wiesel, T. N. [1959]. "Receptive Fields of Single Neurons in the Cat's Stratiate Cortex," *J. of Physiology*, vol. 148, no. 3, pp. 574-591.

Huertas, A. and Medione, G. [1986]. "Detection of Intensity Changes with Subpixel Accuracy using Laplacian-Gaussian Masks," *IEEE Trans. Pattern. Anal. Machine Intell.*, vol. PAMI-8, no. 5, pp. 651–664.

Huffman, D. A. [1952]. "A Method for the Construction of Minimum Redundancy Codes," *Proc. IRE*, vol. 40, no. 10, pp. 1098–1101.

Hufnagel, R. E. and Stanley, N. R. [1964]. "Modulation Transfer Function Associated with Image Transmission through Turbulent Media," *J. Opt. Soc. Amer.*, vol. 54, pp. 52–61.

Hughes, J. F. and Andries, V. D. [2013]. *Computer Graphics: Principles and Practice*, 3rd ed., Pearson, Upper Saddle River, NJ.

Hunt, B. R. [1973]. "The Application of Constrained Least Squares Estimation to Image Restoration by Digital Computer," *IEEE Trans. Comput.*, vol. C-22, no. 9, pp. 805–812.

IEEE Trans. Comm. [1981]. Special issue on picture communication systems, vol. COM-29, no. 12.

IEEE Trans. Information Theory [1992]. Special issue on wavelet transforms and mulitresolution signal analysis, vol. 11, no. 2, Part II.

IEEE Trans. Image Process. [1994]. Special issue on image sequence compression, vol. 3, no. 5.

IEEE Trans. on Image Process. [1996]. Special issue on vector quantization, vol. 5, no. 2.

IEEE Trans. Pattern Analysis and Machine Intelligence [1989]. Special issue on multiresolution processing, vol. 11, no. 7.

IEEE Trans. Signal Processing [1993]. Special issue on wavelets and signal processing, vol. 41, no. 12.

IES Lighting Handbook, 10th ed. [2011]. Illuminating Engineering Society Press, New York.

ISO/IEC JTC 1/SC 29/WG 1 [2000]. ISO/IEC FCD 15444-1: *Information technology—JPEG 2000 image coding system: Core coding system*.

Jain, A. K. [1989]. *Fundamentals of Digital Image Processing*, Prentice Hall, Englwood Cliffs, NJ.

Jain, J. R. and Jain, A. K. [1981]. "Displacement Measurement and Its Application in Interframe Image Coding," *IEEE Trans. Comm.*, vol. COM-29, pp. 1799–1808.

Jain, R., Kasturi, R., and Schunk, B. [1995]. *Computer Vision*, McGraw-Hill, New York.

Jain, R. [1981]. "Dynamic Scene Analysis Using Pixel-Based Processes," *Computer*, vol. 14, no. 8, pp. 12–18.

Ji, L. and Yang, H. [2002]. "Robust Topology-Adaptive Snakes for Image Segmentation," *Image and Vision Computing*, vol. 20, no. 2, pp. 147–164.

Jones, R. and Svalbe, I. [1994]. "Algorithms for the Decomposition of Gray-Scale Morphological Operations," *IEEE Trans. Pattern Anal. Machine Intell.*, vol. 16, no. 6, pp. 581–588.

Kak, A. C. and Slaney, M. [2001]. *Principles of Computerized Tomographic Imaging*, Society for Industrial and Applied Mathematics, Philadelphia, PA.

Kass, M., Witkin, A., and Terzopoulos, D. [1988]. "Snakes: Active Contour Models," *Int'l J. Comp. Vision*, Kluwer Academic Publishers, Boston, MA, pp. 321–331.

Kaushik Roy, K., Bhattacharya, P., and Suen, C. Y. [2012]. "Iris Segmentation Using Game Theory," *Signal, Image and Video Processing*, vol. 6, no. 2, pp. 301–315.

Kerre, E. E. and Nachtegael, M., (eds.) [2000]. *Fuzzy Techniques in Image Processing*, Springer-Verlag, New York.

Kirsch, R. [1971]. "Computer Determination of the Constituent Structure of Biological Images," *Comput. Biomed. Res.*, vol. 4, pp. 315–328.

Klette, R. and Rosenfeld, A. [2004]. *Digital Geometry — Geometric Methods for Digital Picture Analysis*, Morgan Kaufmann, San Francisco, CA.

Kohler, R. J. and Howell, H. K. [1963]. "Photographic Image Enhancement by Superposition of Multiple Images," *Photogr. Sci. Eng.*, vol. 7, no. 4, pp. 241–245.

Kramer, H. P. and Mathews, M. V. [1956]. "A Linear Coding for Transmitting a Set of Correlated Signals," *IRE Trans. Info. Theory*, vol. IT-2, pp. 41–46.

Krizhevsky, A., Sutskever, I., and Hinton, G. E. [2012]. "ImageNet Classification with Deep Convolutional Neural Networks," *Advances in Neural Information Processing Systems 25*, NIPS 2012, pp. 1097–1105.

Langdon, G. C. and Rissanen, J. J. [1981]. "Compression of Black-White Images with Arithmetic Coding," *IEEE Trans. Comm.*, vol. COM-29, no. 6, pp. 858–867.

LeCun, Y., Bengio, Y., and Hinton, G. [2015]. "Deep Learning," *Nature*, vol. 521, pp. 436–444.

LeCun, Y., Boser, B., Dencker, J. S., Henderson, D., Howard, R. E., Hubbard, W., and Jacket, L. D. [1998]. "Backpropagation Applied to Handwritten Code Recognition," *Neural Computation*, vol. 1, no. 4, pp. 541–551.

LeCun, Y., Bottou, L., Bengio, Y., and Haffner, P. [1998]. "Gradient-Based Learning Applied to Document Recognition," *Proc. IEEE*, vol. 86. no. 11, pp. 2278–2324.

LeCun. Y. A., Bottou, L., Orr, G. B., and Muller, Klaus [2012]. "Efficient Backprop," in *Neural Networks: Tricks of the Trade*, G. Montavon et al. (eds.), Springer-Verlag, New York, pp. 9–48.

Le Gall, D. and Tabatabai, A. [1988]. "Sub-Band Coding of Digital Images Using Symmetric Short Kernel Filters and Arithmetic Coding Techniques," *IEEE International Conference on Acoustics, Speech, and Signal Processing*, New York, pp. 761–765.

Li, C., Xu, C., Gui, C., and Fox, M. D. [2005]. "Level Set Evolution Without Re-initialization: A New Variational Formulation," *IEEE Computer Vision and Pattern Recognition Conference*, CVPR-2005, vol. 1, pp. 430–436.

Liangjia, Z., Yi, G., Yezzi, A., and Tannenbaum, A. [2013]. "Automatic Segmentation of the Left Atrium from MR Images via Variational Region Growing With a Moments-Based Shape Prior," *IEEE Trans. Image Process.*, vol. 22, no. 12, pp. 5111–5122.

Lindberg, T. [1994]. "Scale-Space Theory: A Basic Tool for Analyzing Structures at Different Scales," *J. Applied Statistics,* vol. 21, Issue 1–2, pp. 225–270.

Lloyd, S. P. [1982]. "Least Square Quantization in PCM," *IEEE Trans on Inform. Theory,* vol. 28, no. 2, pp.129–137.

Lowe, D. G. [1999]. "Object Recognition from Local Scale-Invariant Features," *Proc. 7th IEEE Int'l Conf. on Computer Vision*, 1150–1157.

Lowe, D. G. [2004]. "Distinctive Image Features from Scale-Invariant Keypoints," *Int'l J. Comp. Vision*, vol. 60, no. 2, pp. 91–110.

Malcolm, J., Rathi, Y., Yezzi, A., and Tannenbaum, A. [2008]. "Fast Approximate Surface Evolution in Arbitrary Dimension," *Proc. SPIE, vol. 6914, Medical Imaging 2008: Image Processing*, doi:10.1117/12.771080.

Mallat, S. [1987]. "A Compact Multiresolution Representation: The Wavelet Model," *Proc. IEEE Computer Society Workshop on Computer Vision*, IEEE Computer Society Press, Washington, DC, pp. 2–7.

Mallat, S. [1989a]. "A Theory for Multiresolution Signal Decomposition: The Wavelet Representation," *IEEE Trans. Pattern Anal. Mach. Intell.*, vol. PAMI-11, pp. 674–693.

Mallat, S. [1989b]. "Multiresolution Approximation and Wavelet Orthonormal Bases of L2," *Trans. American Mathematical Society*, vol. 315, pp. 69–87.

Mallat, S. [1989c]. "Multifrequency Channel Decomposition of Images and Wavelet Models," *IEEE Trans. Acoustics, Speech, and Signal Processing*, vol.37, pp. 2091–2110.

Mallat, S. [1998]. *A Wavelet Tour of Signal Processing*, Academic Press, Boston, MA.

Mallat, S. [1999]. *A Wavelet Tour of Signal Processing*, 2nd ed., Academic Press, San Diego, CA.

Mamistvalov, A. [1998]. "n-Dimensional Moment Invariants and Conceptual Mathematical Theory of Recognition [of] n-Dimensional Solids," *IEEE Trans. Pattern Anal. Machine Intell.*, vol. 20, no. 8, pp. 819–831.

Marquina, A. and Osher, S. [2001]. "Explicit Algorithms for a New Time-Dependent Model Based on Level-Set Motion for Nonlinear Deblurring and Noise Removal," *SIAM J. Sci. Comput.*, vol.22, no. 2, pp. 387–405.

Marr, D. [1982]. *Vision*, Freeman, San Francisco, CA.

Matas, J., Chum, O, Urban, M. and Pajdla, T. [2002]. "Robust Wide Baseline Stereo from Maximally Stable Extremal Regions," *Proc. 13th British Machine Vision Conf.*, pp. 384–396.

Maurer, C. R., Rensheng, Qi, R., and Raghavan, V. [2003]. "A Linear Time Algorithm for Computing Exact Euclidean Distance Transforms of Binary Images in Arbitrary Dimensions," *IEEE Trans. Pattern Anal. Machine Intell.*, vol. 25, no. 2, pp. 265-270.

Max, J. [1960]. "Quantizing for Minimum Distortion," *IRE Trans. Info. Theory*, vol. IT-6, pp. 7–12.

McCulloch, W. S. and Pitts, W. H. [1943]. "A Logical Calculus of the Ideas Imminent in Nervous Activity," *Bulletin of Mathematical Biophysics*, vol. 5, pp. 115–133.

McFarlane, M. D. [1972]. "Digital Pictures Fifty Years Ago," *Proc. IEEE*, vol. 60, no. 7, pp. 768–770.

Meyer, Y. (ed.) [1992a]. *Wavelets and Applications: Proceedings of the International Conference, Marseille, France*, Mason, Paris, and Springer-Verlag, Berlin.

Meyer, Y. (translated by D. H. Salinger) [1992b]. *Wavelets and Operators*, Cambridge University Press, Cambridge, UK.

Meyer, Y. (translated by R. D. Ryan) [1993]. *Wavelets: Algorithms and Applications*, Society for Industrial and Applied Mathematics, Philadelphia.

Meyer, Y. [1987]. "L'analyses par ondelettes," *Pour la Science*, Paris, France.

Meyer, Y. [1990]. *Ondelettes et opérateurs*, Hermann, Paris.

Minsky, M. and Papert, S. [1969]. *Perceptrons: An Introduction to Computational Geometry*, MIT Press, Cambridge, MA.

Mitchell, J., Pennebaker, W., Fogg, C., and LeGall, D. [1997]. *MPEG Video Compression Standard*, Chapman & Hall, New York.

Mohanty, S., et al. [1999]. "A Dual Watermarking Technique for Images," *Proc. 7th ACM International Multimedia Conference*, ACM-MM'99, Part 2, pp. 49–51.

Montavon, et al. [2012]. *Neural Networks: Tricks of the Trade*, Springer-Verlag, New York.

Montgomery, D. C. and Runger, G. C. [2011]. *Applied Statistics and Probability for Engineers*, 5th ed., Wiley, Hoboken, NJ.

Netravali, A. N. [1977]. "On Quantizers for DPCM Coding of Picture Signals," *IEEE Trans. Info. Theory*, vol. IT-23, no. 3, pp. 360–370.

Netravali, A. N. and Limb, J. O. [1980]. "Picture Coding: A Review," *Proc. IEEE*, vol. 68, no. 3, pp. 366–406.

Nie, Y. and Barner, K. E. [2006]. "The Fuzzy Transformation and Its Applications in Image Processing," *IEEE Trans. Image Process.*, vol. 15, no. 4, pp. 910–927.

Nielsen, M. A. [2015]. *Neural Networks and Deep Learning*, Determination Press. (Only available online at http://neuralnetworksanddeeplearning.com/index.html.)

Nilsson, N. J. [1965]. *Learning Machines: Foundations of Trainable Pattern-Classifying Systems*, McGraw-Hill, New York.

Nixon, M. and Aguado, A. [2012]. *Feature Extraction and Image Processing for Computer Vision*, 3rd ed., Academic Press, New York.

Noble, B. and Daniel, J. W. [1988]. *Applied Linear Algebra*, 3rd ed., Prentice Hall, Upper Saddle River, NJ.

Odegard, J. E., Gopinath, R. A., and Burrus, C. S. [1992]. "Optimal Wavelets for Signal Decomposition and the Existence of Scale-Limited Signals," *Proceedings of IEEE Int. Conf. On Signal Proc.*, ICASSP-92, San Francisco, CA, vol. IV, 597–600.

Oppenheim, A. V., Schafer, R. W., and Stockham, T. G., Jr. [1968]. "Nonlinear Filtering of Multiplied and Convolved Signals," *Proc. IEEE*, vol. 56, no. 8, pp. 1264–1291.

Osher, S. and Sethian, J. A. [1988]. "Fronts Propagating with Curvature-Dependent Speed: Algorithms Based on Hamilton-Jacobi Formulations," *J. Comp. Phys.*, vol. 79, no. 1, pp. 12–49.

Otsu, N. [1979]. "A Threshold Selection Method from Gray-Level Histograms," *IEEE Trans. Systems, Man, and Cybernetics*, vol. 9, no. 1, pp. 62–66.

O'Neil, J. B. [1971]. "Entropy Coding in Speech and Television Differential PCM Systems," *IEEE Trans. Info. Theory*, vol. IT-17, pp. 758–761.

Padfield, D. [2011]. "The Magic Sigma," *Proc. of the IEEE Comp. Vision and Pattern Recog. Conf. (CVPR)*, 2011, pp. 129–136.

Paez, M. D. and Glisson, T. H. [1972]. "Minimum Mean-Square-Error Quantization in Speech PCM and DPCM Systems," *IEEE Trans. Comm.*, vol. COM-20, pp. 225–230.

Parhi, K. and Nishitani, T. [1999]. "Digital Signal Processing in Multimedia Systems," Chapter 18: *A Review of Watermarking Principles and Practices*, M. Miller, et al. (eds.), pp. 461–485, Marcel Dekker Inc., New York.

Pennebaker, W. B., Mitchell, J. L., Langdon, G. G., Jr., and Arps, R. B. [1988]. "An Overview of the Basic Principles of the Q-coder Adaptive Binary Arithmetic Coder," *IBM J. Res. Dev.*, vol. 32, no. 6, pp. 717–726.

Perez, A. and Gonzalez, R. C. [1987]. "An Iterative Thresholding Algorithm for Image Segmentation," *IEEE Trans. Pattern Anal. Machine Intell.*, vol. PAMI-9, no. 6, pp. 742–751.

Petrou, M. and Petrou, C. [2010]. *Image Processing: The Fundamentals*, John Wiley & Sons, New York.

Pitas, I. and Vanetsanopoulos, A. N. [1990]. *Nonlinear Digital Filters: Principles and Applications*, Kluwer Academic Publishers, Boston, MA.

Poynton, C. A. [1996]. *A Technical Introduction to Digital Video*, John Wiley & Sons, New York.

Pratt, W., Chen, W., and Welch, L. [1974]. "Slant Transform Image Coding," *IEEE Trans. on Comm.*, vol. COM-22, no. 8, pp. 1075–1093.

Pratt, W. K. [2001]. *Digital Image Processing*, 3rd ed., John Wiley & Sons, New York.

Pratt, W. K. [2014]. *Introduction to Digital Image Processing*, CRC Press, Boca Raton, FL.

Prewitt, J. M. S. [1970]. "Object Enhancement and Extraction," in *Picture Processing and Psychopictorics*, Lipkin, B. S., and Rosenfeld, A. (eds.), Academic Press, New York.

Prince, Simon J. D. [2012]. *Computer Vision: Models, Learning, and Inference*, Cambridge Univ. Press, Cambridge, UK.

Proc. IEEE [1980]. Special issue on the encoding of graphics, vol. 68, no. 7.

Proc. IEEE [1985]. Special issue on visual communication systems, vol. 73, no. 2.

Rabbani, M. and Jones, P.W. [1991]. *Digital Image Compression Techniques*, SPIE Press, Bellingham, WA.

Rajala, S. A., Riddle, A. N., and Snyder, W. E. [1983]. "Application of One-Dimensional Fourier Transform for Tracking Moving Objects in Noisy Environments," *Comp., Vision, Image Proc.*, vol. 21, pp. 280–293.

Ramachandran, G. N. and Lakshminarayanan, A. V. [1971]. "Three Dimensional Reconstructions from Radiographs and Electron Micrographs: Application of Convolution Instead of Fourier Transforms," *Proc. Nat. Acad. Sci.*, vol. 68, pp. 2236–2240.

Shapiro, L. G. and Stockman, G. C. [2001]. *Computer Vision*, Prentice Hall, Upper Saddle River, NJ.

Shepp, L. A. and Logan, B. F. [1974]. "The Fourier Reconstruction of a Head Section," *IEEE Trans. Nucl. Sci.*, vol. NS-21, pp. 21–43.

Shi, J. and Malik, J. [2000]. "Normalized Cuts and Image Segmentation," *IEEE Trans. Pattern Anal. and Machine Intell.*, vol. 22. no. 8, pp. 888–905.

Shi, J. and Tomasi, C. [1994]. "Good Features to Track," *9th IEEE Conf. Computer Vision and Pattern Recog.*, pp. 593–600.

Shi, Y. and Karl, W. C. [2008]. "A Real-Time Algorithm for the Approximation of Level-Set-Based Curve Evolution," *IEEE Trans. Image Process.*, vol. 17, no. 5, pp. 645–655.

Simon, J. C. [1986]. *Patterns and Operators: The Foundations of Data Representations,* McGraw-Hill, New York.

Sklansky, J., Chazin, R. L., and Hansen, B. J. [1972]. "Minimum-Perimeter Polygons of Digitized Silhouettes," *IEEE Trans. Comput.*, vol. C-21, no. 3, pp. 260–268.

Sloboda, F., Zatko, B., and Stoer, J. [1998]. "On Approximation of Planar One-Dimensional Continua," in *Advances in Digital and Computational Geometry*, R. Klette, A. Rosenfeld, and F. Sloboda (eds.), Springer, Singapore, pp. 113–160.

Smith, J.O., III [2003]. *Mathematics of the Discrete Fourier Transform*, W3K Publishing, CCRMA, Stanford, CA. (Also available online at http://ccrma.stanford.edu/~jos/mdft).

Snowden, R., Thompson, P, and Troscianko, T. [2012]. *Basic Vision: An Introduction to Visual Perception*, Oxford University Press, Oxford, UK.

Snyder, W. E. and Qi, Hairong [2004]. *Machine Vision*, Cambridge University Press, New York.

Sobel, I. E. [1970]. "Camera Models and Machine Perception," Ph.D. dissertation, Stanford University, Palo Alto, CA.

Soille, P. [2003]. *Morphological Image Analysis: Principles and Applications*, 2nd ed., Springer-Verlag, New York.

Sokic, E., & Konjicija, S. (2016). "Phase-Preserving Fourier Descriptor for Shape-Based Image Retrieval," *Signal Processing: Image Communication*, vol. 40, pp. 82-96.

Solari, S. [1997]. *Digital Video and Audio Compression*, McGraw-Hill, New York.

Srivastava, N. et al. [2014]. "Dropout: A Simple Way to Prevent Neural Networks from Overfitting," *J. Machine Learning Res.*, vol. 15, pp. 1929–1958.

Sussner, P. and Ritter, G. X. [1997]. "Decomposition of Gray-Scale Morphological Templates Using the Rank Method," *IEEE Trans. Pattern Anal. Machine Intell.*, vol. 19, no. 6, pp. 649–658.

Sze, T.W. and Yang, Y. H. [1981]. "A Simple Contour Matching Algorithm," *IEEE Trans. Pattern Anal. Mach. Intell.*, vol. 3, no. 6, pp. 676–678.

Theoridis, S. and Konstantinos, K. [2006]. *Pattern Recognition*, 3rd ed., Academic Press, New York.

Thurley, J. M. and Danell, V. [2012]. "Fast Morphological Image Processing Open-Source Extensions for GPU Processing With CUDA," *IEEE J. Selected Topics in Signal Processing*, vol. 6, no. 7, pp. 849–855.

Tizhoosh, H. R. [2000]. "Fuzzy Image Enhancement: An Overview," in *Fuzzy Techniques in Image Processing*, E. Kerre and M. Nachtegael (eds.), Springer-Verlag, New York.

Toro, J. and Funt, B. [2007]. "A Multilinear Constraint on Dichromatic Planes for Illumination Estimation," *IEEE Trans. Image Process.*, vol. 16, no. 1, pp. 92–97.

Tou, J. T. and Gonzalez, R. C. [1974]. *Pattern Recognition Principles*, Addison-Wesley, Reading, MA.

Trussell, H. J. and Vrhel, M. J. [2008]. *Fundamentals of Digital Imaging*, Cambridge University Press, Cambridge, UK.

Umbaugh, S. E. [2010]. *Digital Image Processing and Analysis*, 2nd ed., CRC Press, Boca Raton, FL.

Vetterli, M. and Kovacevic, J. [1995]. *Wavelets and Suband Coding*, Prentice Hall, Englewood Cliffs, NJ.

Vincent, L. [1993]. "Morphological Grayscale Reconstruction in Image Analysis: Applications and Efficient Algorithms," *IEEE Trans. Image Process.*, vol. 2. no. 2, pp. 176–201.

Walsh, J. L. [1923]. "A Closed Set of Normal Orthogonal Functions," *Am. J. Math.*, vol. 45, no. 1, pp. 5–24.

Wang, Ruye [2012]. *Introduction to Orthogonal Transforms*, Cambridge University Press, New York.

Weinberger, M. J., Seroussi, G., and Sapiro, G. [1996]. "The LOCO-I Lossless Image Compression Algorithm: Principles and Standardization into JPEG-LS," *IEEE Trans. Image Process.*, vol. 9, no. 8, pp. 1309–1324.

Welch, T. A. [1984]. "A Technique for High-Performance Data Compression," *IEEE Computer*, vol. 17, no. 6, pp. 8–19.

White, J. M. and Rohrer, G. D. [1983]. "Image Thresholding for Optical Character Recognition and Other Applications Requiring Character Image Extraction," *IBM J. Res. Devel.*, vol. 27, no. 4, pp. 400–411.

Whittaker, R. T. [1998]. "A Level-Set Approach to 3D Reconstruction from Range Data," *Int'l. J. Comp. Vision*, vol. 29, no. 3, pp. 203–231.

Widrow, B. and Stearns, S. D. [1985]. *Adaptive Signal Processing*, Prentice Hall, Englewood Cliffs, NJ.

Wiener, N. [1942]. *Extrapolation, Interpolation, and Smoothing of Stationary Time Series*, MIT Press, Cambridge, MA.

Witten, I. H., Neal, R. M., and Cleary, J. G. [1987]. "Arithmetic Coding for Data Compression," *Comm. ACM*, vol. 30, no. 6, pp. 520–540.

Wolberg, G. [1990]. *Digital Image Warping*, IEEE Computer Society Press, Los Alamitos, CA.

Woods, R. E. and Gonzalez, R. C. [1981]. "Real-Time Digital Image Enhancement," *Proc. IEEE*, vol. 69, no. 5, pp. 643–654.

Xiang, Z., Zou, Y., Zhou, X., and Huang, X. [2016]. "Robust Vehicle Logo Recognition Based on Locally Collaborative Representation with Principal Components," *Sixth Int'l Conference on Information Sci. and Tech.*, Dalian, China, pp. 487-491.

Xintao, D., Yonglong, L., Liping, S., and Fulong, C. [2014]. "Color Balloon Snakes for Face Segmentation," *Int'l J. for Light and Electron Optics*, vol. 126, no. 11, pp. 2538–2542.

Xu, C. and Prince, J, L. [1988]. "Snakes, Shapes, and Gradient Vector Flow," *IEEE Trans. Image Process.*, vol.7, no. 3, pp. 359–369.

Yu, H., Barriga, E.S., Agurto, C., Echegaray, S., Pattichis, M.S., Bauman, W., and Soliz, P. [2012]. "Fast Localization and Segmentation of Optic Disk in Retinal Images Using Directional Matched Filtering and Level Sets," *IEEE Trans. Information Tech and Biomedicine*, vol. 16, no. 4, pp. 644–657.

Zadeh, L. A. [1965]. "Fuzzy Sets," *Inform. and Control*, vol. 8, pp. 338–353.

Zadeh, L. A. [1973]. "Outline of New Approach to the Analysis of Complex Systems and Decision Processes," *IEEE Trans. Systems, Man, Cyb.*, vol. SMC-3, pp. 28–44.

Zadeh, L. A. [1976]. "A Fuzzy-Algorithmic Approach to the Definition of Complex or Imprecise Concepts," *Int. J. Man-Machine Studies*, vol. 8, pp. 249–291.

Zahn, C. T. and Roskies, R. Z. [1972]. "Fourier Descriptors for Plane Closed Curves," *IEEE Trans. Comput.*, vol. C-21, no. 3, pp. 269–281.

Zhang, Q. and Skjetne, R. [2015]. "Image Processing for Identification of Sea-Ice Floe Size Distribution," *IEEE Trans. Geoscience and Remote Sensing*, vol. 53, no. 5, pp. 2913–2924.

Ziv, J. and Lempel, A. [1977]. "A Universal Algorithm for Sequential Data Compression," *IEEE Trans. Info. Theory*, vol. IT-23, no. 3, pp. 337–343.

Ziv, J. and Lempel, A. [1978]. "Compression of Individual Sequences Via Variable-Rate Coding," *IEEE Trans. Info. Theory*, vol. IT-24, no. 5, pp. 530–536.

Index